DR. CATHY BURNS

Sharing
212 E. 7th St. (#B)
Mt. Carmel, PA 17851-2211

First Printing: November 2001
Second Printing: June 2002

All Scripture quotations are from the King James Version of the Holy Bible.

ISBN: 1-891117-17-3

TABLE OF CONTENTS

1. LET'S MEET SOME OF BILLY'S FRIENDS

Billy Graham is one of the best-known as well as one of the best-loved individuals of the 20th century. He has been in the listing of "most admired men" for 36 consecutive years—more than any other person.[1] Chuck Colson states that he is the "greatest evangelist of this century—perhaps the greatest since Paul...."[2] Others refer to him as "the world's best-known evangelist,"[3] "the world's most beloved evangelist,"[4] "the most honored evangelical alive,"[5] "the nation's pastor,"[6] or "America's pastor."[7]

Knowing that Graham was so well respected and revered, and hoping to help our community hear the gospel of Jesus Christ, I took the responsibility for trying to bring Graham's films to our school—and succeeded. Even though I was still in high school, I felt a burden to reach out to others and tell them about Jesus. At that time, I thought Graham's films would be one of the best methods available and I was even one of the counselors after the film was aired. Since that time, Graham's popularity has only increased.

Little by little I started hearing about some aspect of Graham's ministry with which I didn't agree, but I'd just shrug my shoulders and ignore it. Eventually, those "little things" started to add up to quite a large number of difficulties. As I started to research some of these issues, I found more and more—and even more problems—problems far worse than I could have possibly imagined. I started noticing Graham's own words in his autobiography and compared that with other sources. I read many biographies on Graham—most of which were authorized by Graham himself and/or published by Graham's ministry (under World Wide Publications). Since I'd been researching the New Age and related movements for the past 19 years, I noticed some names with which I was familiar. As I continued to dig and research, unbelievable associations were uncovered—and some things started to fall into place. I started to understand many things I had not comprehended before. I am now sharing this extensive research with you—and hope you will continue to **do your own research** as well.

This first chapter, especially, may be a little difficult to read and digest, but I feel it is necessary in order to lay a framework for the succeeding chapters. This was not an easy book to write but, as I think should be evident, it has been extensively researched and documented. Many people will not like what has been uncovered—but I believe the truth should be shared with others. Many will want to hold to their cherished beliefs (no matter how false they are)—but I just ask you to read it and then check out the facts for yourself.

Remember, it is better to be disturbed by truth than to be deceived by falsehood. Proverbs 27:6 notes: "Faithful are the wounds of a friend; but the kisses of an enemy are deceitful." Galatians 4:16 asks: "Am I therefore become your enemy, because I tell you the truth?"

Since he is esteemed and revered in the eyes of so many, I think it's very important to look at Billy Graham himself, some of his close friends, as well as some of those he invited to share the platform with him at his Crusades. While I'm sure that Graham would not be in agreement with the views (political, spiritual, or even otherwise) of all those encouraged to sit on his platform, his words of praise for many of them certainly give the impression that he considers these people to be fellow Christians and individuals to be respected and admired. It is one thing not to make a disparaging remark about someone; it is quite another thing to heap praise on a person.

It is obvious that someone in Graham's position does not want to be "negative" about people because he would lose many friends, but does he need to unnecessarily brag up people who are flaunting open sins? For instance, on *Larry King Live,* Graham said that although he has been friends with Bill Clinton for years, he has not and would not bring up the issues of homosexuality or abortion to him. Graham said that if he did that, he "would not be invited back to the White House."[8] (As John 12:43 says: "[T]hey loved the praise of men more than the praise of God.") Silence in a case like this is bad enough, but a few months later, in an interview with *U. S. News and World Report* on May 3, 1993, he said about Clinton: "I am quite impressed with his charisma and with some of the things he believes. If he chose to preach the gospel instead of politics, he would make a great evangelist."[9] He also said: "From a biblical point of view, we should be **headed in the direction of goodness and righteousness, away from crime and immorality** and towards one's neighbors who are in need. **I'm encouraged by the emphasis President Clinton and Hillary are putting on that.**"[10]

Graham says Bill and Hillary are leading us in the direction of goodness and righteousness, yet Clinton was recently photographed at a Democratic fund-raiser with Hugh Hefner, the founder of *Playboy.* The photo then appeared in the May 2000 issue of *Playboy.*[11] This is hardly a righteous influence! Clinton had also "appointed over a score of homosexuals to his staff."[12]

Graham also said that he forgives (and seems to excuse) Clinton's sexual misconduct: "I forgive him. Because I know the frailty of human nature, and I know how hard it is, and especially a strong, vigorous, young man like he is; he has such a tremendous personality. I think the ladies just go wild over him."[13] It's great to have man's forgiveness, but that is not sufficient. Clinton needs to ask for God's forgiveness for only God can cleanse the heart.

In Graham's autobiography, *Just As I Am,* he mentions that he was with President **Clinton** on May 1, 1996. He states: "It was a time of **warm fellowship** with a man who has not always won the approval of his **FELLOW CHRISTIANS** but who has in his heart a desire to serve God and do His will."[14] [Emphasis mine throughout.]

> "At a luncheon for 500 newspaper editors at their annual convention in Washington, D.C., Graham said that the President's personal life and character are 'irrelevant.' At the luncheon...**he promoted Clinton as a man of God.** He explained that he and Clinton had been close friends for many years and stated, 'I believe Bill has gone to his knees many times and asked God to help him.'"[15]

The praises flow both ways, however. At a dinner in Washington with about 650 people in attendance, Clinton praised both Billy and Ruth Graham.[16]

When people consider someone like Clinton (who is a sex pervert, pro-homosexual, pro-abortion, etc.) to be a Christian, we are in desperate spiritual trouble! When someone like Graham does so, we are even in a more profound dilemma since multiplied thousands look up to Graham as a spiritual advisor and man of God.

JOHN FOSTER DULLES

Let's meet another one of Graham's friends: John Foster Dulles. It was **Dulles who was involved in helping to open doors for the 1954 Graham Crusade in London.**

In *A Prophet with Honor,* which Billy Graham had asked William Martin to write, we find: "Secretary of State John Foster Dulles...would also be 'using his considerable prestige to help by writing letters to all of his friends and contacts in England.' Perhaps at Dulles's recommendation, American ambassador to Great Britain, **Winthrop Aldrich, promised his assistance as well."**[17]

Aldrich, by the way, was a brother-in-law to John D. Rockefeller, Jr.[18]

Many people know who John Foster Dulles was but for those who don't, **Dulles was a founder of the Council on Foreign**

Relations[19] (CFR) and a relative (through marriage to Janet Pomeroy Avery) to the Rockefeller family.[20] He served as a **chairman of the board of the Rockefeller Foundation and the Carnegie Endowment.**[21] It was Dulles himself who chose **Communist** Alger Hiss[22] to be president of the Carnegie Endowment for International Peace.[23] We need to remember that the kind of peace the Carnegie Endowment has in mind is different from the peace that you have in mind. This organization said: "[W]e shall have peace through constant warfare!"[24] Not a very peaceful peace, is it?

Dulles and Hiss were friends for a long time. Furthermore, **"Mr. Dulles and Mr. Hiss worked together in The Federal Council of Churches** and...both were chairmen of important committees of the Council."[25]

> "In September 1916, [President Woodrow] Wilson appointed a 'brain trust' of 150 to draw up a charter for **world government**. The League of Nations Covenant was prepared for a new **socialist one-world** to follow WWI. The group included college professors, graduate students, lawyers, economists and writers. Individuals on the committee included Walter Lippman (columnist), Norman Thomas (head of the American **Socialist** Party), Allen Dulles (later head of CIA), **John Foster Dulles** (later Secretary of State) and Christian A. Herter (former Secretary of State)."[26]

Dulles advocated "global <u>inter</u>dependence"[27] and was also a founding member of the United Nations[28] (UN) and helped to prepare the United Nations Charter[29] which states: "The present Charter represents a conscientious and successful effort to create the best **world organization** which the realities permit."[30] Dulles wrote: "I have never seen any proposal made for collective security with 'teeth' in it, or for **'world government'** or for 'world federation,' which could not be carried out either by the United Nations or under the United Nations Charter."[31]

> "The founders of the UN were 16 Communists led by Alger Hiss, and 43 members of the Council on Foreign Relations (CFR).
>
> "Since the UN was founded, to produce peace for all the world, there have been 157 wars [up to 1991]. The UN has yet to prevent a war, stop a war or win a war. On key issues the UN has voted against the U. S. about 85% of the time."[32]

The story of the land where the UN is situated is interesting, too.

> "The UN stands on a piece of land called by the **Manhattan** Indians, Turtle Bay. Their legend was that **floods of blood would drench that place** but that there would come a time when many

tribes will meet here to make peace. It happens that for many years the slaughter houses of Manhattan stood here and floods of blood were lost by hundreds of thousands of animals. When Mr. John Rockefeller bought the land, he got the slaughter houses destroyed and offered the grounds to the UN, the meeting place of many tribes. One could also add that the UN was born from the blood of the 30 million humans who died in World War II. These are the Earth vibrations noticeable at the UN."[33]

Dulles had been hired by Joseph Stalin to act as Russia's legal council in the United States[34] and he was also closely associated with J. P. Morgan.[35] Morgan "was instrumental in forcing our country into World War I. He and his associates funded the Bolsheviks and the Nazis, and he helped organize the Council on Foreign Relations. Occult writers tell us he based his investment strategy on astrology."[36]

"John Foster Dulles and Allen Dulles became senior partners of Sullivan and Cromwell. That firm was chief legal counsel to J. Henry Schroeder Bank which **helped finance Hitler's rise to power** initially aided by the Warburg-controlled Mendelsohn Bank of Amsterdam. Chase National, Equitable Trust, Mechanics and Metals, Bankers Trust and Kuhn Loeb & Co. financed Germany's launching of World War I on the basis of a deal made with Kaiser Wilhelm through their agents—the Warburgs."[37]

SIX PILLARS OF PEACE

It was **John Foster Dulles who dominated the Federal Council of Churches**[38] (FCC) which had been founded, in part, by the **Communist Harry Ward** in 1908.[39] In fact, **John D. Rockefeller, Jr.** was among those who **helped to finance the Federal Council of Churches.**[40] For many years no conference or meeting of the Council was complete without an address by Dulles or one of the Rockefellers.[41]

Since Dulles was involved in both the United Nations and the FCC (later renamed the National Council of Churches), it's no surprise to see the following news item: "Christians should vigorously support efforts to strengthen the United Nations—even at the risk of leaving the United States outvoted, the National Council of Churches decided last night."[42]

In Dulles' book, *War or Peace,* he stated:

"The churches took a strong lead in favor of international organization. The Federal Council of Churches of Christ in America already, in December, 1940, had acted to set up a

Commission on a Just and Durable Peace, of which I [Dulles] was chairman. Our Commission held its first full meeting in September, 1941, just after the promulgation of the Atlantic Charter. We immediately launched a campaign to educate United States public opinion to the **need for world organization.** Most of the Protestant churches of the country set up 'study groups' on **world order.** The Commission conducted 'national missions on world order' which took leading ministers and laymen to the principal cities of the United States. It issued a 'Six Pillars of Peace' statement which set out briefly and cogently the **need for world organization** and the tasks it should assume."[43]

"John Foster Dulles and his many supporters in the church now took their case to the nation. Beginning with a convocation in the **Cathedral of St. John the Divine** in New York, they fanned out across America, ultimately visiting 102 cities."[44]

The report:

> "**called for a world government** of delegated powers, strong immediate **limitations on national sovereignty,** international control of all armies and navies, an international court with adequate jurisdiction, a **universal system of money,** progressive elimination of all tariff and quota restrictions on world trade, an **international bank, and worldwide freedom of immigration.**"[45]

It was **Dulles** who was instrumental in getting the FCC to support the United Nations as well as its UNESCO (United Nations Educational, Scientific and Cultural Organization) program.[46] "Skull and Bones member Archibald MacLeish wrote the UNESCO Constitution and several Freemasons helped create the organization."[47] MacLeish belonged to the Council on Foreign Relations.[48] He, along with Adlai Stevenson, "worked to establish the United Nations and drafted the preamble to its charter."[49] "A fervent international, MacLeish strongly advocated One Worldism...."[50] He was also cited for being involved in at least 12 Communist front organizations and/or activities.[51] In fact, his "FBI file ran to over six hundred pages."[52] He "argued vigorously for a left-wing press in the United States, if only because it advanced views contrary to those of the majority."[53]

Dulles was former President Eisenhower's Secretary of State[54] and in 1950, when the Federal Council of Churches changed its name to the National Council of Churches, **Rockefeller** donated a large parcel of land for its headquarters. It was Eisenhower who laid the cornerstone for the National Council of Churches (NCC) in Masonic style.[55]

Interestingly, President Eisenhower read a prayer at his inauguration in January 1953. When copies of the prayer were checked it was discovered that he had not mentioned the name of Jesus Christ in the entire prayer[56] (just like in Masonry). In the Masonic Lodge the chaplains are repeatedly told not to pray or end their prayers in the name of Jesus.[57]

By the way, the NCC just happens to be across the street from the Rockefellers' Riverside Church and the two buildings are connected by an underground tunnel.[58] Also, Rockefellers gave a $50 million endowment to Riverside Church.[59] "To symbolize the interdenominational spirit and its further reconciliation of religion and science, the tympanum arching the main portal contained the figures of non-Christian religious leaders and outstanding heroes of secular history, Confucius and Moses, Hegel and Dante, Mohammed and even the dread Darwin."[60] Also, this "church building sports stone statues of Gargoyles on its Cathedral as well as statues of the Merovingian King Clovis....John D. Rockefeller, Jr. is chairman of the Building Committee."[61]

Another famous building with gargoyles is **St. John the Divine Church.** One author reveals:

> "Grotesque-looking gargoyles are chiseled from stone and set in place on the Cathedral, jeering down and sticking tongues out at the onlookers. Funding for the two-century-long project has been supplied through gifts, including some quite large—like the one for over a million dollars from international financier and philanthropist **J. P. Morgan."**[62]

Gargoyles "are weird stone figures, half-human and half-animal or half-bird, placed on the edges of cathedrals, palaces, and other buildings."[63]

"Riverside was previously pastored by **Harry Emerson Fosdick.** This was the same Fosdick who was accosted by William Jennings Bryan for heresy—denying the virgin birth."[64] Fosdick declared: "Of course **I do not believe in the Virgin Birth,** or in that old fashioned substitutionary **doctrine of the Atonement;** and **I do not know any intelligent Christian minister who does."**[65]

"Bryan and the fundamentalists tried to excommunicate Fosdick but who do you suppose came to Fosdick's defense?—none other than **John Foster Dulles!**"[66]

GRAHAM FOLLOWS NCC WITH GREAT INTEREST

Fosdick belonged to at least 7 **Communist** front groups.[67] He claimed that "Jesus was as much 'divine' as his own mother."[68] He was also a leader in the **National Council of Churches.**[69] Additionally, Fosdick wrote articles for Margaret Sanger's *Birth Control Review.*[70]

In spite of the apostasy in the leadership of the NCC, **Graham** visited the NCC headquarters on August 27, 1991 and remarked: "There's no group of people in the world that I would rather be with right now than you all. Because I think of you, I pray for you, and **we follow with great interest the things you do."**[71] Graham's connections to the NCC go back to at least **1958.**

Getting back to John Foster Dulles: Not only did Dulles play a large role in the Federal Council of Churches, but he was also involved with the World Council of Churches (WCC).[72] At one of the WCC's meetings, Dulles said: "There is no inherent incompatibility between the Christian view of the nature of man and the practice of economic communism or state socialism."[73]

> "It should be recognized, he suggested, that the long-range social ends which Soviet leaders professed to seek were in many respects similar to the ends which Christian citizens sought—'a higher productivity of labor, abolition of exploitation of man by man, **"from each according to his abilities, to each according to his needs."'** There was nothing in these long-term ends, he thought, irreconcilable with what Christians wanted. 'Most of them have been sought by Christians long before there was a Communist party,' he declared."[74]

REDISTRIBUTION OF WEALTH

As early as 1939 **Dulles said** that there must be **"some dilution of sovereignty,"**[75] and "the establishment of a common money."[76]

On October 28, 1939 Dulles proposed "that America lead the transition to a new order of less independent, semi-sovereign states bound together by a league or federal union."[77]

As mention, in 1942 **he was the chairman of a meeting of the Federal Council of Churches (FCC)** "which **called for a world government,"**[78] etc.

> "The report also called for **world-wide redistribution of wealth.** It held that a 'new order of economic life is both imminent and imperative.' **It accepted Marxian concepts** by denouncing various defects in the profit system as being responsible for breeding war, demagogues, and dictators."[79]

Dulles also stated:

> **"The fundamental fact is that the nationalist system of wholly independent, fully sovereign states is complete in**

> **its cycle of usefulness....Today, more than ever before, are the defects of the sovereign system magnified, until now it is no longer consonant with either peace or justice. It is imperative that there be a transition to a new order. This has, indeed, become inevitable; for the present system is rapidly encompassing its own destruction. The real problem is not whether there will be a transition, but how can transition be made, and to what."**[80] [Emphasis in the original.]

In one of the statements he authored for the Federal Council of Churches, Dulles wrote:

> "...Communism as an economic program for social reconstruction has points of contact with the social message of Christianity as in its avowed concern for the underprivileged and its insistence on racial equality...neither state socialism nor free enterprise provide a perfect economic system; each can learn from the experience of the other...the free enterprise system has yet to prove it can assure steady production and employment...."[81]

In *War or Peace,* Dulles wrote: "Fundamentally, world peace depends upon world law, and world law depends upon a consensus of world opinion as to what is right and what is just."[82]

Dulles, along with John D. Rockefeller III, "created the Population Council, in November 1952. They warned of the need to stop expansion of the world's non-white population."[83] Dulles was also among several Council on Foreign Relations members who **knowingly brought Communist Fidel Castro to power in Cuba.**[84]

Remember, this is the same **John Foster Dulles** who was instrumental in getting **Billy Graham** open doors for a crusade in London in 1954 and **"who designated himself a Christian Communist."**[85] Could Dulles have sincerely been interested in having the Gospel preached? It doesn't seem likely! I might add that Dulles "also gave him a bit of political advice, perhaps hoping Graham would not make statements that ran counter to U. S. foreign policy."[86]

TEMPLETON PRIZE

Billy Graham is so popular that he was selected as the recipient of the Templeton Prize in 1982.[87] In the address that Templeton gave during this ceremony he said: "Every person is created by God, is a child of God and the Holy Spirit dwells within **each** human being."[88] He continued:

> "This afternoon, His Royal Highness Prince Philip presented the Templeton Prize for 1982 to the Reverend Dr

Graham, founder of the Billy Graham Evangelistic Association. Evangelism is a duty for every person who worships **God in any form.** Dr Graham has originated more new ideas in evangelism than any living person. He has given the Church around the world a new hope and has contributed vastly to the wider vision and meaning of evangelism. **His co-operation with all denominations** to involve the statesmen of the world in evangelism has left an indelible mark on Christian history."[89]

Templeton also explained:

"The recipient of the award has been **selected by distinguished judges from all five major religions** worldwide and who serve for a three year period. The **Buddhist judge is the Dalai Lama.** Mr Justice P. N. Bhagwati of the Supreme Court of India is a **Hindu.** The Honourable Philip N. Klutznick, former Secretary of Commerce of the United States, is President of the **World Jewish Congress.** Senator Orrin Grant Hatch, United States Senator, is a **Mormon** from Utah. Her Royal Highness The Grand Duchess Josephine of Luxembourg is a **Roman Catholic.** The Most Reverend Stuart Blanch, Archbishop of York, and Dr Arthur Robert Peacocke, Dean of Clare College, Cambridge, are **Anglicans.** Other Christian judges are The Right Honourable Lynden O. Pindling, Prime Minister of the Bahamas, Charles Rickett Fillmore, Chairman of the **Unity School of Christianity,** and Senator Mark O. Hatfield, United States Senator from Oregon."[90]

NEW WORLD ORDER

Since Hatfield was one of the judges,[91] let's briefly look at him. Hatfield is a 33° Mason[92] and he, along with Ted Kennedy, joined together in 1981 "in proposing a **nuclear freeze** resolution to the Senate."[93] Hatfield "insisted that the murderous Ho Chi Minh was simply a 'nationalist.'"[94] He was one of the signers of the traitorous "Declaration of **Inter**dependence" which states in part:

"Two centuries ago our forefathers brought forth a new nation: now we must join with others to bring forth a **new world order....**

"To establish a **new world order** of compassion, peace, justice and security it is **essential** that mankind free itself from the **limitations of national prejudice....**

"Narrow notions of **national sovereignty must not be permitted** to curtail that obligation."[95]

He stated in the August 24, 1980 issue of the *Washington Post* that "it was possible to be both a political liberal and a conservative, evangelical, born-again Christian."[96]

Of course, born-again Christians don't vote for funding for the pornographic displays put out by the National Endowment for the Arts, but Hatfield voted in favor of funding the NEA.[97]

Hatfield has been a prominent member of the Norman Thomas Endowment at the New School for Social Research which is described as a **Humanist-Socialist** institution.[98] In fact, one of the co-founders for this organization was **John Dewey.**[99] Some of the professors were **W. E. B. DuBois,** a **Mason and Communist,**[100] **ACLU** founder **Roger Baldwin,** and **humanist Corliss Lamont.** New Ager and one-world government promoter, **Norman Cousins,** had been a sponsor of the Norman Thomas Endowment at this school. Other members of the Endowment include Supreme Court Justice William O. Douglas, John Kenneth Galbraith, Julian Huxley, Rev. Theodore Hesburgh, and Gunnar Myrdal.[101]

ZERO POPULATION

One author writes:

> "The New School for Social Research, which operates as an accredited educational institution, has been sold to the general public as an independent and politically neutral institution. Actually the *New School* was cited as: 'established by men who belong to the ranks of near-Bolshevik Intelligentsia, some of them being too radical in their views to remain on the faculty of Columbia University.' When the above characterization was made by the New York State Legislative Committee (1920), the New School Fabian socialist nature was not too well defined but its extremism was recognizable even then. **The list of its faculty, lecturers and directors from its origin in 1919 to the present day, reads like a Who's Who of the socialist and communist movement."**[102] [Italics in the original; boldface added.]

Not surprisingly, the Rockefeller Foundation has donated large sums of money to the New School for **Social** Research.[103]

Mark Hatfield was a member of the radical-extremist Institute for Policy Studies.[104] He is also

> "a **promoter of the New Age** and his endorsement is on the back cover of the New Age book, *Earthkeeping.* Hatfield has also written enthusiastic endorsements for many New Age-oriented 'Christian' books. **Hatfield introduced zero population**

growth legislation into the United States Senate and supports the New Age group *Friends of the Earth* which promotes genocidal global de-population."[105] [Italics in the original.]

In the April 1984 *New Options Newsletter,* "Hatfield had one of the top four scores in the United States Senate for voting affirmatively on New Age issues."[106]

In 1991 **he voted to use taxpayer dollars to fund abortion.**[107] In 1992 he **voted to allow fetal tissue from aborted babies to be used for medical research.**[108] In 1993 he voted for the nominations of **lesbian Roberta Achtenberg** and **Joycelyn Elders,**[109] and for funding of the National Endowment for the Arts (NEA) and their pornographic displays.[110] (For more information on the NEA, see Chapter 6.) In 1995 **he voted in favor of taxpayer funds for homosexuality.**[111]

This is the person Billy Graham called **"a devout evangelical"**[112] and **"a great Christian leader"**[113] and suggested that Nixon make him his running mate.[114] Graham said: "I believe he would be a devoted and loyal vice president....He certainly would appeal to the strong Christian vote, Catholic as well as Protestant."[115] He told Nixon: "He's been an educator and **has taken a more liberal stand on most issues** than you, and I think **the ticket needs that kind of a balance."**[116]

Another person that Billy Graham suggested to Nixon (in 1960) for a running mate was **Walter Judd,** a Congressman from Minnesota.[117] He was a **Mason**[118] and belonged to the **World Federalists.**[119] Graham felt that if Nixon would have listened to him, he could have possibly won the election instead of losing to John F. Kennedy.[120]

"WONDERFUL FELLOWSHIP WITH ALL"

Returning to Hatfield, we find that in the *Chicago Tribune* article announcing Graham's acceptance of the Templeton Prize, that

> "Billy **Graham gives credit to Senator Mark Hatfield** of the United States for **indoctrinating him with the pacifist and disarmament stances** which he has recently swung around to and which he is now agitating for **in his sermons** and, particularly, on his recent visit to the KGB-controlled religious conference held in Moscow...."[121]

So, it was this group of judges including Hatfield, a Mormon, a Buddhist, a Jew, a Science of Mind promoter, and a Hindu, among others, that selected Billy Graham for the Templeton Prize!

Perhaps this is why when Larry King interviewed Billy Graham on January 21, 1997 and asked him: "What do you think of the other [churches]...like Mormonism? Catholicism? Other faiths within the Christian concept?,"[122] Graham could respond: "Oh, I think I have a **wonderful fellowship** with **all** of them."[123] Perhaps, too, this is why, in a *Reader's Digest* ad, he could urge the readers to buy the Mormon Tabernacle Choir records.[124] Of course, the Mormon bookstore, Deseret Book outlet, carries Billy Graham's autobiography![125]

King then asked Graham: "Well, are you comfortable with Judaism?"[126] He responded: "Very comfortable....In New York, they have had me to the Rabbinical Council to...talk with them and Rabbi Tannenbaum (sic), who was a great friend...he gave me more advice and more counsel, and **I depended on him** constantly, **theologically and spiritually and in every way."**[127] How can a Rabbi who doesn't believe in Jesus as the Son of God give **SPIRITUAL** advice to Graham? I can understand that Tanenbaum may be a friend, but for Graham to depend on an unsaved man for SPIRITUAL advice is dangerous!

RABBI TANENBAUM

Who is Rabbi Marc H. **Tanenbaum?** He is with the American Jewish Congress.[128] He is also **a sponsor of the New Age, occult group, Lucis Trust,**[129] as well as being on the board of advisers for the National Peace Institute Foundation.[130] Surprisingly, he is also on the board of advisers for the People for the American Way (PAW).[131] **PAW was founded by** Norman Lear[132] through a $40,000 **grant from Hugh Hefner's Playboy Foundation**[133] and has been supported by several grants since then from Playboy Foundation.[134] "The March 1983 issue of *Playboy* carried a full-page ad from PAW."[135] Needless to say, PAW is a liberal, humanistic, anti-Christian, pro-occult, pro-gay, pro-evolution, pro-abortion group whose aims are to defeat the Christian Right.[136] They have fought for the National Endowment of the Arts' "'right' to fund blasphemous pornographic and homosexual 'art' with taxpayer dollars."[137] They were one of the groups that endorsed the 1993 **homosexual** march in Washington.[138] They also endorsed an **occult** curriculum called "Impressions."[139] A

> "number of the lessons in 'Impressions' require the children to participate in the religious activities of Wicca, or modern **witchcraft.** These include activities generally identified with the New Age movement or the occult, such as sitting in circles and chanting, creating and casting spells and charms to accomplish some purpose, astral projection, role playing as witches and other occult characters, and similar activities."[140]

Below are just 2 of the selections from this curriculum:

✿ "Have the children sit in a circle, pass around an imaginary candle, close their eyes and blow out the candle. Tell the children that by blowing out the candle, they have been transported to a different land. Tell the children that you've forgotten the special chant that will transport everyone back to the classroom. Have the children prepare a magical chant that might return them to the classroom. Have each child hold an imaginary candle in front of him. Have them close their eyes and blow out the candles. When the children open their eyes, they will have returned to the classroom. The magic will have worked.

✿ "Have the children practice being the witches (from a 3rd grade story). They can role-play the hero meeting the witch for the first time (where the witch tells the hero 'You deserve to die for [seeing the witch ceremony—ed.]. But I will spare your life on one condition. Bring me the hearts of your mother and sister, and you shall live. If you do not come, I shall see to it that your wife skins you alive.')"[141]

In addition to the witchcraft, there are stories "about monsters eating children and pigs eating excrement [which] are contained within the readers. Poems about children who show apparent disregard for family life are shown in Xenobia Phobia. The main character hates everything including her father, mother, sister and baby brother."[142]

This is the type material promoted by the group that Tanenbaum belongs to and Tanenbaum is one person to whom Billy Graham goes for **SPIRITUAL** help! Amazing, isn't it?! Graham called Tanenbaum the "best friend I had in the Jewish world."[143] He added that he "did more to bring about understanding and friendship between Christians and Jews than any clergyman I ever knew."[144]

In an interview on Good Morning America, "Graham told host Charles Gibson that **Muslims and Jews can be saved by finding God in their own worship systems."**[145] As far back as **1983** Graham had the Jewish Rabbi, Edgar Magnin, lead in prayer at his Los Angeles, California crusade.[146] Robert Schuller and Paul Crouch also "sat in the front row of prominent platform personalities...."[147] At the 1990 Long Island, New York crusade, a rabbi was sitting on his platform.[148]

A number of years after this crusade, Robert Schuller asked Graham: "...what do you think is the future of Christianity?" Graham's response was:

"Well, Christianity and being a true believer you know, I think there's the body of Christ. This comes from all the Christian groups around the world. Outside the Christian groups, I think everybody who knows Christ, **whether they are conscious of it or not,** they're members of the Body of Christ."

He went on to say,

"...**whether they come from the Muslim world, or the Buddhist world, or the Christian world, they are members of the Body of Christ,** because they've been called by God. **They may not even know the name of Jesus,** but they know in their hearts that they need something that they don't have, and I think they turn to the only light they have, and I think they are saved, and that they are going to be in heaven with us."

Schuller queried: "What, what I hear you saying is that it's possible for Jesus Christ to come into human hearts and soul and life even if they've been born in darkness and never had an exposure to the Bible. Is that a correct interpretation of what you are saying?"

Graham replied: "Yes, it is, because I believe that...."[149]

On the January 2, 2000 program on Fox News, Graham said: "I have never targeted Muslims. I have never targeted Jews."[150]

A few years ago Graham attended a prayer breakfast in which Clinton participated.

"Senator Kerry read Jn. 3:1-21 (skipping verse 16) and said Christ was speaking of 'spiritual renewal' and that 'in the spirit of Christ **Hindu, Buddhist, Muslim, Jew, Christian'** were meeting and 'there is renewal with a new President and Vice President.' **Billy Graham** added, **'I do not know a time when we had a more spiritual time than we've had today.'"**[151]

In *McCall's* magazine (January 1978), in an article entitled "I Can't Play God Any More," we find:

"Graham once believed that Jews, too, were lost if they did not convert to Christianity. Today Graham is willing to leave that up to God....Billy is particularly opposed to evangelical groups such as 'Jews for Jesus' who have made Jews the special target of their proselytizing efforts....'If a person wants to convert to Christianity, that is his own freewill decision,' Billy declares....'I would never go after someone just because he is a Jew, which is why I have never supported the Jewish missions.'"[152]

Graham has also bragged: "The **ecumenical movement** has broadened my viewpoint and I recognize now that **God has his people in all churches."**[153]

TEMPLE OF UNDERSTANDING

In Graham's acceptance speech for the Templeton Award, he said:

> "I feel highly honoured to be here today and to have received the Templeton Award....
>
> "I feel today that **I am in illustrious company with those who have been past recipients."** [154]

One of these past recipients of the Templeton Award was Sarvepalli Radhakrishnan.[155] He was one of the founding friends, along with the Dalai Lama (a Buddhist) and others, of the ungodly **Temple of Understanding** in 1960[156] and he also belonged to the **World Brotherhood.**[157]

The Temple of Understanding (c/o The **Cathedral of St. John the Divine** where at one time a naked female "Christ," called Christa, was hung on the cross[158]) brags:

> *"The purpose of The Temple of Understanding is the worldwide promotion of interfaith dialogue and education, to achieve understanding and harmony among the people of the world's religions and beyond.*
>
> *"The Temple of Understanding maintains a strong commitment to the integrity of each religion or faith tradition and believes that each can better remain true to itself by honoring the truths inherent in all traditions."*[159] [Emphasis in the original.]

The pamphlet adds: "The Temple of Understanding is a Non-Governmental Organization **affiliated with the United Nations....**We have been asked to sponsor an **interfaith** service for heads of state and religious leaders at the **Cathedral of St. John the Divine** on the opening day of the 50th anniversary celebration [of the United Nations]."[160]

The Fall 1998 *Temple of Understanding Newsletter* explains "interfaith" like this:

> "Interfaith is most fundamentally **respect.** At the bottom line it is **respecting different traditions, different religions, different faiths.** It is coming to understanding, knowledge, and appreciation of them. And then **most important, it's coming to a love of them.** You can be Jewish and you can really fall in love with Buddhism. You can be a Buddhist and you can really fall in love with Christianity. You can be a Mohawk Indian and you can really fall in love with Islam.

> "So maybe a slogan we can have is **not conversion, but communion,** communion with compassion."[161]
>
> "The Temple of Understanding periodically organizes events such as 'The Buddhist Experience' featuring **Dr. Bernard Tetsugen Glassman** and **Dr. Robert A. F. Thurman** and 'Religious Harmony in a Pluralistic World' by **Dr. Karan Singh** as well as presentations and discussions by such other distinguished presenters as **Dr. Suheil Bushrui, Prebendary Marcus Braybrooke, Dr. Hans Kung, and Thich Nhat Hanh."**[162] [Emphasis in the original.]

Another person in this "illustrious company" who had received the Templeton Award prior to Billy Graham was Ralph Wendell Burhoe (in 1980), a Unitarian,[163] who is founder and editor of *Zygon.*[164] "He sees the 'theory of **evolution** once considered the enemy of religion, as actually demonstrating the inevitable necessity of religion!' Indeed, Burhoe states that, 'Religion is basic to the evolutionary emergence of civilized society!'"[165]

In fact, in an article that Burhoe wrote which appeared in *Religious Humanism,* we find:

> "For life in a 'global village' in an age of science we must revitalize and modernize the efforts of individuals like Joseph Priestly to interpret religion credibly in the light of the sciences....
>
> "There has been a very significant production in recent years by such Unitarian Universalists as Sophia Fahs, Jack Kent, John Ruskin Clark, Donald Szantho Harrington, and many others. Unitarians historically have played a significant role in moving toward new, more rational, and scientific levels of religious thinking for the future—but we still have a long way to go."[166]

Yet another recipient of this Templeton Prize was Cardinal **Joseph Suenens** who received it in 1976.[167] He was intensely involved with the charismatic movement[168] as well as being "chosen by Pope John XXIII to be one of the chief architects of the Vatican II meetings in the mid-1960s, and served on all four of its major committees."[169] Suenens stated:

> "Since I have had this [charismatic] experience, my allegiance to the Holy Father as the Vicar of Christ in the world has been heightened and strengthened. My appreciation for **Mary as the co-redemptress and mediatoress of my salvation** has been assured. My appreciation of the mass as the sacrifice of Christ has now been heightened."[170]

Even though **Suenens** was a Catholic, he was also a **Mason,** being initiated on June 15th, 1967.[171]

Suenens also "hosted and gave the opening speech at the Second World Conference on Religion and Peace" at Louvain, Belgium in 1974[172] which, according to one researcher, "has nothing to do with true religion or peace, but is a **communist** front."[173] This meeting

> "received Pope Paul VI's blessing. Delegations were particularly impressed with the important role that religious unity will play in establishing the coming world government. A continual call was sounded for **'a new world order.'** Under Catholic leadership, the Louvain Declaration stated:
>
> "'Buddhists, Christians, Confucianists, Hindus, Jains, Jews, Muslims, Shintoists, Sikhs, Zoroastrians and still others, we have sought here to listen to the spirit within our varied and venerable religious traditions....
>
> "'We appeal to the religious communities of the world to inculcate the attitude of **planetary citizenship.'**"[174]

One other Templeton recipient that would be included in Graham's "illustrious company," would be the 1979 winner, Nikkyo Niwano,[175] a Buddhist.[176] In a book about the Templeton Prize, we find:

> "*Nikkyo Niwano* is Founder and President of the lay Buddhist Organisation, Rissho Kosei-Kai, which is the largest Buddhist organisation in the world with a membership of over four million. Mr Niwano is a founding President of the World Conference on Religion and Peace and takes a leading role in interfaith dialogue. He founded the Niwano Peace Foundation to promote peace through religion."[177] [Emphasis in the original.]

Rissho Kosei-Kai

> "came into being in 1938, when Niwano Nikkyo and Naganuma Myoko seceded from Reiyukai. Mrs Naganuma had a reputation for her **psychic powers** and her healing gifts. These gained great publicity for her and **she was regarded as a living Buddha.** Since her death in 1957 the shamanistic elements have not been so prominent, and emphasis has been rather placed upon the *hoza* (counselling groups) and upon the attempt to present Buddhism in modern dress, as a creed that brings about peace and goodwill. Hence, in her popular commentary on the Lotus Sutra, **Niwano speaks of people looking to the attainment of buddhahood,** when 'the black cloud' of error will be done away. Men (sic) and women's daily life is to manifest an acceptance of Buddha's command, for only so can a person show the true repentance that will enable the *karma*

to be broken. The life of faith will mean union with the Buddha, which is union with the 'great life of the universe' and an entrance into the Buddha-world."[178] [Italics in the original; boldface added.]

Niwano is also associated with the *Global Forum of Spiritual and Parliamentary Leaders on Human Survival,* "a major New Age, occult, globalist organization,"[179] and Thanksgiving Square.[180]

JOHN MARKS TEMPLETON

To further understand the Templeton Award which **Billy Graham** has received, we need to look at its founder, **John Marks Templeton.** Templeton went to Yale University,[181] earned a Phi Beta Kappa key,[182] and is a **Rhodes Scholar.**[183] The "John Templeton Foundation hosted four key sessions" at the State of the World Forum in 2000. The theme was **"Shaping Globalization:** Convening the Community of Stakeholders."[184] Some of the participants were Mikhail Gorbachev, Queen Noor of Jordan, George Soros, Dr. Jane Goodall, Colin Powell, Ralph Nader, and South African President Thabo Mbeki.[185]

Says Templeton: "No one should say that God can be reached by only **one** path."[186] Jesus, however, proclaimed: "I am the way, the truth, and the life: no man cometh unto the Father, **but by Me"** (John 14:6).

Templeton is also a leading advocate of the heresies of the mind science cults like Religious Science, Science of Mind, Unity, Christian Science, etc.[187] In fact, Templeton's book, *Discovering the Laws of Life,* is pure Science of Mind.[188] This book is published by Continuum and in the January/February 1997 issue of Templeton's magazine, *Progress in Theology,* we find:

> "On December 10, 1996, Sir John Templeton, John M. Templeton, Jr., M.D., and the trustees of the John Templeton Foundation announced the inauguration of the Templeton Foundation Press, which will publish books in the areas of religion and science, moral education, and the scientific verification of basic spiritual principles. Joanna Hill, formerly **marketing manager at the Swedenborg Foundation,** has been named director of publications."[189]

"'Templeton Foundation Press is dedicated to the same principles as the Templeton Foundation and the Templeton Prize for Progress in Religion,' said Sir John Templeton on the launch of the publishing venture, held in New York City."[190] By the way, the

Swedenborg Foundation is an **occult** organization![191] Sadly, *Christianity Today,* a magazine founded by **Billy Graham**[192] and his father-in-law, Nelson Bell, devoted the entire back cover of its April 25, 1994 issue to an ad promoting this heretical work which was endorsed by **Norman Vincent Peale** (who wrote the foreword[193] and said that Templeton was the "greatest layman of the Christian church in our time"[194] and who was also a former judge for the Templeton Prize[195]), **Robert Schuller, J. Peter Grace** (another former judge for the Templeton Prize[196]), who was also the former head of the **Knights of Malta,** and New Ager **Theodore M. Hesburgh,**[197] who is on the Advisory Council for **Planetary Citizens,**[198] the Advisory Council for the Global Education Associates,[199] and an Advisory Board Member of the **World Federalist Association.**[200] Another ad appeared in the January 8, 1996 issue of *Christianity Today.*[201]

WHO ENDORSED BOOK ON BUDDHISM AND HINDUISM?

There was one other person who endorsed this book which "quoted and promoted the teachings of Christianity, **Buddhism** and **Hinduism."**[202] Who was this endorser? It was none other than **Billy Graham!**[203] Of this book he said:

> "Truly a legend in our time, John Templeton understands that the real measure of a person's success in life is not financial accomplishment but moral integrity and inner character. In this book he **draws upon a variety of sources**—including the Bible—**to reveal** the moral and **spiritual principles** which have shaped his own life and work."[204]

Since Graham endorsed this book, let's take a peek inside the cover to see what Templeton says. He writes:

✔ "[T]he basic principles for leading a 'sublime life'...may be derived from **any** religious tradition—Jewish, Muslim, Hindu, Buddhist and others as well as Christian."[205]

✔ "Astronauts traveled into outer space and did not bring back any evidence of heaven. And whereas drills had penetrated the earth, they found oil, not hell, so spiritual theorists conceive of **heaven and hell right here on earth as states of mind."**[206]

✔ "We have the power to create whatever we need in our life...the power of the mind....Through our choices and attitudes **we create our own heaven or hell right here on earth."**[207]

✔ "Our innate goodness is an essential fact of our existence."[208]

✔ "Be honest. Be true. Love all parts of yourself...the **godhood within you**—the goodness within you—is in a state of becoming perfect."[209]

Does Billy Graham believe these things? I don't know, but if he doesn't, **WHY** did he **endorse** the book and why did the magazine founded by Graham, *Christianity Today,* allow the ad to appear at a very prominent place (the back cover) not just one time but at least **two** times?

Of course, Templeton and Graham seem to agree on one issue. Robert Schuller's 1986 *Possibilities* magazine had Templeton's photo on the cover. "The lead article quoted Templeton that 'nothing exists except God' (that's pantheism) and that 'the **Christ spirit dwells in every human being whether the person knows it or not'** (that's universalism)."[210]

Remember what Graham told Schuller during his interview? He said: "Outside the Christian groups, I think everybody who knows Christ, **whether they are conscious of it or not,** they're members of the Body of Christ." He went on to say, "...**whether they come from the Muslim world, or the Buddhist world, or the Christian world, they are members of the Body of Christ,** because they've been called by God."[211] Did you get what Graham said?

Templeton is also involved with the Center for World Thanksgiving.[212] According to **Thanksgiving Square's** own literature, we find:

> "The Center for World Thanksgiving **celebrates the oneness of all people** in expressing gratitude to God, and explores the healing and uniting power of gratitude. The spirit of Thanksgiving inclines one Godward. It cuts across the differences of culture, creed, sect, rank and wealth with the promise of the healing touch of reconciliation in human relationship. To bring people together in gratitude at special times and occasions, the Center has elected Fellows of World Thanksgiving from **many religions** and countries who pioneer new frontiers of thanksgiving....
>
> "The Center for World Thanksgiving sponsors Convocations of World Thanksgiving every few years. It is the intent of these convocations to ask great religious minds of this age to speak 'Words of Thanksgiving' to the whole human family. The first Convocation in 1981 heard these words from Franz Cardinal Konig, Archbishop of Vienna, a man respected in **world religions** East and West. At the second Convocation in 1984, His Holiness, Tenzin Gyatso, the XIV Dalai Lama, shared these words from the wisdom and depth of the **Tibetan**

Buddhist tradition. The third Convocation in 1989 offered knowledge and insight from two great leaders: the Most Reverend Robert Runcie, Archbishop of Canterbury, and **Sir John Templeton,** founder of the Templeton Prize for Progress in Religion."[213]

In August 2000 an ad appeared in *The Christian Science Monitor* for a book entitled *Worldwide Worship: Prayers, Songs, and Poetry.* It states:

> "The collection begins with prayers drawn from such sources as **Celtic, Native American, Christian, Jewish, and Muslim traditions,** among others....From this rich mixture of prayer, song, and poetry comes a confirmation of the life-affirming **universality of the human spirit.** The universal sphere of worship that is evident when these works are read in relation to one another **bridges the gaps between religions,** cultures, and peoples."

It was published by the **Templeton Foundation Press** and edited by **John Marks Templeton.**

NORMAN VINCENT PEALE

As mentioned earlier, **Norman Vincent Peale** wrote the foreword to one of Templeton's books. Here is another man that needs to be discussed, not only because of his connection to Templeton but because of his close friendship with **Billy Graham.** Graham and Peale had a friendship of about 35 or 40 years. In 1957 at the Madison Square Garden Crusade **Graham had Peale on the platform with him.**[214] In fact, Graham said that Peale was very supportive of his meetings, but there's probably a reason why. Almost 400 decision cards were turned over to Peale for follow-up and nearly 100 of these people later joined his church. No other church had received as many cards as Peale did.[215] In fact, "Peale's church received more cards (373) than **ALL** of the 14 Conservative Baptist churches **COMBINED** (311)."[216]

According to *A Prophet with Honor,* we find that there were 55,000 recorded decisions for Christ during this crusade.[217] With 1700 churches participating,[218] that's an average of 32 cards per church. Peale got **more than 11 times** that amount!! Interesting!

In 1960 Graham invited Peale to address a group of evangelical leaders in Switzerland.[219]

Peale, of course, was a New Ager, a Shriner, a 33° Mason, and Knight Templar.[220] He had already been a Mason for over 30 years and had also been the Grand Chaplain of the Grand Lodge of New

York for several years[221] **before** he sat on the platform with Graham. Peale boasts: "My grandfather was a Mason for 50 years, my father for 50 years, and I have been a Mason for 60 years. This means that my tie with Freemasonry extends back to 1869 when my grandfather joined the Masons....I am proud of my involvement."[222]

"To me, Freemasonry is one form of dedication to God and service to humanity. I am proud to walk in fraternal fellowship with my Brethren,"[223] says Peale.

"In 1973, Dr. Peale was awarded the Gourgas Medal [a Masonic award], the highest honor bestowed by the Northern Jurisdiction, and in 1987 received the Grand Cross from the Southern Jurisdiction."[224]

One article appearing in the Masonic magazine, *The Scottish Rite Journal,* in September 1995, was written by Ruth Stafford Peale, Norman's wife. She wrote: "Being a Freemason was an important part of the life of Norman Vincent Peale, and the Scottish Rite meant a great deal to him. He passed away on December 24, 1993, but I am keeping his message flowing out through both Peale Center and *Guideposts* magazine."[225] (For more information on Masonry, their beliefs, and symbolism, please see the following books: *Hidden Secrets of Masonry; Hidden Secrets of the Eastern Star; Mormonism, Masonry, and Godhood;* and *Masonic and Occult Symbols Illustrated.)*

PEALE'S RESPONSE TO OCCULT LETTERS

Not only was Peale a Mason, but he had endorsed the ungodly **channeled messages** called *The Jesus Letters* written by Jane Palzere and Anna Brown. In an article titled "Psychic Records Letters from Jesus" we are told:

> "Part-time Newington secretary Jane Palzere said each of the messages in the book—entitled *'The Jesus Letters'*—was written by her hand through the **psychic phenomenon** known as inspirational writing [automatic-writing].
>
> "The amazing **holy letters** were written one each day over a two-year period that began on a morning in 1978. She said the **letters were dictated by a 'nonliving spirit'** who identified Himself through her pen as Jesus Christ.
>
> "The first of the divine letters was written after an **eerie** experience that unfolded as she sat at her desk writing.
>
> "'I was holding a pen and the pen was knocked from my hand,' she explained. 'My hand went numb. At first, I thought I was having a stroke.'

"She said she picked up the pen, but it was again knocked from her hand.

"'"It happened two or three times before a sentence appeared on the paper. It read: "You are going to be the channel for the writing of a book." Then (the pen) put down the words, "Love Jesus."

"'"The next message was that there is a comma after the word "Love."

"'"At that point, I realized that Jesus was a signature!'...

"For the next two years, Mrs. Palzere was totally wrapped in a labor of love and trust. Each day, the **spirit communicating** with her dictated a new and revealing message. The result was *'The Jesus Letters,'* now available through direct mail....

"One message instructed her to collaborate with another person on publication of the letters. She quickly enlisted the help of **Anna Brown, a woman she had met while taking a course in ESP.**"[226]

The "Jesus" of *The Jesus Letters* claims that heaven is for all and that every person (including the heathen) has Christ within. The authors (one of whom is a Theosophist) insist that there are many "Christs." Of course, the book also endorses spirit mediums and channelers.[227]

What was Peale's response to this **occult** book? He wrote: *"What a wonderful gift to all of us from you is your book, THE JESUS LETTERS.... You will bless many by this truly inspired book.*"[228] He adds: "It little matters if these writings come from Jesus of Nazareth or Jesus of Jane [Palzere], they are all the same consciousness and that consciousness is God. I am part of God, and Jane and Anna are part of that same God."[229]

Another book is called *Explore Your Psychic World.* A New Age brochure describes this book as

"one of the most thorough overviews of the **psychic** aspects of life in print today. **It examines auras, astral travel, communication with discarnates, clairvoyance, possession, psychic attack, and dreams.** When first published, it was **hailed by Norman Vincent Peale as 'a great piece of work.'**"[230]

In *Psychic* magazine Peale, speaking of the occultist Kreskin, stated: "All he's doing is dramatizing what I've been preaching in my writing for years."[231]

I guess Peale had a penchant for endorsing occultic books dealing with spirit communication. Another book, *The Dead Are Alive! They Can and Do Communicate with You,* was also promoted by Peale.[232] He gushed: "A masterpiece!...I hope it will be widely read."[233]

"The book's author is Harold Sherman, a **psychic and spirit medium** who also wrote a companion book, *You Live After Death.*"[234]

The Bible clearly warns us in Deuteronomy 18:10-12:

> "There shall not be found among you any one that maketh his son or his daughter to pass through the fire, or that useth divination, or an observer of times, or an enchanter, or a witch, Or a charmer, or a **consulter with familiar spirits** [a psychic, channeler, or medium], or a wizard, **or a necromancer** [one who speaks with the dead]. For **all** that do these things are **an abomination** unto the Lord...."

Dr. Bernie Siegel also has a spirit guide that supposedly communicates with him. In one of his books, *Love, Medicine and Miracles,* he tells how George (his spirit guide) appeared to him. This book also promotes and deals extensively with **visualization, hypnosis, and meditation.** One researcher reminds us that "the development of the imagination through 'visualization' exercises is one of the most ancient and widely used **occult** techniques for expanding the mind and opening up the psyche to new (and forbidden) areas of consciousness."[235] (For more information on visualization see my article "What Is Visualization?" For more information on hypnosis, see my booklet "Hypnosis: Cure or Curse?") Siegel writes: "Beliefs that lean heavily on guilt, original sin, and predestination are of little use for healing."[236] This obviously means that Christianity is "of little use for healing."

Siegel also states: "I think of God as the same potential healing **force**—an intelligent, loving energy or light—in **each** person's life."[237]

Would you believe that this book was also **endorsed by Norman Vincent Peale?**[238]

CHRIST IS ONE OF MANY WAYS

Peale himself writes: "Who is God?...God is vitality. God is life. God is energy. **As you breathe God in, as you visualize His energy,** you will be reenergized! You will live longer, you will live better, you will have greater health, you will have dynamic energy."[239]

Since Peale's "God" is equated with energy, it's no wonder that he "denied the virgin birth, deity, resurrection and vicarious satisfaction of Jesus Christ. He did not believe that Jesus Christ is the only way to heaven."[240]

Yet another book endorsed by Peale is *Healing Energies of Music.* Peale says: "I am sure your book will indeed be a blessing to all who read it."[241] This book is sold through Quest Books, which is the Theosophical Publishing House.[242] Theosophy is, according to the *Masonic Quiz Book,* a **"MYSTIC CULT."**[243] It is also a religious system that stresses **OCCULT** practices and theories such as **CLAIRVOYANCE, TELEPATHY,**[244] **EVOLUTION, KARMA, REINCARNATION,**[245] **MYSTICISM, AND SPIRITUALISM.**[246] It is also claimed to be a **"TECHNIQUE FOR ACHIEVING SALVATION"**[247] and "used for the invocation of the angels."[248]

The Theosophical Society was founded on October 20, 1875,[249] by the medium,[250] mystic,[251] occultist,[252] and Satanist,[253] Madame Helena Petrovna Blavatsky.[254] "According to *The Theosophical Glossary* (by H. P. Blavatsky), 'its avowed object was at first the specific investigation of psychic or so-called "spiritualistic" phenomena....'"[255] The Theosophical Society's publication was called *Lucifer.*[256]

They sell books by such New Age and occult authors as: Annie Besant, Helena Petrovna Blavatsky, Don G. Campbell, the Dalai Lama, Evelyn Eaton, Serge King, Jack Kornfield, Dolores Krieger, D. Scott Rogo, Dane Rudhyar, J. Krishnamurti, Ken Wilber, and Huston Smith,[257] yet Peale endorses a book sold through this organization.

On a 1984 Phil Donahue program, Peale said: "It's not necessary to be born again. You have your way to God: I have mine. I found eternal peace in a Shinto shrine....**Christ is *one* of the ways.** God is everywhere."[258]

Shintoism is a religion of Japan which believes in many gods and goddesses as well as mysticism.[259] It is a religion of ancestor worship.[260] "Stones and Rocks are also objects of veneration in Shinto."[261]

Of course, I guess a statement like this wouldn't really bother Billy Graham. You see, in **1956** (which was a year **prior** to the New York Madison campaign), **Graham** went to Japan and "**demanded** that both conservatives and modernistic **pro-Shinto believers** unite for the purpose of evangelism. Kagawa, a noted Japanese liberal and **opponent of Bible truth,** appeared on the platform with Graham."[262] Toyohiko Kagawa, by the way, was also a **Socialist**[263] and a pacifist.[264]

Returning to Peale, we find that he was the main speaker at a Mormon president's birthday festivity in 1980 and praised Mormon leaders.[265] He called Mormon President, Spencer W. Kimball, "a great man of God and a true prophet of Jesus Christ."[266] (For information on Mormonism please see my book *Mormonism, Masonry, and Godhood.*)

Even though Peale denied Christ's virgin birth, deity, and resurrection,[267] Graham said on December 6, 1966, at a National Council of Churches luncheon, "I don't know anyone who has done more for the kingdom of God than Norman and Ruth Peale, or have meant any more in my life—the encouragement they have given me."[268]

Over 30 years later (and after Peale had died), Graham was **still** praising him.[269] In his 1997 autobiography he noted: "...Dr. Peale was warmly supportive of the meetings [at Madison Square Garden in 1957]. Although our emphasis in preaching differed, **I found him a deeply committed believer** with a genuine concern that men and women give their lives to Christ."[270] Oh, by the way, **Graham received $75,000 from John D. Rockefeller, Jr. for this 1957 Crusade.**[271] Others who gave large sums of money and/or support for this crusade were the Vanderbilts, Whitneys, Goulds, Dodges, and Phelpses.[272]

I might also add that by this time (1957),

> "the staff of the Billy Graham Association in Minneapolis (headquarters) had grown to 125 persons and the rented space could not handle any more expansion. It was then that Graham was offered the purchase of **STANDARD OIL COMPANY'S** office building in Minneapolis (a *Rockefeller* business)."[273] [Boldface and caps in the original; italics added.]

Also, Billy Graham's *Christianity Today* magazine "has been able to get millions of dollars from foundations...."[274] Very interesting!

It is true that Peale **claims** to have accepted Jesus Christ as his personal Savior (at least according to the June 21, 1993 issue of *Christianity Today,* which was founded by Billy Graham), but Peale quickly adds: "...I am absolutely and thoroughly convinced that **it is my mission never to use this language** in trying to communicate with the audience that God has given me."[275] We must remember, however, that **Peale has redefined these words to fit his own occultic, New Thought ideas.** For instance, Peale said in an interview with *Modern Maturity* that Christ was "the nearest thing to God...."[276] The Bible, on the other hand, teaches that Christ **is** God. Peale teaches that "Christ is **one** of the ways"[277] but Christ said that He was the **only** way: "I am the way, the truth, and the life: no man cometh unto the Father, **but by Me"** (John 14:6). Peale said: "It's not necessary to be born again,"[278] but Jesus declared: "Except a man be born again, he cannot see the kingdom of God....Ye **must** be born again" (John 3:3, 7). Peale denies Christ's virgin birth,[279] but Matthew 1:23 says that "a virgin shall be with child, and shall bring forth a son, and they shall call His name Emmanuel, which being interpreted is, God with us." Peale denies Christ's resurrection, but I Corinthians 15:14 reveals: "And if Christ be not risen, then is our preaching vain, and your faith is also vain." I Corinthians 15:17 reiterates: "And if Christ be not raised, your faith is vain; ye are yet in your sins." Therefore, if Peale denies Christ's resurrection, then he is not saved and still in his sins, according to the Bible.

Belief in the virgin birth of Christ and His resurrection are vital ingredients in our salvation. If Christ was just another human being (regardless of how perfect He may have been), His sacrifice on the cross would have been insufficient for salvation. Also, if Christ did not resurrect from the dead, then our "faith is vain," as Paul reminds us.

MODERNIST'S DICTIONARY

David Cloud comments:

> "The problem was that Peale's Jesus was not the Jesus of the Bible, but the Jesus of his own creation. Peale's Jesus was a Jesus that did not condemn sin; a Jesus that was not born of a virgin; a Jesus that was not the eternal God; a Jesus that did not die and shed His blood for man's sin.
>
> **"Peale used the fundamentalist's vocabulary, but he used the modernist's dictionary.** This is why so many were deceived by the man. Peale's god was not the God of the Bible, but the god of self. His faith was not faith in the Jesus Christ of the Bible, but faith in faith. His gospel was not the gospel of repentance from sin and faith in the blood of Jesus Christ, but a gospel of self-esteem, self-help, and self-recovery."[280]

I ask: How can someone who endorses **channeled** and occultic materials, denies Christ's virgin birth, deity, and resurrection, who says that he "found eternal peace in a Shinto shrine" and that **"Christ is *one* of the ways"** be considered a "deeply committed believer"? There is not only a problem with Norman Vincent Peale but also with Billy Graham!! Remember, Peale is the man who received almost 400 decision cards from the Billy Graham crusade![281] Both Graham and Peale seem to have a mutual benefit from their friendship. Graham sends "converts" to Peale's church but then Peale endorsed a biography for Graham.[282] However, the Bible warns in James 4:4: "[K]now ye not that the friendship of the world is enmity with God? whosoever therefore will be a friend of the world is the enemy of God."

How could anyone who is truly concerned about souls being saved even think of sending a person to such a church as Peale's? Of course, Peale is just one of many liberals who has been bragged up and promoted by Graham.

WHO GETS THE DECISION CARDS?

As far back as **1955** Dr. James E. Bennet and Rev. Jack Wyrtzen met with Billy Graham. Graham told them "that if some minister, who was a **modernist,** sent 50 of his people to Graham's meetings, and they were saved, he (Billy) would not tell them not to return to that modernistic church, because it would be unfair to the pastor!"[283]

The Bible says that we are to "have **no fellowship** with the unfruitful works of darkness, **but rather reprove them"** (Ephesians 5:11). We are not to invite them on our platforms and praise them as "deeply committed believers" when they don't even believe (much less obey) the Bible.

A letter from the Billy Graham Evangelistic Association (written by W. H. Martindale) dated February 29, **1968** stated: "Mr. Graham, under no conditions, suggests affiliating with those who are, in their doctrines, contrary to the Scriptures."[284] Yet **11 years prior** to this letter, Graham had had Norman Vincent Peale on his platform. Peale had written 46 books, the first one published in 1937.[285] His book, *The Power of Positive Thinking,* had already been in print for several years so his viewpoint was well-known.[286]

It should also be mentioned that the committee for the **1957** New York Crusade was made up of about 120 modernists and unbelievers compared to about 20 fundamentalists. The Executive Committee was comprised of about 15 modernists and only 5 fundamentalists.[287] Many of those on the committees denied the virgin birth, bodily resurrection of Christ, a literal heaven and a literal hell, the inspiration of Scripture, etc. The sad part is that those who went forward at this meeting were turned over to these modernist churches. After all, Graham usually only gives decision cards to those who participate in his meetings. (One exception was in the 1970s when Graham turned over decision cards to a Catholic diocese who had no official involvement in the crusade.[288]) Therefore, all the fundamentalists who do not participate do not get any of the names. In other words, Graham's crusades only end up helping the liberal and unscriptural churches to prosper and grow. Can this be pleasing to God?

Graeme Keith, chairman of the Carolinas Billy Graham Crusade Committee, is quoted in the *Charlotte Observer* (March 1, 1996) as saying:

> "'We have Jewish, Catholic, Protestant and **other** denominations represented on the committee....Our goal is to make it

the finest crusade Dr. Graham has ever conducted.' Graham has even gone further afield on occasion. At his **1966** World Congress on Evangelism in Berlin, Ethiopian Emperor Haile Selassie, who is head of the Coptic Orthodox Church, was featured. The Coptic Church is a blend of Christianity, Judaism, **animism and paganism.**"[289]

I have a copy of a letter that the Billy Graham Evangelistic Association sent to an inquirer in **1968.** Rev. W. H. Martindale, writing for Billy Graham, stated:

> "There are many aspects of the Christian life that Mr. Graham does not touch upon because he does not believe that they are the duty and responsibility of the evangelist. Mr. Graham believes that **we are saved through the blood of Christ,** <u>however</u>, **this aspect of Christian doctrine he does not emphasize in his messages.** This is the **duty and prerogative of the pastors.** Every effort is made to see that the inquirers are oriented in a Bible preaching church."[290]

The last sentence simply **IS NOT TRUE!** The inquirers **ARE NOT** sent to Bible-believing churches in **most** cases. "Cases are documented to show that some ministers have actually gone forward at the invitation and then into the counselor's room and their cards have been sent to **liberal churches** in their community which they, the ministers, have opposed from their own pulpits."[291] For example, in Graham's **1952** Pittsburgh crusade, the *Pittsburgh Sun-Telegraph* reported that Graham said:

> *"Many of the people who reach a decision for Christ at our meetings have joined the Catholic Church and we have received commendations from Catholic publications for the revived interest in their Church following our campaigns. This happened both in Boston and Washington. After all, one of our prime purposes is to help the churches in a community. If after we move on, the locl* (sic) *churches do not feel the efforts of these meetings in increased membership and attendance, then our crusade would have to be considered a failure."*[292] [Emphasis in the original.]

Did you notice that Graham was only interested in a church's increased membership—but nothing was said about a person receiving Christ as his or her personal Lord and Savior. **This** is what is important—not church membership! Church membership could increase a 1000-fold but if people are not being saved, then all is in vain.

Graham also gave a boost to the Catholic Church (in **1952)** when he added that he *"hoped to hear Bishop Fulton J. Sheen at one of the* *masses at St. Paul's Cathedral tomorrow."*[293] [Emphasis in the original.]

> "In **1968,** Graham was in a meeting in San Antonio, Texas. He said that the Roman Church had given 'tremendous cooperation' in areas where he had held crusades. He added, 'A great part of our support today comes from Catholics. **We never hold a crusade without priests and nuns being much in evidence in the audience.'"**[294]

By 1973 nuns were singing in the choir at Graham's crusades.[295]

Continuing on with Graham's ecumenical outlook, the June 10, 1966 issue of *Time* said that volunteers "will tactfully receive those stepping forward to make a decision for Christ, [and] steer them to the nearest **church of their chosen denomination...."**[296]

In Poland in 1978, "Graham taught nuns and priests how to evangelize. A **picture** taken at the famous Polish Shrine of the Black Madonna **shows Graham welcoming pilgrims to the worship of their Virgin."**[297]

NO ASSURANCE OF SALVATION

In 1983, *The Florida Catholic* reported that 600 people were turned over to the Catholic Church from the Orlando crusade.[298] "On the evening of June 9, 1982, the names of 2100 inquirers were given to priests at Pope John XXIII Seminary in Weston, Massachusetts."[299] During the June 1992 Crusade in Philadelphia,

> "[a]pproximately 1,200 Catholics in the Archdiocese and about 700 Catholics from elsewhere took steps...in response to Dr. Graham's 'altar calls.' The individuals...were referred to about 250 parishes, said sister Josephine Kase, I. H. M., Assistant Director of the Archdiocesan Office for Ecumenical and Interreligious Affairs."[300]

In 1987 at the Denver crusade, 500 individuals were referred to the St. Thomas Moore Roman Catholic Church from just one service![301] One Catholic who went forward at this meeting didn't know how to express his feelings but the Catholic counselor, Donald Willette, was there to help out. He said: "Catholics have trouble with the expression 'Born again.'...I try to help people understand what this experience means, **in light of the teaching of the [Catholic] church."**[302] So, even if Graham were definitely preaching the true Gospel of Christ, by allowing his sermon to be "reinterpreted" by the counselors, would negate all the good that would have been done. The "reinterpretation" is done in light of the Catholic Church's teaching—not in accordance with the Scriptures.

> "A Catholic nun, Macrina Scott, director of the Catholic Biblical School in Denver, says she trained about 80 counselors and Bible teachers to assist Billy Graham's Rocky Mountain Crusade last July [1987]."[303]

> "By September 1992, the **Catholic diocese** of Portland, Oregon, had set a goal to **supply 6,000 of the 10,000 counselors needed for the Graham crusade.** All Catholics responding to the altar call were channeled to Catholic churches."[304]

Surprisingly, around 1993 a retired missionary wrote to Graham's organization asking if he was sending new converts back to the Catholic Church. T. W. Wilson (who died on May 25, 2001[305]), a member of the Graham team, responded: "I do not know where you got your information—but **I'm sure you have been misinformed."** Isn't it amazing how they are still trying to conceal this plain fact?

"At the 1996 Charlotte Crusade held by Evangelist Billy Graham, the decision cards of 1700 Catholic responders to his invitation to commit their lives to Christ were given to the local Catholic Diocese for follow up."[306]

The Catholic priests do not believe in salvation by faith. They teach that **salvation is obtained through infant baptism.** "Catholic teaching states that anyone who claims to have the assurance of salvation through God's power or mercy has committed the sin of presumption...."[307] According to the Catholic paper, *Our Sunday Visitor,* we are told that "Presumption is a sin against hope. It is a rash confidence of obtaining eternal salvation....**A person who says that he or she is assured of salvation is presuming...."**[308] This is in direct contradiction to God's Word: "These things have I written unto you that believe on the name of the Son of God; that **ye may know that ye have eternal life,** and that ye may believe on the name of the Son of God" (I John 5:13). I John 2:5 says: "But whoso keepeth His word, in Him verily is the love of God perfected: **hereby know we that we are in Him."**

"Converts" are also turned over to the Jewish synagogues. The Rabbis do not believe in Jesus. Other inquirers are sent back to the liberal Protestant ministers (like New Ager and Mason, Norman Vincent Peale) who deny the atonement of Jesus Christ and the literal meaning of the Scriptures.

Since the Bible clearly teaches that we are only saved through the blood of Christ and His atonement and Graham **"does not** emphasize" this doctrine, how many of these inquirers are **actually** being saved? Notice that Martindale also says that this doctrine (as well as others) is the **prerogative** of the pastors, yet these individuals are not being sent back to churches (in most cases) where the pastor, priest, or rabbi will teach this doctrine. This is spiritual suicide for these people.

WE BECOME CHRIST?

Sounding blasphemous to me, **Graham is quoting as saying: "I stand at the door of the kingdom of Heaven and say, Come in.** And when they come in, they go by way of their particular church."[309]

> "The **June 19, 1969,** issue of the *New York Times* contained a half-page article on Graham follow-up techniques: 'After inquirers are dealt with by "counselors" and cards on each are filled out, a "Co-Labor Corps" sits at long tables until midnight each night counting and sorting the cards and licking envelopes that will go out in the morning mail to ministers of about 1,000 churches.
>
> "'The "Corps" sifts through maps and phone books, finding the church nearest the addresses on the cards, **regardless of whether or not they are liberal,** conservative, Protestant, Catholic or Jewish....'"[310]

When the new convert goes to a **liberal** church (whether it be Catholic, Protestant, or Jewish), he will not hear the Word of God preached. In fact, he will often hear the Bible denounced as "fairy tales," or "myths." For example, in the *Catechism of the Catholic Church* we find: "The account of the fall in *Genesis* 3 uses **figurative language,** but affirms a primeval event, a deed that took place at *the beginning of the history of man.*"[311] "The **parable** of the poor man Lazarus and the words of Christ on the cross to the good thief, as well as other New Testament texts speak of a final destiny of the soul—a destiny which can be different for some and for others."

This *Catechism* also teaches that we are gods! It states: "For the Son of God became man so that **we might become God."** "The only-begotten Son of God, wanting to make us sharers in his divinity, assumed our nature, so that he, made man, might **make men gods."**[312] "Marvel and rejoice: **we have become Christ."**[313] "...through the anointing of his Spirit who flows from the head to the members, **he makes us other 'Christs.'**[314] "So then you who have become sharers in Christ **are appropriately called 'Christs.'"**[315]

Yet, in **"1963** Billy Graham said that he had a Roman Catholic bishop stand beside him and bless the 'converts' as they came forward in Sao Paulo, Brazil."[316] In 1979 almost 3,500 decision cards were turned over to the Catholic Church.[317] In another instance,

> "[t]he Graham Organization and his co-operating churches in the San Francisco Crusade appointed Dr. Farrah to follow up the 'converts' and report on the same. He reported that of over 1,300 Catholics who came forward, 'practically all remained Catholic, continued to pray to Mary, went to Mass and confessed to the priest.'"[318]

In fact, the counselors are specifically warned: "There is to be no proselytizing...."[319] At the Quebec crusade in 1990 it was "made clear to all staff and volunteers [that] there is to be no proselytizing...(and) counselling offered to those who come forward in response to Graham's invitation will not include **any** criticism of the church a person may be attending."[320] What if the person is a Mormon or a New Ager or a witch or a Satanist? This may sound far-fetched but it isn't. Are they to return to their church or coven? After all, there will be **no** "criticism of the church a person may be attending."

> "A disturbed Roman Catholic wrote Graham about some of the changes going on in the Catholic Church. In his answer, Graham wrote, 'Above all, **don't pull out of the church! Stay in it,** stay close to the Lord, and use these experiences as an opportunity to help your church be what God intends and what the world needs.'...This was published in his newspaper column, 'My Answer.'"[321]

Incidentally, it was through Billy Graham's intervention that former President Reagan set up an ambassador to the Vatican.[322] He has been the linking agent from the White House to Rome.[323] Graham wrote:

> "Reagan was the first American President to appoint a full ambassador to the Vatican. Before he made that appointment, he asked my view. I told him I thought it would probably be a good thing—in spite of a number of potential problems concerning the separation of church and state—and wrote an extended confidential letter outlining my reasons. Among other things, I told him I did not think it necessarily violated the separation of church and state. For whatever reasons, Mr. Reagan went ahead with the plan. Later my letter was leaked to the press. It caused some consternation among my Baptist friends."[324]

There are a number of churches in which a new convert may be told that there is no heaven to gain and no hell to shun. The new convert may be led into occultic practices (such as those promoted by Norman Vincent Peale). He could hear a speaker such as Faye Wattleton who was a past president of Planned Parenthood Federation of America when she spoke at Peale's church several years ago (although Peale was no longer head of the Marble Collegiate Church at that time).[325] Or, the new convert could join the Gays/lesbians in Fellowship at the Marble Collegiate Church.[326]

If the new convert was a Jewish person, he or she would be told to return to the synagogue. However, a new convert who returns to the Jewish synagogue will most likely be told that Jesus is not the Messiah. The Jewish *Talmud* teaches "that Mary, the Mother of Jesus Christ, was a whore and an adulteress who bore Jesus by a Roman soldier named Pandera."[327] According to the "uncensored" text of the Talmud we find that Jesus' mother (called Miriam) had sex with many men.[328] The *Talmud* also teaches that "Jesus is now burning in hot excrement in Hell!"[329] Matthew 23:15 states: "Woe unto you, scribes and Pharisees, hypocrites! for ye compass sea and land to make one proselyte, and when he is made, **ye make him twofold more the child of hell than yourselves."**

The Bible also clearly tells us: **"Whosoever denieth the Son [Jesus], the same hath not the Father:** but he that acknowledgeth the Son hath the Father also" (I John 2:23).

THE WOLF SCATTERS

The list could go on and on, yet these liberal churches are the main churches that benefit from Graham's crusades. In Graham's own autobiography he tells how Willis Haymaker joined the Graham team in **1950.** Haymaker "would also **call on the local Catholic bishop** or other clerics to acquaint them with Crusade plans and invite them to the meetings; they would usually appoint a priest to attend and report back. This was years before Vatican II's openness to Protestants, but **we were concerned to let the Catholic bishops see that my goal was not to get people to leave their church...."**[330]

Billy bragged how Haymaker was the one

> "who urged us to drop the word *Campaign* in favor of *Crusade*. The word *Campaign*, Willis pointed out, had been used for many years by evangelists, and was associated in the public mind with outmoded (or even sensationalist) ways of doing things. A new word was needed, he felt, and we agreed on *Crusade.*"[331] [Italics in the original.]

John Christian comments:

> "Billy forgot to mention, the reason why genuine Christian evangelists previously had shunned using the word 'Crusade' in their ministries, was that the term previously applied to the eight military expeditions organized from the 11th Century to the 13th, under the banner of the pagan Cross of Roman

> Catholicism, for the recovery of the Holy Land from the hands of the Saracens."[332]

In **1957** Graham branded the Catholic gospel as "a stench in the nostrils of God,"[333] yet Graham was quoted by several newspapers as having explicitly said **(as early as 1956)** that "we'll send them to their own churches—Roman Catholic, Protestant or Jewish....The rest will be up to God."[334] If Graham truly felt that the Catholic Church was a "stench in the nostrils of God," why would he send people back to this church? This would be equivalent to me giving someone arsenic and then saying that it's up to God to let him live. Certainly God can work in spite of circumstances, but we are also accountable for what we do. God never wants the lambs sent to the wolves.

The Bible tells the shepherd to care for the flock, not to leave them defenseless against vicious attacks. Paul warned that wolves would enter in and the church was to be on guard and try to resist this onslaught. They were not to send the new converts to the wolves but to protect them from the wolves.

> "Take heed therefore unto yourselves, and to all the flock, over the which the Holy Ghost hath made you overseers, to feed the church of God, which He hath purchased with His own blood. For I know this, that after my departing shall grievous wolves enter in among you, **not sparing the flock.** Also of your own selves shall men arise, speaking perverse things, to draw away disciples after them. Therefore watch, and remember, that by the space of three years I ceased not to warn every one night and day with tears" (Acts 20:28-31).

Jesus said: "I am the good shepherd: the good shepherd giveth His life for the sheep. But he that is an hireling, and not the shepherd, whose own the sheep are not, seeth the wolf coming, and leaveth the sheep, and fleeth: and the wolf catcheth them, and scattereth the sheep" (John 10:11-12).

When Paul preached in Ephesus and throughout Asia, he **never** sent his converts back to their pagan temples. He told them to **turn away** from such vain practices as idolatry. He didn't say, "I'll send the converts back to their pagan worship. The rest is up to God." **NO!** Paul told them to worship God and Him alone and to leave their pagan rituals behind them, not to return to them.

One minister was talking to my mother about the ecumenical movement and trying to justify it. He said that if her home were on fire and a Satanist rescued her child, she wouldn't care that the rescuer could be a Satanist. That is true—to a point. I wouldn't care if a Satanist rescued my child, but I certainly would be greatly concerned and worried if that Satanist took my child and raised him to be a

Satanist. There is a big difference being rescued by a Satanist and being trained and indoctrinated by him. Some individuals were saved through unbelievers or backsliders. Some have been convicted of sin while in a bar, but once the person is saved, then he or she needs to get into a Bible-believing church. It is almost impossible for a convert to grow in grace without proper spiritual teaching. An individual may be truly saved at a Billy Graham crusade but if that person is sent to an ungodly church (and many are), it won't take long for the person to wither and die spiritually or for his or her spiritual growth to be greatly hindered.

HENRY LUCE

Another one of Graham's friends is **Henry Luce.** One day in 1950 while Graham was staying at the governor's mansion in South Carolina with Governor **Strom Thurmond,**[335] a 33° Mason, he received a call saying that Henry Luce wanted to come and spend a few days with him. According to Billy, he said that it appears as though **Bernard Baruch** was reading his sermons out of a newspaper which carried them, after which he contacted Henry Luce.[336] Luce had already been carrying articles about Graham in his magazines *Time* and *Life.*[337] After he heard Graham, he was even more supportive of Graham's ministry and did a feature article for *Life.*[338] Graham said that an "enduring friendship" was born after meeting Luce.[339]

Luce and Graham were playing golf together at the Biltmore Country Club in Phoenix as far back as 1953.[340] It was here that Mrs. Davis introduced Graham to her son-in-law, Ronald Reagan.[341]

Who was Henry Luce, the man who gave magazine space to promote Graham?

Luce's magazines included *People, Life, Fortune, Money,* and *Sports Illustrated.* His board of directors included several members of the **Council on Foreign Relations** (CFR).[342]

> "As far back as 1943, Henry Luce had suggested to his editors that the main function of any future world organization (Do you suppose he knew that the United Nations would be formed just years later?) should be 'to search out, to extemporize, to test, to articulate the common law of mankind.' He approved of a 'world order' which could be found in the concept of **'natural law.'** That is, man-made law outside of the laws of God."[343] [Emphasis in the original.]

Luce spoke before the Connecticut Bar Association in 1956 where he said:

"'If rulers feel they must appear lawful then to an extent they must be lawful...the challenge to be lawful is the most effective challenge at the bar of **world** opinion.' Then he emphasized the need for repeal of the Connally Amendment which limited participation in the **World Court.** He pursued the destruction of American sovereignty with the words: **'World law** can grow only...through the accretion of precedent and example. To the extent that we set the example we shall have added to the precedents which help **extend world order** under the rule of law.'"[344] [Emphasis in the original.]

Fortune and the *Journal of the American Bar Association* reprinted Luce's speech which helped found the **World Peace Through Law** movement. Then in September 1965 the World Peace Through Law conference was held and Luce

"prophesied that world government (the New World Order) might become fact....**'The world we are determined to have** is a world characterized by the **rule of law...**which binds the pride of nations to the common good and which protects the individual from the arrogance of governments....' (That is—the arrogance of a sovereign nation with a sovereign constitution like that of the United States of America!)"[345] [Emphasis in the original.]

The same year in which he spoke to the Connecticut Bar Association (1956), **Luce put John D. Rockefeller on the cover of *Time*** and called the feature story "The Good Man." He called Rockefeller "an authentic American hero."[346]

"*Time* first covered the abortion issue in 1965 with an openly sympathetic article in the medicine section....By 1967, it had burst out of the closet and declared itself 'unequivocally in favor of the repeal of restrictive abortion laws.' From that day forward, *Time* has remained resolutely in the Planned Parenthood vanguard with the rest of the mega-press."[347]

Henry Luce was a graduate of Yale and belonged to Skull and Bones (Class of 1920),[348] the Council on Foreign Relations,[349] and the Knights of Malta.[350] He was one of the founders of the Aspen Institute for Humanistic Studies which is now called the Aspen Institute.[351] Obviously, the Aspen Institute is a humanistic think tank as well as a New Age/world government organization.[352] They have

"solid ties to the CFR, TLC [Trilateral Commission], and the United Nations through its membership. This group's financial supporters include the Rockefellers, the Carnegie Corporation, the Ford Foundation, and others. Its trustees include Robert McNamara and Henry Kissinger. In an interview, Joseph Slater, then president of Aspen Institute, proposed 'that there be a council of wise persons that can figure out how to restructure national government and achieve economic and social values.'"[353]

Luce also belonged to the World Brotherhood[354] (which changed its name to the Conference on World Tensions in 1961[355]).

> "According to an official publication, World Brotherhood was 'founded in 1950 at a conference at UNESCO House in Paris' and 'evolved from the educational programs of the National Conference of Christians and Jews, which has been serving the cause of brotherhood in the United States and Canada since 1928.' Its supporters and members included President Eisenhower, **John Foster Dulles,** Allen W. Dulles (ex-Central Intelligence Agency chief), **Henry R. Luce** (owner of *Time* and *Life*), Herbert H. Lehman, Paul G. Hoffman, George Meany, Norman Thomas, Mrs. Eleanor Roosevelt, John F. Kennedy, John J. McCloy, Adlai Stevenson, Chief Justice Warren, ex-Prime Minister John Diefenbaker of Canada and Canada's liquor multimillionaire Samuel Bronfman, Konrad Adenauer (German ex-Chancellor), Paul-Henri Spaak (ex-NATO Secretary General), Trygve Lie (ex-UN Secretary General), Paul Reynaud (French ex-Prime Minister), Marcus Wallenberg (Swedish Bank President whose family at one time controlled the Nobel Prize awards), Prince Bernhard of the Netherlands and ex-head of the Bilderberg Group, Madame Pandit and Dr. S. S. Radhakrishnan of India, the Shah of Iran, Carlos P. Romulo of the Philippines and Sir Zafrulla Khan of the International Court of Justice (and former President of the UN General Assembly), movie mogul Spyros Skouras of the USA, the late Prime Minister of Canada Lester B. Pearson, ex-External Affairs Minister of Canada Paul Martin, Lady Barbara Ward Jackson of Britain, Nobel Prize winner Lord Boyd Orr, etc., etc."[356]

One person whom Luce held in "high regard" was **John Foster Dulles.**[357] "The **Federal Council of Churches,** Dulles assured Luce, **supported 'world government** as an ultimate ideal....'"[358] No wonder both Luce and Dulles could belong to the World Brotherhood.

SOCIALIZE

Luce was often considered to be an anti-Communist, yet he was tolerant of the Communist cell group that operated openly at *Time-Life.*[359] He also bitterly opposed those individuals who could possibly fight the Communist subversion in the United States.[360]

> "In the late Fifties, Henry Luce switched from the 'World Government to oppose Communism' line to the 'peaceful coexistence and World Government with Communism' line, and *Life* went back to glorifying the Soviet Union as it had done during World War II. In 1966, Luce took a group of 43 U. S. businessmen behind the Iron Curtain to promote aid and trade with the enemy."[361]

Another organization that Luce was affiliated with was the **Atlantic Union.** This group believed that "regional government is a necessary way (sic) station on the road to total World Government."[362] One author explains:

> "The idea of Atlantic Union had its origin in the fertile brain of an Englishman named **Cecil Rhodes,** whose dream was to see the United States reannexed to the British Empire. To this end he established the Rhodes Foundation, providing for the education in England of bright young Americans.
>
> "In 1939, a Rhodes Scholar named Clarence Streit wrote a book called *Union Now,* which advocated a gradual approach to final world union by way of regional unions, starting with the union between the U. S. and Britain. Committees were set up all over America, and Mr. Streit reported that over two million Americans had signed petitions asking for union with Britain.
>
> "In Streit's own words, **Atlantic Union,** now expanded to include Western Europe, **was the first step towards total world government:** 'It [Union Now—G.A.] proclaimed the **need of world government** and insisted that no country needed this more urgently than the United States.'
>
> "Streit, who has been a close associate of Communists and socialists all his adult life, has no hostility towards collectivism. He said in *Union Now:* 'Democracy not only allows mankind to choose freely between capitalism and collectivism, but it includes Marxist governments.'
>
> "In his pamphlets Streit asks the question: 'Does the rise of socialism in some Western European democracies prevent our federating with them?' He answers with an emphatic 'No!'"[363]

Of course, the Communists themselves

> "had a similar plan which they specified in their 1936 Communist International. Their three-stage plan for world government was:
>
> "1. Socialize the economies of all nations

"2. Bring about federal unions of various groupings of these socialized nations

"3. Amalgamate the regional unions into a world union of socialist states."[364]

Then in 1949 the Atlantic Union Committee was set up and headed by former Supreme Court Justice Owen J. Roberts.[365] Roberts stated that "in joining the Atlantic Union, the U. S. government would have to surrender its rights and powers to coin money, to levy taxes and tariffs, to regulate immigration, to enact citizenship laws, to declare war, and to maintain standing armies."[366]

Almost fifty years ago the *Los Angeles Examiner* proclaimed what effect the Atlantic Union would have on America:

"They [the nations of Western Europe—G.A.] would **impose their socialism in place of our republican self-government,** extract taxes from us as they pleased, draft our men for their armies and our women for their factories, appropriate the bulk of our productive wealth for their own enrichment."[367]

"An Atlantic Union Resolution which would, in effect, repeal the Declaration of Independence, was first introduced in Congress in 1949. It has been reintroduced every year since, but until recently never received much attention—despite its endorsement by such Rockefeller-CFR stalwarts as Richard Nixon, Hubert Humphrey, George McGovern, Dwight Eisenhower, Adlai Stevenson, **John Foster Dulles,** Jacob Javits, William Fulbright, Eugene McCarthy, and Henry Kissinger."[368]

By 1960, "over half of the members of the Atlantic Union Committee [were] also members of the CFR...."[369]

COMMUNISTIC OBJECTIVES

Of course, world government advocates knew **EXACTLY** what they were promoting. One such advocate, George W. Blount, brags:

"Dr. Luther Evans, president of World Federalists, U. S. A. reminds Federalists that they should not be discouraged. He cites the fact that during the past quarter century (since 1945) World Federalism has spawned a goodly number of world law organizations. He lists the following: The Institute for International Order, The Stanley Foundation, the **World Peace Through World Law** of the American Bar Association, the Parliamentarians for Federation of Democratic Nations, **Atlantic Union,** the American Movement for World

Government, the World Association of World Federalists, the International Peace Academy, the World Constitutional Group. Also there are related organizations, the United Nations Association, U. S. A., The Commission to Study the Organization of Peace, **Council on Foreign Relations,** Foreign Policy Association. **ALL THESE WORK TOWARD THE GOAL OF WORLD PEACE UNDER WORLD LAW."**[370]

Not only did Henry Luce belong to the Atlantic Union but he was also a trustee of the **Institute of Pacific Relations (IPR).**[371]

A little background on the IPR is needed at this point. David Allen Rivera explains:

> "In 1925, Lionel Curtis, **established** the **Institute of Pacific Relations** (IPR) in 12 countries, **in order to steer America towards Communism.** The Round Table finger organization was financed by the **Rockefeller Foundation,** the Carnegie Corporation, the Carnegie Endowment for International Peace, and the Ford Foundation. The American branch received funding from Standard Oil, Vacuum Oil, Shell Oil, International General Electric, Bank of America, National City Bank, **Chase National Bank,** International Business Machines, International Telephone and Telegraph, **Time Magazine,** and J. P. Morgan.
>
> "The IPR was led by Professor Owen Lattimore, head of Johns Hopkins University School of Diplomacy, who, during a 1951-52 investigation of the IPR, was identified as a Soviet operative. **The Senate found the group to be 'a vehicle toward Communist objectives.' Men from the IPR (who were all communist or pro-communist) were placed in important teaching positions, and dominated the Asian Affairs section of the State Department.** After a four year battle, their tax exempt status was revoked from 1955-1960.
>
> "Their publications were used by the armed forces, colleges, and close to 1,300 public school systems. They published a magazine called *Amerasia,* whose offices had been raided by the FBI, who found 1,700 secret documents from various government agencies, including the Army and Navy, that were either stolen, or given to them by traitors within the State Department. The Senate Internal Subcommittee concluded that the American policy decision which helped establish Communist control in China (by threatening to cut-off aid to Chiang Kai-shek unless he went communist), was made by IPR officials acting on behalf of the Soviet Union. Besides Lattimore, they also named Laughlin Curry (an Administrative

Assistant to the President, who was identified as a Soviet agent by J. Edgar Hoover), **Alger Hiss,** Joseph Barnes, Philip Jessup, and Harry Dexter White, as **Communist** sympathizers. While he was Assistant Secretary of Treasury, Harry Dexter White provided Russia with the means of printing currency. He became Director of the International Monetary Fund in 1946, but resigned in 1947, when Whittaker Chambers accused him of being pro-communist, which he denied. In November, 1948, after White's death, Whittaker produced five rolls of microfilmed documents, which included eight pages of U. S. military secrets which had been written by White."[372]

Even Carroll Quigley wrote: "The influence of the **Communists in IPR** is well established...."[373] Remember that it was Lionel Curtis who established the IPR.[374] Curtis published a book, *World Order (Civitas Dei),* in 1938.[375] "This 985-page volume will be called the foundation of all thought on the design of a new order. It examines human society and concludes that a working system must mean the organization of all human society into one commonwealth."[376]

The Institute of Pacific Relations also published P. E. Corbett's *Post-War Worlds* in 1942 in which was stated the following:

> "A **world association** binding together and coordinating regional groupings of states **may evolve toward one universal federal government,** as in the past loose confederations have grown into federal unions. Such evolution will bring with it increasing security and peace and social progress. **World government is the ultimate aim,** but there is more chance of attaining it by gradual development....First it must be recognized that the law of nations takes precedence over national law....There is much to be said for constituting a Supreme World Court....**Nationalism threatens to be a continuing obstacle to general progress....**it may be impossible to 'indict a whole people,' but quite possible to indict and to coerce, when necessary, its leaders....Steps will need to be taken to stop the preaching of the supremacy of the state. The process will have to be assisted by the deletion of the nationalistic material employed in educational textbooks and its replacement by material explaining the benefits of wider association....Men engaged in practical affairs, as well as many theorists, are looking to something in the nature of a federal organization with a common police, a supreme court, a legislative and governing body, and common economic agencies for advice and control....An Economic and Financial Organization, embracing Trade, Development, and Migration Commissions, and a Central Bank. The function of these institutions...would be to regulate the production and distribution of raw materials

and food, control the flow of interregional investment and migration, etc."[377]

So the Institute of Pacific Relations is just one of the organizations that Henry Luce was associated with. It should also be noted that **Luce was a strong supporter of the United Nations** (UN) even after convicted Communist Alger Hiss' role in the establishment of the UN was revealed.[378] (Hiss was the first secretary-general of the UN.[379])

Luce was also carrying on a relationship with Mary Bancroft while he was married to Clare Booth Luce.[380] It was this man, Henry Luce, with whom Billy Graham had a deep friendship. Of course, **Billy Graham has been a supporter of the United Nations** for a long time, so perhaps this is why Luce and Graham could be good friends.[381]

WHO WAS EIGHTH PERSON CHOSEN?

Let's look at just one more item of interest concerning Henry Luce. *Life* magazine "enlisted eight distinguished Americans to respond to what Luce called 'a summons, of some urgency' on the **national purpose.**"[382] [Emphasis in the original.] These men were: **Adlai Stevenson,** a Council on Foreign Relations (CFR) member who presided at the United Nations; **Archibald MacLeish,** a member of The Order of Skull & Bones as well as the head of UNESCO which promotes world government; **David Sarnoff,** another CFR member; **Walt Lippman,** a CFR member, president of the Harvard chapter of the Intercollegiate **Socialist** Society, a British Fabian Society member, an apologist for Fidel Castro, founder and manager of the League for Industrial Democracy and the Students for a Democratic Society, who was "appointed by Woodrow Wilson to draw up a charter for **world government**";[383] **Clinton Rossiter,** who was appointed to head a "team of scholars to study the effects of bringing Communism into various aspects of American life";[384] **John W. Gardner,** a CFR member; and **Albert Wohlstetter,** a CFR member. Oh, the 8th person chosen was none other than **Billy Graham!!**[385] Why would Graham be selected to serve along with a number of Council on Foreign Relations members and/or Communists?

DAVID SARNOFF

David Sarnoff was just mentioned. Billy Graham, in his autobiography, tells how he "accidentally" met Sarnoff. Graham writes:

> "When we were on the ship returning us from Japan and Korea in early 1953, we met a Jewish businessman named Jack

> Lewis. He invited us to a party he was giving, during which **a woman performed a hula dance.** When she found out who I was, she apologized, fearing that she had offended me. I told her I had been to Hawaii before and knew that the hula was part of their ancient culture. It turned out that she was the wife of the owner of Honolulu's morning newspaper. After our arrival in the islands, she invited me to a dinner party at their home. General [David] Sarnoff and his wife were there, and afterward they offered to take me back to the hotel. On the way, the general asked, 'Is there anything I can do for you?'
>
> "'Yes, sir.' I could tell he was surprised at my quick answer. 'I'd like to go on NBC with my radio program.'
>
> "'I'll see what I can do,' he said.
>
> "Apparently true to his word, we soon were on NBC every Sunday evening."[386]

Who is Sarnoff? He was born in Russia.[387] He was also a Mason.[388] Additionally, Sarnoff was a member of the Council on Foreign Relations.[389] He was chairman of the board of Radio Corporation of America (RCA) and known as the "Father of American television."[390]

> "The RCA building in New York was the headquarters of M16 chief British Intelligence officer, Sir William Stephenson. RCA's directorate is composed of British-American establishment figures who figure prominently in organizations such as the CFR, NATO, the Club of Rome, the Trilateral Commission, Freemasonry, Skull & Bones, Bilderbergers and the Round Table."[391]

Other groups represented by RCA's directorate are the "Milner Group, Cini Foundation, Mont Pelerin Society, and the Jesuits-Aristotle Society."[392] "...**Chase Manhattan Bank** controls 6.7 percent of its [ABC's] stock—enough to give it a controlling interest. Chase, through its trust department, controls 14 percent of CBS and 4.5 percent of RCA."[393]

BERNARD BARUCH

We've just looked a little bit at Henry Luce, but it was Bernard Baruch who introduced Luce to Billy Graham in the first place.[394]

A book specially **printed by the Billy Graham organization** states this:

> "Graham's address was read at home by the late **Bernard Baruch,** the aging Jewish financier, **confidant of Churchill**

and former colleague of F. D. Roosevelt. Baruch drew it to the attention of **Henry R. Luce,** his house guest at Yeamans Hall near Georgetown. On the morning of Thursday March 9 **Billy Graham** learned that Luce would stay that night at the executive mansion and would attend the crusade."[395]

Graham's own autobiography brags:

> "In late winter of 1950, we held our first major southern Crusade in Columbia, South Carolina. Governor **Strom Thurmond** invited Ruth and me to come and stay in the governor's mansion as his guests.
>
> "One day while there, we received a call from a Mr. Howland, the head of the Atlanta office of *Time* and *Life*, saying that the founding editor and publisher, **Henry Luce,** wanted to come down and spend two or three days with us. Mr. Luce, it seemed, had received a letter from his friend, senior statesman and financier **Bernard Baruch,** who was vacationing at Hobcaw Barony, his plantation near Charleston. The morning newspaper in Columbia, the *State*, was carrying my sermons each day, and Mr. Baruch had been reading them. He had told Mr. Luce that this was something he thought America needed and that he should send some of his people to get acquainted with me. Henry Luce decided to come himself."[396]

Who was **Baruch?** Well, he was the person who convinced Winston Churchill (a Mason[397]) to join the Illuminati conspiracy. He was also one of many who **gave money for the founding of the Council on Foreign Relations** in 1921.[398] In fact,

> "The Council on Foreign Relations (CFR) became the American headquarters for the Illuminati. Led by [Colonel Edward Mandell] House, who wrote the Charter, they were financed by Paul Warburg, Jacob Schiff, William Averell Harriman, Frank Vanderlip, **Bernard Baruch,** Nelson Aldrich, J. P. Morgan, Otto Kahn, Albert H. Wiggin, Herbert H. Lehman, and John Rockefeller."[399]

Baruch was also the confidant of Franklin D. Roosevelt and one of the biggest contributors to Woodrow Wilson's campaign for presidency.[400] Baruch was then "named by President Wilson to head the War Industries Board where he controlled all domestic war material contracts. 'It was widely rumored in Wall Street that out of the war to make the world safe for international bankers he netted $200 million for himself,' wrote Allen."[401]

Baruch was the United States representative for the United Nations' General Assembly in 1946.[402]

He was also involved with the Royal Institute of International Affairs (RIIA). The RIIA branch in America is known as the CFR.[403]

On August 7, 1918 **Baruch** said:

> "Every man's life is at the call of the nation and so must be every man's property. We are living today in a highly organized state of socialism. The state is all; the individual is of importance only as he contributes to the welfare of the state. His property is only as the state does not need it. **He must hold his life and his possessions at the call of the state."**[404]

Baruch was involved with the Rothschild bankers and in 1913 he, along with others, "brought in Lev Trotzky to New York and paid for the recruiting and training of 300 Russian Jews, who became the leadership in the **Communist** revolution of Russia in 1917."[405]

John Foster Dulles tells us that "Mr. Bernard M. Baruch had, at times, cordial social relations with Mr. Gromyko when they were working together on the Atomic Commission."[406] Gromyko was the Soviet foreign minister and a **Communist** who bragged: "Believe me, I sit here as one who helped to draft the U. N. Charter, and I had a distinct part in drafting this part of the charter with my own hands."[407]

When Gromyko visited the United States, the first man he met with was none other than **David Rockefeller.**[408]

Now, isn't it amazing that **Baruch,** a man who helped bring communism to Russia and who was **involved in bringing in a one world government,** would be **interested in Billy Graham** and thought that Graham's message was needed by America? Of course, Baruch's friend, **Gromyko, also met with Billy Graham.** Graham tells us in his autobiography: "In recognition of our presence, the Kremlin arranged for us to be received by the longtime foreign minister, Andrey Gromyko."[409]

WILLIAM RANDOLPH HEARST

Another man that needs to be looked at is **William Randolph Hearst.** He was a publisher who had the *San Francisco Examiner, Los Angeles Examiner, Boston Sunday Advertiser, New York Morning Journal, New York Evening Journal, Chicago Herald-American, Boston American, Chicago Examiner, New York Daily Mirror, New York Journal-American, Cosmopolitan, Town and Country, Harper's Bazaar, Good Housekeeping,* plus about a dozen or so other magazines.[410] **Hearst was the first one who put Billy Graham in the limelight.**[411] Graham writes in his autobiography about that event in 1949. He states:

"When I arrived at the tent for the next meeting, the scene startled me. For the first time, the place was crawling with reporters and photographers. They had taken almost no notice of the meetings up until now, and very little had appeared in the papers. I asked one of the journalists what was happening.

"'You've just been kissed by William Randolph Hearst,' he responded.

"I had no idea what the reporter was talking about, although I knew the name. Hearst, of course, was the great newspaper owner. I had never met the man, but like most Americans I had read his papers. The next morning's headline story about the Campaign in the *Los Angeles Examiner,* followed by an evening story in the *Los Angeles Herald Express*—both owned by Hearst—stunned me. The story was picked up by the Hearst papers in New York, Chicago, Detroit, and San Francisco, and then by all their competitors. Until then, I doubt if any newspaper editor outside the area had heard of our Los Angeles Campaign....

"Supposedly, he had sent a message to his editors, **'Puff Graham.'..."**[412]

In fact, the night **BEFORE** the rally an editorial written by Hearst said: "Of all great assemblies to take place in the Los Angeles area **this year, none,** perhaps, will be **more significant** and with more far-reaching effects than the Billy Graham rally in the Pasadena Rose Bowl **tomorrow evening."**[413] How did Hearst know? Was there an orchestrated plan to promote Graham?

Not only did Hearst "puff Graham" in his newspapers, he also financed the first three years of Graham's crusades![414]

When *Bookstore Journal* asked Graham in 1991: "What has been the **highlight** of your ministry so far?," he responded:

"I always think my most recent crusade is the highlight, but there have certainly been high points. One was our meetings in Los Angeles in 1949. We were supposed to be there three weeks, but we stayed for eight or 10. Mr. **Hearst, the publisher, became interested in the meetings**—how, I don't know. Before his involvement, we didn't get any coverage at all in any paper, except for maybe a little note on a Saturday-edition page saying that the meetings were continuing.

"Then, all of a sudden, we were on the front pages of both of Hearst's local papers every day—and we were in all of his papers across the country. Of course, the other papers have to pay attention then. *Time* magazine did an article, and I think that was before it had a religion section. That was a turning point."[415]

CHRISTIANS EVERYWHERE

Graham continued:

"Another significant thing happened in the early '50s in Boston. *The Pilot*—which is the diocesan paper—put 'Bravo Billy' on the front cover. That made news all over the country. He and I became close, wonderful friends. That was my first real coming to grips with the whole Protestant/Catholic situation.

"I began to realize that there were Christians everywhere. They might be called **modernists,** Catholics, or whatever, but they were Christians. Jesus taught, 'By this all men will know that you are my disciples, if you love one another.' And that love is more important than anything else. I don't think I've ever departed from that [realization—Ed.]."[416]

Who was Hearst and why would he promote Graham? One researcher says this:

"Hearst had built a **newspaper empire,** which he **used to influence political events** in the United States. He used his papers to demand war with Spain, which broke out in 1897. Five months prior to the assassination of president William McKinley on September 6, 1901, Randolph Hearst printed an editorial in his newspaper, which approved political assassination under extreme circumstances."[417]

"In an editorial dated August 28, 1933, William Randolph Hearst wrote, in part: 'A politician will do anything to keep his job—even became a patriot.'"[418]

"Hearst was not only deeply involved in *dirty politics* and *dirty tricks,* but in his private life he lived in adultery for some 30 years by having movie actress Marion Davies as his mistress. He built a fabulous castle on the California coast at San Simeon, where he entertained the rich and the famous people, particularly inviting decadent actors and actresses from Hollywood to come and stay as guests and flaunt their sinful way of living.

"Hearst never repented of his sins to become a Christian, but he became intensely interested in the Youth for Christ movement, and began to promote it through his papers. The official reason for this *strange behavior* of a rich sinful man, is given by the Billy Graham Association in the authorized biography of Billy Graham by John Pollock, page 35:

"*'Hearst had become interested in Youth for Christ, which flourished exceedingly in his home city of Los Angeles, and promoted it by several editorials in his national chain of newspapers, not for religious reasons but because it provided moral standards for youth and was an answer to the growing problem of juvenile delinquency.'*

"In retrospect, it becomes clear that Hearst was not interested in Youth for Christ as an organization, but his focus was on Billy Graham, who was the *shining star* of this move of God....

"On March 18, 1946 Torrey Johnson organized a tour to launch Youth for Christ to a war devastated Europe. Among the people who went on this trip was Billy Graham. But there were two other men on this trip who would greatly influence Graham. One was the Toronto Youth for Christ director, Charles Templeton, a former newspaper cartoonist. Templeton was an intellectual and had great difficulty in believing that the Bible was the Word of God. A few years later, he made an official decision of rejecting the Bible as the infallible Word of God.

"Here is what Billy Graham said of Templeton: *'He helped me tremendously to broaden my whole vision.'*

"The second man was Wesley Hartzell, a journalist on Hearst's Chicago American. He had been assigned by Hearst to travel with the Gospel team and write articles dealing with the success of the meetings, which were to be featured by the International News Service, reaching into nearly all American cities and large towns. At that time no one in the Christian community knew that the World Government had begun to build '**AN ICON,**' that later would be accepted by large masses of people as *'A HOLY MAN'* speaking for God. The team stayed in Great Britain for three weeks."[419] [Emphasis in the original.]

"PUFF YFC"

Billy Graham asserts that he doesn't know why Hearst gave him publicity since he claims that he and Hearst never met, but earlier in his autobiography he admitted that **Wesley Hartzell, a Hearst newspaperman,** traveled with Youth for Christ and Graham to Great Britain.[420] *A Prophet with Honor,* which Graham asked William

Martin to write, says basically the same thing.[421] Listen to his story. He said that Torrey Johnson, Graham, and a few others were

> "accompanied by Wesley Hartzell, a reporter for William Randolph Hearst's Chicago *Herald-American.* Hartzell...was assigned to this trip on an editor's inspired **hunch that 'Graham might turn out to be a top newsmaker.'** Hearst had already shown considerable interest in YFC [Youth for Christ], apparently because he liked its patriotic emphasis and felt its high moral standards might help combat juvenile delinquency. Not incidentally, he also figured that any movement attracting nearly a million people to rallies every Saturday night might help him sell some newspapers. According to Johnson, who never had any direct contact with Hearst, the reclusive publisher sent his Chicago editor a telegram shortly after the Soldier Field rally. It contained only two words: 'PUFF YFC.' A short time later, all twenty-two Hearst papers carried a full-page story on the YFC movement. Further coverage followed, and other papers picked up the story....As the old titan **[Hearst]** watched the organization grow, he apparently **realized that Graham and Templeton were its two brightest stars and decided to assign someone to chronicle their ascent.** Hartzell's reports of the British trip appeared not only in the Hearst papers but on the International News Service wire as well, providing potential exposure to virtually every significant newspaper in America."[422]

William Martin continues:

> "Accounts of Graham's career have typically portrayed the **Hearst endorsement as a complete surprise,** unsought and unexpected. **The reality was less dramatic.** All the Hearst papers had boosted YFC—Hearst had sent his 'Puff YFC' telegram in 1946—but none had done more for the organization than the Los Angeles *Examiner,* the largest West Coast newspaper at the time. Its publisher, R. A. **Carrington, though not particularly religious himself,** admired the organization, gave its activities good coverage in the newspaper, did much of its printing free of charge, and arranged for the paper to sponsor various YFC projects. Most notably, Carrington had given YFC leader Roy McKeown a weekly column in the Sunday *Examiner* to report on YFC activities for a five-state region. A committee member for the revival, McKeown contacted **Carrington to ask if the paper might give Graham and the meetings special attention.** Carrington met with Graham then telephoned 'the chief' (Hearst), and the rest was publicity....The next morning, the *Examiner* and the city's other Hearst paper, the *Herald,* gave him banner headlines, and twelve

other papers in the Hearst chain also gave the campaign extensive coverage. Within days the Associated Press, the United Press, and the International News Service picked up the story, and *Time, Newsweek,* and *Life* followed soon afterward with major feature stories."[423]

Several of those in leadership at Hearst's publications were Masons such as Frank F. Barham, Vice President and Director of Hearst Publishing Company;[424] Harry O. Davis;[425] William DeBeck;[426] William Franklin Knox, General Manager;[427] Merrill C. Meigs, Vice President and later President of Hearst Corporation in Chicago;[428] Frank J. Nicht, Director;[429] and Fred A. Walker.[430]

AIDS PRAYER

The William Randolph Hearst Foundation (in 1984) gave $10,000 to **Planned Parenthood** (which encourages abortions).[431] Also funded (in part) by the Hearst Corporation was a Pulitzer Prize-winning play called "Angels in America: A Gay Fantasia on National Themes" which was held at **St. John the Divine Cathedral** about 1994. This play contained an "AIDS prayer" which says in part:

> "Let us pray. God: A cure would be nice....Enlighten the unenlightened: The Pope, the cardinals, archbishops and priests, even John [Cardinal—Ed.] O'Connor, teach him how Christ's kindness worked: remind him, he's forgotten, make them all remember, replace the ice water in their veins with the blood of Christ, let it pound in their temples....Your silence, I must tell you, so steadfastly maintained, even in the face of our appalling need is outrageous....So many have died this year alone: In case you were absent, God, or absent-minded....Where, God, are you?...So a cure for AIDS. For racism too. For homophobia and sexism, and an end to war, to nationalism and capitalism, to work as such and to hatred of the flesh....Don't expect that we will forgive you if you allow us to be endangered....Be thou more sheltering, God. Pay more attention."[432]

A few other sponsors of this blasphemous play were Chase Manhattan Bank (controlled by the **Rockefellers**[433]), Donald Trump, Prudential Insurance Company, Colgate-Palmolive Company, Philip Morris Companies, Robert de **Rothschild, David Rockefeller,** Mary C. Rockefeller, **Mr. and Mrs. Laurance Spelman Rockefeller,** Mr. and Mrs. Laurance Rockefeller, Rockefeller Center Properties, Inc., the Rockefeller Group, Inc., and Mr. and Mrs. Steven C. Rockefeller.[434] Steven Rockefeller just presented the Earth Charter for approval at the Millennium World Peace Summit in late August 2000. He said that "the biosphere is in us, and we are in the biosphere."[435]

Hearst is also into book publishing now and has published so-called Christian, pro-gay, occultic, and Satanic books.[436] One of these books was *The Relaxation Response* by Herbert Benson which promoted the occultic technique of yoga (although under a different name).[437] The publisher, William Morrow, was purchased by the Hearst Corporation a number of years ago.[438] About five years ago, William Morrow published a book by Peter Gomes who is a homosexual.[439] Prior to this, they printed Ruth Montgomery's book on Jeane Dixon (an astrologer[440]) as well as *The Book of Predictions*[441] and *The Eye of Shiva.*[442] Oh, another book published by William Morrow was *A Prophet with Honor: The Billy Graham Story* (a book which is very favorable to Graham and which he asked to be written).

What is amazing is that Hearst would take an interest in someone like **Billy Graham** in the first place. As was already mentioned, Hearst was not a Christian and was living in adultery, yet he was drawn to Graham.

William Randolph Hearst, Jr. was even instrumental in helping out with Graham's 1957 Crusade in Madison Square Garden. *A Prophet with Honor* states:

> "Seldom, if ever, has a crusade been able to boast of more competent and influential leadership. The crusade committee, chaired by Roger Hull, vice-president of Mutual of New York, included in its number **Chase Manhattan's George Champion, Norman Vincent Peale,** longtime Graham backers Russell Maguire and J. Howard Pew, corporate executives Walter Hoving, Eddie Rickenbacker, and Jeremiah Milbank, *Reader's Digest* senior editor Stanley High, and media moguls **Henry Luce, William Randolph Hearst, Jr.,** *Herald Tribune* editor Ogden Reid, and ABC president Robert Kintner. With this kind of clout at the top, and with solid encouragement from members of the **Dodge, Phelps, Vanderbilt, Gould, and Whitney families,...**finance chairman Howard Isham, vice-president and treasurer of U. S. Steel, found it relatively easy to raise a large portion of the projected $600,000 budget."[443]

The liberal press has helped Graham in more ways than one. One author reveals:

> "Apparently, Billy Graham has a special tie-in with the liberal media as well since they covered up a report that his nephew, Kevin Graham Ford, pleaded guilty for exposing

himself to two teenaged girls. There was also a story about a $23 million slush fund scandal [see Chapter 7 for more about this] which briefly threatened the Graham empire, but that also suddenly disappeared from mention in the national media."[444]

The World Book Year Book mentioned that "Graham drew criticism from some of his supporters for having concealed the existence of a $23-million educational fund."[445] This book adds: "There were also charges in the publishing world that Graham's best-selling *How to Be Born Again* reproduced, without acknowledging it, a great portion of one of his earlier books, issued by a different publisher."[446]

It sure has paid Graham to have friends in "high places."

BROOKS HAYS

Another individual in "high places" was Brooks Hays. Hays was a Congressman from Arkansas, a **Mason,**[447] and an assistant to the late President Kennedy.[448] He was also a **Council on Foreign Relations** member.[449] Additionally, he was one of the people who sponsored the ungodly **Temple of Understanding** (which will be covered later).[450] Hays states: "I must say at the outset that I do not accept all of the Bible as literally true....[the literal inerrancy position of inspiration is—D.W.C.] anti-biblical—for it tends to make an idol of printed pages...[it is—D.W.C.] Bibliolatry...as dangerous as any other form of idolatry."[451]

What does Graham think of Hays? He writes in his autobiography: "I called my old **Christian friend** Congressman Brooks Hays from Arkansas and asked his advice."[452] Sadly, Hays' statement about the Bible sounds a little bit like what Billy Graham told the *Saturday Evening Post* in April **1963:** "I am not a literalist....If you try to accept the literal meaning of every word in the Bible, you get into all sorts of trouble."[453] Unfortunately, Graham will get into far more trouble on judgment day by not believing the Bible!

PRESIDENTS AND ROYALTY

Just briefly, let's look at some of Graham's friendships with leaders around the world. **The following quotations are taken from Graham's autobiography *Just As I Am.***

☞ "During the eight years of **Reagan's** administration, we saw each other a number of times. I especially appreciated his kindness in inviting Ruth and me to several state dinners for visiting foreign leaders....

"In November of 1985 he invited us again to a state dinner, this one in honor of **Prince Charles and Princess Diana....**

"In December 1987, the Soviet Union's General Secretary **Mikhail Gorbachev** and his wife, Raisa, visited Washington for a summit conference. We were invited to some of the festivities. During the welcoming ceremony on the White House lawn, Ruth and I [were] standing next to **Henry Kissinger....**

"In November 1988, President Reagan's last official guest for a state dinner was Prime Minister **Margaret Thatcher** of England; in 1981 she had been his first such guest. He had invited us then, and he invited us again."[454]

☞ "We first met **George and Barbara Bush** some years earlier, before he became prominent in national politics. I had met his father, Senator **Prescott Bush,** several times during my visits to Washington; I got to know him better after his retirement from the Senate, as a **golfing partner** at Hobe Sound, Florida. I also got acquainted with his wife, Dorothy Bush, a delightful and devout woman who was very supportive of our work across the years."[455]

☞ "The second White House state dinner during the Bush years was in honor of the **Gorbachevs** in 1990. I was seated next to Raisa Gorbachev, with President Bush at her other side."[456]

☞ "I became good friends with **R. Sargent Shriver,** head of the Peace Corps, and later we made a documentary film together on the problem of poverty in the Appalachian Mountains. One day he offered to pick me up in Montreat. He showed up with a helicopter and landed in our front yard...."[457]

☞ **"...Nixon** came to Charlotte on October 15, 1971, honoring me by attending 'Billy Graham Day' there—an event sponsored by the city. He and I stood in an open convertible that moved slowly through town."[458]

☞ "One day Ruth and I attended a Father's Day luncheon at the Waldorf-Astoria Hotel, where I was honored as Father of the Year in the field of religion. I had the opportunity to meet **Mickey Mantle,** the great baseball player. I sat down beside him, and we got to know each other for the first time."[459]

☞ "I enjoyed meeting Generalissimo and Madame **Chiang Kai-shek** in Taipei, Formosa, and **Prime Minister Hatoyama** in Tokyo, where he postponed his appearance at a session of Parliament for a half-hour in order to accommodate me."[460]

☞ "...we were invited to several social events in Washington. On one occasion, at one of the dinners during Ford's presidency, I sat beside **Grace Kelly,** Princess Grace of Monaco."[461]

☞ "From 1955 to 1960, I met with several dozen heads of state, from the prime minister of Japan to the prime minister of Israel. (In fact, in connection with our international ministry, I have continued to meet a wide spectrum of leaders over the years, including virtually every prime minister of Japan and chancellor of Germany.)"[462]

☞ "Since so much of our ministry has been spent in Great Britain, we have had more opportunities to meet a wide spectrum of people in leadership positions there, including almost all of the prime ministers since 1954."[463]

☞ "On March 3, 1983, we were privileged to accept an invitation to such a dinner in San Francisco. The guests of honor were Britain's **Queen Elizabeth and Prince Philip....**During the evening, someone was sent to invite us on behalf of the Queen to a reception the next night on board the royal yacht *Britannia.* We accepted...."[464]

☞ "It may sound impressive to say that we have been with Her Majesty Queen Elizabeth II on a dozen different occasions—but those twelve occasions have been spread over forty years."[465]

☞ "On one occasion when I was in Great Britain, the Queen was preparing her annual Christmas address to be broadcast on television around the world. To illustrate a point, she wanted to toss a stone into a pond to show how the ripples went out farther and farther. She asked me to come and listen to her practice the speech by the pond and give my impressions, which I did."[466]

☞ "I also had the privilege of meeting **Prime Minister Nehru.** This assisted us in other ways, because once you have been received by the head of state in a country like India, mayors and governors are more likely to welcome you to their area."[467]

☞ "At Nixon's second inauguration in 1973, **Bill Marriott** [a Mormon], founder and head of the Marriott hotel and restaurant chain, was chair of the gala affair, as he had been in 1969. He had become **one of my closest friends** and had appointed me honorary chair of the inauguration symphony concert at the Kennedy Center. For that event, Ruth and I dressed up in our best. We arrived early, for a small preconcert reception, and sat with the Agnews and the Charlton Hestons for a while."[468] (Incidentally, Marriott hotels are "America's biggest seller of alcoholic beverages...." Also, "Marriott Hotel will continue selling porno movies because the money is good."[469])

☞ "Knowing of Ruth's deep interest in China, President Reagan invited us in July of 1985 to a state dinner honoring the Chinese president, **Li Xiannian....**the President thoughtfully seated Ruth on his left at the dinner, with President Li on his right. I have no doubt this helped us when we began negotiations for our trip to China three years later."[470]

☞ "One trip to India, in 1972, deserves more than passing mention for several reasons.

"President Nixon, at the request of the American consul in New Delhi, had personally asked me to seek an interview with Prime Minister **Indira Gandhi,** in part to find out from her what kind of ambassador she wanted from America. He asked me to notice every single thing about her—the movement of her hands, the expression on her face, how her eyes looked. 'When you've finished the interview,' he said to me, 'go to the American embassy and dictate your report to me.'

"And so, when I visited with Mrs. Gandhi in the Indian capital, I put the question to her. She told me she wanted someone who understood economics, who had the ear of the President, and who had influence in Congress. This I reported to the President. He later appointed Daniel Patrick Moynihan. Whether my report influenced the President's decision, I never learned....

"Later, during a visit to Washington, I heard a late-night knock on my hotel-room door. It was Daniel Patrick Moynihan.

"'I want to thank you for appointing me ambassador to India,' he said.

"'I didn't have you appointed,' I protested. 'I just passed on to Mr. Nixon a message from Mrs. Gandhi.'

"'I'm sure you had me appointed,' Moynihan insisted. 'I'm a Catholic,' he went on...."[471]

☞ "Shortly before leaving the United States for India—and just a half-year after that meeting with Jack [Dain]—I was able to meet with Secretary of State **John Foster Dulles** for a briefing on relations between the United States and India. He felt that it was especially important for me to know that the visit to India of Soviet leaders Khrushchev and Bulganin two months earlier had had as its sole purpose drawing India into closer ties with the Communist bloc."[472]

☞ "On my return to the United States, I went through Washington and brought **President Eisenhower** and Vice President Nixon up to date on the details of my visit to India....

"'I want you to talk to Dulles about it,' said the President....

"...Dulles kept me a long time because he wanted to hear every detail of our visit to Asia as well as my impressions of India and Nehru. He also wanted to talk with me on a personal matter."[473]

Another source reports: "Johnson invited him [Graham] to the White House twenty-three times, five of those for overnight....The truth was that **Billy knew more of the inner workings of Johnson's White House than Nixon's.**"[474]

The above is just a small sampling of those with whom Graham has rubbed shoulders. In fact, he bragged:

> "Over the years, I have met so many of the rich and famous in many countries that it's impossible to mention—or even remember—them all.
>
> "But I have crossed paths with a wide spectrum of leaders from all kinds of fields—politics, religion, business, education, entertainment, sports. **Richard Nixon once told an interviewer that I knew more international leaders than he did.**"[475]

GRAHAM WONDERS IF HE'S PLEASING GOD OR MAN

Graham said that he was reluctant to talk about all the famous people he had met but that "reluctance" certainly didn't stop him from spending a good amount of the over 700 pages referring to such acquaintances in his autobiography! It also didn't stop him from flaunting picture after picture of himself meeting with various Presidents and royalty. He also pays a lot of attention to the public-opinion polls. In fact, one of Graham's biographers noted that Graham "admitted that he may pay more attention to public-opinion polls than he ought to...."[476] Said Graham: "I wonder sometimes if I'm pleasing God or man...."[477]

> "[Lyndon] Johnson once acknowledged that he often contacted Graham to 'get a new injection' of confidence and optimism, recalling that during one particularly difficult period 'when I was being called a crook and a thug and all,' he invited Graham to spend a weekend with him, and **'we bragged on each other.** I told him he was the greatest religious leader in the world and he said I was the greatest political leader.'"[478]

I've heard it stated that it's wonderful that Graham can be around all these world leaders and witness to them about Jesus. This certainly would be wonderful—**IF** that's what he would do, but I think it's obvious that he isn't really witnessing for Jesus. When he is asked to take messages from world leader to world leader and give reports of his overseas visits to Presidents, he is acting in the realm of **politics**—not religion. Graham denies being involved in politics, but anyone who reads his autobiography can see that he is **heavily** involved in the political arena. As mentioned in this chapter, it was through Graham that Reagan appointed an ambassador to the Vatican. Moynihan thanked Graham for influencing Nixon to appoint him as ambassador to India. Nixon asked for Graham's advice in selecting a running mate.

Below is another quote to show you Graham's influence in the **POLITICAL** realm.

> "One morning Billy got a phone call from the White House. The President **[Eisenhower] had been consulting him for some time on racial matters.** Ike respected moral authority based on the Bible. And Billy knew the Bible. But **this time Ike sought more.** He wanted to know what a moral white southerner thought of the situation in Little Rock. Ike was feeling Billy out about sending troops to Little Rock.
>
> "'Do it, Mr. President.'
>
> "Within an hour, Vice President Nixon called Billy to ask the same question.
>
> "'Do it,' answered Billy.
>
> "That afternoon the 101st Airborne Division entered Little Rock. Central High School was desegregated."[479]

It's true, that Graham has also functioned in the role of the nation's pastor. "In 1968, Billy Graham gave the benediction at both the Democratic and Republican conventions in Chicago and Miami"[480] as well as in 1988.[481]

"In March, 1969, Billy was called to Walter Reed Hospital in Washington, D.C. Ike [Eisenhower] was in bed, ghostly white with nothing left but a trace of the famous grin. He had been there for almost a year, dying. He had asked for Billy."[482]

When Reagan was shot, "the White House sent out an emergency call for Graham, and the evangelist came immediately to the capital to comfort and pray with Mrs. Reagan."[483] When the Oklahoma City bombing took place, Clinton called on Graham for the memorial service.[484] When the diaster occurred at the Twin Towers of the World Trade Center, a national day of prayer was called and Graham was the speaker for the interfaith service with included a Rabbi and a Muslim imam. On this occasion, one clergyman offered a prayer which began with "God of Abraham, Mohammad, and Jesus Christ...."

When George Bush, Sr. decided on the Persian Gulf War, he sent a message to Graham which read: "Come. We need you."[485] He also had Graham preach the sermon. This sermon, however, was quite interesting. Graham said: "Perhaps, out of this war will come a new peace and—as been stated by the President—a **new world order."**[486]

Of course, students of Bible prophecy know that the Antichrist will be the ruler of this new world order.

Could Graham's endorsement and acceptance of the **new world order** be why he has been able to meet with heads of state over the past 50 or so years? Yes, it would be wonderful if Graham would take the message of Jesus Christ to these leaders but he isn't doing it. How could Graham witness to Presidents, etc., when he already believes that people such as Richard Nixon,[487] Lyndon Johnson,[488] Gerald Ford,[489] Jimmy Carter,[490] Bill Clinton,[491] Mother Teresa,[492] John Kennedy, Jr.,[493] Elvis Presley,[494] etc., were Christians. (Some of these people will be covered more thoroughly later on.)

How could Graham preach the **true** gospel of Christ to these people and tell them to repent when he doesn't believe the Jews need Jesus[495] and the pagans can be saved through nature?[496]

How can Graham present a salvation message to those in leadership when he himself disobeys the Bible by having fellowship with apostates and unbelievers[497] (which will be documented in the next several chapters)? The Bible says "have **no fellowship** with the unfruitful works of darkness, **but** rather **reprove** them" (Ephesians 5:11).

I'm sorry to disappoint those who thought Graham was taking the message of salvation to those in leadership, but it just isn't so. Oh, he may mention words like "God," "Christ," and even "Jesus" from time to time—but that isn't sharing the gospel. Witches and occultists also mention those words. It takes more than just mouthing some Christian words. Remember, the Bible says: "Not every one that saith unto Me, Lord, Lord, shall enter into the kingdom of heaven; but he that **doeth the will of My Father** which is in heaven" (Matthew 7:21). Jesus said: "This people draweth nigh unto Me with their mouth, and **honoureth Me with their lips; <u>but</u> their heart is far from Me"** (Matthew 15:8).

Besides, where are the changed lives of those in leadership if Graham is taking the message of Christ to them? The Bible says: "Therefore if any man be in Christ, he is a new creature: old things are passed away; behold, all things are become new" (II Corinthians 5:17). "But if they had stood in My counsel, and had caused My people to hear My words, then **they should have turned them from their evil way,** and from the evil of their doings" (Jeremiah 23:22). Yet, many leaders continue to lie, steal, commit adultery, swear, and live the same sinful life as before they met Graham.

Yes, Graham would be in a wonderful position to reach some leaders for Christ, but remember, if he would point out their sin to them, he wouldn't be in that position very long. Graham himself admitted that if he would bring up issues of homosexuality or abortion to Clinton, Graham "would not be invited back to the White House."[498]

If Graham called out about the filth of Hollywood, do you think he would have a star on the Hollywood Walk of Fame?[499] (See Chapter 7 for more about this.)

GOD'S TRUE PROPHETS WERE PERSECUTED

When the prophets of old called out against sin in high places of leadership, they were put in prison, ostracized, persecuted, tortured, and killed. For instance, John the Baptist was beheaded for telling King Herod that it was unlawful for him to have his brother's wife (Matthew 14:3-10). Jeremiah was thrown in a dungeon (Jeremiah 38:6), the apostles were martyred (Acts 12:2-3; John 21:18-19; Matthew 23:31-34), Stephen was stoned to death (Acts 7:57-8:1), and Paul was beaten (Acts 16:23-37; 21:32; 22:25; II Corinthians 11:23, 24, 25), stoned (Acts 14:19; II Corinthians 11:25), and jailed (Acts 23:29; 25:14; 26:29; II Corinthians 11:23; Ephesians 6:20; Philippians 1:7-16; Colossians 4:3; II Timothy 1:8; 2:9; Philemon 1:10, 13). Yes, Paul came before rulers but he was in chains (Acts 26:28-29). Jesus came before Pilate and Herod—and was crucified (Matthew 27:22-31).

History tells us that Isaiah was inserted into a hollow log and sawn in half. Hebrews says:

> " [O]thers were tortured, not accepting deliverance; that they might obtain a better resurrection: And others had trial of cruel mockings and scourgings, yea, moreover of bonds and imprisonment: They were stoned, they were sawn asunder, were tempted, were slain with the sword: they wandered about in sheepskins and goatskins; being destitute, afflicted, tormented; (Of whom the world was not worthy:) they wandered in deserts, and in mountains, and in dens and caves of the earth" (Hebrews 11:35-38).

These people were not wined and dined and invited back again and again. The **Gospel,** many times, **is an OFFENSE.** "As it is written, Behold, I lay in Sion a stumblingstone and rock of offence..." (Romans 9:33; Isaiah 8:14). I Peter 2:7-8 says: "Unto you therefore which believe He is precious: but unto them which be disobedient, the stone which the builders disallowed, the same is made the head of the corner, And a stone of stumbling, and a rock of offence, even to them which stumble at the word, being disobedient...."

Paul said: "[W]e preach Christ crucified, unto the Jews a stumblingblock, and unto the Greeks foolishness" (I Corinthians 1:23).

II Timothy 3:12 says: "Yea, and all that will live godly in Christ Jesus shall suffer persecution," but Graham only gets praises, a Congressional Gold Medal (with unanimous approval of Congress),[500] honorary degrees,[501] the Presidential Medal of Freedom,[502] the Templeton Prize for Progress in Religion,[503] a highway named after him, and a "Billy Graham Day" to honor him.[504]

The Bible warns: "Woe unto you, when all men shall speak well of you! for so did their fathers to the false prophets" (Luke 6:26). "[K]now ye not that the friendship of the world is enmity with God? whosoever therefore will be a friend of the world is the enemy of God" (James 4:4).

The true Christian is not loved by the world—but **HATED.** Listen to God's Word:

✞ "And ye shall be hated of all men for My name's sake: but he that endureth to the end shall be saved" (Matthew 10:22; Mark 13:13; Luke 21:17). (If Graham were really preaching about Jesus and the cross, the Bible clearly tells us that he would be hated!)

✞ "Then shall they deliver you up to be afflicted, and shall kill you: and ye shall be **hated of all nations** for My name's sake" (Matthew 24:9). (Yet the nations of the world cater to Graham!)

✞ "If the world hate you, ye know that it hated Me before it hated you. If ye were of the world, the world would love his own: but because ye are not of the world, but I have chosen you out of the world, therefore the **world hateth you.** Remember the word that I said unto you, The servant is not greater than his lord. If they have persecuted Me, they will also persecute you..." (John 15:18-20).

Amos 3:3 asks: "Can two walk together, except they be agreed?"

In the next chapter we are going to take a closer look at some more individuals that Graham has endorsed.

2. MORE LIBERAL FRIENDS

Gerald Kennedy was an apostate, leftist, Methodist Bishop who denied many fundamentals of the faith such as the virgin birth.[1] "Kennedy wrote a book entitled *God's Good News* in which he eloquently denies the deity of Christ."[2] He endorsed Nels Ferre's book which states "Jesus never was nor became God."[3] Ferre, a graduate of the Union Theological Seminary[4] (which will be covered in the next chapter), wrote another book entitled *The Christian Understanding of God.* "In this book he said, 'We have no way of knowing, even, that Jesus was sinless.' In this book he promotes the theory that Jesus may have been the son of a German soldier."[5]

"Ferre denied practically every tenet of Bible Christianity, including the perfect inspiration of Scripture, the deity and virgin birth and substitutionary atonement of Jesus Christ, the bodily resurrection, and the second coming."[6] He says that Jesus was not sinless and he thinks "that He probably picked up some of His teachings from the mystics of the Orient and the Middle East during His wanderings in the silent years of His life."[7]

Ferre also stated:

> "According to the very meaning of sovereign love, however, God both can and will have **all to be saved....**Among the numberless **unthinking people** an **immature** and unworthy **eschatology espousing eternal hell is unfortunately still prevalent,** visiting Christian ethics at its very heart."

You see, Ferre belonged to at least six **Communist** front organizations, so it's no wonder that he denied the fundamentals of the Christian faith.[8] Yet, sadly, leaders in the National Council of Churches have called him "one of the great theologians of the day."[9]

In 1966, **Billy Graham "donated about $65,000 toward a stadium at Vanderbilt University,** an extremely liberal Methodist institution, on whose faculty the blasphemous **NELS FERRE** was then serving."[10]

"[Gerald] Kennedy further revealed in his public statements his denial of a literal hell and said that his religion was not a religion based on a book [the Bible]."[11] In his own book, *The Christian and His America,* he brags: "One of my favorite pulpits is in a **Unitarian** church in Pennsylvania."[12]

The name "Unitarian" developed because they don't believe in the Trinity.[13] "In 1785, King's Chapel in Boston revised its prayer book, omitting all references to the Trinity. It thus became the first

Unitarian church in America. In 1796, Philadelphians founded the first church to use the name Unitarian in its title."[14]

Additionally, Unitarians "do not accept the deity of Jesus Christ, the virgin birth, the blood atonement nor the inspiration of the Scriptures."[15]

> "They profess that Jesus Christ is little more than a wonderful teacher, and assert that the **Bible is only one of many sacred writings** available from all the great religions. Naturally, for such a liberal body, concepts such as heaven and hell are considered ridiculous and the Christian doctrine that Jesus Christ died on the cross for our sins is scoffed at and summarily dismissed."[16]

One Unitarian Universalist minister, Leonard Mason, wrote the following poem:

> "Come, return to your place in the pews,
> and hear our heretical views:
> You were not born in sin so lift up your chin,
> you have only your dogmas to lose."[17]

When asked if Unitarian Universalists believe in God, the answer given by Unitarian Christopher Gist Raible, was:

> "In their churches are agnostics, humanists, even atheists—as well as nature worshipers, pantheists, and those who affirm a personal God. All recognize, however, that the word **'God' is a stumbling block to religious communication** for many people because it has so many meanings. All know also that there is no special virtue in being able to declare, 'I believe in God.'"[18]

He further admits: "Many Christian churches refuse to accept them as Christian because they cannot pass the theological 'test' of acknowledging Jesus Christ as 'Lord and Savior.'"[19]

MOTHER GODDESS

Unitarians also support abortion,[20] **active euthanasia,**[21] **and homosexuality.**[22] In fact, they admit that "[t]here are Unitarian Universalists, clergy and laity, who are homosexuals or bisexuals...."[23]

> "Unitarians have produced many 'sex education' materials including a film showing people in the act of heterosexual sex, male homosexuals and also lesbians having sex. They have shown this to fifth grade children. In April of 1997 at Wellesley High School, an assembly that was required of all students

> featured the lesbians' senior minister of Arlington Street Church, Boston (headquarters of Unitarians). She said casual sex is good for teenagers, including homosexual sex. She said, 'It's important to remember that sexuality happens along a long, broad continuum, with the exclusive heterosexuality at one end and exclusive homosexuality at the other. There's a great movable feast in between. Choose for yourself.'"[24]
>
> "Worship of the Mother Goddess is also prevalent in such churches as Unity and **Unitarian.** How could the Unitarian Church be otherwise with its legacy of being intertwined with **The Order of Skull & Bones.** Antony Sutton in his book on the American branch of the Illuminati, *America's Secret Establishment,* reports that, 'The Order [of Skull & Bones] has long-standing and significant links to the relatively small Unitarian Church.' In fact, former President William Taft, whose father co-founded The Order, was President of the Unitarian Association in his time....
>
> "Benjamin Creme is another New Ager linked with Unity and **Unitarian** Church leaders."[25] [Emphasis in the original.]

"Unitarian Universalist Association (UUA) President William F. Schultz says compatibility with paganism 'fits very neatly with our tradition....For us, a religion grounded in nature is part and parcel of our heritage...we have gone too far on this side of rationalism.'"[26]

Actually, Unitarians are moving closer to wicca (or witchcraft) all the time.[27]

> "Witch Starhawk confirms the cohesion between the Unitarian Church, the Order of Skull & Bones, and Witchcraft: '...I participated in a Witchcraft service organized by women of San Francisco's first Unitarian Church....I gave a series of four evening talks at the same church, culminating in a ritual....I was asked to lead a service at a Unitarian Church in Palos Verdes, and to speak to a Unitarian discussion group in Long Beach—We do have friends out there!'"[28]

Starhawk was also featured at the Unitarian Universalist Association's Conference in June 1989 which included a workshop for "a 'midnight summer solstice ritual' on the Yale University Campus where incantations were chanted to the 'earth goddess.' 1,200 of the 3,200 delegates from the assembly attended" Starhawk's session.[29]

Two years ago the Unitarian Universalist Association sent out an ad announcing that the minister and his assistant "will be offering Paganism 101 this Spring [1999]. It will consist of 9 or 10 sessions.

In the class we will discuss Unitarian Universalist Paganism and the history of paganism. We will also be doing ritual."[30]

FOUR ELEMENTS

A Unitarian Universalist (UU) congregation in Princeton has a group known as the Covenant of Unitarian Universalist Pagans (CUUPS).[31] "They're dedicated to enabling pagan and UU networking and promoting **INTERFAITH** dialogue."[32] Four times a year they have the Sunday service at the UU church. Pagan Elissa Hoeger explains:

> "'During the Sunday services, we also do create sacred space pagan-style. This means lighting candles, having a child sweep the circle, as well as doing things which the congregants are familiar with,' she says. In addition, pagans 'call the quarters' in their services—the four directions of the compass, which correspond to the four basic elements: air, fire, earth and water. They also invoke a male deity—and most importantly—a female goddess to guard the sacred space."[33]

She adds: "Drumming, singing, dancing, burning things, holding hands, and eating and drinking together all serve to draw the rest of one's being...into the worshipful act."[34]

According to the December 1929 issue of *The New Age Magazine,* the founder of the Universalist Church, Hosea Ballou, was a Mason.[35]

I have a book in my library dealing with the occult spirit religion called **Santeria** where animal sacrifices are offered to the gods. The copyright page mentioned that this book from Beacon Press was "published under the auspices of the Unitarian Universalist Association of Congregations."[36]

Of course, Unitarians do not only embody the pagan tradition. A survey was conducted by *Free Inquiry,* a secular humanist magazine.

> "The editors found views from naturalistic humanist and pagan to spiritualist, pantheist, New Age, mystic and Buddhist. They conclude that 'although humanism is a strong strand of the UUA, there are many other strands, and humanism seems to be diminishing in influence as a spiritualistic concern begins to be felt more strongly.'"[37]

"When asked to categorize their ministers' belief, 29 said they were Christian; 70 said theist; four said atheist; 11 agnostic; and 82 said humanist."[38]

"A significant **bond between the Unitarians and the Humanists** is evident upon further examination of the first *Humanist Manifesto.* Nearly 25 per cent of the original signers were Unitarians. The point is also made by a past director of the AHA [American Humanist Association] Edwin H. Wilson, that the AHA 'stemmed largely from Unitarianism as a movement of **Religious Humanists.'** The Unitarians can still be found at the core of the Humanist movement; in fact, 170 Unitarian-Universalist ministers were signers of *Humanist Manifesto II* in 1973.

"Among notable past and present Unitarian-Universalists are found the names of many prominent persons, including Chester Bowles, Albert Camus, Sigmund Freud, Dag Hammarskjold, Arthur M. Schlesinger, Jr., Bernard Shaw, Adlai Stevenson, and Senators Joseph Clark, Norris Cotton, Paul Douglas, Maurine Neuberger, Robert Packwood, Leverett Saltonstall, and Harrison A. Williams."[39]

This is the kind of church that Gerald Kennedy seems to feel at home in since he said: "One of my favorite pulpits is in a **Unitarian** church in Pennsylvania."[40]

In **1950** Billy Graham held a Crusade at Boston. Listen to what he says about the Unitarian church:

"At that time, Protestantism in New England was weak, due in part to theological differences within some denominations, the influence of **Unitarian** ideas in other denominations, and the strength of the Roman Catholic Church. In spite of all that, a number of Roman Catholic priests and **Unitarian clergy,** together with some of their parishioners, came to the meetings along with those from evangelical churches. With my limited evangelical background, this was **a further expansion of my own ecumenical outlook.** I now began to make friends among people from many different backgrounds and to **develop a spiritual love for their clergy.**"[41]

Did you notice that over **50 years ago** Graham had developed "a **spiritual** love" for the **Unitarian** clergy?!

Returning to Gerald Kennedy, we find that he belonged to several **Communist** front organizations.[42]

In spite of this, **Kennedy was allowed to chair Graham's 1963 Los Angeles Crusade as well as serving on the executive committee.**[43]

In a book which Graham asked William Martin to write, we find some revealing information:

"In Fundamentalist eyes, the Los Angeles campaign set another, less glorious record, when Graham acquiesced in the choice of Methodist bishop **Gerald Kennedy as the chairman of the crusade's general committee....His theology was frankly liberal**—he had once ventured that **he doubted the deity of Christ** and admitted he had **never believed in the Virgin Birth.** Fundamentalist critics also charged him with **leftist** political views 'of the rankest sort,' noting that **he belonged to such 'Communist front' organizations as the National Council of Churches and the Methodist Federation for Social Action.** Allowing such a man to have a prominent public role in an evangelistic crusade, critics charged, marked 'the farthest reach yet into the apostasy for Crusade leadership.' **Graham chose not to trouble himself with Fundamentalist carpings,** but Robert Ferm, his chief apologist, pointed out that...he found it difficult to believe Kennedy would have accepted the post 'if he did not believe in the basic Christian truths.'"[44]

"Despite Kennedy's **known** record, [Billy] Graham sent a telegram to the First Methodist Church of Shreveport, Louisiana, congratulating them on selecting Bishop Kennedy to conduct an 'evangelistic effort.' It stated that **'We know and respect these men** [Bishop Kennedy and song-leader Bill Mann] **very highly.** May God give you a time of spiritual renewal.' He further had the telegram printed as an advertisement in the *Shreveport Times,* March 7, 1965, so all could see his support of Bishop Kennedy."[45]

"In fact, **Graham said** on August 21, 1963, **'Bishop Kennedy is one of the ten greatest Christian preachers in America.'"**[46]

MINOR DISAGREEMENTS

In an article for *Christian Century,* Graham said:

"[A]fter a decade of intimate contact with Christians the world over I am now aware that the family of God contains people of various ethnological, cultural, class, and denominational differences. I have learned that there can even be minor disagreements of theology, methods, and motives, but that within the true church there is a mysterious unity that overrides all divisive factors."[47]

While it is true that there can be **"minor** disagreements of theology" between those in the family of God, it is also true that one is not in God's family if he denies the fundamentals of the faith as Gerald Kennedy did. In 1952 Graham wrote to Dr. Bob Jones, Sr. stating: "We have never had a man on our [crusade] committee that denied the virgin birth, the vicarious atonement, or the bodily resurrection."[48] Also, Graham had said in 1958 in *Eternity:* "If a man blatantly denies the deity of Christ or that Christ has come in the flesh, we are not to bid him godspeed. Thus, the Scriptures teach that we are to be separated from those who deny the deity of our Lord Jesus Christ....I am to treat him as an Antichrist and an enemy of the cross."[49] Yet, just 5 years later, Graham had such a man chairing his Crusade, and he bragged that he knew and **respected Kennedy "very highly."**[50]

Could have Graham's endorsement been a lack of discernment or a "slip up" in this case? Obviously not, because Graham had been **warned** about Kennedy's theology and Communistic leanings by concerned Fundamentalists but, as just quoted, **"Graham chose not to trouble himself with Fundamentalist carpings...."**[51]

You see, in that same issue of *Eternity* "Graham had reduced the doctrine of verbal inerrancy to the status of mere 'theory,' and denied that 'this particular theory of inspiration' was even essential to Christian orthodoxy, let alone grounds for the breaking of Christian fellowship."[52]

AN IMPOSSIBLE GOD

Besides, Kennedy is not the only such apostate that Graham has endorsed and promoted. In fact, Kennedy wasn't even the first apostate endorsed by Graham! "In his 1959 San Francisco Crusade, Graham honored the notorious **Bishop James A. Pike** by having him lead in prayer."[53] "Pike would also have been involved in Graham's 1957 New York Crusade, as he was the dean of the extremely modernistic **Cathedral of St. John the Divine** in New York from 1952 to 1958."[54]

"In 1960, Graham had Bishop James A. Pike offer prayer at his Detroit Crusade."[55] Who was Bishop Pike? Well, he also denied major doctrines of the faith such as the incarnation, the virgin birth, and the Trinity.[56] "He spoke of the **'myth** of the Garden of Eden.' He said, 'the virgin birth...is a myth which churchmen should be free to accept or reject...."[57] The very **same year** that Graham had Pike pray at his Crusade, Pike wrote in the *Christian Century:* "The Bible seems to indicate that no one is saved except through Christ....To say no one is saved except through the earthly Jesus Christ would be impossible."[58] This article also stated:

> "'But the kind of a god I first believed in, who would limit salvation to a select group of people who happen to have heard the news and heard it well...is an impossible god. As to this god, I am now an atheist.' He continues this incredible line by

stating: **'I have preached** more and more in the past decade **on the values of atheism and agnosticism.** Atheists debunk the small god. I have found that in almost every case the atheist is opposing a concept of God which I myself disbelieve. As to the agnostic, he often has doubts about things I have doubts about. There has to be a large measure of agnosticism in true religion.'"[59]

In the November 1960 issue of the *Pacific Churchman,* Pike basically said that those who **opposed** Communism were servants doing the bidding of hell.[60] By 1961 he was trying "to abolish the congressional investigations into Communist activities in the United States."[61]

Pike was an alcoholic.[62] "Three times Pike was picked up by San Francisco police while he was wandering around in a drunken, confused state late at night. He spent four years in intensive psychoanalysis."[63] He was also an adulterer having been "twice divorced, thrice married, and had at least three mistresses."[64]

PIKE AND THE OCCULT

"A biography about Pike noted that 'never before in the history of the Episcopal Church had a Solemn Requiem Mass been offered for a bishop in the **presence of three surviving wives.'**"[65]

"One of his mistresses committed suicide; one of his daughters attempted suicide. His eldest son committed suicide in 1966 at age 20 (associated with homosexuality)...."[66] It was his son's suicide that lead **Bishop Pike into the world of the occult.**[67] Pike himself "died a tragic death from his involvement in spiritism."[68]

Since he participated in something forbidden by the Bible, he had to "reinterpret" the Biblical passages to try to fit his sinful involvement. He wrote in his book, *The Other Side*:

> "The injunctions in the Old Testament against consulting mediums, such as Leviticus 19:31, are dismissed as the words of 'Jewish religious professionals—the priests and prophets'—who 'had to protect their own roles as those who could reveal and interpret the Word of God, so they were quick to denounce with vehemence any competitors, like mediums and foretellers of the future. In this regard, **those scriptural injunctions are of little help to us today, for our world view is so different.'**"[69]

After Pike's son had committed suicide, the Bishop consulted several mediums in order to try to contact him.[70] "While on television in Toronto, Canada, **Pike met with famous medium, Arthur Ford,** who through his spirit-guide gave the Bishop"[71] a message from his son. Another medium, Ena Twigg, also gave Pike a message from his son. The son said: "'Don't ever believe that God can be personalized. He is the Central Force.' As for Jesus, young Jim's spirit allegedly declared: 'They talk about him—a mystic, a seer, yes, a seer. Oh, but Dad, they don't talk about him as a Saviour.'"[72]

Pike was a promoter of situation ethics.[73] He had taught at the New Age, human potential center, Esalen.[74] He also had sponsored the ungodly Temple of Understanding (which is covered elsewhere).[75]

Of course, the Temple of Understanding is housed in **St. John the Divine Cathedral** and Pike just happened to have been dean of St. John the Divine before becoming bishop.[76]

Even *Newsweek* stated: "Bishop James **Pike,** who **died in 1969, rejected orthodox Christianity** (he dismissed the Trinity as a 'committee god') but was never brought to trial [by the Episcopal Church]."[77]

In spite of his rejection of Christianity, Pike was also asked to address the National Council of Churches' Division of Christian Education which was held in Dallas, Texas. He spoke on "The **New Theology,** the **New Morality** and Christian Education."[78]

Not only did **Graham** invite him to pray at his Crusade, but he **called Pike a "great spiritual leader!"**[79] Pike reciprocated by inviting Graham to pray at his Grace Cathedral in 1960.[80]

> "Graham was no stranger to Grace Cathedral for he was one of the honored guests on May 15, 1958, with a seat on the front row when Dean Pike was consecrated as a bishop. Moreover, **Dr. Graham praised him highly from the platform** of the Cow Palace the same night. He had him on the platform to read a prayer on May 24 before a nationwide TV audience."[81]

A year **before** Graham had praised him, Pike was one of the panelists on the **Playboy Panel** published in the June **1957** issue of *Playboy.*[82]

SKINNY DIPPING AND *PLAYBOY*

Shouldn't *Playboy* bother a Christian minister as Graham is supposed to be? I would think so, but Graham's biographer writes: "For one thing...**Graham is a regular guy who can skinny dip with Lyndon Johnson or flip through Playboy at a barber shop without embarrassment.**"[83] Martin also reveals:

"In 1983, shortly after actress Jean Collins appeared in a widely publicized **nude** spread in *Playboy,* Graham and Collins were booked onto the Merv Griffin show on the same day. His staff was worried. Larry Ross pointed out that 'everything she stood for was a complete about-face from what Mr. Graham stands for. For example, she talked about how to raise a thirteen-year-old daughter with a live-in boyfriend. Several times the audience booed some of her statements, just because of the values they represented. I didn't know what to do. I thought, "This is good television, but it's going to be a real shifting of gears." I thought Mr. Graham may not know everything she stands for. So I told him. He said, "Yes, I know." Well, when he went on, the first thing Merv said was, "Billy, were you aware that Joan Collins has appeared in *Playboy?"* Mr. Graham said, "Yes, I've seen it. Someone showed it to me in the barbershop." Right on national television he said that!'"[84]

Remember, this was in a book very **favorable** to Graham and one which he had asked Martin to write!! This **IS NOT** coming from a source trying to discredit Graham.

Graham himself, while speaking about his friendship with Dulles and Hubert Humphrey, said: "I make every effort not to let it appear that I favor one party over another, I count Secretary Dulles a friend, but Senator Humphrey is also a good friend of mine, [who he met]...when we were both **swimming nude** at the YMCA pool in Minneapolis where he was running for mayor."[85]

When Graham was asked if he saw any X-rated movies, he hedged a bit and then said that he has been to R-rated movies. Although he did not answer in the affirmative, he did not deny seeing the X-rated ones!

LESLIE WEATHERHEAD

In 1966 Graham reminisced about an earlier London crusade where Leslie Weatherhead was on his platform. Graham says: "I remember during our London Crusade in **1954,** I preached a sermon....Dr. **Leslie Weatherhead sat on the platform that evening** and to my surprise commended my sermon."[86] In Graham's autobiography, *Just As I Am,* we find:

"The world-famous Methodist minister Dr. Leslie Dixon Weatherhead wrote a generous newspaper article giving his impressions after attending the first week of the Crusade [in London in 1954]. In that article, he pledged his own prayers for us and urged critics to go to the services and 'listen without prejudice.'"[87]

Why would someone like Weatherhead be on Graham's platform and commend his sermons? That is a very good question. You see, "Weatherhead was a notorious blasphemer who wrote in his book, ***The Christian Agnostic,*** that the Lord Jesus Christ was born an illegitimate child, and that Mary was no virgin, but a temple prostitute."[88]

"[T]oward the end of his life [he] wrote a final book expressing the view that **Jesus was perhaps a spirit reincarnated many times....**Weatherhead in a sermon entitled 'Is Christianity the Only Way to God?' said: 'To my mind **Christianity is certainly not the only way to God.'"**[89]

LONDON SCHOOL OF ECONOMICS

Graham added that during this visit to Britain that he "was also invited to address the various schools and colleges of the University of London, including the **London School of Economics."**[90] When he was introduced, the professor said: "This is the first time a minister has been on this platform....This school was founded on secularism...."[91]

This school certainly was a secular school! One researcher explains about the London School of Economics:

> **"The Fabian Socialists establish[ed] the London School of Economics [in 1895]...as part of their plan to further Socialism. Beatrice Webb was a founder of the Fabians and in Beatrice Webb: A Life 1858-1943, she is quoted as saying: 'We can now feel assured that with the London School of Economics as a teaching body, the Fabian Society as a propagandist organisation, the London City Council Progressives as an object lesson in (our) electoral success, our books as the only elaborate and original work in economic fact and theory, no young man or woman who is anxious to study or to work in public affairs can fail to come under our influence.'"**[92] [Emphasis in the original.]

Another book states:

> "The Fabian socialists had founded the London School of Economics in 1895 to train Socialists for the government bureaucracy (and elsewhere) to gradually put into place their plan to *'manage'* society via rules and regulations. It was described as a slowly executed *'plot'* by Fabian Socialist H. G. Wells in New Worlds for Old (1908)."[93] [Emphasis in the original.]

"Fabians believed that socialism could be achieved through mass education and a series of reforms achieved through capture of Parliament."[94]

> "In fact, the question of tactics was about the only difference between Fabian socialists and communists. Where communists desired to establish socialist governments through revolution, the Fabians were content to slowly move toward socialism through propaganda and legislation."[95]

"The Fabian Socialists had adopted the military tactics of the Roman general Quintus Fabius, who taught that one should not engage the whole enemy at one time in one place but rather should **lure him out piece by piece until he is utterly destroyed.**"[96]

The London School of Economics' "early funding came from the very wealthy: from the Rockefeller Foundation, the Carnegie United Kingdom Trust Fund, and from Mrs. Ernest Elmhirst, the widow of J. P. Morgan partner Williard Straight, amongst others."[97]

> "Some of the illustrious students who attended the School were: Joseph Kennedy Jr., the son his father Joseph Kennedy Sr. wanted to become the first Catholic President of the United States; John Kennedy, who later became President; David Rockefeller; Robert Kennedy, Jr., the son of Robert Kennedy; Senator Daniel Moynihan; Jomo Kenyatta, who was later to form the African terrorist group known as the Mau-Maus who would butcher thousands of their fellow Africans; and Eric Sevareied, CBS broadcaster."[98]

ABOLISH THE U. S.

> "Though the Fabians are dominated by an intellectual elite, and The Group is dominated by a financial elite, they both believe in a **Socialist relationship between government and the masses of people,** who should be led and cared for by an elitist-controlled government. Though the Fabians and The Group have differences of opinion which are significant, The Group will come to greatly influence the London School of Economics."[99]

The "Group" refers to the Round Table Group which came into being through Lord Alfred Milner, Cecil John Rhodes, Lord Waldorf Astor, Lord Nathan Rothschild, Lionel Curtis, Arnold Toynbee, and others.[100] Other names for the "Group" are: Milner's Kindergarten, Rhodes crowd, *The Times* crowd, the secret society of Cecil Rhodes, dream of Cecil Rhodes, All Souls group, the Chatham House crowd, and the Cliveden set.[101]

"The Round Table was dedicated to establishing a **world government** whereby a clique of super-rich financiers would **control the world** under the guise of **socialism.** It wielded great influence because it controlled the immense Rhodes Trust and the chief avenues by which the general public obtains information of public affairs, among other things. The Group adopted a deliberate **policy of secrecy** by organizing as a series of overlapping circles, or 'ring within rings,' hidden behind formally organized groups of no obvious political significance. **The Round Table later was extended into the Royal Institute of International Affairs (RIIA),** in England, under Lionel Curtis, **and the Council on Foreign Relations (CFR),** in the United States, semi-secret front groups which still exercise unopposed control for the **new world order** over foreign and monetary policy in both the United States and Great Britain and appear to be autonomous organizations. The Round Table Group's published quarterly was originally called the *Empire Review,* later called *The Round Table.*"[102]

"The **CFR, originally financed by the Rockefeller Foundation,** is composed of the most elite names in the government, the military, labor, business, finance, the media, the foundations, and the academies, and is the most influential, semi-public organization in the United States in the field of foreign policy....

"Internationalist in viewpoint, CFR members believe national boundaries should be obliterated and one-world rule established. Their goal is simply to abolish the United States with its Constitutional guarantees of liberty, and they don't even try to hide it (see *Study No. 7,* published by the CFR 11/25/59)....

"The CFR's first task was to infiltrate and develop effective control of the US State Department, which it did years ago. The CFR designed the United Nations—the first major successful step on the road to a World Superstate. The CFR headquarters building on the southwest corner of Park Avenue and 68th Street sits across the way from the Soviet Embassy to the UN, in New York City. It publishes *Foreign Affairs,* with editorial offices at 58 East 68th Street, New York, NY 10021."[103]

Isn't it fascinating to know that Billy Graham was the **first** minister to speak at the London School of Economics—especially after knowing about the background and funding of such an institution? Remember that the school was founded in 1895 and no minister spoke there until 1954.

Also remember that the **Rockefellers have funded** this school, **the Council on Foreign Relations, the Institute of Pacific Relations,**[104] the Population Council,[105] the Population Reference Bureau,[106] Columbia University Center for Policy Research,[107] the Environmental Law Institute,[108] the Population Crisis Committee,[109] the Population Institute,[110] numerous Communistic fronts and causes (such as the Highlander Research and Education Center, **Union Theological Seminary, United Nations,** African National Congress, New School for Social Research,[111] etc.), the "Building America textbook series, which played up Marxism, and sought to destroy 'traditional concepts of American government,'"[112] the sex pervert, sado-masochistic homosexual, **Alfred Kinsey**[113] (who is called the "father of the sexual revolution"[114]), as well as the Federal, National, and World Council of Churches—**and, of course, Billy Graham!**

Graham also preached at the Episcopal Washington Cathedral. This church "has had everything from rock and roll in the aisles to serving bananas and Coca Cola for Communion...."[115]

MALCOLM MUGGERIDGE

Let's look at some other speakers that Graham has promoted. At Graham's **1974** International Congress on World Evangelization, **Malcolm Muggeridge** was featured and received a standing ovation.[116] Muggeridge also denies the fundamentals of the faith. For instance, in his **1969** book, *Jesus Rediscovered,* he wrote: "To imagine this deity [that is, God] having a son in any particular sense, and this son to have been born of a virgin, and to have lived on earth for thirty years or so as a man; then to have died and to have risen from the dead, is, as far as I am concerned, beyond credibility."[117] In **1988** in an article in the *Conservative Digest,* "he said he sees the virgin birth 'as an artistic truth rather than an historical truth.' And, addressing Jesus, he asked, 'Did You live and die and rise from the dead as they say? Who knows, or, for that matter, cares?'"[118]

Muggeridge then adds:

> "I even prefer to suppose that some body snatcher, accustomed to hanging about Golgotha...finds out where the corpse [of Jesus] has been laid, drags the stone away, and then, making sure no one is watching, decamps with the body....
>
> "The man contemptuously abandons the body to the vultures, who in their turn leave the bones to whiten in the sun—those precious, precious bones!"[119]

The Bible tells us that Christ's body did not see corruption (or decay) because He rose again. Acts 2:31 states: "He seeing this before spake of the resurrection of Christ, that His soul was not left in hell, neither His flesh did see corruption." (See also: Psalm 16:10; 49:9; Acts 2:27; 13:35.)

Muggeridge "said he has found 'a resting place in the Catholic Church' [which he joined in 1981] and says Mother Teresa was a major influence in his decision." So, both **before** and **after** Billy Graham had Muggeridge featured at the International Congress on World Evangelization, Muggeridge openly and blatantly denied the fundamentals of the faith.[120]

MARTIN LUTHER KING, JR.

Let's move on to another person by the name of **Martin Luther King, Jr.** As many people already know, **King was a flagrant womanizer,[121] and a "participant in sex orgies."[122]**

> "Rev. **Ralph David Abernathy,** who was King's closest aide and confidante devotes one chapter of his 610-page book to King's extra-marital affairs and reveals that King spent parts of the night before his assassination with two women and then fought physically with a third the following morning, knocking her across a bed, according to Abernathy's memoirs."[123]

Abernathy himself was an adulterer.[124]

King was also a plagiarizer.[125] He had plagiarized someone else's work to obtain his Ph.D.[126]

> "According to writer Michael Hoffman, a King sympathizer, the Reverend Doctor's first sermon, given in 1947, was plagiarized from a homily written by the Protestant minister Harry Emerson Fosdick. Further, King's first published book, *Stride Toward Freedom,* was plagiarized from many unattributed sources.
>
> "Further, 'only 49 percent of the sentences,' in King's doctoral dissertation, 'contain five or more words that were King's own.' This admission is from the *Papers of Martin Luther King, Jr.*, a publication of the official organization which owns King's estate and writings.
>
> "Just recently, a committee of researchers at Boston University stated, 'There is no question but that Dr. King plagiarized in the dissertation.' But the committee concluded that it 'would serve no purpose' to revoke King's doctoral degree."[127]

Additionally, King was a Marxist sympathizer.[128] A pamphlet from the Socialist Party brags: "When Martin Luther King made his famous 'I Have a Dream' speech, **he shared the platform with two prominent Socialists:** black labor leader A. Philip Randolph, and presidential candidate Norman Thomas."[129]

Michael Harrington, who is referred to as "the best known socialist,"[130]

> "advised both Martin Luther King Jr. and Jesse Jackson. As the co-chair of Democratic Socialists of America, he sought to move the Democratic Party toward its truest populist and egalitarian tradition....Harrington described his political position as 'the left wing of the possible.'"[131]

Folk singer, Pete Seeger, "has never denied being a hard core Stalinist Communist. He and **Martin Luther King, Jr.** often based their speeches on the **same Communist** flimflam and even **appeared together at meetings sponsored by the Communist Party-USA."**[132]

It's no wonder, then, that King hired many Communists such as Jack O'Dell, a top Communist Party member, and Bayard Rustin, who was organizer and fund-raiser for the Young Communist League.[133] Both men had prestigious positions with King's organizations. Another close friend of King's was Dr. James Cone, who is called the father of Black Theology.[134] Cone said that King admitted he was a Marxist.[135]

CHILD MOLESTER HIRED

King himself

> "had connections with over 60 communist front organizations. Nine of his closest aides were high ranking communist activists and one of those later became an aide to Rev. Jesse Jackson. Stanley Levison, who had been a King advisor since 1956, had been involved with the Communist Party up to 1955, and brought other known communists onto King's staff."[136]

Jesse Jackson, a 59-year-old Baptist minister, made a lot of headlines recently when it was revealed that he had fathered a child out of wedlock to a 39-year-old woman who was a top staffer of his Rainbow/PUSH Coalition.[137] His affair occurred at the same time he was counseling Bill Clinton about his affair with Monica Lewinsky![138] "The press has often noted that the Rev. Jesse Jackson has been similarly unfaithful to his wife. The latest expose is just the last in a long line of affairs."[139]

Recently Jackson hired a child molester as a consultant. This person was then pardoned by Bill Clinton before he left office.[140]

RAINBOW COALITION

Jackson, of course, is following in the Communistic footsteps of King. He was one of the staff members of the **Southern Christian Leadership Conference.**[141] His "PUSH (People United to Save Humanity) is an outgrowth of King's earlier Operation Breadbasket—as is the Rainbow Coalition—but the Rainbow is also the logical extension of the Poor People's Campaign."[142]

When some radical students at Stanford University protested a course in Western civilization, Jackson led a march to fight the course while chanting "Hey, hey, ho, ho, Western culture's gotta go."[143]

The February 1995 *AFA Journal* noted "that his political organization, the National Rainbow Coalition, has named '60s radical Angela Davis as its new executive director. Davis served on the Communist Party, USA's Central Committee, and ran for v-p of the U. S. on the Communist Party ticket in 1984."[144] Jack O'Dell (also known as Hunter Pitts O'Dell and J. H. O'Dell[145]), was also a leader in Jackson's Rainbow Coalition and one of his key aides.[146]

"Jackson was the keynote speaker at a 1985 commemoration of the 10th anniversary of 'the liberation of Vietnam' **sponsored by the Communist Party USA,** according to the *Daily World,* May 7, 1985 edition."[147]

When Jackson went to another country, he held up his clenched fist and said: "Long live Fidel Castro."[148]

Obviously, the Communists were quite pleased that Jackson was running for President in 1988.[149]

> "The Communist Party, USA, has not only admitted that they 'have been actively involved in working with these committees (Labor Political Action Committees—PAC's) and coalitions (Rainbow Coalition Units), but that they 'have had a great influence' in them.
>
> "The Communists then state that: 'Without these forms (PAC's and Rainbow Units) we cannot effectively influence the congressional and senatorial races.'
>
> "The Communist Party was also working under the Democratic Party Machine backing the Jesse Jackson presidential campaign in 1988."[150]
>
> "The *All-People's Front* and the Communist's electoral efforts got a major boost from—and contributed to—Jesse Jackson's campaign for the Presidency. The lead editorial in the November 4, 1983 *Daily World* [a Communist newspaper]

> said: 'Jackson's candidacy represents a crucial component of the emerging independent political front.'"[151]

"The co-founder of the Democratic Socialists of America (DSA), a leftist political organization that roughly mirrors the labor and social democratic parties in Europe, points with great delight to the success of Jesse Jackson."[152] Jackson's Rainbow Coalition's Vermont chapter helped Bernie Sanders, a socialist, run for governor in 1986.[153]

> "Jackson continues to contribute to the Communist cause. In February 1989 he visited Moscow and proclaimed, 'Coexistence is the only path to progress.' The two key words in his statement—'coexistence' and 'progress'—have special significance for Communists. Jackson's statement ran as the banner headline on the front page of the Communist *People's Daily World* for February."[154]

One of his former economic advisors was socialist Derek Shearer, a Rhodes scholar, who also advised Bill Clinton (another Rhodes scholar[155]), Tom Hayden and Jane Fonda.[156] He wants to redistribute the wealth and eliminate private property.[157] "Shearer is a key mover and shaker within the Marxist think tank of the Institute for Policy Studies (I. P. S.), an institute that even the F. B. I. has accused of being funded by the K. G. B."[158]

GAYS AND LESBIANS FOR JACKSON

Jackson was also on Mikhail Gorbachev's guest list for "a special luncheon at the Soviet Embassy during the Bush-Gorbachev summit."[159] Some other guests included Jane Fonda, Ted Turner, Armand Hammer, John Kenneth Galbraith and Henry Kissinger.[160]

The gays and lesbians were also very supportive of Jackson.[161] Gay activist, Allen Roskoff, bragged: "He is the only candidate who makes gays and lesbians feel like they're part of the national agenda. We're part of the official campaign apparatus and we're treated with the same respect as other constituency groups."[162] "Gays and Lesbians for Jackson has been holding fundraisers and is planning a major rally April 15 at the Gay and Lesbian Community Center which Jackson will attend."[163]

Jackson had

> "a full-time gay and lesbian affairs desk headed by Randy Miller, who helped organize the gay and lesbian march on Washington [in 1987]....Jackson has endorsed every position advocated by the homosexual lobby. He opposed restrictions on the ability of gays and lesbians to gain child custody or

become foster parents. He is for granting homosexual couples the same rights married couples have to benefits, including spousal health care coverage, and he is for opening positions in government security agencies to homosexuals."[164]

In fact, the pro-Socialist book, *Encyclopedia of the American Left* states: "To date, the Reverend Jesse Jackson is the only leader of national prominence who has embraced the [gay and lesbian] movement's full agenda, including spousal rights, the rights of gay and lesbian parents to claim custody of their children, and the decriminalization of sodomy."[165]

In spite of Jackson's past, Andrew Young (who will be covered shortly) said after Jesse's first presidential campaign that he was "the **moral** voice of our time."[166]

Jackson is also a member of the Council on Foreign Relations[167] as well as a 33° Mason.[168] He was on the board of directors of SANE[169] and a member of the World Constitution and Parliament Association (WCPA),[170] an organization working toward world government.[171]

Not only is Jackson a Mason, an adulterer, pro-Communist, pro-abortion[172] pro-gay, etc., but he "has clearly repudiated historic Christianity, and his Christ is not the Christ of the Bible."[173] He claims that the story of Adam and Eve is a myth.[174] At the Democratic Convention, he said: "'Remember, Jesus was born to a homeless couple....He was the child of a single mother.' He thus implied that Jesus was born out of wedlock (illegitimate) as Jackson was. But Joseph, a carpenter, was Mary's husband, and they were neither homeless nor jobless."[175]

In spite of Jackson's obviously blasphemous remarks about Christ, the *Jesus Film* Project, which is a ministry of Bill Bright's Campus Crusade,[176] had "A Millennial Tribute to Jesus" and used celebrities to record a "tribute to Jesus."[177] Who were some of these celebrities? Jesse Jackson, Jimmy Carter, Gerald Ford, Andrew Young, Pope John Paul II, and **Billy Graham!**[178] How could Jackson, for instance, give a tribute to Jesus when he implies that He was born out of wedlock? Furthermore, why would the director of the Jesus Film, Paul Eshleman,[179] even consider people like Jackson and Young to bring such a message?

Perhaps it should also be noted that the person who played the role of Jesus in the *Jesus Film,* Brian Deacon, admits that he is not a Christian.[180] "He calls himself 'a lapsed Catholic who hasn't practiced his faith.'"[181] He adds: "I've always found it difficult to know how truth can be proclaimed to others; to me it's more of a private matter."[182]

FOMENT RACIAL TENSION

Returning to King, we find that

> "James Dombrowski was another member of the Communist Party who was a close friend and adviser to 'Martin Luther' King. There exists a photocopy of a cancelled check made out to King from the officially identified Communist front, the Southern Conference Educational Fund (S.C.E.F.). The check was signed by Dombrowski and one Benjamin Smith, an officially identified agent of Fidel Castro. A letter from King to Dombrowski is in the possession of government investigators in which King wrote: 'Dear Jim: We were more than happy to have you in our home, the fellowship was very rewarding.... Sincerely yours, Martin.'"[183]

Dombrowski is considered to be a "Christian Socialist."[184] It was through Dr. Harry F. Ward at Union Theological Seminary that Dombrowski became an organizer.[185] He later joined the Highlander Folk School[186] and then went on to found the Southern Conference Educational Fund.[187]

> "Carl and Anne Braden have both been longtime, notorious members of the Communist Party, working in the Louisville area. They were officers of the S.C.E.F. and were also among the 'Louisville Seven'—a group that purchased a house in an all-white neighborhood in Louisville, sold it to a Negro family, and then, on June 27, 1954, dynamited it in order to foment racial trouble. These facts have been established both by a grand jury and a court trial. Yet in 1959, that apostle of nonviolence, 'Martin Luther' King, wrote a letter to the Bradens urging them to become permanently associated with his **Southern Christian Leadership Conference.** And in 1962, a photograph taken at the 6th annual meeting of the S.C.L.C. shows King, Carl and Anne Braden, and Dombrowski; writing on the reverse side describes King as 'responding to Anne Braden's speech.'"[188]

In 1958, the Bradens were asked to testify in court but Carl said:

> "'My beliefs and my associations are none of the business of this committee,' and refused to testify based on his right of freedom of speech and association contained in the First Amendment....Rev. Martin Luther King, Jr., and other black leaders held a dinner honoring Braden and Wilkinson before they entered prison to begin serving ten months of a year's prison sentence for contempt of Congress."[189]

The Bradens

> "steadfastly worked with and supported Communists and others on the Left and stated their own socialist beliefs when they thought them relevant to the struggle at hand.

"Anne received the 1989 Roger Baldwin Medal of Liberty from the American Civil Liberties Union, for 'outstanding commitment to the cause of civil liberties.'...The American Civil Liberties Union in Louisville likewise honored her on her seventieth birthday in recognition of her fearless work in the South."[190]

"Mrs. Julia Brown was an undercover agent for the F.B.I. and said, '...Mr. King was one of the worst enemies my people ever had.'...She added, '...the Communists loved Martin Luther King. He was one of their biggest heroes....He carried out their orders just as slavishly as Party members....'"[191]

Brown, a former Communist, said the Communist Party was

"told to promote Martin Luther King to unite Negroes and whites behind him....'He was taking directions from Communists. I know for a fact the Communists would never have promoted him, financed him, and supported him if they couldn't trust him. I am certain as I can be that he knew what he was doing!'"[192]

"The May, 1968 issue of *Political Affairs,* the voice of the **Communist Party, wrote** after the death of Rev. Martin Luther King, Jr.: 'The Reverend Martin Luther King, Jr., the voice, inspiration and symbol of the Negro people's struggle for freedom and equality, is dead....The man who, more than anyone else, personified the heroic determination of the Black people to win their liberation now. **One of humanity's great leaders** has been silenced forever....We must see that his memory not be desecrated. We must not fail to do all in our power to realize the dream for which he died.'"[193]

The Guardian, an "independent radical newsweekly,"[194] wrote: "Considering his last acts—his adoption of a class analysis of social issues, his commitment to workers and his growing internationalism—to suggest he was a 'socialist-on-the-path' may be the fairest appraisal of King's final philosophical position."[195] Interestingly, this article had originally appeared in the British journal *Marxism Today.*[196]

RIVERSIDE CHURCH

"One year before his death in Memphis, King ascended the pulpit of the **Riverside Church** in New York City to flay the United States as 'the greatest purveyor of violence in the world today.' He orated that U. S. military forces 'may have killed one million South VietNamese (sic) civilians—mostly children,' and he praised Communist North Viet Nam dictator Ho Chi Minh as the only true leader of the VietNamese (sic) people."[197]

Riverside Church is the church that the Rockefellers attend. By the way, the Rockefellers were some of King's main supporters.[198] Just recently (September 2000) Fidel Castro (who *"demanded a 'new world order'"*[199]) spoke at this church for four hours.[200]

The Rockefellers were supporters of eugenicist Margaret Sanger,[201] the founder of Planned Parenthood, as well.[202] She is credited with coining the term "birth control" in 1912[203] and later was known as "the Mother of Birth Control."[204] She also founded the Euthanasia Society of America, Inc. in 1938.[205]

Not only was she the 1957 "Humanist of the Year,"[206] but she joined the Socialist Party and attended its functions.[207] She was friends with Julius Hammer who was a co-founder of the Communist Party in America.[208] Sanger "went from one lover to another, sometimes several times in a single day....She began to dabble in the occult, participating in seances and practicing Eastern meditation. She even went so far as to apply for initiation into the mysteries of Rosicrucianism and Theosophy."[209] She belonged to Unity,[210] a New Age, New Thought group[211] and was a sponsor of the occult Temple of Understanding.[212] Additionally, she was addicted to both drugs and alcohol.[213]

> "Because of her Malthusian and Eugenic connections, she had become closely associated with the scientists and theorists who put together Nazi Germany's 'race purification' program. She had openly endorsed the euthanasia, sterilization, abortion, and infanticide programs of the early Reich. She published a number of articles in *The Birth Control Review* that mirrored Hitler's Aryan-White Supremacist rhetoric."[214]

In Sanger's book, *Women and the New Race,* "she declared that 'the most merciful thing that the large family does to one of its infant members is to kill it.'"[215]

This is the kind of person that Martin Luther King honored in an article he wrote[216] which appeared in Planned Parenthood, entitled "Family Planning: A Special and Urgent Concern."[217]

MARCH ON WASHINGTON

King, along with Rev. Ralph David Abernathy,[218] and Bayard Rustin, all Communists, founded the Southern Christian Leadership Conference (SCLC).[219]

> "The **[Rockefeller] Foundation contributed money to the** pro-communist New School for Social Research in New York City, and funded projects for the **communist-staffed Southern Christian Leadership Conference, led by Rev. Martin Luther King, Jr.** Rep. Cox said that the Rockefeller Foundation has 'been used to finance individuals and organizations whose business it has been to get communism into private and public schools of the country, to talk down to America, and play up Russia.'...The Foundation also funded the Kinsey Report, which heralded a new era of sexual immorality."[220]

Abernathy, one of SCLC's founders and one of King's top aides, visited **Communist** East Germany. There he said, "What we are still fighting for in the U. S. A. is what has already been achieved... (here)."[221] **Abernathy later became President of the SCLC.**[222]

In 1957 Rustin (who was a **self-proclaimed Communist** as well as a homosexual[223]) attended the Communist Party's national convention. It was just one month after this that the SCLC was founded![224] At this time, Rustin was also a member of the American Forum for **Socialist** Education, which "was officially cited as a Communist Front."[225]

Rustin had

> "served time in a Federal penitentiary during World War II as a draft dodger and went to jail in 1953 after pleading guilty to a charge of sex perversion. Rustin has said that the only hope for the Negro is to 'go left,' and while in Richmond, Virginia, he told an audience that 'more bloody Negro suffering should be encouraged so that the squeamish Northern Negroes would be horrified into line.'"[226]

> "In 1958 Comrade Bayard was one of five Americans sent to Moscow by a 'pacifist' opposed to nuclear weapons. Upon his return, he helped Martin Luther King organize a 'March on Washington,' which *The Worker* [a Communist newspaper] described as a **Communist** project. In 1963, under the supervision of veteran Communist-Fronter A. Philip Randolph, Rustin coordinated the 'March on Washington for Jobs and Freedom.'"[227]

> "Bayard Rustin's enthusiasm for Leftist and pro-Communist causes, is also made clear by his affiliations with the socialist League for Industrial Democracy, the pacifist Committee for Nonviolent Action, the pro-Castro Emergency Committee for Disaster Relief to Cuba, and the Monroe (N.C.) Defense Committee. The latter group was established to defend

> Communist Robert Williams, the Negro revolutionary who fled to Cuba and then Red China when sought by the F.B.I. on a kidnapping charge. For several years Williams has been in the pay of Communist governments and inciting American Negroes to open rebellion against law and order. He recently returned to this country with the blessing of the American government."[228]

Rustin also belonged to the Fellowship of Reconciliation.[229] Of course, King referred to Rustin as a "brilliant, efficient, [and] dedicated" individual.[230] When King went to Oslo to get the Peace Prize in 1964, he took Rustin along for companionship.[231]

Rustin remained King's secretary until 1960 when he was replaced by another Communist, Hunter Pitts O'Dell.[232]

O'Dell was with the **Southern Christian Leadership Conference** and worked as King's staff consultant during the 1960s.

> "During this very period, O'Dell was a member of the National Committee of the Communist Party. After the *St. Louis Globe Democrat* on October 26, 1961 revealed that O'Dell had been twice officially identified as a **communist organizer,** King announced that he had discharged O'Dell. But a few months later it was discovered that O'Dell had not been fired, but promoted, and was actually supervising King's New York office. When this fact was published, King claimed to have discharged O'Dell a second time. Subsequently, a check was made by the United Press International, which determined that Communist Party member O'Dell was still employed for King."[233]

Another of King's secretaries was Rev. Uriah J. Fields. He wrote: **"King helps to advance Communism. He is surrounded with Communists.** This is the major reason I severed my relationship with him during the fifties."[234]

LIQUOR AND PROSTITUTES

> "Karl Prussion, an FBI agent who infiltrated the Communist Party, and for five years attended meetings in California, testified in 1963: 'I further swear and attest that at each and every one of the aforementioned meetings, one Reverend Martin Luther King was always set forth as the individual to whom Communists should look and rally around in the Communist struggle on many racial issues.'"[235]

King used the funds of the Southern Christian Leadership Conference for some strange activities. William C. Sullivan is an FBI agent. He

> "has stated the FBI records indicate **King routinely embezzled and misapplied funds contributed to the civil rights movement. King used SCLC funds to buy liquor and numerous prostitutes,** both black and white, who were taken to his hotel rooms, usually two at a time, for **drunken sex parties** normally lasting several days. Evidence indicated this practice was **habitual** for King during his organizational and speaking tours across the country."[236]

"In Las Vegas, King's aids (sic) paid $100 each to prostitutes to join him in orgies."[237]

"King enjoyed slapping women around, and—get this!—he was a bisexual who actually favored men over women in bed!"[238]

Charles D. Brennan had served as Assistant Director of the FBI. He

> "stated that he had personally been involved in the FBI surveillance of King and knew from first-hand observation the truth about King's sexual conduct—conduct that Mr. Brennan characterized as 'orgiastic and adulterous escapades, some of which indicated that King could be bestial in his sexual abuse of women.' He also stated that 'King frequently drank to excess and at times exhibited extreme emotional instability as when he once threatened to jump from his hotel room window.'"[239]

> "In Norway, King was nude when stopped by police while chasing a woman down a hotel corridor. In Los Angeles a dentist supporter of King was outraged when he discovered his wife engaged in weird sexual acts with the civil rights leader. King was forced to flee the city after the dentist threatened to kill him. This escapade was taped on February 20, 1968. Is this the kind of man we want to hold up before our children to be honored as a national hero?"[240]

I don't know what kind of liquor King bought with SCLC funds, but an ad from Anheuser-Busch Companies bragged that they actively support groups like the SCLC![241] They add: "Anheuser-Busch salutes outstanding African Americans who have made significant contributions to American history. By honoring heroes and heroines like Dr. Martin Luther King, Jr.,...we hope to enrich and perpetuate African-American pride."[242]

Even though King is now deceased, the SCLC has continued to promote liberal causes. For instance, the SCLC was one of several groups that endorsed the 1993 homosexual march in Washington.[243] Also, a list compiled with the assistance of the National Gay and Lesbian Task Force, listed the SCLC as one of the groups "promoting

Democratic rights, civil liberties, social justice, equality and pluralism."[244]

Since King was a Communist it is no surprise to learn that even though he was a Baptist preacher, he denied the fundamental doctrines of Christianity.[245] For instance, he denied the virgin birth, Christ's deity and the resurrection of Christ.[246] He remarked in the January 1961 issue of *Ebony*: "I do not believe in hell as a place of a literal burning fire."[247]

King nominated Thich Nhat Hanh for the 1967 Nobel Peace Prize.[248] Hanh is a Zen Master and Buddhist monk who teaches occultic meditation practices![249]

One of Hanh's verses includes:

> "Before starting the car,
> I know where I am going.
> **The car and I are one**
> If the car goes fast, I go fast."[250]

The New Age movement regularly teaches the theory of "at-one-ment" which is what Hahn was referring to when he said: "The car and I are one."

Recently (October 9, 1999) Hahn was a speaker at the Grand Opening ceremonies of EXPLORIS. There he stated:

> *"I would propose that every morning we practice Seven Steps....Breathing in, I am aware of Mother Earth....It would be wonderful if everyone of us on earth could make steps like that...to massage the earth with our feet, with our love, with our understanding....Understanding is the fruit of meditation.... We should walk in such a way that the...land of Buddha is available in the here and now."*[251] [Emphasis in the original.]

Hahn was also a participant at the 1995 globalist gathering called the State of the World Forum.[252]

King was well aware of Hahn's religious orientation because he said: "I do not personally know of anyone more worthy of the Nobel Peace Prize than this gentle **Buddhist monk** from Vietnam...."[253]

GRAHAM AND KING

With all the Communist activities of Martin Luther King, Jr., how does **Billy Graham** feel about him? Well, in Graham's autobiography, he writes: "One night civil rights leader Dr. **Martin Luther King, Jr.,** whom I was **pleased to count a friend,** gave an eloquent opening prayer at the service; he also came **at my invitation** to one of our Team retreats during the Crusade to help us understand the racial situation in America more fully."[254] Graham was the one who invited King to pray.[255] Graham even tells us that he was the person who had introduced King at this Crusade in 1957[256] and he publicly endorsed him![257] "In his introduction he said, 'A great social revolution is going on in the United States today. Dr. King is one of its leaders, and we appreciate his taking time out of his busy schedule to come and share this service with us tonight.'"[258]

King also gave the opening prayer at Graham's crusade in 1959. Graham said that "a **great social revolution** is going on in America today and he is **one of its most illustrious leaders."**[259]

In 1960, Graham had traveled with King to and from the Baptist World Alliance.[260] A 1963 interview with the *New York Times* quoted **Graham referring to King as his "good personal friend."**[261]

From the book, *A Prophet with Honor,* written at the request of Billy Graham, we read:

> "Billy Graham was letting both whites and blacks know that he was willing to be identified with the revolution and its foremost leader, and Martin Luther King was telling blacks that **Billy Graham was their ally.** According to both Graham and [Howard] Jones, King also told the evangelist that 'your crusades do more with white people than I could do. **We help each other.** Keep on.'"[262]

Ralph Reed (who wrote favorably about King) stated: "Billy Graham had a friendship relationship with King."[263]

A few weeks before Graham's Madison Garden Crusade he did an interview with *The New York Times.* In reference to racial tensions, he

> "stressed that the most effective action would be 'setting an example of love,' then added, **'as I think Martin Luther King...has done in setting an example of Christian love.'** Given the time and his constituency, this **on-the-record endorsement of the controversial civil rights leader** was a notable step for the cautious evangelist."[264]

Graham reveals:

> "Early on, Dr. King and I spoke about his method of using non-violent demonstrations to bring an end to racial segregation. He urged me to keep on doing what I was doing—preaching the Gospel to integrated audiences and **supporting his goals by example**—and not to join him in the streets. 'You stay in the stadiums, Billy,' he said, 'because you will have far more impact on the white establishment there than you would if you

> marched in the streets. Besides that, you have a constituency that will listen to you, especially among white people, who may not listen so much to me. But if a leader gets too far out in front of his people, they will lose sight of him and not follow him any longer.' **I followed his advice.**"[265]

Listen to what else Graham says:

> "Knowing a great number of people has its poignant side also, as I hear of the death of **someone whose friendship I have valued** and realize I will not see that person again. Sometimes their passing is tragic, and I feel it very sharply. **I think, for example, of the death of Martin Luther King, Jr.,** in 1968....
>
> "...I was almost in a state of shock. Not only was **I losing a friend** through a vicious and senseless killing, but **America was losing a social leader and a *prophet*,** and I felt his death would be one of the greatest tragedies in our history."[266]
>
> "Unable to return home for the funeral, he [Graham] sent telegrams and flowers and gave the press a muted tribute to King: 'Many people who have not agreed with Dr. King can admire him for his non-violent policies and in the eyes of the world **he has become one of the greatest Americans.'"**

Christianity Today, a magazine founded by Billy Graham, also mentions King in a favorable light. The article is a book review for *Parting the Waters: America in the King Years, 1953-1963,* written by Taylor Branch. It states:

> "Among the most tantalizing details Branch records are the **friendly contacts King had with** a fellow Southern preacher who, though white, had rejected segregation—**Billy Graham.** King was tremendously impressed by Graham's crusade evangelism with its careful preparation months in advance, and **he met several times with Graham and his aides** to learn their techniques. King dreamed of a Graham-and-King crusade that would convert racially mixed audiences, first in the North and eventually in the South. 'These dreams floundered,' Branch says, 'on the question of emphasis between politics and pure religion.' The two men remained privately friendly, and Graham's aides gave considerable practical advice to King's organization, but their paths remained separate....
>
> "Martin Luther **King,** Jr., was not a perfect man, as he himself was deeply aware. But reading this book one cannot escape the conviction that he **was a great man, and that our**

nation would be far poorer if he had never lived and preached to us."[267]

A year after King's death, **Graham had the Communist Ralph Abernathy, King's closest aide and an adulterer, as one the featured speakers at his 1969 Congress on Evangelism.**[268] Remember, Abernathy is also "an avowed Marxist revolutionary...."

> "One report of the event stated that Abernathy's 'presence was a surprise and shock to many of the delegates because of his well known radical stand.' Graham, however, did not object. Nor did he offer an apology to the 5,000 delegates after Abernathy unleashed a predictably vicious tirade against the Christian churches and the United States."[269]

JAMMING IN THE DOME

King's death did not stop Graham's friendship with the Kings. In 1994 Graham had a youth rally in Atlanta, Georgia.[270] "Dr. Billy Graham said on TV prior to the opening of his crusade here in Atlanta...that they (Christians, Jews and **Moslems**) were going to build a spiritual wall around Atlanta."[271] His

> "recent five-day Georgia Dome crusade featured such big names as Jimmy Carter, Andrew Young, **Coretta Scott King,** Joseph Lowery, Robert Schuller, Charles Stanley, and Greg Laurie. But the biggest attraction was a Saturday night 'Jamming in the Dome' youth rally that drew 78,000 people....It featured two hip-hop religious **rock groups:** DC Talk rappers (with roots in Jerry Falwell's Liberty University[272]), and Take 6 (Seventh-Day Adventists!). Andrae Crouch performed. The BGEA [Billy Graham Evangelistic Association] ran frequent 'MTV-style' commercials on six Atlanta TV stations."[273]

Billy Graham said: "We use their music to get our message across."[274] This "high-tech light and laser show was produced by **Scott DeVoss** who **has produced similar acts for Rolling Stones, Madonna and Michael Jackson."**[275]

Graham himself wrote:

> "It was Saturday evening, October 29, 1994. On the stage of Atlanta's vast Georgia Dome, a **high-energy rap musical group** called dc-Talk was belting out a number at top volume, to the obvious delight of the 78,000 fans packing the stadium, almost all of whom were under the age of twenty-one. A high-tech light show flashed and pulsed from a sixty-foot-high truss

> overhead, part of nine trailer-loads of equipment brought in especially for the production.
>
> "As I stepped onto the platform, I couldn't help but recall the rock concert I had attended in Miami twenty-five years before. But this was a musical event with a difference. All the artists were Christians. 'Jammin' in the Dome,' as it was called, was a special youth-night outreach we had planned as part of our Atlanta Crusade."[276]

Some people do not believe that Graham would do this. All they can picture are his Crusades with George Beverly Shea singing the old-time gospel hymns. This is no longer true. Oh, Shea does still make his appearance, but more and more **Graham is adding at least one night of rock music.**[277] He's had such concerts in Cleveland, Ohio (1994);[278] Toronto, Canada (June 1995);[279] Portland, Oregon (1992);[280] Charlotte, North Carolina (1996);[282] Minneapolis, Minnesota (1996);[282] San Antonio, Texas (April 1997);[283] Indianapolis, Indiana;[284] Tampa, Florida (October 24, 1998);[285] and Jacksonville, Florida (November 2000).[286]

At the **Minnesota Crusade,** one news report states that some older people "were taken back by the **ear-shattering rock music."**[287] The reason some people are unaware of these rock concerts at Graham's crusades is that **such an event is not usually televised.** "Graham's TV director Roger Flessing said that the Saturday event may be the only one **not** televised. 'We don't know if the wider audience is ready for this yet.'"[288] This way the majority of Graham's supporters will never know what is really going on unless they actually attend the Crusade on the night that the rock concert is being performed.

RUNIC SYMBOLISM ON "CHRISTIAN" RECORD

Who were the performers at the Minnesota Crusade? They were **dc Talk, Michael W. Smith, and Amy Grant.**[289]

The *Wall Street Journal* tells us that **Smith was using marijuana, LSD, and cocaine at the same time as he was penning gospel songs.**[290]

> **"Michael W. Smith** was seen as a hot number by the *Wall Street Journal* when it learned that **his sexy, steamy, sensuous video** was produced by the same company that produces the rocker formerly known as Prince. **'I know if I am too blatant about my Christianity and talk about Jesus I won't succeed.** But, hey, I'm not an evangelist. I'm a singer.'"[291]

Smith even has **occultic** runic symbols (runes) on his one record album and the flip side has Smith's name written backwards! (For more information about runes, see my book *Masonic and Occult Symbols Illustrated.* This book shows the runic symbols used on Michael W. Smith's album!) "Writing reversal is a SATANIC principle. Master satanist Aleister Crowley taught his disciples to walk backwards, talk backwards, think backwards, speak backwards, write backwards and even listen to phonograph records backwards to gain insight into the future."[292]

It is also interesting to note that in this "Christian" album by Smith the name of Jesus is only mentioned ONE time![293]

"MADONNA" OF GOSPEL ROCK

As some readers already know, **Amy Grant** was called "The 'Madonna' of Gospel Rock" by *Family Circle* in their September 9, 1986 issue.[294] She swam in the nude with a friend.[295] Here's the report from *Ladies Home Journal:*

> "[In 1984] she **took all her clothes off on what she thought was a nude beach** in Africa....
>
> "'My girlfriend and I wondered why the boys had their clothes on,' Amy remembers, 'so we swam way out in the ocean and stayed there. Later we learned it was *not* a nude beach. But no big deal. **It was a liberating experience.** It felt unbelievably crazy to take off all my clothes and play in the sun. I've not had that much fun in so long...."[296] [Italics in the original.]

Remember, she made her first **"Christian"** music record in 1978—six years **before** this incident.[297]

She also thinks it's fun to use foul language with friends.[298] "Both *Rolling Stone* Magazine and *USA Today* have reported that she uses off-color crude vulgarisms."[299] She said: "I have a healthy sense of right and wrong, but sometimes, for example, using foul, exclamation-point words among friends can be good for a laugh."[300] The Lord is not laughing. The Bible clearly tells us: ""**Let no corrupt communication proceed out of your mouth,** but that which is good to the use of edifying, that it may minister grace unto the hearers...Let all bitterness, and wrath, and anger, and clamour, and evil speaking, be put away from you..." (Ephesians 4:29, 31). Colossians 3:8 warns: "But now ye also put off all these; anger, wrath, malice, blasphemy, **filthy communication out of your mouth."**

"The 12/22 *Woman's Day* says that during a therapy and counselling process, she and her husband, on their way to a movie, 'had this huge fight, **screaming obscenities** at each other.'"[301] "She talks about her feelings, even sexual ones, to her audience...."[302] Both Amy and her former husband, Gary Chapman (a cocaine user[303]), are now divorced and remarried.[304]

After she "crossed over" into the mainstream rock scene back in 1991, "some 'Christian' stations refused to play Grant's songs. Her MTV behavior, and video showing her cavorting with a male model also caused problems."[305] "[S]he favors flashy leopard-skin jackets and leg-huggy black tights"[306] which *Family Circle* "says are worn in a 'sensual' manner."[307]

"She openly admits that her album covers and posters contain sensually oriented pictures of herself in an attempt to sell records."[308] When asked about petting before marriage, she replied: "Petting happens. It's part of growing up, finding out who you are, how men and women work. As a teenager, when I gave part of me to someone, I knew I was just going to flirt, have a little fun, and do whatever I could rationalize, but go no further, because there is only one *first* time."[309] [Emphasis in the original.]

Grant also states: "I'm not going to say too often that **I like a cold beer** while watching a football game. That might bother some of my fans."[310] In another interview she admits: "I love a nice glass of wine."[311] Grant has even been sponsored by beer companies. There was an advertisement in the *Fresno Bee* that "said Grant was being sponsored by Budweiser beer."[312] Also, "on several occasions Grant has appeared with a number of other musical acts in a concert series sponsored by a beer company. On those occasions, the advertising agreements were made between the beer company and the local concert promoter, not between the beer company and Grant."[313]

No wonder Grant says: "I'm a singer, not a preacher...I'm not looking to convert anybody."[314] If she has no intention of converting anyone, what would be the purpose of Billy Graham using her? Of course, Grant has nothing Christian to convert anyone to, anyway!

GRANT SPEAKS IN TONGUES

On a recent album, Grant gave the following notice to the radio stations: "As far as the lyrical content is concerned, **there's no evangelical bent, no mention of God.** If the music you play has to have either of those two elements, you might not want to play it."[315]

Part of Grant's inspiration for her songs came from John Denver. "Denver is an occult lover and nature worshipper, who believes that nature and human beings are actually God. Denver, in reality, is a pantheist. He 'prefers pot to alcohol' and knows in a certain sense that 'I am God.' He is involved in EST, pantheism, transcendental meditation and 'new age' occultism...."[316] How much of this occult influence was manifested through Amy Grant's songs (although perhaps subtly) at Graham's crusades?

Incidentally,

> "St. John's University gave its highest award to rock star Amy Grant [in 1994]....She is the third woman to receive the Pax Christi award, often called a jewel in the crown of the Roman Catholic Church. Pax Christi is the radical International Catholic Peace Movement. Grant, a charismatic [yes, she has received her 'prayer language' and speaks in tongues[317]], was called 'a **contemporary Christian role model for today's generation'** and **praised for the 'Christian values' in her life** and music career."[318]

I might add that many Satanists, witches, occultists, and unsaved people also speak in tongues, so this certainly is not a sign that a person is a Christian.

In the 20 plus years that Grant's been on the music scene, "she has garnered five Grammys and 22 Dove Awards, has been named Artist of the Year four times, and has seen her 14 albums sell over 20 million copies worldwide."[319] The Bible doesn't recognize worldly success. The Bible asks a somber question: "For what is a man profited, if he shall gain the whole world, and lose his own soul? or what shall a man give in exchange for his soul?" (Matthew 16:26; Mark 8:36; and Luke 9:25). In fact, the one album that received a Dove Award didn't even mention the name of Christ **ONE** time! How can this be "Christian" music without Christ?!

HEAD BANGING AND BODY SURFING

Let's look at some other rock singers used by Billy Graham in his crusades. Below is a lengthy quote that appeared in the secular and liberal paper, *The Sacramento Bee.*

> "Old-line Christian evangelism was married with **raw rock 'n' roll** passion Saturday night **as the Billy Graham Crusade cranked up its amps** and celebrated Youth Night in a crowd that was Arco Arena's biggest ever.
>
> "More than 45,000 **people danced, stomped, shouted and swayed to the grunge rock of DC Talk, a band Graham has called his 'translators to a younger generation.'...**

> "When he took the podium at 8:30 p.m., 15 minutes later than usual to accommodate the ear splitting music of *DC Talk,* Graham thanked the Sacramento fire marshal for permitting what the evangelist said were more people than local fire code allowed....As forceful as Graham was, there seemed little doubt that the crowd size was largely attributed to *DC Talk,* one of the most popular Christian bands in the nation. *'I don't understand all that they're singing, but I have the words. And I appreciate all these people. DC Talk has been a guest at my home,* and I know them all and I love them. *I speak their language a little bit, and they're beginning to understand a little of mine. So we get along fine,'* Graham said.
>
> "On the floor in front of the band, hundreds of kids jammed in tightly near the stage tossing paper airplanes, dancing and shouting....**They even formed a mosh pit**—a sea of shaking humanity where bodies were lifted in the air and passed from hand to hand....It was *Youth Night, Rock Your World,* and the only difference between this extravaganza and an arena rock show were the Christian lyrics and the absence of alcohol and marijuana smoke."[320] [Italics in the original.]

Graham likes dc Talk (as is obvious by the above quote), but their role models come from **secular** rock bands like U2, Davie Bowie, The Police, and the Beatles[321] "and they sometimes include a Beatles or Doobie Brothers song in their shows."[322] At one so-called "Christian" concert, dc Talk even used drug addict Jimi Hendrix's song *Purple Haze.* The song title itself is a reference to drugs![323] One observer at the Rapid City Civic Center noted:

> "Each time either band [DC Talk or Audio Adrenaline] did anything secular the amount of body surfing increased as well as other behavior unbecoming of Christians. That should suggest that the majority of the crowd was there for the 'rock' music and the Christian aspect had nothing to do with it.
>
> "Let's not forget—the members from both bands encouraged the behavior and took part in it! Two of the **DC Talk** band members jumped off stage into the crowd and the third band member jumped off sound equipment that sat on the stage which made his jump higher....
>
> "In fact, **DC Talk** says in their promotional video, 'we want to get a good mosh pit going and some head-banging.' As to the bodysurfing, well, the band participates! Does this sort of behavior align to Scripture?"[324]

Andrae Crouch was also used at Graham's Atlanta Crusade. One researcher reports:

"Just previous to this event, *World* magazine, August 13, 1994, reported that 'Mr. Crouch and his choir have popped up on everything from albums by Michael Jackson and Madonna to the soundtrack of *The Lion King.*' From Michael Jackson and Madonna to singing for Christ? What a fine Christian model for young people!?"[325]

ROCK MUSIC FOR AN ALTAR CALL

Another group used by Graham at his Crusades is the Charlie Daniels Band. In an interview with Daniels by the *Huntsville Times* (July 31, 1994), they "quoted him using profanity."[326] A former witch says that this "band is famous for its song about a violin duel between a man and the devil for the man's soul. This is an ungodly and worldly band, and to associate the precious blood of Jesus to such a country-western perversion is inexcusable!"[327] Yet this is the band who was chosen to play country rock before the altar call![328]

At Graham's St. Louis Crusade held from October 14-17, 1999, once again we find that the "[m]usical guests included Michael W. Smith, the Charlie Daniels Band, Kirk Franklin, dc Talk and CeCe Winans."[329]

Graham's June 2000 Crusade in Nashville, Tennessee also featured groups like the "Jars of Clay, dc Talk, Kirk Franklin, and Steven Curtis Chapman."[330] Graham had previously used Jars of Clay in his October 1998 crusade in Tampa, Florida,[331] and in his Quebec, Canada crusade in June 1998,[332] as well as most recently in his Jacksonville, Florida crusade in November 2000.[333] By the way, **"Jars of Clay,** currently [1997] the most popular Christian band, patterns their music after the Beatles and other secular groups."[334] Shortly **before** Graham had them perform in his crusades, **this group had "recorded for an R-rated film loaded with 'live-in' lovers, nudity, graphic violence, and 83 obscenities."**[335] The lead vocalist from this band said: "We don't want to be called a 'Christian band' because it is a turn-off."[336] Jerry Huffman perceptively added: "Don't worry, we would not accuse it of such!"[337]

Billy Graham's son, Franklin, is now taking over "the administrative and management burden" of Graham's ministry and will replace him when he retires.[338] One researcher notes:

> "In succeeding his father Billy Graham, Franklin has to keep up with the times, reconfigured some of the outer trappings of the crusades. George Beverly Shea has 'deferred to the grittier, rowdier (and hunkier) Michael W. Smith, says the 4/5 *Christianity Today.* The shorter attention span of today's audience

forces the younger Graham to keep his message to 15 minutes. Video clips keep the audience entertained between speakers. CT reports: 'Franklin no longer calls them *crusades*—"that's a **church** word." They are *festivals*—"that's a **secular** word."' For baby boomers, this evokes images of Woodstock. This is called being 'seeker sensitive,' but might also be called 'pragmatism,' 'watering down,' 'men-pleasing,' 'compromise,' or catering to the world."[339] [Italics in the original.]

Franklin, too, uses the so-called "Christian" rock to attract the crowds.

"*The Charlotte Observer*, September 28, 1994, reported that '10,000 came Monday to hear Christian rock followed by Graham's **updated** call to confess sins.' Later, the same article reported: 'Franklin had rock group Audio Adrenaline pump up the volume on heavy metal with a Gospel twist. "This is Christian Led Zeppelin," crusade emcee Jim Branch shouted to teenagers....'

"*Time*, May 13, 1996, reports that Franklin Graham desires to 'make the crusade's musical component less churchy and more accessible.' (The Quick and the Dead, a Christian punk band, has played at one of his crusades, singing: 'I'll dress like a woman. Bare my b— But sometimes I wish I was me.')"[340]

How can groups like this possibly reach the youth with the gospel of Jesus Christ? They can't, and since they can't, why have them perform? It's not only a waste of time, it's also a waste of money that was sent to the Grahams' organizations to reach lost souls.

One researcher gives the following story:

"The folly of putting Christian lyrics to rock was brought home by an incident related to me by one of my former students. Doug's parents, Elmer and Ruth Warkentin, serve as missionaries in Kalimantan. One day his sister Jan received a visitor...from the United States. Jan's friend had brought along some of the latest **Christian contemporary albums.** The walls of Kalimantan homes are not noted for their 'soundproofness,' and as one of these songs was being played in the living room, the music floated out into the street. Some members of the local congregation happened to be walking by and heard the strange sound coming from the missionary's house. Wide-eyed and bewildered, they rushed to the house and asked excitedly, **'Why are you calling on the spirits with your music?'** They had no way of knowing that what they were hearing was not the music of the medicine man, but merely the latest 'Christian' music from America. To them this meant only that the missionary had left his senses and was communicating with demons."[341]

Although the rock music night at Graham's crusades has been going on for almost a decade, **over 30 years ago** in 1969 "Graham announced that, as a **supplement** to the nightly rallies, a **new feature** in the form of a huge coffee house would be set up in nearby Manhattan Center, where the young can gather afterward and talk in an atmosphere of **psychedelic lighting and amplified folk-rock music."**[342] Most adults never knew that such a thing was taking place since it was held at another place!

The Bible tells us that we edify ourselves "in psalms and hymns and **spiritual** songs, singing and making melody in [our] heart to the Lord..." (Ephesians 5:19).

Furthermore, some of the counselors for Graham's crusades are not living for Christ, even though some of them profess to be Christians. When **Graham** was in Las Vegas in 1978, he **refused to condemn gambling** and one of his counselors, Larry Trumber, was a casino employee. Trumber continued to work at the casino and claimed that "[w]hile he is dealing the cards for the gaming tables...he witnesses for Christ!"[343]

CORETTA SCOTT KING

Let's return to Coretta Scott King. (Remember, she was on the platform with Graham at his Atlanta Crusade.) She and Graham were also the Co-Chairs for the International Summit of Baptists Against Racism.[344] *Newsweek,* however, mentioned that some people think Graham is hypocritical on the issue of racism because of "his decades-old membership in the all-white Biltmore Forest club near his hometown of Montreat, N.C."[345]

Mrs. King just happens to be one of the "first endorsers" of the New Age group called Planetary Citizens.[346] She is listed among the officers and trustees of the globalist, New Age organization, the World Constitution and Parliament Association.[347] She has also endorsed a New Age book entitled *Happiness Is a Choice.*[348]

Furthermore, Coretta Scott King serves on the Advisory Council of SANE, a nuclear disarmament organization.[349] She was also a speaker at the "Spirit of Peace" conference in March 1985—along with Buddhists, New Agers, a shaman, a Bilderberger, a Zen Master, and others.[350] She has even been a speaker for Sun Myung Moon's organization.[351] Moon is the founder of the cultic (and occultic) Unification Church (better known as the "Moonies") and has had help from the Rockefellers. "Also of interest is that the prominent political figures that have endorsed Moon are those with ties to the NWO [new world order], and include Ted Kennedy, Mason Mark O.

Hatfield, Mason Jesse Helms, [and] Illuminatus William F. Buckley, Jr."[352]

Let's spend just a few minutes looking at some of the other personalities who were **on the platform along with Coretta Scott King and Graham.** One of them was **Joseph Lowery.** He was President of the leftist **Southern Christian Leadership Conference**[353] which we've already covered. He is one of Jesse Jackson's close friends and he excused Jackson's extramarital affair as just a "human frailty" and discouraged Jackson from withdrawing from public life.[354]

ANDREW YOUNG

Andrew Young was also there with Graham. He was the former U. S. Ambassador to the United Nations,[355] three-term Congressman[356] and the former mayor of Atlanta.[357] On April 13, 1970, Young proclaimed that *"it may take the destruction of western civilization to allow the rest of the world to really emerge as a free and brotherly society...."*[358] [Emphasis in the original.]

He is a **Council on Foreign Relations** member[359] and a **Trilateralist.**[360] "The Trilateral Commission is a group with the goal of hastening the era of World Government and promoting an international economy controlled behind the scenes by the Secret Brotherhood."[361] Young is also a **Freemason.**[362]

Young is on the Advisory Board of the National Peace Institute Foundation[363] and the Board of Directors of Habitat for Humanity (HFH).[364] The founder of Habitat, Millard Fuller,[365] states:

> "'**Habitat is in sympathy with the efforts of the World Council of Churches** and other groups to influence churches and God's people to cooperate and work together....[It—J.H.] **is in agreement with the general purpose of the National Council of Churches....**Our desire is that we be even more of a unifying force, bringing more churches...to work together....' He adds, 'So get out your hammers, Catholics and Protestants, liberals and conservatives, Reform and Orthodox, Unitarians and Trinitarians, Gentiles and Jews. We have some houses to build to the glory of God! "The theology of the hammer" binds us together in **common** ministry.'"[366]

In March 2001, the officials of the NCC and Habitat met together and "signed a memorandum of understanding about mutual goals."[367]

> "More than 25,000, or 18 percent, of the NCC's 140,000 affiliated churches have supported local Habitat affiliates. 'Our formal partnership agreement will give us the opportunity to

> make even more of these churches' members feel connected to Habitat for Humanity,' said Sister Betsy Van Deusen, director of church relations for Habitat. 'This agreement makes perfect sense.'"[368]

"The NCC official expects the joint work will foster spiritual growth in the churches as well as produce physical buildings constructed through volunteer efforts with Habitat...."[369]

Fuller was the keynote speaker at a March 4-5, 2001 meeting at Duke University. There he stated: "We don't have doctrine. The only doctrine we have is that if you don't have a Habitat bumper sticker on your car, you're living in sin."[370]

"Former President Jimmy Carter, Chuck Colson, **Amy Grant, Madonna,** and Cedarville College have all assisted Habitat in recent years."[371]

Also, Habitat has recently joined hands with the **Masonic Lodge** in Tennessee.[372] In 1996 Fuller "addressed the Plenary Session of HABITAT II at Istanbul on the subject of sustainable housing, etc."[373] "He expressed a kinship with the United Nations Habitat."[374]

One editor concludes: **Habitat for Humanity** "is rooted in ecumenism, centered in ecologism, and **slanted toward socialism.**"[375]

In fact, Habitat for Humanity is one of the groups that has participated in occult/New Age World Goodwill's World Service Forum.[376]

Fuller is also on the editorial board of *Green Cross,* an environmental magazine.[377] He has signed the "Cry for Renewal" document.[378] This document, says David Kanz,

> "is, in fact, one of the best examples of the ideology and agenda of the ecumenical 'Christian Left,' and I use the term 'christian' very loosely. Evangelicals for Social Action is the spring-board of the initiative, however, **signers and endorsers include:** Steve Hayner, President of InterVarsity, Pete Hammond of InterVarsity, and **basically every Left-wing/global socialist operative from the World Council and National Council of Churches** and the Catholic church."[379]

It was written by Jim Wallis and Tony Campolo[380] as an **alternative** to the Christian Right.[381]

Jerry Huffman states: "Some have described radical *Sojourners* editor **Jim Wallis as Jane Fonda's male clone.** He was pro-Viet Cong (communists) during the Vietnam War. He passes for an evangelical and heads the Call to Renewal...."[382] Campolo is a liberal (to say the least!) who is for "gay rights."[383] In his book, *20 Hot Potatoes Christians Are Afraid to Touch,* he advocates "homosexual covenants" "in which males trying to alleviate loneliness vow to live together in celibacy."[384] Campolo thinks it's okay for two men to cuddle with each other in bed[385] but he does imply that it wrong for them to marry.[386] (Tony Campolo's wife, Peggy Campolo, however, is a big proponent of homosexual marriages.[387]) He believes that the majority of homosexuals are "born that way."[388]

He is one of the "spiritual advisors" to former President Clinton[389] and calls him a "brother."[390] He added that Clinton is "an evangelical Christian who wants to be religious."[391]

MANY WAYS TO HEAVEN

Of course, regardless of who the person is, Campolo believes that Jesus lives in every one—whether or not that person is a Christian.[392] He said that Christ "actually is present" in each one.[393] In his one book he states:

> "That little boy was more than a starving child....**That little boy was Jesus....**The resurrected Jesus...is in every person....I do *not* mean that others *represent* Jesus for us. I mean that Jesus *actually* is *present* in each other person....Forgetting **our divinity...**is responsible for a host of maladies that plague our contemporary society....There are those who would limit Jesus to being present only in those who acknowledge Him as Lord and Savior, but I will not accept that limitation. I believe that Jesus is present even in...those who refuse Him."[394] [Italics in the original.]

He adds:

> **"We affirm our divinity by doing what is worthy of gods,** and we affirm our humanity by taking risks only available to mortals. God had to become one of us before He could be heroic....Isn't God's message to sinful humanity that **He sees in each of us a divine nature** of such worth that He sacrificed His own Son so that **our divine potentialities** might be realized?"[395]

During a visit to New Zealand, Campolo told a large group of teenagers: *"Jesus is everywhere and in everyone. When you go out there today and you witness to a prostitute, the Jesus in you will be witnessing to the Jesus that is already in her."*[396] [Italics in the original.]

With such statements, it's not surprising to find that Campolo does not believe that Jesus is the only way to God. Says Campolo: "I believe going to heaven is like going to Philadelphia....There are many ways....It doesn't make any difference how we go there. We all end up in the same place."[397] To help him defend this statement, surprisingly (or not so surprisingly), he quotes Billy Graham who says that "on Judgment Day, there may be people who enter the Kingdom who have not called themselves Christians."[398]

Even though Campolo's analogy about going to Philadelphia is a poor one (not to mention an unscriptural one!), common sense tells a person that not just ANY road will get you to Philadelphia. Furthermore, as a person gets closer and closer to the city, the choice of roads drastically diminishes. Although going to Philadelphia cannot begin to be compared with going to heaven, there's still not "many" ways to get there.

Regardless of what Campolo and Graham teach, Jesus explicitly said: **"I** am the way, the truth, and the life: **no man** cometh unto the Father, **but by Me"** (John 14:6).

Christianity Today (CT), Graham's magazine, has had favorable reviews on Campolo's books and has defended him and his heresies.[399] In fact, *CT* even defends Campolo's **evolutionary** views. One person writes: "While **he accepts an evolutionary view** of the origin of man and the universe (albeit not Darwin's version), he holds that **this is consistent with Scripture** that teaches only the fact (not the method) of Creation."[400]

Furthermore, Campolo has referred to God as a "she." My friend went to hear Campolo in 1994 and he was telling about God making a daisy and then jumping up and down and clapping, etc. Campolo said that God made another one, and another one, and then **SHE** made another one.[401] He also claims that one-third of the Trinity is female because he believes that the Holy Spirit is feminine.[402]

Since Campolo is promoting New Age ideas, it's no surprise to see that he also promotes New Agers as well as the New Age environmental agenda.[403] He favorably refers to Pierre Teilhard de Chardin, Martin Buber, St. Francis,[404] Mahatma Gandhi, and Martin Luther King, Jr.[405]

He brags about his visit to the New Age, occult church at St. John the Divine. He writes:

> "I was **pleasantly surprised** during a visit to New York City when I happened upon a special **day of blessings for animals** at the **great Cathedral of St. John the Divine.** Once a year, a Sunday afternoon is designated for people to bring their animals to this Episcopal church in order to receive blessings and prayers from the pastors. All kinds of people bring all kinds of animals so that the clergy might lay hands on these

special creatures in the name of Christ. What made this service particularly amazing to me was that, in addition to an array of the expected house pets, a variety of New York Zoo animals, ranging from a camel to sheep and goats, were on hand to be blessed. Some tourists visiting the church that afternoon were amused. But others, perhaps for the first time in their lives, considered the special place that animals hold in God's scheme of things.

"This unusual church service was a **brilliant educational tool....**Other denominations should pick up this idea and make it a regular part of church life. We must explore all ways to raise the awareness of church people to the reality that animals have a right to a blessed life and have a uniquely ordained role to play in worshiping God that stands apart from any utilitarian function they perform for us humans."[406]

ANIMALS IN US

Campolo goes so far as to refer to C. S. Lewis' strange view of animals in regard to human beings. He writes:

"According to Lewis, animals can be so much a part of our lives they become part of who we are. As such, our resurrection must encompass their resurrection too. When we 'humanize' animals by making them our pets, they are *in* us. They share in our personhood. They enter into the spiritual depths of our being. Accordingly, Lewis believed our resurrection would be less than it ought to be if our animals did not share it with us. Their future is tied up with the people who love them. Their only resurrection is in relationship with those who have made them part of their lives. We 'save' animals, Lewis claimed, by training them and incorporating them into our own destiny....

"Animals are 'in' us in a way Lewis claimed is analogous to the way we are 'in' Christ. Thus even as our eternal life is 'in Him,' so the resurrection of the animals is tied up with our resurrection."[407] [Italics in the original.]

What blasphemy! Campolo also states:

"What is needed is repentance....I believe we should repent of those sins we have committed against the environment.

"It would not be a bad idea for us to set aside a day once a year to confess our sins of environmental terrorism. It would be good for us to periodically acknowledge that because of sins against the environment, we have limited nature's power to magnify and worship the Lord."[408]

Campolo also declares that the **Communistic theory of liberation theology** has influenced him.[409] Even the March 1992 issue of *Charisma* magazine refers to his belief as "Christian **socialism.**"[410] Campolo has also helped to promote Habitat for Humanity[411] and he has spoken for the National Council of Churches[412] (which will be covered in Chapter 4). In one of Campolo's books, he **"praised communist heroes** such as James Cone and Martin Luther King, the blasphemous German theologian Dietrich Bonhoffer (sic) and fellow new evangelical radical Ronald Sider."[413]

Campolo and Wallis are the individuals who drafted the "Call to Renewal." Sadly, Billy Graham's magazine, *Christianity Today,* advertised this conference in the April 8, 1996 issue.[414] The same ad appeared in the *New Age Journal!*[415] Of course, David Neff, the executive editor at *Christianity Today* was one of the featured speakers[416] and J. I. Packer, senior editor with *Christianity Today*[417] and a speaker at Billy Graham's Amsterdam 2000 meeting in 2000,[418] was also a signer to this document.[419]

Tony Campolo has even been sponsored by the **World Affairs Council** (which is an arm of the **Council on Foreign Relations!**[420]) as far back as 1981 to speak on terrorism.[421] The World Affairs Council (WAC) in Philadelphia is the same group for which the Declaration of Interdependence (mentioned in Chapter 1) was written in 1975.[422] The WAC gave Rhodes scholar Dean Rusk its **"World Citizen Award"** in 1994.[423] Would you believe that Billy Graham was also awarded the **World Citizen Award** by the WAC in 1990? *The News and Observer* stated: "The award will honor the evangelist for 'promoting and fostering international understanding and world peace.'"[424]

BETTER WORLD SOCIETY

Returning to Andrew Young, we find that he signed the 1993 interfaith Declaration of World Thanksgiving—along with those of other faiths such as the Baha'is, Buddhists, and Muslims.[425]

Young is also involved with the Better World Society (along with "such celebrated figures as Paul Newman, Carl Sagan, Theodore Hesburgh, Joanne Woodward, Yoko Ono, John Denver, Dr. Bernard Lown, Mario Cuomo...and Jane Alexander"[426]) which is working for population control, environmental issues, nuclear disarmament, etc. (Ted Turner is the chairman of the Better World Society.[427] If you remember, he called Christians "bozos" and "losers."[428])

One of the Better World Society's brochures, "Increase and Multiply," states: "Support your local chapter of Planned Parenthood, Zero Population Growth, Audubon Society, or other organizations concerned about international population issues. Help educate your community about population growth."[429] They then list about a dozen addresses of such groups.

Young also signed a SIECUS (Sex Information and Education Council of the United States) **ad** which appeared in the October 16, 1969 issue of *New York Times.*[430] (SIECUS is discussed later in this book.)

Like Mrs. King, **Young** sits on the Advisory Council of SANE/FREEZE.[431] He was also **one of the Vice Presidents for Americans for Democratic Action (ADA).**[432] This is a **leftist** organization[433] also working for nuclear disarmament.[434] The ADA "has 'distinguished' itself for its support of the homosexual movement."[435]

Even the *Los Angeles Times* reported the following:

> "The **ADA** members...are as an organization **strikingly like the British Fabian Socialists....** The Fabians stood for non-Marxian evolutionary **socialism,** to be achieved not by class war but by ballot....
>
> **"ADA** is not an organization for subversive violence like Marxist-Leninist communism....**The socialism they want to bring about** would be quite as total, **industrially,** as that in Russia, but they would accomplish it by legislation...not by shooting, and, of course, **by infiltrating the executive branch of the government....**"[436]

GRAHAM FAVORS DISARMAMENT

Andrew Young is the new President of the liberal **National Council of Churches** (NCC).[437]

> "Young led a NCC delegation to China in October, and, despite overwhelming evidence to the contrary, he found 'no evidence of excessive punitive treatment of Christians that we would use the word "persecution" to describe.'...The very week he delivered his report to the NCC General Assembly in Chicago, the AP reported that the Chinese had beaten and arrested over 140 underground church members."[438]

Young is also a board member of Archer, Daniels, Midland (ADM). ADM has given grants and contributions to the Council on Foreign Relations[439] and is a Corporate Member of the CFR.[440] Its

Chairman, Dwayne Andreas,[441] "was described by the *Wall Street Journal* as 'Moscow's favorite businessman.'"[442] "When questioned about ADM's reprehensible use of financial contributions" to influence politicians and recruit the government bureaucracy on its behalf, ADM Chairman Dwayne Andreas made this startling admission: "People who are not in the Midwest do not understand this is a *Socialist country.*"[443] [Emphasis in the original.]

ELIAN AND THE NCC

Young, as President of the NCC and board member of ADM, has an interesting connection to the Elian Gonzalez case. As some people may be aware, the NCC was profoundly involved in returning Elian to Cuba.[444] A leader in the NCC "was instrumental in raising $50,000 in legal fees for Juan Gonzales' legal fees."[445] (Where's the so-called separation of church and state when the liberals are involved?!)

One reporter writes:

> "By now, anyone who has followed the saga of Elian Gonzalez knows that the NCC is deeply involved in the story. NCC officials were instrumental in convincing Greg Craig, the Washington lawyer whose previous clients have included Bill Clinton and John Hinckley, to represent Elian's father, Juan Miguel Gonzalez. The NCC chartered the jet that flew Juan Miguel to Washington. From its offices in New York, the NCC press office has issued statement after statement demanding that the U.S. government return Elian to Cuba. At every point, the NCC's positions on the case have been indistinguishable from those of the Cuban government, down to its insistence that the boy not be given American citizenship.
>
> "Why would a church group spend so much time and money propagandizing on behalf of an atheist government famously intolerant of religious expression? The official NCC explanation makes vague references to 'human rights.' The more accurate answer might be: habit. The National Council of Churches has long gone far beyond the call of fashionably liberal Protestantism in its defense of Fidel Castro."[446]

While NCC leaders have verbalized their esteem for Fidel Castro,[447] there is an fascinating twist. You, see,

> "Archer, Daniels, Midland has invested $65 million in a so-called molasses refinery in Cuba through a subsidiary, which makes it actually an illegal venture. Rum is made from sugar

> cane molasses, so this is actually an alcoholic liquor distillery. What makes this interesting is that Andrew **Young,** president of the National Council of Churches, is a **board member of ADM.** Young sends a so-called woman NCC preacher to get the child back to Castro and protect ADM's investment. Clinton's lawyer, **Gregory Craig,** who is the lawyer for the child's father (a Castro policeman) **is also the lawyer for ADM.** ADM has plans to make other so-called refineries in Cuba. Clinton and Reno got an illegal warrant to break into a citizen's home and kidnapped a young child whose mother died to get him to America, possibly to keep Castro from taking over ADM's illegal distillery, and they then cry about the 'rule of law.'"[448]

Young has also gone so far as to call the Communist Nelson Mandela "as close to being a saint as can be."[449]

Another person Young likes a lot is Joshua Nkomo from Rhodesia's Patriotic Front, which is a coalition of terrorists. Nkomo said: "I will not rest until the rivers of Zimbabwe (Rhodesia) run red with the Blood (sic) of every white man, woman and child, and every African who supports them."[450]

Just recently Young was at a Presbyterian Church (USA) meeting where he "reiterated his support for homosexual rights."[451]

Oh, I might add that **Andrew Young was "a former assistant to Martin Luther King, Jr.** (as was Jesse Jackson[452]) in the riot-provoking days of King's Southern Christian Leadership Conference."[453] It's obvious to see that **Young is very sympathetic to Communist causes but Graham proudly had Young and Mrs. King on his platform!!**

Coretta Scott King and Andrew Young aren't the only ones in favor of disarmament. Billy Graham also favors this! In the September 1962 issue of Graham's magazine, *Decision,* he wrote: "I support the United Nations and I certainly support the disarmament conference."[454]

On March 29, 1979, Graham was on the CBS Evening News. Jed Duvall asked him about disarmament and Graham responded: **"I'm in favor of disarmament** and I'm in favor of trust. I'm in favor of—of having **agreements** not only to reduce but **to eliminate."**[455] In 1980, Graham "gave glowing approval to the [National Council of Churches'] extensive research and advocacy work for the cause of disarmament."[456]

By 1982 Graham had been invited "to address a Soviet-sponsored peace and disarmament conference"[457] in the Soviet Union (which will be covered later).

ROBERT SCHULLER

Returning to Graham's 1994 Atlanta Crusade, we find that Robert Schuller, pastor of the Crystal Cathedral, was also there on the platform with him. Schuller has the largest TV audience of all the televangelists,[458] yet he promotes the **occult** practice of visualization. He wrote an editorial encouraging **visualization** in his *Possibilities* magazine.[459] He also promoted this technique when he wrote the foreword to Paul (David) Yonggi Cho's book.[460] Cho is a former Buddhist who is now supposedly a Christian but he still uses occult practices.[461]

Schuller's mentor was Norman Vincent Peale[462] (who has already been covered in this book). In fact, Schuller "has been referred to as the 'Norman Vincent Peale of the West Coast.'"[463] He said that Peale was the "man who had the greatest influence upon his theology and ministry."[464] Since Peale was a heretic as far as the fundamentals of the faith, then we can also expect to find the same thing to be true of Schuller since Peale was his mentor and had an "influence upon his **theology.**"[465] "Schuller teaches there is <u>no</u> need for one to recognize his own personal sin, <u>no</u> need for repentance, and <u>no</u> need for the crucifixion of self."[466] [Emphasis in the original.]

A spirit guide (actually a demon) says somewhat the same thing: "Sin does not exist"[467] and "No one is punished for sins [and you—J.A. and J.W.] are not sinners."[468]

Some of Schuller's heresies can be found in his book entitled *Self-Esteem: The New Reformation.* For instance, he reinterprets what it means to be born again. He writes: "To be born again means that we must be changed from a negative to a positive self-image—from inferiority to self-esteem, from fear to love, from doubt to trust."[469]

On the very next page he writes: "And we can pray, 'Our Father in heaven, honorable is *our* name.'"[470] [Emphasis in the original.] Here Schuller is trying to "improve" the Lord's Prayer. Jesus' disciples had come to Him and asked Him to teach them how to pray. Jesus told them: "After this manner therefore pray ye: Our Father which art in heaven, Hallowed be **Thy** name" (Matthew 6:9). Jesus clearly taught them how to pray and it can be seen that ONLY God's name is to be honored (or hallowed)—not OUR name. In this statement, Schuller attempts to do the same thing that Lucifer did when he said: "I will make myself like the most High" (Isaiah 14:14b). Saying that OUR name is as honorable as GOD'S name is BLASPHEMY! Isaiah 42:8 declares: "I am the Lord: that is My name: and MY GLORY WILL I NOT GIVE TO ANOTHER...."

Once again a **spirit guide** echoes Schuller's statement (or is it Schuller who is echoing the spirit guide?!): "God's Name is holy, but no holier than yours. To call upon His Name is but to call upon your own."[471]

SCHULLER LOSES HIS COOL

Schuller goes even further in his assertion that we are gods. He writes in his *Possibilities* magazine that "nothing exists except God" and "The Christ spirit dwells in every human being whether the person knows it or not."[472] Of course, this means that even Satan is God (or good) since "nothing exists except God." This view is very prevalent in the New Age movement today. William Warch, a New Ager, tells us: "You are made up of the same stuff God is, and that is nothing but Good. You are Good. You are not evil. No one is evil."[473] New Ager, Barbara Marx Hubbard who channels a demon spirit by the name of Christ, claims: *"I [Christ] did not...rise again on the third day to show you what I could do, but what* ***you*** *can do. Yours is the power. Yours is the glory!"*[474] [Emphasis in the original.]

A few more quotes from Schuller's book follow:

❃ "What do I mean by sin? Answer:...'Sin is any act or thought that robs myself or another human being of his or her self-esteem.' And what is 'hell'? It is the loss of pride that naturally follows separation from God—the ultimate and unfailing source of our soul's sense of self-respect....A person is in hell when he has lost his self-esteem."[475]

❃ "What we need is a theology of salvation that begins and ends with a recognition of every person's hunger for glory."[476]

❃ "Christ is the Ideal One, for he was Self-Esteem Incarnate."[477]

❃ "Yes, what we need in the worldwide Christian church today is nothing less than a new reformation. Where the sixteenth-century Reformation returned our focus to sacred Scriptures as the only infallible rule for faith and practice, the new reformation will return our focus to the sacred right of every person to self-esteem! The fact is, the church will never succeed until it satisfies the human being's hunger for self-value."[478]

❃ "The most serious sin is the one that causes me to say, 'I am unworthy.'"[479]

❃ "'...And follow me?' What does this mean? It means daring to dream a great dream!"[480]

This certainly isn't how Jesus explains this passage of Scripture.

> "Then said Jesus unto His disciples, If any man will come after Me, let him deny himself, and take up his cross, and follow Me. For whosoever will save his life shall lose it: and whosoever will lose his life for My sake shall find it. For what is a man profited, if he shall gain the whole world, and lose his own soul? or what shall a man give in exchange for his soul?" (Matthew 16:24-26. See also: Mark 8:34-37 and Luke 9:23-25.)

Schuller also wrote: "Christianity with its doctrine of salvation is a faith by God for the glory of the human being for the greater glory of God. Because of this we can pray, 'O God, I am great.'"[481]

> "Schuller contends that the most destructive thing that can be done to a person is to call him a sinner. In an article in *Christianity Today,* October 5, 1984, Schuller said, 'I don't think anything has been done in the name of Christ and under the banner of Christianity that has proven more destructive to human personality and, hence, counterproductive to the evangelism enterprise than the often crude, uncouth, and unchristian strategy of attempting to make people aware of their lost and sinful condition.'"[482]

The Bible, however, states: "This is a faithful saying, and worthy of all acceptation, that Christ Jesus came into the world to save sinners" (I Timothy 1:15). "God commendeth His love toward us, in that, while we were yet sinners, Christ died for us" (Romans 5:8). Jesus said: "They that are whole have no need of the physician, but they that are sick: I came not to call the righteous, but sinners to repentance" (Mark 2:17; Matthew 9:13; Luke 5:32). "Let him know, that he which converteth the sinner from the error of his way shall save a soul from death" (James 5:20).

There is nothing more loving than telling a lost sinner that Christ can save him, but Schuller thinks that this has been "destructive" and "counterproductive."

In 2000 Schuller, an "advisor" to President Clinton,[483] pushed his greatness a little bit too far. Schuller, who had been drinking alcohol, was on a airplane when he assaulted a flight attendant. The attendant said that Schuller "shook him vigorously, causing injuries and pain."[484] Dr. Allen P. Dickerson remarked: "Schuller 'who has such a loving ministry that he will never preach on the wrath of God for fear of driving people away from God and will never call lost people sinners, lost his cool....'"[485]

In spite of Schuller's reinterpretation (and misinterpretation) of Scripture and his endorsement of *"all forms of Eastern meditation* such as TM, Zen Buddhism and yoga as valid methods for 'the harnessing, by human means, of God's divine laws...'",[486] editors from *Christianity Today* said they examined his theology and have concluded that he is not a heretic but that he "believes all the 'fundamental' doctrines of traditional fundamentalism. He adheres to every line of the Apostles' Creed with a tenacity born of deep conviction."[487] I guess this isn't surprising since *Christianity Today* was founded by Billy Graham.

> "In 1972 Schuller 'invited Catholic Bishop Fulton J. Sheen to his pulpit and joined with Catholic bishops at their Mass at the Annual Mary's Hour at the Los Angeles Sports Arena.'...**That same year Billy Graham made Schuller a leader in his Anaheim Crusade.** Graham said, 'There is no one in all the world I love in Christ more than I do Bob Schuller....He has done some of the greatest things for the kingdom of God of any man in our generation.'"[488]

Remember, "Billy Graham has frequently appeared with and praised Schuller. In 1983, Schuller sat in the front row of distinguished guests invited to honor Graham's 65th birthday. In 1986 **Schuller was invited by Graham** to speak at the International Conference for Itinerant Evangelists in Amsterdam."[489]

On one program "Schuller boasted to a pleased Graham that 'thousands of pastors and hundreds of rabbis and...over a million Muslims a week' watch his Hour of Power. Imagine the ingenious tightrope-walking it takes to please this divergent audience!"[490]

In fact, Schuller "no longer wants to be called a 'Christian' because it cuts him off from Hindus and Muslims...."[491]

A DIFFERENT JESUS

Schuller's Crystal Cathedral actually houses the offices for a group called "Christians and Muslims for Peace" (CAMP).[492] Schuller told Imam Alfred Mohammed of the Muslim American Society he wouldn't be bothered if he came back in 100 years and found that his descendants were Muslims.[493] In fact, Schuller has recommended and written a foreword to the book *More in Common Than You Think,* which "declares that Christians and Muslims are all one in our true worship of God."[494] He even had the author appear on his August 28, 1999 program.[495]

Bill Baker, the founder of CAMP and a Schuller associate, says that "CAMP hopes to help Christians and Muslims discover the **common ground** shared by both great religions."[496]

What **common ground** is there between Christians and Muslims? It is true that some Muslims believe that Jesus was a wonderful person. In one Islamic pamphlet is the question: "What

Do Muslims Think of Jesus?" The answer is: "Muslims think highly of Jesus (P) and his worthy mother, Mary....God's other gifts to him included healing the blind and the sick, reviving the dead, making a bird out of clay and most importantly, the message he was carrying. These miracles were given to him by God to establish him as a prophet." That doesn't sound too bad (although it is not completely Scriptural), but then he adds: "According to the Quran, **HE WAS NOT CRUCIFIED** but was raised into Heaven."[497] The Bible tells us in dozens of places that Jesus was crucified (Matthew 26:2; 27:22, 23, 26, 35, 38, 44; 28:5; Mark 15:15, 24, 25, 32; 16:6; Luke 23:23, 33; 24:7, 20; John 19:16, 18, 20, 23, 32; Acts 2:23, 36; 4:10; I Corinthians 1:23; 2:2, 8; 13:4; Galatians 2:20; 3:1; and Revelation 11:8), so the Jesus the Muslims revere is a **DIFFERENT** Jesus.

Another Islamic paper states: "WE BELIEVE THAT **JESUS** (PBUH) WILL COME BACK TO THIS WORLD AND PROCLAIM HIMSELF TO BE A MUSLIM AND THEN HE WILL DIE AND BE RESURRECTED WITH ALL OF US ON THE DAY OF JUDGMENT."[498] [Emphasis in the original.] It is further emphasized:

> "FOR A MUSLIM THE BIRTH OF **JESUS** (PBUH) IS NO MORE THAN ONE OF THE CREATION OF GOD AS TOLD IN THE QURAN: 'THE SIMILITUDE OF **JESUS** BEFORE GOD IS THAT OF ADAM; HE CREATED HIM FROM DUST, THEN SAID TO HIM "BE" AND HE WAS.'...
>
> "MUSLIMS DO NOT BELIEVE **JESUS** (PBUH) IS GOD, OR SON OF GOD, OR GOD INCARNATE."[499] [Emphasis in the original.]

Many people believe that Jesus lived on earth as a human. The problem is not in believing in Christ's existence, but in believing that Jesus is the "only begotten Son" of God (John 3:16) and that "there is no salvation in any other: for there is none other name under heaven given among men, whereby we must be saved" (Acts 4:12). Admitting that the Scriptures teach this is where the problem comes in. In fact, there are many who name the name of Christ who are not saved. Matthew 7:21-23 forewarns us: "Not every one that saith unto Me, Lord, Lord, shall enter into the kingdom of heaven; but he that doeth the will of My Father which is in heaven. **MANY WILL SAY TO ME IN THAT DAY, LORD, LORD, HAVE WE NOT PROPHESIED IN THY NAME? AND IN THY NAME HAVE CAST OUT DEVILS? AND IN THY NAME DONE MANY WONDERFUL WORKS?** And then will I profess unto them, I never knew you: **DEPART FROM ME, YE THAT WORK INIQUITY."**

As one author has wisely stated:

"We should never respect those views which the Bible teaches are morally wrong. They are from Satan....

"Today, Christians are asked to 'respect the views' of those who practice other religions, or we are considered intolerant....

"It is not what we have in common with other religions that is important, but what Christianity has that is different which is essential to salvation. It is the death of Christ for our sins and His resurrection which are important, and we must tell those of other faiths this fact, because without their acceptance of Jesus as Lord and Savior, they will not be saved....

"The Word of God, given us in the Bible, is the only religious 'view' a Christian should respect, for it is the only Truth, and there can be no other."[500]

"WE'RE CLOSER TO ISLAM"

Billy Graham himself has said that Mohammed Ali's beliefs in Islam "are something we all could believe."[501] Maybe we can all believe these ideas, but will they lead us to heaven? That is the important question.

On May 30, 1997, on the David Frost program, Graham said: "...I think Islam is misunderstood, too, because Mohammed has a great respect for Jesus, and he called Jesus the greatest of the prophets except himself. And I think that we're closer to Islam than we really think we are."[502]

Returning to Schuller, we see that on December 17, 1999, he gave a speech at the Abou Nour Mosque in Damascus, Syria. The Crystal Cathedral Ministries reports that this is "the first time a Christian leader has been invited by the Grand Mufti to speak at the holy mosque."[503] Schuller said, "We have all failed, Christians and Muslims, to treat each other with respect and dignity, but now that must change."[504]

After this speech, Schuller did an interview with Larry King for his Christmas Eve 1999 program which was broadcast live from the Mormon Tabernacle in Salt Lake City.[505] Schuller himself was in Bethlehem for this program. Referring to meeting with the Grand Mufti, Schuller bragged: "I have seldom met with a man [with—D.H.] whom **I felt an immediate kinship of spirit and an <u>agreement of faith</u> and philosophy** quite like I have with the Grand Mufti of the [Muslim] faith."[506]

Schuller said that he was hoping to get the Jewish Rabbi and the Muslim Grand Mufti to meet together.[507] When Larry King asked him if Bethlehem gave him encouragement, he responded:

> "Oh, absolutely....When the Chief Rabbi of Israel wants to meet with the top Christian and Muslim leaders...this is marvelous. When the Grand Mufti would invite me...to preach the sermon in his mosque on Holy Day...that he would sit and often hold my hand while I was talking, and here was the Roman Catholic patriarch, the patriarch of the Orthodox church and the patriarch of the Syrian Orthodox Church and the Protestant minister of the town—this is a remarkable thing that's happening."[508]

Schuller then added: "[W]e religious leaders [must—D.H.] begin to say, 'I'm...not trying to convert other religious people to my viewpoint.'"[509]

HOW DO WE COME HOME?

Schuller also promotes and fellowships with other false cults beside Islam. For instance, "Schuller has appeared as a main speaker for the Unity School of Christianity's (New Age) annual conference ridiculing evangelical Christianity, at Unification Church (Moonies) functions with Sun Myung Moon, and at an **interfaith** prayer breakfast at the Mormon Tabernacle."[510] He even dedicated a new Unity Temple in Warren, Michigan.[511]

When the Pope went to Los Angeles, California in 1987, Schuller said: "It's time for Protestants to go to the shepherd [Pope] and say 'what do we have to do to come home?'"[512]

Later Schuller "made a special trip to Rome to ask the Pope's blessing on the building plans for his Crystal Cathedral."[513]

In 1998 Schuller once again met with the Pope "hand-to-hand, heart-to-heart at the Vatican."[514] This was his fourth visit to see Pope John Paul II.[515]

Schuller has had New Agers like Norman Cousins and Gerald Jampolsky on his program,[516] as well as pro-Communist Armand Hammer.[517] "It was Dr. Armand Hammer who first opened the doors for Robert Schuller in Russia in 1989. Dr. Schuller was the first foreign pastor to preach to the Russian people on television on December 24, 1989."[518] The *Los Angeles Times* (May 23, 1987) reported that on Hammer's 87th birthday party, Schuller said: "This is the kind of birthday party the Lord would throw **if He could afford it."**[519] Was Schuller trying to infer that Christ wasn't as wealthy as Hammer was?

Schuller also interviewed Communist Mikhail Gorbachev.[520] On the October 22, 2000 "Hour of Power" program, "Schuller pressed him to acknowledge that he is not an atheist, but the avowed Leninist/atheist Gorbachev would not do so."[521] Schuller later remarked that Gorbachev "calls himself an atheist, but 11 years ago, as one of the most powerful men in the world, **God used this atheist in a mighty way.**"[522]

At the end of this interview an interesting handshake took place. Schuller and Gorbachev gave an extended handshake which appeared to be Masonic in nature.[523] This really isn't surprising to me since Schuller's mentor was 33° Mason Norman Vincent Peale. Schuller himself is a 33° Mason.[524] Also, Schuller has had Burl Ives on his program. He, too, was a DeMolay,[525] a 33° Mason,[526] and a Communist.[527] On that "Hour of Power" program, Schuller asked Ives "'of all the great honors and awards that you have received in your long and successful career what do you hold as the highest.' Brother Ives replied 'WHEN THEY MADE ME A MASTER MASON.'"[528] [Emphasis in the original.] One Masonic brochure added about this "Hour of Power" program: "It is one of the finest testimonials Masonry has ever had."[529]

He even had **Satanist** Sammy Davis on his program.[530] "Davis was such a fervent member [of the Church of Satan] that, for a time, he wore a Satanic Baphomet medallion on stage and actively proselytized the cause, setting up dinner meetings at his Los Angeles home between [Anton] LaVey and various movie and entertainment personalities."[531]

Schuller's advisory board (1989-1990) included a Mormon (George Romney), Masons (Norman Vincent Peale and Clement Stone), and New Agers (such as John Templeton), etc.

In 1997, more "than 80 gay and lesbian pastors and lay leaders from the Metropolitan Community Churches participated in [the]...Robert Schuller Institute for Successful Church Leadership at Schuller's Crystal Cathedral."[532]

Also, Schuller "does not believe that Jesus Christ is the only way to heaven"[533] and he "maintains that Jews and other non-Christians can get to heaven without saving faith in Jesus Christ."[534]

GREAT MAN OF GOD

In an article entitled "Is Robert H. Schuller a Heretic?" by Dr. Joseph Chambers, we find: "His [Schuller's] is nothing but dressed-up humanism. Religious humanism is much worse than secular humanism because of the religious language used to convey the message. It is seductive and evil."[535]

Does any of this seem to bother Billy Graham? Apparently not! Remember (as mentioned earlier), **Graham himself said of Schuller:** "There is no one in all the world I love in Christ more than I do Bob Schuller....**He has done some of the greatest things for the kingdom of God of any man in our generation."**[536] About 20 years later, Graham was still singing Schuller's praises: **"Robert Schuller is a great man of God, whose shoes I am not worthy to stoop and loose."**[537]

In fact, Graham encouraged Schuller to start his own TV program, "Hour of Power."[538] An interview with Schuller appeared in *USA Today*. When he was asked "How did you begin televising your services?," Schuller responded: "In September 1969, Billy Graham had a crusade in Anaheim which he was televising. I found that fascinating, and out of that came his suggestion that we start doing it week to week for the benefit of people who couldn't come out and attend church."[539]

"Graham made a personal appearance on Schuller's 1000th anniversary program, relating how he had encouraged Schuller 20 years earlier when he said, 'Bob, why don't you think of telecasting your services.'"[540]

When *USA Today* asked Schuller what was the secret to his success, he remarked: "We know the things the major faiths can agree on. We try to focus on those without offending those with different viewpoints...."[541] This **sounds** plausible, but remember, only Christianity accepts Jesus Christ as the **"only** begotten Son of God." All other religions deny this. Jesus said: "I am the way, the truth, and the life: no man cometh unto the Father, but by Me" (John 14:6). Again, other religions oppose this doctrine. For Schuller to find "common ground" with Jews, Hindus, Muslims, Buddhists, etc., he **CANNOT** preach the Gospel of Jesus Christ because then he would offend "those with different viewpoints."

Of course, Graham tries to find his own common ground. In an interview with Charles Gibson on Good Morning America in 1998, he told Gibson "that Muslims and Jews can be saved by finding God in their **own worship systems."**[542] A few years prior to this, Graham had gone to India and he assured the Indians that he was "not going to proselytize any Hindus."[543] I thought Graham's crusades were for the purpose of winning lost souls to Christ, but if he is only preaching to the Christians in India, what is the reason for all the expense that goes into a crusade?

Since Graham and Schuller both straddle the fence, I guess it's no surprise to find that **Graham** invited Schuller to speak at Amsterdam '83. Worse yet, he **allowed Schuller to present copies**

of his *Self-Esteem* book (some excerpts were given earlier) "to the thousands of evangelists who attended the conference."[544]

JIMMY CARTER

We've covered several of the individuals who were on the platform with Graham at Graham's Atlanta Crusade. They were Coretta Scott King, Andrew Young, Joseph Lowery, and Robert Schuller. Another person who was there was Jimmy Carter. Carter claims that the most important factor in his life is his relationship with God, but when asked if he would give up politics for Christ he responded with "No."[545]

> "Carter has been extremely active in his Southern Baptist church since he joined at the age of ten. He was a Sunday School teacher when he was sixteen and a deacon in his twenties. And yet he says he was not 'born-again' **until 1967**—more than thirty years after becoming a local Christian leader. **Carter does not accept the inerrancy of the Bible**—a basic doctrine of Southern Baptists....He is, emphatically, not a fundamentalist."[546]

As a politician, **Carter was a supporter of the feminist Equal Rights Amendment.** The July 1976 issue of *Playgirl* magazine calls Jimmy their "feminist candidate" because "he has pledged to support virtually every issue of importance to the women's movement."[547] Although he claims to be against abortion, "he has even refused to oppose the federal funding of abortions."[548] In fact, after his election, "Carter appointed a pro-abortion activist, Sarah Weddington, to the position of assistant to the president. Weddington was lead attorney in the Roe v. Wade, which resulted in legalization of abortion in America and the murder of millions of unborn babies."[549]

Carter said that he didn't want to legalize marijuana but went on to say that he favored decriminalizing it, which meant that someone possessing the drug for personal use would not be considered a criminal.[550]

One author summed up Carter's 1976 campaign like this:

> "The Carter platform is, in fact, tailor-made to bring **socialism** to America. And while the vast body of voters has no idea this is true, one group has seen through the pap being ground out for the masses to the lean Marxist meat on the inside. Three days after the amazing Mr. C. [Carter] tied a bright-red bow around the Democratic convention, the **Socialist Party of America** (now marching under the more acceptable banner of Social Democrats USA) **endorsed 'the forward-thinking**

> **ticket' of Jimmy Carter and Walter Mondale.** Indeed, so enthusiastic were the **socialists** by the Carter promise that they decided *against* running any national ticket this year—urging their members instead to campaign for the peanut politico."[551] [Italics in the original.]

"Tom Hayden told a CBS reporter that, while he himself didn't know much about the peanut vendor, his 'close friends' say Honest Jim [Carter] is **'one hundred times more liberal** than he appears to be.'"[552]

Tom Hayden, by the way, is a **leftist** and is the ex-husband of **socialist** Jane Fonda.[553] He said: **"Communism is one of the options that can improve people's lives."**[554] [Emphasis in the original.] He belonged to the Communistic group called Students for a Democratic Society.[555] It's **his** friends who knew that Carter was a radical liberal!

> "Jimmy Carter's religious convictions are as puzzling as the strange dichotomy between his words and his deeds in the political arena. He is a 'born-again' Christian whose favorite theologian is the ultra-modernist **Reinhold Niebuhr,** former **professor at Union Theological Seminary,** who was a **founder of Americans for Democratic Action, had a list of Communist-front affiliations** as long as your arm, and who openly derided 'born-again' believers. Niebuhr denied the inerrancy of the Bible, the Divine conception of Christ, His virgin birth, and His bodily resurrection as the Son of God. For Carter to call himself a 'born-again believer' whose favorite theologian is Reinhold Niebuhr is like a rabbi saying his favorite politician is Hitler."[556]

KARL BARTH

"Carter also admired Karl Barth (who said the Bible was 'fallible,' and filled with 'historic and scientific blunders,' and 'theological contradictions'), Paul Tillich, and Soren Kierkegaard, all **liberals** who led the **'God is Dead'** movement during the 1960's."[557] Barth also denied the virgin birth.[558]

Not only did Barth reject the doctrines of Christianity but he had a mistress, Charlotte Kirschbaum, whom he moved "into his house over the strenuous objections of his wife and also lived with Charlotte in a mountain cabin every summer....Barth betrayed his loyal followers in Eastern Europe and told them to submit to the authority of the Communists. He and his lovely assistant, Charlotte, had been reds all along, as the historical documents show."[559] **In spite of Barth extolling Communism, Billy Graham has praised him!**[560]

A person greatly influenced by Barth was Dietrich Bonhoeffer[561] and since we are told that Billy Graham was affected by Bonhoeffer,[562] it would do us good to see what Bonhoeffer believed.

Rick Miesel writes:

> **"Bonhoeffer's writings are credited with helping to father the 'Death of God' theology** which was popularized by the Anglican bishop, John A. T. Robinson, in the 1960s decade. Bonhoeffer was in reality a practical atheist and a religious humanist who denied virtually every cardinal doctrine of the historic Christian faith....
>
> "Declaring that it was impossible to know the objective truth about Christ's real nature and essence, Bonhoeffer proclaimed that **God was dead....**
>
> "His religious terminology may appear to be evangelical but its substance was existential."[563]

From Bonhoeffer's books we discover that:

> "He questioned the Virgin Birth, and in reality denied it....
>
> "He denied the deity of Christ; he advocated that 'Jesus Christ Today' is not a real person and being, but a 'corporate presence.'...
>
> "He denied the sinlessness of Christ's human nature and further questioned the sinlessness of His earthly behavior....
>
> "He believed that Christianity is not exclusive, i.e., that Christ is not the only way to God....
>
> "He was an evolutionist...and believed that the book of Genesis was scientifically naive and full of myths....
>
> "He had no faith in the physical resurrection of Christ. He believed that the Resurrection was one of the 'mythological' elements of Christianity that 'must be interpreted in such a way as not to make religion a pre-condition of faith.' He also believed that 'the Resurrection is not the solution of the problem of death,' and that such things as miracles and the ascension of Christ were 'mythological conceptions' as well...."[564]
>
> "Under Dietrich Bonhoeffer's name in the 'Dictionary of the Ecumenical Movement' published by the World Council of Churches, 1991, there are 29 page listings referring to him and his contributions to the **Ecumenical** Movement."[565]

After reading the next chapter, you will probably not be surprised to learn that Bonhoeffer had studied theology at **Union Theological Seminary (UTS).**[566]

One of the professors at UTS was Paul Tillich (who was admired by Carter).[567] "His Communist-front associations may be found listed in the *Cumulative Index* of the Committee of Un-American Activities."[568] He was also a signer of a letter to repeal the McCarran Act which was printed in the *Daily Worker,* the official mouthpiece of the Communist Party.[569]

On October 27, 1999, Carter was on the NBC "Today" show. He said that "many of us who are not Christians worship the same God."[570] In "alluding to his having once met with Israel's Begin and Egypt's Sadat, he adds that they were all 'compatible' since 'we worship the same God....In fact, all the Muslims revere Christ....Jesus said he shouldn't condemn anyone.'"[571]

In Carter's book, *Living Faith,* he wrote: "Of course, the fellowship of faith is even larger than the Christian world."[572]

Carter's November 22, 2000 letter mentioned The Carter Center, which he brags was "attended by members of over 20 Christian denominations, diverse Jewish groups, Muslims, Hindus, Buddhists, Baha'is, and members of many other faiths."[573] These different groups found **common ground** in "establishing peace and preventing human suffering."[574]

In *Living Faith* he also states that he has no problem believing that "the earth is ancient, and **human beings have evolved from primitive ancestors."**[575]

Carter, like Coretta Scott King, has endorsed a New Age book from Barry Kaufman.[576]

In his inaugural address for Governor he proclaimed a Martin Luther King, Jr. Day in Georgia and he also announced that he'd "hang a portrait of King in the capitol building."[577] On another occasion he remarked: "I would not be where I am if it were not for Martin Luther King, Jr."[578]

Carter also belonged to the Better World Society,[579] the Council on Foreign Relations (CFR), and the Trilateral Commission (TC).[580] These groups are working for a one world government. As President, Carter filled his cabinet with CFR members. His National Security Advisor, Zbigniew Brzezinski, was both a CFR and TC member. In fact, Brzezinski was the founding Director of the TC.[581] In his book, *Between Two Ages: America's Role in the Technetronic Era,* Brzezinski wrote:

> "**Marxism** represents a further vital and creative stage in the maturing of man's universal vision. Marxism is simultaneously a victory of the external, active man over the inner, passive man and a victory of reason over belief....The

> nation-state is gradually yielding its sovereignty....Further progress will require greater American sacrifices. More intensive efforts to shape a new world monetary structure will have to be undertaken, with some consequent risk to the presently favorable American position."[582]

GRAHAM DEFENDS ALCOHOL USE

"In the infamous *Playboy* magazine interview, Carter said: 'I've looked on a lot of women with lust. I've committed adultery in my heart many times.'"[583]

Carter was also known for using expletives (profanity and cursing) when things didn't go his way.[584]

Joshua Nkomo, the man who wants to see the death of every white person, was considered a **moderate** by Jimmy Carter![585]

Carter "said that while homosexuality is a sin, he **sees nothing wrong with a 'Christian' homosexual being ordained."**[586] "In 1992, Carter agreed to serve as the honorary co-chair of the Human Rights Campaign, a **homosexual** advocacy group."[587]

So how does Billy Graham feel about Carter? He writes: "I grew to like him as a person and to **respect** both his intelligence and **his genuine and unashamed Christian commitment."**[588] He said that Carter was "a leader we can trust and follow."[589] Graham also said: **"A man of faith and sterling integrity,** he was undoubtedly one of our most diligent Presidents, persistent and painstaking in his attention to his responsibilities."[590] He adds: "Since leaving office, Mr. Carter has continued to carry out his responsibilities as a **Christian...."**[591]

> "In **1966** Carter had chaired a small crusade built around showing Billy's film *The Restless Ones*....After each showing of the film, Carter himself explained the Gospel and invited the audience to the altar. In 1973, Carter chaired the full-fledged crusade in Atlanta and invited Billy for an overnight stay at the governor's mansion."[592]

Graham then goes on to explain: "When my plans for another Crusade in Atlanta in 1994 first began to take shape, Jimmy Carter gladly agreed to serve as the honorary chairman. He was on the platform the opening night in October, in the new Georgia Dome, and spoke for several minutes to the audience."[593]

As just mentioned, **Carter "gave the invitation every night for people to come to receive Christ"**[594] during Graham's **1966** evangelistic outreach in Americus, Georgia,[595] yet Carter says he wasn't even saved until **1967!**[596]

When Carter was criticized for drinking highballs, Graham went to his defense!! He stated: "I do not believe the Bible teaches teetotalism. I can't believe that."[597] Graham

> "not only continued to defend and repeat his earlier statement but acknowledged that he used alcohol himself from time to time, and that he knew something of its effects. 'Once in a while I will have a sip of wine before I go to bed,' he told a reporter. 'I only have to drink a little wine and my mind becomes foggy and I don't like it. After all, a clear mind is what I have been striving for all my life.'"[598]

Now we can see why Graham defended Carter's use of alcohol! The Bible, however, warns: "Wine is a mocker, strong drink is raging: and **whosoever** is deceived thereby is not wise" (Proverbs 20:1). "Look not thou upon the wine when it is red, when it giveth his colour in the cup, when it moveth itself aright. At the last it biteth like a serpent, and stingeth like an adder" (Proverbs 23:31-32).

Graham has even "attended cocktail parties given for the [Hollywood] stars, the most notable having been given by Richard Nixon at his San Clemente home on Sunday evening, while church services were in progress in the area."[599]

DAG HAMMARSKJOLD

Before moving on to another topic, I think it would be profitable to look at one more of Billy Graham's friends. His name is **Dag Hammarskjold.** Hammarskjold, a speaker at the 1954 **World Council of Churches** assembly,[600] was the second Secretary-General of the United Nations.[601] He was "a Swedish **socialist** who openly pushed **communist** policies."[602] "At the age of thirty, Hammarskjold became Undersecretary of the Swedish Ministry of Finance. At the Ministry **he worked under the Fabian socialist** economist Ernst Wigforss, whom he once said he considered his second father. Sweden has long been the leading socialist state of Western Europe, taxing its citizens at a 75% rate."[603]

In spite of his socialist inclination, he was a mystic[604] who also believed that the world needed a **"spiritual** rebirth."[605] He said: *"We can only succeed in achieving world peace if there is a* ***spiritual*** *renaissance on this planet."*[606] [Italics in the original; boldface added.]

Two New Agers, Corinne McLaughlin and Gordon Davidson, tell us that Hammarskjold

> "was instrumental in redesigning the **UN meditation room....**The room is a place of quiet stillness and has been

> referred to as one of the **holiest of holies** on the planet....It is the focus for the **energies** of a unified planet and humanity, and for right relations among all kingdoms of life. When Gordon worked for the UN for four years with World Goodwill, an NGO there, he meditated daily in this room and experienced a very powerful energy helping to support the **synthesis** of nations and the emergence of the Soul of humanity."[607]

This **meditation room** came "into existence through the efforts of the Laymen's Movement for a **Christian** World."[608] Although this may **sound** like a Christian group, we need to remember that some of the speakers for this group have included New Ager/occultist Norman Cousins, Ralph Bunche, William Ernest Hocking, Frank P. Graham, and Kirtley F. Mather of Harvard.[609] One researcher notes that **ALL** of the speakers just mentioned **"have communist-front records."**[610]

John D. Rockefeller, Jr. was a big supporter of this group from its inception and gave yearly grants for many years.[611]

Dr. Robert W. Laidlaw was active in this group yet "he was also a trustee of the American Society for **Psychical Research,** with a special interest in **mediumship."**[612] He was a director of SIECUS[613] and a director of the Association for Voluntary Sterilization.[614] He spoke at an abortion conference in 1955 where he "likened abortion surgery to operating on a ruptured appendix."[615] He was also with the Temple of Understanding.[616] Others involved with the Laymen's Movement for a Christian World were Frank P. Graham, J. C. Penney, Frank Laubach, and Warren Austin.[617]

Briefly, Frank P. Graham was a Vice President of the League for Industrial Democracy which "is the power house of the Fabian Socialists in the United States."[618] He is a former U. S. Senator from North Carolina and former President of the University of North Carolina. He was also a speaker for the NCC's Study Conference on the Churches and **World Order.**[619]

J. C. Penney was a 33° Mason.[620]

Frank Laubach was a Mason.[621] In his book on prayer, he wrote: "While on a train or bus, fancy your spirit walking over to others and touching them on the shoulder...."[622] Another book was titled *Letters of a Modern Mystic.*[623] He was a Union Theological Seminary (UTS) graduate.[624] (UTS will be covered in the next chapter.) Laubach was also a Wainwright House affiliate.[625] The Temple of Understanding has its executive offices at the Wainwright House[626] which is "where most of the high-level plotting for pantheism and syncretism takes place."[627] The Wainwright House is a "participating organization" with the Planetary Initiative for the World We Choose[628] as well as a supporting/endorsing organization with the New Age Chinook Learning Center.[629] New Ager, Daniel Martin, is the "director of the Institute for Global Issues at Wainwright House in Rye, New York...."[630]

When the Laymen's Movement for a Christian World (LMCW)

> "first sought to secure Wainwright House for its headquarters in 1951, **John D. Rockefeller, Jr.,** gave $5,000.00 of the $25,000.00 needed....
>
> "When the Friends of the Meditation Room agreed to raise $15,000 to pay for the redecoration of the Room, **John D. Rockefeller, Jr.** gave $5,000 of the amount sought....**Dag Hammarskjold** personally raised another $10,000 from the Marshall Field family for the cost of the fresco in the Room....
>
> "Wainwright House has its own Meditation Room, on its second floor. The room contains the agba wood altar first used in the U. N. Meditation Room, and the cherry wood chairs and drapes from that room, presented to the Friends by the U. N. in 1957....The [Wainwright] House also contains a large library centered around the Thomas Sugrue Memorial Library, a sixteen hundred dollar collection of books on religion and **occultism**—where one may read up on spiritualism, Zen, Taoism, Yoga, Judaism, etc."[631]

Incidentally, Leighton Ford, Billy Graham's brother-in-law, led a devotional retreat for the Billy Graham Team at the Wainwright House![632]

Warren Austin (with the LMCW) was a Mason, U. S. Representative to the United Nations, and a U. S. Senator.[633] He said that

> "all of us today need...the far vision in world affairs....We must look far ahead to our final goal of **world peace under law:** that introduces **World Federation....World government could not be accepted without radical change** of national outlook....It will take a long time to prepare peoples and governments of most nations for acceptance of and participation in a **world government....**If we expect this future world government to be created by agreement and not by force or conquest, we will have to be willing to work patiently until peoples or governments are ready for it."[634]

Obviously, there was nothing "Christian" about the LMCW.

Alan Morrison writes:

> "In case readers may be wondering what kind of 'spirituality' Dag Hammarskjold advocated, a leaflet about the

United Nations Meditation Room written under the direction of Mr. Hammarskjold stated that the eerie lodestone altar within it *'is dedicated to the God whom man worships under many names and in many forms.'*'"[635] [Emphasis in the original.]

What do the United Nations Meditation Room, the Egyptian Pyramids, the Temple of Understanding, and the Prayer Room in the United States Capitol **have in common** with the Great Seal of the United States?[636] **The all-seeing eye of Lucifer,** of course! (For more information on the all-seeing eye, see my book entitled *Masonic and Occult Symbols Illustrated.*)

SATAN'S TRAPEZOID

Texe Marrs gives some details about the Meditation Room which was redesigned by **Hammarskjold.**[637]

> "Perhaps the best way to comprehend what the all-seeing eye represents is to examine the architecture of the Meditation Room of the United Nations Building in New York City. The Meditation Room is...shaped as a **pyramid** without the capstone. Inside, the room is dimly lit, but coming from the ceiling is a narrow but concentrated pinpoint beam of light which radiates down to a bleak stone altar.
>
> "On the wall straight ahead is a breathtaking, modernistic mural that is dynamically endowed with **occult symbolism,** containing twenty-seven triangles in various configurations, a mixture of black and white and colored background, and a snakelike vertical line. **At the center is the all-seeing eye,** which grips the millions of annual U. N. visitors with its stark, beckoning image of suspicion and omnipresence."[638]

"The Meditation Room faces north north-east. To enter the room one must proceed from darkness to light."[639] Anyone familiar with Masonry should recognize the implication of this. (For more information on Masonry, see my book *Hidden Secrets of Masonry.)*

A pyramid without a capstone results in a shape which is called a **trapezoid.** "The trapezoid has long been regarded by occultists as the most satanic of shapes, **especially adapted to enhance demonic manifestation.** Indeed, the middle order of the **satanic brotherhood** is called 'The Order of the Trapezoid.'"[640] Anton LaVey, the founder of the Church of Satan, refers to an occult principle known as the "Law of the Trapezoid."[641] "His writings underscore the existence of a magical science of geometric angles and spaces [which is very prevalent in the mural in the Meditation Room]....**LaVey says architecture can enhance an evil, <u>spiritual</u> atmosphere.**"[642]

"The bottom line of all this is that the consummate architectural form of the Satan-worshiper is the trapezoid; and that he believes that this shape will create a spiritual 'cloud-chamber' of sorts across which he may track the hoofprints of the demons he wishes to invoke. It is believed to be the perfect atmosphere for the manifestation of the unholy and the cursed."[643]

SATAN'S ALTAR

A former witch, David Meyer, saw this room when he visited the United Nations. He wrote:

"I stood in the **meditation room,** which contains Satan's altar....The room was designed by the late Secretary General of the UN, **Dag Hammarskjold,** who said that the black stone monolith or block is 'every man's god.' The room is **18** feet wide at the entrance, which in numerology is **3 sixes.** The room is also **33** feet long and tapers inward to form a truncated pyramid. There is an abstract **mural** on the front wall, which is **full of witchcraft symbols,** and in the middle of the room, is a black stone block, which weighs exactly 6.5 tons or **13,000** pounds. The black stone block has a certain kind of magnetism about it, and when I walked into the room with my praying wife, I could sense the **intense presence of an evil force beyond description.** This is where the world leaders and Illuminati masterminds go to meditate, which is why it is open to the public **only** in the mornings. Once the sun moves from antemeridiem to post meridiem only the adept in witchcraft are allowed into that room, for that is witchcraft doctrine regarding meditation. As the sun gives way to waning light and the female power of the moon goddess, the meditation room at the UN becomes off-limits to what they call the 'profane.'"[644]

Furthermore, the New Ager and former Assistant Secretary General of the United Nations, Robert Muller, has dedicated one of his books to Dag Hammarskjold, whom he considered to be his "spiritual master."[645]

Muller has said: "We must move as quickly as possible to a one-world government; **A ONE-WORLD RELIGION;** under a one-world leader."[646] He has also stated: "My great personal dream is to get a tremendous **ALLIANCE BETWEEN ALL MAJOR RELIGIONS AND THE UN."**[647] Muller is an ardent follower of the occultist/New Ager, Alice Bailey,[648] and he has a spirit guide (which is actually a demon) by the name of Djwhal Khul, also known as the Tibetan.[649] This is the same spirit guide that directed Bailey to write many of her own occultic books.

Muller refers to himself as a humanist[650] and is one of the editorial advisors for the New Ager's Marilyn Ferguson's *Brain/Mind Bulletin.* He is also on the advisory boards of The Center for Attitudinal Healing[651] (another New Age organization), the Institute for Educational Studies, and The Temple of Understanding,[652] where he is listed as one of the "Founding Friends." He is on the Board of Trustees of the Global Education Associates.[653] Muller also is on the Board of Directors of Planetary Citizens[654] and was one of the co-founders of this group, as well as a board member of the Planetary Initiative for the World We Choose,[655] another New Age group. Moreover, "Muller has encouraged the work of **Benjamin Creme,** of the Tara Center, which has placed ads in leading newspapers of the world proclaiming: 'THE CHRIST IS NOW HERE.'"

Muller, like Hammarskjold, speaks of a **spirituality,** but it has nothing to do with Christianity. In one of Muller's speeches, he claimed: "We need a *World* or *cosmic spirituality*...religious leaders will get together to define before the end of this century the cosmic laws which are *common to all their faiths*....They should tell the politicians what the cosmic laws are, what *God,* or the *gods,* or the *cosmos* are expecting from humans."[656] [Emphasis in the original.]

Interestingly, the **Luciferian** organization, Lucis Trust, which was originally named **Lucifer Publishing Company,**[657] publishes the works of the occultist Alice Bailey. They have also maintained this **United Nations Meditation Room** which was redesigned by **Dag Hammarskjold!**[658]

GRAHAM AND HAMMARSKJOLD

So, what does **Billy Graham** think of Hammarskjold? He writes in his autobiography, *Just As I Am:*

> "In the **1950s,** when I was in New York City, I would occasionally slip by to visit **Dag Hammarskjold,** secretary-general of the United Nations, and have prayer with him. He was a very thoughtful, if lonely, man who was trying to make a difference for world peace, in large part because of his <u>**Christian**</u> **convictions.**"[659]

How can Graham call a New Age mystic and socialist a Christian?! Of course, this is just one more person in a long list of Communists, socialists, and liberals that Graham has referred to as a Christian. Where is his spiritual discernment?

There's also another interesting connection with Muller, the man who dedicated a book to Hammarskjold. Al Dager writes:

> **"Robert Muller was a mentor of Jay Gary,** a major **link between the New Age** teachings of Muller **and today's neo-evangelical leaders.**
>
> "Gary is the founder of the Global Service Office, which is the parent organization of BimillEnnial Global Interaction Network (B.E.G.I.N.), whose letterhead bore the name of Robert Muller. **Gary called Muller a 'key person'** in that organization's bimillennial plans."[660]

A videotape entitled *The Power of A.D. 2000,* distributed by Adopt-A-People in Colorado Springs, Colorado, features Jay Gary. On this video, which was a presentation to a live audience of **Christian** leaders, Gary recommends some astonishing books. One of the books recommended was *The Reimagination of the World* written by **David Spangler** and William Irwin Thompson.[661]

Gary declared:

> "This book, called *Reimagination of the World,* might as well have been entitled, 'The New Age is Dead, Long Live the New Age.' Because these are written by veteran and pioneer New Agers who are looking now at the year 2000, and the New Age movement, reflecting on it after 20 years or more—and more history than that—not as just a mystical experience, but as a metaphor for understanding personal transformation and societal transformation, particularly the dawn of the year 2000.
>
> "This is subtitled, *A Critique of the New Age, Science and Popular Culture.* **AND IT'S ONE OF THE BEST."**

LUCIFER AND CHRIST

If this book is "one of the best," it would be a good idea to check it out. So, how does Spangler view Christ? He writes: **"Lucifer and Christ are twin sides of the demiurgic power of the manifest universe...."**[662] In another of Spangler's books he states:

> **"Lucifer prepares man in all ways for the experience of Christhood** and the Christ prepares man for the experience of God....But **the light that reveals to us the presence of the Christ,** the light that reveals to us the path to the Christ **comes from Lucifer. He is the light giver.** He is aptly named the Morning Star because it is his light that heralds for man the

> dawn of a greater consciousness. He is present when that dawn is realized. He stands no longer as the tester or the tempter but as the great initiator, the one who hands the soul over to the Christ and from the Christ on into ever greater realms."[663]

Says Spangler: **"Christ is the same force as Lucifer** but moving in seemingly the opposite direction."[664]

In *Emergence: The Rebirth of the Sacred,* Spangler reveals that he had "a background of psychic and mystical experiences during childhood."[665] He has several demonic spirit guides that he contacts.[666] In fact, he has "channeled everything from nature spirits, to fairies, to elves, to the Greek god 'Pan,' to angels, to 'God.'"[667] Is it any wonder that the back cover of Spangler's book remarks that he "has been called the shaman of the New Age movement"?[668] He was also a former student of Alice A. Bailey, an occultist.[669]

How does Spangler feel about God's Word? He wrote: "We can take all the **scriptures** and all the teachings, and all the tablets, and all the laws, and all the marshmallows and **have a jolly good bonfire** and marshmallow roast, because **that is all they are worth."**[670]

This is the type person who wrote the book that Jay Gary calls "one of the best"!

Yet, Jay Gary is also heavily involved in the **evangelical** movement.

> "In 1978 Gary went to serve with Ralph D. Winter's U.S. Center for World Mission [USCWM] in Pasadena, California. It is **Jay Gary who developed USCWM's *Perspectives*** study program for world evangelization.
>
> "Under Gary's headship, the *Perspectives* course became an eclectic mix of writings gleaned from extreme ends of the philosophical spectrum. **The course became a platform for ecumenicism and liberation theology** to infiltrate the missions movements of previously evangelical organizations.
>
> "As we've said, the *Perspectives* program is at the heart of the World Christian Movement's evangelization efforts, being utilized by thousands of churches, Christian educational establishments, and missions organizations worldwide."[671]

(For an extensive report on Jay Gary and his New Age/occult connections, see my 40-page article entitled "Jay Gary: The Millennium Doctor.")

Now listen to what Billy Graham says about Gary's *Perspectives* course: "There is no volume of which I know that will inform, inspire, and motivate Christians for world evangelization like the *Perspectives* course....It will stretch your mind, warm your heart, and stir your will."[672]

The list doesn't end here. There are many, many other individuals Graham has endorsed—as we shall discover in the next chapter.

You may be wondering if a man of God can be deceived or have poor judgment. Of course, he can. For instance, Joshua was deceived by the Gibeonites' **appearance** and didn't ask God's counsel (see Joshua 9:14-21). However, when he found out what happened and what the Gibeonites did to deceive him, he **remedied** the situation as much as possible. He **didn't continue** to make more agreements with them.

Billy Graham, on the other hand, has been caught up with the liberal and Communistic crowd over and over and over again. When he is told about his connections, he goes right on ignoring the warning—and he DOES NOT try to remedy the situation. Yes, a man of God can be deceived—but not time after time after time!

3. UNION THEOLOGICAL SEMINARY

The Circuit Riders was an independent group of Methodist clergy and laymen. They were concerned about the Communist influence in the church. "The Circuit Riders compiled and published names of over **7000 ministers and theological school professors who have supported Communist fronts and causes.** Not only is this bad enough, but where do you suppose these traitors are? Stormer, in *None Dare Call It Treason,* shares our worst nightmare: 'In typical Fabian and Communist fashion they had positions of influence and control far out of proportions to their number.' **They make up the hierarchy!'"**[1]

Manning Johnson, a former Communist official, explained one of the tactics that the Communists used which was to **infiltrate the church.**[2] He stated:

> "Once the tactic of infiltrating religious organizations was set by the Kremlin, the actual mechanics of implementing the 'new line' was a question of following the general experiences of the **living church movement** in Russia where the Communists discovered that the destruction of religion could proceed much faster through infiltration of the church by Communist agents operating **within the church itself....**In the earliest stages it was determined that with only small forces available it would be necessary to concentrate Communist agents in the **seminaries and divinity schools.** The practical conclusion, drawn by the Red leaders, was that these institutions would make it possible for a small Communist minority to influence the ideology of future clergymen in the **paths most conducive to Communist purposes....**The plan was to make the seminaries the neck of a funnel through which **thousands** of potential clergymen would issue forth, carrying with them (in varying degrees) an ideology and slant which would aid in **neutralizing the anti-Communist character of the church** and also to use the clergy to spearhead important Communist projects. **This policy was successful beyond even Communist expectations!**"[3] [Emphasis in the original.]

One such school was Union Theological Seminary (to which we will return in a moment).

One of the earlier liberals promoted by Billy Graham was Dr. Henry Pitney Van Dusen. Van Dusen served on the committee for Graham's New York crusade in 1957.[4] He had been Professor of Systematic Theology as well as President of the extremely liberal **Union Theological Seminary.**[5] One author reveals: "Graham affectionately promoted Van Dusen as one of Billy Sunday's converts."[6] In fact, "Dr. Van Dusen is considered by Graham as a GREAT RELIGIOUS LEADER."[7] [Emphasis in the original.] Van Dusen, however, was barely "able to receive ordination in the Presbyterian Church when the judicial commission of that denomination challenged **his denial of the virgin birth** of Christ. Only by asserting the rights of the liberal New York Presbytery was he finally ordained."[8] His lawyer was none other than **John Foster Dulles!**[9] Van Dusen "was a Modernist, who in his book *Liberal Theology* clearly **denies the deity of Christ** and defends Modernism. **Van Dusen and his wife later entered into a successful suicide pact."**[10]

Van Dusen "was a prominent clerical advocate of the 'social gospel,' and a liberal Protestant activist whom Henry Luce greatly respected."[11] We've already covered Luce and his connection to Billy Graham in Chapter 1. I might add that Luce's father, Harry, went to Union Theological Seminary (UTS).[12]

To comprehend this situation better, we need to take a look at UTS where Van Dusen taught[13] and which he later headed. We are told that this seminary "is the leading and most influential **liberal** seminary in the U. S."[14] *U. S. News* mentioned that UTS was "one of the most LIBERAL and LEFT-WING schools in America."[15] [Emphasis in the original.] **John D. Rockefeller, Jr.** helped choose the site for this building. In 1922 he launched an endowment drive and gave a gift of $1,083,333, which was about 25% of the goal.[16] In fact, over the years, Rockefeller, Jr. "had donated more than $50 million to Riverside Church, **Union Theological Seminary,** and International House alone."[17]

UTS "has had a reciprocal educational relationship with Columbia University."[18] This is quite interesting knowing that the Rockefellers have funded both of these organizations.[19]

Columbia University and Columbia Teachers College (also funded by the Rockefellers and part of the Columbia University) have been the main sources of influence for our educational system. **John D. Rockefeller** donated $100,000 to Teachers College to establish an International Institute there.[20] "Today, twenty percent of all American school superintendents and forty percent of all teacher college heads have advanced degrees from Columbia where [John] Dewey spent many years as the Department head."[21] In 1953 about one-third of the presidents and deans at accredited teacher training schools had been educated at Teachers College.[22]

> "To better understand how the process began and who was involved, it might be helpful to look at several of the alumni of Columbia University and Teachers College after **[John] Dewey**

arrived in 1904. George Betts became a professor of education at Northwestern University; Lotus Coffman became dean of the College of Education at the University of Minnesota (and later its president); Elwood Cubberly became dean of the School of Education at Stanford University; Edward Elliott became president of Purdue University; Walter Jessup became president of the University of Iowa and president of the Carnegie Foundation for the Advancement of Teaching; William H. Kilpatrick became professor at Teachers College; Bruce Payne became president of the famous educational George Peabody College in Nashville; David Snedden became Commissioner of Education for Massachusetts; and George Strayer became professor at Teachers College and president of the NEA in 1918-1919. These individuals, along with ten others, became known as the 'Educational Trust,' holding annual meetings known as the Cleveland Conference (because the first meeting was in Cleveland in 1915). Among the other individuals were James Angell, a colleague of Dewey and later a trustee of the Rockefeller Foundation; Leonard Ayers, director of the Russell Sage Foundation; Abraham Flexner, director of the Rockefeller Institute; Paul Hanus, who with the help of the Rockefeller's General Education Board established Harvard University's Graduate School of Education; Frank Spaulding, who received his Ph.D. at Leipzig and became a member of Rockefeller's General Education Board; Paul Monroe, who founded the World Federation of Education Associations; and Dewey colleague Edward Thorndike. The leader of the 'Educational Trust' was Dewey colleague Charles Judd, who had received his Ph.D. from Wilhelm Wundt in Leipzig in 1896."[23]

ATHEIST CLUB

John Dewey is called the "Father of American Education"[24] or the "Father of Progressive Education."[25] He was a **socialist** as well as the former head of the National Education Association (NEA).[26] According to the *Encyclopedia of the American Left* we find:

> "There are strong similarities between Dewey's philosophy and that of Karl Marx....These include a common heritage in Hegel, a strong historical sense, a repudiation of individualism as anathema to democracy, a rejection of all dualistic categories, and a belief in evolution and naturalism (self-realization through interaction with nature). Such parallels have led many writers to seek a rapprochement between the two thinkers. Philosopher Sidney Hook has gone so far as to argue that **Deweyism is the genuine fulfillment of Marxism.**"[27]

Intriguingly, Dewey wrote an article where he mentioned that the **Bolsheviks were engaged** in "'a most interesting sociological experiment,'...and using progressive educational ideas and practices **to '...counteract and transform...**the influence of **home and Church.'**"[28]

Not only was Dewey one of the 34 signers of the *Humanist Manifesto* in 1933 but he also helped to author this document.[29] Additionally, he was the president of the Fabian Socialist League for Industrial Democracy which was formerly called the Intercollegiate Socialist Society (ISS).[30] In fact, he was one of the founders of the ISS.[31] It was under his system called "progressive education" that virtually every school in the country has been influenced.[32]

> "In 1897, Dewey wrote *My Pedagogic Creed,* and in 1899, *The School and Society,* in which he spelled out how the schools should be the instrument to construct an American socialist society. In these schools, psychology would be used, and the academic basic would be deemphasized."[33]

In the July 1908 *Hibbert Journal,* he wrote: "Our schools...are performing an infinitely significant **religious** work. They are promoting the social unity out of which in the end genuine **religious unity must grow.**"[34]

Since Rockefellers fund these organizations, they also maintain some control over the decisions and teachings that emanate from them. In the 1946 Annual Report of the Rockefeller Foundation we find this: "The challenge of the future is to make this world **one world**—a world truly free to engage in common and constructive intellectual efforts that will serve the welfare of mankind everywhere."[35]

Interestingly, at least 18 of those in leadership (professors, president, directors, etc.) at Columbia University belong to the Council on Foreign Relations.[36]

As previously mentioned, Union Theological Seminary has also been funded by Rockefeller.[37] UTS is a school that is supposed to train clergy yet "a Union Theological student was able to join the on-campus **Atheists Club** if he so chose."[38] How many church pulpits were filled by students who belonged to this club?

Union Theological Seminary is so liberal that it is known as the "Red Seminary."[39] Of course, there's a reason for that label! Over 500 "faculty members, students and graduates of the Seminary have had affiliations with **Communist-front** enterprises."[40] Texe Marrs adds that "this seminary has long been a safe harbor and breeding ground for **Marxist activists** and supposed 'Christian' professors who teach that all paths and all religions are the same, and that

Christianity is not unique."[41] This seminary was part of an investigation for Communist infiltration.[42]

In 1919 the New York State Joint Legislative Committee to Investigate Seditious Activities was set up. Their report of "the infiltration of subversive forces" was published on April 24, 1920 and said this:

> "There are two **dangerous centers of Revolutionary Socialist** teaching of a university type in ecclesiastical institutions. One is the **Union Theological Seminary** of New York, where Christian Ethics are taught by **Dr. Harry F. Ward;** the other is St. Stephen's College at Annandale, N.Y., where the president is the Rev. Iddings Bell, and the professor of economics the **Socialist,** Dr. Edwards."[43]

> "Rhodes Scholar Basil Blackwell wrote, 'As of 1955, there were 17 colleges and universities in which their **presidents were Rhodes Scholars,' which included Union Theological Seminary,** Atlantic Christian College, Oberlin College, Columbia Theological Seminary, Purdue, the University of Maryland, and Swathmore, to name a few."[44]

HENRY SLOANE COFFIN

Henry Sloane Coffin, a **Skull and Bones** member (initiated in 1897) "was Professor of Practical Theology at Union from 1904 to 1926 and **President of Union Theological Seminary...**from 1926 to 1945."[45] Coffin was the former moderator of the Presbyterian Church in the USA (PCUSA).[46] In 1923, "the General Assembly of the Presbyterian Church U.S.A. reaffirmed five essential doctrines."[47] One of these doctrines was that it "is an essential doctrine of the Word of God and our standards that Christ offered up Himself a sacrifice to satisfy Divine justice and to reconcile us to God."[48]

> "[I]mmediately 1,292 preachers attacked these doctrines, saying they were not essential as standards of ordination. They called them theories. The document in which they attacked these doctrines has been known historically as the famous Auburn Affirmation, because it was drawn up in Auburn, New York. One of the leading promoters of this Bible-attacking, Christ-denying document is none other than **Dr. Henry Sloane Coffin....**"[49]

He wrote in *The Meaning of the Cross:* "Certain...hymns still perpetuate the theory that God pardons sinners because Christ purchased that pardon by His obedience and suffering....**There is no cleansing blood which can wipe out the record of what has been.... The Cross of Christ is not a means of procuring forgiveness.**"[50]

Coffin was a leader in the **National Council of Churches**[51] and belonged to at least 10 **Communist front** organizations.[52] This is the man, who along with **John Foster Dulles,** helped to found the pro-Communist **World Council of Churches.**

His son, Henry Sloane Coffin, Jr. was also a member of the **Skull and Bones** and he "was one of the Boston Five indicted on federal conspiracy charges."[53] He eventually took over the Riverside Church, which is Rockefeller's church.[54] Coffin was a former Yale chaplain and was only the fourth senior minister at Riverside

> "since **John D. Rockefeller Jr.** built and endowed the church 60 years ago. Coffin, renowned as a promoter of liberal causes and the model for Gary Trudeau's comic strip preacher in Doonesbury, had led the church into deep financial trouble before he resigned. According to published reports, over the last 15 years Coffin spent more than half the original endowment on liberal causes. Since he left in 1987 the church's deficit of $1.4 million has been brought 'under control,' church leaders say."[55]

> "After divorcing his first wife, the left wing peace maker Coffin became involved in a bitter divorce with his second wife when he delivered her a karate chop. Hospital doctors found a hairline fracture. Sloan's wife in the divorce case charged that the great left wing **peace** demonstrator was **anything but peaceful in his own home."**[56]

The minister who succeeded Coffin at Rockefeller's ultra-liberal Riverside Church was James Forbes, Jr.[57] He, too, had been a professor at **Union Theological Seminary.**[58]

Forbes was one of the speakers for "The Summit on Ethics and Meaning" held in April 1996.[59] The ad for this summit stated: "The politics of meaning is **a strategy to counter the Right...."**[60] Other speakers included an assortment of New Agers, lesbians, abortion promoters, leftists, etc., such as Matthew Fox, Paul Hawken, Larry Dossey, Bernie Siegel,[61] Marianne Williamson, Naomi Wolf, Roberta Achtenberg, Jesse Jackson, Jr., Urvashi Vaid, Joan Chittister, Ben Cohen, and Tony Campolo.[62] Additionally, Forbes signed "The Cry for Renewal" statement in 1996.[63] He is also a contributing editor to the liberal, leftist magazine, *Sojourners.*[64]

HARRY F. WARD

Another one of the teachers at Union Theological Seminary was **Harry F. Ward.**[65] He also taught "Christians Ethics" at a theological seminary in Boston.[66] The interesting thing is that **Ward was**

identified under oath as a member of the Communist Party.[67] Manning Johnson, an ex-Communist, said: "I would say that he is the Red Dean of the Communist Party in the religious field."[68] Johnson referred to Dr. **Ward** as **"the chief architect for Communist infiltration and subversion in the religious field."**[69]

Benjamin Gitlow, a former Communist vice presidential candidate, testified that the "Comitern leaders were of the opinion that clergymen with Dr. Ward's point of view, **using the cloak of religion,** could render service of **inestimable value to the Communist Cause** in China and to Soviet interests."[70]

Ward

> "was a crony of **Eugene Debs,** founder of the U. S. Socialist Party and **Wm. Z. Foster** former head of the U. S. Communist Party. *Ward* traveled to Russia in 1924 and 1931 where he studied Marx and Lenin. Teaming up with Wm. Z. Foster in a radio broadcast in Feb. 1946 he declared that Russia's slave labor camps were in reality nothing more than rehabilitation programs."[71] [Italics in the original.]

"Leonard Patterson confirmed that Dr. Ward was not only a Communist with whom he had personally worked but 'a very important member of the Communist party.'"[72]

"At the ninth national convention of the Communist Party, Earl Browder, former head of the [Communist] Party, poured extravagant accolades on the head of Dr. Ward saying that he would 'always receive the unstinted recognition and support of the Communist Party.'"[73]

Ward was one of the founders of the American Civil Liberties Union (ACLU) and he served as the chairman of this group from 1920 to 1940.[74] Other co-founders of the ACLU were Felix Frankfurter, a member of the Council on Foreign Relations (CFR) and the Intercollegiate Socialist Society;[75] Roger Baldwin,[76] a Humanist,[77] a **nudist,**[78] Fabian and front-man for the Communist Party; Elizabeth Gurley Flynn,[79] a top Communist Party official who was associated with the *Daily Worker* (a Communist newspaper[80]); Scott Nearing, a Communist and member of the Socialist Party;[81] Norman Thomas, Socialist Party Chairman;[82] Morris L. Ernst, also on the national executive board of the National Lawyers Guild, "cited as a Communist front which 'is the foremost legal bulwark of the Communist Party, its front organizations, and controlled unions' and which 'since its inception has never failed to rally to the legal defense of the Communist Party and individual members thereof, including espionage agents;'"[83] and **William Z. Foster,** then **head of the U. S. Communist Party.**[84]

GOD WILL BE BANISHED

In Foster's 1932 book, *Toward Soviet America,* he wrote:

> "Among the elementary measures the American Soviet government will adopt to further the cultural revolution are the following: the schools, colleges and universities will be coordinated and grouped around the National Department of Education and its state and local branches. The studies will be revolutionized, being **cleansed of religious,** patriotic, and other features of the bourgeois ideology. The students will be taught on the basis of **Marxian dialectical materialism, internationalism** and the general ethics of the new Socialist society....**The churches will remain free to continue their services, but** their special tax and **other privileges will be liquidated. Their buildings will revert to the State. Religious schools will be abolished and organized religious freedom for minors prohibited. Freedom will be established for anti-religious propaganda....God will be banished from the laboratories as well as from the schools....**"[85]

Foster, along with some others, "developed a strategy that came to be known as 'boring from within.'...The boring-from-within strategy, endorsed by Lenin, had a major impact on early Communist trade union policy."[86]

As most Christians know, the ACLU has consistently advanced an anti-Christian agenda and promoted a new world order.

> "Today, the ACLU supports legalization of child pornography, drugs, polygamy, and prostitution; abortion on demand, busing, mandatory sex education, and tax exemption for satanists. It opposes: Church tax exemption, home schooling,...parental consent laws, voluntary school prayer, prison terms for criminals, and public religious displays.... Supreme Court Justice Ruth Ginsburg was a women's rights attorney for the radical pro-abortion, pro-homosexual ACLU in the 1970s."[87]

"COMMUNISM IS THE GOAL"

The "ACLU has served as legal defense for citizens who aid Fidel Castro, for flag burners, and for the Communist DuBois Clubs; and the ACLU attorney, Humanist William Kunstler, was cited in 1970 by the House Internal Security Committee as Communist-oriented."[88]

Of course, it's no wonder since one of ACLU's founders, Roger Baldwin, had declared in 1935: **"I am for socialism, disarmament,** and ultimately for abolishing the State itself as an instrument of violence and compulsion. I seek the **social ownership of property,** the **abolition of the propertied class** and social control of those who produce wealth. **Communism is the goal."**[89] "Baldwin also wrote in defense of Joseph Stalin."[90]

Baldwin wrote a letter in August 1917 to Louis Lochner who was head of the Bolshevik People's Council of America in which he stated:

> "Do **steer away from making it look like a Socialist enterprise.** Too many people have already gotten the idea that it is nine-tenths a Socialist movement. You can of course, avoid this by bringing to the front people like Senator Works, Miss Addams, and others, who are known as substantial Democrats....**We also want to look like patriots** in everything we do. We want to get a lot of good flags, talk a good deal about the Constitution and what our forefathers wanted to make of this country."[91]

Did you notice the **deception** that he was using? He wanted to make it appear **on the surface** as a patriotic, Constitutional movement all the while that he was trying to destroy the Constitution.

> "Although Baldwin has been affiliated with at least thirty-five **Communist** fronts and causes, he is perhaps best known for a statement made before the Fish Committee, to the effect that 'the American Civil Liberties Union upholds the right of aliens or nationals to advocate murder, assassination, and overthrow of our Government by force and violence.'"[92]

The source just quoted mentioned 35 Communist fronts and causes that Baldwin belonged to. Harry Ward, his co-founder, belonged to approximately 269 Communist front organizations![93]

COMMUNIST FRONT WAS ROCKEFELLER-FUNDED

Baldwin was also active in the Intercollegiate Socialist Society at Harvard. The Intercollegiate Socialist Society later changed its name to The League for Industrial Democracy[94] which was a leading Fabian Socialist group.[95]

In addition to the names just mentioned, other Communists were on the original National Committee of the American Civil Liberties

Union. In fact, since "the 1920's **80%** of its National Committee members **had Communist connections."**[96]

Even a Federal legislative committee explained:

> "'The American Civil Liberties Union is closely affiliated with the Communist movement in the United States, and **fully 90% of its efforts are on behalf of communists** who come into difficulty with the law.' The California Senate Fact Finding Committee supported this estimate of '90%' and said, 'The **American Civil Liberties Union** may be definitely classed as a **communist front** or "Transmission Belt" organization.'"[97]

Returning to Harry F. Ward we find that in 1907 he founded the Methodist Federation for Social Service (later changed to the Methodist Federation for Social Action[98]) which was an officially-cited Communist-front group[99] and was its General Secretary from 1911 to 1944.[100] "The Methodist Federation for Social Services is listed as subversive in the U. S. Government's booklet, 'Guide for Subversive Organizations and Publications.'"[101] **Money for this Communist-front organization came from John D. Rockefeller.**

> "...Ward's job was to teach bright young men to become, so-called, ministers of Christ and to place them as pastors of churches. While teaching them to become ministers, the Reverend Ward also taught them how to subtlely (sic) and craftily preach to their congregations that the entire story of **Christ was a myth** to cast doubts on the divinity of Christ, to cast doubts about the virgin Mary, in short; to **cast doubts on Christianity** as a whole. **It was not to be a direct attack, but** much of it to be **done by crafty insinuation** that was to be applied, in particular, to the youth in the Sunday schools."[102]

Then in 1908 the Federal Council of Churches (FCC) was founded and its "Social Creed" was written by Ward.[103] According to one source,

> "Dr. Ward visited Stalin in Moscow in 1920, and they worked together to form the basis of the Social Gospel, now openly proclaimed by the NCC [National Council of Churches]. This gospel was to increase emphasis on the materialistic side and **decrease emphasis on theology** so **that in due time Marxism and the Social Gospel may become one and the same."**[104]

Ward claimed that "the social program and the social hopes of the prophets were fulfilled in Jesus." He adds: **"Jesus** was not a mere social reformer. He **has been called the first Socialist."**[105] Ward also states:

"The next step in the social expression of religion was the work of that group, some of whom called themselves **Christian Socialists,** who prove once again that the wider social outlook is more invariably the condition for the prophetic gift. The men of our own age who have had something of the prophets' vision and power of language and inspiration have nearly all had the social enthusiasm and faith in the reconstructive power of Christianity. **Maurice and Kingsley, Ruskin and Carlyle, Lamennais and Mazzini, and Tolstoy** were in their measure **true seers of God,** and they made others see."[106]

GIUSEPPE MAZZINI

Can you imagine Ward calling individuals like Frederick Maurice, Charles Kingsley, Giuseppe Mazzini and John Ruskin Christians? For those who do not know who these people are, I'll briefly fill you in. Maurice and Kingsley started the **Christian SOCIALIST Movement.**[107] Mazzini was the founder of the "Young Italy" party.[108] He was a Mason,[109] an Illuminist,[110] and belonged to the Carbonari[111] (which was a secret society[112] that influenced the Illuminati[113]).

"Mazzini was associated with Karl Marx and Masonic leader Albert Pike, the latter of whom delivered a lecture to the Grand Lodge of Louisiana in 1858 titled, 'The Meaning of Masonry,' in which he stated, *'There is no...independent and self-existent Evil Principle in rebellion against God....Evil is merely apparent; and all is in reality good and perfect.'*"[114]

"Mazzini, with Pike, developed a plan for three world wars so that **eventually every nation would be willing to surrender its national sovereignty to a world government.** The first war was to end the czarist regime in Russia, and the second war was to allow the Soviet Union to control Europe. The third world war was to be in the Middle East between Moslems and Jews and would result in Armageddon."[115]

Helena Petrovna Blavatsky (a medium,[116] mystic,[117] occultist,[118] and Satanist[119]) was initiated in the Carbonari by Mazzini.[120]

Albert Pike drew up rituals for a Luciferian organization called the Palladium Rite which openly worshipped Lucifer. This was done at the insistence of **Mazzini!**[121] "When Pike sent him a copy of his Luciferian rituals, Mazzini was full of an enthusiastic praise for his colleague's work...."[122]

"In 1860, Mazzini had formed an organization called the 'Oblonica,' a name derived from the Latin 'obelus,' which means: 'I beckon with a spit (dagger).' Within this group, he established an inner circle called the Mafia."[123] "Although most people know what the Mafia is, few people realize it was founded as a Sicilian **Masonic terrorist** organization. The name Mafia emerged around 1860 and is an acronym for **Mazzini autorizza furti, incendi, avvelenamenti**—Mazzini authorizes thefts, arson and poisoning."[124]

No wonder Mazzini was known as the "Evil Genius of Italy,"[125] yet Ward refers to him as a **Christian!**

JOHN RUSKIN

John Ruskin was another person that Ward referred to as a Christian. Ruskin was a "socialist, racist and ardent nature worshipper."[126] Ruskin said: "I am myself a Communist of the old school—reddest of the red."[127] He "called 'pagan faith' admirable in itself"[128] and he also belonged to the Society for Psychical Research, an occult organization.[129] He was influenced by the writings of occultist Madame Blavatsky.[130] His grave has a swastika on it.[131]

"Ruskin's ideas had their origin in the occult beliefs of **Plato** and **Karl Marx.**"[132] [Emphasis in the original.] He "read Plato every day (e.g., Plato's *Republic,* a 'Republic of Philosophers') and believed in government by the elite who would control means of production and distribution."[133] Plato's *Republic* "outlined his ideal society....It included the elimination of marriage and the family, and introduced selective breeding by the government, who would destroy all inferior offspring. In Plato's utopia, sexual equality dictated that women would fight alongside the men in times of war."[134]

Ruskin gave a lecture that inspired **Cecil John Rhodes.**[135] Rhodes, a homosexual[136] and a Mason[137] (whose library was filled with erotic materials[138]), espoused the view of a **world government**[139] and established the **Rhodes scholarships** with this end in mind.[140] He had received some financial help from the Rothschilds![141]

Men like Ruskin and Mazzini are the kind of individuals that Harry F. Ward thinks are "true seers of God." **Remember, Ward is the man who wrote the "Social Creed" for the Federal Council of Churches!**

No wonder that in 1927

> "Congressman Arthur M. Free described the group [Federal Council of Churches] as 'a Communist organization aimed at the establishment of a state church.' From 1926-29, **John D. Rockefeller** contributed over $137,000 to them, and **donated**

> **the triangle-shaped building that houses the National Council of Churches.** In 1935, they were identified by the Office of Naval Intelligence, as being one of the several organizations which 'give aid and comfort to the **Communist movement** and Party.' Labor that year, Admiral William H. Standley, Chief of Naval Operations, publicly accused the Federal Council of Churches of collaborating with the Communists. In 1942, **their platform called for 'a world government,** international control of all armies and navies, a universal system of money, and a democratically controlled international bank.'"[142]

Ward "also was a co-founder of the 'American League against War and Fascism' which, under [Earl] Browder, became the 'Communist Party of the United States.'"[143]

Additionally, Ward

> "wrote more than fifteen books, many of them hammering the Soviet and domestic Communist line. In 1924 he went to the Soviet Union and spent 1925 touring China with a series of pro-Soviet speeches. He spent 1931 in Russia and came home to write his book, *In Place of Profit.* In the '30's he was the founder and leader in the People's Institute of Applied Religion, cited by the Attorney General as a **Communist** front and subversive organization."[144]

No wonder that by November 24, 1931, Reinhold Niebuhr could write to his girlfriend and say: "Had a letter from [Harry—U.N.] Ward today. He is a **complete communist** by now....I just wonder what he will be like when he comes back."[145] This comment came from a man who was a socialist himself!

COMMUNISM SPREAD FROM PULPITS

One Communist, Karl Prussion, told how that

> "Ward came to a cell meeting to which Prussion belonged and instructed him as member of the Party to enroll at **the Union Theological Seminary** so he could be ordained a protestant (sic) minister. Prussion stated that the Party subsequently decided to send him to San Francisco instead, but this experience impressed him with the technique the [Communist] Party was using in an effort to **infiltrate** protestant (sic) churches."[146]

Speaking at **Union Theological Seminary, Earl Browder, then head of the Communist Party** in the USA, bragged: "You must be interested in knowing that **we have preachers,** preachers **active in churches,** who are members of the Communist Party....There are churches in the United States where the **preachers preach Communism from the pulpits....**"[147]

In spite of (or perhaps, because of) Ward's Communist affiliations, the National Council of Churches (which will be covered in Chapter 4) decided to celebrate his 90th birthday (on October 15, 1953). On the letterhead it was revealed

> "that the committee was sponsored by seventy-two leading clergymen, **twenty-two of whom were in leadership positions in the National Council of Churches.**
>
> "Now, each one of these gentlemen, including Bishop James C. Baker, **Dr. John C. Bennett,** Dr. Harold A. Bosley, Professor W. Russell Bowie, Bishop Matthew Clair, Jr., Bishop Fred Pierce Corson, Bishop A. Raymond Grant, Professor Frederick C. Grant, Professor Paul T. Lehmann, Bishop John Wesley Lord, Dr. John A. MacKay, Dr. Benjamin E. Mays, Dr. Walter G. Muelder, Bishop Marshall R. Read, Reverend William Scarlett, **Dr. Ralph W. Sockman,** Reverend Alfred W. Swan, **Dr. Henry P. Van Dusen,** Bishop William J. Walls, Professor Leroy Waterman, Bishop Lloyd C. Wicke, **knew** the colorful [meaning Communistic] background of Dr. Harry F. Ward."[148]

In fact, *The Worker,* a **Communist** paper here in America,[149] wrote this about Ward's birthday party celebration:

> "Dr. **Ward is a link between the Christian Socialist preachers** of the late nineteenth century, who sought to end the Church's neutrality in the class struggle....He helped set up the American Civil Liberties Union in 1920....He became **a firm advocate of friendship with the Soviet Union.** We are going to be at Carnegie Hall this Tuesday evening, October 15, to wish **this grand man** many more birthdays. We are sure we will see you there."[150]

G. BROMLEY OXNAM

> "One of Harry Ward's pupils at the **Union Theological Seminary** was Bishop **G. Bromley Oxnam.** Oxnam authored a book titled *Personalities in Social Reform* and he devotes several chapters in this book to what he calls 'social reformers.' In Chapter One, 'The Scholar as Social Reformer,' he identifies

> 'the scholar' as the husband-and-wife team of Sidney and Beatrice Webb, the Fabian Socialists of England. Chapter Two is entitled 'The Minister as Social Reformer.' The minister is identified as Walter Rauschenbusch. Chapter Three is entitled 'The Administrator as Social Reformer.' The administrator is David E. Lilienthal, former head of the T.V.A. Chapter Four is entitled 'The Saint as Social Reformer,' and, surprisingly enough, the saint turns out to be Mohandas Gandhi of India, who denied the deity of Christ."[151]

In Oxnam's book, *Preaching in a Revolutionary Age,* he told a story of a boy who hated the God of the Old Testament and called God a "dirty bully." Oxnam then added:

> "We have long since rejected a conception of reconciliation associated historically with an ideal of Deity that is loathsome. God, for us, cannot be thought of as an angry, awful, avenging Being who because of Adam's sin must have his Shylockian pound of flesh. No wonder the **honest** boy in **justifiable repugnance** could say, **'dirty bully.'**"[152]

Of course, Oxnam had received the 33° of Masonry on September 28, 1949.[153] Additionally, he was connected to a multitude of left-wing activities.[154] One author stated that his "record of Communist activities was only slightly shorter than the Manhattan telephone book....It would be difficult to find a Communist Front to which he **didn't** belong."[155] He wrote several pro-Communist books.[156]

> "In a 1927 book entitled *Russian Impressions,* G. Bromley Oxnam tells us, '...it is fair to say that **Soviet Russia has as the object of its collective endeavor the creation of a new order** wherein all men, rendering service to the state shall have a full and complete life. The objective is abundant living.'"[157] [Emphasis in the original.]

Oxnam testified before the Committee on Un-American Activities on July 21, 1953. He had been asked about a **pro-Communistic book that he had sent out to 22,000 Methodist ministers** which he suggested that the ministers read. Along with the book was a statement issued by the **Federal Council of Churches.** In his testimony he stated:

> "I said that I thought if this book went out it ought to be accompanied by the statement, at least by the statement that was issued by The Federal Council of Churches of Christ in America on American-Soviet Relations. *I* had chaired that committee that had drafted this statement. It is no secret, however, that *it was written by Mr. John Foster Dulles.*[158] [Emphasis in the original.]

In other words, the letter that was sent out with this pro-Communistic book was written by **John Foster Dulles.** Remember, this is the same John Foster Dulles who was instrumental in getting doors to open for Billy Graham to hold a crusade in London in **1954** and **"who designated himself a Christian Communist."**[159] Part of the letter stated: "Moreover **communism** as an economic program for social reconstruction **has points of contact with the social message of Christianity** as in its avowed concern for the underprivileged and its insistence on racial equality."[160]

WALTER RAUSCHENBUSCH

In Oxnam's book, *Personalities in Social Reform,* the minister was **Walter Rauschenbusch.** "Rauschenbusch's publications became the canon for the **Social Gospel,** and he became a highly sought speaker across the country....President Theodore Roosevelt consulted him on social policy, promising to **borrow the good from socialism** while leaving out the bad."[161]

"Influenced by Rauschenbusch, Teddy Roosevelt denounced accumulated wealth as an affront to working people...."[162]

Rauschenbusch "replaced the Bible-based belief that man was individually responsible to God for his own salvation with a concept of 'social salvation.'"[163]

His "ideas helped propel the formation in 1908 of the **Federal Council of Churches,** which was the forerunner to the National Council of Churches, the enormous alliance of churches that would gain prominence later in the century."[164]

It was Rauschenbusch "who articulated and provided a theological foundation and rich intellectual tradition for the social concerns" of Communist Martin Luther King[165] and his **"condemnation of capitalism** found fertile ground in a man like King...."[166]

James Cone, the father of Black Theology and a **Communist,** was another one of King's friends.[167] He is a **professor at Union Theological Seminary.**[168] In 2000 he signed a declaration (the "Religious Declaration on Sexual Morality, Justice, and Healing") sponsored by SIECUS (covered later in this chapter) "calling for same-sex unions, ordination of homosexuals and abortion rights."[169]

As mentioned previously, Oxnam's teacher, Harry Ward, was the founder of the Communist-front group called the Methodist Federation for Social Service.[170] Oxnam was the Vice President of this group.[171] He was also **one of the presiding officers of the**

National Council of Churches. Additionally, he was **president of the American Federal Council of Churches** from 1944-1946 as well as "the **first American president of the World Council of Churches"** from 1948-1954.[172]

Oxnam was "one of the founders of Protestants and Other Americans United for Separation of Church and State, of which he is a vice president...."[173] By the way, "about eighty percent of the funding for the predecessor of Americans United for Separation of Church and State came from Masons."[174] Their address is the very same address as that of the Masonic Service Association. In fact, a former Executive Director, Dr. Glenn L. Archer, and a former Associate Director, Dr. C. Stanley Lowell, were both 33° Masons.[175] (For more information on Masonry, see my book *Hidden Secrets of Masonry.*)

RELIGIOUS RIGHT MUST BE STOPPED

Americans United (AU) is against creation being taught in the classroom and they are for abortions, contraceptives, and sex education. A letter received from Barry Lynn, the Executive Director of AU, declares:

> "Now I'm asking you to join with Americans United as we prepare for a massive clash with the Religious Right.
>
> "I don't know about you, but personally I have seen enough, heard enough and read enough about the powerful new political influence of the revamped Religious Right. There's no point in mincing words: <u>they must be stopped</u>! And the sooner the better.
>
> "If the Religious Right prevails, they will destroy our wondrous American mosaic. They'll thumb their noses at pluralism and stifle diversity. They'll inject their own moral code into our personal lives. <u>We cannot</u>—<u>must not</u>—<u>let them do that</u>!
>
> "That's why I'm writing today to ask you—to <u>urge</u> you, really—to join Americans United and play a personal role in our battle against the Religious Right."[176] [Emphasis in the original.]

On Reformation Day (October 30, 1949) Oxnam gave an address at an interdenominational rally held at the ungodly, New Age **Cathedral of St. John the Divine.**[177] A Masonic publication, *The New Age Magazine,* called this speech "another one of [Oxnam's] masterly addresses....”[178] This meeting was sponsored by the **Protestant Council of New York City.**[179]

I think it is interesting to note that this is the **SAME COUNCIL** who sponsored Billy Graham’s Madison Square Garden Crusade just 8 years later (1957).[180] A book **favorable** to Graham says this:

> “But about the same time he took the first steps to found *CT [Christianity Today],* Graham dashed those hopes and severed whatever threads of unity remained between the New Evangelicals and old Fundamentalists by accepting an invitation from the **Protestant Council** of the City of New York, **an affiliate of the liberal National Council of Churches,** to hold a crusade in Madison Square Garden during the late spring of 1957.
>
> **“Graham had turned down invitations to come to New York in 1951 and 1954, both times because he felt the group offering the invitation was too heavily weighted with Fundamentalists** and therefore did not represent the broad spectrum of the city’s Protestant churches. The Protestant Council represented 1,700 churches, 94 percent of all Protestant bodies in the metropolitan area. In fact...the idea received strong support from some wealthy and influential constituents, including Chase Manhattan Bank chairman **George Champion,** a southern Evangelical layman who chaired the council’s Department of Evangelism, and Mrs. Cleveland Dodge...as well as some of the city’s leading clergymen, including **Norman Vincent Peale.”**[181]

It should be noted that Cleveland Dodge was a director of Rockefeller’s National City Bank in New York.[182]

About a decade earlier (January 31, 1945) **John D. Rockefeller had addressed the Protestant Council.**[183]

GRAHAM RECEIVED ROCKEFELLER MONEY

Remember, too, **Graham received $75,000 from John D. Rockefeller, Jr.** for this 1957 Crusade.[184] This funding came from Rockefeller around the same time as Rockefeller’s funding to Planned Parenthood which he started financing in 1952.[185]

Graham sure must have appreciated his invitation from the Protestant Council because after “the 1957 New York City Crusade, he [Graham] **gave $67,618 to the Protestant Council** of New York City, an affiliate of the apostate NCC.”[186] Just a few years later, at the New York World’s Fair, this **same Protestant Council** showed a picture entitled “The Parable.” It **portrayed Jesus as a CLOWN.**[187]

(For those of you who have supported Graham in the past, are you happy with how he has spent your money? Do you want **your** donation being given to liberal organizations like the Protestant Council?)

Graham gave the check to the President of this group, **Dr. Gardner C. Taylor.** He was a member of the National Council of Churches[188] (which will be covered in the next chapter). He was also "an outstanding liberal and a promoter of **left-wing projects.**"[189] **Taylor** was one of the sponsors for the Emergency Civil Liberties Committee which was launched in 1951 by the **Communist Party** and was "the most active **Communist** organization in the United States" at **that** time![190] One researcher tells us more about Taylor:

> "But here is an even more fantastic incident in the recent career of the Rev. Dr. Gardner Calvin Taylor. The incident took place in the Concord Baptist Church of Brooklyn, of which Mr. Taylor is pastor. The funeral service of **one of this country's most prominent Communist leaders** was held in that church with its pastor, the Rev. Dr. Taylor, delivering the funeral sermon. **Dr. Taylor was reported to have paid homage to this outstanding Communist leader 'as one who dared to dream and work for the new world every good person desires.'**
>
> "The deceased Communist Party leader, who was the subject of this high praise from the head of New York City's **Protestant Council,** was Edward E. Strong.
>
> "The **National Committee of the Communist Party, U.S.A., issued an official statement on the death of Edward E. Strong** which read, in part, as follows: 'Returning from his service in World War II, **Ed Strong became a leader of the Communist Party.** As a member of its national committee, as chairman of the Eastern Pennsylvania District, as Southern Regional Secretary, **he enriched the Party with high quality of leadership** which had won the admiration and respect of scores of thousands in the youth movement....Above all, he was a man of sterling personal character. **He was a fitting prototype of the new Communist man.'** That was the official eulogy of the Communist Party, U. S. A. And, to that eulogy, the Protestant leadership of New York City added that he was one who 'dared to dream and work for the new world.'"[191]

Since Taylor can eulogize a Communist, it shouldn't come as a surprise that he is on the Board of Directors of The Interfaith Alliance. This group brags that **one of their main goals is to provide** "people of faith with **an alternative voice to that of the radical religious right."**[192] Remember, Taylor is the man to whom Graham gave over $67,000 in **1957!**

GEORGE CHAMPION

As previously mentioned, George Champion was also one of those who was instrumental in helping with this Crusade.[193] Listen to Billy Graham's explanation of how he received the notice from Champion:

> "Taking a brief break from the June 1955 Paris Crusade, Grady [Wilson] and I were playing a few holes of golf on a course near Versailles. He looked at his watch. We were running late for a meeting back in Paris, so we cut our game short, hurried back to the locker room, and changed our clothes. As we were running out to the car, I heard someone calling my name.
>
> "'Dr. Graham, I heard you on television last night,' he said, 'and my wife and I were very interested. I'm playing golf, and we have only two in our party. Would you and your friend like to join us?'
>
> "'Sir, I would like to very much,' I replied.
>
> "It was the Duke of Windsor....
>
> "'But unfortunately I have a commitment in town,' I added. 'Let me call to see if I can get it postponed.'
>
> "When I called Bob Evans, I discovered that my commitment *could not* be changed. As I went back to apologize to the duke, someone handed me a cable that apparently had been forwarded to the golf club. It was **George Champion,** vice president of the Chase Manhattan Bank, **who headed the evangelism department of the Protestant Council of New York.** The council had voted to extend an invitation to us to hold a Crusade in New York during the summer of 1957."[194] [Italics in the original.]

I think an obituary notice gives some interesting information about Champion:

> "A commercial banker for 40 years, he retired as **Chairman of the Board of the Chase Manhattan Bank** in 1969. At about that time, **he had been president of the Protestant Council of the City of New York,** Treasurer of the United Negro College Fund, a trustee of the Independent College Funds of America,

> board member of the Freedom Foundation in Valley Forge and cofounder of the *Dartmouth College Review*....In 1969, he became the president of the Economic Development Council of NYC....
>
> "As **President** and later Chairman **of the Chase bank,** he won a reputation as probably the nation's foremost authority on lending practices and money market operations. Chase bank was, in the 60's and is still today, the largest commercial bank in the United States. George Champion was one on the nation's greatest bankers."[195]

This obituary goes on to say that he **"personally organiz[ed] the Rev. Billy Graham's first major Manhattan crusade...."**[196]

Champion is reported to be a member of the super secret Illuminati group called the Pilgrim Society,[197] as well as one of the Honorary Board of Directors for the Thomas Jefferson Research Center[198] (TJRC) and is listed as a "Jefferson Associate" for the Jefferson Center for Character Education.[199] (TJRC's name was changed to Thomas Jefferson Center in 1989.[200])

This organization is a **New Age** group[201] and has been "listed as a resource in a number of New Age/globalist directories."[202] It has produced

> "character education material that suggests the use of the infamous 'Lottery' story, and which will emphasize Abraham Maslow's (father of Humanistic 'Third Force' Psychology) hierarchy of needs toward self-actualization. The material's reference resources...include New Age networkers Jean Houston and Jack Canfield. The Center...[is] listed by Maslow in his Eupsychian Network, and as a member and cooperating organization in Unity-In-Diversity Council's *Directory For A New World,* which lists groups and individuals fostering 'the emergence of a new universal person' and 'a global civilization.'"[203]

The Teacher's Guide for the TJRC "utilizes guided fantasy, guided imagery, self-hypnosis, breathing and relaxation exercises, and stress management...."[204]

Remember, the same man (George Champion) that promoted this New Age propaganda (through his association with TJRC) also supported Billy Graham's crusade! Recall, too, that the Chase Manhattan Bank is a **Rockefeller-controlled** enterprise.[205]

RALPH SOCKMAN

Dr. Ralph W. Sockman, a Methodist, was twice President of the same **Protestant Council** that Champion once headed.[206] By the way, Sockman was also a graduate of **Union Theological Seminary.**[207] When asked if the Methodists believe in heaven and hell, Sockman replied:

> "The concepts of heaven and hell vary widely, according to the educational and religious background of the believers. Some have very concrete ideas of golden streets in heaven and fiery furnaces in hell.
>
> "But **the majority of Methodists are emancipated from the pre-scientific view of a physical heaven 'up there' and a physical hell 'down there.'** They trust the promise of Christ: 'I go to prepare a place for you.' **Heaven is the realm of mind and spirit** where the redeemed keep company with God and His Risen Son, Jesus Christ. **Hell is the state where such fellowship is absent."**[208]

Notice carefully that Sockman only referred to hell as a "state" and not a "place." Accordingly, heaven is only "the realm of mind and spirit." Notice also that Sockman claims **today's Methodists** are now **emancipated** (freed, liberated, loosed from) the "pre-scientific" view of a **PHYSICAL** heaven and hell!

The Bible, however, does teach a physical heaven. Jesus explained in John 14:2-3: "In My Father's **house** are many **mansions:** if it were not so, I would have told you. I go to prepare **a place** for you. And if I go and prepare a **place** for you, I will come again, and receive you unto Myself; that where I am, there ye may be also." Likewise, hell is a real place. Jesus cautioned us in Luke 12:5: "But I will forewarn you whom ye shall fear: Fear Him, which after He hath killed hath power to cast into hell; yea, I say unto you, Fear Him." Luke also tells the story of the rich man who died and went to hell and "in hell he lift up his eyes, being in torments, and seeth Abraham afar off, and Lazarus in his bosom" (Luke 16:23).

Heaven and hell are not states of mind but are real places and each one of us will spend eternity in one of these two places. We need to prepare **now** by accepting Jesus Christ as our **personal** Savior if we intend to spend eternity in heaven. (For a more thorough explanation of the Biblical doctrine of hell, see my book *A Scriptural View of Hell.)*

GRAHAM'S "GODLY MEN"

Remember that **Sockman,** who denied a literal heaven and hell, **was on the committee to celebrate Communist Harry Ward's 90th birthday.**[209] Sockman's

"Communist-front associations have been the American Youth Congress; the Emergency Peace Mobilization; board chairman of the Inter-Church Committee of the American Russian Institute; the Methodist Federation for Social Action; greetings sent on the occasion of the 31st Anniversary of the Russian Revolution (Communist) under auspices of the National Council of American-Soviet Friendship; [and] World Youth Conference (sponsor)."[210]

Does any of this seem to bother Billy Graham? Apparently not, because **Sockman and Henry Van Dusen** (covered earlier in this chapter) were among those who **served on Graham's Crusade Committees.**[211] Additionally, **Graham referred to Sockman and Jesse Bader as "godly men."**[212]

Bader was secretary of the National Council of Churches[213] and the Director of Evangelism for the NCC.[214] He was also a Mason.[215] Graham said that Bader was one of his "very close advisers and friends"[216] and he would seek advice from Bader.[217]

Another of Graham's friends is Tom Allan. He is "a **socialist** from Scotland, who said that 'Billy Graham has one of the most acute and social consciences of any man I ever met.'"[218] Billy Graham himself explains:

"A few years after we began publication of *Christianity Today*, we became involved in two magazines in Britain.

"I had heard that the *Church of England Newspaper,* which leaned toward the evangelical point of view, was going to close because of a lack of finances. It was a stock company, and I asked Jerry Beavan to see if he, acting on my behalf, could purchase the majority stock; he did so. My plan was to sell it to a group of evangelicals or to a wealthy evangelical businessman. We didn't publicize our involvement, and later Sir Alfred Owen took over our interest.

"We then purchased a struggling magazine in Great Britain called *The Christian.* Our goal was to make it similar to *Christianity Today.* It had been started in the previous century and covered extensively Dwight L. Moody's ministry in Britain; by 1962 it was on the point of being closed by its owners, the publishers Marshall, Morgan, and Scott. **Tom Allan, our friend from Glasgow, briefly came on as editor and also manager of our London office,** but soon he suffered a heart attack from which he never recovered."[219]

Not only was this **socialist** Graham's friend, but he was **editor** of one of Graham's magazines and he also managed Graham's office in London! Interesting!

A few pages later in Graham's autobiography, we find:

> "Most days began to follow a routine pattern....I often spoke three or four times a day in addition to the Crusade service in the evening—perhaps a luncheon with business leaders, a visit to a university, **a meeting at the United Nations,** a gathering in someone's home designed to reach out to neighbors or friends with the Gospel, a tour of the Bowery, with its tragic clusters of men whose lives had been wrecked by alcohol. Since New York also hosted scores of conventions, I often was invited to speak to them. Opportunities seemed limitless, and our Team—augmented by a number of well-known ministers, including Paul Rees, **Tom Allan,** and **Samuel Shoemaker**—spoke in almost every kind of situation."[220]

SAMUEL SHOEMAKER

The previous sentence brings up another name that should be briefly noted—Sam Shoemaker. Shoemaker was at one time the pastor of the Calvary Church in New York, an Oxford Group member, and the founder of the group Faith at Work. According to *The Greenwood Encyclopedia of American Institutions: Social Service Organizations,* we find that alcoholics, homeless men, and other deviants (including Bill Wilson, the founder of Alcoholics Anonymous [AA]), would go to the Calvary Church's mission to hear lectures on **SPIRITUAL-ISM!**[221] In 1958 Wilson even wrote to **Shoemaker** about occult practices, bragging:

> "Throughout A.A., we find a large amount of **PSYCHIC PHENOMENA,** nearly all of it spontaneous. Alcoholic after alcoholic tells me of such experiences and asks if these denote lunacy—or do they have real meaning? These **PSYCHIC** experiences have run nearly the full gamut of everything we see in the books. In addition to my ORIGINAL MYSTICAL experience, I've had a lot of such phenomenalism myself."[222]

Of course, that's not all. **Shoemaker** was also involved (along with Bill Wilson) in **LSD experimentation!** From AA's own book we read:

> "He [Bill Wilson] invited many of his closest associates to join him in the experience. Those invited included Father Dowling, who accepted, Dr. Jack [Norris], who did not, and **Sam Shoemaker.** Bill reported to Shoemaker: 'You will be highly interested to know that Father Ed Dowling attended one of our **LSD sessions** while he was here recently. On that day, the material was given to one of the Duke precognition

researchers, a man now located in New York. The result was a most magnificent, positive **spiritual** experience. Father Ed declared himself utterly convinced of its validity, and volunteered to take LSD himself.'"[223]

(To learn more about Alcoholics Anonymous and the occult connection, see my book *Alcoholics Anonymous Unmasked.)*

So, here we have a man (Sam **Shoemaker) who was openly taking LSD with others and giving lectures on spiritualism,** yet Billy Graham was using him, along with a **socialist** (Tom Allan), as two of his speakers. When Shoemaker died, Graham stated: "I doubt that any man in our generation has made a greater impact for God on the Christian world than did Sam Shoemaker."[224]

JOHN C. BENNETT

Another President and Professor of **Union Theological Seminary** (1964-1971) was **John C. Bennett.**[225] Bennett "had an extensive record of espousal of **Marxist** causes while President of Union Theological Seminary in New York City, [and] has long printed a host of anti-American and socialistic causes in its pages by familiar advocates of and participants in such causes."[226] Even before becoming President of Union Theological Seminary (UTS), **Bennett was known for his support of Communism and Fascism.** For instance, in 1935 **Bennett "praised Fascism** for its 'constructive value in a stage of the development of a **new economic order.'"**[227]

"John C. Bennett is the author of several books which discuss Communism favorably, including *When Christians Make Political Decisions,* which is a resource book specified in the New Curriculum for youth of the Church of Jesus Christ...."[228]

> "Appearing on the David Susking television program, 'Open End,' December 10, 1961, Dr. Bennett said that 'the Church should not fight Communism.'...In 1955 he was an initiator of a petition seeking amnesty for Communist Party leaders who were convicted under the Smith Act...."[229]

In his book, *Foreign Policy in Christian Perspective,* written in 1966, he stated:

> "Communism has proved to be the instrument by which this nation has been united....
>
> "Say what you will about the cost of the revolution, the cost of allowing old social conditions to go unchanged needs to be weighed over against it. Communism needs to be seen as

the instrument of modernization, of national unity, of greater social welfare. The brainwashing, the cruel dealing with the opposition, and the political totalitarianism are the cost. At this stage, it is not for us to say whether we would or would not choose the effects of this cost."[230]

Writing in *Theology Today,* Bennett asks:

> "Why must they conclude that there is a conflict between Christianity and communism?...Certainly **we cannot find the difficulty in the Communist economic system or in Communist social goals.** There is much overlapping between Communist goals and Christian goals....*I do not believe that American Christians could condemn communism because of its belief that revolution, even violent revolution, is sometimes necessary."*[231] [Italics in the original.]

While he was a **professor at UTS** in 1952, he wrote: **"Communism** wins power because it **has much truth in its teachings...**as he (the Christian) studies communism he finds many things to approve in it...."[232] In 1959 he remarked: "Today I am convinced that our country is handicapped by the fact that there has been so little of the Socialist impulse in our tradition."[233] These quotes by Bennett had appeared in issues of the liberal *Christian Century.*

The *Christian Century* had originally been called *Christian Oracle.*

> "Eight years after the magazine had become THE CHRISTIAN CENTURY, it would have died, had not a young Disciples [of Christ] pastor named Charles Clayton Morris picked up its $1,500 mortgage.
>
> "Morrison, who had studied philosophy under **John Dewey** at the University of Chicago, then became its editor. He made it a 'undenominational' organ in 1916 and guided it until his retirement in 1948."[234]

Of course, the *Christian Century*

> "has been a strong supporter of the United Nations and world government. The April 16, 1947, issue said the UN 'cannot hope to survive on any lesser terms than as an actual **world government.'** The Jan. 14, 1948, issue stated: 'We believe that the crisis of humanity demands that the **churches...** shall once again **declare their faith in a world government...** and shall throw themselves with all the resources they can command into the crusade to set up such a government.'"[235]

Christian Century also supported the communist dictator Fidel Castro.[236]

Since the *Christian Century* and Bennett had so much in common, it's no wonder that the *Christian Century* could brag that John C. Bennett gave a "strong endorsement of our magazine...."[237]

MORE UTS CONNECTIONS

A Unitarian, Dr. Holland Lee Hendrix, was installed as President of **Union Theological Seminary** in 1991.[238] Hendrix "believes that Union and other seminaries need to work for global environmental awareness and to bring about world peace."[239]

Another Unitarian Universalist is F. Forrester Church. He sits on the board of UTS. His name was in the news frequently about a decade ago when he admitted that he was having an adulterous affair with one of his parishioners and he was planning to marry her. His church, the Unitarian Church of All Souls, voted 372-136 to retain him.[240]

> "[Former] Catholic priest Rev. Matthew Fox, a popular speaker on the New Age circuit; Sallie McFague, an environmentalist and feminist; and Dr. Ismar Schorsch, the chancellor of the Jewish Theological Seminary were speakers at the **Union Day** exercises held at James Chapel on the [UTS] campus. After the lectures a 'Carnival: Festival of Creation' was held with worshipers meditating to the strumming of a dulcimer and pouring libations to the ancestors."[241]

Professor Douglas John Hall has written books in which he denies "such doctrines as the vicarious satisfaction and resurrection of Jesus Christ."[242]

> "The idea of a God who substitutes his innocent son for an indeterminate number of guilty men and women is literally a fantastic notion. Not only does it present the spectacle of a deity that only sadomaschoists could lead to appreciate (as Abelard already felt), but it offers as salvation an act of transfer that is physically and rationally already most impossible for the modern mind to grasp, writes Douglas John Hall in *Profession The Faith—Christian Theology in a North American Context.*"[243]

In a more recent book, Hall wrote: **"Communism** itself, contrary to the criticism of capitalist inspired forms of Christendom, **was not a bad vision...."**[244]

Oh, "Hall received his Th.D. from **Union Theological Seminary** in New York City in 1960 and serves as professor of Christian Theology at McGill University in Montreal. He is an ordained minister of the United Church of Canada."[245]

"GOD IS DEAD"

Dorothee Soelle was another **professor at UTS** from 1975 to 1987.[246] She claims: "God is known variously as 'Allah. Great Mother, the Eternal, Nirvana, and the Unsearchable.'"[247] She "defends Marxism and rejects the biblical view of property. She calls for the redistribution of wealth. According to Soelle, man is as much of a 'creator' as her god. Man is a co-creator....She rejects God's standards of morality and promotes homosexuality."[248] Soelle goes so far as to call Karl Marx a "church father."[249] She is known for her statement that "God is dead, red, and a woman,"[250] yet the **World Council of Churches** had her for one of their speakers in 1983.[251]

Explaining her "God is Dead" position, she writes:

> "So I proceeded to write a book titled *Ein Kapitel Theologie nach dem Tode Gottes* (A Chapter of Theology After the Death of God)—because I genuinely felt that this heavenly being did not exist anymore and that we had to take seriously the trend in philosophy (as in Nietzsche, for example) that had abolished this being and regarded him as dead. I then developed a radically Christocentric theological position, **following Dietrich Bonhoeffer's lead** and beginning with the **powerless Christ** who died on the cross, who had no legions behind him, no power that could rescue him or free him. In this theology, God himself, a God who acts and speaks, is inaccessible to us. The only guide we have is this **nonauthoritarian, powerless Christ** who has nothing but love, who exerts no power, has no armies to call on, shouts no one down, as God did Job out of the whirlwind, who has nothing with which to save us but his love.... We are not his because he sired us, created us, made us. We are his because love is his weaponless power, and that power is stronger than death."[252]

With professors like this, no wonder our ministers in the pulpit are so powerless and wishy-washy. No wonder they cannot preach about the power of Christ to save a lost sinner from sin, cleanse him, and make him into a new creature in Christ Jesus (see II Corinthians 5:17).

Phyllis Trible is a professor of sacred literature at **Union Theological Seminary.** In her book, *God and the Rhetoric of Sexuality,* she writes: "Personal growth for either wife or husband may well require intimate friendships besides that with the partner....Intercourse cannot arbitrarily be excluded."[253] In other words, she is encouraging extra-marital affairs!

Beverly Wildung Harrison, professor of Christian Social Ethics at **Union Theological Seminary,** has "decried the demise of socialism and the spread of free market economics. 'Capitalism destroys religion,' she declared. 'It eats everything in our culture that does not bow to the bottom line.'"[254]

At a ReImagining Conference "she credited capitalism with enslaving people [and] destroying communities...."[255]

A workshop Harrison led for Kirkridge (a New Age organization) from March 31-April 4, 1986 focused "on morality for married and unmarried people, celibacy, homosexuality, abortion and reproductive control, the integration of sexuality and spirituality—within the context of biblical, psychological, sociological, and political perspective."[256] Oh, by the way, the title of a book she wrote is *Our Right to Choose (Toward a New Ethic of Abortion).*[257]

SAME SEX UNIONS

Just recently Harrison signed the "Religious Declaration on Sexual Morality, Justice, and Healing."[258] This statement, released on January 18, 2000, supports homosexual marriage and abortion and opposes "unsustainable population growth."[259] It calls for the "[f]ull inclusion of women and sexual minorities in congregational life, including their ordination and the **blessing of same sex unions"** and a "faith-based commitment to sexual and **reproductive rights,** including access to voluntary contraception, **abortion,** and HIV/STD prevention and treatment" among other issues.[260]

Other signers of this document are: Ann Hale Johnson, Dr. George M. Landes, Randall Styers, Kathleen Talvacchia, Barbara K. Lundblad, Dr. Emilie M. Townes, and Joseph Hough—**ALL from Union Theological Seminary.**[261] In fact, Hough is the President of UTS.

Another professor at **Union Theological Seminary** is Delores Williams.[262] She declares: "I don't think we need a theory of atonement at all. I think Jesus came for life and to show us something about life....I don't think we need folks hanging on crosses and blood dripping and weird stuff."[263] At the 1993 ReImagining Conference (to be covered shortly), **sponsored by the World Council of Churches,**[264] she stated: "Jesus in reality was not God....Jesus was human like us, and also, like us, he was infused with God, with sacred spirit, and in that sense was divine, and he had a clue."[265]

At the 1998 ReImagining Conference she "described the emerging community as a 'context of the sacred' where no sexuality is unclean: 'In the heart and soul of the deities, we are all loved, and it doesn't matter who we're sleeping with,'... she declared."[266]

On June 27, 2000, as the leader of the ReImagining God movement, Williams said "that the Bible is not reliable and that the stories of today's women need to be added to the canon."[267]

The 1993 ReImagining Conference was a gathering of over 2000 women from so-called

> "mainline churches in 49 states and 27 countries [who] came together in Minneapolis to **reimagine God,** themselves, their sexuality, and the world. Funded in part by their Presbyterian, Methodist, Baptist, and Lutheran denominations, the four-day gathering sent shock waves through the church....
>
> "Seated in intimate Native American 'talking circles' around the tables, the assembly imagined the faces of their god. 'What does your god sound like, taste like, look like?' they asked each other, while the sounds of a water drum throbbed in the air. 'Tell each other....**Re-imagine your God.** Name! Tell! Imagine!'"[268]

"Conference **participants worshiped the divine in each other by marking red dots on their foreheads to signify their divinity,** and then bowing to each other in an act of reverence."[269]

These women also chanted:

> "Sophia, Creator God, let your milk and honey flow.... Shower us with your love....We celebrate sensual life you give us....We celebrate our bodiliness...the sensations of pleasure, our oneness with earth and water...."[270]
>
> "During the conference, a group of roughly 100 'lesbian, bisexual, and transsexual women' gathered on the platform and were given a standing ovation by many in the crowd. They were 'celebrating the miracle of being lesbian, out, and Christian.'"[271]
>
> "The lesbian theme was heard repeatedly from major speakers. In a workshop called 'Prophetic Voices of Lesbians in the Church,' Nadean Bishop, the first 'out' lesbian minister called to an American Baptist church, claimed that Mary and Martha in the Bible were lesbian 'fore-sisters.' She said they were not sisters, but lesbian lovers. Janie Spahr, a self-avowed lesbian clergywoman in the Presbyterian Church USA...claimed that her theology is first of all informed by 'making love with Coni,' her lesbian partner. Judy Westerdorf, a United Methodist clergywoman from Minnesota, told the workshop that the church 'has always been blessed by gays and lesbians... witches...shamans.' In a seminar on 'Re-Imagining Sexuality-

Family,' lesbian theologian Mary Hunt said, 'Imagine sex among friends as the norm.'"[272]

CHUNG HYUN KYUNG

The person who seemed to draw the most attention was a Korean woman by the name of Chung Hyun Kyung who was a graduate of the **Union Theological Seminary.**[273] Chung was "a professor at Korea's Ewha Women's University, the world's largest university for women, with 20,000 students"[274] and is a feminist and liberation theologian.[275]

She said: "The three goddesses I want to share with you are Kali [Hindu], Kwan-in [Buddhist], and Enna [Philippines]...my new trinity."[276] She added: "The Christian church has been very patriarchal. That's why we are here together, in order to destroy this patriarchal idolatry of Christianity."[277]

Since she would like to see that "patriarchal idolatry of Christianity" destroyed, it's no wonder she can speak fondly of Communism. In *Inheriting Our Mothers' Gardens: Feminist Theology in Third World Perspective,* she reveals: "... a Marxist view of Jesus gives the Gospels afresh both to Christians and to atheists and so provides each group with new insights of itself and the other. Such readings contribute responsibly and beneficially to global issues."[278]

Elsewhere Kyung explains:

> "I came from...a Shamanist, Buddhist and Confucian and Taoist and Christian tradition....When I look at our history of religion, we have more than 5000 years of Shamanism, more than 2000 years of Taoism, and almost 2000 years of Buddhism, and 700 years of Confucianism and only 100 years of Protestantism in Korea. Therefore, whenever I go to temples...and look at Buddha, I feel so young....Buddha died in his 80s and Jesus died when he was 33. Maybe...Jesus should be called 'Too young to understand.'...
>
> "'I feel like my bowel is Shamanist, my heart is Buddhist, my right brain is Confucianist, and my left brain is Christian,' Kyung continued. 'I call it a family of gods and...they are together.'"[279]

Kyung also said:

> "We believe that this life-giving energy came from god and it is everywhere. It is in the sun, in the ocean, it is from the

ground, and it is from the trees....If you feel very tired and you feel you don't have any energy to give, what you do is sit in silence, maybe you go to big tree and ask...'give me some of your life energy.' Or you ask the sun to give you some life energy."[280]

SPIRITS OF THE DEAD SUMMONED

One author adds:

"Chung, who is in great demand as a speaker, gave a plenary address at the Seventh **World Council of Churches** (WCC) International Conference in Australia in 1992 (sic). One trembles even to quote her diatribe against God the Father and the Holy Spirit and her wicked perversion of Christianity. Yet the **WCC delegates gave Chung a standing ovation.** Ecumenical Press Service reported,

"Combining verbal fireworks with a performance by Korean and aboriginal dancers, Chung rendered a dramatic evocation of a **female Holy Spirit...**[which] she linked...to that of Hagar...'exploited and abandoned by Abraham and Sarah.' Chung then burned bits of paper bearing the names of other exploited spirits—which she said were full of 'han,' the Korean word for anger....Chung said, 'I also know that I no longer believe in an omnipotent, Macho, warrior God who rescues all good guys and punishes all bad guys....'

"Eighteen times **Chung summoned the spirits of the dead** who have suffered injustices and claimed that 'without hearing the cries of these spirits, we cannot hear the voice of the **Holy Spirit....**Don't bother the Spirit by calling **her** all the time.' Added Chung, 'I hope the presence of all our ancestors' spirits here with us shall not make you uncomfortable.'"[281]

As mentioned earlier, Kyung was a graduate of **Union Theological Seminary** (UTS). Was the seminary embarrassed by her remarks? Of course not! They responded to her heresies and blasphemy by accepting her as a faculty member of the school! **She is now a professor at UTS.** She, too, has signed the "Religious Declaration on Sexual Morality, Justice, and Healing."[282]

Kyung was also a speaker at the **World Council of Churches** in Harare, Zimbabwe in November 1998 where she performed a sensual dance.[283] "In a private conversation after her performance, Dr. **Kyung declared that to witness about Jesus Christ to another person is in reality 'an act of violence.'** When reminded that Jesus said in John 14:6 that He is the only way, Kyung said Jesus 'was mistaken.'"[284]

Two more **members of the Communist Party** were Rev. Joseph S. Nowak, former pastor of the Portage Park Presbyterian Church, and Rev. John A. Hutchinson. They had gone to the Communist Party headquarters in 1935, right after their graduation from the **Union Theological Seminary** "where they had been 'well grounded in Marxism.'"[285]

Norman Thomas, an "American **Socialist** party leader[286] and six-time candidate for the U. S. presidency,"[287] was another person who was educated at the **Union Theological Seminary**[288] and ordained by UTS.[289] "After the Socialist leader Eugene Debs died in 1926, Thomas was regarded as the leader of the Socialist party in America."[290] In a pamphlet put out by the Socialist Party, Thomas was listed as a candidate for President. This notation was added: *"Martin Luther King called him 'The bravest man I ever met.'"*[291] [Emphasis in the original.] As King was flying to Norway to accept the Nobel Peace Prize, he sent a taped message to Thomas which said: "I can think of no man who has done more than you to inspire the vision of a society free of injustice and exploitation.... Your example has ennobled and dignified the fight for freedom, and all that we hear of the Great Society seems only an echo of your prophetic eloquence."[292]

Thomas was the editor of *The World Tomorrow,*[293] which was the publication for the liberal, pacifist Fellowship of Reconciliation[294] (FOR) as well as the associate editor of *The Nation,* another liberal magazine.[295] He was the codirector of the League for Industrial Democracy from 1922 to 1935.[296] Thomas also helped to found the American Civil Liberties Union in 1920.[297] He was ordained as a Presbyterian minister in 1911 but resigned in 1931. It was during this time **as a minister** that he **joined the Socialist Party** in 1918.[298]

He stated: **"The American people will never knowingly adopt Socialism, but under the name of Liberalism they will adopt every fragment of the Socialist program until one day America will be a Socialist nation without knowing how it happened."**[299] [Emphasis in the original.]

Even though Thomas was a socialist, he, too, was one of the sponsors of the Temple of Understanding[300] (which was covered earlier).

REINHOLD NIEBUHR

Yet another individual at **Union Theological Seminary** (from 1928-1960[301]) was **Reinhold Niebuhr.**[302] He was Professor of Applied

Christianity, the Dean of UTS from 1950-1955,[303] and the Vice President from 1955-1960.[304] Needless to say, **Niebuhr was "an active member of the Socialist party...."**[305] He wrote articles for *The Nation*[306] and *The World Tomorrow*[307] (which he edited[308]). He also supported the **SOCIALIST** Norman Thomas in his campaign for the Presidency in 1932.[309]

A letter to his girlfriend shortly before they were married, shows that he was involved in a number of **socialist** organizations. Niebuhr wrote:

> "I have been elected president of the Fellowship of Reconciliation, a job I'd really like to accept, but I told them I would do so only if I could relinquish my chairmanship of the League for Industrial Democracy. I have put it up to Norman Thomas. I think the F.O.R. would be the most ideal organization for me to keep in contact with the outside world and its problems, something as [Harry—U.N.] Ward does through the American Civil Liberties."[310]

Less than a month earlier he had written to her: "Tomorrow I am going to try and revamp my Ethics course and then work out a **socialist** speech for Tuesday night when I must speak at some **socialist** rally."[311]

After they were married, he wrote another letter stating: "I may even have to cancel some of my engagements in order to go to Buffalo for the organization meeting of the State Committee of the **Socialist Party."**[312]

Additionally, he was editor for *Christianity and Society* and *Christianity and Crisis,*[313] of which he was the founder.[314] A few years ago I received a notice to subscribe to this magazine. They support abortion, gay rights, feminism, etc.[315]

In the last chapter we mentioned the Americans for Democratic Action (ADA). Niebuhr was one of the top officials in ADA[316]

> "along with Hubert H. Humphrey [a Mason[317]], Jacob K. Javits, John Kenneth Galbraith, Herbert H. Lehman and Arthur Schlesinger, Jr. Here are a few of the policies which the ADA openly and vigorously advocated in 1961:
>
> "1. Abolition of the House Committee on Un-American Activities...
>
> "3. Total disarmament under United Nations control
>
> "4. U. S. recognition of Red China
>
> "5. Admission of Communist Red China to the United Nations, in place of Nationalist China

> "6. Federal aid to all public schools
>
> "7. Drastic overhaul of our immigration laws, to permit a more 'liberal' admission of immigrants
>
> "8. Urban renewal and planning for all cities."[318]

Most of these socialist policies have now been implemented.

In 1951, *The City of Man: A Declaration on World Democracy,* was co-authored by Reinhold Niebuhr and others. This book states:

> "Universal peace can be founded only on the **unity of man under one law and one government....**All states, deflated and disciplined, must align themselves under the law of the world-state...the new order...when the **heresy of nationalism** is conquered and the absurd architecture of the present world is finally dismantled....And there **must be a common creed...**or ethico-religious purpose."[319]

Several decades ago a social gospel group was set up at the **Union Theological Seminary** by Niebuhr which he called the Fellowship of **Socialist** Christians.[320] Needless to say, Niebuhr was pro-Communist[321] and had received 12 citations for participation in Communist fronts, activities, campaigns, etc.[322]

In fact, the **Chairman** of the executive committee of the Fellowship of **Socialist** Christians **was a Communist,** Francis Henson.[323] Another member of this committee was **John C. Bennett,** former President of Union Theological Seminary.[324] Yet another member was **Henry P. Van Dusen,** also a former President of UTS.[325] Remember, Van Dusen was active in Graham's New York crusade—and **was promoted by Graham!**

"The Fellowship of Socialist Christians published a magazine called *Radical Religion,* under the editorship of Reinhold Niebuhr. The magazine is still published under the more ambiguous title, *Christianity and Society.*"[326] The Fellowship of Socialist Christians "became the Frontier Fellowship and, in 1951, Christian Action."[327]

LEAGUE FOR INDUSTRIAL DEMOCRACY

Niebuhr was also the treasurer of the Intercollegiate Socialist Society which later changed its name to the League for Industrial Democracy (LID).[328]

In 1967 the LID published a book, *American Power in the Twentieth Century,* which called for redistribution of wealth.[329] Another book, *Why Do We Need Socialism in America,* written by the LID's chairman, Michael Harrington, "has a picture of Karl Marx superimposed over the United States flag" on its front cover.[330]

The LID is the parent organization for Students for a Democratic Society which is another pro-Communist group.[331]

No wonder Reinhold Niebuhr could announce: "If, as Bertrand Russell prophesies, some form of oligarchy, whether capitalistic or communistic, be inevitable, in a technological age...the **communistic oligarchy would seem preferable in the long run to the capitalistic one."**[332]

Niebuhr was involved in the World and Federal Council of Churches.[333] In one letter to his girlfriend, he penned: "Tonight I am trying to get some of my course material in shape because I must run from one thing to another tomorrow. **Federal Council of Churches meeting, socialist,** dentist, dinner with Francis Henson [a **Communist],** etc., etc."[334] Did you notice that he mentions the FCC and the socialist meeting in the same breath?! Niebuhr was the dominant voice behind the Federal Council of Churches' Dun Commission's report on **disarmament.**[335] He was also a speaker at the World Council of Churches[336] and was a member of the American delegation at the founding of the WCC in 1948.[337]

In a letter he wrote to his wife concerning the meetings, he added this note: "Last night we went to a nearby pub and [Karl] Barth, Bishop [Stephen] Neil [assistant to the archbishop of Canterbury, [Willem Visser] t'Hooft (sic), Pierre Maury, and Bill Pauck and I had some beer."[338] Instead of spending time in prayer, here are these so-called "Christian" leaders drinking beer at a pub.

WCC leaders no longer have to visit the barroom. The barroom is now brought to them. Dr. Ralph Colas, a Christian who attends WCC meetings as an observer and to warn others of its apostasy, "declined a special invitation from WCC leaders to all accredited press members to a press party where 'wine, beer and other beverages' was (sic) to be served."[339]

Don't ever try to say that the WCC was founded on Christianity and God's Word!

HIGHLANDER RESEARCH AND EDUCATION CENTER

"In 1932 theologian Reinhold Niebuhr wrote an initial fund-raising letter for something called the Southern Mountain School, a project initiated by his former student Myles Horton. After a few years of study at **Union Theological Seminary** and the University of Chicago, Horton, a native Tennessean, had become inspired to return to Tennessee and begin an experimental school specializing in education for fundamental social change. The idea developed into the **Highlander Folk School,** now called **Highlander Research and Education Center."**[340]

Horton was the director of this Center from its founding until 1973.[341]

Leftist researchers state:

> "As a seminarian [at Union Theological Seminary], **Horton encountered the ideas of Christian socialism and Marx,** other equally serious southerners, the Danish Folk High School movement, and Dr. Harry F. Ward's unremitting calls for ethical service and labor. Horton returned to Tennessee dedicated to teach a **social gospel** blending these influences. With other southerners, including Don West, James A. Dombrowski, and John Thompson, he founded Highlander Folk School in 1932 at Monteagle, Tennessee. His propelling impulse was a mixture of Christ's teachings with **socialist** theories."[342]

Don West himself was a pro-Communist poet and a so-called "Christian" minister.[343] Also, because of "Dr. Harry F. Ward at Union Theological Seminary in New York, and the social turbulence of the 1920s, Dombrowski became an organizer."[344]

"WE SHALL OVERCOME"

The book, *The Marxist Minstrels,* gives a little more information about this school.

> "The Highlander Folk School was organized by Don West and Myles Horton. West was identified under oath as having been a district director of the **Communist Party** in North Carolina. Myles Horton was identified by John P. Frey, president of the Metal Trades Department of the AFL, as one of the persons who 'attended a secret convention in North Carolina, at which time plans were made for spreading the revolutionary theories throughout the South.' When asked to become a member of the Communist Party, Horton replied, 'I am doing you just as much good now as I would if I were a member of the Communist Party.'
>
> "Also closely associated with West and Horton was Dr. James Dombrowski, a protege of identified Communist Dr. Harry F. Ward and himself identified as having been a high-ranking member of the Communist Party."[345]

> "James Dombrowski...was included in the Highlander board of directors and [then] the head of the Southern Conference Educational Fund, a Communist outfit based in New Orleans."[346]

> "Significant also is the fact that all three, West, Horton and Dombrowski, were graduates of **Union Theological Seminary,** New York, and **disciples of Harry F. Ward.** Also of interest is the fact that the counsel for Dr. Dombrowski when he appeared before the Senate Internal Security Subcommittee was Benjamin E. Smith, a member of the subversive National Lawyers Guild and at present registered under the Foreign Agents Registration Act as an agent for Fidel Castro."[347]

In *Encyclopedia of the American Left,* we find:

> "Toward the end of 1934 and in the early part of 1935, Birmingham **Communists** drew up a 'united front agreement' **with** a handful of southern **Socialists, most of whom were affiliated with the Highlander Folk School** and were **openly supportive of the left wing Revolutionary Policy Committee within the Socialist Party.** Although most state Socialist leaders denounced the agreement, a good portion of rank-and-file Socialists joined the Communist Party soon afterward."[348]

The civil rights movement's theme song, "We Shall Overcome,"[349] was popularized at Highlander. Myles Horton explains:

> "'We Shall Overcome' was just one of the many songs that were (sic) brought to Highlander. It came from Charleston, South Carolina, where the American Tobacco workers were on strike. Like a lot of people, they made up songs based on their hymns. And they brought to **Highlander** a pretty rough-hewn song they'd made up. With my wife Zilphia's encouragement, that song grew. It had something to it that people just kept singing it. When **Martin Luther King Jr.** heard it, he said, 'This has got to be the **hymn of the civil rights movement.'** Zilphia collected such songs and put out music books that spread all over the South and were used during the civil rights movement and the labor period."[350]

One researcher claims that Zilphia Horton was even more pro-Communist than her husband.[351]

What is interesting is that "Fidel Castro's official slogan for the Communist regime in Cuba is precisely 'Venceremos,' i.e., 'We Shall Overcome.' Fidel Castro closes every public speech with, 'Patria o muerte, venceremos' (Fatherland or death, we shall overcome), and his captive mobs dutifully chant, 'Venceremos.'"[352]

Martin Luther King, Jr., Rosa Parks, and others held workshops at the Highlander Folk School (HFS).[353]

> "The Augusta, Georgia, *Courier* of July 8, 1963, printed a picture of Mr. King at the Highlander Folk School in Monteagle, Tennessee during the Labor Day weekend of 1957. This school had an intriguing history. After King visited there, the school was closed by the Tennessee Legislature in 1960 after having conducted hearings into its true nature. **The school was cited as being a 'meeting place for known Communists and fellow travelers,' and as a 'Communist Training School.'"**[354]
>
> "Shown in the photograph sitting adjacent to King are Abner Berry, a correspondent for the **Communist Party** newspaper, the *Daily Worker,* Aubrey Williams, identified as a member of the CPUSA [Communist Party, USA] and President of SCEF [Southern Conference Educational Fund, a **Communist** organization[355]]; and Myles Horton...."[356]
>
> "Paul Crouch, who had been district organizer for the state of Tennessee for the **Communist Party,** described in his testimony the uses of the HFS for the Party as they were developed in a conference that included himself, Horton, and Dombrowski: 'The purpose of the conference was to work out a plan by which the *Daily Worker* would be purchased by the school. They would be made accessible to the students, that everywhere possible the instructors should refer to the *Daily Worker,* to news that had come in it, to encourage the students to read it, and it was agreed that the Communist Party should have a student, a leader, sent there as a student whose job it would be to look around for prospective recruits and Mildred White, now in Washington, D.C., was selected to **attend the Highlander Folk School for the purpose of recruiting for the Communist Party and carrying the Communist Party line among the student body there.'"**[357]

By 1962, "Martin Luther King, Jr. was listed as a sponsor of the Highlander Center on its letterhead."[358]

Even though Myles Horton died on January 19, 1990, the center's new director was John Gaventa, a **Rhodes scholar!**[359] He said: **"The issues change, but the philosophy remains the same...."**[360]

Interestingly, the Rockefeller Foundation is one of the supporters of the Highlander Research and Education Center.[361]

Closely connected to Highlander was an organization called **Southern Christian Leadership Conference (SCLC)** which King headed.[362]

"The Joint Legislative Committee on Un-American Activities, reported that his **Southern Christian Leadership Conference was 'substantially under the control of the Communist Party** through the influence of the Southern Conference Educational Fund and the communists who manage it.' **King had connections with over 60 communist front organizations. Nine of his closest aides were high ranking communist activists** and one of those later became an aide to Rev. **Jesse Jackson.** Stanley Levison, who had been a King advisor since 1956, had been involved with the **Communist Party** up to 1955, and brought other known communists onto King's staff."[363]

"Leftist influences, however, had been present in King's movement from its very genesis. Rosa Parks, the woman whose refusal to move to the back of the bus set off the Montgomery boycott, had previously attended training classes at the radical Highlander Folk School, and a major boycott organizer, E. D. Nixon, had been a lifelong associate of A. Philip Randolph. SCLC would have continuing contacts with Highlander and with Left support groups such as the Southern Conference Educational Fund...any local campaign was likely to include radical veterans of battles in which the **Communist Party had played a major role.**"[364]

E. V. HILL AND GRAHAM

One minister who belongs to Southern Christian Leadership Conference is **E. V. Hill.**[365] Martin Luther King, Jr. was his very close friend.[366]

In spite of the affiliations of these men, Billy Graham has used them in various situations. Graham writes in his own autobiography:

"One night civil rights leader Dr. **Martin Luther King, Jr., whom I was pleased to count a friend,** gave an eloquent opening prayer at the service; he also came **at my invitation** to one of our Team retreats during the Crusade to help us understand the racial situation in America more fully."[367]

In 1984 **E. V. Hill endorsed Jesse Jackson** for the Democratic nomination for president.[368] **He was also a speaker at Billy Graham's Amsterdam '83 Conference,** and was listed as a speaker for Billy Graham's 1992 "School of Evangelism" in Wheaton, Illinois.[369] Additionally, **he is on the board of directors of the Billy Graham Evangelistic Association** (BGEA)![370]

If Hill serves on Billy Graham's board of directors, it would be profitable to know more about him. Hill is the black pastor of the Mt. Zion Missionary Baptist Church in the Watts section of Los Angeles.[371]

> "His church is affiliated with the National Baptist Convention, which is a part of the **National Council of Churches.** His doctor's degree (or, at least one of them) is from Oral Roberts University in 1985. Dr. Hill has a strange list of credentials. The *Fundamental Information Service Bulletin* for September 15, 1982 quoted the *Wheaton College Bulletin* for March 1977 as stating that Dr. Hill was on the Billy Graham Association board of directors, the board of the Los Angeles Urban League, [and] the Los Angeles NAACP...."[372]

"*Christian Life* for March 1982 indicated that Dr. Hill appeared with Rev. [Jesse] Jackson at a Campus Crusade sponsored conference in Chicago called 'Chicago '81.'"[373]

Hill has been a Promise Keepers speaker[374] and he also was a big supporter of the Rev. Henry Lyons, the former President of the National Baptist Convention.[375] Lyons has been shown to be "an adulterer, liar, and thief,"[376] yet Hill promoted him. The July 2000 issue of *Charisma* showed a picture of Hill with false prophet Benny Hinn. Hill was the speaker for Hinn's August Mission for the New Millennium conference.[377]

Below is an eye-witness account by someone who attended the North American Congress on the Holy Spirit and World Evangelization from July 22-26, 1987 where E. V. Hill was also a speaker. He reports:

> "Now consider this. E. V. Hill sat for about two and a half hours before he actually got up to speak. What did he see and hear? He listened to the loud **babble of tongues** during the 'worship' times, and the unspeakably confusing time of **'holy shouting.'** He heard **rock music** as loud as at a secular rock concert, **watched the dancing girls** of the 'drama' teams, **heard prophecies** which were delivered in the first person as from Jesus Christ Himself, **heard a woman Roman Catholic preach about** growing in the fullness of salvation and **halos and icons and St. Xavier,** watched Catholic Kevin Ranaghan and Pentecostal Vinson Synan hug each other twice and speak of how wonderful it is for Catholics and Pentecostals finally to get together. For more than two hours Hill looked out over a crowd of 35,000, half of which were Catholics. After this experience, E. V. Hill walked up to the podium and said what?

> What should a man say after experiencing such things, a man who claims to be a fundamental Bible-believer, a man who speaks in fundamental Baptist churches? If he were a prophet of God, he would have plenty to say and it wouldn't have been music to the ears of those creating this doctrinal confusion! But what did he say? Hill stood for a moment, calmly looking around, then said, 'WOW! If you're not on fire by now, your wood is wet! If your bell isn't ringing, your clapper is broken!'"[378] [Caps in the original.]

No wonder Jerry Huffman could state that "left-wing/social action promoter" Hill "apparently has never seen an ecumenical forum he didn't like—be it charismatic/Catholic/NCC, or Promise Keepers."[379]

BILLY GRAHAM'S STAFF

It should be profitable to look at a few others who serve on Billy Graham's staff. William M. Watson was the director of the BGEA. He

> "is a **Freemason,** and he is also President of Occidental Petroleum Corporation. Chairman of Occidental was **Armand Hammer.** Watson is also a member of the development council of the Masonic run Baylor University....He also was a member of the Southwestern Baptist Theological Seminary in Ft. Worth which had at least three **Freemasons** on its board of trustees, and likely more."[380]

Another director of the BGEA was David M. McConnell. He "is a **Freemason.** He was also U. S. ambassador to the United Nations (1968-69), business associate with Illuminatus Charles Gambrell, in Belk Stores of Charlotte, North Carolina."[381]

Arthur Lee Malory was the co-chairman of the Billy Graham Crusade Advisory Committee for the St. Louis Crusade in 1973. He is a 32° **Mason.**[382]

Also, an interesting tidbit is that for the 1992 Portland, Oregon Billy Graham Crusade only **Shriner** clowns were allowed to perform.[383] **To become a Shriner, a person must first be a 32° Mason!** There were other clowns available, but they were not allowed to perform. That seems quite odd, doesn't it? Is Graham subtly trying to get a message across?

E. V. Hill, as previously mentioned, belongs to the Communistic Southern Christian Leadership Conference.[384] This is the same Southern Christian Leadership Conference which **sponsored the 1993 Gay**

Rights march on Washington![385] This march was also sponsored by the National Association for the Advancement of Colored People (NAACP),[386] another group to which Hill belongs.[387]

Remember, the Southern Christian Leadership Conference is connected to Highlander Folk School and Highlander was founded by Myles Horton who had been a student at **Union Theological Seminary** and Niebuhr had been his teacher.

> "Reinhold Niebuhr's socialism, more than his theology, has influenced the thinking of thousands of Protestant clergymen. From Niebuhr's Fabian socialism to Harry Ward's Marxism has been an easy step for many of the students and graduates of **Union Theological Seminary.** I note in passing that **504 faculty members, students and graduates of the Seminary have had affiliations with Communist-front enterprises.** Arnold Johnson, one of the convicted so-called second-string Communist Party leaders, is a graduate of Union Theological Seminary, class of 1932, and a protege of Harry Ward."[388]

No wonder that Niebuhr was among those who were members of the National Committee to Abolish the House Un-American Activities Committee which was a group trying to expose Communist activities.[389] Some other members of this group were: **Dr. John C. Bennett** (National Council of Churches), **Martin Luther King,** Carl Braden, Dr. John A. MacKay, James A. Dombrowski, and Linus Pauling.[390]

Of course, Niebuhr's theology is a far cry from fundamentalism. He denies the inerrancy of the Bible.[391] He calls the creation story in Genesis and the resurrection a myth.[392] He also denies the virgin birth of Christ.[393] Niebuhr remarked: "My view is that the virgin birth doesn't make a bit of difference. I can't get angry at anybody for holding it, but on the other hand I certainly don't hold it myself."[394]

UNESCO

Niebuhr was a co-founder of UNESCO.[395] UNESCO is an organization trying to influence our children to accept a **world government.** Julian Huxley, former director of UNESCO[396] and 1962 **Humanist of the Year,** was an atheistic philosopher, a member of the Communistic Colonial Bureau of the British Fabian Society,[397] and a signer of the *Humanist Manifesto II.*[398] In 1948 Huxley wrote:

> "'In its education program (UNESCO) can stress the ultimate **need for world political unity** and familiarize all peoples with the implications of the **transfer of full**

sovereignty from separate nations to a world organization.... Political unification in some sort of **world government will be required.'** Tasks for the media division of UNESCO [will be—D.L.C.] to promote the growth of a common outlook shared by all nations and cultures....to help the emergence of a single world culture....Even though it is quite true that any radical eugenic policy will be for many years politically and psychologically impossible, it will be **important for UNESCO to see that the eugenic problem is examined with the greatest care,** and that the public mind is informed of the issues at stake so that much that now is unthinkable may at least become thinkable."[399]

UNESCO's own material explains:

"If UNESCO is attacked on the grounds that it is helping to prepare the world's people for world government, then it is an error to burst forth with apologetic statements and denials. Let us face it: **the job of UNESCO is to help create and promote the elements of world citizenship**. When faced with such a 'charge,' let us by all means affirm it from the housetops."[400] [Emphasis in the original.]

"...Huxley angered some American officials by appointing communists and communist sympathizers in key posts. For example, the chief of the Soviet Ministry of Education served as an early director of UNESCO's secondary education department."[401]

"Furthermore, according to Huxley UNESCO would assist in the process of 'values clarification' on a global level. Because none of the religious traditions was adequate to the needs of a world government, a new world morality would have to be summoned into existence, and it would be UNESCO's task to do the summoning: 'It will be one of the major tasks of the philosophy division of UNESCO to stimulate...the quest for a restatement of morality that shall be in harmony with modern knowledge and adapted to the fresh functions imposed on ethics by the world of today.' Instilling this new world morality in schoolchildren would be UNESCO's most important task."[402]

CONTRACEPTIVES FOR MINORS

"Under Huxley's guidance, the United Nations prepared a guidebook for teachers. This guidebook reminds them that the DESTRUCTION of a child's love of country and patriotism is the FIRST STEP in educating that child for WORLD CITIZENSHIP."[403]

(For more information on UNESCO, see my book entitled *A One World Order Is Coming.)*

Niebuhr, UNESCO's co-founder, even signed a SIECUS ad which appeared in the October 16, 1969 issue of *New York Times.*[404] SIECUS stands for Sex Information and Education Council of the United States.[405] This group promotes extensive sex education in schools. SIECUS Position Statements reveal the following:

> "It is the position of SIECUS that contraceptive services should be available to all—including minors who should enjoy the same rights of free and independent access to... contraceptive care as do others....It is the position of SIECUS that the use of explicit sexual materials (sometimes referred to as pornography) can serve a variety of important needs in the lives of countless individuals...."[406]

Perhaps it isn't surprising to find out that the Playboy Foundation granted the initial "seed money" for SIECUS.[407] (For more information on SIECUS, see my book *Masonic and Occult Symbols Illustrated.)*

How does Billy Graham feel about Reinhold Niebuhr? In Graham's booklet, *Evangelism and the Church Today,* he writes: "The **great theologians** of today are Rudolph Bultmann, **Karl Barth, Emil Brunner, Reinhold Niebuhr, Paul Tillich,** and Carl Henry."[408] This booklet was sent to Los Angeles ministers prior to Graham's crusade in that area.[409]

Brunner denied "the infallible inspiration of Holy Scripture and many other cardinal doctrines,"[410] yet Graham writes: "When I was in Zurich with Emil Brunner, whose stature as a theologian was next to Barth's, he was warm, friendly, and **supportive."**[411]

Brunner's and Barth's theology

> "was variously called neo-orthodoxy, dialectical theology, the theology of paradox, crisis, or despair. In America where it was called Christian existentialism or Christian realism, its foremost exponents were, and are, **Reinhold Niebuhr, John C. Bennett, Paul Tillich,** Robert Calhoun, and William M. Horton."[412]

Brunner, Barth and Niebuhr were all speakers at the World Council of Churches[413] (which is covered in the next chapter). Brunner, in fact, was one of the founders of the WCC.[414]

PAUL TILLICH

> "Paul Tillich was a modernist who did not believe in the virgin birth, the sinless life and the bodily resurrection of Christ.

> Since his death, Tillich's second wife has written a book telling about his illicit relationships with his secretary and other women who came to him for counselling. A former student of Tillich's has written a book that tells of Tillich's immoral relationship with his student's fiancee."[415]

Yet, according to Graham, men like Tillich and Niebuhr are "great theologians"! As a "great theologian," Tillich should be familiar with I Corinthians 6:9-10 which warns:

> "Know ye not that the unrighteous shall not inherit the kingdom of God? Be not deceived: neither fornicators, nor idolaters, **nor adulterers,** nor effeminate, nor abusers of themselves with mankind, Nor thieves, nor covetous, nor drunkards, nor revilers, nor extortioners, **shall inherit the kingdom of God."**

Tillich, too, was a professor at **Union Theological Seminary** from 1933 to 1955.[416]

In 1985 William Martin received a letter from Billy Graham asking him to write a book about Graham's life.[417] In this **very favorable** book, *A Prophet with Honor: The Billy Graham Story,* we find:

> "As a further sign he **was veering to the left,** Graham began to accept invitations to speak at **liberal** seminaries. At Colgate Rochester Divinity School, he **attempted to bridge the differences between his own theology and that of the eminent neo-orthodox theologian and social critic, Reinhold Niebuhr.** When he spoke of 'the central need for a personal experience of Jesus Christ,' he added, as if they were synonymous conceptions, 'or what Niebuhr would call an encounter with the living God.' A Fundamentalist reporting on this event objected that 'no one in his right mind would believe for a moment that what the neo-orthodox Niebuhr means by "an encounter with the living God" and what Jesus Christ defined as being "born again" are one and the same.' At New York's **Union Theological Seminary,** Graham had the temerity to say kind words about 'known liberals,' including his old friend Chuck Templeton, who was then serving as an evangelist for the National Council of Churches....To make matters worse, **he had invited** some prominent American liberals, including New York pastor **John Sutherland Bonnell,** who <u>**publicly**</u> **acknowledged that he did not believe in the Trinity, the Virgin Birth, the Resurrection, the inerrancy of Scripture, or heaven and hell,** <u>**to sit on the platform with him**</u> during some of the services at Kelvin Hall. When Scottish reporters tried to pin down Graham's location on the contemporary

spectrum, he declared, in a statement that mightily offended his conservative critics, 'I am neither a fundamentalist nor a modernist.' To make matters worse, he told another reporter, **'The ecumenical movement has broadened my viewpoint** and I recognize now that God has his people in **all** churches.'"[418]

JOHN SUTHERLAND BONNELL

Was Graham aware of Bonnell's viewpoint? One researcher reveals this:

> "John Sutherland **Bonnell,** pastor of the Fifth Avenue Presbyterian Church in New York City, wrote an article that was published in LOOK [March 23, **1954]** magazine. He **stated** in this article that **it was not necessary** for a Presbyterian minister **to believe in the virgin birth. Graham knew about the article** and professed to a friend that he was offended by it. However, later on when he held his New York Crusade, **Bonnell was on the executive committee** and was **honored by Graham on the platform** of the Crusade."[419]

Not only did the *Look* article reveal that Bonnell did not believe in the virgin birth, but it stated that Bonnell did not believe in the inspiration of Scripture or a literal heaven and hell. He said that he and most other Presbyterians "do not conceive of heaven as a place with gates of pearl and streets of gold. Nor do they think of hell as a place where the souls of condemned are punished in fire and brimstone."[420]

In another article, when asked if Presbyterians believe in the resurrection, Bonnell responded: "Yes," but then he went on to explain: "With few exceptions, Presbyterians do not interpret the phrase in the Apostles' Creed 'the resurrection of the body' as meaning the *physical* body."[421] [Emphasis in the original.] In other words, he **does not believe in a literal, bodily resurrection,** which the Bible clearly teaches.

Graham was well aware of Bonnell and his beliefs yet he had used Bonnell **TWICE** on his platform (once in Scotland in 1955 and in New York in 1957)—both events which occurred **AFTER** Bonnell's article appeared in *Look.*[422]

In fact, Graham writes the following in his autobiography:

> "Before the meetings [in Scotland in 1955] began, I was to address a gathering of clergy, theological professors, and theological students. That was a bit intimidating. **I asked Dr. John Sutherland Bonnell, the distinguished Scottish-born pastor of Fifth Avenue Presbyterian Church in New York,**

> **<u>to accompany me</u>.** As he looked over the crowd, he leaned over and whispered, 'This is probably the greatest gathering of theological minds in modern Scottish history.' That didn't help me to relax!"[423]

David Martyn Lloyd-Jones met with Graham and talked with him for about three hours in 1963 and discussed the issue of Graham using a **known** liberal, John Sutherland Bonnell. In response, "...Graham replied that he could have more 'fellowship' with Bonnell than with a number of evangelicals...."[424]

As just mentioned, Graham bragged that **"The ecumenical movement has broadened my viewpoint** and I recognize now that God has his people in **all** churches."[425]

At the Madison Square Garden Crusade in **1957,**

> "Graham honoured Dr. Robert J. **McCracken,** Fosdick's successor at Riverside Church, by having him **sit on the platform and** having him **lead in prayer** before the crusade audience. Yet, **McCracken is an infidel** like Fosdick, and **does not believe in the virgin birth, the blood atonement, Christ's bodily resurrection or the inspiration of the Bible."**[426]

STAN MOONEYHAM

Stan Mooneyham was a Billy Graham Evangelistic Association (BGEA) executive.[427] Mooneyham was divorced and remarried and was survived by both of his wives at his death in 1991.[428] He was head of the National Association of Evangelicals (NAE),[429] was on the board of directors for the **liberal** organization, Bread for the World,[430] and held a position in the Evangelical Press Association[431] and was also a former president of World Vision.[432]

> "The March 1981 issue of World Vision magazine featured an extensive lead article on Mother Teresa. The June-July 1984, issue of World Vision magazine included a glowing account of a visit with Mother Teresa by Joseph Ryan, director of World Vision's Northwest Regional Office. **World Vision has given thousands of dollars to Mother Teresa.** Mooneyham has appeared on television appealing for $10,000 for Mother Teresa.... **The proceeds for the Jesus '81 rally at Anaheim Stadium in Los Angeles went to Mother Teresa's Indian work...."**[433]

(In Chapter 8 we will look closer at Mother Teresa and her beliefs.)

Mooneyham wrote a book entitled *What Do You Say to a Hungry World.* Although he has long enjoyed great prominence in the

Christian world, his book advocates much of the political program of the New Agers. Mooneyham says:

> "Now another theme. Population. That's a touchy one. No one likes to be told how many little feet can patter around in his own house. But just that is the big question. How many feet per square foot can this world support?
>
> "If you see this program as critical where you live, then it would be profitable to investigate the availability of family planning services in your community. Press for adequate facilities, if necessary.
>
> "Insist on open forum discussion on birth control, *abortion, artificial insemination, genetic control* and *death control* in your church or club program. *Some of these subjects, unfortunately, seem to be outside the orbit of evangelical Christian concern."*[434] [Emphasis in the original.]

CONDOM DISTRIBUTION

Since Mooneyham was head of the NAE and World Relief (WR) is an arm of the NAE, it's no surprise to see that the WR is involved in condom distribution. According to the March 28, 1998 issue of *World* we find:

> "'World Relief receives more than 60 percent of its overseas budget from Uncle Sam and helps advance Washington's family-planning objectives.' The article stated, 'This raises a hard question: What role does condom distribution play in the fulfillment of the Great Commission?' A WR official says his agency is involved in sterilization of women and 'all forms of family planning.' But WR officials in the U.S. say, 'The only contraceptive that World Relief makes available to women is the condom.' The lure of government funds can be a diversive snare."[435]

Also in Mooneyham's book we find that he **favors a one-world government.** He "quotes Julius Nyerere of Tanzania with approval: 'Unfortunately, there is no world government which would tax the rich nations for the benefit of the poor nations; there is no international equivalent of social security payments. Instead, we have an acknowledgement of the need for "international aid."'"[436] He also called for "an International Joseph With an International Plan."[437]

> "Similarly to the Alice Bailey books and 'Tibetan' predictions, Mooneyham recommends a 'turning inward' combined

with revolutionary changes in the present world order. He approvingly quotes Mahbub ul Haq, a senior economic advisor at the World Bank, as follows: 'The developing countries have no choice but to turn inwards, much the same as Communist China...and to adopt a different style on life, seeking a consumption pattern more consistent with their own poverty—pots and pans and bicycles and simple consumption habits— without being seduced by the life styles of the rich. This requires a **redefinition of economic and social objectives** which is of privileged groups and vested interests which may only be **achieved through revolutions** rather than through an evolutionary change.

"'This is strong medicine, but he is not the only one prescribing it.'"[438]

Of course, since Mooneyham promotes New Age methods, it should come as no surprise to see him approvingly quoting several New Agers—but **WHY** would Billy Graham have him on his executive committee?

A SPIRITUAL UNITED NATIONS

One **interfaith** organization is called the Temple of Understanding. The *World Goodwill Newsletter* states:

"Founded by Juliet Hollister in 1960, the Temple of Understanding has as one of its goals the creation of **'a spiritual United Nations.'** In its work to promote understanding between religions on the basis of the **oneness of the human family,** the Temple has numbered amongst its members and supporters such influential world servers as U Thant, Eleanor Roosevelt, Thomas Merton, Jawaharlal Nehru, Anwar el Sadat, S. Radhakrishnan. In addition to the main centre in New York, where it is based at the **Cathedral of St. John the Divine,** the Temple has active chapters in India and the UK and representatives in Africa, Latin America, Asia and the Middle East.

"The major work of the Temple has been a series of influential Spiritual Summit Conferences at which leaders of the major world religions have come together to consider world problems from a spiritual perspective."[439]

Although Juliet Hollister died in 2000, "the Temple of Understanding continues to produce educational programs, is considered to be the first real **interfaith** organization, and remains what Eleanor Roosevelt called 'a **spiritual** United Nations.'"[440]

What is interesting is that the Temple of Understanding

> "was the brainchild of a wealthy American woman who had studied comparative religion at **Union Theological Seminary** in New York. By 1963, it had been sponsored by six thousand politicians, **occultists,** celebrities, **one-world religion advocates** and multinational companies, including Robert McNamara (then U. S. Secretary of Defence; later head of the World Bank), financier **John D. Rockefeller IV,** Dr. Henry A. Smith (President, Theosophical Society of America), Walter N. Thayer (President, *New York Herald Tribune),* James Linen (President, Time-Life Inc.), Milton Mumford (President, Lever Bros.), Barney Balaban (President, Paramount Pictures), Thomas B. Watson Jnr. (President, IBM), Richard Salant (President, CBS News), Cary Grant (Hollywood actor), Dr. Martin Israel (now an Anglican vicar and renowned teacher in the Church of England); the Presidents of Egypt, India and Israel; representatives of Methodist, Unitarian, Episcopalian, 'Spiritualist,' Lutheran and Presbyterian churches; various U.N. officials; and many others."[441]

Yes, this **interfaith** organization was founded by Mrs. Hollister who had attended **Union Theological Seminary!**[442] Even though Hollister attended a theological seminary, she "is herself a Shinto."[443]

Also, listed among one of the founding friends of the Temple of Understanding was **S. Radhakrishnan,**[444] a Hindu.[445] Please recall that he was one of the **past recipients of the Templeton Award**[446] when Billy Graham bragged: "I feel today that **I am in illustrious company with those who have been past recipients."**[447]

Another interfaith organization is the Council for a Parliament of the World's Religions (CPWR). They introduced the 1999 Parliament in a meeting at (where else?!) **Union Theological Seminary** in New York.[448] The September 13, 1999 meeting had Native American leaders as well as leaders from Christianity, Baha'i, Buddhism, etc.[449] "Rev. Dr. Joseph C. Hough, Jr., **president of Union Theological Seminary,** and the Very Rev. James Parks Morton, president of the Interfaith Center...open[ed] the gathering."[450] In 1985 Morton, former Dean of the Cathedral of St. John the Divine,[451] became President of the Temple of Understanding.[452]

PEBBLES INSTEAD OF BREAD

In Chapter 2 we looked at Bishop Pike's involvement with the occult and his denial of the fundamentals of the faith. Part of his apostasy may be due to the teaching he received when he went to **Union Theological Seminary.** Pike told Francis Schaeffer: "When I turned from being agnostic, I went to **Union Theological Seminary,** eager for and expecting bread; but when I graduated, all that it left me was a handful of pebbles."[453]

So much more could be said about Union Theological Seminary (UTS), their presidents and professors. For instance, Donald Woods Shriver, Jr. was a Professor of Christianity at UTS as well as its President.[454] He is also a member of the Council on Foreign Relations[455] as well as a member of the Board of Trustees for the New Age, one world order organization, Global Education Associates.[456]

Raymond Brown is a liberal Catholic priest who has "rejected the Bible's inerrancy, and was active in the World Council of Churches. He went to New York's liberal Union Seminary in 1971 and became its first tenured RC [Roman Catholic] professor...."[457] He "said Jesus was not the all-knowing God and was in error."[458] In spite of such comments, *Christianity Today,* a magazine founded by **Billy Graham,** "highly recommended" Brown's book and said that he "provides an excellent synthesis of contemporary New Testament scholarship."[459]

PSYCHIC PHENOMENA

Lawrence LeShan has been a lecturer and research psychologist at **Union Theological Seminary** and is involved in the examination of parapsychology (the study of **psychic phenomena** which is occultic).[460] He has written a book entitled *How to Meditate.* The inside front cover of this book explains: "Drawing upon the meditational practices of such disciplines as Zen, Sufi, Yoga, and Christian and Jewish mysticism, LeShan describes specific exercises and programs, both structured and unstructured, ranging from breath-counting and simple mantras to group movement and sensory awareness....A practicing psychotherapist, LeShan also explores such intriguing fields as the role of meditation in psychotherapy and the relation of meditation to the paranormal."[461]

Many of the men mentioned in this chapter (such as G. Bromley Oxnam, Harry Ward, John C. Bennett, Reinhold Niebuhr, Jesse Bader, Henry Van Dusen, etc.) were members of the World Council of Churches (WCC) and/or the National Council of Churches (NCC).[462] **In fact, it was during a meeting at Union Theological Seminary in 1894 that a committee was appointed "to consider the practicability of organizing a Federate Council of the Churches in New York City."**[463] Therefore, we need to take a closer look at the WCC and the NCC—which we will do in the next chapter.

Remember, too, that several of the liberals and Communists covered in this chapter (Van Dusen, Niebuhr, Bonnell, Sockman, and King) have been **PRAISED BY GRAHAM** and some have even been invited **BY HIM** to sit on the platform at some of his crusades! How could a true man of God have such poor discernment over and over and over again? Granted, any one of us can slip up and make mistakes. Any one of us could endorse someone and then discover that we should not have done so. However, when one person **CONSTANTLY** and **CONSISTENTLY** endorses liberals and Communists, it appears to be far more than a case of poor discernment. Jeremiah 50:6: "My people hath been lost sheep: **their shepherds have caused them to go astray,** they have turned them away on the mountains: they have gone from mountain to hill, they have forgotten their restingplace." The Bible clearly warns in II Corinthians 6:14: "Be ye not unequally yoked together with unbelievers: for what fellowship hath righteousness with unrighteousness? and what communion hath light with darkness?" Is Billy Graham a "prophet with honor" or is he a wolf in sheep's clothing?

4. FCC, NCC, AND THE WCC

The *Congressional Record* for December 9, 1987 revealed an FBI report on *Soviet Active Measures in the United States*. One section was called "The Soviet Campaign to Influence Religious Organizations," which stated: **"It is clear...that the Soviet Union is increasingly interested in influencing and/or manipulating American churches, religious organizations, and their leaders within the United States...."**[1] The report went on to say that "the campaign 'has targeted the members and leaders of a broad range of religious organizations within the United States' and uses several channels for its campaign of disinformation."[2]

In this chapter we will look at some of these "religious organizations and their leaders."

The Federal Council of Churches (FCC) was founded on December 2, 1908.[3] It originally consisted of 31 major American denominations. By 1950 "it represented 144,000 local congregations and a total membership of 32,000,000."[4] It was formed by men such as **Communist Harry F. Ward and Socialist Walter Rauschenbusch.**[5] We've already looked at Harry F. Ward, so let's briefly examine Rauschen-busch's background.

Rauschenbusch was a Baptist and a graduate of the Rochester Theological Seminary.[6] He had also taught at this seminary.[7]

One group in England, started by Frederick Denison Maurice and Charles Kingsley, was called the Christian **Socialist** Movement.[8] **"It sought to bring the kingdom of God upon earth** by social legislation that would give men economic and social as well as political democracy."[9] They did not believe in eternal punishment in hell and believed that no one would be lost (universalism). They also claimed that each one should recognize his or her sonship.[10]

It was this group that had some influence on Rauschenbusch.[11] He developed these ideas and soon became one of the main leaders in what was called the **"Social Gospel."**[12]

> "Analyzed, the 'social salvation' which collectivist theologians teach is basically a restatement of the **Marxian** dogma of Economic Determinism—'change the economic environment and man will be transformed.' A theology based on the message of Christ teaches that through true acceptance of Him and His teachings, man is changed, and can, in turn, change the world and correct its ills."[13]

Rauschenbusch wrote: "...we **differ** from many Christian men and women who believe that if only men are personally converted wrong and injustice will gradually disappear from the construction of society. It does not appear such to us."[14] The Bible, on the other hand, states: "Therefore if any man be in Christ, he is a new creature: old things are passed away; behold, all things are become new" (II Corinthians 5:17).

In 1892 he was instrumental in organizing a group called the Society of Jesus which was later changed to the Brotherhood of the Kingdom.[15]

He belonged to the British **Fabian Society.**[16] The Society's "purpose was to gradually move the world toward **socialism** through political **synthesis** or **syncretism.**"[17] "In 1907, the Fabians began a weekly review called *New Age.* Their coat-of-arms is a **wolf in sheep's clothing....**"[18] The dictionary gives this definition for syncretism: "Reconciliation or **fusion** of **differing systems of belief,** as in philosophy or religion, especially when success is partial...." This definition should have more significance by the end of this chapter!

Rauschenbusch "called upon Christians to build a just social order **based on moral law** [not God's law!]....He thought that **Christians had failed to** carry out Christ's command to **build a kingdom of God on earth....**"[19]

He also wrote:

> "In Socialism...we recognize an aspiration after this higher social order and an attempt to prefigure it in economic forms.... As such an aspiration Socialism is distinctly a moral protest against existing disorders....We believe that whatever better social order is coming in on the earth will come as an evolution. We are evolutionists, not revolutionists....In this sense **we are Socialists,** Socialists in the spirit rather than the letter....We follow the methods by which Jesus Christ applied His principles. It is after His pattern that we would be **Christian Socialists.**"[20]

Rauschenbusch wrote in 1893: **"The only power that can make socialism succeed, if it is established, is religion. It cannot work in an irreligious country."**[21] [Emphasis in the original.] Another author wrote about Rauschenbusch: "Socialism, thus was his first concern. **Religion was only a means towards achieving socialism."**[22] You see, the "Communists know they can't destroy religion so they have organized to **infiltrate** it."[23]

This is a **very important** statement—especially in light of the fact that Rauschenbusch was one of the founding members of the **Federal Council of Churches.** Since he believed that socialism could only succeed through religion, it's no wonder that he started a

religious organization (the FCC) to help promote his goal of socialism.

In fact, the social creed influenced the Federal Council of Churches which adopted several aims that have become known as the "Social Creed of the Churches."[24] These aims "reflected the influence of such writers as Josiah Strong [a social Darwinist[25]], **Shailer Mathews,** Washington Gladden [father of the Social Gospel movement[26]], Francis G. Peabody, Frank Mason North, **Walter Rauschenbusch,** Charles Stelzle, and **Harry F. Ward....**"[27]

We will now look at a number of individuals who had prominent roles in the FCC, NCC, and/or WCC.

SHAILER MATHEWS

Shailer Mathews, one of the early Presidents of the FCC and a liberal Baptist,[28] didn't believe in Christ's substitutionary atonement[29] and also denied a literal and personal return of Christ. "The true Second Coming, Mathews insisted, was the triumph of the ideals of Jesus in human affairs."[30] Mathews would mock biblical teachings and in an address to the Religious Education Association (published in 1910), he said: "Whereas Calvinists spoke of God's election of man, the democrat speaks of **man's election of God.** The democratic spirit of the age is demanding that the church abandon sovereignty as the controlling concept of its theology and leaven itself with democracy."[31]

The NCC "made headlines by coming to the defense of radicals such as the communist anarchist Angela Davis, supporting the treasonous Panama Canal giveaway, opposing the Vietnam war, and promoting the 'inclusive language' for both human beings and God."[32]

Earl F. Adams was the administrative secretary of the National Council of Churches, director of the Washington office of the NCC, and the chairman of the Field Department of the FCC. He also was associated with the American Youth Congress, a **Communist-front** organization.[33]

Luther A. Weigle was the President of the FCC[34] and helped to organize the NCC. He was head of the committee which was responsible for producing the *Revised Standard Version* of the Bible.[35] His **leftist** affiliations were: "Committee on Militarism in Education; Coordinating Committee to Lift the Spanish Embargo; National Religion and Labor Foundation; North American Committee to Aid Spanish Democracy; World Tomorrow Poll, which called for socialism (signer); War Resistors League."[36] Additionally,

> "Dr. Weigle collaborated with Professor Starbuck in preparing a series of textbooks for **UNITARIAN** Sunday schools. Unitarians reject the Christian doctrine of the Trinity; they do not believe that Jesus Christ is the Second Person of the Trinity or that the Holy Spirit is the Third Person of the Godhead. Unitarians reject altogether the deity of Jesus Christ and do not believe the Bible to be infallible."[37]

"Dr. Weigle is involved also in a translation of the apocryphal writings."[38]

Roswell P. Barnes was the associate general secretary of the FCC.[39] His **leftist** affiliations were

> "Associated Film Audiences (member of the Executive Board); Committee on Militarism in Education (secretary); Committee for Norman Thomas; Norman Thomas Campaign Committee (secretary); Emergency Peace Campaign (national sponsor); Fellowship of **Socialist** Christians (secretary); National Religion and Labor Foundation; North American Committee to Aid Spanish Democracy; United China Relief; War Resistors League, and World Youth Congress (sponsor)."[40]

The Federal Council of Churches' vice chairman of Commission on Worship and later the vice chairman of the Department of Worship and Art, W. Russell Bowie, belonged to the following **leftist** affiliations:

> "American Committee for Non-Participation in Japanese Aggression; American Committee to Save Refugees; American Committee for Protection of Foreign Born; Church Emergency Committee for Relief of Textile Strikers; Church League for Industrial Democracy; Attack the American Legion Lobby in Washington; Citizens Congress; Committee on Militarism in Education; Coordinating Committee to Lift the Spanish Embargo; Emergency Committee for Strikers Relief; Friends of Italian Democracy; Greater New York Emergency Conference on Inalienable Rights; Harry Bridges Defense Committee; National Citizens Political Action Committee; National Citizens Committee on Relations with Latin America; National Council of the Arts, Sciences and Professions; National Emergency Conference for Democratic Rights; National Federation for Constitutional Liberties; Non-Intervention Citizens Committee; North American Committee to Aid Spanish Democracy; Open Letter on Harry Bridges (signer); Open Letter to President Roosevelt protesting Bridges' deportation (signer); *The Protestant* **(pro-Communist** magazine; signed petition); Schappes Defense Committee; War Resistors League; Washington Committee to Lift the Spanish

Embargo, and World Tomorrow Poll, which called for **socialism.**"[41]

PLANNED ECONOMIC SYSTEM

Samuel McCrea Cavert was the general secretary of the FCC as well as the general secretary of the NCC. His **leftist** affiliations were:

"North American Committee to Aid Spanish Democracy (sponsor); *The Protestant* (pro-Communist magazine; signed appeal, and sponsor of *The Protestant* dinner); War Resistors League (endorsed pamphlet, 'Military Training in the Schools and Colleges of the U. S.,' an attack upon the reserve officers' training program)."[42]

"In its many official pronouncements, the **Federal Council attacked free enterprise, capitalism and the American way of life, and boldly advocated Socialism.** In an official report in 1932, the Federal Council stated: 'The Christian ideal calls for hearty support of a planned economic system....It demands that cooperation shall replace competition as a fundamental method.'

"At a full meeting in Indianapolis in December 1933, the Federal Council adopted unanimously this Socialist creed: 'The churches should stand for social planning and control of the credit and monetary system and the economic processes.'"[43]

To help the FCC carry out these plans, funds were necessary. Although the member churches provided some of the income for the FCC, about two-thirds of its money came from other sources. Some of these sources in 1948 were:

"The Julius Rosenwald Fund made a contribution of $30,229.56; the Arbuckle-Jameson Foundation gave $16,975.47; the **Russell Sage Foundation** gave $2,959.00; the Lewis J. and Mary E. Horowitz Foundation, Inc., gave $2,000.00; The **Henry Luce Foundation,** Inc. (of *Time, Life,* and *Fortune* fame), gave $1,000.00; the **Rockefeller Brothers Fund,** Inc., contributed $1,000.00; the Adeline and Carl Loeb Foundation gave $250.00; the Bulova Foundation for the Department of Race Relations gave $150.00; The Gastonia-Jewish Welfare Fund contributed $50.00.

"Of special importance is the fact that The Federal Council of Churches had secured a tax-exempt status."[44]

One of the above sources, the **Russell Sage Foundation,** has been a funder of **Communist** causes[45] as well as a supporter of **Planned Parenthood.**[46]

WORLD PEACE THROUGH WORLD GOVERNMENT

Andrew Carnegie, the richest man in the world at the time,[47] "gave large amounts of money to the Federal Council of Churches to further his goal of **world peace through world government."**[48] In 1914, Carnegie

> "offered to establish an endowment of two million dollars to finance a peace program of the churches, on the condition that the Federal Council of the Churches of Christ in America should share in the income and cooperate in the promotion of an international peace conference. To administer the fund, the Church Peace Union was founded in New York."[49]

Dr. Stanley Monteith states: "Carnegie was a **socialist,** but the socialism he envisioned created a ruling class. After selling U. S. Steel, he funded several foundations with instructions that their power was to be used to transform society and **promote world government."**[50]

Elsewhere Dr. Monteith writes: "Andrew Carnegie and Cecil Rhodes were friends. The directors of the Carnegie Endowment for International Peace planned World War I....They **financed Lucis Trust** and have worked to establish a world government. **Andrew Carnegie was a spiritualist."**[51]

> "Andrew Carnegie records in his Autobiography how he chanced to read Darwin and certain works of Herbert Spencer: 'I remember that light came as in a flood and all was clear. Not only had **I got rid of theology** and the supernatural, but I had **found the truth of evolution.'"**[52]

One large contributor to the Federal Council of Churches was **John D. Rockefeller.**[53] From 1926 to 1929 he had contributed over $137,000 to them, which was about ten percent of the FCC's total income from all sources.[54] Of course, the **Federal Council of Churches** "partially repaid the support of the wealthy when, in 1942, it **issued a platform calling for 'a world government, international control of all armies and navies, a universal system of money, and a democratically controlled international bank.'"**[55]

Also, the FCC

> "was used routinely by the Rockefellers to further their personal interests in church circles. Rockefeller donated to the Federal Council's Department of Church and Economic Life and promoted the concept of an **international** church. This is how 'ecumenism' got its beginning as Rockefeller became the most important financier of liberal and ecumenical Protestantism."[56] [Emphasis in the original.]

Rockefeller's

> "idea was that 'another crusade was needed to bring the warring factions of Christianity together.' Rockefeller promoted universal *ecumenism* by stating in December 1917: 'Would that I had the power to bring to your minds the vision as it unfolds before me! *I see all denominational emphasis set aside....* **I see the church molding the thought of the world** as it has never done before, leading in all great movements as it should. **I see it literally establishing the Kingdom of God on earth.'"**[57] [Boldface in the original.]

CHANGE THE NAME

During this time, knowledge of the FCC's Communist activities was growing. "In 1927, Congressman Arthur M. Free introduced a resolution in the House of Representatives describing the **Federal Council of Churches as a 'Communist organization** aimed at the establishment of a state-church....'"[58] The FCC was "pronounced by U. S. Naval Intelligence in 1936 as one of the most dangerous, subversive organizations in the country."[59]

In 1933, a past president of the FCC, Rev. Albert W. Beaven, "signed with forty-four others a letter to President Roosevelt urging him to **socialize** America. It read: 'We hold that there can be no recovery so long as the nation depends on palliative legislation inside the capitalistic system.'"[60]

> "Sworn testimony before the Special House Committee on Un-American Activities headed by Congressman Martin Dies in the 1930s revealed: 'The radical affiliation of the Federal Council of Churches of Christ is a subject of extensive discussion. Apparently, in lieu of primarily promoting Christianity among its several members it more represents a **huge political machine** and appears to meddle in **radical politics.** Its directorate indicates that **it interlocks with many of the most radical organizations**.'"[61] [Emphasis in the original.]
>
> "Among these organizations, such as the **American Civil Liberties Union,** its relationships were closer than they were with the denominations which it professed to represent. This was because its political program was coordinated with their activities through strategic interlocking directorates with them.
>
> "These political activities included promotion, among other worthy causes, of the slacker's oath, League of Nations propaganda, recognition of Soviet Russia, protection of aliens

in America, cancellation of foreign debt, and reduction of tariffs. These objectives generally were **advocated by the Socialists.**"[62]

"When **Communist organizations** are exposed for their radical activities they routinely **change their name,**"[63] so, likewise, the FCC's name was changed. On November 29, 1950 the Federal Council of Churches, along with about a dozen other interdenominational agencies, merged to become the National Council of the Churches of Christ (NCC).[64] By 1951, 29 churches belonged to the NCC and included about two-thirds of the Protestant and Orthodox membership in the United States.[65]

> "Some 40 years ago an Air Force Manual rightly noted that **many NCC churchmen** were or had been **members of Communist front organizations.** The Lutheran Church—Missouri Synod's **Lutheran Witness** referred to the Federal Council of Churches, the predecessor of the NCC, as 'the most vicious agency in Protestantism.'"[66]

> "As for NCC's religious fervor, a survey of the views of its leadership published in *Newsweek* on June 26, 1967, showed that 'over one-third could not state they have a firm belief in God...over 40% do not believe Jesus Christ was divine...only one in six accepts the Bible doctrine of man's sinful nature. Slightly more than 60% of the delegates look forward to a life after death.' Little wonder, then, that **NCC supported and commended the Supreme Court decision that removed prayer and Bible reading from the public schools.**"[67]

Of course, the NCC followed in the same footsteps as the FCC. Gus Hall, the General Secretary of the Communist Party, USA, seemed pleased with the liberal church for in the July 15, 1968 issue of *Approach* he mentioned that the Red (or **Communistic**) goals for America were **"almost identical** to those espoused by the **Liberal Church.** We can and we should work together for the same things."[68] Hall is the person who said:

> "I dream of the hour when the last Congressman is strangled to death on the guts of the last preacher—and since the Christians seem to love to sing about the blood, why not give them a little of it? Slit the throats of their children and drag them over the mourner's bench and the pulpit, and allow them to drown in their own blood; and then see whether they enjoy singing these hymns."[69]

With a statement like that, isn't it somewhat unsettling to see that the Communists' goals are "almost identical" with the liberal church's goals?

POPULATION CONTROL

The **Rockefellers,** who are interested in liberal "Christianity," had provided funds for the Federal Council of Churches—and the National Council of Churches was no different.[70] The Rockefellers even donated the land for the NCC and supplied "the initial capital to fund a wide-ranging study of organizational structures for the new group...."[71] Additionally, a "fifteen-story Interchurch Center would rise on this plot as the headquarters of the principal Protestant denominations in America, their Home and Foreign Missions, and their National Council."[72]

John D. Rockefeller, Jr., was a big contributor to the World Council of Churches as well.[73]

His son, John D. Rockefeller III, was a member of the Council on Foreign Relations. He was also the Chairman of the Commission on Population Growth and the American Future, which strongly promotes population control.[74] In his acceptance speech for this appointment, he declared: "The average citizen doesn't appreciate the social and economic implications of population growth and what it does to the quality of all our lives. Rather than think of **population control** as a negative thing, we should see that it **can be enriching.**"[75]

Did you notice that we are enriched by abortions?!

> "One of the earlier reports of the Rockefeller Commission recommended 'that present state laws restricting abortion be liberalized along the lines of the New York State Statute, such abortions to be performed on request by duly licensed physicians under conditions of medical safety.'...And even though Mr Rockefeller is a 'religionist,' as a zealous supporter of the National Council of Churches, he says, 'Religious preconceptions must be overcome.'
>
> "The ideal New York State model **abortion law was passed** under the leadership of **John Rockefeller's brother, Nelson.** In fact, the Rockefellers financed the establishment of one of the first abortion factories. The first large scale abortion center opened by Planned Parenthood—New York City was established in the summer of 1971. It was a prototype for the development of additional centers throughout the city, state, and country. The initial funds to establish the abortion mill came from a $200,000 pledge from the Rockefeller Brothers Fund."[76]

HUMANISM PROMOTED

In the Rockefeller Foundation (RF) publication, *RF Illustrated,* we find: "The RF will continue to work in the less-developed world as well as to intensify its efforts in the United States, but **will seek an even greater integration of *humanistic* and scientific disciplines to achieve its goals.”**[77]

> “Over the years, the [Rockefeller] Foundation has granted large sums of money to propagate the **Humanist** philosophy of Professor **John Dewey** and such Humanist-oriented institutions and groups as the **National Council of Churches,** the **Union Theological Seminary** of New York, the **London School of Economics** (British educational headquarters of the **Fabian Socialists),** and its American counterpart, the **New School for Social Research.** Nor is it pure coincidence that the Rockefeller brothers have invested scores of millions to promote **one-world government,** and donated the land for the **United Nations** complex in New York City.”[78]

In the book, *United Nations: The First Fifty Years,* we read:

> “On December 11, 1946, U. N. Ambassador Warren Austin, the former senator from Vermont who succeeded Stettinius, informed the U. N. that John D. Rockefeller Jr. had offered it $8.5 million to buy the Turtle Bay slum area. The General Assembly accepted the offer by a vote of forty-six to seven. The U. N. complex, including the thirty-nine-story Secretariat Building for the Security Council on eighteen acres of land, was designed mainly by Wallace K. Harrison, the architect for Rockefeller Center.”[79]

Since the Rockefellers fund Communistic and humanistic groups and one of these groups is the NCC, it doesn’t take any great imagination to realize that the NCC is not a Christian group.

Rockefellers’ church is the Riverside Church (also called “the Rockefeller Church”[80]). “An affiliated arm of the WCC, called the American Friends of the World Council of Churches, is headquartered at the liberal Riverside Church at 475 Riverside Drive, New York City, where Vietnam war resister Rev. William Sloane Coffin (Skull & Bones class of ’49) pastored.”[81] Coffin later became the President of **SANE/FREEZE,**[82]

> “a **socialist, internationalist group** pushing for a United Nations military force and general disarmament of national armies, naval, and air forces. Coffin has now added the environmental issue to his left-wing activist agenda. He is also a big supporter of and has been a keynote speaker for the **World Federalists Association,** the group begun by the late writer Norman Cousins to lobby for a One-World Government and the end of American sovereignty and independence.”[83]

HARRY EMERSON FOSDICK

Another former pastor at Riverside was Harry Emerson Fosdick.[84] He, too, was a leader in the NCC[85] as well as a former President of the Rockefeller Foundation.[86] He didn't believe in the deity of Christ.[87] He said: "Of course, I do not believe in the Virgin Birth, or in that old-fashioned substitutionary doctrine of the Atonement; and do not know any intelligent minister who does...."[88] It was in May 1922, when he

> "preached a now-famous sermon entitled, 'Shall the Fundamentalists Win?' In the sermon **he declared all-out war on Bible-believing Christianity and those who upheld it....** Shortly thereafter he became pastor of the immense Riverside Church in New York City (built largely with Rockefeller money), and continued teaching his unbiblical views there."[89]

In the April 4, 2001 issue of *The Christian Century* was an ad seeking for a minister of "Mission and Social Justice" at the Riverside Church. The ad said that the ideal candidate will possess "Experience working with denominations that are members of The **National Council of Churches and other ecumenical alliances."**[90]

Soon after the National Council of Churches was organized, a formal constitution called the Document of Record was written. One representative from each of the 29 churches signed the official book. "**Eleven** of these 29 signers of the official book have public records of **affiliation with pro-communist enterprises....**There were 358 clergymen who were voting delegates to the constituting convention.... Of these clergymen, **123 (or 34 percent) have had affiliations with Communist projects and enterprises. That represents a high degree of Communist penetration."**[91]

No wonder the Communists have bragged that they are filling our pulpits!

Over forty years ago (in 1960), Richard Arens, from the House Committee on Un-American Activities reported:

> "Thus far of the **leadership of the National Council of Churches of Christ in America,** we have found **over 100 persons in leadership capacity with either Communist-front records or records of service to Communist causes.** The aggregate affiliations of the leadership, instead of being in the hundreds as first indicated, is now, according to the latest count, into the **thousands,** and we have yet to complete our check, which would certainly suggest, on the basis of authoritative sources of this committee, that the statement that there is infiltration of fellow travelers in churches and educational institutions is a complete understatement."[92]

Since the FCC was involved in Communistic causes and activities, it's not surprising to see that the NCC is also involved in such endeavors. You see, many "of the liberal leaders of the Federal Council became prominent leaders of the new organization."[93]

NCC'S READING LIST

> "Further, a 1957 reading list published by NCC recommended works by Herbert Aptheker (leading theoretician for the **Communist Party, USA),** W. E. B. DuBois [a Mason[94]], his wife Shirley G. DuBois, and Victor Perlo, **all well-known Communists;** Gordon Allport, E. Franklin Frazier, and Ruth Benedict, who are **Communist** fronters; and **pro-Marxist** Gunnar Myrdal."[95]

Let's look at some of these authors for a few minutes.

> **"Aptheker...**was in 1960 director of the Faculty of Social Science, the major open Communist Party school in the U. S. He also has edited *'Political Affairs,'* the Communist Party's official monthly theoretical organ, having been appointed to this position by the National Committee of the Communist Party in July, 1957.
>
> "He has been associate editor of *'Mainstream'* a Communist Party cultural monthly.
>
> "Testifying in 1952 as a defense witness for top Communist Party leaders, he stated, that he had **joined the Communist Party** in 1939. In later proceedings he stated that the Soviet Union and Red China were on the side of peace, but that he believed the Government of the U. S. was 'the center of war danger in the world.'"[96]
>
> "During the 1960s, Aptheker was often invited to college campuses to represent the views of the Communist Party. From December 1965 to January 1966 at the invitation of North Vietnam, he took Tom Hayden and Staughton Lynd to North Vietnam. Upon their return from this trip, the group spoke frequently at protests against the war and in numerous forums.... He founded the American Institute for **Marxist** Studies in New York and edited its newsletter and series of publications for many years."[97]

Aptheker had three books that were published by the Communist publishing house called International Publishers.[98]

His name was added as a signer to a letter which said: "We see these struggles as inseparable from the path to a socialist U. S. A."[99]

"DuBois has served on the faculty of the Communist Party's Jefferson School of Social Sciences.

"He has been a contributing editor to numerous Communist Party magazines.

"He has been actively associated with over 75 Communist fronts and causes. He was denied admission to Canada in 1952, and also was refused a passport by the U. S. Government until the time of the Kent-Briehl decision by the Supreme Court....

"In a speech in Red China, DuBois heaped praise on Red China and the Soviet Union. He urged the people of Africa to arise and turn to the U. S. S. R., following the example of China. He also attacked churches and the clergymen, and defamed the United States which he branded as an enemy of Africa."[100]

"Dubois wrote in a public letter to Gus Hall, chairman of the Communist Party U. S. A., on October 1, 1961; **'In the end Communism will triumph. I want to help bring that day.'"**[101]

SHIRLEY GRAHAM DUBOIS

DuBois' wife, Shirley Graham DuBois,

"has six books on the recommended reading list [of the NCC].

"She has been a contributing editor to *'Masses and Mainstream,'* a Communist Magazine."[102]

She was also with the paper, *Freedomways,*[103] which was established with the Communist Party's assistance.[104]

"In 1950, she served as a marshal in the Communist Party's May Day parade.

"She has an extensive record of affiliation with Communist fronts and causes, and has been identified by Louis Budenz as a member of the Communist Party."[105]

Victor Perlo's book, *The Negro in Southern Agriculture,* is on the NCC reading list. This was published in 1953 by International Publishers, which is the major publishing firm for the **Communist Party.**[106]

"According to a 1945 document of a U. S. intelligence agency, Perlo had served as the head of the second most important espionage group in the U. S. Government.

"He has also been described by the Senate Internal Security Subcommittee as 'an open propagandist for the Soviet world conspiracy.'

"His book, *'American Imperialism'* contains vicious smears of the U. S. and was highly praised by the **Communist** press."[107]

One of E. Franklin Frazier's books, *The Negro in the United States,*

"so **promoted the Marxist cause** that it was **advertised in the Communist Workers Book Shop** catalogs for 1949 and 1950, after also receiving **favorable reviews in the Communist publications** *Daily Worker* and *People's World.* This book, as well as others by Frazier, **appears on the recommended reading list of the National Council of Churches,** and the **National Education Association's** book list for American Negro History."[108]

"He has headed departments at Communists (sic) schools, contributed to Communist magazines, lectured on their behalf and has been associated with several dozen Communist fronts and causes."[109]

Ruth Benedict "was dismissed from Columbia University in 1953 after she accused the U. S. Government of waging germ warfare in Korea. She took the Fifth Amendment on the subject of her membership in the Communist Party."[110]

She "had been associated with over 35 Communist fronts."[111]

Gunnar Myrdal's book, *An American Dilemma,* which is on the NCC's reading list, "defames the Founding Fathers of our country and attempts to discredit the U. S. Constitution...."[112]

"Myrdal, now deceased, had also been a Rockefeller fellow, a Spelman Fund fellow, and among the first endorsers of **Planetary Citizens."**[113]

LANGSTON HUGHES

Langston Hughes is a black poet who has nine books on NCC's list.[114] Some of his poetry was printed in the **Leftist** magazine, *Anvil.*[115]

"He spent a year (1932-1933) in the Soviet Union, to which he had gone to help make a film (soon abandoned) about American race relations. Warmly received, he wrote several radical poems, including 'Good Morning Revolution' and 'Goodbye Christ,' as well as a short book, *A Negro Looks at Soviet Central Asia* (1934), in praise of the Soviet treatment of its darker peoples. In 1934 he wrote 'One More "S" in the U.S.A.' (to make it Soviet) for a national Communist Party convention. The same year, he was elected president of the Communist-backed League of Struggle for Negro Rights."[116]

His poem, "Good Morning Stalingrad," "showed deep admiration of the Soviet people, and now and then he defended the American Left in his weekly column in the *Chicago Defender.*"[117]

Hughes' poem "Goodbye Christ" is on the NCC's reading list.[118] This poem goes like this:

> *"Listen Christ, you did alright in your day, I reckon, but that day's gone now. They ghosted you up a swell story, too. Called it the Bible, but it's dead now. The Popes and the preachers 've made too much money from it. They've sold you you (sic) to too many kings, generals, robbers, and killers, even to the Tzar and the Cossacks, even to Rockefeller's church, even to the Saturday Evening Post. You ain't no good no more. They've pawned you till you've done wore out. Good-by (sic). Christ Jesus Lord God Jehovah, beat it on away from here now. Make way for a new guy with no religion at all, a real guy named Marx, Communist Lenin, Peasant Stalin, Worker ME, I said ME! Go ahead on now, You're getting in the way of things, Lord, And please take Saint Gandhi with you when you go, And Saint Pope Pius, And Saint Aimee McPherson, And big black Saint Becton of the Consecrated Dime. And step on the gas Christ! Move! Don't be so slow about movin'! The world is mine from now on, and nobody's gonna sell ME to a king, or a general, or a millionaire. Good-by (sic) Christ, good morning Revolution!"*[119] [Emphasis in the original.]

In 1961 the North American Ecumenical Youth Assembly put on a play entitled "For Heaven's Sake." It was **sponsored** by the **National Council of Churches.** This blasphemous play, in reference to Christ, said that "he was a flop at 33."[120]

Many of the National Council of Churches leaders are also against capitalism.

> "A number of NCC executives feel a just society is impossible under capitalism. In 1975, an Ecumenical Consultation on Domestic Hunger sponsored by the NCC passed a statement that said there was a basic **contradiction** between capitalism 'and biblical justice, mercy, stewardship, service, community and self-giving love.' Warren Day, the NCC's Director of News and Information, points out that such statements do not reflect the 'official' view of the NCC. Nonetheless, the statements passed by such conferences are revealing of attitudes prevalent among the NCC staff members

that organize them. Similar antagonistic views toward the American economic system are evident in the publications of the NCC's Friendship Press and in NCC-sponsored films."[121]

NCC SUPPORTS TERRORISTS

As mentioned the NCC "made headlines by coming to the defense of radicals such as the communist anarchist Angela Davis, supporting the treasonous Panama Canal giveaway, opposing the Vietnam war, and promoting the 'inclusive language' for both human beings and God."

In just two years the **NCC sent hundreds of thousands of dollars** to "groups supporting the Palestine Liberation Organization [PLO], the governments of Cuba and Vietnam, the pro-Soviet totalitarian movements of Latin America, Asia and Africa, and several violence-prone fringe groups in the United States."[122]

In 1982 *"the NCC had funneled $5.5 million to Communist terrorists in Zimbabwe, Naminia, Mozambique, and Angola...."*[123] [Emphasis in the original.]

In 1983 it was discovered that the **NCC was channeling money to the Communist guerrillas** in El Salvador and promoting the Sandinistas in Nicaragua as well as the Communist FRELIMO government in Mozambique.[124] They also endorsed Daniel Ortega,[125] a **Marxist Communist** and former Sandinista dictator,[126] who was "deeply **involved in satanism and witchcraft.** Indeed, Ortega's wife in 1989 sponsored and participated in a worldwide witch's convocation held in Nicaragua's capital of Managua."[127] (Needless to say, the Riverside Church also welcomed Ortega to its pulpit.[128])

When shown pictures of starving children, many people's sympathy is aroused and they are ready to give money to help such children. Sadly, many groups take advantage of such situations and use the children to solicit funds for causes that do not help these children. The National Council of Churches is one such group.

> "The Domestic Hunger Network coordinated by the NCC has much more to do with changing society than with feeding the hungry. It consists of 105 projects and in 1980 received over $650,000 raised from churchgoers responding to hunger appeals by their churches, which typically show a photograph of needy children. As Mary Ellen Lloyd, director of the project, points out, 'This isn't just funding a bag of groceries.' Some of the money from hunger appeals, how much she could not say, does go for emergency help, but **a significant portion of it is funding political activists."**[129] [Emphasis in the original.]

SIECUS

Not only is the NCC involved with Communistic activities,[130] but they are promoters of sexual materials. For example, in 1961, the NCC published a pamphlet entitled *Called to Responsible Freedom: Meaning of Sex in the Christian Life.* The pamphlet told the young people:

> "For the Christian there are no laws, no rules, no regulations....Life is a series of grays and not pure blacks and whites.... You are now bound by detailed rules of behavior, telling you that it is 'all right' to go so far in expressing affection for a member of the opposite sex, and 'all wrong' to go further. No one outside yourself can tell you that—not really....
>
> "You have to make up your own mind....what your standards of conduct are going to be....There just aren't any rules, you do whatever strikes your fancy."[131]

Dr. William Graham Cole, the author of this pamphlet and a proponent of **situation ethics,** later became a director of Sex Information and Educational Council of the United States (SIECUS).[132] (For more information on SIECUS and their promotion of nudity and pornography, see my book *Masonic and Occult Symbols Illustrated.*)

> "The SIECUS influence within the National Council of Churches does not end here. Other individuals who are either past or current members of NCC's Commission on Marriage and Family include SIECUS board members Evelyn Duvall and Clark Vincent, as well as Humanist Mary Calderone, SIECUS executive director. Of further interest is the fact that NCC's president from 1969 to 1973, Cynthia Clark Wedel,[133] is also associate director of the Center for a Voluntary Society of the National Education Association's National Training Laboratories in Washington, D.C., a pioneer in sensitivity training."[134]

In addition to **Calderone belonging to SIECUS**[135] and speaking on sex education to the First North American Conference on Church and Family which was convened by the NCC,[136] she also held membership in **Planned Parenthood-World Population,** the International Fertility Association, the Committee on Human Reproduction of the American Medical Association, the American Society for the Study of Sterility, and the World Health Organization.[137] She was also chosen as the **"Humanist of the Year"** in 1974.[138]

In a TV interview in 1968 with Alexander Cohen, Calderone remarked:

> "'I accept and advocate masturbation as part of the evolutionary sexual development of the individual.' A more recent interview by *Playboy* magazine brought forth this comment on whether or not the topic should be incorporated into the school curriculum: 'Yes, if it's done calmly and objectively, with the teacher simply pointing out that masturbation is almost universal, doesn't hurt anyone, and it is useful as a release from tension....'"[139]

Here are a few more quotations from her:

✷ "*Sexology* magazine is no more pornographic than the Bible."[140]

✷ "The adolescent years are, among other things, for learning how to integrate sex usefully and creatively into daily living, therefore, we must accept that adolescent **sexual experimentation is** not just inevitable, but **actually necessary for normal development."**[141]

✷ "An extra-marital affair that's really solid might have very good results."[142]

Calderone was known for using four-letter words.[143] She also sent her daughter to the **socialist** New School for Social Research for her education.[144]

Cynthia Clark Wedel was also just mentioned in connection with SIECUS and the National Council of Churches. She was a former President of the National Education Association,[145] former President of the WCC, as well as an endorser of Thanksgiving Square.[146]

When one group wrote a report recommending that pornography laws be lifted, 25 organizations endorsed it. One of these groups was none other than the **National Council of Churches!**[147] The NCC is also in favor of decriminalizing marijuana.[148]

As you read the rest of this chapter, try to keep in mind that the WCC's doctrinal statement claims: "The World Council of Churches is a fellowship of Churches which **confess the Lord Jesus Christ as God and Saviour according to the Scriptures** and therefore seek to fulfill together their common calling to the glory of the one God, Father, Son and Holy Spirit."[149] Of course, just two paragraphs later it adds: "Since the World Council of Churches is not itself a church, it passes no judgment upon the sincerity with which member churches accept the basis."[150] It then admits: "Some...liberal churches do not accept the trinitarian formula."[151] In other words, WCC members sign the agreement with reference to the Trinity, yet they deny the Trinity. Obviously, these people are lying by attaching their signature and agreeing to this statement—yet knowing full well that they don't believe it. Sadly, it doesn't seem to bother them.

WILLIAM TEMPLE

It was mainly through the leadership of **William Temple,** the **left-wing** Archbishop of Canterbury[152] (and a member of the Labour Party[153]) that the **World Council of Churches** and the British Council of Churches came into being. He was the first president of the World Council "in process of formation" in 1938.[154] Christian researcher, Alan Morrison, reveals that Temple

> "was a **lifelong socialist** and **champion of the 'Social Gospel'**—the idea that the preaching of the Gospel can be best fulfilled through social activism and the promotion of societal change. Significantly, William Temple's theological position has been described by one reputable source as *'Hegelian Idealism.'* He was rector of St. James' Church, Piccadilly, London from 1914 to 1917. This so-called 'church' was to become—and is still to this day—the principal centre for **syncretism, occultism** and libertarian politics in the Church of England."[155] [Italics in the original.]

Temple did not believe in a literal hell with torment:

> "One thing we can say with confidence: Everlasting torment is to be ruled out. If men had not imported the Greek and unbiblical notion of the nature indestructibility of the individual soul, and then read the New Testament with that already in their minds, they would have drawn from it [the New Testament—Eds.] a belief, not in everlasting torment, but in annihilation."[156]

JOSEF L. HROMADKA

Josef L. Hromadka was a founding member of the WCC's Central Committee. He was an **admitted Communist** and a Communist Party member![157] In his speech in January 1959 he stated:

> "Communism is no embodiment of evil, no 'murder of souls' as some people in the West believe. It is our task to demonstrate that this view is mistaken. Communism has grown out of the humanitarian efforts of many philosophers and poets who desired to create a more just and happy human society."[158]

> "In Helsinki, Finland, on July 23, 1951, Professor Hromadka spoke at a **Communist** rally publicly using his important place in The **World Council of Churches** to give weight to his Communistic utterances. The rally was sponsored by an organization called 'The World Peace Partisans,' a Communist

organization, and was an attempt to line up the Finns behind the current Communistic peace propaganda. The Finnish Communist newspaper *Vapaa Sana (The Free Word)* quotes Professor Hromadka as follows: 'In this peace effort the Christian and non-Christian, Communists and non-Communists, can stand together because our efforts are the same; therefore, I urge all Finnish Christians to join our work for the peaceful and generous world.'"[159]

At the WCC conference in Prague, Czechoslovakia in 1948, Hromadka said: "The answer is for the West to acknowledge its defeat and adjust itself to **cooperate with the Communist movement."**[160] One author wrote: "One could not see in his address anything but revolution and violence...."[161]

"In February, 1956, Dr. Hromadka was quoted as having said while on a visit to Australia that 'if you mean by communism a certain method of political action and reconstruction on a socialist basis, I believe it is possible to be both a communist and a Christian.'"[162]

> "He explained that Czechoslovakia was 'not a communistic or Marxist state, according to its constitution,' but was 'presently led by the communist party,' which felt 'a strong mission to lead the nation toward a new classless society,' and admitted that he had 'very much to say in favor of this aim.' He defended the view that Christians might well discuss their problems with Marxists in a friendly way."[163]

"For Hromadka, socialism and communism as practiced in Russia, China and Eastern Europe are shining ideals worthy of every necessary sacrifice on the part of Christian people to achieve, and something to be striven for devoutedly."[164]

Hromadka is a chairperson for the Inter-Religious Federation for World Peace (IRFWP). This group was founded by Sun Myung Moon, an occultist, who claims he is the Messiah.[165]

COMMUNISM AND THE WCC

> **"Communism has gained a strong foothold in the World Council of Churches....**Patriarch Alexis of the Russian Orthodox Church has the approval of the Communist regime. It is recognized that at least ten robed ecclesiastics of the Russian Church delegation to the Council at New Delhi were Communists in clerical garb. To top it all off, and to show that the WCC not merely tolerates, but also approves such activity, Patriarch German of Yugoslavia was elected at Uppsala in 1968 as one of the six presidents of WCC! This man's record of

brutality and murder against faithful Christians, and of his faithfulness to the whole Communist Regime is beyond dispute. The United States Internal Security Subcommittee in 1965 published a report which exposed him and his activities."[166]

Metropolitan Nikodim (also spelled Nicodim) was one of the six WCC Presidents who served in 1975.[167] "He had been repeatedly identified as an actual KGB agent by many Russian refugees."[168] "Nicodim in his many speeches and statements carried the same communist propaganda to the platform of the WCC."[169] He said: "I should also like to say that Christians in the Soviet Union...have not only accepted the socialist revolution that took place in our country, but have and are active builders of a classless, socialist society...."[170]

Another co-President of the WCC was **T. C. Chao.** He was the Dean of Yenching University School of Religion in China. This school was funded, in part, by the **Rockefellers.** "When the Communists were taking over China, Chao and his students welcomed their actions, and he was later given an official position in the Red Chinese government."[171] He "said that a Christian could be a communist in China."[172] *Time* (October 16, 1950) revealed some of Chao's Communistic endeavors.[173] While Chao was co-president of the WCC "he tried to justify Mao's house arrests of missionaries, compulsory indoctrination, etc. He said Christians should curse and oppose America because 'Jesus Christ commanded us to oppose sin.'"[174]

"Dr. Chao has written a book, *The Life of Jesus,* in which he denies all the miracles of the New Testament, states that Jesus Christ did not walk on the water, did not raise people from the dead, and did not turn water into wine. **Jesus Christ, writes Dr. Chao, was a revolutionist and a Socialist.** The World Council of Churches leaders knew what Dr. Chao's theology was when they elevated him to high office."[175]

KGB AGENT ON WCC COMMITTEE

One person involved with the WCC mentioned that the WCC was accused of having Communists (or those sympathetic to Communism) on their Assembly and Council.[176] He personally felt that there was just a "small percentage of them."[177] He then admitted:

"Actually, they were, for the most part, **socialists** or collectivists, who, while rejecting its ideology, accepted as essentially Christian its professed theoretical objects of a classless society and economic equality. They believed that the cure for the defects of both Marxian communism and capitalism was more socialism. They had the doctrinaire assurance that

> the churches and the state would be able, working together in complementary ways, to control the 'welfare order' which they envisaged and fix its bounds at any degree of leftness they might determine, and so to avoid the danger that the increasing momentum of socialism might deliver the world into the hands of communism. In ruling capitalism out as an adequate substructure for democratic political liberty, they were so sure of themselves that they saw no need to consider its usefulness even as a brake against possible sudden and uncontrollable veerings leftward."[178]

Metropolitan Filaret of the Russia Orthodox Church in the Soviet Union was on the Central Committee of the WCC.[179] In 1986-87 the FBI report named "him as the government representative and **KGB agent** who is running the churches."[180] In fact, Filaret has three different names by which he is known: "Denisenko (real last name), Filaret (church name), and 'Antonov' (secret KGB code name)."[181]

When Gorbachev signed the INF treaty, "he brought Metropolitan Filaret with him on his plane and several other of these religious agents....The world saw Shultz welcoming Gorbachev at the steps of the plane but the media suppressed these agents with him."[182]

PETE SEEGER

In Uppsala, Sweden in 1968, **Pete Seeger** was the honored guest and entertainer of the **World Council of Churches.**[183] Who is Pete Seeger? Seeger "has been identified under oath by an FBI undercover agent as having been a member of the Communist Party. His actions over the years would hardly disprove the charge."[184] According to the *Encyclopedia of the American Left,* Seeger had **joined the Communist Party** in 1942.[185]

In April 1992 Seeger told the Marxist publication, *Crossroads,* that "I will continue to call myself a Communist"[186] and in December 1994 he bragged: "I am still a Communist."[187]

One researcher states:

> "His biography over the past few decades reads like a Who's Who in Communist Activity. *News and Views* for July, 1965, listed over ninety Communist fronts and activities of Pete Seeger, but even this is a partial listing of his hundreds of pro-Communist activities over the past thirty years....
>
> "He provided the entertainment, according to the *Daily Worker* of June 20, 1947, for the Allerton Section of the Communist Party's housewarming....

> "Seeger provided the entertainment, according to the *Daily Worker* of April 30, 1948, for the Essex County Communist Party's May Day Rally.
>
> "He entertained the Cultural Division of the Communist Party of New York at a May Day show, according to the *Daily Worker* of May 4, 1949. This same *Worker* identified Seeger as a member of the Music Section of the Cultural Division of the Communist Party along with two other members of The Weavers' singing group....
>
> "Pete marched in the Communist Party of New York May Day parade in 1950. He also marched in the May Day parade in 1952....
>
> "He entertained at the rallies of the subversive National Council of American-Soviet Friendship in 1958, 1960 and 1962."[188]

Hours after Seeger reiterated that he was a Communist, former President Clinton "praised Seeger as 'an inconvenient artist who dared to sing things as he saw them.' Alluding to troubles caused by Seeger's Communist ties, the President said, 'He was banned from television. Now that's a badge of honor.'"[189]

Seeger is also a Planetary Citizen member.[190]

In spite of such a record, the

> "W.C.C. leadership had already declared Pete Seeger, Joan Baez and Phil Ochs as the new hymn writers for the coming new day. It seems our present hymns are too 'individualist.' Instead, our new hymns will taste something like the following [published by the World Council of Churches]:
>
> "It was on a Friday morning that they took me from the cell
> "And I saw they had a carpenter to crucify as well
> "You can blame it onto Pilate, you can blame it on the Jews,
> "You can blame it on the Devil, It's God I accuse.
> "It's God they ought to crucify instead of you and me
> "I said to the carpenter a hanging on the tree."[191]

No wonder Dr. Morrison, a WCC leader, asserts that **"to bring the hidden church into existence the BIBLE MUST BE REMOVED FROM ITS STATIC POSITION AS A CONSTITUTION OF THE CHURCH."**[192] [Emphasis in the original.]

> "In the U.S. Congressional Record of January 10th 1963, forty-five worldwide goals of Communism were listed, many of which are now being fulfilled. Goal No. 27 reads: **'Infiltrate**

> **the churches** and **replace revealed religion** with "social" religion. **Discredit the Bible** and emphasise the need for intellectual maturity which does not need a "religious crutch.""""[193]

Certainly this **Communistic** goal has been accomplished through the Federal, National, and World Council of Churches.

The *Chicago Daily News* (June 1, 1963) announced a "Pentecost Service of Christian Unity" where "Clergymen from 33 Christian communions will join in reading the 'New Delhi Statement of Unity' adopted by the World Council of Churches at its Third Assembly in New Delhi, India, in 1961."[194] The article went on to report: "The ecumenical nature of the event will be strengthened by the fact that a member of the **Billy Graham evangelistic team,** Dan Piatt, and a prominent theologian, the Rev. Dr. Franklin H. Littell of Chicago Theological Seminary, will speak."[195] By the way, "Franklin Littell has been one of the most radical modernists in the United States and has a record of affiliation with various **Marxist** front organizations and causes."[196]

S. PARKES CADMAN

S. Parkes Cadman was president of the FCC from 1924-1928. He was a **Mason** and the grand chaplain of the Grand Lodge of New York for 28 years.[197] Masonic author, William R. Denslow, stated that Cadman "was noted for his broad and liberal attitude with regard to the religious opinions of others."[198]

He was instrumental in founding the National Conference of Christians and Jews in 1928 along with Charles Evans Hughes, a member of the **Council on Foreign Relations.**[199]

Cadman wrote a book entitled *Robbing Youth of Its Religion.* In this book he listed a number of things that people believe which he claims is not the truth. Some of these items are:

> "They have taken for truth the dogma of an infallible Bible....
>
> "They have taken for truth the dogma of the virgin birth....
>
> "They have taken for truth the deity of Jesus—the dogma that Jesus is very God....
>
> "They have taken for truth the historicity of the miracles of Jesus....
>
> "They have taken for truth a veritable host of things which manifestly are not truth...."[200]

The inscription on this book read: "To the young people of America, engaged in a great intellectual and spiritual adventure—that of breaking the shackles of the past and interpreting the religion of Jesus in terms of the spirit of a **NEW AGE."**[201] [Emphasis in the original.] This was written in 1927—while he was President of the FCC!

Also in 1927 he referred to the Bolshevists as being people "with advanced ideas."[202]

Another president of the FCC was Ivan Lee Holt. He, too, was a **Mason**[203] as well as a **Communist.**[204] In fact, listen to what the Communist paper, the *Daily Worker,* wrote about him:

> "The Methodist Young People's Conference, with 5000 delegates in attendance, took _a sharp turn to the Left_ in its closing sessions. *The Soviet Union was highly praised by Ivan Lee Holt, president of the Federal Council of Churches....*
>
> "Dr. Holt defended the Soviet Union from attack. He declared that the aim of the dictatorship of the proletariat in Russia was the establishment of a better life. The Russian government does not purport to do this through exploiting someone else, but through raising the general level of all. It is difficult to find youth anywhere in this world more devoted to the cause of Christ than you'll find in Russia devoted to 'Stalin and his **new order.'**
>
> "He warned the older generation that 'amongst most of the youth of the world today there is a desire for a change, many preferring revolution. Youth is willing to die for a **new order....'"**[205] [Boldface in the original.]

Some other **Masons** who were involved in the various Council of Churches were: George C. Barber (President of the Australian Council of the WCC from 1950-1951);[206] Levi Gilbert (FCC);[207] Perry E. Gresham (WCC);[208] Joseph C. Hazen (FCC);[209] John B. Lennon (FCC);[210] William C. Martin (former NCC President from 1952-1954);[211] McGruder Ellis Sadler (FCC);[212] Henry St. George Tucker (former FCC President from 1942-1944);[213] and Hugh I. Evans (WCC).[214]

We've already covered Oxnam in some detail. He was a former President of the Federal Council of Churches, one of the presiding officers at the founding of the National Council of Churches and the first American President of the World Council of Churches from 1948-1954.[215] He was also a 33° Mason.[216] He said "that one day there would be, 'only two groups, the Protestant and Catholic, and they will unite to form the Holy Catholic Church.'"[217]

E. STANLEY JONES

"Another Federal Council leader, preacher and speaker, **E. Stanley Jones,** stated: 'When the Western world was floundering in an unjust and competitive order...God reached out and put his hand on the Russian Communists to produce **a juster order** and to show a recumbent church what it has missed in its own gospel.'"[218] [Emphasis in the original.]

He also said:

> "We have yet to see the folly of trying to change the individual and leaving him in an unchanged, selfish, corporate life. Life on a collective scale must be born again. Cannot be done? Absurd. The Russians have done it. She (Russia) has had a secular new birth. The very basis of her life has been changed and changed profoundly, and the result of that change has been as startling that John Gunther, in the penetrating book, 'Inside Europe' ends the book by saying, 'Give Russia ten years more of peace and she will be the most powerful nation on earth.' Why? Because she has hold of a higher principle, co-operation, and it is working out in higher results than we can work out of a lower principle, competition."[219]

It's no surprise that Jones would defend Communism—especially since he belonged to at least 4 Communist front organizations.[220]

"Jones denied the virgin birth of Christ, the verbal inspiration of the Scripture, the triune Godhead and other doctrines."[221]

Jones was a Methodist missionary in India for many years and met Mahatma Gandhi while there.

> "Instead of Dr. Jones influencing Gandhi toward Christian conversion, the reverse took place. Dr. Jones admits this in his book *Mahatma Gandhi.* Dr. Jones became a disciple of *Satyagraha,* or pacifist resistance, as practiced by Gandhi and his followers.
>
> "Dr. Jones went so far as to ask Gandhi to come to the United States and organize the people in a resistance movement against military preparedness. He called Gandhi 'God's trump card' and the man through whom God was working in the twentieth century. He admits that Gandhi would not accept the Christ or the God of the Bible; but the fact that Gandhi was a pacifist made him a 'natural Christian' instead of an 'orthodox' one."[222]

How does Billy Graham feel about Jones? In his 1963 Los Angeles Crusade he "took ten minutes to **eulogize** [praise] Dr. E. Stanley Jones...."[223] At one crusade **Graham introduced Jones with**

these words: "I now present my good friend and trusted advisor...."[224]

PHILIP POTTER

Philip Potter was the General Secretary of the WCC.[225] He, too, advocates Communist activities (and **violent** ones, at that[226])! He said in *Newsweek* (August 28, 1972): "We are at a stage in the **ecumenical movement** where we have to become involved in difficult activities. Ultimately, **I am prepared to face chaos and anarchy,** if that is what it takes to bring about the necessary change."[227]

In 1969 Potter

> "quoted from a 1969 WCC Central Committee directive as follows: 'We call upon the churches to move beyond charity, grants and traditional programming to relevant and sacrificial action leading to new relationships of dignity and justice among all men and to become THE AGENTS FOR THE RADICAL RECONSTRUCTION OF SOCIETY.' He also made it perfectly clear what this involved when he said, 'But the conflict has become intense when it has been perceived that A RADICAL CHANGE OF ECONOMIC, SOCIAL AND POLITICAL STRUCTURES ARE (sic) NEEDED AND NOT THE MERE PRUDENTIAL TRANSFER OF RESOURCES AND TECHNOLOGIES.' Another WCC document stated: 'In the developed countries it means changes in the production structure and employment policies which will ONLY BE POSSIBLE THROUGH A CERTAIN "SOCIALIZATION" of decisions that have so far been taken autonomously on the basis of interests of the private sector.'"[228] [Emphasis in the original.]

In 1977 he "praised the communist victory in Vietnam."[229] He even admitted that he "may sometimes be more radical than most Marxists."[230]

Potter, a disciple of Reinhold Niebuhr, Richard Niebuhr, Paul Tillich, and Karl Barth,[231] believes that individuals in non-Christians religions are not lost.[232] He stated: "Indeed, the world is already a redeemed world so that, whether men discern their true condition or not, and even if they deny it, they are still the heirs of God's redemption."[233]

In 1981 the NCC had Potter as an honored guest. He remarked: "Of course, the apostle Paul was somewhat of a prude and a sexist."[234]

Potter sent an invitation for Billy Graham to speak at the WCC in 1983. Due to other engagements, Graham was unable to do so, but he wrote a nice letter to Potter expressing his regret.[235] He said: "This will be only the second general assembly of the WCC that I have had to miss. I will certainly miss seeing you and many other old friends and **fellowshipping** with those from all over the world."[236]

Graham also wrote about this invitation:

> "A number of people will be going directly to Vancouver from this Conference, including several members of **my organization** who will be there as observers. **It has been my privilege to be at every Assembly of the World Council except Nairobi,** as an observer or visitor....I cannot help but recall that **I was present in 1948 when the World Council of Churches was formed here in Amsterdam,** in large part out of the desire of many for a new thrust in evangelism and world missions. **The World Council has its roots deep in biblical evangelism."**[237]

It is true that **officially** the WCC called "itself 'a fellowship of Churches which accept Jesus Christ Our Lord as God and Saviour' but in reality it is strongly pro-Communist and syncretist."[238]

At this 1983 WCC Assembly in Vancouver, Canada, "major speeches were given by a Buddhist, a Hindu, a Sikh, and a Canadian Indian who worships spirits!"[239] (More about this shortly!)

BROTHERS IN CHRIST

We've seen how Graham feels about the WCC, but how does he feel about Potter? In 1957 at the Madison Square Garden he had Potter lead in prayer.[240] Later, he called Potter "a brother in Christ!"[241] If Potter is really Graham's "brother in Christ," are you serving the same "Christ" as Billy Graham is?!

At a press conference in 1974, Graham was asked about his relationship with the WCC, to which he replied: "As far as I know, **we have** nothing but **the warmest relationships with the World Council of Churches."**[242] The Bible warns us in Ephesians 5:11: "And have no fellowship with the unfruitful works of darkness, but rather reprove them."

"The **Singapore government expelled the WCC** leaders who were holding an office for their Far Eastern Council [the Christian Conference of Asia] **because of their communism,"**[243] yet people like **Graham** can brag that they "have nothing but the warmest relationships" with the WCC. Doesn't it appear as though something must be wrong somewhere?!

C. D. MacFarland, former Secretary of the Federal Council of Churches claimed: "The incarnation was in man that it might be in men. O child of God, as God lived in his Son, so would he live in his sons and children."[244]

In the last chapter mention was made of the blasphemous Re-Imagining conference. One participant was Mary Ann Lundy. She joined "in a milk and honey ritual with lesbian activist Jane Spahr...and others at the **ReImagining** conference. This ceremony included prayers to 'Sophia, Creator God.'"[245] Although the Presbyterian Church (USA) pressured her to resign in June 1994, the **World Council of Churches** opened their arms and appointed her as their Deputy General Secretary in 1995.[246] In 1997 she gave a speech in which she said: **"We are learning that to be ecumenical is to move beyond the boundaries of Christianity. You see, yesterday's heresies are becoming tomorrow's Book of Order."**[247] [Emphasis in the original.]

ATHEISTS IN HEAVEN

Archbishop Ramsey was a former President of the WCC. He commented: "I can foresee the day when all Christians might accept the Pope as Bishop of a World Church."[248] He also denied the virgin birth.[249] "In the London *Daily Mail* for Feb. 10, 1961, Ramsey said: "Heaven is not a place for Christians only. I expect to see many present day atheists there." Another source gives this quote from Ramsey: **"Those who led a good life on Earth but found themselves unable to believe in God will not be debarred. I expect to meet present-day atheists in heaven."**[250] [Emphasis in the original.] The Bible, however, says that **"without faith it is impossible to please Him:** for **he that cometh to God <u>must believe that He is</u>,** and that He is a rewarder of them that diligently seek Him" (Hebrews 11:6).

> "In 1966, Ramsey had an audience with Pope Paul VI at the Vatican. He addressed the Pope as 'Your holiness' and expressed his desire for closer unity with Rome. As Ramsey and the other Anglican clergy were departing they bowed and kissed the Pope's ring. Speaking about this papal visit a year later, Ramsey testified that he and the Pope walked arm and arm out in St. Peter's Basilica and dedicated themselves to the task of unifying 'all Christendom and all the churches of all the world into one church.'"[251]

"In November 1968 the Archbishop of Canterbury, Dr. Michael Ramsey,[252] said in London, 'It is in the dealings of man with his neighbours that we shall find transcendence. **We must join hands with humanists, atheists and agnostics in the service of mankind.'"**[253] Oh, is that so? My Bible tells me: **"Be ye not unequally yoked together with unbelievers:** for what fellowship hath righteousness with unrighteousness? and what communion hath light with darkness?" (II Corinthians 6:14).

> "In September 1970 the WCC decided to donate $200,000 to guerrilla organizations sending terrorists into Rhodesia, Angola, Mozambique, and South Africa. **The decision was taken at a meeting in London at which the co-chairman was Dr. Ramsay,** late Archbishop of Canterbury. In the same year the WCC decided to give $70,000 annually for three years helping American draft dodgers escape from the USA into Canada."[254]

In spite of such actions and comments, Billy Graham calls Ramsey "a giant of a man"[255] and added: "We were friends for many years."[256]

Another Archbishop of Canterbury, **Geoffrey F. Fisher,** was a **Mason**[257] as well as a speaker for the World Council of Churches.[258]

> "As president of the **World Council of Churches** (1946-54), he was a vigorous proponent of **ecumenism.** In 1960 he traveled to meet with the Orthodox patriarchs of Jerusalem and Constantinople. He also visited Pope John XXIII, becoming the first archbishop of Canterbury to visit the Vatican since 1397."[259]

A member of the WCC staff, Stanley Samartha,[260] announced in 1971: **"Because Christians cannot claim to have a monopoly of truth, we need to meet men of other faiths and ideologies as part of our trust and obedience to the promise of Christ."**[261] [Emphasis in the original.]

Dr. David Gill, a representative of the WCC, told the British Broadcasting Corporation "that the most important aim of the W.C.C. for 1974 would be to **'De-Protestantize the Churches.'"**[262] [Emphasis in the original.]

MARTIN NIEMOELLER

Martin Niemoeller was President of the WCC from 1961-1968.[263] He

> "had personally welcomed the coming to power of the Nazis in 1933. In that year his autobiography, *From U-Boat to Pulpit,* had been published. The story of how this submarine commander in the First World War had become a prominent Protestant pastor was singled out for special praise in the Nazi

> press and became a best seller. To Pastor Niemoeller, as to many a Protestant clergyman, the fourteen years of the Republic had been, as he said, 'years of darkness' and at the close of his autobiography he added a note of satisfaction that Nazi revolution had finally triumphed and that it had brought about the 'national revival' for which he himself had fought so long—for a time in the free corps, from which so many Nazi leaders had come.

"He was soon to experience a terrible disillusionment..."[264] and later became a foe of Nazism and denounced its racial views.[265] Niemoeller, however, was an advocate of international **disarmament** and he is listed as a "First Endorser" of **Planetary Citizens,** a New Age organization.[266]

Paulos Mar Gregorios was a past President of the World Council of Churches.[267] He attended the ungodly Parliament of the World's Religions in Chicago in 1993 along with the Buddhist Dalai Lama, witches, Muslims, Hindus, and pagans of all stripes.[268] He is also on the Board of Advisors for the Temple of Understanding (which was mentioned earlier in this book).[269] He is on the Advisory Council for the Whole Earth Papers[270] as well as the Advisory Council for the New Age Global Education Associates.[271] William Swing, the promoter of a United Religions Initiative, visited Gregorios in the hospital in 1996 and asked him what he thought about such a proposal as a "United Religion." Swing said that "[n]ot only did he endorse the proposal, he promised to alert others, worldwide, to the initiative. He said that a United Religions would be more than a symbol. It would be an agent of global unity."[272]

ARNOLD TOYNBEE

As far back as 1949, Dr. Arnold Toynbee was a representative for the World Council of Churches.[273] In the July 1956 issue of *The Ecumenical Review* (put out by the WCC) were articles on "various aspects of the **Christian** responsibility for a peaceful and just international order." John Foster Dulles, Ralph Bunche, Dag Hammarskjold, Luther A. Weigle, and Toynbee were some of the contributing authors.[274] Who was Toynbee? He was a historian and the ex-director of Studies of the **Royal Institute of International Affairs** (RIIA).[275] The RIIA is the British equivalent to the **Council on Foreign Relations** and was **founded in 1919 as part of Cecil Rhodes' plan for world domination.**[276]

Toynbee was one of the "First Endorsers of the **Planetary Citizens**[277] and he had taught at the New Age/human potential center known as Esalen.[278] He leaned towards **Buddhism**[279] and was called 'an apostle of an amalgam of Christianity and Mahayanian Buddhism.'"[280]

Not surprisingly, he is also a big **advocate of world government.** In 1931, Fabian socialist Toynbee gave a speech in which he remarked:

> *"We are at present working discreetly with all our might to wrest this mysterious force called sovereignty out of the clutches of the local nation states of the world.* ***All the time we are denying with our lips what we are doing with our hands,*** *because to impugn the sovereignty of the local nation states of the world is still a heresy for which a statesman or publicist can perhaps not quite be burned at the stake but certainly be ostracized and discredited."*[281] [Italics in the original.]

In 1971 he wrote a book, *Surviving the Future,* in which he announced:

> "I expect that the World is going to be united politically in the teeth of nationalistic resistance....The people of each local sovereign state will have to renounce their state's sovereignty and subordinate it to the paramount sovereignty of a literally world-wide world government....**I want to see a world government established."**[282]

Toynbee was also an **evolutionist**[283] who was involved with the **environmental** movement. He basically blamed the ecological problems on Christians.[284] In one article he wrote:

> "If the cogent evidence for divinity were really power, **Dionysus and Demeter and Zeus and Poseidon,** who are now re-asserting their power, **would be more credible gods than Yahweh;** for they are demonstrating to present-day man that he cannot pollute soil, air, and water with impunity."[285]

TOTEM POLE

Two witches reveal:

> "Recent books...have...been calling for a return to the worship of the Mother. So many wistful comments made by writers such as Merlin Stone, Mary Daly, James Lovelock, Judy Chicago, Dolores LaChapelle, Rene Dubos, Daniela Gioseffi, Paolo Soleri, Elizabeth Gould Davis, and **Arnold Toynbee** reflect a craving for such a religious revival. The truth is that such a revival has been going on for some time now—since the early 1960's—in the form of what we call the Neo-Pagan movement (from Latin *paganus*—peasant or country dweller—Paganism now refers to all nature religions). The new Paganism encompasses many Nature-oriented groups such as Feraferia,

> Church of All Worlds, Madrakara, Bear Tribe, Venusian Church, Pagan Way, Church of the Eternal Source, Reformed Druids, and Holy Order of Mother Earth. The largest contingent of modern Goddess-worshippers, however, is found in Witchcraft, or Wicca. Wicca is a pre-Christian European Pagan magical tradition....The Neo-Pagan movement and especially Feminist Witchcraft, has recently been joined by increasing numbers from the Women's Spirituality movement....If Witches can be priestesses of feminism, then Neo-Pagans are the chaplains of the ecology movement."[286]

No wonder Toynbee wrote about a "New Universal Church."[287] He also remarked:

> "I believe that in the twenty-first century human life is going to be a unity again in all its aspects and activities. I believe that, in the field of religion, **sectarianism is going to be subordinated to ecumenism;** that in the field of politics **nationalism is going to be subordinated to world government;** and that, in the field of human affairs. (sic) specialization is going to be subordinated to a comprehensive view."[288]

The WCC has been comfortable with non-Christians for quite some time already. In **1983** the WCC included "religious leaders from Buddhism, Hinduism, Islam and Judaism on the platform...."[289] They also set up "a Canadian Indian spirit house with a sacred flame which is really a pagan altar"[290] and they received an **occultic totem pole** which was "to be shipped for erection at WCC headquarters in Geneva."[291] In fact, **Philip Potter** (the person who sent the invitation for **Billy Graham** to speak **this same year!)** helped to raise the totem pole into an upright position.[292]

Brad Gsell explains what this **totem pole** represented—from the literature given out at the WCC:

> "The **official program** which was distributed at the pole-raising ceremony gave a description of what the carvings on the pole described. One section reads: 'Our Totem Pole shows man, born first as spirit, then shows Raven, pictured as mother nature finding man coming from the sea in the clam shell and for centuries he roamed the earth and worshipped nothing.' This is contrary to Scripture, which states that God created man *as* man, and that the first man knew God. The text concludes, 'Our pole shows the picture of man's travel through his history from the sea to where he is now, Spiritual evolution in picture form.' Prior to this, the text describes how man at first worshipped serpents, bulls, etc., then progressed to worshipping the stars and eagles. Finally man realized that there

was 'a force greater than anything on earth.' The Bible says that man has *always* known of God and has always had the choice of serving Him or rejecting Him for idols and deities."[293] [Italics in the original.]

One of the speakers this year **(1983)** was Pauline Webb, a **socialist** who serves on the WCC executive committee.[294] This is also **the same year** that Dorothee Soelle (who claimed that "God is dead, red, and a woman") spoke.[295]

In 1975 they had invited Professor **K. L. Seshagiri Rao** to present a paper to the WCC Assembly. He was the **Hindu representative** of 750 million Hindus[296] and is "the editor of a magazine called *Insight,* published by a syncretist organisation known as the 'Temple of Understanding.'"[297] He is also the chief editor of the *New Encyclopedia of Hinduism.*[298] Rao is on the International Board of Advisors for the Temple of Understanding[299] as well as being involved with Thanksgiving Square.[300] He is on the Board of Advisors for the International Religious Federation for World Peace (IRFWP),[301] Sun Myung Moon's group.[302] In 1989 Rao once again addressed the World Council of Churches.[303] He called "the invitation to people of other faiths to participate in this meeting a 'great breakthrough.'"[304]

In 1988, Selena Fox, a **witch,** bragged: "As we go to press, I am off to Canada. The **World Council of Churches has invited Margot Adler and me as Wiccan priestesses** to take part in a weeklong International Women's **Interfaith** Dialoguing Conference being held in Toronto."[305]

Paganism was also manifested at the "Ecumenical Moment '88" which was sponsored by the National Council of Churches and the World Council of Churches. **Philip Potter,** Wesley Ariarajah, and other WCC leaders were present at this meeting which also started with a heathen ritual.[306] The "celebration" was held outdoors at a garden pond where prayers and water libations were offered "to the Seven Spirits of the seven directions of the universe ('O Spirit of the North, blow upon us...O Spirit of the East...West...South...Above... Below...Center...')."[307]

MILLION MINUTES OF PEACE

A "Million Minutes of Peace" was held from September 16 to October 16, 1986 as a project for the United Nations International Year of Peace.[308]

"The promoters stated that people were prepared to commit themselves to link with others in thought, **regardless of belief,** tradition or political differences. On page two of their first issue, they talked about the 'hundredth monkey' concept....

"The **list of groups and individuals,** which either **endorsed** this event or actively worked for its success, included Lucis Trust Eileen Caddy (co-founder of Findhorn), His Holiness the Dalai Lama, Institute of Noetic Sciences (Willis Harman), Friends of the Earth, Planetary Citizens, Brahma Kumaris World Spiritual Organization, author Sydney Sheldon, Rt. Hon. Bishop Desmond Tutu, author/lecturer Marilyn Ferguson, Sen. Edward Kennedy, the **president of the World Council of Churches,** the Church of Religious Science, Unity-in-Diversity Council, and the Human Unity Institute, to name just a few.

"The Appeal climaxed at a Peace Concert that was held at **St. John the Divine Cathedral...."**[309]

Again, this paganism in the NCC and WCC has been going on for a long time. For the World Day of Prayer in **1956,** the NCC used a prayer by an Indian chief which started out with "O Great Spirit."[310]

In fact, the **"National Council of Churches and the World Council of Churches are listed in the Lucis Trust publications as part of the new group of world servers."**[311]

Furthermore, the Swedenborgian Church of the New Jerusalem is a full member of the NCC and WCC.[312] The Swedenborgian Church denies the deity of Jesus Christ.[313] Of course, the founder of this "church" (also called the New Church[314]) was **Emmanuel Swedenborg.**[315] He has been called "perhaps the greatest **occultist** of his time."[316] He was a **Mason,** even having a Masonic rite called the Swedenborg Rite.[317] According to one book, Swedenborg was also associated with the Illuminati.[318] He practiced clairvoyance,[319] astral travel, automatic writing, and consulted mediums.[320] Texe Marrs writes: "Many say that Swedenborg can rightly be called the **'Father of Spiritualism.'"**[321]

He continues:

"Generally, Swedenborgians believe that Swedenborg's writings were divinely inspired. Among their teachings: that there is a state, much like the Catholic's purgatory, where after death the individual goes to prepare for heaven or hell. Another teaching is that Jesus did not shed His blood for our sins but simply died on the cross after 'a life of service.' Moreover, the Holy Spirit is not a personality, say the Swedenborgians, and Jesus Christ is not wholly God, for God is a force that can be called the 'Divine Essence.'

> "Like their founder, Emmanuel Swedenborg, modern-day Swedenborgians believe that the Old Testament is of little value. They are also opposed to almost anything written by the Apostle Paul....
>
> "In a recent issue of *Chrysalis,* a journal of the Swedenborg Foundation, a Swedenborg group in New York City, we find articles on reincarnation, the I Ching, and other occultic subjects."[322]

The Church of the New Jerusalem (the Swedenborgian Church) is also a member of the Council for a Parliament of the World's Religions along with other groups such as: American Buddhist Congress, American Islamic College, Spiritual Assembly of the Baha'is, Brahma Kumaris World Spiritual Organization, Buddhist Council of the Midwest, Catholic Theological Union, Sri Chinmoy Center, Evangelical Lutheran Church in America, Guru Gobind Singh Foundation, Hindu Temple of Greater Chicago, Institute for Twenty-First Century Studies, Interfaith Ministries, Muslim Community Center, Presbyterian Church (U.S.A.), The Temple of Understanding, Theosophical Society in America, Unitarian Universalist Association, Federation of Zoroastrian Associations of North America, and the First Baptist Church of Evanston, Illinois.[323]

Lois Wilson is a feminist[324] and the past President of the World Council of Churches.[325] She asserts: "Christianity, as practiced in today's world, demonstrates more of a nightmare than a vision."[326] "In a report in the Ecumenical News Service of the WCC...[Wilson] made this statement: 'And then there is the "Virgin Mary." IN MY VIEW, THE FACT OF HER VIRGINITY HAS NOTHING TO DO WITH HER SEXUAL BEHAVIOUR.'"[327] [Emphasis in the original.] She was one of the speakers at the sacrilegious **ReImagining** Conference which was covered in the last chapter.[328]

ABORTION AND HOMOSEXUALITY

Joe Leonard was a senior official at the NCC. He endorsed a Planned Parenthood sex education video called "Talking About Sex." This "video kit calls **abortion 'safe' and homosexuality 'fulfilling,'** and seems to ok unmarried sex."[329]

In 1996 there was legislation that would have banned "partial birth" abortions in which "a baby is but inches and seconds from birth. The abortionist partly extracts the baby feet first then suctions out its brain to let the head pass through the birth canal."[330] When Bill Clinton vetoed this legislation several liberal church groups such as the Presbyterian Church in the USA (PCUSA), Episcopal, United

Church of Christ, and Methodist "praised Clinton by letter for the veto."[331] Oh, the National Council of Churches' leader also supported the veto![332]

Concerning homosexuality, the President of the NCC, Andrew Young (who was covered in detail earlier), said: "When I worked at the National Council of Churches, **most of my colleagues were gay. I should have been talking about sex on their behalf,** but I didn't know what to say except 'judge not that you be not judged.'"[333] Many people seem to forget that the Bible also says that we are to "judge righteous judgment" (John 7:24). I Corinthians 6:2-3 asks: "Do ye not know that the saints shall judge the world? and if the world shall be judged by you, are ye unworthy to judge the smallest matters? Know ye not that we shall judge angels? how much more things that pertain to this life?"

> "Dr. **Gwynne Guidbord,** a leader in the predominately **homosexual** Universal Fellowship of Metropolitan Community Churches, was warmly received as a speaker at the recent **National Council of Churches'** General Assembly. At least half of assembled NCC delegates gave her a standing ovation.... She actually blamed opposition to homosexuality for forcing young people into prostitution, drugs, and alcohol abuse. Some NCC leaders, including NCC President Craig Anderson, favor accepting the UFMCC as a member denomination."[334]

Guidbord has recently been elected President of the California Council of Churches.[335] She "is also president-elect of a pro-abortion group named 'Mobilization for the Human Family.'"[336]

An article in *More Light Update* reports:

> "Even more recently, a coalition of gay and lesbian religious organizations has decided to give an annual award to a heterosexual religious leader who has served as an outspoken advocate of 'homosexual rights.' The Paul H. Sherry Leadership and Courage award is named after its first recipient, Paul Sherry who recently retired as president of the United Church of Christ. **The Interfaith Assembly of Lesbian Gay, Bisexual and Transgender Caucuses and Affirming Organizations will distribute the award each year at the National Council of Churches' (NCC) general assembly meeting.** Both Eileen Lindner, associate general secretary of the NCC and Gwynne Guidbord, ecumenical officer of the Universal Fellowship of Metropolitan Community Churches (UFMCC—a primarily homosexual and lesbian denomination), told Ecumenical News International (ENI) that the UFMCC 'has been making quiet inroads within the Unites (sic) States **ecumenical** movement.' Lindner said, 'Informally there have been great advances....'"[337]

CANAAN BANANA

Canaan Banana was the former President of Zimbabwe and an official in the WCC. He holds anti-Scriptural and **Marxist** views.[338] "At the 1980 Australian WCC meeting the outright denunciation and **overthrow of Capitalism was demanded,** by Rev. Canaan Banana."[339] He says: "When I look at a guerrilla, I see Jesus Christ. The guerrilla dies that we may live."[340] He also noted: "As for me, I am not ashamed of the revolution, for it is the power of the people unto salvation."[341] What a misrepresentation of Scripture! The Bible says in Romans 1:16: "For I am not ashamed of the **gospel of Christ:** for it is the power of God unto salvation to every one that believeth...."

Banana also said:

> "In the final analysis it is not so much a social struggle as a class struggle: poor against rich, oppressed against oppressor... each historical situation will determine the choice of the method the poor will use to achieve their **ultimate goal of** changing the system and **building socialism."**[342]

Recently Banana was found guilty of 11 counts of sodomy and attempted sodomy with his bodyguards, cooks, and gardeners while he was President.[343]

Dr. William Paton was a co-secretary of the WCC. He remarked: "Collectivism is coming, whether we like it or not."[344]

Brian Wenham, an Australian pastor, attended the WCC's Conference on World Mission and Evangelism which was held in Melbourne, Australia in 1980. He wrote, "At this conference **Marxism permeated everything**—the liturgy, the songs, the addresses, the questions, the bookstall, the voluminous free literature—everything! Revolution was in the atmosphere."[345]

> "One of Pastor Wenham's friends also having his first personal look at the WCC, commented, 'Had I not seen the sign, **World Council of Churches,** on the gate, and had I not known what I was visiting, I would have thought I had strayed into a **Communist Party** workshop.' Wenham concluded, 'In every session, every paper and almost every brochure and poster, I was being peppered, even pounded with **marxist** philosophy!'"[346]

BENJAMIN CHAVIS

Benjamin Chavis was a former Vice President of the NCC as well as the former Executive Director of the National Association for the Advancement of Colored People (NAACP).[347] He was also a member of the Clinton-Gore transition team. He "is a pioneer in what has been called 'environmental racism.'"[348]

Chavis, like Jackson, King, Lyons, etc., has had "his own hijinx with women and money."[349] He bragged that his ministry "has always been **ecumenical** and **interfaith.** There is a linkage between Judaism, Christianity and Islam and I [Chavis] believe that there should be a greater trialogue, not a dialogue, but a trialogue between these three great revealed religions."[350] In 1997 he "announced he is converting to Islam and becoming a member of Rev. Louis Farrakhan's Nation of Islam."[351] He claims that he still believes in Jesus Christ but he "expects his announcement to shock many of his Christian friends and fellow members of the clergy...."[352] He also insists that he really hasn't changed. He states: "If you pour water from one glass to another glass, the composition of the water is the same. I am who I am...." "And there is but one God. The God of Judaism is the God of Christianity is the God of Islam. So if we all serve the same God why can't we all work together?"[353]

The problem is, however, that we are not serving the **SAME** God. The God of Islam differs drastically from the God of Christianity. The Islamic God is called Allah. He was the moon god, who married the sun goddess. "Together they produced three goddesses who were called 'the daughters of Allah.' These three goddesses were called Al-Lat, Al-Uzza, and Manat."[354]

The *Encyclopedia of Religion* mentions that "'Allah' is a pre-Islamic name...corresponding to the Babylonian Bel."[355] Bel (or Baal), by the way, is another name for **SATAN.**[356]

The Jesus Christ of Islam is also different. Muslims do not believe that Jesus was the Son of God[357] or that He was crucified.[358]

In spite of the differences between Christianity and Islam, "a Muslim leader addressed the National Council of Churches" for the first time in 1996.[359]

Also, Chavis claims that when water is poured from one glass to another, it remains the same. However, if the glass into which the water is poured is dirty, the water will also become dirty. If the water itself is dirty, it will make a clean glass dirty. Just suppose I had a glass of pure water in my hand and you are holding a glass of muddy water. It wouldn't hurt you to compromise with me by mixing your water with mine, **BUT** it would matter greatly to me to compromise with you by mixing my water with yours. Instead of a glass of pure water and a glass of contaminated water, we would now have two glasses of contaminated water. When a person knows the truth of God's Word, he or she can never compromise and be the same as before the compromise! Jesus and His Word are the true waters of life (see John 4:14; Revelation 21:6; 22:1, 17). We **cannot** mix this water with the polluted streams of Islam, Hinduism, Buddhism, New Age thought, psychology, paganism, witchcraft, etc. When we start to dialogue with these people and start to make concessions, we are forsaking the pure water of life. Compromise for the Christian **always** leads them further from the truth—it **never** leads them closer to the truth. The only party who gains in the dialogue is the non-Christian. They have nothing to lose by compromise—but the Christian has everything to lose by compromise. Jeremiah 2:13 says: "For **My people have committed two evils; they have forsaken Me the fountain of living waters,** and hewed them out cisterns, broken cisterns, that can hold no water."

Proverbs 5:15-17: **"Drink waters out of thine own cistern,** and running waters out of thine own well. Let thy fountains be dispersed abroad, and rivers of waters in the streets. **Let them be only thine own, and not strangers' with thee."** II Corinthians 6:17 warns: "Wherefore come out from among them, and **be ye separate,** saith the Lord, and **touch not the unclean thing;** and I will receive you."

We have an instance in the Bible where King Ahab wanted to "dialogue" with Naboth about his vineyard. He said that he wanted to buy Naboth's inheritance. The offer he made **seemed** very reasonable and fair. Ahab offered him a choice of a **better** vineyard or to pay the worth of it in money (I Kings 21:2). Naboth wouldn't lose out on the deal—or would he? What was wrong with this offer? Just one problem: "Naboth said to Ahab, **The LORD forbid it** me, that I should give the inheritance of my fathers unto thee" (I Kings 21:3). For Naboth, the issue was settled. The Lord forbid the selling of one's inheritance and no amount of dialogue or tempting offer could change God's command. This refusal cost Naboth his physical life for Queen Jezebel got two false witnesses to lie about, and testify against, Naboth. These witnesses accused Naboth of blaspheming God (I Kings 21:13). Doesn't Satan always reverse things? Naboth was **OBEYING** God but the false witnesses maligned him and said that he blasphemed God, so Jezebel had him put to death. She then went in to Ahab and told him to take possession of the vineyard.

Yes, Naboth lost his physical life but he gained eternal life. Ahab gained a physical possession but he ended up in hell. "[T]hese shall go away into everlasting punishment: but the righteous into life eternal" (Matthew 25:46). To the world, it seems as though Naboth may have been a fool to risk losing his life, but Paul reminds us that "we look not at the things which are seen, but at the things which are not seen: for the things which are seen are temporal; but the things which are not seen are eternal" (II Corinthians 4:18). For the Christian, this world is not the end. "But now they desire a better country, that is, an heavenly: wherefore God is not ashamed to be called their God: for He hath prepared for them a city" (Hebrews 11:16).

EMILIO CASTRO

Dr. Emilio Castro was one of "four outstanding Latin American advocates of **Liberation Theology** [who] held high ranks at WCC....."[360] Castro, a graduate of **Union Theological Seminary,**[361] was serving as the General Secretary of the WCC[362] when he "referred to the writings of Karl Marx as including *'hopes and dreams about a new humanity and a future transformed for the better.'* He then went on to state that *'Marxists and Christians in significant measure share a common source for such longings, which makes it possible for them to do much together.'*"[363] [Emphasis in the original.]

No wonder when Castro was elected as the General Secretary of the WCC[364] "a KGB memo confirms that its agents supported Castro as 'a candidate acceptable to us.'"[365]

At the 1980 Melbourne, Australia Conference of the Commission on World Mission and Evangelism we find that Castro "presented many heresies under the false theme of 'Your Kingdom Come' including false teaching that Christ's Kingdom is already here. **Communism was proposed as the answer to the poor** 'since **Christianity had failed.'"**[366]

Castro, in 1982, remarked: "The philosophical basis of **capitalism is evil,** totally contrary to the Gospel."[367]

In July 1989 the World Council of Churches Central Committee met in Moscow. There Emilio Castro commented: "I might be tempted to quote some of the most beautiful pages of Karl Marx, dreaming of the New Man, the new creature. He was dreaming out of the same biblical traditional from which we come. In that common dream, we hope that between us we will have many steps to take in common."[368] Karl Marx's "new man" certainly was different than what the Bible reveals to us in II Corinthians 5:17: "Therefore if any man be in Christ, he is a new creature: old things are passed away; behold, all things are become new."

This same year (1989) Castro signed the "Declaration of World Thanksgiving" from the Center for World Thanksgiving.[369] Without going into detail, suffice it to say that this is an ungodly, New Age, interfaith organization which includes Muslims, Buddhists, Jews, Protestants, Catholics, etc.[370]

He also attended the World Day of Prayer for Peace where "Hindus, Buddhists, African tribal witchdoctors, Togo snake handlers, and others, met in Assisi, Italy, and prayed together for world peace."[371] Welcoming this assortment of occultists and New Agers on this occasion was none other than Pope John Paul II![372]

Castro has "specifically called upon the churches to support 'the guerrilla movements.' This refers to **communist** terrorist groups such as the African National Congress (ANC) and the South African Communist Party."[373] In fact, Castro called for the WCC to funnel more money to these terrorist groups.[374]

How does Billy Graham feel about Emilio Castro? Well, in Graham's autobiography he writes that when he was in Uruguay in 1962 that **Castro was the vice chairman of his Montevideo Crusade.** Graham adds: "He stayed by my side throughout our visit, taking me everywhere in his little car....In later years, after Emilio Castro became prominent in the World Council of Churches, we did not always agree on all **theological** points. On **social affairs and social conscience, though, he did sharpen my thinking."**[375] Do you understand what you just read? Graham states that Castro and he did not always agree theologically, but that Castro's **SOCIAL** (meaning Communistic) awareness sharpened his thinking!

During this crusade **Graham** asked Castro to lead in prayer and **referred to his as "my great friend Castro."**[376] This is a man who believes that the God of the Buddhist is the same as our God[377] and who "said it was very possible that man came from a monkey."[378]

Just two weeks **before** Graham's crusade in Montevideo, **Castro** was on a panel discussion on TV where he **kept excusing abortion,** yet the **following week** Castro was once again on TV—this time **announcing the Billy Graham Crusade!** Castro was greatly rewarded by receiving **40%** of all the decision cards turned in![379] This was way back in **1962!**

Furthermore, we've seen some of Castro's beliefs on Communism, yet in 1953 Graham declared: "The matter of Communists among the clergy has largely been greatly exaggerated. All of this talk of Communism in the church is undermining the confidence and faith of the people of the church. While there may be some left-wing sympathizers, **I do not personally know any Communist sympathizer in the ranks of the clergy."**[380]

> "In the February, 1986 issue of THE NORTH INDIA CHURCHMAN, the World Council's declaration made at Zimbabwe was published. On the cover of that issue of the CNI's periodical was a photo of a 'worship' service held during the Zimbabwe meetings. In the photo **Emilio Castro,** head of

the WCC, is seen in the foreground, with members of the consultation in the background, their arms held in the air and **fists clenched in the traditional salute of international communism.** The caption under the photo says, 'Behind Emilio Castro, General Secretary, WCC, members of the South African delegation raising their fists in solidarity with the suffering black people in South Africa....'"[381]

NELSON MANDELA

Nelson Mandela is another person who uses the **clenched fist.**[382]

> "The media fails to tell us that Mandela's **clenched-fist salute is the symbol of international communism.** From media reports, one would gather that this salute is some kind of harmless, chic image! Rather, it is the proud symbol of international communism, the same philosophy which is responsible for countless millions of murders and abominations against mankind. The **clenched-fist salute** is the salute of the Castros, of the Lenins, of the Stalins, of the Maoists, and of the butchers of North Korea. This is Mandela's crowd."[383]

Another meeting was convened in Zimbabwe in February 1990 (less than a week after Nelson Mandela was released from prison) by the World Council of Churches. At this meeting Emilio

> "Castro described the subsequent release of Mandela as 'yet another act of courage' by the South African president....his release is a significant achievement."[384] In fact, "the call for Mandela's unconditional release has been a critical aspect of the WCC's strategy of 'mass mobilization against apartheid,' said Castro...."[385]

> "In a letter inviting Mandela to visit WCC headquarters in Geneva, Castro expressed gratitude to God, 'who has called you to this moment and to this task—of negotiating the end of apartheid in order to bring to fruition the hopes of a new democratic and non-racial South Africa.'"[386]

Mandela also spoke at the 50th anniversary of the World Council of Churches in Zimbabwe in December 1998.[387]

Who is this **Nelson Mandela** that the World Council of Churches has called for his release from prison and who has been their speaker?[388] For one thing, he is **not** a political prisoner as has been reported but he is a **convicted terrorist.**[389] "When he was arrested in 1962 at a farm in South Africa, police found 210,000 hand-grenades, 48,000 land mines, 50 tons of high explosives, the plans of 107 buildings and installations to be blown up, and a hand-written document entitled 'How To Be a Good Communist.'"[390]

After he was released from serving a 27 year sentence, his first public speech was in Capetown, South Africa, where the balcony

> "was draped with a flag bearing the **communist symbol of the hammer and the sickle.** He repeatedly referred to his fellow ANC [African National Congress] members as 'comrades' and he praised the South African Communist Party and the memory of the 'great Communists' he said would be cherished for years to come."[391]

It is interesting to note that this Communist credits Maitreya, the New Age "Christ," for helping him to be released from prison![392]

MANDELA—"THE NEW CHRIST"

In Mandela's document, *How to Be a Good Communist,* he states:

> "We Communist Party members are the most advanced revolutionaries in modern history and are the contemporary fighting and driving force in changing society and the world.... The people of South Africa, led by the South African Communist Party, will **destroy capitalism and build in its place socialism.** The **transition from capitalism to socialism** and the liberation of the working class cannot be affected by slow changes or by reforms, as reactionaries and liberals often advise, but by **revolution.** One must, therefore, be a revolutionary and not a reformist."[393]

Shortly after Mandela's release, one writer noted:

> "In recent weeks we have seen Nelson Mandela called 'a cold-blooded communist killer,' an 'unrepentant adulterer' who left his first wife and children, an 'unrepentant terrorist,' a 'hard-line communist' and a 'Marxist' who refuses to renounce violence.
>
> "**Mandela,** in his own handwriting, in a document at his 1964 trial for sabotage and treason, **called himself a communist** and revolutionary....Over half of his ANC's ruling council are communist party (SACP) members. Yet this man was accorded a hero's welcome in his 8-city tour of the U. S. He was honored by City Councils, praised by mayors, received by our President and addressed the UN and our Congress....
>
> "Our **National Council of Churches** gave him $200,000 to 'be used for the glorification of humanity.'...
>
> "The NCC president said: 'We are committed to being with you, Mr. Mandela....' WCC head **Emilio Castro** praised him

> as a man 'who happens to love democracy.'...The WCC has funded the ANC. **At Riverside Church** [Rockefellers' church], Mandela was called 'God's servant,' the 'moral leader of the world,' 'our bright and morning star' and 'the black pope.'
>
> "But 'the Rev.' Jesse Jackson's praise of this comrade of Arafat, Qaddafi and Castro topped all this blasphemy. He called Mandela 'the new Christ.' He compared his prison 'witness' to the Apostle John's Patmos vision; his faith and courage to Daniel and the three Hebrews; his release, to Jesus' resurrection; and his suffering to Isaiah 53's 'suffering servant.'"[394]

One big promoter of Mandela and his African National Congress (ANC) is none other than **David Rockefeller** who has been backing the ANC for more than a decade![395] In fact, one of Mandela's first stops in New York was to Rockefeller's **Riverside Church.**[396] (Another of his stops was a pilgrimage to the grave of **Martin Luther King, Jr.**[397]) On one of Mandela's recent trips to the US, "he called several times for **'a new world order'** and advocated a combined religion consisting of "Christians, Jews, Moslems, Hindus and even Animists."[398]

WCC FUNDS TERRORIST GROUP

Would you believe that between 1980 and 1985 the World Council of Churches had given $362,000 to the ANC which is headed by Nelson Mandela?[399] By 1992, the WCC had given the ANC over $1.3 million in grants.[400] This money was given "in spite of the fact that the ANC has a military arm which has openly and brazenly murdered hundreds of blacks in its terrorist movement to overthrow the nation's government. It is the ANC that uses the method of **'necklacing'** to burn to death those who oppose communist plans for South Africa."[401] "Necklacing has often been the preferred way of murder by ANC terrorists...."[402] Necklacing

> "is a hideous torture and terror method devised by the ANC communists in which an automobile tire filled with gasoline or diesel is placed around the neck of the victim, whose hands have been either chopped off or wired behind their backs. The necklace is then set aflame, and, as the poor victim writhes in pain, the mob dances the toyi toyi and stabs, stones, and kicks him or her. The ANC is publicly on record, in their radio broadcasts and their literature, endorsing this barbaric practice. Over the last several years around a thousand black men, women, and young children even have suffered this horrible death at the hands of the ANC mobs."[403]

Mandela's former wife, Winnie, said: "Together, hand in hand with our boxes of matches and our necklaces, we shall liberate this country."[404]

> "On Oct. 24, 1993, the African National Congress (ANC) held a festival featuring 32 **witchdoctors** who called on the spirits of the ancestors to 'bless' Nelson Mandela, President of the ANC. This *kushisha impepho* ceremony, in order to be valid, requires a ritual with human blood and flesh. 'This is the reason for many of the ritual murders in which body parts are removed,' said reporter Ed Cain. 'The same is true for other forms of occultic practices and Satanic worship.'...Mandela has endorsed **Islam,** received communion from the **Roman Catholic** archbishop, and took part in a **Hindu** festival...."[405] [Italics in the original.]

The three people that Mandela admires are Yasser Arafat, Moammar Qaddafi, and Fidel Castro.[406] He remarked: "'During all my years in prison,' Cuba 'was an inspiration and comrade Fidel Castro a tower of strength.' 'There is one thing where that country (Cuba) stands out head and shoulders above the rest—that is in its love for human rights and liberty.'"[407]

In another speech he commented: "There are those who say to us, 'Why don't you renounce Castro?' Mandela said. 'No freedom fighter with integrity can desert friends who assisted him during the difficult times.'"[408] "Mandela also stated on the ABC network that 'Stalin, Lenin and Mao were the greatest leaders in history.'"[409] "Mandela...stated upon his release from prison, 'I salute the South African Communist Party for its sterling contribution to the struggle for democracy.'"[410]

After all that's been said about Mandela, can you believe that an article in ***Christianity Today* (Billy Graham's magazine) called Mandela a Christian?!**[411]

At Mandela's inauguration as President of South Africa on May 10, 1994, were such individuals as Hillary Clinton, Al and Tipper Gore, and **Fidel Castro.**[412] "Reportedly, the U. S. chipped in $35 million toward the festivities, a down payment on an initial $180 million to launch Mandela's regime."[413]

How does Billy Graham feel about Mandela? Graham himself has

> "said that Mandela's victory and the events surrounding the election 'are a testimony to us all of this great man's resiliency in the face of 27 years of imprisonment; his faith in his country; his ability to command the respect of the people of all races in that country; and the **ultimate triumph of good.'...**

> "He concluded, 'I offer President Mandela not only my heartfelt **congratulations** but also my prayers for his government, that it may be strong and just, that he will have wisdom from God as he champions this nation's efforts to bring equality to a nation that has suffered for many years under apartheid.'"[414]

Andrew Young (who was covered earlier) is the new President of the **National Council of Churches.** He was **"installed** Nov. 11 in the **Catholic** Cathedral of St. John the Evangelist in Cleveland."[415] He said that Mandela is "as close to being a saint as can be."[416]

The World Council of Churches has also given $85,000 to Marxist Robert Mugabe's Patriotic Front in Zimbabwe.[417] Joshua Nkomo (mentioned in Chapter 2) was also with this group.[418] "More than 600 farms have been under attack by government-backed squatters, who have murdered and beaten farmers and workers, set afire farm buildings and added to a national panic and economic crisis."[419] Mugabe has called these white farmers the "enemies of the state."[420] "According to *Time* and *Newsweek,* Mugabe's guerrillas murdered Catholic and Pentecostal missionaries as well as Rhodesians defending the former regime."[421]

In addition to the funding of Mugabe's organization by the World Council of Churches, we find that at the WCC's 50th anniversary, they "gave Mugabe a center stage and its leaders continued to applaud his government."[422] One of the speakers at this celebration was Julius Nyerere. He is a Communist and was the former President of Tanzania.[423]

PROGRAM TO COMBAT RACISM

Since 1970, the Program to Combat Racism, a program under the auspices of the WCC, "has distributed over $10 million to more than 130 organizations in some 30 countries—about half to revolutionary **Marxist** movements in Africa."[424]

Returning to other World, Federal, and National Council of Churches leaders, we find that Dr. John C. Bennett, a member of the NCC[425] and the WCC's Executive Committee, said the following about Red China:

> "We cannot use our usual moral standards in assessing Red China. It deserves our reverence rather than our condemnation. **Communism is to be seen as an instrument of modernization of national unification and increasing social welfare. Red China is the new savior for the poor nations of the earth."**[426]

The "NCC under the leadership of such men as Dr. John Bennett voted 90 to 3 in 1966 to encourage the United Nations to accept Red China, which had slaughtered so many innocent people."[427]

Bennett also said: "The tendency to consign non-Christians to eternal punishment is one of the worst abominations in Christian history."[428] Remember that Bennett was the former President of the Union **Theological** Seminary.

Eduard C. Lindeman is a member of the FCC's Commission on Research. He noted: **"The Christian religion is not a suitable religion for today."**[429] [Emphasis in the original.]

George Buttrick, a former President of the Federal Council of Churches (1940-1942),[430] remarked: "A God who punishes men with fire and brimstone through all Eternity would hardly be Godlike. He would be almost satanic in cruelty and childlike in imagination—like a nasty little boy pulling off the wings of a fly."[431]

In Buttrick's book, *Christian Fact and Modern Doubt,* he wrote:

> "The future is hidden. We must be faithful to our ignorance.... Jesus **apparently** conquered death....But **we do not know,** why pretend we do....We covet the chance to say to God hereafter, **if God there be;** Lord, they told us to grab the present gain, but there was more gain in staking life on a grand Perhaps."[432]

Buttrick believes that the Bible is full of contradictions and that "the story of Adam and Eve is a myth,...that the book of Daniel is a fraud,...[and] that Christ did not die to save sinners, that man is not a fallen creature who needs to be born again, that God did not require an atoning Saviour."[433]

Lesslie Newbigin was the first director of the Division of World Missions and Evangelism for the World Council of Churches.[434] Newbigin leaned toward the belief in universalism where all people will be saved.[435] Obviously, he believed that there is salvation in non-Christian religions.[436] In his book, *The Open Secret,* we find: "Christians then, in dealing with men and women who do not acknowledge Jesus as Lord, will meet them and share with them in a common life, not as strangers, but as those who live by the same life-giving Word, and in whom the same life-giving light shines."[437]

Newbigin also criticized capitalism,[438] yet in spite of Newbigin's unbiblical viewpoint, **Billy Graham** praised him at the NCC meeting in Miami in 1966.[439]

VIRGINIA RAMEY MOLLENKOTT

Since many in leadership positions of the FCC, NCC, and WCC don't believe the Bible, it's not hard to see why they have been instrumental in translating it to better fit their lifestyle and beliefs. One of these versions was the *Inclusive Language Lectionary* produced by the NCC which addresses **God in feminine terms.**[440] A New Age group called the Cosmic Study Center wrote:

> "Portrayal of a non-sexist deity by changing the language of the Bible from 'Father' to 'Mother and Father' in the *Inclusive Language Lectionary,* produced under the direction of the National Council of Churches, is **an important change** and the **prelude to further clarification** prophesied in The New Revelation by the Revelator Himself (1959) through William Ferguson."[441] [Underlining in the original.]

Virginia Ramey Mollenkott served on this committee[442] and was its editor.[443] She also "was a consultant for the *NIV* translating committee."[444] This "Bible" "has eliminated the most obviously genderized language for God: *Lord* becomes *Sovereign, Son of Man* becomes *the Human One,* and the references to God as *he* or *him* are eliminated by the repetition of the word *God.* "[445] [Italics in the original.]

Mollenkott is a self-professed **lesbian.**[446] She has held workshops for Kirkridge called "Gay, Lesbian and Christian"[447] as well as authored a book named *Sensuous Spirituality: Women, Men, and the Bible.*[448] This book tells of her **spirit guide** and her contact with her dead mother (which is necromancy). It also mentions her involvement with Tarot cards and the I Ching[449] (which is divination and forbidden by Deuteronomy 18:10-12).

She mentions her lesbianism and concludes that "in a very physical sense we are all gay, we are all lesbian, we are all heterosexual, we are all bisexual—because we are all one."[450] "Her view of the kingdom of God on earth is a society in which 'lesbian women, bisexual people, and gay men are going to be accepted as first-class citizens in the church and in society as a whole.'"[451]

In 1994 she published *The Divine Feminine: The Biblical Imagery of God as Female* (which is sold by the blatantly occultic bookstore, Samuel Weiser[452]). This book states: that "because God is woman-like—women are Godlike."[453] She also "suggests that 'the Lord's prayer might be addressed to Our Father/Mother who is in Heaven.'"[454]

MOLLENKOTT AND THE OCCULT

Another book she wrote is entitled *Is The Homosexual My Neighbor?*[455] In this book (co-authored with Letha Scanzoni) she openly "talks about her lesbianism and monistic beliefs in a **female God.**"[456]

> "The book argues that the Sodom account in Genesis does not teach the evil of homosexuality, but the evils of violent gang rape and inhospitality to strangers. The book also claims

> that 'the idea of a life long homosexual orientation or "condition" is never mentioned in the Bible'...and that Romans 1 does not 'fit the case of a sincere homosexual Christian.'"[457]

Sadly, this book "received **favorable reviews** in ***Christianity Today*** [Billy Graham's magazine], *The Christian Century, The Journal of the Evangelical Theological Society,* and *The Christian Ministry.*"[458] As late as 1992, *Christianity Today* referred to Mollenkott as an **"evangelical** author"![459] Remember, that **PRIOR** to this date, Mollenkott was

> "'born again' into a new spiritual freedom using I Ching (pagan Chinese divination), Tarot Cards and the study of the New Age text, *A Course in Miracles.* She calls her experience of enlightenment both a coming out from fundamentalism, and 'one distinct "holy instant" (a notion taken from the *A Course in Miracles,* as she admits)...like my Elder Brother, Jesus, I am a sinless Self travelling through eternity and temporarily having human experiences in a body known as Virginia Ramey Mollenkott....Perhaps my Self has been on earth before in other bodies [reincarnation], perhaps not.'"[460]

Mollenkott's involvement with the homosexual and lesbian movement goes back to at least 1979 when she attended a conference at the largely gay Universal Fellowship of Metropolitan Community Church. "In a report which was published by the *Christian Century,* September 26, 1979, Mollenkott stated, 'This was the most grateful celebration of Christ I had ever attended....'"[461]

In 1985 she openly admitted that she was a lesbian. "In October of that year, her signature appeared on a statement supporting homosexuality which was published in the *Sojourners* magazine."[462]

> "In 1987 Mollenkott wrote an article claiming that refusal to ordain homosexual 'clergywomen' is unscriptural discrimination. She wrote: 'To ask lesbians and gay men to pretend they are like the majority is to deny the self-identification and affirmation that is the natural legacy of every healthy adult. Forcing gay Christians into silence also denies them the opportunity to celebrate in gratitude to God for their authentic nature and for their life-enriching mutual relationship with a loving partner.'"[463]

In June 1991 she stated: "My lesbianism has always been a part of me....I tried to be heterosexual. I married myself off. But what I did ultimately realize was that God created me as I was, and that this is where life was meaningful."[464] The first time **she publicly admitted**

that she was a lesbian was before none other than the Governing Board of the National Council of Churches![465]

Yet the very next year (1992) *Christianity Today* tried to convince us that Mollenkott is an evangelical!!

When TV's *Ellen* announced her lesbianism, Mollenkott said:

> "I came of age in the 1940's and 1950s, discovering my own sexuality at a time when only negative information was available to me....I was one of the many gay teenagers who have attempted suicide because we cannot fit in—one of those to whom Ellen dedicated her dual coming-out. When the show ended, I sat thinking about the parties...all over the country...I thought of the many gay women and men celebrating perhaps the most public affirmation we had ever received."[466]

Just last year she signed a declaration called the "Religious Declaration on Sexual Morality, Justice, and Healing" (which was briefly covered in the last chapter) sponsored by SIECUS "calling for same-sex unions, ordination of homosexuals and abortion rights."[467]

MOLLENKOTT AND THE NIV

Since Mollenkott is so vocal about her lesbianism, it's no surprise to find that the *New International Version (NIV)* for which she was a stylist,[468] reflects her bias. I'll list just a few examples. Deuteronomy 23:17 warns: "There shall be no whore of the daughters of Israel, nor a **sodomite** of the sons of Israel." The *NIV* changes this to: "No Israelite man or woman is to become a **shrine prostitute."** I Kings 14:24 reads: "And there were **sodomites** in the land...." The *NIV* states: "There were even **male shrine prostitutes** in the land...."

The *NIV* goes so far as to condemn to hell those who call out **against** homosexual behavior. In the *King James Version (KJV)* in I Corinthians 6:9 we find: "Know ye not that the unrighteous shall not inherit the kingdom of God? Be not deceived: neither fornicators, nor idolaters, nor adulterers, nor effeminate, nor abusers of themselves with mankind?" This verse tells us that the effeminate (or homosexuals) cannot enter heaven, but the *NIV* declares: "Do you not know that the wicked will not inherit the kingdom of God? Do not be deceived: neither the sexually immoral nor idolators nor adulterers nor male prostitutes nor **homosexual offenders...."** Did you catch that? Those who OFFEND the homosexuals ("homosexual offenders") are the ones who cannot enter heaven! That's the Christians who are barred from heaven—at least according to the *NIV.*

Mollenkott is pro-abortion and promotes adultery.[469] Mollenkott also claims that **Jesus was a woman.**[470] In fact, during "a news conference at the National Council of Churches' governing board, she said, 'You might be interested to know that...Jesus remained chromosomally female throughout life.'"[471]

"GOD HERSELF"

At the 1993 ReImagining Conference (covered in the last chapter) where Mollenkott was one of the speakers,[472] she said that "Women would worship **'god herself,'** give 'honor to every world religion,' and agree that 'everything that lives is holy.'"[473] She "claimed that **Jesus' death was the ultimate in child abuse** and a model for human child abuse. 'As an incest survivor, I can no longer worship in a theological context that depicts **God as an abusive parent** and Jesus as the obedient, trusting child,' she declared."[474]

A speech given to the International CLOUT Gathering (Christian Lesbians Out Together) by Mollenkott was entitled "Whore-ishly Implementing the Political Vision of the Christ-Sophia." She stated: "We are the whores of Jesus the Christ-Sophia's place and time; and Jesus received us, depended upon our assistance, and broke bread with us."[475]

In 1998, former General Secretary[476] and WCC President,[477] Konrad Raiser, had "urged acceptance of the homosexual agenda at [the] conference in Amsterdam, a center of homosexuality...."[478] Raiser, incidentally, is also supportive of the Program to Combat Racism which gives millions of dollars to Communist and violent groups.[479]

Regarding other religions, he remarked: "We as Christians have to be humble and listen to the wisdom of eastern religions, especially Buddhism, which has had much to say on peace and non-violence."[480] He was also a signer of "A Universal Declaration of Human Responsibilities."[481]

> "[Raiser] warns against aggressive evangelism by missionaries and says they ought to focus instead on 'being agents of reconciliation.'
>
> "Aggressively seeking conversions to Jesus Christ, Raiser said,...has led to conflicts between Christians and Muslims and people of other faiths."[482]

Raiser wants to continue the ecumenical dialogue with the Roman Catholic Church but he added that "the WCC does not agree with the pope on moral issues such as abortion and euthanasia...." "In April 1996, Raiser met with Pope John Paul II at the Vatican and said a 'fresh spirit' exists between the WCC and the Roman Catholic Church."[483]

Dr. Eugene Stockwell was the associate general secretary for overseas ministries with the NCC[484] and the chairman of the WCC's Commission on World Mission and Evangelism.[485] In 1989, at the WCC's World Conference on Mission and Evangelism in San Antonio, Texas, where he gave the keynote address, "Stockwell was rejoicing in the fact that, for the first time, **religious leaders from several religions were present as consultants, not visitors. These included Two Hindus, Two Muslims, Two Jews, A Buddhist, A Sikh, A Jain, and Three People of Traditional Religions."**[486] [Emphasis in the original.] He believes that people from non-Christians religions will receive eternal life. His response to the question "Is Christ the Only Way?" was: "No, **Jesus is not the only way,** if that is taken to mean that all who do not name the name of Jesus have lost the way, have no passport to heaven."[487] He adds that

> "Muslim, Buddhist, Hindus, Jews, Zoroastrians, Jains etc.,...are not created by another God than the one we worship. They are our sisters and brothers, flesh of our flesh, life of our life. Time and time again they espouse great ideals and live by them, something we Christians often fail to do."

IS JESUS THE ONLY WAY?

S. Wesley Ariarajah is a director of the WCC.[488] He, too, answered the question "Is Jesus the Only Way?" His reply was:

> "Jesus makes no claims to divinity or to oneness with God. He does not suggest himself to be a meditator, much less the only mediator between God and men. Thus, can a Christian turn around and say to the Buddhist that he or she is misguided?...We have no grounds to do so."[489]

The Bible clearly teaches that Jesus was God. John 10:30 says: "I and My Father are one." After Jesus said this, the Jews were ready to stone Him. The reason they gave was that they were going to stone Him for "blasphemy; and because that Thou, being a man, makest Thyself God" (John 10:33). They obviously understood Jesus' statement to mean that He was God but Ariarajah asserts that "Jesus makes no claims to divinity or to oneness with God."

Paul tells us in I Timothy 2:5 that "there is one God, and **one mediator** between God and men, the man **Christ Jesus."** Jesus Himself also said: **"I am the way,** the truth, and the life: **no man cometh unto the Father, but by Me"** (John 14:6).

Since Ariarajah doesn't accept Jesus as the only way, it's no surprise to see that he has signed the "Declaration of World

Thanksgiving"[490] and that he was "especially interested" in a "United Religions" organization.[491]

At the 1998 WCC meeting in Harare, Zimbabwe, "an Anglican priest told the group that one of the young people in his church, whom he had trained 25 years ago is now a Buddhist monk. 'I am delighted that one of my parishioners became a Buddhist. That shows that he is growing,' he declared."[492]

There was also a meeting place for discussion on gay and lesbian issues. The session "was led by two homosexual leaders who summarized their research on sexual orientation, recounted a sexual orientation history from the homosexual point of view, and divided the participants into small groups to share their gay/lesbian experiences."[493] One of the booths set up at the WCC defended and promoted lesbianism.[494]

A Bible study booklet, used as a guideline for the participants, was given to everyone in attendance.

> "One chapter was titled 'We May Be Called Dogs But....' Its setting is an imaginary discussion that Jesus had with six women, one of whom was the Syrophenician woman who had a daughter with great needs. This **woman rebuked Jesus** and said that she felt sad and ashamed after Jesus said 'It is not meet to take the children's bread and cast it unto the dogs.' She asked Jesus, 'Why did you call me a dog?' According to the author of the Study Guide, **Jesus responded, 'I am sorry** I said that. I was brought up in such a discriminatory society I used that kind of language without thinking. I am a man and because of my privilege **I did not realize how insulting was my comment.** But I was afraid. I had to be careful of the powerful religious leaders, the priests, the scribes and Pharisees who wanted to find fault and judge me. So I had to watch what I said.' **He then apologized for abusing this Syrophenician woman."**[495]

The booklet also had **Jesus saying** to the woman: **"I repent of my indifference, my weakness, my fear, my pride, my unkind behavior and my exclusive language in front of you. Thank you for teaching me."**[496]

> "The WCC refused to criticize homosexuality and the Zimbabwean government did decide to allow into their country WCC delegates who were part of the Gay and Lesbian Organizations. But the discussion about this continued to come to the surface. At a press conference, Dr. Kosuke Koyama, a leader of the WCC's Faith and Order Commission, and also a

> **professor at Union Theological Seminary** in New York, was questioned by one of the young ladies who was present. Identifying herself as a student at Union Theological Seminary, she challenged the professor regarding his failure to chastise the 'sin of heterosexuality which made me feel out of place as a lesbian.' The response from those participating at the press conference was that 'sexual preference is part of one's identity.' Dr. Koyama later revealed that **he had at least 15 homosexuals in his classes at Union Theological Seminary!"**[497]

"When some WCC leaders were asked to define 'sin,' the answers were, 'discrimination against lesbians is sin,' and 'racism is a sin,' but nothing of the definition God gives in His Word was ever offered."[498]

In the Spring 2001 issue of *CLOUTreach* (standing for "Christian Lesbians OUT), we see that Mab Segrest is a lesbian and a founding director of North Carolinians Against Racist and Religious Violence. Oh, she also "served as coordinator of the Urban-Rural Mission, a program of the **World Council of Churches."**[499]

ONGOING REVELATION

Marga Buhrig was involved in the **feminist** movement as well as one of the co-presidents of the World Council of Churches.[500] She said that most male theologians "are afraid to admit that the Bible might not be the only source of revelation—that there is also an ongoing revelation. They are afraid of women claiming their power."[501] She also brags:

> "In recent years, I've grown more focused on bringing together the questions of women and minorities with gay and lesbian concerns, refugee concerns, peace concerns—I'm a member of Women for Peace in Switzerland. These questions all belong together. We must always try to make connections between the different areas where oppression takes place."[502]

At one forum where the focus was on women, Buhrig was one of the women who was honored, along with Faye Wattleton (former President of Planned Parenthood[503] and 1986 "Humanist of the Year"[504]), Jane Goodall, Marian Wright Edelman (who is active in the National and World Council of Churches,[505] the ACLU,[506] the Student Nonviolent Coordination Committee,[507] former Director of the Americans for Democratic Action,[508] a CFR member,[509] plenary speaker at Gorbachev's 1996 State of the World Forum,[510] signer of the Cry for Renewal document,[511] and President of the leftist Children's Defense Fund[512] and whose son is a Rhodes Scholar[513]), etc.[514]

"Each participant and media representative at the Forum was given a **charm** called 'Women's Night Dance' with a cord to thread it on and hang around one's neck. **The pendant showed a circle of female witches dancing naked in the moonlight** —'a primal symbol of female energy,' according to the attached card. 'The moon is female and Her phases echo the phases of life. The Stars are also female, as is the Night itself. A women's ceremony, acted out under the Sky's protective energy, is still an important way to summon the primordial energy of feminine power.'"[515]

In 1984 the WCC, Lutheran World Federation, World Student Christian Federation, and the World Young Women's Christian Association (YWCA) jointly published a book called *No Longer Strangers.* The book contains poems which repeatedly refer to God as a woman. For instance, in "Blessing the Bread," we find:

"In the beginning was God
"In the beginning, the source of all that is
"In the beginning, God yearning
"God, moaning
"God, labouring
"God, rejoicing
"And God loved what **SHE** had made
"And God said, 'It is good.'"[516]

In "I Believe," reference is made to the "Mother-Father Spirit." God is again mentioned in the feminine sense where God is called "Baker**woman.**"[517]

In 1995 there was a UN World Conference and NGO Forum on Women held in Beijing.[518] This

"Conference outlined a pseudosexuality in which men were portrayed as villains, patriarchy (including biblical male headship) assaulted in seminar after seminar, lesbian rights pushed with no official resistance, and access to abortion and birth control promoted with zeal.

"The writing of the platform document for the Conference was supervised by former U. S. member of Congress Bella Abzug. An archfeminist, Abzug also led a workshop in Beijing which was observed by a reporter from the *Washington Times*: 'Mrs. Abzug, in one of the more than 350 workshops on the second day of the forum, joined hands with other women in a prayer tribute to "Mother Earth" that mocked orthodox Christian belief. "Give thanks for the fruits of life," said a Brazilian delegate who led the group in prayer. "Thanks to Mother Earth, for you give life. Thanks for water. People from

> my community decided no more Crucifixion. We believe in life. We celebrate life, not the Crucifixion. We are power." Mrs. Abzug and several dozen women holding hands then thrust their hands into the air, chanting, "I am power. I am power. I am power.""""[519]

Workshops for the Beijing Conference included "Lesbianism for the Curious," "Spirit and Action: Lesbian Activism from an Interfaith Perspective," "Lesbian Flirtation Techniques," and "Beyond the Trinity Creator."[520] Another seminar was "Women, Religion, and Culture." This seminar was

> "on how to fight fundamentalism, [and] labeled Christianity 'imperialistic, patriarchal, colonialist, capitalistic, egocentric, racial, and homophobic.' The leader of the **WCC (World Council of Churches) seminar** added, 'This is a religion so corrupted I call it religious fundamentalism.'"[521]

> "A Presbyterian (USA) staffer at a workshop **sponsored by the WCC** claimed that 'messages from the Bible, from church tradition, and authorities helped to perpetuate and justify domestic violence, incest, child abuse, and sexual exploitation of girls and women by clergy.' She suggested that 'any element of Christian tradition that denies the full humanity of women *must be discarded,* ignored, or transformed.'"[522] [Italics in the original.]

At a recent session of the United Nations General Assembly in Geneva, Esther Camac Ramirez, a member of the **ecumenical** team of the **World Council of Churches,** included **polytheism** and "Mother Earth" in her speech.[523] She said: "For us, the world is a place where **gods,** sacred places, big rocks, great rivers, mountains, plants and animals are to be found. This is where the sun rises, with the solar rays fertilizing the Earth so that she can give life."[524]

> "Our re-encounter with Mother Earth is central to our identity, it helps us formulate the concepts of autonomy and self-sufficiency in relation to nature and the cosmos....we affirm that this balance starts at home,...and in our belief that our Mother Earth is a woman who gave birth to us, and from whom we receive the gift of life....And nature belongs to the **gods....**"[525]

JOHN BRADEMAS

John Brademas was a member of the Central Committee of the WCC.[526] He was also a Mason,[527] Rhodes Scholar,[528] CFR member,[529] Trilateralist,[530] Bilderberger,[531] "chairman of the board of directors of the Rockefeller Foundation and the Aspen Institute for Humanistic Studies. Additionally, he was President of New York University, a member of the Federal Reserve, and a trustee of the Committee for Economic Development (CED)."[532]

One official of the NCC was **Arthur S. Flemming.** He was a former Secretary of the Department of Health, Education and Welfare (HEW). He was also an active council member of Planned Parenthood and a member of the Population Crisis Committee. "Both of these organizations are Humanist-dominated and are working for eventual world **population control....**It is also noteworthy that Flemming is a recipient of the Alexander Meiklejohn Award for Academic Freedom, which is named in honor of a prominent Humanist of an earlier day."[533]

After a

> "lobbying effort by Planned Parenthood, the Committee on Marriage and the Home of the **Federal Council of Churches**—a precursor to the National Council [of Churches]—became the **first major ecclesiastical institution in the history of Christendom to affirm the language, philosophy, and ethical methodology of 'choice.'**"[534]

What does **Billy Graham** think about Arthur Flemming? He had him on his platform "for **honor** and Christian recognition as" a leader "worthy of trust and confidence"![535]

ANOTHER COMMUNIST FRONT

Dr. Stanley Stuber "has done extensive public relations work for the National Council of Churches....He is a member of the United Nations Association of the U. S. A., and has been affiliated with at least six organizations cited by agencies of the federal government as either 'Communist' or 'Communist fronts.'"[536]

The Director of International Affairs for the WCC is Dr. Nina Koshy. She, too, advocates Communism when she states:

> "To a large number of Christians in all parts of the world, the social and political **message of Marxism has been** a challenge and even **inspiration....**This has also led to active collaboration between Christians and Marxists in liberation movements, in struggles for peace and justice in revolutionary situations and in building socialism together."[537]

One author explains about this "collaboration between Christians and Marxists." He writes that the collaboration

> "was formalized by the 1988 visit of Konstantin Kharchev to the World Council of Churches headquarters in Switzerland. Kharchev was chairman of the State Council for Religious

Affairs in the Council of Ministers of the USSR. He met with the general secretaries and top staff of the World Council of Churches, World Alliance of Reformed Churches and the Lutheran World Federation.

"Kharchev as the top religious official in the Soviet Union told the assembled church leaders that while he disagrees with the belief that God exists, 'I respect and must respect the other point of views.'

"After giving a glowing report about new freedoms for religion under 'perestroika,' Kharchev then noted that...

"...the arrival of 'full communism' will mean an end to religion, but such a day is far off. **For now and the foreseeable future, Communists and religious believers need to live in mutual respect and build a good life for people together on earth.**

"The World Council of Churches response to this official reaffirmation that communism will eventually abolish all religion was to go to Moscow for its July 1989 Central Committee meeting."[538]

"The FBI report identified the Christian Peace Conference as a **Communist** front whose president is Karoly Toth of communist Hungary, also a member of the Central Committee of the World Council of Churches. **The communists have their men** in these top key places to **pose as fine Christians** and thus **deceive** those with whom they affiliate."[539]

GRAHAM SETTLES FOR MAO'S PRINCIPLES

"A 1972 WCC 'Salvation Today' Conference in Bangkok published a series of essays by such **Marxist** authors as Julius Nyerere, Roger Garaudy and Ignazio Silone. One essay told how to substitute Mao's *Little Red Book* for the Bible."[540] This essay reminds me somewhat of a quotation from Billy Graham which appeared in a Tokyo newspaper.

"In the May 28, 1973, *Mainichi Daily News,* published in Tokyo, Graham declared, 'I think communism's appeal to youth is its structure and promise of a future utopia. **Mao Tse-tung's eight precepts are basically the same as the Ten Commandments.** In fact, if we can't have the Ten Commandments read in our schools, **I'll settle for Mao's precepts.'"**[541]

Read this paragraph again and remember that these are **Graham's OWN WORDS!**

> "When news of Graham's statements got back to the United States press, which carried it from coast to coast, a storm of protest arose across America in regard to Graham's equating the Ten Commandments with Communist China's leader Mao Tse-tung's eight precepts.
>
> "When Graham attempted to deny that he had said exactly this to Maureen D'Honau during their interview, Miss D'Honau promptly replied that **Graham had said EXACTLY that** and her notes said that **THIS WAS A DIRECT QUOTATION FROM HIM."**[542]

Claude C. Williams, another **Federal Council of Churches** member as well as a Communist Party member and the Director of the People's Institute of Applied Religion, said: "Denominationally, I am a Presbyterian; religiously a Unitarian; and politically, **I'm a Communist.** I'm not preaching to make people good or anything of the sort. **I'm in the church because I can reach people easier that way and get them organized for Communism."**[543]

Another FCC member, Jerome Davis, asked: "Is it not probable that the greatest event of the 20th Century thus far is the Soviet Revolution and all it has meant to human welfare?"[544]

Dr. Ernest Lefever was the former Associate Director of the NCC and he attended the founding meeting of the WCC in 1948. He was involved with the Maryland Values Education Commission and has "a lengthy history of activity in **Leftist** causes...."[545]

> "His long career has included stints as research associate in the School of Advanced International Studies of Johns Hopkins University; as an instructor in political science at Maryland University; as consultant on foreign relations to the United States Senator Hubert Humphrey in 1959-1960; consultant to the **leftist**-oriented Council on Religion and International Affairs from 1958 to 1963; since 1964 as a research analyst for the Foreign Policy Division of the Brookings Institution; as a consultant to President John F. Kennedy's Task Force on Arms Control; and as a consultant to the International Affairs Division of the **leftist**-oriented Ford Foundation!"[546]

He was also the Director of the Ethics and Public Policy Center at Georgetown University.[547]

Joe Agne is the former Racial Justice Program Director for the National Council of Churches and an outreach coordinator for *Sojourners.* In a 1996 article in *The Witness,*[548] he referred to himself and others as "We on the **Left...."**[549]

"The socialist message of the NCC was emphasized even more in May, 1972, when a religious **ecumenical** assembly of 400 Americans met as the **'Christians for Socialism.'** The May 4th edition of the *New York Times,* said that the newly organized group called for the purpose of achieving socialism throughout Latin America (since) socialism appears to be the only acceptable alternative for bringing an end to the exploitation of the class society."[550]

Is it any wonder that at "the NCC convention in Miami in 1972, 72% of the delegates **did not** believe in the Virgin Birth"?[551]

EUGENE CARSON BLAKE

Dr. **Eugene Carson Blake,** former General Secretary,[552] former delegate and President[553] of the WCC,[554] as well as a former President of the NCC from 1954 to 1957,[555] has participated in the World Conference on Religion and Peace (WCRP) as well as giving the inaugural address at the Second Spiritual Summit Conference organized by the **Temple of Understanding.**[556] His speech was well received by the **pagans** in attendance. In fact,

"Sir Muhammad Zafrulla Khan, President of the International Court of Justice at the Hague, ex Foreign Minister of Pakistan and President of the 17th Session of the UN, said, 'Dr. Blake did not stress any single value which I, as a Muslim, could not wholly and eagerly embrace and endorse....'"[557]

Blake was a former judge for the **Templeton Prize for Progress in Religion** (which was covered earlier).[558] Blake also belonged to the **Planetary Citizens.**[559] This is a New Age organization. Some people on the board of Planetary Citizens are also listed on the letterhead of the World Government of World Citizens. This group has an application form to register to be a WORLD CITIZEN. They write in a letter accompanying the registration form, that they issue WORLD passports, WORLD identity cards, WORLD citizen cards, and WORLD birth certificates.[560] Also included is the "Credo of a World Citizen." The "Pledge of Allegiance," to which the applicant affixes his signature, says, in part:

"I, the undersigned, do hereby, willingly and consciously, declare myself to be a Citizen of the World. As a WORLD CITIZEN, I pledge my planetary civic commitment to WORLD GOVERNMENT, founded on three universal principles of One Absolute Value, One World, and One Humanity, which constitute the basis of WORLD LAW. As a WORLD CITIZEN I acknowledge the WORLD GOVERNMENT as having the right and duty to represent me...."[561]

A letter from Planetary Citizens reveals that it

> "was founded in 1974 by **Norman Cousins, U Thant** and **Donald Keys,** to assist in stimulating global awareness and a conscious identification with humanity as a whole, as stated in **its motto, 'ONE EARTH, ONE HUMANITY, ONE DESTINY.'** The organization was predicated on the realization that adjustment of international relations and the achievement of global peace would require, above all else, emergence of a 'global patriotism' or a sense of belonging to the human family, and the **embrace** of all its parts and **diversity."**[562]

As any Christian knows, not everyone will have the same destiny. Our destiny depends on our relationship with Christ. If we are saved, our destiny will be heaven. If we are not saved then our destiny is hell.

In Planetary Citizen U Thant's address to the World Association of World Federalists, he mentioned *"world citizens as they work steadfastly to usher in the new world order."*[563] [Emphasis in the original.] U Thant wrote that **Lenin's "ideals** of peace and peaceful coexistence among states have won widespread international acceptance and they **are in line with the aims of the United Nations Charter...."**[564]

LUCIFERIC INITIATION

Also of note is that David Spangler, a well-known New Ager, is a leading figure in the Planetary Citizens.[565] He wrote:

> "**LUCIFER** works within each of us to bring us to wholeness, and as we move into a **NEW AGE,** which is the age of man's wholeness, each of us in some way is brought to that point which I term the **LUCIFERIC INITIATION,** the particular doorway through which the individual **MUST PASS IF** he is to come 'fully' into the presence of his light and his wholeness."[566]

He adds: **"LUCIFER came to give us the final gift of wholeness.** If we accept it then he is free and we are free. That is the **LUCIFERIC INITIATION.** It is one that many people now, and in the days ahead will be facing, for **it is an initiation into the NEW AGE."**[567]

The Bible foretold that the time would come when the Antichrist will cause "all, both small and great, rich and poor, free and bond, to receive a mark in their right hand, or in their foreheads: And that NO MAN might BUY OR SELL, save [except] he that had the mark, or the name of the beast, or the number of his name....and his number is six hundred threescore and six [666]" (Revelation 13:16-18).

There is one major problem about taking this **"LUCIFERIC INITIATION"**—the Bible tells us that **ANYONE** who receives this "mark of the beast" is doomed (Revelation 14:9-11). By accepting the mark of the beast you will literally make your choice to worship Satan (Lucifer) rather than God. You will be saying a final "NO" to God and a "YES" to Satan.

Yet this is the kind of organization and people that **Eugene Carson Blake** is willing to be associated with! One author notes:

> **"One of the most blasphemous ecumenicists** in the Presbyterian Church was then pastor at the Pasadena Presbyterian Church. Dr. **Eugene Carson Blake** was one of the Presbyterian General Assembly. He was to be the author of the apostate Confession of 1967 which replaced the Westminster Confession of Faith."[568]

Blake "was co-conspirator, with the unbelieving Episcopal Bishop **James Pike,** of the Blake-Pike church merger proposals."[569]

> "In a 1960 sermon in Grace Cathedral in San Francisco, Mr. Blake called for a reunion of American Protestant bodies. The call developed into the Consultation on Church Union, an effort by 10 U. S. Protestant church bodies to form a united church. 'I don't believe it is God's will to have so many churches in the United States,' he said.
>
> "The late Rt. Rev. James E. Pike, who at that time was bishop of the Episcopal Diocese of California, called Mr. Blake's plan 'the most sound and inspiring proposal for unity of the church' ever enunciated in the United States."[570]

"'The **tent should be spread <u>as broad as possible</u>,'** he said. 'It is the key to the ultimate purpose of the churches—not to make people **sectarian,** but to try to make them Christian.'"[571]

"He was a notable apologist for Russia."[572] No wonder Blake was the recipient of the Lenin Peace Prize![573]

Blake also "views the Socialist experiment in Chile as a sign of encouragement and stimulus to many other countries who share similar difficulties and similar hopes,"[574] reported the World Council of Churches in 1971. Allende is a Marxist who "has pledged to transform Chile into a socialist state."[575]

"Mr. Blake was credited with bringing thousands of white Christians into the **civil rights** movement and helping to change the attitudes of white churchgoers toward the efforts of the **Rev. Martin Luther King Jr."**[576]

In 1974 the National Council of Churches launched a U. S. Bicentennial initiative.

> "Among the initial sponsors of the program, using the Bicentennial as an excuse to promote liberal **ecumenicity,** were: **Mrs. Martin Luther King, Jr.;** liberal editor **Norman Cousins;** Rev. W. Sterling Cary, black President of the National Council of Churches; Vernon Jordan, Director of the National Urban League; **Dr. Eugene Carson Blake,** radical modernist and retired General Secretary of the World Council of Churches; and evangelist **BILLY GRAHAM.**"[577]

Norman Cousins (mentioned in the last paragraph) was an evolutionist who endorsed all kinds of mind control techniques, including transcendental meditation. He was also a humanist.[578] As already mentioned, he co-founded the **Planetary Citizens.**[579] Additionally he was a member of the American Civil Liberties Union,[580] Council on Foreign Relations,[581] Club of Rome,[582] People for the American Way,[583] Population Crisis Committee,[584] Planetary Initiative for the World We Choose,[585] Americans United for World Government,[586] World Council of Wise Persons,[587] the co-founder of United World Federalists,[588] former President of the World Association of World Federalists,[589] and former President of the World Federalist Association.[590]

Cousins stated: "World government is coming, in fact, it is inevitable. No arguments for or against it can change that fact."[591] He also remarked that *"humanity needs a world order. The fully sovereign nation is incapable of dealing with the poisoning of the environment....The management of the planet, therefore...requires a world-government."*[592] [Emphasis in the original.]

This is the kind of person (along with **Billy Graham, Mrs. Martin Luther King, and Eugene Carson Blake),** who sponsored the NCC's Bicentennial program!

WILLEM VISSER 'T HOOFT

Another WCC leader is Dr. Willem Visser 'T Hooft who is known as the "father of the World Council of Churches."[593] He was the first General Secretary of the WCC (1948) and held this position until 1966.[594] He "declared that the **Communist** social principle, 'From each according to his ability, to each according to his need,' *has its roots in the teaching of Jesus."*[595] [Emphasis in the original.] Of course, this phrase is not found in the teachings of Jesus.

Visser 'T Hooft

> *"emphasizes the fact that today the ancient religions of the Buddhists, Muslims, Hindus, Jews, and others are continuing*

to influence religious thought and must be included—even along with pagans—in any conversations about the spiritual well-being of man. All religious and ideological families must learn that they cannot serve the world as long as they persist in their own monologue about their pious wishes for the future of society."[596] [Emphasis in the original.]

In the September 9, 1964 issue of *Christian Century,* Visser 'T Hooft remarks: "The WCC as it is today is only **an instrument for Christian unity.** It must disappear in its present form when the unity of the Church becomes a reality....The time is hidden in the wisdom of God when the whole flock will be gathered together under one Shepherd."[597]

No wonder the banner over the stage of the World Council of Churches on August 23, 1948 read: "One World—One Church."[598] In fact, their slogan is "One Church for One World."[599] This slogan was announced by **Communist** and **Mason** G. Bromley Oxnam.[600]

Visser 'T Hooft started the WCC **Ecumenical** Institute in Geneva which was financed with a **MILLION DOLLAR** grant from **John D. Rockefeller, Jr.**[601] New Agers were also enamored with Visser 'T Hooft because he was supporting **world order.**[602] They bragged:

> "Visser 't Hooft, then, is a Christian voice supporting world order. But more importantly, he is a witness to the fact that not only individual Christians, but a whole Christian movement—**the ecumenical movement**—has for decades **supported** the movement for the establishment of a responsible **world order** and will continue to do so in the future."[603]

The article also said: "As we have seen, **the ecumenical movement and the world-order movement have been interrelated and share common characteristics.** But let us underscore the notion of ecumenical support for world order."[604]

Dr. Jan Pronk, speaking to the Sixth WCC Assembly, also declared: "So the **only promising option** is one which would enable us to cope with the problems....You may call it a New International Economic Order, or international democratic socialism, or life in unity or a just, participatory and sustainable society...."[605] [Emphasis in the original.]

The above list of men and women is just **some** of those in leadership in the FCC, NCC, and WCC. There are many, many others that could also be listed, but I'm sure enough has been given to show that these organizations are far from godly institutions. They are basically Communistic groups dressed in sheep's clothing so that they can deceive and beguile unsuspecting individuals.

BILLY GRAHAM AND THE WCC

Now, since this book is mainly about Billy Graham, we need to look at what Graham thinks about these unholy councils.

Graham attended the formation assembly of the WCC as a observer.[606] He admitted that "some **extreme theological liberals**—persons who would not hold all the tenets of the Apostles' Creed, which was my own basic creed—had been **given prominence.** Nevertheless, **I was impressed** by the **spiritual depth** and commitment of many of the participants."[607] He also said about this meeting: *"One of the most thrilling experiences of my life up to that moment."*[608] [Emphasis in the original.] He had been **invited** to attend by Dr. Willem Visser 'T Hooft (who was promoting **world order).**[609]

"Graham's own magazine, *Christianity Today* (November 13, 1995), reports that Graham had attended major assemblies of WCC since 1948 and 'professed to be "thrilled at the whole process of seeing world churchmen sitting down together, praying together, discussing together."'"[610]

In Graham's own words, we find:

> "Perhaps an event that occurred a few months before that Campaign, in late summer, had given me a **greater desire to work with as many churches as possible. I had attended the founding session of the World Council of Churches in Amsterdam.** Christianity was taking on a new worldwide dimension for me."[611]

By 1960, **Graham was one of the speakers for the World Council of Churches** in Geneva. He then went to San Francisco for the National Council of Churches' 50th Anniversary which was held from December 4-9, **1960.**[612]

Dr. Edwin T. Dahlberg, a former President of the NCC, conducted the NCC Assembly.[613] He's been identified with 25 **Communist and left-wing activities,**[614] yet **Billy Graham had him on his platform** and **honored** him as a leader "worthy of trust and confidence."[615]

One speaker and vice chairman of the Protestant Radio Commission of the FCC[616] was Dr. Truman B. Douglass who "delivered an address which was the answer to a Communist dream as it extolled the virtues of materialism."[617] Another speaker (December 6th) was Bishop **Oxnam, a Mason and a Communist** who was connected with at least 45 Communist activities.[618]

Yet another speaker was **Billy Graham.** He was

> "listed with **Eugene Carson Blake,** Franklin Clark Fry, **G. Bromley Oxnam, Henry P. Van Dusen,** and **James A.**

Pike—<u>not a conservative believer in the crowd</u>. Psalm 1 says 'Blessed is the man that walketh not in the counsel of the ungodly, nor standeth in the way of sinners, nor sitteth in the seat of the scornful.'"[619]

One author states:

"Dr. Graham's NCC address was given on December 4 [1960] at 3 p.m. from the pulpit of Grace Cathedral, **at Bishop Pike's invitation.** Let it be remembered that Pike is the gentleman who wrote in the *Christian Century,* 'The Bible seems to indicate that no one is saved except through Christ....To say no one is saved except through the earthly Jesus Christ would be impossible.' Graham was no stranger to Grace Cathedral for he was one of the honored guests on May 15, 1958, with a seat on the front row when Dean Pike was consecrated as a bishop. Moreover, **Dr. Graham praised him highly from the platform of the Cow Palace the same night. He had him on the platform to read a prayer on May 24 before a nationwide TV audience....**

"In his closing prayer, Dr. Graham offered a special petition for the success of the current assembly of the National Council of Churches, and prayed that 'out of this meeting there may come a great message to the Christian world,' according to the official NCC news release. The main prayer of the service was by Dr. Dahlberg. The benediction was given by Bishop Pike. This is the same bishop who said so recently, 'This means that I am more liberal in theology than I was ten years ago...the biblical evidence and the theological implications seem to be in favor of assuming that **Joseph was the human father of Jesus.**'"[620]

Is that **REALLY** what the Bible says? Which version is Pike reading? My Bible clearly declares:

"Now the birth of Jesus Christ was on this wise: When as his mother **Mary** was espoused to Joseph, **<u>before</u>** they came together, she **was found with child of the Holy Ghost.** Then Joseph her husband, being a just man, and not willing to make her a publick example, was minded to put her away privily. But while he thought on these things, behold, the angel of the Lord appeared unto him in a dream, saying, Joseph, thou son of David, fear not to take unto thee Mary thy wife: for **that which is conceived in her is of the Holy Ghost.** And she shall bring forth a son, and thou shalt call His name JESUS: for He shall save His people from their sins. Now all this was done, that it might be fulfilled which was spoken of the Lord by the prophet, saying, Behold, **a <u>virgin</u> shall be with child,** and shall

> bring forth a son, and they shall call His name Emmanuel, which being interpreted is, God with us. Then **Joseph** being raised from sleep did as the angel of the Lord had bidden him, and took unto him his wife: And **knew her not till she had brought forth her firstborn son:** and he called his name JESUS" (Matthew 1:18-25 including a prophecy from Isaiah 7:14).

In spite of Pike's obvious denial of God's Word, this is the person that Graham **PRAISED** and allowed on his platform to say a prayer![621] In fact, **Graham called Pike** a "great **spiritual** leader."[622] (Pike was covered in detail in a previous chapter.)

PRAYERS FOR THE DEAD

On December 7, 1960, the **National Council of Churches prayed for the dead.**

> "[B]efore Bishop Pike spoke to the NCC, the crowd was led in an orthodox Catholic worship service by Father Altounian, Father Sempadian and Bishop Verjebedian, in which the Only-Begotten Son 'who didst design to become incarnate through the *Holy Mother-of-God* and ever virgin' was recognized. While the bishop was making the sign of the cross over the people, the deacon prayed 'for the souls of them that are at rest and fallen asleep in Christ in the true and orthodox faith, let us beseech the Lord.'"[623]

The World Council of Churches also had a service where they included a prayer for the dead. "Another day everyone was instructed on the correct way to make the sign of the cross."[624]

The Bible plainly tells us that "it is appointed unto men once to die, but after this the judgment" (Hebrews 9:27). Prayers for the dead are useless for if the person is a Christian, he is "absent from the body, and...present with the Lord" (II Corinthians 5:8). If he is unsaved, then the person goes immediately to hell as did the rich man in Luke 16:22-23. Jesus Himself taught that "beside all this, between us and you there is **a great gulf fixed: so that they which would pass from hence to you cannot; neither can they pass to us, that would come from thence"** (Luke 16:26). Our destiny is settled at death and no amount of prayers can change that destiny. "[B]ehold, now is the accepted time; behold, **now** is the day of salvation" (II Corinthians 6:2).

Returning to Graham's December 4th NCC address, we find:

> "The NCC press release further reported: 'Dr. Graham did not close his message with the usual altar call, but he did ask

> for heads to be bowed and urged those who wanted to make a **deeper commitment** of their lives to God to raise their hands.' **He assumed they were Christians.** One of the stock excuses given by the backers of Dr. Graham for participating in ecumenical evangelism is to give the message to the modernists who need it so badly. Here he had a golden opportunity to get some of them saved by pressing home the decision, but there was no invitation. In fact, there was little Gospel. When he had the modernists before him, as at Union [Theological] Seminary and Rochester-Colgate Seminary, he didn't give them an opportunity to respond."[625]

APOSTASY AT COW PALACE

Earlier we learned that the extremely liberal **Protestant Council of New York** had invited Graham to speak at Madison Garden in 1957. It should be noted again that **this Council was affiliated with the National Council of Churches.**[626]

Also, remember that **Graham received $75,000 from John D. Rockefeller, Jr.** for his 1957 Crusade[627] and then afterwards Graham **gave $67,618 to the Protestant Council.**[628]

The next year (April and May **1958**), Graham held a seven-week crusade in San Francisco at the Cow Palace.[629] He chose Mrs. William Lister Rogers, an American Baptist, who was **President of the San Francisco Council of Churches,** to be the chairperson of the Billy Graham San Francisco Bay Crusade finance committee.[630]

> **"Mrs. Rogers was originator of the United Nations Festival of Faith,** held in June **1955**. The *Outlook*, **official publication of the NCC,** said in its report immediately following the event: 'They **called God by different names,** speaking to Him in different tongues, but the dream in their hearts was the same....High point of the prayer meeting was the recitation together of the Responsive Reading composed of sentences from the sacred books of the six faiths represented—Christian, Jewish, Moslem, Buddhist, Hindu and Confucian. **The initial idea for the service came from Mrs. William Lister Rogers, council president.'"**[631]

Remember, Rogers had organized this meeting 3 years **BEFORE** Graham had her as the chairperson of his finance committee!

This **interfaith** meeting was also held at the San Francisco Cow Palace (June 19, 1955) and was in commemoration of the **United Nation's** 10th anniversary. The representative for the National Council of Churches **and** the World Council of Churches was none other than **John Foster Dulles!**[632] He spoke on the subject of "The Moral Foundations of the United Nations."[633]

> "This was the same year (1955) that Erich Fromm's The Sane Society was published, in which he predicted that *'the theistic concepts are bound to disappear in the future development of humanity....A new religion will develop...the most important feature of such a religion would be its universalistic character...it would embrace the humanistic teachings common to all great religions of the East and of the West....The same suggestion for a new humanistic religion has been made by Julian Huxley in "Evolutionary Humanism....*" ' "[634] [Emphasis in the original.]

"Dulles was a member of World Brotherhood and the Council on Foreign Relations (as was his CIA brother Allen). John Foster Dulles' son Avery Dulles is now an influential Jesuit priest."[635]

The Bible explicitly warns true Christians: **"Be ye not unequally yoked together with unbelievers:** for what fellowship hath righteousness with unrighteousness? and what communion hath light with darkness?" (II Corinthians 6:14).

The Bible also specifically commands us to "come out from among them, and **be ye separate..."** (II Corinthians 6:17), but Graham not only has fellowship with unbelievers but he invites them on his platform!

Going even further against Scriptural commands, Graham **PRAISES** unbelievers. For instance, he visited the National Council of Churches headquarters on August 27, 1991.

> "Among other words of praise Graham had for these false teachers were these amazing words, quoted from the NCC Press Release of August 27, 1991: **'There's no group of people in the world that I would rather be with right now than you all.** Because I think of you, I pray for you, and we follow with great interest the things you do....I don't speak to too many church assemblies any more because **I consider myself as belonging to all the churches.** And I love everybody equally and **I have no problem in fellowship with anybody who says that Jesus Christ is Lord.** This has been a great relief to me to come to that conclusion about 20 some years ago.' "[636]

Remember that Matthew 7:21-23 points out that many who call Jesus "Lord, Lord" were "workers of iniquity."

We are to preach the Gospel but at the same time we are to also "**earnestly contend for the faith** which was once delivered unto the saints" (Jude 1:3). If we are not contending for the faith, then we are not truly exemplifying the Gospel. The Bible cautions: "Be not deceived: evil communications corrupt good manners" (I Corinthians 15:33).

LET'S CONTROL THE PRESS

The National Council of Churches has virtually controlled the field of religious broadcasting. One researcher commented way back in 1958:

> "Committee members or representatives of the Council get together with the Federal Communications Commission and press upon them the idea that religious time should not be purchased from the major broadcasting systems but rather that the networks should grant free time equally to the three major religions in the United States: Protestantism, Catholicism, and Judaism. Then the Council representatives, posing as the Voice of Protestantism, seek to convince the Federal Communications Commission, the heads of the broadcasting chains, and the local radio stations, that since the Council represents the majority of the Protestants in the United States, it should be given sole disposition of the free time granted to Protestants. Hundreds of local evangelical ministers who have refused to join the Federal or National Council have been forced off the air by representatives of local councils of churches. Several major broadcasting chains have been highly partial to the Federal-National Council and have refused to give independent groups an equal voice on these chains. *The Council has even succeeded in putting some of its own representatives in official positions in the networks to manage the chains' sections on religious broadcasting.*
>
> "The Federal Council's 1946 Biennial Report, in the chapter entitled 'National Religious Radio,' says: 'For the past two years in particular, recognition should be given to the vision and leadership of the 59 clergymen whose names are listed herewith. Without their cooperation, religious radio programs sponsored by The Federal Council of Churches would not have afforded the spiritual inspiration so vitally needed.'"[637] [Emphasis in the original.]

It was difficult for fundamentalists to have their own radio and TV programs, yet remember the story (in Chapter 1) of how Graham "accidentally" met David Sarnoff, the "Father of American television,"[638] and soon was on NBC TV.[639]

Also, shortly after Graham's radio program, *The Hour of Decision,* starting airing, the *Chicago-Tribune-New York News* wanted him to write a syndicated column which is called "My Answer."[640] This column soon had daily circulation with over 20 million readers, brags Graham.[641]

On October 30, 1976, the *Chicago Tribune* reported that "Forest Boyd, White House correspondent for the Mutual Broadcasting System, ha[d] been appointed Director of Communications for the Billy Graham Evangelistic Association."[642] How convenient!

Obviously, not all preachers on large radio and TV stations are associated with the liberal NCC but many of them certainly are not orthodox Christians. I John 4:1, 5-6 warns us:

> "Beloved, believe not every spirit, but try the spirits whether they are of God: because many false prophets are gone out into the world....They are of the world: therefore speak they of the world, and the world heareth them. We are of God: he that knoweth God heareth us; he that is not of God heareth not us. Hereby know we the spirit of truth, and the spirit of error."

5. BIBLES FOR BETRAYAL

In a previous chapter we took a long look at the Union Theological Seminary (UTS), known as the "Red Seminary"[1] because of its many Communistic faculty members.[2] Another person who attended UTS was **Bishop K. H. Ting**[3] (Bishop Ding Guangxun[4]). He is one of the Presidents of the World Conference on Religion and Peace[5] (which is covered later in this book). He is also the Principal of Nanking (or Nanjing) Theological Seminary,[6] but, like so many others from UTS, he promotes a **Communistic** agenda.[7]

Ting's wife declared in the February 23, 1977 issue of *Christian Century:* "We love Chairman Mao [Tse-tung] for all he has taught us."[8] She also remarked: "As Chinese Christians we do not see Christianity and Socialist China as opposed to each other. It is God working, whether in his name or not."[9] Bishop Ting has also praised Mao Tse-tung[10] and his revolutionaries by referring to them as "honest, sincere, good men!"[11] He said: "[T]hank God for them (the **Communists)** and **we want to learn from them** through what they do."[12]

On September 23, 1984 Ting spoke at Rikkyo University. His lecture was then reprinted in the *International Bulletin of Missionary Research* in July 1985.[13] In reference to the revolutionaries, he said: "They were certainly not the monsters and rascals they were said to be, but quite normal human beings with idealism, serious theoretical interests, and high ethical commitment."[14]

Under the Communist regime in China (up to 1971) somewhere between 34,300,000 to 63,784,000 lives were lost.[15] One author wrote: "China's communist leader Mao Tse Tung established one of the most brutal dictatorships under the sun. Not only did he take away the basic human liberties of the Chinese people, he was directly responsible for the murder of millions."[16] Even the *Guinness Book of World Records* states that the greatest massacre in human history occurred during the rule of Mao Tse-tung between 1949 and 1965.[17]

Referring to Mao and his fellow Communists, Ting remarks: "And, although they had no high regard for religion at all, they did not attempt to persecute or liquidate religion either...."[18] Oh, really? Let's look at a few facts. Before the end of the 1950s, the

> "200 churches in Shanghai were reduced to 23. Peking had only 4 churches open rather than 65 as in years past. The zealous Communists (under the banner of the **Three-Self Movement)** went on to dissolve the Jesus Family communities and took over (or closed) 3 Catholic universities, 189 secondary

schools, 2,011 primary schools, and 2,243 prayer schools—involving 30,000 students in all. The Union Theological Seminary in Canton was also closed down....Some have estimated that by 1959 **approximately 80 percent of the churches in China were closed....**

"A former missionary to China, M. E. Loewen, declared that 'I know...that within a few years of the communist takeover in 1949, nearly three out of four of all professed Christians abandoned ship....Hundreds of thousands of Christians vanished. Most were presumed dead. The survivors are underground.'"[19]

Yet Ting tells us that Mao did not try to liquidate religion in China!!

SOCIALISM IS NOT A LOSS OF FREEDOM

In spite of this inhumane, savage, and ruthless behavior, Ting thinks these murderers had a **"high ethical** commitment!" In fact, "Ting described the communist enslavement of China as 'the people's **liberation** movement with all its goodness and beauty!'"[20]

Of course, **Ting** himself "was an adulterer and a murderer," according to the *Christian News.*[21]

In Ting's opening address to the Third Chinese National Christian Conference, he stated: "We give thanks to God in our prayers for the achievements of **socialist** New China."[22]

He also announced: **"Socialism** seems to me to be a society that organizes people for mutual benefit. It is not a loss of freedom; it **is a gain of freedom."**[23]

Below are a few more quotations from Ting (taken from statements he made in 1977).

➢ "In the new China the life of the people has improved a great deal. No one needs to worry about starvation, medical help, etc."[24]

➢ "We returned to China in 1951. People in Europe were very concerned about our coming back. They felt I would be killed or put in a **concentration camp.** I am still alive, and **I do not believe that there is any such camp.** We do not need it. I have been engaged in religious work all these years. **I believe in the honesty of the communists concerning the policy of religious freedom."**[25]

➢ "[T]he missionary movement was part of a system. Missionaries were tools of imperialist aggression."[26]

"Ting says that it was the Communist 'party that made a correct analysis of the root cause of China's suffering and misery—imperialism and feudalism.'"[27]

In a speech Ting gave in 1980, he said: "New China is the people's China. It exists for the broad masses of the people. **It has brought liberation, benefits and happiness to its people. It is revolutionary** and progressive."[28]

Just recently he declared that **"socialism is the best social system which has appeared in human history."** He indicated that "any theology that is 'incompatible with socialism should not be preached.'"[29] In 1999 he "said that **all Christians in China should be socialists."**[30] One writer notes:

> "What most people do not realize is that **Bishop K. H. Ting** was the major Protestant leader who **sold out to the communists** when they took over China. **Ting's sell-out was believed responsible for the deaths of many true believers** who refused to bow to godless Red atheists when they took control of China."[31]

"It has been said, and correctly so, that no other man has as much authority in any other communist country as Ting does in China."[32]

In the August 29-September 5, 1979 issue of *Christian Century* was an article about Ting.

> "The article admits that **Ting is a member of the communist People's Consultative Assembly** and even concludes by admitting that Ting represents that part of the Christian movement in China that sought modes of accommodation with the government of the People's Republic (Red Government). In spite of this knowledge, the article treats Ting as though he were a true Christian instead of the apostate traitor he really is. Incidentally, Ting was in the USA for the recent World Conference on Religion and Peace [which has nothing to do with true religion or peace, but is a communist front—Ed.] after which he was **given a 'Red Carpet' tour by the National Council of Churches."**[33]

Ting has bragged:

> "The year **1949 was a special year for China.** From one standpoint the United States 'lost' China in that year and, from another, in that same year the **Chinese people got their liberation.** For us Chinese Christians that liberation marks the beginning of a process in our church known as the **Three-Self Movement."**[34]

Of course, **1949 was the year that the Communists took over China.**[35] To Ting, this was a "liberation" for the Chinese people but what else can we expect from a Marxist?[36] Notice also that he said that this "liberation" was the start of what is now known as the **Three-Self Movement.**

THREE-SELF PATRIOTIC MOVEMENT

Ting was the head of the Three-Self Patriotic Movement (TSPM) from its inception until recently.[37] (He is now the honorary chairman.[38]) The term "Three-Self" refers to China's policy for the churches to be "self-supporting," "self-governing," and "self-propagating."[39]

In China, the **TSPM is the official church and is officially sanctioned by the Chinese Communistic government.**[40] There are also the **unofficial** churches (not sanctioned by the government) known as **house churches, which are illegal in China.**[41] Many pastors who refuse to join the TSPM are either arrested or made fugitives.[42] "With China celebrating its 50th anniversary of Communist rule [in 1999], house church Christians face stiff labor camp sentences for meeting in homes and refusing to join the state registered and controlled church."[43] In spite of these persecutions, there are reasons why the house church Christians do not want to join the TSPM. One writer explains about the TSPM:

> "The Communist government organized the Religious Affairs Bureau (RAB) to **control religion.** In 1951 the **Three-Self Patriotic Movement (TSPM)** was organized under the control of the RAB to direct the affairs of the Protestant churches. **All churches were to be brought under the control of the TSPM** and **detailed files were kept on all church leaders and their activities.** By 1958 the churches were firmly under the government's control. **Christian leaders who refused to submit to the TSPM were publicly accused and sentenced to prison.** At the Shang-hai Conference in 1981 it was stated, **'To be anti-TSPM is to be anti-government, for religion must be organized and under control.'** It is evident that the government controls the TSPM and that the TSPM seeks to control all the churches in China. **They designate what buildings can be used for church services, which pastors can preach, and what areas can be traveled to spread religion. The TSPM has recently called on the Public Security Bureau to close the meeting of the house churches, arrest the house church leaders, and arrest traveling evangelists. The clergy in the Three-Self churches are all on the government payroll, and their salaries are much higher than the average wage earner in China."**[44]

I'm sure it would not come as any surprise that the head of the Religious Affairs Bureau is an atheist.[45]

> "Those with ultimate power for controlling religion in China are atheists—**they are required to be so by Communist**

> **Party regulations.** State religious policy, as explained by Chinese president Jiang Zemin in the March 14, 1996, edition of the *People's Daily,* is to 'actively **guide religion so that it can be adapted to socialist society.'**"[46]

PATRIOTIC COVENANT

Since the TSPM-controlled churches have several limitations and restrictions, many true Christians realize that they are unable to fulfill the Great Commission of Mark 16:15 to go "into all the world, and preach the gospel to every creature." Some of the prohibitions for Christians in the "Patriotic Covenant" include:

> "1) A prohibition on evangelizing and baptizing children under 18; 2) a prohibition on church activities that conflict with work; 3) a prohibition on listening to foreign radio broadcasts; 4) a prohibition on receiving literature from abroad; 5) a prohibition on unauthorized contact with foreigners; 6) a prohibition on construction of churches; and 7) a prohibition on criticism of the government. **Moreover, the TSPM church must agree to uphold and promote the teachings of Marxism."**[47]

The churches are also forbidden to preach from the book of Revelation.[48]

Furthermore, there are a number of unwritten instructions which the Three-Self Patriotic Movement gave to pastors in Fuzhou. They are forbidden to preach on the return of Christ, the suffering of Christ, casting out of demons, healing the sick, or "love not the world."[49] Other taboo topics are abortion and the marriage between unbelievers and believers.[50]

Another report tells of other restrictions upon the Christian believers in another village.

> "Four of the rules are that believers can only read Bibles and books printed by the Three-Self Patriotic Movement (TSPM)—**any other books must be turned in to the authorities;** believers may not have contact with itinerant preachers who are not a part of the TSPM; **house meetings are forbidden;** and **those under 18 years old are not allowed to attend religious meetings."**[51]

Yet another report states: "Privately published books and Bibles, mimeographed by house church leaders, have been confiscated by local authorities and used in court as evidence of producing and distributing 'anti-revolutionary' materials."[52]

Many times when the Christians violate (or do not espouse) these prohibitions, the TSPM reports them to the Public Security Bureau.

> "The question frequently asked by many is, 'Why don't Chinese house church Christians register with the state controlled Three Self Patriotic Movement (TSPM) and thus end all the government's persecution? After all, wouldn't registering with the state offer a legal advantage that would permit believers to enjoy freedom of religion?' First, registration with the Chinese government most certainly will not end the persecution of the church, which has already been clearly evident. Estimated to number about 70 million, house church believers throughout China have since long distrusted the pastors of the TSPM churches. Since the early 1950s, **many pastors were arrested and imprisoned because of the betrayal of TSPM pastors who had served as informants for the government** in repeated efforts by the government to oppress and control the church. Certainly, not all TSPM pastors are traitors or government agents. In fact today some TSPM pastors share a close relationships (sic) with the pastors of house churches. Nevertheless, the general attitude remains the same and betrayals continue to occur."[53]

According to a 1994 report, some house churches in the cities of Fuzhou and Shanghai did register with the Three-Self Patriotic Movement. Did the persecution stop? No! The house churches were ordered to stop their meetings.

> "According to information received by this Center from a recent traveler to these two cities, TSPM officials sent notices to house church leaders that their people must attend the open churches in those cities. In Fuzhou, a notice was received in mid-March that registered meeting points in the city must close. Only meetings with less than five persons would be permitted. These orders in effect applied to the twenty to thirty registered house churches in Fuzhou as well as the eight registered groups, since all meetings would be restricted to five persons....Fuzhou has only two open churches."[54]

BIBLE IS ANTI-REVOLUTIONARY MATERIAL

As mentioned, the only literature that Christians are permitted to read is to be printed by the TSPM. To have legally printed materials available and to solicit funds from Christians around the world, the Amity Foundation (which established the Amity Press in 1985[55]) was founded by **Bishop K. H. Ting** and his associate **Han Wenzao** (also spelled Wensao).[56] **The Amity Press is licensed by the China Christian Council (CCC) which was also headed by Bishop Ting** until recently.[57] (Ting is now the honorary chairman of the CCC.[58]) Are you getting the picture? Ting heads the China Christian Council which licenses the Amity Press (headed by Ting) which publishes the material for the TSPM (also headed by Ting). As already noted, Ting has had high praise for the Communist butcher, Mao Tse-tung.[59] Although Ting has recently retired, the China Christian Council is now headed by Han Wenzao who helped Ting found the Amity Press[60] and who had been the vice president under Ting.[61] Both Ting and Wenzao are Communists as well as promoters of China's pro-abortion, one-child policy.[62] The CCC has also been accepted as a full member of the **World Council of Churches** as of 1991.[63]

As also mentioned, **Ting attended the Union Theological Seminary** (from 1947-1949).[64] He repudiates the fundamentals of the Christian faith, denies that the Bible is the inspired Word of God, rejects the physical resurrection of Christ, and is a modernist.[65] He does not believe that sinful humans will face judgment. He does believe, however, that we should see the logos (Christ, who is the Word in John 1:1) in everyone. He also praises liberation theology.[66] Ting leans towards universalism and thinks that there is light in all religions.[67] He does not think that nonbelievers will go to hell.[68]

Ting was also the president of the China Christian Council's Nanjing Seminary, and "turned it into a hotbed of theological heresy."[69]

> "Studies at the modernistic Nanjing Seminary are permeated with **Marxist** philosophy. They include **classes in socialism and international Communism.** 'A Western observer who visited the Union Seminary and interacted with students reports that the course on the history of Christianity in China vilified all major Protestant missionaries. Apart from the regular courses, occasional courses on Jews in Chinese History (in which Jews were attacked as capitalists, etc.), Theological Abstracts, and Evolution of Theology in China ("rethinking" theology to fit Marxist philosophy) were also offered, as were courses on comparative religious studies in China, government, religious policy, and "questions most commonly asked by foreign visitors"—public relations training enabling students to correctly answer those from outside China.'"[70]

One of the conditions for entry into this seminary is "political awareness" which "refers to submission to **communist** dogma."[71] A person who visited the seminary said that "their curriculum included a class on the TSPM (its history and philosophy) and a class on patriotism (the teachings of Mao)."[72]

"Evangelicals...also report that the TSPM is reasserting its own brand of theology within China's seminaries—a mixture of Marxism, New Age ideas and Biblical teachings."[73]

Additionally,

> "Bishop Ting of Red China has been in **ecumenical** waters on behalf of the Communists of Red China as far back as 1955. He attended the meeting of the WCC's Executive Committee in Communist Hungary, just before the uprising there, and has his picture on the front page of the WCC's official organ, *The Outlook*. He has backed the Communists all through these years. He is a member of one of their governing bodies, The Chinese People's Political Consultative Conference. When the Communists established China's council of churches, he was placed in full charge. **He is a Communist, a thorough-going Marxist, using the cover of Christianity for his deception."**[74]

In 1956 Ting informed the Central Committee of the WCC,

> "before which he appeared **by invitation,** that Chinese Christians did not regard the rise of the People's Republic as an act of God's wrath but of his love. He said they would not wish to end the new regime if they could. Christians in China did not pretend to agree with communists in their views on religion, he declared, but this did not prevent their recognizing the value of the good things the People's government was doing. They were humbled and gave thanks to God for their **improved** circumstances."[75]

WHY A FULL COLOR PRINTING PRESS?

Now, why would Communists like Wenzao and Ting want to print Bibles and Christian literature? One author states:

> "Many Lutherans and Christians around the world are to be commended and thanked for their desire to replace the millions of Bibles destroyed by Mao's Red Guards. The only weak link in this chain was that **the same people who had destroyed those 10 million Bibles, the Communists, were now in charge of the Bible production to replace those Bibles that they had destroyed....**
>
> **"Ting worked with the Communists who destroyed 10 million Bibles. Ting worked with the Communist security**

> **police in helping them to raid churches and arrest and jail pastors and their members—and in one case murdered a member."**[76]

So, the answer to why the Communists want to print Bibles is simple but two-fold. Christians want to help their fellow Christians, especially those in Communist countries such as China. When we hear of an opportunity to get Bibles to believers who do not have Bibles, many Christians are more than willing to open their hearts (and their purses) to provide money to purchase the Bibles. This, then, becomes a "fund-raiser" for the Communists. By playing on our sympathy (and our desire to distribute the Gospel to as many as possible), the Communists are able to get money that should be used for the work of Christ and **divert** it into their own coffers to print Communistic literature. You see, the **Amity Printing Press** wants a full-color press and has solicited money for this purpose. There is a catch, however. The **Bible only needs to be printed in black and white** but about 95% of the **Communistic literature requires color.**[77] Therefore the "need" for a color press—not for Bibles (as is often advertised) but for **Communistic** literature.

Ting admitted that the $6.7 million press (which was supplied by the United Bible Societies[78]) would not be used exclusively for Bibles.

> "In a letter to Hong Kong *Christian Weekly* dated April, 1986 and released the following May, the Amity Foundation gave the following clarifications.
>
> "'The press will be jointly run by the Amity Foundation and the Nanjing Teachers University. **It will undertake all kinds of printing projects, not limited to Bibles.** If the churches inside or outside of China commission/contract to print Bibles, the press will do its best to give priority to this project. **The churches have to pay for the services** in order to maintain the self-supporting principle.
>
> "'The quantity of the Bibles printed is to be decided by the commissioning/contracting party and the press. It is not to be decided by the United Bible Societies.'
>
> "What is the reality of the situation here? China will have a $6.7 million dollar printing press, on which 'hopefully' Bibles will be printed.
>
> "However, there is no formal guarantee that a single Bible will be printed on the Nanjing press."[79]

BIBLES—FOR EXPORT

Of course, there are some Bibles being printed on this press. However, most of the Bibles that are actually printed here are in the English (not Chinese!) language and are **FOR EXPORT,**[80] so the Communist government is making money by collecting for the press as well as making money selling the Bibles to other English-speaking countries, but the Chinese people, for the most part, are not getting these Bibles. Moreover, when a Chinese Christian does get a Bible, the cost is exorbitant for the average worker. "The born-again Chinese are 85 per cent rural, country or farmers where **their entire year's income would pay for one of the Bibles** on sale at the government-sponsored registered church."[81] If generous people were supplying the press plus the money to print the Bibles, wouldn't you think that the Bibles could be given away free—or at least sold at a reasonable price?

Not only is Communistic literature being printed on this press but there is a second, even more sinister, reason why the Communists are printing Bibles. When a Chinese **house church Christian** orders a Bible, he **must register his name, address, church affiliation, and other Christian history!**[82] Many Chinese Christians refer to these Bibles as the "dolu-hebi" or "poison-snake" Bibles.[83] Why? Because the **Bibles are being used as bait** and when a person tries to purchase a **legal** Bible, **he is often arrested** since the government has now obtained the person's name and church affiliation.[84] The government knows that a Bible is precious to a Christian. Therefore the Communists offer something of value in order to entrap Christians—and make them pay money on top of it.

Here is one example of what took place in China.

> "A little country church ordered and **paid** for 500 of these Bibles to be sent to them over a thousand miles away. They paid for them in advance. The 500 Bibles came to the designated railway station. **When the Christians went to pick them up, they were all arrested and put in jail.**"[85]

Does this sound safe? Yet, an ad for Ned Graham's East Gates International appeared in the October 26, 1999 issue of *Christianity Today* with Billy Graham saying: "These Bibles...are hard bound and printed LEGALLY IN CHINA. Because these Bibles are printed and distributed legally, there is not the associated risk to the Chinese believers as with smuggled Bibles."[86] Really? If there are no risks, then why are so many believers arrested after purchasing a **LEGAL** Bible?

Pastor Li Dexian, a house church leader in China, has been arrested so many times in the past two years that he has lost count.[87] He said that the Public Security Bureau (PSB) officials

> "stormed into a house church meeting, confiscated hymnals and Bibles, and prevented the service from continuing.
>
> "'They confiscated and destroyed Bibles that we had **LEGALLY** purchased from the government,' said Li.
>
> "Last year, PSB officials also confiscated Li's church and welded the doors shut, and in early November in the city of Wenzhou, Zhejiang Province, they reportedly blew up and demolished at least 450 churches, temples and shrines. Government officials said religious leaders had built the churches and temples illegally."[88]

Obviously, then, even the **LEGAL** Bibles are not safe from confiscation in China.

One person writes:

> "The head of a famous worldwide church group in Hong Kong told me that he and other Chinese pastors went to visit Ting. He said: 'Bishop Ting, I have friends who have not been able to get a Bible in three years. Can we not send Bibles from Hong Kong?' Bishop Ting replied: 'NO, BUT YOU CAN SEND THE CASH.'"[89] [Emphasis in the original.]

Even though Ting and Wenzao Han do not want Christianity to flourish in China, they are both very receptive to the idea of a "United Religions"[90] (which will be covered in Chapter 6).

Now, after all that was said about Bishop **Ting**—his **Communistic** ties, his pro-**abortion** stance, his **praise of Mao Tse-tung,** and his printing press that is used to **arrest Christians,** would you believe that a **favorable article appeared in Graham's *Christianity Today*** (September 6, 1985) and the Chinese edition of his *Decision* magazine (December 1985)? The article was written by Tom Goosmann and Edward E. Plowman and seemed to present Ting's **Three-Self Patriotic Movement** as an **evangelical** organization. In referring to a conference held at Nanjing in the early 1980's, the authors quoted from Werner Burklin who said he sensed "a strong **evangelical** spirit among all those who attended. They came across as **men and women without guile...**my prejudices softened after meeting **Ting. I was overwhelmed** by his humility, his spirit, and **by his <u>spiritual</u> insight."**[91] In this short article, Burklin's name was mentioned four times. He just happens to be "the Executive Director of the 1986

Amsterdam Conference of Itinerant Evangelists sponsored by the Billy Graham Evangelistic Association."[92]

> "Most unfortunately, Burklin and Sam Wolgemuth, President emeritus of Youth for Christ, drafted an 11-point statement addressed to believers outside of China. It called on Christians not to criticize the Church in China [i.e. TSPM—J.C.]. It exhorted Christian broadcasters to pay attention to [TSPM—J.C.] Christian leaders, and it **urged evangelicals to cooperate with the TSPM.**"[93]

The article went on to say that "there was a strong support among church leaders for a preaching visit by evangelist Billy Graham."[94] It seems that this story was written in order to soften the Americans' criticism of Billy Graham's soon-to-come visit to China in the 1980s.[95]

A MAN OF PEACE

Now let's see how **Billy Graham** himself feels about Ting. In **Graham's autobiography,** *Just As I Am,* he brags:

> "In 1985 a preliminary **invitation had arrived from Bishop K. H. Ting,** head of the China Christian Council, whom Ruth had met during her 1980 trip. After a series of negotiations, a firm invitation arrived, asking us to preach in churches in several cities in September of 1987. **I promised to give the invitation priority,** pending further research into the details of the invitation....
>
> "Our formal invitation, as I said, came from the **China Christian Council,** which was **officially recognized by the government** and also **was affiliated with what was known as the 'Three-Self Patriotic Movement.'...**
>
> **"We were given a red-carpet welcome at the airport by our two official hosts, Ambassador Zhang Wenjin and Bishop K. H. Ting,** president of the China Christian Council. Ambassador Zhang...was president of the Chinese People's Association for Friendship with Foreign Countries, a title that did not begin to describe his courtesy and helpfulness. He was often described as 'Mr. Integrity,' and was among those who had negotiated with **Henry Kissinger** in **confidential** talks some years before. The association's vice president, Liu Gengyin (whom Ruth had met in 1980), was also there.
>
> "In addition to **Bishop Ting,** the China Christian Council was represented by its vice president, **Han Wenzao.** American

> Ambassador **Winston Lord** was on hand too, to remind us that we were not out of touch with home....
>
> "I sat at a huge round table beside Ambassador Zhang amid other **distinguished officials, including Bishop Ting, Zhao Puchu of China's Buddhist Association, and Ambassador Lord.** In the introductory remarks, Ruth was called 'a daughter of China' and I 'a man of peace.'"[96]

Before moving on, a few comments are in order. Han Wenzao was there. We've covered a little bit about Wenzao previously. He is the **Communist** who has now replaced Ting as head of the China Christian Council and also helped Ting found the Amity Press.[97] When Graham met with the officials, he explained "that Christians were good citizens, illustrating with Romans 13 that the Bible instructed Christians to **obey authorities.**"[98] It is true that Christians are to obey the authorities but when those in leadership demand a Christian to do something **against** God's will, our first obligation is to obey God. The apostles were jailed for preaching but an angel opened the prison doors and told them to preach in the temple.

> "Then came one and told them [the priests], saying, Behold, the men whom ye put in prison are standing in the temple, and teaching the people....And when they had brought them [the apostles], they set them before the council: and the high priest asked them, Saying, **Did not we straitly command you that ye should not teach in this name?** and, behold, ye have filled Jerusalem with your doctrine....Then Peter and the other apostles answered and said, **We ought to obey God rather than men"** (Acts 5:25, 27-29).

In Communist countries, many Christians are disobeying the authorities just by attending a worship service, but Graham seemed to give the Communistic officials the impression that the "Christians" he would speak to would obey the government rather than God.

Graham admitted in his autobiography that the China Christian Council (CCC) was affiliated with the Three-Self Patriotic Movement and that the CCC was officially recognized by the government. In other words, **he was not entering into this proposition ignorantly!** He was **fully aware** of the problem between the house churches and the government. He even wrote:

> "On the other hand, millions of Chinese Christians worshiped either as single family units or in so-called house churches, meeting as regularly as possible. These groups of believers were sometimes referred to as 'meeting-point Christians.'

> **Many of the house churches were not affiliated with the officially sanctioned Three-Self Patriotic Movement. In many instances, they rejected the leadership of that body and its churches because of their ties to the government.**"[99]

SKULL AND BONES

Notice also that **Winston Lord** was present with Graham, Ting, and Wenzao. Lord is a member of the **Council on Foreign Relations** (CFR),[100] the **Trilateral Commission,**[101] and on the steering committee of the **Bilderbergers!**[102] In fact, he was the editor the CFR's journal, *Foreign Affairs,*[103] as well as the President of the CFR for a number of years.[104]

Despatch Magazine explains: "Virtually every American member of the Bilderbergers is a current or former member of the CFR....It has been described as ***'a training and orientation school for prospective world government administrators.'***"[105] [Emphasis in the original.]

Lord was the former director of planning and coordination for the State Department[106] and President Clinton's Assistant Secretary of State for East Asian and Pacific Affairs[107] and the chairman of the National Commission on America and the New World, Carnegie Endowment for International Peace.[108]

On September 29, 1992, Lord gave a speech called "Changing Our Ways: America and the New World." He said:

> "To a certain extent, we are going to have to **yield some of our sovereignty,** which will be controversial at home....(Under) the North American Free Trade Agreement (NAFTA)...some Americans are going to be hurt as low-wage jobs are taken away....We **encourage the development of international law** so that the international community is able to intervene across national borders in cases of large-scale human rights abuses, by force if necessary."[109]

Furthermore, **Lord was a member of the Skull and Bones**[110] (also called the Brotherhood of Death, the Order, or the American Establishment[111]). The Skull and Bones initiates "lay naked in coffins and tell their deepest and darkest sexual secrets as part of their initiation."[112] It is interesting to note that Anton LaVey, the founder of the Church of Satan, wrote in his book, *The Satanic Rituals:* "The ceremony of rebirth takes place in a large coffin....This is similar to the coffin symbolism that...is found in most lodge [Masonic, etc.] rituals."[113]

The Lord family has a long involvement in the Skull & Bones. For instance,

> "Oswald Bates Lord (initiated 1926) married Mary Pillsbury of the Pillsbury flour family and Charles Edwin Lord II (initiated 1949) became acting Comptroller of the Currency in 1981. The son of Oswald Bates Lord and Mary Pillsbury is **Winston Lord** (initiated 1959) who was chairman of the **Council on Foreign Relations** in 1983 and today cavorts with **David Rockefeller** in creating friendly business relations with the 'world community,' **especially Communist China.**
>
> "The Lord family legacy goes back much farther than 1926. Since 1854, at least six members of the Lord family have been initiated into **The Order of Skull & Bones.** In 1854 George Deforest Lord was initiated into The Order. He became a New York lawyer."[114]

Under President Reagan, Lord was appointed Ambassador to China.[115] This was the time when Graham went to China to visit Ting.

While in China in 1988, Graham said that he and Ruth

> "met with members of the diplomatic and international community at a luncheon at Ambassador Lord's residence; several **religious leaders** were there also, **including** China's leading **Buddhist,** Zhao Puchu....Ambassador Lord's wife, the well-known writer Bette Bao Lord, returned from the United States just in time to be hostess at the luncheon; she was a delightful and knowledgeable conversationalist."[116]

Like her husband, Mrs. Lord belongs to the Council on Foreign Relations[117] and the Bilderbergers.[118] The head of the Bilderbergers, Prince Bernhard, declared: "It is difficult to reeducate the people who have been brought up on nationalism to the idea of relinquishing part of their sovereignty to a supranational body...."[119]

Mrs. Lord is also Chairman of the Board for the **Freedom House,** which is a **CFR front.**[120] Bayard Rustin (a **Communist** who was covered earlier) was the executive committee chairman for the Freedom House.[121] Mrs. Lord is also on the Board of Trustees for The Freedom Forum.[122]

When **David Rockefeller** returned from China in 1973, the *New York Times* published his observations in which he stated:

> "One is impressed immediately by the sense of national harmony...there is a very real and pervasive dedication to Chairman Mao and Maoist principles. Whatever the price of the Chinese Revolution, it has obviously succeeded not only in producing more efficient and dedicated administration, but also in fostering high morale and community purpose. General social and economic progress is no less impressive....The

enormous social advances of China have benefitted greatly from the singleness of ideology and purpose....The social experiment in China under Chairman Mao's leadership is one of the most important and successful in history."[123]

ARMAND HAMMER AND BILLY GRAHAM

Another person connected to Billy Graham was Armand Hammer.[124] He was "able to get Billy Graham into any country."[125]

> "On November 1 [1990], Hammer met with Rabbi Daniel Lapin of the Pacific Jewish Center to plan one final event: his belated bar mitzvah ceremony. He had denied his Jewish heritage for most of his life. When he had gone to Russia in the 1920s, he had identified himself as an atheist. When he had gone to Saudi Arabia and Libya in search of oil in the 1960s, he had given his religion as Unitarian. Even in Los Angeles in the 1980s, he had listed himself on hospital records as Protestant or WASP. But now, with only weeks left to live, he planned to return to Judaism in a dramatic way: by the initiation into manhood. This ceremony traditionally takes place when a boy turns thirteen...."[126]

Hammer was a **Council on Foreign Relations** member,[127] as well as on the **World Federalist Association's** National Advisory Board in 1989.[128]

In 1919, Armand performed an abortion in his home and the woman died shortly afterwards. His father, **Julius Hammer,** ended up taking the rap for this death and served time in prison for first-degree manslaughter[129] (although he was able to be released before finishing his time[130]). Julius himself was a **co-founder of the Communist Party in America** and remained a member throughout his life.[131] In fact, he held party card 1.[132] "When his first child was born in 1898, he named him Armand for the arm-and-hammer symbols of the proletarian revolution."[133]

Armand himself was very closely associated with the Communists although he claims he never officially joined the Communist Party.[134] However, Boris Reinstein, who was "one of Lenin's chief Americanologists"[135] and secretary of the Profintern in Russia,[136] wrote a report in which he stated that Julius and Armand Hammer were "convinced Communists and sincere comrades...."[137]

Also, according to the June 11, 1992 issue of the London *Daily Mail,* we find:

> "American oil tycoon **Armand Hammer was a Soviet agent** in the Twenties, secret Communist Party documents have

> revealed. He worked as a courier, delivering money for the Soviet-sponsored Communist International 'Izvestia' newspaper reported yesterday...the newspaper said party documents showed Hammer 'was a Comintern agent in 1921,' delivering money during frequent trips to the Soviet Union."[138]

"...Armand Hammer became friends with Lenin (and other Soviet leaders), to the extent that on November 10, 1921, Lenin autographed a portrait for Hammer, which said 'To **comrade** Armand Hammer.'"[139] This was "an appellation that Lenin almost always used for a **fellow Communist** and one that he applied to no other Western businessman."[140] When Hammer wanted a concession in Russia,

> "Lenin instructed his secretaries to 'make note of *Armand* Hammer and *in every way help* him on my behalf if he applies.' Lenin also ordered Grigory Y. Zinoviev, the head of the Petrograd Soviet, to provide **'Comrade Hammer'** with special care and 'issue orders at once to see that there is no red tape.'...The man chosen to make the full assessment on Hammer was Boris Reinstein."[141] [Italics in the original.]

Texe Marrs reveals:

> "Armand Hammer's Marxist leanings were demonstrated in the 1920s as he became a fanatical follower of communism's founder, V. I. Lenin. To prove his fidelity, the industrialist made many trips to Moscow over the years, even during the bleakest days of the Cold War, meeting privately with hardline dictators Lenin, Stalin, Khrushchev, Brezhnev, and finally, Gorbachev. On occasion, he was given briefcases full of U. S. dollars by the Russian KGB—money intended for Gus Hall, head of the Communist Party U. S. A. Strangely, U. S. customs officials looked the other way."[142]

HAMMER'S "GOPHER"

On Hammer's 80th birthday, Brezhnev honored him with "the Soviet Union's Lenin Order of Friendship Among the Peoples, which no other American capitalist had been, or will ever be awarded...."[143] Also, in honor of his 90th birthday, the Soviet Union aired "a laudatory hour-long television documentary on him...."[144] He then "flew to Moscow, where he had been invited by Gorbachev to be an 'observer' to the Reagan-Gorbachev summit—the only private citizen in the world so honored."[145]

Another researcher writes:

> "Billionaire Armand Hammer helped to finance Samuel Rubin who was an elite member of the Communist Party. The

Rubin Foundation funded the **Peace Research Institute** which became the Marxist-Communist **Institute for Policy Studies.** The Rubin Foundation is a client of the law firm of *Winston Lord....* "[146] [Boldface in the original; italics added.]

The Institute for Policy Studies (IPS)

> "is a violence-prone group of extremists intent on changing America into a Marxist-socialist society by, '*...Dismantling the capitalist economic order and reshaping public-sector institutions in ways that give the Left political power thus far denied by the electoral process.*' IPS has firm ties to anti-American terrorists and militant Marxists worldwide; and IPS has firm ties to Bill and Hillary Clinton also....
>
> "Individuals who have been identified as CP [Communist Party] members...have participated in IPS functions. IPS representatives have also affiliated with known communists."[147] [Emphasis in the original.]
>
> "The FBI reports that IPS personnel are linked to the *'pro-communist and anti-U. S.'* SDS group, the *'Weathermen'* terrorist group which was involved in *'strategic sabotage,'* and the *'Progressive Labor Party* [which—D.M.P.] was founded...*by individuals expelled from the Communist Party USA, for following the Chinese Communist Line.*'"[148] [Emphasis in the original.]

"The FBI has compiled some 2705 pages of information which document how IPS is a violent and subversive organization."[149]

Armand Hammer, along with **World Vision,** following the Armenian earthquake in 1987, presented "a $1 million relief gift to **Mikhail Gorbachev....**"[150]

Al Gore, Sr. was also involved with Armand Hammer and was known as "Hammer's gopher."[151]

Remember, it was Hammer who was able to get Graham into other countries and Winston Lord (whose client was financed by Hammer) was also a friend of Billy Graham. It's a small world, isn't it?

POISON BIBLES

A few pages after Graham tells about the luncheon he attended at Lord's residence, he goes on to boast:

> "It gives Ruth and me special joy that our younger son, Ned, has become deeply committed to China. He now heads a small organization based in the Seattle area called East Gates Ministries International, devoted to assisting the Church in

China through training, literature, and Bible distribution. As I write this, East Gates has been given **official permission** to print several million Bibles at the **Amity Printing Press** in Nanjing, a **joint project of the China Christian Council and the United Bible Societies.** These are **earmarked for legal distribution to house churches** throughout China—groups that have had no reliable **legal** source of Bibles in the past."[152]

Do you realize what you've just read?! Graham's son, with the blessing of Billy and Ruth Graham, is involved in getting the "poison-snake" Bibles printed by the Communistic Amity Press.

Furthermore, according to one article, we are told:

> "The Amity Foundation [headed by K. H. Ting—D.W.C.], a Christian organization which works with foreign church-related organizations which want to assist cultural, educational, and social service programmes in China, issued a statement last month on such relationships. It says such **aiding groups should be in 'general sympathy with China's socialist modernization...be willing to abide by the laws and customs' of China, and 'respect the Three-Self** [the Three-Self movement is also headed by K. H. Ting—D.W.C.] **principle' of Chinese church life.** The foundation opposes 'random distribution of Christian literature, fund-raising for church building and other work, the use of funds for the training of Chinese church workers...and similar practices which are carried on without the expressed consent of proper Chinese church authorities.'"[153]

So, to even be allowed to do what the Grahams are doing, would mean that the **organization should be in sympathy with socialism and also respect the Three-Self Patriotic Movement!** Would the Lord be pleased with such compromise in order to *supposedly* be able to distribute His Word?

LESS THAN 12%

Ruth Graham (and a few others) started East Gates Ministries in 1989 but in 1991 Ned became President.[154] In 1997, the Billy Graham Evangelistic Association gave Ned Graham's organization almost $1 million.[155]

One article relates:

> "East Gates public-relations materials emphasize the organization's distribution of Bibles for people in China without ready access to them. Documents filed with the IRS show that in 1996 East Gates **spent $494,515 on Bible purchases and distribution,** and $504,497 on other ministries (in China and

> on donated food to North Korea valued at $300,000), not including all associated costs, **out of a total income of $42,076,533.** Other expenses included an item for 'building relationships with governmental agencies and individuals.'
>
> "In 1997, East Gates reported that it spent **$268,890** on Bible purchases and distribution....In 1998...it spent **$178,000** on Bibles...."[156]

Notice how the amount for Bibles keeps dwindling over the last few years.

Ned's May 1999 letter stated:

> "In the coming years, **East Gates will continue our Bible and Christian literature distribution** as well as develop new projects that benefit and assist the Church in China. **These endeavors would be impossible without the prayers and financial support of partners such as you.** Even though East Gates is a relatively small organization, we are putting your resources to the greatest strategic work possible in China....
>
> "Your partnership is critical in our endeavors. Thank you for helping us love China for Christ."[157]

Doesn't it seem like the money you give is **supposed** to go for Bibles and projects to help the Chinese people? However, in 1997, East Gates spent **less than 12%** of the money they collected for Bibles and distribution, and **less than 5%** for food, etc., yet many people who are giving their money to East Gates probably are under the impression that this money is being used for Bibles and food. Of course, even when the money is used for Bibles, it often leads to arrests for the house church Christians.

Nevertheless, Ned Graham's January-March 2000 newsletter, *East Gates Connection,* shows a picture with this caption: "Dr. **Han Wenzao,** President of the China Christian Council, signs new Bible contract with Ned Graham in Beijing."[158] Remember, Wenzao is a **Communist!**

Ned also admits that he knows about the house churches. He wrote:

> "In September 1989, shortly after the June 4th Tiananmen Square incident, a courageous Christian named Chen from an **unofficial House Church** ventured into a government approved Three Self Church to purchase a **'legal'** Bible. **He had been cautioned not to do this because he may have been required to sign his name and give his identity card number.** Yet **Chen took the risk** and successfully obtained a legal Bible."[159]

This quote from Ned clearly shows that many Christians in China are afraid to purchase the **LEGAL** Bibles because of giving their name, etc. Notice also that Ned admits that "Chen took the risk," yet Billy Graham claimed in a 1999 ad in *Christianity Today* that purchasing a legal Bible does not have "the associated risk to the Chinese believers as with smuggled Bibles."[160] If you read enough of Billy's and Ned's literature, you will begin to see discrepancies and contradictions.

The Grahams claim they don't see persecution in China[161] yet the quote just given hints that there is persecution or Chen and the other house church Christians would not have been concerned about giving their name or with taking a risk to obtain a Bible.

I'm sure you've seen pictures of Christians from China and other Communist countries where the people's faces (or eyes) are covered so that they will not be able to be identified by others. This is for their protection since, if they are identified, they could easily be arrested and tortured for admitting that they are believers. Ned also shows pictures of Chinese Christians. One of the pictures he clearly labels as *"A House Church family in Jiangxi Province...."*[162] [Emphasis in the original.] There are three indiscriminations here: First, he mentions that it is a "House Church family." The house churches are **illegal** in China, so they are committing a "crime." Second, he tells which province they are from. Third, he shows the family without any features covered up and, worse of all, he shows them close-up. Another picture shows Ned teaching in a house church and, once again, the people could be identified. Was this done intentionally? Is he trying to get them arrested? I don't know, but he should definitely know better and I can only wonder why he did what he did.

COMMUNIST ENTOURAGE

Of course, the Grahams are quite friendly with the Chinese government officials. Below is part of an article that appeared in the November 6, 1999 issue of *World.*

> "Diplomatic activities are an unusual section of Mr. [Ned] Graham's ministerial portfolio, but not a new one. During his tenure as president of East Gates, **Mr. Graham has had frequent contact with high-level Beijing officials.** Last year at the Washington Hilton he had to deal with a crisis when the four-star hotel booked Mr. Graham and an entourage of Chinese government religious-affairs specialists on the same floor as the official delegation from Taiwan.

"For Mr. Graham—whose **coast-to-coast tour with Beijing officials** was coming to a climax in the nation's capital—this was a nightmare come true. Mainland China and Taiwan are technically at war with each other, and the room placement would anger some of the bureaucrats with whom Mr. Graham had built up good rapport.

"Mr. Graham prevailed upon his Hilton hosts to move the Taiwan delegation, he later told aides—and **bragged** to staff members about the switch, according to a former employee. The employee also said that Mr. Graham took particular relish in relating that many of the Taiwanese were moved to a floor with fewer amenities and had complained. Other Taiwanese were moved to another hotel; one Taiwan official, Vincent Yao, recalled, 'We were told there were not enough rooms.'

"Maneuvers of that sort helped Ned Graham build good relations with the Chinese Communist Party's religion-control officials. Three of those officials—**Ye Xiaowen, director of the Religious Affairs Bureau; Wenzao Han, president of the China Christian Council; and Deng Fucun, vice-chair and secretary-general of the Three-Self Patriotic Movement**—seem particularly influential, and all three were on the tour. (TSPM is the organization created by **Communist** leaders in the 1950s to oversee Protestant churches; it answers to the Religious Affairs Bureau.)

"They visited East Gates headquarters south of Seattle, Wheaton College near Chicago, and attractions in New York and Washington, D.C. **They met with Billy Graham and his wife Ruth at the Graham home in North Carolina, and attended a seminar on DVD technology at the nearby Billy Graham study center.**

"Cost of the tour for these leaders and staff members was $36,000, Mr. Graham told WORLD. He said that the trip's 'primary purpose was to focus on the need for solid, foundational, theological training at all levels in China.' But Rich Cizik of the National Association of Evangelicals said of the **Chinese officials, 'They were clearly on a propaganda campaign.'"**[163]

EAST GATES AIDS COMMUNISTS

Did you notice how Ned Graham had the power to allow the Chinese officials better hotel accommodations than the Taiwanese officials received? Did you also notice how these **Communists** toured Ned's ministry (East Gates), Wheaton College (which will be covered in Chapter 7), and also spent time in Billy and Ruth Graham's home and how they were given a seminar on DVD technology at Billy Graham's center?! Finally, for those of you who are giving money to the Grahams for their "outreach," I want to ask you: "Are you pleased that **<u>YOUR</u>** money may have been used to give these **Communist** officials royal treatment?"

Furthermore, Ned brags in his newsletter:

> "East Gates has had the privilege of assisting in the building of the largest church in Huaiyin. When completed in mid-2000, it will seat over 4000 worshippers. This will make it one of the largest churches in China. In 1998, East Gates assisted with the construction costs. Recently, we helped to pay for 50% of the pews and sound system."[164]

Ned explained that his mother was born in Huaiyin and that is where her father, Dr. L. Nelson Bell, had served as a surgical missionary.[165] Ned brags in his April 2001 newsletter that in "the past four months alone, we've been able to help refurbish or build churches in Hunan, Jiangsu and Zhejiang Provinces."[166] Graham is helping to build churches in the very provinces where they are being destroyed by the Communists—and where he had previously claimed there was no persecution!

Before saying "Praise the Lord," we need to once again notice a few things. It would be wonderful if churches were being built in China where the Gospel of Jesus Christ could be preached and souls could be saved. The frustrating truth is that no such thing can happen with the church that Graham helped to build with God's money and people's often sacrificial gifts. Why? Simply because the church that Ned helped to build has to be a **GOVERNMENT** church! You see, the **house churches meet in small groups in people's homes.** They also meet **in secret** so that they can preach, teach, and share God's Word with others. Of course, in China, this is **illegal.** "The TSPM teaching is that Jesus was a good teacher, with many wise things to say, but true salvation comes from the Communist party. Preaching on the resurrection and return of Christ is forbidden. They even forbid the mention of God outside of a TSPM building."[167] So, when Graham brags that this will be one of the **largest churches** in China, we know that it has to be a **registered** church affiliated with the Three-Self Patriotic Movement. It also has to be **under government control,** which includes not being allowed to preach from the book of Revelation.

NO EVANGELIZING

We are told: "The Red Chinese **communists** own church properties and **permit no evangelizing** off church properties."[168]

Another writer reminds us: "THERE ARE NO FREE CHURCHES IN CHINA. ALL VISIBLE CHURCH BUILDINGS ARE UNDER THE COMMUNIST CONTROL OF THE RELIGIOUS AFFAIRS BUREAU."[169] [Emphasis in the original.]

Bishop Ting himself said that "the work of evangelism and church-building in China is the responsibility and task of us Chinese Christians ourselves, and that no group outside of China regardless of skin and colour should undertake any work of this nature in China **without first consulting the China Christian Council."**[170] Remember, Ting was head of the China Christian Council![171]

Of course, **Ting** "advocates New Age concepts that de-emphasize the importance of faith in Jesus Christ, for salvation, **questions the divine inspiration of Scripture, and says evangelism is not necessary** because God does not require people to believe in Him...."[172]

Please remember that the

> "clergy in the Three-Self churches are all on the government payroll, and their salaries are **much higher** than the average wage earner in China. A pastor of a Three-Self church told me that in some places their sermons have to be shown first to the government authorities before they can be preached, and in other places the authorities visit their churches to see who attends and to check on what is said."[173]

Once again, we can see that the **money** that **people give to East Gates** is not going to help the poor Chinese Christians but rather it **is going to aid and abet the Communists!**

BELL RECEIVED ROCKEFELLER GRANT

Also of interest is the mention of Ruth Graham's father, **L. Nelson Bell.** Without going into detail, I'll briefly mention that an **authorized** biography of Bell published for the Billy Graham Evangelistic Association in 1971 entitled *A Foreign Devil in China,*[174] with a foreword written by Billy Graham, reveals that Bell had received a grant in surgery from the **Rockefeller Foundation!**[175] Later on, he "enlisted help from the Rockefeller Foundation in Peking and from a government organization."[176] (I mentioned the "Rockefeller connection" with Billy Graham in an earlier chapter, but it appears as though the association with the Bell and Graham families has gone on for quite a long time!) Bell was also related to President **Woodrow Wilson.**[177] "He paraded in Washington at the Presidential Inauguration of his distant cousin Woodrow Wilson in March 1913."[178]

Bell attended the Medical College of Virginia where he was **"initiated** into the medical fraternity, Omega Upsilon Psi, and went to live in the fraternity house on Grace Street between the college and Jefferson's graceful capitol."[179] This biography also mentions: "Bell's popularity with students was proved by **his election to the coveted fraternity of the Skull and Keys, 'a right wild bunch,'** although the members knew he would not join the more uproarious of their proceedings."[180]

Bell also performed abortions and he explained his reasoning to Billy Graham.[181] In 1989 and 1992, on CNN, and May 1997 on "20/20," **Graham advocated abortion** in cases of "rape or incest or any of those things."[182] He "has also stated that he does not complain about abortion because, 'No one really knows when life begins.'"[183] No one knows when life begins? Obviously, this is just an excuse to clear a guilty conscience because common sense alone tells a person that without life there can be no growth. If the baby in the womb is growing and has a heartbeat, there **has** to be life.

Even if a young lady is raped, it does not give her a right to kill the innocent child that may be conceived as a result. The Bible says that God hates "hands that shed innocent blood" (Proverbs 6:16-17). Two wrongs do not make a right and aborting a child is murder no matter how the child was conceived.

Now consider this: The Rockefeller Foundation gave L. Nelson Bell a grant. They gave funding for Graham's crusade and Rockefeller financed Planned Parenthood. Is there a connection? Has Rockefeller money perverted Bell's and Graham's viewpoints **OR** did Rockefeller fund them because of their viewpoints in the first place?

One researcher points out:

> "Even a large number of prominent Evangelical leaders from around the world yielded to the temptations of Planned Parenthood's logic. Meeting under the auspices of *Christianity Today* [Billy Graham's] magazine and the Christian Medical Society, and led by the highly esteemed Carl F. H. Henry, the Evangelicals engaged in debate and exchanged papers for several days before they drafted a consensus report. Published later in the magazine, the report said in part:
>
> "'Changes in the state laws on therapeutic abortion should be encouraged.

> "'Suitable cases for abortion would fall within the scope of the American College of Obstetricians and Gynecologists Statement on Abortion.
>
> "'As to whether or not the performance of an **induced abortion** is always sinful we are not agreed, but about the **permissibility for it** under certain circumstances we are in accord.
>
> "'The **Christian physician will advise induced abortion** only to safeguard greater values sanctioned by Scripture. These values should include individual health, family welfare, and **social responsibility.**
>
> "'Much human **suffering can be alleviated by preventing the birth of children where there is a predictable high risk of genetic disease or abnormality.** This appears to be a reasonable Christian objective.'"[184]

Wow! That is a fairly inclusive statement to allow for abortions for almost **any** reason. Notice that the mother's life does not need to be at risk for the abortion to take place, but an abortion can be performed for "family welfare" or "social responsibility." Can you think of any abortion that **would not** be covered under this definition?!

Nelson Bell also seemed to be somewhat involved in politics. In the book, *Billy Graham: The Great Evangelist,* we find:

> "He [Billy] drove to Grandmother Bell's house in the Asheville area, not more than two hours west of Charlotte. Ruth's parents were there....He [Dr. Nelson **Bell]** confided to Billy he **was going to Washington, D.C., to warn the State Department that the Japanese planned a war with the United States."**[185]

How was he privy to this information?

As an aside, Nelson Bell's son, Clayton Bell, pastors the Highland Park Presbyterian Church in Dallas, Texas. One of his members is **Ross Perot.**[186] Billy Graham also mentioned that he has been Perot's houseguest.[187]

Let's return to Ned Graham. In his January-March 2000 newsletter he stated:

> "When we first started traveling extensively to China in 1990, less than a year after the Tiananmen Square incident, Western missionary activity was almost completely underground. The only notable 'open' involvement was the **World Council of Churches, which had established diplomatic ties of sorts with the Three-Self Patriotic Movement and the United Bible Societies, which had funded the Bible printing press in Nanjing known as Amity."**[188]

It is interesting to observe that the "only notable 'open' involvement" was with the WCC. Of course, I've already covered the Communistic leanings of the WCC, so it's no surprise to me that the **WCC was working with the Communistic government of China.** In 1975 some writings by the WCC staff were published in which they favorably quoted Joseph Needham, a believer in communism, when he proclaimed: "China is the only truly Christian country in the world in the present day, in spite of its absolute rejection of all religion."[189]

What may be a surprise to some, however, is that **Ned Graham is able to work so freely with the same Communistic authorities.**

UNITED BIBLE SOCIETIES

We also need to notice that the United Bible Societies (UBS) is helping to fund Amity Press and is in a joint venture with them.[190] Of course, we have to wonder what kind of Bible is being produced on this press. One author states:

> "Not only is the United Bible Societies corrupt ecumenically, but the Bibles they are producing are corrupt as well. First, their translations are based on a Greek text which deletes thousands of words and many entire verses. You will look in vain in UBS Bibles for these verses: Matthew 12:35; 17:21; 18:11; 21:44; 23:14; Mark 7:16; 9:44; 9:46; 11:26; 15:28; Luke 17:36; 22:20; 23:17; 24:12; 24:40; John 5:4; Acts 8:37; 28:29; Romans 16:24; and 1 John 5:7-8.
>
> "Further, most new UBS translations follow the 'common language' paraphrasing principles. An example of this type of 'translation' is the *Today's English Version* copyrighted by the American Bible Society. The widespread usage of common language methodology was admitted to me in a letter dated July 31, 1987, from Philip Stine, Translations Research Coordinator for the United Bible Societies. He said, 'It is probably fair to say that of the 570 languages in which we are currently working that all but 15 or 20 of them would meet our definition of common language translations.' It is impossible to produce a pure Bible by using common language principles."[191]

The person who popularized the dynamic equivalency was Eugene Nida.[192] He was originally with Wycliffe Bible Translators and then worked with the UBS as the Executive Secretary of the Translations Department from 1946 to 1980.[193]

> "Dr. Nida was also Translation Research Coordinator for the **United Bible Societies** from 1970 to 1980.

> "While now retired, Nida retains his relationship with the ABS [American Bible Society] and UBS as a Special Consultant for Translations, and is active in research, writing and lecturing."[194]

Of course, Nida does not believe the fundamentals of the Christian faith. He is a "theological liberal."[195] Here are a few of Nida's beliefs:

➽ "God did not give eternal truths, says Nida, but granted communication."[196]

➽ "Nida states emphatically that the biblical revelation is not 'absolute.'..."[197]

➽ "The only absolute in Christianity is the triune God. Anything which involves man, who is finite and limited, must of necessity be limited, and hence relative. Biblical culture **relativism is an obligatory feature** of our incarnational religion, for without it we would either absolutize human institutions or relativize God."[198]

➽ "According to Nida, Jacob's struggle with the angel is being interpreted **psychoanalytically** or **mythologically...."**[199]

➽ Nida also denies the blood atonement.[200]

Remember Nida is the person who was the Executive Secretary of the Translations Department for several decades and also worked with the American Bible Society.

Another person with the ABS is Barclay M. Newman. He denies that Adam and Eve were real people.[201]

Obviously, the views of these people will eventually find their way into the Bible translations. For instance, *Today's Dutch Version* changes Philippians 2:6 which reads: "Who being in the form of God, thought it not robbery to be equal with God" to "Although he had a divine form, **he did not value being like God."**[202] What a difference of meaning! Clearly both versions cannot be correct!

"Translations such as the NASV [New American Standard Version] differ from the KJV 36,000 times in the N. T. [New Testament] *alone!"*[203] [Emphasis in the original.]

The United Bible Societies just happens to be an affiliate of the American Bible Society[204] and the ABS is an affiliate of the National Council of Churches.[205] "According to an EP News Service report of August 18, 1984, the United Bible Societies produce nearly 80% of the world's Scriptures. In 1983 the Bible Societies disseminated more than 497 million copies of the Scriptures (EP News Service, May 5, 1984)."[206] The American Bible Society pays almost one-half of the

United Bible Societies' budget[207] and the ABS holds the copyright to the *Good News Bible* (also known as *Today's English Version* or *TEV)* which was an extremely popular Bible.

> "The chief translator was Robert Bratcher, a modernist who does not believe that Jesus Christ is God, nor that Jesus Christ was born of a virgin, nor that the blood of Jesus Christ is necessary to atone for sin. The *TEV* reflects these wicked views. For example, in 16 key passages which deal with the blood atonement of Jesus Christ, the *TEV* deletes the word 'blood.'"[208]

Bratcher has also stated:

"Jesus Christ could not enjoy omniscience. That is an attribute of God....Jesus did not claim He and the Father to be one—which would be absurd."[209] He has also remarked: "Only willful ignorance or intellectual dishonesty can account for the claim that the Bible is inerrant and infallible....To invest the Bible with the qualities of inerrancy and infallibility is to idolatrize it, to transform it into a false god."[210]

These are the views of a man who is the translator for the *Good News Bible/Today's English Version!* Yet **Billy Graham has made this version popular** by being one of the first to distribute it throughout his organization. **Graham claimed that it was an excellent translation** and promoted it on nation-wide TV during his campaign in Anaheim, California.[211]

"We now see New York rappers featured in an ABS interactive computer program that translates Bible stories into language and images appealing to teenagers....A version of Mark 5:1-20 that 'would be at home on MTV' has **cursing,** rap music, and violent images."[212]

I guess it should not be a surprise to discover that the first secretary of the American Bible Society, John Pintard, was a **Mason.**[213] Also, John T. Manson was the President of the ABS for a while. He, too, was a Mason.[214] "The American Bible Society presented the [Masonic] Grand Lodge [of Ohio] with a copy of the Holy Scriptures."[215] We also find that **John Marks Templeton, a Rhodes scholar**[216] who was awarded the Norman Vincent Peale Award for Positive Thinking in 1992,[217] has been a board member[218] and a trustee of the ABS.[219] Ruth Peale, whose husband was a 33° Mason, was a member of the Board of Managers of the ABS.[220]

BIBLE CONTAINS LEGENDS

Another board member of the ABS is Professor **Bruce Metzger.**

> "He served on the committee which produced the *RSV [Revised Standard Version]* and the *New RSV.* He was chairman for the butchered *Reader's Digest Condensed Bible. O Timothy* Editor David Cloud says...: 'Bruce Metzger is a Liberal. He piously claims on one hand that the Bible is the inspired Word of God; but out of the other side of his mouth he **claims the Bible is filled with myth and lies.** He denies the Bible's history, its miracles, and its authorship....'"[221]

"Metzger rejects the Mosaic authorship of the Bible and the inerrancy of Holy Scripture. He says that the Book of Jonah is 'a popular legend' and Job an 'ancient folktale.' According to him the known Eighth Century Prophet **Isaiah did not write Isaiah 40-66."**[222] He claims that the Bible "is not to be read 'with a dull prosaic and **literalistic mind!'"**[223]

"The publication of the *Revised Standard Version* of the Bible was authorized in 1951 by the **National Council of Churches** of Christ...."[224] Metzger was just one person out of 96 individuals[225] who helped with the *RSV.* A few other individuals were Walter Russell Bowie, Henry J. Cadbury (Harvard), George Dahl (Yale), Leroy Waterman (University of Michigan), and Fleming James.[226] The five men just listed and 25 others from this committee had "records of support for **COMMUNIST** causes...."[227] Bowie was affiliated with 33 **Communist** fronts and causes, Cadbury had 9 affiliations, Dahl had 18, Waterman had 20, and James had 25 connections with Communist ties![228] Bowie, Cadbury, Dahl, and Waterman "were all affiliated with the *National Federation of Constitutional Liberties* (NFCL). The House Committee on Un-American Activities officially reported: **'<u>The NFCL is one of the viciously subversive organizations of the Communist Party</u>.'"**[229] [Emphasis in the original.]

Of course, men like this don't believe the Bible. For instance, Bowie wrote in *Great Men of the Bible:*

> "According to the enthusiastic traditions which had come down through the FOLKLORE of the people of Israel, Methuselah lived 969 years; Methuselah has become, not only a LEGEND, but a proverb....The story of Abraham comes down from ancient times; and HOW MUCH OF IT IS FACT AND HOW MUCH OF IT IS LEGEND, NO ONE CAN POSITIVELY TELL."[230] [Emphasis in the original.]

> "Referring to Jacob's night of wrestling with the Angel of God, he says, 'The man of whom these words were written (Genesis 32:31) belongs to a time so long ago that IT IS UNCERTAIN WHETHER ITS RECORDS ARE HISTORY

> OR LEGEND.' Explaining away the miraculous in the account of the burning bush, he comments, 'One day he (Moses) had a vision. In the shimmering heat of the desert, beneath the blaze of that eastern sun, he saw a bush that SEEMED on fire, and the bush was not consumed.' He makes the fact of Elijah's mighty victory on Mt. Carmel out to be a mere legend something like KING ARTHUR AND THE KNIGHTS OF THE ROUND TABLE....'It is not strange that in the atmosphere of tradition and LEGEND which gathers around heroic figures there should be this reflected light. But the central matter is independent of these miraculous occurrences.' Concerning the three Hebrew children in the fiery furnace, he says, 'And then the old story tells the TRADITION of their miraculous deliverance.'"[231] [Emphasis in the original.]

JESUS WAS CONCEITED AND INSANE

Cadbury authored *Jesus, What Manner of Man?* in which he implies that Jesus was conceited "and perhaps just a little insane."[232] He wrote: "Indeed, as is well known, the emphasis of orthodoxy... upon his messianic claims and messianic consciousness led some psychiatrists to doubt his sanity....He [Jesus—P.F.R.] was given to overstatements, in his case, not a personal idiosyncrasy, but a characteristic of the oriental world."[233] In *The Peril of Modernizing Jesus,* he suggested that there was a fairy tale factor that crept into the Gospels.[234]

Fleming James co-authored a book with Frederick C. Grant entitled *The Beginnings of Our Religion,* in which we are told that the first five books were pieced together from several sources, two of which cannot be called history.[235]

> "Regarding the crossing the Red Sea he writes: 'WHAT REALLY HAPPENED AT THE RED SEA WE CAN NO LONGER KNOW....THE SAME MAY BE SAID OF THE ACCOUNT OF THE PLAGUES.' With reference to Elijah in II Kings 1, he writes: 'The narrative of calling down fire from heaven upon the soldiers sent to arrest him is PLAINLY LEGENDARY.'"[236] [Emphasis in the original.]

Grant remarked: "We may admit at once that the older view of Jesus' life and ministry WAS NOT ENTIRELY HISTORICAL."[237] [Emphasis in the original.] He also believed in purgatory and told us to continue to pray for those who have died.[238] Concerning purgatory, I must ask, if salvation is a **free gift** (as the Bible teaches) then how can there be such a place as purgatory where one has to **pay** for his sins? Psalm 49:7 says: "**None** of them can **by any means** redeem his brother, nor give to God a ransom for him." "Forasmuch as ye know that **ye were not redeemed with corruptible things, as silver and gold,** from your vain conversation received by tradition from your fathers; But with the precious blood of Christ, as of a lamb without blemish and without spot" (I Peter 1:18-19).

Isn't it interesting to note that while "less than three per cent [as of 1964] of Protestant ministers have affiliated in any way with **communist fronts** and causes, on this one important project [writing the *Revised Standard Version* of the Bible] **nearly 30% of the participants have been so affiliated."**[239]

DEMONS ARE DELUSIONS

Let's spend a few more minutes to examine some of the other translators' beliefs. Edgar J. Goodspeed wrote a book, *A Life of Jesus.* In this book he removes the deity of Christ.[240]

> "Goodspeed also describes the 'demons' of the Bible as 'delusions.' He writes: 'My name is Legion!' cried this man, "for there are many of us." This was clearly the man's own conviction of his emotional instability; he felt himself to be in the control of a multiple personality....Jesus humored him, and the man's cries and movements so frightened the animals that they rushed in panic over the edge of the cliff into the lake.' Actually the Bible teaches that the swine had listened to 'the man's cries and movements' for years without running in panic over the cliff. It was only when the man ceased his maniacal screamings that they became 'panic stricken.'"[241]

He denies the **physical** resurrection when he writes: "That he is to be with them always, to the very end, shows that IT IS NOT AS A PHYSICAL PRESENCE THAT HE HAS COME BACK TO THEM, BUT AS A SPIRITUAL ONE."[242] [Emphasis in the original.]

The Bible is very specific that Christ had a physical resurrection. Here are just a **few** verses:

† "And when they had fulfilled all that was written of Him, they took Him down from the tree, and laid Him in a sepulchre. But **God raised Him from the dead:** And He was seen many days of them which came up with Him from Galilee to Jerusalem, who are His witnesses unto the people" (Acts 13:29-31).

† "And we are witnesses of all things which He did both in the land of the Jews, and in Jerusalem; whom they slew and hanged on a tree: **Him God raised up the third day, and shewed Him openly"** (Acts 10:39-40).

† "This Jesus hath God raised up, whereof we all are witnesses" (Acts 2:32).

† "God, having raised up His Son Jesus, sent Him to bless you, in turning away every one of you from his iniquities" (Acts 3:26).

† "The God of our fathers raised up Jesus..." (Acts 5:30).

† "Knowing that He which raised up the Lord Jesus shall raise up us also by Jesus..." (II Corinthians 4:14).

The issue of the resurrection is vital to the Christian's belief. "[I]f thou shalt confess with thy mouth the Lord Jesus, and shalt **believe** in thine heart that **God hath raised Him from the dead, thou shalt be saved"** (Romans 10:9). Paul then reminds us in I Corinthians 15:17: "[I]f Christ be not raised, your faith is vain; ye are yet in your sins." Without believing in Christ's resurrection, no one can be saved.

In another book Goodspeed wrote, *How to Read the Bible,*

> "he calls Genesis the product of an 'oriental story teller at his best'; describes Ruth as a little idyll belonging to 'Israel's FICTION, rather than to its history, and should be read among its tales and stories'; the book of Job is 'religious FICTION'; and of Jonah he says: 'Jonah is the first missionary book in the world. If people would RECOGNIZE IT AS FICTION, they might get from it its meaning, which was never more needed than today.'"[243] [Emphasis in the original.]

BIBLE "ALTOGETHER UNRELIABLE"

Julius A. Brewer is another translator for the *RSV.* In his book, *The Literature of the Old Testament,* he claims that the "dates and figures found in the first five books of the Bible turn out to be ALTOGETHER UNRELIABLE."[244] [Emphasis in the original.] James Moffatt ("who published his own translation of the Bible"[245]) wrote *The Approach to the New Testament,* in which he claimed: "The writers of the New Testament MADE MISTAKES in interpreting some of the Old Testament prophecies."[246] [Emphasis in the original.] William F. Albright doesn't accept the Gospel of John as "a historical source."[247]

Clarence T. Craig asserts:

> "It is to be remembered that there were no eyewitnesses of the resurrection of Jesus. No canonical gospel presumed to describe Jesus emerging from the tomb. The mere fact that a tomb was found empty was capable of many explanations. The

very last one that would be credible to a modern man **would be the explanation of a physical resurrection of the body.**"[248]

He denies the second coming of Christ in these words: "In other words the **coming of Christ** is to the hearts of those who love him. It **is not a hope for some future time,** but a present reality to faith."[249]

Willard L. Sperry doesn't believe that the Gospel of John is accurate in recording the words of Jesus.[250] In *Outline of Biblical Theology,* Millar Burrows states: "We cannot take the Bible as a whole and in every part as stating with divine authority what we must believe and do."[251]

Another translator of this *Revised Standard Version,* William A. Irwin, writes in his book, *The Problem of Ezekiel,* that much of Ezekiel is false. He said that Ezekiel often declared "Therefore thus saith the Lord." Irwin then remarked: "This phrase is an almost unfailing mark of SPURIOUSNESS [falseness]."[252] [Emphasis in the original.]

> "In his revision of J. M. Powis' book on THE PROPHETS AND THEIR TIMES he says: 'Only bigotry could bring us to deny an equal validity with the prophets of Israel in the religious vision of men such as Zoroaster or Ikhnaton or, on a lower level, the unnamed thinkers of ancient Babylonia.' He also teaches progressive revelation coming from men rather than from God: 'The prophets were forced by the disasters that befell to do some hard and painful thinking. They were forced by the history of their own times to revise their messages again and again in order to keep up with the progress of the age. THE ASSYRIANS AND BABYLONIANS FORCED THEM TO REVISE THEIR CONCEPTION OF YAHWEH FROM TIME TO TIME UNTIL THEY FINALLY MADE HIM GOD OF THE UNIVERSE.'"[253] [Emphasis in the original.]

CHRIST'S DEITY ATTACKED

With such liberals and non-Christians on the Bible translation committee, it's no surprise to find many important doctrines such as Christ's deity attacked. For instance, Isaiah 7:14 changes "a **virgin** shall conceive" to "a young woman shall conceive."[254] This is no big deal as young women conceive every day but **ONLY ONE** woman conceived as a **VIRGIN.** There is a vital difference—a difference with **eternal** consequences, for if Christ is not virgin-born, then He could not save us for He, too, would have been born in sin as all humanity is. Romans 3:23 tells us that "all have sinned, and come short of the glory of God." Romans 5:12 explains: "Wherefore, as by one man sin entered into the world, and death by sin; and so death passed upon all men, for that all have sinned." "But when the fulness of the time was come, God sent forth His Son, made of a woman, made under the law, To redeem them that were under the law, that we might receive the adoption of sons" (Galatians 4:4-5).

Since many of the translators didn't believe in the resurrection, it's no wonder they changed Job 19:26. The *King James Version* states: "And though after my skin worms destroy this body, yet **in my flesh** shall I see God." The *RSV* reads: "And after my skin has been destroyed, then **WITHOUT MY FLESH** I shall see God."[255] [Caps in the original; boldface added.]

This version (as well as most versions since this one) leaves out entire verses. For example, the entire passage from John 7:53 to John 8:11 and Mark 16:9-20 are missing as well as Mark 15:28; Matthew 17:21; Mark 9:44, 46; Matthew 12:47; Mark 11:26; Romans 16:24; Mark 21:44; and Acts 8:37.[256]

Many verses omit references to Christ's blood. Colossians 1:14 states: "In whom we have redemption THROUGH HIS BLOOD, even the forgiveness of sins," but the *RSV* has: "In whom we have redemption, the forgiveness of sins."[257] John 3:16 omits the word "begotten" in "His only **begotten** Son."[258] Perry F. Rockwood explains:

> "In Romans 3:25, I John 2:2 and I John 4:10 the word 'propitiation' has been changed to 'expiation.' The word 'propitiation' carries with it the thought that the Cross-work of Christ gained the pleasure of God in place of wrath for those who receive Christ as personal Saviour. The word 'expiation' carries with it the thought that Christ died a 'martyr's' death rather than as the sinner's Redeemer. It is another direct attack on the vital ministry of Christ on Calvary's Cross....
>
> "In Luke 2:33 they change the words 'And JOSEPH and his mother' to 'And his FATHER and his mother.' In verse 43 they have changed 'And Joseph and his mother' to 'his parents.' In both places the Greek text contains the word 'IOSEPH' which means Joseph, and is translated Joseph by these same 'scholars' in each of the thirty-three times it is found in the New Testament [except the two instances above—Ed.]. This is another wicked attempt directed against the virgin birth of Christ."[259] [Emphasis in the original.]

A footnote in the *RSV* for Matthew 1:16 says:

> "Other ancient authorities read: Joseph to whom was betrothed the virgin Mary, **was the father of Jesus** who is called Christ. *The footnote did not appear in the New Testament issued in 1946. Neither does it appear in the cheap paper-bound issues. It is found only in the better bound issues since **1952.**"*[260] [Italics in the original; boldface added.]

These are only a few of the changes and omissions.

GRAHAM PROMOTES *RSV*

So, how does Billy Graham feel about the *Revised Standard Version* produced by many pro-Communist "theologians"?

> "In **1952** Billy Graham accepted a copy of the modernistic *Revised Standard Version* and told a crowd of 20,000 people: 'These scholars have probably given us the **most nearly perfect translation** in English. While there may be room for disagreement in certain areas of the translation, yet this new version should supplement the *King James Version* and make Bible reading a habit throughout America.'"[261]

Let's return to the Amity Press, UBS, and ABS and their Bible printing. Since many in leadership roles in the UBS and ABS do not believe in the inerrant Word of God, do you want your money going to such organizations in order for them to print Bibles? Are these corrupt Bibles the ones being printed on the Amity Printing Press? In addition to the Communists using the Bibles as bait, could the term "poison-snake" also refer to corrupt versions of God's Word?

Remember, the Amity Printing Press "was organized with the help of the United Bible Society in the United States when **Dr. Oswald Hoffmann** (well-known Lutheran Hour Speaker) was President of the U. B. S....Funding for the Amity Press from the USA was directed through the American Bible Society."[262] The UBS is "the group that controls **all** of the Bible Societies in the world."[263]

Oh, by the way, Billy Graham wrote a foreword to Hoffmann's book.[264] Hoffmann is also on the Board of Directors of *Christianity Today,* a magazine started by Billy Graham.[265] It's a small world, isn't it?

UNIVERSALISM

Do you recall that I just mentioned that the ABS (affiliated with the UBS which was headed by Hoffmann who helped to organize the Amity Press) holds the copyright to the *Today's English Version (TEV)* of the Bible? "...Graham has distributed thousands of copies of the *TEV* through his crusades."[266] This is the Bible that denies the blood atonement of Christ in 16 places.[267]

In fact, the wording of several of these verses gives the impression that because Christ died, **all** are saved. For example, Ephesians 1:7 in the *TEV* says: "For by the DEATH of Christ we are set free, and our sins are forgiven." However, the *King James Version* explains that it is through Christ's BLOOD that we have redemption and the forgiveness of sins. Without accepting His atonement for us, we cannot be saved. There is a condition to having our sins forgiven. We are not automatically forgiven just because Christ died. We must accept His provision for us.

Returning to the Amity Press, I ask, isn't it strange that the **COMMUNIST** government would not allow any Bibles to be distributed in China yet they allow "legal" Bibles to be printed by Amity Press? Obviously, there is a catch somewhere. Furthermore, in November 1999, a contract was signed with Deng Fucun, the Vice-Chairman of the **Three-Self Patriotic Movement** (who is also President of the Zhejiang Christian Council), "for the publishing and distribution of Billy Graham's sermons."[268] By the end of 2000 Ned Graham was hoping that Billy's book, *Just As I Am* (already in the translating stage), would be available to the Chinese.[269]

Ned and Billy Graham are not the only Grahams working in China with the **Communist** government. Franklin Graham, Billy's son, also has connections with them. In his January 2000 *Samaritan's Purse* newsletter he mentioned that there was a major breakthrough in China. He notes:

> "A Korean, Benhur Lee, has obtained **official permission** from the **Chinese government** to open a Christian school for children. Lee was saved in a **Billy Graham Crusade** in Seoul, South Korea, in 1973 and has committed his life to spreading the Gospel.
>
> "The International Academy opened in the capital city of Beijing this fall....
>
> "My mother, whose parents were missionaries to China, had to go to a missionary school in North Korea. Now Christian professionals can send their children to a **government-sanctioned** Christian school in the heart of China."[270]

Franklin adds: *"Dr. Benhur Lee,...president of the International Academy of Beijing, and Elmer Kilbourne,...our Samaritan's Purse representation to China, worked to establish the government-sanctioned school."*[271] [Emphasis in the original.]

MISSIONARIES ARE THE ENEMY

A **Christian** school in China would be wonderful and we should thank the Lord for it—**IF** it were true, but once again we need to take notice that the school is **GOVERNMENT-SANCTIONED.** I think it is also interesting to note that the person who was able to receive permission for this school just happened to have been "saved" at a Billy Graham Crusade and is now President of the school! What a "coincidence"! Note also that just recently the President of China (who is head of the Communist Party) said: **"Our enemy is** not those with guns, but **missionaries with Bibles."**[272] Do you **honestly** think that such a person would grant permission for a **Christian** school?

Of course, the Grahams repay the Communists for such privileges.

> "According to the *Chicago Tribune,* April 6, 1970, 'Graham said that he also refused to discuss communism...."For years I have not spoken about that," he said, "I cannot go around the world and say who is right and who is not right."' J. Edgar Hoover once warned 'If a minister can be influenced to keep silent about the dangers of communism, the Party has gained.'"[273]

Not only have Ned and Billy Graham catered to these Communists by giving them a tour of their facilities, etc., but the Grahams promoted the PNTR (formerly known as the Most Favored Nation or MFN[274]) and Ned has even "testified before the Senate Finance Committee concerning the U. S. granting China *Permanent Normal Trade Relations* (PNTR)."[275] Probably due, at least in part, to Graham's speech, this bill passed the House on May 24, 2000.

> "On a 237-197 vote, the House voted to grant permanent normal trade relations to Beijing and to end 20 years of turbulent annual reviews.
>
> "That was 19 more than the 218 votes needed for passage, a far more comfortable margin than either side had predicted.
>
> "Clinton appeared in the Rose Garden moments later to applaud the action...."[276]

One author remarks:

> "Increased American trade with China through the granting of **Permanent Normal Trade Relations** or the ascension of China to the WTO [World Trade Organization] **will simply further** Jiang Zemin's goal of **'perfecting' socialism** in China. Do we, as a nation, really want to have a hand in helping the Chinese Communists achieve this goal? Previous attempts to 'perfect' socialism in China have resulted in genocide on a scale never previously seen."[277]

In 1999, the Chinese Premier, **Zhu Rongji (a Communist**[278]), toured the U. S. and the White House had a state dinner honoring him. **Billy and Ruth Graham were among the guests** who attended. Graham said: "I think he [Zhu—Ed.] has turned China around."[279] (Rongji, by the way, was also a speaker at one of the **Council on Foreign Relations** meetings in 1990[280] and was invited as a participant in Gorbachev's State of the World Forum.[281]) Dr. Stanley Monteith says: "Gorbachev's State of the World Forum meetings **always** have an underlying theme of **occultism.**"[282] Of course, the Grahams already knew Rongji since they had met in China in 1988 and 1994.[283]

GRAHAMS SUPPORT MFN FOR CHINA

Ned and Billy Graham have been strong proponents for granting China "Most Favored Nation" (MFN) status for several years already. Remember that China is a nation which practices infanticide and persecutes Christians.[284] A few years ago, when legislators were hesitant to grant China MFN status, Billy Graham wrote a letter to them in support of the bill. Many legislators who were on the fence voted in favor of the bill after receiving his letter.[285] Also, when Li Peng, the butcher of Tiananmen Square,

> "passed two **laws against Christians,** Dr. **Graham sent out a letter of support for him.** The two laws in violation of the religious freedoms of the Chinese Constitution made it **a crime** for foreigners **to give out Bibles** or do missionary work in China **and for** China's 100 million **house church Christians to hold their secret house church worship services."**[286]

Since then, things in China have deteriorated even more according to one U. S. State Department official who said: "It hasn't been this bad since the early '90s just after Tiananmen."[287]

Yet **Ned Graham states that he knows of no persecution in China**[288] and after **Billy's trip to China** he stated that China is open and **he also failed to see the persecution of the Christians.**[289] Ned Graham just returned from China in mid-2000 and he said: "China has changed and is continuing to change at a rapid pace. The **main problem now faced by the Church is no longer general persecution** mandated by the government, as many would think...."[290] In Ned's May 1999 letter he brags:

> "East Gates has also had the privilege of working at the highest levels in China to educate Chinese leaders as to the benefits of its growing Christian population. Because of **East Gates' positive engagements with China's leadership,** <u>several religious policies have been changed</u>, clarified and published, <u>creating improved conditions for China's Christian</u>

population. **We continue to work with governmental authorities** towards improvement in these challenging arenas."[291]

PERSECUTION CONTINUES

The Grahams must have missed the news report in November 1998 where over 140 Protestants were arrested and their leaders beaten. This was just **ONE MONTH** after China signed a United Nations treaty **protecting freedom of religion.**[292] Between February and June 1996 in just the Zhejiang province alone, it is reported that "police have destroyed **at least fifteen thousand** unregistered temples, churches and tombs."[293]

> "Chinese newspapers have reported a crackdown on unauthorized worship in the coastal city of Wenzhou, an area isolated from government control. Over 1,000 temples, churches, and ancestral halls in the areas have been shut down since November [2000], and many were demolished....The heavy-handed actions come less than a month after China agreed to resume human rights talks with the U.S."[294]

Dr. Noah Hutchings has taken Bibles and other Christian literature into China throughout the years. In 1996 he was arrested (again) for doing so. He wrote: "On January 14, 1996, the communist Central Committee **criminalized all Christian activity outside the Three-Self Church.** I could not place a direct call to a church or visit a church without a government permit."[295]

In 1997, the Chinese police were "circulating an arrest warrant that bears the names of **three thousand evangelical preachers.**"[296] On December 27, 1999 five more house church leaders were arrested in the Henan province.[297] One house church leader reported: "The last six months have been the toughest in years for house churches.... we have experienced vastly increased surveillance and interference."[298] On August 23, 2000 another 130 Christians were arrested in the Henan province.[299] On September 4, 2000, a 19-year-old was arrested and beaten so badly that he died.[300] Back in May 2000, 13 house church members were also arrested.[301]

Around the same time, many churches were closed down in the Guangdong province and at least 10 leaders of underground Christian groups were arrested.[302] One official said: **"Unregistered** or illegal **groups may be punished** according to the relevant regulations...."[303]

Soon after Billy's visit to China, the following story appeared in the evangelical press about the crackdown on China's independent churches:

> "At a time when many facets of Chinese society are experiencing greater freedom, **members of house churches across China are facing the worst repression since the end of the Cultural Revolution.** For about a year, **reports of increased arrests and harassment** have filtered out of China. In the last six months, such reports have snowballed. China watchers are alarmed by the recent proliferation of regulations on Christian activities....Action against Christians has been especially harsh in Anhui and Henan, provinces where the church has grown fastest...."[304]

According to the U. S. State Department's 2000 report on religious persecution, the Chinese Christians face "harassment, extortion, prolonged detention, physical abuse, and incarceration in prison or in 'reeducation through labor' camps."[305]

MORE ARRESTS

In 1999 there was a report which stated:

> "Eight house church leaders are still being detained among the **31 Christians that were arrested in August.** The eight are currently being held by the Public Security Bureau in Nanyang, Henan Province....**The government has recently carried out a number of executions as part of a campaign to control any form of dissent.**
>
> "Among the eight house church leaders presently detained, two of them are signers of the *Confession of Faith* that was signed in November 1998. The *Confession* included a statement that appealed to the government to recognize the house churches and to cease persecuting them."[306]

With numerous reports of persecution hitting some newspapers, Ned has finally admitted that some persecution **MAY** exist, but he also quickly explains that the reason this may be so is because "believers do not interpret Scripture correctly, act upon erroneous teachings from outsiders or do not use wisdom in expressing their faith. This only invites scrutiny and misunderstanding of the Christian faith and its followers."[307] However, if China has religious freedom, as the Grahams try to make us believe, then it really doesn't matter (to the government, that is) if the group interprets Scripture correctly or not. Besides, how would a Communistic, anti-God, atheistic government know how to interpret Scripture correctly?! This is just another ploy for the Grahams to side with the **Communistic** Chinese government while **at the same time** trying to satisfy their readers' inquiries about the persecution—and keep the funds coming in to their ministries.

"BILLY GRAHAM OF CHINA"

There's an interesting story about an arrest that took place in 1988 **WHILE** Billy Graham was in China. The report states:

> "A prominent house church leader from Henan Province was arrested in Beijing two weeks ago by China's Ministry of State Security. The man, Xu Yongze, 48, had gone to the capital **hoping to meet with visiting American evangelist Billy Graham on April 17.** However, according to a traveler who came out from China last week, **Xu was arrested around 4 p.m. on April 16** in the Yuetan (Altar of the Moon) Park in Beijing.
>
> "Xu Yongze is a leader of a house church group in central China which has established over 3,000 churches since 1980. He and several of his co-workers went to Beijing on April 13 at the invitation of a fellow house church pastor in order to hear Billy Graham preach on Sunday, April 17. **Word had been circulated that Dr. Graham would also meet with house church pastors and have communion with them in a certain believer's home on that day.**
>
> "On April 15, Xu Yongze stayed at the home of a relative who lives in a residence owned by a particular government agency. The following day Xu and two of his cousins went for a stroll in the nearby Yuetan Park. While the two cousins went into a pavilion...Xu remained outside alone. This is when he was arrested....
>
> "Many evangelists with Xu Yongze's group (and other groups doing similar work) have been arrested or detained over recent years. Over eighty evangelists are reported to be in detention at present in just one area in Shaanxi Province.
>
> "Most detainees, many of whom are young rural evangelists in their late teens or early twenties, are interrogated, sometimes with physical abuse, kept in detention for several weeks and then released. Key leaders are treated more seriously, however. In one area of Anhui Province, the local Public Security Bureau offered a reward of 4,000 yuan (around US $1,000) for information leading to the arrest of two female evangelists."[308]

That is not all of the story, however. You, see:

> **"Xu had written a letter to a friend in Beijing telling him of his intention to see Billy Graham.** It appears that this letter was intercepted by the authorities, resulting in his arrest. According to his co-workers, who spoke after the arrest to the bearer of this report, Xu had intended to tell Billy Graham about the phenomena of church growth, revival and **persecution** in rural China....
>
> "In the nature and impact of his work, Xu Yongze can rightly be called the Billy Graham of China, so **it is ironic that he was arrested on the eve of his meeting with Graham."**[309]

Perhaps, as was suggested, the authorities did intercept the letter—or could it be that the letter reached Graham and he turned it over the authorities?—as he **previously** had done when he gave the Russian KGB a list of names of persecuted Christians (which will be covered shortly).

> "More recent news from Henan Province has revealed that several associates of Xu were arrested there two days after his detention in Beijing. Several of their church meeting points were raided and closed down. Indications are, therefore, that the **arrest of Xu was part of a planned and coordinated operation."**[310]

In 1997, Yongze was again sentenced to 10 years in prison for "illegal activities" which included refusing to have his church registered.[311] "During this imprisonment, he was beaten hundreds of times and often tortured after interrogation sessions. Xu reported that once both arms were handcuffed to different iron gates. When the gates were opened, he was stretched off the ground in a crucifixion position."[312]

Han Wenzao claims that Yongze is "'basically not a Christian,' since his views were 'heretical.'" You see, Yongze was preaching the world would soon end, which is heresy to the Communists,[313] but does it really matter what Yongze teaches if there is **religious freedom** as claimed by the Grahams, Ting, and Wenzao?

GRAHAM BETRAYS PERSECUTED CHRISTIANS

A similar incident occurred in Russia.

> "[D]uring his visit there, persecuted Christians gave Graham, on written notes, their names and pleas addressed to Graham to help them get the message out to the world of their persecution and dreadful agony. Instead of taking pity on

tortured Christians, **Graham turned those handwritten, scribbled, pitiful smuggled notes to the KGB!"**[314]

Do you realize what you've just read? Graham **BETRAYED** the confidence of these persecuted Christians and turned their notes over to the **Communistic** KGB!!

Persecuted Christians who thought they would find a friend in Billy Graham were sadly mistaken. After all, the Grahams don't really think (or admit) that there is persecution taking place there.[315] In a book entitled *A Prophet with Honor: The Billy Graham Story,* which **Graham asked William Martin to write,**[316] we are told that if Graham were to visit Russia,

> "it would be imperative for him to visit the six Siberian Pentecostals who, claiming to be victims of religious persecution, had sought asylum in the U. S. Embassy in 1978 and had been living in its basement ever since....
>
> "The Siberian Six ('Seven' before one of their number went on a hunger strike and had to be removed to a hospital) had become a vexing source of tension between the Soviet and U. S. governments, and a cause celebre for champions of religious freedom around the world. Soviet authorities persistently claimed the Pentecostals were not sincere religionists persecuted for their faith but opportunists using religion as a means to force the government to allow them to leave the country, as they had been trying to do for over twenty years. **Several Graham associates eventually came to share this view...."**[317]

Dr. Alexander Haraszti, Billy Graham's "point man,"[318]

> "explained that if Graham returned to America and said the Soviet government had not allowed him to see the Siberians, it would reflect badly on the government and on the peace conference. **If he said he had freely chosen not to see them, he would suffer an enormous loss of respect in America, either because he lacked compassion or commitment to religious freedom or because he was lying.** And if he said the Pentecostals had not wanted to receive him, Americans would scoff, charging him with swallowing obvious propaganda. Uncomfortable as it might be for all concerned, Graham had to see the Siberians."[319]

I'm sure you noticed that **Graham only visited the Siberian Six** out of pressure and **to keep from losing the Americans' respect for him** (but not out of concern for the people). However he did nothing to help them and only **sided with the Russian government in claiming that they were not being persecuted for their religious**

faith. In fact, "[d]uring his visit to Moscow, Billy Graham made this amazing statement: 'I have seen **no signs of oppression of the believers in the Soviet Union.'"**[320]

Concerning the Siberian Six, he said: "One of the Soviet officials I spoke with did indicate that he thought the problem would be resolved in due time. But they viewed the Pentecostals as lawbreakers, not as refugees, he said."[321]

This is the normal Communist line whether in Russia or China: Any Christians in jail are there because they have broken the law, but it just so happens that to be a Christian and witness to someone else is against the law.

> "When asked about the Christians in China who have been jailed by the communists, **Ting's** usual answer is that 'they have broken the laws.' He tries to make the faithful Christians appear as common criminals, whereas **their only 'crime' is their decision to obey Christ rather than communism.** Yes, those Christians under communism who are in prison have indeed broken the laws, but what laws? They have **broken communist laws which forbid public preaching of the Gospel.** They have **broken communist laws which forbid the religious training of the children.** They have broken communist laws whereby the local church is put under the authority of the state rather than allowed to have the freedom to exercise its ministry under its one and only Head, the Lord Jesus Christ. Yes, many Christians in communist lands have broken such laws and been severely persecuted for it."[322]

A leading Hong Kong newspaper quoted Bishop Ting as saying: "If there are Christians in jail in China, it is not because of their faith, but because they are criminals."[323] Han Wenzao said the same thing.[324] Remember, however, that being a house church Christian in China **IS** a crime, so Christians are considered to be criminals! The same thing is true in the Soviet Union.

GRAHAM WON'T CRITICIZE SOVIET GOVERNMENT

While in Russia, Graham commented that he didn't have time to visit the unofficial groups because the Russians had his time scheduled hour by hour, yet the *Chicago Sun-Times* revealed: "Graham's schedule, however, showed he had **no events** Tuesday night, Wednesday morning or all day Thursday."[325] Was Graham being truthful?

Of course, **Graham admitted that he refused "to criticize the Soviet government in public."**[326] He even claimed that there was "'a measure of freedom' in the Soviet Union...."[327] He then bragged:

> **"As it turned out, the May 1982 trip to Moscow was a signal to other Communist-dominated countries that they could now invite us without risking a frown from the Kremlin.** During the summer, invitations arrived from East Germany and Czechoslovakia, among the most restrictive governments in that part of the world."[328]

It is easy to see that Graham was richly rewarded for keeping quiet about the persecution of Christians in Russia and elsewhere.

In Franklin Graham's book, *Rebel with a Cause,* he mentioned that on one of his father's trips to Russia, which was **orchestrated by the Communists,** that **Billy Graham**

> **"thanked Lenin** for 'converting the Orthodox church' by taking its property and stripping it of its power so it 'turned to God.' Franklin said, 'Communist officials carefully controlled Daddy's schedule during that trip, but never hindered his preaching....' Why? **'Daddy never spoke against Communism in his sermons.'"**[329]

Interestingly, Billy Graham "admitted that he had sought advice of **Vatican** officials on what they believed to be the most effective approach in dealing with the Soviets during his trip" to Moscow.[330]

Graham also had a crusade in Moscow in 1991. He remarked: "Things are more open now in the Soviet Union than ever before.... People are able to take the Gospel and distribute Bibles in schools, prison—even the military."[331]

GRAHAM RECEIVES HONORARY DEGREE

On January 6, 1981, Graham "received an honorary degree from the Christian Theological Academy in Warsaw, Poland....At this time, Mr. Tadeusz Dusik, Deputy Director of the State Office of Religious Affairs (a **communist),** said, 'This distinction is a symbol of **our great respect and warmth for you.'"**[332] David Cloud writes:

> "Though there is some semblance of freedom of worship, the **communist government of Poland** seeks to control all religious activity. For example, a 1984 official ruling **forbids the display of crosses in any public buildings.** The Polish government strictly controls the printing of all Christian literature, and 'allows only one evangelical Christian book to be printed every year!'...When the Polish workers attempted in 1981 to form a simple labor union independent from the

government sanctioned and controlled ones, the leaders of the movement were imprisoned and the movement was violently crushed by the Polish military. This was the same year that Billy Graham was honored by Polish authorities—the very same authorities who rule the Polish people with an iron fist!"[333]

Graham had also bragged up the "religious freedom" he saw in 1977 in Hungary, another Communist country.[334] In 1981, Graham again went to Hungary to receive another honorary degree from a **Communist-controlled** seminary.[335] "...Imre Miklos, Secretary of State for Church Affairs **(communist party)** and Bishop Bartha (apostate red puppet **World Council of Churches** leader) co-hosted his visit and praised him warmly."[336]

Graham himself wrote that Miklos "had been extremely helpful to us during our 1977 visit"[337] and was once again his co-host for his honorary degree.[338] He added:

> "At a formal academic ceremony steeped in centuries-old tradition, Bishop Bartha conferred the degree on me. The event was in the academy's main auditorium, with the faculty in full academic regalia (as was I). The audience included not only students and pastors but also **a number of Communist officials.** The American ambassador had driven from Budapest for the ceremony."[339]

> "Several times during the '80s, Graham made trips to speak in various Communist countries. Again, he accommodated the atheistic governments and the religious powers of these lands. The *Charlotte Observer* reported in its January 19, 1989, issue that '[Graham's—B.K.G.] trip this July to Budapest is **cosponsored by the [Communist] government** and the Roman Catholic Church.'"[340]

GRAHAM ARRANGES TRIP

Recently,

> "three prominent American clergymen were touring China by agreement of President Clinton and Chinese leader Jiang Zemin. Mr. Cizik, who accompanied the group, believes the **Graham-arranged trip** was a deliberate, if less promoted, counterpoint.

> "The trip included public pronouncements by Mr. Ye of the Religious Affairs Bureau, which oversees government-sanctioned religious activities. At press conferences in New York and Washington, Mr. Ye told journalists that reports of

religious persecution in China 'may be a case of general ignorance.' Mr. Ye defended the imprisonment of some Chinese Christians: **'I can tell you in all seriousness they are in prison not because of their religious beliefs but because they broke the law.'** In China, meeting for worship without government permission is illegal.

"The delegates met with 17 members of Congress, according to China's Xinhua news agency, 'some of whom had voted against president Clinton's decision to extend China's most-favored-nation trade status while others had criticized religious freedom in China.' The news agency said the delegation 'has provided a very good opportunity for people of various circles of the United States to fully, correctly, and objectively understand the religious situation in China.'

"This past June [1999], during congressional debate over China's trade status, Mr. **Graham spoke** at a policy forum in Washington sponsored by the Cato Institute. He offered prepared remarks as part of a three-man panel **touting the benefits of expanding commercial ties with China.**

"Then he was asked to talk about the situation of Christians in China. **Mr. Graham responded by stating that intellectuals have been persecuted more than 'religious practitioners' in China.** He said 'there are still instances of individuals encouraged to be aborted or forced to be aborted, but not as prevalently as some people would have you believe.' **He concluded, 'I have not in my experience encountered individuals who have recently been detained or interrogated or persecuted simply for their faith structure of beliefs.'** Cato's Dan Griswold, organizer of the forum, said Mr. **Graham 'almost left the impression that believers are as free in China as they are here.'"**[341]

WEED OUT EXTREMISTS

In Ned's November 2000 letter, he again downplays the persecution. Let's look at several sentences in the letter along with a few comments. He writes: "Our East Gates team continues to work hard to serve the indigenous Christians across China. As you know, **East Gates works with <u>all</u> Christian groups as long as their focus is on the fundamentals of evangelical Christianity."**[342] That sounds fairly good, does it not? However, the very next sentence says: "We generally **do not work with the extreme Fundamentalists,** Pentecostals or liberal groups **because of their divisive and**

separatist activities."[343] Excuse me, but don't the "extreme Fundamentalists" believe in the "fundamentals of evangelical Christianity"?

Ned Graham continues:

> "The vast majority of Christians in China are evangelical and their focus is on serving God, each other and **evangelism.** The fringe groups, however, tend to get a lot of attention from some overseas ministries that report their activities for fundraising purposes. Because **these fringe groups frequently violate Chinese law,** it is reported that they are persecuted when in fact the Chinese authorities are oftentimes doing their best to **weed out the extremists while protecting legitimate religious activities."**[344]

Most people will read over these few sentences without analyzing what Graham has just said. He is using "double-speak" and justifying the Chinese government's persecution. Notice that he said that the "vast majority" of Chinese Christians are involved in **evangelism.** Of course, this is an **ILLEGAL** activity in China, yet he refers to the "fringe groups that violate Chinese law." If his statement is true (and there's no reason to doubt it), then this makes the **vast majority** of Chinese Christians **criminals,** not just the fringe groups. Of course, by saying that there are fringe groups and extremists which the Chinese government is trying to weed out, he sides with the **Communist** government in their persecution of Christians. Notice that Ned says that some people are reporting that Christians are persecuted, when in fact he thinks **the government is "doing their best to weed out the extremists."** He continues that the Communist government is "**protecting legitimate religious activities."** This just isn't true, and remember, evangelism is not a **"legitimate** religious activit[y]."

Contradictions like this are necessary for Graham to be able to cater to the Communists **while at the same time** trying to convince American Christians to continue sending their money to him. If only people would stop and think about what is being said instead of just quickly glancing over the surface, they would not be so quick to support Ned Graham's ministry.

Yes, Billy and Ned Graham want China to have the Permanent Normal Trade Relations (PNTR). After all, Ned admits that the PNTR trading system will **help his East Gates ministries.**[345] He adds: "My concern is that if the U. S. does not grant China PNTR before China's accession into WTO, China will retaliate by restricting U. S. access to China's markets. If this were to happen, **it could harm <u>our</u> work,** especially in the area of publishing."[346]

BILLY AND RUTH DEFEND NED

At this point, **Ned** needs to worry about his work being harmed—but not from not granting PNTR status to China. His own personal life is in a total disarray. His wife,

> "Carol Graham, in a November 10, 1998, affidavit filed in court, accused her husband of **infidelity, domestic violence, and drug and alcohol abuse.** Ned and Carol Graham were then members of Grace Community Church in Auburn, Washington, where Mr. Graham had been an elder and associate pastor. Church elders met with him for two hours in mid-December 1998. They discussed not only the accusations in the divorce complaint but also Mr. **Graham's rare church attendance during the preceding three years,** according to Bruce Ker, chairman of the church's elder board....
>
> "The church subsequently stopped supporting East Gates (at $500 a month), revoked Mr. Graham's ministerial license, and told him to stop using the title 'Rev.' since he had never been ordained."[347]

Ned Graham claimed in September **1999:**

> "'I **never** personally used the title Reverend and East Gates no longer uses the title Reverend in reference to me.' But a **1997** letter he wrote to members of Congress is signed **'Rev.** Ned Graham.' The East Gates website at least until mid-October included a photograph of Mr. Graham holding a bible, with the photo captioned **'Rev.** Ned Graham.' (The site has since been changed; 'President' replaced 'Rev.')"[348]

This is just **one** of the lies that Ned's been caught in!

When *World* asked about his treatment for an alcohol-related condition, Graham would only reply that he "took Board-approved time away in June of 1998" but he didn't deny being treated for it.[349]

> "In response to a question about alleged involvement with a woman who was not his wife, Mr. Graham wrote, **'during our marriage and before the divorce** I had never been alone in a woman's home or apartment and had never been alone in my home with any woman other than my wife. [What about being alone in a motel with another woman? Also, what about **since** the divorce?] To directly answer your implied question—I was **faithful to my wife for 18 years** without exception. **At the time of the divorce filing, Ned and Carol Graham had been married for 19 years and 2-1/2 months.** They have two sons, ages 11 and 13.

"WORLD gave Mr. Graham an opportunity to amend his answer. An aide replied by e-mail: 'Please very carefully note that Mr. Graham's answers were factually correct.'"[350]

If his answer is **factually** correct, then he **lied** about being faithful to his wife in the last year of their marriage!

"At least six of the 10-member East Gates staff resigned in the first six months of this year [1999]. Three of the five members of the East Gates board of directors resigned at a December 1, 1998, telephone-conference-call board meeting. Three new board members came on at that meeting: **Mr. Graham's sister** Ruth Graham McIntyre, his **brother-in-law** Stefan Tchividjian, and motivational speaker **Peter Lowe.** Mr. Graham informed the Evangelical Council for Financial Accountability in a January 8, 1999, letter that East Gates was voluntarily withdrawing its membership since it had fallen out of compliance with ECFA's standard that **family members** should not constitute a majority of a board."[351]

"East Gates bylaws require all board members and employees to be 'in a pattern of...personal and corporate accountability.'... They are expected 'to put into their family life the time needed for the well-being of the family unit.' Mr. Gordon cited **'fraternization' with a woman employee as another of Mr. Graham's bylaw violations."**[352]

Additionally, his wife said that Ned has used pornographic materials.[353]

Right after these accusations, **Billy and Ruth Graham wrote** a letter in defense of Ned and had it published in *Christianity Today.*[354] They said:

"...Ned has our full and complete confidence and support. **We are very proud of Ned** and the **honesty** and integrity he has demonstrated in dealing with these difficult issues.

"We respect Ned for continuing to be faithful to God's calling in his life to serve the growing church in China. We also continue to fully support the ministry of East Gates and its various projects in China."[355]

It is natural to come to a family member's defense but we must be **honest** when we do so. To claim that Ned has been honest in dealing with these issues just is not true!

As an extra note, Ned also practiced karate and other martial arts—at least as a young person. In Billy Graham's book, *Unto the Hills,* he mentioned that Ned had "much practice" in the martial arts.[356]

For those we may not be aware of it, I'll just briefly point out that the martial arts come right out of Buddhism. Karate (which is a generic term that encompasses all kinds of styles that utilize different hand and foot blows) was handed down by a Zen Master to a Buddhist monk by word of mouth. Everything that is done in karate can be traced back to some principle of **Zen Buddhism.** Zen Buddhism is a pagan religion which believes in reincarnation, no hell, meditation, yoga, special breathing exercises (taken from yoga), and many other ideas that are foreign and contradictory to Biblical teachings.

PETER LOWE

As just mentioned, Ned Graham's one new board member is **Peter Lowe,** a motivational speaker. Lowe's organization is described as

> "a business seminar featuring **some of the best and most effective speakers** in America today. What you probably didn't know is that the organization promoting SUCCESS 1996 is a self-supporting, non-profit **Christian** ministry which is effectively **reaching the business world for Christ.** Many of your church members work beside men and women who are not Christians, and struggle with how to approach them about their relationship to the Lord, and how to invite them to church. We believe we can assist you in this endeavor."[357]

The announcement bragged that several thousand people have made first-time decisions for Christ through his SUCCESS seminars.[358] Some of the speakers for 1996 were Lady Margaret Thatcher, Ozzie Smith, Bob Costas, William J. Bennett, Jack Groppel, Paul Harvey, Zig Ziglar, Tom Hopkins, and **Mikhail Gorbachev.**[359] Gorbachev, of course, is a **Communist,**[360] yet he was one of the speakers at this seminar.

Lowe's April 29, 1998 SUCCESS seminar included such speakers as **Muhammad Ali, Christopher Reeve, Barbara Bush, Larry King,** and **Henry Kissinger.**[361] These seminars have been featured in such magazines as *Christianity Today, National and International Religion Report, Ministries Today,* and *New Man* (which was the Promise Keepers' magazine at that time).[362] They boasted that they were featured in these magazines "because of the highly effective way we are **reaching secular business people for Christ."**[363] How can unsaved speakers lead others to Christ?!

The October 16, 2001 SUCCESS seminar has scheduled Zig Ziglar, Marie Osmond (a Mormon), Mike Krzyzewski, Peter Lowe, Dale Jarrett, Dr. Earl Mindell, Dean Smith, and once again, **Mikhail Gorbachev.**[364]

As just mentioned, Gorbachev is a Communist. On November 2, 1987 he stated: "We are moving towards a new world, the world of Communism; we shall never turn off that road."[365]

In a speech before the Politburo in November 1987, Gorbachev said:

> *"Gentlemen, comrades, do not be concerned about all you hear about glasnost and perestroika and democracy in the coming years. These are primarily for outward consumption. There will be no significant internal change within the Soviet Union, other than for cosmetic purposes. Our purpose is to disarm the Americans and to let them fall asleep. We want to accomplish three things: One, we want the Americans to withdraw conventional forces from Europe. Two, we want them to withdraw nuclear forces from Europe. Three, we want the Americans to stop proceeding with Strategic Defense Initiative."*[366] [Emphasis in the original.]

He added that "perestroika is no retreat from Communism but rather a step towards the final realization of a Marxist-Leninist utopia; a continuation of Lenin's ideas. Those who expect us to give up Communism will be disappointed."[367]

In yet another speech to Russian students on November 15, 1989, he declared:

> "We are for Lenin, who is alive...in the building of our future we are basing it on the gigantic intellectual and moral potential of the Socialist idea united with the theory of Marxism-Leninism....We see no rational reason to give up the **spiritual** riches of **Marxism.** To achieve this the Communist Party of the Soviet Union must return to the roots and principles of the Bolshevist Revolution, to the ideas of Lenin on the building of a new society."[368]

Of course, we need to remember that **Gorbachev's idol, Vladimir Lenin,**[369] wrote a letter to the Politburo on March 19, 1922, stating that **"the more representatives of the clergy we manage to shoot the better**—now is the time to teach the lesson that for many decades the people will not dare even to think of resistance."[370] Anybody showing resistance to Communism's tenets doesn't stand a chance with the Communists. How then can **Billy Graham** be so well accepted by these same people?!

"NATURE IS MY GOD"

On December 9, 1987 **"Gorbachev hosted** 100 'intellectual leaders' at a breakfast reception in the Soviet Embassy. Evangelist

Billy Graham was among the chosen few."[371] Graham commented: "I have read that he [Gorbachev] has cold eyes....I never saw those cold eyes. His eyes were always warm or they were dancing. He has a tremendous sense of charisma about him."[372] **"[H]e impressed me as being sincere."** This was **just one month** after his November 1987 speech where Gorbachev boasted that they would never leave the road of Communism!

Even *Time* magazine (who selected Gorbachev as the "Man of the Decade" in 1990[373]) revealed: "Some people regard Gorbachev as a hero because they believe he is presiding over the demise of a loathsome ideology. But **he does not mean to abolish Communism.** On the contrary, **he wants to save it** by transforming it."[374]

The very next year the August 19, 1991 issue of *Christianity Today* bragged that

> "Graham's fifth visit to Moscow also included a 40-minute meeting with Soviet leader **Mikhail Gorbachev.** Most of the conversation was behind closed doors and covered various topics, 'including moral and spiritual concerns,' Graham said, declining to divulge details.
>
> "At the conclusion of his School of Evangelism, Graham also met with **Boris Yeltsin.** Meeting with the evangelist was **one of Yeltsin's first official appointments** following his inauguration as president of the Russian republic. Graham described the meeting as one of the best he has ever had with any political leader. Their conversation dealt almost entirely with spiritual topics, he said."[375]
>
> "Graham clearly doubted that the Soviet leader [Gorbachev] was a committed atheist, pointing out that 'when he got off the plane, if you remember, he said, "May God help us." And then in his talk to that group at the embassy, an hour and a half where I was sitting right in front of him, he used the word **spiritual** three times.'"[376]

Remember that just 2 years prior to this, Gorbachev remarked about the **"spiritual riches of Marxism,"**[377] so it's not a big deal that he would use the word "spiritual" again.

Then, on March 11, 2001, a news report revealed that Gorbachev is back on the international scene and is "promoting what amounts to a **Marxist version of world government.**"[378]

It is true that Gorbachev does not **seem** to be an atheist although he is a Communist. On "The Charlie Rose Show" on October 23, 1996, Gorbachev proclaimed: "We are part of the Cosmos. Cosmos is my God. Nature is my God....The future society will be a totally new civilization which will **synthesize** the experience of Socialism and Capitalism...."[379]

Some people don't understand the seeming contradiction, but we need to also realize that Lenin's theory was that he "had to **do and say whatever** was necessary to advance the image of a nonthreatening and potentially profitable Soviet Russia—**even when such measures deviated from, or contradicted, Marxist ideology.** The **end still justified the means** where the survival of the revolution was at stake."[380] This is why we hear some in leadership professing a **spirituality while maintaining an atheistic viewpoint** or professing to be a Christian while embracing the occult, etc. Just because a person claims to be a Christian does not make him or her a Christian. Titus 1:16 reminds us: "They **profess** that they know God; **but in works they deny Him,** being abominable, and disobedient, and unto every good work reprobate." "This people draweth nigh unto Me with their mouth, and **honoureth Me with their lips;** but their **heart is far from Me"** (Matthew 15:8; Mark 7:6; Isaiah 29:13).

Remember, "Christian talk is no substitute for the Christian walk."[381]

GORBACHEV IS A COMMUNIST

One researcher reminds us:

> "Gorbachev is **still** a professed Communist. Communism, a Masonic tool, has long been involved in forming the one-world religion. In fact, Communism, which is a form of pantheism, has been promoted as the basis for a one-world religion and world unity. **Communists have been attending international interfaith conferences for years,** even whilst they were the 'enemy.'"[382]

Also, according to Wayne Peterson, the former director of the Fulbright Scholarship Program and an U. S. diplomat, **"Gorbachev was one of the first to work with Maitreya."**[383] He said that Gorbachev "doesn't mind his name used publicly with Maitreya's emergence—seeing Him as the reappeared Christ."[384] He added: "I was not surprised to learn this about Mr. Gorbachev, since I had heard much earlier of his involvement with Maitreya from a Pentagon official. I had also heard, from people I place much confidence in, that Mrs. Gorbachev had been to India several times to see the Avatar Sai Baba."[385] Yet, as mentioned earlier, Gorbachev refused to acknowledge that he was not an atheist on Schuller's *Hour of Power* program.[386]

Most of my readers will probably be aware of Maitreya but for those who may not know, Maitreya is supposed to be the Messiah. According to this esoteric (occult) doctrine, "Jesus was a disciple of Maitreya. And the Lord Maitreya took over the body of Jesus for three years, from the baptism to the crucifixion...."[387]

The spokesman for Maitreya is Benjamin Creme. He wrote:

> "All the great religions hold before humanity the idea of a further revelation which will be given by a future Teacher or Avatar. Christians hope for the Christ's return, the Buddhists look for the coming of another Buddha, the Lord Maitreya, while the Muslims await the coming of the Imam Mahdi, the Hindus, the Bodhisattva or Krishna, and the Jews the Messiah. Each of them expects a Coming One, a Revealer of new Truths and a Guide into the future."[388]

He adds:

> "If you really believe it, then tell everyone you meet, everyone who will listen, that you believe that the Christ is in the world—that Maitreya is in the world. **It depends to whom you are talking:** if you are talking to Jews you will call Him the Messiah. If you are talking to Christians you will call Him the Christ. To Hindus you will call Him the Bodhisattva; to Buddhists, the Lord Maitreya; to Moslems, the Imam Mahdi."[389]

"If you are a Christian and prefer to call Maitreya **Jesus Christ,** that is perfectly fine with him. Maitreya, **however,** makes it very clear that **HE IS NOT THE SAME MAN AS IN ROMAN TIMES."**[390] Notice that the terminology is changed—depending on whom you are speaking to. This way the **deception** can be hidden behind a name change!

In fact, Alice Bailey states:

> "The Christ Who will return **WILL NOT BE LIKE THE CHRIST** Who (apparently) departed. He will not be a 'man of sorrows'; He will not be a silent, pensive figure; He will be the enunciator of spiritual statements which will not necessitate interpretation (and give rise to misinterpretation) because He will be present to indicate the true meaning.
>
> "He has been for two thousand years the supreme Head of the Church Invisible, the spiritual Hierarchy, composed of disciples of all faiths. He recognises and loves those who are not Christian but who retain their allegiance to their Founders—the Buddha, Mohammed, and others. He cares not what the faith is, if the objective is love of God and of humanity. **If men**

> **look for the Christ Who left His disciples centuries ago they will fail to recognise the Christ Who is in the process of returning.** The Christ has no religious barriers in His consciousness. It matters not to Him of what faith a man may call himself.
>
> "The Son of God is on His way and He cometh not alone. His advance guard is already here and the Plan which they must follow is already made and clear. Let recognition be the aim."[391]

"'I have not come to create followers,' says Maitreya. **'Each of you should continue to develop within your own religious tradition.** A real disciple is one who will respect the traditions. **Respect your own religions, your own ideologies,** in brief, your own thoughtform, and you will experience the Master.'"[392] (Doesn't this sound a little bit like Billy Graham's idea that each person should be returned to his own church—Catholic, Jewish, or Protestant?)

"MAN IS AN EMERGING GOD"

"Do not try to worship Me, Maitreya counsels. If you worship Me you are trying to lower yourself. I do not want this. *I want you to be equal.* You are a spark of the Supreme Being. Do not think you are below Me."[393] [Emphasis in the original.]

Maitreya claims: **"Man is an emerging God....**My plan and My Duty is to reveal to you a new way...which will permit the divine in man to shine forth."[394]

Maitreya also declares:

> "'Men must see themselves **as One.'** This is the **essential first step** to all future progress: on the fulfilment of that condition everything else depends. The first task of Maitreya and His group will be to show men that this is so, that only then can self-destruction be avoided, that only then can the sleeping potential of man be unleashed for its next and great achievement."[395]

How can an atheistic Communist, like Gorbachev, accept the "Messiah"? In *Encyclopedia of the American Left* we find:

> "Other spiritualist figures—journalistic spokespersons, practitioners, and poetry or fiction writers, often the same individuals—continued to affirm the centrality of radical reform or **socialism to spiritualist expectations of a New World ahead.** As late as 1879, a less controversial president of the American Spiritualist Association asserted, in the semiofficial

> *Banner of Light,* that 'if spiritualism has been under a cloud because of its connection with freeloveism, it is destined to pass under a still darker cloud—but that one has a golden lining. This cloud is called SOCIALISM'; **furthermore, 'spiritualism...will spring up unbidden in the very center of the socialistic camp.'"**[396]

The answer may also be in the following statement by Benjamin Creme: "Thus will the new age be built by **MAN HIMSELF** under the guidance of Maitreya and His Group....From **WITHIN MAN HIMSELF** will come the urge for betterment, a testimony of the divinity inherent in us all."[397]

We are also told: "The Master **(Maitreya)** has awakened the communist leaders and told them that **communism is not evil.** It has certain qualities that democracy does not have. **Democracy has certain destructive elements** which create rich and poor, the haves and have-nots."[398]

Maitreya says: "Disarmament is essential for world peace."[399] New Ager and occultist, Alice Bailey, writing through the intervention of her demon spirit guide, the Tibetan, declared:

> "In the preparatory period for the **new world order** there will be a steady and regulated **disarmament.** It will not be optional. No nation will be permitted to produce and organise any equipment for destructive purposes or to infringe the security of any other nation. One of the first tasks of any future peace conference will be to regulate this matter and gradually see to the disarming of the nations."[400]

Disarmament is one of the main goals of the Communists as well.[401] The **Socialist Party** states:

> **"We call for general and complete disarmament,** initiated unilaterally [one-sided!], with zero nuclear weapons. We are not afraid for the U. S. to take the first step toward disarmament....
>
> "The **Socialist Party** is a member of the International Peace Bureau...**working for disarmament** and a non-interventionist foreign policy."[402]

Gorbachev, too, would like to see America disarmed. Of course, **Graham also is for disarmament.**[403] Tom Sine (a very liberal "Christian") states: **"Billy Graham has recently put himself on the line as a leading advocate for nuclear disarmament,** declaring, 'The present arms race is a terrifying thing and it is almost impossible to overestimate its potential for disaster.'"[404] Vernon Grounds, President

Emeritus of Denver Theological Seminary, also "praised Evangelical leaders Senator Mark Hatfield and evangelist **Billy Graham for their opposition to the arms race and their advocacy of a nuclear moratorium [disarmament]....**"[405]

Graham and Gorbachev have the same goal of disarmament and Gorbachev is the person that Peter Lowe invited to speak at his seminar and Lowe now sits on Ned Graham's board of East Gates International. East Gates is the organization that is funding the Amity Press (headed by Communist K. H. Ting), which supplies the Bibles to the Chinese who must then supply their names and addresses and who often end up being arrested shortly afterwards. Amity Press is also being funded by the United Bible Societies whose President was Oswald Hoffmann. Hoffmann was on the Board of Director of *Christianity Today* which is Graham's magazine and Graham wrote a foreword to his book! Some interesting connections, wouldn't you agree?

One cannot help but wonder why Graham turned over the names of persecuted Christians to the Communist KGB; why he gets along so well with all the Communists; why he meets privately with them so often; why he was so intent on China receiving "Most Favored Nation" status; why he is for nuclear disarmament, etc., etc. Could it be that he is a wolf in sheep's clothing? Matthew 7:15-16 warns: "Beware of false prophets, which come to you in sheep's clothing, but inwardly they are ravening wolves. Ye shall know them by their fruits."

6. THE ENVIRONMENT, ASTROLOGY, AND HOMOSEXUALITY

The environment is a big issue today. The National and World Council of Churches are both involved in promoting the environmental agenda.[1]

> "In the 1960s at the World Council of Churches meeting in New Delhi Dr. Joseph Sittler first pointed out the importance of environmental ethical concerns. By the late 1980s the secular conservation and environment movements and the ethical and religious concerns for social development and environmental values more systematically began to merge."[2]

In 1990 a Global Forum was held in Moscow where over 1,000 participants gathered. Then-Senator Al Gore, gave a plenary address in which he

> "declared that **ecological problems could only be solved through a '<u>new spirituality</u>' common to all religions.** (Gore's 'new' ecumenical spirituality is revived paganism.) The 'Moscow Declaration' signed by participants called for 'a global council of spiritual leaders' and the 'creation of an inter-faith prayer...a new **communion with Nature....'**"[3]

The NCC then established an office on environmental and economic justice in 1991.[4] In May 1992, **"so-called** leading **evangelicals** joined a coalition of science and religion sponsored by the 'Joint Appeal by Religion and Science for the Environment.' Joint Appeal is based at New York's godless Episcopal **Cathedral of St. John the Divine,** a bastion of New Age/ecumenical/Antichrist deception."[5] Remember, St. John the Divine is where a naked female "Christ" was hung on the cross.[6]

This agreement says, in part:

> "We are people of faith and of science who, for centuries, often have traveled different roads. In a **time of environmental crisis,** we find these roads converging. As this meeting symbolizes, our two ancient, sometimes antagonistic, traditions now reach out to one another in a common endeavor to preserve the home we share....
>
> "At the same time, the human community grows by a quarter of a million people every day, mostly in the poorest nations and communities. That this crisis was brought about in part through inadvertence does not excuse us. Many nations are responsible.

> The magnitude of this crisis means that it cannot be resolved unless many nations work together. **We must now join forces to that end.**
>
> "Our own country is the leading polluter on Earth, generating more greenhouse gases, especially CO_2, than any other country. Not by word alone but by binding action, our nation has an inescapable moral duty to lead the way to genuinely effective solutions. We signers of this declaration—leaders in religion and science—call upon our government to change national policy so that the United States will begin to ease, not continue to increase, the burdens on our biosphere and their effect upon the planet's people.
>
> "We believe that **science and religion, working together, have an essential contribution** to make toward any significant mitigation and resolution of the world environmental crisis....Insofar as our peril arises from a neglect of moral values, human pride, arrogance, inattention, greed, improvidence, and a penchant for the short-term over the long, **religion has an essential role to play.** Insofar as our peril arises from our ignorance of the intricate interconnectedness of nature, science has an essential role to play."[7]

Some of the signers to this appeal are: James Parks Morton (then Dean, Cathedral of St. John the Divine), Thomas Berry (who "places the blame for environmental ills squarely on the shoulders of Christianity"[8]), Elizabeth Bowen (of the Baha'is), William J. Byron (President of the Catholic University of America), Joan Campbell (then General-Secretary, **National Council of Churches of Christ),** Benjamin F. Chavis, Jr., Steven C. Rockefeller (Professor of Religion, Middlebury College), Carl Sagan, Theodore M. Hesburgh (President Emeritus, University of Notre Dame), Roberta Hestenes (then President, Eastern College, and Chair of the World Vision International), Richard D. Land (Executive Director of the Christian Life Commission of the Southern Baptist Convention), Oren Lyons, Barbara Bellows Rockefeller (Professor of History, Middlebury College), Arthur Simon,[9] and Ronald Sider (Executive Director of Evangelicals for Social Action[10] [ESA], a radical, **leftist** group[11]). Sider brags: "I would be quite willing to join a coalition to oppose the nuclear arms race that includes Marxists, provided the coalition is not dominated by Marxists."[12] ESA

> "strongly opposes nuclear war as contrary to God's will, and it has endorsed a nuclear freeze....In addition, ESA calls Christians to work for structural changes to combat poverty and **redistribute wealth,** to oppose discrimination of **any** sort, to work for the protection of human rights around the world,

and to uphold a responsible life style and stewardship of the environment."[13]

UNEQUALLY YOKED

Sider seems willing to work with a variety of New Age groups as well. ESA and the Evangelical Environmental Network (to which Sider is also connected[14]) are associated with the Interfaith Voice for Peace and Justice. This group lists "hundreds of New Age, heathen and/or anti-Christ organizations"[15] on their web site "each supporting and recommending the other"[16] including:

✘ *Christian New Age Quarterly*

✘ Council for a Parliament of the World's Religions

✘ Islamic Information Office

✘ Margaret Sanger's Supporters

✘ Temple of Understanding

✘ UUA Office of Bisexual, Gay, Lesbian and Transgender Concerns

✘ World Muslim Congress

✘ EarthSpirit[17]

Some "Christian" groups linked to this site are:

✘ Habitat for Humanity International

✘ Vatican II Center

✘ World Council of Churches

✘ Floresta

✘ Call to Renewal

✘ National Catholic Conference for Interracial Justice

✘ National Association of Evangelicals[18]

Al Dager reminds us that

> "while the World Christian Movement links arms with unbelievers for one cause (i.e., environmentalism), it will also be linked to many who are actively pursuing abortion as a means to control world population. **When one allies oneself with the devil in a common cause for 'good,' he will find himself compromised in all other areas."**[19]

EVANGELICALS FOR SOCIAL ACTION

"ESA traces its beginnings back to 1973, when about forty evangelical leaders gathered in Chicago to discuss the need for more social concern in the churches. John Alexander, Jim Wallis, Carl Henry, Rufus Jones, and Ronald Sider were among those who drew up the **Chicago Declaration** of Evangelical Social Concern. From that came a proposal for an organization called Evangelicals for Social Action."[20]

The **Chicago Declaration calls for** the New Age/Communistic view of **disarmament and the redistribution of the wealth:**

> *"We must attack the materialism of our culture and the maldistribution of the nation's wealth and services....Before God and a billion hungry neighbors, we must rethink our values regarding our present standard of living and promote more just acquisition and distribution of the world's resources...."*[21] [Emphasis in the original.]

In Sider's book, *Rich Christians in an Age of Hunger,* he admits: "For example, in mid-1975 **David Rockefeller** of Chase Manhattan Bank and about one hundred other members of the intellectual and business establishment of the industrial world met in Japan to grope for a way through the contemporary crisis. This established elite **called for more equal sharing of the world's wealth** and political power,"[22] and he proudly endorses the very same thing. Sider has also urged the United States to **unilaterally disarm** even though other nations are not doing so.[23]

Sider, who has a degree from Yale[24] and who was on the World Council of Church's program in Vancouver,[25] has written some books which "are full of **Marxist** terminology such as 'economic violence,' 'exploitation,' 'proletariat,' 'social justice,' 'structural change,' and 'new international economic order.' He even entitles a section in *Rich Christians* **'Is God a Marxist?'"**[26]

> "Sider has kind words for the former Marxist president of Chile, Allende, and criticizes no governments except those of the United States, Brazil, South Korea, and Chile. He apparently sees no problem with the communist governments of the world, or if he does, he does not think it important enough to criticize them."[27]

Jerry Huffman states:

> "Sider launched an Evangelicals for McGovern group, which led to the **Chicago Declaration** of 1973. Critics call him a **socialist.** He is a pacifist and advocated (in a 1982 IVP [InterVarsity Press] book) that the U.S. totally disarm, allow Soviet Communists to invade, endure the slaughter of one or two million Americans, and see world peace emerge."[28]

> "When President Reagan in Orlando in 1983, appearing before the National Association of Evangelicals, spoke of the Soviet Union as an 'evil empire' and the 'focus of evil,' it was Ron Sider, a member of the NAE, who led the assembled evangelicals not to endorse or even commend the President's statement concerning the destructive nature of Communism."[29]

FREEDOM OF RELIGION

Sider also signed the Cry for Renewal statement,[30] yet in spite of Sider's leftist views, *Christianity Today* (founded by Billy Graham) featured him on its April 27, 1992 cover and had a five-page article on him.[31] The magazine claims that Sider "'is a heartland **evangelical,** deeply committed to an inspired Bible, to a passionate communication of the gospel, and to a transforming personal faith.' 'In short, Sider is no flaming radical.'"[32] Not only does *Christianity Today* feature Sider, but he is one of the magazine's corresponding editors![33]

Contradicting this analysis, Dr. John W. Robbins, explains:

> "Sider's message is **not** the message of the Bible; neither his economics nor his ethics can be called Christian. He has misled many through his selective citing of statistics and Scripture. He believes that governments may violate the Eighth Commandment whenever they act for the 'common good.' he (sic) dislikes personal charity and generosity. Like many advocates of the socialist gospel before him, he twists the Scriptures to his own destruction. Unfortunately, that destruction is not merely his own, but all those who follow him."[34]

For instance, in 1982 "pro-Sandinista mobs stormed and occupied some 20 churches in Nicaragua." What does Sider think about this? He asserts: "There's enormous **religious freedom to worship,** to evangelize in public places, and to distribute Christian literature freely. Virtually all the evangelical leaders we talked to said the situation had improved dramatically and the crisis was over."[35]

Yet missionary John Ashley Whitehouse, said that he was warned "not to preach in this now Communist nation, nor to even visit the city of Managua [in Nicaragua]."[36] He says "the Castro-Russian troops and agents are thick as flies (there) and exporting their propaganda and arms to other central American nations."[37]

Doesn't **Sider's** "freedom of religion" in Nicaragua sound very much like Graham's insistence that China has "freedom of religion"? Maybe this is why the "official 'Chicago declaration' **book was endorsed on the back cover by Billy Graham** with the phrase, 'I could identify with most of the recent **Chicago Declaration.'"**[38] Please remember that this was the **declaration that called for disarmament and redistribution of wealth!**[39]

MUTUAL RESPECT AMONG RELIGIONS

As far back as August 1979 the liberal *Sojourners* magazine (which is endorsed by Ron Sider[40]) had Graham featured on its front cover. The caption read: *"Billy Graham: Preaching Against the Arms Race."*[41] By 1982 Graham had been invited "to address a Soviet-sponsored peace and **disarmament** conference"[42] in Moscow. One researcher explains:

> "Billy Graham participated in 'The World Conference of Religious Leaders for Saving the Sacred Gift of Life from Nuclear Catastrophe.' That **the meeting was entirely a lying propaganda ploy of the Soviet Union** in their ongoing **effort to disarm** the NATO nations was evident to all. In spite of this, **Graham attended and spoke on the same agenda with leaders from Buddhism, Zoroastrianism, Hinduism, Judaism, Muslim, Sikhism, Shintoism, and apostate Christianity.** In a speech delivered before all of those attending the conference, Dr. **Graham said: 'We need to reaffirm our commitment to mutual respect among religions, such as we are practicing here.'"**[43]

When Graham called for "mutual respect among religions," he was well aware that many non-Christian religions were present. He admits in his autobiography that this conference "would draw to Moscow several hundred representatives from **all the major world religions,** not just Christianity."[44]

On this visit Graham was also able to show one of his films. A newsman from Finland described the showing of this film as "THE BEST PROPAGANDA THE COMMUNISTS COULD WANT."[45] [Emphasis in the original.]

> "This newsman pointed out that such a film was much more valuable to the Reds than one which they could produce themselves. It left the false impression that religion is doing well under communism. It presented communism in the best possible light. And, coming from one of the world's top religious leaders, it carries a tremendous amount of weight with millions of people who are unaware of the real situation."[46]

Additionally, the **Communists were quite pleased with Graham's disarmament speech** and in the July 1982 issue of *The*

Soviet Land they bragged that Graham "made an eloquent speech against the enemies of peace who are threatening to engulf the world in a nuclear catastrophe."[47] Graham himself stated: "The speech seemed to be well received; the audience responded with applause that grew into a standing ovation."[48] Just imagine, **Graham got a standing ovation from some Communists!**

Perhaps a part of his speech that pleased the Communists was when he declared that "we should urge all governments to respect the rights of religious believers as outlined in the **United Nations A Universal Declaration of Human Rights."**[49] In fact, **Graham** said himself that when he **read a draft of his message to Henry Kissinger that Kissinger** "urged me to make a more forceful statement on human rights. I gratefully accepted his suggestion."[50]

You see, the **New Agers, occultists, and atheists** just love this declaration. The occult newsletter, *Thoughtline,* insists: *"This is recommended reading for all members of the new group of world servers, and can be found in its whole form on the United Nations web page on the internet...."*[51] [Emphasis in the original.] The writer of the document was Dr. John Humphrey, a past President of the World Conference on Religion and Peace (WCRP) in Canada.[52] "The WCRP is a UN Non-Governmental Organization, headquartered at the United Nations in New York, with chapters in several countries. It works closely with the UN, UNICEF and UNESCO."[53]

UNIVERSAL DECLARATION OF HUMAN RIGHTS

World Goodwill (a New Age, world order group) encourages people and nations to accept the Universal Declaration of Human Rights. In the 1998 issue of *World Goodwill Newsletter* we find:

> **"The Universal Declaration of Human Rights is a wonderful example** of the upward human aspiration towards the revelation and manifestation of freedom, specifically 'freedom to.'...The extent to which brotherhood will manifest is in direct proportion to the extent to which the awareness of humanity becomes increasingly **inclusive."**[54]
>
> "It is here that the work of that pioneering group which [occultist] Alice Bailey calls 'the new group of world servers' comes in. This group is composed of all those whose first allegiance is to the human race as a whole. **Seeing no divisions between people** on the basis of race, class or creed, their main concern is to bring into being a world of unity, justice and

peace; **a world where the Universal Declaration of Human Rights is a lived reality;** a world where everyone enjoys the Four Freedoms—freedom of speech, freedom of worship, freedom from fear and freedom from want."[55]

New Agers Corinne McLaughlin and Gordon Davidson claim that this statement is a **"consecration to the sanctity of the Individual."**[56] [Emphasis in the original.] Robert Muller, an occultist, also says this is "a new magnificent consecration of the individual...."[57] He adds that a **child** has a "right to economic, social, moral and spiritual development...."[58] The ungodly **Temple of Understanding** and the **United Religions** are also behind this declaration.[59]

Even atheists and agnostics such as the writers of the *Humanist Manifesto* regard this declaration. *Humanist Manifesto II* contends: "We would safeguard, extend, and implement the principles of human freedom evolved from the *Magna Carta* to the *Bill of Rights,* the *Rights of Man,* and the *Universal Declaration of Human Rights.*"[60] Isn't this just wonderful? New Agers, occultists, and atheists all agree that Christians should be free to practice their faith and that even life is sacred—or do they? The very same paragraph of the *Humanist Manifesto* where they want to implement this declaration we find:

> "To enhance freedom and dignity the individual must experience a full range of *civil liberties* in all societies. This includes freedom of speech and the press, political democracy, the legal right of opposition to governmental policies, fair judicial process, religious liberty, freedom of association, and artistic, scientific, and cultural freedom. It also includes a recognition of **an individual's right to die with dignity, euthanasia, and the right to suicide."**[61] [Italics in the original.]

"The right to birth control, **abortion,** and divorce should be recognized."[62] Oops, I guess the baby in a mother's womb doesn't have the freedom that this declaration is supposed to be guaranteeing.

OUTMODED FAITH

A few pages earlier in the *Humanist Manifesto II* we see:

> "As in 1933, humanists still believe that traditional theism, especially **faith in the prayer-hearing God,** assumed to love and care for persons, to hear and understand their prayers, and to be able to do something about them, **is an unproved and outmoded faith. Salvationism,** based on mere affirmation, **still appears as harmful,** diverting people with false hopes of heaven hereafter. Reasonable minds look to other means for survival."[63]

Also:

¤ **"In place of** the old attitudes involved in **worship and prayer** the humanist finds his religious emotions expressed in a heightened sense of personal life and in a cooperative effort to promote social well-being."[64]

¤ "It follows that there will be no uniquely religious emotions and attitudes of the kind hitherto associated with belief in the supernatural."[65]

¤ "We believe, however, that **traditional dogmatic or authoritarian religions that place revelation, God, ritual, or creed above human needs** and experience **do a disservice to the human species....**We find insufficient evidence for belief in the existence of a supernatural; it is either meaningless or irrelevant to the question of the survival and fulfillment of the human race. As nontheists, we begin with humans not God, nature not deity."[66]

¤ "Promises of immortal salvation or fear of eternal damnation are both illusory and harmful."[67]

¤ "Certainly religious institutions, their ritualistic forms, ecclesiastical methods, and communal activities **must be reconstituted as rapidly as experience allows,** in order to function effectively in the modern world."[68]

¤ **"Religions the world over are under the necessity of coming to terms with new conditions** created by a vastly increased knowledge and experience."[69]

Freedom of religion is only within certain guidelines—and true, Bible-believing Christianity will not fit this scheme.

FREEDOM LIMITED BY UN

Even the Universal Declaration of Human Rights admits that "a common understanding of these rights and freedoms is of the greatest importance for the full realization of this pledge...."[70] Article 28 reads: "Everyone is entitled to a social and **international order** in which the rights and freedoms set forth in this Declaration can be fully realized."[71] Article 29 adds:

> "In the exercise of his rights and freedoms, everyone shall be subject only to such **limitations as are determined by law** solely for the purpose of securing due recognition and respect for the rights and freedoms of others and of meeting the just requirements of morality, public order and the general welfare in a democratic society."[72]

Article 29 continues: "These rights and freedoms may **in no case be exercised contrary to the purposes and principles of the United Nations."**[73]

Oh, so even though we are **supposedly** guaranteed freedom of worship and religion, we can not have any independence, freedom, or liberty that is "contrary to the purposes and principles of the United Nations." Now you can see why the New Agers, occultists, atheists, etc., can all promote this document. They believe in a **"freedom" of religion that is in agreement with the United Nations!** I can understand why these people would support this declaration—but **why would Billy Graham?!**

Maitreya, a false "Christ," states:

> "The **UN is the major hope of the world.** In its interrelationships we can see democracy writ large—the symbol for that expression of God's Will that men call goodwill.
>
> "With the advent of the Christ [who is called Maitreya] this goodwill will bring all men and all nations into correct relationship and create the necessary circumstances for the expression of that **synthesis** which will be the outstanding keynote of the coming civilization.
>
> "In this vast enterprise **the UN will play a major role."**[74]

Humanist Manifesto 2000 is subtitled "A Call for **a New Planetary Humanism."**[75] This document states: "We should be tolerant of cultural diversity **except** where those cultures are themselves **intolerant or repressive.** It is time to rise above narrow tribalism to **find common ground."**[76] Remember, a true, Bible-believing Christian is considered to be intolerant!

The same year as Graham's disarmament conference, the **"WCC** Central Committee **called for total nuclear disarmament."**[77] A book written that same year (1982) was entitled *The Idea of Disarmament!* In its "Call to Action," the signers pledged:

> "—to **support the role of the UN in disarmament** negotiations and such international forums as the Special Session on Disarmament and other initiatives in this field....
>
> "—to support **ecumenical** programmes concerned with disarmament, especially the World Council of Churches Programme for Disarmament and Against Militarism and the Arms Race; and to cooperate with other non-governmental programmes for disarmament.

> "—to express readiness to unite our efforts for peace and disarmament with the followers of **all religions and all persons of goodwill."**[78]

Signers of this declaration included at least 10 people associated with the NCC and WCC.[79]

DISARMAMENT

The topic of disarmament has long been on the National and World Council of Churches' agenda[80] and the WCC "was a founding member of the International Action Network on Small Arms...."[81] One New Age group reminds us:

> "From the beginning, the **World Council,** through its Commission of the Churches for International Affairs, gave helpful criticism and **support to the United Nations** on issues such as **human rights,** international peace and security, **disarmament,** refugees, economic and social development, and decolonization."[82]

The **NCC** is a member of the Coalition for a New Foreign Policy which **promotes "arms control and disarmament."**[83] Other members include: Americans for Democratic Action; Democratic Socialists of America, Fellowship of Reconciliation; Friends of the Earth; Gray Panthers; National Office of Jesuit Social Ministries; OXFAM America; Pax Christi, U.S.A.; Quixote Center; SANE/FREEZE; Unitarian Universalist Association; Unitarian Universalist Service Committee; War Resistors League; and the World Federalist Association.[84]

Jerry Huffman explains: **"Disarmament is a first step toward a communist-type dictatorship."**[85]

In 1983, just one year after Graham's Soviet-sponsored disarmament conference in Moscow, he had a meeting called "Amsterdam '83." This conference, says one researcher,

> "GAVE A PLATFORM FOR **COMMUNIST** PROPAGANDA by **representatives of the following communist nations:** USSR, Bulgaria, Cuba, Czechoslovakia, German Democratic Republic (Communist East Germany), Hungary, Poland, Romania, Armenia and Yugoslavia. **They were all there because Billy Graham wanted them there.** True, this platform was that of a workshop rather than the main assembly, but the deceptiveness was heightened by the fact that it was listed under the title, 'Resistant Peoples and Difficult Areas—Marxists.' The obvious impression was that this workshop

> would present suggestions for reaching people for Christ in Communist countries. Instead, **it really amounted to a defense of communism and a criticism of anti-communism.** In addition, this workshop was personally chaired by Dr. Walter H. Smyth who is the chief executive officer in Graham's organization....Smyth went out of his way to present the most favorable image possible for the first speaker from the Russian Orthodox Church, Metropolitan Vladimir, referring to 'the great and rich tradition of Orthodoxy.'...[T]he **Orthodox Church** in Communist countries is not only a **chief apologist for communism** but is under God's curse for preaching 'another gospel.'"[86] [Caps in the original.]

NATIONAL RELIGIOUS PARTNERSHIP FOR THE ENVIRONMENT

Returning to the Joint Appeal by Religion and Science for the Environment, we find that by 1993 it changed its name to the National Religious Partnership for the Environment[87] (NRPE) and "announced its $5 million program...'to underscore the connection between addressing issues of poverty and the environment.'"[88] The Partnership is a formal agreement among the U. S. Catholic Conference, National Council of Churches of Christ (NCC), Coalition on the Environment and Jewish Life, and the Evangelical Environmental Network (EEN).[89]

"The Partnership grew out of a two-year process of consultation, strategic planning, and pilot programs enacted by senior religious leaders in collaboration with eminent scientists, and a bipartisan congressional group...."[90]

> "**Founded** in 1993 **by** Vice-President **Gore,** the National Religious Partnership for the Environment, also **based at St. John the Divine,** has distributed tens of thousands of packets containing ecologically oriented prayers, sermon ideas and Sunday-school lessons to Catholic, Protestant, Jewish, and evangelical congregations across the country. Its director is convinced that the eco-crisis will transform 'what it will mean to be religious in the 21st century.'"[91]

"The purpose of the NRPE is <u>to merge science and religion—paganism—and to recruit volunteer labors for the State, while turning millions of congregants into a spiritual/political action force for Mother Earth</u>."[92] [Emphasis in the original.]

> "Read carefully the statement issued by the Partnership. **'Ancient faith communities are hereby resolving to**

> **integrate a new world historical challenge throughout all dimensions of religious life....This is not only a contribution to global justice and sustainability but an affirmation of what it must mean from now on to be truly and fully religious.'"**[93] [Emphasis in the original.]

Before moving on, let's look briefly at NRPE's co-founder, **Al Gore.** As a senator, in 1989, "he co-sponsored a bill in Congress to **use tax monies to study New Age and occult methods such as ESP, biofeedback, visualization, transcendental meditation, Zen, yoga, and other forms of Eastern Mysticism."**[94] He is an

> "[o]fficial member of the executive committee of the New York-based *Global Forum of Spiritual and Parliamentary Leaders on Human Survival,* a major New Age, occult, globalist organization, along with Buddhist Nichiko Niwano, Hindu Karan Singh, ultra-liberal rabbi Gwarham Soetendorp, Islam's Vigar Hamdani, native American tribal leader Oren Lyons, Catholic Franz Koenig of Austria, and others. *Global Forum* is co-sponsor of the *World Parliament of Religions,* a gala event that promotes population control....*Global Forum* is also working with Russia's Mikhail Gorbachev to establish him as head of a new environmental organization to be called the *International Green Cross."*[95]

CONGRESSIONAL CLEARINGHOUSE ON THE FUTURE

Gore was Chairman of the Congressional Clearinghouse on the Future for a number of years.[96]

> "The Congressional Clearinghouse on the Future (founded 1976) publishes a newsletter titled *What's Next* (now reprinted by the Congressional Institute for the Future). The Congressional Clearinghouse has invited many New Age networkers for discussions, 'providing a forum for Members of Congress.' During the years when Albert Gore, Jr. was Chairman or on their Executive Committee, there were discussions by Marilyn Ferguson, Isaac Asimov, Norman Cousins, Willis Harman, and others. When Chairman, Gore arranged for a number of Members of Congress to participate in sessions of the Fourth General Assembly of the WORLD FUTURE SOCIETY. He welcomed attendees at the Assembly and moderated a session which included Barbara Marx Hubbard and Willis Harman speaking on transformation, governance, and networking. Among others speaking at the Assembly were: Donella

> Meadows, co-author of *The Limits to Growth* and *Groping in the Dark: The First Decade of Global Modeling;* Fritjof Capra, author of *The Turning Point* and *The Tao of Physics;* Lester Brown, author of *Building A Sustainable Society* and president of Worldwatch Institute; James Channon, First Earth Battalion; Jean Houston on 'Religion and the Future of Human Consciousness'; Harlan Cleveland, author of *Management of Sustainable Growth* and *The Third Try at World Order;* and Marilyn Ferguson, author of *The Aquarian Conspiracy.* One panel discussion theme was 'Networking Toward a New Age.'"[97] [Emphasis in the original.]

The *U. S. News & World Report* mentions that the Congressional Clearinghouse on the Future has provided "a forum that has given some **psychics** a platform in the capital."[98]

A paper from the World Future Society (WFS) bragged that they helped to establish the Congressional Clearinghouse on the Future.[99] WFS explains: "Often these conferences serve as forums for world leaders to announce their plans. You can get an exclusive advance view. For example, at our 1989 conference, then-Senator Albert Gore Jr., now the vice president, spelled his views on the environment and population."[100]

Gore also was a participant in the State of the World Forum.[101]

GORE PRAISES HOMOSEXUAL GROUP

As Vice President, in March 1995, Al Gore and his wife, Tipper, opened their home "to 150 **homosexual** political activists and praised the leadership of the Human Rights Campaign Fund, possibly the largest gay lobby."[102] Gore said: "It's a wonderful thing to do what you're doing, and that's devoting your lives to others."[103] He remarked: "This dedication is an outgrowth of the way you live your entire lives."[104] Tipper Gore added: "We very deeply share your vision of a society that is fair and free of discrimination for [gays—J.H.]."[105]

More recently, he "endorsed the *'Ellen'* coming out episode and said it forced millions of Americans 'to look at sexual orientation in a more favorable light.'"[106]

As Senator, Gore voted to continue funding the National Endowment for the Arts (NEA) so that the NEA could proceed with their pornographic filth.[107] That very year (1991) the "NEA received $174,083,000 in **taxpayer funding** from the federal government...."[108] I think most of my readers are aware of the trash that the NEA funds with **your** tax dollars, but for those who are not familiar with this, I'll list a few items.

✍ **Karen Finley,** who calls herself "Queen of the Dung Dynasty,"[109] received NEA funds for her performances which included **witchcraft** and obscene props.[110] She appeared "nude on stage, smeared [herself] with chocolate, screaming 'God is dead,' while she burned several American flags before a wildly cheering audience."[111] She has received at least four grants from the NEA.[112]

✍ "NEA grantee **Holly Hughes** works to advance **lesbianism.** Her stage performance includes a scene in which she inserts her hand into her genitals and speaks of seeing 'Jesus between mother's hips.'"[113]

✍ The producers of "Poison" received $25,000. "This movie has graphic homosexual scenes. The main character, Broom, is a young thief. In prison he is shown being raped by a fellow inmate, fondling another male's genitals, brutalized and ultimately shot to death as he attempts to escape from prison."[114]

✍ In a newsletter from the Wise Woman Center, whose head is a **witch,** we discover that a "Sacred Sex" workshop (for **women only**) with "The Red Witches," **Annie Sprinkle and Jwala** (who are also **lesbians),** was to be held in 1990.[115] The workshop would draw "upon Tantric, Taoist, and Native American teachings...[and] will introduce you to 'firebreath orgasm,' the sensuous intoxication of living in nature, group rebirthing, 'the wave,' and the mystery of the **sacred slut.** We'll climax with an ecstatic Tantric ritual."[116] Sprinkle said: *"Sex is my spiritual discipline, expertise, politics, favorite subject matter, source of my income, foremost conversational topic, and the key to my health and happiness. I live as if I were making love every moment."*[117] She had starred in more than 150 X-rated movies,[118] yet the NEA gave Sprinkle a grant.[119] In fact, in 1990, she was featured "in an exhibition called 'Annie Sprinkle: Post Porn Modernist' in which she invited the audience to inspect her vagina and cervix with the aid of a flashlight. In that exhibition, she said: 'I usually get paid a lot of money for this, but [tonight] it's **government-funded.'"**[120] "The show involved on-stage masturbation with a variety of 'sex toys' and urination."[121]

✍ "'Artist' **Andres Serrano** got a $15,000 National Endowment for the Arts grant for his display of a crucifix in a jar of his own urine. It was called 'P—s Christ.'"[122]

✍ "The NEA also provided $30,000 in tax money for a traveling display of homo-erotic photographs. The unbelievable display included a picture of one man urinating into another man's mouth. The rest of the display showing perverted homosexual acts was so pornographic and sick that it can not be described. Congressmen opposed to further financing of such 'art' were prohibited from bringing the photos into the halls of Congress—even though the 'art' had been paid for with tax money."[123]

✍ "NEA gave a $70,000 seasonal support grant to Artists Space to put on a show called 'Degenerate with a Capital D' which included 'Alchemy Cabinet' by **Shawn Eichman,** featuring the remains of the **artist's own aborted baby."**[124]

✍ "NEA gave a $20,000 writing fellowship to **Minnie Bruce Pratt** who stated in the *Washington Blade,* a homosexual newspaper, that 'the material I sent to the NEA was **explicitly lesbian** and it was homoerotic. That's the material they read, and they decided to give me the award **after** they read it.'"[125]

✍ The NEA gave $15,000 to the University Galleries where "Tongues of Flame" was shown. "This picture shows **Christ as a drug addict** in the process of injecting drugs into his arm via a syringe. The tightly wound cord around his upper arm is used by addicts to raise veins in order to make injection easier."[126]

✍ **Joel-Peter Witkin** received $20,000 from the NEA. "His sick photographs include Testicle Stretch, Woman Castrating a Man, the Maquette for Crucifix. His picture of a corpse's head sliced in two sold for $27,000 at Sotheby's in 1990."[127] This was his fourth NEA grant![128]

✍ "The National Endowment for the Arts, in an act clearly insulting to millions of Christians, has helped fund a book which contains a poem about **Jesus sodomizing a six-year-old boy."**[129]

✍ Corpus Christi was "an off-Broadway play about a homosexual Jesus character (Joshua) who has sexual relationships with characters resembling the twelve disciples—most especially Judas." They received $125,000 in government grants from the National Endowment for the Arts.[130]

The list could go on and on, but these are just a few of the grants given right before and right after Al Gore voted to continuing using our tax money to fund these perversions.

Gore, as already mentioned, is a big supporter of the environment and "also a major force behind Earth Day 1990."[131] He wrote *Earth in the Balance,*[132] which promotes the false theory of **evolution.**[133] This book also sanctions all kinds of pagan earth and goddess worship.[134] In fact, Samantha Smith writes:

> "By now, many people also know that Al Gore is a member of the Watermelon Gang—green on the outside and red in the center. Even worse, in his book *Earth In The Balance,* we find Mr. Gore promoting a return to goddess-worshipping pagan religions, as a means to both personal and planetary salvation—all the while claiming to be a Southern Baptist."[135]

Gore admits:

"My treatment of spirituality and the environment is based in part on a series of dialogues that I have organized, along with Dean **James Morton** of the **Cathedral of Saint John the Divine** in New York City and Carl Sagan, with active help from my colleague Senator Tim Wirth. These dialogues, between scientists and religious leaders, have been aimed at exploring the **common ground** between these two worlds."[136]

(We'll discuss Morton shortly.) No wonder the editors of the **witchcraft** magazine, *The Green Egg,* stated:

"'Few pagans would change much more than a pronoun.'...

"Gore's philosophy of the Earth, say the witchcraft magazine's editors in ecstatic tones, is 'music to our ears.'"[137]

GORE BLAMES CHRISTIANITY

Dave Hunt noted that **Gore**

"praises goddess worship and **blames Christianity** for wiping out 'the last vestige of organized goddess worship.' He praises Islam, Hinduism, Sikhism and Baha'i as well as heretical Catholic priest Teilhard de Chardin, known as the father of the New Age. The book, in his own words, confirms the fact that Gore, who was one of the speakers at 'Global Forum' in Moscow, a veritable New Age Summit, is a zealous New Ager who advocates 'a new faith in the future' which will be a return to paganism's worship of the earth as sacred."[138]

Another author states:

"In his book, Gore endorses Eastern and Mystery religions, the worship of the ancient goddess, Hinduism, Buddhism, and Islam. But he blasts Christians who he says, 'are afraid to open their minds to teachings first offered outside their own system of belief.' **Gore dislikes fundamental Christians** who truly believe the Bible. He says that because Christians refuse to believe that the earth is our sacred mother, that **Christians are a threat** to the survival of humanity. **He calls Christians a blight on the environment.** He also states that to believe in Bible prophecy is unforgivable. He said, 'Not only is this idea heretical, it is an appalling self-fulfilling prophecy of doom.' Gore says he is friendly with the Dalai Lama, the Tibetan Buddhist who claims to be a reincarnated god on earth. Gore is a favorite speaker at New Age conferences and last year he spoke on the environment and spirituality for 'Common

> Boundary,' a globalist New Age group. Other speakers at the seminar promoted witchcraft and goddess themes."[139]

Gore also said that the patriarchal system of Christianity "was responsible for dysfunctional families."[140]

According to Gore, the environmental problem is a **spiritual** problem.[141] He also believes that *"Nature, in its fullest, is God."*[142] [Emphasis in the original.] In his "sermon" at **St. John the Divine Cathedral,** he "declared that God is not separate from the earth."[143]

GRAHAM AND THE ENVIRONMENT

In spite of Gore's heresy, occult beliefs, and New Age orientation, **Billy Graham** met with him in February 1995. Alicia C. Shepard commented that "Graham had a two-hour candlelight dinner with Vice President Al Gore, spending a third of the session talking about the environment—Gore's signature issue. Afterwards, **Graham said he would speak publicly on 'ecology** and our responsibility to the environment' after meeting with environmental experts."[144]

After this meeting with Gore, Cal Thomas asked Graham: *"You've been reluctant to speak out on the top social issue of our time, abortion. Why?"* to which Graham responded: *"I think the top social issue of our time may be ecology (the environment). I think that's more dangerous...and I'm going to start speaking out on that."*[145] [Emphasis in the original.]

On another occasion Graham said: **"We Christians have a responsibility to take a lead in trying to take care of the Earth."**[146] [Emphasis in the original.]

Graham's emphasis on the environment reminds me somewhat of what the former General-Secretary of the National Council of Churches, Joan Brown Campbell,[147] said. She claims that "the goal is to make **global warming 'a litmus test for the faith community.'"**[148] Campbell, by the way, is on the board of the National Religious Partnership for the Environment[149] and one of the Presidents of the World Conference on Religion and Peace.[150]

> "The World Conference on Religion and Peace (WCRP) is dedicated to promoting cooperation among the world's religions for peace. A worldwide movement based on **respect** for religious differences, WCRP has members in over 100 countries. Accredited to the **United Nations,** WCRP engages in vigorous peace promoting initiatives throughout the world on a multi-religious basis. Leaders and believers of the following religions regularly participate in WCRP: Baha'ism; Buddhism; Christianity; Confucianism; Hinduism; Taoism; Traditionalism

of the indigenous cultures of Africa, the Americas, Australia, and Oceania; and Zoroastrianism."[151]

> "WCRP provides a potent base on local, national, regional, and global levels for a variety of peace related activities. Examples include: promoting religious tolerance;...working for disarmament;...encouraging equitable and sustainable development;...and sponsoring environmental projects."[152]

To give you a better idea of what Campbell stands for, a few years ago she met with the gay and lesbian Metropolitan Community Churches (UFMCC). She went so far as to **rearrange** her travel plans in order to participate in the UFMCC gathering and show her support for civil rights for them.[153] Of course, the **NCC has been showing support for homosexuals** for quite some time already. Over 20 years ago, the National Gay Task Force received support from the NCC.[154] Also, when Senator Paul Tsongas planned to introduce a gay rights bill, support once again came from the NCC.[155] The NCC's support for gays even includes large monetary gifts. For instance, the "Church World Service, an arm of the National Council of Churches, donated $30,000 to the UFMCC for its program with Cuban homosexuals."[156]

Returning to Campbell, we find that in September 1995, she spoke before the United Nations and "condemned the privatizing of life which inspires resistance to the United Nations concept of a **global neighborhood.** She condemned those preoccupied with "my family, my property, my children" and said such "selfishness calls us away from building a **world community.**"[157]

CAMPBELL'S TRIP TO CUBA

In 1999, Campbell took

> "one of her many trips to Cuba. At a rally in Revolution Square in Havana, **Campbell shared a stage with Fidel Castro.** At one point she addressed the crowd of 100,000. Characteristically, Campbell used her platform to make a call for freedom—not from totalitarianism in Cuba, but from the tyranny of its capitalist neighbor. 'We ask you to forgive the suffering that has come to you by the actions of the United States,' she said. The crowd cheered."[158]

Not surprisingly, Campbell "denies that the Bible is the infallible Word of God...."[159]

Campbell signed the Cry for Renewal statement[160] and is also on the Board of Directors of a group called the Interfaith Alliance.[161] Their mission statement says:

> "The Interfaith Alliance is a nonpartisan, **ecumenical** organization committed to three main goals: **promoting the positive role of religion** as a healing and constructive force in public life, encouraging the renewal of values within our families and communities, and **providing people of faith with an alternative voice to that of the radical religious right."**[162]

Oh, yes, another group listed as an alternative to the "religious right" is the **NCC!**[163] Also listed is the **Southern Christian Leadership Conference,**[164] the Communistic group founded by Martin Luther King, Jr.[165]

These groups may be ecumenical but they certainly aren't tolerant of the "religious right." In 1995, the Iowa state chapter of the Interfaith Alliance was afraid that some conservatives would be elected to the school board. They came up with a pledge that the candidates were asked to sign. The candidates "had to promise to 'affirm the religious diversity of this country' and 'reject any political group which preaches or practices exclusion and intolerance, including any assertion that votes for its candidates are "votes for God."'"[166] A New Age magazine proudly added: "The pledge tactic worked: Suspected Christian right candidates failed to sign it, and more progressive forces prevailed."[167]

The NCC even helps humanists and atheists. When Madalyn Murray O'Hair went to the Supreme Court to get prayer and Bible reading removed from the schools, the NCC lent their support to her case![168]

Some tolerance! There's tolerance for pagans, New Agers, occultists, Communists, one-world government proponents, liberals, etc., etc., but **NO TOLERANCE** for true Christians. Incidentally, the NCC is one of the groups that has participated in the National Coalition Against Censorship (NCAC)![169] Supposedly the NCC is against censorship, but they advocated **removing** the Bible from the schools. Isn't this censorship?!

Of course, the NCAC want to see books in the school library such as *Heather Has Two Mommies* and *Daddy's Roommate* which are "intended for children 2 to 8" years old![170] "The reason: both are stories about daily lives of **homosexual** families—Heather and her Mama Kate and Mama Jane and a little boy, his divorced Daddy and Daddy's roommate, Frank."[171] When concerned parents wanted these books moved to the adult section, the NCAC fought to have them stay in the children's area.[172]

The NCAC is also for nude displays in libraries, etc. They write:

> "Should a nude painting be permitted in an art exhibit in a public library?...Public libraries sometimes specify in their

exhibition guidelines that nude paintings are not acceptable, presumably to 'protect' children who have access to the library from viewing visual material library directors or board members consider inappropriate. **Such restrictions put a chill on creativity and raise questions of the integrity** of exhibits that are limited by content guidelines unrelated to artistic worth."[173]

NO CENSORSHIP

Remember, the NCAC is against censorship. They want books promoting homosexuality and nude art displays. If we didn't have them, that would be censorship—according to them. But wait! The Bible shouldn't be in the school. That's a dangerous and harmful book to these people.[174] Jacob L. Moreno, who "developed psychodrama and sociometry using role-playing or 'God-playing,' as he called it,"[175] proclaimed: **"My job is to destroy the GOD-SYNDROME and the concepts of right and wrong which is the cause of ALL PSYCHOLOGICAL ILLNESS."**[176] In Moreno's book, *Who Shall Survive?,* "he indicated that religions such as Christianity and Judaism were limited, and he **proposed a new 'religion'** modified by science."[177] Paul Brandwein declares: "Any child who believes in God is MENTALLY ILL."[178] Remember, the *Humanist Manifesto* states:

> "As in 1933, humanists still believe that traditional theism, especially **faith in the prayer-hearing God,** assumed to love and care for persons, to hear and understand their prayers, and to be able to do something about them, **is an unproved and outmoded faith. Salvationism,** based on mere affirmation, **still appears as harmful,** diverting people with false hopes of heaven hereafter. **Reasonable minds look to other means for survival."**[179]

Yet, the National Council of Churches is one of the groups that has joined together with people of this ilk and the NCAC in fighting "censorship."

GAIA WORSHIP

The WCC, like the NCC, is involved in environmental issues. The World Council of Churches has "decreed that environmental consciousness is a better test of 'orthodoxy' than a belief in the resurrection."[180] At Au Sable, "[s]cientists and theologians from a variety of Christian traditions gather...to discuss the **church's responsibility toward the environment."**[181]

Since the NRPE is a partnership of four religious groups, the churches are obviously being targeted with the environmentalist message.

> "Each of the four partner organizations has developed its own **Environmental Education/Action Kit.** The kits are designed to assist congregations in studying how **environmentalism is a religious issue** in their own faith tradition, and to enable people of faith to engage in concrete activities that reflect their environmental concerns. Additional resources are also available."[182] [Emphasis in the original.]

One researcher writes:

> "The National Religious Partnership for the Environment (NRPE) is currently providing 'education and activity' kits to 67,300 American congregations which minister to more than 100 million members. The 'education' contained in these kits flows from an 'enlightenment' empowered by a belief in gaia as the giver of all life. The 'activity' encouraged in these kits is political activity in support of legislation and regulations that will force individuals to modify behavior to comply with the tenets of gaia worship."[183]

> "The **objectives of the NRPE are nothing less than the transformation of social order into a global society** organized around the notion that the earth itself is the giver of life, and that all the world's religions are evolving into a state of enlightenment that recognizes Gaia as the true source of life and spirituality, and is the only relevant object of worship."[184]

With that in mind, it is interesting to look at some of the names on the letterhead from the NRPE. Some of these names (among others) are: Rev. James Parks Morton; Dr. Carl Sagan; Bishop Vinton R. Anderson, President, World Council of Churches; Rev. Joan Campbell, then General-Secretary, National Council of Churches of Christ; and Paul Gorman, Executive Director of the National Religious Partnership for the Environment.[185]

WITCHES AND NATURE WORSHIPPERS

James Parks Morton, one of the co-founders of the NRPE,[186] stated that all religious groups are "increasingly being called to realize that **the body of Christ is the earth**—the biosphere—the skin that includes all of us."[187]

Morton, who has a bronze head of **Buddha** on his desk,[188] was dean of the **Cathedral of St. John the Divine Church** in New

York,[189] the largest Gothic cathedral in the world.[190] This is a New Age church, as even David Spangler himself admits.[191] (Remember, David Spangler is the person who said that we must take a "Luciferic Initiation" if we wish to enter into the New Age.[192])

Morton stated: "The challenge before the religious community in America is to **make every congregation...truly 'green'—a center of environmental study and action....This is their religious duty."**[193] On St. Francis Day, thousands of people flock to this church for the "Blessing of the Beasts," "which ends with a procession of elephant, camel, llama, pony, eagle, rat, cockroach, and a flask of 10 trillion algae down the nave to the altar to be blessed by the clergy."[194]

Morton belongs to the New Age group called **Planetary Citizens** as well as the Planetary Initiative for the World We Choose (PI).[195] Planetary Initiative's theme is "think globally, act locally."[196] The PI had a Congress which focused on the following concerns: "pioneering and **bridging** among consciousness and cause groups, the traditional and **new age, the religious and secular."**[197]

One researcher writes:

> "The Planetary Initiative for the World We Choose is a New Age, globalist organization which numbers among its luminaries such notables as Reverend James Park Morton, dean of the New Age-oriented Cathedral of St. John the Divine in New York City; political organizer Donald Keys; and science fiction writer Isaac Asimov (now deceased). On the staff of this organization is Gerhard Elston, former executive director of Amnesty International. Elston has also been a member of the board of directors of such groups as Bread for the World, Clergy and Laity Concerned, and the ultra-liberal American Civil Liberties Union (ACLU). Elston is active in the Lutheran World Federation and previously served on the staff of the **National Council of Churches."**[198]

Morton is also co-chair of the Global Forum Council.[199] When the Global Forum met in 1988,[200] Morton noted that "this meeting was only **the beginning in paving the way for this emerging coalition of religious and political leaders....**[201] Remember, too, that Al Gore is involved with this group and it's this group that was working with **Mikhail Gorbachev."**[202] In fact, Gorbachev's Green Cross International is an offspring from the Global Forum.[203]

Morton was also a former President of the Temple of Understanding and now a member of the Board of Directors.[204] While he was President of the Temple of Understanding in 1988, Morton held a Thanksgiving Day service at St. John the Divine Cathedral

> "in which 4,000 children and adults joined with American Indians, tribal leaders, medicine men, witches, nature worshippers and other anti-Christian elements in a 'Circle dance' of religious friendship and unity. Morton said the purpose of the dance was to 'redefine' Thanksgiving. He also declared that part of the impetus for the ceremony was to create 'a heightened consciousness of the **necessity of different religions working together to save our planet.'"**[205]

It's not surprising to note that Morton "openly supports Benjamin Creme, David Spangler and Shirley MacLaine."[206]

RELIGIOUS LIBERTY

Another name on the letterhead for the National **Religious** Partnership for the Environment was Carl Sagan. In fact, he was on the Board of Trustees for the NRPE.[207] Sagan, who gave an endorsement for Al Gore's book, *Earth in the Balance,*[208] is often referred to as Sagan the **Pagan,**[209] yet his name is on a so-called **RELIGIOUS** organization.

Sagan, who died on December 20, 1996,[210] was on the Board of Directors of the American Civil Liberties Union[211] (ACLU) and was a member of the Council on Foreign Relations,[212] a group promoting a one-world government.[213] In his keynote address at the Oxford Conference in 1988, **he "called for an end to** 'jingoist (chauvinistic) **nationalism,'** predicted a coming 'paradigm shift' and expounded his belief that 'we are all one.'"[214]

Sagan was an evolutionist,[215] whose evolutionary beliefs were promoted through his TV series, *Cosmos,*[216] seen by over 500 million people.[217]

He also espoused **humanism**[218] and was the 1981 "Humanist of the Year."[219] **Sagan** said that "he **opposed the spread of Christianity"** and in the March 18, 1996 issue of *U. S. News & World Report,* he stated that "the Bible is demonstrably wrong in areas of science."[220] In the March 10, 1996 issue of *Parade* he said: "I cannot conceive of a god who rewards and punishes his creatures...."[221]

He "participated in Gorbachev's Fall 1995 'State of the World Forum: Toward a New Civilization,' which was loaded with New World Order or New Age speakers...."[222] Sagan was also a trustee of Gorbachev's International Green Cross.[223] They "have pledged to wear tiny green crosses on their lapels to signify their concern for the environment."[224]

In spite of his atheistic,[225] humanistic, evolutionistic leanings, he was also the co-founder of the Planetary Society and served on its

Board of Directors.[226] This group "is seeking to **make contact with extraterrestrials,** [and was] funded in part by a $100,000 gift from Steven Spielberg."[227] Furthermore, Sagan was on the Advisory Board of Americans for Religious Liberty.[228] What kind of "religious liberty" does this group advocate? They want evolution taught in the schools "undiluted by pseudoscience or sectarian religion."[229] Their literature also states: "A free and secular democratic state secures personal freedom and privacy....It makes abortion and sexual behavior between consenting adults issues of personal choice."[230]

This is the kind of person who wants to unite science and religion. "Together with other scientists, Sagan has led a strong effort to encourage religious leaders to become involved with environmental problems."[231] He said: *"...separately, neither science nor religion could solve the problem of redeeming the environment from the shortsightedness of the last few decades."*[232] [Emphasis in the original.] He believes that the **"environmentalist crusade should be considered a <u>religious</u> crusade."**[233]

He regards the earth as sacred (as do many New Agers and pagans).[234] At the Global Forum he stated: "As scientists, many of us have had profound experiences of awe and reverence before the universe. We understand that what is regarded as sacred is more likely to be treated with care and respect. Our planetary home should be so regarded."[235] You see, the "environmental crisis is the vehicle upon which the New Age movement, the New World Order...plan...to move the world to global government..."[236] and they are trying to engage in this process. Gorbachev, too, has said that **we need an environmental crisis.**[237]

REWRITE THE TEN COMMANDMENTS

Gorbachev is the brainchild (along with New Ager Maurice Strong and Stephen Rockefeller) of the new Earth Charter which he is hoping the United Nations will adopt by the year 2002.[238]

> "Once adopted, the Charter would be the basis for new global, national, and even local laws. Steven Rockefeller, chairman of the Rockefeller Brothers Fund is supporting Earth Charter activities in 10 Third World countries. Global Education Associates and the Temple of Understanding—interfaith organizations that actively support the URI [United Religions Initiative]—also promote the Earth Charter."[239]

This charter mentions increased population and calls for the "equitable distribution of wealth."[240] On December 30, 2000,

Gorbachev wrote a letter to President-elect Bush in which he clearly told him that America's standard of living is not justifiable as long as other countries live in poverty.[241] What he doesn't mention is that other countries could have American's standard of living if Communism was not in control of these countries. He continued:

> "It is also difficult to believe that, under present circumstances, relations between the United States, on the one hand, and China, India and all the rest of the earth that lives in abject poverty, on the other, could develop a positive direction....
>
> "The present leadership of Russia appears ready to cooperate with the United States in framing a **new agenda** for relations....If we truly want to **build a new world order** and further European unity, we have to recognize that this will not be possible without an active role for Russia....Sooner or later, international policy, including that of the United States, will have to come to terms with that variety."[242]

Gorbachev's Earth Charter also claims that the Earth is alive (a New Age/occult viewpoint).[243]

> "Gorbachev views the proposed Earth Charter as ***'a kind of Ten Commandments, a "Sermon on the Mount," that provides a guide for human behavior toward the environment in the next century and beyond.'*** Strong says, ***'The real goal of the Earth Charter is that it will in fact become like the Ten Commandments, like the Universal Declaration of Human Rights.'***"[244] [Emphasis in the original.]

Gorbachev, at press conferences, etc., has said: "We are going to rewrite the Ten Commandments and replace them with a new set of ten or fifteen and in that paradigm man will no longer have dominion over the earth as God sets out in the book of Genesis."[245]

Notice that Strong claims the goal of this Earth Charter is to become "like the Universal Declaration of Human Rights." Remember, this is the declaration that Billy Graham referred to when he was in Russia and received a standing ovation.[246]

Tying religion and the environment together, the

> "United Nations Environment Programme [UNEP] publishes 'An Environmental Sabbath-Earth Rest Day Guide,' titled *Our Children Their Earth: Playing For Keeps,* in which one finds a *'Mount Olympus'* exercise where a group of students meets *'the **gods** or the Lords of the Universe.'* The students are supposed to 'try to win over (persuade) the **gods** to save

the planet—and the human race' instead of destroying everyone with global warming or a disease.

"This Guide indicates that *'it is designed as a practical and moral road map to the Environmental Sabbath, to be used in conjunction with the UNEP Sabbath booklet, Only One Earth.'* The Environmental Sabbath was originated by Dr. John Kirk (of Montclair State University, New Jersey) who was chairman of an advisory committee with UNEP to establish (in 1987) an **inter-faith** Environmental Sabbath as **a way to meld spiritual values with environment science."**[247] [Italics and underlining in the original; boldface added.]

EARTH IS SACRED

New Agers Corinne McLaughlin and Gordon Davidson[248] also view the earth as sacred. They have been associated with Findhorn[249] (where Luciferian David Spangler also was[250]). In fact, Spangler wrote the foreword to their book, *Builders of the Dawn.*[251] They are followers of the occultist Alice Bailey and the demonic spirit guide called Djwhal Khul.[252] Corinne was "was the first Task Force Coordinator for President Clinton's Council for Sustainable Development. She also **taught her theosophical mediation strategies at the Department of Education, the Pentagon, and the EPA."**[253] She has also "taught transformational politics at American University in Washington DC."[254] Gordon "worked four years for the United Nations with World Goodwill"[255] at Lucis Trust.[256]

In their book, *Spiritual Politics* (with a foreword by the Dalai Lama[257]), they state:

"The environmental crisis is motivating humankind to change its attitude about taking nature for granted and thereby 'fouling its own nest.' The deeper significance of this crisis is to help humanity recognize its purpose of incarnating Spirit on earth by renewing our bond with the natural world and seeing it once again as part of the sacred circle in which all life is one. We then see our role as a co-creator with nature, rather than as a dominator of the earth.

"Pollution may also serve as a catalyst in bringing together the nations of the world to develop joint policies to cope with environmental threats."[258]

They add: "International cooperation and coordination will develop from the compelling need to find global solutions to our world environmental crisis, for it cannot be solved by any one nation or bloc of nations."[259]

BOB EDGAR

> "One of the leading figures in this particular crisis is [former] Congressman **Bob Edgar,** [former] chairman of the Congressional Clearing House on the Future and a member of the Members of Congress for Peace through (*World*) Law. Edgar argues that the **environmental problem lies in national sovereignty and that only a world government can now 'save' the environment.** Specifically, he claims that the present U.S. governmental system is faulty because members are responsible to only one country, and for only a four year period. He claims that 'a system such as this cannot be expected to deal with long-term international problems such as acid rain.'"[260]

Edgar, a minister,[261] served as a Pennsylvania Congressman for 6 terms.[262] During that time he **signed** the traitorous document called a **Declaration of <u>Inter</u>dependence.**[263] He is now the General Secretary of the **National Council of Churches.**[264] In this position in 2000, he signed the Christian Declaration of Marriage.[265] This declaration "defines marriage as 'a holy union of one man and one woman' and calls for 'a stronger commitment to this holy union.'"[266] That sounds like a decent statement to sign. But wait—"later in the week Edgar released a statement saying his support for marriage between a man and a woman has been misconstrued, and has nothing to do with same-sex unions."[267] He went on to add that

> "there is unanimity among us in our longstanding advocacy for full civil rights for gay, lesbian, bisexual, and transgendered persons. Through our dialogues, we have come to celebrate the gifts and the challenges they present to us. We stand with them in our common battle against hatred and violence and the pain of exclusion. In our dangerously fragmented society, I regret and will resist any attempt to interpret support for one beleaguered segment of society as an attack on another."[268]

The day after Edgar met with the NCC's gay caucus, he went so far as to have his name **removed** from the declaration and **apologized to the gay community** for having signed it in the first place.[269] He "said he was removing his name because he personally favors gay marriages and gay union blessings and the statement refers only to marriage between a man and a woman."[270]

Edgar has been a liberal for a long time. His voting record on key moral issues on the conservative Congressional Report Card was only 8%,[271] yet the liberal,[272] leftist,[273] pro-homosexual[274] Americans for Democratic Action gave him a 93%.[275] He is also connected with the World Future Society, a New Age, one world government organization.[276]

THE ENVIRONMENT AND WORLD GOVERNMENT

Remember, the environment is being used as an inroad to bring everyone together so that a world government can be realized. We must all join together, they claim, so that we will not destroy our environment. Even Pope John Paul II approves this concept:

> "Science can purify religion from error and superstition, religion can purify science from idolatry and false absolutes. Each can draw the other into a wider world, a world in which both can flourish....Such bridging ministries must be nurtured and encouraged. Nowhere is this more clear than in the current **environmental crisis....**It has the potential to *unify and renew religious life.*[277] [Italics in the original.]

The Global Forum's Declaration declares that *"the environmental crisis has an inner, spiritual dimension...."*[278] [Emphasis in the original.]

It should be obvious by now that the environmental movement is just another strategy to entice the church into joining and promoting New Age and occult doctrines and beliefs. When you see the people involved in starting the NRPE, etc., and when you discern their agenda, you know that this is something that the church of Jesus Christ cannot condone and support, yet church leaders like **Billy Graham** and others, have jumped on their bandwagon. Sadly, the wagon is heading over the cliff and those who are on board will perish together.

Carl Sagan has gone so far as to suggest: "If we must worship a power greater than ourselves, does it not make sense to revere the Sun and stars?"[279] One researcher responds to this question like this:

> "No, it does not. Reverence does not pertain to *things* but to *persons.* To reverence the impersonal creation instead of the personal God who created us is a perversion designed for escaping moral accountability to the Creator. God indicts those who worship the creation instead of its Creator (Rom 1:18-23); and warns of the corruption of morals and behavior which results (24-32)."[280] [Emphasis in the original.]

Sagan's worship of the stars leads to astrology, so let's look at that topic for a few minutes.

ASTROLOGY

Astrology is a practice in which a person consults the sun, moon, stars, and planets to foretell future events. The astrologers claim that the position of these heavenly bodies at the exact time of one's birth will influence this person's entire life including his personality, romance, and career. Given the exact time and location of one's birth, astrologers can then determine which days will be "lucky" and which days will be "bad." These good and bad days supposedly differ from person to person.

Many people read their horoscopes or consult astrologers hoping to gain insight into their future. Astrology, however, is not a science but an **OCCULT** practice. *The World Book Encyclopedia,* under "OCCULT," reveals: "The best-known of the old **OCCULT** subjects included **ASTROLOGY,** alchemy, necromancy, and magic."[281] Under "ASTROLOGY" we find: "Judicial astrology is the astrology of today. It was and still is closely related to other **pseudo** [false] sciences and superstitions such as palmistry, numerology, and the use of charms and magic."[282] Related articles under "MAGIC" include: **ASTROLOGY,** clairvoyance, divination, evil eye, exorcism, hypnosis, necromancy, shaman (witch doctor), telepathy, trance, voodoo, and witchcraft![283]

An ad for a book entitled *A Treasury of Witchcraft,* says this:

> "Source book of the magic arts covers the history and practice of **witchcraft in all of its forms, incl[uding]** divination and **astrology,** lycanthropy and necromancy, more. Complete with specific spells, charms, invocations, **satanic pacts** and descriptions of occult practices."[284]

There are many problems with astrology. For instance, not everyone is born with a horoscope.[285] (For more information on Astrology, see my booklet *Astrology and Your Future.)* In spite of this, many people put their faith in astrological readings and plan their day accordingly. One person who has consulted astrologers was Nancy Reagan.[286] Her involvement in astrology was extensive. The President's schedule was controlled by astrological charts and timing. In fact, Nancy had several different astrologers doing work for her. At one time Jeane Dixon was her astrological advisor and then Nancy shifted to Joan Quigley.[287] It was reported that Reagan was paying Quigley $3000 a month for these services. There was also a man who did astrological work for Mrs. Reagan.[288]

According to Donald Regan's book, *For the Record: From Wall Street to Washington,* "virtually every major move and decision" made by former President Reagan during his two terms in office was affected by astrological timing.[289] Joan Quigley brags that she "briefed the President through Nancy for every meeting with Gorbachev in Geneva," and was asked advice about members of Congress who had a key vote in a bill Reagan wanted passed. She even claimed to be responsible for the timing of **all** presidential conferences, State of the Union addresses, and the Reagan-Carter debate.[290]

Reagan's

> "first major economic address as president, for example, was scheduled exactly on the Taurus full moon—a good time for focusing on issues of money and security. His major press conferences were often scheduled for perfect astrological timing. The signing of the INF Treaty was scheduled at exactly 1:30 P.M. on December 8, 1987, at Nancy Reagan's insistence, as Jupiter was ascending. This is commonly held by astrologers to be a good time to begin new partnerships or activities."[291]

Even though Mrs. Reagan's involvement was **extensive,** Billy Graham tries to excuse it. In his autobiography, Graham rationalizes: "I had never seen her as a gullible or experimental person in her **spiritual** understanding and could not help but feel **it was a momentary lapse caused by anxiety and stress."**[292] When **Graham** was asked about Nancy Reagan's involvement in astrology on the BBC radio program, *Sunday,* he **replied: "Astrology is alright as long as it is not taken too seriously."**[293] Instead of Graham telling his listeners that the Bible forbids the practice of astrology, he seems to imply that it's okay to "dabble" in astrology for fun—just as long as the person does not take it "too seriously." I wonder how many people have played around with astrology only to find themselves deeply ensnared in the occult. Such advice can have harmful **eternal** consequences.

PRESIDENTIAL MEDAL OF FREEDOM

Of course, former President Reagan had already given Graham a high honor. Graham writes:

> "While he was President, Ronald Reagan bestowed on me one of the highest honors I could ever imagine. On February 23, 1983, he presented me with the Presidential Medal of Freedom, the highest civilian honor our government gives to an American, for service to the nation. I felt unworthy of the honor, and still do. But whatever else it means, it will always remind me of the generosity and friendship of a remarkable man and a warm and enduring personal friend, Ronald Wilson Reagan."[294]

Just recently (April 5, 2000) Nancy Reagan presented Graham with the Ronald Reagan Freedom Award.[295] Republican National Committee Chairman, Jim Nicholson, said:

> "It's a pleasure to join with so many leaders to honor one of the world's greatest spiritual leaders....In everything he has done, Rev. Billy Graham has been a healer, bringing people together and spreading God's word around the globe. I can think of no one more deserving of this award for all he has done on behalf of religious freedom."[296]

"The Ronald Reagan Freedom Award is presented annually by the Ronald Reagan Presidential Foundation. Previous winners include General Colin Powell, Lady Margaret Thatcher, Mikhail Gorbachev, and Yitzhak Rabin."[297]

There may be another reason why Graham won't call out against astrology. You see, Alice Braemer worked with the psychic/astrologer **Jeane Dixon** for seven years.[298] "She obtained many pictures of our presidents, congressmen, Oral Roberts and other famous people consulting Jeane Dixon."[299] She said that a man from Billy Graham's office would pick up a check each month from the Dixons' office. In fact, on September 29, 1979, she even wrote a letter to *Christianity Today* (which was started by Billy Graham) and told Harold Myra about these things. I have a copy of that letter in which she asked:

> "Wouldn't it be wonderful if **Billy Graham** looked straight into the television camera and said: 'Yes, I did say nice things about Jeane Dixon on television back in 1966. I did keep in touch with her over the years. Yes, a man from my office did pick up a check each month from the Dixon office...from Mr. Dixon's private office. Yes, the man chatted with Mr. Dixon each time—for a little while.'"[300]

GRAHAM ENDORSES STAPLETON

Billy Graham has also endorsed Ruth Carter Stapleton, Jimmy Carter's sister, who was an **occultist.** Stapleton was

> "a featured speaker at the 13th Annual World Festival of the International Cooperation Council, held in Santa Monica, California, on January 22, 1978. This gathering of Eastern mystics, mind-science practitioners, and assorted esotericists from around the world billed itself as a Synergy Conference—'a cooperative effort on the part of all philosophies to unite in common setting to exchange ideas,' and 'a creative process moving from the individual to the cosmos.'"[301]

The conference brochure stated:

> "The International Cooperation Council is an association of approximately 200 organizations which foster the **emergence of a new universal person and civilization** based on **unity in diversity** among all peoples....The council seeks to provide a framework within which the efforts of all become highly significant in **helping to bring about the emerging world civilization."**[302]

Of course, this refers to a **new world order.**

"BORN AGAIN" IN AN ART MUSEUM

Here's how Stapleton explains what it means to be "born again":

> "You know, it's really strange, but every single human being can **experience being born again in a way that's unique with them.** I've known those who were in an art museum, and they looked at a beautiful picture, hanging on the wall, by one of the great masters, and all of sudden, for the first time in their life, something exploded inside, and there was the reality of truth: God is. That consciousness that we call the consciousness of Christ...it would flood their being; and then, from then on they knew that there was more than just two dimensions in life, but there was that dimension of the spirit, and a knowing of that Oneness. Sometimes I've known people that experienced this when they were listening to one of the great composers in music."[303]

That certainly is not the **Biblical** explanation of being "born again"!

On February 26, 1978 at Christ Universal Temple in Chicago, **Stapleton declared: "God is wholeness and you are God."**[304]

In an interview with *Christianity Today* (November 4, 1977), Stapleton remarked: "The Bible **does not** teach that **we experience hell** after we die, we experience it **<u>before</u> we die."**[305]

STAPLETON USES OCCULT PRACTICES

Stapleton has used guided meditation and the occult technique of visualization.[306] In fact, her 1977 book, *The Experience of Inner Healing,* deals extensively with the **occult method of meditation.**[307] (For more information on visualization, see my articles "What Is Visualization?" and "A Look at Inner Healing.") Stapleton also described a case where **Jesus <u>failed</u> to bring healing** "so Mary was called upon, and she was successful."[308]

She explains how one should use **repetition** to attain the state of concentration.[309] She suggests repeating a phrase such as "I am one with God" over and over again.[310]

Stapleton, who learned "inner healing" from Agnes Sanford,[311] tells the following story. A young woman, hating herself so much because she was an illegitimate child, got caught up in a life of drugs and crime. To heal her bad concept of herself, Ruth took "the young woman back in 'a guided meditation' in which Christ was visualized as 'present' during the act of fornication that caused her conception and [made] it 'holy and pure, an act of God...ordained by her heavenly Father.'"[312] This IMAGINARY Christ who is conjured up through VISUALIZATION not only condones the sinful act of her parents' fornication but actually blesses this sin by pronouncing it "holy and pure, an act of God...ordained by her heavenly Father." The Jesus of the Bible certainly WILL NOT BLESS or put His approval on something that He has already told us is SIN.

Let's stop here for a moment and think about the VISUALIZATION of this young woman. Mrs. Stapleton had her VISUALIZE Christ as being present when she was conceived. Do you realize that this lady COULD NOT POSSIBLY VISUALIZE this event WITHOUT actually MAKING IT UP in her IMAGINATION? After all, this event took place approximately 9 months BEFORE she was even born! This woman is not actually visualizing the event AS it took place but AS she THINKS and IMAGINES it took place. Most Inner Healing is based on a person's PERCEPTION of a situation rather than an ACTUAL situation! We also find that those who promote Inner Healing develop many ideas that are foreign and contrary to the Scriptures.

Stapleton claims "to have led [pornography] magnate Larry Flynt into a 'born again' experience. (As it turned out, his religious 'conversion' resulted in nothing more than his *Hustler* magazine being published with a new twist: placing graphic sex in religious settings.)"[313]

She even accepts homosexuality "if engaged in with proper motives...."[314] She states: **"If** it is evil, it is only so because of how they use it. If they choose to exploit persons for their own gratification and to ignore their own need to grow emotionally and spiritually that **attitude is wrong...."**[315] The **attitude** of exploitation is wrong, not the act of homosexuality, according to Stapleton.

So how does **Billy Graham** feel about Stapleton's book which promotes **OCCULT MEDITATION,** visualization, etc., etc.? Well, it's not hard to find out, since the following **ENDORSEMENT** is on the back cover of Stapleton's book, *The Experience of Inner*

Healing: **"Thank God for someone like Ruth, who goes about the country exalting the name of Jesus Christ, the way she does in her ministry."** Yes, Billy Graham has his endorsement on her book!

I also think it's interesting to note the day chosen for Graham's wedding. In his autobiography, he writes: "We were married there in August, on the night of **Friday the thirteenth** [1943], with a **full moon** in the sky."[316] This was the only Friday the thirteenth the entire year of 1943. Was it intentionally selected? I don't know, but Graham does seem to have a fascination with the moon. When he referred to the night his father was saved, he quoted his father as saying it was a "moonlit night."[317] Also, Graham's Global Mission '95 was held from March 16-18, 1995. Each of the three nights of the meeting he specifically referred to the **full moon.**[318] March 17th was the night of the full moon. In fact, one researcher has mentioned that he "has observed the majority of his [Graham's] major experiences and Crusades have been 'synchronized to major Satanic Feasts and phases of the Moon.'"[319]

GRAHAM AND HIS DOG

In Graham's autobiography he shows a picture of his dog. What's the dog's name? None other than Belshazzar.[320] In the book of Daniel we find that the **pagan** King Nebuchadnezzar's son's name was Belshazzar. This name means **"prince of Bel,"**[321] or "Bel protect the king."[322] Bel was the male god of the Phoenicians and Canaanites and was worshipped with self-torture and human sacrifices.[323] Not only was Bel the sun-god[324] but he was also known as the "King of the Underworld" (hell)![325]

Bel, by the way, is just another name for Baal.[326] The **Bible condemned Baal worship** on numerous occasions. Whenever the Israelites forsook the true God, they turned their worship to false gods, usually Baal. They went so far as to even burn their children as sacrifices to Baal: "They have built also the high places of Baal, to burn their sons with fire for burnt offerings unto Baal, which I commanded not, nor spake it, neither came it into My mind" (Jeremiah 19:5). Some other verses that deal with the abomination of Baal worship are: Judges 2:11, 13; 3:7; 8:33; 10:6, 10; I Samuel 7:4; 12:10; I Kings 16:30-33; 18:18; 22:53; II Kings 17:16; 21:2-3; II Chronicles 17:3; 24:7; 28:2; 33:3; Jeremiah 11:13, 17; 23:13; 32:29, and 35.

BAAL IS ALSO A SYNONYM FOR THE DEVIL,[327] so it isn't surprising that another title of Bel was "the Bright One" or the "god of light."[328] Satan often appears as an "angel of light" as II Corinthians 11:14 warns us: "Satan himself is transformed into an angel of light."

One has to wonder **why Billy Graham** would give his dog a name that would have such a connotation! Even if Graham was unaware of the paganism of such a name, he certainly should not be unaware that a pagan king had this name in the Bible. According to Daniel 5 we see that **Belshazzar** made a feast for 1000 lords and **was having a drunken orgy.** He commanded that the golden and silver vessels from the temple in Jerusalem be brought so that he and his wives could drink out of them.

> "They drank wine, and **praised the gods of gold, and of silver, of brass, of iron, of wood, and of stone.** In the same hour came forth fingers of a man's hand, and wrote over against the candlestick upon the plaster of the wall of the king's palace: and the king saw the part of the hand that wrote. Then the king's countenance was changed, and his thoughts troubled him, so that the joints of his loins were loosed, and his knees smote one against another. The king cried aloud to **bring in the astrologers,** the Chaldeans, **and the soothsayers.** And the king spake, and said to the wise men of Babylon, Whosoever shall read this writing, and shew me the interpretation thereof, shall be clothed with scarlet, and have a chain of gold about his neck, and shall be the third ruler in the kingdom" (Daniel 5:4-7).

None of the king's men could read the interpretation but the Queen remembered that Daniel had interpreted dreams for Nebuchadnezzar, so he was called. Daniel reminded Belshazzar about what happened to Nebuchadnezzar when he became proud and how the Lord brought him down. He then added:

> "And thou his son, O Belshazzar, hast not humbled thine heart, **though thou knewest all this;** But hast **lifted up thyself against the Lord of heaven;** and they have brought the vessels of his house before thee, and thou, and thy lords, thy wives, and thy concubines, have drunk wine in them; and thou **hast praised the gods** of silver, and gold, of brass, iron, wood, and stone, which see not, nor hear, nor know: and the God in whose hand thy breath is, and whose are all thy ways, hast thou not glorified" (Daniel 5:22-23).

Daniel then read the handwriting on the wall: "This is the interpretation of the thing: MENE; God hath numbered thy kingdom, and finished it. TEKEL; **Thou art weighed in the balances, and art found wanting.** PERES; Thy kingdom is divided, and given to the Medes and Persians....In that night was Belshazzar the king of the Chaldeans slain" (Daniel 5:26-28, 30).

What a sad commentary! Would **YOU** want your dog's name to be Belshazzar?!

STEVIE NICKS

Graham seems comfortable with those who embrace paganism. The inaugural week for Bill Clinton's presidency was filled with perversion and witchcraft. The Lesbian and Gay Band of America was scheduled to march at the Inaugural Parade.[329] "The Clinton inaugural planners reportedly invited the homosexual musical ensemble....The December 18 *Washington Blade,* 'The Gay Weekly of the Nation's Capital,' reports that 13 open 'Gays' are on Clinton's presidential transition team."[330]

> "Then there were the gala parties and balls which the dynamic quadruplet—Bill, Hillary, Al, and Tipper—attended. The performers included Bill's favorite rock band, *Fleetwood Mac,* with self-proclaimed **witch, Stevie Nicks,** on the vocals.... Immersed in ecstasy, the dynamic quadruplet literally drank and danced the nights away."[331]

While Nicks was working in a spirit-haunted French chateau for her 1982 "Mirage" album, she "experienced direct demonic manifestations."[332] *Rolling Stone* referred to Nicks as "Rock's blond priestess of the **occult."**[333] On Fleetwood Mac's album, *Rumours,* Nicks can be seen holding a crystal ball.[334]

Here are some other facts you should know about Nicks:

> "Halloween is her favorite night of the year. She would like to build her own pyramid, and someday retire to a 'little witch house' by the sea. Her publishing company is 'Welsh Witch Music.' She has been photographed wearing occult jewelry like the crescent, pyramid and crescent/star necklaces. She believes in reincarnation and says she was a monk in a former life."[335]

As recently as 1998 she said: "I totally believe in magic."[336] "Stevie Nicks often dedicates a song or concert to 'all the **witches** of the world.' On the album *Bare Trees* a special thanks is given to Mrs. Scarrot for her readings (fortune telling)."[337]

Nicks' "admission concerning her use of sorcery has been a well-known fact in the rock press for years."[338]

> "A feature length film based on her hit single 'Rhiannon' was produced with a setting in ancient times and included gods, goddesses, magic and of course the Welsh witch, Rhiannon. The song tells of a mythical Welsh goddess who defied her 'heavenworld,' leaving the higher plane for earth and marriage and to be a human."[339]

Stevie believes that she is the reincarnation of Rhiannon.[340]

"Nicks also uses Hindu symbolism on her first solo album, 1981's *'Bella Donna.'*...The crystal ball endorses divination (knowing the future). The tambourine represents the porthole of perception into the spirit world, and the three roses indicate the power of the pyramid."[341]

The album's title *"Bella Donna,"*

"itself has satanic significance. Not only is this wild plant a deadly poison, it is also burned at devil worship ceremonies to put the witches into a proper state of mindlessness!...

"In 1983, she released a record titled, *'The Wild Heart,'* whose cover featured Nicks dressed in a hooded robe, her hands held out in a strange form of 'signing.'"[342]

Jeff Godwin, who had played in a rock band for 7 years before becoming a Christian,[343] tells more about Nicks and *Fleetwood Mac:*

"When *'Rumours'* was released in 1977, almost overnight *Fleetwood Mac* became the most popular group in America. The album sold over 15 [now 25] million copies as single after single spun its way into the Top 10. On one of the songs, Nicks' 'Gold Dust Woman,' as the final chorus winds down with one last keening wail from Stevie's sandpapery throat, something very strange takes place. Mick Fleetwood's drumming abruptly changes. Instead of the laid back, unforced style maintained throughout the song, he instantly double times until the tom-toms throb with a tribal beat like something straight out of the jungles of Haiti. Her voice shimmery and distant, Stevie very slowly and deliberately recites a **witchcraft** incantation:

"'Great shadow of demon
"'Black widow
"'Hail shadow of dragon...'

"In the occult, the word 'hail' means 'come forth.' So Stevie has just called up demons on this record. And every time you play your copy of *'Rumours,'* those same demons are called into your room with you."[344]

McCalls says that the band's song, "Don't Stop," "became an anthem for the Clinton campaign after the group performed it **at the inaugural [1993].**"[345] Yet this same year she was so badly addicted to drugs that she checked herself into a detox center—again. (She had previously been addicted to cocaine.[346])

WE ARE ALL BROTHERS AND SISTERS

So, for Clinton's inauguration he was surrounded by lesbians and homosexuals and a witch who was addicted to drugs at the very time she was performing for Clinton. Yet Graham said (as mentioned in Chapter 1): "From a biblical point of view, we should be **headed in the direction of goodness and righteousness, away from crime and immorality** and towards one's neighbors who are in need. **I'm encouraged by the emphasis President Clinton and Hillary are putting on that.**"[347]

He also said that Clinton "has not always won the approval of his **FELLOW CHRISTIANS** but who has in his heart a desire to serve God and do His will."[348] Since when is it right to condone perverse and occultic behavior? The Bible clearly teaches:

* **"Them that sin rebuke before all,** that others also may fear" (I Timothy 5:20).

* "Preach the word; be instant in season, out of season; **reprove, rebuke,** exhort with all longsuffering and doctrine" (II Timothy 4:2).

* "And **have no fellowship with the unfruitful works of darkness, but rather reprove them.** For it is a shame even to speak of those things which are done of them in secret" (Ephesians 5:11-12).

One writer asked: "How can he [Graham] stand on a platform with President Clinton who marched into Washington for his inauguration ceremony officially accompanied with practicing homosexuals and lesbians?"[349] Good question!

Texe Marrs gives a little more detail about the 1993 inauguration. After Clinton's speech,

> "...Mother Earth religious poet Maya Angelou arose to give an original poetry reading. Angelou, a darling of the New Age crowd, wowed an international TV audience with dreamy, spiritually-oriented lyrics which had human beings talking to rocks, trees, forests, and rivers. The poem also stated something to the effect that the Earth and its people 'are one.'...
>
> "Maya Angelou told *People* magazine (Jan. 25, 1993) that she prepared for the inauguration by checking into a hotel room with only her pen, a writing pad, a bottle of sherry, and a Bible."[350]

The poem referred to "the rabbi, the priest, the sheik, the **gay,** the straight."[351]

Marrs continues:

> "She related to *U. S. A. Today* (Dec. 15, 1992, p.D-1) that she is a constant church-goer, adding that it didn't matter *which church* she attends. Angelou proudly explained that she frequents Moslem mosques, Jewish synagogues, Buddhist temples, and pro-gay Protestant churches with equal enthusiasm....

> "Ms. Angelou was interviewed back in 1990 by *Magical Blend* (Issue 26, April 1990), a popular New Age magazine. In that interview, she discussed her friendship with the late Malcolm X, the Black Muslim leader who often referred to caucasians as 'white devils.' Angelou also reminisced about the time she was in Accra, Ghana, in Africa, participating in a demonstration against the American Embassy. Here is how she described her part in that radical event: *'We in fact were marching against the American Embassy. About just after dawn two soldiers came out of the building and walked with the folded flag to the flagstand.... We started shouting.'*
>
> "Isn't it fascinating that Bill Clinton, who especially chose Maya Angelou to be his inaugural poet, himself once led anti-American demonstrations overseas against this very same flag—the stars and stripes. Clinton did this first in Oxford, England and then later in communist Russia, in Moscow."[352]

Angelou wrote the controversial book *I Know Why the Caged Bird Sings.* This book is offensive and endorses sexual perversion. In facts, parts of the book could not be aired on public television.[353]

> "Following poet Maya Angelou's pantheistic Mother Earth stanzas, famed evangelist **Billy Graham** got up and prayed, asking God's blessings on the president and the country.
>
> "As soon as Graham's short prayer of benediction ended, the huge and enthusiastic crowd went wild. Gay men and lesbians were seen warmly embracing their partners, kissing and stroking each other's body parts. At the podium, behind a virtually invisible bullet-proof glass shield, Bill, Hillary, and Chelsea Clinton stood, smiled, and waved to the throng."[354]

Before making an excuse for **Graham** and saying that he probably didn't know about the witch and Maya Angelou being on the platform with him, we need to remember that he said in *Parade* magazine as well as his own autobiography that **he has told each President** who invited him to give the prayer that **they should have other religions represented as well.**[355]

The October 20, 1996 issue of *Parade* has Graham saying:

> "'Each time a President has asked me to lead the Inaugural prayer, **I have argued that I should not do it alone, that leaders of other religions should be there too,'** he said. **'We are a multireligious nation, and it would be good to reflect that at this important ceremonial occasion....**
>
> **"'We are <u>all</u> brothers and sisters in our hearts,'** he stressed. 'We ought to love each other.'"[356]

OTHER PATHS TO GOD

We've already covered the paganism of Unitarians, so I found it interesting to see a letter in *The News and Observer* by a Unitarian Universalist minister in response to the above quotation from Billy Graham. Robert Murphy wrote:

> **"What a wonderful proposal!...**If Christians and Jews, Muslims and Hindus, and Buddhists and Native American traditionalists could stand together for even a moment on Inauguration Day, it would send a powerful message to all of America and to every nation in the world. I hope that Inauguration Day planners will honor this suggestion. This is the time for some healing."[357]

As Christians, we are to love each other but we do not condone, promote, and respect others' sin and pagan belief systems. There is a big difference! I have non-Christian friends and family members and while I love them and pray for them, I certainly have no intention of inviting them on a platform and asking them to lead others in prayer!

Graham also stated that "as an American, **I respect other paths to God**—and, as a Christian, I am called on to love them."[358] Interestingly, a **New Ager says:**

> "This same theme of **practical love is found at the core of the New Age teachings** presented by Blavatsky and Bailey. Djwhal Khul, the Tibetan Master [a demonic spirit guide] whose ideas were expressed by Alice Bailey, repeatedly affirmed that the **only real sin was a sense of separation—or lack of love**—among people and between people and God."[359]

Also notice that Graham referred to "other paths to God." Here is "America's greatest evangelist" saying that there **other paths to God.** I wonder how many times he has read the Bible for the Bible certainly does not teach this. **Jesus said: "I am the way,** the truth, and the life: **no man cometh unto the Father, but by Me"** (John 14:6). I Timothy 2:5 clearly reveals: "For there is one God, and **one mediator** between God and men, the man **Christ Jesus."** "Let no man deceive you with vain words: for because of these things cometh the wrath of God upon the children of disobedience" (Ephesians 5:6).

As an aside, the *Parade* article also stated: "Regarding politics, Graham said: 'Most people think I'm a Republican, because of my close friendships with Republican Presidents. But I have close friends in both parties. Actually, **I'm a Democrat**—that's my political identification.'"[360] This article was conveniently printed about 2 weeks before the Presidential election of Nov. 5, 1996 when his friend Bill Clinton, a Democrat, won the election.

Of course, Graham has been begging Presidents for decades to have other faiths represented at the inauguration. Richard Nixon asked Graham to pray for the 1969 inauguration.[361] Graham writes about this event in his autobiography:

> "Nixon wanted me to do all the prayers at the swearing-in ceremony, but I objected.
>
> "'Dick, you've got to have **all faiths represented,** or you're going to have trouble.
>
> "'No, I just want you,' he insisted.
>
> "Eventually, Nixon gave in to the **ecumenical** idea, and I suggested other clergy, including my friend and supporter Rabbi Edgar Fogel Magnin, of the large Jewish synagogue on Wilshire Boulevard in Los Angeles."[362]

In fact, according to *A Prophet with Honor,* we are told that Graham said:

> "I told him, 'You cannot leave the Jewish people out. You cannot leave out the Catholics and the Orthodox.' But he said, 'No, I want you, and I want you to take ten minutes.' I told him, 'No, Sir, I can't do that.' Finally, someone did persuade him that he had to have all the major religious groups...."[363]

Graham also insisted on George Bush having **ecumenical** prayers.[364] Graham writes:

> "At his inauguration in 1989, George Bush invited me to lead the various prayers during the public ceremony. **I protested at first, pointing out that it was customary to have clergy from other traditions participate** also (often a Jewish rabbi, a Catholic priest, and perhaps an Orthodox leader). He remained adamant, however, saying he felt more comfortable with me; besides, he added, he didn't want people to think he was just trying to play politics by having representatives of different faiths."[365]

PRAY FOR THOSE IN AUTHORITY

I'm sure some people are saying that it's wonderful that someone like Graham can lead prayers for those in authority. After all, we are to pray for those in authority (I Timothy 2:1-3). It is true that we are to pray for those in leadership, but we are not to **fellowship** with those of other faiths who don't even acknowledge that Jesus is the

Messiah or who are not Christians. The Bible clearly warns us in II John 1:9-10: "Whosoever transgresseth, and abideth not in the doctrine of Christ, hath not God. He that abideth in the doctrine of Christ, he hath both the Father and the Son. If there come any unto you, and bring not this doctrine, receive him not into your house, **neither bid him God speed."** Praying blessings upon those who are willfully committing sins is not Scriptural.

When Paul was at Athens he came across an altar with an inscription on it "to the unknown god" (Acts 17:23). Can you imagine Paul calling in the rabbis as well as idol worshippers to give their opinion of this god? Can you envision him asking non-Christians to offer a prayer to this "god"? Of course, he didn't do any such thing. He clearly told them that this "unknown god" was the Lord of heaven and that they needed to repent. He didn't insinuate that the Athenians' god was the same as the God he worshipped. He certainly didn't believe that all paths led to the one true God.

HOMOSEXUAL INVITES GRAHAM

Billy Graham spoke at Harvard University in October 1999 at the request of **Peter Gomes,** a homosexual chaplain[366] and a professor of Christian Morals,[367] who said: "I am a Christian who happens as well to be gay."[368] Two years prior to Graham's invitation, Gomes announced that the Harvard University Memorial Church "has decided to allow same-sex marriage."[369]

Graham had also spoken at Harvard in 1982. *Christianity Today* reported on that visit with Tom Minnery recounting the following: "In fact, if there was a reason for Graham's success with the Harvard students, it was his forthright admission that he does not have all the answers, and for his gentle approach to the Gospel, **minus the fire and damnation."**[370]

We need to remember that Jesus spoke more of hell than of heaven. I don't think Graham can say with the apostle Paul: "For **I have not shunned to declare unto you <u>all</u> the counsel of God"** (Acts 20:27).

GRAHAM PRAISES THE DALAI LAMA

Graham even goes beyond the Judeo-Christian faiths. Although Graham said the way to God is through Jesus Christ, he also "expressed **tolerance for other religions."**[371] Additionally, he "lauded the **Buddhist Dalai Lama** for peace efforts...and emphasized the **similarities between the Christian and Islamic scriptures."**[372]

For those who are not aware of who the Dalai Lama is, he was a former judge for the Templeton Prize[373] and is a **BUDDHIST**[374] who is supposed to be a reincarnation of a god.[375] "To the Himalayan Buddhists, the Dalai Lama, the Kun-don or Holy One, is the holiest of holy men."[376] He "is acknowledged as one of the greatest living Buddhist teachers"[377] and "is the Supreme Head of all Buddhists in Tibet."[378]

Although he is accepted as a holy man, he advocates the sexual practice of Tantric yoga.[379] He also is involved with spirit mediums and "regularly consults with the Nechung Oracle, said to be a spirit deity who takes over the body of a chosen Tibetan Buddhist."[380]

The Dalai Lama was among the "First Endorsers" of the New Age group called Planetary Citizens[381] and an endorser of the Planetary Initiative for the World We Choose.[382]

A few months prior to Graham's praise, the Dalai Lama published his book, *Ethics for the New Millennium.* In this book he said that religion is not always necessary: "'Whether or not a person is a religious believer does not matter much,' he said in his book. 'We humans can live quite well without recourse to religious faith.'"[383] The Dalai Lama is a founding member of the Temple of Understanding[384] (which was covered earlier) and gave the keynote address in 1984.[385] He said: "I appreciate any organization or individual people who sincerely make an effort to promote harmony between humanity, and particularly **harmony between the various religions.** I consider it very sacred work and very important work."[386] He also strongly supports the idea of a "United Religions."[387] William Swing, the man behind the United Religions Initiative,[388] stated that the Dalai Lama

> "quickly saw the need for a United Religions in the face of rising militant fundamentalism. More important in his mind, he saw the United Religions as a focus of the best of our past traditions and the best representation for the hope of unity among various world peoples and a place where we can act in concert."[389]

Yes, **Graham praised the Dalai Lama for his efforts for peace,** but just a few weeks **BEFORE** this, the Dalai Lama

> "held a 12-day seminar in Bloomington, Indiana to lead disciples through the Kalachakra Initiation, a revered **Buddhist teaching designed to foster peace....**
>
> "Religious practice is a way to achieve peace, but **faith, says the Dalai Lama, is not necessary.** Rather, the world needs 'secular ethics' of compassion and loving-kindness."[390]

The Dalai Lama talked more about the kind of peace he is working for in a speech he made entitled "A Human Approach to World Peace." He stated:

> "There are two primary tasks facing religious practitioners who are concerned with **world peace.** First, **we must promote better interfaith understanding** so as to **create a workable degree of unity among all religions.** This may be achieved in part by **respecting** each other's beliefs and by emphasizing our common concern for human well-being.
>
> "Second, we must bring about a viable consensus on basic spiritual values that touch every human heart and enhance general human happiness: We practitioners of **different faiths can work together for world peace** when we view different religions as essentially instruments to develop....
>
> "I believe that **all of the major religions of the world can contribute to world peace** and work together for the benefit of humanity, if we put aside subtle metaphysical differences, which are really the internal business of each religion."[391]

"BUDDHISM IS THE BEST RELIGION"

In accepting the Hollister Award from the Temple of Understanding, the Dalai Lama declared:

> "For me **Buddhism is the best religion**—for me, the best; but that does not mean Buddhism is best for everyone. For my Christian brothers and sisters, Christianity is the best. For my Muslim brothers and sisters—the Muslim tradition is the best. I feel there should be a variety of religious traditions so that the variety of people get more benefit."[392]

Yet, in spite of the Dalai Lama's seeming tolerance for all religions, on January 25, 2001 he joined with the Hindus in their festival. This particular Hindu group has been "dedicated to persecuting Christians and Muslims."[393] The Dalai Lama also rebuked "Christians for trying to convert others to their religions."[394] So much for his tolerance for all religions!

The Dalai Lama has been a participant in many **interfaith** activities such as signing the "Declaration of World Thanksgiving."[395] He participated in the World Parliament of Religions where pagans, occultists, voodoo high priests, shamans, Zoroastrian sun-god worshippers, witchcraft devotees wearing images of Venus, druid priests, etc. were in attendance.[396] He also participated in Thanksgiving Square,[397] the Global Conference of Spiritual and Parliamentary Leaders on Human Survival,[398] the World Day of Prayer for Peace where "Hindus, Buddhists, African tribal witchdoctors, Togo snake handlers, and others, met in Assisi, Italy, and prayed together for world peace,"[399] and the United Religions Initiative (URI).[400]

UNITED RELIGIONS INITIATIVE

The URI is an organization that is trying to unite all religions and is patterned after the United Nations.[401] *"The purpose of the United Religions Initiative is to birth in June, 2000 a global organization of the world's religions and spiritual traditions, to be known as the United Religions."*[402] [Emphasis in the original.] The signing of the United Religions' charter took place, as planned, on June 26, 2000. This was the anniversary of the day that the United Nations' charter was signed.[403] In a speech given by William Swing, he said:

> "The purpose of the United Religions Initiative 2000 is that there would be **one central, interfaith global body** primarily constituted to strive permanently and daily for peace among religions for the sake of peace among nations and wholeness for the entire created order."[404] [Underlining in the original.]

Swing bragged to the *San Francisco Chronicle:*

> ***"I've spent a lot of time praying with Brahmins, meditating with Hindus, and chanting with Buddhists. I feel I've been enormously enriched inwardly by exposure to these folks. I've gone back and read our own scriptures, and it's amazing how they begin to read differently when you're exposed to more truth from more people in other parts of the world."***[405] [Emphasis in the original.]

The intriguing thing is that the headquarters for the **URI** is at the **Presidio.** This is also the headquarters for the **Gorbachev Foundation.**[406] One researcher points out:

> "It is interesting to note that the word **'Presidio'** is Spanish for 'fortress.' We also know that the word **'Kremlin'** means 'fortress.' We also know that an executive committee in the Soviet Union serving as a permanent organ of a larger governmental body, was called a 'Presidium.' What an amazing place for the headquarters of the new 'World Church,' and yet not so amazing when you understand Illuminism, and that Satan is behind the entire thing!"[407]

The head of the Gorbachev Foundation is Jim Garrison.[408] Garrison is an occultist and was head of the New Age Esalen Institute,[409]

> "a mind-control organization involved in conducting experimental psychological techniques in American school classrooms. Garrison is also President of the Shevardnadze International Foreign Policy Association, which he runs from the same office in the Presidio, the closed U.S. military base in San Francisco."[410]

In *The San Francisco Weekly* in 1995, was an article entitled "One World, Under Gorby" in which Garrison stated: "Over the next twenty to thirty years, **we are going to end up with world government. It's inevitable....**There's going to be conflict, coercion and consensus. That's all part of what will be required as we give birth to the first global civilization."[411]

WHAT IS INTERFAITH?

"The Dalai Lama actively promotes 'a spiritual New World Order and the unity of all faiths, religions and sects.'"[412] In the same issue of the *Temple of Understanding Newsletter* that tells about the Dalai Lama receiving the Hollister Award, it also gives a definition of "interfaith." This article asks:

> "What is interfaith? Interfaith is most fundamentally respect. At the bottom line it is **respecting** different traditions, different religions, different faiths. It is coming to understanding, knowledge, and **appreciation** of them. And then most important, it's coming to a **love** of them. You can be Jewish and you can really fall in love with Buddhism. You can be a Buddhist and you can really fall in love with Christianity. You can be a Mohawk Indian and you can really fall in love with Islam."[413]

As can be seen by the Dalai Lama's own words, the "peace" he is working for starts by bringing all the religions together, yet **Graham praises the Dalai Lama for his peace efforts!** Why?

Graham has long pushed the ecumenical movement and he **BRAGS** about this in his autobiography. The sad thing is, the New Age movement is also working towards the ecumenical/interfaith movement. In fact, it is **NECESSARY** to have an **interfaith** endeavor in order for the Antichrist to come on the scene. The Antichrist will never be accepted in an atheistic world. He needs a religious and "spiritual" society in order to foster his plans. He wants **WORSHIP** but an atheistic community is not ordinarily interested in worship. To be able to encourage worship, the society must be prepared in advance. This is part of why we are seeing so much interest in the **spiritual** aspect. Unfortunately, **a spiritual society is not necessarily a Christian society.**

For instance, the Dalai Lama gave a speech in the Hawaiian Islands in 1994. He explained:

> "When I say **Spirituality,** I am **not thinking** in terms of **religious** belief. A religion, if you have one, is good. It is very useful. But even without religions, we can manage. There can be a happy person even without religion. So, therefore, when I

say that spirituality, or internal spiritual development, it means the basic human good qualities. That is, Human affection; the human sense of community; and a sense of responsibility. These are, I believe, the basic internal spiritual values....

"So it is very important to know that it is our Nature that is the base of reality. So to me various different religious traditions are actually about strengthening basic human good qualities. Sometimes I describe religion, not out of disrespect, but sometimes I describe it as 'a luxury asset item.' If you have it, very good! But, without it we can survive."[414] [Italics in the original; boldface added.]

WHAT IS SPIRITUALITY?

Joseph Fort Newton, a well-known Mason, also explains his view of **"spirituality."** He writes:

"Many kinds of life have to be lived, and we must have a care when we call one type of life spiritual and another not. What is spirituality? Who is spiritual? When is a man spiritual and when not? Audubon studying birds was not less spiritual than Jonathan Edwards pondering theology. John Woolman, the Quaker saint, was not more spiritual than Washington at Valley Forge, fighting for the liberty of his people. Music is not more spiritual than mathematics. An 'interior' meditative life is not necessarily more spiritual than an 'exterior' life of social ministry. A sanctuary and a laboratory may be equally spiritual, since in both men seek the truth. In short, spirituality is not only a sacred awe, a reverence, an inward aspiration; it is also insight, action, doing or suffering the will of God. It is not one type of temperament."[415]

The Universal Fellowship of Metropolitan Community Churches (UFMCC) is a large denomination consisting mainly of gays and lesbians.[416] They, too, have a **spirituality** but they are not Christians. *The New Age Journal* had an article about the MCC in 1985 which said:

"On this particular Sunday morning, the service at the Metropolitan Community Church in downtown Los Angeles isn't too different from any other Protestant assembly taking place in the city. There is a rousing choir, an emotional laying-on of hands, some spirited preaching. New members from MCC churches in other states are introduced to the congregation.

"But you can't miss the difference when the worshippers line up at the altar rail for communion: a few wear black leather vests; couples of the same sex go to the front holding hands.

The minister solemnly performs a 'blessing of intention'—an MCC rite similar to the Roman Catholic posting of marriage bans—for two women as they kneel in front of the congregation.

"Services like this are taking place at more than two hundred gay Metropolitan Community Churches [as of 1985! There are now more than 300 congregations.[417]] across the U.S. and Canada, and even as far away as Australia, Denmark, and Africa....

"Behind the facade is a fifteen-year-old quiet prairie fire of a movement, a well-kept secret that the fastest growing organizations in the gay world have been **religious and spiritual in nature."**[418]

The article continues:

"The gay **spiritual path** is taking many forms....Gays have been prominent in the **neopagan and goddess worship** movements; they also form a sizable conclave within the following of San Diego minister Terry Cole-Whittaker, whose preachings do not touch on the issue of sexual preference, but whose 'you're-perfect-as-you-are' motto has an appeal to a group accustomed to damnation."[419]

A NEW SPIRITUALITY

Don Lattin, writing in the *San Francisco Chronicle* stated: "The **'new spirituality'** is 'happening **outside** the religious mainstream.'..."[420]

"Lattin writes that homosexuals' **spiritual** search is also leading them to new age teachings and practices such as channelling, positive thinking, and meditation and visualization. The New Age healing tapes and books of Louise Hay and the esoteric 'Christian' *Course in Miracles* books are among the most popular in the AIDS community."[421]

The UFMCC even has an **ECUMENICAL** ministry that they engage in.[422] They ask:

"WHY DOES UFMCC WANT TO ENGAGE IN ECUMENICAL MINISTRY?...

"Those of us active in UFMCC's ecumenical ministry like to say that 'to know us is to love us.' We mean that it is in the sharing and **working together** that other Christians come to know and love the people of the Universal Fellowship. And with that love comes healing and <u>change</u>."[423] [Underlining in the original.]

This group has applied for admittance to the National Council of Churches.[424] While the NCC was not quite ready at that time to accept the UFMCC into membership, the then-General Secretary, Joan Brown Campbell, let it be known that she and the NCC supported "civil rights for all."[425] **Campbell went so far as to join the homosexual demonstration** on June 24, 1994. "Campbell explained why she joined the protest: 'Our churches are very united on civil rights for gays and lesbians, and there are places where we can be supportive. We don't go as far as the MCC wants us to go, but there is a fair distance that we can go, and that needs to be made visible.'"[426]

In fact, the magazine for the NCC, *Eculink,* reveals: "Upon learning of the UFMCC event, which coincided with **Campbell's** scheduled return flight from a trip to Moscow, **she rearranged her travel plans in order to participate...."**[427]

This is the person who said about **Billy Graham** in 1991:

> "'It is indeed a high honor for the NCC to have in our midst this man of faith. His purpose in coming is to become better acquainted with the general secretary and to discuss **common interests and concerns.'**
>
> "She told Religious News Service that she hopes the meeting would contribute to the perception that Graham and the 32-denomination organization **have much in common."**[428]

Again, we see that Graham returned the praise. When Graham met with Campbell in 1991, he said that he had "no problem in fellowshipping with anybody who calls Jesus Christ Lord."[429] What would a Bible-believing person really have in **common** doctrinally with the National Council of Churches? As one author reminds us, a

> "great percentage of **NCC leaders deny the deity, virgin birth, blood atonement, and resurrection of Jesus Christ.** In fact it would be a difficult task to find a leader in the NCC who believes the Bible is the perfect, inspired Word of God. They have had **witches** speak at their meetings, and they are in dialogue with the homosexual Metropolitan Community of Churches. They are syncretistic and work hand-in-hand with heathen religions. They are given over to liberation theology, and put the vast part of their energy and finances into projects to bring about a **new world government** and religion."[430]

GRAHAM AND THE NCC

Of course, Graham has had connections to the NCC for many **decades.** For instance, in "one of his speeches before the National

Council of Churches, he said, 'My wife is a Presbyterian. Her denomination is in the National Council so perhaps I am here by marriage.'"[431] On August 27, 1991, he praised the NCC with these words:

> "There's no group of people in the world that I would rather be with right now than you all. Because I think of you, I pray for you, and we follow with great interest the things you do....I don't speak to too many church assemblies any more because **I consider myself as belonging to all the churches.** And I love everybody equally and I have no problem in fellowship with anybody who says that Jesus Christ is Lord. This has been a great relief to me to come to that conclusion about 20 some years ago."[432]

The Bible, however, doesn't agree. Matthew 7:21-23 says:

> "Not every one that saith unto Me, Lord, Lord, shall enter into the kingdom of heaven; but he that **doeth** the will of My Father which is in heaven. **MANY WILL SAY TO ME IN THAT DAY, LORD, LORD, HAVE WE NOT PROPHESIED IN THY NAME? AND IN THY NAME HAVE CAST OUT DEVILS? AND IN THY NAME DONE MANY WONDERFUL WORKS?** And then will I profess unto them, I never knew you: **DEPART FROM ME, YE THAT WORK INIQUITY."**

Notice that these individuals had done miracles, cast out devils, and prophesied in Jesus' name, yet Jesus told them that He did not know them. It is possible to use Jesus' name and do "wonderful works" and yet not be His child.

Another example is given in Luke:

> "When once the master of the house is risen up, and hath shut to the door, and ye begin to stand without, and to knock at the door, **saying, Lord, Lord,** open unto us; and He shall answer and say unto you, I know you not whence ye are: Then shall ye begin to say, **We have eaten and drunk in Thy presence,** and Thou hast taught in our streets. But He shall say, I tell you, **I know you not** whence ye are; **depart from Me, all ye workers of iniquity.** There shall be weeping and gnashing of teeth, when ye shall see Abraham, and Isaac, and Jacob, and all the prophets, in the kingdom of God, and **you yourselves thrust out"** (Luke 13:25-28).

The Pharisees called Jesus "Master," but they were seeking a sign from Him. (See Matthew 12:38.) The Herodians said "Master," but they were trying to ensnare Christ in His speech so that they could find fault with Him (Matthew 22:15-21; Luke 20:20-26). The Sadducees also approached Jesus by calling Him "Master" (Matthew 22:24; Luke 20:28), but they, too, were trying to trap Him. Likewise, Judas referred to Jesus as "Master," but then he betrayed Him with a kiss. (See Matthew 26:25, 49; Mark 14:45.)

Jesus asked: **"Why call ye Me, Lord, Lord, and do not the things which I say?"** (Luke 6:46). One command is found in II Thessalonians 3:6: "Now we command you, brethren, in the name of our Lord Jesus Christ, that ye **withdraw yourselves from every brother that walketh disorderly,** and not after the tradition which he received of us."

In Acts we find a specific case where unsaved people called upon Jesus—with disastrous results:

> "Then certain of the vagabond Jews, exorcists, took upon them to call over them which had evil spirits **the name of the Lord Jesus,** saying, We adjure you by Jesus whom Paul preacheth. And there were seven sons of one Sceva, a Jew, and chief of the priests, which did so. And the evil spirit answered and said, Jesus I know, and Paul I know; but who are ye? And the man in whom the evil spirit was leaped on them, and overcame them, and prevailed against them, so that they fled out of that house naked and wounded" (Acts 19:13-16).

We need to remember that Paul warned about "another Gospel" (Galatians 1:6-9) and "another Jesus" (II Corinthians 11:4).

I cannot say with Graham that "I have no problem in fellowship with anybody who says that Jesus Christ is Lord"[433]—especially when such is said about the ungodly National Council of Churches. Titus 1:16 reminds us: "They profess that they know God; but in works they deny Him, being abominable, and disobedient, and unto every good work reprobate."

COMMON GROUND

Even homosexual groups are comfortable with Graham (and Graham with them). In 1995, the River City Metropolitan Community Church planned to send representatives to Graham's crusade. *The Sacramento Bee* a **"socialist** oriented newspaper...owned by the McClatchy family,"[434] reported **positively** on this: "Whatever their differences, everyone can find **common ground** in Graham's message, members of various churches said."[435]

> "Freda Smith is a female **homosexual pastor** of the Sacramento Metropolitan Community Church, which is part

> of the nationwide denomination of homosexual churches in the United States. **Smith and her church were participating in the Billy Graham crusade, which means that some of the counselors receiving people who were coming forward were homosexuals.** Thus **some people coming forward were counseled by openly proclaimed homosexuals.** This gave Smith and her church a ripe mission field to use, to try to seduce people seeking salvation and Jesus Christ. **That this homosexual church was allowed to participate in the crusade was not advertised by the Billy Graham people."**[436]

This isn't the first time that the homosexuals welcomed Graham. In 1992, "Oregon's lesbian and gay newsmagazine,"[437] *Just Out,* had an article about the then-upcoming Graham crusade which was entitled "A powerful (and surprising) **ally** is coming to Oregon." The article stated:

> "We did some investigating and at every turn became more and more impressed with the integrity of the Billy Graham Crusade organization....
>
> "Fearing that the impending Billy Graham Crusade in September would whip the fanatic 'religious' right into a frenzy of gay-bashing, *Just Out* decided to contact the crusade headquarters and see just what Billy Graham preaches.
>
> "We talked to Tom Phillips, the senior crusade organizer, about some of our fears and concerns regarding the crusade coming to Portland. He was very receptive to us. Phillips stated, 'The Billy Graham Crusade does not target groups. Billy Graham's message is about the love of God through Jesus Christ.' There seems to be no room in the crusade organization for people who do not have that level of loving acceptance of all people....
>
> **"The crusade does not teach a sectarian doctrine or in any way try to influence people toward a specific church or denomination....**
>
> "Preaching love, acceptance and diversity to people is what Oregon desperately needs right now. We can only hope that Billy Graham's message is able to heal the hate-torn 'Christians' who are turning themselves inside out trying to annihilate everyone who doesn't agree with their dogma."[438]

At the time of Graham's visit, Oregon was scheduled to vote on Measure 9 which would have declared homosexuality as abnormal.[439] When asked about this measure, Graham said that "there are **good Christians on both sides** of the measure."[440] Talking to reporters,

Graham said that he stays out of all politics[441] (which is not true—but it allows him to sit on the fence and cater to both sides)!

"IT'S IN THEIR GENES"

In the August 6, 1994 issue of *TV Guide* Graham was asked about homosexuality. He did say that he thought it was a sin but he quickly added: "In my judgment, it's not that big."[442] Later that year, on "the Larry King Live show in December 1994, **Billy Graham said homosexuals are born that way and that 'it's in their genes.'"**[443]

Graham, as usual, tries to please both sides but it doesn't just work out Scripturally. If homosexuality is a sin and homosexuals are born that way (as Graham claims), then God is the author of sin. Obviously, this is not true. First of all, homosexual relationships do not produce offspring, therefore homosexuality cannot be in the genes and cannot be passed on to the next generation. Furthermore, if homosexuality were in the genes, then a person would not be responsible for his lifestyle, but God clearly tells us that homosexuality is an abomination. I Corinthians 6:9-10 explains:

> "Know ye not that the unrighteous shall not inherit the kingdom of God? Be not deceived: neither fornicators, nor idolaters, nor adulterers, nor effeminate, nor abusers of themselves with mankind, Nor thieves, nor covetous, nor drunkards, nor revilers, nor extortioners, shall inherit the kingdom of God."

WE WANT YOUR CHILDREN

In a 1987 issue of *Gay Community News* we find this quote:

> "We shall sodomize your sons....We shall seduce them in your schools, in your dormitories, in your gymnasiums, in your locker rooms, in your sports arenas, in your seminaries, in your youth groups, in your movie theater bathrooms, in your army bunkhouses, in your truck stops, in your all-male clubs, in your houses of Congress, wherever men are with men together. Your sons shall become our minions and do our bidding. They will be recast in our image. They will come to crave and adore us....All laws banning homosexual activity will be revoked. Instead, legislation shall be passed which engenders love between men. All homosexuals must stand together as brothers; we must be united artistically, philosophically, socially, politically, and financially. We will triumph only when we present a common face to the vicious heterosexual enemy....We will unmask the powerful homosexuals who masquerade as

> heterosexuals. You will be shocked and frightened when you find that your presidents and their sons, your industrialists, your senators, your mayors, your generals, your athletes, your film stars, your television personalities, [are not—Ed.] your civic heterosexual figures you assumed them to be. We are everywhere; we have infiltrated your ranks. Be careful when you speak of homosexuals because we are always among you; we may be sitting across the desk from you; we may be sleeping in the same bed with you....We shall conquer the world because warriors inspired by and banded together by homosexual love and honor are invincible as were the ancient Greek soldiers. The family unit will be abolished....Perfect boys will be conceived and grown in the genetic laboratory....All churches who condemn us will be closed. Our holy gods are handsome young men....We shall rewrite history, history filled and debased with your heterosexual lies and distortions. We shall portray the homosexuality of the great leaders and thinkers who have shaped the world. We will demonstrate that homosexuality and intelligence and imagination are inextricably linked....We shall be victorious because we are fueled with the ferocious bitterness of the oppressed who have been forced to play seemingly bit parts in our dumb, heterosexual shows throughout the ages. We too are capable of firing guns and manning barricades of the ultimate revolution."[444]

Does this quotation sound like homosexuality is "in the genes" (as Billy Graham claims) or does it sound like perversion as the Bible says it is? Romans declares:

> "For this cause God gave them up unto vile affections: for even their women did change the natural use into that which is against nature: And likewise also the men, leaving the natural use of the woman, burned in their lust one toward another; men with men working that which is unseemly, and receiving in themselves that recompence of their error which was meet.... Who knowing the judgment of God, that they which commit such things are worthy of death, not only do the same, but have pleasure in them that do them. Therefore thou art inexcusable..." (Romans 1:26-27, 32-33).

In 1997 Graham once again welcomed the homosexuals:

> "'Whatever your background, whatever your sexual orientation, we welcome you tonight.'...Billy followed this up by telling the smiling and happy liberal media: 'What I want to preach about in San Francisco is the love of God. People need to know that God loves them no matter what their sexual orientation.'"[445]

Homosexuals should be welcome in our churches, but they should never be given a position of leadership or be used as a counselor (as in Graham's crusade). They should be invited to our churches, but in most cases, they will not be comfortable if the preacher preaches about sin. Of course, the Gospel is not designed to make a sinner feel contented. It is intended to draw us to the cross where we confess—and **forsake**—our sins. Proverbs 28:13 says: "He that covereth his sins shall not prosper: but whoso confesseth and forsaketh them shall have mercy." Then and only then should we feel secure in Christ. If sinners (whether homosexual or otherwise) can attend service after service in a church and not feel condemned, there is a good probability that the preacher is not proclaiming the Word of God as it was meant to be conveyed.

Are the homosexuals uncomfortable with Graham's message?

> "According to the *San Francisco Chronicle & Examiner* (October 10, 1997), after hearing Graham's latest milktoast (sic) sermon, Brian Jackie, a gay San Francisco Catholic, praised the evangelist. 'Graham is a man of integrity,' said Jackie, adding that Billy Graham always has a 'positive message.'
>
> "Jackie's friend, the Reverend Bill Byrd, **homosexual pastor** of the San Francisco Evangelical Gay Church, heartily agreed. **'I have no problem with Graham's preaching,'** said the Reverend Byrd, 'Billy Graham brings people together.'"[446]

"I HAVE SO MANY GAY FRIENDS"

Graham has said: "I have so many gay friends, and we remain friends."[447] One of these friends is Mel White. White ghostwrote books for many "evangelicals"[448] such as Pat Robertson,[449] Jim Bakker,[450] Billy Graham,[451] D. James Kennedy,[452] and Jerry Falwell,[453] as well as speeches for Ollie North.[454] He was even a Fuller Seminary professor for 14 years.[455] In 1992 he came "out of the closet" and announced that he was a homosexual.[456] In 1993 he was installed as dean of the Cathedral of Hope Metropolitan Community Church in Dallas, with 14,000 congregants, the world's largest gay and lesbian congregation.[457] White lives with his male lover, Gary Nixon, in Dallas. He says: "I am gay, I am proud, and God loves me without reservation."[458] Someone who knew White asked him if he knew he was sinning by being a homosexual. He said that knew it but he added, "Once saved, always saved," so he thought he had nothing to worry about.[459]

I guess he thinks he can also murder and still be a "Christian." "White, who in 1990 helped to poison a man infected with AIDS calls on sodomites to build networks with godless organizations such as the NAACP, ACLU, NOW, and People for the American Way to advance their cause."[460]

White was one of the signers of the "Religious Declaration on Sexual Morality, Justice, and Healing" which calls "for same-sex unions, ordination of homosexuals and abortion rights."[461] He was an endorser of the "Stop the Hate" vigil.[462] He was also awarded the National Civil Liberties Award by the left-wing American Civil Liberties Union.

"He rejects the 'Christian' label and says this word 'now stands for the enemy.'"[463] "The problem, White insists, is that what the television evangelists sincerely believe is that they ought to rid society of anyone who disagrees with their theological views."

So, how does White feel about Graham? **"White exempts evangelist Billy Graham from his accusations."**[464] In his book, *Stranger at the Gate: To Be Gay and Christian in America,* White explains the difference between Graham and others of the Christian right.[465] How interesting! Furthermore, Philip Yancey, an editor of *Christianity Today,* Graham's magazine, has even **endorsed** White's pro-gay book![466]

Isaiah 5:20 warns: "Woe unto them that call evil good, and good evil; that put darkness for light, and light for darkness; that put bitter for sweet, and sweet for bitter!"

7. QUOTABLE QUOTES AND OTHER NOTES

In *McCall's* magazine (January 1978), in an article entitled "I Can't Play God Any More," Graham declared: "I used to think that pagans in far-off countries were lost—were going to hell—if they did not have the Gospel of Jesus Christ preached to them. I no longer believe that....I believe there are **other ways** of recognizing the existence of God—**through nature,** for instance—and plenty of other opportunities, therefore, of saying yes to God."[1] If the pagans don't need Christ because they can discover Him through nature, etc., then why does Billy Graham continue to hold crusades in pagan countries? Is there another agenda?

A Prophet with Honor, written at Graham's request,[2] elaborates on the above statement: Graham

> "did not automatically consign to hell all who never heard the Christian gospel preached. 'They are in the hands of a God of love and mercy and grace,' he said. 'I don't think I can play God.' He was willing to venture, however, that he doubted a righteous God would consign an Albert **Schweitzer, who denied the deity of Christ** but gave his life to good works, to the same fate reserved for such consummately evil men as Hitler and Eichmann. **'Hitler and Schweitzer should not be in the same place.'"**[3]

In the April 10, 1983 issue of *The Orlando Sentinel,* Graham was asked about why many Americans don't accept the concept of hell. He responded:

> "I think that hell essentially is separation from God forever. And that is the worst hell that I can think of. But I think people have a hard time believing God is going to allow people to burn in literal fire forever. I think the fire that is mentioned in the Bible is a burning thirst for God that can never be quenched."[4]

In July 1983, in a book written by Graham and

> "distributed at his International Conference for Itinerant Evangelists in Amsterdam, he wrote: 'Hell is not the most popular of preaching topics. I don't like to preach on it. But I must if I am to proclaim the whole counsel of God. We must not avoid warning of it. The most outspoken messages on hell, and the most graphic references to it, came from Jesus Himself....Jesus used three words to describe hell....The third word

that He used is 'fire.' Jesus used this symbol over and over. This could be literal fire, as many believe. Or IT COULD BE SYMBOLIC....I'VE OFTEN THOUGHT THAT THIS FIRE COULD POSSIBLY BE A BURNING THIRST FOR GOD THAT IS NEVER QUENCHED. What a terrible fire that would be—never to find satisfaction, joy, or fulfillment!'"[5] [Emphasis in the original.]

In the November 15, 1993 issue of *Time,* he stated: "When it comes to a literal fire, I don't preach it because I'm not sure about it."[6]

When interviewed on television in England he was asked about hell and replied: "I do not believe in a literal hell now."[7]

"Dr. Graham further claims that we cannot take the Bible teachings on Hell in a 'literalist' manner because not enough is known about the subject of eternal punishment."[8]

JESUS WENT TO HELL

"In 1975 Paul E. Billheimer wrote a book titled *'Destined for the Throne'* in which he puts forth E. W. Kenyon's heresy that **Jesus** lied on the cross when He said 'It is finished' and He **had to go to hell to suffer and be tortured by Satan** and his demons."[9] He wrote:

> *"Because He* [Jesus] *was 'made sin,' impregnated with sin, and became the very essence of sin, on the cross He was banished from God's presence as a loathsome thing. He and it were made synonymous....[I]t was not sufficient for Christ to offer up only His physical life on the cross. His pure human spirit had to 'descend' into hell....His spirit must not only descend into hell, but into the lowest hell....The Father turned Him over, not only to the agony and death of Calvary, but to the satanic torturers of His pure spirit as part of the just dessert of the sin of all the race. As long as* ***Christ*** *was 'the essence of sin,' He* ***was at Satan's mercy*** *in that place of torment....While Christ identified with sin,* ***Satan and the hosts of hell ruled over Him as over any lost sinner.*** *During that seemingly endless age in the nether abyss of death, Satan did with Him as he would, and all hell was 'in carnival.'"*[10] [Italics in the original.]

Would you believe that **Billy Graham** wrote the foreword to this book?[11] Isn't it strange that Graham does not believe in a literal hell with fire and torment, yet he could write a foreword to a book that claims that Jesus went to hell and was tormented? Graham says that this "book is inspiring and has a fresh interpretation of the Scriptures and its principles should be applied to the readers (sic) life."[12] On Graham's October 30, 1999 program he mentioned "that the Lord Jesus Christ suffered in hell...."[13]

When Christ went to hell, it was to **triumph** over Satan. Colossians 2:14-15 states: "Blotting out the handwriting of ordinances that was against us, which was contrary to us, and took it out of the way, nailing it to His cross; And **having spoiled principalities and powers,** He made a shew of them openly, **triumphing over them** in it." Jesus was **AT NO TIME** under Satan's control or at his mercy. On the cross, Jesus said: "Father, into Thy hands I commend My spirit: and having said thus, He gave up the ghost" (Luke 23:46). His spirit did not go to hell to be tortured by Satan, yet Graham endorses such a blasphemous book and says that the principles in the book should be applied to the reader's life!

VIRGIN BIRTH NOT NECESSARY

> "In an interview with a United Church of Canada publication in 1966, Graham gave the following reply to a question about the virgin birth of Christ:
>
> "Q. Do you think a literal belief in the Virgin birth—not just as a symbol of the incarnation or of Christ's divinity—as an historic event is necessary for personal salvation?
>
> "A. While I most certainly believe that Jesus Christ was born of a virgin, **I do not find anywhere in the New Testament that this particular belief is necessary for personal salvation....**
>
> "In his zeal to appease the apostates in the United Church of Christ (its current moderator, Bill Phipps, denies that Jesus Christ is God), Graham tells an absolute lie. How would it be possible for a saved person to deny the virgin birth of Jesus Christ? If Jesus Christ were not virgin born, he was a sinner; and if he were a sinner, he could not have died for our sins. Further, if Christ were a sinner and if He were not virgin born, He was a liar for making such claims and the Bible that records those claims is a blatant and wicked lie, and the Bible-believing Christian is a deceived and foolish person whose faith has no authoritative foundation. Therefore, apart from the virgin birth there is no Gospel and no Salvation and no authoritative Bible. Billy Graham is dead wrong. The virgin birth of Christ is 'fatal' doctrine, meaning it is crucial for salvation. The entire Gospel stands or falls on the virgin birth."[14] [Emphasis in the original.]

If Jesus Christ had not been born of a virgin, then His sacrificial death on the cross of Calvary could not have atoned for our sins. This is an important doctrine.

INFANT BAPTISM

> "I still have some personal problems in this matter of infant baptism, but all of my children with the exception of the youngest were baptized as infants. I do believe that something happens at the baptism of an infant, particularly if the parents are Christians and teach their children Christian truths from childhood. We cannot fully understand the mysteries of God, but I believe that a miracle can happen in these **children** so that they **are regenerated, that is, made Christian, through infant baptism.** If you want to call that baptismal regeneration, that's all right with me."[15]

If Graham is correct (which he isn't), then children could be "made Christian" by baptism and all children should be baptized as infants. That way, in just a few short years, we can have an entire Christian world. Of course, belief in infant baptism is not Scriptural. Jesus was DEDICATED (not baptized) as a 40-day-old infant (see Luke 2:22). Scriptural baptism always takes place **AFTER** an individual has accepted Jesus Christ as his or her personal Saviour (Colossians 2:12; Matthew 3:6; Mark 1:5; Acts 2:38; 8:13, 36-38; 10:47; 16:33; 18:8; 19:4-5; Romans 6:4; etc.). Baptismal regeneration is taught by the Catholic Church (and some Protestant churches as well) but IT IS NOT a **Scriptural** doctrine.

NOAH'S FLOOD NOT WORLDWIDE

Graham doubts if Noah's flood was worldwide—even though the Bible clearly says that it was.[16] For instance, look at Genesis 6:17 where God said: "I, even I, do bring a flood of waters upon the earth, to **destroy all flesh,** wherein is the breath of life, from under heaven; and **every thing that is in the earth shall die."** Also, Genesis 7:4: "[E]very living substance that I have made will I destroy from off the face of the earth."

Dave Hunt writes:

> "God's instructions to Noah to bring two of every species into the ark only make sense if the flood was worldwide. God promised never to destroy the *earth* by water again (Gen 9:11), yet there have been many great *regional* floods. The future destruction of the world prophesied by Peter would be merely a local fire if the flood, to which he compares it (2 Pt 3:6-7), were local. Finally, Jesus likens His future worldwide judgment of all mankind to the flood (Mt 24:38-41)."[17] [Italics in the original.]

TUNE IN, TURN ON, DROP OUT

Graham said that when hippies "talk about tune in, and turn on, and drop out, [that] this is almost Biblical language. When they call their boots 'Jesus boots,' when they wear their hair long...this is, in my judgment, a subconscious longing for Jesus. This is our image of Jesus.'"[18]

"Tune in, turn on, and drop out"[19] **IS NOT** "almost Biblical language." This phrase was coined by Timothy Leary, a former Harvard professor who popularized acid and LSD usage.[20]

In 1971 Graham said: "I would not say a woman has to wear a bra, or should not wear a minishirt (sic). There is nothing in the Bible that says a woman must conceal the fact that she is a woman."[21]

Perhaps Graham should look up the following verses: "In like manner also, that women adorn themselves in modest apparel...(which becometh women professing godliness) with good works" (I Timothy 2:9-10).

In 1991 Graham endorsed a teenage hotline which was known for its frank discussion of sex. He wrote that teenagers "need help as they grow into mature, responsible young men and women....I believe that Straight Talk will provide valuable help to many of our North Carolina teens."[22]

However, when Deborah McRary called the hotline she was in for a surprise. She said that the messages "were more or less encouraging kids to go into masturbation, sexuality and alcohol...."[23]

> "'Hand stimulation is the safest way to masturbate,' the Straight Talk message says. It urges further discussion with a parent, priest, minister, counselor or rabbi.
>
> "'For most young people, masturbation is a good and safe substitute for having sex with another person,' the recorded message says."[24]

Finally, in 1993, A. Larry Ross, a spokesman for the Billy Graham Evangelistic Association said that Graham had withdrawn.[25] This is good news—if it is true. But why was his endorsement on this hotline in the first place?!

JESUS WAS SEXUALLY TEMPTED

On **Graham's** program in June 2000, "he said when He was on earth, the Lord **Jesus was sexually enticed by Mary Magdalene."**[26] This is not the same Jesus I serve for my Bible tells me that Christ "knew no sin" (II Corinthians 5:21), "did no sin," (I Peter 2:21) and that "He was manifested to take away our sins; and in Him is no sin" (I John 3:5). Jesus also said: "But I say unto you, That whosoever looketh on a woman to lust after her hath committed adultery with her already in his heart" (Matthew 5:28).

Since Graham thinks that Christ was sexually tempted, that may be the reason why he refused to criticize the vulgar and blasphemous movie *The Last Temptation of Christ* which mocked Jesus. This movie portrayed Jesus having graphic sexual desires.[27]

The author of the novel, Nikos Kazantzakis, had fully embraced **Marxism** and he felt that "Lenin and his message had come to represent the highest form of truth."[28] He "was motivated by a very deep-seated hatred of God and Jesus Christ, and he attempted to vent that hatred directly at the character of the Son of God by portraying him as a demented lunatic, a liar, a reluctant leader, and an unrestrained gigolo."[29] A gigolo is "a man who has a continuing sexual relationship with and receives financial support from a woman."[30]

From an **admirer** of Kazantzakis' work we read:

> "Kazantzakis's novel carried a stunning theological theme: Jesus was a man, a man struggling with great faults, a paranoid, guilt-ridden dreamer, a man who lusted after Mary Magdalene, who resisted the vocation of Messiah so desperately that he left Jerusalem before the Jews and the Romans could kill him, who married and live happily in Bethany with darling little Jesuses all around him. Of course the marriage turned out to be a dream. But at the very least Kazantzakis made the old story fresh. Kazantzakis's Christ had sweat, mistakes, sexuality and surprise.
>
> "Kazantzakis's Jesus was also divine, but in the novel there is no parthenogenesis [virgin birth] (Kazantzakis's Matthew, constantly scribbling notes on the life of his master, invents this), no walking on the water (Peter dreams the famous miracle), and no appearance of the risen Lord (Jesus' last word on the cross is the last word in the book). Jesus heals, but seems surprised at his own power, and when his power is focused on the supreme miracle of the raising of Lazarus, the resurrection is frightening and incomplete: Lazarus is still covered with earth, he smells of decay, his legs and arms are swollen and green, worms are crawling over his body, and he has grass in his hair."[31]

From this novel, Martin Scorsese put these blasphemous ideas into a movie.[32] Many Christian leaders were quite upset over this and vocally said so—but not Billy Graham. "...CNN talk show host Larry King reported in *USA Today* that he had personally talked with Billy Graham about the movie. King noted that unlike most other evangelical Christian leaders, *Billy Graham refused to criticize the movie.*"[33] [Italics in the original.]

BIRTHDAY BASH

Speaking about movies, how many know that Graham has his name engraved on the Hollywood Walk of Fame?[34] The October 14, 1989 issue of the *News-Herald* carried the following story:

> "The world's best-known evangelist tomorrow will have his name and the likeness of an old-fashioned radio microphone engraved on the 1900th star along the Hollywood Walk of Fame....
>
> "'I'm not sure a clergyman belongs in that group of entertainers,' Graham said sheepishly, noting that his star will be near those honoring Wayne Newton, Buster Crabbe, John Travolta, Judy Holliday, Julie Andrews, Olivia Newton-John and Greta Garbo....'A star was offered to me 30 years ago,' he said, 'and I said, No then. But **I've changed my views.'**"[35]

Isn't it strange that the Hollywood crowd would want a preacher listed among them? Stranger yet, Graham was received by a **UNANIMOUS** vote. The paper reported:

> "'I doubt there is anyone in Hollywood who has been seen, heard or enjoyed by more people than Billy Graham,' said Johnny Grant, Hollywood's honorary mayor and chairman of the Walk of Fame Committee. Grant said that the **committee voted unanimously** to give Graham the honor **after he was nominated last year by friends who paid the $4,800 fee."**[36]

John Ashbrook comments: "This is the way the accommodation game is played. I won't protest your filth if you don't protest my star."[37]

It's also interesting to note that the "Druid priests had magical wands made out of 'Holly-wood'—hence the name 'Hollywood.'"[38]

Of course, Graham seems to be comfortable among the Hollywood crowd. For instance, look at the following news item from the 1998 *People* magazine:

> "At the 75th-birthday bash for TIME magazine in Manhattan, a zebra-striped **Sharon Stone...**offered a toast with a feminist slant to Betty Friedan. Stone thanked the veteran women's liberationist 'for the shocking freedom with which

> I've been able to move through my life.' Meanwhile, **President Clinton...**gala-vanted (sic) about, chatting with **Mary Tyler Moore, Rev. Billy Graham** and **Lauren Bacall."**[39] [Emphasis in the original.]

The picture accompanying this item shows Graham sitting between two women, one of whom has a very low neckline.

As mentioned in Chapter 2, Graham has "attended cocktail parties given for the [Hollywood] stars...."[40]

PRINCE OF EGYPT

When the *Prince of Egypt* movie came out, Graham

> "gave the film two thumbs up, expressing special appreciation for what he called its accurate portrayal of the miracles of the Passover, which shows God protecting the lives of the Jewish infants. Mark Pattison, media editor for Catholic News Service, said, 'Catholics will probably consider "Prince of Egypt" to be a spiritually uplifting film.' David Koch, editor of *Wireless Age,* a magazine covering Christian media, praised the film's biblical accuracy...."[41]

In fact, this film received "the near-unanimous consensus of the hundreds of religious leaders who have viewed portions of the film over the past three years, along with dozens of religious journalists who have screened the finished project...."[42]

This film seems to have support

> "from liberal Christians to conservatives Jerry Falwell and Pat Robertson to Rabbi Norman Lamm, president of Yeshiva University, and Muslim leader Maher Hathout. 'Hollywood got this one right,' Falwell says, (sic) Evangelist Robert Schuller has even laid hands on [Jeffrey] Katzenberg and blessed him."[43]

DreamWorks, the producer of the film,[44] "has commissioned seven study guides (Muslim, Catholic, Jewish, Protestant, and so on) for parents and Sunday schools to use in conjunction with the film."[45]

"Dr. Ted Baehr of the Christian Film and Television Commission says, 'I think this is an extraordinary event. It's very good news because we're starting to **build a bridge between the church and Hollywood.'"**[46]

With all the so-called "Christian" leaders (including Billy Graham, Dr. James Dobson and Charles Swindoll[47]) promoting this film, it would seem as though the movie would be Bible-based, right? **WRONG!** For example, many religious leaders claimed that the film was an **accurate** story but the film portrayed Rameses II of the 13 century B.C. This is the incorrect Pharaoh if we are to accept the inerrancy of the Bible and the messianic prophecy dating from the Exodus.[48]

Since Muslims were also invited to view and comment on the film, we see that their input must have been considered. For instance, the Bible tells us that **Pharaoh's daughter found Moses** but the film shows Pharaoh's **wife** finding him.[49] What most people are not aware of is that the Muslims teach that it was actually Pharaoh's wife—and not his daughter—who found Moses.[50] One preacher's wife always thought that Pharaoh's daughter found Moses but after watching this movie she thought that **she** had been mistaken. Do you see how subtle a movie like this (or any other movie, for that matter) can be?!

Also, to please the feminists, YHWH says (in the book—not the movie): "I am the God of your ancestors Abraham, Isaac, and Jacob; the God of Sara, Rebecca, Rachel and Leah."[51]

When Moses' mother put Moses in the basket to place him at the river's edge, the movie portrays her as singing this prayer: "River, O river...Such precious cargo you bear. Do you know somewhere he can live free? River, deliver him there...."[52] Moses' mother would not have prayed such a pagan prayer by addressing the river as a god. She would have prayed to Jehovah God.

Furthermore, the film shows Pharaoh giving Moses his wife[53] instead of Reuel (or Jethro), Zipporah's father, giving her—as the Bible clearly states in Exodus 2:18-21.

When Moses fled from Pharaoh, he came to the well where Jethro's daughters were watering their flock. The movie shows these daughters as children. It also made the story "politically correct." Al Dager points out:

> "In today's movies, women cannot be saved from peril by men, at least not without contributing in some way their own saving. Since Jethro's daughters in reality needed Moses to stand up for them, today's movie makers had to portray them as little children. Women today must be portrayed as strong, self-sufficient and able to take down men with their bare hands. Often, women are seen saving men from peril. And if a man does save a woman, it is always reciprocated. In this case, after standing up for the girls, Moses loses his balance and falls into the well. Zipporah comes by to help the girls pull him out."[54]

This movie also portrays the occult as something that is exciting. One report states:

> "...DreamWorks presents Egyptian occultism as fun, exciting and empowering rather than as serious evil. In the movie, the entertaining Egyptian priests or shamans soften the evil of their ritual with their funny performance. Fun times are good for us, but the song inviting children to learn the names of pagan gods and sing along is no laughing matter:
>
> "By the power of Ra, Mut, Nut, Khnum, Ptah...
> "So you think you've got friends in high places
> "With the power to put us on the run
> "Well, forgive us these smiles on our faces
> "You'll know what power is when we are done...
> "Ev'ry spell and gesture
> "Tells you who's the best...
> "By the might of Horus...."[55]

Steven Spielberg admitted that the film was not a true Bible story but was "deliberately crafted to appeal to **ALL** faiths."[56] In spite of all these errors, so-called "Christian" leaders claim that the movie was fairly accurate!

Additionally, one report mentioned that this movie had "some suggestive clothing, one shot up a man's tunic revealing underwear; one shot of buxom woman behind veil who turns out to be a servant who was bound and gagged."[57]

Graham has done his own film productions for many decades already. Almost 40 years ago Graham's World Wide Pictures had determined "to be thoroughly competitive with the contemporary cinema...."[58] One of their productions was called *Two A Penny* about

> "a young art student who is dabbling in drugs....The film was planned to be shown in a theater like any secular feature and to go on commercial circuit. No concessions are made to decorous Christians. The *Cincinnati Post* wrote: 'Hang on to your cushioned seats, folks. Billy Graham has come up with a blockbuster. **The film contains conflict, sex, irreverence—even some blasphemy.** In other words, it's a rather accurate portrayal of the human condition.
>
> "'And it swings. It's obviously aimed at today's young people. Some on the far side of the Generation Gap are going to leave the theater shaking their heads in bewilderment asking: 'What made Billy Graham produce a film like this?' **Cliff Richard as Jamie is not even converted at the end:** 'I just need to know if You are there,' he is singing. 'Show me the

way, For I long to see. If you are real, Lord, Be real to me.' **The pagan in the audience does not feel preached at."**[59]

Did you catch what a **secular** paper said about this film?! Sex... irreverence...blasphemy—and the film ends without the actor being converted. What purpose does such a film fulfill? Remember, the Bible warns us: "Let no corrupt communication proceed out of your mouth, but that which is good to the use of edifying, that it may minister grace unto the hearers" (Ephesians 4:29). Also: "[P]ut off all these; anger, wrath, malice, blasphemy, filthy communication out of your mouth" (Colossians 3:8). How can someone who professes to be a Christian even play a character who blasphemes and is irreverent? Consider the following verses:

✞ "But let your communication be, Yea, yea; Nay, nay: for whatsoever is more than these cometh of evil" (Matthew 5:37).

✞ "Teaching us that, denying ungodliness and worldly lusts, we should live soberly, righteously, and godly, in this present world" (Titus 2:12).

✞ "That ye put off concerning the former conversation the old man, which is corrupt according to the deceitful lusts" (Ephesians 4:22).

✞ "Be not deceived: evil communications corrupt good manners" (I Corinthians 15:33).

PRINCE OF DARKNESS

Billy Graham has also been friends with the news media and people like Rupert Murdoch. In his biography Graham wrote:

> "It was in Adelaide [in 1959] that I met **Rupert Murdoch** for the first time. He was virtually unknown outside Australia and was just starting his career in publishing, but his quiet intensity impressed me. We later became friends, and **he has been very supportive of our work** through his publications in many parts of the world."[60]

A few years ago Murdoch bought Zondervan for $56.7 million dollars[61] and Pat Robertson's International Family Entertainment for $1.9 billion.[62] He also is financing Robert Schuller's TV program in Europe,[63] but don't let that fool you into thinking that Murdoch is a Christian. You see, he is also a **pornography magnate** "whose tabloids in Britain profit from their lurid, bare pictures of beautiful young women."[64] Some of his other holdings include Harper and Collins Publishers,[65] Twentieth Century Fox Film Corporation, Fox Broadcasting Company, Fox Television Stations, Inc., Harper-Collins, *New York Post, TV Guide, Elle, Daily Racing Form, Good Food,*

The Times, The Sunday Times, Today, Sun, News of the World, Seventeen, etc.[66] The new *Seventeen* "magazine is described as 'flashy, racy, titillating, hip, jazzy, flirty, glamourous and sexy.'"[67] *U. S. News & World Report* mentioned that Rupert's *Sun* magazine built "its 3.5 million circulation with a steady diet of upper-crust scandals, royalty's gaffes and foibles, and **pictures of topless models."**[68] His Harper-Collins company publishes books such as *The New Joy of Gay Sex.*

Interestingly, *"The Chicago Tribune* referred to Murdoch as "the Prince of Darkness" and *"Time* magazine called him one of the four most powerful men in the world...."[69] He was also at Gorbachev's State of the World Forum,[70] yet he is supportive of Graham. Fascinating!

LOWELL THOMAS AWARD

About 1991, Capital Cities/ABC Inc. (which owns Word, Inc.) honored Graham with the Lowell Thomas Award for Distinguished Achievement for his book *Hope for the Troubled Heart.*

First of all we need to see what Capital Cities/ABC is. ABC "is owned by Standard Oil, which is owned by **David Rockefeller,** who is owned by Philippe Rothschild...."[71] This is not the first time that ABC has been involved with Graham. Robert Kintner, ABC President in 1957, was one of the members of the Madison Square Garden Crusade.[72]

In 1985 American Broadcasting Companies (ABC) merged with Capital Cities. They are listed as a "Corporate Member" of the **Council on Foreign Relations** (CFR).[73] The Chairman of Capital at the time the award was presented to Graham was Thomas Murphy.[74] He, too, is a CFR member.[75]

"The Lowell Thomas Award recognized Dr. Graham for his contributions as an evangelist, author, moral statesman, and counselor to heads of state world-wide."[76]

Who was Lowell Thomas? He was a traveler, an author, and the associate editor of *Asia Magazine.*[77] He was the major owner of Capital Cities Communication.[78] Thomas was also a member of the Bohemian Grove[79] (which is a place that is known for holding occultic rituals[80]) as well as the President of the American Society for **Psychical** Research,[81] an occult organization. Oh, he was also a Mason.[82]

"The luncheon guest list," for Graham to receive the award,

> "was a veritable roll call of Who's Who in business, government, entertainment, and the media. The luncheon was attended by such media notables as Hugh Downs, Peter Jennings, Dan Rather, Diane Sawyer, and former Lowell

> Thomas Award winner Paul Harvey. Also present were New York City Mayor David Dinkins, Pepsico Inc.'s Don Kendall, chairman and CEO of News Corporation (Fox Television) Rupert Murdoch, as well as CEOs of NBC and CBS."[83]

This list is more than a "Who's Who" in media, etc. It's also a list of many Council on Foreign Relations (CFR) members, Bilderbergers, and/or DeMolay members. Dinkins,[84] Kendall,[85] Rather,[86] and Sawyer[87] are all **CFR** members. Rather also has written for the American Humanist Association[88] as well as being a co-sponsor of various events for the National Lesbian and Gay Journalists Association.[89] Sawyer, on September 22, 1995, "glorified the value of voodoo in Haiti as a realistic answer the problems of a society out of control. To demonstrate the effectiveness of voodoo, Sawyer showed the voodoo witch doctor butchering the throat of a bull tied to a post for sacrifice, then drinking and washing his face in its blood."[90] Even through Kendall is a CFR member, when Graham was invited to go to Russia for "The World Conference of Religious Leaders for Saving the Sacred Gift of Life from Nuclear Catastrophe," he contacted Kendall and asked his advice. Kendall, as well as then-President Nixon, Rupert Murdoch, and Henry Kissinger (a CFR member[91]) all gave their approval and urged Graham to go.[92]

GAG ORDER

Jennings is a **Bilderberger**[93] as is Kendall.[94] Dinkins, who was mayor of New York City, was responsible for appointing "three lesbians to municipal judgeship posts as part of his first four judicial appointments"[95] and served as one of the hosts for Lambda (a gay and lesbian organization) to present its first award.[96] He supported the New York City schools in their efforts to distribute free condoms.[97] He is also a member of the Democratic **Socialists** of America[98] and had strong **Communistic** support when he was elected as Mayor in 1989.[99] Downs was on the host committee of the **World Federalist Association** when an award was presented to Walter Cronkite[100] who promotes **world government.**[101] In his speech he said: "*We must strengthen the United Nations as a first step toward a World Government.... We Americans will have to yield up some of our sovereignty.*"[102] [Italics in the original.] He is also a DeMolay member[103] as well as a Bohemian Grove member.[104]

Harvey approvingly read a letter in 1998 which advocated global religion, universalism, evolution, and God as **MOTHER** and Father.[105] This worldview is promoted by Masonry and Harvey[106] as well as Rather[107] are Senior DeMolays. (The DeMolays is a **Masonic** organization for young boys but they also have Senior members.)

GRAHAM ENDORSES DEMOLAYS

Of course, Billy Graham has bragged up the DeMolay organization. In a Masonic book, *The Clergy and the Craft,* in which the author states "*The* ***clergy*** *represented in this volume are proud to be* ***both Masons and Ministers*** *of God*[108] [Italics in the original; boldface added.] we find this statement by Graham: "There are the young people upon which the hope of America's future rests and DeMolays are part of this group....**May God richly bless all DeMolays as they continue their good work.**"[109]

One DeMolay member that is a good friend of Graham's is Bill Clinton.[110] We've already seen some of the praise that Graham gave to Clinton in Chapter 1. What was not mentioned then was that Graham first met Bill Clinton when he was governor of Arkansas. They met again during Graham's 1989 Crusade in Little Rock.[111] **Governor Clinton was honorary chair of that Crusade.** Bill and Hillary gave a luncheon for Graham along with a few of the Crusade's strongest supporters and leaders of the state who were invited, including former governor Orval Faubus.[112] Faubus, by the way, is also a Mason.[113]

We need to remember that Clinton was a Rhodes Scholar.[114] "According to Rhodes' biographer Sarah Millin, *'The government of the world was Rhodes' simple desire.'* Thus, it seems unlikely that his scholars would be individuals who were not 'one-worlders.'"[115] Clinton has also belonged to the Council on Foreign Relations[116] and the Trilateral Commission[117] as well as attending the Bilderberger meetings.[118] All of these groups are one-world in outlook. Additionally, Clinton presented Communist Nelson Mandela with the Congressional Medal of Honor on September 23, 1998.[119] Both Clintons have been admirers of Communist Jane Fonda[120] (before her supposed "conversion"). Hillary funded the pro-Marxist Institute for Policy Studies and other Communist organizations in her position for the New World Foundation in 1987-1988.[121] This was just **ONE YEAR** before Graham's Little Rock Crusade of which Bill Clinton was the honorary chair!

Around 1996, Bill Clinton said that he wanted all military chaplains to refer to him as "Master."[122] The article explained "that Clinton has ordered the Pentagon to put **a 'gag order' on all chaplains who oppose partial birth abortions** and make it known. The prohibition applies to all pastoral duties, sermons, teaching and counseling, and if they do not comply, they are threatened with prison."[123] Yet Graham is comfortable with Clinton and Clinton is acceptable to Graham. Hmmm!

Several years ago Eric Barger wrote:

"Make no mistake. Bill Clinton and his team are extreme far-left socialist, New Age and as globally minded in orientation as anyone could imagine....[F]rom Hillary Clinton's alleged contacting of the spirit of Eleanor Roosevelt, to Al Gore's Mother Earth goddess advocacy, Clinton is surrounded by, and is himself no small advocate of a New Age-New World Order based on collective communism. It appears that Clinton is destined to set the dubious record as the U. S. President with the most extreme socialist, one-world orientation, complete with the staff to inflict it upon the American citizenry."[124]

SOME PEOPLE GRAHAM EXPECTS TO SEE IN HEAVEN

Among those Graham looks forward to seeing in heaven is Elvis Presley. Graham said: "I never met him, but **I believe I will see him in heaven, because Elvis was very deeply religious,** especially in the last two or three years [of his life.]."[125] This was originally reported in the *San Francisco Chronicle* on October 8, 1977, but was also repeated in *A Prophet with Honor.* Anyone who has looked at Presley's life knows that he was not a Christian. He was heavily involved in **occultic** activities including numerology, spiritualism,[126] the New Age,[127] and the teachings of Madame Blavatsky. He had a substantial library of occult books. At concerts he would read from Blavatsky's book *The Voice of Silence* to indoctrinate his audiences. Albert Goldman said it was from the inspiration of *The Voice of Silence* that Elvis was to name his gospel group "Voice."

One issue of *Parade* "reported that this immoral King of Rock Music even had an affair with the wife of Billy Stanley, his third stepbrother."[128] Elvis frequented orgiastic parties at his home, healed with psychic power, and used and dispensed various drugs.[129] His ex-wife "recalls her first visit to Graceland—she was 17—when Elvis dosed her with enough Placidyl to knock her out for 48 hours."[130] He needed drugs to wake up and drugs to sleep and at the time of his death from a drug overdose, there were at least 10 different drugs in his body.[131] Dr. Eric Muirhead was the pathology chief who helped perform the autopsy on Elvis and he said: "Elvis 'was a drug addict.... We knew he was a drug addict because he had been at Baptist to be treated for that....' His death 'was clearly a result of "polypharmacy," or death from drug interaction,' Dr. Muirhead added."[132]

When his girlfriend, Ginger Alden, and medical investigators found him, they also "found a how-to sex manual with an astrological theme near Elvis' body."[133]

"In another revelation, former girlfriends, a personal valet and other intimates say Elvis seldom bathed, relying on a Swedish formula that was supposed to cleanse from within. But it didn't work. Those close to Elvis were often relieved when he passed out from drugs because it gave them a chance to put him in the shower, where they could scrub him, with the excuse that they were trying to revive him."[134]

Delbert "Sonny" West served as Presley's bodyguard and confidant for 16 years.[135] He wrote:

"Presley's drug habit was so severe that he had to take pills for everything, to get up in the morning, to perform, to go to sleep....

"Presley believed that he was a 'supernatural power' put on earth as a kind of modern-day Jesus, and felt that he had psychic healing powers....

"Presley had ordered his bodyguards to kill the man who took his wife from him, and on one occasion, ordered his bodyguards to produce a drug-pusher for Presley himself to execute. Presley was a lonely, brooding man who would often stay in his room for weeks, eating enormous quantities of food, taking drugs and refusing to come out."[136]

In spite of this, Billy Graham is looking forward to meeting Elvis in heaven! Something is drastically wrong—especially when Graham felt that about 85% of those who have been baptized are not saved[137] yet he thinks Elvis will be in heaven.

When John Kennedy, Jr. and the Bessette sisters were killed, Billy Graham ministered to the family. Graham then told Larry King on CNN that he believes all three victims are "resting in heaven."[138] He said that the Kennedys were at his home and he talked about John, Jr.'s faith. He said: "I think JFK, Jr. had a strong faith, and I think Carolyn had a strong faith."[139] Kennedy was far from a moral person, even posing practically nude in his magazine, *George,* yet Billy Graham thinks he's in heaven today. Where is his spiritual and Scriptural discernment?

GRAHAM AND NIXON

Billy Graham was very close to Richard Nixon. Perhaps it should be noted that Nixon attended Norman Vincent Peale's church when he was in New York City and his daughter, Julie Nixon, had been married by Peale in 1968. Graham was also asked to participate in the wedding but he had other engagements at the time.[140]

"At a Portland crusade in May [1968], he introduced Julie and Tricia Nixon to the assembly, noting that there is 'no American I admire more than Richard Nixon.'"[141]

A Prophet with Honor states:

> "Graham never imagined for a moment that Nixon's values varied from his own or doubted that Richard Nixon was God's man for that critical hour in American history. In a handwritten note near the end of the President's second year in office, Graham wrote, 'My expectations were high when you took office nearly two years ago but you have exceeded [them] in every way! **You have given moral and spiritual leadership to the nation** at a time when we desperately needed it—in addition to courageous political leadership! Thank you!' He signed the letter 'With Affection.'"[142]

Graham said in his autobiography that **"Nixon held such noble standards of ethics and morality for the nation."**[143] He also said that he had a "deep personal faith in God....Although he doesn't flaunt his faith publicly, **I know him to be a deeply religious man."**[144]

Even though Graham admits that he was distressed over the Watergate tapes and the vulgar language that Nixon used,[145] at Richard Nixon's funeral Billy Graham indicated that "Nixon was at that very moment in the presence of his wife Pat who had preceded him in death."[146]

Graham said: "The world has lost a great citizen, America has lost a great statesman, and those of us who knew him have lost a personal friend...."[147] He went on to add:

> "For the believer who has been to the Cross, death is no frightful leap into the dark, but is an entrance into a glorious new life....
>
> "For the believer, the brutal fact of death has been conquered by the resurrection of Jesus Christ.
>
> "For the person who has turned from sin and has received Christ as Lord and Savior, death is not the end.
>
> "For the believer there is *hope* beyond the grave....
>
> **"Richard Nixon had that hope,** and today that can be our hope as well."[148] [Emphasis in the original.]

Graham believed that both Nixons were enjoying the presence of Christ. The Bible, however, plainly says: "Let no corrupt communication proceed out of your mouth, but that which is good to the use of edifying, that it may minister grace unto the hearers"

(Ephesians 4:29) and "put off all these; anger, wrath, malice, blasphemy, filthy communication out of your mouth" (Colossians 3:8). Need I say any more?

Graham, writing about Gerald Ford, a Mason and CFR member, proclaimed:

> "I knew him to be a professing Christian, and we had several times of prayer together. He was always warm, friendly, and outgoing to me.
>
> "A lot of us Christians saw him as a **spiritual** leader as well as a political one."[149]

LYNDON JOHNSON

Lyndon Johnson attended Graham's 1965 Houston Crusade. "Graham praised Johnson and publicly supported his programs, including poverty and civil rights efforts"[150] which were referred to as Johnson's "Great Society" programs.[151] Johnson said: "We are going to try to take all of the money that we think is unnecessarily being spent and take it from the 'haves' and give it to the 'have-nots' that need it so much."[152] Ralph Epperson called Johnson a "closet Communist" and states:

> "Those who know President Lyndon Johnson, the speaker of the words above, and his 'Great Society,' know that this was indeed **his goal: to redistribute wealth** from the wealthy to the poor. Few, however, will fare to compare **Johnson's governmental philosophy with** the writings and **teachings of Marx.** But the **comparison is inevitable:** the action and its results are the same, no matter whether it is called the 'Great Society,' or Marxist Communism. Both seek to use government to divide wealth."[153]

The liberal (and Rockefeller-funded[154]) Brookings Institute wrote Johnson's **"Great Society" programs.** One researcher notes:

> "Although Brookings wrote the programs, they were, in every detail, **simply lifted from Fabian Socialist papers** drawn up in England. In some instances, Brookings did not even bother to change the titles of the Fabian Society papers. One such instance was using 'Great Society,' which was taken directly from a Fabian Socialist paper of the same title."[155]

Not surprisingly, Norman Thomas (a **Communist** who was covered earlier), "was **pleased with Johnson's Great Society:** 'I ought to rejoice and I do. I rub my eyes in amazement and surprise. His war on poverty is a **Socialistic** approach....'"[156]

Isn't it amazing that **Billy Graham** could brag up the same **socialistic** programs as a **Communist?!** Furthermore, "Graham described President Johnson as a man whose 'spiritual roots are deep in Texas' religious history, 'a man reared in the deep religious faith that has prevailed in this Southwest country since the beginning.'"[157] When Johnson died, Graham spoke at his funeral.[158]

Does the following item from the *U. S. News and World Report* sound like Johnson had a deep religious faith? The article states: "Lyndon Johnson would ask his aides about a young woman joining the staff, 'Will she shuck her pants?'"[159] The *Knoxville News-Sentinel* discloses that Graham was a "regular guy who can **skinny dip** [swim in the nude] with Lyndon Johnson or **flip through Playboy at a barber shop without embarrassment.**"[160] Also, Johnson had a number of mistresses, one of whom bore him a son. She was his mistress for 21 years.[161]

Yet another person Graham expects to see in heaven is Catholic Archbishop Fulton J. Sheen. Graham wrote in his autobiography:

> "It has also been my privilege to meet a number of the outstanding Christian leaders of our time, many of whom I have already mentioned in these pages. One whom I have yet to mention—and with whom I felt a special affinity—was the Roman Catholic preacher Bishop Fulton J. Sheen....I had watched his television program *Life Is Worth Living* from time to time and greatly admired his gifts as a preacher and communicator. So did many other Protestants."[162]

When they finally met on a train, Graham told Sheen that he was grateful for his ministry.[163] He added: "We talked further and we prayed; and by the time he left, I felt as if I had known him all my life. Our paths crossed a number of times after that, and we became good friends."[164]

One time when Graham was sick, Gerald Beaven "stayed at his bedside and read to him from Bishop Fulton Sheen's *Peace of Soul* and Rabbi Joshua Loth Liebman's *Peace of Mind.* From that experience, Graham began to consider writing a book on the same theme. Published in 1953, it bore the title, *Peace with God.*"[165]

When Graham spoke at Notre Dame University in 1977 "he altered his sermons mainly by adding references to Bishop Fulton Sheen and Mother Teresa..." says Graham's biographer, William Martin.[166] *Christianity Today*

> "reported that one priest had taken off his collar as he came forward, telling a counselor he was accepting Christ for the first time, but Graham required no such renunciation of past

allegiance. On the contrary, **he assured Catholics that he was not asking them either to break or to form a relationship with a particular denomination.** And as one measure of the impact of his ecumenism on his own team, Robert **Ferm, who had often assured anxious supporters that Mr. Graham would never compromise the gospel by consorting with Catholics,** addressed the faculty and students at the Notre Dame seminary prior to the crusade."[167]

The invitation he gave at Notre Dame was: "Many of you want to come tonight and **reconfirm your confirmation.** You want to **reconfirm the decision that you made when you joined the church."**[168] Notice carefully that he was **NOT** telling these people **HOW** to be saved. He only offered for them to reconfirm their confirmation or their joining of the church! Joining a church (**ANY** church) **WILL NEVER SAVE YOU.** A person can only be saved by **repenting** of his sins and accepting the sacrifice of Christ upon the cross of Calvary. How many people went forward during that meeting but were never saved?

WHO'S GOING FORWARD?

Another thing that needs to be mentioned is that those people you see on TV who flock to the front to supposedly "accept" Christ are not all inquirers or seekers after salvation. A large number of them are the counselors and choir members themselves. According to David Altheide and John Johnson, we are told:

> "At the moment of Graham's invitation to 'come forward to Christ,' counselors and choir members begin moving forward....To a naive member of the audience or a television viewer, this movement **creates an illusion of a spontaneous and mass response** to the invitation. Having been assigned seating in strategic areas of the auditorium or arena and given instructions on the **staggered time-sequencing for coming forward,** the counselors move forward in such a fashion as to **create the illusion of individuals 'flowing' into the center of the arena** from all quarters, in a steady outpouring of individual decision. Unless an outsider or observer of these events has been instructed to look for the name tags and ribbons worn by those moving forward, it is all too easy to infer from these appearances the 'charismatic' impact of Graham and his invitation."[169]

> "David Briggs, an Associated Press reporter, wrote concerning the 9/22/91 Billy Graham New York City Crusade that 'many of those who answer the call at the end of his crusade

have been swayed by techniques such as having the **ushers come forward to give the impression there is a groundswell of people committing to Christ.'"**[170]

While I am not saying that this is necessarily sinful or wrong, it must be noted that a large number "going forward" are not really getting saved. People who support Graham will quickly point you to the "fact" that multitudes are accepting Christ—just look at all the "converts" that go forward, they say. The fact is, **VERY FEW** going forward are going to be saved. For instance, at the Crusade in Tennessee in 1970, there were three options on the decision card. "The choices were 'acceptance' of salvation, 'rededication,' and 'assurance of salvation.'"[171] Almost two-thirds selected the later two choices, leaving only about one-third to select acceptance of salvation. How many out of that group were then truly saved? Only God knows, but when these people are sent back into liberal Protestant, Catholic, and Jewish churches and synagogues, how much hope is there that these individuals will ever have the assurance of salvation?

Furthermore, a sociology professor, McCurdy Lipsey, did a number of interviews for Graham's Knoxville Crusade back in 1970. He said: "In one interview I was told the **local community had to guarantee $125,000 to the Billy Graham Association."**[172] So, according to this, a Graham crusade can be quite profitable—to the Billy Graham Evangelistic Association!

Returning to Sheen, we find that

> **"Billy [Graham]** became fascinated by the famous Bishop and **referred noticeably to Fulton Sheen in sermons.** The friendship grew and Sheen continued to influence the evangelist until his death on December 9, 1979.
>
> "The Associated Press contacted the evangelist the night of the television prelate's death. Billy Graham called Sheen's death *'a great loss to the nation and both the Catholic and Protestant churches. He broke down many walls of prejudice between Catholics and Protestants. I mourn his death and look forward to our reunion in heaven.'*"[173] [Emphasis in the original.]

One researcher writes:

> "Sheen was a Catholic traditionalist who upheld Rome's dogmas. He was a staunch enemy of the New Testament faith.... Sheen's hope was in Mary, not in Christ's completed atonement. Unless he repented and turned wholly to Christ on his deathbed, there is no reason to believe Sheen will be in heaven...."[174]

"As a bishop, Sheen proved obedient to the spirit of Vatican II...."[175] Not only did he welcome Vatican II but he avidly participated in it.[176]

SHEEN—A LOVER OF MARY

Sheen was

> "a great lover of the Catholic Mary. In his biography, Sheen devoted an entire chapter to Mary, 'The Woman I Love.' He said, 'When I was ordained, I took a resolution to offer the Holy Sacrifice of the Eucharist every Saturday to the Blessed Mother....All this makes me very certain that when I go before the Judgment Seat of Christ, He will say to me in His Mercy: "I heard My Mother speak of you." During my life I have made about thirty pilgrimages to the shrine of Our Lady of Lourdes and about ten to her shrine in Fatima.'"[177]

Concerning purgatory, Sheen wrote: "The necessity of purgatory is grounded upon the absolute purity of God....If there be no purgatory, then the justice of God would be too terrible for words, for who are they who would dare assert themselves pure enough and spotless enough to stand before the Immaculate Lamb of God?"[178] It is true that in ourselves we are not worthy but "Christ hath redeemed us from the curse of the law, being made a curse for us..." (Galatians 3:13). Colossians 1:10 says: "That ye might walk worthy of the Lord unto all pleasing, being fruitful in every good work, and increasing in the knowledge of God" and I Thessalonians 2:12: "That ye would walk worthy of God, who hath called you unto His kingdom and glory." Luke 20:35 refers to "they which shall be accounted worthy to obtain that world, and the resurrection from the dead..." and Luke 21:36 commands: "Watch ye therefore, and pray always, that ye may be accounted worthy to escape all these things that shall come to pass, and to stand before the Son of man."

Referring to Christ's death in the Catholic Mass, "Sheen declared, 'It is something that is **still happening...**it is **a drama as actual <u>now</u> as <u>then</u>,** *and so it will remain as long as time and eternity endure.*'"[179] The Bible, however, clearly reveals that Christ died **ONCE FOR ALL:** "Who needeth **not daily,** as those high priests, to offer up sacrifice, first for His own sins, and then for the people's: for this **He did once,** when He offered up Himself" (Hebrews 7:27). "Neither by the blood of goats and calves, but by His own blood **He entered in <u>once</u>** into the holy place, **having obtained eternal redemption for us"** (Hebrews 9:12). "So **Christ was once offered** to bear the sins of many; and unto them that look for Him shall He appear the second time without sin unto salvation" (Hebrews 9:28).

One Catholic, Mr. Roche, "wrote a chapter about priests. The book reveals the **revolutionary actions of Bishop Fulton Sheen.** A popular American writer, speaker and T.V. celebrity with his own program, **Sheen is listed among *Left Wing Catholics*** that included a radical (Father)

James Groppi."[180] As a "left wing" Catholic, it may seem strange, but according to the *Catholic Digest* we find that he "drove new Cadillacs, dined at fashionable restaurants, and built a mansion in Washington, D.C."[181] "For most of his adult life, Sheen associated with—and famously converted—the rich and celebrated, receiving and giving away millions with an abandon that worried his admirers."[182]

Additionally, according to the *Encyclopedia of American Religions,* Fulton Sheen is one of those credited with helping to propagate the New Thought movement[183] (which includes "Christian Science, Visualisation techniques, the power of Positive Thinking, Prosperity Consciousness, Possibility Thinking, and other uses of 'mind-power'"[184]). Also, a video catalog that was advertised as **"'Your One-Stop Shop for New Age Products, Audio & Video'"**[185] [Emphasis in the original.] listed Fulton Sheen under "Famous Teachers, Leaders, Artists & Visionaries" along with other New Agers and occultists such as Frank Alper, Sri Anandamayi Ma, Leo Buscaglia, Edgar Cayce, Sri Chinmoy, Benjamin Creme, Dalai Lama, Salvador Dali, Jane Fonda, Matthew Fox, Louise Hay, Buckminster Fuller, Stephen Levine, Ram Dass, Ken Keyes, Joanna Macy, Theodore Rozsak, Swami Satchidananda, Jean Houston, Barbara Marx Hubbard, Bernard Jensen, Martin Luther King, Swami Kriyananda, John Lennon, Sufi Sam Lewis, Pope John Paul II, Elizabeth Clare Prophet, Bhagwan Shree Rajneesh, Nicholas Roerich, Sathya Sai Baba, Jack Schwartz, Bernie Siegel, Sun Bear, Mother Teresa, Willis Harman, Huston Smith, Shakti Gawain, Patricia Sun, Virginia Satir, Joseph Campbell, Stanislav Grof, Joseph Chilton Pearce, Rupert Sheldrake, Kenneth Pelletier, Stanley Krippner, Helen Palmer, Fritjof Capra, Frances Vaughan, Edith Fiore, George Leonard, Michael Murphy, Kevin Ryerson, Judith Skutch Whitson, Alan Vaughan, Alan Watts, Terry Cole-Whittaker, and Yogi Amrit Desai.[186]

TEILHARD DE CHARDIN

Sheen was interested in Teilhard de Chardin,[187] a French Jesuit priest[188] who was a Catholic heretic,[189] eugenicist,[190] Marxist[191] (he was "a great admirer of the Communist system in China"[192]), pantheist,[193] evolutionist[194] (he "was heavily involved in the 1912 forgery that was called 'Piltdown Man'"[195]), humanist,[196] and a proponent of a one-world government.[197] He was also known as "The Father of the New Age."[198] "Teilhard dreamed of humanity merging into 'God' and each realizing his own godhood at the Omega point. This belief has inspired many of today's New Age leaders."[199] "In fact, Chardin is one of the most frequently quoted writers by leading New Age occultists."[200]

As just mentioned, Chardin was involved in the "Piltdown Man" fraud.

> "In 1912, outside Piltdown, England, Charles Dawson and Arthur Keith discovered a so-called 'ape-man,' a missing link in the chain of evolution. Teilhard de Chardin and Sir Arthur Woodward came to assist in the work. For forty-one years, the 'Piltdown Man' was displayed in the British Museum as positive proof of evolution. In 1953 (two years before Teilhard's death), scientists John Winer and Samuel Oakley discovered that **'Piltdown Man' was an intentional hoax!** Through careful examination, they found that the skull was a modern man, the jawbone was from an ape, and human teeth had been filed deliberately to look as if they belonged to an ape. Additionally, the jawbone had been treated with bichromate of potassium and iron salt to appear fossilized. It only seems logical to question the theology of a man who would participate in such a fraud to support his beliefs."[201]

A few of Chardin's quotes follow:

✽ "It is a law of the universe that in all things there is prior existence. Before every form there is a prior, but lesser evolved form. **Each one of us is evolving towards the godhead."**[202]

✽ "What I am proposing to do is to narrow that gap between pantheism and Christianity by bringing out what one might call the Christian soul of Pantheism or the pantheist aspect of Christianity."[203]

✽ "...I can be saved only by becoming one with the universe."[204]

✽ "I believe that the Messiah whom we await, whom we all without any doubt await, is the universal Christ; that is to say, the Christ of evolution."[205]

✽ "A general convergence of religions upon a universal Christ who fundamentally satisfies them all: that seems to me the only possible conversion of the world, and the only form in which a religion of the future can be conceived."[206]

Even though Chardin was declared a heretic by the Catholic Church, Pope John Paul II likes him. One Catholic paper said: "From the early days of his Pontificate, John Paul quoted and honored Teilhard de Chardin with a reverence which was disturbing to many."[207]

POPE JOHN PAUL II

Of course, there are **many** problems with Pope John Paul II. Since the Pope admired Chardin who was an evolutionist, it's probably no surprise to discover that the Pope also promotes evolution.[208] According to *U. S. News & World Report,* we find that

> "the pope declared that evolution is 'more than just a theory' and is fully compatible with the Christian faith. But in

a letter to the Pontifical Academy of Sciences, he also reaffirmed church teachings that while the human body may have evolved gradually, the soul 'is immediately created by God' in each person.

"The pope's statement may rankle biblical fundamentalists, who take the Genesis creation story literally, but it is likely to have little impact on the **Roman Catholic Church, which has long looked favorably on evolution.** In 1950, Pope Pius XII called evolution a 'serious hypothesis' worthy of study. And as early as the fifth century, **St. Augustine warned against a literal reading of the Genesis creation account.** But John Paul II went further than previous popes in declaring that a 'convergence' of scientific evidence gathered in the past 50 years makes 'a significant argument in favor of this theory.'"[209]

The Vatican's Pontifical Academy of Sciences **honored Charles Darwin** on the 100th anniversary of his death and said: "[M]asses of evidence render the application of the concept of evolution...beyond serious dispute."[210]

Cardinal John O'Connor told worshippers at St. Patrick's Cathedral that "Adam and Eve may have been 'some other form' than human, and it is possible that the first living creature was a lower animal."[211] He added:

"It is possible that when the two persons we speak of as Adam and Eve were created, it was in some other form, and God breathed life into them, breathed a soul into them—that's a scientific question....

"Perhaps the spirit of God that breathed forth life into the Earth was a lower animal...."[212]

Some Catholics were quite concerned about the Pope's view of evolution as well as evolution being taught in the schools. One Catholic magazine, *Soul,* tried to set these people straight. Franklyn McAfee wrote:

"Too many Catholics, I fear, are taking a position on this issue which is a conservative Protestant position and not a Catholic one.

"The **Catholic Church never has taught** that the biblical account of creation found in **Genesis happened exactly as it is recounted.** As far back as Saint Augustine, the Church cautioned against interpreting the word 'day' literally in the creation account. In fact, Saint Augustine himself developed a form of evolutionary theory....But the **Church has been careful not to condemn evolutionary theories** which allow for a creation from nothing *(ex nihilo)* and which do not deny the direct creation of the human soul."[213] [Italics in the original.]

EVOLUTION

One Catholic, Amy Welborn, writing in *Our Sunday Visitor,* announces: "There's not a thing wrong with the idea of evolution itself—God can use any means He wishes to create, and perhaps He did use an evolutionary process of sorts."[214] She adds that "whoever brought the Book of Genesis together wasn't writing a scientific text. If so, he really botched the job...."[215]

Amy is certainly wrong about Genesis being "botched" up.

> "Did you know that for years the Science Research Bureau, headed by the late Dr. Harry Rimmer, publicly offered a reward of one thousand dollars to any person who could prove the existence of a scientific blunder in the Bible? Although that offer was made in twenty-seven different countries, the thousand dollars is still uncollected. In November of 1939 a suit was brought against Dr. Rimmer by a Mr. William Floyd of New York. Mr. Floyd thought that he had found several bonafide (sic) scientific blunders in the Bible. The judge, Honorable Benjamin Shalleck of the Fourth District Municipal Court heard both sides of the case and awarded his decision in favor of the Bible....More recently Dr. John Grebe, formerly director of both Nuclear and Basic Research at Dow Chemical, Midland, Michigan, has offered a one thousand dollar reward along similar lines."[216]

After the Pope sanctioned evolution, Graham's magazine, *Christianity Today,* supported his position.[217] This is not surprising since Billy Graham has "agreed that God may have used evolution to create man."[218] Graham's biographer, William Martin, mentioned that Graham had given a positive assessment of a controversial book by Bernard Ramm entitled *The Christian View of Science and Scripture.* Ramm "challenged the belief that the Bible could be taken as authoritative on scientific matters and left open the possibility that a **divinely guided form of evolution might have played a role in the origin of species** and the development of humankind."[219]

In fact, on Graham's January 2, 2000 program he mentioned "that God had not changed in a million years, promoting evolution...."[220]

NO LITERAL HELL

Returning to Pope John Paul II, we find that he, like Graham, doesn't believe in a **literal** hell.[221] He said: "Hell is not a punishment imposed externally by God, but the **condition** resulting from attitudes and actions which people adopt in this life." He added, **"Hell exists, [but] not as a place...."**[222] The Bible, on the other hand, warns us that hell is a **place** where there is eternal torment (Luke 16:23, 28; Matthew 25:46), "fire that shall never be quenched" (Mark 9:43, 45, 47), with "wailing and gnashing of teeth" (Matthew 8:12; 13:42, 50; 22:13; 24:51; 25:30; Luke 13:28). (For more information on hell, see my book *A Scriptural View of Hell.)*

The Pope also denies that heaven is a literal place. According to *The Sunday Telegraph,* we find that

> "the Pope told pilgrims in Rome that **heaven was neither an actual location nor an abstract concept,** but an ineffable 'union with God.' Paradise, 'is not an abstraction nor a physical place in the clouds, but a living and personal relationship of unity with the Holy Trinity,' he said, 'it is important to always maintain a certain moderation in describing these 'ultimate realities' as any description of them is always inadequate.'"[223]

In spite of believing that heaven is not a literal location, the Pope said on December 6, 2000 that

> "all who live a just life will be saved even if they do not believe in Jesus Christ and the Roman Catholic Church. He said, 'The gospel teaches us that those who live in accordance with the Beatitudes—the poor in spirit, the pure of heart, those who bear lovingly the sufferings of life—will enter God's kingdom.'...He said Heaven is open to all as long as they are good. This contradicts that Jesus is the only way to heaven (John 14:6) and is a false gospel."[224]

According to the news report from Vatican City, we are told: "The pontiff, addressing some 30,000 pilgrims gathered in St. Peter's Square for his weekly general audience, **strongly reasserted the liberal interpretation of the Bible's teaching on salvation that emerged from the Second Vatican Council."**[225]

MARK OF SHIVA

If, as the Pope believes, those who do not believe in Jesus Christ can be saved, then it's perhaps not surprising to find out that in 1998 John Paul II

> "allowed a **Shiva priestess to create the traditional Shiva mark on his forehead.** Of course, this event will cause any person to sit up and take notice, [especially] those of us who literally believe Biblical prophecy. In the Book of Revelation,

> the False Prophet, the leader of the new global religion of Antichrist, causes all people in the world to take a mark, either in the forehead or in the right hand. Therefore, it is a big deal when a Pagan priestess causes a mark to be made in the forehead of the Pope!"[226]

To understand this gesture a little better, it is important that you know just who Shiva (or Siva) is. According to *The Satanic Bible,* **Shiva is a synonym for Satan!**[227] He is also called the "Lord of Death."[228] "Siva carries a snake around his neck. Snakes always surround his image, and a snake is coiled around his phallus (*linga*)."[229]

The spot on the forehead where the priestess marked the Pope is called the **"third eye"** in the occult world. Occult writer, Robert Hieronimus, remarks: "The single eye also has been identified with the **third or spiritual eye** and therefore with **clairvoyance.** The **esoteric** tradition relates the single eye to the inner light, intuitive power, illumination, and the philosopher's stone...."[230]

> "In the Hindu/yoga world of 'reality,' they believe, as do much of the occult and New Age meditators, that the body contains seven basic energy centers, known as chakras. When these centers are properly aligned by practicing **yoga and meditation,** there will then occur a 'merging' of the spinal chakra (the serpent of Kundalini) together with **Shiva, located in the frontal chakra (psychic third eye)** and this 'spiritual union' is believed to **increase extrasensory and psychic powers."**[231]

Many authors recognize that **clairvoyance is gained through use of the third eye.** For instance, a book entitled *The Third Eye,* describes how T. Lobsang Rampa "entered Chakpori Lamasery, the Temple of Tibetan Medicine where he learned **clairvoyance, levitation and astral projection** by learning to **open the third eye."**[232]

Alice Bailey, an occultist, declared: "Through the practice of the power of visualization the **third eye** is developed."[233] Bailey also wrote:

> "No man is a magician or worker in white magic until the third eye is opened, or in process of opening, for it is by means of that eye that the thought form is energised, directed and controlled, and the lesser builders are swept into any particular line of activity....
>
> "The *'Eye of Shiva'* in the human being has its position...in the centre of the forehead, between the two physical eyes."[234] [Emphasis in the original.]

CROSS REPLACED WITH BUDDHA

Pope John Paul II has been involved with many other pagan religions in the recent past. For example, it was the Pope who orchestrated the "Day of Prayer for World Peace" at Assisi, Italy in 1986.[235] There

> "John Paul II joined in a circle to pray and meditate with snake handlers from Togo, shamans and tribal witchdoctors from West Africa, Hindu gurus from India, Buddhist monks from Thailand, and liberal protestant clergymen from Great Britain, as all joined hands in 'pray[ing] to their gods for "peace."' The Pope also announced in Assisi that there are 'many paths to God.'"[236]

On this occasion, "the pope allowed his good friend the Dalai Lama to **replace the cross** with **Buddha** on the altar of St. Peter's Church in Assisi and for him and his monks to perform their **Buddhist worship there."**[237] [Emphasis in the original.]

> "Again in 1986, in Fiji, 'the Pope quaffed a potent island liquor, accepted three whale's teeth and watched a spear dance during an ancient welcoming ceremony dating back to when the Fijians practiced cannibalism....[Fijian tribal] chiefs handed the Pope a mud-colored, alcoholic drink called kava [a drink condemned by early missionaries to Fiji as devil worship]... [which] he downed in a single gulp.' At the Pope's next stop in Auckland, New Zealand, 15 elders of the Maoris tribe pressed noses with the Pope, 'to exchange each other's breath, which is the life force.'"[238]

> "On January 9-10, 1993, the Pope again hosted the Dalai Lama of Tibetan Buddhism and representatives of many other false and ungodly religions. It was an incredible sight to see these weird persons, 'holy books' in hand, all standing serenely, side-by-side with the Pope. In the 2/10/93 issue of the official Vatican newspaper, *L'Osservatore Romano*, the Pope said he recognizes within the devil worship sect of Voodoo, 'God's riches...the seed of the Word...solidarity among believers...for... human liberation.'"[239]

Later in 1993 the Pope

> "held meetings with a number of voodoo practitioners and sorcerers.
>
> "The *Associated Press* gave an account of the pope's visit to the African country of Benin with the following headline:

> 'Pope Meets With Voodoo Believers.' The newspaper reported, **'Pope John Paul II** on Thursday **sought common ground with the believers in voodoo, suggesting they would not betray their traditional faith by converting to Christianity.'** In other words, they could retain their voodoo while joining the Catholic church! Voodoo worshipers believe in many deities and use snake rituals. Incredibly, Pope John Paul explained to the voodoo witch doctors that as they worship their ancestors, Christians also revere their 'ancestors in the faith, from the Apostles to the missionaries.' According to the Associated Press account, voodoo priests warmly welcomed the pope."[240]

No wonder the Pope could tell a Hindu leader, "Your gospel and my gospel are the same"[241]—but it is **not** the Gospel of Jesus Christ.

Pagans and non-Christians can and do **WORSHIP.** We find many non-Christian worshippers in the Bible. Cain, Balaam and Korah all *worshipped* or served the Lord—but they wanted it **on their own terms.** Cain offered a sacrifice unto the Lord but it was HIS kind of sacrifice (Genesis 4:3-4). The Bible tells us that "without shedding of blood is no remission" (Hebrews 9:22), yet Cain offered a bloodless sacrifice of "the fruit of the ground" but "unto Cain and to his offering He [God] had not respect" (Genesis 4:5). Isn't it strange that Cain did not offer an animal sacrifice but he could kill his brother? (Doesn't this sound like the New Agers today? They claim they are vegetarians because they don't want to hurt an animal but then they go and perform the most horrific partial-birth abortions and rip the limbs off the tiny babies in their mothers' wombs.)

Balaam, too, sought the Lord and even blessed the Israelites (Numbers 22-24) but II Peter 2:15 says that he "loved the wages of unrighteousness." He told the King of Moab how to infiltrate and ruin the Israelites through intermarriage (see Numbers 25:1-3 and 31:16 with Revelation 2:14). (Isn't Billy Graham committing spiritual intermarriage by promoting the ecumenical movement?) Korah was another person who served the Lord but he wanted a better position (Numbers 16). His sin brought about the first earthquake (Numbers 16:30, 32).

A man named Simon became a believer and when he saw the power that the apostles had, he wanted to buy this power himself (Acts 8:13-24). "But Peter said unto him, Thy money perish with thee, because thou hast thought that the gift of God may be purchased with money" (Acts 8:20). (Incidentally, this is where the word "simony"—the buying of ecclesiastical pardons or offices—comes from.)

Uzziah, a king of Judah, served the Lord and even offered incense (II Chronicles 26:16) but there was a problem. Only the consecrated priests could lawfully burn the incense (II Chronicles 26:18). His sin resulted in him becoming a leper (II Chronicles 26:21). Likewise, King Saul worshipped the Lord but he offered the sacrifice that was only lawful for the priests and his sin resulted in the kingdom being turned over to David (I Samuel 13:12-14).

You see, **worship in itself is not enough**—even if the true God is the object of our worship. The Bible says that we must worship in SPIRIT and in **TRUTH** (John 4:23-24). Isaiah 48:1 refers to those "which swear by the name of the LORD, and make mention of the God of Israel, but not in truth, nor in righteousness." "There is a way which seemeth right unto a man, but the end thereof are the ways of death" (Proverbs 14:12, 16:25).

Jesus said: "This people draweth nigh unto Me with their mouth, and honoureth Me with their lips; but their heart is far from Me. But **in vain they do worship Me, teaching for doctrines the commandments of men"** (Matthew 15:8-9; Mark 7:7).

POPE HONORS OCCULTIST

> "*The Philippine Star* of 8/25/94 reported that Jose Silva, founder of the world-famous Silva Method, received the Special Apostolic Blessing bestowed on him by Pope John Paul II on the occasion of his 80th birthday. Reports reaching Silva International say the Vatican has given its approval to the Silva training course."[242]

Without going into detail, suffice it to say that the Silva Method (formerly called Silva **Mind Control**[243]) is an occult practice in which a person makes contact with spirit guides (which are actually demonic entities[244]). A former New Ager, Randall Baer, took the Silva Method. He wrote:

> "In a seminar taught over the span of two weekends, I learned an amazing array of mind power techniques for doing things like: **acquiring inner spirit guides,** intuitively diagnosing the health problems of any stranger, dream control, 'mind-over-matter' techniques, **psychic powers,** using thought-power to control reality, trance-induction methods, and much more....
>
> "What I didn't realize at the time was that everything in Silva Mind Control was based on **occult** philosophy."[245]

Silva claims that his methods came from "a Chinese **spirit guide sitting in Yoga position in the astral plane** whom he met in the early days when he was learning how to have **out-of-body-experiences."**[246]

The Silva Method finances the New Age magazine called *Magical Blend.*[247] In one issue was an article by Christopher Hyatt which labeled **fundamentalists as "The Shadow** emerging in society."[248] "He predicted, however, that the fundamentalist forces will be overcome. There will be a 'changing of the guards.'"[249]

I can only wonder why the Pope honored someone like Silva.

So, how does Billy Graham feel about Pope John Paul II? Said Graham: "Of course, I'm a great admirer of his. He gives **moral** guidance in a world that seems to have lost its way."[250]

When Graham was on the Phil Donahue Show in 1979, he said (concerning the Pope's visit to the United States):

> "I think the American people are looking for a leader, a moral and spiritual leader that believes something. And he (meaning the pope) does. He didn't mince words on a single subject. As a matter of fact, his subject in Boston was really an evangelistic address in which he asked the people to come to Christ, to give their lives to Christ. I said, **'Thank God I've got somebody to quote now with some real authority.'"**[251]

I wonder if Graham would want to quote **Pope John Paul II** when he "said **Rome must always be the center of all Christianity and the pope must be the head"?**[252]

Graham reveres this present Pope so much that he has even written the foreword to the book, *Pope John Paul II, A Tribute.*[253]

In an article in *Time* magazine (1979), Graham remarked:

> "No other man in the world today could attract as much attention on moral and spiritual subjects as John Paul. He is articulating what Catholic and Protestant churches have traditionally held, the **moral values from the Ten Commandments** and the Sermon on the Mount. The country is responding in a magnificent way. It shows there's a great spiritual hunger. The Pope has reached millions of Protestants."[254]

Graham said that the Pope is articulating the values from the Ten Commandments. Doesn't your Bible state in Exodus 20:3: "Thou shalt have **no other gods** before Me"? In Exodus 20:4-5 we find: "Thou shalt not make unto thee **any graven image,** or any likeness of any thing that is in heaven above, or that is in the earth beneath, or that is in the water under the earth: **Thou shalt not bow down thyself to them,** nor serve them: for I the LORD thy God am a jealous God...." Yet I have seen numerous pictures where the Pope is kneeling before a statue (or graven image) of Mary.[255] On October 8, 2000, the Pope once again knelt before the idol and placed the Catholic Church in

Mary's hands. He said: "Today we wish to entrust to you the future that awaits us, and we ask you to be with us on our way....Here we stand before you to entrust to your maternal care ourselves, the Church and the entire world."[256]

One Catholic newspaper reported:

> "The entrustment was made against the background of the Fatima apparitions, in which the Blessed Virgin Mary requested that the whole world be consecrated to her Immaculate Heart....
>
> "The act of entrustment following Catholic doctrine regarding the Blessed Virgin...and **Marian consecration as the 'quickest way to Christ'** as was taught by St. Louis de Montfort, the great theologian of consecration....
>
> "At the end of the Mass the great crowds of the faithful were given their chance to react to the entrustment and **pay their respects to the statue** of Our Lady, which was brought from Fatima for the occasion.
>
> "As four Vatican ushers carried the 3-foot-tall statue—which contains the bullet that was removed from John Paul following the attempt on his life in 1981—the faithful followed the customs of pilgrims to Fatima, waving white handkerchiefs and singing *Ave Maria.*"[257]

Yet again, on June 3, 2001, the Pope "entrusted 'the whole Church' to the intercession of Mary and 'placed in her hands the expectations of peace and justice of the world.' He called her the 'queen of heaven.'"[258] He added: "...let us invoke [pray to or entreat] her with confidence."[259] The "queen of heaven" is mentioned in Jeremiah. There the Lord said: "The children gather wood, and the fathers kindle the fire, and the women knead their dough, to make cakes to the **queen of heaven,** and to pour out drink offerings unto other gods, that they may **provoke Me to anger."** (Jeremiah 7:18. See also Jeremiah 44:17, 18, 19, 25.) The worship of the queen of heaven was very displeasing to God. In fact, God told Jeremiah that because the people worshipped the queen of heaven that Jeremiah should "pray not...for this people, neither lift up cry nor prayer for them, neither make intercession to Me: for I will not hear thee" (Jeremiah 7:16). How, then, could the Pope fulfill the Ten Commandments when he doesn't even obey them?

Reverence for statues was evident on Mother Angelica's program in October 1995. The listeners were told how to sell their home quickly: "Put a **statue of St. Joseph** in a bottle or masonjar (sic) and bury it in the front yard (head first), thereby guaranteeing a quick sale of the home. After the sale, the seller is to dig up St. Joseph, put him in a prominent place in the new residence, and **pray to him....**"[260]

"DUMB IDOLS"

The Bible gives a good description of these idols:

> "Their idols are silver and gold, the work of men's hands. They have mouths, but they speak not: eyes have they, but they see not: They have ears, but they hear not: noses have they, but they smell not: They have hands, but they handle not: feet have they, but they walk not: neither speak they through their throat. **They that make them are like unto them; so is every one that trusteth in them"** (Psalm 115:4-8; 135:15-18).

The Bible refers to them as "dumb idols":

> "What profiteth the graven image that the maker thereof hath graven it; the molten image, and a teacher of lies, that the maker of his work trusteth therein, to make **dumb idols?** Woe unto him that saith to the wood, Awake; to the **dumb stone,** Arise, it shall teach! Behold, it is laid over with gold and silver, and there is no breath at all in the midst of it." (Habakkuk 2:18-19. See also I Corinthians 12:2.)

"[W]e ought **not to think that the Godhead is like unto gold, or silver, or stone, graven by art and man's device.** And the times of this **ignorance** God winked at; but **now commandeth all men every where to repent"** (Acts 17:29-30).

The Israelites were not only forbidden to make or worship graven images but they were instructed to cut them down, destroy them, and burn them with fire when any images were encountered. (See Deuteronomy 7:5, 25; 12:3; Exodus 34:13; II Chronicles 31:1; Ezekiel 6:6; Isaiah 30:22; Micah 1:7.)

The Bible goes so far as to pronounce a curse on anyone who makes a graven image or an idol: **"Cursed be the man that maketh <u>any</u> graven or molten image, an abomination unto the LORD,** the work of the hands of the craftsman..." (Deuteronomy 27:15). "I am the LORD: that is My name: and My glory will I not give to another, neither My praise to graven images" (Isaiah 42:8).

While many Catholics will tell you that they do not **worship** the idol,[261] we need to remember that the Bible also forbids us to **BOW DOWN** to them. Furthermore, the Second Council of Nicaea said: "The Christians should not only serve and honor **images,** but **adore and worship them."**[262] Pope Pius IV stated: "I most firmly assert, that the images of Christ, and of the mother of God, ever virgin, and also of the other saints, are to be had and retained; and that one honour and veneration are to be given to them."[263]

One former Catholic, in referring to idols, asks a simple question. "My friends, our Lord and Saviour...is ***alive!*** Would you talk to a picture of your dad if you could pick up the phone and call him? Well, that's what Catholic praying is. Please think about this."[264] [Emphasis in the original.]

Most, if not all, pagan religions worship and bow before idols. I realize that Catholics will say that their idols **represent** Mary, Jesus, and the saints and not pagan gods. However, what the average Catholic is not aware of, is that the **"saints"** they are worshipping **are really the same pagan gods and goddesses of the occultists.** For instance, historian Will Durant, reveals:

> "Paganism survived...in the form of ancient rites and customs condoned, or accepted and transformed, by an often indulgent [Catholic] Church. An intimate and trustful worship of **saints replaced the cult of pagan gods....Statues of Isis and Horus were renamed Mary and Jesus;** the Roman Lupercalia and the feast of purification of Isis **became** the Feast of the Nativity; the Saturnalia were **replaced** by Christmas celebration...an ancient festival of the dead by All Souls Day, **rededicated** to Christian heroes; incense, lights, flowers, processions, vestments, hymns which had pleased the people in older cults were domesticated and cleansed in the ritual of the Church...soon people and priests would **use the sign of the cross as a magic incantation** to expel or drive away demons."[265]

> "The Virgin was given the title Queen of Heaven and is depicted wearing a blue robe decorated with stars and standing on a crescent Moon. **This image is almost identical to pagan representations of the goddess of love Ishtar** who was worshipped by the Babylonians. The statues of the Madonna holding the infant Jesus in her arms, which were erected in Catholic churches, are **almost exact copies of the effigies of Isis suckling her baby son Horus,** found in Egyptian temples."[266]

SAME IDOLS, TEMPLES, AND FAVORS

One researcher comments:

> **"Pagan gods were made Christian saints.** Bacchus became St. Bacchus, and Dionysius became St. Denys or Denis. The rustic festival of Dionysius was called *Festum Dionysii Eleutherei Rusticum,* and the ignorant Christians thought these names were of saints or gods, so they made St. Eleuther and

St. Rustic. They made a St. Delphin because Delpheus was the name of the universal womb, which name came from the dolphin, the fish of Venus. Tammuz, the Hebrew form of the Accadian Tam-zi, the sun god, or Dum-zi, became St. Thomas the Doubter. Bodisat (the title of the future Buddah or Buddha), was Yudasatf in Arabic. He became finally St. Joseph. Some nuns once acquired a box of bones from the catacombs, with a date and word, *espedito,* on the containing box, not knowing that *espedito* meant 'sent off.' They made a saint, San Espedito, and altars are dedicated to him in Italy today. In the Church of the Apostles in Florence was an altar adorned with the picture of this saint, who really never lived at all, but the church finally removed him from its calendar after the fraud was exposed."[267] [Italics in the original.]

Another researcher has found basically the same situation:

"As paganism and Christianity were merged, sometimes a saint was given a similar sounding name as that of the pagan god or goddess it replaced. The goddess Victoria of the Basses-Alpes was renamed as St. Victoire. Cheron as St. Ceranos, Artemis as St. Artemidos, Dionysus as St. Dionysus, etc. The goddess Brighit (regarded as the daughter of the sun god and who was represented with a child in her arms) was smoothly renamed as 'Saint Bridget.' In pagan days, her chief temple at Kildare was served by Vestal Virgins who tended the sacred fires. Later her temple became a convent and her vestals, nuns. They continued to tend the ritual fire, only it was now called 'St. Bridget's fire.'"[268]

One person, while studying for the Catholic priesthood, also made a disturbing discovery. He writes:

"The modern Pontifex Maximus (the Pope of Rome), supposed successor of St. Peter, the Vicar of Jesus Christ, resembled the 'Pontifex Maximus' of the great republic of Rome like two drops of water. **Our pope preserved the name, the attributes, the pageantry, the pride, and even the garb of that high <u>pagan</u> priest.** Was not the worship of the saints absolutely the same as the worship of the demigods of olden time? Was not our purgatory minutely described by Virgil? Were not our prayers to the Virgin and to the saints repeated, **almost in the same words,** by the worshipers before the images of their gods, just as we repeated them every day before the images in our churches? Was not our holy water in use among the idolaters, and for the **same purpose?**

"We knew by history the year in which the magnificent temple consecrated *to all the gods,* bearing the name of

Pantheon, had been built at Rome. Words cannot express the shame we felt on learning that the Roman Catholics of our day, under the very eyes and with the sanction of the pope, still prostrated themselves before the SAME IDOLS, in the SAME TEMPLE, and to obtain the SAME FAVORS!

"When we asked, 'What is the difference between the religion of heathen Rome and that of the Rome of today?' more than one student would answer: 'The only difference is in the name. Instead of calling this statue Jupiter, we call it Peter; and instead of calling that one Minerva or Venus, it is called St. Mary. It is the old idolatry coming to us under Christian names.'"[269] [Caps in the original; boldface added.]

The Vatican even houses many pagan idols. A naked statue of Aion (except for a Masonic-type apron) was unearthed in a Roman villa and it is now preserved in the Vatican.[270] In St. Peter's is a large statue of "Peter" whose foot has been kissed so frequently that the toes are just about worn away. One picture shows Pope John XXIII (to be covered shortly) about to kiss the statue's toes. One problem, however, is that this is not really Peter but a statue of **Jupiter** whose **name was changed** to **Peter!**[271] By the way, the practice of **kissing a statue comes directly out of paganism.** Remember the Bible story of Elijah and the prophets of Baal? Elijah thought he was alone in serving God but God reminded him, saying: "I have left Me seven thousand in Israel, all the knees which have not **bowed** unto Baal, and every mouth which hath not **kissed** him" (I Kings 19:18). Hosea 13:2 also refers to images being kissed: "And now they **sin** more and more, and have made them molten images of their silver, and idols according to their own understanding, all of it the work of the craftsmen: they say of them, Let the men that sacrifice **kiss** the calves."

HILL OF DIVINATION

In the book, *Inside the Vatican,* we find some interesting information. In 1949 Pope Pius XII visited the **Vatican Grottoes** and told Monsignor Carlo Respighi to try to find St. Peter's tomb. The first find of this excavation was somewhat surprising. The author explains why:

"A **statue of Bacchus,** the god of wine and sensuous pleasures, was lying near the place where St. Peter's tomb was supposed to be. Pius XII, who had disregarded Clement's taboo, was not shocked by Bacchus' vine leaves. Not only did he encourage the archeologists to go on but when they ran out of money he financed the excavations out of his personal funds.

> "Little by little the bowels of the earth yielded their secret. The **excavators found a road flanked by two rows of pagan tombs** belonging to upper middle-class Roman families of the second century. These tombs were extremely well-preserved, almost intact. The explanation is this: When Emperor Constantine decided to build the first basilica of St. Peter, the ground of the Vatican Hill had to be raised on one side to make a level foundation. Constantine's architects **did not bother to demolish the pagan tombs that stood there, but just made a hole in the roof of each of them, filled them with earth and debris and did their building on top of them.** The tombs were thus sealed away for sixteen centuries."[272]

With all the paganism that has been prevalent in Catholicism, I guess it isn't surprising that when the excavators ran into trouble with some water problems, they called in a water diviner or a dowser.[273] This is an **occult practice** which is often **called water witching.** (For more information on dowsing, see my booklet "Dowsing Is in the Bible.")

The word "basilica" was just mentioned. It is interesting to note that this word comes from the same root word as "basilisk." The *American Heritage Dictionary* says that a basilisk is a "legendary serpent or dragon with lethal breath and glance."[274] The image "is clearly **infernal in character,** as is shown by its threefold attributes (its three-pointed crest and trifurcated tail) since they are an **inversion of the qualities of the Trinity;** and also by the predominance of **evil components,** such as the toad and the snake. It is one of the many 'keepers of treasure' mentioned in legend."[275]

George Oliver, in his Masonic book, *Signs and Symbols,* says:

> "Egypt was the great conservator of ancient idolatry.... Cneph was the Serpent-god of this people; he was the second person of the sacred Triad, and said to be the Creator of the world. He was usually represented by a hooded snake, sometimes called **Basiliscus,** or the Royal Serpent."[276]

PETER WAS JUPITER

Another word connected to Rome (and Washington, D.C.!) is "Capitol." The dictionary tells us that this word comes from "Capitolium" which was the **"temple of Jupiter at Rome** on the Capitoline Hill."[277] Capitoline, according to *Webster's,* means "of or relating to the smallest of the seven hills of ancient Rome, the temple on it, or the **gods** worshipped there."[278] This is especially intriguing since we've already been told that the statue of Peter was **ORIGINALLY** Jupiter![279]

We need to also look at the name "Vatican." It means "hill of divination" in Latin![280]

You see, **"Vatican Hill was once the major center of worship for the mother-goddess Cybele."**[281]

An article entitled "Which Goddess Is Which?" explains that Cybele

> "was called 'Virgin, pure and undefiled, supposedly had the power to wash away sin, was claimed to have resurrected bodily to heaven, and was served by an emasculated priesthood.
>
> "Rome's Virgin later supplanted Cybele and wherever Cybele had been worshiped, so too did worship of Rome's Virgin prosper.
>
> "One of Rome's claims for their Virgin is most telling. 'An inscription (found under "St." Peter's Basilica) portrays Mary as Protectrix for the departed and their Mediatrix.' (*Dictionary of Mary,* Catholic Book Publishing Co., 1985).
>
> "The **inscription is dated 100-200 A.D.** But **Cybele's temple occupied the site of St. Peter's until the 4th century A.D.** Cybele was the Empire's top deity.
>
> "Furthermore, historical records tell of bull's testicles being obtained at Cybele's shrine for use in magic in 160 A.D. the very time that Rome says the inscription *to the Catholic Virgin* is dated!
>
> "Obviously, the inscription was referring to Cybele, who bears the same titles as the Roman Catholic Virgin...and whose headquarters were located in the same place as today's goddess.
>
> "There is no difference. One virgin-mother goddess is the same as the next."[282] [Italics in the original; boldface added.]

Peter and Patti Lalonde toured the Vatican and surrounding areas. Their guide

> "pointed out to us two 'Christian' churches, built in honor of Mary, on each side of three columns that had been left standing from an ancient temple of **Venus.** Throughout the city there are remains of temples built in honor of some Roman god or goddess. Even the **Vatican museum houses pagan statues** and replicas of ancient times."[283]

David Cloud also toured the Vatican. He wrote:

> "I toured the Vatican in 1992 and was astounded at how **pagan** the place is. It reminded me of the many temples we

toured during our years of missionary work in Asia. Fitting to the home of the man who claims the titles and position of Jesus Christ and who accepts worship, the **Vatican** is a monument to idolatry and blasphemy. There are **statues of all sorts of pagan gods and goddesses....**In fact, the Vatican is one gigantic idol. The great altar over the supposed tomb of St. Peter is overwhelmed by gigantic golden spiraling columns which look for all the world like coiling serpents."[284]

I know many Catholics would never think of bowing down before a statue of Buddha but they don't think twice about bowing before a statue of Mary. It's sad that they have never been taught that the statue before whom they are bowing was once a pagan goddess. If they knew the truth, I wonder how many people would leave the Catholic Church.

Of course, Graham doesn't want that to happen. Instead of warning about the idolatry, etc., Graham brags up the Pope. He has called the Pope a "great evangelist,"[285] the "greatest religious leader of the modern world and one of the greatest moral and spiritual leaders of this century."[286] "On another occasion, he said that he believed the Pope to be 'God's instrument for revival in our generation.'"[287] No wonder Graham could brag that the Pope was interested in Graham's ministry.[288]

GRAHAM AND POPE ARE BROTHERS

Graham and the Pope are so close that in 1990 when Graham was with John Paul II, "the Pope reportedly complained [to Graham!] about aggressive evangelicals trying to draw Latins away from the Catholic faith," says *Christianity Today.*[289]

Prior to this,

> "Graham spoke about a meeting with Pope **John Paul II:** 'There was a pause in the conversation; suddenly the Pope's arm shot out and he grabbed the lapels of my coat, he pulled me forward within inches of his own face. He fixed his eyes on me and said, **"Listen Graham, we are brothers...."**' Graham said that that was a great happening in his life."[290]

In 1994 when *Time* magazine named the Pope as "Man of the Year," Graham said: "He'll go down in history as the greatest of our modern popes." "He's been the strong conscience of the whole Christian world."[291]

Graham's magazine, *Christianity Today,* even carried a full-page ad for "'Six Inspirational Video Sets,' one of which was entitled

'Pope John Paul II.' Concerning this, the ad reads: 'This inspiring video collection invites you to join one of the most beloved religious leaders....'"[292]

> "In a recent interview with Associated Press (AP) reported Richard Ostling, world-renowned evangelist Billy Graham said if he were to choose a 'man of the century,' he would probably choose Pope John Paul II. Graham told the AP that the current pope 'has brought the greatest impact of any pope in the last 200 years.' He added, 'I admire his courage, determination, intellectual abilities and his understanding of Catholic, Protestant and Orthodox differences, *and the attempt at some form of reconciliation.*'"[293]

Reconciliation? With whom? Pagans, Buddhists, Hindus, witches, shamans? Remember this is the **same Pope who has arranged interfaith meetings with the occultists!** From October 24-28, 1999 **the Pope**

> **"summoned representatives of the world's religions to the Vatican** for one last try during this millennium at cooperation to solve common problems of the world's peoples....
>
> "Participants at the **interfaith** meeting included Jews, Hindus, Muslims, Buddhists, Shintoists, and Baha'is, to name only a few. Representatives from Orthodox, Anglican, Lutheran and evangelical churches attended and participated as well. **Joining the pope on the platform during his speech was the Dalai Lama, Tibet's exiled spiritual leader."**[294]

John Paul II has even gone so far as to call the Dalai Lama "a great **spiritual** leader."[295]

FUNDAMENTALIST APPROACH IS DANGEROUS

The Pope, according to Graham, is "God's instrument for revival," yet

> "Pope John Paul II criticizes 'Bible-only' thinking in one of his encyclical letters, *'Faith and Reason' (Fides et Ratio).* The pope, a one-time philosophy professor, warns against 'fideism,' the idea that rational knowledge has little value for faith. He condemns 'biblicism' as 'one currently widespread' symptom of the problem. John Paul defines biblicism as the tendency 'to make the reading and exegesis of scripture the sole criterion of truth.'"[296]

What the Pope condemns is a good description of a Bible-believing Christian as the Bible is the Christian's **sole** guide for living!

> "In 1994, the **Vatican officially criticized a literal interpretation of the Bible** and said the fundamentalist approach to Scripture was 'a kind of intellectual suicide.' The document said fundamentalism 'refuses to admit that the inspired Word of God has been expressed in human language...by human authors possessed of limited capacities and resources.' The 125-page document, 'The Interpretation of the Bible in the Church,' was written by the Pontifical Biblical Commission, a group of scholars who assist the pope in the study of Scripture. **'The fundamentalist approach is dangerous,** for it is attractive to people who look to the Bible for ready answers to the problems of life,' the document said. 'Fundamentalism actually invites people to a kind of intellectual suicide.'"[297]

Almost 800 years ago at the Council of Toulouse in 1229, we find that the Catholic Church said: "We **prohibit** also that **the laity** should be permitted **to have the books of the Old or the New Testament....**"[298]

In *Rome Has Spoken...* we read: *"For much of [Catholic] church history, Scripture was not directly accessible to the faithful, not only because of widespread illiteracy, but—especially after the Council of Trent—because* ***church officials discouraged Scripture reading,*** *fearing interpretations that might not accord with church doctrine."*[299] [Italics in the original; boldface added.]

> "The Bible contains much fiction, myth, and embellishments says an early-1997 issue of *Notre Dame Magazine*. The publication of the (Roman Catholic) University of Notre Dame quotes various Notre Dame professors as attacking such fundamental doctrines of historic Christianity as the deity of Christ. The publication is in general agreement with the Roman Catholic professors. Kerry Temple, managing editor of *Notre Dame Magazine*, claims that the story of Jesus in the Bible 'is more like poetry' than 'a news report or documentary film that presents historical events literally and factually.'...She also quotes Albert Schweitzer: 'The Jesus of Nazareth who came forward publicly as the Messiah, who preached the ethic of the Kingdom of God, who founded the Kingdom of Heaven upon earth, and died to give his work its final consecration never had any existence.'
>
> "'Less credence is given to claims for other kinds of miracles. "Anything involving changes of nature," says Notre Dame's John Collins, "we are more inclined to regard as

theological fictions." The purposes of these legends, scholars believe, are to give insight into Jesus's teachings, to demonstrate his supernatural powers, to affirm his divinity and to reinforce faith. Among theologians today the consensus seems to be: Don't count on the miracles to prove that Jesus was God. "These nature miracles," says Thomas Sheehan in the highly controversial book *The First Coming*, "are simply legends which arose among early Christians and which were projected backward, under the impact of faith, into the life of the historical Jesus."'"[300]

Remember, Notre Dame had Billy Graham as one of their speakers.[301]

TOSS THE BIBLE

Since the Catholic Church does not accept the Bible as the inerrant Word of God, I guess it's no surprise that a question in *The Jesuits Catechism* asking "What if the Holy Scriptures command one thing, and the Pope another contrary to it?," has this answer: **"The Holy Scriptures must be thrown aside...."**[302]

This book also asks "What is the Pope?" The answer starts with this response: "He is the Vicar of Christ, King of Kings, and Lord of Lords, and **there is but one and the same Judgment-Seat belonging to God and the Pope...."**[303]

Recently the Vatican issued a document entitled *Dominus Iesus*. According to the *National Catholic Register*, the document "said that while others can be saved through a special grace, **the Catholic Church is necessary for their salvation."** It also says that "that the Church of Christ exists fully only in the Catholic Church."[304] Pope John Paul II declared that the document has his personal approval.[305]

Explaining that the Catholic Church is still open for dialogue, Archbishop Ivan Dias indicated:

> "While salvation comes through Christ alone...through other religions 'the Spirit leaves tracks which eventually lead to Christ.'
>
> **"'The ways which lead to Jesus are different,** but there is no other mediator' between humanity and God...."[306]

It's amazing how tolerant the Pope can be of other religions—all except Bible-believing Christians, that is. For instance, one researcher informs us:

> "Angry at Christian Bible-believers and others who refuse to acknowledge his spiritual leadership, Pope John Paul II and Vatican cronies have called for an all-out war.

"As reported in the *Associated Press,* with the Tibetan god-man, the Dalai Lama, sitting at his right side, this October [1999] in Rome the Pope presided at a special council of some 200 religious leaders of various faiths, sects, and cults.

"The Pontiff told the assembled Buddhist monks, Zoroastrian priests, Catholic cardinals, Hindu gurus, American Indian shamen (sic), Jewish rabbis, and ecumenical clergy that all must join in *condemning* the Christian fundamentalists who 'abuse speech' and whose efforts at converting others 'incite hatred and violence.'

"The Pope further directed that the religious leaders promote 'tolerance,' mutual understanding, and respect for *all* religions and faiths, not just their own.

"Newspaper sources called the meeting 'remarkable,' noting incredible scenes ranging from a ritual in which an American Indian blessed the four corners of the earth from the heart of Rome, to a Moslem Mufti and his followers kneeling toward Mecca and praying.

"All present were in accord on two key points: (1) Pope John Paul II was endorsed by consensus as the planet's chief spiritual guide and overseer; and (2) **Religious fundamentalists who refuse to go along with the global ecumenical movement are to be silenced.** They must also be denounced as 'dangerous extremists' full of hate."[307] [Italics in the original.]

Such an effort is being carried out. For instance, in the June 15, 2001 issue of *Calvary Contender* we find:

"Catholic leaders in San Nicolas, Mexico, a town of some 4,000 people, are telling 36 evangelical families they **must** leave town within 90 days 'or be kicked out.'...Their water and sewer services were cut off Mar. 28. A San Nicolas spokesperson said, 'What the town wants is for the evangelicals to stop spreading their religion to more people and to stop having their meetings....'"[308]

It's incredible how tolerant people can be of all the false religions (including paganism, witchcraft, and even Satanism), but how unbelievably intolerant they are when it comes to those who believe the Bible! Wilson Ewin wrote: "Such action is in perfect harmony with Catholic philosophy which teaches 'When I am in the minority you must tolerate me for I am right; when I am in the majority I must persecute you for you are wrong.'"[309]

GRAHAM CONSULTS POPE

Graham has been consulting with the Pope on various issues. For instance, after "receiving honors from communists in Eastern Europe in January 1981, Graham visited the pope. Prior to his journey to Moscow in 1982, Graham again visited the pope for counsel!"[310]

In 1992 **Graham** went to the **Communist** country of North Korea where he preached in a Protestant and a Catholic church with **government** approval.[311] He also delivered a message from the Pope to the Communist dictator, Kim Il Sung,[312] and Kim gave him a return message for the Pope.[313]

Graham even called Kim a "great leader"[314] and praised this Marxist leader's call for "reconciliation and peace,"[315] and added that he has "learned to appreciate Korea's long struggle to preserve its national sovereignty."[316]

In Graham's own autobiography he writes:

> "I had just been to Pyongyang for the second time and had spent several hours with President Kim Il Sung. President Kim had been very warm to me personally, in spite of our differences in background, and I felt that he sincerely wanted to move forward in establishing better relations. I told Mr. Carter this and urged him to go. I felt that his warm personality would meet with a positive response from President Kim, and it did."[317]

Later in the book we find that Graham once again met with Kim:

> "Early on Saturday, January 29, 1994, we got word the President Kim Il Sung would receive us that morning. We journeyed through the now-familiar countryside to the same residence where we had been received in 1992; and I found him just as alert and friendly as before. **He embraced me** and then, with the press corps still present, **greeted me with words that deeply touched me, particularly given the differences in our points of view: "I consider it a great honor to have a friend like you in the United States. You have become like a member of our family.**
>
> "After the journalists were dismissed, we discussed a number of topics of a general nature, including the possibility of a visit by Ruth. Then we adjourned for a private meeting, accompanied only by our interpreters. I conveyed to President Kim the message President Clinton had asked me to extend to him. In turn he asked me to convey a confidential message to my President.

> "Unlike the brief message he had asked me to give to President Bush during our previous visit, however, the one to President Clinton was fairly extensive. Several times Steve, who was interpreting for me, stopped to discuss the exact meaning of certain phrases with President Kim's interpreter to be sure there was no misunderstanding. The message included a specific proposal that President Kim felt would **break the logjam in the difficult discussions over the nuclear issue.**"[318]

Franklin Graham wrote that his father's "visit helped open the doors in many ways for friendlier relations with the West."[319]

In case you hadn't noticed, Graham was carrying messages to the Communist dictator from both Republican and Democratic Presidents—Carter, Bush, and Clinton.

One researcher added:

> "Billy Graham has long been a water carrier and an errand boy for the Rockefellers, the Presidents, and other political and financial bigwigs. His recent scam, helping Communist China at President Clinton's behest, is just the latest in a string of political favors that Graham has tendered his influential and powerful friends in high places."[320]

Remember, Graham is **supposed** to be a preacher who claims that he **is not** involved in politics. Why, then, does he deliver **political messages** to heads of state?

IS HE SENILE?

When I was discussing some of Graham's actions and compromise, someone suggested to me that perhaps he was going senile. This person said it's so sad to see him on TV as his health is failing. Could his Parkinson's disease or senility be the reason for his compromise? Hardly! Do you think that heads of state like the U. S. President, the North Korean President, or the Pope would entrust a senile man to carry secret messages to other heads of state? Do you think a senile man would be asked to give an invocation at the Presidential inauguration? Do you think someone lacking mental facilities would meet privately with Mikhail Gorbachev, etc.? Do you think a senile man would be entrusted with the awesome responsibility of meeting with heads of state and then giving a report to the U. S. President on his meeting? Of course not! Besides, Graham's compromise has not just taken place in recent years. As has been extensively documented in this book, he's been compromising for almost 50 years! There's no way one can honestly believe that Graham's compromise is due to senility.

Billy Graham was also an admirer of other Popes preceding John Paul II. In 1978, while in Poland, Graham said: "I praise the greatness of the present Pope Paul VI."[321] Paul VI was one of the founding members of the ungodly Temple of Understanding[322] (which was covered in an earlier chapter). Some Catholics considered him to be an "impostor Pope" since he embraced the Communists.[323] **Paul VI's secretary was a Jesuit named Tondi, a Communist who had attended the Lenin School in Moscow.**[324]

Paul VI was the first Pope to visit the Western Hemisphere. His first visit was to none other place than the United Nations headquarters on October 4, 1965[325] where he gave a secular humanistic speech.[326] "After the speech, Pope Paul VI went to the Meditation Room of the U. N."[327]

POPE VI AND U THANT

Occultist Robert Muller said that Paul VI "was a dear friend of former Secretary-General U Thant, whom I often heard speak of him with great fondness and admiration. Pope Paul was one of the few people, a group of very special persons, with whom U Thant was in constant **spiritual** communion."[328] Remember, U Thant said that **Lenin's "ideals** of peace and peaceful coexistence among states have won widespread international acceptance and they **are in line with the aims of the United Nations Charter...."**[329] Also, in an address to the World Association of World Federalists, he mentioned *"world citizens as they work steadfastly to usher in the new world order."*[330] [Emphasis in the original.] Paul VI was so much enamored by U Thant that he went so far as to give "the Papal ring of diamonds and rubies, and his pectoral cross of diamonds and emeralds...and the tiara, the triple crown that denotes the Trinity, the authority, and the spiritual powers of the Church...to the **Buddhist** U Thant, then Secretary-General of the United Nations."[331]

Cardonnel, a member of the Dominican Order, was called "the God's death theologian" because of his extremely anti-Christian expressions.[332] Catholic author, Piers Compton, states: "He boasted of the title, left his Order and finally the Church, and **became a hardened devil-worshipper.** In a typical outburst he likened the Christian God to Stalin, to a beast, and finally to Satan."[333] Amazingly, **Paul VI admired Cardonnel's work,** "and although he ignored requests from Catholics who wished to safeguard their religion, he made a special point of writing to Cardonnel, **congratulating him and sending good wishes."**[334]

Another person Paul VI was impressed with was Saul Alinsky.[335] **Alinsky was a Marxist[336] who gave an acknowledgement to Lucifer** in his book *Rules for Radicals.*[37] Alinsky was known as the "Apostle of Permanent Revolution."[338] Paul VI was so inspired by Alinsky that "the two spent a fortnight together, discussing how best to bring the demands of the Church, and those of the Communist unions, into line with each other...at the end of their talks Montini [who became Paul VI] declared that he was pleased to call himself one of Alinsky's best friends...."[339] In this book, Alinsky states: "...I have always believed that birth control and abortion are personal rights to be exercised by the individual."[340] Isn't it strange that the Pope would consider Alinsky one of his "best friends"?

In another one of Alinsky's books, he criticized "narrow nationalism."[341]

While we're briefly discussing Alinsky, it should be noted that his book with the acknowledgement to Lucifer has also been called the National Education Association's "bible."[342]

Also, denominations belonging to the National Council of Churches "have paid hundreds of thousands of dollars to Saul Alinsky and his Area Foundation Inc."[343] The Pope hasn't been the only one enamored with this Marxist!

TWISTED CROSS

Paul VI

> "made use of a sinister **symbol, used by Satanists** in the sixth century, that had been revived at the time of Vatican Two. This was a **bent or broken cross,** on which was displayed a repulsive and distorted figure of Christ, which the **black magicians and sorcerers** of the Middle Ages had **made use of to represent the Biblical term 'Mark of the Beast.'** Yet not only Paul VI, but his successors, the two John-Pauls, carried that object and held it up to be revered by crowds, who had not the slightest idea that it stood for anti-Christ."[344]

"Within a few days of Paul's return to Rome,...Pope Paul let it be known that Rome...was ready to take a new look at secret societies."[345] In fact, many of those close to Paul VI were Masons such as Monsignor Pasquale Macchi who was Paul VI's private secretary (initiated April 23, 1958),[346] Monsignor Mario Rizzi (initiated September 16, 1969),[347] Cardinal Ugo Polatti (initiated February 17, 1969),[348] and Monsignor Franceso Marchiasano (initiated February 4, 1961).[349] Paul VI himself has been purported to be a Mason.[350]

In 1964 Paul VI presented Dr. Radhakrishnan with the Golden Spur, the highest Vatican honor.[351] Keep in mind that Radhakrishnan was one of the founding members of the Temple of Understanding[352] and he also belonged to the World Brotherhood.[353] He was also a Hindu.[354] Could this be why Paul VI could say: "The Hindu life and the Christian life shall go together. Your message and my message are the same."[355]

Paul VI also "wrote a Papal Encyclical that **called on the nations to abandon sovereignty to form a world government."**[356] When the Pope issued his "Pastoral Constitution on the Church in the Modern World," on December 7, 1965,

> "he spoke of *'the birth of a new humanism, one in which man is defined first of all by this responsibility to his brothers and to history.'*...In his pastoral letter, the pope went on to talk about such things as 'service to the common good,' 'economic equity,' 'international order and brotherhood,' and 'universal authority.'"[357]

On March 26, 1967 Paul VI wrote:

> "Who can fail to see the need and importance of thus gradually coming to the establishment of a world authority capable of taking effective action on the juridical and political planes?...Delegates to international organizations, public officials, gentlemen of the press, teachers and educators—all of you must realize that you have your part to play in the construction of a **new world order."**[358]

One researcher stated:

> *"The growing involvement of the Vatican and its allies in politics and religion reminds one of Alice Bailey's [Luciferian, New Age leader] prediction that the **new world order would be ushered in with the help of a universally-accepted church.** Bailey explained that the New Age would rest upon the foundation of a newly interpreted and enlightened Christianity...being universal in nature."*[359] [Italics in the original; boldface added.]

NOT SURE OF HEAVEN

Interestingly, "Pope Paul VI was asked whether he was sure he was going to heaven when he died. He responded that he couldn't know he was going straight to Heaven, but there would be 600 million Catholics praying for him. If a Catholic says he is sure of heaven, it is the sin of presumption, a mortal sin."[360] The Bible, on the other hand, tells us that we can know:

> "And this is the record, that God hath given to us eternal life, and this life is in His Son. He that hath the Son hath life; and he that hath not the Son of God hath not life. These things have I written unto you that believe on the name of the Son of God; that **ye may know that ye have eternal life,** and that ye may believe on the name of the Son of God" (I John 5:11-13).

At the end of his life the apostle Paul could say: "I have fought a good fight, I have finished my course, I have kept the faith: Henceforth there is laid up for me a crown of righteousness, which the Lord, the righteous judge, shall give me at that day: and not to me only, but unto all them also that love His appearing" (II Timothy 4:7-8).

Yet, sounding a little bit like Pope Paul VI (whom Graham said he admired), Graham was asked this question by Tony Snow on January 2, 2000: "When you get to Heaven, who's going to speak first, you or God?" Graham's reply was:

> "'When I get there, I'm sure that Jesus is going to say that he will welcome me. But I think that he's going to say: "Well done, our good and faithful servant." Or he may say: "You're in the wrong place."' SNOW: **'You really worry that you may be told you're in the wrong place? GRAHAM: Yes, because I have not—I'm not a righteous man.** People put me up on a pedestal that I don't belong (sic) in my personal life. And they think that I'm better than I am. **I'm not the good man that people think I am.** Newspapers and magazines and television have made me out to be a saint. I'm not. I'm not a Mother Teresa. And I feel that very much.'"[361]

SEX IN HEAVEN?

Sadly Graham doesn't seem to have any assurance of salvation! In fact, as you will see from the following quote, Graham seems to believe that some people are too good for evangelism. In a pre-crusade television interview in 1993,

> "Graham said (speaking of the people of Columbus, Ohio): 'You're too good, you don't need evangelism. In fact, that's what kept us from coming [to Columbus] for so long.' A TV news reporter said Graham didn't care what faith you were from, that 'the idea is to bring you back to your faith, **no matter what it is,** and to use the Crusade as a catalyst to **bring you back to that faith.'**"[362]

My Bible teaches that **"ALL** have sinned, and come short of the glory of God" (Romans 3:23). **NO** community is too good as each community is made up of individual people—each in need of a Saviour.

Of course, Graham also has a wrong view of heaven as can be seen in the following interview with Larry King in 1998. On King's Christmas program he asked Graham what paradise would be like. Graham responded: "People say that the Bible teaches there's no sex in Heaven. If sex is necessary for our happiness and fulfillment, it'll be there....If certain other things that we think are pleasurable—it'll be there."[363] Again the Bible gives the answer to this—but it's just the opposite of what Graham claimed. Jesus Himself said: "Do ye not therefore err, because **ye know not the scriptures,** neither the power of God? For when they shall rise from the dead, they **neither marry, nor are given in marriage;** but are as the angels which are in heaven" (Mark 12:24-25).

Prior to King's interview, Graham had an interview with David Frost. "Frost asked: 'What do you think Heaven will be like?' Graham said: 'It'll be where Jesus is....A place where we'll work....[**God**—Ed.] **may send us to other planets to help in the redemption** of other planets, I don't know....I think there's life on other planets.'"[364] Does Graham really believe that we are co-redemptors?

HOW'S THAT AGAIN?

Graham also has a strange interpretation for the following passage found in Revelation 14:18-20:

> "And another angel came out from the altar, which had power over fire; and cried with a loud cry to him that had the sharp sickle, saying, Thrust in thy sharp sickle, and **gather the clusters of the vine** of the earth; for **her grapes are fully ripe.** And the **angel** thrust in his sickle into the earth, and **gathered the vine of the earth, and cast it into the great winepress of the wrath of God.** And the winepress was trodden without the city, and blood came out of the winepress...."

Revelation 14 takes place during the tribulation, but regardless of one's viewpoint of eschatology (and regardless if you think it's literal or symbolic), I think anyone reading these verses can see that when the grapes are gathered, they are being gathered for **destruction.** However, here's what Billy Graham says about this:

> "I ask you to seriously pray for our upcoming Crusade in Sacramento, California (October 18-22, 1995). Sacramento is located near the heart of Northern California's **vineyards,** and it is the capital of the most populous state in the country. People will be coming from all over California, and we will have an opportunity to touch the entire state. It seems that we hear the

challenge from Revelation 14: 'It is harvest time. Earth's harvest is ripe for reaping...the grapes are bursting with ripeness.' Pray with us for a **great harvest of conversions** through this Crusade."[365]

How Graham can believe this refers to a "great harvest of **conversions** rather than the "winepress of the **wrath** of God" is beyond me.

"I ADMIRE POPE JOHN XXIII"

Yet one other Pope that Graham praised was John XXIII. When John XXIII died, the June 2, 1963 issue of *Michigan City News-Dispatch* quoted Graham as saying: "I admire Pope John XXIII tremendously....I felt he brought a new era to the world. It is my hope that the cardinals elect a new Pope who will follow the same line as John. It would be a great tragedy if they chose a man who reacted against John."[366] Just who was this Pope? He was born Angelo Roncalli but when he became Pope he took the name John XXIII. Strangely, in the early **1400's,** during the period known as the "Great Western Schism" in the Catholic Church,[367] there was **another Pope** who took the name **John XXIII.** He

> "was accused by thirty seven witnesses (mostly bishops and priests) of fornication, adultery, incest, sodomy, simony, theft, and murder! It was proved by a legion of witnesses that he had seduced and violated three hundred nuns. His own secretary, Niem, said that he had at Boulogne, kept a harem, where not less than two hundred girls had been the victims of his lubricity."[368]
>
> "A **Vatican record** offers this information about his immoral reign: 'His lordship, **Pope John,** committed perversity with the wife of his brother, incest with holy nuns, intercourse with virgins, adultery with the married, and all sorts of sex crimes...wholly given to sleep and other carnal desires, totally adverse to the life and teaching of Christ...he was **publicly called the Devil incarnate.'**
>
> "To increase his wealth, Pope John taxed about everything—including prostitution, gambling, and usury. He has been called 'the most depraved criminal who ever sat on the Papal throne.'"[369]

Yet another source reveals:

> "Until recent years, and according to Piers Compton who was for fifteen years literary editor of the Roman Catholic

weekly, 'The Universe,' his portrait appeared in the *Annuario Pontifico,* the Church's year book. Compton wrote of this earlier John XXIII *'We know nothing to his credit, for his only recorded achievement, if the word of such a precious reprobate as himself can be believed, was to have seduced more than two hundred women, including his sister-in-law.'*"[370] [Emphasis in the original.]

With John XXIII leaving such a "legacy," why would **any** Pope want to take the exact same name and number? Why didn't Roncalli at least select number XXIV instead of XXIII?

Roncalli served "as the Vatican's first permanent observer at the United Nations Educational, Scientific, and Cultural Organization (UNESCO) for nineteen months in 1951 and 1952."[371] UNESCO (already covered in Chapter 3) is an organization trying to influence our children to accept a **world government.**[372] Roncalli was also "a **friend of socialists** [and] a man able to get along with the Nazis...."[373] "Even the **Communists trusted him** and said he understood them."[374] In fact, one researcher states:

> "John's strategy was to win the world on two fronts—the religious with syncretism and ecumenism, and the ideological with Communism....
>
> **"John was a left winger....**In *'The Vatican Moscow Washington Alliance'* Avro Manhattan makes it clear that John, a Socialist Humanist, was a man for his time, not to be welcomed by the Protestants, but a Pope to put Rome back in favour with the winning side, one to make a Moscow Alliance instead of the Washington Alliance that had preceded him. He was out to win back the favours of the greatly increased Communist world."[375]
>
> "In 1963, Pope John XXIII, welcomed Soviet Premier Nikita Khrushchev's daughter and son-in-law to the Vatican.
>
> "In 1972, a **Vatican publication** suggested that the teachings and philosophy of Mao Tse-tung 'reflected' Christian values. This surprising statement was noted widely in the world's press.
>
> "Soon after, in Geneva, a Vatican diplomat publicly praised the Chinese Communist 'social system.'
>
> "In June 1973, a delegation of ecumenists from the Vatican issued a statement affirming that there 'is a strong tendency toward some form of "socialism" in many parts of the world.'"[376]

RONCALLI'S RED HAT

A former priest, Bartholomew F. Brewer, explains that after World War II Roncalli

> "became an advisor of the pope [Pius XII]....The pope, who was now ardently pro-American, didn't trust Roncalli, however, and **Roncalli** also deplored the pope's pro-American attitude. He worked behind the scenes, careful never to defy the pope, but wherever he could he **showed favor toward socialists and communists.** The pope soon learned of Roncalli's actions, however, and finally had enough of him. In order to get him out of the Vatican and appease the church liberals, he gave Roncalli the red hat of a cardinal and sent him to a minor post in Vienna. He expected Roncalli to attend to his duties quietly, drop out of politics, and die peacefully.
>
> "Pope Pius died first, however. Cardinals from all over the world gathered in Rome to elect a new pope. Most of the left-leaning nations favored Roncalli to be pope; so did a large number of liberal cardinals, most of whom were Italian....
>
> "Who would be the new pope? At first it didn't seem that Cardinal Roncalli had a chance, but after ten ballots, the cardinals seemed unable to agree on anyone else. Roncalli seemed to be a good 'compromise candidate.' He was seventy-seven years of age, overweight, a heavy smoker, and not expected to live very long. Most important of all, he was an experienced Vatican administrator and a skilled diplomat. In a world freighted with troubles and uncertainty, he seemed to be an expedient choice.
>
> "Roncalli, elected on the eleventh ballot, became Pope John XXIII. He was thought of as a sort of 'care-taker' pope who would serve until a more widely acceptable candidate emerged.
>
> "What a shock the Vatican was in for! The cardinals could hardly have been more wrong in thinking of the new pope as a mere caretaker. He launched a revolution in the church such as had not been seen since the Reformation. He was a zealous reactionary against the policies and practices of his predecessor, Pope Pius XII. **Pope John XXIII can properly be called 'the first pink pope.'"**[377]

Another researcher also calls John XXIII a "pink" Pope:

> "Revolutionary changes became visible within the structure of the entire [Catholic] Church. Foremost among those most

responsible, there stands the late 'pink' Pope John XXIII. **His liberal encyclical,** *Pacem in Terris,* **called for world government, disarmament and socialism—the identical program of International Communism.** In fact, the *New York Times* reported, April 13, 1963, 'The Communist camp where atheism is a basic tenet has given a rousing welcome to Pope John XXIII's encyclical, *Pacem in Terris.* Without waiting for word from Moscow, **the major Communist Parties of Western Europe greeted the Pope's call for peace and disarmament.'"**[378]

*"...**Pope John XXIII, was a socialist at heart** and brought a storm of liberalism into the Church of Rome. In the words of Jesuit Malachi Martin, this had the effect 'of hurling it towards Communism.' **Pope John's leftist encyclicals,** 'Mater et Magistra' and 'Pacem in Terris,' **reveal a strong influence of Marxist-Leninist ideology.** The result became evident as the Church gradually **adopted a New World Order strategy."**[379]* [Italics in the original; boldface added.]

From the book, *Inside the Vatican,* we find that Roncalli liked exquisite foods and offered his guests excellent wines, renowned liqueurs, and choice cigars.[380]

"He never failed to visit all the pavilions of the Art Show, including those where the **nudest of nudes** were shown, without making any comment. As regards the Film Festival, while obviously he did not attend the actual projections, he each year gave a splendid and luxurious reception at his Palace, to which were invited indiscriminately Soviet producers and actors and several film stars who had been the center of shocking scandals."[381]

MASONIC POPES?

It is also alleged that Roncalli was a member of the secret society of the Rosicrucians.[382]

"In his book *The Broken Cross,* Piers Compton, an ex-editor of the Catholic newspaper *The Universe,* has traced the alleged infiltration of the Roman Church by the Illuminati. He cites as evidence the use of the Illuminist symbol of the eye in the triangle by leading Catholics. It has been used by the Jesuits, it has appeared as the seal of the Philadelphia Eucharistic Congress in 1976 and featured on a special issue of Vatican stamps in 1978. Compton further claims that Pope John XXIII, who died in June 1963, used the symbol on his personal cross."[383]

Furthermore, it has been reported that Pope John XXIII (as well as Pope Paul VI) were Masons.[384] Of course, John XXIII, like Paul VI, was one of the founding members of the Temple of Understanding.[385]

This Pope also employed New Ager Norman Cousins (who was already covered in Chapter 4) for several diplomatic missions for the Vatican![386]

It was Roncalli (John XXIII) who initiated Vatican II.[387] A former priest writes:

> "It [Vatican II] met from October 11 to December 8, 1962, and again under Pope Paul VI sporadically from September 29, 1963, to December 8, 1965. Its key aim was to prepare the church for the leadership of **all world religions in an ecumenical church.** To make itself more widely acceptable, it used the Council to **appear to give up offensive beliefs** and practices **without actually doing so."**[388]

While many older and traditional Catholics are highly against Vatican II and feel that the Church has been compromised by this council, it must be stated that both "John XXIII and Paul VI, in convening Vatican II, made it clear that **they were guarding the doctrinal assertions of Trent."**[389] Said John XXIII: "I do accept entirely all that has been decided and declared at the Council of Trent."[390]

LET HIM BE ANATHEMA

What was decided at Trent? This council, held from 1545-1563, released hundreds of anathemas with over 100 of them being against Bible-believing Christians.[391] A former priest explains: "To be 'anathema' means to be cursed, damned, excommunicated, and consigned to Hell."[392]

Who is consigned to hell? Let's look at a few of these items from the Council of Trent that put a curse on individuals and which are **still** in force today.[393] If you fit even just **ONE** of these categories, you are destined for hell—at least according to the Catholic Church!

▼ "If anyone shall say that the ungodly man is **justified by faith only** so as to understand that nothing else is required...**let him be accursed."**[394] In other words, if you believe that salvation is by **faith alone and not earned by works,** then you are assigned to hell by the Catholic Church.

▼ "...if anyone shall say that man is absolved from his sins and justified...and that by **faith alone** absolution and justification are perfected: **let him be anathema."**[395]

▼ "If anyone says that **God always pardons the whole penalty** together **with** the guilt and that the satisfaction of penitents is **nothing else than the faith** by which they perceive that Christ has satisfied for them, **let him be anathema."**[396]

▼ **"If anyone says that** the sacraments of the New Law are not necessary for salvation but are superfluous, and that without them or without the desire of them **men obtain from God through faith alone the grace of justification,** though all are not necessary for each one, **let him be anathema."**[397]

▼ "If anyone says that in the Roman Church, which is the mother and mistress of all churches, there is **not the true doctrine concerning the sacrament of baptism, let him be anathema."**[398]

▼ If anyone says "that by means of **the images which we kiss and before which we uncover the head and prostate ourselves,** we adore Christ and venerate the saints whose likeness they bear....**if anyone should teach or maintain anything contrary to these decrees, let him be anathema."**[399]

▼ The Catholic Church **"condemns with anathema** those who say that *indulgences are useless* or that **the Church does not have the power to grant them."**[400] [Boldface in the original; italics added.]

Jesus said: "This people draweth nigh unto Me with their mouth, and honoureth Me with their lips; but their heart is far from Me. But **in vain they do worship Me, teaching for doctrines the commandments of men"** (Matthew 15:8-9; Mark 7:7).

▼ "If anyone denieth, either that sacramental **confession [to a priest]** was instituted, or **is necessary to salvation,** of divine right; or saith, that the manner of confessing secretly to a priest alone, which the Church hath ever observed from the beginning, and doth observe, is alien from the institution and command of Christ, and is a human invention; **let him be anathema."**[401]

In spite of this anathema, *Catholic Digest* reports: "In 1993, 66% of Catholics told the Gallup Poll that they thought one could still be a good Catholic without going to yearly Confession. And in 1995, sociologist James D. Davidson Jr. found that 57% of people who described themselves as Catholics say they never, or almost never, go to Confession."[402] Without realizing it, over half of the Catholics polled are headed for hell by their own Church's anathema!

▼ "If anyone does not receive the entire books [including the Apocrypha] with all their parts as they are accustomed to be read in the Catholic Church, and in the old Latin *Vulgate* Edition, as sacred and canonical...let him be anathema."[403] "It is from the *Vulgate* that our English [Catholic] *Douai Version* comes..."[404] and the "Latin *Vulgate* Bible is the **only translation** ever decreed by the Church to be error-free."[405]

Surprisingly, the Catholic scholar, St. Jerome, who translated the Scriptures for the *Vulgate,* did not consider the Apocryphal books as part of the canon of Scripture.[406] Even Pope Leo I in 447 A.D. condemned the apocryphal books and said that they "form a nursery-ground for many falsehoods"[407] and added that they "are not only to be proscribed [outlawed], but also taken away altogether and burnt to ashes in the fire."[408]

Yet the anathema from the Council of Trent said that **anyone** who didn't accept the apocryphal books was damned. **This anathema would also apply to most Catholics** as many Catholics no longer use the *Douai (Douay)* version! For proof, you just need to look at the November-December 2000 issue of a Catholic magazine, *Be.* The question was asked "Which Bible translation is best for me?" to which the following answer was given:

"The best translation for you is the one you will read....Some people prefer the modern language of recent translations such as the ***New American Bible* (the one used most commonly at Mass).** Others prefer older, more formal translations, such as the *Douay-Rheims.* I suggest you purchase several translations in cheap paperback editions. Try each for a week or two, and then buy a hardback copy of the translation you prefer."[409]

In fact, the 1988 edition of the *New American Bible* is now the **OFFICIAL** Catholic translation in the United States.[410]

▼ "If anyone says that in the sacred and holy sacrament of the Eucharist the substance of the bread and wine remains conjointly with the body and blood of our Lord Jesus Christ, and **denies that** wonderful and singular **change** of the whole substance of **the bread into the body** and the whole substance of **the wine into the blood,** the appearances only of bread and wine remaining, **which change the Catholic Church most aptly calls transubstantiation, let him be anathema.**"[411]

TRANSUBSTANTIATION

More and more Catholics no longer believe that the Eucharist is the actual, literal body and blood of Jesus (transubstantiation). All those who do not believe this, are consigned to hell by the Council of Trent.[412]

Jeff Mardis writes:

> "'Do not ye yet understand, that **whatsoever** entereth in at the mouth [the Eucharist] goeth into the belly, and is **cast out** into the draught?' (Matt. 15:17) Now, if (according to the Roman Catholic Church) Jesus Christ dwells in the transformed Eucharist (and he does); and 'whatsoever' enters in at the mouth goes into the belly (and it does); and 'whatsoever' goes into the belly is eventually 'cast out into the draught' (and it is), then this can ONLY mean that Jesus the Wafer is ultimately...."[413] [Emphasis in the original.]

Although Mardis doesn't finish the sentence, the message is quite obvious. This is not meant to be sacrilegious. You see, according to former priest, Bartholomew Brewer, we find that if

> "the consecrated Host is dropped and a mouse or other animal snatches the wafer away, the priest is given a forty-day penance to perform....If the priest vomits after consuming the bread or the wine, it is **recommended** that he **consume the vomit,** provided that he can do it without creating an embarrassing scene. The alternative is to burn what he vomited. And such things have happened many times; I myself recall times that mass was being said on tossing Navy ships and the priest became seasick."[414]

The wafer-God is so important that if it is vomited up, the vomit should be consumed (or burned). Yet only a few short hours later that same wafer will pass through the body and no one seems to even care. At what point does "Jesus" no longer become "Jesus"?

Former priest, Charles Chiniquy, was faced with trying to rescue his "Jesus" from worse than vomit. At one point Chiniquy had mistakenly left his silver box which contained the Host at a person's home. The woman, wondering what was inside, opened the box and out fell the Host—right into the vessel which contained the bodily wastes—and sank down in it. About the time, Chiniquy, realizing he had forgotten his container, returned to the home. There he found the woman in a fit of hysteria, tearing her hair, and foaming at the mouth. The emotional husband finally was able to tell Chiniquy what had happened. As a priest, Chiniquy knew what was required of him. He wrote:

> "I felt struck with such unspeakable horror at the thought that the body, blood, soul and divinity of my Saviour, Jesus Christ, was there, sunk into that vessel that I remained speechless, and for a long time did not know what to do. At first it came into my mind to plunge my hands into the vessel and try to get my Saviour out of that sepulchre of ignominy. But I could not muster courage to do so.

> "At last I requested the poor desolated family to dig a hole three feet deep in the ground, and deposit it, with its contents, and I left the house, after I had forbidden them from ever saying a word about that awful calamity."[415]

The "Jesus" (the Host) of Catholicism is made with hands and decays, yet my Bible says in Acts 2:31 that Christ's "soul was not left in hell, **neither His flesh did see corruption.**" (See also Psalm 16:10; Acts 2:27; 13:35, 37.)

NO CAFETERIA STYLE

Former Catholic, T. A. McMahon, reminds us:

> "Considering all the laws of the Church (a task most lawyers would find overwhelming), it's doubtful that even the most zealous Catholics know and obey every one of them. Catholics more often than not take a 'cafeteria' approach to their religion, picking and choosing what laws they want to obey. For example, many reject the Church's teachings and regulations regarding contraception (even abortion!), marriage to a non-Catholic, divorce and remarriage, annulments, etc....Some Catholics don't believe that transubstantiation actually changes the communion wafer into the real body, blood, soul and spirit of Jesus Christ, and some refuse to believe that purgatory is a reality. **Regardless of what individual dissenting Catholics think, they are condemned by their Church for rejecting its teachings."**[416]

In 1302 Pope Boniface VIII said: "We declare, affirm, and define as a **truth necessary for salvation** that **every human being is subject to the Roman Pontiff."**[417]

If the Pope is infallible and the doctrines of the Catholic Church are valid, one must accept them **in their entirety** to get to heaven. If the doctrines are not valid and the Pope is fallible, then **NO ONE** is under the obligation to believe and abide by the doctrines put forth by the Church. With the Catholic Church, it is not an "either/or" situation, it is "all or nothing."

Elsewhere McMahon adds:

> "The Catholic Church imposes damnations (more than 100 specific anathemas are listed) upon Catholics who decided *not* to accept some of its teachings and practices. While liberal, lax, and even biblically leaning Catholics attempt to justify their contrary-to-official-belief views, they are mutinying against their Church which (according to Roman Catholic dogma) is their only means to heaven. The laws of the Roman

> Catholic Church, however, explicitly condemn those who hold 'mutinous' beliefs. In other words, if a Catholic hopes to gain eternal life as a Catholic, he *must* abide strictly by his Church's proclaimed infallible rules. This manmade religious system does not tolerate a pick-and-choose approach to its faith."[418] [Italics in the original.]

AN UNBLOODY SACRIFICE

Additionally, according to the *Catechism of the Catholic Church* we find that the

> "Eucharist is thus a **sacrifice** because it *re-presents* (makes present) the sacrifice of the cross....
>
> "In this divine sacrifice which is celebrated in the Mass, the same Christ who offered himself once in a bloody manner on the altar of the cross is contained and is **offered in an unbloody manner.**"[419] [Italics in the original.]

Also: "We believe that the Mass which is celebrated by the priest in the person of Christ in virtue of the power he receives in the Sacrament of Order...**is indeed the Sacrifice of Calvary sacramentally realized on our altars.**"[420]

Another Catholic source reveals: "At Mass, we are not only present at **Jesus Christ's actual death and resurrection, <u>prolonged</u> through time and space.** We also really take part in them to the extent we want to."[421]

First of all, Hebrews 10:12 says that Christ "had offered **ONE** sacrifice for sins **forever,** sat down on the right hand of God...."

Christ "needeth not daily, as those high priests, to offer up sacrifice, first for His own sins, and then for the people's: for this He did **ONCE,** when He offered up Himself" (Hebrews 7:27), yet the Catholic Church insists (according to Canon 904) "that the **work of <u>redemption</u> is <u>continually</u> accomplished in the mystery of the Eucharistic Sacrifice....**"[422]

> "Further, according to official Roman Catholic doctrine, Jesus Christ is **immolated** on the Roman Catholic altar every time mass is offered, as Vatican Council II states, 'For in the sacrifice of the Mass Our Lord is **immolated** when he begins to be present sacramentally as the spiritual food of the faithful under the appearances of bread and wine.'"[423]

The word "immolate" means to "kill as a sacrifice" or "destroy." Hebrews explains clearly that Christ was not to be offered "often" but **only one time:**

> "For Christ is not entered into the holy places made with hands, which are the figures of the true; but into heaven itself, now to appear in the presence of God for us: **Nor yet that He should offer Himself often,** as the high priest entereth into the holy place every year with blood of others; For then must He often have suffered since the foundation of the world: but now **ONCE** in the end of the world hath He appeared to put away sin by the sacrifice of Himself" (Hebrews 9:24-26).

"By the which will we are sanctified through the **offering of the body of Jesus Christ once for all"** (Hebrews 10:10). "For by **one offering** He hath perfected for ever them that are sanctified" (Hebrews 10:14).

Additionally, the mass is supposed to be "offered in an unbloody manner,"[424] but Hebrews 9:22 says that "without shedding of blood is **no remission."**

KILL THE HERETIC

Augustin Bea, who was made a cardinal by John XXIII,[425] reminds us:

> "'No Catholic of education will believe that the council [Vatican II] can or would change even a single dogma. The Supreme Pontiff and the Council have a duty inherent in their ecclesiastical authority to preserve whole and entire the doctrine passed to them by tradition, and no love for the separated brethren can induce us to lay even the lightest hand on the sacred deposit of the faith.'"[426]

He also stated:

> "The Roman Catholic Church would be gravely misunderstood if it should be concluded that her present ecumenical adventuresomeness and openness meant that she was prepared to re-examine any of her fixed dogmatic positions. What the church is prepared to do is to take the responsibility for a more imaginative and contemporary presentation of these **fixed positions."**[427]

Pope Leo XIII added his own anathema: "Anathema on the one who says: The Holy Spirit does not want us to kill the heretic."[428] He also "stipulated that acceptance of the **primacy of the pope was a necessary condition of Christian reunion."**[429]

Regardless of what ecumenical Protestants like Billy Graham and Chuck Colson, etc., may claim, the theme of "papal primacy" is **still** a requisite! There was an interview in the July 29, 2001 issue of

Our Sunday Visitor, in which Cardinal Edward I. Cassidy, former top ecumenical officer for the Vatican,[430] was asked: "Would the Catholic church be prepared to modify its own understanding of papal primacy for the sake of agreement with the Orthodox?" He responded: "Certainly, I don't think we could abandon papal primacy in its essence. It's part of our understanding of the Church; so why would we do something disloyal to our very understanding of the truth?"[431] He did add that **how** that primacy would be exercised could be open to discussion, but the primacy itself is not negotiable![432]

MARY IS THE CENTER

Vatican II, however, was the instrument that helped the Vatican open up the door to the ecumenical movement.[433] New Ager and occultist, Robert Muller, bragged: "There is no doubt that Paul VI, together with John XXIII and John Paul II, will be remembered as the three great Popes of Peace, pioneers of a momentous **transcendence of the Catholic Church into the New Age."**[434]

In spite of this, the **Billy Graham organization recommended the biography of John XXIII** which "contained hundreds of pages of the Pope's devotion to Mary and the saints, worship of the Eucharistic wafer, and his trust in the sacraments for salvation...."[435] Graham "commended it in ads as 'a classic in devotion.'"[436]

Pope John XXIII remarked: "Mary is the center of all things in the sight of God."[437] He also said: "Mary is the center and light of all theology. Without Mary's light, theology is in darkness, in heresy. Without Mary, and if it were not for Mary, God would not have made the world.'"[438]

Graham himself said in 1966: "I find myself closer to Catholics than the radical Protestants."[439]

Cardinal Cushing, a Roman Catholic from Boston, made an interesting comment to the press in the **early 1950's** that "if he had half a dozen Billy Grahams, he would not worry about the future of his [Catholic] church!"[440] In fact, Graham bragged: "No ranking member of the Catholic hierarchy spoke out against the [1957 New York Madison Square Garden] Crusade, and I suspect many Catholics knew of my friendship with various Catholic leaders."[441]

> "In **1964,** Graham spent forty-five minutes with Richard Cardinal Cushing, Catholic Archbishop of Boston. Cushing gave unqualified support for Graham. The *Cleveland Plain Dealer* for Oct. 8, 1964, reported Cushing's words: 'I am 100% for the evangelist. I have never known a religious crusade that

> was more effective than Dr. Graham's. I have never heard the slightest criticism of anything he has ever said from a Catholic source.'
>
> "Graham returned the favor by saying: 'I feel much closer to Roman Catholic tradition than to some of the more liberal Protestants....'"[442]

Graham confessed: "My goal, I always made clear, was not to preach against Catholic beliefs or to proselytize people who were already committed to Christ within the Catholic Church."[443]

He added: "I was grateful for the statement one U. S. Catholic newspaper made as it reviewed our first South American trip: 'Never once, at least in our memory, has [Billy Graham—B.G.] attacked the Catholic Church.'"[444]

The July 1972 issue of *The Catholic Digest,*

> "presented a feature article lauding Billy Graham. The Jesuit author wrote, 'Billy Graham is orthodox. I have read nothing by him that is contrary to Catholic faith.' In some places priests are being instructed to become familiar in the use of 'evangelical' terminology like 'getting saved' or being 'born again.'"[445]

In 1978 Graham stated: "I found that **my beliefs are essentially the same as those of orthodox Catholics."**[446]

"The *Detroit Free Press* for Sept. 29, 1991, quoted Graham as saying, 'The Roman Catholics know that I'm not against them, and in my thinking, rightly or wrongly, I represent **all** the churches.'"[447]

Not only does Graham not attack the falseness in the Catholic Church but he even protects the wrong. For instance,

> "around **1961,** Billy Graham bought the rights to *Halley's Pocket Bible Handbook.* The original *Halley's,* up until the 22nd edition (1959), warned about the Jesuits. There are chapters about the Roman Papacy and the Jesuits. According to Mrs. Halley, Mr. Halley spent years working on those chapters and never would have permitted the book to be changed. However, when he died, Billy Graham bought the rights, and **removed all the research and warning about the Jesuits** in the editions Billy Graham printed."[448]

NOTHING BUT "RUMORS"

As news of Graham's coziness with Catholicism started to surface, people would write to the Graham headquarters and ask if what they were hearing was true.

> "In **1964,** Graham's aide, George Edstrom, wrote: 'Mr. Graham has never preached in a Catholic Church, and he does not agree with them in the joining of one church. If you heard this, it is nothing but false rumors.' Yet, as early as **1963,** one year **prior** to the above statement, Graham had spoken at the Roman Catholic Belmont Abbey in North Carolina."[449]

By **1966,** William Manseau, a Catholic priest "noted approvingly that a Catholic publication in England recently suggested that some day the Catholic Church may canonize the Baptist evangelist, making him 'St. Billy....'"[450]

In **1967** Graham was given an honorary degree from Belmont Abbey, a Catholic school. He said that he

> "'knew of no greater honor a North Carolina preacher, reared just a few miles from here, could have than to be presented with this degree. I'm not sure but what this could start me being called "Father Graham,"' he facetiously added....
>
> "'The gospel that built this school and the gospel that brings me here tonight is still the way to salvation.'"[451]

David Cloud responds:

> "This is simply amazing. Does Billy Graham really believe that the sacramental gospel that built Belmont Abbey is the way of salvation? If so, why does Graham preach that salvation is entirely of grace? If so, why does he remain a Baptist rather than joining the Catholic church? On the other hand, if Graham does not believe Rome's gospel is true, why did he say what he did? Why does he fellowship with Rome? The evangelist tries to have it both ways, but it is impossible. This is why Graham has been called 'Mr. Facing Both Ways!'"[452]

"The United States Congress of Evangelism was held in Minneapolis, Sept. 8-13, **1969.** Billy Graham was the sponsor and included Roman Catholics in the program. A priest, John J. Okeefe, led the Thursday morning devotions...."[453]

> "On April 21, **1972,** Billy Graham was awarded the International Franciscan Award by the Catholic Franciscan friars for 'his contribution to **true ecumenism'** and 'his sincere and authentic evangelism....' In acknowledging the award, Graham said: 'While I am not worthy to touch the shoe laces of St. Francis (a Roman Catholic saint who believed in salvation by works), yet this same Christ that called Francis in the 13th century also called me to be one of His servants in the 20th century....'"[454]

No wonder Graham could say (as reported in *U. S. News & World Report)*:

> "'World travel and getting to know clergy of all denominations has helped mold me into an **ecumenical being.** We're separated by theology and, in some instances, culture and race, but **all of that means nothing to me any more.'** A phone call to Billy Graham's headquarters confirmed the accuracy of this amazing admission."[455]

GRAHAM PRAYS FOR THE DEAD

> "In Milwaukee on Oct. 21, 1973, Graham said, 'This past week I preached in a great Catholic Cathedral a funeral sermon for a close friend of mind who was a Catholic [publisher James Strohn Copley], and they had several bishops and archbishops to participate, and as I sat there going through the funeral Mass that was a very beautiful thing and certainly straight and clear in the gospel, I believe, there was a wonderful little priest that would tell me when to stand and when to kneel and what to do.'"[456]

While in Belfast, Ireland, Billy Graham even prayed for the dead. He writes in his autobiography about an explosion that took place when he was there:

> "We tried to bring some measure of comfort to the chaotic scene. Several of the people recognized me. I was not wearing clerical garb, of course, but they insisted on calling me 'Father,' begging me to **give the last rites to the dead** and the dying. It was not a time for theological distinctions: **I knelt by each one and prayed for them.** One woman said I was the first Protestant clergyman she had met. Many thanked us for coming."[457]

> "In Aug. **1988,** the Billy Graham Evangelistic Association co-sponsored A National Festival of Evangelism called Congress '88 in Chicago, Illinois. The congress was cosponsored by the Catholic Archdiocese of Chicago. **Joseph Cardinal Bernardin,** Catholic Archbishop of Chicago, was a plenary speaker."[458]

Bernardin, by the way, was a **Council on Foreign Relations** member[459] and a former chairman for the Templeton Prize in 1993.[460] He was on the Board of Directors of the **disarmament** group called the Arms Control Association[461] as well as sponsoring the Anti-Ballistic Missile Treaty which is also for reducing nuclear arms.[462] He was the founder of The Catholic Common Ground Initiative.[463]

Bernardin was also a plenary **speaker at the Parliament of the World's Religions in 1993**[464] where

> "[m]ore than 500 seminars were held, with such titles as 'The Role of the High Priestess in the Temple of Isis,' 'Euthanasia,' 'Human Abduction by UFOs—Its Significance for the Future,' 'Humanism—The Modern Alternative to Traditional Religion,' 'The Return of the Goddess,' 'AIDS as Social Symbol,' 'Christian Reflections on the Bhagavad Gita,' and 'Spiritometry—the Scientific Step Towards God.' There was a variety of 'interfaith celebrations, meditations and contemplative vigils,' coupled with 'sacred art, music, dance, poetry and theatre.' There were 'Neo-Pagan' concerts, Theravada Buddhist group chantings and other exotic entertainment. Ta'i Ch'i and Hindu meditations were held before breakfast each morning; and in every nook and cranny of the hotel during that week, characters could be found posing in meditational *asanas* from every tradition imaginable!"[465] [Emphasis in the original.]

No wonder **Bernardin** labelled parts of the New Testament as "problematic" and

> **"called on Christianity to** confront its anti-Semitic past and **consider reinterpreting parts of the Bible.**
>
> "Bernardin, in an hour long speech at Hebrew University, said the Gospel according to John is 'generally considered among the most problematic of all the New Testament books in its outlook toward Jews and Judaism.' Bernardin, in his speech, cited John 8:44, in which John 'placed on the lips of Jesus' the belief that Jews are the children of the devil. 'Christians today must come to see that such teachings, while an acknowledged part of their biblical heritage, can no longer be regarded as definitive teaching,' Bernardin said."[466]

When Bernardin was suffering with cancer, he blasphemously said: "I offer up my sufferings for the **redemption** of mankind."[467] This is the man Graham had as a speaker in 1988!

ONE MERGED CHURCH

By **1992,** "*The Oregonian,* the largest newspaper in the state of Oregon...quoted Billy **Graham** at a news conference in Portland as **calling for 'a One Merged church.'"**[468]

However, anyone like Billy Graham and a host of others who think that Protestants and Catholics can join together in evangelism, needs to stop and think again. Bernardin believes that Catholics must reject "any approach that would ignore the 'living magisterium of the church exercised by the bishops and the chair of Peter'"[469] In other words, the Catholic Church and the Pope must be recognized as superior to all others.

For instance, Keith Fournier, a so-called "evangelical Catholic" who dedicated his book to Chuck Colson,[470] solemnly reminds us:

> "As a Catholic Christian, I believe the Eucharist is the sacrament of unity. And because the church is divided, **I embrace my church's position** that **I cannot participate in the Eucharist with Christians of other traditions.** We are **not** one. We must long to be one, and it should grieve our hearts that we cannot go to a common table. Our hunger for unity should lead us to impassioned prayer and aggressive relationship building. But we cannot pretend there aren't differences in our understandings of the Eucharist, or the Lord's Supper. There are differences, and they are real and important."[471]

One person asked this question: "Occasionally I visit Protestant churches, usually with Protestant friends who invite me. Is it okay for me to receive communion at those churches?" The answer was:

> "No, it is not permissible. **No Protestant church** has valid priestly orders, and that means no Protestant church **has a valid Eucharist.** If you were to receive communion at a Protestant church, you would be indicating that you think that church has the Real Presence, which it does not. At the Protestant church the bread and wine remain just bread and wine. They do not become the body and blood of Christ. **Therefore, to treat Protestant communion as if it were Catholic Communion would be an act of idolatry."**[472]

Pius XI said: "The Apostolic See has never allowed Catholics to attend meetings of non-Catholics; the **union of Christians can only go forward by** encouraging the dissidents to **return to the one true church."**[473]

Do you realize what you've just read? Yes, Rome wants us all to be one—but it must be on **HER CONDITIONS!**

> "This sacred Council urges the faithful to abstain from any frivolous or imprudent zeal, for these can cause harm to true progress toward unity. Their **ecumenical activity cannot be other than fully and sincerely Catholic,** that is, loyal to the truth we have received from the Apostles and the Fathers, and **in harmony with the faith which the Catholic Church has always professed."**[474]

In 1864 the Catholic Church said:

"Of course, nothing is more important for a Catholic than that schisms and dissensions among Christians be radically abolished and that all Christians be united....But **under NO circumstances** can it be tolerated that faithful Christians and ecclesiastics be under the leadership of heretics [which is anyone outside of the Catholic faith]...."[475]

INVITE THEM TO BECOME CATHOLICS

About 100 years later, Pope Paul VI, referring to the **ecumenical movement,** wrote:

"The **restoration of unity among all Christians** is one of the principal concerns of the Second Vatican Council. Christ the Lord founded one Church and one Church only....For it is only **through Christ's Catholic Church,** which is 'the all-embracing means of salvation,' that they can benefit fully from the means of salvation....

"When such actions are undertaken prudently and patiently by the Catholic faithful, with the attentive guidance of their bishops, they promote justice and truth, concord and collaboration, as well as the spirit of brotherly love and unity. This is the way that, when the **obstacles to perfect ecclesiastical communion have been gradually overcome, all Christians will at last,** in a common celebration of the Eucharist, **be gathered into the one and only Church in that unity which Christ bestowed on His Church from the beginning.** We believe that this **unity subsists in the Catholic Church as something she can never lose,** and we hope that it will continue to increase until the end of time....

"Now that **we have briefly set out the conditions for ecumenical action** and the principles by which it is to be directed, we look with confidence to the future. This Sacred Council exhorts the faithful to refrain from superficiality and imprudent zeal, which can hinder the real progress toward unity. Their **ecumenical action must be fully and sincerely Catholic,** that is to say, faithful to the truth which we have received from the apostles and Fathers of the Church, in harmony with the faith which the Catholic Church has always professed, and at the same time directed toward that fullness to which Our Lord wills His Body to grow in the course of time."[476]

In the *Catholic Twin Circle* of September 29, 1985 we find:

"Jesus **Christ established one Church** solely during the time of His earthly sojourn. **That Church is the Roman Catholic**

Church, which is His Mystical Body. The only Church in existence today, and for all time, is the Roman Catholic Church. Other churches are allied to that by way of extension or some kind of partial participation in the one Church established by Jesus, the one which has the successor of Peter, the Pope, as its visible head....**The ultimate goal of ecumenism is the reunion of separated Christians around the Chair of Peter;** thus, enjoying the fullness of the truth and grace which Jesus Christ conferred exclusively on His Mystical Body, the Roman Catholic Church...."[477]

At "Indianapolis '90" Tom Forrest, a Catholic, held a training session. He said:

> **"Evangelization for us Catholics,** evangelization into the Catholic church **means leading someone into the** local church, leading someone to become a member, active, practicing member, of a **Catholic parish,** a parish where they can be pastored into deep, spiritual ongoing communal growth....
>
> "'No, **you don't just invite someone to become a Christian. You invite them to become Catholics.** You invite them to come with you as a new parishioner of your Catholic church.'"[478]

SEPARATED BRETHREN

As recently as September 5, 2000 a Catholic document entitled *Dominus Iesus* was issued by Joseph Cardinal Ratzinger and confirmed and ratified by Pope John Paul II.[479] This statement, carrying the full authority of an official Vatican decree, "declares the Roman Catholic Church to be the **only** 'instrument for the **salvation of all humanity.'"**[480] Karl Keating, a very prominent Catholic,[481] assures us that

> "there is **no new teaching in it.** It was **issued as a reminder** of the Church's constant teaching. The most controversial part concerns the fact that **non-Catholic churches are 'defective'** in one or more ways. The Protestant churches, for example, do not have five of the seven sacraments, while the Eastern Orthodox churches, while having all seven sacraments, do not acknowledge the role of the papacy. These rightly are called 'defects' because they are things 'left out.' They are omissions from the original deposit of faith. True **ecumenism** demands that we view ourselves and others clearly, without blinders. This means we need to keep in mind that, while **other Christian**

bodies adhere to many truths, **each of them is missing something.**"[482]

In order to reach out to the "separated brethren" (those outside the Catholic Church), some priests are now "being instructed to become familiar in the use of 'evangelical' terminology like 'getting saved' or being 'born again.'"[483]

You see, the Pope is not about ready to relinquish his position. As Paul IV reveals: "[T]he pope is doubtless the most serious obstacle on the path of ecumenism."[484] As Catholic writer, Paolo Ricca, mentions:

> "The unique paradox of the papacy is that on the one hand it is 'principle and foundation' of Catholic unity and would like to be so for Christian unity. **Union with the bishop of Rome is an 'essential requisite' for Catholic unity** and, according to the encyclical, should also be the essential condition for ecumenical unity....The structure which is the basis of Catholic unity—the papacy—and which should serve Christian unity is the very thing that in fact prevents that unity."[485]

Some of the titles applied to the Pope are: His Holiness, Holy Father, Vicar of Christ, Sovereign, Keeper of the Keys, Head of the Church, Prince of the Apostles, Head of the Bishops, Supreme Pastor, Universal Ruler of the Truth, Infallible Ruler, Father of all Christians, Supreme Teacher of the Universal Church, Father of Princes and Kings, Ruler of the Round Earth, Viceroy of Jesus Christ,[486] Bishop of Rome, Supreme Pontiff of the Universal Church, Sovereign of the Vatican City State, and Rector of the World upon Earth.[487]

After the Pope is elected, he is crowned with a triple tiara. According to the *Catholic Dictionary* the

> "first circlet symbolizes the Pope's universal episcopate, the second his supremacy of jurisdiction, and the third his temporal supremacy. It is placed on his head at his coronation by the second cardinal deacon, with the words, 'Receive the tiara adorned with three crowns and know that thou art Father of princes and kings, **Ruler of the world, Vicar of our Saviour Jesus Christ!**'"[488]

> "The **triple crown** the Pope wears **symbolizes his authority in heaven, on earth, and in the underworld**—as king of heaven, king of earth, and king of hell—in that through his absolutions [pardons] souls are admitted to heaven, on the earth he attempts to exercise political as well as spiritual power, and through his special jurisdiction over the souls in purgatory and

> his exercise of 'the power of the keys' he can release whatever souls he pleases from further suffering and those whom he refuses to release are continued in their suffering, the decisions he makes on earth being ratified in heaven...."[489]

Also, on the fish-shaped hat which the Pope wears are the words in Latin "Vicarirs Feleii Dei" which means **"substitute for the Son of God"!**[490]

In spite of all this supposed papal supremacy, would you believe that the Pope must confess his sins to another priest?! Here is the "infallible" person who has dominion over heaven, earth, and hell, yet he needs to go to someone **under him** to confess his sins! Clement VIII's confessor was Cesare Baronius;[491] Pius XII confessed to a Jesuit, Augustin Bea,[492] and John XXIII confessed to Monsignor Alfredo Cavagna.[493] The "personal preacher" to Pope John Paul II and to the papal household is Raneiro Cantalamessa.[494] According to the July-August 2001 issue of the Catholic magazine, *Be,* we find: "The **popes** of the last one hundred years, it has been reported, commonly **went to confession at least weekly;** some of them went daily. They **confessed to regular priests** assigned to the papal household."[495]

The Bible, however, tells us that "there is one God, and **one mediator between God and men,** the man **Christ Jesus"** (I Timothy 2:5). Romans 14:11 says: "As I live, saith the Lord, every knee shall bow to Me, and **every tongue shall confess to God."** (See also Isaiah 45:23.) Philippians 2:10-11 states: "That **at the name of Jesus** every knee should bow, of things in heaven, and things in earth, and things under the earth; And that every tongue should confess that Jesus Christ is Lord, to the glory of God the Father."

GORDON-CONWELL THEOLOGICAL SEMINARY

Let's move on to another topic. Billy Graham is chairman of the Board of Trustees at the Gordon-Conwell Theological Seminary (G-C).[496] Jerry Huffman says: "Liberals and radicals are featured as speakers"[497] at this seminary. One of these speakers was James Forbes of **Union Theological Seminary**[498] (which was covered earlier). Another trustee just happens to be Mrs. Mary French Rockefeller.[499] Her husband, billionaire Laurance Spelman Rockefeller, has been a big promoter of New Age causes and a funder of UFO research and alien abduction.[500] He also gives an **annual** grant of $100,000 to New Ager Maurice Strong's Manitou Foundation[501] as well as funding ecological groups[502] such as the Green Earth Foundation which is headed by Terence McKenna.

> "McKenna scouts the globe collecting psychoactive plants [such as LSD], which he is permitted to cultivate in Hawaii. One of McKenna's theories is that psychoactive substances used by native cultures in religious ceremonies induce telepathic links with alien cultures. He believes the patriarchal 'dominator' cultures of the past few thousand years have failed us and the earth, and calls for an 'archaic revival,' which requires a return to humanity's last 'sane' moment 15,000 years ago on the plains of Africa 'rocked in the cradle of the great horned mushroom goddess.'"[503]

Yet another group which is a recipient of Laurance's money is the Human Potential Foundation (HPF).

> "According to Dick Farley, who worked for the organisation for about three years, Rockefeller's interest in HPF seemed to be the promotion of 'alternative religious and psychiatric/psychological paradigms, including so-called "UFOs" and "abductions," having "Global Mind Change" potentials. Rockefeller put more than $700,000 through the "HPF" from 1991 to 1994, as *Common Cause Magazine* recently reported.'"[504]

HPF had conferences with people like occultist Ruth Montgomery[505] (who died on June 10, 2001[506]).

> "Laurance Rockefeller owned the very inn, Woodstock in Vermont, where the Bilderbergers had one of their meetings. Also, a famous resort in Williamsburg, Virginia, owned by the Rockefeller family was yet another site of a Bilderberger conference."[507]

Lindisfarne Institute, founded by William Irwin Thompson in 1973,[508] is another recipient of Rockefeller's funding.[509] This place "features such distinguished faculty members as Luciferian guru David Spangler."[510]

> "The *Encyclopedia of Occultism and Parapsychology* indicates that Thompson developed his concept of a new 'planetary culture' involving a synthesis of science, art, and spiritual awareness...after visiting Findhorn community in Scotland. According to the encyclopedia, he *'regarded Lindisfarne as typifying a historic clash between esoteric Christianity and ecclesiastical Christianity, between religious experience and religious authority.'*"[511] [Emphasis in the original.]

In Chapter 1 it was mentioned that a blasphemous/homosexual play called "Angels in America: A Gay Fantasia on National Themes" was held at **St. John the Divine Cathedral** about 1994. This play was funded in part by Mr. and Mrs. Laurance Rockefeller![512] Laurance has also given a grant to the occultist Matthew Fox so he could write his heretical book, *The Coming of the Cosmic Christ,*[513] which "proclaims that Jesus is a god of the past and that man must worship other gods in the new era of Aquarius."[514] He also funded another occult book by Barbara Marx Hubbard[515] and the New Age magazine *Creation.*[516]

YWCA

Additionally, Laurance and Mary French Rockefeller were dedicated supporters of the Young Women's Christian Association (YWCA).[517] Although the word "Christian" is in YWCA's and YMCA's names, they are **NOT** Christian groups. One researcher states that

> "the YWCA has been actively pressing for sex education since 1900. Since then, and with the gradual influx of secularism into its ranks and those of the YMCA, the two 'Y's' have become just two more cogs in the socialist-Humanist wheel.
>
> "For example, veteran Communist-fronter Kirtley F. Mather labored in the highest echelons of the 'Y,' from 1948 through 1960, holding such positions as president of the YMCA's National Council, executive committee member of the World Alliance of YMCA's, and Alliance representative at the United Nations. (Mather is also affiliated with the American Civil Liberties Union, having been an official of the Civil Liberties Union of Massachusetts.) Another exemplar of secularism in the ranks of the 'Y' is Louis Gomberg, who serves on the board of managers of the Golden Gate Branch of the YMCA in San Francisco. Gomberg is also a member of the board of directors and a former president of the American Humanist Association of San Francisco."[518]

Dr. Calderwood, a YMCA executive "was the primary author of the X-rated Unitarian-Universalist Association sex education series, *About Your Sexuality,* which is currently being used in training programs for some 'Y' leaders."[519] Oh, Laurance Rockefeller was also a former president of the YWCA and was also on the Board of Trustees[520] as well as Mary being a former vice president of the YWCA.[521]

> "Radical endeavors of the formerly traditionalist YWCA include forming coalitions for the purpose of public demonstrations with such controversial groups as the National Organization for Women (women's lib), the Black Panther Women, the Attica Brigade, World Federalists U.S.A., the Women's International League for Peace and Freedom, the American Civil Liberties Union, and various lesbian organizations.

"Local YWCA programs are not without their share of internationalist orientation. Members are escorted on prearranged trips to the United Nations or urged to join and participate in the activities of the 'Y's' World Fellowship Committee. The 'Y' is further linked to the UN though Mrs. Richard Persinger, a member of both the YWCA National Board and the United Nations Association of the U.S.A. Both the World Young Women's Christian Association and the World Alliance of Young Men's Christian Associations are allied with the United Nations as 'Non-Governmental Organizations with Consultative Status.'

"And finally...the **YWCA** has further demonstrated its close alliance with the forces of secularism by its consistent **support** of such Humanist causes as **the movement to legalize abortion."**[522]

Laurance Rockefeller is on the Board of Advisors for the John Templeton Foundation[523] and Mrs. Rockefeller was on John Templeton's Humility Theology Information Center's Advisory Board.[524] I guess it's not surprising, then, to find that one of Gordon-Conwell's faculty members, Dr. John Jefferson Davis, was honored with the 1996 Templeton Foundation's Humility in Theology prize for a paper he wrote.[525] Another G-C faculty member, Dr. Kurt Richardson, received the Templeton Foundation Exemplary Article Award in 1995.[526]

Incidentally, one of G-C's graduates, Rev. John B. Loudon, "is serving as Imperial Chaplain of the **Shriners Fraternity** for 1996-97, and in that capacity he sits on the board of the Shrine Hospitals for Children."[527] This item of interest appeared in G-C's own paper, *Hilltop.* (Remember, to become a Shriner, one must first be a 32° Mason!)

At least two Professors (Richard Lovelace and Stephen Mott) as well as former President Cooley have signed "An Evangelical Declaration on the Care of Creation."[528]

Lovelace also signed the Chicago Call (which was a radical conference which took place in 1977[529]) and Mott signed an anti-nuclear declaration which called for the United States to disarm unilaterally.[530] Needless to say, many modernists, radicals, revolutionaries and Marxist sympathizers also signed this statement.[531]

ROCKFELLER AND GRAHAM

The Gordon-Conwell Theological Seminary further honored Mrs. Rockefeller by establishing the Mary French Rockefeller

Endowed Chair in New Testament Studies![532] One newsletter from Gordon-Conwell shows a picture of **Mrs. Rockefeller along with** George Bennett, former G-C President Robert E. Cooley, and yes, **Billy Graham.**[533] Cooley "has also served as senior editor of *Christianity Today,*"[534] which is Graham's magazine.

Although G-C is supposed to be a Protestant seminary, many of their recent graduates have become Catholics "and helped lead nearly 150 of their fellow Protestant pastors into the [Catholic] Church."[535] One Catholic paper proudly mentioned that before Billy Graham bought Gordon-Conwell it was a "Carmelite boys' school with the purpose of producing vocations for the [Catholic] Church."[536] Is there a connection here?

By the way, the **Billy Graham Evangelistic Association (BGEA) has given $4 million to Gordon-Conwell in just 5 years!**[537] Is this where **YOU** want **YOUR** money to go when you support Billy Graham's organization?! Says Graham: "I am convinced this school is being used by God to help fulfill the Great Commission."[538]

Other funding for Gordon-Conwell has come from Lilly Endowment, Inc.[539] (almost half a million dollars) and Pew Charitable Trusts with a $2.27 million grant.[540]

WHEATON COLLEGE

While we are discussing seminaries, perhaps it would be good to look at Wheaton College where Graham attended.[541] According to Graham's autobiography he said that the President of Wheaton College approached him about a site for Graham's archives and, says Graham, not "only did they promise a site, but Wheaton College agreed to raise the necessary funds."[542] Graham said the BGEA board gave its approval. He continues:

> "In time, plans were expanded to include within the same building not only the archives but a library and museum devoted to evangelism, seminar facilities, and space for the Wheaton College Graduate School....
>
> "While construction was still under way, Wheaton determined that it was unable to raise sufficient funds for the project and could not carry through on its commitment to us after all. This presented us with a dilemma, partly because several members of the BGEA board were also members of the Wheaton College board. We found ourselves pulled in two directions, therefore, but in the end the BGEA board agreed to make it a joint effort, with most of the resources for construction

and maintenance raised by us. The building is owned by Wheaton College, and a BGEA liaison committee consults with the center as it develops programs in the history and theology of evangelism and evangelistic strategy....

"Groundbreaking for the project took place in **1977....**"[543]

"SLUSH FUND"

The President of Wheaton College then launched "a major fund-raising drive to pay for the Graham Center."[544] There's a strange twist to this story, however. We are told that Wheaton was going to raise the funds but, according to Graham, they was unable to do so, so Graham's ministry agreed to help out. Graham, nonetheless, had already given more than $1 million to Wheaton for this Billy Graham Center between the years 1971 and 1975, yet the groundbreaking never took place until 1977![545] But, in **1977,** a *Chicago Tribune* headline read: "$23 MILLION GRAHAM FUND DISCLOSED."[546] The article stated:

"An arm of Billy Graham's ministry has amassed almost $23 million over the past **seven years** in land, stocks, bonds and cash holdings, in a **fund that has been shielded from public view,** the *Charlotte Observer* reported in its Sunday edition....

"It [the fund] **was not included** in the list of Graham organizations compiled by the *Observer* last Fall that a Graham associate told the newspaper **was complete.**

"Mr. Graham told the *Observer* that 80% to 90% of the Fund's receipts had come from the Billy Graham Evangelistic Association, the main arm of the Graham ministry."[547]

People were giving support to Graham thinking it was being used for radio and television time as well as ministry expenses to reach the lost. If they would have known that he was accumulating **large amounts of money to invest in land and stocks and to give away to other organizations,** do you think they would have continued to support him? So, he needed to "hide" this extra cash under another name which was called the World Evangelism and Christian Education Fund (WECEF) and located in Texas.[548]

"Though he used WECEF money, the *Observer* reported, [Jerry John] Crawford [the Dallas attorney] did not mention Graham or any of his organizations while making the purchase. Further, when owners of land next to the tract asked if Graham

> or any of his people owned the land, they had been told **no** as recently as the spring of 1977. That WECEF was a Graham organization was beyond question. Almost all of its funds had been funneled into it from BGEA. Nine of its eleven board members were also directors of BGEA; the other two were Ruth Graham and her brother, Clayton Bell."[549]

Additionally, the land that was purchased was at a highly inflated price "without so much as getting an appraisal or haggling over the premium,"—and was purchased from someone who had connections to several of Graham's relatives and close friends.[550]

> "Graham never told the contributors to the Billy Graham Evangelistic Association that he was going to start a special fund-raising drive to build a building on the campus of Wheaton College, nor did he tell those same contributors (two million on his mailing list) that he would divert money solicited for 'evangelism' to erect such a building to be named for himself."[551]

Further, when Graham's association was requested to make a full disclosure of his ministry's financial assets, this fund was not included.[552]

As already mentioned, groundbreaking for the Graham Center

> "took place in 1977; two years later, the cornerstone was laid. In September 1980, the five-story colonial-style building was completed.....
>
> "The **main speaker** at the dedication was Ambassador Charles Malik, a Lebanese Christian who had been **president of the United Nations General Assembly."**[553]

Graham calls Malik a Christian, but I found **Charles Malik's** name on the letterhead of the **Planetary Citizens**—a New Age, occultic, one-world order organization![554] Malik was also a representative for the **World Council of Churches.**[555] Not only was he the President of the United Nations General Assembly[556] but he was also Chairman of the United Nations Commission on Human Rights.[557]

Anyway, in 1979, after Graham's hidden money became public, he decided to start the Evangelical Council for Financial Accountability (ECFA).[558] "The organization's stated purpose is 'to enunciate, maintain and manifest a code of financial accountability and reporting which is consistent with enlightened and responsible Christian faith and practice.'"[559]

Billy Graham was also able to accumulate plenty of money for another building project. He "spent $50 million dollars in building the Cove, a Christian retreat in North Carolina."[560]

GRAHAM BOYS CAN'T MEET DAD'S GUIDELINES

Interestingly, **BOTH** of Graham's boys, Franklin and Ned, ran afoul of the ECFA guidelines in recent years and had to discontinue their membership in this group. Ned voluntarily withdrew in late 1999.[561] Franklin, who also overstepped his bounds, is now taking over "the administrative and management burden" of Graham's ministry and will replace him when he retires.[562]

I have heard several ads on the radio telling people to make sure that the organization they support belongs to ECFA. Of course, just because an organization belongs to ECFA doesn't give any real guarantee that the ministry can be trusted with your gifts and donations. About 100 or so ministries which belonged to ECFA were taken into a get-rich, Ponzi-type scam about 6 years ago by **New Era.**[563] Organizations were promised that their investment (of $500,000 or more) would be doubled in just 6 months. [564] Out of over 500 clients, almost 200 of them were from evangelicals groups[565]—and about half of them belonged to ECFA!

The ministries were "lured" into this scam because it was headed by John Bennett—a man promoted by Billy Graham and John Templeton![566]

> "In 1992 Billy Graham invited Bennett to speak at a Graham crusade in Philadelphia. *The Philadelphia Inquirer* (May 21, 1995) quoted John G. Templeton, Jr. as recalling how Bennett 'gave a testimony at Billy Graham's crusade that was very powerful, very uplifting.' According to Templeton, Bennett was 'very involved' in the Billy Graham crusade.
>
> "We see, then, a major reason why so many gullible Christian leaders fell victim to Bennett's flim-flam operation. They thought that if Billy Graham endorses this guy, he must be legit. The Graham factor looms as a key reason for the success of the scam."[567]

Jerry Huffman states:

> "When New Era filed for bankruptcy in May and the donors did not exist, it sent shock waves throughout much of the evangelical world. What caused Christian organizations to ignore caution was the 'impeccable reputation' of New Era's creator, John G. Bennett (8/95 *Charisma*). He was well-connected—**Laurance Rockefeller** was a supporter [this should have raised a red flag!—J.H.]. Despite Bennett's reputation as a man of

integrity...*[Christianity Today]* revealed that Bennett gave away, unsolicited, over $20 million to organizations that had not placed money with New Era such as Harvard University and **Planned Parenthood.**"[568]

The name "New Era" (meaning "New Age") should have also been a red flag to evangelicals--but it didn't seem to make a difference.

"MISS" KATHRYN KUHLMAN

Returning to Wheaton, we find that in 1987, the Billy Graham Center at Wheaton had a month-long exhibit titled "Ministry of Kathryn Kuhlman Exhibit."[569] Kuhlman, as many already know, was a famous so-called charismatic "healer."[570] Since Kuhlman was usually referred to as **"Miss** Kuhlman," many people did not realize that she was also an adulterer.[571] Burroughs Waltrip had left his wife and family in a deplorable situation and then divorced his wife to marry Kuhlman.[572] About six years later Kuhlman and Waltrip then divorced.[573]

Kuhlman was known for her "flamboyant lifestyle, her love for expensive clothes, precious jewels, luxury hotels and first-class travel"[574] yet "her employees worked at starvation wages."[575] She also outrightly lied about her age.[576] Additionally, she had an audience with Pope Paul VI on October 11, 1972 and promoted him until her death. Of her visit with the Pope she said: *"When I met Pope Paul there was a oneness. He had an interpreter there, but we needed no interpreter."*[577] [Emphasis in the original.] The "Pope told this adulterer: 'You're doing an admirable job. You not only have my blessing, you have my prayers.'"[578]

By the way, "Miss Kuhlmann (sic), the healer, died at Oral Roberts' medical center in Tulsa where even healer Oral Roberts was not even able to heal her."[579]

This is the person who was given a month-long exhibit at the Billy Graham Center.

Additionally, in the Billy Graham Museum at Wheaton College there are nine 20-foot tall banners "depicting various alleged fathers of evangelism. Museum literature says, 'each banner bears an individual witness selected from Christian history and was chosen on the merit of revelation of Christ as Lord and Savior.'"[580] Among these 9 banners are 2 Catholics fathers—Gregory VII (also known as Gregory the Great) and St. Francis of Assisi. "Gregory held to the standard Catholic heresies such as infant baptism, baptismal regeneration, prayers to Mary, veneration of relics, etc."[581]

It was Pope Gregory who proposed that, in addition to heaven and hell, there was "a *third* state—a place for the purification of souls before their entrance into heaven."[582] This idea of purgatory, however, did not become an actual dogma of the Catholic Church until the Council of Florence in 1439.[583]

Gregory was the one responsible for bringing the pagan/Druid/ Satanic holiday of Halloween into the church.[584] He also said that "the truth shines forth from the Catholic Church alone...."[585] I wonder if he'd be comfortable in this museum if he knew he was placed among several Protestants.

WE ARE THE MOTHER OF CHRIST

The other banner was of Francis of Assisi who

> "was the founder of the Franciscans, that Catholic order of monks who, together with the Dominicans, brutally persecuted Bible believers during the Dark Ages. The pope was Innocent III, the very father of the wretched and bloody Inquisition. While Innocent III sent out his henchmen to hunt out and torment the heretical Waldenses, Francis of Assisi was his loyal subject."[586]

Francis said: "We are the mother of Christ when we carry him in our heart and body by love and a pure and sincere conscience. And we give birth to him through our holy works which ought to shine on others by our example."[587] Obviously, this is not true. We certainly are not the mother of Christ and we can't give birth to Him—no matter how holy our works are.

Francis is famous for his "Canticle of the Sun"[588] which says in part:

> "**Praise to You,** my Lord, **through our Brother Sun,** through whom You give us light....
>
> "**Praise to You,** my Lord, **through Sister Moon** and all the stars, you formed them clear and precious and beautiful.
>
> "**Praise to You,** my Lord, **through Brother Wind,** and through the air, cloudy and serene, and every kind of weather.
>
> "**Praise to You,** my Lord, **through Brother Fire,** through whom You light the night and he is beautiful and playful and robust and strong.
>
> "**Praise to You,** my Lord, through Sister **Earth, our Mother,** who sustains and governs us, and who produces various fruits, colored flowers and herbs."[589]

If you notice carefully, the praise to "my Lord" is through the sun, moon, wind, etc. Also, by referring to the elements as our brothers and sisters, he is showing that he is a panentheist. Even Matthew Fox, a New Ager, recognizes this. He said: "With deep reverence for all of life, **a true panentheist,** Francis sought to rectify church corruption with a movement of friars who would espouse Lady Poverty. **He was strongly influenced by Celtic spirituality and no little bit by Sufism."**[590]

Panentheism, says Fox, "means that 'God is in all things and all things are in God.'"[591]

Because of Francis' connection with nature, Pope John Paul II named him the patron saint of ecology.[592] It is on St. Francis Day that thousands of people flock to St. John the Divine Cathedral for the "Blessing of the Beasts"[593] (mentioned in Chapter 6).

Also, occultist Robert Muller informs us that Francis has "been declared patron saint of the United Nations."[594]

Remember, Francis is the person Graham referred to when he received the Franciscan Award and said: "...I am not worthy to touch the shoe laces of St. Francis...."[595]

GRAHAM SELECTS AUTHORS AND BOOK SUBJECTS

Graham's influence even carries into an arena that most people would not suspect. Back in 1978 Graham was being paid $39,500 **per year** as a consultant to Word Books.[596] He would advise them of potential authors and would even choose the book subjects that should be published. Do you realize the amount of control and influence this type of activity would entail? If Graham didn't relish a certain topic, he could advise against books being printed on this subject. If he liked a particular author, that individual could be catapulted to fame. In such a position, Graham could literally control, to a large extent, the books and authors people would read (at least from Word)—and he could do so at quite a generous fee!

BIBLE VERSIONS

Graham has a tendency to promote one new Bible version after another—and he has been doing this for the past **49 years.** He

> "popularized the liberal *Revised Standard Version [RSV]* which was produced by the apostate National Council of Churches of America. He advertised it in his crusades and recommended it highly....Many of those who worked on this

> version denied Christ's virgin birth, deity, and bodily resurrection, as well as most of the Bible's miracles."[597]

(For more info on the *RSV* and the beliefs of those who were on this committee, as well as their Communistic affiliations, refer back to Chapter 5.)

J. B. Phillips was author of *The New Testament in Modern English.* In his autobiography he said that Graham spoke highly of his work as early as 1952.[598]

David Cloud reveals: "J. B. Phillips was a heretic, and his translation was a wretched perversion of God's Word. I have many of Phillips' books in my library, and they are filled with heresy."

Let's look at what heresy is before continuing with Phillips. One writer explains:

> "Apostasy is a rejection of truth. **Heresy is a perversion of truth.** Of the two, heresy is in many ways the more dangerous...because it is harder to detect. By its very nature, heresy is closer to the truth than apostasy. The closer to the genuine the counterfeit becomes, the more insidious it becomes. No genuine believer would be tempted to embrace apostasy, but many have succumbed to the threat of heresy. For this very reason God clearly commands us to reject the unrepentant heretic."[599]

Now, continuing with Phillips, Cloud states:

> "J. B. Phillips was a universalist, believing that all men are children of God....
>
> "J. B. Phillips denied that Hell is a place of eternal torment. [He said:] 'Jesus surely used it **symbolically** to mean, not a place of torture, but the place for useless rubbish. The real danger is, not that we might be tortured for endless ages, but that we might be found to be useless and only fit, so to speak, for the celestial rubbish dump.'...
>
> "J. B. Phillips believed that demons are merely the 'storm center of the personality.'...
>
> "J. B. Phillips denied the Blood Atonement, claiming that Jesus could have accomplished the same work had he died in a gas chamber or an electric chair....
>
> "J. B. Phillips did not believe the Bible is faultless and he denied verbal inspiration. 'I should like to make it quite clear that I could not possibly hold the extreme "fundamentalist" position of so-called "verbal inspiration."'

"J. B. Phillips did not believe that Satan is a real creature. 'If our critics mean that we believe in the permanent existence of Satan, the Devil or the powers of evil, they are wrong, for we do not.'

"J. B. Phillips called the ascension of Christ a PARABLE...."[600] [Caps in the original.]

"READS LIKE A NOVEL"

Graham promoted *The Living Bible* which is only a paraphrase and not a literal translation.[601] One researcher explains:

"Graham almost single-handedly rescued the *Living Bible* from oblivion. 'The *Living Bible* might be called "The Billy Graham Bible," for it was he who made it the success that it is. According to *Time* magazine, July 24, 1972, Billy Graham ordered 50,000 copies of the Epistles, and a short time later ordered some 450,000 more, and still later ordered 600,000 special paperback versions for his autumn television crusade in 1972. From that time on, orders began to pour in.'

"That was only the beginning of Graham's love affair with the *Living Bible.* At Amsterdam '86, Graham allowed Living Bibles International to distribute free copies of the *Living Bible* in 40 differed (sic) languages to the 8,000 evangelists in attendance....

"Graham distributed 10,000 copies of the *Living Bible* to people who attended his Mission England Crusade....In 1987, Graham appeared in television ads for *The Book,* a condensed version of the *Living Bible.* He said it 'reads like a novel.'"[602]

Would you like a sample of a few of the verses in this "Bible"?

✣ "Saul boiled with rage. You son of a b——! he yelled at him. Do you think I don't know that you want this son of a nobody to be king in your place, shaming yourself and your mother?" (I Samuel 20:30).

✣ "You illegitimate bast-rd, you! they shouted. Are you trying to teach us? And they threw him out" (John 9:34). This is a reference to our Lord and Saviour, Jesus Christ.

✣ "About noontime, Elijah began mocking them. You'll have to shout louder than that, he scoffed, to catch the attention of your god! Perhaps he is talking to someone, or is out sitting on the toilet, or maybe he is away on a trip, or is asleep and needs to be wakened!" (I Kings 18:27).

✣ "God even protects him from accidents" (Psalm 34:20). This is so different from the *King James Version* which reads: "He keepeth all His bones: not one of them is broken." This verse is a Messianic prophecy which was fulfilled at Christ's crucifixion and it is quoted in John 19:36. Kenneth Taylor's rendering of this verse destroys the prophecy.

Another prophecy Taylor tampers with is in Zechariah 13:6: "And one shall say unto Him, what are these wounds in Thine hands? Then He shall answer, those with which I was wounded in the house of My friends." Taylor changes this verse to: "And if someone asks then, what are these scars on your chest and your back, you will say, I got into a brawl at the home of a friend." He then adds a footnote saying that this is not referring to Christ.

✣ Revelation 13:18 reads in the *KJV:* "Here is wisdom. Let him that hath understanding count the number of the beast: for it is the number of man; and his number is Six hundred threescore and six **[666].**" The *Living Bible* adds a footnote to this which says: "Some manuscripts read **616.**"[603]

Perry F. Rockwood notes:

> "Over and over again *THE LIVING BIBLE* changes the word 'Lord' to 'sir' or 'master' weakening the Lordship of Christ: Matthew 8:2, 8, 21; 14:28; 15:25; 16:22 (a small s); 17:4; 18:21; 20:30; 25:11, 22, 24 and 37.
>
> "'Lord' is omitted entirely in Matthew 8:6; 13:51; 15:27; 20:31; 25:20; 26:22; 28:6 and many other passages."[604]

Yet Graham claims that *The Living Bible*

> "speaks the language of the hour....I read with renewed interest the age-abiding truths of the Scriptures, as though they had come to me direct from the Lord....I believe that these paraphrased epistles communicate the message of Christ to our generation."[605]
>
> "'*The Living Bible:* Widely praised for its easy readability by all ages. **[It is] accurate and fluent.** One of the largest selling editions of the Bible ever published, this paraphrase communicates the Lord's message to our generation,' says Billy Graham."[606]

When the *New Living Translation* came out, Graham said: "'*The Living Bible* has been used by God around the world for many years to introduce people to the Scriptures. Now I am pleased to recommend the *New Living Translation* for even greater readability and accuracy.'"[607]

BAD NEWS FOR MODERN MAN

Graham was there to promote *Good News for Modern Man.* This "Bible," too, destroys or corrupts most all of the "references to the deity of Christ and replaces the word 'blood' with 'death' in speaking of Christ's atonement."[608] This version eliminates the words "redeem," "redeemed," and "redemption" in 16 of the 20 passages where it occurs.[609]

"Graham praises the new unreliable paraphrase by Eugene Peterson, *The Message,...* and has distributed a special edition of it."[610] In a letter I received from Graham's organization in 1995, he wrote:

> "P.S. The Message is one of the most dynamic recent versions of the New Testament that I have seen—and I want to send it to you free! Children can easily understand it, and veteran Bible readers will see Christ's words in a fresh light.
>
> "Our special edition, which you can't get anywhere else, has many explanations that I've written to help you understand what the New Testament says. This would be a wonderful New Testament for you to read, or give to your family or a friend."[611] [Emphasis in the original.]

Rick Miesel writes:

> "*The Message* teaches a different gospel and a different morality than the Bible (as well as a worldly/warm fuzzy view of life). For example...in Romans 1:26-27, the words 'God gave them over...' are deleted in *The Message* and words that qualify homosexuality are added, thereby providing a loophole for committed homosexuals who 'love' each other. Thus, in *The Message,* lust becomes the sin, not the choice of a same-sex partner. There are hundreds of examples like these in *The Message.*"[612]

Why would Graham want to use and promote such perverted revisions of the Bible which belittle our precious Lord and Savior? Why would Graham favor a "Bible" that excuses immoral behavior? Could there be a hidden agenda?

WESTCOTT AND HORT

Most of today's Bible versions are based on the Greek text of Brook Foss Westcott and Fenton John Anthony Hort.[613] They mainly used the *Vaticanus* and *Sinaiticus* manuscripts which vary from the *Textus Receptus* (or the "Received Text") from which the *King James Version* comes.[614]

Since most modern versions are mainly based on the Westcott-Hort translation, it would be good to take a look at some of their beliefs. For instance:

❋ Westcott believed that the devil was only a power and not a personality.[615]

❋ "I suppose I am a communist by nature," said Westcott.[616]

❋ Westcott believed that men could be divine in some way.[617]

❋ Westcott believed in the Fatherhood of God.[618]

❋ Westcott questioned the pre-existence of Jesus Christ.[619]

❋ Westcott explained away some of Christ's miracles.[620]

❋ Hort stated: **"Evangelicals seem to me to be perverted** rather than untrue"[621] and "Westcott spoke of **Evangelical believers as dangerous and unsound."**[622] [Emphasis in the original.]

❋ Hort wrote: "I had no idea till the last few weeks of the importance of texts, having read so little Greek Testament, AND DRAGGED ON WITH THE **VILLAINOUS** [evil] TEXTUS RECEPTUS....THINK OF THAT **VILE TEXTUS RECEPTUS...."**[623] [Caps in the original.]

❋ Neither Westcott nor Hort believed in a literal resurrection of Jesus Christ.[624]

❋ Both men believed that Heaven was only a "state" rather than a "place."[625]

❋ Both denied the deity of Jesus Christ.[626]

❋ They held to a heretical view of the vicarious sacrifice of Christ.[627] Hort wrote the following to Westcott: "I entirely agree...with what you there say on the Atonement....The popular doctrine of **substitution, is an immoral** and material **counterfeit.** Certainly nothing can be more **unscriptural** than the modern limiting of **Christ's bearing our sins** and suffering to His death; but indeed that is only one aspect of an almost universal heresy."[628] Hort, in a letter to John Ellerton concerning the redemption through the blood of the Lamb, penned: LANGUAGE CANNOT ACCURATLEY (sic) DEFINE THE TWINGE OF SHRINKING HORROR WHICH MIXES WITH MY THOUGHTS WHEN I HEAR THE POPULAR NOTION ASSERTED."[629] [Emphasis in the original.]

❋ Both Westcott and Hort believed in evolution.[630] Hort wrote: "But the book which has most engaged me is Darwin. Whatever may be thought of it, it is a book that one is proud to be contemporary with. I must work out and examine the argument more in detail, but at present my feeling is strong that the theory is unanswerable."[631] Westcott remarked: "No one now, I suppose, holds that the first three chapters of Genesis, for example, give a literal history."[632]

❋ Both men belonged to **occult societies** such as the **Ghostly Guild**[633] (which "evolved into the infamous **Society for Psychical Research**"[634]), **Hermes Club** (which was founded by Westcott "which he named after the Graeco-Egyptian deity, Hermes Trismegistus"),[635] **Ghost Society,**[636] **Company of Apostles,**[637] and **Eranus**[638] (which was founded by Westcott, J. B. Lightfoot, and Hort).

BIBLE IS FLAWED

The modern versions which Graham endorses are mainly based on the translation from these 2 men! Of course, the list of Bibles that Graham has endorsed could go on, but we should be able to see that Graham doesn't really believe in the inerrancy of the Scriptures.[639] It's too bad that Graham's can't honestly quote II Corinthians 2:17: "For we are not as many, which corrupt the word of God: but as of sincerity, but as of God, in the sight of God speak we in Christ."

Interestingly, Benjamin Creme, speaking for Maitreya, who is supposed to be the "New Age Christ" (and who was covered in Chapter 5), was asked this question: "I wonder if, in this new age, our Christian Bible will be used or will there be something to replace it?" He replied:

> "Within the Christian churches, the Bible will continue to be used for some time. It is obvious, however, that the presence in the world of the Christ and the Masters—including the Master Jesus—will necessitate a **profound reinterpretation** of the meanings of that **symbolical work.** Much will be **discarded** but much will be found to be **relevant when correctly interpreted.** It will be the task of the Master Jesus to guide the Christian churches into the light of the new dispensation. Eventually, **Maitreya will inaugurate a new world religion** based on the esoteric science of initiation."[640]

Dr. Shirley Correll tells about an educational conference she attended nearly 30 years ago. She writes:

> "...it was discussed that the UN was to be a worldwide peacemaking agency. War was to be a thing of the past, and those things which had contributed to wars would be examined and abolished (the rhetoric sounds good, but an honest evaluation shows that since the inception of the UN there have been more wars in this period than at any time in the history of the world). We were told at this conference that religions had caused many wars, and that in order to avoid wars in the future, **<u>only one universal Bible was to be permitted</u>, which would avoid the differences leading to wars."**[641] [Emphasis in the original.]

One person writes:

> "It isn't important to Satan that everyone believes the same thing or belongs to the same religious institution. All that's necessary is that the **Gospel be diluted sufficiently so as to render it ineffective....**
>
> "This disregard for doctrine, and subsequent acceptance of every aberration that goes by the name of Christian, is necessary for the eventual unification of all religious thought. Therefore, opposition to deception in the Church is being stifled under the pretense that those who expose deceivers are sowing discord among brethren and hindering unity."[642] [Emphasis in the original.]

Remember: "Men do not reject the Bible because it contradicts itself, but because it contradicts them."[643]

Unfortunately, these new Bible versions are preparing the way for the coming "new world religion."

ACCEPTABLE LOSSES

There is so much more that could have been said about Billy Graham. I had intended on writing a small book about Graham but once I started, information pertaining to this subject seemed to come in almost daily. Knowing what information to insert and what not to was difficult. This book could probably be twice the present size if I had included everything, but I think that any person who has an open mind before God can easily see that there is a problem with Graham and his ministry—and there has been almost since the very beginning. Because he originally came under a conservative banner and preached about Jesus, many people accepted him. As Graham's message became more and more watered down, excuses were made for him. A number of people went to him personally and talked with him, but Graham rebuffed them. A few people wrote tracts and articles pointing out Graham's downward slide, but, for the most part, these warnings went unheeded. Even when some individuals were no longer enthralled with Graham's techniques, they would still point to the large number of "converts" going forward and feel that God was blessing his ministry. Anyone who would dare to talk about Graham would often be met with the admonition: "Touch not God's anointed."

We need to remember, however, that even if Graham were God's anointed, he is not above reproof and rebuke. Peter was one of God's anointed but when he withdrew himself and did not eat with the Gentiles (as he had done previously), Paul reprimanded him. He said:

"But when Peter was come to Antioch, I withstood him to the face, because he was to be blamed" (Galatians 2:11).

As far as the great number of "converts" in Graham's meeting, we now know that a large number of them are counselors and ushers who are going forward. Furthermore, about only a small number of those who go forward mark "acceptance of salvation" on their cards. About two-thirds mark "rededication" or "assurance of salvation." Also, when Graham tells people to come forward to renew their confirmation vows, these people are not going forward to receive Christ as their Lord and Saviour. We do thank God and rejoice for every person who has received Christ through Graham's crusades, but the number is far less than most people have ever imagined.

You may ask, "If Graham were not serving God why would he even give an altar call?" That is a good question—and it deserves an answer. First of all, most fundamentalists and evangelicals would never have accepted Graham's ministry as legitimate if he had not done so. At first, Graham was very dependent on fundamentalist support to get started, so he needed to do something that would gain and merit that support. Secondly, there is, in military terms, was is known as **"acceptable losses."** A former career air force officer explains this technique.[644] He said before going into war, it is decided how many men they can risk **losing** and still consider the war a success. They may decide that they can lose 30%—or even 50% or more—depending on the circumstances. Ideally, of course, no one's life would be lost, but that's not how war is won. Satan does the same thing. Obviously, Satan doesn't want to lose one person to the Lord Jesus Christ, but it would be worth losing some (by having them accept Christ and be born again), **IF** he could win a larger cause. What would even several **thousand** souls be to him **IF** he could push 6 **billion** people into the ecumenical movement and who would ultimately accept and worship the Antichrist? What would a few thousand souls be **IF** the majority of people were so compromised and spiritually lulled to sleep that they wouldn't even notice the danger involved in the ecumenical movement? Yes, these **"acceptable losses" are tolerated** so that the final goal of a one-world religion can be achieved.

I'm not saying that Billy Graham is doing Satan's bidding—at least not necessarily knowingly, but I am saying that Satan does come as an **angel of light,** therefore it would not be a surprise to see altar calls being given although there may be an ulterior motive. II Corinthians 11:13-15 states: "For such are **false apostles,** deceitful workers, **transforming themselves into the apostles of Christ.** And no marvel; for **Satan himself is transformed into an angel of light.**

Therefore it is no great thing if **his [Satan's] ministers also be transformed as the ministers of righteousness;** whose end shall be according to their works."

DID YOU NOTICE?

Before proceeding to the next chapter, let's briefly recapitulate a few items that have already been covered. (Each of these features has been previously footnoted, so I'm not including that information here.) For instance, did you notice that Graham:

— had his **1957 crusade** partially funded by Rockefeller?

— sent almost 400 converts to Peale's church? Remember Peale promoted occultic techniques, denied the fundamentals of the faith, and was a 33° Mason.

— praised Norman Vincent and Ruth Peale by saying: "I don't know anyone who has done more for the kingdom of God than Norman and Ruth Peale, or have meant any more in my life—the encouragement they have given me"?

— attends cocktail parties?

— has gone swimming in the nude (skinny-dipping)?

— can flip through *Playboy* without embarrassment?

— doesn't believe in literal fire in hell?

— had **known Communists** such as Martin Luther King, Jr. and Ralph Abernathy on his platform almost **40 years ago?**

— has had several Masons in leadership positions in the Billy Graham Evangelistic Association and has used many Masons in his meetings?

— **betrayed** the persecuted Russian Christians by giving their names to the Communistic KGB?

— has praised the DeMolays, the Masonic organization for boys?

— accepts abortion in the case of rape, incest, etc., because, "No one really knows when life begins"?

— praised the occultist Ruth Carter Stapleton and endorsed her book?

— insists that other faiths be represented and their leaders pray at Presidential inaugurations since the **1960s?**

— said that he wasn't worthy to loose Schuller's shoes? Remember, Schuller is a Mason and promotes occultic techniques as well as denying many fundamentals of the Christian faith. Graham also said that he wasn't worthy to loose St. Francis' shoes.

— received the **World Citizen Award** from the World Affairs Council which is an arm of the Council on Foreign Relations?

— had the heretic and occultist Bishop Pike lead in prayer in his **1960 crusade?**

— received the Templeton Prize for Progress in Religion?

— was awarded the International Franciscan Award by the Catholic Franciscan friars for "his contribution to true ecumenism"?

— endorses modern Bible versions that weaken the Lordship of Christ?

— has a star on the Hollywood Walk of Fame?

— had liberals and apostates who denied the fundamentals of the faith such as Gerald Kennedy, Ralph Sockman, Henry Van Dusen, etc., on his platform and crusade committees and referred to many of them as "godly men"?

— said that he respects "other paths to God"?

— uses rock musicians for his crusades (and has done so for many years)?

— expects to see Elvis Presley, John Kennedy, Jr., the Bessette sisters, Richard Nixon, etc., in heaven?

"For the preaching of the cross is to them that perish foolishness; but unto us which are saved it is the power of God" (I Corinthians 1:18).

"There is a way which seemeth right unto a man, but the end thereof are the ways of death" (Proverbs 14:12; 16:25).

"For the time will come when they **will not endure <u>sound</u> doctrine;** but after their own lusts shall they heap to themselves teachers, having itching ears; And they shall **turn away their ears from the truth,** and shall **be turned unto fables"** (II Timothy 4:3-4).

8. AMSTERDAM 2000

Amsterdam 2000 was a conference sponsored by the Billy Graham Evangelistic Association (BGEA), and was held from July 29 to August 6, 2000. The conference included 10,000 evangelists and church leaders from 209 nations and more than 900 plenary and teaching sessions were scheduled to be conducted by some of the world's top "Christian" leaders.[1] The cost for this conference was around $35 to $40 **million** dollars.[2]

Although Billy Graham himself was unable to attend due to being hospitalized, he did send greetings to those in attendance. I think it would be of interest to look at a few of the speakers selected to speak at this conference.

The first speaker we'll look at is John Stott.[3] Stott claims that he believes in hell but he doesn't believe in eternal punishment.[4] At a conference sponsored by the National Association of Evangelicals in the late 1980's, Stott "revealed that he was a **proponent of conditional immortality, or annihilationism,** a view that denies eternal punishment in hell for the unsaved."[5] In the January 8, 1996 issue of *Christianity Today,* a magazine founded by Billy Graham, is an interview with Stott. Stott refers to his book, *Evangelical Essentials,* and suggests that "'eternal punishment' may mean the ultimate **annihilation of the wicked** rather than their eternal conscious torment. I would prefer to call myself agnostic on this issue....In my view, the biblical teaching is not plain enough to warrant dogmatism. There are awkward texts on both sides of the debate."[6] Elsewhere he stated that "the language of destruction means to destroy but can be a metaphor when the Bible speaks of the Lake of Fire."

Stott is a strong supporter of the liberal, pro-Communist National Council of Churches.[7] No wonder he writes: "The fundamentalist is like a caged bird, unable to escape at all."[8]

He is also a contributing editor to the liberal, left-wing publication,[9] pro-abortion,[10] pro-homosexual,[11] and pro-feminist[12] magazine, *Sojourners.*[13] I guess this isn't really all that surprising since Stott has said: *"We must engage in a double listening, both to the voice of feminists and to the voice of God."*[14] [Emphasis in the original.]

Sojourners joined the Unitarian Universalist Association, the Jewish Reconstructionist Federation, the New Age *Utne Reader,* and *Tikkun* (among other groups) for "The Summit on Ethics and Meaning" on April 14-16, 1996. Among the speakers were New Agers such as Paul Hawken, Bernie Siegel, Ben Cohen, Marianne

Williamson, Larry Dossey, and Matthew Fox. Another speaker was Urvashi Vaid from the National Gay and Lesbian Task Force Policy Institute[15] as well as lesbian activist, Roberta Achtenberg.[16] Pro-Communists Pete Seeger, Jesse Jackson, Jr., and Tom Hayden were also speakers.[17] Michael Lerner, who "formerly described himself as a 'revolutionary Marxist,'"[18] was also there.

Of course, *Sojourners* "is famous for its vicious anti-America attacks and its complimentary phrases for Liberation Theology and Marxist Communism."[19]

Here are a few quotes from previous issues of *Sojourners:*

→ **"Marxist analysis needs to be the main guide."**[20] (*Sojourners,* October 1982, p.37-38)

→ **"Karl Marx proceeded logically with an agenda of history and destiny dependent upon humanitys'** (sic) **reality rather than its illusions."**[21] (*Sojourners,* November 1981, p.14)

→ **"As the practitioner and teacher of a subversive practice Jesus is a political messiah....Jesus would not hesitate to employ violence [today—Ed.] to bring it about."**[22] (*Sojourners,* February 1982, p.37-38)

One of the contributing editors for *Sojourners* (besides John Stott) is Richard Barnet,[23] a co-founder of the Institute for Policy Studies (IPS).[24] "The FBI has compiled some 2705 pages of information which document how IPS is a violent and subversive organization."[25] The "money to found the IPS came from Communist Party member Rubin and was administered by Rubin's daughter Cora [Weiss]...."[26]

"...Richard Barnet used his IPS status to *personally* assist and instruct Communist Nicaragua's dictator Daniel Ortega on how to establish a Marxist government in Nicaragua."[27] [Emphasis in the original.]

> "Richard J. Barnet, who is also a member of the World Government promoting group, Institute for World Order, has written about a 'very different kind of world order' which he would like to see. Barnet reveals, 'revolution is the only answer' to bring about this new 'world order'—which he hopes will be based on Red China, Cuba, and the old Soviet Union."[28]

(Incidentally, the Institute for World Order is now called World Policy Institute.[29])

With Barnet as a contributing editor, no wonder *Sojourners* "has been called 'a religious arm of the Institute for Policy Studies.'"[30]

Barnet is also a member of the Council on Foreign Relations (CFR).[31]

RELIGIOUS RIGHT IS AN ABERRATION

Other pro-Communists are also contributing editors to *Sojourners.*[32]

The March/April 1995 issue contained an ad for the one-world organization—the World Constitution and Parliament Association.[33] This same issue states: "The Religious Right in America is indeed an **aberration.**"[34] Other issues contain ads for the pro-homosexual, New Age organization, Kirkridge,[35] and they sell New Age books.[36] One of their publications refers to the "human weakness of the Bible."[37] Another one states: "Therefore, we ought to **re-think our doctrine of the Trinity,** which traditionally has been pictured as totally masculine. And there is biblical precedent for understanding the masculine and **feminine elements of the Trinity.**"[38]

This is the kind of magazine that "evangelical" and Billy Graham speaker, John Stott, writes for. Stott probably is at home with the pro-Communists since *Christian News* refers to Stott as a "socialist."[39] Stott has just written a foreword to a new book on Billy Graham as well.[40]

> "From April 14-18, 1977, John Stott was chairman of the Second National Evangelical-Anglican Congress in Nottingham, England. Addressing the 2,000 evangelicals in attendance, Stott said, 'The visible unity of all professing Christians should be our goal...and **evangelicals should join others in the Church of England in working toward full communion with the Roman Catholic Church.**'"[41]

Dennis Costella, however, cautions us: "Unity at the expense of purity is a concept diametrically opposed to the Bible-based position of Fundamentalist Christians."[42]

> "John Stott is also a vice-president of the **United Bible Societies.** This is significant, because this position brings him into close fellowship with other leaders of the United Bible Societies, some of whom are Roman Catholic leaders. The United Bible Societies are committed to working closely with the Roman Catholic church in its Bible translation projects, and 'it was reported that out of a total of 590 translation projects of the United Bible Societies, as many as 390 were of the interconfessional type' [meaning those translated in fellowship with Rome—Ed.]."[43]

We've already discussed the United Bible Societies (UBS) in a previous chapter. Remember that Billy Graham wrote that the Bibles supposedly being printed on the Amity Printing Press was "a **joint project of the China Christian Council and the United Bible Societies.**"[44]

"Second, as a vice-president of the UBS, Stott also plans and prays with **Dr. Francis Arinze,** who is not only a Roman Catholic archbishop (of Onitsha in Nigeria) but has also recently been made a Cardinal by the Pope."[45]

HEAVEN WITHOUT JESUS?

Many people seem to think that Cardinal Arinze will be the next Pope.[46] He is the President of the Pontifical Council for Inter-Religious Dialogue[47] as well as being

> "on the Congregations for the Doctrine of the Faith, the Causes of Saints, the Evangelization of Peoples, the Oriental Churches; the Pontifical Councils for Promoting Christian Unity, for the Laity, and for Culture; and the Pontifical Committee for International Eucharistic Congresses, the Cardinals' Committee for Jubilee 2000, the Postsynodal Council for the African Synod, and the Preparatory Council for the Lebanese Synod."[48]

In October 1998 the **Vatican** called for a **dialogue between the Christian and Hindu communities.** "Dialogue leader **Cardinal Francis Arinze** said while following separate spiritual paths, **both could work together** to offer hope to humanity. He said increased friendly ties between Christians and Hindus, especially in India, should facilitate a dialogue based on **mutual respect** for religious traditions...."[49]

Of course, the Hindus are not the only religious group that Arinze (and the Vatican) is trying to work with. On October 25, 1999, representatives

> "of more than 20 of the world's religions gathered at the Vatican...for four days of dialogue aimed at asserting the **values they hold in common** at the start of the new millennium....
>
> "Arinze said the Vatican called the interreligious assembly in the spirit of Pope John Paul II's 1986 meeting with religious leaders at Assisi, the hill town north of Rome where St. Francis was born, to mark the World Day of Prayer for Peace.
>
> "The 200 delegates who gathered at the Vatican included representatives of the Jewish, Muslim, Mandaean, Hindu, Buddhist, Zoroastrian, Sikh, Jain, Shinto, Confucian, Baha'i, Tenrikyo, Miochikai, Rissho Kosei-Kai and Ennokyo faiths and traditional religions of India, Africa and North America."[50]

I might add that the World Council of Churches also participated in this interfaith "prayer" meeting.[51]

Arinze is also involved with Thanksgiving Square.[52] This New Age, interfaith organization was covered briefly earlier. In January

1995, there was a four day meeting of the Thanksgiving World Advisors at Thanksgiving Square where **common ground** was being sought among Christianity, Judaism, Hinduism, Buddhism and Islam.[53] Of course, Arinze took part in this meeting as well as many others of like nature.

In one conversation with Arinze, Dr. Joseph Tyson, and Robert Ashley, Dr. Tyson said: "It seems to me that one of the barriers to interreligious dialogue, at least on the Christian side, is the kind of exclusivistic claim—that in fact if you don't believe in Jesus Christ, you will not be in the right with God..." to which Arinze responded: "[A document from the Second Vatican Council—Ed.] says that God's grant of salvation includes not only Christians, but Jews, Muslims, Hindus and people of good will." He added: "If a person were to push what you said a little further and say that if you're not a Christian you're not going to heaven, we'd regard that person as a **fundamentalist...**and **theologically wrong."**

He continued:

> "I met in one place in Pakistan a **Muslim** [who—Ed.] lived alone, and people would go to him....He had a wonderful concept of the Koran....We were like two twins that had known one another from birth. And I was in admiration of this man's wisdom. I think that man **will go to heaven....**
>
> "There was a **Buddhist** in Kyoto, Japan. This man, a good man, open, listening, humble—I was amazed. I listened to his words of wisdom and said to myself, 'The **grace of God is working in this man.'"**

Mr. Ashley then asked: **"So you can still get to heaven without accepting Jesus?"** to which Arinze responded: **"Expressly, yes."**[54]

Arinze, who specifically believes that people can go to heaven without accepting Jesus, is the man who serves **along with John Stott,** a Billy Graham speaker, on the **United Bible Societies.**

Arinze even "issued joyful greetings to **Buddhists** for their feast of Vesakh on June 1st...."[55]

WCRP

In July 1997, Arinze was at the World Conference on Religion and Peace (WCRP) held in Melbourne, Australia.[56]

One researcher writes:

> "The usual hodgepodge of would-be leaders of the global spirituality of the next millenium showed their true colours

when they joined together in a 'prayer' containing elements of fire worship, pantheism, occultism, agnosticism and atheism. At the conference dinner, in a darkened room illuminated only by a candle at each table, the approximately 250 attendees bowed their heads as this 'Prayer for Togetherness' was recited: 'Let us focus on the candle, the small quivering fire, the light in the darkness, the call to evening prayer, the call to thanksgiving...for our togetherness, for our unity, as sons and daughters of the earth in this vast and ancient land, this sacred soil of the Dreamtime.

"'In the presence of the ineffable Other, the Holy Being of Infinity, the Numinous Beyond, the One and the Ultimate, the Alpha and the Omega, the Unknown and the Unknowable, Lord of the Cosmos, Centre of Creation God, the God of power and righteousness, we pray to you in the immensity and grandeur of the world.'...

"Fundamentalism and absolutism were severely attacked at the Melbourne conference. When the speakers were accused of persecuting Christians for their creation beliefs, Cardinal Arinze 'supported the rights of all religions to believe and teach their own creation stories.'...He 'also had severe criticism of those who demand that their religion is "superior" to others, and want their countries to have "one religion." We live in a "global village,"' Arinze insisted. 'We should have **"Unity and Diversity."'"**[57]

"The WCRP is a UN Non-Governmental Organization, headquartered at the United Nations in New York, with chapters in several countries. It works closely with the UN, UNICEF and UNESCO. Dr. John Humphrey, a past president of the Canadian chapter, wrote the UN's Universal Declaration of Human Rights."[58]

Remember, Billy Graham urged "all governments to respect the rights of religious believers **as outlined** in the **United Nations A Universal Declaration of Human Rights."**[59]

The WCRP had met earlier (on November 3, 1994) at the **Vatican.** At that meeting there were representatives from religions such as Islam and Buddhism.

"The conference theme was 'Healing the World: Religions for Peace.' This was the first time an official **interfaith** conference had been convened at the Holy See. In his opening address, the Pope told the 900 representatives of the world's religions assembled in the Synod Hall that 'religious leaders must clearly show that they are pledged to the promotion of

> peace' and religions must 'engage in a dialogue of mutual understanding and peace on the basis of the values they share.' He ended by remarking, 'The Vatican is open to you. I hope you all return soon.'"[60]

The Pope then "listened to Koranic verses and Jewish, Shinto, Buddhist and Hindu invocations for peace...."[61]

The WCRP wrote:

> "WCRP wishes to express its gratitude to H. E. [His Excellency] **Francis Cardinal Arinze,** President of the Pontifical Council for Interreligious Affairs, and Bishop Michael Fitzgerald, the Secretary of the Council, for their immense and always considerate assistance in the Vatican's hosting of the opening session of the Assembly."[62]

They added:

> "In addition to the sponsorship of the Camapana dei Caduti, recognition must be given for the very **generous financial support** of several other organizations. Chief among them are Rissho Kosei-kai, the German Evangelical Church and Evangelisches Missionswerk in Deutschland, WCRP/USA in partnership with the **Rockefeller Foundation,** WCRP/Korea, the Konko Church of Izuo, the Shoroku **Shinto** Yamatoyama, the Singapore **Buddhist** Welfare Association, Mr. Mahalingham of **Shakti** Sugar Companies (for financial support and the Indian cultural events), and WCRP/Japan."[63]

Christians can never have mutual respect for pantheistic and occultic religions. Yes, people are free to practice their religion in our society, but I cannot **RESPECT** (meaning worship, adore, admire, love, revere, appreciate, cherish, honor, value, etc.) their false doctrines.

One person explains:

> "It is better to be divided by truth than to be united in error. It is better to speak the truth that hurts and then heals, than falsehood that comforts and then kills. Let me tell you something, friend: it is not love and it is not friendship if we fail to declare the whole counsel of God. It is better to be hated for telling the truth than to be loved for telling a lie. It is not possible to find anyone in the Bible who was a power for God who did not have enemies and was not hated. It is better to stand alone with the truth, than to be wrong with a multitude. It is better to ultimately succeed with the truth than to temporarily succeed with a lie. There is only one gospel and Paul said, 'If any man preach any other gospel unto you than that which we have preached unto you, let him be accursed.'"[64]

ARCHBISHOP GEORGE CAREY

Another person involved with the Melbourne Conference (along with Cardinal Arinze) was George Carey,[65] now the Archbishop of Canterbury.[66] In fact, he opened the conference and agreed that **"God was unknown and unknowable."**[67] Carey is also a key person in the United Religions Initiative (URI).[68] When Bishop William Swing, who heavily promoted the URI,[69] asked Carey what he thought about the idea, Swing said that Carey

> "spoke about how much greater an investment he has had to make in **interfaith** work in his five years as Archbishop. One of the strong points about a **United Religions** for him is the rapid proliferation of interfaith demands and new groups. One central, coordinating group would be a blessing. Although he had many questions and reasonable cautions, he was sincerely involved in our dialogue and personally **most supportive."**[70]

Carey, too, is involved with the Thanksgiving World Assembly through Thanksgiving Square.[71] Announcing the one meeting, *Dallas Morning News* reported:

> "The Spirit of thanksgiving forms a foundation for **practically all religions** in the world, so the **United Nations** decided to build on this common denominator by declaring 2000 the 'International Year of Thanksgiving.'
>
> "What's more, word of this global message falls on receptive ears in Dallas, where there already exists an institution, the **Thanks-Giving Foundation, dedicated to the very goals promulgated by the United Nations."**[72]

Carey had

> "been named by Queen Elizabeth II to succeed Robert Runcie as archbishop of Canterbury....
>
> "He is also an ardent environmentalist (he once said that 'God is green')."[73]

In his position as Archbishop he is the "spiritual leader" of 70 million Anglicans, including the Episcopal Church. When the issue of homosexuality came up in early 1997, he called on the church members to be **tolerant** and said that Anglicans are "a people who live with diversity and differences."[74] He added: "Let us never be among those who separate from other Christians because of our disagreements with them over matters to do with discipline or doctrine."[75]

One writer states:

> "Carey is the head of the Anglican and Episcopal churches, and as such he is in close fellowship with every sort of heresy and moral abomination. There are thousands of homosexual Anglicans, many of whom boldly march in public to demand their 'rights.' There are many homosexual 'clergy' within the Anglican denominations. Many Anglican clergy deny and question the virgin birth, vicarious atonement, and resurrection of Jesus Christ."[76]

Carey himself wrote in *Jesus 2000:* "Unlike the birth of Christ and the crucifixion, **Christians cannot know** with the same certainty **that He was resurrected."**[77] This book also says: "I can tell you frankly that while we can be absolutely sure that Jesus lived and that He was certainly crucified on the Cross, **we cannot know that He was raised by God from the dead."**[78]

Remember, the Archbishop of Canterbury also said: **"Those who led a good life on Earth but found themselves unable to believe in God will not be debarred. I expect to meet present-day atheists in heaven."**[79] [Emphasis in the original.]

Ephesians 5:6-7 says: "Let no man deceive you with vain words: for because of these things cometh the wrath of God upon the children of disobedience. Be not ye therefore partakers with them."

No wonder Carey

> "has severely criticized Anglican pastors who have persevered in evangelical efforts to preach the gospel of Jesus Christ to **Hindus, Jews, Buddhists,** and other non-Christian groups. Incredibly, in a demonstration of the spiritual bankruptcy of the Church of England, Archbishop Carey has instructed his ministers that nonbelievers in Jesus Christ are just 'fellow travelers' on the road to spiritual enlightenment, and therefore they **must not be evangelized!** In addition, the archbishop declared that he plans a trip to Rome in the near future to discuss how to remove obstacles to ecumenical interfaith unification."[80]

THE RETURN OF THE GODDESS

He also

> "condemned fundamentalists who place the Bible 'above and beyond human enquiry.' He said the Bible stood as 'the enduring foundational document of the church' but maintained that it was not beyond research or critical analysis....Carey also noted, 'The Anglican Church is a broad church and there is

room in our fellowship for great variety—for traditionalists, evangelicals, Anglo-Catholics, liberals, and charismatics.'"[81]

George Carey was in favor of the Parliament of the World's Religions in Chicago in 1993.[82]

> "Over 4,500 delegates from all over the world attended, including representatives of Orthodox, Protestant and Roman Catholic 'Christianity,' and those of Baha'ism, Buddhism, Confucianism, Hinduism, Jainism, Judaism, Islam, Native American Shamanism, **Wicca (witchcraft),** Shintoism, Neo-Paganism, the polytheistic Native African Yoruba cult, Sikhism, Taoism, Unitarianism, Zoroastrianism, etc....One of [the 'blessings'] was brought by a High Priestess of the pagan Temple of Isis, whose devotions were given *'in the name of the 10,000 names, the spirits, the birds, reptiles and trees.'"*[83] [Italics in the original.]

(Refer back to Chapter 7 for more about this meeting.)

Yet, Carey gave his sanction to such paganism by stating: *"Few things are more important to our world today than the growth of mutual respect and understanding between different faith communities."*[84] [Emphasis in the original.] He also "believes that **Hindus share a common spiritual walk with Christians."**[85]

In June 2000, senior Church of England clergy joined together in a conference with Druids, wiccans, and shamans which was "designed to 'help reconcile' their 'traditions.' The conference is called Spirit of the Land 2000 and is described as 'a **Christian-Druid dialogue and reconciliation** meeting for the New Millennium....'"[86]

In an earlier chapter we looked at the apostasy of the World Council of Churches. Carey was one of the WCC speakers in 1991 and the denomination of which he is the head, is a member of the WCC.[87] The theme that year was "Come, Holy Spirit—Renew the Whole Creation."[88] The keynote speaker was Chung Hyun Kyung (who was also covered earlier).[89]

The following is part of the invocation that was delivered that year:

> "...I would like to invite all of you to get on the Holy Ground with me by taking off your shoes while we have dancing to prepare the way of the spirit. With humble heart and body, let us listen to the cries of creation and the cries of the Spirit within.
>
> *"Come.* The spirit of Hagar....
>
> *"Come.* The spirit of Joan of Arc, and of the many other women burnt at the 'witch trials.'...

"*Come.* The spirit of Mahatma Ghandi (sic), Steve Biko, Martin Luther King Jr., Malcolm X, Victor Jara, Oscar Romero, and many other unnamed women freedom fighters who died....

"*Come.* The spirit of the Amazon rain forest now being murdered every day.

"*Come.* The spirit of Earth, Air, and Water, raped, tortured and exploited....

"Without hearing the cries of these spirits we cannot hear the voice of the Holy Spirit.

"I hope the presence of all our ancestors (sic) spirits here with us shall not make you uncomfortable....Because of them we can feel, touch and taste the concrete bodily historical presence of the Holy Spirit in our midst....Here, in Australia, we are gathered from every part of our mother earth to pray for the coming of the Holy Spirit to renew the whole creation. Indeed it is a happy occasion, a big family gathering."[90] [Emphasis in the original.]

The Religious News Service described more of this conference:

"Aboriginal men girded in loincloths and feathers, their bodies painted in tribal decoration, danced around an altar and beat drums in a tradional (sic) purification ceremony that opened the Seventh Assembly of the World Council of Churches here February 7. Standing near them at the altar were aboriginal women clothed in traditional black and red dresses and colorful aboriginal clergymen garbed in western vestment."[91]

"An Ecumenical Press Service report gives more details of the **heathen purification ceremony** which **opened the WCC Assembly.** 'The congregation entered the tent by passing through smoke made by burning leaves—a traditional cleansing process for Aborigines in Australia....Before worship began, a traditional Aboriginal **"message stick"** was carried to the worship tent by an Aboriginal runner. In that actions (sic), WCC General Secretary **Emilio Castro** [who was covered earlier] asked permission for the council to enter the land. Gathered in the tent were Aboriginal elders, who ritually granted permission, whereupon the WCC worship leaders walked in procession into the tent.'

"The Aboriginals involved in this rite were **almost naked,** and the entire thing was an abomination to God. The supposed spirituality of the Aboriginals was applauded by the WCC Assembly, but the Bible condemns it as heathen idolatry."[92]

"A huge banner in the main tent showed the Mother Earth with a serpent around her pregnant belly. The New World Order propaganda was everywhere."[93]

Is it any wonder that in the 1930s Francis Younghusband, founder of The World Congress of Faiths, stated that *"a religious basis is essential for the new world order"?*[94] [Emphasis in the original.]

Carey has recently

> "accepted an invitation to become a patron of the Ecumenical Society of the Blessed Virgin Mary. In his letter of acceptance, Dr. Carey wrote, 'The ESBVM has had an important place in the ecumenical landscape for many years and has made a significant contribution to the unity of God's Church. I am very pleased to be associated with this important work.' He recalled how he had once spent three weeks at the new Anglican Centre in Rome, and then later returned for private study of the Roman Catholic teaching on the Virgin Mary. He said this time [at the Centre] had changed his ecumenical outlook."[95]

In a letter from Pope John Paul II, we find:

> "I greet with particular affection His Grace the Archbishop of Canterbury, the Most Reverend Dr. **George Carey,** who together with you has called this special gathering. On several occasions I have had the joy of meeting His Grace, most notably when **he visited Rome in 1996 and when we opened together the Holy Door of the Basilica of Saint Paul's Outside the Walls in Rome on 18 January this year** [2000]. On each occasion we prayed fervently for the restoration of the full visible unity which is Christ's will for his followers."[96]

"...Carey has already agreed for his part that recognizing 'the universal primacy of the pope' is essential to unity."[97]

PRINCESS DIANA'S FUNERAL

Carey was the officiator at Princess Diana's funeral where a **homosexual** and his partner were there and John Elton took part.[98] One researcher noted:

> "I was extremely disturbed to hear **Carey pronounce almost a universal salvation message** at the end of that trying service. One would have thought that any of those thousands of people out there in the streets of London could have gone straight to heaven, just by repeating the 'Lord's Prayer.' What an opportunity for a real Christian to humbly, gently, sensitively and faithfully preach Christ and His Sacrifice! Carey had two

> and a half billion people who were listening, and he confirmed them in their sin, by not even showing a little bit of light on the true condition of the lost, or what Christ has done for the world which must be responded to in order to be safe in God's love."[99]

Soon a new "Bible" will be released which is written in Cockney slang.

> "It is written in a sort of 'rap' format, as the story of Jesus feeding the 5,000 as follows: *'Jesus made a Jim Skinner dinner for 5,000 geezers with just five loaves of Uncle Fred bread and two Lillian Gish fish.'* Another passage says, *'Noah built a bloomin' massive nanny boat, from nanny goat.'*"[100] [Italics in the original.]

This "Bible" has the backing of none other than Dr. George Carey![101]

As we've already seen, Carey believes he will meet atheists in heaven and he said that we can't know that Christ was raised from the dead, but Billy Graham had Archbishop George Carey as one of his speakers at Amsterdam 2000!![102]

Also featured at Amsterdam 2000 was a "drama team from Bill Hybels' Willow Creek Community Church [which] had a prominent role at the meeting. One presentation dealt with the woman taken in adultery. In acting out the part, she said, 'Jesus said to me, "You are not condemned."' She failed to add that Jesus also said, 'Go and sin no more.'"[103]

It is interesting to note that in 1946, the Federal Council of Churches had a Biennial Report on the subject of "Worship." One subhead was "Drama in Religion" and called for "drama **within** the church." Drama had been used for hundreds (and perhaps thousands of years), but it is only recently that drama is being used as a substitute for worship and is taking place inside church buildings.[104]

BILLY KIM

Another speaker at Amsterdam 2000 was Billy Kim.[105] He was the interpreter for Billy Graham in 1973 when Graham went to Seoul, Korea.[106]

At the conference, Kim "favorably quoted Martin Luther King, Jr., who, according to Kim 'pricked America's conscience and gave America a dream.'"[107]

Kim, a Promise Keepers speaker,[108] was the vice president and is now the president, of the liberal Baptist World Alliance (BWA).[109]

About three weeks **prior** to Kim speaking at Amsterdam 2000, the BWA had a "very important" and "excellent" several hour meeting with Cuban communist dictator, **Fidel Castro.**[110] Castro was the guest speaker for the BWA's General Council meeting in July.[111] Kim even had a **private** visit with Castro.[112]

> "The BWA resolution that gained the most publicity was the **unanimous** resolution calling for the end of the blockade of medicine and food products to Cuba. A BWA report says 'Baptists of the world stated very clearly that they thought it was unfair to punish the poor people of Cuba by such a blockade.' Why not a resolution against Castro's 'unfair' denial of freedom to poor Cubans?"[113]

The BWA leaders also "boldly stated that **evangelism is more important than doctrine and faithfulness to the truth.** Outgoing BWA President Nilson Fanini stated in an interview that 'theology sometimes divides us, but evangelism and missions bring us all together.'"[114]

> "The BWA is an **ecumenical alliance** of 191 Baptist denominations in more than 140 countries. It promotes the false teaching that **unity is more important than doctrinal truth.** In decades past **it has been strongly influenced by communists, and it supports new age one-world organizations such as the United Nations (UN).** At the 15th Baptist World Alliance meeting in 1985, the **BWA commended the UN** and challenged Baptists 'to make a new commitment of prayer for the UN, promote interest and support for its programmes, and encourage world-wide rededication to the principles and purposes of its charter.'...
>
> "Among the denominations which are united under the BWA umbrella are the American Baptist Convention and the Baptist Union of Great Britain, both of which are **permeated with the most blasphemous and heretical modernism** under the sun."[115]

BWA AT PAGAN-FEST

The BWA was represented at the 1986 Day of Prayer for World Peace in Assisi, Italy, along with "mantra-mumbling Buddhists, Shiva-loving Hindus, spirit-worshipping Indians invoking the Great Spirit of the Sky, Shintos, Bahais, Jainists, African animists calling on The Great Thumb, fire-worshipping Zoroastrians, Sikhs, [and] Moslems crying to Allah."[116] This event, by the way, was organized by **Pope John Paul II!**[117]

What happened at Assisi? The Associated Press reports:

"Chants, temple bells and pagan spells echoed around the **Roman Catholic shrines** of Assisi yesterday as Pope John Paul II and his 200 guests from the world's 12 main religions prayed for world peace....

"The medicineman of the Crow Indians [spirit worshipers—D.W.C.], Chief John Pretty-on-Top, offered to cast out evil spirits. Many came forward, among them a young Franciscan monk.

"In a chapel down the road, the head of the Zoroastrian church in Bombay prayed before a fire that symbolized his God.

"Next door, six turbanned Sikhs—all Italian converts—sat chanting their prayers in the lotus position to gramophone music.

"At an old Roman temple, shoeless Moslems sat on prayer mats.

"The 14th Dalai Lama, exiled god-king of Tibet, headed the strong Buddhist contingent, mumbling sutras amid tinkling bells at the Basilica of St. Peter.

"In the gardens outside, a Shinto sect called Tenrikyo, in black kimonos, swayed to temple music.

"African animists, their togas the envy of any designer, invoked the spirits of trees and plants to come to the aid of peace...."[118]

"Two tribal animists from Africa intoned, 'Almighty God, the Great Thumb we cannot evade in tying any knot, the Roaring Thunder that splits mighty trees, the All-Seeing Lord up on high who sees even the footprints of an antelope on a rock mass here on earth...you are the cornerstone of peace.'

"Smoking a ceremonial peace pipe, John Pretty-on-Top, a Crow Indian medicine man [witchdoctor] from Montana, in full-feathered headdress, recited, 'O Great Spirit, I raise my pipe to you, to your messengers the four winds, and to mother earth, who provides for your children...I pray that you bring peace to all my brothers and sisters of this world.'"[119]

CHRISTIAN-MARXIST DIALOGUE

Paganism isn't the only attraction for some of the BWA leadership. In 1960, Jakov Zhidkov "preached the Communist line before the Baptist World Alliance and offered Khrushchev's disarmament program as the one behind which all Christians should unite."[120]

> **"Bychkov,** leader of the **communist-controlled** All Union Council of Evangelical Christians-Baptists, was also **identified as a KGB agency** by the FBI. April 17-23 [1988] Ecumenical Press Service reports that Bychkov met recently with the Southern Baptist Foreign Mission Board in Richmond, Virginia. This infiltrator **is also a member of the Executive Committee of the Baptist World Alliance,** whose largest supporter is the Southern Baptists."[121]

This really isn't surprising since at BWA's 15th World Congress in 1985 they decided to **dialogue with heathen religions and communists.** Dr. Glenn A. Igleheart (sic) wrote a report entitled "Why Baptists Dialogue with Others" in which he stated:

> "The situation in the world outside the churches demands dialogue take place. Other world religions have entered a resurgent missionary phase in their history, and Baptists should join with other Christians in utilizing dialogue as a means of truly entering into relationship with representatives of these faiths. **Dialogue may cause Christians to rethink their perceptions of these and other faiths and to revise their approaches** to them. In addition to other world religionists, **Christians need to enter into Christian-Marxist dialogues** in order to know how to cope with the followers of that ideology."[122]

Iglehart, by the way, serves on a commission in the **National Council of Churches.**[123]

As Christians, we are not to dialogue with other faiths. The Bible tells us that we should "mark them which cause divisions and offences contrary to the doctrine which ye have learned; and **avoid them"** (Rom. 16:17). I Timothy 6:3, 5 states: "If any man teach otherwise, and consent not to wholesome words, even the words of our Lord Jesus Christ, and to the doctrine which is according to godliness;... Perverse disputing of men of corrupt minds, and destitute of the truth... **from such withdraw thyself." "[S]hun** profane and vain babblings..." (II Timothy 2:16). II John 1:10-11 warns: "If there come any unto you, and bring not this doctrine, **receive him not into your house,** neither bid him God speed: For he that biddeth him God speed is partaker of his evil deeds." Finally, II Corinthians 6:14, 17 cautions us:

> "Be ye not unequally yoked together with unbelievers: for what fellowship hath righteousness with unrighteousness? and what communion hath light with darkness?...Wherefore **come**

out from among them, and be ye separate, saith the Lord, and **touch not the unclean thing;** and I will receive you."

"We are to BELIEVE sound doctrine, Titus 1:9. We are to PREACH sound doctrine, II Timothy 4:2. We are to ADORN sound doctrine, Titus 2:10. All three of these are important."[124] [Emphasis in the original.]

In a previous chapter I mentioned that Graham had traveled with **Communist sympathizer, Martin Luther King, Jr.,** to and from the **Baptist World Alliance.**[125] From 1955 until at least 1993, Graham had given the closing address at each BWA Congress.[126] After speaking at the BWA meeting in 1980, **Graham "joined** in a rousing **applause accorded the Russian hammer and sickle** during the traditional Parade of Flags."[127]

Additionally, Graham "encourages everyone to support the BWA. In 1995 the BWA honored Graham with a special award...."[128] In 1999, the *Baptist World* (BWA's magazine) "had an article praising Billy Graham as the 'greatest evangelist of this century,' and termed as 'Twentieth Century prophets' the likes of Bonhoeffer, King, and Oscar Romero."[129]

Another person who attended a BWA meeting and spoke was none other than **Han Wenzao,** the Chinese **Communist,** who was discussed earlier. When he presented his appeal he mentioned the **"socialist** modernization in Mainland China."[130]

Several of the past presidents of the BWA have been **Masons** such as William R. Tolbert, 33°,[131] George W. Truett, 32°,[132] and former vice president Louie D. Newton, 32°.[133]

Billy Kim pastors the 10,000-member Central Baptist Church in Korea,[134] and "has traveled/spoken with David Yonggi Cho, the Assembly of God pastor of the world's largest church who has been said to use **occultic mind techniques."**[135] (In spite of Cho's occultic inclination, Billy Graham has had Cho as one of his main speakers at Amsterdam '83![136] Graham was the main dedication speaker for Cho in 1973 when a new auditorium was added.[137])

BISHOP TUTU

"The apostate **BWA featured socialist Bishop Tutu** at a 1998 BWA meeting...."[138]

Tutu, a "proponent of **leftist** revolution in South Africa,"[139] is a former Anglican Archbishop[140] and a Nobel Peace Prize winner.[141] He was one of the ten Presidents of the **World Conference on Religion and Peace** (WCRP),[142] a **New Age** organization working to bring in the **new world order.**[143] In *Religion for Peace,* a newsletter from the WCRP, we find that the *"WCRP/International is actively seeking staff on loan from Buddhist, Hindu, Muslim and other religious bodies to serve on the Secretariat."*[144] [Emphasis in the original.]

Tutu also attended the "Spirit of Peace" conference[145] along with people like

> "Marilyn Ferguson leading proponent of the New Age movement; Prince Bernhardt (sic) of the Netherlands, commonly known as a leader of the one-world secret elitist society, the Bilderbergers; 'His Holiness' Tenzin Gyatso, the XIV Dalai Lama of Tibet; Zentatsu Richard Baker-Roshi, co-founder and second abbot of San Francisco Zen (Buddhist) Center; Helen Caldicott, president of 'Physicians for Social Responsibility,' an organization favoring U. S. unilateral disarmament;...and Robert Muller, [former] Ass't Secretary General of the U. N., in charge of co-ordinating the work of 32 specialized agencies and world programs."[146]

Tutu is very supportive of the **United Religions Initiative**[147] and he also participated in (and was a co-chairman, **along with Mikhail Gorbachev,**[148] of) the **State of the World Forum,** an organization also working for a **one world order.**[149] He was one of the speakers for the Council on Foreign Relations in 1990.[150]

In 2000 Tutu joined several prominent theologians

> "to urge religious leaders to work together to **find a new image of God** for the 21st century.
>
> "'No religion can claim to have the whole truth about the mystery' of faith, Tutu said....
>
> **"Tutu also urged Christians to embrace other faiths."**[151]

TUTU CALLS FOR ORDINATION OF HOMOSEXUALS

Tutu has been a speaker for the New Age, one-world World Constitution and Parliament Association[152] and he is a member of the Club of Rome (along with the Dalai Lama, Mikhail Gorbachev, and Robert Muller).[153]

He is the highest ranking Anglican to **call for the ordination of practicing homosexuals,** and has warned that rejecting homosexuals is "nearly the ultimate blasphemy."[154] He even wrote the foreword to a book that is a collection of "Christian" liturgies for gays.[155] At a

Windsor meeting in March 1995, Tutu said: "THE CHURCH MUST NOT EXCLUDE PEOPLE ON THE BASIS OF gender, culture, ethnic origin or SEXUAL ORIENTATION."[156] [Emphasis in the original.] He added: "Let ours be inclusive communities, welcoming and embracing."[157] On February 9, 1996, Tutu signed a public message in support of the Lesbian and Gay Christian Movement.[158]

Tutu is a Marxist.[159] In 1983, he said: "I find capitalism quite horrendous and unacceptable. I am a socialist."[160] When he received the Nobel Peace Prize, he bragged: "I receive the Nobel Peace Prize on behalf of Nelson Mandelas, the Walter Sisulus, the Goven Mbekis, the Winnie Mandelas, the Albertina Sisulus."[161] We've already taken a look at Mandela and his **Communist** connections,[162] so you have an idea of what kind of people Tutu finds inspiring!

You will get a better idea of who Tutu is by looking at a few of his quotations:

➻ "Imagine what would happen if only 30 percent of domestic servants [in the white households—Ed.] would poison their employers' food."[163] (Remember, this statement comes from a Nobel **Peace** Prize winner!)

➻ "I hate capitalism."[164]

➻ "Mandela is my leader."[165]

➻ "The West can go to H-ll."[166]

➻ "I think I would use Marxist insights."[167]

➻ "When young people take up arms, I will not condemn them." (ABC Interview, October 16, 1984.)[168]

➻ "In terms of the New Testament, the Jews must suffer. Therefore, we will put it into practice if we will be in charge and there will be no sympathy for the Jews when the blacks take over."[169]

➻ "I am glad I am not Christian."[170]

➻ "Some people thought there was something odd about Jesus' birth. It may be that Jesus was an illegitimate son."[171]

So much more could be said about Tutu and his socialistic and un-Christian viewpoints, but this is the man who has spoken at the Baptist World Alliance of which Billy Kim, a Graham speaker at Amsterdam 2000, is now President!

Tutu also spoke at the World Council of Churches in 1993 and drew a standing ovation.[172]

II Peter 2:1-3 warns:

> "But there were false prophets also among the people, even as there shall be false teachers among you, who privily shall bring in damnable heresies, even denying the Lord that bought

them, and bring upon themselves swift destruction. And many shall follow their pernicious ways; by reason of whom the way of truth shall be evil spoken of. And through covetousness shall they with feigned words make merchandise of you: whose judgment now of a long time lingereth not, and their damnation slumbereth not."

Also, Romans 16:18: "For they that are such serve not our Lord Jesus Christ, but their own belly; and by good words and fair speeches deceive the hearts of the simple."

BILL BRIGHT

Let's move on to another Amsterdam 2000 speaker—Bill Bright.[173] Although Bright has probably done much good in his earlier days, he has more recently aligned himself with many questionable people and organizations. For example:

✢ He signed and publicly endorsed the unscriptural and ecumenical document called "Evangelicals and Catholics Together."[174]

✢ Roy Rogers, 33° Mason (now deceased), Johnny Cash, Paul (David) Yonggi Cho, Jay Gary, Jesse Helms, 33° Mason, Bruce Larson, Norman Vincent Peale, 33° Mason (now deceased), Robert Schuller, 33° Mason, Michael W. Smith, Jack Van Impe, and dozens of others were/are part of the Campus Crusade for Christ's International Committee of Reference.[175] (Incidentally, Billy Graham also used Mason Roy Rogers and Dale Evans in his crusade.[176] Graham also honored Rogers and Evans for "their 50 years in show business."[177] Additionally, Graham has also used Burl Ives, another 33° Mason[178] and a Communist in his crusade!)

✢ Bright mentioned that he could feel God's presence in the Toronto Blessing ("Holy Laughter").[179] (For more information on this movement, see my article "Unholy Laughter.")

✢ He is a speaker and promoter of Promise Keepers and a contributor to a Promise Keepers book *(Seven Promises of a Promise Keeper)* published by Focus on the Family in 1994.[180]

✢ He was a member of the National Honorary Committee of Clement Stone's Religious Heritage of America (RHA).[181] Stone, a 33° Mason,[182] is a promoter of the occultic theory that God is a metaphysical power that can be tapped into.[183]

✢ Bright has endorsed Hugh Ross and/or his books.[184] Ross is a theistic evolutionist/progressive creationist. Ross states: "'Bipedal, tool-using, large-brained hominids roamed the earth at least as long ago as **one million years.** New evidence indicates that the hominid species may have gone extinct before, or as a result of, the appearance of man. Starting about 2 to 4 million years ago, **God began creating man-like mammals.'** Although some of these creatures looked completely human (e.g., Cro-Magnon, Neanderthal), 'used tools, buried their dead, and painted on cave walls,' **they were actually animals and 'had no spirits.'** He has stated that the major difference between men and hominids is that humans were 'the first spirit creatures.'"[185] "In time, all these man-like creatures went extinct. Then, about 10 to 25 thousand years ago, **God replaced them with Adam and Eve."**[186]

Billy Graham, as well as the Pope, have also "agreed that God may have used evolution to create man."[187]

✢ Bright, nominated by Chuck Colson,[188] was the 1996 recipient of the Templeton Prize.[189] We've already covered Templeton and his prize earlier. Remember that a "committee made up of leaders from the world's five major religions ('Christianity,' Hinduism, Buddhism, Islam and Judaism) meet annually to choose a recipient for this prize worth over" one million dollars.[190] Templeton is described as a "New Age pantheist/science-of-mind Universalist/investment guru."[191] Templeton, an evolutionist, believes that the Bible does not "accurately record the words of Christ."[192] He also states: "I am hoping we can develop a body of knowledge about God that doesn't rely on ancient revelations or scripture [such as the Bible!—D.H.]...that is scientific... and is not disputed because of division, between religions or churches or ancient scripture or liturgy...."[193]

Even though Templeton "openly rejects the Bible as the unique Word of God, he served on the Board of Managers of the American Bible Society for fifteen years...and on the Board of Princeton Theological Seminary."[194] "By accepting this prize, Bright now joins the ranks of Buddhist, Muslim and Hindu leaders, together with liberal theologians and atheists"[195] who have received this prize in the past.

✢ Bright was involved in Washington for Jesus '88.[196]

✢ He served on the National Advisory Board of the March for Jesus.[197] (For more information on March for Jesus, see my article "March for Jesus.")

✢ He has endorsed (and re-endorsed!) Jay Gary's book, *The Star of 2000*.[198] (For more information on Jay Gary and his New Age connections, see my article "Jay Gary: The Millennium Doctor.")

✢ Bright is a promoter of so-called "Christian" rock music and has spoken at the "Fishnet '91" rock concert.[199] He was on ZTV's advisory board. ZTV is a major 24-hour music video network targeting the 12 to 34 year olds.[200]

Bright brags: "I can work with anyone who calls Jesus Lord."[201] When someone pointed out to Bright that many who call Jesus "Lord, Lord" were "workers of iniquity" (Matthew 7:21-23), "[h]e made no answer and walked from the room in silence."[202] Incidentally, Bright can also work with people who **DO NOT** call Jesus "Lord." For example, he was at an **interfaith** meeting with Muslims and Jewish Rabbis. In his prayer he referred to the "God of **OUR** fathers."[203] The god of the Muslims **IS NOT** the same God I serve.

✢ Not only is Bright very ecumenical in his outreach but he also gives a watered-down Gospel message. A former Campus Crusade worker wrote: "One reason why the Campus Crusade message is so popular is that Campus Crusaders are taught either by design or by default not to use 'Christian jargon' like witness, repent, converted, blood, hell, sin, save, holiness, and apostasy....Granted these are not 'soft,' 'cool' or easily received words, but the world's words and ways are always at odds with God's. II Timothy 1:13 commands us to 'hold fast the form of sound words.'"[204] The Bible also warns us: "Cursed be he that doeth the work of the Lord deceitfully" (Jeremiah 48:10).

✢ In addition, *"The Jesus Film,"* which was released in 1979 by Campus Crusade for Christ, has been viewed by some 700 million people. But, "*Charisma* magazine, September 1995, reported in an article entitled 'Playing God' that Brian Deacon, the actor who played Jesus in this film, is not a Christian. He calls himself a 'lapsed Catholic who hasn't practiced his faith.'

> "Deacon testified, 'I've always found it difficult to know how truth can be proclaimed to others; to me it's more of a private matter.'...
>
> "The Jesus film also focuses too much on the human side of the Lord Jesus and not enough on His deity. Jesus is depicted, typically, with long, straggled, hippie-type hair. The Lord Jesus was not under a Nazarite vow not to cut His hair, and there is no reason to believe that He had long hair. In fact, the Bible plainly says long hair on a man is shameful (1 Cor. 11:14). Interestingly, Christ's disciples are depicted in the Jesus film with short hair."[205]

It is claimed that "41 million people have made professions of faith after watching the film."[206] If this were true, where are all the changed lives that the Bible tells us will occur when a person gets saved (see II Corinthians 5:17)?

CHUCK COLSON

Let's move on to another speaker at Amsterdam 2000—Chuck Colson.[207] At this meeting Colson remarked: "We must hold **what we have in common** so we can stand together against secular naturalism and it was Billy Graham who helped us break down the walls."[208]

Colson is a Baptist who is divorced and remarried.[209] His present wife is a Roman Catholic,[210] so it's not too surprising to see that he was a co-writer (along with Richard John Neuhaus) of the "Evangelicals and Catholics Together" (ECT) document.[211] Colson wrote:

> "...do we accept everyone who says he is a Christian? No. Those who **deny the fundamentals, such as the bodily resurrection of Christ, cannot be part of the confessing body.** When we encounter this kind of dis-belief (sic), the church must correct, discipline, or **disfellowship.** Or, as some traditions call it, 'excommunicate.'"[212]

Good words—except that Colson doesn't practice what he preaches.

Before we look at Colson we need to see the type of person he worked with to write ECT. **Richard Neuhaus** was a Lutheran who became a Catholic priest in 1990.[213] He is a **"universalist** who rejects the Christian doctrine of justification by faith in the merits of Jesus Christ alone, the inerrancy of the Bible and the Christian doctrine of Hell...."[214] He also **denies "the virgin birth of Christ** was divinely revealed. **Neuhaus says** that this and other **miracles,** such as that of the loaves of bread and the fish, **are myths."**[215] He believes that the **Bible contains errors** and that **evolution is true.**[216] He also **denies the resurrection of Christ.**[217] Additionally, he claims that the "Jews do not need Jesus Christ and that they can still go to heaven while rejecting Jesus as Lord"[218] as well as Muslims and other non-Christians.[219]

Richard Neuhaus has promoted Marxist civil rights causes and demonstrated against the war in Vietnam.[220] He maintained that **Communist sympathizer Martin Luther King, Jr. was a saint.**[221]

Why would Chuck Colson co-author a document with such a man?! He said someone who denies the resurrection should be excommunicated or disfellowshipped but Colson did not do this. Instead, he yoked up with Neuhaus!

In his foreword to Catholic Keith Fournier's book, *Evangelical Catholics,*[222] Colson wrote: "But at root, those who are called of God, whether Catholic or Protestant, are part of the same Body. What they share is a belief in the basics: the virgin birth, the deity of Christ, His bodily resurrection, His imminent return, and the authority of His infallible Word."[223] Doesn't it seem strange that if Colson believes what he wrote, that he would join together with someone like Neuhaus who denies these fundamentals of the faith?

COLSON GIVES NEUHAUS AWARD

In his book, *The Body,* Colson brags: "Father Richard John Neuhaus has also been a tremendous inspiration. He has one of the keenest minds we've ever known. He writes with weight and gritty substance and profound insight."[224]

In 1998 Colson honored Richard John Neuhaus with Prison Fellowship's Wilberforce Award.[225] Recently Colson turned over the control of Prison Fellowship (PF) to Michael Timmis, a Roman Catholic.[226] By the way, over 70% of Colson's PF chaplains are Catholics.[227]

Of course, Colson is not the conservative that many people think he is. Granted, he is a powerful speaker and has some very good points, but he also has some dangerous viewpoints as well. In 1979 he attended a Catholic/charismatic renewal meeting "which featured a **Marxist** priest, a mass celebrated by Cardinal Cooke, and a healing service led by **Ruth Carter Stapleton...."**[228] Stapleton, as mentioned earlier, was an **occultist!**[229]

Colson declared: "I'm proud Mother Teresa is my sister in Christ"[230] and he claims she is "an example of holy living."[231] He wrote:

> "I can't tell you how many letters I've received over the years protesting my use of Mother Teresa as an example of holy living. Many even suggest that I visit her so I can give her the plan of salvation. To me this reaction is astounding. How could anyone deny this woman's **faithful witness?...**Who knows how many souls have come into the kingdom through her witness...."[232]

Graham has also mentioned Mother Teresa's **"Christian** love" in his autobiography[233] and Franklin Graham, too, says that she is an "example of the woman God uses."[234]

MOTHER TERESA

While Mother Teresa seemed to be doing a good work in some areas, she was by no means a Christian. She was the first recipient of the Templeton Prize in 1973.[235] She is also a **New Ager** and does not believe in being born-again and "considers Buddhism, Hinduism, Islam and other religions to be acceptable ways to God...."[236]

Mother Teresa has said:

> "If in coming face to face with God we accept Him in our lives, then we are converting. **We become a better Hindu,** a better **Muslim,** a better Catholic, a better **whatever** we are....What approach would I use? For me, naturally, it would be a Catholic one, for you it may be Hindu, for someone else, Buddhist, according to one's conscience. What God is in your mind you must accept."[237]

When someone asked Mother Teresa if she converted, she replied: "Of course I convert. I convert you to be a better Hindu or a better Muslim or a better Protestant. Once you've found God, it's up to you to decide how to worship him."[238] She has also bragged: "We prayed with the Jews, the Armenians, the Jains, the Buddhists, the Hindus. It was extraordinary. All hearts united in prayer to the one true God."[239]

"The April 7-13, 1990 issue of *Radio Times* tells the story of Mother Teresa sheltering an old Hindu priest. 'She nursed him with her own hands and helped him to die reconciled with his own gods.'"[240]

William Swing visited Mother Teresa and asked her about the **United Religions Initiative.** He wrote that she was **"thrilled by the prospect** and promised to get her female and male colleagues praying for the United Religions. Promised also to speak to the Pope about it. **Full endorsement."**[241]

Mother Teresa was involved with the **Temple of Understanding** and was one of their speakers.[242] She has also signed the "Declaration of World Thanksgiving"[243] along with Hindus, Buddhists, and pagans of all stripes. In 1985 Mother Teresa attended a conference sponsored by the United Nations University of Peace whose featured agenda was a call to bring about the **New World Order.**[244] In her speech to the UN, she said: "We gather to thank God for the 40 years of the beautiful work of the United Nations for the good of people. No color, no religion, no nationality should come between us—**we are <u>all</u> children of God....**When we destroy an unborn child, we destroy God."[245]

While abortion is murder and is wrong in God's sight, when an unborn child is destroyed, **God** is not being destroyed. By what Mother Teresa said, she is insinuating that we are God! The first one to propagate this teaching was Satan in the Garden of Eden. He told Eve that if she would eat of the tree of knowledge of good and evil, she would be as a god (Genesis 3:5). Of course, this is a typical New Age teaching, so it isn't surprising to see Mother Teresa espousing such a belief.

Even though Mother Teresa may have done many good works, we need to remember that the Bible teaches us in Titus 3:5 that it is **"[n]ot by works of righteousness** which we have done," but by God's mercy that we are saved. Isaiah 64:6 also reminds us that **"all our righteousnesses are as filthy rags;** and we all do fade as a leaf; and our iniquities, like the wind, have taken us away." Paul tells us in Ephesians 2:8-9 it is "by grace [that] are ye saved through faith;

and that not of yourselves: it is the gift of God: **Not of works, lest any man should boast."** Also in Philippians 3:9 we find that Paul said that he was to be found in Christ **"not having mine own righteousness,** which is of the law, but that which is through the faith of Christ, the righteousness which is of God by faith." Romans 10:3 adds: "For they being **ignorant of God's righteousness,** and **going about to establish their own righteousness,** have not submitted themselves unto the righteousness of God."

Good works are necessary and those who are saved will produce them, but good works are not enough and will never save us. Jesus Himself said in Matthew 5:20: "For I say unto you, That **except your righteousness shall exceed** the righteousness of the scribes and Pharisees, ye shall in **no case enter into the kingdom of heaven."** Unsaved people can perform good works. Even Satan comes as an angel of light and some of those who follow in his footsteps act as ministers of **righteousness!** II Corinthians 11:13-15 warns:

> "For such are **false apostles, deceitful workers,** transforming themselves into the apostles of Christ. And no marvel; for **Satan himself is transformed into an angel of light.** Therefore it is no great thing if **his ministers also be transformed as the ministers of righteousness;** whose end shall be according to their works."

WITCHES, DRUIDS, PAGANS—AND CHUCK COLSON

It's sad when someone like Colson believes that just because some good works were done, the person is a Christian. Not only does Colson call Mother Teresa his "sister in Christ," but he also accepted the $1 million Templeton Prize for Progress in Religion[246] (as has Mother Teresa[247]). The selection committee that picked Colson consisted of James H. Billington, a Council on Foreign Relations member;[248] a Bilderberger;[249] and a Rhodes Scholar;[250] Otto von Habsburg, a member of one of the top 13 Illuminati bloodlines; a Unity church official; and a Muslim.[251]

This particular year (1993) the prize was given at the Parliament of World Religions.[252] When concerned Christians wrote to Colson[253] about this, he sent out a letter saying that the prize was **not** part of the Parliament of World Religions and was being given **prior** to the Parliament.[254] This, however, was not completely true—and Colson had to have known it wasn't true.

> "The 'Twenty-First Presentation of the Templeton Prize for Progress in Religion' is listed in the preview of major events

of the Parliament titled 'glimpses of the 1993 Parliament' contained in the official packet sent to all registrants. It does not *precede* the Parliament, but, according to the official schedule of events, take place on the *6th evening* of the 8-day Parliament—Thursday, September 2, 1993. The *CPWR* [Council for a Parliament of the World's Religions—D.H.] *Journal* of June, 1993, indicates that Sir John Marks Templeton, founder of the prize, is a 'CPWR Board Member' actively involved in planning and promoting the Parliament. He is also a major donor for the underwriting of Parliament expenses."[255]

I might add that the National Council of Churches,[256] as well as the Rockefellers,[257] were also co-sponsors and supporters of this ungodly and pagan gathering.

Texe Marrs explains:

"Among the 'distinguished' attendees scheduled to be with **Chuck Colson** there in Chicago are Chidananda Saraswati, a **Hindu swami;** Hans Kung, a liberal Roman Catholic theologian; Omar Naseef, secretary-general of the **Muslim** World League; and the **Dalai Lama of Tibetan Buddhism.** Also attending: Joan Campbell, feminist director of the Marxist-oriented National Council of Churches, officials of Lucis Trust (formerly *Lucifer Publishing*), **Zoroastrian sun god worshippers, witchcraft priestesses, santeria/voodoo high priests,** apostate Christians, **Freemason** higher-ups, **serpent charmers,** and **druid priests.** In all, occultists and false religionists from over 130 countries will trek to Chicago to celebrate their **'Unity in Diversity.'...**

"In press releases, Chuck Colson announced his pleasure in being selected for the 'John S. Templeton Progress in Religion Prize' with its cash reward of one million dollars. He noted that Mother Teresa and Billy Graham were past recipients of the prize. However, Colson failed to mention that *other* **past recipients include India's Hindu guru Baba Amte, Japanese Buddhist teacher Nikkyo Niwano, and the secretary-general of the World Muslim Congress, Dr. Inamullah Khan....**

"Funded mainly with Rockefeller money, the *Parliament of World Religions* will be held in Chicago August 28-September 4 [1993]. It will kick off a 7 year New Age Plan first formulated by the *Club of Rome,* a key planning group under the control of the Illuminati hierarchy."[258] [Italics in the original; boldface added.]

Perhaps Colson needs to look at Ephesians 5:11-12 again: "And **have no fellowship** with the unfruitful works of darkness, **but rather**

reprove them. For it is a shame even to speak of those things which are done of them in secret."

In 1993 Colson

> "sent out a computer-generated, fundraising letter to his thousands of followers. In the letter, Colson tearfully appealed for an immediate $800,000 or, he claimed, Prison Fellowship wouldn't be able to pay its summer bills. *This letter was sent just* ***after*** *Colson's group had pocketed over $1 million he had received in May from the Sir John Templeton Prize Committee.*"[259] [Emphasis in the original.]

(The money was given in May but the speech by Colson and the official presentation of the Award was presented at the Parliament of the World's Religions.)

Colson's Prison Fellowship was listed as an organization "IN **ACTIVE SUPPORT** OF THE PLANETARY COMMISSION AND WORLD HEALING DAY."[260] [Caps in the original; boldface added.] John Randolph Price was the founder of the Planetary Commission and Quartus Foundation for Spiritual Research. His stated objective is "to continually document the truth that man is a spiritual being possessing all the powers of the spiritual realm...that **man is indeed God individualised,** and that as man realises his true identity, he becomes a Master Mind with dominion over the material world."[261]

Price believes in reincarnation,[262] communication with spirit guides[263] (two of which are "Quartus" and "Asher"[264]), evolution,[265] the New Age,[266] and the divinity of man.[267] In fact, when Price was asked how he defined the **antichrist,** he responded: **"Any individual or group who denies the divinity of man...."**[268] By this definition, I, as well as all true Christians, would be the antichrist!

Price repeatedly claims that we are God. Here are just a few of his quotations:

❊ "I see myself as God being me!"[269]

❊ "...you are God individualized...."[270]

❊ *"I am the Self-Expression of God. I am the Presence of God where I am. I am the Christ, Son of the Living God."*[271] [Emphasis in the original.]

❊ "God is expressing as me now. I am the expression of God. I am the Christ."[272]

❊ **"I am one with the Universe. I am the Universe. I and my Father are one. All that the Father is, I am. I am the Spirit of the Living God."**[273] [Emphasis in the original.]

❊ "Remember, you are the Christ of God. Therefore, you will walk as the Christ, sit as the Christ, stand as the Christ. Your body language will reflect the Christ. Your facial expressions will reflect the Christ. And you will see everyone else as you see yourself...as the Christ of God...God in individual expression."[274]

Strangely, Price teaches that we are Christ, yet he claims that **Christ,** the "God-Man had become hu-man...an **animal man."**[275] Seems like he has his priorities mixed, doesn't it?

Along with the Planetary Commission, Price was the mastermind behind the World Healing Day (also called the World Instant of Cooperation,[276] Global Mind-Link,[277] and World Meditation Day) starting on December 31, 1986 and continuing every December 31st.[278] The World Healing Meditation contains blasphemous phrases. "First the user calls upon the 'One Presence and Power of the Universe,' invoking that oneness be restored to the world and decreeing that mankind be returned to 'Godkind.'"[279] Some of the phrases from this meditation are:

> **"I am a co-creator with God,** and it is a new Heaven that comes....
> "I begin with me.
> "I am a living soul and the spirit of God dwells in me, as me.
> "I and the Father are one, and all that the Father has is mine.
> "In Truth, **I am the Christ of God.**
> "I am one with the Light....
> "I am the Light of the world....
> "Let mankind be returned to Godkind."[280]

This is the meditation for the World Healing Day that Colson's Prison Fellowship supported!

POINTS OF LIGHT

Colson "has also enthusiastically promoted George Bush's 'Thousand Points of Light' program, which has proven to be a project of the Secret Brotherhood...."[281]

Colson also wrote the foreword for the book entitled *You Can Be a Point of Light.*[282] In it, sounding like many New Agers, he penned: "Before the phrase was ever coined, I saw that the world's darkness is illuminated not by grand spotlights, but by **a thousand points of light** flickering in the night: individual Christians, living out Christ's love among those in need."[283]

Colson said that he saw the darkness was illuminated by points of light **before** the phrase was coined. However, **before** Colson was even born this phrase was used by **occultists.** For instance, the *New Age Almanac* states:

> "The Arcane School and the books of Alice Bailey have contributed heavily to the concept and language of the New

> Age Movement. **As early as 1920,** she introduced the idea of **'points of light'** and 'light groups' which channel the higher spiritual forces necessary to build the New Age. She also introduced the concept of full-moon meditations. This was based on her belief that periods of the full moon were especially auspicious times for the transmission of energy from the hierarchy....The school publishes a magazine, *The Beacon.*"[284]
>
> "To accomplish such work, Bailey initiated the Triangles Program in **1937.** This program brought together people in groups of three who united daily to radiate energy into the world. The spiritual work of radiating energy provided the context in which to speak the Great Invocation. Bailey considered the **Great Invocation** a most helpful tool when repeated while visualizing the movement of energy through the group and to the world. The text as follows is now used widely in **New Age** settings: 'From the **point of Light** within the Mind of God Let Light stream forth into the minds of men. Let Light descend on Earth.'"[285]

The Great Invocation is referred to as **"A MANTRAM FOR THE NEW AGE AND FOR ALL HUMANITY."**[286] [Emphasis in the original.] The October 1982 edition of the *Reader's Digest* had a full-page ad for this "prayer."[287]

One New Age paper tells us:

> "When you say the first line: **'From the point of Light...,'** visualise...the Buddha, the Embodiment of Light or Wisdom on the planet. Visualise Him sitting in the Lotus posture, saffron robe over one shoulder, hand raised in blessing, and see emanating from the heart centre, the ajna centre (between the eyebrows), and the upraised hand of the Buddha, a brilliant golden light. See this light enter the minds of men everywhere.
>
> "When you say the line: 'Let Light descend on Earth,' visualise the sun, the physical sun, and see emanating from it beams of white light. See this light enter and saturate the Earth."[288]

In Bailey's book, *Discipleship in the New Age,* we find: "The **points of light** become the many lines or rays of light; these lines then merge and blend until the lighted Way appears before the eyes of each tired **pilgrim** on that Way. He walks in light. He **is himself the light,** the light upon the Way. He is the Way and always walks thereon."[289] This message was given in **1936.**

A spirit guide (actually a demon) called Djwhal Khul said in **1939:** *"The world today is in such a distressing condition that the major need in every country is the appearance of 'steadily shining*

points of light' *which can illuminte the way for others."*[290] [Italics in the original; boldface added.]

In World Goodwill's October 1973 commentary, we are told:

> *"It is the hearts and minds of men and women throughout the world that need to be transformed.... Unlike the* ***repressive and puritanical misapplication of spiritual values*** *in the past, these* ***new values*** *can then be recognized as a liberating and fulfilling way of life. The individual whose livingness is expressed daily in terms of right values can be thought of as a* ***point of light....*** *When there are enough men and women of goodwill actively expressing the new value, the world will be aflame with the possibilities of transformation."*[291] [Italics in the original; boldface added.]

In another of Bailey's book, she writes:

> "In all the teaching given to the aspirant and to the disciple in the early stages of their training, **the emphasis has been upon the 'point of light'** which must be discovered, brought into full illumination, and then so used that the one in whom the light shines becomes a **light-bearer** in a dark world. This, the aspirant is taught, becomes possible when contact with the soul has been made and the light is found. This is familiar teaching to many and is the essence of the progress to be made by aspirants and disciples in the first part of their training."[292]

In *A Treatise on White Magic,* Bailey reminds us:

> "Humanity is the planetary **light bearer,** transmitting the light of knowledge, of wisdom, and of understanding, and this in the **esoteric** sense....In man's achievement and spiritualization is the hope of the world. **Mankind itself is the world Saviour,** of which all world Saviours have been but the symbol and the guarantee."[293]

One Christian researcher adds:

> "Then, in perhaps the most revealing book Bailey ever wrote, 1957's *The Externalization of the Hierarchy,* she tells us that the **'Points of Light' refers to the men who comprise the occult leadership group** known as the *New Group of World Servers.* These individuals, she remarks, are in *service* to 'the work of the Brotherhood...the Forces of Light.' They are the ones who are to usher all of mankind from the darkness of outmoded Christianity and faded nationalism into the bright and shining 'New World Order.'
>
> "How amazing that in 1957, 31 years **before** George Bush uttered those words in New Orleans, one of the world's top

occultists, a woman who first named her organization **Lucifer Publishing,** originated not only the phrase **'points of light'** but also that vague term said by his closest advisors to be George Bush's own invention, the **'New World Order.'**"[294] [Italics in the original.]

So many occult and New Age materials refer time and again to "points of light."[295]

Although Alice Bailey may have popularized the occult phrase **"points of light,"** this expression was actually used by Masons Alexander Hamilton and George Washington as far back as September **1788.**[296] "The 19th century revolutionary Mazzini had been referred to at that time as an *'established* ***point of light*** *when rays traversed the world.'*"[297] I find it intriguing that Colson uses the same phrase!

Bailey's group, World Goodwill/Lucis Trust, was located at the United Nations.[298] In the 1995 *World Goodwill Newsletter* we find:

> "Since the earliest days of the United Nations, World Goodwill has consistently voiced its support for the Organisation as the hope of humanity.... World Goodwill's support is rooted in the belief that the UN represents the single most outstanding opportunity for humanity to move forward on the path towards an era of unity and right relations."[299]

Bailey even dreamed of the United Nations as "a new church of God."[300]

Interestingly, Colson also has "connections with the United Nations."[301]

COLSON BLASTED PRO-LIFERS

The liberal *Washington Post* asked

> "Colson to write a guest article. In the article, **Colson blasted pro-life Christians,** accusing them of 'inflammatory rhetoric.' Pro-lifers, said Colson, must **'seek common ground' with the abortionists.** Moreover, 'the Religious Right,' Colson wrote, 'must accept the fact that America is a pluralist nation.'"[302]

In addition to Colson claiming that we need to seek common ground with the abortionists, he (along with Dr. James Dobson and a few others) were participants in a conference which was held at the Vatican in November 2000 to "discuss the potential and actual effects of **globalization** on the family."[303] One writer bragged:

> "Over two hundred people attended the conference, which was quite a success, particularly as **it encouraged dialogue**

> **between Catholics and Protestants** on a topic of mutual concern: the important role of the family in **establishing** the moral and cultural foundation of a **humane globalization process.** The Institute's involvement in this conference also demonstrated its continued commitment to promoting freedom and virtue, particularly in our world's increasingly **interdependent** and sophisticated economic context."[304]

While we are talking about Colson and the Vatican, let's also look at a claim in Colson's book, *The Body,* that "indulgences are no longer part of Catholicism."[305] He wrote: "The Reformers, for example, assailed the corrupt practice of **indulgences; today they are gone."**[306] This just isn't true. Around the same time that Colson was claiming that indulgences were gone, I was taking a course in Catholicism on indulgences from the Knights of Columbus. The course explained indulgences like this:

> "An indulgence, then, is a grant whereby the Church in a sort of matching-grants program adds a portion of her reserved satisfaction to that acquired by the good works of individual members. Thus, for example, when one performs the good work of giving help to someone in need of food or clothing, this work in itself merits a degree of satisfaction which the charitable one may retain for his own spiritual benefit or offer in favor of those in Purgatory.
>
> "In either case, under certain conditions, the Church will add a share of satisfaction also, thereby enhancing the value of the good works performed. The effect of this combined satisfaction will be the remission in whole or in part of the debt of satisfaction attaching sins already forgiven."[307]

There was a question asked in the *Catholic Twin Circle* (November 4, 1990) about indulgences. The following answer was given by Priest Benjamin Luther: **"The Church still believes in indulgences and always will."**[308]

Vatican II allocates 18 pages to dealing with indulgences and *"anathematizes anyone who rejects that doctrine."*[309] Listen to Vatican II:

> "Indulgences are...the taking away of the temporal punishment due to sins when their guilt has already been forgiven....In granting an indulgence the Church uses its power as minister of Christ's Redemption....It teaches and **commands that the usage of indulgences**—a usage most beneficial to Christians and approved by the authority of the Sacred Councils—should be kept in the Church; and it **condemns with**

> **anathema [a curse] those who say that indulgences are useless** or that the Church does not have the power to grant them."[310]

The **official** *Catechism of the Catholic Church* also deals with this topic.[311] For instance: "Through indulgences the faithful can obtain the remission of temporal punishment resulting from sin for themselves and also for the souls in Purgatory"[312] and "Since the faithful departed [the dead] now being purified are also members of the same communion of saints, one way we can help them is to obtain indulgences for them, so that the temporal punishments due for their sins may be remitted."[313]

Just recently Pope John Paul II "declared the millennial year [2000] as a 'jubilee,' complete with the issuing of indulgences (for time off in purgatory)."[314] It was a 29-page degree and the "edict includes ways of earning indulgences to help get to heaven faster, including by abstaining from smoking and drinking (for even one day is rewarded) during the Holy Year and by giving to charity...."[315]

One researcher points out:

> "There are a lot of things written down on paper that show the Roman Catholic estimation of the Bible....The pope gave an indulgence to those who would read the Bible. Back in the days when they gave numerical value to partial indulgences, you could get **300 days indulgence if you read the Gospels for 15 minutes.** That means they **gave 20 days for each minute they read the Bible.** In the forewords (sic) of the Confraternity Roman Catholic edition, they give you a prayer to the Holy Spirit that you can recite. That prayer takes **less than a minute.** The indulgence for saying this prayer is **5 years.** That makes it **over 90 times as powerful as Bible reading.**"[316]

INDULGENCES GENERATE FRAUD

The Catholic Encyclopedia admitted that the idea of indulgences (declared a dogma by Clement VI in mid-1300s[317]) led to many abuses. It says that because indulgences are linked with money, "the practice was fraught with grave danger, and soon became a fruitful source of evil...a means of raising money...indulgences were employed by mercenary ecclesiastics as a means of pecuniary gain... abuses were widespread."[318]

Indulgences are so much of an issue for Catholicism today that on February 9-10, 2001, "Catholics, Lutherans and Reformed held an ecumenical theological consultation on the theme of INDULGENCES."[319] [Emphasis in the original.] The meeting took place in Rome by the invitation of the Pontifical Council for Promoting Christian Unity.[320]

Furthermore, Vatican II adds:

> "The faithful who use with devotion an object of piety (crucifix, cross, rosary, scapular or medal) after it has been duly blessed by any priest, **can gain a partial indulgence.** But if this object of piety is blessed by the Pope or any bishop, the faithful who use it with devotion can also gain a **plenary indulgence** on the feast of the apostles Peter and Paul....When one of the faithful is in danger of death and no priest in available to administer the sacraments to him with the apostolic blessing... holy Mother Church still grants a plenary indulgence to be gained at the moment of death, on condition that they are properly disposed and have been in the habit of reciting some prayers during their lifetime. The practice of using a crucifix or cross while gaining this plenary indulgence is praiseworthy."[321]

So much for **Colson's false claim** that indulgences are gone!

MADELEINE L'ENGLE

Chuck Colson has "encouraged Christians to read the works of fiction writer Madeleine L'Engle, in spite of the fact that **L'Engle's writings are laced with occultism and New Age imagery."**[322] These writings are also full of heresy and even blasphemy. For instance, consider the following quotations taken from some of L'Engle's books.

✧ "The **Bible** is not a moral book. It is not an ethical book. It is a magnificent story book. It **doesn't give any answers,** it just tells more stories."[323]

✧ "We are not called to be Christians; we are called Christs."[324]

✧ "Contradictions start in the first chapter of Genesis. There are two Creation stories, two stories of the making of Adam and Eve."[325]

✧ L'Engle contends that "limited literalism which demands that the Bible's poetry and story and drama and parable be taken as factual history is one of **Satan's cleverest devices."**[326] In other words, L'Engle claims that to take the Bible literally is one of Satan's devices!

✧ In one of her books she has Dennys talking about the flood: "Listen, it's a stupid story....They're just like whoever wrote the silly ark story, seeing things only from their own point of view, using people."[327]

✧ "Some churches remain stuck in the old literal representations of heaven and hell....They are still good metaphors, but no longer to be taken literally."[328] L'Engle's book that contains this quotation is part of the Wheaton Literary Series![329] We've already covered a little bit about Wheaton College in Chapter 7.

✧ "Heaven is not a place name. Heaven is wherever God's will is being done. When, occasionally, it is done on earth, then there is heaven."[330]

✧ "No matter how many eons it takes, he [God] will not rest until all of creation, **including Satan,** is reconciled to him...."[331]

✧ "For me Gandhi is a Christ figure. I'll be perfectly happy to go wherever he goes. If you want to call that hell, that's your problem."[332]

✧ "The story of Gideon [in the Bible] was a favorite **fairy tale** for me...."[333]

✧ "In the language of prayer I sometimes refer to my Maker as Abba/Amma (Amma being the intimate feminine for mother, mama, as Abba is father, daddy). Abba/Amma is much softer and far more personal than Father/Mother."[334]

✧ **"Jesus** is also **the true princess,** and the true princess is within each one of us, too."[335] (Notice the feminine reference to Jesus as a princess—not a prince!)

✧ *"How many people visualize God as looking like Moses—long beard, white nightgown—and Moses in a bad temper at that? Male. Chauvinist. Punitive."*[336]

✧ At one point she refers to the God of the Old Testament as the "paternalistic male chauvinist pig Old Testament god."[337] The book that has this statement in it was "published as part of the Wheaton Literary Series!"[338]

✧ "When I am informed that Jesus of Nazareth was exactly like us except sinless, I block. If he was sinless he wasn't exactly like us....I want Jesus to be like us because he is God's show and tell, and too much dogma obscures rather than reveals the likeness."[339]

✧ "Elijah, like Ezekiel, is a **mythic figure,** larger than life....At the end of Elijah's life, a chariot of fire appears, and horses of fire, and *Elijah went up to heaven in a whirlwind.* What a wonder!

"Strong stuff. **Mythic** stuff....

"Jesus, like Elijah, stands *on the mountain in the presence of the Lord* and takes with him Peter and James and John, and extraordinary things, incomprehensible things, come to pass. Jesus' clothing becomes shining, and Elijah himself appears to Jesus in the brilliance, and so does Moses, and the three talk together, breaking ordinary chronology into a million fragments. And then a cloud over-shadows them, as it over-shadowed Moses on the mount, and the voice of God thunders out of the cloud.

"Strong stuff. **Mythic stuff. Story."**[340] [Italics in the original.]

✧ "When I receive **Communion** I am partaking in **the most sacred myth** and ritual of the Christian church...."[341]

✧ She said that "the **Ascension** is freed to move to the **realm of myth.**"[342]

✧ In *Camilla,* L'Engle writes: "You know **what we need is a new God....**I mean what we need is a God people like me, or David, or you, or our parents, could really believe in. I mean, look at all the advances we've made scientifically since—oh, well, since Christ was born if you want to put a date on it....But you take God. God hasn't change any since Jesus took him out of white nightgown and long whiskers....So what we need again now is a new God. The God most people are worshipping in churches and temples hasn't grown since Christ's time. He's deteriorated....We need a God who's big enough for the atomic age."[343]

We don't need a new God. My God says: "For I am the LORD, I change not..." (Malachi 3:6). Hebrews 1:10-12 (taken from Psalm 102:25-27) states:

> "Thou, Lord, in the beginning hast laid the foundation of the earth; and the heavens are the works of Thine hands: They shall perish; but Thou remainest; and they all shall wax old as doth a garment; And as a vesture shalt Thou fold them up, and they shall be changed: but **Thou art the same,** and Thy years shall not fail."

✧ "The methods of contemplative prayer are similar in all traditions. Sit quietly, preferably comfortably...having found the physical context, breathe slowly, rhythmically, deeply. Fit the words of your **mantra** to this rhythm. And don't be afraid of the word, **mantra.**"[344]

VAIN REPETITIONS

Any Christian who knows anything about the New Age movement and **occult meditation** can easily recognize that L'Engle has just described this very state! Furthermore, Christians **SHOULD** be afraid of the word "mantra"! I have hundreds upon hundreds of references to mantras—all from New Age and occult sources. Mantras or "words of power"[345] are often used by occultists to enter into an **ALTERED STATE of consciousness** or a **TRANCE-LIKE state.**[346] According to occultists, the word **mantra means "incantation"**[347] **or "a magic utterance."**[348] In a Christian book, *Psychic Forces and Occult Shock,* we find:

> "Mantras are special words believed to be imbued with occult powers and used in eastern meditation. Almost always they have corresponding *devas* (gods or spirits) which

accompany them and help the meditator accomplish his purposes of gaining power, wealth, control over others, etc....The mantra is used to empty the mind, attract the spirit, and when he is possessed, the magician bids the spirit to do his will. In this case, the spoken mantra itself has no power, but the spirit who places himself behind it. The mantra has become a focalization for occult power."[349] [Emphasis in the original.]

A New Age source states:

"Through adequate *mantras* any sort of being can be evoked. *Mantras* are therefore the key to all rituals in all religions and are also used in most forms of magic....

"Each deity is represented by a distinct *mantra,* and it is only through these mysterious sounds that images can be consecrated and become 'alive.' It is the power of the *mantra* which brings down the deity and makes it enter the image....

"'Hindu life is pervaded by *mantras.* The entire existence of a peasant or a prince is regulated by them. The purposes of *mantras* are numerous; they are used for: (1) attaining liberation, (2) worship of the manifest forms of divinity, (3) worship of the lesser gods and genii, (4) communicating with deities, (5) the acquisition of superhuman powers, (6) the feeding of Ancestors and gods, (7) communicating with ghosts and spirits, (8) warding off evil influences, (9) exorcising devils, (10) the cure of diseases, (11) preparing curative water, (12) destroying plants, animals, or men, (13) eliminating poisons from the body, (14) influencing others' thoughts and actions, (15) bringing men, beasts, lesser deities, and ghosts under control, (16) the purification of the human body.'"[350] [Emphasis in the original.]

These "words of power" are REPEATED OVER AND OVER again until this trance-like condition is achieved. In this state, the mind is opened to all kinds of demonic activity and influence because the person's rational, thinking ability has been set aside by the REPETITION of the words he or she has spoken. Is it any wonder that the Bible warns us not to use "VAIN REPETITIONS, as the HEATHEN do..." (Matthew 6:7)? God knew that the use of repetitious words would open us up to demonic influence and, therefore, He warned us not to do this.

In spite of biblical warning NOT to use REPETITIOUS words and phrases, so-called "Christian" leaders (such as L'Engle) are now telling us to use a word or phrase OVER AND OVER again so that what we say can register in our subconscious minds and become reality in our lives.

L'Engle believes in evolution and refers to Adam and Eve as **"mythic** ancestors."[351] She even "puts down those who believe the Genesis creation account—comparing them to fools who still think the world is flat."[352]

"She acquaints the reader with the Hindu concept that God is within everyone or, more precisely, that everyone is God. She describes the Hindu greeting of *Namaste,* 'I salute the God within you,' and calls it beautiful."[353]

She also "teaches the New Age heresy that we realize godhood by acquiring the 'gifts' of the past: necromancy, mediumship, astral travel, ESP, witchcraft...and these are just a...few."[354] No wonder her "books are populated with dozens of New Age occult symbols, witches, unicorns, pegasus, crystal balls, rainbows, demons, all seeing eyes, dragons, and the powers of the mind."[355] She "continually exalts those acts that God forbids, promoting homosexuality, witchcraft, occult practices, Druids, and premarital sex. In fact, *House Like a Lotus* contains a graphic sex scene in which a sixteen-year-old loses her virginity—for children to read and enjoy."[356]

> "When witches gather in covens, they use certain rituals for creating altered states of mind and for practicing magic. Miriam Starhawk, who calls herself a goddess-worshipping pagan witch, has written a book called *Spiral Dance* in which she gives the four basic skills every young **witch** needs to master for magic. Those skills are: 1) relaxation, 2) concentration, 3) visualization, and 4) projection or manifestation. It is interesting that **L'Engle teaches these same four steps in her books."**[357]

Readers also need to understand that **L'Engle "is the librarian at St. John the Divine.** This **New Age** cathedral achieved notoriety in recent years by **displaying a life-sized crucifix with a shapely, female Christ and by housing a Buddha."**[358]

L'Engle's son-in-law happens to be Alan Jones, the Dean of Grace Cathedral.[359] The Grace Cathedral had a "Spirituality Series" in 1997 with such occultists/New Agers as: Huston Smith, Frances Vaughan, Ram Dass, and Christina Grof.[360] Jones was one of the participants at Gorbachev's State of the World Forum[361] and is also involved with the United Religions Initiative.[362]

So much more could be said about L'Engle and her ungodly books, but in spite of all the evil, heresy, and occultism, so-called "Christians" continue to endorse her works and open their pulpits to her. Billy Graham's magazine, *Christianity Today,* has admiringly quoted from L'Engle.[363] "She was a featured speaker at Bill and Gloria Gaither's 'Praise Gathering' in Indianapolis [in 1991]. She also lectures on Christian college campuses across the nation."[364] Wheaton College gave her an honorary doctorate degree[365] and her "writings are housed in a special collection in Wheaton's library, placing a mark of rare significance upon them."[366] Interestingly, if I were to leave the Wheaton College library and drive down the road a few miles, I would arrive at the occult/New Age Theosophical Society—where I could purchase L'Engle's books![367] The occultists certainly seem to be aware of the contents of her works. It's sad that the so-called "Christian" leaders can't see this—or are they intentionally trying to lead naive Christians into occult practices?

Not only does Colson promote L'Engle, but in his May 1992 *Breakpoint* he urged people to buy C. S. Lewis' **occult fantasy** video, *The Chronicles of Narnia.*[368] He wrote:

> "There's a fantasy world where animals talk, where children are kings and queens, where an evil spell means it's always winter but never Christmas. Where a noble, talking lion breaks the evil spell and spring comes at last to the frost-bound land....
>
> "What puzzles me a bit is that I never heard about these excellent videos through Christian channels. Are any Christian organizations distributing them? Here's a rare opportunity for Christians to applaud **secular** broadcasting for a **product we can wholeheartedly approve....**
>
> "Buy the videos and watch them with your children."[369]

GREEK GOD OF LUST

In Colson's book, *The Body,* he once again brags up these occult fantasy books and then adds that they "present the entire history of redemption...."[370] He adds that "Lewis's science fiction trilogy—*Out of the Silent Planet, Perelandra,* and *That Hideous Strength*—tells the same story for adults."[371] Well, I've read *Perelandra* and I found it disgusting! It certainly didn't seem to explain the gospel to me. I might add that it also contained swearing and curse words.

Perelandra "promotes the concept of the entire planet as the 'Green Lady.'"[372] The New Agers says this "refers to the Goddess of the pagan mythologies. Indeed, New Agers have even established the *Perelandra Community* based on the writings of C. S. Lewis."[373]

The founder of Perelandra, Machaelle Small Wright, "welcomes visitors to the community but one cannot become a resident until Wright is satisfied that the person has read Lewis' novel *Perelandra.*"[374]

Wright "teams up the devas and nature spirits with mankind to heal the planet and maintain balance and harmony."[375] An article in the New Age magazine, *Connecting Link,* says that "Wright is a gifted **channel** [a medium] with whom the nature intelligences have been working to create the Perelandra garden, a research project which stands as a model to the Earth's farming community."[376] Wright herself reports: "As you probably know, there is a huge volume of traditional literature around nature spirits and **Pan.** Usually nature spirits are portrayed as cute and Pan is portrayed as powerful and **demonic."** Of course, she denies that Pan is demonic but she feels that he is "in charge" of the nature spirits. She continues:

> "Pan is everywhere and available to us all. Whenever I wish to be connected to the nature spirit level in a general manner for whatever reason, I connect with Pan. If I have a question regarding an issue around spirit and form and I don't know which specific nature spirit to contact for help, I go to Pan."[377]

What Wright fails to tell you is that Pan happens to be another name for **Satan.**[378] For instance, the **occult** catalog, *International Imports,* states: "In Greek mythology **Pan** was the **god of nature.** In astrology he is one aspect of Saturn. He **is also equated with Satan** and life's baser aspects."[379] Pan is normally pictured as a goat or half-goat, half-man[380] and "is usually represented with horns...and with legs covered with hair...."[381] In *The Satanic Bible* Pan is called the "Greek god of lust" who was "later relegated to devildom."[382] Another name for Pan is Baphomet![383] (For more information on Baphomet, see my book entitled *Hidden Secrets of the Eastern Star.)*

PERELANDRA MEANS "VENUS"

"Pan was the patron saint of sexual pastimes"[384] and was known for his "sudden sexual forays against girls and boys alike."[385] "He often tried to capture women, and because of his lustfulness, they lived in such fear of him that his name is still associated with fear, in the adjective 'panicky' and the noun 'panic.'"[386] Since Pan is represented with horns it is no wonder that he is called the "Horned God" by the witches.[387] Aleister Crowley, a black magician, Satanist, and Mason, wrote a *Hymn to Pan* and had it recited at his funeral service.[388]

> "In Rhode Island, the Church of Pan exists. The members are involved with a nudist campground....
>
> "The logo for the Magical Childe occult store in New York is of a Pan figure. This store was formerly called the **Warlock Shop."**[389]

This is the deity that helps Wright in her Perelandra community. Now what does Perelandra mean? "...the word 'perelandra' means

'venus, planet of perfection.'"[390] Occultists believe that Lucifer, who they envision as a "good" being, came from the planet Venus about 18 to 19 million years ago.[391] In fact, **Venus is another name for Lucifer!**[392] Occultist Helena Petrovna Blavatsky wrote in *The Theosophical Glossary:* "Lucifer....The planet Venus, as the bright Morning Star."[393] Masonic writer, John Robinson, concurs: "In Roman astronomy, Lucifer was the name given to the morning star (the star we now know by another Roman name, Venus)."[394] Another New Ager states: "Scholars agree that the name Lucifer originally denoted the planet Venus, the morning star and bringer of light...."[395] Masonic writer, Arthur Edward Waite, remarks that the morning star is Lucifer.[396] Additionally, the Association for Research and Enlightenment (ARE), as well as other New Age groups, believe that Lucifer (or Venus) is the bright and morning star.[397] Revelation 22:16 reveals that **JESUS** is the Bright and Morning Star, but Lucifer has always wanted to take God's place (Isaiah 14:12-14). Since he is a liar and the father of lies (John 8:44), it is no surprise that he also takes a name that does not belong to him.

The *Short Dictionary of Mythology* states: **"Lucifer,** a name of the planet Venus. It is called Lucifer when it appears in the morning before the sun; when it appears after sunset it is called Hesperus."[398] [Emphasis in the original.] Interestingly, this same book, under the word **"goat"** says **"see** Iphigenia, **Mendes, and Venus."**[399] Remember that Pan (Satan or Lucifer) is portrayed as a goat-god and also called **Baphomet** or the Goat of Mendes,[400] as well as the "god of the witches."[401] The book, *The Occult Conspiracy,* ties these names together when it states:

> "On the forehead of the **Baphomet** figure, marking the physical site of the pineal gland or **third eye,** is the magical sign of the **pentagram** or five pointed star which represents humankind in its unperfected state. It is also a symbol of the **morning star, Venus,** which was associated with Ishtar and Astarte. The morning star was also a title given to **Lucifer...."**[402]

Can you guess the new title of Lewis' *Perelandra* when it was reprinted as a **PAN** paperback in 1953?[403] It was issued as *The Voyage of **Venus.***[404] Just a little "coincidence," right?!

As already mentioned Pan was a god of lust.[405] Venus, too, is the goddess of erotic love and represented lust.[406] In the rites of Venus, "the men offer sacrifices to her in woman's attire, the women wearing male garments, because the same goddess is esteemed both male and female."[407] She was also the goddess of prostitution.[408] With that in mind, it's interesting to note that the word "venereal disease" was derived from the name "Venus."[409]

JESUS WAS THE FULFILLMENT OF MYTH

Without going into much detail, suffice it to say that **Lewis was an occultist.**[410] "He was a Theosophist before he turned to the Anglican Church,"[411] but he took his occultic ideas with him.

"C. S. Lewis was most fond of expressing a belief in Jesus, followed by a clarifying exclamation, 'Jesus was the fulfillment of **myth.'** According to Lewis, Jesus deserved worship because he was, 'the **myth** that had come true.'"[412]

"...Lewis also taught in his novels, the *Chronicles of Narnia* series, that all service done by a person on behalf of Lucifer and the dark side was, in fact, also credited by God as service to him!"[413]

Albert Dager writes:

> "Many of Lewis's fans see the great lion, Aslan, as Christ. This [is] because Aslan lays down his life to free the children from the curse of the evil witch (believed to represent Satan). He possesses knowledge of a greater 'magic' than that of the witch—a magic that brings him back to life and destroys the witch's power.
>
> "It is argued that, in presenting a blend of fantasy with analogy to Christian truth, Lewis hoped to encourage his readers to search out the truth further. This, however, was **not** Lewis's intention in writing his fantasies. Rather, he was genuinely enamored of mythology and believed the 'Story' to take precedence over any preconceived moral. In Lewis's own words, 'Some people seem to think that I began by asking myself how I could say something about Christianity to children; then fixed on the fairy tale as an instrument; then collected information about child-psychology and decided what age group I'd write for; then drew up a list of basic Christian truths and hammered out 'allegories' to embody them. This is all pure moonshine. I couldn't write in that way at all. Everything began with images; a faun carrying an umbrella, a queen on a sledge, a magnificent lion. **At first there wasn't even anything Christian about them;** that element pushed itself in of its own accord.'
>
> "So we see that *Narnia* was not by design, Christian allegory."[414]

Dager further notes:

> "In any case, it is dangerous to present evil as good, and magic as synonymous with the miracle-working power of the Holy Spirit (Isaiah 5:20; Acts 8:9-23).

> "Many of Lewis's characters in his fantasies, depicted as 'good,' are in reality associated with witchcraft, pagan mythology, and in Norse mysteries. They are, in fact, **gods of nature.** And magic in these stories is used for either 'good' **OR** 'evil' purposes depending upon the source of that magic."[415]

For instance, the Satan clone (a faun in the form of **Pan)** in *The Chronicles of Narnia* is a "good" character who helps the children.[416] Listen to Lewis' description of this being:

> "He was only a little taller than Lucy herself and he carried over his head an umbrella, white with snow. From the waist upwards he was like a **man,** but his legs were shaped like a **goat's** (the hair on them was glossy black) and instead of feet he had **goat's hoofs.** He also has a **tail,** but Lucy did not notice this at first because it was neatly caught up over the arm that held the umbrella so as to keep it from trailing in the snow. He had a red woollen (sic) muffler round his neck and his skin was rather reddish too. He had a strange, but pleasant little face, with a short pointed beard and curly hair, and out of the hair there stuck two **horns,** one on each side of his forehead."[417]

Lewis' books contain curse words and take the name of the Lord in vain.[418] The Bible warns: "Thou shalt not take the name of the Lord thy God in vain" (Exodus 20:7; Deuteronomy 5:11).

Interestingly, **occult** stores carry *The Chronicles of Narnia* and other books by Lewis.[419] "The 'Books of Light' New Age Bookclub has chosen C. S. Lewis' novels as main selections. One New Age publisher actually named their company *Aslan Publishing,* after the main character, the god-lion Aslan, in C. S. Lewis' *Chronicles of Narnia.*"[420]

Dr. Shirley Correll shares this important tidbit: "It would be difficult to go to any occult book store and not find the *Chronicles of Narnia* promoted. One such occult book store owner told this author [Dr. Correll] and others that he became involved in the occult as a result of reading the *Chronicles of Narnia.*"[421]

> "**Jean Houston,** of the New Age's The Mystery School, has also **highly commended C. S. Lewis'** mythological book *Perelandra.* In a recent brochure sent out by The Mystery School she exclaims: 'The fictional works of visionary writers like Lewis Carroll (*Alice in Wonderland*)...and the fantasies of **C. S. Lewis** (*Perelandra*) and **Madeleine L'Engle** (*A Wrinkle in Time*) and many others may serve to inspire our creation of the new **myth.'** In the New Age, the 'new myth' is a cult phrase for the New Age kingdom on planet earth."[422]

WE ARE GODS

One **occult** organization wrote:

> "C. S. Lewis originally wrote the *Chronicles of Narnia* for children. However, the books were discovered by students of **mystical metaphysics** because they truly convey an inspirational feeling of sacred dimensions parallel to the physical plane. Enter Narnia and you experience magical lands and enchanted happenings."[423]

Occultists recognize the esoteric aspect of these books, but people such as Chuck Colson think they represent Christian ideas—which they definitely do not!

"In Lewis' nonfiction writings, we discover his belief in evolution, in the Catholic version of Mary, and in the odd notion that in our 'next lives,' Christians may just become planets, stars, or other heavenly objects."[424]

Moreover, Lewis believed the Bible to be flawed,[425] "denied the depravity of man, the inerrancy of Scripture, and the substitutionary Atonement of Jesus Christ."[426] He suggested that **"Jesus was an ignorant prophet,** regrettably tied to the Jewish messianic myth. Lewis further suggested that Jesus' prophecies had failed to come to pass."[427]

Lewis wrote: "I have the **deepest respect for Pagan myths,** still more for **<u>myths</u> in the Holy Scriptures."**[428]

He accepted the belief in purgatory[429] but he rejected the literal resurrection of the body. "His contention that some pagans may 'belong to Christ without knowing it' is a destructible heresy....Lewis never believed in a literal hell, but instead believed hell is a state of mind one chooses to possess...."[430]

In *Mere Christianity* Lewis wrote that God said in the Bible

> "that we were 'gods,' and He is going to make good His words. If we let Him—for we can prevent Him, if we choose—**He will make the feeblest and filthiest of us into a god or goddess,** dazzling, radiant, immortal creature, pulsating all through with such energy and joy, and wisdom and love as we cannot now imagine.'"[431]

Lewis' books teach enough Mormon doctrine that Deseret Book stores carry a number of his books.[432]

> "The book *Mormons on the Internet* lists a C. S. Lewis home page with the description: 'Yeah, yeah, so he wasn't technically LDS [Latter-day Saint or Mormon]. But his personal

theology continues to speak to LDS beliefs to such a degree that he certainly deserves the status of honorary member.'"[433]

I find it strange that Mormons are willing to accept Lewis as an "honorary member" in light of the fact that he "was a heavy beer drinker and strongly addicted to tobacco—rarely being seen without his pipe."[434] You see, Mormons are supposed to avoid alcoholic beverages, tobacco, and even caffeine.[435] (For more information on the teachings of Mormonism, please see my book *Mormonism, Masonry, and Godhood.)*

These were the beliefs of the author of books that Colson has urged people to read! Lewis' influence has been continued in the Evangelicals and Catholics Together document. Charles Colson contributed to the book entitled *Evangelicals and Catholics Together: Working Towards a Common Mission.* In it he "tells us that C. S. Lewis was a **major influence** which led him to form the movement (Billy Graham was another!). In fact Colson says that *Evangelicals and Catholics Together* seeks to **continue the legacy of C. S. Lewis** by focusing on the core beliefs of all true Christians."[436]

HARRY POTTER

Just recently Colson bragged up, and highly recommended, the **occultic** Harry Potter books to his radio audience. "Harry and his friends 'develop courage, loyalty, and a willingness to sacrifice for one another—even at the risk of their lives,' says Colson. 'Not bad lessons in a self-centered world.'"[437]

He also states: "It may relieve you to know that the magic in these books is purely mechanical, as opposed to occultic. That is, **Harry and his friends cast spells, read crystal balls, and turn themselves into animals**—but they don't make contact with a supernatural world."[438] Of course, this just isn't true. If Harry Potter doesn't "make contact with a supernatural world," how does his broomstick fly? How can he and his friends turn into animals, etc.? Former occultists know that the Harry Potter books are **REAL WITCHCRAFT.**

> "The hero namesake of the [Harry Potter] books is a young **wizard,** the son of a murdered wizard and witch. His adoptive parents, who are not witches, are depicted as foolish and cruel; but he escapes to attend the Hogwarts wizard's school.... Textbooks at the wizard school have titles like 'The Standard **Book of Spells.'** The directors of the school are **ghosts** who died gruesome deaths. One is named Near Headless Nick; he was killed by being struck 45 times in the neck with a blunt ax. There is a 'Sorceror's (sic) Stone' that has the power to give immortality.

> "The world of **witchcraft is depicted as exciting and desirable. Witches are intelligent** and caring; whereas **non-witches,** called Muggles in the books, **are dull and uncaring. Harry Potter and his wizard friends lie, steal, break rules, disobey authority figures, and take revenge. Harry Potter also makes and uses drug potions,** including the psychedelic drug thujone, which has been banned in the United States since 1915. The wizards practice Hindu-type meditation 'to clear the Inner Eye.' There is swearing and violence. A three-headed dog mangles the leg of a professor; a mysterious figure drinks blood from a unicorn carcass; children are attacked and paralyzed; a dead cat is hung upside-down by its tail. There are creatures called Dementors that 'suck out people's souls.' There are ghosts who haunt bathroom toilets. In the second volume, a monster speaks to Harry through the walls of a castle, saying, 'Come...come to me....Let me rip you....Let me tear you.... Let me kill you.' When Harry kills the monster, its eyes are punctured and 'a sudden shower of dark blood spattered the floor.' The fourth volume contains a **torture scene** and two deaths. The final battle scene is 'bloody and frightening. Voldemort's servant must exhume the bones of the Dark lord's father, draw Harry's blood, and **sacrifice his own hand** in order to restore Voldemort's body.'"[439]

Harry Potter and the Prisoner of Azkaban teaches astral travel and necromancy, which is communication with the dead.[440] The Bible warns in Deuteronomy 18:10:

> "There shall not be found among you any one that maketh his son or his daughter to pass through the fire, or that useth divination, or an observer of times, or an enchanter, or a **witch,** Or a charmer, or a consulter with **familiar spirits,** or a **wizard,** or a **necromancer.** For *all that do these things are an abomination unto the LORD....*"

Another book, *Harry Potter and the Sorcerer's Stone,* teaches that *"death is but the next great adventure."*[441] [Emphasis in the original.] The Bible, however, tells us that death is an **enemy** (I Corinthians 15:26). This Harry Potter book also explains: *"There is no good and evil."*[442] [Emphasis in the original.] The Bible, on the other hand, teaches that good and evil do exist and warns: "Depart from evil, and do good; seek peace, and pursue it." (Psalm 34:14. See also Psalm 37:27; Amos 5:14-15.)

"In the books we see young Harry lying, breaking rules, making fun of and mocking adults, and seeking revenge. To defeat his foes, Harry uses magic and witchcraft rituals and methods. On his forehead, notably, is the rune symbol of the satanic lightning bolt."[443]

Psalm 52:3 seems appropriate: "Thou lovest evil more than good; and lying rather than to speak righteousness." Remember, I Corinthians 15:33 forewarns: "Be not deceived: evil communications corrupt good manners."

Since the Harry Potter books are on the market, the membership of the Young Magicians Club has increased by 25%.[444] "The Pagan Society claims it gets over 100 calls a month from children wanting to become witches."[445] "Phyllis Curott, a **witch** interviewed by ABCNews.com, observed that the books depict wizards and witches as 'positive,' 'friendly,' and 'good'; therefore the books 'might change the way people feel about us.'"[446] Yet such books are **highly recommended** by Chuck Colson! He said: **"This is an admirable message...."**[447]

CT PROMOTES OCCULT BOOKS

Of course, Colson isn't the only "evangelical" promoting the Harry Potter books. *Christianity Today (CT)* also promotes these **occultic** books. It states: "We think you should read the Harry Potter books to your kids."[448] *CT* also said that this series was a "'Book of Virtues' with a pre-adolescent funny bone. Amid the laugh-out-loud scenes are wonderful examples of compassion, loyalty, courage, friendship and even self-sacrifice."[449]

The April 23, 2001 issue of *CT* also extolled **C. S. Lewis** and called him "'the 20th century's greatest Christian apologist' and praised his mythical works."[450] David Cloud states: "*Christianity Today* says, 'In Aslan [a mythical lion in Lewis' *Narnia* series], Christ is made tangible, knowable, real.' As if we can know Jesus Christ best through a **fable** that is vaguely based on biblical themes."[451]

Graham, as well as his family, were also enthralled with Lewis' works. In *Billy Graham: The Great Evangelist* we find:

> "When he [Billy Graham] fretted and gnawed his fingernails, as he always did, the children dubbed him 'Puddleglum,' a lovable but constantly pessimistic character in *The Silver Chair* by **C. S. Lewis.** 'Is the King dead? Has the enemy landed in Narnia?' giggled the children. They had read all the 'Narnia' books by Lewis. So did Ruth. And she branched out into the realm of Lewis, reading his adult books and his taste in other writers: George MacDonald and G. K. Chesterton. She even collected discarded first editions signed by them.
>
> "'Someday maybe these **saintly authors** will be appreciated,' she told Billy."[452]

Remember, *Christianity Today* is the magazine that **Billy Graham** started—and still has some control over to this day. In the December 4, 2000, issue Harold Myra, Corporate Editor, bragged:

> **"*Christianity Today* has a rich heritage of leadership, starting with our founder, Billy Graham, and his early colleagues.**
>
> "'As of this issue, Billy appears on our mastheads as both founder and honorary chairman. He served as our chairman for many years and throughout the life of **Christianity Today** International has been its guiding light and vital resource. For more than five decades, he has recruited board members, encouraged and admonished us, and modeled a positive gospel. As health allows, he will continue to share his wisdom and vision.'"[453] [Emphasis in the original.]

Who were some of these recruits? Graham himself gives the answer in his autobiography: "As for the contributing editors, I suggested to Carl [Henry] a lot of people I had met in my travels throughout the world—people he wouldn't necessarily have known. **Among these were** English and Australian leaders and **World Council of Churches people...."**[454]

Colson is listed in *Christianity Today* as one of its contributing editors (along with John R. W. Stott).[455] Richard Neuhaus, Colson's co-author of "Evangelicals and Catholics Together," is also an advisory editor for *Christianity Today.*[456] Oh, Neuhaus' *First Things* also supports the Harry Potter books.[457]

COMMON GROUND

One senior editor for *Christianity Today* is J. I. Packer.[458] He has signed the Evangelicals and Catholics Together document.[459]

> "Of this participation with Evangelicals and Catholics Together he concluded, 'I remain glad to endorse it.' At a meeting in Dublin, Ireland, on July 31, 1998, Packer referred to Pope John Paul II as 'a fine Christian man.'"[460]

He also met the Pope at John Cardinal O'Connor's residence in New York.[461]

Not surprisingly, Packer has endorsed Colson's book, *The Body.*[462] Both Colson and Packer have also endorsed a book by Peter Kreeft, a Catholic.[463] In this book Kreeft claims that

> "'*Muslims and Christians preach and practice the same First Commandment;* Islam, total surrender submission of the

> human will to the divine will. We fight side by side not only because we face a common enemy but above all because *we serve and worship the same divine Commander.'*
>
> "...Kreeft has the audacity to call all pagans as well. Only these are no longer pagans—they're anonymous Christians!
>
> "Finally even atheists and agnostics, if they are of good will and intellectual honesty and still believe in objective truth and objective morality, are on our side in the war against the powers of darkness.'"[464] [Emphasis in the original.]

One of Kreeft's suggestions is: "Consecrate your life to the Immaculate Heart of Mary. She is the one who will win this war. She is the one (as the Bible says) who triumphs over Satan."[465] The Bible says no such thing—but that doesn't seem to matter to either Packer or Colson.

Of course, Packer doesn't believe what the Bible teaches about hell, either. In a *Christianity Today* article he stated that he doesn't believe that "the essence of hell is grotesque bodily discomfort."[466]

Packer has joined with Catholics on several occasions **but he criticizes the fundamentalists** and states that "it is the way of fundamentalists to follow the path of contentious orthodoxism, as if the mercy of God in Christ automatically rests on persons who are notionally correct and is just as automatically withheld from those who fall short of notional correctness...."[467] Leigh Adams responds to Packer's criticism like this:

> "[Packer's] railing accusation does not bode well for this noted theologian and expositor. Sadly, it appears he has chosen to walk with the crowd rather than follow the clear teaching of the Word of God to separate from error. Obedience to the Word of God cannot be defined as 'the path of contentious orthodoxism.'"[468]

I guess we should not be surprised that **Packer dislikes fundamentalists** as he was one of those who attended a meeting in Washington a few years ago to **protest the religious right.**[469] He also signed "The Cry for Renewal"[470] statement which was drafted by Tony Campolo and Jim Wallis—"two leaders widely known as religious liberals," says the *Philadelphia Inquirer.*[471] Additionally, Packer was one of the signers of "An Evangelical Declaration on the Care of Creation"[472] (as were Ronald Sider and John Stott[473]).

Packer, like Colson, loves the **occultist C. S. Lewis** and referred to him as **"our patron saint."**[474]

Would it surprise you to learn that Packer was one of the speakers at Billy Graham's Amsterdam 2000?[475]

THE ALPHA COURSE

Packer is also an endorser of the Alpha program that has been recently sweeping the world.[476] **"Alpha...is being seen as a means of drawing together both Protestants and Catholics...." "Alpha bids to focus on common ground."**[477] [Boldface in the original; underlining added.] Jerry Huffman warns about "the highly controversial and dangerous Alpha Course. It was started by Holy Brompton, London, a large charismatic Anglican church. Anglican priest **Nicky Gumbel** began teaching it in 1990....Its philosophy is said to be New Age, leading to experiences rooted in the occult. **C. S. Lewis** is the first author recommended."[478] Elsewhere Huffman adds:

> "It promotes humanism, ecumenism, and Charismaticism (tongues-speaking, Toronto Blessing, etc.). Conversion is mentioned but it is conversion to a Christian lifestyle, not conversion to Christ....This is spreading like wildfire among Catholics, Baptists, and others, so Christians should be warned, be wise, beware!"[479]

David Cloud reminds us "that C. S. Lewis has exerted a major influence on the Alpha course, and that it quotes or refers to him almost ad nauseum. Could not the Alpha course be renamed the 'Mere Christianity' course?"[480]

Wendy Howard cautions us:

> "Being involved with Alpha will bring the church-goer into a full blown ecumenical movement which is rapidly heading down the **One World Church trail, under the Vatican and the United Nations.** There is no way that the Alpha organisation will avoid full inclusion into the politically-motivated One World and its government, it cannot because it is already so far advanced into the NWO [new world order]. When people are moving along with Alpha, feel so much a part of it, revere such leaders as Nicky Gumbel, they will move easily and happily into the next step—UNION within Christendom and with non-Christian religious groups....The New Age experience-orientated global religiosity will be seen as merely another example of a search for God."[481] [Emphasis in the original.]

A **New Age** group also tells us: "As we have seen, the **ecumenical movement and the world-order movement have been interrelated and share common characteristics."**[482]

PANDAEMONIUM

The Alpha course gained prominence because of the so-called "holy laughter," "laughing revival," and "Toronto blessing" movement.[483] (For more information on this movement, see my article entitle "Unholy Laughter.") **Nicky Gumbel** explains in his video:

> ***"We went to their house....where a group of leaders of their church was meeting....Ellie Mumford told us a little bit of what she had seen in Toronto....it was obvious that Ellie was just dying to pray for all of us....then she said 'Now we'll invite the Holy Spirit to come,' and the moment she said that, one of the people there was thrown, literally, across the room and was lying on the floor, just howling and laughing... making the most incredible noise....I experienced the power of the Spirit in a way I hadn't experienced for years, like massive electricity going through my body....One of the guys was prophesying. He was just lying there prophesying...."***[484] [Emphasis in the original.]

When he returned to the Holy Trinity Brompton church, Gumbel

> "apologised for being late for a meeting due to what had happened. Asked to close this meeting in prayer he says, ***'I prayed "Lord, thank you so much for all you are doing and we pray you'll send your Spirit" and I was just about to say "in Jesus name. Amen" and go out the door, when the Spirit came on the people who were in the room. One of them started laughing like a hyena....'"***[485] [Emphasis in the original.]

The August 15, 1994 edition of *Time* reported:

> "Though pathetically tiny flocks of Londoners attend many Anglican services, Holy Trinity Brompton has a standing room only turnout of 1500....After the usual scripture readings, prayers and singing, the chairs are cleared away. Curate Nicky Gumbel prays that the Holy Spirit will come upon the congregation. Soon a young woman begins laughing. Others gradually join her with hearty belly laughs. A young worshiper falls to the floor, hands twitching...within half an hour there are bodies everywhere as supplicants sob, **roar like lions,** and strangest of all, **laugh uncontrollably...**this frenzied display has become known as the **laughing revival,** or Toronto blessing."[486]

Many people in the United States may be familiar with Stephen Hill and the "Brownsville Revival." Hill "claims he received his anointing and ability to 'slay in the Spirit' from Holy Trinity Brompton."[487]

His pastor at the Brownsville Assembly of God is John Kilpatrick. He

> *"admitted that there was pandemonium in the church at Brownsville. In fact, he actually condoned such activity. 'God*

> *sent pandemonium in the church,' he said. 'I think it's time that we have grand pandemonium in the Baptists, in the Lutheran, the Episcopal, the Assembly of God [churches]. God sent pandemonium!' Kilpatrick exclaimed. It is interesting to note that the word 'pandemonium' was coined by John Milton in 1667 in his epic Paradise Lost.* ***'Pandaemonium' was the name of the capital of Hell, the 'high capital of Satan and his peers.' The word literally means 'place of all the demons.'*** *Today, the word is generally defined as 'any place of wild disorder, noise or confusion.' Is that what was happening at Brownsville? Yes it was. Is that what God condones in his church? Absolutely not."*[488] [Italics in the original; boldface added.]

Interestingly, Benjamin Creme, the person who is representing Maitreya (or the New Age "Christ"), was recently asked about the Toronto Blessing (TB). "His response was that **he thought the TB was a good thing:** it is, according to him, the method being used by his spiritual Masters to soften up Christian Fundamentalists to accept the New Age Christ when he appears."[489] [Emphasis in the original.]

What is fascinating to me is that the **occult** movement also has an **"Alpha Course."** One ad reads:

> "Ed Moret is a highly skilled, high energy, **psychic;** teacher; visionary artist; illustrator; world traveler and certified Reiki healer. He has served for 10 years as a **psychic** consultant and is a dynamic workshop leader....Ed Moret will present his well-known **ALPHA COURSE,** during the **Psychic** Discovery Cruise Workshops. This includes: **telepathy, auras, past life regressions, psychometry, meditation, healings and chakra balancing."**[490] [Caps in the original; boldface added.]

Many New Agers have written about alpha.[491] For instance, Laurie Cabot, a witch, explains:

> "The science of **Witchcraft** is based on our ability to enter an **altered state of consciousness** we call **'alpha,'** where brain waves register at seven to fourteen cycles per second. As mentioned earlier, this is a state of consciousness associated with relaxation, meditation, and dreaming.....
>
> "In **alpha** the mind opens up to nonordinary forms of communication, such as **telepathy, clairvoyance, and precognition.** Here we also may experience **out-of-the-body** sensations and psychokinesis, or **receive mystical, visionary information** that does not come through the five senses. In alpha the rational filters that process ordinary reality are

weakened or removed, and the **mind is receptive to nonordinary realities."**[492]

She continues:

> "Almost all cultures have used **altered states of consciousness,** such as **alpha,** for **communal religious rituals,** personal **spiritual** rites, divination, and healing work....
>
> "In an **alpha state** wonderful changes take place. Our egos are less dominant so that we can process information in terms other than our own personal security and survival....**Alpha alters our perceptions** so that we are freed from those time-space constructs and can draw in experience from other times and places. For all these reasons **Witches do most of their magical work in alpha....**
>
> "This basic procedure for entering alpha is the key to all future work in the Craft [witchcraft]."[493]

VISUALIZATION IS HYPNOSIS

I'm not saying that **Nicky Gumbel** took an occult concept for his course name—but I do think the correlations are fascinating. You see, **Gumbel does use the occult technique of visualization** in his course work.[494] One esoteric/occultic book states that **visualization is "a form of self-hypnosis widely used by Buddhists...."**[495] Gumbel even admits that visualization can involve shamanism (witchcraft)[496] so he tells the participants to visualize Jesus.[497] Visualizing Jesus, however, **DOES NOT** Christianize the occult!

Michael Harner is a shaman (a witchdoctor). He admits:

> "The burgeoning field of holistic medicine shows a tremendous amount of experimentation involving the reinvention of many **techniques long practiced in shamanism, such as visualization, altered state of consciousness,** aspects of psychoanalysis, hypnotherapy, meditation, positive attitude, stress-reduction, and mental and emotional expression of personal will for health and healing."[498]
>
> "Most of the people being seduced into the practice of visualization—especially those within the Church—have not the faintest conception of the occultic aim which lies at its root. In spite of the attractions and harmless benefits put forward by its advocates, **visualization is a primary gateway for demonic infiltration** into human consciousness—a deception currently being worked on a truly grand scale."[499]

A psychologist, Michael Yapko, explains: “Many times therapists aren’t even aware that they’re doing **hypnosis.** They’re doing what they call **guided imagery [which is visualization] or guided meditation,** which are all very mainstream **hypnotic** techniques.”[500]

One Christian researcher reveals:

> “Between 8 and 13 vibrations, **visualization** is able to take place. Vibrations at this frequency are called ***alpha*** *rhythms.* In his very popular book *Celebration of Discipline,* Richard Foster points out that meditative visualization, in addition to catapulting one into a divine/human encounter, maintains a consistent alpha-level brain-wave pattern.
>
> “The **‘alpha state’** is associated with other interesting phenomena. The hypnotic trance exists within the alpha level. Because of this, the **visualization technique is included within material offering self-hypnosis. The occult trances of Edgar Cayce are found within alpha.** A ‘truth serum’ drug such as sodium Pentothal causes a person to lapse into the alpha state....
>
> “In order to initiate visualization, a state of ‘centered’ relaxation requiring a passive mental process is necessary. A person is not able to concentrate upon the images in the imagination without being ‘centered.’ While some inner-healing teachers may claim that they do not use breathing exercises or other techniques to enter into the ‘visualization prayer,’ the issue is merely academic. If I instruct a person to relax, close his eyes, and visualize some event from the past, **bringing the image of Jesus into the event,** I am of necessity **leading him down to alpha.** While functioning at **alpha level produces visualization,** engaging in visualization will cause one to function at alpha.”[501] [Italics in the original.]

GUIDANCE FROM VOICES

Remember, witch Cabot says that in the alpha state one can **“receive mystical, visionary information** that does not come through the five senses. In alpha the rational filters that process ordinary reality are weakened or removed, and the **mind is receptive to <u>nonordinary</u> realities.”**[502]

Now, compare the “Christian” phenomena mentioned in the July 2000 issue of *The Day Drawing Near* with what happens under the **occultic** alpha level. The newsletter reports:

> “A close look at the materials and teaching of ALPHA reveals the excesses of the Charismatic movement: tongues,

> words of knowledge, healing, and **guidance from visions, voices, and dreams.** The ALPHA course is referred to as a 'Holy Spirit Weekend.' Supporters say the out-of-control emotionalism is the work of the Holy Spirit. Critics say the emotions are the result of self-hypnosis, suggestion and altered states of consciousness perhaps demonic in nature. ALPHA also promotes Kingdom Now Theology (Dominionism) with its focus on health, wealth and earthly power."[503] [Caps in the original.]

In spite of the occult-like and unscriptural phenomena in Alpha, *Christianity Today* carried a full-page ad for Alpha in its April 27, 1998 issue.[504] Furthermore, **Billy Graham invited Nicky Gumbel** to be one of the speakers at his Amsterdam 2000 conference.[505] Graham wrote to Gumbel: "Your experience and expertise as a leader will be a **great asset to the conference,** and participants will gain invaluable knowledge and insight from the content of the workshop."[506]

Nicky, however, has some very flawed teachings. For instance, he states that Jesus was so attractive and magnetic that people were drawn to Him.[507] My Bible, though, says just the opposite. For instance, turn to Isaiah 53:2b-3: "He hath no form nor comeliness; and when we shall see Him, there is no beauty that we should desire Him. He is despised and rejected of men; a man of sorrows, and acquainted with grief: and we hid as it were our faces from Him; He was despised, and we esteemed Him not." Isaiah 52:14 mentions that "His visage was so marred more than any man, and His form more than the sons of men." Also, John 6:66 reminds us: "From that time many of His disciples went back, and walked no more with Him." Yes, Jesus did draw the crowds as long as He healed their sick and fed them, but when He gave His teachings, many could not handle it and went back from following Him.

MIXING THE TRUTH

Gumbel teaches that "Jesus had evil thoughts" and he implies that Jesus was fallible.[508] He also claims:

> "The fact that Jesus is the only way to God does not mean that we simply write off all **other** religions as misguided or demonic. Jesus said, 'I am the Truth.' In him, **ultimate** truth is to be found....But this does not mean that parts of the truth cannot be found in other religions...only in Jesus Christ do we find **infallible** truth....By putting other religions alongside

God's revelation in Jesus Christ, we see that they contain both **truth** and error."[509] [Emphasis in the original.]

No wonder Amos 8:11-12 reminds us

"Behold, the days come, saith the Lord GOD, that I will send a famine in the land, not a famine of bread, nor a thirst for water, but of hearing the words of the LORD: And they shall wander from sea to sea, and from the north even to the east, they shall run to and fro to seek the word of the LORD, and shall not find it."

If other religions contain truth and error, then they **are** misguided. How would you like someone to hand you a map and tell you that a magnificent treasure is to be discovered by following the directions on the map? The person then proceeds to tell you that some of the directions are not correct, but adds that it's okay because the treasure is still available. How would you know which directions to follow and which ones to ignore? The person can tell you that an infallible map exists but you'll have to discover it for yourself—and then compare your map to the true map. This example, however, pales in comparison to trifling with the "truth" and errors of other religions. Unless an individual knows that the Bible is God's infallible Word, they have no guidelines to follow in detecting truth from error.

Additionally, picking out the "good" in false religions is extremely dangerous. If you mix a batch of cookies and add a little poison, how can you separate the good from the bad? Besides, if you were taking a true/false test in school, and 99% of the question was true and 1% of it was false, the **entire** answer must be marked false! If you select the good in the question and mark it true, you would be incorrect. Selecting a wrong answer on a test may not be that big of a deal, but when your eternal welfare is at stake, there's no room to play around and take chances. Matthew 7:13 cautions us: "Enter ye in at the strait gate: for wide is the gate, and broad is the way, that leadeth to destruction, and many there be which go in thereat."

Jerry Huffman asks "What killed the rat?" and then answers:

"The thing that killed the rat was 98 percent hamburger. Only 2 percent of the mixture was poison but the rat died....**A mixture of truth and falsehood is usually far more deadly than pure falsehood which can be isolated and discerned.** Yet today, Christians often say, 'But there's so much GOOD in it!' ALL false systems contain elements of truth—in fact, the more truth mixed with deadly error, the more dangerous it is for deception. To be effective, a deception must **appear** to be essentially true. Over 90 percent of what is conveyed to the 'target' must be true. Even in deceptive days, Christians have no excuse for being deceived. God's Word and Spirit are sufficient to expose error/errorists of our day (Isa. 8:20)."[510]

The Bible commands "they that worship Him [God] must worship Him in spirit **AND IN TRUTH"** (John 4:24).

Continuing with the Alpha Course we find that it then brags up Clark Pinnock and says that he "is to be saluted...for having done much to lead the evangelical wing of Christianity **away from** the old **exclusivism,** which believes that **only Christians are saved...."**[511] [Emphasis in the original.] Pinnock writes:

> "'As an **inclusivist** [i.e. someone who denies that Christianity is the only way to be saved—E.M.], I acknowledge my debt to the Catholic Church for its leadership in this regard.' He goes on to say, **'I welcome** the Saiva Siddhanta literature of **Hinduism,** which celebrates a personal God of love, and the emphasis on grace that I see in the Japanese **Shin-Shu Amida sect.** I also **respect** the **Buddha** as a **righteous** man (Matt 10:41) **and Mohammed** as a prophet figure in the style of the Old Testament.'"[512] [Emphasis in the original.]

LEIGHTON FORD

Other endorsers of the Alpha Course are: Charles Colson,[513] Bill Bright,[514] Tony Campolo,[515] Jack Hayford,[516] Cardinal William H. Keeler (Archbishop of Baltimore),[517] Richard Foster,[518] Bill Hybels,[519] Pat Robertson,[520] Luis Palau,[521] George Gallup, Jr.,[522] David Yonggi Cho,[523] Billy Kim,[524] Paul Cedar[525] (a frequent speaker at the Billy Graham School of Evangelism[526]), Robert Schuller,[527] and Leighton Ford[528] (Billy Graham's brother-in-law[529] and a former Vice President of the Billy Graham Evangelistic Association[530]).

Ford signed the Evangelicals for Social Action's statement "challenging materialism, racism, militarism and totalitarianism."[531]

He has "praised Mother Teresa, whom he had...visited in Calcutta, though she constantly prays the Rosary for her own salvation and considers Buddhism, Hinduism, Islam and other religions to be acceptable ways to God...."[532] No wonder Ford declared that Christians shouldn't "be so negative as to refuse to endorse or work with those who belong to a group that proclaims a different gospel."[533]

The Bible, however, gives this warning about "another gospel" in Galatians 1:6-8: "I marvel that ye are so soon removed from Him that called you into the grace of Christ unto another gospel: Which is not another; but there be some that trouble you, and would pervert the gospel of Christ. But **though we, or an angel from heaven,**

***preach any other gospel* unto you than that which we have preached unto you, *let him be accursed.*"** Ford, on the other hand, tells us that we can endorse and work with those who have another gospel.

Of course, Graham himself asked: "Wouldn't it be great if we could forget our denominations and just be people of God?"[534] [Emphasis in the original.] He added "that **all** denominations and backgrounds 'have the same God.'"[535] The context of this quote was after his Oakland, California crusade in which **over 100 denominations** participated.[536]

In the October 2, 2000 issue of *Christianity Today,* Ford

> "says his new ministry is 'spiritual direction,' mentoring, etc., which seems dangerously akin to **New Age** mysticism. In 1993, he heard Princeton Seminary's Diogenes Allen speak about the Benedictine discipline of *lectio divina,* a very ancient Catholic art which involves 'a slow contemplative praying of the Scriptures which enables the Bible to become a means of union with God.' Ford is now said to be 'simply walking in people's souls' and finding out what God is doing there."[537] [Italics in the original.]

Ford also signed the "Chicago Declaration"[538] (which was covered earlier).

One researcher wrote:

> "The [New Age] Planetary Initiative For The World We Choose is the organization which came up with the catchy slogan now echoed by almost every globalist environmental group active today: **'Think globally, act locally.'** In their ignorance (hopefully!) a number of Christian organizations, and even Dr. **Leighton Ford,** the top lieutenant to Billy Graham, have pushed this **same slogan** as a real neat idea for the church to demonstrate its concern for **world environmentalism."**[539]

NEGATIVITY ISN'T ALWAYS BAD

Briefly, let's return to Ford's statement about not being "so negative." Being negative, however, is not always bad. For instance, consider a traffic light. Green would be positive—or go. Yellow is neutral and red is negative—or stop. What would happen if the light were always green—from all four sides?! The red (negative/stop) is a deterrent to bedlam, commotion, and chaos. It is necessary to have restrictions in order to have freedom. Paul asked: "For if the trumpet give an uncertain sound, who shall prepare himself to the battle?" (I Corinthians 14:8). In Bible days, the trumpet was used in order to gather the people together. Different sounds and the number of trumpets would indicate the purpose for the gathering (Exodus 19:13; Leviticus 25:9; Numbers 10:2, 4, 9; Joshua 6:5; Judges 3:27; II Samuel 15:10; Nehemiah 4:18, 20; Psalm 81:3; Jeremiah 4:19; 6:17; Ezekiel 33:3; Joel 2:15, etc.). If the trumpet didn't give a precise sound, the people would not know what to do. Certainly war is "negative," but if a country is being invaded, the people have a right to know about it in order to be able to prepare themselves as much as possible. Yes, the warning is "negative" and yet it is "positive" because it is for the individual's own good. If I had a dreaded disease and the Dr. didn't warn me about it, how could I know what to do to try to ease it or cure it? The Dr. would be "negative" in warning me, yet his negativity is far more loving and beneficial than someone who would remain "positive" (or neutral)—and let me die a painful and agonizing death.

During Old Testament times, a watchman was appointed to warn the people. In Ezekiel we are told:

> "If when he seeth the sword come upon the land, he blow the trumpet, and warn the people; Then whosoever heareth the sound of the trumpet, and taketh not warning; if the sword come, and take him away, his blood shall be upon his own head. He heard the sound of the trumpet, and took not warning; his blood shall be upon him. But he that taketh warning shall deliver his soul. But if the watchman see the sword come, and blow not the trumpet, and the people be not warned; if the sword come, and take any person from among them, he is taken away in his iniquity; but his blood will I require at the watchman's hand. So thou, O son of man, I have set thee a watchman unto the house of Israel; therefore thou shalt hear the word at My mouth, and **warn** them from Me" (Ezekiel 33:3-7).

Leighton Ford, Graham, and many others try to be so positive. For example, Graham claims to be neutral in so many situations because he wants to keep friends on both sides of an issue, but at times, it is necessary to name sin. Proverbs 27:5 says: "Open rebuke is better than secret love." "It is better to hear the rebuke of the wise, than for a man to hear the song of fools" says Ecclesiastes 7:5. "And they come unto thee as the people cometh, and **they sit** before thee **as My people,** and they hear thy words, but they will not do them: for **with their mouth they shew much love,** but **their heart goeth after their covetousness"** (Ezekiel 33:31). "And have **no fellowship** with the unfruitful works of darkness, **but** rather **reprove** them" (Ephesians 5:11).

We also need to remember that we can't begin with what we have in common. We need to begin with the Gospel. When the Gospel says that Jesus is the **ONLY** way, I can't have common ground with pagans. When the Bible says that "[a]ll have sinned and come short of the glory of God" (Romans 3:23), I can't accept the tenet that **all** will be saved.

CAREY, ALPHA, AND GRAHAM

Yet another **Alpha** endorser is Archbishop **George Carey.**[540] Carey even "singled out the Alpha course for special mention during a keynote speech"[541] at **Billy Graham's Amsterdam 2000** Conference. He added: "That's why I want to give a plug for one of your workshops tomorrow. Alpha's great success lies in its ability to take evangelism out of the church into the home and to bridge the gulf between church and community."[542]

Alpha News bragged:

> "Seven hundred of the world's leading evangelists attending Billy Graham's major conference Amsterdam 2000 in August attended official events where major presentations of the **Alpha course were given top billing....**
>
> "As well as this, Sandy Millar was invited to speak to 500 parachurch leaders about the course during one of their special sessions.
>
> "An Alpha stand in the conference's main Exhibition Hall was mobbed throughout the week of the event, with vast amounts of material handed out."[543]

UNITY AND DIVERSITY

I'm sure that many readers will recognize that a number of those promoting the Alpha course were speakers at Graham's Amsterdam conference. There is another problem, however. Nicky Gumbel stated that the

> "differences between Protestants and Catholics are ***'totally insignificant compared to the things that unite us...we need to UNITE around the death of Jesus, the resurrection of Jesus; the absolute essential things at the core of the Christian faith on which we are all agreed. We need to give people liberty to disagree on the things which are secondary.'***"[544] [Emphasis in the original.]

How can we "unite around the death of Jesus, the resurrection of Jesus," etc., when people like George Carey and Richard Neuhaus don't even believe in the resurrection?! We need to remember what Carey said: "I can tell you frankly that while we can be absolutely sure that Jesus lived and that He was certainly crucified on the Cross, **we cannot know that He was raised by God from the dead."**[545]

Carey was at the World Conference on Religion and Peace[546] (which was covered earlier in this chapter). "The Interfaith conference stressed the need for **unity and diversity** amongst ALL the religions of the world, not just the denominations of Christendom."[547] [Caps in the original; boldface added.]

Maybe we should now look at the theme of Amsterdam 2000. The subtitle of the conference was none other than **"Unity in Diversity!"**[548] Wow. That's a popular concept in the **New Age/occult** movement[549] but it's nothing new to Graham! About 25 years ago already Graham had urged evangelicals to "'accept **unity in diversity**' and **avoid divisiveness** over such matters as Biblical inerrancy, charismatic phenomena, and political activism."[550]

We need to remember that the word **"unity"** is mentioned only **3** times in the Bible. On the other hand, the word **"truth"** is mentioned **235** times! This alone should tell us that the truth of God's Word is far more important than unity—especially a **false** unity. Ephesians 4:13 mentions "the unity of the faith" and the next verse adds: "That we henceforth be **no more** children, **tossed to and fro, and carried about with every wind of doctrine,** by the sleight of men, and cunning craftiness, whereby they lie in wait to deceive."

I well remember one banking class I had taken. When the teacher asked a question I raised my hand and gave my answer. He then asked the rest of the class how many thought I was wrong and EVERYONE raised their hands. Since I had studied the lesson I KNEW I was correct but NOT ONE of the other students would agree with me. The teacher then told the class that I was correct and they were all wrong. Now, what would have happened had I changed my mind and gone along with the majority? Would that have made me right because EVERYONE else thought they were correct? No, instead of ONE person being correct, NO ONE would have been correct. In fact, had I gone along with the majority I would have been even more wrong than they were because I knew the truth and would have compromised what I had known to be right to be accepted by the majority. But I stood firm and it paid off. What made the difference? I STUDIED the book and KNEW what I had studied and even though the ENTIRE class was in disagreement with me I could STAND FIRM on my answer. It was also a great feeling to hear the teacher say that I was right. This is one reason why Paul writes: "STUDY to show thyself approved unto God, a workman that needeth not to be ashamed" (II Timothy 2:15). We can stand firm even though most people will disagree with us and then one day we will hear our Master say "Well done, thou good and faithful servant: thou hast been faithful over a few things, I will make thee ruler over many things: enter thou into the joy of thy lord" (Matthew 25:21, 23). So, by studying and knowing the Word of God (our lesson book) we will be better able to keep the **UNITY OF THE FAITH.**

IS DOCTRINE IMPORTANT?

We are also to work at keeping "the **unity OF THE SPIRIT"** (Ephesians 4:3). Notice carefully that Christians are only to keep the unity **IN ACCORDANCE WITH THE SPIRIT.** We ARE NOT to keep or maintain unity IF there is a conflict with God's Word. Paul further verifies this point in Romans 15:5 where he says: "Now the God of patience and consolation grant you to be LIKEMINDED one toward another **ACCORDING TO CHRIST JESUS."**

This "unity of the faith," according to Jude 3, is to be EARNESTLY CONTENDED for. The Greek word for "contend" is "epagonizomai" and means to strive, labor fervently, or fight for the faith. Our English word "agony" comes from this word, thus giving us an idea that A STRUGGLE WILL BE INVOLVED IN MAINTAINING THIS UNITY of the faith. But how can a Christian contend for the faith UNLESS he knows what he is to contend for? Because of this, a Christian MUST CAREFULLY STUDY God's Word in order to be able to know what the Bible says about different doctrines and issues. Once a Christian has sure footing on the Solid Rock, Christ Jesus, he won't be "tossed to and fro, and carried about with every wind of doctrine" (Ephesians 4:14).

Just how important is doctrine? Below are a few verses that should answer this question:

⁕ "Till I come, **give attendance** to reading, to exhortation, **to doctrine"** (I Timothy 4:13).

⁕ **"Take heed** unto thyself, and **unto the doctrine; continue in them:** for in doing this thou shalt both save thyself, and them that hear thee" (I Timothy 4:16).

⁕ "But **speak** thou the things which become **sound doctrine"** (Titus 2:1).

⁕ "Preach the word; be instant in season, out of season; reprove, rebuke, **exhort with all** longsuffering and **doctrine"** (II Timothy 4:2).

⁕ "Whosoever transgresseth, and abideth not in the **doctrine of Christ,** hath not God. He that abideth in the doctrine of Christ, he hath both the Father and the Son. If there come any unto you, and **bring not this doctrine, receive him not** into your house, neither bid him God speed" (II John 1:9-10).

⁕ "For the time will come when they will not endure **sound doctrine;** but after their own lusts shall they heap to themselves teachers, having itching ears; And they shall turn away their ears from the truth, and shall be turned unto fables" (II Timothy 4:3-4).

One author who was sympathetic to the Unitarian doctrine bragged that Unitarianism was able to survive because of a mood of **COMPROMISE.** This writer noted: "THEY LOVED TO EMPHASIZE THE POINTS OF AGREEMENT RATHER THAN THE POINTS OF DIFFERENCE. THEY WERE WILLING TO MAKE CONCESSIONS FOR THE SAKE OF THE PEACE OF THE CHURCHES." Isn't that a good description of what is happening in the churches today? So many will say, "Let's forget doctrine. Let's not discuss theological issues. Let's just agree on the points we have in common."[551]

In a short time the Bible is practically thrown out so as to keep peace with all those in attendance.

As Christians who are contending for the faith, we are involved in a warfare and we must actually fight, struggle, and strive to keep this unity. Unity, for the Christian, IS NOT a passive thing. We are to work and labor to maintain the kind of unity Jesus maintained even though division may follow. There is an action and EFFORT involved and sometimes this fight for right causes a **DIVISION.**

You may ask, "How can there be division when we are working for unity?" Actually, there HAS TO BE some type of division and separation to maintain the BIBLICAL unity of the Spirit and unity of the faith. While Christians are to endeavour to keep the unity, we also find that we will cause division. "But," you may say, "the Bible says 'mark them which cause division and AVOID them' and if someone is causing division shouldn't we avoid him?" The Bible does say to avoid those who cause division but let's correctly read the passage from Romans 16:17. It states: "...mark them which cause divisions and offences **CONTRARY TO THE DOCTRINE WHICH YE HAVE LEARNED;** and avoid them." Those who are causing division for the sake of the gospel ARE NOT to be avoided but rather we are to avoid those who are bringing in unscriptural doctrines and activities that are CONTRARY to God's Word. Jude tells us that "certain men crept in unawares" (Jude 4). The word "crept" in the

Greek means "to slide in alongside of." It is people like this—those who insidiously come into the church and try to change the standards, doctrines, and "the faith which was once delivered unto the saints" (Jude 3)—that we are to avoid.

BEWARE OF FALSE PROPHETS

Division is not necessarily bad! Are you aware that one of the first things God did when He began His creation of the world was an act of DIVISION? In Genesis 1:4 we read: "And God saw the light, that it was good: and God DIVIDED the light from the darkness." This division between light and darkness, good and evil, must continue. Satan saw that he could not destroy God's church, so he has tried to infiltrate the church with false teachers. Satan comes as an "angel of light" and he also sends some of his ministers forth under the guise of "apostles of Christ" and "ministers of righteousness" (II Corinthians 11:13-15). These false ministers creep into the church "unawares" and Christ warns us: "Beware of false prophets, which come to you in sheep's clothing, but inwardly they are ravening wolves. Ye shall know them by their fruits" (Matthew 7:15-16). This is another reason why we must know the Bible so we can tell if the fruit these people are bearing is in accordance with God's Word. We are to try to maintain unity but **NEVER** at the price of COMPROMISING what the Bible teaches.

Jesus, the very Son of God, caused division time and time again and even said that He came to divide. In Luke 12:51 Jesus asks: "Suppose ye that I am come to give peace on earth? I tell you, Nay; but rather DIVISION." We read of Jesus: "So there was a division among the people because of Him" (John 7:43); "And there was a division among them" (John 9:16); and "There was a division therefore AGAIN among the Jews for these sayings" (John 10:19). Divisions will occur whenever there are rebellious people who do not want to follow God's Word. This is why there will be divisions within the church. There will be a division between those who want to do what the Bible teaches and those who are unwilling to submit to Christ's authority. There will be those who will stand by the Word of God and there will be others who will want their own way REGARDLESS of what the Bible says.

The "word of God is quick, and powerful, and sharper than any two-edged sword" (Hebrews 4:12). A sword is an instrument that is used to divide and Hebrews 4:12 goes on to say that God's Word does divide. Each Christian is to be equipped with this sword for part of a believer's armor is "THE SWORD OF THE SPIRIT, which is the word of God" (Ephesians 6:17). This means that there may be times when believers will be engaged in a battle and will have to use their swords (the Word of God) thus causing a division between right and wrong. Paul frequently refers to the Christian life as a life of warfare. He charged Timothy to "FIGHT the good fight of faith....keep this commandment WITHOUT SPOT, unrebukeable, UNTIL the appearing of our Lord Jesus Christ..." (I Timothy 6:12, 14). Times may have changed but God's Word has not.

Jesus prayed: "They are not of the world, even as I am not of the world. Sanctify them through Thy truth: Thy word is truth" (John 17:16-17). The word "sanctify" means "set apart" and all believers are to be a sanctified (or "set apart") people.

Remember, however, that Christians will not be the only ones causing division. Sinners will separate us from their company: "Blessed are ye, when men shall hate you, and when **they shall separate you from their company...for the Son of man's sake"** (Luke 6:22). Those who usually cry the loudest for "unity" are also causing division because they do not want to be bound by what the Word of God has to say. The world's cry for unity usually means that a Christian is supposed to condone EVERYTHING a worldly-minded person is doing, but this has NOTHING to do with the Biblical command to maintain the unity OF THE FAITH. In trying to keep the unity of the faith, we must remember that "All scripture is given by inspiration of God, and is profitable for doctrine, for reproof, for correction, for instruction in righteousness: That the man of God may be perfect, throughly furnished unto all good works" (II Timothy 3:16-17).

UNITY BRINGS A NEW WORLD RELIGION

Now, let's look at a few instances of **"unity in diversity"** (which was the **theme of Graham's Amsterdam 2000** Conference) from a **New Age** perspective. In *One Country,* we find:

> **"World citizenship** begins with an acceptance of the **oneness of the human family** and the **interconnectedness of the nations** of 'the earth, our home.' While it encourages a sane and legitimate patriotism, it also insists upon a wider loyalty, a love of humanity as a whole....**Its hallmark is 'unity in diversity.'"**[552]

The *World Goodwill Newsletter* states: "Through these relatively new steps taken by humanity to realise a greater **interrelatedness,** an **essential** pattern and vision can be seen to be emerging—one characterised by **unity in diversity,** which **must** eventually be manifested as a living, **global reality."**[553]

Another issue of the *World Goodwill Newsletter* bragged:

"It would have to be a very special conference [referring to the Oxford Conference] to draw such eminent leaders as the Dalai Lama, Mother Teresa, Archbishop Runcie, Carl Sagan, members of the Central Committee of the Soviet **Communist** Party, the Chief Rabbi of Romania, the High Priest of the Sacred Forest of Togo, the Metropolitan of the Russian Orthodox Church in Moscow, Sri Lankan development leader A. T. Ariyaratne, senators, cabinet ministers and influential members of the media from every region of the world. And a very special conference it most certainly was....

"Unity in diversity was surely the message."[554]

Another report informs us:

"The unity we seek is in no way related to uniformity. Rather to be of real and lasting value it is essential to achieve **unity-in-diversity.** The **new world order** must accommodate the diverse cultures of the world thereby retaining the richness of expression of our common humanity."[555]

The United Religions (UR) drafted a charter which explains:

"Imagine a world...where there is peace among religions, where people from a <u>diversity of religions</u> and spiritual traditions and from all sectors of society gather at <u>common tables</u> all over the world to pursue justice, healing and peace with reverence for all life, where there is a <u>United Religions</u>, an inclusive, decentralized organization, a <u>spiritual partner of the United Nations</u>, where local actions are connected to form a global presence, where the wisdom of faith traditions is revered, where the deepest values of people are respected and put into action for the good of all.

"The United Religions is a dream whose time has come....

"The UR will take action to promote dialogue and a theology of acceptance to help the world's people explore <u>common ground</u>, awareness of <u>unity within diversity</u>, and ever-increasing kinship....We believe that all religions derive their wisdom from that ultimate Source."[556] [Boldface and italics in the original; underlining added.]

Dan Wheatley writes:

"As a Baha'i I see myself as a **world citizen** and I strongly believe that the world is moving closer to a **united global community,** a human family....

> "**Unity in diversity** may sound like just another sound-bite, a trite piece of verbal cosmetics in an age where content is less important than presentation. The reality is that the concept of **unity in diversity is a deeply spiritual concept, it is a key tenet of the Baha'i faith** and it is an essential concept to bear in mind when trying to find solutions to a wide range of global problems."[557]

MYSTERIES WILL UNIFY ALL FAITHS

Two authors, Corinne McLaughlin and Gordon Davidson, both followers of the occultist Alice Bailey, tell us:

> "Fundamentalist Christians have great fear of any movement toward a world government, such as the United Nations, or toward 'oneness,' such as the New Age movement. They see this as the work of the devil....A helpful way for fundamentalists to overcome their fear is to remember the **'unity in diversity'** theme, which forms the basis of the work of both the United Nations and the New Age movement—respecting diversity and uniqueness while focusing on the underlying unity."[558]

Leland P. Stewart, founder of the Unity-and-Diversity World Council,[559] said:

> "The meaning of **unity-and-diversity** in this arena is to serve both the synthesis, which we call the **unity,** and also to pay close attention to the **diversity,** which each aspect of the unity represents....Diversity is not something to be feared, so long as there is mutual respect between differing points of view."[560] [Boldface in the original; underlining added.]

He explains:

> "I discovered that Synthesis is a very important term in the Alice Bailey teachings. For her, the Aquarian age is primarily an age of synthesis, a time for bringing together all of the seemingly disjointed parts of our society and the world as a whole. In these teachings, the Buddha represents **light,** the Buddha being 'the illumined one.' The Christ represents **love,** 'the energy of consciousness.' The central goal of these teachings is to help give birth to a **new world religion.** All of these dimensions resonate with our work [of Unity-and-Diversity World Council]."[561] [Boldface in the original; underlining added.]

Carol Houst agrees: "**Synthesis is the ideal at the heart of the Unity and Diversity movement,** and what the Unitarian Universalist Church seeks to support and encourage. It is at the center of all of the UN challenges around the world."[562]

One book, *Toward a Maitreyan Revolution,* explains that this

> "**New universal religion...**will be nondogmatic...a **synthesis of mysticism, occultism, humanism, theism, pantheism, and idealism,** all related to a glorious search for cosmic consciousness. There will be new temples arising where the symbols of every religion will be seen as part of one architectural and geometrical reality of the cosmos....The **new religion** will have its prayers, mantras, and invocations, plus acknowledging the value and expression of those from the religions and teaching of the past."[563]

"God works in many ways through many faiths and many religious agencies. The universal platform of the **new world religion** will be built by **emphasizing the unity** and fellowship of the spirit,"[564] says World Goodwill, an **occult** organization. The platform of the new world religion will be built by religions working together—and Billy Graham, Chuck Colson, Pope John Paul II, etc., are helping to bring about this new world religion by supporting and promoting the ecumenical movement.

> "Today, slowly, the concept of a **world religion** and the need for its emergence are widely desired and worked for. The **fusion of faiths is now a field of discussion.** Workers in the field of religion will formulate the **universal platform of the new world religion.** It is a work of loving **synthesis** and will **emphasise the unity and the fellowship** of the spirit....The **platform of the new world religion will be built by many groups,** working under the inspiration of the [New Age] Christ....
>
> "God works in many ways, through many faith and religious agencies; this is one reason for the **elimination of non-essential doctrines."**[565]
>
> "...other steps will also be taken in this department of religions and of education, over which the Christ rules, and He will move to restore the ancient spiritual landmarks, to **eliminate that which is nonessential,** and to reorganise the entire religious field—again in preparation for the restoration of the Mysteries. These Mysteries, when restored, will **unify all faiths."**[566]

SACRIFICE DOCTRINES

New Ager, Natalie Banks, states:

"Looking below the seething surface of outer events we become aware of the spreading move towards the **elimination of sectarian separativeness** and an increasing **distaste for reliance on hard and fast doctrine and dogma.** At the same time there is an intensified search for a deeper understanding of the inner teachings and their application to the enormous problems of today."[567]

"J. P. Morgan, the Rothschild's representative in the United States, set up a trust fund to **unite the various Christian denominations.** [Charles Taze] Russell [founder of the Jehovah Witnesses] praises this in his Jan. 1, 1911 *WT [Watch Tower],...* 'Mr. Morgan's well-known business capacity, exhibited in connection with financial trusts, encourages many to believe that he will accomplish the desired end in connection with the movement. More and more all denominations are craving a religious trust or federation and are **becoming more and more willing to sacrifice doctrines and principles formerly held dear,** in order to accomplish the federation....Evidently this federation is near at hand; the Scriptures have long foretold the Federation, as we have been pointing out therefrom for thirty years. It is to us one of the special signs of our day, one of the special indications marking the end of the Gospel age and the inauguration of Messiah's kingdom.'"[568]

Alice Bailey, an occultist, remarked:

"The day is dawning when **all religions** will be regarded as emanating from one great spiritual source; all will be seen as **unitedly** providing the one root out of which the **universal world religion** will inevitably emerge. Then there will be neither Christian nor heathen, neither Jew nor Gentile, but simply **one great body of believers,** gathered out of all the current religions. **They will accept the same truths,** not as theological concepts but as essential to spiritual living; they will **stand together on the same platform of brotherhood** and of human relations; they will recognise divine sonship and will seek unitedly to co-operate with the divine Plan....Such a *world religion* is no idle dream but something which is definitely forming today."[569] [Italics in the original.]

Occultist and Mason, Manly Palmer Hall, says: **"Freed of limitations of creed and sect,** [the Mason] stands **master of all faiths...."**[570]

"Thus the expressed aims and efforts of the **United Nations** will be eventually brought to fruition and **a new church of God,** gathered out of all religions and spiritual groups, will unitedly **bring to an end the great heresy of separateness.** Love, unity, and the Risen Christ will be present, and He will demonstrate to us the *perfect life.*"[571] [Italics in the original.]

James Wardner writes:

"Naturally the **World Council of Churches** fits right into the plan. New Ager Lola Davis says: 'The World Council of Churches...has potential to serve as a source of **unity among the diversity of religions.** The West is becoming more familiar with the Eastern religions because of the efforts of some of their spiritual leaders.'"[572]

A NEW SPIRITUALITY

William Irwin Thompson, a New Ager,

"indicates that the **<u>form</u>** of the church in the New Age will remain the same; thus, churchgoers are less likely to notice that there has been a change in the message. He says, 'The new spirituality does not reject the earlier patterns of the great universal religions. Priest and church will not disappear; they will not be forced out of existence in the New Age, *they will be absorbed* into the existence of the New Age.'"[573] [Boldface and underlining in the original; italics added.]

In 1991 Thompson declared:

"We have **<u>a new spirituality</u>,** what has been called **<u>the New Age movement</u>.** The **<u>planetization of the esoteric</u>** has been going on for some time....The esoteric tradition of the New Age has been going on for a long time....The independent sovereign state, with the sovereign individual in his private property are over just as *the Christian fundamentalist days are about to be over.* We are fast becoming a **<u>planetary culture</u>.**"[574] [Boldface and underlining in the original; italics added.]

One flyer maintains:

"This is a time of preparation not only for a NEW CIVILISATION and culture in a **NEW WORLD ORDER,** but also for the coming of a **NEW SPIRITUAL DISPENSATION....**

"Preparation by men and women of goodwill is needed to introduce **NEW VALUES** for living, **NEW STANDARDS** of behaviour, **NEW ATTITUDES of non-separateness and cooperation,** leading to right human relations and a world at peace. The coming **WORLD TEACHER** will be mainly concerned, not with the result of past error and inadequacy but with the **REQUIREMENTS of a NEW WORLD ORDER** and with the **REORGANISATION of the social structure."**[575]

Today's church world certainly seems to have **NEW STANDARDS.** When people who profess to be Christians and those who don't are compared, there is very little difference between them. The church has taken on the "values" of the world and is no longer a separated—and a holy—people. For instance, George Gallup "compared the behavior of churched and unchurched in a variety of categories—people who called in sick when they weren't, people who puffed their resumes, people who cheated on tax deductions—and found 'little difference in the ethical views and behavior of the churched and the unchurched.'"[576]

I Timothy 4:1-2 warns: "Now the Spirit speaketh expressly, that in the **latter times** some shall **depart from the faith, giving heed to seducing spirits, and doctrines of devils;** Speaking lies in hypocrisy; having their conscience seared with a hot iron."

Also, II Timothy 3:1-5:

> "This know also, that in the **last days perilous times shall come.** For men shall be lovers of their own selves, covetous, boasters, proud, blasphemers, disobedient to parents, unthankful, unholy, Without natural affection, trucebreakers, false accusers, incontinent, fierce, **despisers of those that are good,** Traitors, heady, highminded, lovers of pleasures more than lovers of God; **Having a form of godliness, but *denying the power thereof:* from such turn away."**

CHURCHES HAVE BEEN INFILTRATED

In a recent Barna survey, "60% of adults said they believe the **Bible** to be **completely accurate in everything it says."**[577] Yet, "65% believe the Holy Spirit to be merely a symbol of God's presence, and 58% believe that Satan doesn't really exist."[578] Worse yet, 55% of those who profess to be born again Christians "reject the existence of the Holy Spirit."[579] How can anyone claim that the Bible is completely accurate while at the same time declaring that Satan and the Holy Spirit don't exist?

Yet another poll showed that

> "while most Americans assert that Jesus Christ was the Son of God, many doubt His divinity. Not only did 40 percent

> of all adults state that when Jesus Christ was on earth that He made mistakes, but an even larger proportion (42 percent) believe that when He lived on earth **'Jesus Christ was human and committed sin,** just like other people.'"[580]

Among those who profess to be born again, 25% "believe that Jesus committed sins during His life on earth."[581]

The church has been already so infiltrated that "while 80 percent of Americans profess to be Christian, about half of all Americans believe in ESP, more than a third in mental telepathy, one-quarter in reincarnation, and one out of five say they have been in touch with the dead!"[582]

> "The Barna Research Group reported that 49 percent of professing born-again Christians believe: 'All good people, whether they consider Jesus Christ to be their Savior or not, will live in heaven after they die.' They also reported that 43 percent of born-again Christians agree: 'It does not matter what religious faith you follow because all faiths teach similar lessons about life.' They also stated: '71 percent of American adults believe there is no such thing as absolute truth, a view shared by 64 percent of born-again Christians and 40 percent of evangelical Christians.'"[583]

Proverbs 20:12 warns: "There is a generation that are pure in their own eyes, and yet is not washed from their filthiness."

With a lot of professing (but not possessing) "Christians" accepting the world's standards, it is not hard to see how many of these same people will not only accept, but also promote, the coming one world religion and one world government.

No wonder the question is asked in the Bible: "Nevertheless when the Son of man cometh, shall He find faith on the earth?" (Luke 18:8).

SHEEP AND GOATS

Robert Muller, a Catholic in name but an occultist who follows the Alice Bailey writings[584] and her demonic spirit guide, Djwhal Khul,[585] writes:

> "The world's major religions must **speed up dramatically their ecumenical movement** and **recognize the unity** of their objectives **in the diversity** of their cults. Religions must actively cooperate to bring to unprecedented heights a better understanding of the mysteries of life and of our place in the universe. **'My religion, right or wrong,' and 'My nation, right or wrong' must be abandoned forever in the planetary age."**[586]

To show the twisted viewpoint of Bailey, we only need to look at her book *Discipleship in the New Age* (which was "Dedicated to the Master Djwhal Khul"[587]). She states:

> "I would like to point out that the distinction between the 'sheep and the goats' is mainly hierarchical. The term 'goats' is esoterically applied to initiated disciples and to those who have climbed the mountain of initiation. The term **'sheep'** is applied to those who are **following blindly** the inner urge of their souls and who are groping their way (in relatively large numbers) toward the Hierarchy. For them still has to come the great revelation that the 'kingdom of God is within you.' Such is the word for them at this stage in humanity's history."[588]

You can see that Bailey believes that the "sheep" are dumb and the "goats" are the advanced ones. The Bible, however, reveals:

> "When the Son of man shall come in His glory, and all the holy angels with Him, then shall He sit upon the throne of His glory: And before Him shall be gathered all nations: and **He shall separate them one from another, as a shepherd divideth his sheep from the goats:** And He shall set the **sheep on His right hand,** but the **goats on the left.** Then shall the King say unto them on **His right hand, Come, ye blessed of My Father,** inherit the kingdom prepared for you from the foundation of the world....Then shall He say also unto them on the **left hand, Depart from Me, ye cursed, into everlasting fire,** prepared for the devil and his angels....And these shall go away into everlasting punishment: but the righteous into life eternal" (Matthew 25:31-34, 41, 46).

Elsewhere Djwhal Khul remarks that

> **"Jesus was wrong** about the dividing of the sheep and the goats: 'It has been thought that the **sheep went to heaven and the goats went to hell.** <u>**It is the other way around**</u>**.** The goat in Capricorn is the initiate and from a certain esoteric angle the **goats do go to heaven** because they function in the spiritual kingdom....The **sheep remain on earth...**until they become goats.'...
>
> "'Entrance into heaven,' declares Djwhal Khul, 'is entrance into the Aquarian Age...and Piscean **(Christian) forces will be receding rapidly.'"**[589]

The School for Esoteric Studies, a group working towards establishing a **new world order,** reveals:

> "The New Age will not be ushered in and find true expression of its latent energies through the medium of old and patched

> up forms, or through the preservation of ancient techniques and attitudes. It will come into being through entirely new forms and by means of the intelligent **DISCARDING OF OLD MODES OF RELIGION,** government and economic and social idealisms."[590]

CHANGE OR DIE

Now, let's look at what some of the goals of this one world government and one world religion entail. World Goodwill, a New Age organization, explains:

> **"The churches and the world religions should indicate the unity** within all facets of truth which will provide a UNIVERSAL platform, one to which **ALL** men everywhere could give allegiance. Such a platform should include:
>
> "The truth that...**all men are divine.**
>
> "The truth that **evolution governs the growth of the human being...."**[591]

Muller's dream is "to get a tremendous **ALLIANCE BETWEEN ALL MAJOR RELIGIONS AND THE UN."**[592] He thinks that religions should "create **common world religious institutions"** and "display the U. N. flag in all houses of worship."[593]

He also said (as previously mentioned): "We must move as quickly as possible to a **one-world government; A ONE-WORLD RELIGION;** under a **one-world leader."**[594]

To accomplish this goal, **some changes must be made.** For instance, World Goodwill relates that the "Church today is in many ways the tomb of truth....Modern youth is not interested in the virgin birth or in the historicity of the birth of Jesus Christ."[595] They do brag, however, that many "churches, and particularly their theological seminaries, are beginning to SHAKE OFF THE CHAINS OF THE PAST and attempt to bring a **new unity** and livingness into religion...."[596]

It is easy to see that the New Age will accept liberal theology but they do not want to be bothered with the "chains of the past" or with a religion that teaches the Virgin Birth of Christ. World Goodwill explicitly states:

> "This radiant light [the message of Christ] **CANNOT** have **ANYTHING** to do with the somber teachings of the churches based on death, crucifixion, agony, eternal Hell and the wrath of a vengeful God....

"To build a new civilisation based on the emerging 'new consciousness' in humanity, the church organisations, **IF THEY WANT TO SURVIVE,** will have to **ADJUST** to the spiritual Hierarchy [the demonic leadership of the New Age]...."[597]

What is to happen to those Bible-believing Christians (and others) who cannot go along with this amalgamation of religion? Democratic Vice Presidential nominee for 1984 and Executive Director of the World Future Society, Barbara Marx Hubbard, doesn't mince words when she informs us:

"Humanity will not be able to make the transition from Earth-only to universal life **UNTIL** the chaff has been separated from the wheat....

"No worldly peace can prevail until the self-centered members of the planetary body **EITHER CHANGE or DIE.** That is the choice....They must surely DIE, or CHANGE....

"This act is as horrible as killing a CANCER cell. It **MUST** be done for the sake of the future of the whole....

"There have always been **DEFECTIVE SEEDS.** In the past they were permitted to die a 'natural death.'...We, the elders have been patiently waiting until the very last moment before the quantum transformation, to take action to CUT OUT this corrupted and corrupting element in the body of humanity. It is like watching a CANCER grow; something **MUST** be done before the whole body is destroyed...."[598]

MISFITS REMOVED

Djwhal Khul, speaking through Alice Bailey, announces:

"A violent **streptococcic germ** and **infection** has menaced the life of humanity....The **germ...**makes it presence felt in infected areas in the body of humanity.

"Another **SURGICAL OPERATION** may be necessary... to dissipate the infection and **GET RID** of the fever....let us never forget that...when a [life] form proves inadequate, or too diseased, or too crippled for the expression of that purpose, it is...no disaster when that form **HAS TO GO. DEATH IS NOT A DISASTER** to be feared; the work of the destroyer is not really cruel or undesirable....

"Therefore, there is **MUCH DESTRUCTION PERMITTED** by the Custodians of the Plan and much evil turned into good...."[599]

Bible-believing Christians are referred to by the New Agers with such derogatory terms as "unfit," "undesirable elements," "cancer," "infection," "germs," etc. Of course, who wants to let cancer or infection go unchecked? The best thing to do is to **REMOVE** the infected area before the infection spreads and this is just what the New Agers and humanists plan to do with the Christians.

Removing a person's cancer, no matter how painful, is doing him a favor and the New Agers also believe that removing those who disagree with them is doing a FAVOR to both the individual and the group as a whole. They teach that those who are killed will be sent to a special place where they will learn to cooperate with the New Age ideas. It is "a demonstration of the BENEFICENT will of God, [that] this potent energy [of Shamballa] tends to DESTROY ALL FORMS that HINDER the emergence of a new and better world...."[600]

These hindrances "will be brought under the care of Great Ones who will nurse them back to a healthy state. This can be done much better and more quickly WITHOUT the physical body."[601] Ruth Montgomery says that "souls...will have passed on into SPIRIT to RETHINK their attitudes...."[602] In another book by Montgomery she mentions

> "the unpleasant reminder of the ENORMOUS LOSS OF LIFE, as we think of it, that the Guides foresee when the earth shifts on its axis. To them, of course, it IS NOT a LOSS of life, BUT GRADUATION from Schoolhouse Earth to a HIGHER DIMENSION OF LIVING...."[603]

A former New Ager, Randall Baer, states that those who refuse the mark of the beast will be targeted "for EXTERMINATION in what would euphemistically be called RE-EDUCATION CENTERS of love and RELOCATION, that is, death camps in disguise."[604]

S. Radhakrishnan (a Templeton Prize winner[605]) bluntly comments that man "MUST CHANGE or PERISH."[606] One man from India who purports to be the Messiah, R. P. Lawrie Krishna, warns us:

> "A period of EXTREME TRIBULATION and UNPRECEDENTED MISERY is soon to cover the entire world....All events coming to light are pointing directly towards the end.... Such wholesale **DESTRUCTION of the UNDESIRABLE ELEMENTS** from the surface of the earth comes into effect at different places through different causes. It may be through storms and flood, through famine and diseases, through wars, through MASSACRES or through heavenly calamities like

> volcanic upheavals, etc....My Master also speaks: 'Signs are evident that the DESTRUCTION of the UNDESIRABLE ELEMENTS in the world has already commenced. There should be ENORMOUS BLOODSHED all over the world and the LOSS OF LIFE through various causes shall be so great that the world population shall be CONSIDERABLY REDUCED.... The old order shall be changed and a new [order] shall be born. The new structure of the coming world shall stand on BONES AND ASHES."[607]

You may be asking, "How do you know FOR SURE that they are REALLY referring to the Christians?" The answer is simple: their own testimonies reveal it! Mortimer J. Adler explains: "World peace is impossible without world government. World government is impossible to establish and, even if established, it would not long endure and prosper without world community. And World Community requires a certain degree of cultural **unity,** a condition that certainly does not exist at present."[608] *The Omega-Letter* expounds on this:

> "Simply stated, Adler argues that we will not be able to attain world peace until we attain cultural unity. But, Adler argues that there is ONLY ONE OBSTACLE to this unity—CHRISTIANITY....
>
> "Adler's point is simple—CHRISTIANITY claims 'supernatural knowledge' and 'divine revelation' that is divisive and not open to rational debate, and therefore, SHOULD NOT BE TOLERATED."[609]
>
> "'The CHRISTIAN Churches,' writes Rothschild in *'Reality and Illusion,'* 'must also **kill out all separativeness** and learn to **COOPERATE with ALL the other faiths...**whose Scriptures are of EQUAL VALUE and beauty as the New Testament.'"[610]

Further identifying the Christians, Alice Bailey admits that the "enlightened people...will not tolerate authoritarianism in any church or totalitarianism in any political system; they WILL NOT ACCEPT or PERMIT the rule of any body of men who undertake to tell them what they must believe in order to be saved...."[611] In other words, any church or doctrine that teaches that Jesus is the **only** way through which humankind can be saved **WILL NOT BE TOLERATED!** Surgery must be performed and the **"infection" of Christianity MUST BE REMOVED.**

Yes, Christians are misfits to the New Agers.

CHANGING OF THE GUARDS

Robert Muller, speaking at the Parliament of World Religions, declared:

> *"Do not worry if not all religions will join the United religions organization. Many nations did not join the UN at its beginning, but later regreted* (sic) *it and made every effort to join. It was the same with the European community and it will be the case with the world's religions because* ***whoever stays out or aloof will sooner or later regret it."***[612] [Italics in the original; boldface added.]

Dr. Christopher Hyatt refers to Christian fundamentalists as "The Shadow emerging in society."[613]

> "He predicted, however, that the fundamentalist forces will be overcome. There will be a 'changing of the guards.'
>
> "Hyatt went on to reveal just how this 'changing of the guards' will take place. 'I see,' he stressed, 'that the Earth still requires some blood before it is ready to move into new and different areas....
>
> "'I see it [the New Age] as requiring...a lot of blood, disruption, chaos, and pain for a mass change to occur.'"[614]

Yes, **true Christianity is considered to be EVIL** and full of misery. With this in mind, it is no wonder that in the Great Invocation (a New Age "prayer" to their "Messiah," Maitreya) is found this phrase: "And may it seal the door where EVIL dwells." In fact, Alice Bailey tells us: "The Forces of Evil [Bible-believing Christians] are defeated, though not yet 'sealed' behind the door where humanity can put them...."[615] The very next page of Bailey's booklet advises: "There must be NO...distress over the DISAPPEARANCE of the old order. 'The good, the true and the beautiful' is on its way, and for it MANKIND IS RESPONSIBLE, and not some outer divine intervention."[616] Many other New Age writers say that when the old order is removed, there should be no regret, and at least one writer encourages a great rejoicing when the old ways are destroyed.

Maharishi Mahesh Yogi says that to "kill in love" is justified if it is done "in support of the purpose of evolution."[617]

Amazingly, Jesus foretells us that "the time cometh, that whosoever killeth you will think that he doeth God service. And these things will they do unto you because they have not known the Father, nor Me. But these things have I told you, that when the time shall come, ye may remember that I told you of them" (John 16:2-4). Jesus also said that Christians would be persecuted and "hated of all nations for [His] name's sake" (Matthew 24:9; Mark 13:13; Luke 21:17). This is what is happening today. Those who hold to the inerrant Word of God are being persecuted. We are looked on as being "unenlightened," "ignorant," and "undesirable elements." After all, claim the New Agers, ANYONE who is so FOOLISH as to believe the Bible has not kept up with the times. They are still living in the "Dark Ages."

The apostle Paul remarked that "we are made as the FILTH of the world, and are the OFFSCOURING of all things" (I Corinthians 4:13).

LOVE NOT THE WORLD

The "kind," "loving," "gentle," "tolerant," "let's-all-get-together" New Agers are not about ready to permit those into their world order who believe that Jesus is the **ONLY** way to heaven. Oh, no! They must get rid of the infection (Christians) so that they will be able to implement their world religion and world government. You see, Christians are misfits. Webster tells us that a misfit is "something that fits badly" or "a person poorly adjusted to his environment." This definition implies that misfits are "out of place" in their surroundings and they are different from those around them. Misfits have different standards and beliefs than the majority of the people. Actually, this is a good description of a Christian. In the prayer Jesus prayed shortly before His crucifixion, He said: "They [the Christians] are not of this world [the world system], even as I am not of this world" (John 17:16). The writer of Hebrews reminds us that we are "strangers and pilgrims on the earth" (Hebrews 11:13b).

The Greek word for "pilgrim" is "parepidemos" which is "an adjective signifying 'sojourning in a strange place, away from one's own people....'"[618]

We live in the world but we are not to partake of the evil which surrounds us. I John 2:15 clearly states: "Love not the world, neither the things that are in the world. If any man love the world, the love of the Father is not in him." James asks: "Know ye not that the friendship of the world is enmity with God? whosoever therefore will be a friend of the world is the enemy of God" (James 4:4). As Christians we are to "live soberly, righteously, and godly, in this present world" (Titus 2:12) in spite of the wickedness around us. Those who do live righteously, however, are in the minority, and, therefore, can easily be termed as "misfits."

As misfits we do not conform to this world (Romans 12:2). In fact, one synonym for "misfit" is "nonconformist." Peter declared that the world would "think it strange that [we] run not with them to the same excess of riot" (I Peter 4:4), and because we won't conform to their worldly standards, they will speak evil of us (I Peter 4:4). Jesus remarked that the world would hate us because we are not of the world (John 17:14). John plainly tells us: "Marvel not, my brethren, if the world hate you" (I John 3:13). In speaking to His disciples, Jesus reminded them: "If ye were of the world, the world would love his own: but because ye are not of the world...therefore the world hateth you" (John 15:19).

The story of Cain and Abel comes to mind. Abel offered a proper sacrifice to God, but Cain was rebellious and offered a sacrifice of HIS own choosing. When God accepted Abel's offering but refused Cain's oblation, Cain became jealous and angry. Instead of repenting, Cain decided to get rid of his brother, Abel. After all, when he looked at Abel it was only a reminder of his own disobedience and Abel's submission. So, Cain killed Abel. The apostle John asks: "And wherefore slew he him?" The answer John gives is: "Because his own works were evil, and his brother's righteous" (I John 3:12b). John also indicated that "men loved darkness rather than light, because their deeds were evil. For every one that doeth evil hateth the light, neither cometh to the light, lest his deeds should be reproved" (John 3:19b-20). Even though we are hated, we are to rejoice.

> "Blessed are they which are persecuted for righteousness' sake: for theirs is the kingdom of heaven. Blessed are ye, when men shall revile you, and persecute you, and shall say all manner of evil against you falsely, for My sake. REJOICE, and be exceeding glad: for great is your reward in heaven: for so persecuted they the prophets which were before you" (Matthew 5:10-12).

"If ye be reproached for the name of Christ, happy are ye; for the spirit of glory and of God resteth upon you: **on their part He is evil spoken of, but on your part He is glorified"** (I Peter 4:14).

Many other Bible verses forewarn Christians that they will be hated and persecuted because they live righteously and are different from the world. To the world, the Christian is the "monkey wrench in the machinery." Actually, the Christian's righteous life is an indictment of the world's sin and wrongdoing. If the Christian could only be removed, the world would be left to do "its own thing" without suffering from a guilty conscience. Like Cain, the world wants to get rid of the Abels.

We are told that fundamentalism is hazardous to one's mental well-being. New Ager, Dick Sutphen, feels that **fundamentalism "is EXTREMELY DANGEROUS** to the future of this planet and the potential for a New Age."[619] One newsletter informs us: "We also need to continue telling the public how the fundamentalist experience can be a SERIOUS MENTAL HEALTH HAZARD to millions."[620] In fact, one of the Fundamentalists Anonymous' goals is "to help people make a successful transition from fundamentalism to a HEALTHIER lifestyle...."[621]

One New Ager changes the word "Christendom" into "Christian-dumb."[622] Paul Brandwein declares: "Any child who believes in God is MENTALLY ILL."[623]

There are numerous quotations from New Agers, occultists, humanists, and even church leaders that reiterate time and time again that the Bible-believing Christians stand in their way. Christians are aware that a one world government will be controlled by the antichrist and, therefore, they do not support it. For the New Agers to accomplish their diabolical plan, the Christians must be silenced.

RELIGION AS A COVER-UP

The Antichrist will be a religious man. He will come announcing that he is God and he will accept worship as such. Paul warned us about this in 2 Thessalonians 2:4: "Who opposeth and exalteth himself above all that is called God, or that is worshipped; so that he as God sitteth in the temple of God, shewing himself that he is God." The false prophets don't mind pretending to be religious. Jesus warned His disciples that "many shall come in my name, saying, I am Christ" (Matthew 24:5). It is through the **guise of religion** and the working of miracles, signs, and wonders that the Antichrist and false prophets will deceive many (Matthew 24:5, 24; Mark 13:6, 22; Luke 21:8; Revelation 13:13-14; 19:20).

From the beginning Satan has wanted to be worshipped as God. Isaiah described this ambition of Satan: "For thou hast said in thine heart, I WILL ascend into heaven, I WILL exalt my throne above the stars of God: I WILL sit also upon the mount of the congregation, in the sides of the north: I WILL ascend above the heights of the clouds; I WILL BE LIKE THE MOST HIGH" (Isaiah 14:13-14). We also see Satan's desire to be worshipped when he tempted Christ in the wilderness.

> "Again, the devil taketh Him up into an exceeding high mountain, and sheweth Him all the kingdoms of the world,

> and the glory of them; And saith unto Him, All these things will I give Thee, if Thou wilt fall down and worship me. Then saith Jesus unto him, Get thee hence, Satan: for it is written, Thou shalt worship the Lord thy God, and Him only shalt thou serve" (Matthew 4:8-10).

The psalmist exclaimed of the true God: "O God, who is like unto Thee!" (Psalm 71:19). He stated further: "Among the gods there is none like unto Thee, O Lord; neither are there any works like unto Thy works." (Psalm 86:8. See also Psalm 89:8 and 113:5.) The Antichrist, however, will gladly accept worship and all those who are not saved will worship him (Revelation 13:4, 8, 15). His followers will cry in amazement "Who is like unto the beast?" (Revelation 13:4).

Not only do the followers of the Antichrist wonder who is like unto their leader, but they add: "Who is able to make war with him?" (Revelation 13:4). They may feel that the Antichrist is invincible, but they will be sorry that they asked this question, for in Revelation 19 we see that Christ is coming to make war with the Antichrist: "And I saw heaven opened, and behold a white horse; and He that sat upon him was called Faithful and True, and in righteousness He doth judge and make war....And the armies which were in heaven followed Him upon white horses, clothed in fine linen, white and clean" (Revelation 19:11, 14). The apostle John continues: "And I saw the beast, and the kings of the earth, and their armies, gathered together to make war against Him that sat on the horse, and against His army" (Revelation 19:19).

WAR AGAINST CHRIST

The Antichrist is so arrogant that He seems to believe that he will be able to win a war against Christ. He will persecute the followers of Christ and overcome them (Revelation 13:7; Daniel 11:32-35) so he will attempt to also overcome Christ, but the outcome will be that the Antichrist is defeated. Paul tells us that he will be destroyed "with the brightness of [Christ's] coming" (II Thessalonians 2:8) and John reveals that "These shall make war with the Lamb, and the Lamb shall **overcome** them: for He is Lord of lords, and King of kings: and they that are with Him are called, and chosen, and faithful" (Revelation 17:14).

In spite of all the Antichrist's imitations and disguises to appear like Christ, it will eventually become evident that he is not what he has appeared to be, but by the time many discover his deception it will be too late for them. The true Christian, however, does not need to live in fear and worry about falling into his trap IF we are living for the Lord, for His Word is our guideline and we are told that "we are not ignorant of [Satan's] devices" (II Corinthians 2:11). The Bible tells us in advance that "there shall arise false Christs, and false prophets, and shall shew great signs and wonders; insomuch that, if it were possible, they shall deceive the very elect" (Matthew 24:24), but it also adds: "Wherefore if they shall say unto you, Behold, he is in the desert; go not forth: behold, he is in the secret chambers; believe it not" (Matthew 24:26).

"For we are not as many, which corrupt the word of God: but as of sincerity, but as of God, in the sight of God speak we in Christ" (II Corinthians 2:17).

Are **YOU** going to obey the Word of God or follow ecumenical leaders such as Billy Graham? Peter tells us that the Scriptures can be twisted: "[T]hey that are unlearned and unstable **wrest** [twist], as they do also the other **scriptures, unto their own destruction.** Ye therefore, beloved, seeing ye know these things before, **beware** lest ye also, being led away with the error of the wicked, fall from your own stedfastness" (II Peter 3:16b-17).

WHOSE BRIDE ARE YOU?

Christ has a bride, the church, which is supposed to be holy. Paul refers to this bride in Ephesians 5:25-27: "Christ also loved the church, and gave Himself for it; That He might sanctify and cleanse it with the washing of water by the word, That He might present it to Himself a glorious church, not having spot, or wrinkle, or any such thing; but that it should be holy and without blemish." The Antichrist, too, will have a bride, but instead of being pure and spotless, she will be a whore (Revelation 17:1, 15, 16).

Are you waiting for Christ or the Antichrist? Which person are you following? If you claim you are following Christ, does your life match your profession? We are admonished by Peter: "But as He which hath called you is holy, **so be ye holy** in all manner of conversation" (I Peter 1:15). "The fruit of the Spirit is love, joy, peace, longsuffering, gentleness, goodness, faith, Meekness, temperance" (Galatians 5:22-23). On the other hand, the fruits of the flesh are: "Adultery, fornication, uncleanness, lasciviousness, Idolatry, witchcraft, hatred, variance, emulations, wrath, strife, seditions, heresies, Envyings, murders, drunkenness, revellings, and such like: of the which I tell you before, as I have also told you in time past, that they which do such things shall not inherit the kingdom of God" (Galatians 5:19b-21). "In this the children of God are manifest, and the children of the devil: whosoever doeth not righteousness is not of God, neither he that loveth not his brother" (1 John 3:10). "They that are Christ's have crucified the flesh with the affections and lusts" (Galatians 5:24).

Regardless of what man may say, the Bible is our final authority. No church can save you. Only Jesus Christ can do that. Even though you may be a moral and honest person, if you have never invited Christ into your heart as your own **PERSONAL** Savior, you, too, need to repent. Maybe you are not committing a blatant sin, but the Bible tells us that **"ALL** have sinned and come short of the glory of God" (Romans 3:23). The **"ALL"** includes both you and me, and "the wages of sin is [eternal] death; but the gift of God is eternal life through Jesus Christ our Lord" (Romans 6:23). God's gift to us is eternal life, but we must **accept** this gift to make the transaction valid. If I had a gift to give to you and you refused to accept it, that gift would do you no good. You must **RECEIVE** this gift for it to become effective.

SOME GOOD NEWS

Even though **ALL** of us are born in sin, the good news is that "Christ Jesus came into the world to save sinners" (I Timothy 1:15). If you have never accepted Christ as your **PERSONAL** Savior and would like to do so, the first step is to be born again. John 3:3 emphasizes: **"EXCEPT** a man be born **AGAIN,** he **CANNOT** see the kingdom of God." How can one be born **AGAIN?** We all know that we were born once, our physical birth, but can we enter into our mother's womb and be born the second time (see John 3:1-17)? No. The second birth comes by being born into the family of God. John 3:16: "For God so **LOVED** the world [that includes **YOU!**] that He **GAVE** His only Begotten Son, that **WHOSOEVER** [that includes **YOU] BELIEVETH** [trusts, clings to, relies on] Him [God's Son, Jesus] should not perish [in hell], but have everlasting life."

All you need to do is sincerely believe with all your heart that Jesus is the Son of God and to be willing to turn from your sins, whatever they are—big or small. Ask Jesus to come into your heart and help you to live for Him, and He **WILL** do it. "He that covereth his sins shall not prosper: but whoso **CONFESSETH AND FORSAKETH** them shall have mercy" (Proverbs 28:13). John 6:37 promises: "Him that cometh to Me I will **IN NO WISE** cast out." Romans 10:9 states: "If thou shalt **CONFESS** with thy mouth the Lord Jesus, and shalt **BELIEVE** in thine heart that God hath raised Him from the dead, thou **SHALT** be saved [born again]."

If you would like to be born again, pray your own prayer or sincerely pray the following:

> *Dear Jesus, I realize that I am a sinner. I believe that You died for my sins. Please forgive me of my past sins and come into my heart. Save me for Your sake, and help me to live for You. I ask this in Your name. Amen.*

If you sincerely prayed and asked Jesus to forgive you of your sins, you will have the assurance that you are now a child of God. John 1:12 reveals: "But **AS MANY AS RECEIVED HIM,** to them gave He power to become the sons of God, even to them that **BELIEVE** on His name." Read your Bible **EVERY** day (start with the book of John), and find a Bible-believing church where you can worship God with other born again believers.

"Therefore being justified by faith, we have peace with God through our Lord Jesus Christ" (Romans 5:1), "and the peace of God, which passeth all understanding, shall keep your hearts and minds through Christ Jesus" (Philippians 4:7). "If the Son [Jesus Christ] therefore shall make you free, ye shall be free indeed" (John 8:36).

ENDNOTES

1. LET'S MEET SOME OF BILLY'S FRIENDS

[1] *Christian News* (January 3, 2000, Vol. 38, No. 1). See also: William Martin, *A Prophet with Honor: The Billy Graham Story* (NY: William Morrow and Company, Inc., 1991), p.303; William P. Grady, *Final Authority: A Christian's Guide to the King James Bible* (Knoxville, TN: Grady Publications, Inc., 1993), p.185.

[2] Chuck Colson with Ellen Santilli Vaughn, *The Body* (Dallas, TX: Word Publishing, 1996 Edition), p.300. See also: "The Prodigal Graham," *New Man* (October 1996, Vol. 3, No. 7), p.12.

[3] John E. Ashbrook quoting from *The News-Herald* in *New Neutralism II: Exposing the Gray of Compromise* (Mentor, OH: Here I Stand Books, 1992), p.31, 35; "Graham Promotes BWA" quoting from *Baptist World* in *Calvary Contender* (August 15, 1997, Vol. 14, No. 16), p.1; Jack T. Chick, *Smokescreens: Who Is the "Whore" of Revelation? A Biblical and Historical Answer* (Chino, CA: Chick Publications, 1983), p.58.

[4] "Billy Graham Does Political Favor for President Clinton," *Flashpoint* (September 1997, Vol. 97-9). See also: "Modernists Among 'Greatest Preachers,'" *Calvary Contender* (January 15, 2000), p.2.

[5] *The Berean Call* (February 1999).

[6] Bill Broadway, "Franklin Graham Set for Bush Invocation," *The News and Observer* (January 16, 2001), p.7A.

[7] Rick Miesel, "Billy Graham: General Teachings/Activities" (Biblical Discernment Ministries, Revised January 1994).

[8] Texe Marrs, "Heroism and Cowardice in the Lion's Den," *Flashpoint* (April 1994), p.2; J. W. Wardner, "Billy Graham, Freemasonry & the Communists," *Despatch Magazine* (September 1998, Vol. 10, No. 3), p.28; "Billy Graham Praises Clinton," *Christian View of the News* (October 10, 1994, Vol. 19, No. 19), p.2; James W. Wardner, *Unholy Alliances* (n.p., 1996), p.138; "Billy Graham Praises Bill Clinton," *Flashpoint* (April 1994), p.2.

[9] James W. Wardner, *Unholy Alliances* (n.p., 1996), p.139. See also: *Ibid.;* Miesel, *op. cit.;* "Billy Graham Praises Clinton," *Christian View of the News* (October 10, 1994, Vol. 19, No. 19), p.2; J. W. Wardner, "Billy Graham, Freemasonry & the Communists," *Despatch Magazine* (September 1998, Vol. 10, No. 3), p.28; "Church Leaders Praise Bill Clinton's 'Spirituality,'" *Christian News* (November 13, 2000, Vol. 38, No. 42), p.2.

[10] "Church Leaders Praise Bill Clinton's 'Spirituality,'" *Christian News* (November 13, 2000, Vol. 38, No. 42), p.2; Miesel, *op. cit.*

[11] Caption under picture in *Christian News* (January 22, 2001, Vol. 39, No. 4), p.11.

[12] "Clinton: Saint, or Socialist?," *Calvary Contender* (May 15, 1994, Vol. 11, No. 10), p.1.

[13] NBC's *Today,* 3/5/98. See also: "Billy Graham Is a Great Deceiver," *Flashpoint* (May 1998, Vol. 98-5), p.1; "Clinton's Cynicism Toward Repentance," *Calvary Contender* (September 15, 1998, Vol. 15, No. 18), p.1.

[14] Billy Graham, *Just As I Am: The Autobiography of Billy Graham* (Harpers Collins Worldwide, 1997), p.656; "Clinton Desires to Serve God," *Christian News* (May 12, 1997, Vol. 35, No. 19), p.11.

[15] Wardner, *Unholy Alliances, op. cit.,* p.138; "Clinton: Saint, or Socialist?," *op. cit.;* J. W. Wardner, "Billy Graham, Freemasonry & the Communists," *Despatch Magazine* (September 1998, Vol. 10, No. 3), p.28; J. W. Wardner, "Unholy Alliances—The Order—The Illuminati Pedigree," *Despatch Magazine* (September 1998, Vol. 10, No. 3), p.29.

[16] Adelle M. Banks, "Clinton, Others Praise Graham at Washington Dinner," *Christian News* (May 13, 1996, Vol. 34, No. 20), p.7.

[17] William Martin, *A Prophet with Honor: The Billy Graham Story* (NY: William Morrow and Company, Inc., 1991), p.174.

[18] Peter Collier and David Horowitz, *The Rockefellers: An American Dynasty* (NY: Holt, Rinehart and Winston, n.d.), p.158; Emanuel M. Josephson, *The Truth About Rockefeller* (New York City, NY: Chedney Press, 1964), p.140.

[19] *The Road to Socialism and the New World Order* (Highland City, FL: Florida Pro Family Forum, Inc., 1995), p.23; *Now Is the Dawning of the New Age New World Order* (Oklahoma City, OK: Hearthstone Publishing, Ltd., 1991), p.238; William T. Still, *New World Order: The Ancient Plan of Secret Societies* (Lafayette, LA: Huntington House, Inc., 1990), p.173; Jim Marrs, *Rule by Secrecy: The Hidden History That Connects the Trilateral Commission, the Freemasons, and the Great Pyramids* (New York, NY: HarperCollins Publishers, Inc., 2000), p.33, 127, 140; James W. Wardner, *The Planned Destruction of America* (Debary, FL: Longwood Communications, 1994), p.61; David Allen Rivera, *Final Warning: A History of the New World Order* (Harrisburg, PA: Rivera Enterprises, 1994 Edition), p.98; James R. Patrick, Compiler and Editor, *America 2000/Goals 2000* (Moline, IL: Citizens for Academic Excellence, 1994), p.584.

[20] John A. Stormer, *None Dare Call It Treason* (Florissant, MO: Liberty Bell Press, 1964), p.210, 213; Wardner, *Unholy Alliances, op. cit.,* p.146, 157; Fritz Springmeier, *The Top 13 Illuminati Bloodlines* (Portland, OR: n.p., 1995), p.156; Gary Allen, *The Rockefeller File* (Seal Beach, CA: '76 Press, 1976), p.157; Emanuel M. Josephson, *The Truth About Rockefeller* (1964), p.28, 84, 90, 151.

[21] Collier and Horowitz, *op. cit.,* p.108, 271; Fritz Springmeier, *The Top 13 Illuminati Bloodlines* (Portland, OR: n.p., 1995), p.25, 156; *The Observer* (January 17, 1996); Wardner, *Unholy Alliances, op. cit.,* p.146; James W. Wardner, *The Planned Destruction of America* (Debary, FL: Longwood Communications, 1994), p.61; Emanuel M. Josephson, *The Truth About Rockefeller* (1964), p.84, 151.

[22] "White House Honors Memory of Anti-Communist Chambers," *Christian News* (July 23, 2001, Vol. 39, No. 30), p.13.

[23] Wardner, *Unholy Alliances, op. cit.*, p.146; Berit Kjos, "Conforming the Church to the New Millennium," *Prophecy Corner and the Nosh Box* (November 2000), p.8; James W. Wardner, *The Planned Destruction of America* (Debary, FL: Longwood Communications, 1994), p.61; Berit Kjos, "Conforming the Church to the New Millennium," *Christian News* (February 28, 2000, Vol. 38, No. 9), p.9; Emanuel M. Josephson, *The Truth About Rockefeller* (1964), p.84, 85, 151; "The Rehabilitation of Communism," *The Schwarz Report* (October 2000, Vol. 40, No. 10), p.7; Fritz Springmeier, *The Top 13 Illuminati Bloodlines* (Portland, OR: n.p., 1995), p.25; *The Observer* (January 17, 1996); Edgar C. Bundy, *Collectivism in the Churches: A Documented Account of the Political Activities of the Federal, National, and World Councils of Churches* (Wheaton, IL: The Church League of America, 1958), p.170, 179.

[24] Paul Fisher, "A Syndicated Conspiracy Against God and Man?," *The Observer* (January 17, 1996), p.13.

[25] Edgar C. Bundy, *Collectivism in the Churches: A Documented Account of the Political Activities of the Federal, National, and World Councils of Churches* (Wheaton, IL: The Church League of America, 1958), p.179, 64. See also: Robert E. Herzstein, *Henry R. Luce: A Political Portrait of the Man Who Created the American Century* (New York, NY: Macmillan Publishing Company, 1994), p.306; Fisher, *op. cit.*, p.13; Graham, *Just As I Am, op. cit.*, p.274.

[26] Taken from the Internet.

[27] Robert E. Herzstein, *Henry R. Luce: A Political Portrait of the Man Who Created the American Century* (New York, NY: Macmillan Publishing Company, 1994), p.306.

[28] Wardner, *Unholy Alliances, op. cit.*, p.146; *Intelligence Newsletter* (July-August 1991), p.7; David Allen Rivera, *Final Warning: A History of the New World Order* (Harrisburg, PA: Rivera Enterprises, 1994 Edition), p.166; William T. Still, *New World Order: The Ancient Plan of Secret Societies* (Lafayette, LA: Huntington House, Inc., 1990), p.173; David P. Gaines, *The World Council of Churches: A Study of Its Background and History* (Peterborough, New Hampshire, Richard R. Smith Company, Inc., 1966), p.251; Jim Marrs, *Rule by Secrecy: The Hidden History That Connects the Trilateral Commission, the Freemasons, and the Great Pyramids* (New York, NY: HarperCollins Publishers, Inc., 2000), p.140, 141; James R. Patrick, Compiler and Editor, *America 2000/Goals 2000* (Moline, IL: Citizens for Academic Excellence, 1994), p.663; Fisher, *op. cit.*, p.13.

[29] "John Foster Dulles," Softkey Multimedia Inc., Infopedia (1996).

[30] John Foster Dulles, *War or Peace* (NY: The Macmillan Company, 1950), p.40.

[31] *Ibid.*, p.204.

[32] "Let's Not Follow 'Orders,'" quoting Tom Anderson in *The Christian World Report* (April 1991, Vol. 3, No. 4), p.4.

[33] Robert Muller, *First Lady of the World* (Anacortes, WA: World Happiness and Cooperation, 1991), p.3. See also: Newsletter from Radio Liberty (August 2000), p.6; Texe Marrs, *Circle of Intrigue* (Austin, TX. Living Truth Ministries, 1995), p.58. See also: Alan Morrison, *The Serpent and the Cross: Religious Corruption in an Evil Age* (Birmingham, England: K & M Books, 1994), p.580; *Last Trumpet Newsletter* (August 2001, Vol. 20, Issue 7 [sic]), p.2-3.

[34] David Allen Rivera, *Final Warning: A History of the New World Order* (Harrisburg, PA: Rivera Enterprises, 1994 Edition), p.166.

[35] Des Griffin, *Fourth Reich of the Rich* (South Pasadena, CA: Emissary Publications, 1978), p.138; Wardner, *Unholy Alliances, op. cit.*, p.148; *President Clinton Will Continue the New World Order* (Oklahoma City, OK: Southwest Radio Church, 1993), p.23.

[36] Stanley Monteith, *Brotherhood of Darkness* (Oklahoma City, OK: Hearthstone Publishing, 2000), p.131.

[37] Taken from the Internet. See also: Jim Marrs, *Rule by Secrecy: The Hidden History That Connects the Trilateral Commission, the Freemasons, and the Great Pyramids* (New York, NY: HarperCollins Publishers, Inc., 2000), p.163-164.

[38] Wardner, *Unholy Alliances, op. cit.*, p.146, 157; *The Road to Socialism and the New World Order, op. cit.*, p.23; Graham, *Just As I Am, op. cit.*, p.274; David P. Gaines, *The World Council of Churches: A Study of Its Background and History* (Peterborough, NH: Richard R. Smith Company, Inc., 1966), p.189, 251-252, 559, 934; *Secret Records Revealed: The Men, the Money and the Methods Behind the New World Order* (Oklahoma City, OK: Hearthstone Publishing, Ltd., 1999), p.62; "Books," *Christian Century* (October 22, 1986), p.921; *The Observer* (January 17, 1996); *Intelligence Newsletter* (July-August 1991), p.7; Fritz Springmeier, *The Top 13 Illuminati Bloodlines* (Portland, OR: n.p., 1995), p.156.

[39] *Ibid.*, p.152.

[40] *Ibid.*, p.154; Texe Marrs, *Dark Majesty: The Secret Brotherhood and the Magic of a Thousand Points of Light* (Austin, TX: Living Truth Publishers, 1992), p.206.

[41] *Ibid.*, p.157.

[42] G. Archer Weniger, *Modernism of National Council of Churches* (Murfreesboro, TN: Sword of the Lord Publishers, 1961), p.19.

[43] Dulles, *op. cit.*, p.34. See also: Bundy, *Collectivism in the Churches, op. cit.*, p.163-164, 168, 318, 319; Berit Kjos, "Conforming the Church to the New Millennium," *Prophecy Corner and the Nosh Box* (November 2000), p.7; Herzstein, *op. cit.*, p.306; Leonard Moseley, *Dulles: A Biography of Elmer, Allen, and John Foster Dulles* (1970), p.151; Berit Kjos, "Conforming the Church to the New Millennium," *Christian News* (February 28, 2000, Vol. 38, No. 9), p.9; Robert Sessler, *To Be God of One World: The French Revolution Globalized* (Merlin, OR: Let There Be Light Publications, 1992), p.125.

[44] Herzstein, *op. cit.*, p.306.

[45] *Secret Records Revealed: The Men, the Money and the Methods Behind the New World Order* (Oklahoma City, OK: Hearthstone Publishing, Ltd., 1999), p.62. See also: *The Road to Socialism and the New World Order, op. cit.*, p.23; "American Malvern," *Time* (March 16, 1942); Berit Kjos, "Conforming the Church to the New Millennium," *Christian*

News (February 28, 2000, Vol. 38, No. 9), p.9; Wardner, *Unholy Alliances, op. cit.*, p.158; Stormer, *None Dare Call It Treason, op. cit.*, p.214; Rivera: *op. cit.*, p.226.

[46] Springmeier, *Bloodlines, op. cit.*, p.291.

[47] *Ibid.*, p.291. See also: *Now Is the Dawning of the New Age New World Order* (Oklahoma City, OK: Hearthstone Publishing, Ltd., 1991), p.128; Jim Marrs, *Rule by Secrecy: The Hidden History That Connects the Trilateral Commission, the Freemasons, and the Great Pyramids* (New York, NY: HarperCollins Publishers, Inc., 2000), p.96; Scott Donaldson, *Archibald MacLeish: An American Life* (New York, NY: Houghton Mifflin Company, 1992), Front flap, p.193, 392; Texe Marrs, *Dark Majesty: The Secret Brotherhood and the Magic of a Thousand Points of Light* (Austin, TX: Living Truth Publishers, 1992), p.195; Antony C. Sutton, *How the Order Controls Education* (Phoenix, AZ: Research Publications, Inc., 1983), p.62; "Global Connections," *EFA Today* (January-March 1993, Issue No. 2), p.6; Wardner, *Unholy Alliances, op. cit.*, p.131.

[48] James R. Patrick, Compiler and Editor, *America 2000/Goals 2000* (Moline, IL: Citizens for Academic Excellence, 1994), p.663.

[49] Scott Donaldson, *Archibald MacLeish: An American Life* (New York, NY: Houghton Mifflin Company, 1992), Front flap, p.388.

[50] *Ibid.*, p.363.

[51] Claire Chambers, *The SIECUS Circle: A Humanist Revolution* (Belmont, MA: Western Islands, 1977), p.132, 336, 356.

[52] Donaldson, *op. cit.*, p.xi.

[53] *Ibid.*, p.284.

[54] Carroll Quigley, *Tragedy and Hope: A History of the World in Our Time* (NY: The Macmillan Company, 1966), p.988, 989, 991, 1059; *The Road to Socialism and the New World Order, op. cit.*, p.24; *Now Is the Dawning of the New Age New World Order* (Oklahoma City, OK: Hearthstone Publishing, Ltd., 1991), p.238; Jim Marrs, *Rule by Secrecy: The Hidden History That Connects the Trilateral Commission, the Freemasons, and the Great Pyramids* (New York, NY: HarperCollins Publishers, Inc., 2000), p.33, 127, 141; Edgar C. Bundy, *Billy Graham: Performer?, Politician?, Preacher?, Prophet?* (Wheaton, IL: Church League of America, 1982), p.46; "John Foster Dulles," Softkey Multimedia Inc., Infopedia (1996); "Dwight David Eisenhower," Softkey Multimedia Inc., Infopedia (1996); *Intelligence Newsletter* (July-August 1991), p.7; Graham, *Just As I Am, op. cit.*, p.264; Berit Kjos, "Conforming the Church to the New Millennium," *Christian News*, (February 28, 2000, Vol. 38, No. 9), p.9; "New Red Hats—and the Next Pope?," *Newsweek* (January 22, 2001), p.6; Collier and Horowitz, *op. cit.*, p.271; Gary Allen, *The Rockefeller File* (Seal Beach, CA: '76 Press, 1976), p.157; Wardner, *Unholy Alliances, op. cit.*, p.159; Bundy, *Collectivism in the Churches, op. cit.*, p.64, 174; James W. Wardner, *The Planned Destruction of America* (Debary, FL: Longwood Communications, 1994), p.61; Rivera: *op. cit.*, p.98, 169; David P. Gaines, *The World Council of Churches: A Study of Its Background and History* (Peterborough, NH: Richard R. Smith Company, Inc., 1966), p.934; *Secret Records Revealed, op. cit.*, p.58, 62; *President Clinton Will Continue the New World Order* (Oklahoma City, OK: Southwest Radio Church, 1993), p.16; Patrick, *op. cit.* p.585, 668.

[55] Wardner, *Unholy Alliances, op. cit.*, p.159; Richard N. Ostling, "National Council of Churches Falls upon Hard Times," *Christian News* (November 29, 1999, Vol. 37, No. 44), p.7; "The Right Place for a Mass Murdering Atheist to Speak," *Christian News* (September 18, 2000, Vol. 38, No. 34), p.4.

[56] Bundy, *Collectivism in the Churches, op. cit.*, p.244.

[57] Jim Shaw and Tom McKenney, *The Deadly Deception: Freemasonry Exposed...by One of Its Top Leaders* (Lafayette, LA: Huntington House, Inc.), p.136.

[58] Wardner, *Unholy Alliances, op. cit.*, p.159.

[59] *Ibid.* See also: Collier and Horowitz, *op. cit.*, p.153.

[60] Collier and Horowitz, *op. cit.*, p.154. See also: *Ibid.*, p.149.

[61] Springmeier, *Bloodlines, op. cit.*, p.222.

[62] Brenda Scott and Samantha Smith, *Trojan Horse: How the New Age Movement Infiltrates the Church* (Lafayette, LA: Huntington House Publishers, 1993), p.68.

[63] Siby Moholy-Nagy, "Gargoyle," *The World Book Encyclopedia* (Vol. 7), (Chicago 54, IL: Field Enterprise Educational Corporation, 1961 Edition), p.41.

[64] Wardner, *Unholy Alliances, op. cit.*, p.149. See also: Brad K. Gsell, *The Legacy of Billy Graham* (Charlotte, NC: Fundamental Presbyterian Publication, n.d.), p.2; Bundy, *Collectivism in the Churches, op. cit.*, p.256.

[65] David W. Cloud, "The Attack upon the Blood Atonement," *O Timothy* (1987, Vol. 4, Issue 1), quoting from a letter by Harry E. Fosdick of which a photostat copy appeared in *Christian Beacon*, July 24, 1947, quoted in *The Ethics of Modernism*, by Chester E. Tulga, Challenge Press, 1981, p.40; Perry F. Rockwood, "The Revised Standard Version," *O Timothy* (1985, Vol. 2, Issue 3). See also: "The Right Place for a Mass Murdering Atheist to Speak," *Christian News* (September 18, 2000, Vol. 38, No. 34), p.4; Bundy, *Collectivism in the Churches, op. cit.*, p.257; Joel A. Carpenter, *Revive Us Again: The Reawakening of American Fundamentalism* (New York, NY: Oxford University Press, 1997), p.273. See also: "ELCA Publishes Book by Marxist 'Theological Atheist,'" *Christian News* (June 4, 2001, Vol. 39, No. 23), p.15.

[66] Wardner, *Unholy Alliances, op. cit.*, p.149.

[67] *The NCC/WCC—Communism's Helpers* (Virginia Beach, VA: Good News Baptist Church, n.d.), p.5.

[68] "The Right Place for a Mass Murdering Atheist to Speak," *Christian News* (September 18, 2000, Vol. 38, No. 34), p.4.

[69] Cloud, "The Attack upon the Blood Atonement," *op. cit.;* Perry F. Rockwood, "The Revised Standard Version," *O Timothy* (1985, Vol. 2, Issue 3); "The Right Place for a Mass Murdering Atheist to Speak," *op. cit.*, p.4.

[70] George Grant, *Grand Illusions: The Legacy of Planned Parenthood* (Nashville, TN: Thomas Nelson, Inc., 1998 Edition), p.73.

[71] *Foundation* (June-August 1991), p.34.

[72] Springmeier, *Bloodlines, op. cit.*, p.291.

[73] David P. Gaines, *The World Council of Churches: A Study of Its Background and History* (Peterborough, NH: Richard R. Smith Company, Inc., 1966), p.253.

[74] *Ibid.*, p.253-254.

[75] *Secret Records Revealed, op. cit.*, p.58; *The Road to Socialism and the New World Order, op. cit.*, p.24.

[76] *Ibid. The Road to Socialism and the New World Order, op. cit.*, p.24.

[77] *Now Is the Dawning of the New Age New World Order* (Oklahoma City, OK: Hearthstone Publishing, Ltd., 1991), p.116; *The New World Order: A Critique and Chronology* (Milford, PA: America's Future, Inc., n.d.).

[78] Bundy, *Collectivism in the Churches, op. cit.*, p.165. See also: Berit Kjos, "Conforming the Church to the New Millennium," *Prophecy Corner and the Nosh Box* (November 2000), p.7; Herzstein, *op. cit.*, p.306.

[79] Stormer, *None Dare Call It Treason, op. cit.*, p.214. See also: "American Malvern," *Time* (March 16, 1942).

[80] Patrick, *op. cit.* p.668.

[81] Wardner, *Unholy Alliances, op. cit.*, p.158; Stormer, *None Dare Call It Treason, op. cit.*, p.214. See also: Bundy, *Collectivism in the Churches, op. cit.*, p.176.

[82] Dulles, *op. cit.*, p.187.

[83] Ron Patton, "The Depopulation Agenda," *Endure to the End* (October 1994, Vol. 1, Issue 1), p.5.

[84] John F. McManus, "The Council on Foreign Relations: Early History Shows Its Subversive Designs," *America 2000/ Goals 2000* 1994, p.585; "Needed: America-First Locally Controlled Education" (n.d.), n.p.

[85] Emanuel M. Josephson, *The Truth About Rockefeller* (1964), p.84, 129.

[86] Martin, *A Prophet with Honor, op. cit.*, p.191.

[87] John Templeton, *Possibilities for Over One Hundredfold More Spiritual Information: The Humble Approach in Theology and Science* (Philadelphia, PA: Templeton Foundation Press, 2000), p.199; Graham, *Just As I Am, op. cit.*, p.511; Wilbert Forker, Editor, *The Templeton Foundation Prize for Progress in Religion* (Edinburgh: Scottish Academic Press, 1988), p.85, 89, 280; "Charles Colson to Join Mother Teresa and Pagan Religious Leaders at Parliament of the World's Religions," *O Timothy* (1993, Vol. 10, Issue 6); "The Templeton Prize for Religious Excellence," *Despatch Magazine* (June 2001, Vol. 13:2); "Templeton Is Awarded to Physicist," *Reading Eagle* (March 11, 1995); Harry Bruinius, "Templeton Winner Coaxed Science and Religion to Talk," *Christian Science Monitor* (March 11, 1999), p.18; "Barbour Wins Templeton Prize," *Calvary Contender* (July 15, 1999, Vol. 16, No. 14); "Books of Interest Endorsed by the John Templeton Foundation" (Paper from the John Templeton Foundation dated January 11, 1996), p.1; Joan Veon, *Prince Charles: The* Sustainable *Prince* (Oklahoma City, OK: Hearthstone Publishing, Ltd., 1997), p.102.

[88] Wilbert Forker, Editor, *The Templeton Foundation Prize for Progress in Religion* (Edinburgh: Scottish Academic Press, 1988), p.89.

[89] *Ibid.*, p.89-90.

[90] *Ibid.*, p.89. See also: Edgar C. Bundy, *Billy Graham: Performer?, Politician?, Preacher?, Prophet?* (Wheaton, IL: Church League of America, 1982), p.179.

[91] Templeton, *op. cit.*, p.203; "The New Right" (Part III), *Distant Drums* (March 1981, Vol. 3, No. 1), p.4.

[92] Letter from Mark Hatfield, dated June 4, 1992; *Congressional Record—Senate*, "Nomination of David Bryan Sentelle" (September 9, 1987), n.p.; Wardner, *Unholy Alliances, op. cit.*, p.66, 67, 203.

[93] D. James Kennedy with Norman Wise, *The Great Deception* (Fort Lauderdale, FL: TCRM Publishing, 1985), p.89.

[94] "The New Right" (Part III), *Distant Drums* (March 1981, Vol. 3, No. 1), p.3.

[95] Declaration of Interdependence.

[96] "The New Right," *op. cit.*, p.4.

[97] *Christian Coalition Congressional Scorecard* (1994).

[98] Chambers, *op. cit.*, p.363; "The New Right" *op. cit.*, p.4. See also: "AmerRuss: The Illuminati Plot to Merge the United States and Russia," *Power of Prophecy* (February 2001, Vol. 2001-02), p.2.

[99] *Chronology of Education with Quotable Quotes* (Highland City, FL: Pro Family Forum, Inc., 1994, Updated, bound volume), p.14; *Ibid.*, p.15.

[100] Mari Jo Buhle, Paul Buhle, and Dan Georgakas, Editors, *Encyclopedia of the American Left* (New York, NY: Oxford University Press, 1998, Second Edition), p.199-201; "Rally to the Defense of KFUO," *Christian News* (January 2, 1995, Vol. 33, No. 1), p.9.

[101] *Chronology of Education, op. cit.*, p.14. See also: Chambers, *op. cit.*, p.16; "The New Right," *op. cit.*, p.4.

[102] Zygmund Dobbs, *Keynes at Harvard: Economic Deception As a Political Credo* (West Sayville, NY: Probe Research,

Inc., 1969 Edition), p.46. See also: *Ibid.*, p.14; Chambers, *op. cit.*, p.15.

[103] Chambers, *op. cit.*, p.9.

[104] Wardner, *Unholy Alliances, op. cit.*, p.127-128.

[105] *Ibid.*, p.203.

[106] *Ibid.*

[107] *Christian Coalition Congressional Scorecard, 102nd Congress 1991-1992; Christian Coalition Congressional Scorecard* (1993).

[108] *Ibid; Christian Coalition Congressional Scorecard* (1993).

[109] *Christian Coalition Congressional Scorecard* (1993 Fall Edition); *Christian Coalition Congressional Scorecard* (1994).

[110] *Christian Coalition Congressional Scorecard* (1994).

[111] *Catholic Alliance* (1996); *Christian Coalition Congressional Scorecard* (1996).

[112] Graham, *Just As I Am, op. cit.*, p.446.

[113] Martin, *A Prophet with Honor, op. cit.*, p.352.

[114] Graham, *Just As I Am, op. cit.*, p.446; *Ibid.* See also: Sam Wellman, *Billy Graham: The Great Evangelist* (Uhrichsville, OH: Barbour Book, 1996), p.170.

[115] *Ibid.*

[116] Martin, *A Prophet with Honor, op. cit.*

[117] *Ibid.*, p.271; Graham, *Just As I Am, op. cit.*, p.445; Sam Wellman, *Billy Graham: The Great Evangelist* (Uhrichsville, OH: Barbour Book, 1996), p.148.

[118] William R. Denslow, *10,000 Famous Freemasons* (Vol. II) (n.p., 1958), p.322.

[119] *Distant Drums* (December 1980, Vol. 2, No. 5), p.6., 11.

[120] Graham, *Just As I Am, op. cit.*, p.445.

[121] Edgar C. Bundy, *Billy Graham: Performer?, Politician?, Preacher?, Prophet?* (Wheaton, IL: Church League of America, 1982), p.179.

[122] *The Berean Call* (January 1998), p.2.

[123] *Ibid.*; Texe Marrs, "Has the Entire Christian Establishment Finally Just Gone Berserk?," *Power of Prophecy* (April 2001, Vol. 2001-04), p.2.

[124] *Calvary Contender* (July 1, 1989); "Not Just Another Denomination," *The Omega-Letter* (October 1989, Vol. 4, No. 9), p.3; Letter on file, written to John R. Corts, Vice President of Operations of the Billy Graham Evangelistic Association.

[125] Richard N. and Joan K. Ostling, *Mormon America: The Power and the Promise* (New York, NY: HarperSanFrancisco, 1999), p.xvi.

[126] Texe Marrs, "Has the Entire Christian Establishment Finally Just Gone Berserk?," *Power of Prophecy* (April 2001, Vol. 2001-04), p.2.

[127] *The Berean Call* (January 1998), p.2. See also: Marrs, "Has the Entire Christian Establishment Finally Just Gone Berserk?," *op. cit.*, p.2.

[128] Graham, *Just As I Am, op. cit.*, p.301, 509, 536; Martin, *A Prophet with Honor, op. cit.*, p.370; Jeffrey K. Hadden and Charles E. Swann, *Prime Time Preachers: The Rising Power of Televangelism* (Reading, MA: Addison-Wesley Publishing Company, Inc., 1981), p.147; "The New Right: Part II: The Religious Heritage of America: Instrument of Brotherhood," *Distant Drums* (December 1980, Vol. 2, No. 5), p.6, 11.

[129] "The Cult Awareness Network May Be Hazardous to Your Health," p.8.

[130] Brochure from the National Peace Institute Foundation.

[131] Jeffrey K. Hadden and Charles E. Swann, *Prime Time Preachers: The Rising Power of Televangelism* (Reading, MA: Addison-Wesley Publishing Company, Inc., 1981), p.147.

[132] "White House Ignores NEA Indecency," *The Christian World Report* (April 1990, Vol. 2, No. 4), p.4.

[133] Michael H. Heuer, "People for the American Way: What Is It?," *Faith for the Family* (July/August 1985, Vol. 14, No. 6), p.10; *Ibid.*

[134] *Ibid.*

[135] *Ibid.*

[136] Cal Thomas, *Book Burning* (Westchester, IL: Crossway Books, 1983), p.18; Johanna Michaelsen, *Like Lambs to the Slaughter* (Eugene, OR: Harvest House Publishers, 1989), p.29; Heuer, *op. cit.*, p.10; "Know Your Enemies," http://www.eff.org/pub/groups/bcfe/befenatl.html; Letter from Lowell P. Weicker; Darlene Carter, "A Very Outspoken Interview with Dick and Tara Sutphen," *Self-Help Update* (Issue #31), p.25; "Groups Endorse Homosexual March," *AFA Journal* (June 1993, Vol. 17, No. 6), p.9.

[137] "White House Ignores NEA Indecency," *op. cit.*, p.4.

[138] "Groups Endorse Homosexual March," *AFA Journal* (June 1993, Vol. 17, No. 6), p.9.

[139] "Lawsuit Filed Over 'Impressions' Curriculum," *The Christian World Report* (February 1991, Vol. 3, No. 2), p.16.

[140] "People for the American Way Defends New Age Impressions Curriculum," *Christian Parent Alert* (August 1991, Vol. 1, No. 1), p.7.

[141] *Ibid.*

[142] "'Impressions' Curriculum Angers Parents," *The Christian World Report* (July 1990, Vol. 2, No. 6), p.23.

[143] "1,000 Attend Rabbi's Funeral" (July 11, 1992), p.B4.

[144] *Ibid.*

[145] David R. Barnhart, "Islam: The Cross or the Crescent?," *The Vine and Branches* (Summer 1998, Vol. 13, Issue 3), p.7. See also: John Ashbrook, "Billy Graham—The Mouthpiece of New Evangelicalism," *O Timothy* (1993, Vol. 10, Issue 1).

[146] D. W. Cloud, "Some Frightening Facts About Billy Graham," *O Timothy* (1984, Vol. 1, Issue 4).

[147] *Ibid.*

[148] Miesel quoting from *The Baptist Lighthouse, op. cit.*

[149] Barnhart, "Islam," *op. cit.*, p.7. See also: "Graham and Catholic Universalism," *Calvary Contender* (October 15, 1997, Vol. 14, No. 20), p.2; "New Gospel Emerging," *Media Spotlight* (1997, Vol. 20, No. 2), p.24; Albert James Dager, *The World Christian Movement: A Great Delusion Leading to the Religio-Political State of the Anti-Christ* (Redmond, WA: Sword Publishers, 2001), p.73.

[150] W. W. Mosely, *The Evangelical Methodist* (December 2000, Vol. 78, No. 8), p.5.

[151] Miesel, *op. cit.*

[152] Ashbrook, "Billy Graham," *O Timothy, op. cit.;* Ashbrook, *New Neutralism II, op. cit.*, p.29.

[153] Martin, *A Prophet with Honor, op. cit.*, p.220.

[154] Forker, *op. cit.*, p.97-98.

[155] *The Globalists: The Power Elite Exposed* (Oklahoma City, OK: Hearthstone Publishing, 2001), p.114.

[156] *Despatch Magazine* (September 1994, Vol. 6:3), p.8; Chambers, *op. cit.*, p.434; Letter dated November 1997 from the Temple of Understanding; Brochure from the Temple of Understanding; Scott and Smith, *op. cit.*, p.77.

[157] "The New Right: Part II: The Religious Heritage of America: Instrument of Brotherhood," *Distant Drums* (December 1980, Vol. 2, No. 5), p.11; *Distant Drums* (November 1982, Vol. 4, No. 5), p.11.

[158] Texe Marrs, "Christianity Afflicted with Doctrines of Devils," *Flashpoint* (December 1996, Vol. 96-12), p.2; "Jesus' Image That of a Female," *The Voice of the Nazarene* (November/December 1994, Vol. 31, No. 12), p.10; Wanda Marrs, *New Age Lies to Women* (Austin, TX: Living Truth Publishers, 1989), p.20, 44; Kathleen R. Hayes, "Feminism, Goddess Movement Infect Christendom, Church," *NRI Trumpet* (March 1989); *Bold Truth* (April 1993), p.12; "Planetary Initiative for the World 'They' Choose," *Prophecy Newsletter* (1985, Vol. 1, No. 8), p.11; Dave Hunt, "The Greening of the Cross," *The Berean Call* (July 1997), p.2; Scott and Smith, *op. cit.*, p.69, 75.

[159] Pamphlet from The Temple of Understanding, Unnumbered page.

[160] *Ibid.*

[161] "Second Hollister Awards Ceremony" (excerpted from remarks by The Very Reverend James Parks Morton), *Temple of Understanding Newsletter* (Fall 1998), p.1.

[162] Pamphlet from The Temple of Understanding, Unnumbered page.

[163] David W. Cloud, *Flirting with Rome: Evangelical Entanglement with Roman Catholicism (Volume 4—The Charismatics)* (Oak Harbor, WA: Way of Life Literature, 1993); "Chuck Colson Organization Spreading Misinformation," *O Timothy* (1994, Vol. 11, Issue 2).

[164] *Distant Drums* (March 1981, Vol. 3, No. 1), p.5; Forker, *op. cit.*, p.280.

[165] *Ibid.*

[166] Ralph Wendell Burhoe, "Religion's Importance As Seen in Natural History," *Religious Humanism* (n.d.), p.183-184.

[167] Templeton, *op. cit.*, p.198; Cloud, *Flirting with Rome (Volume 4—The Charismatics), op. cit.; CIB Bulletin,* (September 1990, Vol. 6, No. 9), p.2; John Cotter, *A Study in Syncretism* (Flesherton, Ontario: Canadian Intelligence Publications, n.d.), p.83; "New Right: Part II," *op. cit.*, p.11.

[168] Cloud, *Flirting with Rome (Volume 4—The Charismatics), op. cit.;* "Goal for the Year 2000," (May 2, 1991), p.3; Albert James Dager, *The Vineyard: History, Teachings and Practices* (Redmond, WA: Media Spotlight, 1996), p.12; Dave Hunt, *Global Peace and the Rise of Antichrist* (Eugene, OR: Harvest House Publishers, 1990), p.153; Rene Laurentin (Translated by Matthew J. O'Connell), *Catholic Pentecostalism: An In-Depth Report on the Charismatic Renewal by a Renowned International Theologian* (Garden City, NY: Doubleday & Company, Inc., 1977), p.23; Jim Shaw, "A Pontiff Freemason" (no other info available), p.3; Roy Livesey, *Understanding Deception, New Age Teaching in the Church* (Chichester, England: New Wine Press, 1987), p.154; John W. Robbins, "Contemporary Religion Vs. the Gospel," *Christian News* (April 24, 1995, Vol. 33, No. 17), p.12; Wilson Ewin, *The Spirit of Pentecostal-Charismatic Unity* (Norton, VT: n.p., n.d.), p.5, 33; *CIB Bulletin,* (September 1990, Vol. 6, No. 9), p.2; "Cardinal Suenens Dies at 91," *Calvary Contender* (August 15, 1996, Vol. 13, No. 16), p.1.

[169] Cloud, *Flirting with Rome (Volume 4—The Charismatics), op. cit.* See also: "Global Mind Linking" (Part III), *Bold Truth* (Fall 1991), p.2; Vinson Synan and Ralph Rath, *Launching the Decade of Evangelization* (South Bend, IN: North

American Renewal Service Committee, 1990), p.121; "Cardinal Suenens Dies at 91," *Calvary Contender* (August 15, 1996, Vol. 13, No. 16), p.1.

[170] *Ibid.,* quoting Joseph Suenens.

[171] Jim Shaw, "A Pontiff Freemason" (no other info available), p.3; Piers Compton, *The Broken Cross: The Hidden Hand in the Vatican* (Cranbrook, Western Australia: Veritas Publishing Company Pty. Ltd., 1984), p.78.

[172] *CIB Bulletin,* (September 1990, Vol. 6, No. 9), p.2. See also: "NCEA 1985 'and the Strange Gods of Syncretism,'" *Distant Drums* (June 1985, Vol. 7, No. 2), p.9; John Cotter, *A Study in Syncretism* (Flesherton, Ontario: Canadian Intelligence Publications, n.d.), p.48, 81, 83.

[173] "Ting Has Been a Puppet of Communism from the Beginning," *O Timothy* (1994, Vol. 2, Issue 5). See also: Piers Compton, *The Broken Cross: The Hidden Hand in the Vatican* (Cranbrook, Western Australia: Veritas Publishing Company Pty. Ltd., 1984), p.107 for more about Suenens' Communistic endeavors.

[174] *CIB Bulletin,* (September 1990, Vol. 6, No. 9), p.2; Dave Hunt, *Global Peace and the Rise of Antichrist* (Eugene, OR: Harvest House Publishers, 1990), p.154. See also: John Cotter, *A Study in Syncretism* (Flesherton, Ontario: Canadian Intelligence Publications, n.d.), p.83.

[175] Cloud, *Flirting with Rome (Volume 4—The Charismatics), op. cit.;* "Chuck Colson Organization Spreading Misinformation," *O Timothy* (1994, Vol. 11, Issue 2); John Cotter, *A Study in Syncretism* (Flesherton, Ontario: Canadian Intelligence Publications, n.d.), p.48; "New Right: Part II," *op. cit.,* p.11.

[176] *Ibid.,* "Chuck Colson Organization Spreading Misinformation," *O Timothy* (1994, Vol. 11, Issue 2); Forker, *op. cit.,* p.267, 279; Texe Marrs, "Texe Marrs Asks Chuck Colson: 'Will You Sell Your Soul to the Devil for a Million Dollars?,'" *Flashpoint* (June 1993), p.1; "Pope Praises Buddhist Leader," *O Timothy* (1992, Vol. 9, Issue 4); John Cotter, *A Study in Syncretism* (Flesherton, Ontario: Canadian Intelligence Publications, n.d.), p.48; "New Right: Part II," *op. cit.,* p.11; Texe Marrs, "Texe Marrs Asks Chuck Colson: 'Will You Sell Your Soul to the Devil for a Million Dollars?,'" *Flashpoint* (June 1993), p.1; Texe Marrs, "Al Gore's Hidden Ties with an Occult, Globalist Group," *Flashpoint* (January 1993), p.1; "Religions Cooperating for Peace: The World Conference on Religion and Peace" (Received July 3, 1995), p.4; "WCRP" (Received November 3, 1995), p.5, 6; *Religion for Peace* (February 1995, Issue 65-A), p.1; Virginia Birt Baker,. "Who's Who in the U. S. Government?," *Wisconsin Report* (February 18, 1993, Vol. 18, No. 8), p.4; Geoffrey Parrinder, Editor, *World Religions: From Ancient History to the Present* (New York, NY: Facts on File Publications, 1971, 1983), p.379.

[177] Forker, *op. cit.,* p.267, 279. See also: John Cotter, *A Study in Syncretism* (Flesherton, Ontario: Canadian Intelligence Publications, n.d.), p.48; "New Right: Part II," *op. cit.,* p.11; "Religions Cooperating for Peace: The World Conference on Religion and Peace" (Received July 3, 1995), p.4; Brochure from WCRP (Received November 3, 1995), p.5, 6; *Religion for Peace* (February 1995, Issue 65-A), p.1; Geoffrey Parrinder, Editor, *World Religions: From Ancient History to the Present* (New York, NY: Facts on File Publications, 1971, 1983), p.379; "WCRP Sixth World Assembly Held in Rome and Riva Del Garda, Italy, November 1994," *Religion for Peace* (February 1995, Issue 65-A), p.3.

[178] Geoffrey Parrinder, Editor, *World Religions: From Ancient History to the Present* (New York, NY: Facts on File Publications, 1971, 1983), p.379.

[179] Texe Marrs, "Al Gore's Hidden Ties with an Occult, Globalist Group," *Flashpoint* (January 1993), p.1. See also: Virginia Birt Baker,. "Who's Who in the U. S. Government?," *Wisconsin Report* (February 18, 1993, Vol. 18, No. 8), p.4.

[180] Paper from Thanksgiving Square.

[181] Templeton, *op. cit.,* back cover.

[182] Amy Donohue, "How John Templeton Got Rich," *Philadelphia* (October 1996), p.85; "John Marks Templeton," *Progress in Theology* (June 1996, Vol. 4, No. 2), p.2.

[183] Templeton, *op. cit.,* back cover; *Secret Records Revealed, op. cit.,* p.53; Joan Veon, *Prince Charles: The* Sustainable *Prince* (Oklahoma City, OK: Hearthstone Publishing, Ltd., 1997), p.24; Donohue, *op. cit.,* p.85; Paper from the John Templeton Foundation (January 11, 1996), p.1; "John Marks Templeton," *Progress in Theology* (June 1996, Vol. 4, No. 2), p.2.

[184] Brian R. Hook, "Leaders Explore Globalization at State of the World Forum," *Progress in Theology* (December 2000, Vol. 8, No. 8), p.8.

[185] *Ibid.,* p.8.

[186] "The Templeton Prize for Religious Excellence," *Despatch Magazine* (June 2001, Vol. 13:2).

[187] Dave Hunt, "'Stand Fast in the Faith' I Corinthians 16:13," *The Berean Call* (December 1994), p.1.

[188] *Ibid.*

[189] "Templeton Foundation Press Launched," *Progress in Theology* (January/February 1997, Vol. 5, No. 1), p.1.

[190] *Ibid.*

[191] *The Watchman Expositor* (1998, Vol. 15; No. 5), p.26.

[192] http://www.wheaton.ed/bgc/archives/bio.html, revised 7/29/99; "Christianity Today Is No Longer the Conservative Evangelical Publication It Was When It Began," *Christian News* (April 21, 1997, Vol. 35, No. 16), p.2.

[193] *Christianity Today* (January 8, 1996), back cover; *Christianity Today* (April 25, 1994), back cover; Richard A. Noll, "The Tetelestai Initiative: Paid in Full" (Part IV), *Midnight Call* (July 2000), p.16; *Continuum* (Spring/Summer 1996), p.84; Catalog from the National Institute for Healthcare Research (Received May 7, 1999), p.6; Paper from the John Templeton Foundation (January 11, 1996), p.1. See also: *Continuum* (Fall/Winter 1995/96).

[194] "The Templeton Prize for Religious Excellence," *op. cit.*

[195] Templeton, *op. cit.*, p.204.

[196] *Ibid.*, p.203.

[197] *Christianity Today* (April 25, 1994), back cover; See also: Hunt, "'Stand Fast in the Faith,'" *op. cit.; The Berean Call* (July 1999), p.1.

[198] *Secret Records Revealed, op. cit.*, p.132.

[199] *Breakthrough* (Spring/Summer 1987, Vol. 8, No. 3-4), p.2.

[200] *World Federalist Bicentennial Edition* (1987), p.B-2.

[201] *Christianity Today* (January 8, 1996), back cover.

[202] Barnhart, "Islam," *op. cit.*, p.7.

[203] *Continuum* (Fall/Winter 1995/96), p.6.

[204] Barnhart, "Islam," *op. cit.*, p.7. See also: Catalog from the National Institute for Healthcare Research (Received May 7, 1999), p.6; Catalog from the National Institute for Healthcare Research (Winter-Spring 2000), p.6.

[205] Hunt, "'Stand Fast in the Faith,'" *op. cit.*; Richard A. Noll, "The Tetelestai Initiative: Paid in Full" (Part IV), *Midnight Call* (July 2000), p.16.

[206] Richard A. Noll, "The Tetelestai Initiative: Paid in Full" (Part IV), *Midnight Call* (July 2000), p.16.

[207] Hunt, "'Stand Fast in the Faith,'" *op. cit.; Ibid.*

[208] *Ibid.*; Noll, *op. cit.*

[209] *Ibid.*; Noll, *op. cit.*

[210] *Ibid.*

[211] Barnhart, "Islam," *op. cit.*, p.7.

[212] Paper from Thanksgiving Square; "Gratitude: The Adamant of Existence," *World Goodwill* (2000, No. 4), p.6; David R. Barnhart, *Contending for the Faith* (Eagan, MN: Abiding Word Publications, 1994), p.123-124.

[213] Paper from Thanksgiving Square. See also: Scott and Smith, *op. cit.*, p.79-80.

[214] Allen Dickerson, "Passive Fundamentalism" *O Timothy* (1995, Vol. 12, Issue 6); Miesel, *op. cit.*

[215] Martin, *A Prophet with Honor, op. cit.*, p.238; Miesel, *op. cit.*; "Graham and Masonry," *Christian News* (July 27, 1992, Vol. 30, No. 30), p.8; George Zeller, *Billy Graham: Ecumenical Evangelism* (Middletown, CT: Middletown Bible Church, n.d.), p.7.

[216] Bundy, *Billy Graham, op. cit.*, p.26.

[217] Martin, *A Prophet with Honor, op. cit.* p.236.

[218] Sam Wellman, *Billy Graham: The Great Evangelist* (Uhrichsville, OH: Barbour Book, 1996), p.137.

[219] Graham, *Just As I Am, op. cit.*, p.391.

[220] "Norman Vincent Peale Was Gourgas Medalist," *The Northern Light* (February 1994, Vol. 25, No. 1), p.7; "Peale's 100th Anniversary," *Calvary Contender* (June 15, 1998, Vol. 15, No. 14), p.2; "The Theology of Robert Schuller," *Christian News* (January 22, 2001, Vol. 39, No. 4), p.6; Allen E. Roberts, *Masonic Trivia and Facts* (Highland Springs, VA: Anchor Communications, 1994), p.161; Albert James Dager, *The World Christian Movement: A Great Delusion Leading to the Religio-Political State of the Anti-Christ* (Redmond, WA: Sword Publishers, 2001), p.61; Miesel, *op. cit.; Newsletter from a Christian Ministry* (July 1, 1993, Vol. 2, No. 10), p.40; "Norman Vincent Peale to be Honored on National T.V.," *Christian News* (January 22, 2001, Vol. 39, No. 4), p.7.

[221] *Ibid.*, p.7.

[222] *Freemasonry and Religion* (The Supreme Council, 33°, Ancient and Accepted Scottish Rite of Freemasonry, Mother Jurisdiction of the World, Southern Jurisdiction, U. S. A., 1977), p.3, 5. See also: Norman Vincent Peale, "What Freemasonry Means to Me," *Scottish Rite Journal* (February 1993, Vol. 101, No. 2), p.39.

[223] "Norman Vincent Peale Was Gourgas Medalist," *op. cit.*, p.7.

[224] *Ibid.*

[225] Ruth Stafford Peale, "A Life of Faith and Love: Remembering Norman Vincent Peale 33°, Grand Cross," *The Scottish Rite Journal* (September 1995, Vol. 104, No. 9), p.5.

[226] Sam Fox, "Psychic Letters from Jesus," *Alpha...and Beyond.* Reprinted from the *Weekly World News* April 24, 1984, p.39.

[227] *HRT Ministries Inc. Newsletter* (January/February/March 1991, Vol. 4, No. 1).

[228] Fox, *op. cit.*, p.40.

[229] *Ibid.; The BDM Letter* (October 1993, Vol. 2, No. 8), p.2.

[230] *Four Books on Spiritual Growth* (Brochure from Ariel Press).

[231] *Newsletter from a Christian Ministry* (July 1, 1993, Vol. 2, No. 10), p.40.

[232] *HRT Ministries Inc. Newsletter* (January/February/March 1991, Vol. 4, No. 1); *Free Inquiry* (Winter 1987/88, Vol. 8, No. 1), p.32; Wanda Marrs, *New Age Lies to Women* (Austin, TX: Living Truth Publishers, 1989), p.46.

[233] Texe Marrs, *Mystery Mark of the New Age: Satan's Design for World Domination* (Westchester, IL: Crossway Books, 1988), p.139; *HRT Ministries Inc. Newsletter* (January/February/March 1991, Vol. 4, No. 1); Texe Marrs, *Texe Marrs Book of New Age Cults and Religions* (Austin, TX: Living Truth Publishers, 1990), p.301; Wanda Marrs, *New Age Lies to Women* (Austin, TX: Living Truth Publishers, 1989), p.46.

[234] Texe Marrs, *Texe Marrs Book of New Age Cults and Religions* (Austin, TX: Living Truth Publishers, 1990), p.301.

[235] Martin and Deidre Bobgan, *Hypnosis: Medical, Scientific, or Occultic* (Santa Barbara, CA: EastGate Publishers, 2001), p.28-29; Alan Morrison, *The Serpent and the Cross: Religious Corruption in an Evil Age* (Birmingham, England: K & M Books, 1994), p.426.

[236] Bernie S. Siegel, *Love, Medicine and Miracles* (New York, NY: Harper & Row Publishers, 1986), p.178.

[237] *Ibid.*, p.179.

[238] *Ibid.*, back cover.

[239] Norman Vincent Peale, "No More Stress or Tension," *Plus, The Magazine of Positive Thinking* (Pawling, NY: Foundation for Christian Living, May, 1986), p.22, 23; Albert James Dager, *Out on a Limb* (Costa Mesa, CA: Media Spotlight, 1987), p.3. See also: Wanda Marrs, *New Age Lies to Women* (Austin, TX: Living Truth Publishers, 1989), p.46; *The BDM Letter* (October 1993, Vol. 2, No. 8), p.2; Bobgan, *op. cit.*, p.28.

[240] "Norman Vincent Peale to be Honored on National T.V.," *Christian News* (January 22, 2001, Vol. 39, No. 4), p.7. See also: "The Theology of Robert Schuller," *Christian News* (January 22, 2001, Vol. 39, No. 4), p.6.

[241] Catalog from Quest Books (Fall 1991), p.8.

[242] *Ibid.*

[243] William O. Peterson, Editor, *Masonic Quiz Book: "Ask Me Another, Brother"* (Chicago, IL: Charles T. Powner Company, 1950), p.215.

[244] W. L. Reese, *Dictionary of Philosophy and Religion: Eastern and Western Thought* (Atlantic Highlands, NJ: Humanities Press, Inc., 1980), p.575.

[245] H. M. Kallen, "Theosophist," *The World Book Encyclopedia* (Vol. 17) (Chicago 54, IL: Field Enterprises Educational Corporation, 1961 Edition), p.192.

[246] Colin Wilson, *The Occult: A History* (New York, Random House, 1971), p.332.

[247] Joseph Leon Blau, *The Christian Cabala* (Port Washington, NY: Kennikat Press, Inc., 1944), p.52.

[248] *Ibid.*, p.83.

[249] Erica Carle, "Who Cares About the Constitution?," *The Florida Forum* (Summer 2000), p.24.

[250] Wilson, *The Occult, op. cit.*, p.331; J. Gordon Melton, Jerome Clark, and Aidan A. Kelly, *New Age Almanac* (Detroit, MI: Visible Ink, 1991), p.7, 17; Jan Karel Van Baalen, *The Chaos of Cults* (Grand Rapids, MI: Wm. B. Eerdmans Publishing Company, 1962), p.62; Erica Carle, "Six Generational to Serfdom," *The Florida Forum* (Spring 2001), p.10, 21; Jane Gumprecht, *New Age Health Care: Holy or Holistic* (Orange, CA: Promise Publishing, 1988), p.176; Nat Freedland, *The Occult Explosion* (NY: G. P. Putnam's and Sons, 1972), p.69; Howard Kerr and Charles L. Crow, Editors, *The Occult in America: New Historical Perspectives* (Urbana, IL: University of Illinois Press, 1983), p.3, 4; Clifford Wilson and John Weldon, *Psychic Forces and Occult Shock: A Biblical View* (Chattanooga, TN: Global Publishers, 1987), p.181, 248, 255.

[251] Carle, "Who Cares About the Constitution?," *op. cit.*, p.24.

[252] Nat Freedland, *The Occult Explosion* (NY: G. P. Putnam's and Sons, 1972), p.69.

[253] G. A. Riplinger, *New Age Bible Versions* (Munroe Falls, OH: A. V. Publications, 1993), p.412.

[254] *Now Is the Dawning of the New Age New World Order, op. cit.*, p.45; J. Gordon Melton, Jerome Clark, and Aidan A. Kelly, *New Age Almanac* (Detroit, MI: Visible Ink, 1991), p.xi, 17, 32; Jan Karel Van Baalen, *The Chaos of Cults* (Grand Rapids, MI: Wm. B. Eerdmans Publishing Company, 1962), p.62; Jane Gumprecht, *New Age Health Care: Holy or Holistic* (Orange, CA: Promise Publishing, 1988), p.176; Freedland, *op. cit.*, p.69; Howard Kerr and Charles L. Crow, Editors, *The Occult in America: New Historical Perspectives* (Urbana, IL: University of Illinois Press, 1983), p.2, 3, 7, 111, 116; Lucindi Frances Mooney, *Storming Eastern Temples: A Psychological Explanation of Yoga* (Wheaton, IL: The Theosophical Publishing House, 1976), p.8, 128; Clifford Wilson and John Weldon, *Psychic Forces and Occult Shock: A Biblical View* (Chattanooga, TN: Global Publishers, 1987), p.248, 255; Barbara Aho, "The 19th Century Occult Revival," *The Christian Conscience* (July/August 1997, Vol. 3, No. 6), p.24; John Cotter, *A Study in Syncretism* (Flesherton, Ontario: Canadian Intelligence Publications, n.d.), p.9, 26; *The Watchman Expositor* (1998, Vol. 15, No. 5), p.27; Marrs, *Mystery Mark of the New Age, op. cit.*, p.80; Colin Wilson, *Beyond the Occult: A Twenty Year Investigation into the Paranormal* (New York, NY: Carroll and Graf Publishers, Inc., 1989), p.136; Willy Peterson, *The Leavening: A New Age Primer for Christian Parents* (Linwood, KS: n.p., 1996, Third Edition), p.193; J. Gordon Melton, *The Encyclopedia of American Religions* (Vol. 2) (Wilmington, NC: McGrath Publishing Company, 1978), p.139, 141; Wardner, *Unholy Alliances, op. cit.*, p.235; Nancy Wilson Ross, *Three Ways of Ancient Wisdom* (New York, NY: Simon and Schuster, 1966), p.197; "Magic," *The World Book Encyclopedia* (Vol. 12), (Chicago 54, IL: Field Enterprise Educational Corporation, 1961 Edition), p.46; Gina Cerminara, *Many Lives, Many Loves* (NY: William Morrow and Company, Inc., 1963), p.69, 135; John Godwin, *Occult America* (Garden City, NY: Doubleday and Company, Inc., 1972), p.134; David L. Carrico, *Lucifer—Eliphas Levi—Albert Pike and the Masonic Lodge* (Evansville, IN: Followers of Jesus Christ, 1991), p.14; See also: David L. Carrico, *Manly P. Hall: The Honored Masonic Author* (Evansville, IN: Followers of Jesus Christ, 1992), p.12; Gary Kah, *En Route to Global Occupation* (Lafayette, LA: Huntington House Publishers, 1992), p.89; John Yarker, *The Arcane Schools* (Belfast, Ireland: William Tait, 1909), p.492; Frank Gaynor, Editor, *Dictionary of Mysticism* (NY: Philosophical Library, 1953), p.185; David Carrico, *The Occult Meaning of the Great Seal of the United States*

(Evansville, IN: Followers of Jesus Christ, 1991), p.51, 55; E. M. Butler, *The Myth of the Magus* (NY: MacMillan Company, 1948), p.247; R. Swinburne Clymer, *The Mysteries of Osiris or Ancient Egyptian Initiation* (Quakertown, PA: The Philosophical Publishing Company, 1951, Revised Edition), p.331, 349; Norman MacKenzie, Editor, *Secret Societies* (Holt, Rinehart and Winston, 1967), p.144; Riplinger, *op. cit.*, p.412; "Where Did the New Age Come From?," *The Front Page* (September 1993, Vol. 7, No. 9), p.10; John Algeo, "One Life: A Theosophical View of the Global Challenge," *The Quest* (Autumn 1993, Vol. 6, No. 3), p.43; Richard Leviton, "The Imagination of Pentecost: Rudolf Steiner and Contemporary Spirituality," *The Quest* (Autumn 1993, Vol. 6, No. 3), p.73; *The World Book Encyclopedia* (Vol. 17) (Chicago 54, IL: Field Enterprises Educational Corporation, 1961 Edition), p.192; Pamphlet entitled "Theosophy Simply Stated", p.5; Wilson, *The Occult, op. cit.*, p.332-333; *New Age Journal* (March/April 1987, Vol. 3; Issue 2), p.26; *The Christian World Report* (February 1991, Vol. 3, No. 2), p.8.

[255] Frank Gaynor, Editor, *Dictionary of Mysticism* (NY: Philosophical Library, 1953), p.185. See also: E. M. Butler, *The Myth of the Magus* (NY: MacMillan Company, 1948), p.247, 259.

[256] *Now Is the Dawning of the New Age New World Order, op. cit.*, p.46; Wardner, *Unholy Alliances, op. cit.*, p.235; Arthur Edward Waite, *The Mysteries of Magic: A Digest of the Writings of Eliphas Levi* (Chicago, IL: De Laurence, Scott and Company, 1909), p.xi; William T. Still, *New World Order: The Ancient Plan of Secret Societies* (Lafayette, LA: Huntington House, Inc., 1990), p.45; Rudolf Steiner (Translated by Max Gysi), *The Way of Initiation* (NY: Macoy Publishing and Masonic Supply Company, 1910), p.33; Constance Cumbey, *The Hidden Dangers of the Rainbow: The New Age Movement and Our Coming Age of Barbarism* (Shreveport, LA: Huntington House, Inc., Revised Edition, 1983), p.46; Riplinger, *op. cit.*, p.25, 412, 413; Manly P. Hall, *America's Assignment with Destiny* (Los Angeles, CA: Philosophical Research Society, Inc., 1951), p.27.

[257] Catalog from Quest Books (Wheaton, IL: Fall 1991), back cover.

[258] *Calvary Contender* (July 15, 1998, Vol. 15, No. 14), p.2. See also: Dave Hunt and T. A. McMahon, *The Seduction of Christianity: Spiritual Discernment in the Last Days* (Eugene, OR: Harvest House Publishers, 1985), p.152; Albert James Dager, *The World Christian Movement: A Great Delusion Leading to the Religio-Political State of the Anti-Christ* (Redmond, WA: Sword Publishers, 2001), p.61; David W. Cloud, "Norman Vincent Peale: Apostle of Self-Esteem," *O Timothy* (1994, Vol. 11, Issue 2); Miesel, *op. cit.*; "Schuler (sic) and Gorbachev," *Christian News* (January 22, 2001, Vol. 39, No. 4), p.9; "Peale's 100th Anniversary," *Calvary Contender* (June 15, 1998, Vol. 15, No. 14), p.2; *The BDM Letter* (October 1993, Vol. 2, No. 8), p.2; "Billy Graham Endorser of Evil," *The Perilous Times* (February 1994, Vol. 15, No. 12), p.6.

[259] *New Larousse Encyclopedia of Mythology* (Prometheus Press, 1972 Edition), p.407; *The BDM Letter* (October 1993, Vol. 2, No. 8), p.2; Elizabeth Seeger, *Eastern Religions* (NY: Thomas Y. Cromwell Company, 1973), p.158, 167); See also: Miesel, *op. cit.*; Parrinder, *op. cit.*, p.370, 378.

[260] John Godwin, *Occult America* (Garden City, NY: Doubleday and Company, Inc., 1972), p.294.

[261] *New Larousse Encyclopedia of Mythology, op. cit.*, p.417.

[262] George Zeller, *Billy Graham: Ecumenical Evangelism* (Middletown, CT: Middletown Bible Church, n.d.), p.8; Bundy, *Collectivism in the Churches, op. cit.*, p.158.

[263] Bundy, *Collectivism in the Churches, op. cit.*, p.158.

[264] Ursala Niebuhr, Editor, *Remembering Reinhold Niebuhr* (New York, NY: HarperSanFrancisco, 1991), p.88.

[265] "Peale's 100th Anniversary," *Calvary Contender* (July 15, 1998, Vol. 15, No. 14), p.2.

[266] Dave Hunt and T. A. McMahon, *The Seduction of Christianity: Spiritual Discernment in the Last Days* (Eugene, OR: Harvest House Publishers, 1985), p.68; David W. Cloud, "Norman Vincent Peale: Apostle of Self-Esteem," *O Timothy* (1994, Vol. 11, Issue 2); *Newsletter from a Christian Ministry* (July 1, 1993, Vol. 2, No. 10), p.40.

[267] "Peale's 100th Anniversary," *op. cit.*; *The BDM Letter* (October 1993, Vol. 2, No. 8), p.2.

[268] David W. Cloud, "Norman Vincent Peale: Apostle of Self-Esteem," *O Timothy* (1994, Vol. 11, Issue 2); *The BDM Letter* (October 1993, Vol. 2, No. 8), p.2. See also: "Billy Graham Endorser of Evil," *The Perilous Times* (February 1994, Vol. 15, No. 12), p.6; Miesel, *op. cit.*; David W. Cloud, "Norman Vincent Peale: Apostle of Self-Esteem," *Christian News* (May 12, 1997, Vol. 35, No. 19), p.10.

[269] "Peale's 100th Anniversary," *Calvary Contender* (June 15, 1998, Vol. 15, No. 14), p.2.

[270] Graham, *Just As I Am, op. cit.*, p.315.

[271] Collier and Horowitz, *op. cit.*, p.150. See also: Fritz Springmeier, *The Top 13 Illuminati Bloodlines* (Portland, OR: n.p., 1995), p.135-136; J.W. Wardner, "Billy Graham, Freemasonry & the Communists," *Despatch Magazine* (September 1998, Vol. 10, No. 3), p.27.

[272] Fritz Springmeier, *The Top 13 Illuminati Bloodlines* (Portland, OR: n.p., 1995), p.243; Martin, *A Prophet with Honor, op. cit.*, p.226.

[273] John S. Torell, "Betrayal," *The Dove* (Autumn/Winter 1995, Vol. 16, No. 3), p.14.

[274] "Christianity Today Is No Longer the Conservative Evangelical Publication It Was When It Began," *Christian News* (April 21, 1997, Vol. 35, No. 16), p.2.

[275] Cloud, "Norman Vincent Peale: Apostle of Self-Esteem," *op. cit.*

[276] *Ibid.*

[277] *Calvary Contender* (July 15, 1998, Vol. 15, No. 14), p.2. See also: Dave Hunt and T. A. McMahon, *The Seduction of Christianity: Spiritual Discernment in the Last Days* (Eugene, OR: Harvest House Publishers, 1985), p.152.

[278] *Ibid.* See also: Dave Hunt and T. A. McMahon, *The Seduction of Christianity: Spiritual Discernment in the Last Days*

(Eugene, OR: Harvest House Publishers, 1985), p.152.

[279] *Calvary Contender* (July 15, 1998, Vol. 15, No. 14), p.2.

[280] Cloud, "Norman Vincent Peale: Apostle of Self-Esteem," *op. cit.*

[281] See "Graham and Masonry," *Christian News* (July 27, 1992, Vol. 30, No. 30), p.8; Martin, *A Prophet with Honor, op. cit.*, p.238; Zeller, *op. cit.*, p.7.

[282] Martin, *A Prophet with Honor, op. cit.*, back cover.

[283] Bundy, *Billy Graham, op. cit.*, p.9. See also: David W. Cloud, *Flirting with Rome: Evangelical Entanglement with Roman Catholicism (Volume 1—Billy Graham)* (Oak Harbor, WA: Way of Life Literature, 1993).

[284] Letter on file from the Billy Graham Evangelistic Association, dated February 29, 1968.

[285] Ruth Stafford Peale, "A Life of Faith and Love: Remembering Norman Vincent Peale 33°, Grand Cross," *The Scottish Rite Journal* (September 1995, Vol. 104, No. 9), p.6.

[286] *Ibid.*

[287] Zeller, *op. cit.*, p.7; See also: Martin, *A Prophet with Honor, op. cit.*, p.222.

[288] *The Berean Call* (June 1997), p.4.

[289] Brad K. Gsell, *The Legacy of Billy Graham* (Charlotte, NC: Fundamental Presbyterian Publication, n.d.), p.28.

[290] Letter in my files from W. H. Martindale, Spiritual Counselor for the Billy Graham Evangelistic Association, dated February 29, 1968. See also: David W. Cloud, "Billy Graham's Disobedience to the Word of God" (Updated March 2, 1999), p.9; Ian Paisley, "Billy Graham's Tragic Romeward Run," *O Timothy* (1993, Vol. 10, Issue 9).

[291] Bundy, *Billy Graham, op. cit.*, p.68.

[292] Wilson Ewin, *Under the New World Order: Evangelicals, Catholics and Israel: Conspiracy of the Ages* (Compton, Quebec: Quebec Baptist Missions, n.d.), p.76. See also: David W. Cloud, *Flirting with Rome (Volume 1—Billy Graham)* (Oak Harbor, WA: Way of Life Literature, 1993); Wilson Ewin, *Evangelism: The Trojan Horse of the 1990's* (Compton, Quebec: Quebec Baptist Missions, 1992), p.3; D. W. Cloud, *Is the Roman Catholic Changing?* (1984); "Did You Know?," *The Good Newsletter* (November/December 1996, Vol. 2, Issue 12), p.12; "Graham Team Denies Sending Roman Catholics Back to Romanism," *O Timothy* (1994, Vol. 11, Issue 12).

[293] *Ibid.*; "Did You Know?," *The Good Newsletter* (November/December 1996, Vol. 2, Issue 12), p.12; David W. Cloud, *Flirting with Rome (Volume 1—Billy Graham)* (Oak Harbor, WA: Way of Life Literature, 1993); Wilson Ewin, *Evangelism: The Trojan Horse of the 1990's* (Compton, Quebec: Quebec Baptist Missions, 1992), p.3; "Graham Team Denies Sending Roman Catholics Back to Romanism," *O Timothy* (1994, Vol. 11, Issue 12).

[294] Miesel, *op. cit.*

[295] Wilson Ewin, *Evangelism: The Trojan Horse of the 1990's* (Compton, Quebec: Quebec Baptist Missions, 1992).

[296] "Evangelism," *Time* (June 10, 1966), p.84.

[297] Ewin, *Evangelism, op. cit.*; David W. Cloud, *Flirting with Rome (Volume 1—Billy Graham)* (Oak Harbor, WA: Way of Life Literature, 1993).

[298] David W. Cloud, "Billy Graham's Disobedience to the Word of God" (Updated March 2, 1999), p.3; David W. Cloud, "Evangelical Entanglement with Romanism: How Serious Is the Back-to-Rome Movement?," *Foundation* (January/February 1987), p.5; David W. Cloud, "Evangelical Leaders Befriend the Mother of Harlots," *O Timothy* (1988, Vol. 5, Issue 4).

[299] Wilson Ewin, *The Assimilation of Evangelist Billy Graham into the Roman Catholic Church* (Compton, Quebec: Quebec Baptist Missions, 1992), p.14; "Graham Turned 2,000 Inquirers over to the Catholic Church in New England," *O Timothy* (1992, Vol. 9, Issue 6); Ewin, *Evangelism, op. cit.*; Ian Paisley, "Billy Graham's Tragic Romeward Run," *O Timothy* (1993, Vol. 10, Issue 9); David W. Cloud, *Flirting with Rome (Volume 1—Billy Graham)* (Oak Harbor, WA: Way of Life Literature, 1993).

[300] Christie L. Chicone, "1,900 Catholics Respond to Billy Graham's Call," *The Catholic Standard and Times* (July 16, 1992), p.10; Ewin, *The Assimilation of Evangelist Billy Graham into the Roman Catholic Church, op. cit.*, p.14.

[301] Cloud, "Billy Graham's Disobedience to the Word of God," *op. cit.*, p.3; David W. Cloud, "Evangelical Leaders Befriend the Mother of Harlots," *O Timothy* (1988, Vol. 5, Issue 4); Ewin, *Evangelism, op. cit.* See also: David W. Cloud, *Flirting with Rome (Volume 1—Billy Graham)* (Oak Harbor, WA: Way of Life Literature, 1993).

[302] David W. Cloud, *Flirting with Rome (Volume 1—Billy Graham)* (Oak Harbor, WA: Way of Life Literature, 1993).

[303] David W. Cloud, "Evangelical Leaders Befriend the Mother of Harlots," *O Timothy* (1988, Vol. 5, Issue 4); Ewin, *Evangelism, op. cit.*; *Ibid.*

[304] Cloud, "Billy Graham's Disobedience to the Word of God," *op. cit.*, p.3. See also: Miesel, *op. cit.*; "Billy Graham," *The BDM Letter* (November 1993, Vol. 2, No. 9), p.2; Cloud, *Flirting with Rome (Volume 1—Billy Graham), op. cit.*

[305] "T. W. Wilson, Longtime Associate to Billy Graham Dies at 82," *Christian News* (June 4, 2001, Vol. 39, No. 23), p.2.

[306] "Graham Continues to Send to Catholicism," *The Flaming Torch* (April/May/June 1998, Vol. 39, No. 2), p.5.

[307] "Roman Catholicism: Scripture vs. Tradition," a tract by Mike Gendron. See also: "Salvation by Sanctifying Grace Demo," *Constantly Evolving Catholicism* (September 1995), p.5; Sheedy, "Ask Me a Question," *Our Sunday Visitor* (February 14, 1993, Vol. 81, No. 42), p.20.

[308] Sheedy, "Ask Me a Question," *Our Sunday Visitor* (February 14, 1993, Vol. 81, No. 42), p.20.

[309] Bundy, *Billy Graham, op. cit.*, p.74.

[310] Cloud, *Flirting with Rome (Volume 1—Billy Graham), op. cit.*

[311] *Catechism of the Catholic Church* (New York, NY: Image Books, 1995), p.110.

[312] *Ibid.*, p.129.

[313] *Ibid.*, p.228.

[314] *Ibid.*, p.732-733.

[315] *Ibid.*, p.733.

[316] Cloud, "Some Frightening Facts," *op. cit.;* Cloud, "Billy Graham's Disobedience to the Word of God," *op. cit.*, p.3; Bundy, *Billy Graham, op. cit.*, p.79; David W. Cloud, D. W. Cloud, *Is the Roman Catholic Changing?* (1984); "Billy Graham's Disobedience," *O Timothy* (1995, Vol. 12, Issue 11); David W. Cloud, *Is the Roman Catholic Changing?* (Oak Harbor, WA: Way of Life Literature, 1995 Edition); Ewin, *Evangelism, op. cit.;* Cloud, *Flirting with Rome (Volume 1—Billy Graham), op. cit.;* Cloud, "Evangelical Leaders Befriend the Mother of Harlots," *op. cit.*

[317] Cloud, *Flirting with Rome (Volume 1—Billy Graham), op. cit.;* Gsell, *op. cit.*, p.34; Ashbrook, *New Neutralism II, op. cit.*, p.35; D.W. Cloud, *Is the Roman Catholic Changing?* (1984).

[318] Cloud, "Some Frightening Facts," *op. cit.;* Cloud, *Flirting with Rome (Volume 1—Billy Graham), op. cit.*

[319] Ewin, *Under the New World Order, op. cit.*, p.66, 67.

[320] *Ibid.*, p.67. See also: "The Deception of Billy Graham," *Newsletter from a Christian Ministry* (July 1, 1993, Vol. 2, No. 10), p.39.

[321] Cloud, "Some Frightening Facts," *op. cit.*

[322] "Romanism, Ecumenicalism and Protestantism," *Bold Truth* (November 5, 1993), p.4; Miesel, *op. cit.;* Trish Rector, "Who Is Jay Gary?," *Bold Truth* (February 15, 1993 [sic]), p.8; Ashbrook, *New Neutralism II, op. cit.;* Cloud, *Flirting with Rome (Volume 1—Billy Graham), op. cit.*

[323] *Ibid.*

[324] Graham, *Just As I Am, op. cit.*, p.535.

[325] Letter from James Dobson dated February 13, 1992, p.4.

[326] *Calvary Contender* (July 1, 1993, Vol. 10, No. 13).

[327] David W. Cloud, "What Is Judaism?," *O Timothy* (1988, Vol. 5, Issue 2). See also: "Midrash—What Is It?," *Despatch Magazine* (June 2000, Vol. 12, No. 2), p.82; "Be Informed About the Talmud," *Christian News* (March 5, 2001, Vol. 39, No. 10), p.7; Maureen Fiedler and Linda Rabben, Editors, *Rome Has Spoken...: A Guide to Forgotten Papal Statements, and How They Have Changed Through the Centuries* (New York, NY: The Crossroad Publishing Company, 1998), p.69; "Lieberman, Gore, and God," *Power of Prophecy* (September 2000, Vol. 2000-09), p.2; "Lieberman, The Talmud, The Noahide Laws and Judeo-Christians," *Christian News* (September 18, 2000, Vol. 38, No. 34), p.7; "Noahide Laws: Religion of a New World Order," *GANPAC Brief* (February 1992, No. 112), p.4; Texe Marrs, "Secrets #60," *Power of Prophecy* (June 9, 2001 program).

[328] "Judaism's Strange Gods," *Christian News* (October 9, 2000, Vol. 38, No. 37), p.15.

[329] "Lieberman, Gore, and God," *Power of Prophecy* (September 2000, Vol. 2000-09), p.2.

[330] Graham, *Just As I Am, op. cit.*, p.163.

[331] *Ibid.*

[332] John D. Christian, *Gladiator: A Masterpiece of Nazi Propaganda* (Postscript) (New Zealand, Underground Press, 2001), p.14.

[333] Martin, *A Prophet with Honor, op. cit.*, p.223. See also: Miesel, *op. cit.*

[334] *Ibid.* See also: Bundy, *Billy Graham, op. cit.*, p.9, 10, 25; Ewin, *Under the New World Order, op. cit.*, p.76; David W. Cloud, "Billy Graham's Disobedience," *O Timothy* (1995, Vol. 12, Issue 11); *Christian News* (February 12, 2001, Vol. 39, No. 7), p.16; Ian Paisley, "Billy Graham's Tragic Romeward Run," *O Timothy* (1993, Vol. 10, Issue 9); *The Vine and Branches* (Summer 1998, Vol. 13, Issue 3), p.7; "Did You Know?," *The Good Newsletter* (November/December 1996, Vol. 2, Issue 12), p.12; Cloud, *Flirting with Rome (Volume 1—Billy Graham), op. cit.;* Gsell, *op. cit.*, p.34; Cloud, "Some Frightening Facts," *op. cit.;* Ewin, *Evangelism, op. cit.;* Cloud, "Billy Graham's Disobedience to the Word of God," *op. cit.*, p.3.

[335] Graham, *Just As I Am, op. cit.*, p.162. See also: Wellman, *op. cit.*, p.95.

[336] *Ibid.;* Martin, *A Prophet with Honor, op. cit.*, p.129; John Pollock, *Crusades: 20 Years with Billy Graham* (Minneapolis, MN: World Wide Publications, 1969, Special Billy Graham Crusade Edition), p.77; George Beverly Shea with Fred Bauer, *Then Sings My Soul* (Minneapolis, MN: World Wide Publications, 1968), p.73. See also: http://www.wheaton.ed/bgc/archives/bio.html, revised 7/29/99.

[337] Martin, *A Prophet with Honor, op. cit.*, p.129; George Beverly Shea with Fred Bauer, *Then Sings My Soul* (Minneapolis, MN: World Wide Publications, 1968), p.73.

[338] Wellman, *op. cit.*, p.96.

[339] John Pollock, *Crusades: 20 Years with Billy Graham* (Minneapolis, MN: World Wide Publications, 1969, Special Billy Graham Crusade Edition), p.78.

[340] Martin, *A Prophet with Honor, op. cit.*, p.473.

[341] *Ibid.*

[342] James W. Wardner, *The Planned Destruction of America* (Debary, FL: Longwood Communications, 1994), p.127; Wardner, *Unholy Alliances, op. cit.*, p.132.

[343] Wardner, *Unholy Alliances, op. cit.*, p.140.

[344] *Ibid.*

[345] *Ibid.*, p.140-141.

[346] Collier and Horowitz, *op. cit.*, p.334. See also: Herzstein, *op. cit.*, p.178.

[347] Grant, *op. cit.*, p.182.

[348] Antony C. Sutton, *America's Secret Establishment: An Introduction to the Order of Skull & Bones* (Billings, MT: Liberty House Press, 1986), p.28; Jim Marrs, *Rule by Secrecy: The Hidden History That Connects the Trilateral Commission, the Freemasons, and the Great Pyramids* (New York, NY: HarperCollins Publishers, Inc., 2000), p.90, 94, 97; Newsletter from Radio Liberty (May 2001), p.3; Springmeier, *Bloodlines, op. cit.*, p.150; Wardner, *The Planned Destruction of America, op. cit.*, p.116; *The Road to Socialism and the New World Order, op. cit.*, p.19; Donaldson, *op. cit.*, p.193; Wardner, *Unholy Alliances, op. cit.*, p.132; Torell, *op. cit.*, p.12; Texe Marrs, *Dark Majesty: The Secret Brotherhood and the Magic of a Thousand Points of Light* (Austin, TX: Living Truth Publishers, 1992), p.197.

[349] Texe Marrs, *Dark Majesty: The Secret Brotherhood and the Magic of a Thousand Points of Light* (Austin, TX: Living Truth Publishers, 1992), p.197; Wardner, *Unholy Alliances, op. cit.*, p.132; Gary Allen, *Jimmy Carter, Jimmy Carter* (Seal Beach, CA: '76 Press, 1976), p.76; John Cotter, *A Study in Syncretism* (Flesherton, Ontario: Canadian Intelligence Publications), p.92; David Carrico, *The Occult Meaning of the Great Seal of the United States* (Evansville, IN: Followers of Jesus Christ, 1991), p.78; Jim Marrs, *Rule by Secrecy: The Hidden History That Connects the Trilateral Commission, the Freemasons, and the Great Pyramids* (New York, NY: HarperCollins Publishers, Inc., 2000), p.90, 97; Wardner, *The Planned Destruction of America, op. cit.*, p.127; Gary Allen, *The Rockefeller File* (Seal Beach, CA: '76 Press, 1976), p.72; A. Ralph Epperson, *The Unseen Hand: An Introduction to the Conspiratorial View of History* (Tucson, AZ: Publius Press, 1985), p.238; Stormer, *None Dare Call It Treason, op. cit.*, p.212.

[350] Rick Martin, "The Most Powerful Man in the World? The 'Black' Pope Count Hans Kolvenbach—The Jesuit's General," *Free American Newsmagazine* (July 2000), p.25.

[351] Jim Marrs, *Rule by Secrecy: The Hidden History That Connects the Trilateral Commission, the Freemasons, and the Great Pyramids* (New York, NY: HarperCollins Publishers, Inc., 2000), p.97.

[352] *Global 2000: An Interview with Mr. and Mrs. William Bowen* (Oklahoma City, OK: Southwest Radio Church, 1984), p.37; William T. James, Editor, *Foreshocks of Antichrist* (Eugene, OR: Harvest House Publishers, 1997), p.226; Chambers, *op. cit.*, p.193.

[353] Texe Marrs, *Millennium: Peace, Promises, and the Day They Take Our Money Away* (Austin, TX: Living Truth Publishers, 1990), p.60.

[354] John Cotter, *A Study in Syncretism* (Flesherton, Ontario: Canadian Intelligence Publications), p.16, 17, 92; Stormer, *None Dare Call It Treason, op. cit.*, p.211.

[355] *Ibid.*, p.17.

[356] *Ibid.*, p.16-17.

[357] Herzstein, *op. cit.*, p.306.

[358] *Ibid.*, p.309.

[359] Gary Allen, *The Rockefeller File* (1976), p.72.

[360] *Ibid.*

[361] *Ibid.*, p.73.

[362] *Ibid.*, p.79.

[363] *Ibid.*, p.79-80; See also: *Secret Records Revealed, op. cit.*, p.57, 93; Carroll Quigley, *The Anglo-American Establishment* (New York, NY: Books in Focus, Inc., 1981), p.283.

[364] *Now Is the Dawning of the New Age New World Order, op. cit.*, p.239.

[365] *Ibid.*, p.240; Gary Allen, *The Rockefeller File* (1976), p.80.

[366] *Ibid.*, p.239.

[367] Gary Allen, *The Rockefeller File* (1976), p.80.

[368] *Ibid.*, p.81.

[369] *Now Is the Dawning of the New Age New World Order, op. cit.*, p.240.

[370] George W. Blount, *Peace Through World Government* (Durham, NC: Moore Publishing Company, 1974), p.32.

[371] Wardner, *The Planned Destruction of America, op. cit.*, p.129; Stormer, *None Dare Call It Treason, op. cit.*, p.140.

[372] Rivera: *op. cit.*, p.94. See also: A. Ralph Epperson, *The Unseen Hand: An Introduction to the Conspiratorial View of History* (Tucson, AZ: Publius Press, 1985), p.210-211; "To Socialism by Way of Tax-Exempt Foundations," *The Florida Forum* (Summer 1997), p.1, 22; Rene A. Wormser, *Foundations: Their Power and Influence* (New York, NY: Devin-Adair

Company, 1977 Edition), p.45; Josephson, *op. cit.*, p.27; Quigley, *Tragedy and Hope, op. cit.*, p.132, 582, 935; Gary Kah, *En Route to Global Occupation* (Lafayette, LA: Huntington House Publishers, 1992), p.21, 30, 31, 50; William T. Still, *New World Order: The Ancient Plan of Secret Societies* (Lafayette, LA: Huntington House, Inc., 1990), p.172; *Don Bell Reports* (September 13, 1993, Vol. 40, No. 18), p.1; Carroll Quigley, *The Anglo-American Establishment* (New York, NY: Books in Focus, Inc., 1981), p.192.

[373] Quigley, *Tragedy and Hope, op. cit.*, p.946.

[374] *Ibid.*, p.948.

[375] *Ibid.*, p.146; Carroll Quigley, *The Anglo-American Establishment* (New York, NY: Books in Focus, Inc., 1981), p.282.

[376] *"Secret Records" Revealed: The Men, the Money, and the Methods Behind the New World Order* (Marlborough, NH: Plymouth Rock Foundation, 1994), p.19; *The New World Order: A Critique and Chronology* (Milford, PA: America's Future, Inc.); *Now Is the Dawning of the New Age New World Order, op. cit.*, p.117; *Secret Records Revealed, op. cit.*, p.58.

[377] *Now Is the Dawning of the New Age New World Order, op. cit.*, p.121-122.

[378] Gary Allen, *The Rockefeller File* (1976), p.72; "Update Report: Historic ~ Millennium Summit Sept. 2000," *Despatch Magazine* (September 2000, Vol. 12:3), p.48.

[379] "Update Report: Historic ~ Millennium Summit Sept. 2000," *Despatch Magazine* (September 2000, Vol. 12:3), p.48; Piers Compton, *The Broken Cross: The Hidden Hand in the Vatican* (Cranbrook, Western Australia: Veritas Publishing Company Pty. Ltd., 1984), p.66.

[380] Peter Grose, *Gentleman Spy: The Life of Allen Dulles* (New York, NY: Houghton Mifflin Company, 1994), p.430.

[381] Rivera: *op. cit.*, p.227.

[382] Wardner, *Unholy Alliances, op. cit.*, p.132.

[383] *Ibid.*

[384] *Ibid.*, p.133.

[385] *Ibid.*, p.132-135.

[386] *Ibid.*, p.180-181.

[387] Gary Allen, *The Rockefeller File* (Seal Beach, CA: '76 Press, 1976), p.69.

[388] William R. Denslow, *10,000 Famous Freemasons* (Vol. IV) (n.p., 1961), p.99; Henry C. Clausen, *Masons Who Helped Shape Our Nation* (The Supreme Council, 33°, Ancient and Accepted Scottish Rite of Freemasonry Southern Jurisdiction, U. S. A., 1976), p.44; Wardner, *Unholy Alliances, op. cit.*, p.194; http://www2.linknet.net/masonic/mig1.htm.

[389] Gary Allen, *The Rockefeller File* (Seal Beach, CA: '76 Press, 1976), p.69; Wardner, *Unholy Alliances, op. cit.*, p.132.

[390] Wardner, *Unholy Alliances, op. cit.*, p.194; Denslow (Vol. IV), *op. cit.*, p.99; Henry C. Clausen, *Masons Who Helped Shape Our Nation* (The Supreme Council, 33°, Ancient and Accepted Scottish Rite of Freemasonry Southern Jurisdiction, U. S. A., 1976), p.44.

[391] *Ibid.*, p.132.

[392] John Coleman, *The Conspirators' Hierarchy: The Committee of 300* (Carson City, NV: Joseph Publishing Company, 1994), p.248.

[393] Gary Allen, *The Rockefeller File* (Seal Beach, CA: '76 Press, 1976), p.69-70. See also: Gary Kah, *En Route to Global Occupation* (Lafayette, LA: Huntington House Publishers, 1992), p.56.

[394] Graham, *Just As I Am, op. cit.*, p.162; Martin, *A Prophet with Honor, op. cit.*, p.129; Pollock, *op. cit.*, p.77; George Beverly Shea with Fred Bauer, *Then Sings My Soul* (Minneapolis, MN: World Wide Publications, 1968), p.73; Torell, *op. cit.*, p.12.

[395] Pollock, *op. cit.*, p.77.

[396] Graham, *Just As I Am, op. cit.*, p.162. See also: Martin, *A Prophet with Honor, op. cit.*, p.129.

[397] George R. Adams, *A Trilogy: Inner Journey to the East, Meditations of a Master Mason Along the Way, Masonry for the Millennium* (Glen Echo, MD: SELFormation Corporation, Inc., 1999), p.153; Marrs, *Rule by Secrecy, op. cit.*, p.255.

[398] A. Ralph Epperson, *The Unseen Hand: An Introduction to the Conspiratorial View of History* (Tucson, AZ: Publius Press, 1985), p.196-197.

[399] Rivera: *op. cit.*, p.92. See also: Marrs, *Rule by Secrecy, op. cit.*, p.33, 184.

[400] *Ibid.*, p.49. See also: Marrs, *Rule by Secrecy, op. cit.*, p.184.

[401] Marrs, *Rule by Secrecy, op. cit.*, p.184.

[402] William G. Carr, *One World in the Making: The United Nations* (Ginn and Company, 1946), p.25.

[403] Monteith, *op. cit.*, p.97; Marrs, *Rule by Secrecy, op. cit.*, p.32, 41, 83; Newsletter from Radio Liberty (May 2001), p.4.

[404] *Secret Records Revealed, op. cit.*, p.33-34.

[405] Torell, *op. cit.*, p.12.

[406] Dulles, *op. cit.*, p.66.

[407] David L. Carrico, *The Gulf War, George Bush, the World Order, the Vision of the United Nations Founders* (Evansville, IN: Followers of Jesus Christ, 1991), p.8.

[408] "The Agenda of the Invisible Government," *The Prophecy Newsletter* (1985, Vol. 1, No. 3), p.8.

[409] Graham, *Just As I Am, op. cit.,* p.548.

[410] "William Randolph Hearst," Softkey Multimedia Inc., Infopedia (1996); Ostling, *op. cit.,* p.xvi.

[411] Jeremy Rifkin with Ted Howard, *The Emerging Order: God in the Age of Scarcity* (NY: G. P. Putnam's Sons, 1979), p.167.

[412] Graham, *Just As I Am, op. cit.,* p.149-150. See also: Martin, *A Prophet with Honor, op. cit.,* p.117; *America's Hour of Decision: Revival Campaigns and Life Story of Billy Graham* (Wheaton, IL: Van Kampen Press, 1951), p.98, 108-109; Bundy, *Collectivism in the Churches, op. cit.,* p.72, 90, 91, 113; Robert Sherrill, "Billy Graham," *Collier's Encyclopedia* (1988 Edition), p.271; "Campus Crusade for Christ," *CovertAction Information Bulletin* (Spring 1987, No. 27), p.12; George Beverly Shea with Fred Bauer, *Then Sings My Soul* (Minneapolis, MN: World Wide Publications, 1968), p.68; Eddie Karnes, "Dr. Billy Graham and Dr. Oswald Hoffman, Thank You, But..." (Part I), *Christian News* (February 12, 2001, Vol. 39, No. 7), p.16; Joel A. Carpenter, *Revive Us Again: The Reawakening of American Fundamentalism* (New York, NY: Oxford University Press, 1997), p.225; Torell, *op. cit.,* p.5, 11; M. H. Reynolds, Jr., *Billy Graham, the Pope, and the Bible* (Fundamental Evangelical Association, n.d.), p.3; Hadden and Swann, *op. cit.,* p.20; Jeremy Rifkin with Ted Howard, *The Emerging Order: God in the Age of Scarcity* (NY: G.P. Putnam's Sons, 1979), p.166-167; Jack T. Chick, *Smokescreens: Who Is the "Whore" of Revelation? A Biblical and Historical Answer* (Chino, CA: Chick Publications, 1983), p.53; Wardner, *Unholy Alliances, op. cit.,* p.139; Springmeier, *The Top 13 Illuminati Bloodlines, op. cit.,* p.19, 135-136; http://www.wheaton.ed/bgc/archives/bio.html, revised 7/29/99.

[413] Quote from William Randolph Hearst in *America's Hour of Decision: Revival Campaigns and Life Story of Billy Graham* (Wheaton, IL: Van Kampen Press, 1951), p.98.

[414] Springmeier, *Bloodlines, op. cit.,* p.417.

[415] *Bookstore Journal* (November 1991), p.30.

[416] *Bookstore Journal* (November 1991), p.30. See also: Miesel, *op. cit.;* Ewin, *Under the New World Order, op. cit.,* p.71; Cloud, *Flirting with Rome (Volume 1—Billy Graham), op. cit.;* Wilson Ewin, *Today's Evangelicals Embracing the World's Deadliest Cult* (Compton, Quebec: Quebec Baptist Missions, n.d.), p.55.

[417] Torell, *op. cit.,* p.10.

[418] *The Evangelical Methodist* (2000, Vol. 78, No. 4), p.8.

[419] Torell, *op. cit.* See also: James Hefley, *God Goes to High School* (Waco, TX: Word Books, 1970), p.13, 14, 25, 34; Wellman, *op. cit.,* p.79, 81; Martin, *A Prophet with Honor, op. cit.,* p.95; "Templeton Dies," *Calvary Contender* (August 15, 2001, Vol. 18, No. 16), p.2.

[420] Graham, *Just As I Am, op. cit.,* p.98. See also: Joel A. Carpenter, *Revive Us Again: The Reawakening of American Fundamentalism* (New York, NY: Oxford University Press, 1997), p.166; Wellman, *op. cit.,* p.70.

[421] Martin, *A Prophet with Honor, op. cit.,* p.94-95.

[422] *Ibid.,* p.117.

[423] *Ibid.,* p.117-118. See also: Joel A. Carpenter, *Revive Us Again: The Reawakening of American Fundamentalism* (New York, NY: Oxford University Press, 1997), p.315.

[424] William R. Denslow, *10,000 Famous Freemasons* (Vol. I) (n.p., 1957), p.57.

[425] *Ibid.,* p.290.

[426] *Ibid.,* p.297.

[427] William R. Denslow, *10,000 Famous Freemasons* (Vol. III) (n.p., 1959), p.57; Wardner, *Unholy Alliances, op. cit.,* p.59.

[428] *Ibid.,* p.188.

[429] *Ibid.,* p.269.

[430] Denslow (Vol. IV) *op. cit.,* p.289.

[431] Springmeier, *The Top 13 Illuminati Bloodlines, op. cit.,* p.239; Springmeier, *Bloodlines, op. cit.,* p.418.

[432] "Cathedral Not-So-Divine," *The New American* (January 23, 1995), p.11.

[433] Rivera: *op. cit.,* p.67; Gary Allen *The Rockefeller File* (Seal Beach, CA: '76 Press, 1976), p.27; Softkey Multimedia Inc., Infopedia, "David Rockefeller" (1996); *Newsletter from a Christian Ministry* (October 1992, Vol. 1, No. 8), p.6.

[434] "Cathedral Not-So-Divine," *The New American* (January 23, 1995), p.11.

[435] "World Religious Leaders Meet at UN," *Calvary Contender* (September 15, 2000, Vol. 17, No. 18), p.1. See also: "What Are Other Investigators Saying?," *Despatch Magazine* (June 2001, Vol. 13:2), p.52.

[436] Springmeier, *The Top 13 Illuminati Bloodlines, op. cit.,* p.135; Springmeier, *Bloodlines, op. cit.,* p.221.

[437] Herbert Benson with Miriam Z. Klipper, *The Relaxation Response* (New York, NY: William Morrow and Company, Inc., 1975). This organization was purchased by the Hearst Corporation.

[438] Alvin P. Sanoff with Ron Scherer, "Behind Merger Mania in Book Publishing," *U. S. News & World Report* (December 10, 1984, Vol. 97, No. 24), p.86.

[439] Robin Estrin, "Harvard Preacher Takes New Look at Bible," *Christian News* (January 27, 1997, Vol. 35, No. 4), p.2.

[440] Ruth Montgomery, *A Gift of Prophecy: The Phenomenal Jeane Dixon* (NY: William Morrow & Company, 1965).

[441] David Wallechinsky, Amy Wallace, and Irving Wallace, *The Book of Predictions* (New York, NY: William Morrow and Company, Inc., 1981).

[442] Amaury de Riencourt, *The Eye of Shiva: Eastern Mysticism and Science* (William Morrow and Company, Inc., 1980).

[443] Martin, *A Prophet with Honor, op. cit.*, p.225-226. See also: Collier and Horowitz, *op. cit.*, p.408.

[444] Wardner, *Unholy Alliances, op. cit.*, p.139. See also: Wellman, *op. cit.*, p.185-186; J. W. Wardner, "Billy Graham, Freemasonry & the Communists," *Despatch Magazine* (September 1998, Vol. 10, No. 3), p.28.

[445] "Protestantism, "*The World Book Year Book* (Chicago, IL: World Book—Childcraft International, Inc., 1978), p.450.

[446] "Protestantism," *The World Book Year Book* (Chicago, IL: World Book—Childcraft International, Inc., 1978), p.450.

[447] Denslow (Vol. II) *op. cit.*, p.203; "The Deception of Billy Graham," *Newsletter from a Christian Ministry* (July 1, 1993, Vol. 2, No. 10), p.38.

[448] Cotter, *op. cit.*, p.69.

[449] John A. Stormer, *None Dare Call It Treason...25 Years Later* (Florissant, MO: Liberty Bell Press, 1992), p.211.

[450] Cotter, *op. cit.*, p.69.

[451] David W. Cloud, "Modernism in the Southern Baptist Convention," *O Timothy* (1994, Vol. 11, Issue 1).

[452] Graham, *Just As I Am, op. cit.*, p.201.

[453] Roland Rasmussen, "Back Billy Graham?—Californian Baptist Pastor Says No," quoting from April 13, 1963 issue of *Saturday Evening Post* in *Sword of the Lord* (October 18, 1963).

[454] Graham, *Just As I Am, op. cit.*, p.531-532. See also: Wellman, *op. cit.*, p.199-200.

[455] *Ibid.*, p.587-588.

[456] *Ibid.*, p.593.

[457] *Ibid.*, p.397.

[458] *Ibid.*, p.460.

[459] *Ibid.*, p.314.

[460] *Ibid.*, p.273.

[461] *Ibid.*, p.471.

[462] *Ibid.*, p.685.

[463] *Ibid.*, p.689.

[464] *Ibid.*, p.531.

[465] *Ibid.*, p.683.

[466] *Ibid.*, p.690.

[467] *Ibid.*, p.271.

[468] *Ibid.*, p.456-457.

[469] *Utah Evangel* (March 1987), p.1.

[470] Graham, *Just As I Am, op. cit.*, p.531.

[471] *Ibid.*, p.275-276, 281. See also: Wellman, *op. cit.*, p.172.

[472] *Ibid.*, p.264.

[473] *Ibid.*, p.274.

[474] Wellman, *op. cit.*, p.181.

[475] Graham, *Just As I Am, op. cit.*, p.683.

[476] Ewin, *Under the New World Order, op. cit.*, p.77.

[477] *Ibid.*

[478] Martin, *A Prophet with Honor, op. cit.*, p.303, picture caption between p.320 and p.321.

[479] Wellman, *op. cit.*, p.140.

[480] Pollock, *op. cit.*, p.286.

[481] Wellman, *op. cit.*, p.199-200.

[482] *Ibid.*, p.171-172. See also: Pollock, *op. cit.*, p.283.

[483] Martin, *A Prophet with Honor, op. cit.*, p.474.

[484] Graham, *Just As I Am, op. cit.*, p.653-654.

[485] Norman Langley and Leon Freilich, "What Really Happened Between the President and America's Leading Preacher in the Countdown to War: How Billy Graham Brought Light to George Bush's Darkest Hour," *Star* (February 5, 1991), p.6. See also: Megan Rosenfeld, "Once Again, a President Calls on Billy Graham," *The News and Observer* (January 18, 1991), p.5A.

[486] *Ibid.*, p.6. See also: "Let's Not Follow 'Orders,'" *op. cit.*, p.4; Megan Rosenfeld, "Once Again, a President Calls on Billy Graham," *The News and Observer* (January 18, 1991), p.5A; Miesel, *op. cit.*

[487] Martin, *A Prophet with Honor, op. cit.*, p.279. See also: Jerry D. Knapper, "What Happens to Christians When They Die?," *The Front Page* (October 1993, Vol. 7, No. 10), p.4; Wellman, *op. cit.*, p.206.

[488] Bundy, *Billy Graham, op. cit.*, p.52. See also: Martin, *A Prophet with Honor, op. cit.*, p.311.

[489] Graham, *Just As I Am, op. cit.*, p.466.

[490] *Ibid.*, p.492; "Guardian Angel," *U. S. News & World Report* (May 5, 1997), p.66. See also: Wellman, *op. cit.*, p.183.

[491] *Ibid.*, p.656.

[492] *Ibid.*, p.277. See also: Billy Graham, *Approaching Hoofbeats: The Four Horsemen of the Apocalypse* (Minneapolis, MN: Grason, 1983), p.196-197; Cloud, *Flirting with Rome (Volume 1—Billy Graham), op. cit.*

[493] William Schnoebelen, "The Curse Causeless," *Liberator* (July-August 1999, Vol. 8, No. 4), p.3.

[494] Martin, *A Prophet with Honor, op. cit.*, p.577; Ashbrook, *New Neutralism II, op. cit.*, p.31; "The Worshiping Heathen," *Christian News* (January 18, 1993, Vol. 31, No. 3), p.6; Bundy, *Billy Graham, op. cit.*, p.115; "Heaven: Guess Who's Coming," *Christian News* (February 19, 2001), p.9; Ashbrook, "Billy Graham," *O Timothy, op. cit.* See also: Miesel, *op. cit.*

[495] Barnhart, "Islam," *op. cit.*, p.7. See also: Ashbrook, "Billy Graham," *O Timothy, op. cit.*

[496] "Billy Graham," *The BDM Letter* (November 1993, Vol. 2, No. 9), p.2; "Billy Graham Says 'Pagans Saved Through Nature,'" *Flashpoint* (August 1995), p.1; Ashbrook, "Billy Graham," *O Timothy, op. cit.;* Miesel, *op. cit.;* Bundy, *Billy Graham, op. cit.*, p.119; J. W. Wardner, "Billy Graham, Freemasonry & the Communists," *Despatch Magazine* (September 1998, Vol. 10, No. 3), p.28; Ashbrook, *New Neutralism II, op. cit.*, p.29.

[497] M. H. Reynolds, Jr., *Billy Graham, the Pope, and the Bible* (Los Osos, CA: Fundamental Evangelistic Association, n.d.), p.4.

[498] Marrs, "Heroism and Cowardice in the Lion's Den," *op. cit.;* J. W. Wardner, "Billy Graham, Freemasonry & the Communists," *Despatch Magazine* (September 1998, Vol. 10, No. 3), p.28; "Billy Graham Praises Clinton," *Christian View of the News* (October 10, 1994, Vol. 19, No. 19), p.2; Wardner, *Unholy Alliances, op. cit.*, p.138; "Billy Graham Praises Bill Clinton," *Flashpoint* (April 1994), p.2.

[499] Wardner, *Unholy Alliances, op. cit.*, p.125; Ashbrook, quoting from *News-Herald* in "Billy Graham," *O Timothy, op. cit.;* Ashbrook, *New Neutralism II, op. cit.*, p.31-32.

[500] Graham, *Just As I Am, op. cit.*, p.656; Adelle M. Banks, "Billy, Ruth Graham Receive Congressional Gold Medal," *Christian News* (May 13, 1996, Vol. 34, No. 20), p.6; "People," *U. S. News & World Report* (May 13, 1996, Vol. 120, No. 19), p.21.

[501] *Ibid.*, p.483, 488; Martin, *A Prophet with Honor, op. cit.*, p.491.

[502] *Ibid.*, p.539.

[503] Templeton, *op. cit.*, p.199; *Ibid.*, p.511; Forker, *op. cit.*, p.85, 89, 280; "Charles Colson to Join Mother Teresa and Pagan Religious Leaders at Parliament of the World's Religions," *O Timothy* (1993, Vol. 10, Issue 6); "The Templeton Prize for Religious Excellence," *op. cit.;* "Templeton Is Awarded to Physicist," *Reading Eagle* (March 11, 1995); Harry Bruinius, "Templeton Winner Coaxed Science and Religion to Talk," *Christian Science Monitor* (March 11, 1999), p.18; "Barbour Wins Templeton Prize," *Calvary Contender* (July 15, 1999, Vol. 16, No. 14); "Books of Interest Endorsed by the John Templeton Foundation" (Paper from the John Templeton Foundation dated January 11, 1996), p.1; Joan Veon, *Prince Charles: The* Sustainable *Prince* (Oklahoma City, OK: Hearthstone Publishing, Ltd., 1997), p.102.

[504] Graham, *Just As I Am, op. cit.*, p.460.

2. MORE LIBERAL FRIENDS

[1] James W. Wardner, *Unholy Alliances* (n.p., 1996), p.135; William Martin, *A Prophet with Honor: The Billy Graham Story* (NY: William Morrow and Company, Inc., 1991), p.294; J. W. Wardner, "Billy Graham, Freemasonry & the Communists," *Despatch Magazine* (September 1998, Vol. 10, No. 3), p.27; David W. Cloud, "Billy Graham's Disobedience to the Word of God"; *Distant Drums* (December 1980, Vol. 2, No. 5), p.11; D. W. Cloud, "Some Frightening Facts About Billy Graham," *O Timothy* (1984, Vol. 1, Issue 4). See also: Edgar C. Bundy, *Billy Graham: Performer?, Politician?, Preacher?, Prophet?* (Wheaton, IL: Church League of America, 1982), p.46.

[2] George Zeller, *Billy Graham: Ecumenical Evangelism* (Middletown, CT: Middletown Bible Church, n.d.), p.10. See also: *The BDM Letter* (November 1993, Vol. 2, No. 9), p.2; Brad K. Gsell, *The Legacy of Billy Graham* (Charlotte, NC: Fundamental Presbyterian Publication, n.d.), p.21; Rick Miesel, "Billy Graham: General Teachings/Activities" (Biblical Discernment Ministries, Revised January 1994); John A. Stormer, *The Death of a Nation* (Florissant, MO: Liberty Bell Press, 1968), p.114.

[3] David W. Cloud, "Billy Graham's Disobedience to the Word of God"; D. W. Cloud, "Some Frightening Facts About Billy Graham," *O Timothy* (1984, Vol. 1, Issue, 4); "Billy Graham's Disobedience," *O Timothy,* (1995, Vol. 12, Issue 11); David W. Cloud, "Modernism in the Southern Baptist Convention," *O Timothy* (1994, Vol. 11, Issue 1).

[4] Edgar C. Bundy, *Billy Graham: Performer?, Politician?, Preacher?, Prophet?* (Wheaton, IL: Church League of America, 1982), p.53.

[5] Cloud, "Billy Graham's Disobedience to the Word of God," *op. cit.*; Edgar C. Bundy, *Collectivism in the Churches: A Documented Account of the Political Activities of the Federal, National, and World Councils of Churches* (Wheaton, IL: The Church League of America, 1958), p.161; D. W. Cloud, "Some Frightening Facts About Billy Graham," *O Timothy* (1984, Vol. 1, Issue 4); David W. Cloud, "The Course of This Church Age," *O Timothy* (1985, Vol. 2, Issue 3); David W. Cloud, "Modernism in the Southern Baptist Convention," *O Timothy* (1994, Vol. 11, Issue 1); Bundy, *Billy Graham: Performer?*, *op. cit.*, p.53-54.

[6] David W. Cloud, "Modernism in the Southern Baptist Convention," *O Timothy* (1994, Vol. 11, Issue 1). See also: Edgar C. Bundy, *Collectivism in the Churches: A Documented Account of the Political Activities of the Federal, National, and World Councils of Churches* (Wheaton, IL: The Church League of America, 1958), p.162.

[7] Edgar C. Bundy, *Collectivism in the Churches: A Documented Account of the Political Activities of the Federal, National, and World Councils of Churches* (Wheaton, IL: The Church League of America, 1958), p.162.

[8] *The NCC/WCC—Communism's Helpers* (Virginia Beach, VA: Good News Baptist Church, n.d.), p.5.

[9] Bundy, *Collectivism in the Churches, op. cit.*, p.162.

[10] Bundy, *Billy Graham: Performer?, op. cit.*, p.53.

[11] Brad K. Gsell, *The Legacy of Billy Graham,* (Charlotte, NC: Fundamental Presbyterian Publication, n.d.), p.22.

[12] *Ibid.*

[13] Gil Rugh, *Faithfulness and Conflict: The Church's Battle Against Heresy* (Lincoln, NE: Sound Words Communications, 1990), p.1. See also: Texe Marrs, *Texe Marrs Book of New Age Cults and Religions* (Austin, TX: Living Truth Publishers, 1990), p.328; William G. McLoughlin and Robert N. Bellah, *Religion in America* (Boston, MA: Houghton Mifflin Company, 1968), p.263, 264.

[14] Vic Bovee, "Unitarian Churches," *The World Book Encyclopedia* (Vol. 18) (Chicago 54, IL: Field Enterprises Educational Corporation, 1961 Edition), p.25.

[15] Edgar C. Bundy, *How Liberals and Radicals Are Manipulating Evangelicals* (Miami Shores, FL: Edgar Bundy Ministries, Inc., 1982), p.78. See also: Rugh, *op. cit.*; Texe Marrs, *Texe Marrs Book of New Age Cults and Religions* (Austin, TX: Living Truth Publishers, 1990), p.328; William G. McLoughlin and Robert N. Bellah, *Religion in America* (Boston, MA: Houghton Mifflin Company, 1968), p.267.

[16] Texe Marrs, *Texe Marrs Book of New Age Cults and Religions* (Austin, TX: Living Truth Publishers, 1990), p.328. See also: *The Omega-Letter* (April 1989, Vol. 4, No. 3), p.15; William G. McLoughlin and Robert N. Bellah, *Religion in America* (Boston, MA: Houghton Mifflin Company, 1968), p.267, 268.

[17] Walter Martin, *Kingdom of the Cults.*

[18] William G. McLoughlin and Robert N. Bellah, *Religion in America* (Boston, MA: Houghton Mifflin Company, 1968), p.265.

[19] *Ibid.*

[20] *We Affirm: National Religious Organizations' Statements on Abortion Rights* (Washington, DC: Religious Coalition for Abortion Rights, n.d.), p.8-9; McLoughlin and Bellah, *op. cit.*, p.271.

[21] *Free Inquiry* (Winter 1988/89, Vol. 9, No. 1), p.6.

[22] McLoughlin and Bellah, *op. cit.*, p.271.

[23] *Ibid.*, p.272.

[24] "Unitarians Promote Free Sex!," *Christian News* (January 17, 2000, Vol. 38, No. 3), p.10.

[25] Wardner, *Unholy Alliances, op. cit.*, p.225. See also: Texe Marrs, *Dark Majesty: The Secret Brotherhood and the Magic of a Thousand Points of Light* (Austin, TX: Living Truth Publishers, 1992), p.205-206; Robert Sessler, *To Be God of One World: The French Revolution Globalized* (Merlin, OR: Let There Be Light Publications, 1992), p.139.

[26] "Unitarians Say Paganism Fits Well with Their Tradition," *The Christian World Report* (November 1989, Vol. 1, No. 8), p.12.

[27] "Wicca Stories Are 'Bunk,' Historians Say," *Christian News* (January 29, 2001, Vol. 39, No. 5), p.16. See also: Martin, *Kingdom of the Cults, op. cit.*; "Unitarian Churches Using Wicca Rituals," *Christian News* (February 26, 2001, Vol. 39, No. 9), p.2.

[28] Wardner, *Unholy Alliances, op. cit.*, p.225. See also: Constance Cumbey, *A Planned Deception: The Staging of a New Age "Messiah"* (East Detroit, MI: Pointe Publishing, Inc., 1985), p.137.

[29] "Unitarians Say Paganism Fits Well with Their Tradition," *op. cit.*

[30] Caroline Alexander, "The World of the Occult and Its Infiltration into Modern Society," *The Perilous Times* quoting from the Unitarian Universalist Association ad (July/August 2000, Vol. 22, No. 5), p.7, 9).

[31] Susan Van Dongen, "An Ever-Widening Circle of Light," *TimeOff* (June 30, 2000), p.9.

[32] *Ibid.*

[33] *Ibid.*

[34] *Ibid.*

[35] *The New Age Magazine* (December 1929), p.753; William R. Denslow, *10,000 Famous Freemasons* (Vol. I) (n.p., 1957), p.53.

[36] Joseph M. Murphy, *Santeria: African Spirits in America* (Boston, MA: Beacon Press, 1993 Edition), p.vi.

[37] "New Findings on Religious Behavior and Attitudes," *Christian World Report* (May 1991, Vol. 3, No. 5), p.16.

[38] *Ibid.*

[39] Claire Chambers, *The SIECUS Circle: A Humanist Revolution* (Belmont, MA: Western Islands, 1977), p.82-83. See also: Martin, *Kingdom of the Cults, op. cit.*

[40] Gsell, *op. cit.*, p.22.

[41] Billy Graham, *Just As I Am: The Autobiography of Billy Graham* (Harpers Collins Worldwide, 1997), p.167.

[42] Wardner, *Unholy Alliances, op. cit.*, p.135; William Martin, *A Prophet with Honor: The Billy Graham Story* (NY: William Morrow and Company, Inc., 1991), p.294; J. W. Wardner, "Billy Graham, Freemasonry & the Communists," *Despatch Magazine* (September 1998, Vol. 10, No. 3), p.27.

[43] *Ibid;* Zeller, *op. cit.*, p.10; *The BDM Letter* (November 1993, Vol. 2, No. 9), p.2; Cloud, "Billy Graham's Disobedience to the Word of God," *op. cit.;* Gsell, *op. cit.*, p.21; William Martin, *A Prophet with Honor: The Billy Graham Story* (NY: William Morrow and Company, Inc., 1991), p.293-294.

[44] William Martin, *A Prophet with Honor: The Billy Graham Story* (NY: William Morrow and Company, Inc., 1991), p.293-294.

[45] Gsell, *op. cit.*, p.22. See also: Wardner, *Unholy Alliances, op. cit.*, p.135

[46] Cloud, "Billy Graham's Disobedience to the Word of God," *op. cit.;* D. W. Cloud, "Some Frightening Facts About Billy Graham," *O Timothy* (1984, Vol. 1, Issue 4); David W. Cloud, "Billy Graham's Disobedience," *O Timothy* (1995, Vol. 12, Issue 11).

[47] Martin, *A Prophet with Honor, op. cit.*, p.294.

[48] "Billy Graham: Fellowship with Apostasy," *The BDM Letter* (November 1993, Vol. 2, No. 9), p.2.

[49] *The BDM Letter* (November 1993, Vol. 2, No. 9), p.2; Rick Miesel, "Billy Graham: General Teachings/Activities" (Biblical Discernment Ministries, Revised January 1994).

[50] Gsell, *op. cit.*, p.22. See also: Wardner, *Unholy Alliances, op. cit.*, p.135; Rick Miesel, "Billy Graham: General Teachings/ Activities" (Biblical Discernment Ministries, Revised January 1994).

[51] Martin, *A Prophet with Honor, op. cit.*, p.294.

[52] Rick Miesel, "Billy Graham: General Teachings/Activities" (Biblical Discernment Ministries, Revised January 1994).

[53] David W. Cloud, "Billy Graham's Disobedience to the Word of God" (Updated March 2, 1999), p.5.

[54] *Ibid.*

[55] Gsell, *op. cit.*, p.21; Bundy, *Billy Graham: Performer?, op. cit.*, p.20.

[56] *Ibid.;* Cloud, "Billy Graham's Disobedience to the Word of God," *op. cit.;* Zeller, *op. cit.*, p.9; Bundy, *Billy Graham: Performer?, op. cit.*, p.20-21; D. W. Cloud, "Some Frightening Facts About Billy Graham," *O Timothy* (1984, Vol. 1, Issue 4).

[57] Cloud, "Billy Graham's Disobedience to the Word of God," *op. cit.;* D. W. Cloud, "Some Frightening Facts About Billy Graham," *O Timothy* (1984, Vol. 1, Issue 4); David W. Cloud, "Billy Graham's Disobedience," *O Timothy* (1995, Vol. 12, Issue 11). See also: Zeller, *op. cit.*, p.9.

[58] G. Archer Weniger, *Modernism of National Council of Churches* (1961), p.9, 5.

[59] *Ibid.*, p.27. See also: Gsell, *op. cit.*, p.21.

[60] See: *Ibid.*, p.15.

[61] *Ibid.*

[62] Gsell, *op. cit.*, p.21; Cloud, "Billy Graham's Disobedience to the Word of God" (Updated March 2, 1999), *op. cit.*, p.5, 6.

[63] Cloud, "Billy Graham's Disobedience to the Word of God" (Updated March 2, 1999), *op. cit.*, p.6.

[64] *Ibid.*

[65] *Ibid.*

[66] *Ibid.*

[67] *Ibid.*

[68] John Ankerberg and John Weldon, *The Facts on Spirit Guides: How to Avoid the Seduction of the Spirit World and Demonic Powers* (Eugene, OR: Harvest House Publishers, 1988), p.39.

[69] Johanna Michaelsen quoting from James A. Pike's book *The Other Side,* in *The Beautiful Side of Evil* (Eugene, OR: Harvest House Publishers, 1982), p.170.

[70] William J. Petersen, *Those Curious New Cults* (New Canaan, CT: Keat Publishing, Inc., 1973), p.67.

[71] Josh McDowell and Don Stewart, *Understanding the Occult* (San Bernardino, CA: Here's Life Publishers, Inc., 1982), p.147.

[72] Petersen, *op. cit.* p.67.

[73] Chambers, *op. cit.*, p.19.

[74] J. Gordon Melton, Jerome Clark, and Aidan A. Kelly, *New Age Almanac* (Detroit, MI: Visible Ink, 1991), p.205.

[75] John Cotter, *A Study in Syncretism* (Flesherton, Ontario: Canadian Intelligence Publications), p.69; Brenda Scott and Samantha Smith, *Trojan Horse: How the New Age Movement Infiltrates the Church* (Lafayette, LA: Huntington House Publishers, 1993), p.78.

[76] Melvin E. Schoonover, "William Stringfellow's Quest for Truth," *Sojourners* (December 1985), p.14. See also: Brenda Scott and Samantha Smith, *Trojan Horse: How the New Age Movement Infiltrates the Church* (Lafayette, LA: Huntington House Publishers, 1993), p.67.

[77] Gsell, *op. cit.*, p.21. See also: David W. Cloud, "Billy Graham's Disobedience," *O Timothy* (1995, Vol. 12, Issue 11).

[78] *Christian News* (February 10, 1997, Vol. 35, No. 6), p.18.

[79] Gsell, *op. cit.*, p.21; Bundy, *Billy Graham: Performer?*, *op. cit.*, p.87.

[80] *Ibid.*; Bundy, *Billy Graham: Performer?*, *op. cit.*, p.87; David W. Cloud, "Billy Graham's Disobedience," *O Timothy* (1995, Vol. 12, Issue 11).

[81] Weniger, *op. cit.*, p.9. See also: Cloud, "Billy Graham's Disobedience to the Word of God," *op. cit.*

[82] *Christian News* (February 10, 1997, Vol. 35, No. 6), p.18.

[83] David Briggs, "In Shadow of Armageddon, Preacher at 73 Tiring but Plans to Keep Working," *The Knoxville News-Sentinel* (September 15, 1991), p.A8. See also: Miesel, "Billy Graham: General Teachings/Activities," *op. cit.*; Martin, *A Prophet with Honor, op. cit.*, p.299.

[84] Martin, *A Prophet with Honor, op. cit.*, p.597.

[85] "The Deception of Billy Graham," *Newsletter from a Christian Ministry* (July 1, 1993, Vol. 2, No. 10), p.35; Personal conversation with Texe Marrs on June 25, 2001. See also: Graham, *Just As I Am, op. cit.*, p.449 where Graham refers to Hubert Humphrey as his "longtime friend."

[86] David Bay, "Meet the Real Reverand (sic) Billy Graham—He Is Not the Person Whom You Thought You Knew!" (Received February 10, 2000), p.4.

[87] Graham, *Just As I Am, op. cit.*, p.224.

[88] Bay, *op. cit.*, p.4.

[89] "Leslie Weatherhead, Methodist Modernist," *Calvary Contender* (April 1, 2001, Vol. 18, No. 7), p.2.

[90] Graham, *Just As I Am, op. cit.*, p.225. See also: Sam Wellman, *Billy Graham: The Great Evangelist* (Uhrichsville, OH: Barbour Book, 1996), p.119.

[91] *Ibid.*

[92] *Chronology of Education with Quotable Quotes* (Highland City, FL: Pro Family Forum, Inc., 1994, Updated, bound volume), p.9, 69. See also: "Tavistock and Internationalizing via Education," *The Christian Conscience* (May 1998, Vol. 4, No. 4), p.12; "Tavistock and Internationalizing via Education," *The Florida Forum* (Spring 1998), p.13; "The Vast Left-Wing Conspiracy," *The Christian Conscience* (May 1998, Vol. 4, No. 4), p.37; *Secret Records Revealed: The Men, the Money and the Methods Behind the New World Order* (Oklahoma City, OK: Hearthstone Publishing, Ltd., 1999), p.17, 154, 166-167, 176; Barbara Aho, "The 19th Century Occult Revival," *The Christian Conscience* (July/August 1997, Vol. 3, No. 6); *Now Is the Dawning of the New Age New World Order* (Oklahoma City, OK: Hearthstone Publishing, Ltd., 1991), p.46, 47, 84; "Rockefeller Influence on Education Yesterday and Today," *The Florida Forum* (Spring 1996), p.7, footnote; Newsletter from Radio Liberty (May 2001), p.3; "The Philosophy Behind School-to-Work (and Goals 2000)," *The Florida Forum* (Summer 1997), p.12; *Don Bell Reports* (August 15, 1994, Vol. 41, No. 16), p.4; "To Socialism by Way of Tax-Exempt Foundations," *The Florida Forum* (Summer 1997), p.23; A. Ralph Epperson, *The Unseen Hand: An Introduction to the Conspiratorial View of History* (Tucson, AZ: Publius Press, 1985), p.195; *The Florida Forum* (Fall 1994, Special Edition), p.21; Brian Garling, *Global Checkmate by the New Age-New World Order* (Landsborough, Queensland: Endtime Ministries, 1993), p.30; Carol Woster, *Woster's Religious Almanac* (Columbia Falls, MT: Christian Wall Center, 1999), p.36; Zygmund Dobbs, *Keynes at Harvard: Economic Deception As a Political Credo* (West Sayville, NY: Probe Research, Inc., 1969 Edition), p.26, 33, 42, 102, 128, 144, 156; Eric Samuelson, *Fabian Society* (n.p., n.d.); David A. Noebel, *The Marxist Minstrels: A Handbook on Communist Subversion of Music* (Tulsa, OK: American Christian College Press, 1974), p.107; John A. Stormer, *None Dare Call It Treason...25 Years Later* (Florissant, MO: Liberty Bell Press, 1992), p.6; Wardner, *Unholy Alliances, op. cit.*, p.207; David Allen Rivera, *Final Warning: A History of the New World Order* (Harrisburg, PA: Rivera Enterprises, 1994 Edition), p.84; *"Secret Records" Revealed: The Men, the Money, and the Methods Behind the New World Order* (Marlborough, NH: The Plymouth Rock Foundation, 1994), p.5.

[93] *The Road to Socialism and the New World Order* (Highland City, FL: Florida Pro Family Forum, 1995), p.21.

[94] Mari Jo Buhle, Paul Buhle, and Dan Georgakas, Editors, *Encyclopedia of the American Left* (New York, NY: Oxford University Press, 1998, Second Edition), p.930.

[95] Jim Marrs, *Rule by Secrecy: The Hidden History That Connects the Trilateral Commission, the Freemasons, and the Great Pyramids* (New York, NY: HarperCollins Publishers, Inc., 2000), p.99.

[96] Bundy, *Collectivism in the Churches, op. cit.*, p.100. See also: *Ibid.*

[97] A. Ralph Epperson, *The Unseen Hand: An Introduction to the Conspiratorial View of History* (Tucson, AZ: Publius Press, 1985), p.195-196. See also: "To Socialism by Way of Tax-Exempt Foundations," *The Florida Forum* (Summer 1997), p.23; Eric Samuelson, *Fabian Society* (n.p., n.d.); Emanuel M. Josephson, *The Truth About Rockefeller* (New York City, NY: Chedney Press, 1964), p.29; Gary Allen, *Rockefeller: Campaigning for the New World Order* (n.p., n.d.), p.9; Paper from the Committee of Christian Laymen, Inc. of Woodland Hills (October 16, 1969, No. 181), p.1; David

Allen Rivera, *Final Warning: A History of the New World Order* (Harrisburg, PA: Rivera Enterprises, 1994 Edition), p.84; *Ibid.*, p.51, 99.

[98] *Ibid.*, p.195-196. See also: Marrs, *Rule by Secrecy, op. cit.*, p.100.

[99] *"Secret Records" Revealed: The Men, the Money, and the Methods Behind the New World Order* (Marlborough, NH: The Plymouth Rock Foundation, 1994), p.4. See also: *Secret Records Revealed: The Men, the Money and the Methods Behind the New World Order* (Oklahoma City, OK: Hearthstone Publishing, Ltd., 1999), p.14.

[100] Carroll Quigley, *The Anglo-American Establishment: From Rhodes to Cliveden* (New York, NY: Books in Focus, 1981), p.4-7. See also: Marrs, *Rule by Secrecy, op. cit.*, p.84.

[101] *Ibid.*, p.ix, 4. See also: Virginia Birt Baker, "Who's Who in the U. S. Government?," *Wisconsin Report* (February 18, 1993, Vol. 18, No. 8), p.4.

[102] Virginia Birt Baker, "Who's Who in the U. S. Government?," *Wisconsin Report* (February 18, 1993, Vol. 18, No. 8), p.4.

[103] *Ibid.*

[104] *Secret Records Revealed: The Men, the Money and the Methods Behind the New World Order* (Oklahoma City, OK: Hearthstone Publishing, Ltd., 1999), p.36; Emanuel M. Josephson, *The Truth About Rockefeller* (New York City, NY: Chedney Press, 1964), p.27; David Allen Rivera, *Final Warning: A History of the New World Order* (Harrisburg, PA: Rivera Enterprises, 1994 Edition), p.63, 70, 71; Carroll Quigley, *Tragedy and Hope: A History of the World in Our Time* (NY: The Macmillan Company, 1966), p.951.

[105] Gary Allen, *The Rockefeller File* (Seal Beach, CA: '76 Press, 1976), p.147, 148; Marrs, *Rule by Secrecy, op. cit.*, p.49.

[106] *Ibid.*, p.147.

[107] *Ibid.*

[108] *Ibid.*

[109] *Ibid.*, p.148.

[110] *Ibid.*

[111] *Ibid.*, p.147; Texe Marrs, *Circle of Intrigue* (Austin, TX: Living Truth Ministries, 1995), p.58.

[112] David Allen River, *Final Warning: A History of the New World Order* (Harrisburg, PA: Rivera Enterprises, 1994 Edition), p.70.

[113] Stanley Monteith, *Brotherhood of Darkness* (Oklahoma City, OK: Hearthstone Publishing, 2000), p.52.

[114] Ronald Ray, "Kinsey's Legal Legacy," *The New American* (January 19, 1998), p.31.

[115] Bundy, *Billy Graham: Performer?, op. cit.*, p.146.

[116] Gsell, *op. cit.*, p.22; *Sword of the Lord* (March 31, 1989, Vol. 55, No. 7), p.2A; Dave Hunt, *Whatever Happened to Heaven?* (Eugene, OR: Harvest House Publishers, 1988), p.22.

[117] *Ibid.* See also: *Sword of the Lord* (March 31, 1989, Vol. 55, No. 7), p.2A; Cloud, "Billy Graham's Disobedience to the Word of God" (Updated March 2, 1999), *op. cit.*, p.6.

[118] *Sword of the Lord* (March 31, 1989, Vol. 55, No. 7), p.2A.

[119] Dave Hunt, *Whatever Happened to Heaven?* (Eugene, OR: Harvest House Publishers, 1988), p.23. See also: Dave Hunt, "Time & Eternity," *The Berean Call* (January 1996), p.1.

[120] *Sword of the Lord, op. cit.*

[121] "Turret of the Times," *Christian News* (July 19, 1999, Vol. 37, No. 29), p.2; Wilhelm E. Schmitt, "Some Facts About 'Martin Luther' King, Jr. Ignored by the National Capital Planning Commission," *Christian News* (January 1, 2000, Vol. 38, No. 1), p.7; "Billy Graham's Last Scheduled International Event to Be His Most Technologically Advanced," *Christian News* (June 19, 2000, Vol. 38, No. 25), p.7; Miesel, "Billy Graham: General Teachings/Activities," *op. cit.;* "Catholics May Name King 'Martyr for the Faith,'" *Calvary Contender* (February 1, 2000), p.1; "King's Sexual Orgies" *Christian News* (January 24, 2000), p.11; "News Bits from Here and There," *Voice in the Wilderness* (March 2000), p.13; "King Holiday a Travesty," *Calvary Contender* (February 15, 1992, Vol. 9, No. 4), p.1; Wilhelm E. Schmitt, "Some Facts About 'Martin Luther' King Apparently Missed by a Wheaton College Professor," *Christian News* (October 26, 1992, Vol. 30, No. 39), p.19; Rivera, *op. cit.*, p.76; "Turret of the Times," *Christian News* (February 17, 1991, Vol. 30, No. 7), p.19; "Abernathy Attacked by Blacks for King Revelations," *The Christian World Report* (December 1989, Vol. 1, No. 9), p.11; "Promise Keepers' D.C. Covenant Agenda for Churches Revealed," *Media Spotlight* (1997, Vol. 20, No. 2), p.14; "King No Role Model," *Calvary Contender* (February 15, 1998, Vol. 15, No. 4); "Turret of the Times," *Christian News* (February 5, 2001, Vol. 39, No. 6), p.2; "The Christian Legacy of Martin Luther King," *Christianity Today* (June 16, 1989, Vol. 33, No. 9), p.33; "Ralph Reed/'Christian Coalition' Preaching Another Gospel Which Is Christ Denial,"*Christian News* (January 23, 1995, Vol. 33, No. 4), p.18. (Reprinted from *The Lofton Letter.);* Wilhelm E. Schmitt, "Some Facts About 'Martin Luther' King Apparently Missed by a Wheaton College Professor," *Christian News* (October 26, 1992, Vol. 30, No. 39), p.19; "Turret of the Times," *Christian News* (February 1, 1993, Vol. 31, No. 5), p.2; "Turret of the Times," *Christian News* (February 17, 1991, Vol. 30, No. 7), p.19; Brian Snider, "A Review Article on the 'Stand in the Gap' Promise Keepers Rally in Washington," *Christian News* (December 1, 1997, Vol. 35, No. 44), p.16; "LCMS Pastors and Laymen Asking—Who Invited Neuhaus and Dawn?," *Christian News* (March 28, 1994, Vol. 32, No. 13), p.13; "Praising a Twice Divorced Woman 'Pastor,'" *Christian News* (March 8, 1993, Vol. 31, No. 10), p.9.

[122] Wilhelm E. Schmitt, "Some Facts About 'Martin Luther' King Apparently Missed by a Wheaton College Professor," *Christian News* (October 26, 1992, Vol. 30, No. 39), p.19; See also: "Billy Graham's Last Scheduled International Event to Be His Most Technologically Advanced," *Christian News* (June 19, 2000, Vol. 38, No. 25), p.7.

[123] "Abernathy Attacked by Blacks for King Revelations," *The Christian World Report* (December 1989, Vol. 1, No. 9), p.11. See also: "Turret of the Times," *Christian News* (July 19, 1999, Vol. 37, No. 29), p.2; "Catholics May Name King 'Martyr for the Faith,'" *Calvary Contender* (February 1, 2000), p.1; Rivera, *op. cit.*, p.76; "Quote of the Day: Former Sen. Harris Wofford," *Christian News* (January 15, 2001, Vol. 39, No. 3), p.3; Albert James Dager, "Promise Keepers' D.C. Covenant Agenda for Churches Revealed," *Media Spotlight* (1997, Vol. 20, No. 2), p.14; "Ban Jackson and All Adulterers from the Pastoral Ministry," *Christian News* (January 29, 2001, Vol. 39, No. 5), p.5; "The Christian Legacy of Martin Luther King," *Christianity Today* (June 16, 1989, Vol. 33, No. 9), p.34; Brian Snider, "A Review Article on the 'Stand in the Gap' Promise Keepers Rally in Washington," *Christian News* (December 1, 1997, Vol. 35, No. 44), p.16; "LCMS Pastors and Laymen Asking—Who Invited Neuhaus and Dawn?," *Christian News* (March 28, 1994, Vol. 32, No. 13), p.13; "Turret of the Times," *Christian News* (April 5, 1993, Vol. 31, No. 14), p.2.

[124] "Turret of the Times," *Christian News* (July 19, 1999, Vol. 37, No. 29), p.2; "Praising a Twice Divorced Woman 'Pastor,'" *Christian News* (March 8, 1993, Vol. 31, No. 10), p.9.

[125] "King Holiday a Travesty," *Calvary Contender* (February 15, 1992, Vol. 9, No. 4), p.1; "Ralph Reed/'Christian Coalition' Preaching Another Gospel Which Is Christ Denial," *Christian News* (January 23, 1995, Vol. 33, No. 4), p.18 (Reprinted from *The Lofton Letter.)*; "Quote of the Day: Former Sen. Harris Wofford," *Christian News* (January 15, 2001, Vol. 39, No. 3), p.3; Schmitt, "Some Facts About 'Martin Luther' King Apparently Missed by a Wheaton College Professor," *op. cit.*, p.19; "Billy Graham's Last Scheduled International Event to Be His Most Technologically Advanced," *Christian News* (June 19, 2000, Vol. 38, No. 25), p.7; Jesse Helms, *The King Holiday and Its Meaning* (St. Louis, MO: Council of Conservative Citizens, 1998), p.11; "Turret of the Times," *Christian News* (February 1, 1993, Vol. 31, No. 5), p.2; "Turret of the Times," *Christian News* (February 17, 1991, Vol. 30, No. 7), p.19; Pamphlet titled "The Council of Conservative Citizens' Guide to *Martin Luther King, Jr. Holiday,"* p.4; "Catholics May Name King 'Martyr for the Faith,'" *Calvary Contender* (February 1, 2000), p.1; "Turret of the Times," *Christian News* (April 5, 1993, Vol. 31, No. 14), p.2.

[126] Schmitt, "Some Facts About 'Martin Luther' King Apparently Missed by a Wheaton College Professor," *op. cit.*, p.19; Wilhelm E. Schmitt, "Some Facts About 'Martin Luther' King, Jr. Ignored by the National Capital Planning Commission," *Christian News* (January 1, 2000, Vol. 38, No. 1), p.7; "Catholics May Name King 'Martyr for the Faith,'" *Calvary Contender* (February 1, 2000), p.1.

[127] Pamphlet titled "The Council of Conservative Citizens' Guide to *Martin Luther King, Jr. Holiday,"* p.4-5.

[128] "King Holiday a Travesty," *op. cit.*, p.1; "King No Role Model," *Calvary Contender* (February 15, 1998, Vol. 15, No. 4); Miesel, "Billy Graham: General Teachings/Activities," *op. cit.;* "Turret of the Times," *Christian News* (February 1, 1993, Vol. 31, No. 5), p.2; "Says King Was a Communist Traitor," *Christian News* (January 24, 2000), p.11; Jesse Helms, *The King Holiday and Its Meaning* (St. Louis, MO: Council of Conservative Citizens, 1998), p.5, 7, 17, 43, 44; "LCMS Pastors and Laymen Asking—Who Invited Neuhaus and Dawn?," *Christian News* (March 28, 1994, Vol. 32, No. 13), p.13; Albert James Dager, "Promise Keepers' D.C. Covenant Agenda for Churches Revealed," *Media Spotlight* (1997, Vol. 20, No. 2), p.14; "Turret of the Times," *Christian News* (February 17, 1991, Vol. 30, No. 7), p.19; "What Kind of Man Was Martin Luther King, Jr.?," *Common Sense for Today* (November/December 1995), p.1; "Quote of the Day: Former Sen. Harris Wofford," *Christian News* (January 15, 2001, Vol. 39, No. 3), p.3; Pamphlet titled "The Council of Conservative Citizens' Guide to *Martin Luther King, Jr. Holiday,"* p.6; Schmitt, "Some Facts About 'Martin Luther' King Apparently Missed by a Wheaton College Professor," *op. cit.*, p.19; "Billy Graham's Last Scheduled International Event to Be His Most Technologically Advanced," *Christian News* (June 19, 2000, Vol. 38, No. 25), p.7; W. Cleon Skousen, *The Communist Attack on U. S. Police* (Salt Lake City, UT: The Ensign Publishing Company, 1966), p.21; Epperson, *op. cit.*, p.394; M. Stanton Evans, "Dr. King and the Communists," *Human Events* (February 1, 1986, Vol. 46, No. 5), p.7; "Promise Keepers' D.C. Covenant Agenda for Churches Revealed," *Media Spotlight* (1997, Vol. 20, No. 2), p.14; *The NCC/WCC—Communism's Helpers, op. cit.*, p.5; Rivera, *op. cit.*, p.70, 76; "Communist Mandela Given Hero's Welcome in Canada, U. S.," *The Christian World Report* (July 1990, Vol. 2, No.6), p.3); "Catholics May Name King 'Martyr for the Faith,'" *Calvary Contender* (February 1, 2000), p.1; "LCMS Pastors and Laymen Asking—Who Invited Neuhaus and Dawn?," *Christian News* (March 28, 1994, Vol. 32, No. 13), p.13; Wilhelm E. Schmitt, "Some Facts About 'Martin Luther' King, Jr. Ignored by the National Capital Planning Commission," *Christian News* (January 1, 2000, Vol. 38, No. 1), p.7; *O Timothy* (1995, Vol. 12, Issue 11).

[129] *"A Lot of What's Best in America...Is Socialist"* (New York, NY: Socialist Party, n.d.), p.3. See also: Cotter, *op. cit.*, p.69.

[130] Jim Wallis, "A Life of Commitment and Compassion," *Sojourners* (December 1989, Vol. 18, No. 11), p.7.

[131] *Ibid.*

[132] "Comrades Seeger and King, Our 'Heroes,'" *Christian News* (June 23, 1997), p.16.

[133] "What Kind of Man Was Martin Luther King, Jr.?," *Common Sense for Today* (November/December 1995), p.1. See also: Jesse Helms, *The King Holiday and Its Meaning* (St. Louis, MO: Council of Conservative Citizens, 1998), p.7, 20, 24, 25, 26, 33; Pamphlet titled "The Council of Conservative Citizens' Guide to *Martin Luther King, Jr. Holiday,"* p.6; Schmitt, "Some Facts About 'Martin Luther' King Apparently Missed by a Wheaton College Professor," *op. cit.*, p.19; M. Stanton Evans, "Dr. King and the Communists," *Human Events* (February 1, 1986, Vol. 46, No. 5), p.7; Buhle, Buhle, and Georgakas, *op. cit.*, p.136; "Jackson's 'Rainbow' Includes Pink Adviser," *Human Events* (May 10, 1986), p.5; Wilhelm E. Schmitt, "Some Facts About 'Martin Luther' King, Jr. Ignored by the National Capital Planning Commission," *Christian News* (January 1, 2000, Vol. 38, No. 1), p.7; W. Cleon Skousen, *The Communist Attack on U.S. Police* (Salt Lake City, UT: The Ensign Publishing Company, 1966), p.21, 25; "Bayard Rustin at Notre Dame," *The Review of the News* (December 3, 1969), p.1; "Says King Was a Communist Traitor," *Christian News* (January 24, 2000), p.11.

[134] "Billy Graham's Last Scheduled International Event to Be His Most Technologically Advanced," *Christian News* (June 19, 2000, Vol. 38, No. 25), p.7.

[135] *Ibid.;* "King Holiday a Travesty," *op. cit.*, p.1; "King No Role Model," *Calvary Contender* (February 15, 1998, Vol.

15, No. 4); "Catholics May Name King 'Martyr for the Faith,'" *Calvary Contender* (February 1, 2000), p.1; "Turret of the Times," *Christian News* (February 17, 1991, Vol. 30, No. 7), p.19; *Christian News* (October 28, 1991, Vol. 29, No. 39), p.20; "What Kind of Man Was Martin Luther King, Jr.?," *op. cit.*, p.1; John E. Ashbrook, *New Neutralism II: Exposing the Gray of Compromise* (Mentor, OH: Here I Stand Books, 1992), p.54; "The 'Peace' Prize That the World Gives" *The Christian World Report* (February 1991, Vol. 3, No. 2), p.6; "Bayard Rustin at Notre Dame," *The Review of the News* (December 3, 1969), p.2; "The Right Place for a Mass Murdering Atheist to Speak," *Christian News* (September 18, 2000, Vol. 38, No. 34), p.4.

[136] Rivera, *op. cit.*, p.76. See also: "Christians Interested in Salvation," *Christian News* (May 13, 1996, Vol. 34, No. 20), p.15; Jesse Helms, *The King Holiday and Its Meaning* (St. Louis, MO: Council of Conservative Citizens, 1998), p.7, 19; M. Stanton Evans, "Dr. King and the Communists," *Human Events* (February 1, 1986, Vol. 46, No. 5), p.7; *The Council of Conservative Citizens' Guide to Martin Luther King, Jr. Holiday* (Jasper, AL: n.p., n.d.), p.6; Buhle, Buhle, and Georgakas, *op. cit.*, p.136.

[137] "The Awful Truth About Jesse Jackson (Part I)," *Flashpoint* (March 2001, Vol. 2001-03), p.4; David W. Cloud, "The Preachers Who Influenced Bill Clinton," *Christian News* (March 26, 2001, Vol. 39, No. 13), p.17; Mark Hosenball and Evan Thomas, "Jesse and Al's Food Fight," *Newsweek* (April 9, 2001, Vol. 137, No. 15), p.41; "Progressive National Baptist Convention Affirm Jackson," *The Voice in the Wilderness* (May 2001), p.5.

[138] Lynette Clemetson and Flynn McRoberts, "A Confession from Jesse," *Newsweek* (January 29, 2001, Vol. 137, No. 5), p.38; "Turret of the Times," *Christian News* (February 5, 2001, Vol. 39, No. 6), p.2; "The Jesse Jackson Scandal," *Calvary Contender* (February 1, 2001, Vol. 18, No. 3), p.1; "National Enquirer Bombshell: Jesse Jackson Love Child; Mistress Paid in Cash," *Christian News* (January 22, 2001, Vol. 39, No. 4), p.20; "Jesse Jackson Fathers Child out of Wedlock," *The News-Item* (January 19, 2001), p.3; Jack E. White, "The End of the Rainbow," *Christian News* (February 5, 2001, Vol. 39, No. 6), p.2; "Jackson Returns to Public Stage, Thanks Family, Supporters," *Christian News* (January 29, 2001, Vol. 39, No. 5), p.5; "Jesse Jackson's Confession Shocks America!," *The Sacred Name Broadcaster* (January 2001, Vol. 33, No. 10); David W. Cloud, "The Preachers Who Influenced Bill Clinton," *Christian News* (March 26, 2001, Vol. 39, No. 13), p.17; "Ban Jackson and All Adulterers from the Pastoral Ministry," *Christian News* (January 29, 2001, Vol. 39, No. 5), p.5; "Jackson Needs Leave of Absence," *Christian News* (February 12, 2001, Vol. 39, No. 7), p.20.

[139] "Ban Jackson and All Adulterers from the Pastoral Ministry," *Christian News* (January 29, 2001, Vol. 39, No. 5), p.5; John Lofton, "Could Jackson Be Next?," *Christian News* (January 29, 2001, Vol. 39, No. 5), p.5; Richard Scales, "Allegations Unchallenged," *Christian News* (January 29, 2001, Vol. 39, No. 5), p.6; "Contradictions and Ambiguities," *Christian News* (January 29, 2001, Vol. 39, No. 5), p.6.

[140] *Power of Prophecy* (April 2001, Vol. 2001-04), p.5.

[141] Buhle, Buhle, and Georgakas, *op. cit.*, p.140; Marshall Frady, *Jesse: The Life and Pilgrimage of Jesse Jackson* (NY: Random House, Inc., 1996), p.3.

[142] Herb Boyd, "What King Left Behind," *The Guardian* (April 13, 1988, Vol. 40, No. 28), p.10. See also: Marshall Frady, *Jesse: The Life and Pilgrimage of Jesse Jackson* (NY: Random House, Inc., 1996), p.3.

[143] Rush Limbaugh, *The Way Things Out to Be* (New York, NY: Pocket Books, 1992), p.204.

[144] "Jesse Jackson and Communism," referring to the *AFA Journal* article in *Calvary Contender* (March 1, 1995, Vol. 12, No. 5), p.1; "Contradictions and Ambiguities," *Christian News* (January 29, 2001, Vol. 39, No. 5), p.6.

[145] "Jackson's 'Rainbow' Includes Pink Adviser," *Human Events* (May 10, 1986), p.5.

[146] *Ibid.*; "News & Views," *Plains Baptist Challenger* (May 1993, Vol. 52, No. 5), p.6; John A. Stormer, *None Dare Call It Treason...25 Years Later* (Florissant, MO: Liberty Bell Press, 1992), p.498; "Contradictions and Ambiguities," *Christian News* (January 29, 2001, Vol. 39, No. 5), p.6; Joseph Farah, "Jesse: Black, Blue and Red?," *The Schwarz Report* (May 2001, Vol. 41, No. 5), p.6.

[147] Joseph Farah, "Jesse: Black, Blue and Red?," *The Schwarz Report* (May 2001, Vol. 41, No. 5), p.6.

[148] Texe Marrs, *Power of Prophecy* (February 10, 2001 program). See also: "The Awful Truth About Jesse Jackson," *op. cit.*, p.4; Marshall Frady, *Jesse: The Life and Pilgrimage of Jesse Jackson* (NY: Random House, Inc., 1996), picture on unnumbered page.

[149] John A. Stormer, *None Dare Call It Treason...25 Years Later* (Florissant, MO: Liberty Bell Press, 1992), p.437-438; Peter Svoboda, "Jesse Jackson, the Democrats, and the 1988 Elections," *Solidarity*, p.1-3; Farah, *op. cit.*, p.6.

[150] Robert Sessler, *To Be God of One World: The French Revolution Globalized* (Merlin, OR: Let There Be Light Publications, 1992), p.168-169. See also: "Contradictions and Ambiguities," *Christian News* (January 29, 2001, Vol. 39, No. 5), p.6.

[151] Stormer, *None Dare Call It Treason...25 Years Later, op. cit.*, p.436.

[152] Victoria Irwin, "US Socialist Leader Says He Prefers Jackson But Is Comfortable with Dukakis," *The Christian Science Monitor* (July 21, 1988, Vol. 80, No. 165), p.3.

[153] Kevin J. Kelley, "A Socialist in the House?," *The Guardian* (April 13, 1988, Vol. 40, No. 28), p.4-5.

[154] Stormer, *None Dare Call It Treason...25 Years Later, op. cit.*, p.438.

[155] James Leasor, *Rhodes and Barnato: The Premier and the Prancer* (London, England: Leo Cooper, 1997), p.257; *President Clinton Will Continue the New World Order* (Oklahoma City, OK: Southwest Radio Church, 1993), unnumbered page, p.1; "Who Controls American Education?," *The Blumenfeld Education Letter* (February 1994), p.2, 4; "Time to Rescind North Carolina's Resolution for World Government," *The Citizen* (May 19, 1997), p.8; "Dialectics: Perpetual Process of the Ruling Elite," *Christian Conscience* (September 1995, Vol. 1, No. 8), p.35; *Chronology of Education with Quotable Quotes, op. cit.*, p.10; *"Secret Records" Revealed, op. cit.*, p.2, 5, 42; *Secret Records Revealed, op. cit.*, p.9, 68, 110, 146; "Could It Be Possible That Rush Is a Closet 'Kook?,'" *The Times Leader* (March 23, 1996, Vol. 4, No. 93),

p.4; "Clinton Taps 'Fresh Thinking' Activists," *The Daily Item* (December 12, 1992, Vol. 55, No. 346), p.13; Texe Marrs, "Bill Clinton and the Bilderberger Conspiracy," *Flashpoint* (September 1992), p.1; "The Disarmament of America," *The Florida Forum* (Spring 1996), p.21; "Rockefeller Influence on Education Yesterday and Today," *The Florida Forum* (Spring 1996), p.7; Jessica Lipnack and Jeffrey Stamps, "Networking the World: People, Corporation, Communities, and Nations," *The Futurist*, p.9; Joan Veon, *Prince Charles: The* Sustainable *Prince* (Oklahoma City, OK: Hearthstone Publishing, Ltd., 1997), p.24; Wardner, *Unholy Alliances, op. cit.*, p.128; J. Royce Thomason, "Just What Is a Rhodes Scholarship," *The Voice in the Wilderness* (July 1994), p.7; Rivera, *op. cit.*, p.89; "Who's Who in the Clinton Administration," *Wisconsin Report* (February 18, 1993, Vol. 18, No. 8), p.4; "One More Step Toward World Government," *The Christian World Report* (March 1994, Vol. 9, No. 3), p.7; "Rhodes to the New World Order," *The Christian World Report* (March/April 1993, Vol. 8, No. 2), p.12.

[156] Charles Williams, "The Clinton/Marxist Connections: Derek Schearer (sic) & the Institute for Policy Studies," *Wisconsin Report* (July 8, 1993, Vol. 18, No. 27), p.1.

[157] *Ibid.*

[158] *Ibid.*

[159] "Gorby's Favorites," *The Christian World Report* (September 1990, Vol. 2, No. 8), p.19.

[160] *Ibid.*

[161] Kevin J. Kelley, "Jackson Radically Altering Political Landscape," *The Guardian* (May 4, 1988), p.5; "Democrats Endorse Gay/Lesbian Rights," *Task Force Report* (Winter 1988), p.1; "Jesse's Movement," *The Nation* (April 2, 1988, Vol. 246, No. 13), p.448; Paul Hockenos, "Jackson Spirit Takes Hold in New York," *The Guardian* (April 13, 1988, Vol. 40, No. 28), p.5; *The Omega Letter* (March 1991, Vol. 6, No. 3), p.14; "Jesse Jackson Is the Best Candidate for the Gay and Lesbian Community," *National & International Religion Report* (April 25, 1988, Vol. 2, No. 8), p.1; "For Jesse Jackson and His Campaign," *The Nation* (April 16, 1988, Vol. 246, No. 15), p.522.

[162] Paul Hockenos, "Jackson Spirit Takes Hold in New York," *The Guardian* (April 13, 1988, Vol. 40, No. 28), p.5.

[163] *Ibid.*

[164] "Jesse Jackson Is the Best Candidate for the Gay and Lesbian Community," *National & International Religion Report* (April 25, 1988, Vol. 2, No. 8), p.1. See also: Buhle, Buhle, and Georgakas, *op. cit.*, p.261.

[165] Buhle, Buhle, and Georgakas, *op. cit.*, p.261.

[166] Marshall Frady, *Jesse: The Life and Pilgrimage of Jesse Jackson* (NY: Random House, Inc., 1996), p.5.

[167] *Council on Foreign Relations: Annual Report July 1, 1990-June 30, 1991*, p.184; *Council on Foreign Relations: Annual Report July 1, 1992-June 30, 1993*, p.170; *Council on Foreign Relations: Annual Report July 1, 1994-June 30, 1995*, p.149; Texe Marrs, *Circle of Intrigue* (Austin, TX: Living Truth Ministries, 1995), p.41, 180; Gary Kah, *En Route to Global Occupation* (Lafayette, LA: Huntington House Publishers, 1992), p.79, 83-84.

[168] Mustafa El-Amin, *Freemasonry: Ancient Egypt and the Islamic Destiny* (Jersey City, NJ: New Mind Productions, 1988), p.x, 67; Texe Marrs, *Circle of Intrigue* (Austin, TX: Living Truth Ministries, 1995), p.180; Allen E. Roberts, *Masonic Trivia and Facts* (Highland Springs, VA: Anchor Communications, 1994), p.160; Texe Marrs, "Witchcraft Invades Christianity," Intelligence Examiner (tape); Wardner, *Unholy Alliances, op. cit.*, p.69.

[169] Letter from SANE, p.5.

[170] "Jesse Jackson—A One World Propagandist?," *Flashpoint* (February 1992), p.3; Gary Kah, *En Route to Global Occupation* (Lafayette, LA: Huntington House Publishers, 1992), p.80, 84, 169; *Now Is the Dawning of the New Age New World Order* (Oklahoma City, OK: Hearthstone Publishing, Ltd., 1991), p.389; "The Open Conspiracy," *Don Bell Reports* (February 21, 1986, Vol. 33, No. 8), p.3.

[171] *Ibid.*

[172] "The Awful Truth About Jesse Jackson," *op. cit.*, p.4.

[173] "Jesse Jackson and Communism," *Calvary Contender* (March 1, 1995, Vol. 12, No. 5), p.1.

[174] John E. Ashbrook, *New Neutralism II: Exposing the Gray of Compromise* (Mentor, OH: Here I Stand Books, 1992), p.68.

[175] "'The Rev.' Jesse Jackson Blasphemes," *Calvary Contender* (August 15, 1992, Vol. 9, No. 16), p.1.

[176] Ashbrook, *op. cit.*, p.46; "Facts to Consider Concerning AD 2000 Evangelism," *Foundation* (July-September 1995, Vol. 16, Issue 4), p.26; "Actor in Jesus Film Is Not a Believer," *O Timothy* (1995, Vol. 12, Issue 10); "Creative Partnership Initiatives with the AD2000 Movement," *Mission Frontiers* (July-August 1993, Vol. 15, No. 7-8), p.22.

[177] "Campus Crusade's Ecumenical Tribute to Jesus," *Calvary Contender* (January 15, 2000, Vol. 17, No. 2), p.1.

[178] *Ibid.*

[179] *Ibid.*; Luis Bush, Editor, *AD 2000 and Beyond Handbook* (Colorado Springs, CO: AD 2000 & Beyond Movement, 1993), p.25; Personal letter from John Quam (dated March 20, 1995); Debbie Wood, "Latins Say 'Si' to World Evangelization: Latinoamerica 2000," *Mission Frontiers* (January/February 1997, Vol. 19, No. 1-2), p.43; Letter from Mission American 2000 (dated January 31, 1995); "The Commission: Many Voices, One Calling," Paper put out by The Navigators Commission; Brochure from Fasting & Prayer '95; Rick Wood, "Taking Jesus to the World," *Mission Frontiers* (November-December 1997, Vol. 19, No. 11-12).

[180] "Actor in Jesus Film Is Not a Believer," *O Timothy* (1995, Vol. 12, Issue 10); Dave Hunt, "Why Christ Came," *The Berean Call* (December 1995), p.2; David W. Cloud, "The Positive Jesus," *O Timothy* (1995, Vol. 12, Issue 10).

[181] *Ibid.*

[182] *Ibid.*

[183] Wilhelm E. Schmitt, "Some Facts About 'Martin Luther' King, Jr. Ignored by the National Capital Planning Commission," *Christian News* (January 1, 2000, Vol. 38, No. 1), p.7. See also: *The King Holiday and Its Meaning* (Saint Louis, MO: Council of Conservative Citizens, 1998), p.29.

[184] Buhle, Buhle, and Georgakas, *op. cit.*, p.194.

[185] *Ibid.*, p.195.

[186] *Ibid.*

[187] *Ibid.*

[188] Schmitt, "Some Facts About 'Martin Luther' King, Jr. Ignored by the National Capital Planning Commission," *op. cit.*, p.7. See also: *The King Holiday and Its Meaning* (Saint Louis, MO: Council of Conservative Citizens, 1998), p.29.

[189] Buhle, Buhle, and Georgakas, *op. cit.*, p.102.

[190] *Ibid.*, p.103.

[191] "What Kind of Man was Martin Luther King, Jr.?," *op. cit.*, p.1. See also: Schmitt, "Some Facts About 'Martin Luther' King, Jr. Ignored by the National Capital Planning Commission," *op. cit.*, p.7.

[192] Epperson, *op. cit.*, p.394. See also: Rivera, *op. cit.*, p.76; Schmitt, "Some Facts About 'Martin Luther' King, Jr. Ignored by the National Capital Planning Commission," *op. cit.*, p.7.

[193] Rivera, *op. cit.*, p.76.

[194] *The Guardian* (November 30, 1988, Vol. 41, No. 10).

[195] Boyd, *op. cit.*, p.10.

[196] *Ibid.*

[197] Schmitt, "Some Facts About 'Martin Luther' King Apparently Missed by a Wheaton College Professor," *op. cit.*, p.19. See also: "The Right Place for a Mass Murdering Atheist to Speak," *Christian News* (September 18, 2000, Vol. 38, No. 34), p.4; Jesse Helms, *The King Holiday and Its Meaning* (St. Louis, MO: Council of Conservative Citizens, 1998), p.39, 40.

[198] Gary Allen, *Rockefeller: Campaigning for the New World Order* (n.p., n.d.), p.10.

[199] "Disrespect for Traditional Religion," *The Florida Forum* (Spring 2001), p.4.

[200] "Castro Applauded at Church," *The Voice in the Wilderness* (December 2000), p.13; "Castro Is Applauded at Riverside Church," *Calvary Contender* (October 15, 2000, Vol. 17, No. 20), p.2; Anita Snow, "Harlem Backers Applaud Castro," *The Schwarz Report* (November 2000, Vol. 40, No. 11), p.5; "The Right Place for a Mass Murdering Atheist to Speak," *Christian News* (September 18, 2000, Vol. 38, No. 34), p.4.

[201] George Grant, *Grand Illusions: The Legacy of Planned Parenthood* (Nashville, TN: Thomas Nelson, Inc., 1998 Edition), p.36, 75, 161; "Population Control and the 'New Age Religion," *An American Commentary* (Oklahoma City, OK: Hearthstone Publishing Ltd., 1993), p.54; *Now Is the Dawning of the New Age New World Order* (Oklahoma City, OK: Hearthstone Publishing, Ltd., 1991), p.96; Marrs, *Rule by Secrecy, op. cit.*, p.47.

[202] William M. Bowen, Jr. *Globalism: America's Demise* (Shreveport, LA: Huntington House, Inc., 1984), 39; William Norman Grigg, "Whose Child Is This?," *The New American* (November 28, 1994, Vol. 10, No. 24), p.29; Fritz Springmeier, *The Top 13 Illuminati Bloodlines* (Portland, OR: n.p., 1995), p.239; "Public School Sex Education: A Report," *AFA Journal* (October 1990, Vol. 14, No. 9), p.12; Kimberly Parker, "The Abortion Connection: Linking Schools to Health Care," *The Christian Conscience* (May 1995, Vol. 1, No. 5), p.10; *President Clinton Will Continue the New World Order* (Oklahoma City, OK: Southwest Radio Church, 1993), p.11; Sarah H. Leslie, "The Feminist As Oppressor," *The Christian Conscience* (March 1995, Vol. 1, No. 3), p.29; *Chronology of Education with Quotable Quotes, op. cit.*, p.18; Randy Engle, "The Roots of Sex Education," *Free World Report* (December 1993, Vol. 2, No. 12), p.14; Larry Abraham and Franklin Sanders, *The Greening* (Atlanta, GA: Soundview Publications, n.d.), p.137; F. V. Scott, "The New American Gothic Planned Parenthood," *Passport Magazine* (July-August 1988), p.6; Chambers, *op. cit.*, p.34, 221; William P. Cheshire, "Margaret Sanger: Weeding Out Misfits to Get Thoroughbreds," *Wisconsin Report* (November 14, 1991, Vol. 16, No. 44), p.1; "A Guinea Pig Remembers," *Wisconsin Report* (January 28, 1993, Vol. 18, No. 5), p.7; "Planned Parenthood's Supremacist Roots," *The Christian World Report* (September 1990, Vol. 2, No. 8), p.21.

[203] F. V. Scott, "The New American Gothic Planned Parenthood," *Passport Magazine* (July-August 1988), p.6.

[204] Chambers, *op. cit.*, p.323.

[205] *Ibid.*, p.324.

[206] *Now Is the Dawning of the New Age New World Order* (Oklahoma City, OK: Hearthstone Publishing, Ltd., 1991), p.96; Scott, *op. cit.*, p.6, 8; *Chronology of Education with Quotable Quotes, op. cit.*, p.18; Chambers, *op. cit.*, p.59, 60, 233, 326; *The Globalists: The Power Elite Exposed* (Oklahoma City, OK: Hearthstone Publishing, 2001), p.317.

[207] Grant, *op. cit.*, p.67, 109; "Public School Sex Education: A Report," *AFA Journal* (October 1990, Vol. 14, No. 9), p.12; Larry Abraham and Franklin Sanders, *The Greening* (Atlanta, GA: Soundview Publications, n.d.), p.137; Scott, *op. cit.*, p.6; Chambers, *op. cit.*, p.79, 324.

[208] *Ibid.*, p.67, 109; Armand Hammer with Neil Lyndon, *Hammer* (New York, NY: G. P. Putnam's Sons, 1987), p.71; Joan Veon, *Prince Charles: The* Sustainable *Prince* (Oklahoma City, OK: Hearthstone Publishing, Ltd., 1997), p.46; David Mark Price, *Secret* (1994), p.3; "Watch Al Gore Closely," *The McAlvany Intelligence Advisor* (November 1992), p.6; "Schuller Promotes Pope and Comrade," *Omega-Letter* (March 1988, Vol. 3, No. 3), p.15; Allen, *The Rockefeller File, op. cit.*, p.118; Rivera, *op. cit.*, p.202; Edward Jay Epstein, *Dossier: The Secret History of Armand Hammer* (NY: Random House, 1996), p.20-21, 68, 88; *Omega-Letter* (March 1991, Vol. 6, No. 3), p.16.

[209] *Ibid.*, p.69, 74, 243. See also: *Now Is the Dawning of the New Age New World Order, op. cit.*, p.96; Larry Abraham and Franklin Sanders, *The Greening* (Atlanta, GA: Soundview Publications, n.d.), p.137; Monteith, *op. cit.*, p.81; "Public School Sex Education: A Report," *AFA Journal* (October 1990, Vol. 14, No. 9), p.12; William P. Cheshire, "Margaret Sanger: Weeding Out Misfits to Get Thoroughbreds," *Wisconsin Report* (November 14, 1991, Vol. 16, No. 44), p.1; Scott, *op. cit.*, p.7.

[210] *Ibid.*, p.243; Chambers, *op. cit.*, p.324.

[211] Melton, Clark, and Kelly, *op. cit.*, p.343, 344, 432; Dave Hunt, "Progress in Religion?," *The Berean Call* (May 1996), p.2; "Schuller Speaks for Moonies, Mormons," *Calvary Contender* (January 1, 1999, Vol. 16, No. 1), p.1; "Schuler (sic) and Gorbachev," *Christian News* (January 22, 2001, Vol. 39, No. 4), p.9; *The Watchman Expositor* (1998, Vol. 15, No. 5), p.20, 22, 27; Jane Gumprecht, *New Age Health Care: Holy or Holistic* (Orange, CA: Promise Publishing, 1988), p.ii, v, 100, 111, 191.

[212] Chambers, *op. cit.*, p.34, 324.

[213] Grant, *op. cit.*, p.76; Scott, *op. cit.*, p.6; Chambers, *op. cit.*, p.325.

[214] *Ibid.*, p.75. See also: Scott, *op. cit.*, p.7; Fritz Springmeier, *The Top 13 Illuminati Bloodlines* (Portland, OR: n.p., 1995), p.239; "Planned Parenthood's Supremacist Roots," *The Christian World Report* (September 1990, Vol. 2, No. 8), p.21.

[215] *Ibid.*; "Population Control and the 'New Age Religion," *An American Commentary* (Oklahoma City, OK: Hearthstone Publishing Ltd., 1993), p.54; *Now Is the Dawning of the New Age New World Order, op. cit.*, p.96; Scott, *op. cit.*, p.6.

[216] *Ibid.*, p.64.

[217] *Ibid.*, p.350.

[218] David G. Racer, Jr., *Not for Sale: The Rev. Sun Myung Moon and One American's Freedom* (St. Paul, MN: Tiny Press, 1989), p.15-16; Cotter, *op. cit.*, p.79; Jesse Helms, *The King Holiday and Its Meaning* (St. Louis, MO: Council of Conservative Citizens, 1998), p.31.

[219] Pamphlet titled "The Council of Conservative Citizens' Guide to *Martin Luther King, Jr. Holiday,"* p.6; *The NCC/WCC—Communism's Helpers, op. cit.*, p.9; Jesse Helms, *The King Holiday and Its Meaning* (St. Louis, MO: Council of Conservative Citizens, 1998), p.18; Ralph Reed, *Active Faith: How Christians Are Changing the Soul of American Politics* (New York, NY: Free Press, 1996), p.60; Buhle, Buhle, and Georgakas, *op. cit.*, p.710; "Jackson Needs Leave of Absence," *Christian News* (February 12, 2001, Vol. 39, No. 7), p.20; "King Honored As National Hero," *Sojourners* (May 1986), p.12; "Two United Methodist Leaders Close to MLK Welcome Verdict," *Christian News* (January 1, 2000, Vol. 38, No. 1), p.7.

[220] Rivera, *op. cit.*, p.70. See also: Allen, *Rockefeller: Campaigning for the New World Order, op. cit.*, p.9.

[221] Schmitt, "Some Facts About 'Martin Luther' King, Jr. Ignored by the National Capital Planning Commission," *op. cit.*, p.7; Schmitt, "Some Facts About 'Martin Luther' King Apparently Missed by a Wheaton College Professor," *op. cit.*, p.19; "Two United Methodist Leaders Close to MLK Welcome Verdict," *Christian News* (January 1, 2000, Vol. 38, No. 1), p.7.

[222] Cotter, *op. cit.*, p.79; Martin, *A Prophet with Honor, op. cit.*, p.363; Bundy, *Billy Graham: Performer?, op. cit.*, p.87.

[223] Pamphlet titled "The Council of Conservative Citizens' Guide to *Martin Luther King, Jr. Holiday,"* p.6; Buhle, Buhle, and Georgakas, *op. cit.*, p.710.

[224] Schmitt, "Some Facts About 'Martin Luther' King Apparently Missed by a Wheaton College Professor," *op. cit.*, p.19; "Bayard Rustin at Notre Dame," *The Review of the News* (December 3, 1969), p.1; W. Cleon; Skousen, *The Communist Attack on U. S. Police* (Salt Lake City, UT: The Ensign Publishing Company, 1966), p.21; Pamphlet titled "The Council of Conservative Citizens' Guide to *Martin Luther King, Jr. Holiday,"* p.6.

[225] "Bayard Rustin at Notre Dame," *The Review of the News* (December 3, 1969), p.1.

[226] W. Cleon Skousen, *The Communist Attack on U. S. Police* (Salt Lake City, UT: The Ensign Publishing Company, 1966), p.21. See also: *Ibid.*

[227] "Bayard Rustin at Notre Dame," *op. cit.*, p.2. See also: Bob Waymer, *A. Philip Randolph: A Short Biography* (Atlanta, GA: The Elloree Company, 1990), p.20; Paper from the Committee of Christian Laymen, Inc. (October 16, 1969, No. 181), p.4; Buhle, Buhle, and Georgakas, *op. cit.*, p.710.

[228] *Ibid.*

[229] Buhle, Buhle, and Georgakas, *op. cit.*, p.709.

[230] Schmitt, "Some Facts About 'Martin Luther' King Apparently Missed by a Wheaton College Professor," *op. cit.*, p.19.

[231] "The 'Peace' Prize That the World Gives," *The Christian World Report* (February 1991, Vol. 3, No.2), p.6.

[232] Skousen, *op. cit.*, p.21. See also: ""Bayard Rustin at Notre Dame," *op. cit.*, p.1.

[233] Schmitt, "Some Facts About 'Martin Luther' King Apparently Missed by a Wheaton College Professor," *op. cit.*, p.19. See also: Pamphlet titled "The Council of Conservative Citizens' Guide to *Martin Luther King, Jr. Holiday,"* p.6.

[234] Rivera, *op. cit.*, p.76.

[235] *Ibid.*; Epperson, *op. cit.*, p.394.

[236] Pamphlet titled "The Council of Conservative Citizens' Guide to *Martin Luther King, Jr. Holiday,"* p.3. See also: "King's Sexual Orgies," *Christian News* (January 24, 2000), p.11.

[237] "King's Sexual Orgies," *Christian News* (January 24, 2000), p.11.

[238] Texe Marrs, "The World Is More Queer Than Most People Think," *Power of Prophecy* (June 2001, Vol. 2001-06), p.3.

[239] Jesse Helms, *The King Holiday and Its Meaning* (St. Louis, MO: Council of Conservative Citizens, 1998), p.9-10.

[240] "King's Sexual Orgies," *op. cit.*

[241] *The Crisis* (October 1992, Vol. 99, No. 7), p.11.

[242] Pamphlet titled "The Council of Conservative Citizens' Guide to *Martin Luther King, Jr. Holiday,"* p.3.

[243] "Groups Endorse Homosexual March," *AFA Journal* (June 1993, Vol. 17, No. 6), p.9; Newsletter from the Voice of the Nazarene, p.1.

[244] "Groups Promoting Democratic Rights, Civil Liberties, Social Justice, Equality & Pluralism," p.7.

[245] "King Holiday a Travesty," *op. cit.*, p.1.

[246] "Quote of the Day: Former Sen. Harris Wofford," *Christian News* (January 15, 2001, Vol. 39, No. 3), p.3; "King No Role Model," *Calvary Contender* (February 15, 1998, Vol. 15, No. 4); Schmitt, "Some Facts About 'Martin Luther' King Apparently Missed by a Wheaton College Professor," *op. cit.*, p.19; "LCMS Pastors and Laymen Asking—Who Invited Neuhaus and Dawn?," *Christian News* (March 28, 1994, Vol. 32, No. 13), p.13; Schmitt, "Some Facts About 'Martin Luther' King, Jr. Ignored by the National Capital Planning Commission," *op. cit.*, p.7; Bundy, *Billy Graham: Performer?, op. cit.*, p.16; "Turret of the Times," *Christian News* (July 19, 1999, Vol. 37, No. 29), p.2; Brian Snider, "A Review Article on the 'Stand in the Gap' Promise Keepers Rally in Washington," *Christian News* (December 1, 1997, Vol. 35, No. 44), p.16; "Billy Graham's Last Scheduled International Event," *op. cit.*, p.7; "The Theology of Martin Luther King," *Christian News* (April 13, 1998, Vol. 36, No. 15), p.1, 12; Adelle M. Banks, "Struggling to Honor King in a Shifting Racial Climate," *Christian News* (January 19, 1998, Vol. 36, No. 3), p.14.

[247] "Taking the Fire out of Hell," *Christian News* (September 27, 1999, Vol. 37, No. 35), p.10.

[248] "War and Peace: The Turbulent Times of Thich Nhat Hanh," *New Age Journal* (November/December 1990, Vol. 7, Issue 6), p.45; Linda Ilene Solomon, "Village of Peace," *New Age Journal* (March/April 1992, Vol. 9, Issue 2), p.54.

[249] *Ibid.*; "EXPLORIS: Grand Opening and Connecting the Dots...," *The Florida Forum* (Summer 1999), p.11, 12; "Solstice Library," *Solstice* (May/June 1989, Issue 36), p.62; Linda Ilene Solomon, "Village of Peace," *New Age Journal* (March/April 1992, Vol. 9, Issue 2), p.54; Corinne McLaughlin and Gordon Davidson, *Spiritual Politics: Changing the World from the Inside Out* (NY: Ballantine Books, 1994), p.395; *Mindszenty Report* (March 1996, Vol. 37, No. 3), p.3.; Thich Nhat Hanh, "Every Breath You Take," *New Age Journal* (November/December 1990, Vol. 7, Issue 6), p.44; *New Call to Peacemaking: A Cooperative Program of Brethren, Friends and Mennonites* (Elkhart, Indiana, n.d.), p.7; "Gorbachev to Convene Meeting in S.F. in Fall—Invitees include Bush, Thatcher, Tutu," *San Francisco Chronicle* (February 3, 1995).

[250] Thich Nhat Hanh, "Every Breath You Take," *New Age Journal* (November/December 1990, Vol. 7, Issue 6), p.44.

[251] "EXPLORIS: Grand Opening and Connecting the Dots...," *The Florida Forum* (Summer 1999), p.12.

[252] "State of the World Forum," *Wisconsin Report* (September 21, 1995, Vol. 20, No. 36), p.3.

[253] "War and Peace, *op. cit.*, p.45.

[254] Graham, *Just As I Am, op. cit.*, p.314. See also: Ralph Reed, *Active Faith: How Christians Are Changing the Soul of American Politics* (New York, NY: Free Press, 1996), p.60; Alicia C. Shepard, "Billy Graham Goes Global in 'Capstone' of His Career," *Christian News* (February 27, 1995, Vol. 33, No. 9), p.18; Martin, *A Prophet with Honor, op. cit.*, p.234-235; Rick Miesel, "Billy Graham"; "Billy Graham and Al Gore Team Up to Save the Earth," *Flashpoint* (August 1995), p.2.

[255] Sam Wellman, *Billy Graham: The Great Evangelist* (Uhrichsville, OH: Barbour Book, 1996), p.139.

[256] Graham, *Just As I Am, op. cit.*, p.425.

[257] Briggs, *op. cit.*, p.A8; Miesel, "Billy Graham: General Teachings/Activities," *op. cit.*

[258] Martin,*A Prophet with Honor, op. cit.*, p.235. See also: Graham, *Just As I Am, op. cit.*, p.452.

[259] Bundy, *Billy Graham: Performer?, op. cit.*, p.16.

[260] Martin, *A Prophet with Honor, op. cit.*, p.272; Graham, *Just As I Am, op. cit.*, p.359.

[261] *Ibid.*, p.295. See also: "Billy Graham and Al Gore Team Up to Save the Earth," *Flashpoint* (August 1995), p.2.

[262] *Ibid.*, p.235. See also: Wellman, *op. cit.*, p.141.

[263] Ralph Reed, *Active Faith: How Christians Are Changing the Soul of American Politics* (1996) (New York, NY: Free Press, 1996), p.68. See also: Colin Greer, "'Our Task Is To Do All We Can—Not To Sit And Wait,'" *Parade* (October 20, 1996), p.4; Briggs, *op. cit.*, p.A8.

[264] Martin, *A Prophet with Honor, op. cit.*, p.233.

[265] Graham, *Just As I Am, op. cit.*, p.426.

[266] *Ibid.*, p.696.

[267] "The Christian Legacy of Martin Luther King," *Christianity Today* (June 16, 1989, Vol. 33, No. 9), p.34.

[268] Bundy, *Billy Graham: Performer?, op. cit.*, p.87; Wardner, *Unholy Alliances, op. cit.*, p.136-137; J. W. Wardner, "Billy Graham, Freemasonry & the Communists," *Despatch Magazine* (September 1998, Vol. 10, No. 3), p.28.

[269] Wardner, *Unholy Alliances, op. cit.*, p.136-137; J. W. Wardner, "Billy Graham, Freemasonry & the Communists," *Despatch Magazine* (September 1998, Vol. 10, No. 3), p.28.

[270] "Follow Up on Graham Crusade," *Christian View of the News* (November 10, 1994, Vol. 19, No. 21), p.4.

[271] *Ibid.*

[272] "Falwell's BBF Address," *Calvary Contender* (March 15, 1999, Vol. 16, No. 6).

[273] "Graham Youth Rally in Atlanta," *Calvary Contender* (January 1, 1995, Vol. 12, No. 1), p.2. See also: "Graham's Atlanta Crusade," *Calvary Contender* (November 15, 1994, Vol. 11, No. 20), p.2; "News Alert," *The Berean Call* (January 1995), p.4; "Graham Crusades Now Feature Rock Music," *Calvary Contender* (August 1, 1995), p.1; Gsell, *op. cit.*, p.44; Cloud, "Billy Graham's Disobedience to the Word of God" (Updated March 2, 1999), *op. cit.*, p.9.

[274] "News Alert," *The Berean Call* (January 1995), p.4.

[275] *Ibid.;* "Follow Up on Graham Crusade," *op. cit.*, p.4.

[276] Graham, *Just As I Am, op. cit.*, p.648.

[277] Wellman, *op. cit.*, p.205. See also: "CCM: At The Crossroads," *Calvary Contender* (April 1, 1999, Vol. 16, No. 7), p.1; "Graham's Rock Music Friends Say 'Thanks," *Calvary Contender* (August 15, 2001, Vol. 18, No. 16), p.2.

[278] "Graham Crusades Now Feature Rock Music," *Calvary Contender* (August 1, 1995), p.1.

[279] *Ibid.;* Bob Bettson, "Ailing Graham Still Draws Record Crowds," *Observer* (August 1995), p.26.

[280] Miesel, "Billy Graham: General Teachings/Activities," *op. cit.*

[281] "Graham's Unscriptural Means, Unscriptural Goal," *Calvary Contender* (March 15, 1996, Vol. 13, No. 6), p.2.

[282] "Graham Crusade in Minneapolis Breaks Attendance Records," *The Vine and Branches* (Mid-Summer 1996, Vol. 11, Issue 4), p.8.

[283] Gordon Sears, *Apostasy and Deception in Christian Music* (Coldwater, MI: Song Fest, 1998), p.35.

[284] "Food for Thought on Music," *The Day Drawing Near* (July 2000, Vol. 2, No. 2), p.3.

[285] "Graham's Music at Tampa," *Calvary Contender* (January 1, 1999, Vol. 16, No. 1), p.2.

[286] "Thousands Rock with Evangelist," *The Ledger* (November 6, 2000), p.B6.

[287] "Graham Crusade in Minneapolis Breaks Attendance Records," *op. cit.*

[288] *Ibid.*

[289] *Ibid.* See also: Gsell, *op. cit.*, p.45.

[290] Terence D. McLean, "Whatever Happened to Godly Music?," *Christian News,* quoting from the September 11, 1991 issue of the *Wall Street Journal* (September 29, 1997), p.4.

[291] *Ibid.*

[292] Jeff Godwin, *What's Wrong with Christian Rock?* (Chino, CA: Chick Publications, 1990), p.47.

[293] Jeff Godwin, *Dancing with Demons: The Music's Real Master* (Chino, CA: Chick Publications, 1988), p.251.

[294] Gsell, *op. cit.*, p.45.

[295] Jeff Godwin quoting from *Rolling Stone* in *Dancing with Demons, op. cit.*, p.334; *Ladies' Home Journal* (December 1985), p.100.

[296] *Ladies' Home Journal* (December 1985), p.100.

[297] Steve Rabey, "Christian Singer Appeals to Fans of Secular Pop Music: Is Amy Grant Sending Mixed Messages?," *Christianity Today* (November 8, 1985), p.62.

[298] Jeff Godwin quoting Amy Grant from *Ladies Home Journal* in *Dancing with Demons, op. cit.*, p.333; Texe Marrs, *The Dragon's Hot Breath: Unmasking the Awful Truth About "Christian" Rock Music* (Austin, TX: Living Truth Ministries, n.d.), p.6.

[299] "Where's the Gospel?," *Christian News* (January 11, 1999), p.23.

[300] *Ladies' Home Journal, op. cit.*

[301] "Amy Grant at 'Christian Rock Festival,'" *Calvary Contender* (March 1, 1993, Vol. 10, No. 5).

[302] Gsell, *op. cit.*, p.45.

[303] "Where's the Gospel?," *op. cit.*

[304] "Divorce Rampant Among Contemporary Christian Musicians," *Christian News* (January 15, 2001, Vol. 39, No. 3), p.3; "Amy Grant Remarries, Terry Separates," *Calvary Contender* (April 1, 2000, Vol. 17, No. 7), p.1; "Grant, Gill Marry," *Christian News* (April 3, 2000, Vol. 38, No. 14), p.8; "Amy Grant, Gary Chapman Separate," *Dallas Morning News* (January 9, 1999); "Amy Grant and Husband Separate," *Calvary Contender* (February 1, 1999, Vol. 16, No. 3), p.1.

[305] "Amy Grant at 'Christian Rock Festival,'"*op. cit.* See also: David W. Cloud, "Amy Grant Says Being Sexy Is Good," *O Timothy* (1991, Vol. 8, Issue 10-12).

[306] Gsell, *op. cit.*, p.45.

[307] *Ibid.* See also: "Where's the Gospel?," *op. cit.*

[308] "Where's the Gospel?," *op. cit.*

[309] *Ladies' Home Journal, op. cit.*, p.210; Jeff Godwin, *Dancing with Demons, op. cit.*, p.333.

[310] McLean, quoting from the May 4, 1994 issue of the *Greenville News, op. cit.*, p.4. See also: *Ladies' Home Journal, op. cit.*, p.100; "Where's the Gospel?," *op. cit.*

[311] *Ladies' Home Journal, op. cit.*, p.100.

[312] Rabey, *op. cit.*, p.62.

[313] *Ibid.*

[314] McLean, *op. cit.*

[315] *The ACCC Report* (July 1998), p.3.

[316] "Where's the Gospel?," *op. cit.*

[317] *Charisma and Christian Life* (June 1988, Vol. 13, No. 11), p.82.

[318] "Catholics 'Honor' Amy Grant," *Calvary Contender* (June 1, 1994, Vol. 11, No. 11), p.1; David W. Cloud, "Roman Catholic Church Awards Amy Grant," *O Timothy* (1994, Vol. 11, Issue 6).

[319] "Where's the Gospel?," *op. cit.* See also: Rabey, *op. cit.*, p.62; D. W. Cloud, "The Church and Its Music," *O Timothy* (1984, Vol. 1, Issue 1); David W. Cloud, "Contemporary Christian Music and the Rock Beat," *O Timothy* (1988, Vol. 5, Issue 8).

[320] John S. Torell, quoting from *The Sacramento Bee* in "Betrayal," *The Dove* (Autumn/Winter 1995, Vol. 16, No. 3), p.24-25.

[321] "DC Talk Mixes Secular & 'Sacred,'" *Calvary Contender* (September 1, 1996, Vol. 13, No. 17), p.1; John Beardsley, "DC Talk Examined," *The Christian Conscience* (June 1996, Vol. 2, No. 6), p.54.

[322] *Ibid.* See also: John Beardsley, "DC Talk Examined," *The Christian Conscience* (June 1996, Vol. 2, No. 6), p.55.

[323] John Beardsley, "DC Talk Examined," *The Christian Conscience* (June 1996, Vol. 2, No. 6), p.55.

[324] *Ibid.*, p.57.

[325] Gsell, *op. cit.*, p.44.

[326] "Graham's Music at Tampa," *op. cit.*

[327] *Last Trumpet Newsletter* (April 2001, Vol. 20, Issue 4), p.4.

[328] Gsell, *op. cit.*, p.45.

[329] "Graham Draws Many Back to Christ, Church," *Christian News* (November 15, 1999), p.17.

[330] "Graham's Nashville Crusade," *Calvary Contender* (July 15, 2000, Vol. 17, No. 14), p.2.

[331] "Graham's Music at Tampa," *op. cit.*

[332] "Graham's Quebec Crusade Unites English Protestants, French Catholics," *Calvary Contender* (September 1, 1998, Vol. 15, No. 17), p.2.

[333] "Thousands Rock with Evangelist," *op. cit.*

[334] "Jars of Clay," *Calvary Contender* (February 15, 1998, Vol. 15, No. 4), p.1.

[335] *Ibid.* See also: "Jars of Clay at Creation 97," *Calvary Contender* (February 15, 1997, Vol. 14, No. 4), p.1.

[336] "Jars of Clay No Christian Band," *Calvary Contender* (September 15, 1998, Vol. 15, No. 18), p.1.

[337] *Ibid.*

[338] Graham, *Just As I Am, op. cit.*, p.675; Jim Jones, "Billy Graham's Organization in Good Hands—His Son's," *The News and Observer* (December 8, 2000), p.2F. See also: "Graham Meetings," *Calvary Contender* (January 15, 2001, Vol. 18, No. 2), p.2; "Billy Graham Takes Failing Health in Stride, Plans More Crusades Next Year," *The News and Observer* (November 1, 2000), p.11A; "BBF Gives Graham Book to Preachers," *Calvary Contender* (April 1, 1999, Vol. 16, No. 7), p.2; "Franklin Graham Named CEO of His Father's Evangelical Association," *The Vine and Branches* (Winter 2001, Vol. 16, Issue 1), p.10; Christine Wicker, "The Son Also Rises: Franklin Graham to Preach at First Baptist Church," *The Dallas Morning News*, p.1G; "Franklin Graham to Speak at Liberty," *Calvary Contender* (May 1, 1996, Vol. 23, No. 9), p.2; "People and Events," *Moody* (January-February 2001, Vol. 101, No. 3), p.38; "Franklin Graham Named CEO of Father's Evangelical Association," *Christian News* (November 27, 2000, Vol. 38, No. 44), p.2; Gsell, *op. cit.*, p.46; Adelle M. Banks, "Graham Ministry Spans Half a Century," *Christian News* (May 13, 1996, Vol. 34, No. 20), p.6; "The Prodigal Graham," *New Man* (October 1996, Vol. 3, No. 7), p.12; Wellman, *op. cit.*, p.205.

[339] "Franklin Graham's Ecumenical Festivals," *Voice in the Wilderness* (December 2000), p.14.

[340] Gsell, *op. cit.*, p.46.

[341] David W. Cloud, *Mom and Dad Sleep While the Children Rock in Satan's Cradle* (Oak Harbor, WA: Way of Life Literature, 1991 Edition).

[342] Bundy, *Billy Graham: Performer?, op. cit.*, p.66, 69.

[343] *Ibid.*, p.122.

[344] "BWA Ecumenism," *Calvary Contender* (August 15, 1998, Vol. 15, No. 16).

[345] Eleanor Clift and Elizabeth Ann Leonard, "Playing a Losing Game?," *Newsweek* (May 4, 1992), p.29.

[346] *Now Is the Dawning of the New Age New World Order, op. cit.*, p.269; "Transformation Toward New Age Synthesis," *Distant Drums* (March 1986, Vol. 8, No. 1), p.2; *Secret Records Revealed, op. cit.*, p.131-132; Letter from Planetary Citizens dated April 17, 1985; Letter from Planetary Citizens dated January 1987; Letter from Planetary Citizens dated September 1989; *Global 2000: An Interview with Mr. and Mrs. William Bowen* (Oklahoma City, OK: Southwest Radio Church, 1984), p.44.

[347] "The Open Conspiracy," *Don Bell Reports* (February 21, 1986, Vol. 33, No. 8), p.3.

[348] Catalog from Option Institute (1992), p.1. See also: Catalog from Option Institute (2000), p.6.

[349] Letter from SANE; Brochure from SANE, p.6; Letter from Coalition for a New Foreign Policy; *New Age Journal* (September/October 1987, Vol. 3, Issue 5), p.86.

[350] *The Prophecy Newsletter* (1985, Vol. 1, No. 5), p.6. See also: *Distant Drums* (November 1989, Vol. 11, No. 3), p.8.

[351] Andrew Pollack, "Moon's Church Tied to Bush Sponsor," *The Oregonian* (September 4, 1995), p.A14.

[352] Fritz Springmeier, *Bloodlines of the Illuminati* (Westminster, CO: Ambassador House, 1999), p.221.

[353] "Two United Methodist Leaders Close to MLK Welcome Verdict," *Christian News* (January 1, 2000, Vol. 38, No. 1), p.7.

[354] Cynthia Tucker, "Jackson Needs a Leave of Absence," *Christian News* (February 12, 2001, Vol. 39, No. 7), p.20.

[355] "EXPLORIS, *op. cit.*, p.11, 12; "NCC, Young Find No Persecution in China," *Calvary Contender* (January 15, 1999, Vol. 16, No. 2), p.1; "Champions of Mental Health," *Psychology Today* (June 2001, Vol. 34, No. 3), p.51; Declaration of World Thanksgiving 1993; "The ICCRE Family: News from Around the Country," *The Spirit of the Earth* (Fall 1995, Vol. 3, No. 2), p.2; "Disrespect for Traditional Religion," *op. cit.*, p.5; Robert Gaylon Ross, Sr., *Who's Who of the Elite* (San Marcos, TX: RIE, 1995), p.108; Buhle, Buhle, and Georgakas, *op. cit.*, p.140.

[356] *Ibid.;* Gary Allen *Jimmy Carter, Jimmy Carter* (Seal Beach, CA: '76 Press, 1976), p.22.

[357] *Ibid.;* Brochure from The National Peace Institute Foundation; Brochure from Habitat for Humanity.

[358] "Disrespect for Traditional Religion," *op. cit.*, p.5.

[359] *Council on Foreign Relations: Annual Report July 1, 1990-June 30, 1991,* p.194; *Council on Foreign Relations: Annual Report July 1, 1987-June 30, 1988,* p.187; *Council on Foreign Relations: Annual Report July 1, 1992-June 30, 1993,* p.179; *Council on Foreign Relations: Annual Report July 1, 1994-June 30, 1995,* p.159; Robert Gaylon Ross, Sr., *Who's Who of the Elite* (San Marcos, TX: RIE, 1995), p.108.

[360] Robert Gaylon Ross, Sr., *Who's Who of the Elite* (San Marcos, TX: RIE, 1995), p.108; Marrs, *Rule by Secrecy, op. cit.*, p.26.

[361] Texe Marrs, *Dark Majesty: The Secret Brotherhood and the Magic of a Thousand Points of Light* (Austin, TX: Living Truth Publishers, 1992), p.28. See also: Marrs, *Rule by Secrecy, op. cit.*, p.30; Don McAlvany, *Confronting Our Nation's Problems: The Financial, Political, and Spiritual Decline of America* (Oklahoma City, OK: Southwest Radio Church, n.d.), p.16.

[362] El-Amin, *op. cit.*, p.x, 67.

[363] Brochure from the National Peace Institute Foundation.

[364] Brochure from Habitat for Humanity.

[365] "Habitat for Humanity a Global Religion," *Calvary Contender* (January 1, 1997, Vol. 14, No. 1), p.1; William Braun, Sr., "Habitat's Cash Cow," *Christian Conscience* (July/August 1997, Vol. 3, No. 6), p.8; "Falwell Lends a Hand to Habitat," *Calvary Contender* (November 1, 1999, Vol. 16, No. 21), p.2; Marsha Hamilton and Judith Couchman, "Building Houses with Love," *Christian Life* (May 1987, Vol. 49, No. 1), p.36; "Schuller Has Catholic Speaker," *Calvary Contender* (November 15, 1998, Vol. 15, No. 24), p.2; John L. Palmer, "Vision 2013 and Habitat for Humanity in Tennessee," *The Scottish Rite Journal* (June 1998, Vol. 106, No. 6), p.50; Karen Jenkins, "Home at Last: Habitat Offers the Ultimate Hospitality," *World Christian* (September/October 1987, Vol. 6, No. 5), p.36; "NAE '96 Speakers," *Calvary Contender* (March 1, 1996, Vol. 13, No. 5), p.2; "New Liberal Religious/Political Group Deplores 'False Choices,' Redefines Evangelism," *Christian News* (July 1, 1996, Vol. 34, No. 27), p.23; "Habitat for Humanity Promotes Ecumenical Movement," *Calvary Contender* (December 1, 1994, Vol. 11, No. 21), p.1; Brochure from Habitat for Humanity; "Eastern College," *Calvary Contender* (May 15, 1997, Vol. 14, No. 10), p.2; *Mindszenty Report* (March 1996, Vol. 37, No. 3), p.2; "Habitat for Humanity Is About Money," *Calvary Contender* (September 1, 1997), p.1; Brochure from Renovare (Received November 12, 1996), p.12.

[366] "Habitat for Humanity Promotes Ecumenical Movement," *Calvary Contender* (December 1, 1994, Vol. 11, No. 21), p.1; "Habitat for Humanity a Global Religion," *Calvary Contender* (January 1, 1997, Vol. 14, No. 1), p.1.

[367] "Habitat for Humanity, NCC Join Hands," *Christian Century* (April 11, 2001, Vol. 118, No. 12), p.9. See also: "NCC, Habitat Form New Partnership," *Calvary Contender* (July 15, 2001, Vol. 18, No. 14), p.1.

[368] *Ibid.* See also: Kevin Eckstrom, "NCC, Habitat for Humanity, Launch Partnership," *Christian News* (June 18, 2001, Vol. 39, No. 25), p.21.

[369] "Habitat for Humanity, NCC Join Hands," *op. cit.*

[370] Robert P. Mills, "Habitat for Humanity Builds on Christian Foundations," *The Presbyterian Layman* (March/April 2001, Vol. 34, No. 2), p.11.

[371] "Habitat for Humanity Promotes Ecumenical Movement," *op. cit.*

[372] John L. Palmer, "Vision 2013 and Habitat for Humanity in Tennessee," *The Scottish Rite Journal* (June 1998, Vol. 106, No. 6), p.50.

[373] William Braun, Sr., "Habitat's Cash Cow," *Christian Conscience* (July/August 1997, Vol. 3, No. 6), p.8; "Habitat for Humanity Is About Money," *Calvary Contender* (September 1, 1997), p.1.

[374] "Habitat for Humanity Is About Money," *Calvary Contender* (September 1, 1997), p.1.

[375] "Falwell Lends a Hand to Habitat," *Calvary Contender* (November 1, 1999, Vol. 16, No. 21), p.2.

[376] "Groups Represented," *World Goodwill Newsletter* (1988, No. 4), p.8.

[377] *Green Cross* (Winter 1995, Vol. 1, No. 2), p.2; *Green Cross* (Summer 1995, Vol. 1, No. 3), p.3; *Green Cross* (Winter 1996, Vol. 2, No. 1), p.3.

[378] "New Liberal Religious/Political Group Deplores 'False Choices,' Redefines Evangelism," *Christian News* (July 1, 1996, Vol. 34, No. 27), p.23; *Mindszenty Report* (March 1996, Vol. 37, No. 3), p.2; "The Cry for Renewal: Biblical Faith and Spiritual Politics" (May 23, 1995), p.3.

[379] David C. Kanz, *The New Global Missions Agenda: InterVarsity Christian Fellowship and New Age Politics* (Oak Creek, WI: Logos Communication Consortium, 1996), unnumbered page. See also: "Karen Burton Mains," *Bold Truth* (October 1995), p.4.

[380] Laurie Goodstein, "Christian Leaders Counter Religious Right," *Philadelphia Inquirer* (May 24, 1995). See also: "Sojourners Forms Coalition," *Call to Action News* (March-April 1996, Vol. 18, No. 1), p.2.

[381] *Ibid.;* Jim Wallis, "Biblical Faith and Spiritual Politics," *The Cry for Renewal: Biblical Faith and Spiritual Politics* (May 23, 1995), p.2; "People of Faith: A Call to Action" (Received September 3, 1996), p.1, 2; "New Liberal Religious/ Political Group Deplores 'False Choices,'" *op. cit.,* p.23; Kanz, *op. cit.;* Albert James Dager, "The World Christian Movement—Part 3: Toward the New World Order," *Media Spotlight* (1999, Vol. 22, No. 3), p.7; "Christian Witnessing to an Alternative," *The Witness* (November 1996, Vol. 79, No. 11), p.11.

[382] "Wallis Revitalizes Social Activism," *Calvary Contender* (July 1, 1997, Vol. 14, No. 13), p.2.

[383] Ron Goldwyn, "Clinton's Spiritual Adviser Feeling Fallout from Scandal," *Philadelphia Daily News* (April 9, 1999), p.3; "Moralphobic," *Christian News* (November 11, 1991, Vol. 29, No. 41), p.11; Texe Marrs, "Heroism and Cowardice in the Lion's Den," *Flashpoint* (April 1994), p.1; "Liberal Who Parades As Evangelical," *The Perilous Times* (July 1999, Vol. 21, No. 5). See also: "New Liberal Religious/Political Group Deplores 'False Choices,'" *op. cit.,* p.23.

[384] Tom Watson, *The Evangelical Eroding of the Deity of Christ* (Southlake, TX: Countryside Bible Church, 1996), p.25.

[385] Texe Marrs, *Power of Prophecy* program.

[386] John Lofton, "Tony Campolo's Wife Says We Should 'Celebrate' Homosexual Marriages and That Our Lord Violated God's Law!," *Christian News* (April 11, 1994, Vol. 32, No. 15), p.19.

[387] *Ibid.;* David W. Cloud, "The Preachers Who Influenced Bill Clinton," *Christian News* (March 26, 2001, Vol. 39, No. 13), p.17; "Mrs. Tony Compolo (sic) Promotes Homosexual Weddings," *Christian News* (September 26, 1994, Vol. 32, No. 35), p.6.

[388] Watson, *op. cit.,* p.25; David W. Cloud, "The Preachers Who Influenced Bill Clinton," *Christian News* (March 26, 2001, Vol. 39, No. 13), p.17.

[389] Texe Marrs, "Has the Entire Christian Establishment Finally Just Gone Berserk?," *Power of Prophecy* (April 2001, Vol. 2001-04), p.1; David W. Cloud, "The Preachers Who Influenced Bill Clinton," *Christian News* (March 26, 2001, Vol. 39, No. 13), p.17. See also: "Campolo: Clinton's 'Socialist' Friend," *Calvary Contender* (May 15, 1994, Vol. 11, No. 10), p.1.

[390] Goldwyn, *op. cit.,* p.3; Texe Marrs, "Heroism and Cowardice in the Lion's Den," *Flashpoint* (April 1994), p.1; "Tony Campolo Excoriates Religious Right," *Christian News* (December 19, 1994, Vol. 32, No. 47), p.19.

[391] Texe Marrs, "Heroism and Cowardice in the Lion's Den," *Flashpoint* (April 1994), p.1.

[392] Ashbrook, *op. cit.,* p.52; Dave Hunt, "'Stand Fast in the Faith' I Corinthians 16:13," *Berean Call* (December 1994), p.1; "Campolo's Confusing Attempt to Clarify," *Calvary Contender* (October 1, 1999, Vol. 16, No. 19), p.2; "Campolo Teaches 'Socialism' to So. Baptist Teens," *Calvary Contender* (March 15, 1992, Vol. 9, No. 6), p.2.

[393] *Ibid.,* p.52-53; "Campolo Teaches 'Socialism' to So. Baptist Teens," *Christian News* (October 19, 1992, Vol. 30, No. 38), p.2; Dave Hunt, "'Stand Fast in the Faith' I Corinthians 16:13," *Berean Call* (December 1994).

[394] *CIB Bulletin* (January 1991, Vol. 7, No. 1), p.2. See also: "Campolo Teaches 'Socialism' to So. Baptist Teens," *Christian News* (October 19, 1992, Vol. 30, No. 38), p.2; Joe Schimmel, "Sweet to the Ears—Deadly to the Soul," *CIB Bulletin* (October/November 1992, Vol. 8, No. 10), p.3; "Campolo Teaches 'Socialism' to So. Baptist Teens," *Calvary Contender* (March 15, 1992, Vol. 9, No. 6), p.2.

[395] "News Briefs," *CIB Bulletin* (December 1989, Vol. 5, No. 12), p.4. See also: David W. Cloud, "The Preachers Who Influenced Bill Clinton," *Christian News* (March 26, 2001, Vol. 39, No. 13), p.17.

[396] Marrs, "Has the Entire Christian Establishment Finally Just Gone Berserk?," *op. cit.* See also: "Gone Berserk," *Power of Prophecy* (May 2001, Vol. 2001-05), p.6.

[397] Ashbrook, *op. cit.,* p.53; Dave Hunt, "'Stand Fast in the Faith' I Corinthians 16:13," *Berean Call* (December 1994). See also: "Campolo Won't Say Jesus Only Way to Heaven," *Calvary Contender* (August 15, 1999, Vol. 16, No. 16), p.2; "Campolo Reaffirms Belief in Universalist Theology, Cites Graham to Support His Position," *Foundation* (November-December 1999), p.41; "Campolo Won't Say Jesus Only Way to Heaven," *Prophecy Corner and the Nosh Box* (August 1999, Vol. 4, Issue 8); Transcript from the Charlie Rose Show (Received February 8, 1997).

[398] "Campolo's Confusing Attempt to Clarify," *Calvary Contender* (October 1, 1999, Vol. 16, No. 19), p.2; "Campolo Reaffirms Belief in Universalist Theology, Cites Graham to Support His Position," *Foundation* (November-December 1999), p.41.

[399] See: Ashbrook, *op. cit.,* p.54; Watson, *op. cit.,* p.25.

[400] *Ibid.*

[401] Personal phone conversation on September 6, 1994.

[402] Personal phone conversation on August 8, 1994.

[403] Tony Campolo, *How to Rescue the Earth Without Worshiping Nature* (Nashville, TN: Thomas Nelson Publishers, 1992), Inside Front Cover, p.ix, x, 6, 52-56, 59-60, 130, 140-141, 151, 159, etc.; "Liberal Who Parades As Evangelical," *The Perilous Times* (July 1999, Vol. 21, No. 5); Marrs, "Heroism and Cowardice in the Lion's Den," *op. cit.*

[404] *Ibid.*, p.6, 55.

[405] "Campolo Teaches 'Socialism' to So. Baptist Teens," *Calvary Contender* (March 15, 1992, Vol. 9, No. 6), p.2; "Campolo Teaches 'Socialism' to So. Baptist Teens," *Christian News* (October 19, 1992, Vol. 30, No. 38), p.2; "Book Review," *Christian News* (October 28, 1991, Vol. 29, No. 39), p.20.

[406] Campolo, *How to Rescue the Earth, op. cit.*, p.140-141. See also: Brenda Scott and Samantha Smith, *Trojan Horse: How the New Age Movement Infiltrates the Church* (Lafayette, LA: Huntington House Publishers, 1993), p.66.

[407] *Ibid.*, p.60. See also: Larry Spargimino, "Fido, Come Forth!," *Prophetic Observer* (April 2001, Vol. 8, No. 4), p.1.

[408] *Ibid.* p.130.

[409] "Campolo Teaches 'Socialism' to So. Baptist Teens," *Calvary Contender, op. cit.*; "Book Review," *Christian News* (October 28, 1991, Vol. 29, No. 39), p.20; "Campolo Teaches 'Socialism' to So. Baptist Teens," *Christian News* (October 19, 1992, Vol. 30, No. 38), p.2.

[410] *Ibid.*; "Campolo Teaches 'Socialism' to So. Baptist Teens," *Christian News* (October 19, 1992, Vol. 30, No. 38), p.2.

[411] Ashbrook, *op. cit.*, p.54.

[412] *Ibid.*, p.52, 54; "Campolo Teaches 'Socialism' to So. Baptist Teens," *Calvary Contender, op. cit.*; "Campolo Teaches 'Socialism' to So. Baptist Teens," *Christian News* (October 19, 1992, Vol. 30, No. 38), p.2.

[413] *Ibid.*, p.54; "Book Review," *Christian News* (October 28, 1991, Vol. 29, No. 39), p.20.

[414] Kanz, *op. cit.*

[415] *Ibid.*

[416] Brochure from Call to Renewal (Received August 28, 1996).

[417] Goodstein, *op. cit.*

[418] "Billy Graham's Amsterdam 2000: A Special First-Hand Report by Ralph Colas," *Calvary Contender* (August 15, 2000, Vol. 17, No. 16).

[419] Goodstein, *op. cit.*; *The Cry for Renewal: Biblical Faith and Spiritual Politics* (May 23, 1995), p.2; "Karen Burton Mains," *Bold Truth* (October 1995), p.4; Paul Fisher, "A Syndicated Conspiracy Against God and Man?," *The Observer* (January 17, 1996), p.13; Albert James Dager, "The World Christian Movement—Part 3: Toward the New World Order," *Media Spotlight* (1999, Vol. 22, No. 3), p.7.

[420] Allen, *The Rockefeller File, op. cit.*, p.79; Myron Fagan, Transcript of "Illuminati and the Council on Foreign Relations"; Rivera, *op. cit.*, p.100-101; Gary Allen, *C. F. R.: Conspiracy to Rule the World* (n.p., n.d.), p.20.

[421] "Terrorism and the Moral Majority" (Brochure from The Couples Learning Center advertising a meeting which was held on December 1, 1981), p.8-9.

[422] *Now Is the Dawning of the New Age New World Order, op. cit.*, p.250-251; William T. Still, *New World Order: The Ancient Plan of Secret Societies* (Lafayette, LA: Huntington House, Inc., 1990), p.188; Rivera, *op. cit.*, p.170; Ralph G. Griffin, "Bush Heralds a 'New World Order,'" *The Christian World Report* (March 1991, Vol. 3, No. 3), p.8.

[423] *Secret Records Revealed, op. cit.*, p.104.

[424] "Billy Graham to Get Award in Charlotte," *The News and Observer* (February 1, 1990), p.4B).

[425] Declaration of World Thanksgiving 1993.

[426] Brochure from The Better World Society entitled "Harnessing the Power of Television to Make a Better World," p.5.

[427] Wanda Marrs, *New Age Lies to Women* (Austin, TX: Living Truth Publishers, 1989), p.40. See also: Texe Marrs, *Millennium: Peace, Promises, and the Day They Take Our Money Away* (Austin, TX: Living Truth Publishers, 1990), p.40-41; "Goodwill Games and Ted Turner," *Despatch Magazine* (March 2001, Vol. 13, No. 1), p.26.

[428] *Ibid.*

[429] Brochure from the Better World Society entitled "Increase and Multiply."

[430] Chambers, *op. cit.*, p.430, 432.

[431] Brochure from SANE/FREEZE, p.6.

[432] Letter from Americans for Democratic Action, Inc., dated April 21, 1988).

[433] C. H. 'Max' Freedman, "Hatchet-Job on Wildmon Shows Moral Bankruptcy of His Foes," *AFA Journal* (October 1990, Vol. 14, No. 9), p.12; *"Secret Records" Revealed, op. cit.*, p.23; *Secret Records Revealed, op. cit.*, p.73; Chambers, *op. cit.*, p.63, 239; Enrique Rueda, *The Homosexual Network: Private Lives and Public Policy* (Old Greenwich, CT: The Devin Adair Company, 1982), p.411; John A. Stormer, *None Dare Call It Treason* (Florissant, MO: Liberty Bell Press, 1964), p.146.

[434] Letter from Coalition for a New Foreign Policy; John A. Stormer, *None Dare Call It Treason* (Florissant, MO: Liberty Bell Press, 1964), p.146.

[435] Enrique Rueda, *The Homosexual Network: Private Lives and Public Policy* (Old Greenwich, CT: The Devin Adair

Company, 1982), p.411.

[436] Wardner, quoting the *Los Angeles Times* in *Unholy Alliances, op. cit.*, p.155.

[437] "NCC, Young Find No Persecution in China," *Calvary Contender* (January 15, 1999, Vol. 16, No. 2), p.1; "Big Severance Package to NCC's Former Leader," *Calvary Contender* (July 1, 2001, Vol. 18, No. 13), p.2; "Disrespect for Traditional Religion," *op. cit.*, p.13; Richard N. Ostling, "National Council of Churches Falls upon Hard Times," *Christian News* (November 29, 1999, Vol. 37, No. 44), p.7; "Andy Young Is New President of NCC?," *Calvary Contender* (February 15, 1998, Vol. 15, No. 4), p.1; "NRB Cuts Ties with NAE," *Calvary Contender* (March 1, 2001, Vol. 18, No. 5), p.2; "National Council of Churches Turns to Evangelicals and Roman Catholics," *The Vine and Branches* (2000, Vol. 15, Issue 5), p.13; "NCC: New Leaders, New Woes," *Calvary Contender* (December 1, 1999, Vol. 16, No. 23), p.2; Letter from Noah W. Hutchings dated June 2000.

[438] *Ibid.*

[439] *Council on Foreign Relations: Annual Report July 1, 1994-June 30, 1995,* p.106.

[440] *Council on Foreign Relations: Annual Report July 1, 1992-June 30, 1993,* p.160; *Council on Foreign Relations: Annual Report July 1, 1994-June 30, 1995,* p.140.

[441] Texe Marrs, *Days of Hunger, Days of Chaos: The Coming Great Food Shortages* (Austin, TX: RiverCrest Publishing, 1999), p.109; *Wisconsin Report* (September 21, 1995, Vol. 20, No. 36), p.3.

[442] *Now Is the Dawning of the New Age New World Order, op. cit.*, p.331.

[443] Marrs, *Days of Hunger, Days of Chaos, op. cit.*, p.109-110.

[444] "Disrespect for Traditional Religion," *op. cit.*, p.13.

[445] "Methodist Church to Remain in NCC," *The Vine and Branches* (Summer 2000, Vol. 15, Issue 3), p.12.

[446] Tucker Carlson, "Fidel's National Council of Churches," *The Schwarz Report* (June 2000, Vol. 40, No. 6), p.5-6. See also: "Elian Revisited," *Prophetic Observer* (March 2001, Vol. 8, No. 3), p.3.

[447] "Methodist Church to Remain in NCC," *op. cit.*

[448] Letter from Noah W. Hutchings dated June 2000. See also: "Elian Revisited," *Prophetic Observer* (March 2001, Vol. 8, No. 3), p.3. See also: "Disrespect for Traditional Religion," *op. cit.*, p.13.

[449] "NCC, Young Find No Persecution in China," *op. cit.; Calvary Contender* "Andy Young Is New President of NCC?" (February 15, 1998, Vol. 15, No. 4), p.1.

[450] Des Griffin, *Fourth Reich of the Rich* (South Pasadena, CA: Emissary Publications, 1978), p.112.

[451] "NCC Turns to Evangelicals, Catholics for Financial Help," *Calvary Contender* (September 15, 2000), p.2; "National Council of Churches Turns to Evangelicals and Roman Catholics," *The Vine and Branches* (2000, Vol. 15, Issue 5), p.13.

[452] Frady, *op. cit.*, p.3.

[453] Gary Allen *Jimmy Carter, Jimmy Carter* (Seal Beach, CA: '76 Press, 1976), p.22. See also: Helms, *op. cit.*, p.24; Buhle, Buhle, and Georgakas, *op. cit.*, p.140.

[454] This was taken from "Back Billy Graham?—Californian Baptist Pastor says No" by Roland Rasmussen, published in the "Sword of the Lord," October 18, 1963 (quoting from the September 1962 issue of *Decision,* p.15.

[455] Bundy, *Billy Graham: Performer?, op. cit.*, p.135.

[456] *Ibid.*, p.139.

[457] *Ibid.*, p.149. See also: Billy Graham, *Approaching Hoofbeats: The Four Horsemen of the Apocalypse* (Minneapolis, MN: Grason, 1983), p.133; Graham, *Just As I Am, op. cit.*, p.499-502; Wilson Ewin, *The Emerging 666 Peace and the Abolition of Nuclear War* (n.p., 1984), p.18; D. W. Cloud, "Some Frightening Facts About Billy Graham," *O Timothy* (1984, Vol. 1, Issue 4).

[458] Dave Hunt, "What's Happening to the Faith?," *The Berean Call* (May 1998), p.1.

[459] Dave Hunt, *Beyond Seduction: A Return to Biblical Christianity* (Eugene, OR: Harvest House Publishers, 1987), p.199.

[460] Dave Hunt and T. A. McMahon, *The Seduction of Christianity: Spiritual Discernment in the Last Days* (Eugene, OR: Harvest House Publishers, 1985), p.16.

[461] "Billy Kim a Friend of Cho," *Calvary Contender* (April 1, 1993, Vol. 10, No. 7), p.2; Martin and Deidre Bobgan, *Hypnosis: Medical, Scientific, or Occultic* (Santa Barbara, CA: EastGate Publishers, 2001), p.28.

[462] Hunt, "What's Happening to the Faith?," *op. cit.*, p.1; "May Is the Month of 100th Birthday!!!," *Powerlines* (May 1998), p.3; *Media Spotlight* (Vol. 20, No. 2), p.25; "Hybels Featured at Schuller Meeting," *Calvary Contender* (February 15, 2001, Vol. 18, No. 4), p.2; Albert James Dager, *The World Christian Movement: A Great Delusion Leading to the Religio-Political State of the Anti-Christ* (Redmond, WA: Sword Publishers, 2001), p.75.

[463] "The Theology of Robert Schuller," *Christian News* (January 22, 2001, Vol. 39, No. 4), p.6; David W. Cloud, "Norman Vincent Peale: Apostle of Self-Esteem," *Christian News* (May 12, 1997, Vol. 35, No. 19), p.10.

[464] Hunt, "What's Happening to the Faith?," *op. cit.*, p.1.

[465] "Hybels Featured at Schuller Meeting," *Calvary Contender* (February 15, 2001, Vol. 18, No. 4), p.2.

[466] *The BDM Letter* (October 1993, Vol. 2, No. 8), p.2-3.

[467] Ankerberg and Weldon, quoting from *A Course in Miracles, op. cit.*, p.22.

[468] *Ibid.*

[469] Robert H. Schuller, *Self-Esteem: The New Reformation* (Waco, TX: Word Books, 1982), p.68. See also: David W. Cloud, "Evangelicals and Modernist Robert Schuller," *O Timothy* (1993, Vol. 10, Issue 7); "Schuler (sic) and Gorbachev," *Christian News* (January 22, 2001, Vol. 39, No. 4), p.9.

[470] *Ibid.*, p.69.

[471] Ankerberg and Weldon, *op. cit.*, p.22.

[472] Robert Schuller, quoted in *CIB Bulletin* (July 1987, Vol. 3, No. 7), p.4; "Schuler (sic) and Gorbachev," *Christian News* (January 22, 2001, Vol. 39, No. 4), p.9; "The Templeton Prize for Religious Excellence," *Despatch Magazine* (June 2001, Vol. 13:2), p.48.

[473] Texe Marrs, quoting William Warch in *Mystery Mark of the New Age: Satan's Design for World Domination* (Westchester, IL: Crossway Books, 1988), p.207.

[474] Berit Kjos, *A Twist of Faith* (Green Forest, AR: New Leaf Press, 1997), p.173, 201.

[475] Schuller, *op. cit.*, p.14-15. See also: David W. Cloud, "Evangelicals and Modernist Robert Schuller," *O Timothy* (1993, Vol. 10, Issue 7); "Speakers at Schuller's Institute," *Christian News* (March 19, 2001, Vol. 39, No. 12), p.2.

[476] *Ibid.* p.26-27.

[477] *Ibid.* p.135.

[478] *Ibid.* p.38.

[479] *Ibid.* p.98.

[480] *Ibid.* p.119.

[481] Joseph P. Gudel, "A New Reformation?: The Faulty Gospel of Robert Schuller," *Passport Magazine* (January-February 1988), p.9.

[482] David W. Cloud, "Evangelicals and Modernist Robert Schuller," *O Timothy* (1993, Vol. 10, Issue 7).

[483] "Flight Attendant to Sue Schuller," *Calvary Contender* (October 15, 1997, Vol. 14, No. 20), p.2.

[484] *Ibid.* See also: Texe Marrs, "Global Explosion of Religious Apostasy," *Flashpoint* (July 1998, Vol. 98-7), p.1; "Shame, Shame on the Christian Establishment," World of Prophecy (October 11, 1997); "United Flight Attendant to Sue Schuller for $5 Million," *Christian News* (September 15, 1997, Vol. 35, No. 33), p.11.

[485] *Ibid.*

[486] Hunt, "What's Happening to the Faith?," *op. cit.*, p.1.

[487] Rick Miesel, "Robert Schuller" (Biblical Discernment Ministries); Cloud, "Evangelicals and Modernist Robert Schuller," *op. cit.*

[488] "Schuller and Rome," *Christian News* (October 9, 2000, Vol. 38, No. 37), p.8.

[489] Cloud, "Evangelicals and Modernist Robert Schuller," *op. cit.*

[490] Hunt, "What's Happening to the Faith?," *op. cit.*, p.1. See also: Albert James Dager, *The World Christian Movement: A Great Delusion Leading to the Religio-Political State of the Anti-Christ* (Redmond, WA: Sword Publishers, 2001), p.75.

[491] "Don't Call Schuller a Christian," *Prophecy Corner and the Nosh Box* (August 1999, Vol. 4, Issue 8).

[492] Hunt, "What's Happening to the Faith?," *op. cit.*, p.1; *The Berean Call* (April 1998), p.4; "Well Hello, Dalai," *Endtime* (September/October 1999), p.28; "Christians and Muslims for Peace," *Endtime* (September/October 1999), p.28-29.

[493] *Ibid.; The Berean Call* (April 1998), p.4; "Schuler (sic) and Gorbachev," *Christian News* (January 22, 2001, Vol. 39, No. 4), p.9.

[494] "More in Common Then (sic) You Think," *The Voice in the Wilderness* (November 1999), p.8.

[495] *Ibid.*

[496] "Christians and Muslims for Peace," *Endtime* (September/October 1999), p.29.

[497] Abdul Jalil, "25 Most Frequently Asked Questions about Islam" (Received October 14, 1995), p.3.

[498] Paper from PIOUS, p.9.

[499] *Ibid.*, p.15. See also: Lionel Luckhoo, *The Quran Is Not the Word of God* (Dallas, TX: Luckhoo Ministries, n.p.), p.1-2, 4.

[500] *An American Commentary* (Oklahoma City, OK: Hearthstone Publishing, Ltd., 1993), p.4.

[501] "Billy Graham: Fellowship with Apostasy," *op. cit.*, p.2; Bay, *op. cit.*, p.4; Miesel, "Billy Graham: General Teachings/Activities," *op. cit.*

[502] "Evangelicals and Catholics: Coming Together," *The Day Drawing Near* (March 1999, Vol. 1, No. 6), p.2.

[503] "Robert Schuller Addressed 15,000 Muslim at the Abou Nour Mosque," *Foundation* (January-February 2000, Vol. 21, Issue 1), p.45.

[504] *Ibid.*

[505] Dave Hunt, "A New Christianity," *The Berean Call* (February 2000), p.1.

[506] *Ibid.*

[507] *Ibid.*

[508] *Ibid.*

[509] *Ibid.*

[510] "Schuller Speaks for Moonies, Mormons," *Calvary Contender* (January 1, 1999, Vol. 16, No. 1), p.1. See also: Hunt and McMahon, *The Seduction of Christianity, op. cit.*, p.152. "Schuller, Mother Teresa, and the New Age," *O Timothy* (Vol. 11, Issue 2, 1994); Marrs, "Has the Entire Christian Establishment Finally Just Gone Berserk?," *op. cit.*, p.2.

[511] "Schuler (sic) and Gorbachev," *Christian News* (January 22, 2001, Vol. 39, No. 4), p.9.

[512] David W. Cloud, "Flirting with Rome: Evangelical Entanglement with Roman Catholicism," quoting from *Calvary Contender* in *O Timothy* (1993); D. W. Cloud, "Papal Supremacy," *O Timothy* (1987, Vol. 4, Issue 7); "Schuller Promotes Pope and Comrade," *Omega-Letter* (March 1988, Vol. 3, No. 3), p.15.

[513] *Ibid.*, quoting from *Foundation;* D. W. Cloud, "Papal Supremacy," *O Timothy* (1987, Vol. 4, Issue 7); "Shame, Shame on the Christian Establishment," World of Prophecy (October 11, 1997).

[514] "Schuller Meets with Cho and Pope," *Calvary Contender* (August 15, 1998, Vol. 15, No. 16), p.2.

[515] *Ibid.*

[516] Constance Cumbey, *A Planned Deception: The Staging of a New Age "Messiah"* (East Detroit, MI: Pointe Publishing, Inc., 1985), p.109. See also: Frances Adeney, 'Re-Visioning' Reality," *SCP Newsletter* (June-July 1981, Vol. 7, No. 2), p.3; Wardner, *Unholy Alliances, op. cit.*, p.205.

[517] "Schuller Rides High," *The Omega-Letter* (July 1989, Vol. 4, No. 6), p.16; "Schuller, Mother Teresa, and the New Age," *O Timothy* (Vol. 11, Issue 2, 1994); "May Is the Month of 100th Birthday!!!," *Powerlines* (May 1998), p.3; "Schuller Promotes Pope and Comrade," *Omega-Letter* (March 1988, Vol. 3, No. 3), p.15.

[518] "May Is the Month of 100th Birthday!!!," *Powerlines* (May 1998), p.3. See also: Texe Marrs, "Global Explosion of Religious Apostasy," *Flashpoint* (July 1998, Vol. 98-7), p.1; "Schuler (sic) and Gorbachev," *op. cit.*, p.8; Dave Hunt, "Religious Unity and the New World Order," *The Omega-Letter* (July 1990, Vol. 5, No. 6), p.16; Dave Hunt, *Global Peace and the Rise of Antichrist* (Eugene, OR: Harvest House Publishers, 1990), p.135.

[519] "Schuller as Blasphemer," quoting from *The Los Angeles Times* in *Christian News* (January 22, 2001, Vol. 39, No. 4), p.8.

[520] "Hybels Featured at Schuller Meeting," *op. cit.*, p.2.

[521] "Atheist Speaks at Schuller's Church," *Calvary Contender* (November 15, 2000, Vol. 17, No. 22), p.1. See also: "Gorbachev on Schuller's 'Hour of Power,'" *Prophecy Corner and the Nosh Box* (November 2000), n.p.; "The Theology of Robert Schuller," *op. cit.*, p.7; "Schuler (sic) and Gorbachev," *op. cit.*, p.8; "So, How Much Did Schuller Pay Gorbachev Who Gets $75-$100,000 Per Talk?," *Christian News* (January 22, 2001, Vol. 39, No. 4), p.8.

[522] "Atheist Speaks at Schuller's Church," *Christian News* (October 30, 2000, Vol. 38, No. 40), p.23; "Gorbachev on Schuller's 'Hour of Power,'" *Prophecy Corner and the Nosh Box* (November 2000), n.p.; "'Marketing Christianity' & 'Purpose Driven Church,'" Transcript of Radio Liberty Audio, *Despatch Magazine* (June 2001, Vol. 13:2), p.57.

[523] Picture of Gorbachev's and Schuller's handshake on file.

[524] Texe Marrs, *Power of Prophecy* (June 23, 2001 program); "Kenneth Copeland 33rd Degree Mason Exposed," *Despatch Magazine* (December 1997, Vol. 9:4; "Shame, Shame on the Christian Establishment," World of Prophecy (October 11, 1997).

[525] "DeMolay Hall of Fame," *The Scottish Rite Journal* (March 1994, Vol. 102, No. 3), p.52.

[526] "Turret of the Times," *Christian News* (November 11, 1991, Vol. 29, No. 41), p.2; William Schnoebelen, *Masonry: Beyond the Light* (Chino, CA: Chick Publications, 1991), p.259; "1993 Biennial Session Banquet Honorees," *The Scottish Rite Journal* (January 1994, Vol. 102, No. 1), p.31.

[527] David A. Noebel, *The Marxist Minstrels: A Handbook on Communist Subversion of Music* (Tulsa, OK: American Christian College Press, 1974), p.138; Wardner, *Unholy Alliances, op. cit.*, p.189. See also: Buhle, Buhle, and Georgakas, *op. cit.*, p.340.

[528] *MSA "Freemasonry's Servant": How It Works* (Silver Spring, MD: The Masonic Service Association of the United States, n.d.), p.23.

[529] *Ibid.*

[530] "Schuller Rides High," *op. cit.*, p.16; *USA Today* (March 23, 1989); *The Omega-Letter* (March 1991, Vol. 6, No. 3), p.16.

[531] Arthur Lyons, *Satan Wants You: The Cult of Devil Worship in America* (New York, NY: The Mysterious Press, 1988), p.108. See also: Fritz Springmeier, *The Top 13 Illuminati Bloodlines* (Portland, OR: n.p., 1995), p.35, 94; Springmeier, *Bloodlines of the Illuminati, op. cit.*, p.158.

[532] "Schuller Trains Homosexual Pastors?," *Calvary Contender* (June 15, 1997, Vol. 14, No. 12). See also: *Last Trumpet Newsletter* (October 1997, Vol. 16, Issue 10), p.2.

[533] "The Theology of Robert Schuller," *op. cit.*, p.7.

[534] *Ibid.*

[535] *Ibid.*

[536] "Schuller and Rome," *op. cit.*

[537] *The BDM Letter* (October 1993, Vol. 2, No. 8); "Billy Graham Endorser of Evil," *The Perilous Times* (February 1994, Vol. 15, No. 12), p.7; Miesel, "Billy Graham: General Teachings/Activities," *op. cit.*

[538] *Ibid.* See also: Judy Pinalto, "Unholy Hands on the Bible," American Freedom Network (Guest on Henry Feinberg's June 14, 1996 Program); "New Gospel Emerging," *Media Spotlight* (1997, Vol. 20, No. 2), p.24; Miesel, "Billy Graham: General Teachings/Activities," *op. cit.; CIB Bulletin* (May 1989, Vol. 5, No. 5), p.4.

[539] "Program Is a Platform We Use to Help People," *USA Today* (March 23, 1989).

[540] *The BDM Letter* (October 1993, Vol. 2, No. 8). See also: *CIB Bulletin* (May 1989, Vol. 5, No. 5), p.4; "Schuller Rides High," *op. cit.*, p.16.

[541] "Program Is a Platform We Use to Help People," *USA Today* (March 23, 1989).

[542] *The Vine and Branches* (Summer 1998, Vol. 13, Issue 3), p.7.

[543] Fritz Springmeier, "Billy Graham Is Indeed Popular....," *Christian News* (July 27, 1992, Vol. 30, No. 30), p.8.

[544] David W. Cloud, "The Attack upon the Blood Atonement," *O Timothy* by David W. Cloud (1987, Vol. 4, Issue 1); D.W. Cloud, "Some Frightening Facts About Billy Graham," *O Timothy* (1984, Vol. 1, Issue 4).

[545] Allen *Jimmy Carter, Jimmy Carter, op. cit.*, p.43; Rivera, *op. cit.*, p.199.

[546] *Ibid.*, p.43.

[547] *Ibid.*, p.65.

[548] *Ibid.*, p.62.

[549] David W. Cloud, "Jimmy Carter Leaves the Southern Baptist Convention—Again," *Christian News* (November 6, 2000, Vol. 38, No. 41), p.23.

[550] Allen, *Jimmy Carter, Jimmy Carter, op. cit.*, p.63-64.

[551] *Ibid.*, p.65-66.

[552] *Ibid.*

[553] David Mark Price, *Secret* (Wichita, KS: Sunset Research Group, 1994), p.17; *The McAlvany Intelligence Advisor* (November 1992), p.6; Buhle, Buhle, and Georgakas, *op. cit.*, p.295.

[554] David Mark Price, *Secret* (Wichita, KS: Sunset Research Group, 1994), p.18.

[555] Buhle, Buhle, and Georgakas, *op. cit.*, p.294.

[556] Allen *Jimmy Carter, Jimmy Carter, op. cit.*, p.43. See also: Rivera, *op. cit.*, p.198-199; "Carter Comments on Conversion," *Calvary Contender* (March 15, 1997, Vol. 14, No. 5), p.1; *The NCC/WCC—Communism's Helpers, op. cit.*, p.5; Ursala Niebuhr, Editor, *Remembering Reinhold Niebuhr* (New York, NY: HarperSanFrancisco, 1991), Front flap, p.194, 220, 370, 410; Chambers, *op. cit.*, p.134.

[557] Rivera, *op. cit.*, p.199. See also: Cloud, "Billy Graham's Disobedience to the Word of God" (Updated March 2, 1999), *op. cit.*, p.6-7; David W. Cloud, "Jimmy Carter Leaves the Southern Baptist Convention—Again," *Christian News* (November 6, 2000, Vol. 38, No. 41), p.23.

[558] Cloud, "Billy Graham's Disobedience to the Word of God" (Updated March 2, 1999), *op. cit.*, p.6.

[559] "Thy Strong Word," *Christian News* (October 16, 2000, Vol. 38, No. 38), p.19. See also: "Barth, a Socialist, Praised by Evangelicals," *Calvary Contender* (June 1, 1998, Vol. 15, No. 11); Bundy, *How Liberals and Radicals Are Manipulating Evangelicals, op. cit.*, p.69; Cloud, "Billy Graham's Disobedience to the Word of God" (Updated March 2, 1999), *op. cit.*, p.6.

[560] "Barth, a Socialist, Praised by Evangelicals," *Calvary Contender* (June 1, 1998, Vol. 15, No. 11); Cloud, "Billy Graham's Disobedience to the Word of God" (Updated March 2, 1999), *op. cit.*, p.6; D. W. Cloud, "Some Frightening Facts About Billy Graham," *O Timothy* (1984, Vol. 1, Issue 4).

[561] "Dietrich Bonhoeffer: Heroic Christian Thinker & Martyr or Poor Deceived False Prophet?" (Biblical Discernment Ministries, n.d.), p.1; "Bonhoeffer Lauded by Evangelicals," *Calvary Contender* (June 15, 1998, Vol. 15, No. 12), p.2; "Dietrich Bonhoeffer," *The BDM Letter* (July/August 1995, Vol. 4, No. 4), p.1.

[562] "Dobson Touts Ecumenical Hero Dietrich Bonhoeffer," *Despatch Magazine* (September 1998, Vol. 10, No. 3), p.44.

[563] "Dietrich Bonhoeffer: Heroic Christian Thinker & Martyr or Poor Deceived False Prophet?" (Biblical Discernment Ministries, n.d.), p.2-3; "Dietrich Bonhoeffer," *The BDM Letter* (July/August 1995, Vol. 4, No. 4), p.2-3. See also: Alan Geyer, *The Idea of Disarmament! Rethinking the Unthinkable* (Elgin, IL: The Brethren Press and the Churches' Center for Theology and Public Policy, 1982), p.210; "John MacArthur Update," *The BDM Letter* (March/April 1995, Vol. 4, No. 2), p.2; "Hilary (sic) Clinton's Religious Beliefs," *Christian News* (April 12, 1993), Vol. 31, No. 15), p.14.

[564] "Dietrich Bonhoeffer: Heroic Christian Thinker & Martyr or Poor Deceived False Prophet?" (Biblical Discernment Ministries, n.d.), p.3-6; "Dietrich Bonhoeffer," *The BDM Letter* (July/August 1995, Vol. 4, No. 4), p.3-6. See also: "LCMS Seminary President Praises Fortress Press," *Christian News* (December 4, 2000, Vol. 38, No. 45), p.8; David W. Cloud, "Jerry Falwell Praises Modernist Bonhoeffer," *O Timothy* (1993, Vol. 10, Issue 8); "AAL Helps Create Film on Bonhoeffer," *Christian News* (May 15, 2000, Vol. 38, No. 20), p.6; "Book Review," *Christian News* (October 28, 1991, Vol. 29, No. 39), p.20; "Bonhoeffer Denied Christianity" *Calvary Contender* (July 15, 2000, Vol. 17, No. 14), p.1.

[565] "Dobson Touts Ecumenical Hero Dietrich Bonhoeffer," *Despatch Magazine* (September 1998, Vol. 10, No. 3), p.43. See also: "Dietrich Bonhoeffer," Softkey Multimedia Inc., Infopedia (1996).

[566] "Dietrich Bonhoeffer: Heroic Christian Thinker & Martyr or Poor Deceived False Prophet?" (Biblical Discernment Ministries, n.d.), p.2; "Bonhoeffer Lauded by Evangelicals," *Calvary Contender* (June 15, 1998, Vol. 15, No. 12), p.2; Raymond F. Surburg, "An Evaluation of Dietrich Bonhoeffer's Life and Theology After Half of a Century," *Christian News* (May 15, 2000, Vol. 38, No. 20), p.8; "Dietrich Bonhoeffer," Softkey Multimedia Inc., Infopedia (1996); "Bonhoeffer Denied Christianity" *Calvary Contender* (July 15, 2000, Vol. 17, No. 14), p.1.

[567] Bundy, *Collectivism in the Churches, op. cit.*, p.236, 238.

[568] *Ibid.*, p.236.

[569] *Ibid.* See also: Edward Jay Epstein, *Dossier: The Secret History of Armand Hammer* (NY: Random House, 1996), p.103.

[570] *Christian News* (March 6, 2000, Vol. 38, No. 10), p.3.

[571] *Ibid.*

[572] Jimmy Carter, *Living Faith* (Times Books, 1996), p.36.

[573] Letter from Jimmy Carter, dated November 22, 2000.

[574] *Ibid.*

[575] Carter, *op. cit.*, p.29.

[576] Catalog from Option Institute (2000), p.6.

[577] Allen *Jimmy Carter, Jimmy Carter, op. cit.*, p.21.

[578] *Ibid.*, p.51.

[579] Texe Marrs, *Millennium: Peace, Promises, and the Day They Take Our Money Away* (Austin, TX: Living Truth Publishers, 1990), p.41.

[580] Ross, *op. cit.*, p.101. See also: *Now Is the Dawning of the New Age New World Order, op. cit.*, p.252; Marrs, *Rule by Secrecy, op. cit.*, p.24, 26, 28, 29.

[581] *Now Is the Dawning of the New Age New World Order, op. cit.*, p.244; Allen *Jimmy Carter, Jimmy Carter, op. cit.*, p.75, 77.

[582] *Ibid.; Secret Records Revealed, op. cit.*, p.113-114.

[583] Rivera, *op. cit.*, p.199. See also: Carter, *op. cit.*, p.127-128.

[584] *Ibid.;* Allen *Jimmy Carter, Jimmy Carter, op. cit.*, p.54-55.

[585] Griffin, *Fourth Reich of the Rich, op. cit.*, p.112.

[586] "Carter Cuts SBC Ties," *Calvary Contender* (November 15, 2000, Vol. 17, No. 22), p.2; Todd Starnes, "Carter States Affirmation of Homosexual Ordination," *Christian News* (October 30, 2000, Vol. 38, No. 40), p.19.

[587] David W. Cloud, "Jimmy Carter Leaves the Southern Baptist Convention—Again," *Christian News* (November 6, 2000, Vol. 38, No. 41), p.23.

[588] Graham, *Just As I Am, op. cit.*, p.492; "Guardian Angel," *U. S. News & World Report* (May 5, 1997), p.66. See also: Wellman, *op. cit.*, p.183.

[589] Martin, *A Prophet with Honor, op. cit.*, p.463.

[590] Graham, *Just As I Am, op. cit.*, p.498.

[591] *Ibid.*, p.497.

[592] Wellman, *op. cit.*, p.183-184. See also: *Ibid.*, p.491.

[593] Graham, *Just As I Am, op. cit.*, p.497-498.

[594] Bundy, *Billy Graham: Performer?, op. cit.*, p.98. See also: Graham, *Just As I Am, op. cit.*, p.491; Wellman, *op. cit.*, p.184.

[595] Graham, *Just As I Am, op. cit.*, p.491.

[596] Allen *Jimmy Carter, Jimmy Carter, op. cit.*, p.43.

[597] Martin, *A Prophet with Honor, op. cit.*, p.584. See also: Bundy, *Billy Graham: Performer?, op. cit.*, p.99.

[598] *Ibid.*, p.584. See also: "Graham Admits Alcohol Use," *The Perilous Times* (March 1995, Vol. 17, No. 1), p.7.

[599] Bundy, *Billy Graham: Performer?, op. cit.*, p.51, 64.

[600] David P. Gaines, *The World Council of Churches: A Study of Its Background and History* (Peterborough, New Hampshire, Richard R. Smith Company, Inc., 1966), p.648; Alan Geyer, *The Idea of Disarmament! Rethinking the Unthinkable* (Elgin, IL: The Brethren Press and the Churches' Center for Theology and Public Policy, 1982), p.208-209.

[601] *Last Trumpet Newsletter* (August 1999, Vol. 18, Issue 8), p.1; "Brotherhood of Mormon" (Part II), *Distant Drums* (June 1985, Vol. 7, No. 2), p.10; Albert James Dager, "The World Christian Movement—Part 3: Toward the New World Order," *Media Spotlight* (1999, Vol. 22, No. 3), p.19.

[602] Rivera, *op. cit.*, p.167.

[603] "What the U. N. Doesn't Want You to Know" by Irvin Baxter, Jr., http://www.endtime.com/.

[604] Robert Muller, *New Genesis: Shaping a Global Spirituality* (Garden City, NY: Image Books, 1984), p.xvi, 46; Donald Keys, *Spirituality at the United Nations* (Jersey City, NJ: Aquarian Age Community, n.d.), p.6; Alan Morrison, *The Serpent and the Cross: Religious Corruption in an Evil Age* (Birmingham, England: K & M Books, 1994), p.177.

[605] Robert Muller, *The Birth of a Global Civilization* (Anacortes, WA: World Happiness and Cooperation, 1991), p.27; Robert Muller, "Religions and Spiritual Traditions: The World Needs You Very Much!," *World Goodwill* (1994, No. 1), p.3.

[606] "The Spiritual Work of the United Nations and the Spiritual Welfare of the Planet: The Promise of the New Millennium: Revelation of the Soul in Humanity," Summary Report of April 1, 1999 meeting, p.2.

[607] Corinne McLaughlin and Gordon Davidson, *Spiritual Politics: Changing the World from the Inside Out* (NY: Ballantine Books, 1994), p.318. See also: *Last Trumpet Newsletter* (August 2001, Vol. 20, Issue 7 [sic], p.2; Donald Keys, *Spirituality at the United Nations* (Jersey City, NJ: Aquarian Age Community, n.d.), p.2.

[608] *Ibid.*; Donald Keys, *Spirituality at the United Nations* (Jersey City, NJ: Aquarian Age Community, n.d.), p.2; Robert Keith Spenser, *The Cult of the All-Seeing Eye* (Palmdale, CA: Omni Publications, 1964), p.11.

[609] Robert Keith Spenser, *The Cult of the All-Seeing Eye* (Palmdale, CA: Omni Publications, 1964), p.12.

[610] *Ibid.*

[611] *Ibid.*

[612] Clifford Wilson and John Weldon, *Psychic Forces and Occult Shock: A Biblical View* (Chattanooga, TN: Global Publishers, 1987), p.378.

[613] Chambers, *op. cit.*, p.35, 163, 239, 402.

[614] *Ibid.*, p.239.

[615] Suzanne M. Rini, *Beyond Abortion: A Chronicle of Fetal Experimentation* (Rockford, IL: Tan Books and Publishers, Inc., 1993), p.99.

[616] Chambers, *op. cit.*, p.35.

[617] Donald Keys, *Spirituality at the United Nations* (Jersey City, NJ: Aquarian Age Community, n.d.), p.2.

[618] Paper from the Committee of Christian Laymen, Inc. (October 16, 1969, No. 181), p.4.

[619] Bundy, *Collectivism in the Churches, op. cit.*, p.194.

[620] Kenneth M. Kearns, "A Visit by J. C. Penney, 33°," *The Scottish Rite Journal* (August 1992, Vol. 100, No. 8), p.55, 56; William R. Denslow, *10,000 Famous Freemasons* (Vol. III) (n.p., 1959), p.326.

[621] William R. Denslow, *10,000 Famous Freemasons* (Vol. III) (n.p., 1959), p.60.

[622] Frank C. Laubach, "The Mightiest Force in the World," *Plus: The Magazine of Positive Thinking* (February 1988, Vol. 39, No. 2), p.18.

[623] Spenser, *op. cit.*, p.11.

[624] *Ibid.*

[625] Brenda Scott and Samantha Smith, *Trojan Horse: How the New Age Movement Infiltrates the Church* (Lafayette, LA: Huntington House Publishers, 1993), p.121.

[626] "The Temple of Understanding," *Wisconsin Report* (October 25, 1984, Vol. 9, No. 42), p.4; Cornelia R. Ferreira, "The Global Ethic: From Golden Rule to Common Ground," *Wisconsin Report* (May 14, 1998), p.1.

[627] Cornelia R. Ferreira, "The Global Ethic: From Golden Rule to Common Ground," *Wisconsin Report* (May 14, 1998), p.1.

[628] Letter from Planetary Initiative for the World We Choose, p.2.

[629] Brochure from Chinook Learning Center advertising the international conference entitled "Earth and Spirit: The Spiritual Dimension of the Environmental Crisis," p.8.

[630] *Creation Spirituality* (March/April 1992), p.38.

[631] Spenser, *op. cit.*, p.12.

[632] John Pollock, *Crusades: 20 Years with Billy Graham* (Minneapolis, MN: World Wide Publications, 1969, Special Billy Graham Crusade Edition), p.174.

[633] William R. Denslow, *10,000 Famous Freemasons* (Vol. I) (n.p., 1957), p.40. See also: *Secret Records Revealed, op. cit.*, p.77-78; Peter Collier and David Horowitz, *The Rockefellers: An American Dynasty* (NY: Holt, Rinehart and Winston, n.d.), p.236.

[634] *Secret Records Revealed, op. cit.*, p.78.

[635] Alan Morrison, *The Serpent and the Cross: Religious Corruption in an Evil Age* (Birmingham, England: K & M Books, 1994), p.177, 180, 550. See also: *Last Trumpet Newsletter* (August 2001, Vol. 20, Issue 7 [sic]), p.2; Scott and Smith, *op. cit.*, p.76; Keys, *op. cit.*, p.2.

[636] Marrs, *Mystery Mark of the New Age, op. cit.*, p.102. See also: Spenser, *op. cit.*, p.5; Albert James Dager, "The World Christian Movement—Part 3: Toward the New World Order," *Media Spotlight* (1999, Vol. 22, No.3), p.19.

[637] Albert James Dager, *The World Christian Movement: A Great Delusion Leading to the Religio-Political State of the Anti-Christ* (Redmond, WA: Sword Publishers, 2001), p.193.

[638] Marrs, *Mystery Mark of the New Age, op. cit.,* p.102. See also: Griffin, *Fourth Reich of the Rich, op. cit.,* p.151; Spenser, *op. cit.,* p.10; Albert James Dager, "The World Christian Movement—Part 3: Toward the New World Order," *Media Spotlight* (1999, Vol. 22, No.3), p.19; Dager, *The World Christian Movement, op. cit.,* p.198; Piers Compton, *The Broken Cross: The Hidden Hand in the Vatican* (Cranbrook, Western Australia: Veritas Publishing Company Pty. Ltd., 1984), p.70.

[639] Spenser, *op. cit.,* p.13.

[640] William J. Schnoebelen and James R. Spencer, *White Sepulchers: The Hidden Language of the Mormon Temple* (Boise, ID: Through the Maze, 1990), p.46.

[641] *Ibid.* p.44.

[642] *Ibid.,* p.48.

[643] *Ibid.*

[644] *Last Trumpet Newsletter* (August 1999, Vol. 18, Issue 8), p.1-2. See also: Spenser, *op. cit.,* p.7-9.

[645] David C. Kanz, Ingrid Guzman, and Steven P. Smith, *An Urgent Report: Celebration 2000 and Jay Gary* (Milwaukee, WI: VCY/America Radio Network, 1995), p.2.

[646] Dwight L. Kinman quoting Robert Muller in *The World's Last Dictator* (Woodburn, OR: Solid Rock Books, Inc. 1995), p.81.

[647] *Blueprint for Building the New World Order* (Dearborn, MI: The Omega-Letter/Christian World Report, n.d.), p.21; Kanz, Guzman, and Smith, *op. cit.,* p.2.

[648] Cumbey, *A Planned Deception, op. cit.,* p.34.

[649] *Chronology of Education with Quotable Quotes, op. cit.,* p.77; *Now Is the Dawning of the New Age New World Order, op. cit.,* 272; "Transformation Toward New Age Synthesis," *Distant Drums* (May 1986, Vol. 8, No. 2), p.2; "Dr. Paul Cedar Pulls Endorsement from *Star of 2000,"* Report from Broadcasters United for Revival and Reformation, p.2; *Don Bell Reports* (January 10, 1986), Vol. 33, No. 2), p.3.

[650] Muller, *New Genesis, op. cit.,* p.75.

[651] *The Rainbow Connection* (April 1995), p.3.

[652] Brochure from the Temple of Understanding, (Received March 12, 1991), p.2.

[653] *Breakthrough* (Winter/Summer 1990, Vol. 11, No.2-4), p.2. See also: Rosamond C. Rodman, Editor, *The United Nations in an Interdependent World: Past, Present, Future* (New York, NY: Global Education Associates, 1995), p.2.

[654] Letter from Planetary Citizens dated April 17, 1985.

[655] Sessler, *op. cit.,* p.63.

[656] Texe Marrs, "New Agers Meet to Plan World Takeover," *Flashpoint* (January 1990), p.1; Rhea Fulmer, Teri Jeter, and Wanda Riner, "Robert Muller's Vision for 2000 A. D.," *The Christian Conscience* (May 1995, Vol. 1, No. 5), p.35.

[657] *Now Is the Dawning of the New Age New World Order, op. cit.,* p.53; *Secret Records Revealed, op. cit.,* p.200; William Schnoebelen, *Masonry: Beyond the Light* (Chino, CA: Chick Publications, 1991), p.205; Shirley Correll, "Who Are the Gods of the New World Order and What Is a Spiritual U. N.?" (Part IV), *The Florida Forum* (Spring 2001), p.6; *Battle Cry* (March/April 1991), p.4; Constance Cumbey, *The Hidden Dangers of the Rainbow: The New Age Movement and Our Coming Age of Barbarism* (Shreveport, LA: Huntington House, Inc., Revised Edition, 1983), p.49; Texe Marrs, *Circle of Intrigue* (Austin, TX: Living Truth Ministries, 1995), p.177; Chambers, *op. cit.,* p.34; Scott and Smith, *op. cit.,* p.158.

[658] *Ibid.,* p.53; "The Deceptive New Age 'Service' and 'Light,'" *The Christian World Report* (February 1991, Vol. 3, No. 2), p.8; *Secret Records Revealed, op. cit.,* p.200; Texe Marrs, *Circle of Intrigue* (Austin, TX: Living Truth Ministries, 1995), p.177; Chambers, *op. cit.,* p.34.

[659] Graham, *Just As I Am, op. cit.,* p.685-686.

[660] Albert James Dager, "The World Christian Movement—Part 3: Toward the New World Order," *Media Spotlight* (1999, Vol. 22, No.3), p.15-16.

[661] Videotape entitled *The Power of A.D. 2000,* distributed by Adopt-A-People in Colorado Springs, Colorado.

[662] Kanz, Guzman, and Smith, quoting Spangler and Thompson, *op. cit.,* p.8.

[663] David Spangler, *Reflections on the Christ* (Scotland: Findhorn Publications, 1977), p.43-44.

[664] *Ibid.* p.40. See also: Scott and Smith, *op. cit.,* p.xi.

[665] David Spangler, *Emergence: The Rebirth of the Sacred* (NY: Dell Publishing, 1984), p.24. See also: "Finding Heaven on Earth," *The New Age Journal* (January/February 1988, Vol. 4, Issue 1), p.38.

[666] *Ibid.,* p.65-67.

[667] Elliot Miller, *A Crash Course on the New Age Movement: Describing and Evaluating a Growing Social Force* (Grand Rapids, MI: Baker Book House, 1989), p.157. See also: Findhorn Community, *The Findhorn Garden* (New York, NY: Harper & Row, 1975), p.180.

[668] Spangler, *Emergence, op. cit.,* Back Cover.

[669] Morrison, *op. cit.*, p.107.

[670] *Passport* (October/November 1987). See also: Texe Marrs, *Dark Secrets of the New Age: Satan's Plan for a One World Religion* (Westchester, IL: Crossway Books, 1987), p.181.

[671] Dager, "The World Christian Movement—Part 3," *op. cit.*, p.15-16. See also: Dager, *The World Christian Movement, op. cit.*, p.5, 23, 182; Jay and Olgy Gary, *The Countdown Has Begun: The Story of the Global Consultation on AD 2000* (Rockville, VA: AD 2000 Global Service Office, 1989), p.8; David R. Barnhart, *Contending for the Faith* (Eagan, MN: Abiding Word Publications, 1994), p.123; Albert James Dager, *Media Spotlight* (Received 1995), p.3-4; *Bold Truth* (February 13, 1994), p.8; Kanz, Guzman, and Smith, *op. cit.*, p.2.

[672] "Global Evangelization Course to Be Offered Along the Front Range," *Colorado Christian News* (January 1995, Vol. 6, Issue 6), p.5; "Vision on the Nations" (U. S. Center for World Mission, Received November 28, 1997); Albert James Dager, "The World Christian Movement: Evangelism Vs. Evangelization," *Media Spotlight* (1999, Vol. 22, No. 1), p.10. See also: Pamphlet from Perspectives on the World Christian Movement (Pamphlet received November 28, 1997).

3. UNION THEOLOGICAL SEMINARY

[1] James W. Wardner, *Unholy Alliances* (n.p., 1996), p.160.

[2] *Ibid.*, p.161.

[3] *Ibid.*

[4] David Bay, "Meet the Real Reverend (sic) Billy Graham—He Is Not the Person Whom You Thought You Knew!" (Received February 10, 2000), p.4; David W. Cloud, "Billy Graham's Disobedience to the Word of God" (Updated March 2, 1999), p.5; Edgar C. Bundy, *Billy Graham: Performer?, Politician?, Preacher?, Prophet?* (Wheaton, IL: Church League of America, 1982), p.45.

[5] Brad K. Gsell, *The Legacy of Billy Graham* (Charlotte, NC: Fundamental Presbyterian Publication, n.d.), p.20; David A. Noebel, *Is the NCC Really Soft on Communism?* (Tulsa, OK: Christian Crusade, n.d.), p.16; Joseph Fort Newton, *River of Years: An Autobiography* (Philadelphia, PA: J. B. Lippincott Company, 1946), p.274; Wardner, *Unholy Alliances, op. cit.*, p.154; David W. Cloud, "Billy Graham's Disobedience to the Word of God" (Updated March 2, 1999), p.5; Edgar C. Bundy, *Billy Graham: Performer?, Politician?, Preacher?, Prophet?* (Wheaton, IL: Church League of America, 1982), p.45.

[6] *Ibid.*

[7] Bay, *op. cit.*, p.4.

[8] Gsell, *op. cit.* See also: Edgar C. Bundy, *Billy Graham: Performer?, Politician?, Preacher?, Prophet?* (Wheaton, IL: Church League of America, 1982), p.45-46; David W. Cloud, "Billy Graham's Disobedience to the Word of God" (Updated March 2, 1999), p.5.

[9] Edgar C. Bundy, *Billy Graham: Performer?, Politician?, Preacher?, Prophet?* (Wheaton, IL: Church League of America, 1982), p.45-46.

[10] Gsell, *op. cit.* See also: *Ibid.*, p.45; David W. Cloud, "Billy Graham's Disobedience to the Word of God" (Updated March 2, 1999), p.5.

[11] Robert E. Herzstein, *Henry R. Luce: A Political Portrait of the Man Who Created the American Century* (New York, NY: Macmillan Publishing Company, 1994), p.5, 149.

[12] *Ibid.*, p.25.

[13] *Ibid.*, p.5, 149.

[14] G. Archer Weniger, *Modernism of National Council of Churches* (Murfreesboro, TN: Sword of the Lord Publishers, 1961), p.5.

[15] Bay, *op. cit.*, p.4.

[16] Peter Collier and David Horowitz, *The Rockefellers: An American Dynasty* (NY: Holt, Rinehart and Winston, n.d.), p.155; Wardner, *Unholy Alliances, op. cit.*, p.148.

[17] *Ibid.*, p.315. See also: Gary Allen *Rockefeller: Campaigning for the New World Order* (n.p., n.d.), p.9; Wardner, *Unholy Alliances, op. cit.*, p.149; Edgar C. Bundy, *Collectivism in the Churches: A Documented Account of the Political Activities of the Federal, National, and World Councils of Churches* (Wheaton, IL: The Church League of America, 1958), p.256.

[18] "Union Theological Seminary," Softkey Multimedia Inc., Infopedia (1996); "Columbia University," Softkey Multimedia Inc., Infopedia (1996); Antony C. Sutton, *America's Secret Establishment: An Introduction to the Order of Skull and Bones* (Billings, MT: Liberty House Press, 1986), p.28; Edwin O. Kennedy, "Union Theological Seminary," *The World Book Encyclopedia* (Vol. 18) (Chicago 54, IL: Field Enterprises Educational Corporation, 1961 Edition), p.24.

[19] Rene A. Wormser, *Foundations: Their Power and Influence* (New York, NY: Devin-Adair Company, 1977 Edition), p.142, 167; Robert Sessler, *To Be God of One World: The French Revolution Globalized* (Merlin, OR: Let There Be Light Publications, 1992), p.112; Gary Allen, *The Rockefeller File* (Seal Beach, CA: '76 Press, 1976), p.147.

[20] *Ibid.*, p.145.

[21] A. Ralph Epperson, *The Unseen Hand: An Introduction to the Conspiratorial View of History* (Tucson, AZ: Publius Press, 1985), p.386. See also: "'Progressive' Educators' Plans Fulfilled Today," *The Florida Forum* (Spring 1996), p.18;

Chronology of Education with Quotable Quotes (Highland City, FL: Pro Family Forum, Inc., 1994, Updated, bound volume), p.9; *Now Is the Dawning of the New Age New World Order* (Oklahoma City, OK: Hearthstone Publishing, Ltd., 1991), p.104, 153, 237-238; *Ibid.*, p.145; Paolo Lionni, *The Leipzig Connection: The Systematic Destruction of American Education* (Sheridan, OR: Heron Books, 1993), p.19, 64; Robert Sessler, *To Be God of One World: The French Revolution Globalized* (Merlin, OR: Let There Be Light Publications, 1992), p.108, 111; Gary Allen, *The Rockefeller File* (Seal Beach, CA: '76 Press, 1976), p.46; Claire Chambers, *The SIECUS Circle: A Humanist Revolution* (Belmont, MA: Western Islands, 1977), p.64; Antony C. Sutton, *America's Secret Establishment: An Introduction to the Order of Skull and Bones* (Billings, MT: Liberty House Press, 1986), p.56.

[22] *Now Is the Dawning of the New Age New World Order* (Oklahoma City, OK: Hearthstone Publishing, Ltd., 1991), p.104, 153; "'Progressive' Educators' Plans Fulfilled Today," *The Florida Forum* (Spring 1996), p.18.

[23] *Ibid.*, p.153-154.

[24] Paolo Lionni, *The Leipzig Connection: The Systematic Destruction of American Education* (Sheridan, OR: Heron Books, 1993), p.19. See also: Chuck Colson with Ellen Santilli Vaughn, *The Body* (Dallas, TX: Word Publishing, 1996 Edition), p.155.

[25] *Secret Records Revealed: The Men, the Money and the Methods Behind the New World Order* (Oklahoma City, OK: Hearthstone Publishing, Ltd., 1999), p.19, 47; Newsletter from Radio Liberty (April 2001), p.5; "'Copping a 'Tude,'" *Voice in the Wilderness* (March 2001, Vol. 8, Issue 3), p.13; *NEA: The Grab for Power: A Chronology of the National Education Association* (Oklahoma City, OK: Hearthstone Publishing, 2000), p.11; Carroll Quigley, *Tragedy and Hope: A History of the World in Our Time* (NY: The Macmillan Company, 1966), p.832; Mari Jo Buhle, Paul Buhle, and Dan Georgakas, Editors, *Encyclopedia of the American Left* (New York, NY: Oxford University Press, 1998, Second Edition), p.205.

[26] Shirley Correll, "Will the Communist Plans for America Be Fulfilled in Louisville?," *The Florida Forum* (Winter 2000), p.11.

[27] Mari Jo Buhle, Paul Buhle, and Dan Georgakas, Editors, *Encyclopedia of the American Left* (New York, NY: Oxford University Press, 1998, Second Edition), p.188.

[28] Newsletter from Radio Liberty (May 2001), p.5.

[29] Shirley Correll, "Who Are the Gods of the New World Order and What Is a Spiritual U. N.?" (Part III), *The Florida Forum* (Summer 2000), p.11; *NEA: The Grab for Power: A Chronology of the National Education Association* (Oklahoma City, OK: Hearthstone Publishing, 2000), p.7, 12; Correll, "Will the Communist Plans for America Be Fulfilled in Louisville?," *op. cit.*, p.11; Newsletter from Radio Liberty (April 2001), p.5; *Secret Records Revealed, op. cit.*, p.19, 47; *Now Is the Dawning of the New Age New World Order, op. cit.*, p.102, 103; Claire Chambers, *The SIECUS Circle: A Humanist Revolution* (Belmont, MA: Western Islands, 1977), p.64; *Global 2000: An Interview with Mr. and Mrs. William Bowen* (Oklahoma City, OK: Southwest Radio Church, 1984), p.16.

[30] *Now Is the Dawning of the New Age New World Order, op. cit.*, p.127, 237-238; *Ibid.*; Newsletter from Radio Liberty (April 2001), p.5; Buhle, Buhle, and Georgakas, *op. cit.*, p.364, 365, 428, 800; Newsletter from Radio Liberty (May 2001), p.5; John A. Stormer, *None Dare Call It Treason* (Florissant, MO: Liberty Bell Press, 1964), p.101; Paper from the Committee of Christian Laymen, Inc. of Woodland Hills (October 16, 1969, No. 181), p.4; Paper from the Committee of Christian Laymen, Inc. of Woodland Hills (September 10, 1970, No. 196), p.2.

[31] *Secret Records Revealed, op. cit.*, p.17; *Now Is the Dawning of the New Age New World Order, op. cit.*, p.84; Epperson, *op. cit.*, p.386-387.

[32] Lionni, *op. cit.*, p.64-65; *Ibid.*, p.47; Correll, "Who Are the Gods of the New World Order and What Is a Spiritual U.N.?" (Part III), *op. cit.*, p.12.

[33] *Now Is the Dawning of the New Age New World Order, op. cit.*, p.84.

[34] *Ibid.*, p.384-385; *NEA: The Grab for Power: A Chronology of the National Education Association* (Oklahoma City, OK: Hearthstone Publishing, 2000), p.8; *The Grab for Power: A Chronology of the NEA* (Marlborough, NH: Plymouth Rock Foundation, 1993), p.1.

[35] Robert Sessler, *To Be God of One World: The French Revolution Globalized* (Merlin, OR: Let There Be Light Publications, 1992), p.113.

[36] Robert Gaylon Ross, Sr., *Who's Who of the Elite* (San Marcos, TX: RIE, 1995), p.112-113.

[37] Gary Allen *Rockefeller: Campaigning for the New World Order* (n.p., n.d.), p.9; Fritz Springmeier, *Bloodlines of the Illuminati* (Westminster, CO: Ambassador House, 1999), p.218.

[38] Wardner, *Unholy Alliances, op. cit.*, p.148; Antony C. Sutton, *America's Secret Establishment: An Introduction to the Order of Skull and Bones* (Billings, MT: Liberty House Press, 1986), p.28.

[39] Antony C. Sutton, *America's Secret Establishment: An Introduction to the Order of Skull & Bones* (Billings, MT: Liberty House Press, 1986), p.28.

[40] David A. Noebel, *Is the NCC Really Soft on Communism?* (Tulsa, OK: Christian Crusade, n.d.), p.17. See also: Fritz Springmeier, *Bloodlines of the Illuminati* (Westminster, CO: Ambassador House, 1999), p.137.

[41] Texe Marrs, *Dark Majesty: The Secret Brotherhood and the Magic of a Thousand Points of Light* (Austin, TX: Living Truth Publishers, 1992), p.206.

[42] Sutton, *America's Secret Establishment, op. cit.*, p.28; Wardner, *Unholy Alliances, op. cit.*, p.148.

[43] Edgar C. Bundy, *Collectivism in the Churches: A Documented Account of the Political Activities of the Federal, National, and World Councils of Churches* (Wheaton, IL: The Church League of America, 1958), p.130.

[44] Joan Veon, *Prince Charles: The* Sustainable *Prince* (Oklahoma City, OK: Hearthstone Publishing, Ltd., 1997), p.24.

[45] Sutton, *America's Secret Establishment, op. cit.*, p.28; Wardner, *Unholy Alliances, op. cit.*, p.148. See also: Perry F. Rockwood, "The Revised Standard Version," *O Timothy* (1985, Vol. 2, Issue 3); Ursala Niebuhr, Editor, *Remembering Reinhold Niebuhr* (New York, NY: HarperSanFrancisco, 1991), p.17, 35; Antony C. Sutton, *How the Order Controls Education* (Phoenix, AZ: Research Publications, Inc., 1983), p.31, 62; David W. Cloud, "The Attack upon the Blood Atonement" *O Timothy* (1987, Vol. 4, Issue 1).

[46] Perry F. Rockwood, "The Revised Standard Version," *O Timothy* (1985, Vol. 2, Issue 3).

[47] David W. Cloud, "The Attack upon the Blood Atonement," *O Timothy* (1987, Vol. 4, Issue 1).

[48] *Ibid.*

[49] *Ibid.*

[50] Rockwood, *op. cit.; Ibid.*

[51] Cloud, "The Attack upon the Blood Atonement," *op. cit.; Ibid.*

[52] *The NCC/WCC—Communism's Helpers* (Virginia Beach, VA: Good News Baptist Church, n.d.), p.5.

[53] Sutton, *America's Secret Establishment, op. cit.*, p.28; See also: Wardner, *Unholy Alliances, op. cit.*, p.148.

[54] Wardner, *Unholy Alliances, op. cit.*, p.148; "Charismatic Professor to Pastor Nation's Foremost Liberal Church," *Ministries Today* (May/June 1989), p.82; "The Right Place for a Mass Murdering Atheist to Speak," *Christian News* (September 18, 2000, Vol. 38, No. 34), p.4.

[55] "Charismatic Professor to Pastor Nation's Foremost Liberal Church," *Ministries Today* (May/June 1989), p.82-83.

[56] "The Right Place for a Mass Murdering Atheist to Speak," *Christian News* (September 18, 2000, Vol. 38, No. 34), p.4.

[57] "Charismatic Professor to Pastor Nation's Foremost Liberal Church," *op. cit.*, p.83; "Castro Is Applauded at Riverside Church," *Calvary Contender* (October 15, 2000, Vol. 17, No. 20), p.2; Jacqueline Trussell, "Making a Joyful Noise," *CPWR Journal* (November 1993, Vol. 5, No. 6), p.7; "Baylor Honors Chuck Swindoll," *Calvary Contender* (March 1, 1997, Vol. 14, No. 5), p.2; "New Liberal Religious/Political Group Deplores 'False Choices,' Redefines Evangelism," *Christian News* (July 1, 1996, Vol. 34, No. 27), p.23.

[58] *Ibid.*; "Colson, Palau to Gordon-Conwell Board," *Calvary Contender* (September 15, 1999, Vol. 16, No. 18); "Colson, Palau to Gordon-Conwell Board," *Despatch Magazine* (September 1999, Vol. 11, No. 3), p.39; Brochure from Philadelphia Ministries Conference (1982); *Kirkridge* (Spring/Summer 1988), p.8; Brochure from Seminary Consortium for Urban Pastoral Education (SCUPE) (1988); "Colson, Palau to Gordon-Conwell Board," *Calvary Contender* (September 15, 1999, Vol. 16, No. 18), p.2.

[59] *Christian News* (February 26, 1996, Vol. 34, No. 9), p.17.

[60] *Ibid.*

[61] *Ibid.*

[62] Paper from the Summit on Ethics and Meaning (Received March 14, 1996), p.1. See also: "Campolo a Bad Role Model for Youth," *Calvary Contender* (June 1, 1998, Vol. 15, No. 11), p.2.

[63] "New Liberal Religious/Political Group Deplores 'False Choices,' Redefines Evangelism," *Christian News* (July 1, 1996, Vol. 34, No. 27), p.23; Laurie Goodstein, "Christian Leaders Counter Religious Right," *Philadelphia Inquirer* (May 24, 1995); *The Cry for Renewal: Biblical Faith and Spiritual Politics* (May 23, 1995), p.2.

[64] *Sojourners* (January 1990, Vol. 19, No. 1), p.6; *Sojourners* (October 1989, Vol. 18, No. 9), p.2; *Sojourners* (March/April 1995, Vol. 24, No. 1), p.4.

[65] William McIlhany, "The WCC: A Haven for Marxists?," *Family Protection Scoreboard*, p.21; James W. Wardner, *The Planned Destruction of America* (Debary, FL: Longwood Communications, 1994), p.133; B. F. Collins, "Religious Freedom Restoration Act of 1993: Beware the Greeks Bearing Gifts," *The Florida Forum* (Fall 1994), p.5; Buhle, Buhle, and Georgakas, *op. cit.*, p.31, 195; Epperson, *op. cit.*, p.221.

[66] W. Cleon Skousen, *The Communist Attack on U. S. Police* (Salt Lake City, UT: The Ensign Publishing Company, 1966), p.47.

[67] Epperson, *op. cit.*, p.221; McIlhany, *op. cit.;* Noebel, *Is the NCC Really Soft on Communism, op. cit.*, p.9; Wardner, *Unholy Alliances, op. cit.*, p.152; *Ibid.;* Bundy, *Collectivism in the Churches, op. cit.*, p.103; *Intelligence Newsletter* (July-August 1991); Claire Chambers, *The SIECUS Circle: A Humanist Revolution* (Belmont, MA: Western Islands, 1977), p.27.

[68] Skousen, *op. cit.* See also: Wardner, *Unholy Alliances, op. cit.*, p.152.

[69] Epperson, *op. cit.*, p.221; Noebel, *Is the NCC Really Soft on Communism, op. cit.*, p.9; *Intelligence Newsletter* (July-August 1991); Wardner, *Unholy Alliances, op. cit.*, p.225. See also: Bundy, *Collectivism in the Churches, op. cit.*, p.137.

[70] Paper from the Committee of Christian Laymen Inc. of Woodland Hills (No. 5), p.1. See also: Bundy, *Collectivism in the Churches, op. cit.*, p.113-119. See also: Edward Jay Epstein, *Dossier: The Secret History of Armand Hammer* (NY: Random House, 1996), p.40-41.

[71] *Ibid.* See also: Paper from the Committee of Christian Laymen Inc. of Woodland Hills (February 14, 1965, No. 121); Bundy, *Collectivism in the Churches, op. cit.*, p.124; *The Road to Socialism and the New World Order* (Highland City, FL: Florida Pro Family Forum, Inc., 1995), p.22; James W. Wardner, *The Planned Destruction of America* (Debary, FL: Longwood Communications, 1994), p.133; James R. Patrick, Compiler and Editor, *America 2000/Goals 2000* (Moline, IL: Citizens for Academic Excellence, 1994), p.131; "Who Is Behind the ACLU?," *The Perilous Times* (December 1993,

Vol. 15, No. 10), p.1; *Now Is the Dawning of the New Age New World Order, op. cit.*, p.102; Epperson, *op. cit.*, p.383; Carroll Quigley, *Tragedy and Hope: A History of the World in Our Time* (NY: The Macmillan Company, 1966), p.917; *The New World Order* (Milford, PA: America's Future, Inc., 1992), p.5; Fred C. Schwarz, "The Leninist Use of Force and Violence," *The Schwarz Report* (November 2000, Vol. 40, No. 11), p.4; B. F. Collins, "Religious Freedom Restoration Act of 1993: Beware the Greeks Bearing Gifts," *The Florida Forum* (Fall 1994), p.5; "(Soviet) American Education Today," *The Christian Conscience* (June 1995, Vol. 1, No. 6), p.38; Jay Tower, "ACLU: Its Subversive Past and Evil Vision for America's Future," *Christian Crusade* (May 1993, Vol. 41, No. 5), p.4; Claire Chambers, *The SIECUS Circle: A Humanist Revolution* (Belmont, MA: Western Islands, 1977), p.27; *Chronology of Education with Quotable Quotes* (Highland City, FL: Pro Family Forum, Inc., 1994, Updated, bound volume), p.17; David Allen Rivera, *Final Warning: A History of the New World Order* (Harrisburg, PA: Rivera Enterprises, 1994 Edition), p.77; David A. Noebel, *The Marxist Minstrels: A Handbook on Communist Subversion of Music* (Tulsa, OK: American Christian College Press, 1974), p.iii.

[72] Skousen, *op. cit.*

[73] *Ibid.* See also: Bundy, *Collectivism in the Churches, op. cit.*, p.125.

[74] John A. Stormer, *None Dare Call It Treason* (Florissant, MO: Liberty Bell Press, 1964), p.185; B. F. Collins, "Religious Freedom Restoration Act of 1993: Beware the Greeks Bearing Gifts," *The Florida Forum* (Fall 1994), p.5; McIlhany, *op. cit.; The NCC/WCC—Communism's Helpers, op. cit.*, p.11; Paper from the Committee of Christian Laymen Inc. of Woodland Hills (No. 5), p.1; James W. Wardner, *The Planned Destruction of America* (Debary, FL: Longwood Communications, 1994), p.133; Bundy, *Collectivism in the Churches, op. cit.*, p.124, 131; Noebel, *Is the NCC Really Soft on Communism, op. cit.*, p.9.

[75] *Ibid.; The NCC/WCC—Communism's Helpers, op. cit.*, p.11; Paper from the Committee of Christian Laymen Inc. of Woodland Hills (No. 5), p.1; James W. Wardner, *The Planned Destruction of America* (Debary, FL: Longwood Communications, 1994), p.133; B. F. Collins, "Religious Freedom Restoration Act of 1993: Beware the Greeks Bearing Gifts," *The Florida Forum* (Fall 1994), p.5.

[76] B. F. Collins, "Religious Freedom Restoration Act of 1993: Beware the Greeks Bearing Gifts," *The Florida Forum* (Fall 1994), p.5; Jay Tower, "ACLU: Its Subversive Past and Evil Vision for America's Future," *Christian Crusade* (May 1993, Vol. 41, No. 5), p.4; Buhle, Buhle, and Georgakas, *op. cit.*, p.23, 26, 274, 358, 540; "Who Is Behind the ACLU?," *The Perilous Times* (December 1993, Vol. 15, No. 10), p.1; John A. Stormer, *None Dare Call It Treason...25 Years Later* (Florissant, MO: Liberty Bell Press, 1992), p.556; Claire Chambers, *The SIECUS Circle: A Humanist Revolution* (Belmont, MA: Western Islands, 1977), p.27; *Distant Drums* (March 1986, Vol. 8, No. 1).

[77] *Global 2000: An Interview with Mr. and Mrs. William Bowen* (Oklahoma City, OK: Southwest Radio Church, 1984), p.43.

[78] "ACLU's Attack on God," Interview by Dr. Stan Monteith with William Donahue on August 22, 2000.

[79] Collins, *op. cit.*, p.5; David Allen Rivera, *Final Warning: A History of the New World Order* (Harrisburg, PA: Rivera Enterprises, 1994 Edition), p.77; John A. Stormer, *None Dare Call It Treason...25 Years Later* (Florissant, MO: Liberty Bell Press, 1992), p.556; James W. Wardner, *The Planned Destruction of America* (Debary, FL: Longwood Communications, 1994), p.133; Jay Tower, "ACLU: Its Subversive Past and Evil Vision for America's Future," *Christian Crusade* (May 1993, Vol. 41, No. 5), p.4; "Who Is Behind the ACLU?," *The Perilous Times* (December 1993, Vol. 15, No. 10), p.1; Buhle, Buhle, and Georgakas, *op. cit.*, p.229.

[80] Carroll Quigley, *Tragedy and Hope: A History of the World in Our Time* (NY: The Macmillan Company, 1966), p.923, 946; Buhle, Buhle, and Georgakas, *op. cit.*, p.151, 159, 230; Jay Tower, "ACLU: Its Subversive Past and Evil Vision for America's Future," *Christian Crusade* (May 1993, Vol. 41, No. 5), p.4.

[81] David Allen Rivera, *Final Warning: A History of the New World Order* (Harrisburg, PA: Rivera Enterprises, 1994 Edition), p.77; Noebel, *Is the NCC Really Soft on Communism, op. cit.*, p.9; Buhle, Buhle, and Georgakas, *op. cit.*, p.26, 50, 541.

[82] *Ibid.*; Buhle, Buhle, and Georgakas, *op. cit.*, p.133, 150.

[83] Claire Chambers, *The SIECUS Circle: A Humanist Revolution* (Belmont, MA: Western Islands, 1977), p.29. See also: James W. Wardner, *The Planned Destruction of America* (Debary, FL: Longwood Communications, 1994), p.133.

[84] Collins, *op. cit.*, p.5; Wardner, *Unholy Alliances, op. cit.*, p.166; Buhle, Buhle, and Georgakas, *op. cit.*, p.27, 237; Rivera, *op. cit.;* Paper from the Committee of Christian Laymen, Inc. of Woodland Hills (September 10, 1970, No. 196), p.2; Transcript of "Illuminati and the Council on Foreign Relations" by Myron Fagan; Ray Raehm, "Why Neither George Bush Nor Albert Gore Seems Willing or Able to Derail the Ongoing Cultural Revolution in America," *The Florida Forum* (Fall 2000), p.20; "Federal Agents Confiscate Church and Forcibly Remove Pastor and Members—Fulfilling the Plan of the Communist Internationale," *The Florida Forum* (Winter 2000), p.10; James W. Wardner, *The Planned Destruction of America* (Debary, FL: Longwood Communications, 1994), p.133; Jay Tower, "ACLU: Its Subversive Past and Evil Vision for America's Future," *Christian Crusade* (May 1993, Vol. 41, No. 5), p.4; "Communism, Socialism and the New World Religion," *The Florida Forum* (Winter 1998), p.19; *Now Is the Dawning of the New Age New World Order, op. cit.*, p.167-168; Ursala Niebuhr, Editor, *Remembering Reinhold Niebuhr* (New York, NY: HarperSanFrancisco, 1991), p.41; Fred C. Schwarz, "The Communist Front, *The Schwarz Report* (September 2000, Vol. 40, No. 9), p.5; "Transformation Toward New Age Synthesis," *Distant Drums* (March 1986, Vol. 8, No. 1), p.6; Zygmund Dobbs *Keynes at Harvard: Economic Deception As a Political Credo* (New York, NY: Probe Research, Inc., 1969 Edition), p.19; Raymond Blanton, "In Perils of the ACLU," *The Perilous Times* (December 1993, Vol. 15, No. 10), p.1; *Ibid.*, p.15, 27; John A. Stormer, *None Dare Call It Treason...25 Years Later* (Florissant, MO: Liberty Bell Press, 1992), p.556; "America Subverted by the A.C.L.U.," *Christian World Report* (July 1989, Vol. 1, No. 5), p.4; David A. Noebel, *The Marxist Minstrels: A Handbook on Communist Subversion of Music* (Tulsa, OK: American Christian College Press, 1974), p.127; Noebel, *Is the NCC Really Soft on Communism, op. cit.*, p.9; James W. Wardner, *The Planned Destruction of America* (Debary, FL: Longwood Communications, 1994), p.133.

[85] James R. Patrick, Compiler and Editor, *America 2000/Goals 2000* (Moline, IL: Citizens for Academic Excellence, 1994), p.131; *Chronology of Education with Quotable Quotes* (Highland City, FL: Pro Family Forum, Inc., 1994, Updated, bound volume), p.17; "Federal Agents Confiscate Church and Forcibly Remove Pastor and Members—Fulfilling the Plan of the Communist Internationle," *The Florida Forum* (Winter 2000); p.10; *Now Is the Dawning of the New Age New World Order, op. cit.*, p.102-103; "Communism, Socialism and the New World Religion," *The Florida Forum* Winter 1998), p.19; Correll, "Will the Communist Plans for America Be Fulfilled in Louisville?," *op. cit.*, p.11.

[86] Buhle, Buhle, and Georgakas, *op. cit.*, p.198, 237.

[87] "What the A.C.L.U. Is For and Against," *Christian News* (October 18, 1993, Vol. 31, No. 38), p.2. See also: Chambers, *op. cit.*, p.28.

[88] Chambers, *op. cit.*, p.28.

[89] Rivera, *op. cit.*, p.77. See also: Texe Marrs, *Big Sister Is Watching You* (Austin, TX: Living Truth Publishers, 1993), p.136; "What the A.C.L.U. Is For and Against," *Christian News* (October 18, 1993, Vol. 31, No. 38), p.2; Jay Tower, "ACLU: Its Subversive Past and Evil Vision for America's Future," *Christian Crusade* (May 1993, Vol. 41, No. 5), p.4; John A. Stormer, *None Dare Call It Treason...25 Years Later* (Florissant, MO: Liberty Bell Press, 1992), p.556; "Who Is Behind the ACLU?," *The Perilous Times* (December 1993, Vol. 15, No. 10), p.1.

[90] Texe Marrs, *Big Sister Is Watching You* (Austin, TX: Living Truth Publishers, 1993), p.136; "Who Is Behind the ACLU?," *The Perilous Times* (December 1993, Vol. 15, No. 10), p.1.

[91] *The Road to Socialism and the New World Order* (Highland City, FL: Florida Pro Family Forum, Inc., 1995), p.14; Zygmund Dobbs *Keynes at Harvard: Economic Deception As a Political Credo* (New York, NY: Probe Research, Inc., 1969 Edition), p.44.

[92] Chambers, *op. cit.*, p.31.

[93] Noebel, *Is the NCC Really Soft on Communism, op. cit.*, p.9; *The NCC/WCC—Communism's Helpers, op. cit.*, p.5; Paper from the Committee of Christian Laymen Inc. of Woodland Hills (No. 5), p.1.

[94] *Chronology of Education with Quotable Quotes* (Highland City, FL: Pro Family Forum, Inc., 1994), p.11, 15, 34; *Now Is the Dawning of the New Age New World Order, op. cit.*, 1991), p.27. 237; Buhle, Buhle, and Georgakas, *op. cit.*, p.364, 365, 428, 800; Zygmund Dobbs *Keynes at Harvard: Economic Deception As a Political Credo* (New York, NY: Probe Research, Inc., 1969 Edition), p.42.

[95] Paper from the Committee of Christian Laymen Inc. of Woodland Hills (September 10, 1970, No. 196), p.2.

[96] Rivera, *op. cit.*, p.77.

[97] Skousen, *op. cit.*, p.68. See also: Chambers, *op. cit.*, p.27; Paper from the Committee of Christian Laymen Inc. of Woodland Hills (December 10, 1964, No. 114), p.1.

[98] Paper from the Committee of Christian Laymen Inc. of Woodland Hills (June 30, 1964, No. 102), p.1; Bundy, *Collectivism in the Churches, op. cit.*, p.94, 137.

[99] Wardner, *Unholy Alliances, op. cit.*, p.152. See also: Skousen, *op. cit.*, p.48; *The NCC/WCC—Communism's Helpers, op. cit.*, p.5, 6, 11; McIlhany, *op. cit.*; Paper from the Committee of Christian Laymen Inc. of Woodland Hills (June 30, 1964, No. 102), p.1; Bundy, *Collectivism in the Churches, op. cit.*, p.109, 116-117; Paper from the Committee of Christian Laymen Inc. of Woodland Hills (September 10, 1970, No. 196), p.1; Paper from the Committee of Christian Laymen Inc. of Woodland Hills (No. 5), p.1; Paper from the Committee of Christian Laymen Inc. of Woodland Hills (January 28, 1964, No. 87), p.1; Chambers, *op. cit.*, p.300; Rivera, *op. cit.*, p.224, 225; Edgar C. Bundy, *How Liberals and Radicals Are Manipulating Evangelicals* (Miami Shores, FL: Edgar Bundy Ministries, Inc., 1982), p.32.

[100] Skousen, *op. cit.*, p.48; Rivera, *op. cit.*, p.226; *Ibid.*, p.152, 226.

[101] *The NCC/WCC—Communism's Helpers, op. cit.*, p.11; McIlhany, *op. cit.*

[102] Transcript "Illuminati and the Council on Foreign Relations" by Myron Fagan. See also: Wardner, *Unholy Alliances, op. cit.*, p.225.

[103] *The NCC/WCC—Communism's Helpers, op. cit.*, p.11; Paper from the Committee of Christian Laymen Inc. of Woodland Hills (October 16, 1969, No. 181), p.1; Paper from the Committee of Christian Laymen Inc. of Woodland Hills (No. 5), p.1; Bundy, *Collec-tivism in the Churches, op. cit.*, p.100.

[104] *Ibid.* See also: Paper from the Committee of Christian Laymen Inc. of Woodland Hills (No. 122, revised), p.1.

[105] Bundy, *Collectivism in the Churches, op. cit.*, p.90.

[106] *Ibid.*, p.91.

[107] Clyde L. Manschreck, *A History of Christianity: Readings in the History of the Church from the Reformation to the Present* (Englewood Cliffs, NJ: Prentice-Hall, Inc., 1964), p.413; Earle E. Cairns, *Christianity Through the Centuries: A History of the Christian Church* (Grand Rapids, MI: Zondervan Publishing House, 1954), p.463; David P. Gaines, *The World Council of Churches: A Study of Its Background and History* (Peterborough, NH: Richard R. Smith Company, Inc., 1966), p.30.

[108] Eric Samuelson, *Fabian Society*; John B. Harrison and Richard E. Sullivan, *A Short History of Western Civilization* (NY: Alfred A. Knopf, 1960), p.501; "Satan, the Illuminati and the Destruction of Fatherhood," *Newsletter from a Christian Ministry* (July 1, 1993, Vol. 2, No. 10), p.13; Rivera, *op. cit.*, p.33; Norman MacKenzie, Editor, *Secret Societies* (NY: Holt, Rinehart and Winston, 1967), p.195.

[109] Julius E. Schindler, "Despotism vs. Popular Government," *The New Age Magazine* (November 1929, Vol. 37, No. 11), p.675; "The Mafia," *Newsletter from a Christian Ministry* (September 1, 1993, Vol. 2, No. 12), p.12; "Irrepressible Mussolini," *The New Age Magazine* (July 25, Vol. 33, No. 7), p.390; "Satan, the Illuminati and the Destruction of

Fatherhood," *Newsletter from a Christian Ministry* (July 1, 1993, Vol. 2, No. 10), p.13; John H. Cowles, "Italian Masonry Under Fascist Regime," *The New Age Magazine* (January 1926, Vol. 34, No. 1), p.15; Henry C. Clausen, *To a Non-Mason: You Must Seek Masonic Membership!* (Washington, DC: The Supreme Council, 33°, Mother Council of the World, Southern Jurisdiction, USA, 1977), p.6; Michael Baigent and Richard Leigh, *The Temple and the Lodge* (NY: Arcade Publishing, Inc., 1989), p.192; Wardner, *Unholy Alliances, op. cit.*, p.143; Joseph Fort Newton, *The Builders: A Story and Study of Masonry* (Cedar Rapids, IA: The Torch Press, 1914), p.232; David L. Carrico, *Lucifer—Eliphas Levi—Albert Pike and the Masonic Lodge* (Evansville, IN: Followers of Jesus Christ, 1991), p.30; David Carrico, *The Occult Meaning of the Great Seal of the United States* (Evansville, IN: Followers of Jesus Christ, 1991), p.56; Samuelson, *op. cit.; Chronology of Education with Quotable Quotes, op. cit.*, p.14; *Now Is the Dawning of the New Age New World Order, op. cit.*, p.41, 76; Jim Marrs, *Rule by Secrecy: The Hidden History That Connects the Trilateral Commission, the Freemasons, and the Great Pyramids* (New York, NY: HarperCollins Publishers, Inc., 2000), p.255.

[110] Brian Garling, *Global Checkmate by the New Age-New World Order* (Landsborough, Queensland: Endtime Ministries, 1993), p.19; "The Mafia," *Newsletter from a Christian Ministry* (September 1, 1993, Vol. 2, No. 12), p.12; David F. Webber and N. W. Hutchings, *Satan's Kingdom and the Second Coming* (Oklahoma City, OK: Southwest Radio Church, 1983), p.34-35; "The Vietnamese Syndicate's Connection to the Illuminati," *A Newsletter from a Follower of Jesus Christ* (September 1995, Vol. 4, No. 5), p.39.

[111] *Now Is the Dawning of the New Age New World Order, op. cit.*, p.41, 76; John B. Harrison and Richard E. Sullivan, *A Short History of Western Civilization* (NY: Alfred A. Knopf, 1960), p.501; Michael Baigent and Richard Leigh, *The Temple and the Lodge* (NY: Arcade Publishing, Inc., 1989), p.264; William T. Still, *New World Order: The Ancient Plan of Secret Societies* (Lafayette, LA: Huntington House, Inc., 1990), p.118, 119; Manly P. Hall, *America's Assignment with Destiny* (Los Angeles, CA: Philosophical Research Society, Inc., 1951), p.94; Samuelson, *op. cit.;* Michael Baigent and Richard Leigh, *The Temple and the Lodge* (NY: Arcade Publishing, Inc., 1989), p.264; Rivera, *op. cit.*, p.33.

[112] H. L. Haywood, *More About Masonry* (Chicago 16, IL: The Masonic History Company, 1948), p.50, 200; Jim Marrs, *Rule by Secrecy: The Hidden History That Connects the Trilateral Commission, the Freemasons, and the Great Pyramids* (New York, NY: HarperCollins Publishers, Inc., 2000), p.197.

[113] Jim Marrs, *Rule by Secrecy: The Hidden History That Connects the Trilateral Commission, the Freemasons, and the Great Pyramids* (New York, NY: HarperCollins Publishers, Inc., 2000), p.291.

[114] *Now Is the Dawning of the New Age New World Order, op. cit.*, p.41. See also: Gary Kah, *En Route to Global Occupation* (Lafayette, LA: Huntington House Publisher, 1992), p.116-117; "The Vietnamese Syndicate's Connection to the Illuminati," *A Newsletter from a Follower of Jesus Christ* (September 1995, Vol. 4, No. 5), p.39; William T. Still, *New World Order: The Ancient Plan of Secret Societies* (Lafayette, LA: Huntington House, Inc., 1990), p.138.

[115] *Ibid.*, p.42. See also: *The New Age Adversary Bulletin and Old Time Gospel Advocate* (January 1993, Vol. 8, No. 1), p.12; William T. Still, *New World Order: The Ancient Plan of Secret Societies* (Lafayette, LA: Huntington House, Inc., 1990), p.128; Sessler, *op. cit.*, p.71.

[116] Colin Wilson, *The Occult: A History* (NY: Random House, 1971), p.331; J. Gordon Melton, Jerome Clark, and Aidan A. Kelly, *New Age Almanac* (Detroit, MI: Visible Ink, 1991), p.7, 17; Jan Karel Van Baalen, *The Chaos of Cults* (Grand Rapids, MI: Wm. B. Eerdmans Publishing Company, 1962), p.62; Jane Gumprecht, *New Age Health Care: Holy or Holistic* (Orange, CA: Promise Publishing, 1988), p.176; Nat Freedland, *The Occult Explosion* (NY: G. P. Putnam's and Sons, 1972), p.69; Howard Kerr and Charles L. Crow, Editors, *The Occult in America: New Historical Perspectives* (Urbana, IL: University of Illinois Press, 1983), p.3, 4; Clifford Wilson and John Weldon, *Psychic Forces and Occult Shock: A Biblical View* (Chattanooga, TN: Global Publishers, 1987), p.181, 248, 255.

[117] Erica Carle, "Who Cares About the Constitution?," *The Florida Forum* (Summer 2000), p.24.

[118] Nat Freedland, *The Occult Explosion* (NY: G. P. Putnam's and Sons, 1972), p.69.

[119] G. A. Riplinger, *New Age Bible Versions* (Munroe Falls, OH: A. V. Publications, 1993), p.412.

[120] *Now Is the Dawning of the New Age New World Order, op. cit.*, p.41, 76; Samuelson, *op. cit.*

[121] David L. Carrico, *Lucifer—Eliphas Levi—Albert Pike and the Masonic Lodge* (Evansville, IN: Followers of Jesus Christ, 1991), p.30; David Carrico, *The Occult Meaning of the Great Seal of the United States* (Evansville, IN: Followers of Jesus Christ, 1991), p.56. See also: D. Duane Winters, *A Search for Light in a Place of Darkness: A Study of Freemasonry* p.69-70; William Schnoebelen, *Masonry: Beyond the Light* (Chino, CA: Chick Publications, 1991), p.193; Gary Kah, *En Route to Global Occupation* (Lafayette, LA: Huntington House Publisher, 1992), p.113-114; William T. Still, *New World Order: The Ancient Plan of Secret Societies* (Lafayette, LA: Huntington House, Inc., 1990), p.123.

[122] David Carrico, *The Occult Meaning of the Great Seal of the United States* (Evansville, IN: Followers of Jesus Christ, 1991), p.57; *Ibid.*, p.31.

[123] Rivera, *op. cit.*, p.34. See also: William Schnoebelen, *Masonry: Beyond the Light* (Chino, CA: Chick Publications, 1991), p.76, 192; "The Mafia" *Newsletter from a Christian Ministry* (September 1, 1993, Vol. 2, No. 12), p.12.

[124] William Schnoebelen, *Masonry: Beyond the Light* (Chino, CA: Chick Publications, 1991), p.192. See also: Lew White, *Fossilized Customs: The Pagan Sources of Popular Customs* (Louisville, KY: Strawberry Islands Publishers, 2000), p.54.

[125] Rivera, *op. cit.*, p.34.

[126] Kathleen R. Hayes, "All Rhodes Lead To One World Government" (1993). See also: J. Royce Thomason, "Just What Is a Rhodes Scholarship," *The Voice in the Wilderness* (July 1994), p.7; *The Road to Socialism and the New World Order, op. cit.*, p.3; *Secret Records Revealed, op. cit.*, p.8; *"Secret Records" Revealed: The Men, the Money, and the Methods Behind the New World Order* (Marlborough, NH: The Plymouth Rock Foundation, 1994), p.1; Newsletter from Radio Liberty (September 1999), p.3; "Rhodes to the New World Order," *The Christian World Report* (March/April 1993, Vol. 8, No. 2), p.11.

[127] *Ibid.; President Clinton Will Continue the New World Order* (Oklahoma City, OK: Southwest Radio Church, 1993), p.23; J. Royce Thomason, "Just What Is a Rhodes Scholarship," *The Voice in the Wilderness* (July 1994), p.7; "Rhodes to the New World Order," *The Christian World Report* (March/April 1993, Vol. 8, No. 2), p.30.

[128] Ronald Hutton, *The Triumph of the Moon: A History of Modern Pagan Witchcraft* (Oxford, England: Oxford University Press, 1999), p.13.

[129] *Secret Records Revealed, op. cit.*, p.20; Newsletter from Radio Liberty (April 2001), p.5; *Ibid.*, p.73-74; "The *'One World'* Movement," *The Florida Forum* (Summer 1998), p.6; Samuelson, *op. cit.;* "The President's Letter," *Spiritual Advisory Council Newsletter* (May/June 1989, Vol. 15, No. 5 & 6), p.1.

[130] Marrs, *Rule by Secrecy, op. cit.*, p.85.

[131] *Secret Records Revealed, op. cit.*, p.8; Newsletter from Radio Liberty (May 2001), p.3; *The Globalists: The Power Elite Exposed* (Oklahoma City, OK: Hearthstone Publishing, 2001), p.9.

[132] Newsletter from Radio Liberty (September 1999), p.3. See also: Marrs, *Rule by Secrecy, op. cit.*, p.85.

[133] *Secret Records Revealed, op. cit.*, p.9. See also: *Now Is the Dawning of the New Age New World Order, op. cit.*, p.433; Stanley Monteith, *Brotherhood of Darkness* (Oklahoma City, OK: Hearthstone Publishing, 2000), p.116; William T. Still, *New World Order: The Ancient Plan of Secret Societies* (Lafayette, LA: Huntington House, Inc., 1990), p.151; Marrs, *Rule by Secrecy, op. cit.*, p.85; Rivera, *op. cit.*, p.87; Pat Robertson, *The New World Order* (Dallas, TX: Word Publishing, 1991), p.110.

[134] Rivera, *op. cit.*, p.87.

[135] Hayes, *op. cit.; "Secret Records" Revealed: The Men, the Money, and the Methods Behind the New World Order* (Marlborough, NH: The Plymouth Rock Foundation, 1994), p.36; Newsletter from Radio Liberty (April 2001), p.5; *The Globalists: The Power Elite Exposed* (Oklahoma City, OK: Hearthstone Publishing, 2001), p.9; Marrs, *Rule by Secrecy, op. cit.*, p.85; Stanley Monteith, *Brotherhood of Darkness* (Oklahoma City, OK: Hearthstone Publishing, 2000), p.22; Newsletter from Radio Liberty (September 1999), p.3; Gary Allen *The C.F.R.: Conspiracy to Rule the World* (n.p., n.d.), p.4; Stanley Monteith, "Brotherhood of Darkness," *Prophetic Observer* (January 2001, Vol. 8, No. 1), p.3.

[136] Veon, *op. cit.*, p.21; James Leasor, *Rhodes and Barnato: The Premier and the Prancer* (London, England: Leo Cooper, 1997), p.209-210.

[137] William R. Denslow, *10,000 Famous Freemasons* (Vol. IV) (n.p., 1961), p.29-30; Wes Cook, Editor, *Masonic Curiosa from the Desk of H. L. Haywood* (Fulton, MO: The Ovid Bell Press, Inc., 1968), p.150, 153; *Now Is the Dawning of the New Age New World Order, op. cit.*, p.48, 433; James Leasor, *Rhodes and Barnato: The Premier and the Prancer* (London, England: Leo Cooper, 1997), p.79, 84; *Ibid.;* Fritz Springmeier, *The Watchtower and the Masons* (Portland, OR: n.p., 1992), p.v; Marrs, *Rule by Secrecy, op. cit.*, p.86, 255; Gary Kah, *En Route to Global Occupation* (Lafayette, LA: Huntington House Publishers, 1992), p.22; Fritz Springmeier, *The Top 13 Illuminati Bloodlines* (Portland, OR: n.p., 1995), p.7-8; Michael Baigent and Richard Leigh, *The Temple and the Lodge* (NY: Arcade Publishing, Inc., 1989), p.265.

[138] James Leasor, *Rhodes and Barnato: The Premier and the Prancer* (London, England: Leo Cooper, 1997), p.209.

[139] Michael Howard, *The Occult Conspiracy: The Power of Secret Societies in World History* (New York, NY: MFJ Books, 1989), p.165; "One More Step Toward World Government," *The Christian World Report* (March 1994, Vol. 9, No. 3), p.7; *"Secret Records" Revealed: The Men, the Money, and the Methods Behind the New World Order* (Marlborough, NH: The Plymouth Rock Foundation, 1994), p.1; Newsletter from Radio Liberty (September 1999), p.3; Epperson, *op. cit.*, p.193; Rivera, *op. cit.*, p.89; Gary Kah, *En Route to Global Occupation* (Lafayette, LA: Huntington House Publishers, 1992), p.22.

[140] *President Clinton Will Continue the New World Order* (Oklahoma City, OK: Southwest Radio Church, 1993), p.23, unnumbered page; Newsletter from Radio Liberty (September 1999), p.3; Rivera, *op. cit.*, p.89; Fritz Springmeier, *The Top 13 Illuminati Bloodlines* (Portland, OR: n.p., 1995), p.7-8; "Abraham Flexner and the Rhodes Connection," *The Christian Conscience* (February 1996, Vol. 2, No. 2), p.15; *"Secret Records" Revealed: The Men, the Money, and the Methods Behind the New World Order* (Marlborough, NH: The Plymouth Rock Foundation, 1994), p.2; Leasor, *op. cit.*, p.228, 257, 258; Epperson, *op. cit.*, p.193; Veon, *op. cit.*, p.21; Gary Kah, *En Route to Global Occupation* (Lafayette, LA: Huntington House Publishers, 1992), p.22; Pat Robertson, *The New World Order* (Dallas, TX: Word Publishing, 1991), p.111; "One More Step Toward World Government," *The Christian World Report* (March 1994, Vol. 9, No. 3), p.7; Carroll Quigley, *The Anglo-American Establishment: From Rhodes to Cliveden* (New York, NY: Books in Focus, 1981), p.33.

[141] *Now Is the Dawning of the New Age New World Order, op. cit.*, p.433; Leasor, *op. cit.;* Rivera, *op. cit.*, p.12, 89; Pat Robertson, *The New World Order* (Dallas, TX: Word Publishing, 1991), p.110.

[142] Rivera, *op. cit.*, p.226. See also: Marrs, *Dark Majesty, op. cit.*, p.206.

[143] Transcript of "Illuminati and the Council on Foreign Relations" by Myron Fagan.

[144] Skousen, *op. cit.*, p.48.

[145] Ursala Niebuhr, Editor, *Remembering Reinhold Niebuhr* (New York, NY: HarperSanFrancisco, 1991), p.73.

[146] Skousen, *op. cit.* See also: Paper from the Committee of Christian Laymen Inc. of Woodland Hills (October 16, 1969, No. 181), p.1.

[147] *The NCC/WCC—Communism's Helpers, op. cit.*, p.7. See also: Bundy, *Collectivism in the Churches, op. cit.*, p.133; *IPS Packet* (Independence, MO: Price Publishing Company, n.d.), p.18.

[148] Noebel, *Is the NCC Really Soft on Communism, op. cit.*, p.7-8. See also: Wardner, *Unholy Alliances, op. cit.*, p.154.

[149] David A. Noebel, *The Marxist Minstrels: A Handbook on Communist Subversion of Music* (Tulsa, OK: American

Christian College Press, 1974), p.105, 146; Chambers, *op. cit.*, p.30, 115, 132.

[150] Noebel, *Is the NCC Really Soft on Communism, op. cit.*, p.9-10.

[151] *Intelligence Newsletter* (July-August 1991). See also: Bundy, *Collectivism in the Churches, op. cit.*, p.96.

[152] Rockwood, *op. cit.;* Cloud, "The Attack upon the Blood Atonement," *op. cit.* See also: "Pope Foreseen As Leader of World Church," *Midnight Call* (March 1993), p.20.

[153] William R. Denslow, *10,000 Famous Freemasons* (Vol. III) (n.p., 1959), p.299; "Bishop Oxnam Invites the Pope to Live Our Liberty," *The New Age Magazine* (December 1949, Vol. 57, No. 12), p.716; "The Deception of Billy Graham," *Newsletter from a Christian Ministry* (July 1, 1993, Vol. 2, No. 10), p.38.

[154] Weniger, *op. cit.*, p.6; *The NCC/WCC—Communism's Helpers, op. cit.*, p.5, 12; Paper from the Committee of Christian Laymen, Inc. of Woodland Hills (October 16, 1969, No. 181), p.1.

[155] Wardner, *Unholy Alliances, op. cit.*, p.168. See also: Paper from the Committee of Christian Laymen, Inc. (October 16, 1969, No. 181), p.1.

[156] *The NCC/WCC—Communism's Helpers, op. cit.*, p.12. See also: Rivera, *op. cit.*, p.224.

[157] Wardner, *Unholy Alliances, op. cit.*, p.168.

[158] Bundy, *Collectivism in the Churches, op. cit.*, p.174-175.

[159] Emanuel M. Josephson, *The Truth About Rockefeller* (New York City, NY: Chedney Press, 1964), p.129.

[160] Bundy, *Collectivism in the Churches, op. cit.*, p.175.

[161] Ralph Reed, *Active Faith: How Christians Are Changing the Soul of American Politics* (New York, NY: Free Press, 1996), p.43. See also: McIlhany, *op. cit.;* Jim Fields, "The Changing Face of Christianity," *The Evangelical Methodist* (May 2001, Vol. 79, No. 5), p.2.

[162] *Ibid.*, p.43-44. See also: William G. McLoughlin and Robert N. Bellah, Editors, *Religion in America* (Boston, MA: Houghton Mifflin Company, 1968), p.159.

[163] Sessler, *op. cit.*, p.124.

[164] Reed, *op. cit.*, p.43. See also: McIlhany, *op. cit.*

[165] *Ibid.*, p.58.

[166] *Ibid.*

[167] "King Holiday a Travesty," *Calvary Contender* (February 15, 1992, Vol. 9, No. 4), p.1; "King No Role Model," *Calvary Contender* (February 15, 1998, Vol. 15, No.4; "Catholics May Name King 'Martyr for the Faith,'" *Calvary Contender* (February 1, 2000), p.1; "Turret of the Times," *Christian News* (February 17, 1991, Vol. 30, No. 7), p.19; *Christian News* (October 28, 1991, Vol. 29, No. 39), p.20; "What Kind of Man Was Martin Luther King, Jr.?," *Common Sense for Today* (November/December 1995), p.1; John E. Ashbrook, *New Neutralism II: Exposing the Gray of Compromise* (Mentor, OH: Here I Stand Books, 1992), p.54; "The 'Peace' Prize That the World Gives," *The Christian World Report* (February 1991, Vol. 3, No. 2), p.6; "Bayard Rustin at Notre Dame," *The Review of the News* (December 3, 1969), p.2.

[168] *The Evangelical Methodist* (2000, Vol. 78, No. 2), p.6; "As Mainstream Accepts King, Young Blacks Turn to Malcolm," *Associated Press* (January 17, 1993).

[169] *Ibid.* See also: http://www.religionproject.org/declaration.html, p.1.

[170] Skousen, *op. cit.*, p.48.

[171] Rivera, *op. cit.*, p.224; *The NCC/WCC—Communism's Helpers, op. cit.*, p.12; Bundy, *Collectivism in the Churches, op. cit.*, p.134.

[172] Denslow, (Vol. III), *op. cit.*, p.299; *Ibid.;* "Garfield Bromley Oxnam," Softkey Multimedia Inc., Infopedia (1996); *The NCC/WCC—Communism's Helpers, op. cit.*, p.12; Wardner, *Unholy Alliances, op. cit.*, p.168; "Bishop Oxnam Invites the Pope to Live Our Liberty," *The New Age Magazine* (December 1949, Vol. 57, No. 12), p.716; Rockwood, *op. cit.;* Bundy, *Collectivism in the Churches, op. cit.*, p.134, 232.

[173] "Bishop Oxnam Invites the Pope to Live Our Liberty," *The New Age Magazine* (December 1949, Vol. 57, No. 12), p.716.

[174] *Now Is the Dawning of the New Age New World Order, op. cit.*, p.433.

[175] Henry C. Clausen, *Masons Who Helped Shape Our Nation* (The Supreme Council, 33°, Ancient and Accepted Scottish Rite of Freemasonry Southern Jurisdiction, 1976), p.71.

[176] Letter from Barry Lynn, Executive Director of Americans United for Separation of Church and State (Received February 17, 1993).

[177] "Bishop Oxnam Invites the Pope to Live Our Liberty," *op. cit.*

[178] *Ibid.*

[179] *Ibid.* Bundy, *Billy Graham: Performer?, Politician?, Preacher?, Prophet?, op. cit.*, p.9.

[180] John Ashbrook, *Billy Graham's Catholic Connection;* William Martin, *A Prophet with Honor: The Billy Graham Story* (NY: William Morrow and Company, Inc., 1991), p.221.

[181] William Martin, *A Prophet with Honor: The Billy Graham Story* (NY: William Morrow and Company, Inc., 1991), p.221. See also: *Christian Perspectives* (Fall/Winter 1997, Vol. 10, No. 2), p.3; Fritz Springmeier, *The Top 13 Illuminati*

Bloodlines (Portland, OR: n.p., 1995), p.135-136; Billy Graham, *Just As I Am: The Autobiography of Billy Graham* (Harpers Collins Worldwide, 1997), p.298, 299.

[182] Marrs, *Rule by Secrecy, op. cit.*, p.72.

[183] Fritz Springmeier, *The Top 13 Illuminati Bloodlines* (Portland, OR: n.p., 1995), p.134.

[184] Collier and Horowitz, *op. cit.*, p.150. See also: Fritz Springmeier, *Bloodlines of the Illuminati* (Westminster, CO: Ambassador House, 1999), p.221, 425.

[185] George Grant, *Grand Illusions: The Legacy of Planned Parenthood* (Nashville, TN: Thomas Nelson, Inc., 1998 Edition), p.168.

[186] Gsell, *op. cit.*, p.20-21; Bundy, *Billy Graham: Performer?, Politician?, Preacher?, Prophet?, op. cit.*, p.11, 26.

[187] Paper from the Committee of Christian Laymen, Inc. of Woodland Hills (June 30, 1964, No. 102), p.1.

[188] Bundy, *Billy Graham: Performer?, Politician?, Preacher?, Prophet?, op. cit.*, p.11.

[189] *Ibid.*

[190] *Ibid.*

[191] *Ibid.*, quoting J. B. Matthews, p.12-13.

[192] Letter from The Interfaith Alliance dated April 13, 1995, p.2, 6.

[193] *A Prophet with Honor* p.225-226.

[194] Billy Graham, *Just As I Am: The Autobiography of Billy Graham* (Harpers Collins Worldwide, 1997), p.207-208.

[195] Robert Mateer, "In Memory," *Christian Perspectives* (Fall/Winter 1997, Vol. 10, No. 2), p.3. See also: Collier and Horowitz, *op. cit.*, p.408; Patrick, *op. cit.*, p.462; Judith A. Reisman, *Kinsey: Crimes and Consequences* (Arlington, VA: The Institute for Media Education, Inc., 1998), p.309; Pamphlet from Contemporary Economics and Business Association (Received June 11, 1999); Pamphlet from Contemporary Economics and Business Association (Received January 2, 1999).

[196] *Ibid.*

[197] Fritz Springmeier, *Bloodlines of the Illuminati* (Westminster, CO: Ambassador House, 1999), p.462, 464.

[198] Robert C. Paull, Editor, *Achievement Skills: Guidelines for Personal Growth* (Teacher's Guide) (Thomas Jefferson Research Center, 1984), n.p.

[199] Paper from the Jefferson Center for Character Education (September 11, 1993), n.p.

[200] *Chronology of Education with Quotable Quotes, op. cit.*, p.35.

[201] K. E. Barr, *Unholy Alliances 2000* (Kansas City, MO: Barr Press, 1994), p.35.

[202] Kathy Finnegan, *Goals 2000: Restructuring Our Schools...Restructuring Society* (Oklahoma City, OK: Hearthstone Publishing, Ltd., 1996), p.25.

[203] *Chronology of Education with Quotable Quotes, op. cit.* See also: Shirley Correll, *Body Snatching and the New World "Odor"* (Highland City, FL: Florida Pro Family Forum, Inc., 1995), p.41, 78; *Distant Drums* (December 1983), p.7, 8.

[204] Malcolm Lawrence, "Education Expert Announces 'Lame-Brain Awards,'" *Human Events* (May 3, 1986, Vol. 46, No. 18), p.13.

[205] Rivera, *op. cit.*, p.67; Gary Allen *The Rockefeller File* (Seal Beach, CA: '76 Press, 1976), p.27; Softkey Multimedia Inc., Infopedia, "David Rockefeller" (1996); *Newsletter from a Christian Ministry* (October 1992, Vol. 1, No. 8), p.6.

[206] William G. McLoughlin and Robert N. Bellah, *Religion in America* (Boston, MA: Houghton Mifflin Company, 1968), p.170. See also: Bundy, *Billy Graham: Performer?, Politician?, Preacher?, Prophet?, op. cit.*, p.10.

[207] *Ibid.*

[208] *Ibid.*, p.174.

[209] Noebel, *Is the NCC Really Soft on Communism, op. cit.*, p.7-8. See also: Wardner, *Unholy Alliances, op. cit.*, p.154.

[210] Bundy, *Collectivism in the Churches, op. cit.*, p.49-50.

[211] George Zeller, *Billy Graham: Ecumenical Evangelism* (Middletown Bible Church: Middletown, Connecticut, n.d.), p.7. See also: Allen Dickerson, "Passive Fundamentalism" *O Timothy* (1995, Vol. 12, Issue 6).

[212] Martin, *op. cit.*, p.222.

[213] David W. Cloud, *Flirting with Rome: Evangelical Entanglement with Roman Catholicism (Volume 1—Billy Graham)* (Oak Harbor, WA: Way of Life Literature, 1993); *Ibid.*, p.138, 222; Rivera, *op. cit.*, p.227; Graham, *op. cit.*, p.297.

[214] Bundy, *Billy Graham: Performer?, Politician?, Preacher?, Prophet?, op. cit.*, p.45.

[215] William R. Denslow, *10,000 Famous Freemasons* (Vol. I) (n.p., 1957), p.44.

[216] Cloud, *Flirting with Rome (Volume 1—Billy Graham), op. cit.* See also: Rivera, *op. cit.*, p.227; Bundy, *Billy Graham: Performer?, Politician?, Preacher?, Prophet?, op. cit.*, p.45; Graham, *op. cit.*, p.297.

[217] Martin, *op. cit.*, p.139.

[218] Rivera, *op. cit.*, p.227.

[219] Graham, *op. cit.*, p.293.

[220] *Ibid.*, p.314.

[221] Peter Romanofsky, Editor, *The Greenwood Encyclopedia of American Institutions: Social Service Organizations* (Greenwood Press: Westport, CT: 1978), p.6.

[222] *Pass It On: The Story of Bill Wilson and How the A.A. Message Reached the World* (NY: Alcoholics Anonymous World Services, Inc., 1984), p.374.

[223] *Ibid.*, p.371.

[224] Sam Shoemaker, et. al. *Steps to a New Beginning* (1993), p.32.

[225] John A. Stormer, *The Death of a Nation* (Florissant, MO: Liberty Bell Press, 1968), p.92; Bundy, *Collectivism in the Churches, op. cit.*, p.187, 209, 247; Niebuhr, *op. cit.*, p.35, 81; *WCC Packet* (Independence, MO: Price Publishing Company, n.d.), p.18, 19; Edgar C. Bundy, *How Liberals and Radicals Are Manipulating Evangelicals* (Miami Shores, FL: Edgar Bundy Ministries, Inc., 1982), p.75; Paper from the Committee of Christian Laymen, Inc. (October 16, 1969, No. 181), p.4; Noebel, *Is the NCC Really Soft on Communism, op. cit.*, p.17; Edward Mandell House, *Philip Dru: Administrator* (Appleton, WI: Robert Welch University Press, 1998 reprint), p.vi (Foreword by William Norman Grigg).

[226] Edgar C. Bundy, *How Liberals and Radicals Are Manipulating Evangelicals* (Miami Shores, FL: Edgar Bundy Ministries, Inc., 1982), p.75.

[227] Edward Mandell House, *Philip Dru: Administrator* (Appleton, WI: Robert Welch University Press, 1998 reprint), p.vi (Foreword by William Norman Grigg).

[228] *WCC Packet* (Independence, MO: Price Publishing Company, n.d.), p.19.

[229] *Ibid.*, quoting from *Times*, December 21, 1995, p.19.

[230] Stormer, *The Death of a Nation, op. cit.*, p.92-93.

[231] Bundy, *Collectivism in the Churches, op. cit.*, p.187-188.

[232] "The Christian Century...Mouthpiece for Modernism," *Christian News* (February 10, 1997, Vol. 35, No. 6), p.22.

[233] *Ibid.*

[234] Erica Carle, "Six Generational to Serfdom," *The Florida Forum* (Spring 2001), p.22.

[235] "The Christian Century...Mouthpiece for Modernism," *op. cit.*

[236] Stormer, *None Dare Call It Treason, op. cit.*, p.128.

[237] Undated letter from *Christian Century.*

[238] "Apostasy and Deception," *CIB Bulletin* (November 1991, Vol. 7, No. 11), p.4; "Union Seminary's New Leader Is a Unitarian," *Christian News* (September 9, 1991, Vol. 29, No. 32), p.2.

[239] *Ibid.*

[240] "All Souls Pastor Retained," *The Christian Century* (November 6, 1991, Vol. 108, No. 32), p.1024.

[241] "Apostasy and Deception," *op. cit.*

[242] "ELCA Fills Minds of Youth with Anti-Christian Theology," *Christian News* (September 25, 2000, Vol. 38, No. 35), p.4.

[243] *Ibid.*, quoting Douglas John Hall.

[244] "Christendom Is Ending," *Christian News* (September 25, 2000, Vol. 38, No. 35), p.5.

[245] "ELCA Fills Minds of Youth with Anti-Christian Theology," *op. cit.*

[246] "ELCA Publishes Book by Marxist 'Theological Atheist,'" *Christian News* (June 4, 2001, Vol. 39, No. 23), p.15; "The Strength of the Weak—Toward a Christian Feminism Identity," *Christian News* (June 4, 2001, Vol. 39, No. 23), p.15; "Union Seminary's New Leader Is a Unitarian," *Christian News* (September 9, 1991, Vol. 29, No. 32), p.2.

[247] "Lutherans Publish Book by 'Theological Atheist,'" *Christian News* (July 16, 2001, Vol. 39, No. 29), p.2.

[248] "ELCA Publishes Book by Marxist 'Theological Atheist,'" *op. cit.; Ibid.* See also: "Editor's Testimony to LCMS Convention Committee," *Christian News* (July 16, 2001, Vol. 39, No. 29), p.9.

[249] *Ibid.* "Lutherans Publish Book by 'Theological Atheist,'" *op. cit.*

[250] "ELCA Publishes Book by Marxist 'Theological Atheist,'" *op. cit.*; "Lutherans Publish Book by 'Theological Atheist,'" *op. cit.*

[251] *Ibid.*; "Lutherans Publish Book by 'Theological Atheist,'" *op. cit.*

[252] "The Strength of the Weak—Toward a Christian Feminism Identity," *Christian News* (June 4, 2001, Vol. 39, No. 23), p.15.

[253] *The Presbyterian Layman* (January/February 1999, Vol. 32, No. 1), p.9.

[254] Parker T. Williamson, "Sophia Upstages Jesus at the 1998 ReImagining Revival," *The Presbyterian Layman* (May/June 1998, Vol. 31, No. 3), p.4; *The Presbyterian Layman* (January/February 1999, Vol. 32, No. 1), p.9.

[255] *Ibid.*

[256] *The Other Side* (April 1986, Vol. 22, No. 3, Issue 171), p.53. See also: *Kirkridge* (Spring/Summer 1986).

[257] *Kirkridge* (Spring/Summer 1986).

[258] http://www.religionproject.org/endorsement.html, p.7.

[259] *The Evangelical Methodist* (2000, Vol. 78, No. 2), p.6; http://www.religionproject.org/declaration.html, p.1.

[260] http://www.religionproject.org/declaration.html, p.1.

[261] http://www.religionproject.org/endorsement.html, p.8, 10, 11, 17.

[262] John H. Adams, "Sophia Speaker: Put More Women in Canon," *The Presbyterian Layman* (July/August 1998, Vol. 33, No. 4), p.10; Berit Kjos, *A Twist of Faith* (Green Forest, AR: New Leaf Press, 1997), p.34, 41.

[263] "Liberal Women Try to Create Gods in Their Own Image," *Christian News* (February 28, 1994, Vol. 32, No. 9), p.11; *The Presbyterian Layman* (January/February 1999, Vol. 32, No. 1), p.9; David W. Cloud, "WCC Conference Honors Sophia Goddess, Gives Ovation to Lesbians," *O Timothy* (1994, Vol. 11, Issue 3); Berit Kjos, *A Twist of Faith* (Green Forest, AR: New Leaf Press, 1997), p.23, 34.

[264] "Virginia Mollenkott," *Christian News* (February 17, 1997, Vol. 35, No. 7), p.23.

[265] *The Presbyterian Layman* (January/February 1999, Vol. 32, No. 1), p.9.

[266] Williamson, *op. cit.*, p.4.

[267] Adams, *op. cit.*

[268] William T. James, Editor, *Foreshocks of Antichrist* (Eugene, OR: Harvest House Publishers, 1997), p.58. See also: Berit Kjos, *A Twist of Faith* (Green Forest, AR: New Leaf Press, 1997), p.11, 30.

[269] "Liberal Women Try to Create Gods in Their Own Image," *op. cit.*

[270] Berit Kjos, *A Twist of Faith* (Green Forest, AR: New Leaf Press, 1997), p.11. See also: "WCC Conference Honors Sophia Goddess, Gives Ovation to Lesbians," *The Evangelical Methodist* (June 1994, Vol. 73, No. 6), p.4; Ted Kyle, "Pagan Earth Mother Reemerges As 'Christian' Sophia Cult," *Pulpit Helps* (March 1995, Vol. 20, No. 3), p.16.

[271] "WCC Conference Honors Sophia Goddess, Gives Ovation to Lesbians," *The Evangelical Methodist* (June 1994, Vol. 73, No. 6), p.4; David W. Cloud, "WCC Conference Honors Sophia Goddess, Gives Ovation to Lesbians," *O Timothy* (1994, Vol. 11, Issue 3).

[272] David W. Cloud, "WCC Conference Honors Sophia Goddess, Gives Ovation to Lesbians," *O Timothy* (1994, Vol. 11, Issue 3).

[273] "Liberal Women Try to Create Gods in Their Own Image," *op. cit.;* Kjos, *A Twist of Faith, op. cit.*, p.31; *The Witness* (November 1996, Vol. 79, No. 11), p.18; *Ibid.*

[274] "WCC Conference Honors Sophia Goddess, Gives Ovation to Lesbians," *The Evangelical Methodist, op. cit.*

[275] *The Witness* (November 1996, Vol. 79, No. 11), p.18.

[276] James, *op. cit.*, p.59. See also: Dave Hunt, "The Greening of the Cross," *The Berean Call* (July 1997), p.1; "WCC Conference Honors Sophia Goddess, Gives Ovation to Lesbians," *The Evangelical Methodist, op. cit.;* Kjos, *A Twist of Faith, op. cit.*, p.30.

[277] "Liberal Women Try to Create Gods in Their Own Image," *op. cit.;* Dave Hunt, "The Greening of the Cross," *The Berean Call* (July 1997), p.1; Wardner, *Unholy Alliances, op. cit.*, p.249; Kjos, *A Twist of Faith, op. cit.*, p.53.

[278] *The Presbyterian Layman* (January/February 1999, Vol. 32, No. 1), p.5.

[279] James, *op. cit.;* "WCC Conference Honors Sophia Goddess, Gives Ovation to Lesbians," *The Evangelical Methodist, op. cit.;* "World Council of Churches Ecumenical Women's Decade Festival," *The ACCC Report* (January 1999); Kjos, *A Twist of Faith, op. cit.*, p.31.

[280] Kjos, *A Twist of Faith, op. cit.*, p.33; "Liberal Women Try to Create Gods in Their Own Image," *op. cit.;* "WCC Conference Honors Sophia Goddess, Gives Ovation to Lesbians," *The Evangelical Methodist, op. cit.*

[281] Dave Hunt, "The Greening of the Cross," *The Berean Call* (July 1997), p.1. See also: "W. C. C. Speaker Admits to Syncretism," *Calvary Contender* (April 1, 1992, Vol. 9, No. 7), p.2; David W. Cloud, "World Council of Churches Promotes Female Gods," *O Timothy* (1992, Vol. 9, Issue 1); Joseph A. Harriss, "The Gospel According to Marx," *Christian News* (February 1, 1993, Vol. 31, No. 5), p.12; *World Council of Churches: The Shaky Ship Sails On...* (Los Osos, CA: Fundamental Evangelistic Association, 1999), p.19; David W. Cloud, "World Council of Churches Baptizes Heathenism," *Plains Baptist Challenger* (June 1994), p.1.

[282] http://www.religionproject.org/endorsement.html, p.10.

[283] "World Council of Churches Ecumenical Women's Decade Festival," *The ACCC Report* (January 1999), p.1.

[284] *Ibid.*

[285] Bundy, *Collectivism in the Churches, op. cit.*, p.132-133.

[286] Buhle, Buhle, and Georgakas, *op. cit.*, p.663, 770, 777, 800, 820; Stanley Monteith, *Brotherhood of Darkness* (Oklahoma City, OK: Hearthstone Publishing, 2000), p.48.

[287] "Norman Mattoon Thomas," Softkey Multimedia Inc., Infopedia (1996). See also: Stormer, *None Dare Call It Treason, op. cit.*, p.183; Richard L. Watson, Jr., "Norman Mattoon Thomas," *World Book Encyclopedia* (Vol. 17) (Chicago 54, IL: Field Enterprises Educational Corporation, 1961 Edition), p.201; Lew White, *Fossilized Customs: The Pagan Sources of Popular Customs* (Louisville, KY: Strawberry Islands Publishers, 2000), p.55; Wormser, *op. cit.*, p.159.

[288] Richard L. Watson, Jr., "Norman Mattoon Thomas," *World Book Encyclopedia* (Vol. 17) (Chicago 54, IL: Field Enterprises Educational Corporation, 1961 Edition), p.201.

[289] Buhle, Buhle, and Georgakas, *op. cit.*, p.820.

[290] "Norman Mattoon Thomas," Softkey Multimedia Inc., Infopedia (1996).

[291] *"Are These the Only Choices I've Got?"* (New York, NY: Socialist Party, n.d.), p.6.

[292] Buhle, Buhle, and Georgakas, *op. cit.*, p.821.

[293] *Ibid.*, p.820.

[294] *Ibid.*, p.702.

[295] "Norman Mattoon Thomas," Softkey Multimedia Inc., Infopedia (1996). See also: Watson, *op. cit.*

[296] *Ibid.*

[297] *Ibid.*; "Watson, *op. cit.*

[298] "Norman Mattoon Thomas," Softkey Multimedia Inc., Infopedia (1996).

[299] Stanley Monteith, *Brotherhood of Darkness* (Oklahoma City, OK: Hearthstone Publishing, 2000), p.48; *"Secret Records" Revealed: The Men, the Money, and the Methods Behind the New World Order* (Marlborough, NH: The Plymouth Rock Foundation, 1994), p.13; Epperson, *op. cit.*, p.47. See also: Lew White, *Fossilized Customs: The Pagan Sources of Popular Customs* (Louisville, KY: Strawberry Islands Publishers, 2000), p.55.

[300] John Cotter, *A Study in Syncretism* (Flesherton, Ontario: Canadian Intelligence Publications, n.d.), p.69; *The SIECUS Circle* p.35.

[301] Niebuhr, *op. cit.*, p.xi, xiii.

[302] Collier and Horowitz, *op. cit.*, p.155; Buhle, Buhle, and Georgakas, *op. cit.*, p.31; *Ibid.*, Front flap; D. W. Cloud, "Some Frightening Facts About Billy Graham," *O Timothy* (1984, Vol. 1, Issue 4); Bundy, *Billy Graham: Performer?, Politician?, Preacher?, Prophet?, op. cit.*, p.71; Graham, *op. cit.*, p.301; Foster Stockwell, "Niebuhr: Relevant Theologian," *The World Book Year Book*, (Chicago 54, IL: Field Enterprises Educational Corporation, 1972), p.492; L. J. Trinterud, "Reinhold Niebuhr," *The World Book Encyclopedia* (Vol. 13), (Chicago 54, IL: Field Enterprises Education Corporation, 1961 Edition), p.323.

[303] L. J. Trinterud, "Reinhold Niebuhr," *The World Book Encyclopedia* (Vol. 13) (Chicago 54, IL: Field Enterprises Education Corporation, 1961 Edition), p.323.

[304] "Reinhold Niebuhr," Softkey Multimedia Inc., Infopedia (1996).

[305] *Ibid.* See also: Bundy, *Billy Graham: Performer?, Politician?, Preacher?, Prophet?, op. cit.*, p.71; Buhle, Buhle, and Georgakas, *op. cit.*, p.133; Alan Geyer, *The Idea of Disarmament! Rethinking the Unthinkable* (Elgin, IL: The Brethren Press and the Churches' Center for Theology and Public Policy, 1982), p.201.

[306] Niebuhr, *op. cit.*, p.3.

[307] *Ibid.*, p.40.

[308] Buhle, Buhle, and Georgakas, *op. cit.*, p.133.

[309] Niebuhr, *op. cit.*, p.80, p.92, 93.

[310] *Ibid.*, p.56.

[311] *Ibid.*, p.42.

[312] *Ibid.*, p.90.

[313] Wardner, *Unholy Alliances, op. cit.*, p.154; "Reinhold Niebuhr," Softkey Multimedia Inc., Infopedia (1996); *Ibid.*, p.3, 377.

[314] Niebuhr, *op. cit.*, p.162.

[315] Ad to subscribe to magazine (Received on September 14, 1991).

[316] Niebuhr, *op. cit.*, p.194, 220.

[317] Marrs, *Rule by Secrecy, op. cit.*, p.255.

[318] Wardner, *Unholy Alliances, op. cit.*, p.154-155. See also: Gary Allen, *Jimmy Carter, Jimmy Carter* (Seal Beach, CA: '76 Press, 1976), p.43.

[319] *The New World Order* (Milford, PA: America's Future, Inc., 1992), p.7; *Now Is the Dawning of the New Age New World Order, op. cit.*, p.120.

[320] Rus Walton, *One National Under God* (Nashville, TN: Thomas Nelson Publishers, 1987), p.109; Noebel, *Is the NCC Really Soft on Communism, op. cit.*, p.16, 17; Niebuhr, *op. cit.*, p.80, 245, 377.

[321] Rivera, *op. cit.*, p.198. See also: Alan Geyer, *The Idea of Disarmament! Rethinking the Unthinkable* (Elgin, IL: The Brethren Press and the Churches' Center for Theology and Public Policy, 1982), p.200; McLoughlin and Bellah, *op. cit.*, p.159.

[322] Chambers, *op. cit.*, p.130, 133.

[323] Noebel, *Is the NCC Really Soft on Communism, op. cit.*, p.16.

[324] *Ibid.*

[325] *Ibid.*; Niebuhr, *op. cit.*, p.28.

[326] *Ibid.*, p.17; Niebuhr, *op. cit.*, p.377.

[327] Niebuhr, *op. cit.*, p.377.

[328] *Chronology of Education with Quotable Quotes, op. cit.*, p.11, 15, 34; *Now Is the Dawning of the New Age New World Order, op. cit.*, p.27, 237; Zygmund Dobbs *Keynes at Harvard: Economic Deception As a Political Credo* (New York,

NY: Probe Research, Inc., 1969 Edition), p.42; *Ibid.*, p.56.

[329] Paper from the Committee of Christian Laymen, Inc. of Woodland Hills (September 10, 1970, No. 196), p.2.

[330] *Ibid.*

[331] Buhle, Buhle, and Georgakas, *op. cit.*, p.364, 365; Paper from the Committee of Christian Laymen, Inc. of Woodland Hills (September 10, 1970, No. 196), p.2.

[332] *The NCC/WCC—Communism's Helpers, op. cit.*, p.7.

[333] Alan Geyer, *The Idea of Disarmament! Rethinking the Unthinkable* (Elgin, IL: The Brethren Press and the Churches' Center for Theology and Public Policy, 1982), p.191; Niebuhr, *op. cit.*, Front flap, p.211, 227, 252.

[334] Niebuhr, *op. cit.*, p.55.

[335] Geyer, *op. cit.*, p.191, 200.

[336] David P. Gaines, *The World Council of Churches: A Study of Its Background and History* (Peterborough, NH: Richard R. Smith Co. Inc., 1966), p.244; Niebuhr, *op. cit.*, p.227, 236-237.

[337] Niebuhr, *op. cit.*, p.252.

[338] *Ibid.*, p.259.

[339] "WCC Faith & Order Commission Conference," *Calvary Contender* (September 15, 1993, Vol. 10, No. 18), p.2.

[340] Interview by Danny Collum with Myles Horton, "Building Democracy in the Mountains" *Sojourners* (April 1986), p.26. See also: Skousen, *op. cit.*, p.24-25; Jesse Helms, *The King Holiday and Its Meaning* (St. Louis, MO: Council of Conservative Citizens, 1998), p.37. See also: Niebuhr, *op. cit.*, p.98.

[341] *Ibid.; Distant Drums* (August 1995, Vol. 16, No. 1), p.6.

[342] Buhle, Buhle, and Georgakas, *op. cit.*, p.330.

[343] *Ibid.*, p.674.

[344] *Ibid.*, p.195.

[345] Noebel, *The Marxist Minstrels, op. cit.*, p.174-175. See also: *The Council of Conservative Citizens' Guide to* Martin Luther King, Jr. Holiday (Jasper, AL: n.p., n.d.), p.6; Jesse Helms, *The King Holiday and Its Meaning* (St. Louis, MO: Council of Conservative Citizens, 1998), p.36; *Ibid.*, p.195.

[346] *Ibid.* p.135. See also: Pamphlet titled "The Council of Conservative Citizens' Guide to *Martin Luther King, Jr. Holiday*, p.6; Jesse Helms, *The King Holiday and Its Meaning* (St. Louis, MO: Council of Conservative Citizens, 1998), p.36; Buhle, Buhle, and Georgakas, *op. cit.*, p.195, 785.

[347] *Ibid.*, p.175.

[348] Buhle, Buhle, and Georgakas, *op. cit.*, p.87.

[349] "Clinton Honors 'Best-Loved Commie,'" *AIM Report* (December 1994, 23-24), p.2.

[350] Interview by Danny Collum with Myles Horton, *op. cit.*, p.29. See also: Carol Polsgrove, "Unbroken Circle," *Sierra* (January/February 1992, Vol. 77, No. 1), p.132.

[351] Noebel, *The Marxist Minstrels, op. cit.*, p.173.

[352] *Ibid.*, p.173, 134.

[353] Peter Applebome, "Nurturing New Seeds in a Garden of Hopes," *The New York Times National* (January 29, 1990); Carol Polsgrove, "Unbroken Circle," *Sierra* (January/February 1992, Vol. 77, No. 1), p.130. See also: Skousen, *op. cit.*, p.25; "Rosa Parks: 'She Sat Down and the World Turned Around,'" *U. S. News & World Report* (August 20-27, 2001, Vol. 131, No. 7), p.49.

[354] Epperson, *op. cit.*, p.40. See also: *The Auger News Letter* (January 2000), p.1; Rivera, *op. cit.*, p.76; Jesse Helms, *The King Holiday and Its Meaning* (St. Louis, MO: Council of Conservative Citizens, 1998), p.36.

[355] Noebel, *The Marxist Minstrels, op. cit.*, p.135. See also: Pamphlet titled "The Council of Conservative Citizens' Guide to *Martin Luther King, Jr. Holiday*, p.6; Jesse Helms, *The King Holiday and Its Meaning* (St. Louis, MO: Council of Conservative Citizens, 1998), p.29, 36; Buhle, Buhle, and Georgakas, *op. cit.*, p.195, 785; Wilhelm E. Schmitt, "Some Facts About 'Martin Luther' King, Jr. Ignored by the National Capital Planning Commission," *Christian News* (January 1, 2000, Vol. 38, No. 1), p.7.

[356] Jesse Helms, *The King Holiday and Its Meaning* (St. Louis, MO: Council of Conservative Citizens, 1998), p.36.

[357] *Ibid.*, p.37.

[358] *Ibid.*, p.38.

[359] Applebome, *op. cit.*

[360] *Ibid.*

[361] *The Auger News Letter* (January 2000), p.1.

[362] Martin, *op. cit.*, p.364; Noebel, *The Marxist Minstrels, op. cit.*, p.176; Carol Polsgrove, "Unbroken Circle," *Sierra* (January/February 1992, Vol. 77, No. 1), p.132; Rivera, *op. cit.*, p.76.

[363] Rivera, *op. cit.*, p.76.

[364] Buhle, Buhle, and Georgakas, *op. cit.*, p.137.

[365] "E. V. Hill a PK Speaker," *Calvary Contender* (February 15, 1996, Vol. 13, No. 4), p.2; John E. Ashbrook, *New Neutralism II: Exposing the Gray of Compromise* (Mentor, OH: Here I Stand Books, 1992), p.68.

[366] Martin, *op. cit.* "In Globo Cogitare et in Loco Agree (sic) (Thinking Globally and Acting Locally)" (Part III), *Distant Drums* (May 1983, Vol. 5, No. 2), p.5.

[367] Graham, *op. cit.*, p.314. See also: Reed, *op. cit.*, p.68.

[368] Mike Betancourt, Compiler, "Promise Keepers: Should Fundamentalists Get Involved?," *O Timothy* (n.d.), p.2; John E. Ashbrook, *New Neutralism II: Exposing the Gray of Compromise* (Mentor, OH: Here I Stand Books, 1992), p.68.

[369] John E. Ashbrook, *New Neutralism II: Exposing the Gray of Compromise* (Mentor, OH: Here I Stand Books, 1992), p.68; M. H. Reynolds, "Planting the Seeds of Ecumenical Apostasy in the Name of Evangelism," *Foundation* (1983, Vol. 4, No. 4).

[370] Graham, *op. cit.*, p.427, 674; Martin, *op. cit.*, p.563; *Ibid.;* "E. V. Hill a PK Speaker," *op. cit.;* "E. V. Hill Supports Lyons," *Calvary Contender* (November 15, 1997, Vol. 14, No. 22), p.2; "Promise Keepers," *The BDM Letter* (May/June 1996, Vol. 5, No. 3), p.2; *A Prophet with Honor* p.563.

[371] "Communion Service at Promise Keepers Clergy Conference," *Christian News* (April 1, 1996, Vol. 34, No. 14), p.1; Jefferson M. Angers, Editor, *Council for National Policy Annual Directory 1984-85* (Baton Rouge, LA: Council for National Policy, 1984), p.30; George Archibald, "Conservative Blacks Fault GOP for Not Overcoming Party Image As the Enemy," *The Washington Times* (December 2, 1985), unnumbered page.

[372] Ashbrook, *New Neutralism II, op. cit.* See also: "E. V. Hill Defends Lyons," *Christian News* (September 29, 1997, Vol. 35, No. 35), p.18; "Promise Keepers," *The BDM Letter* (May/June 1996, Vol. 5, No. 3), p.2; "In Globo Cogitare et in Loco Agree (sic) (Thinking Globally and Acting Locally)" (Part III), *Distant Drums* (May 1983, Vol. 5, No. 2), p.5; Jefferson M. Angers, Editor, *Council for National Policy Annual Directory 1984-85* (Baton Rouge, LA: Council for National Policy, 1984), p.30; "Ecumenical Prayer Call," *The Perilous Times* (September 1993, Vol. 15, No. 7), p.4; "Strange Things in New Orleans," *O Timothy* (1987, Vol. 4, Issues 8-9).

[373] *Ibid.*

[374] "Moody Founder's Week Features Ecumenicals," *Calvary Contender* (December 15, 1995), p.1; "E. V. Hill Supports Lyons," *Calvary Contender* (November 15, 1997, Vol. 14, No. 22), p.2; "Four Die Waiting for Healing," *The Voice in the Wilderness* (December 2000), p.13; "Promise Keepers," *The BDM Letter* (May/June 1996, Vol. 5, No. 3), p.2; Mike Betancourt, Compiler, "Promise Keepers: Should Fundamentalists Get Involved?," *O Timothy* (n.d.).

[375] "National Baptists Forgive Lyons," *Calvary Contender* (October 15, 1997, Vol. 14, No. 20), p.2; "Baptist Leader Apologizes but Refuses to Step Down," *Christian News* (December 15, 1997, Vol. 35, No. 46), p.2; "Baptist Leader Surprises Jewelers ," *Christian News* (September 15, 1997, Vol. 35, No. 33), p.11.

[376] "E. V. Hill Supports Lyons," *Calvary Contender* (November 15, 1997, Vol. 14, No. 22), p.2; "E. V. Hill Defends Lyons," *Christian News* (September 29, 1997, Vol. 35, No. 35), p.18. See also: Texe Marrs, "Has the Entire Christian Establishment Finally Just Gone Berserk?," *Power of Prophecy* (April 2001, Vol. 2001-04), p.2; "Convicted Baptist Leader Seeking Divorce," *Christian News* (April 23, 2001, Vol. 39, No. 17), p.17; "Baptist Leader Apologizes but Refuses to Step Down," *Christian News* (December 15, 1997, Vol. 35, No. 46), p.2; "Baptist Leader Denied Two Previous Unions at Time of Third Marriage," *Christian News* (September 15, 1997, Vol. 35, No. 33), p.11.

[377] "Four Die Waiting for Healing," *The Voice in the Wilderness* (December 2000), p.13.

[378] "Strange Things in New Orleans," *O Timothy* (1987, Vol. 4, Issues 8-9).

[379] "Moody Founder's Week Features Ecumenicals," *op. cit.*

[380] "The Deception of Billy Graham," *Newsletter from a Christian Ministry* (July 1, 1993, Vol. 2, No. 10), p.38.

[381] *Ibid.*

[382] *Ibid.*

[383] *Ibid.*, p.36.

[384] Ashbrook, *New Neutralism II, op. cit.*, p.68. See also: "E. V. Hill Defends Lyons," *Christian News* (September 29, 1997, Vol. 35, No. 35), p.18; "Promise Keepers," *The BDM Letter* (May/June 1996, Vol. 5, No. 3), p.2; "In Globo Cogitare et in Loco Agree (sic) (Thinking Globally and Acting Locally)" (Part III), *Distant Drums* (May 1983, Vol. 5, No. 2), p.5; "Ecumenical Prayer Call," *The Perilous Times* (September 1993, Vol. 15, No. 7), p.4; "Strange Things in New Orleans," *O Timothy* (1987, Vol. 4, Issues 8-9).

[385] "E. V. Hill a PK Speaker," *op. cit.;* "Promise Keepers," *The BDM Letter* (May/June 1996, Vol. 5, No. 3), p.2.

[386] David E. Anderson, "Religious Groups Support Gay Rights March," *Christian News* (March 8, 1993, Vol. 31, No. 10), p.1.

[387] Ashbrook, *New Neutralism II, op. cit.*

[388] Noebel, *Is the NCC Really Soft on Communism, op. cit.*, p.17-18. See also: Weniger, *op. cit.*, p.5-6.

[389] Paper from the Committee of Christian Laymen, Inc. (December 18, 1964), No. 115), p.1.

[390] *Ibid.* See also: Helms, *op. cit.*, p.35-36.

[391] Gary Allen, *Jimmy Carter, Jimmy Carter* (Seal Beach, CA: '76 Press, 1976), p.43.

[392] Jan Karel Van Baalen, *The Chaos of Cults* (Grand Rapids, MI: Wm. B. Eerdmans Publishing Company, 1962), p.303.

[393] Rivera, *op. cit.*, p.198; Allen, *Jimmy Carter, Jimmy Carter, op. cit.*

[394] D. W. Cloud, "Some Frightening Facts About Billy Graham," *O Timothy* (1984, Vol. 1, Issue 4).

[395] *Now Is the Dawning of the New Age New World Order, op. cit.*, p.128; Niebuhr, *op. cit.*, Front flap, xii, p.266.

[396] *An American Commentary* (Oklahoma City, OK: Hearthstone Publishing, Ltd., 1993), p.56; *President Clinton Will Continue the New World Order, op. cit.*, p.14; *The Road to Socialism and the New World Order, op. cit.*, p.51; *Secret Records Revealed, op. cit.*, p.16, 77; "The Vast Left-Wing Conspiracy?," *The Christian Conscience* (May 1998, Vol. 4, No. 4), p.36; Berit Kjos, "Character Training for Global Citizens," *The Christian Conscience* (June 1997, Vol. 3, No. 5), p.49; Cotter, *op. cit.*, p.2; David M. Virkler, *The Word and the World Presenting...A Commentary on Secular Humanism* (Towaco, NJ: Dedication Evangelism, Inc., 1984), p.4; Corliss Lamont, *The Philosophy of Humanism* (NY: Frederick Unger Publishing Company, 1949), p.22, 60; William Norman Grigg, "A Global School Board," *The New American* (January 23, 1995), p.22, 24; "The U. N. & Education," *The Florida Forum* (Fall 2000), p.23; Nancy Leigh DeMoss, Executive Editor, *The Rebirth of America* (Arthur S. DeMoss Foundation, 1986), p.122.

[397] Stormer, *None Dare Call It Treason, op. cit.*, p.109. See also: *Now Is the Dawning of the New Age New World Order, op. cit.*, p.128.

[398] Paul Kurtz, *Humanist Manifestos I and II* (Buffalo, NY: Prometheus Books, 1973), p.29.

[399] *Secret Records Revealed, op. cit.*, p.77; *President Clinton Will Continue the New World Order, op. cit.*, p.14; *The Road to Socialism and the New World Order, op. cit.*, p.51; "The U. N. & Education," *The Florida Forum* (Fall 2000), p.23.

[400] Wardner, *Unholy Alliances, op. cit.*, p.131; Peter Lalonde, *One World Under Antichrist* (Eugene, OR: Harvest House Publishers, 1991), p.107.

[401] William Norman Grigg, "A Global School Board," *The New American* (January 23, 1995), p.22.

[402] *Ibid.*, p.23.

[403] Stormer, *None Dare Call It Treason, op. cit.*, p.112.

[404] Chambers, *op. cit.*, p.430, 431.

[405] *Ibid.*, p.v.

[406] *Chronology of Education with Quotable Quotes, op. cit.*, p.37.

[407] Judith A. Reisman and Eunice Van Winkle Ray, "Kaiser Foundation's Sexual Propaganda," *The Florida Forum* (Fall 2000), p.7.

[408] Cloud, "Some Frightening Facts About Billy Graham," *op. cit.;* Bundy, *Billy Graham: Performer?, Politician?, Preacher?, Prophet?, op. cit.*, p.71.

[409] *Ibid.*

[410] "Jimmy Carter Leaves the Southern Baptist Convention—Again," *Christian News* (November 6, 2000, Vol. 38, No. 41), p.23; "Neo-Orthodox Christianity," *The Watchman Expositor* (1998, Vol. 15, No. 5), p.20; McLoughlin and Bellah, *op. cit.*, p.60.

[411] Graham, *op. cit.*, p.694.

[412] McLoughlin and Bellah, *op. cit.*, p.60.

[413] Gaines, *op. cit.*, p.244.

[414] Softkey Multimedia Inc., Infopedia, "World Council of Churches" (1996).

[415] Cloud, "Some Frightening Facts About Billy Graham," *op. cit.*

[416] "Paul Johannes Tillich," Softkey Multimedia Inc., Infopedia (1996).

[417] Martin, *op. cit.*, p.13.

[418] *Ibid.*, p.220. See also: Bundy, *Billy Graham: Performer?, Politician?, Preacher?, Prophet?, op. cit.*, p.10; Gsell, *op. cit.*, p.20; Zeller, *op. cit.*, p.7; Cloud, "Some Frightening Facts About Billy Graham," *op. cit.;* Allen Dickerson, "Passive Fundamentalism" *O Timothy* (1995, Vol. 12, Issue 6).

[419] Cloud, "Some Frightening Facts About Billy Graham," *op. cit.* See also: Graham, *op. cit.*, p.299.

[420] David W. Cloud, "Billy Graham's Disobedience to the Word of God," *O Timothy* (Updated March 2, 1999), p.5.

[421] McLoughlin and Bellah, *op. cit.*, Chapter entitled "What Is a Presbyterian?" by John S. Bonnell, p.205.

[422] Cloud, "Billy Graham's Disobedience to the Word of God,"*op. cit.*

[423] Graham, *op. cit.*, p.249.

[424] An interview by Carl F. H. Henry, *Christianity Today* (February 8, 1980), p.29.

[425] Martin, *op. cit.*, p.220.

[426] Cloud, "Some Frightening Facts About Billy Graham," *op. cit.*

[427] *A Prophet with Honor* p.328. See also: "Stan Mooneyham," *Christianity Today* (July 22, 1991, Vol. 35, No. 8), p.46; Graham, *op. cit.*, p.561.

[428] Stan Mooneyham," *Christianity Today* (July 22, 1991, Vol. 35, No. 8), p.46; Gil Alexander-Moegerle, *James Dobson's War on America* (Amherst, NY: Prometheus Books, 1997), p.174.

[429] "NAE's World Relief Gets Big Bucks from U. S. Government to Distribute Condoms?," *Christian News* (October 5, 1998, Vol. 36, No. 36), p.2; *Ibid.*

[430] Arthur Simon, *Bread for the World* (Grand Rapids, MI: William B. Eerdmans Publishing Company, 1984, Revised Edition), p.217.

[431] "Stan Mooneyham," *op. cit.*

[432] Constance Cumbey, *A Planned Deception: The Staging of a New Age "Messiah"* (East Detroit, MI: Pointe Publishing, Inc., 1985), p.119; John Pollock, *Crusades: 20 Years with Billy Graham* (Minneapolis, MN: World Wide Publications, 1969), p.234; *Ibid;* David W. Cloud, "World Vision and Rome," *O Timothy* (1995, Vol. 12, Issue 2).

[433] David W. Cloud, "World Vision and Rome," *O Timothy* (1995, Vol. 12, Issue 2).

[434] Constance Cumbey quoting Stanley Mooneyham in *The Hidden Dangers of the Rainbow: The New Age Movement and Our Coming Age of Barbarism* (Shreveport, LA: Huntington House, Inc., 1983), p.154.

[435] "NAE's World Relief Gets Big Bucks from U. S. Government to Distribute Condoms?," *Christian News, op. cit.;* "NAE's World Relief Gets Big Bucks from U. S. Government to Distribute Condoms?," *Calvary Contender* (April 15, 1998, Vol. 15, No. 8).

[436] Cumbey, *A Planned Deception, op. cit.,* p.120.

[437] *Ibid.,* p.119.

[438] *Ibid.,* p.120-121.

[439] *World Goodwill Newsletter* (1994, No. 1), p.10. See also: *Now Is the Dawning of the New Age New World Order, op. cit.,* p.143; David R. Barnhart, *Contending for the Faith* (Eagan, MN: Abiding Word Publications, 1994), p.120; "Beware of 'Comparative Religion,'" *Christian News* (September 26, 1998, Vol. 26, No. 35), p.4; Cotter, *op. cit.,* p.68; *Chronology of Education with Quotable Quotes, op. cit.,* p.34; Albert James Dager, *The World Christian Movement: A Great Delusion Leading to the Religio-Political State of the Anti-Christ* (Redmond, WA: Sword Publishers, 2001), p.175; *Despatch Magazine* (September 1994, Vol. 6:3), p.8; *Eco◆Logic* (November/December 1995, No. 29), p.26-27. *Eco◆Logic* (May 1995, No. 26), p.14-15; *Eco◆Logic* (1997), p.3; "Another Major Player: The Ford Foundation," *The Florida Forum* (Summer 1996), p.5; Corinne McLaughlin and Gordon Davidson, *Spiritual Politics: Changing the World from the Inside Out* (NY: Ballantine Books, 1994), p.250; Chambers, *op. cit.,* p.32; *Yoga Vedanta* (October/November/December 1994, Vol. 3, No. 4), p.15; Berit Kjos, "Gorbachev's New Global Pulpit," *The Christian World Report* (July 1993, Vol. 8, No. 5), p.1; *Wisconsin Report* (November 6, 1997, Vol. 22, No. 43), p.6; *Wisconsin Report* (November 1, 1984, Vol. 9, No. 43), p.6; "The Temple of Understanding," *Wisconsin Report* (October 25, 1984, Vol. 9, No. 42), p.4; Wardner, *Unholy Alliances, op. cit.,* p.170; *United Religions* (Fall 1997, Issue 4), p.18; Barbara L. Overby, "Spiritual Philanthropy: A Communist Perspective," *The Bridging Tree* (Winter 2000-2001, Vol. 4, Issue 1), p.2; *The Temple of Understanding Newsletter* (Fall 1995), p.6, 8; *The Temple of Understanding Newsletter* (Summer 1996); Letter from The Temple of Understanding Newsletter (November 1997), *The Temple of Understanding Newsletter* (Fall 1998), p.1; Albert James Dager, "The World Christian Movement—Part 3: Toward the New World Order," *Media Spotlight* (1999, Vol. 22, No.3), p.13; Brenda Scott and Samantha Smith, *Trojan Horse: How the New Age Movement Infiltrates the Church* (Lafayette, LA: Huntington House Publishers, 1993), p.75, 79.

[440] Barbara L. Overby, "Spiritual Philanthropy: A Communist Perspective," *The Bridging Tree* (Winter 2000-2001, Vol. 4, Issue 1), p.2.

[441] Alan Morrison, *The Serpent and the Cross: Religious Corruption in an Evil Age* (Birmingham, England: K & M Books, 1994), p.538. See also: Brenda Scott and Samantha Smith, *Trojan Horse: How the New Age Movement Infiltrates the Church* (Lafayette, LA: Huntington House Publishers, 1993), p.75; "WCC Promotes Left Wing Revolutionary Causes and Universalism," *Christian News* (May 23, 1994, Vol. 32, No. 21), p.9.

[442] Cotter, *op. cit.,* p.68.

[443] *Ibid.,* p.70. See also: *Distant Drums* (June 1985, Vol. 7, No. 2); Piers Compton, *The Broken Cross: The Hidden Hand in the Vatican* (Cranbrook, Western Australia: Veritas Publishing Company Pty. Ltd., 1984), p.69.

[444] Brenda Scott and Samantha Smith, *Trojan Horse: How the New Age Movement Infiltrates the Church* (Lafayette, LA: Huntington House Publishers, 1993), p.77.

[445] Marcus Braybrooke, *A Wider Vision: A History of the World Congress of Faiths* (Oxford, England: Oneworld Publications, 1996), p.41, 43.

[446] *Despatch Magazine* (September 1994, Vol. 6:3), p.8; Chambers, *op. cit.,* p.434; Letter dated November 1997 from The Temple of Understanding.

[447] Wilbert Forker, Editor, *The Templeton Foundation Prize for Progress in Religion* (Edinburgh: Scottish Academic Press, 1988), p.97-98.

[448] "Parliament of World's Religions Event in New York," *Christian News* (September 20, 1999), p.21.

[449] *Ibid.*

[450] *Ibid.*

[451] "A Very Successful Start," *World Goodwill Newsletter* (1988, No. 3), p.3; Albert James Dager, *The World Christian Movement: A Great Delusion Leading to the Religio-Political State of the Anti-Christ* (Redmond, WA: Sword Publishers, 2001), p.178; Scott and Smith, *op. cit.,* p.66.

[452] Albert James Dager, "The World Christian Movement—Part 3: Toward the New World Order," *Media Spotlight* (1999, Vol. 22, No.3), p.15; Albert James Dager, *The World Christian Movement: A Great Delusion Leading to the Religio-Political State of the Anti-Christ* (Redmond, WA: Sword Publishers, 2001), p.179.

[453] *O Timothy* (1994, Vol. 11, Issue 11); "Testimony of a Modernist," *O Timothy* (1994, Vol. 11, Issue 12).

[454] Sean Jacobs, "Forgiveness on the Agenda," *Breakthroughs* (February 2001), p.5; "Navy Chaplains Take on a New Role," *Breakthroughs* (February 2001), p.6; "Apostasy and Deception," *op. cit.;* "Beyond Boundaries: Choices for Community," (Conference held from June 24027, 1997 at the University of Minnesota), p.5.

[455] *Council on Foreign Relations: Annual Report, July 1, 1987-June 30, 1988,* p.184; *Council on Foreign Relations: Annual Report, July 1, 1992-June 30, 1993,* p.176; *Council on Foreign Relations: Annual Report, July 1, 1994-June 30, 1995,* p.156; Ross, *op. cit.*, p.135.

[456] *Breakthrough* (Winter/Summer 1990, Vol. 11, No. 2-4), p.2; *Breakthrough News* (Fall 1994), p.2.

[457] "*CT* Praises Liberal Catholic Theologian," *Calvary Contender* (October 15, 1998).

[458] *Ibid.*

[459] *Ibid.*

[460] Lawrence LeShan, *How to Meditate: A Guide to Self-Discovery* (Boston, MA: Little, Brown and Company, 1974), Inside back cover.

[461] *Ibid.*, Inside front cover.

[462] See: Noebel, *Is the NCC Really Soft on Communism, op. cit.*, p.17.

[463] Bundy, *Collectivism in the Churches, op. cit.*, p.4.

4. FCC, NCC, AND THE *WCC*

[1] James W. Wardner, *Unholy Alliances* (n.p., 1996), p.175.

[2] *Ibid.*, p.175-176.

[3] Clyde L. Manschreck, *A History of Christianity: Readings in the History of the Church from the Reformation to the Present* (Engle-wood Cliffs, NJ: Prentice-Hall, Inc., 1964), p.416, 465; A. Ralph Epperson, *The Unseen Hand: An Introduction to the Conspiratorial View of History* (Tucson, AZ: Publius Press, 1985), p.221; Edgar C. Bundy, *Collectivism in the Churches: A Documented Account of the Political Activities of the Federal, National, and World Councils of Churches* (Wheaton, IL: The Church League of America, 1958), p.3, 92; Paul Fisher, "A Syndicated Conspiracy Against God and Man?," *The Observer* (January 17, 1996), p.13; Peter Collier and David Horowitz, *The Rockefellers: An American Dynasty* (NY: Holt, Rinehart and Winston, n.d.), p.150; David Allen Rivera, *Final Warning: A History of the New World Order* (Harrisburg, PA: Rivera Enterprises, 1994 Edition), p.225; William McIlhany, "The WCC: A Haven for Marxists?," *Family Protection Scoreboard,* p.21; Kenneth Scott Latourette, *A History of Christianity* (New York, NY: Harper and Row, 1953), p.1268, 1342.

[4] *Ibid.*, p.465; David P. Gaines, *The World Council of Churches: A Study of Its Background and History* (Peterborough, NH: Richard R. Smith Company, Inc., 1966), p.34, 938.

[5] David Allen Rivera, *Final Warning: A History of the New World Order* (Harrisburg, PA: Rivera Enterprises, 1994 Edition), p.225; Edgar C. Bundy, *Collectivism in the Churches: A Documented Account of the Political Activities of the Federal, National, and World Councils of Churches* (Wheaton, IL: The Church League of America, 1958), p.4, 93; John A. Stormer, *None Dare Call It Treason* (Florissant, MO: Liberty Bell Press, 1964), p.23, 125; Robert Sessler, *To Be God of One World: The French Revolution Globalized* (Merlin, OR: Let There Be Light Publications, 1992), p.125; Paper from the Committee of Christian Laymen, Inc. (September 10, 1970, No. 196), p.1; Paper from the Committee of Christian Laymen, Inc. (October 16, 1969, No. 181), p.2; *The Florida Forum* (Fall 1994, Special Edition).

[6] John A. Stormer, *None Dare Call It Treason* (Florissant, MO: Liberty Bell Press, 1964), p.125; Kenneth Scott Latourette, *A History of Christianity* (New York, NY: Harper and Row, 1953), p.1264.

[7] Earle E. Cairns, *Christianity Through the Centuries: A History of the Christian Church* (Grand Rapids, MI: Zondervan Publishing House, 1954), p.434; Ralph Reed, *Active Faith: How Christians Are Changing the Soul of American Politics* (New York, NY: Free Press, 1996), p.42; Hartzell Spence, *The Story of America's Religions* (NY: Holt, Rinehart and Winston, 1957), p.32; Kenneth Scott Latourette, *A History of Christianity* (New York, NY: Harper and Row, 1953), p.1264.

[8] Manschreck, *op. cit.*, p.413; *Ibid.*, p.463; David P. Gaines, *The World Council of Churches: A Study of Its Background and History* (Peterborough, NH: Richard R. Smith Company, Inc., 1966), p.30.

[9] Cairns, *op. cit.*, p.434.

[10] Manschreck, *op. cit.*, p.413.

[11] Cairns, *op. cit.*, p.434; Manschreck, *op. cit.*, p.413.

[12] William G. McLoughlin and Robert N. Bellah, Editors, *Religion in America,* "The 'New Breed' in American Churches" by Harvey Cox (Boston, MA: Houghton Mifflin Company, 1968), p.380; "Social Gospel," Softkey Multimedia Inc., Infopedia (1996); "Walter Rauschenbusch," Softkey Multimedia Inc., Infopedia (1996); Stormer, *None Dare Call It Treason, op. cit.*, p.125; Ralph Reed, *Active Faith: How Christians Are Changing the Soul of American Politics* (New York, NY: Free Press, 1996), p.42, 43; Cairns, *op. cit.*, p.450, 463, 464; Manschreck, *op. cit.*, p.415; Kenneth Scott Latourette, *A History of Christianity* (New York, NY: Harper and Row, 1953), p.1264.

[13] Stormer, *None Dare Call It Treason, op. cit.*, p.124.

[14] *Ibid.*, p.124-125.

[15] Manschreck, *op. cit.*, p.416; Edgar C. Bundy, *Collectivism in the Churches: A Documented Account of the Political Activities of the Federal, National, and World Councils of Churches* (Wheaton, IL: The Church League of America, 1958), p.92, 99; "Walter Rauschenbusch," Softkey Multimedia Inc., Infopedia (1996).

[16] Stormer, *None Dare Call It Treason, op. cit.*, p.125; Wardner, *Unholy Alliances, op. cit.*, p.153.

[17] *Now Is the Dawning of the New Age New World Order* (Oklahoma City, OK: Hearthstone Publishing, Ltd., 1991), p.46-47.

[18] *Ibid.*, p.47.

[19] Ralph Reed, *Active Faith: How Christians Are Changing the Soul of American Politics* (New York, NY: Free Press, 1996), p.43. See also: Stormer, *None Dare Call It Treason, op. cit.*, p.125.

[20] Manschreck, *op. cit.*, p.429.

[21] Wardner, *Unholy Alliances, op. cit.*, p.153. See also: Edgar C. Bundy, *Collectivism in the Churches: A Documented Account of the Political Activities of the Federal, National, and World Councils of Churches* (Wheaton, IL: The Church League of America, 1958), p.101; *Don Bell Reports* (August 15, 1994, Vol. 41, No. 16), p.4; Stormer, *None Dare Call It Treason, op. cit.*, p.125; A. Ralph Epperson, *The Unseen Hand: An Introduction to the Conspiratorial View of History* (Tucson, AZ: Publius Press, 1985), p.221; Robert Sessler, *To Be God of One World: The French Revolution Globalized* (Merlin, OR: Let There Be Light Publications, 1992), p.124; *The Florida Forum* (Fall 1994, Special Edition), p.21; Paper from the Committee of Christian Laymen, Inc. (October 16, 1969, No. 181), p.2; Paper from the Committee of Christian Laymen, Inc. (September 10, 1970, No. 196), p.1.

[22] *Ibid.*; Stormer, *None Dare Call It Treason, op. cit.*, p.125.

[23] *The NCC/WCC—Communism's Helpers* (Virginia Beach, VA: Good News Baptist Church, n.d.), p.12.

[24] David P. Gaines, *The World Council of Churches: A Study of Its Background and History* (Peterborough, NH: Richard R. Smith Company, Inc., 1966), p.36; Cairns, *op. cit.*, p.464; Manschreck, *op. cit.*, p.437; "Social Gospel," Softkey Multimedia Inc., Infopedia (1996).

[25] S. Brent Morris, Editor, *Heredom: The Transactions of The Scottish Rite Research Society* (Vol. 5) (Washington, DC: The Scottish Rite Research Center, 1996), p.120.

[26] Charles R. Geisst, *Monopolies in America: Empire Builders and Their Enemies from Jay Gould to Bill Gates* (Oxford, England: Oxford University Press, 2000), p.12.

[27] Gaines, *op. cit.*, p.37; McLoughlin and Bellah, *op. cit.*, p.380. See also: *The NCC/WCC—Communism's Helpers, op. cit.* p.11; John E. Ashbrook, *New Neutralism II: Exposing the Gray of Compromise* (Mentor, OH: Here I Stand Books, 1992), p.12; Max L. Stackhouse, *Public Theology and Political Economy: Christian Stewardship in Modern Society* (Grand Rapids, MI: Wm. B. Eerdmans Publishing Company for Commission on Stewardship, National Council of the Churches of Christ in the U. S. A., 1987), p.116; Jeremy Rifkin with Ted Howard, *The Emerging Order: God in the Age of Scarcity* (NY: G. P. Putnam's Son, 1979), p.159.

[28] John E. Ashbrook, *New Neutralism II: Exposing the Gray of Compromise* (Mentor, OH: Here I Stand Books, 1992), p.12; Edgar C. Bundy, *Collectivism in the Churches: A Documented Account of the Political Activities of the Federal, National, and World Councils of Churches* (Wheaton, IL: The Church League of America, 1958), p.23, 26-27.

[29] Joel A. Carpenter, *Revive Us Again: The Reawakening of American Fundamentalism* (New York, NY: Oxford University Press, 1997), p.273.

[30] *Ibid.*, p.39.

[31] Edgar C. Bundy, *Collectivism in the Churches: A Documented Account of the Political Activities of the Federal, National, and World Councils of Churches* (Wheaton, IL: The Church League of America, 1958), p.27-28.

[32] "NCC a Sinking Ship?," *Calvary Contender* (January 1, 2000, Vol. 17, No. 1).

[33] Bundy, *Collectivism in the Churches, op. cit.*, p.50.

[34] *Ibid.*, p.53.

[35] *Ibid.*

[36] *Ibid.*

[37] *Ibid.*, p.54.

[38] *Ibid.*

[39] See: David A. Noebel, *Is the NCC Really Soft on Communism* (Tulsa, OK: Christian Crusade, n.d.), p.16-17.

[40] Bundy, *Collectivism in the Churches, op. cit.*, p.50.

[41] *Ibid.*, p.50-51.

[42] *Ibid.*, p.50.

[43] Gary Allen, *The Rockefeller File* (Seal Beach, CA: '76 Press, 1976), p.47-48.

[44] Bundy, *Collectivism in the Churches, op. cit.*, p.41. See also: Texe Marrs, *Circle of Intrigue* (Austin, TX: Living Truth Ministries, 1995), p.58.

[45] Pat Robertson, *The New World Order* (Dallas, TX: Word Publishing, 1991), p.143.

[46] Fritz Springmeier, *The Top 13 Illuminati Bloodlines* (Portland, OR: n.p., 1995), p.240; Fritz Springmeier, *Bloodlines of the Illuminati* (Westminster, CO: Ambassador House, 1999), p.419.

[47] Geisst, *op. cit.*, p.63.

[48] http://www.sounddoctrine.com

[49] Gaines, *op. cit.*, p.41.

[50] Stanley Monteith, "Brotherhood of Darkness," *Prophetic Observer* (January 2001, Vol. 8, No. 1), p.2. See also: Stanley Monteith, *Brotherhood of Darkness* (Oklahoma City, OK: Hearthstone Publishing, 2000), p.16.

[51] Stanley Monteith, *Brotherhood of Darkness* (Oklahoma City, OK: Hearthstone Publishing, 2000), p.131.

[52] Erica Carle, "Six Generational to Serfdom," *The Florida Forum* (Spring 2001), p.21.

[53] Fritz Springmeier, *Bloodlines of the Illuminati* (Westminster, CO: Ambassador House, 1999), p.222; A. Ralph Epperson, *The Unseen Hand: An Introduction to the Conspiratorial View of History* (Tucson, AZ: Publius Press, 1985), p.221; Springmeier, *The Top 13 Illuminati Bloodlines, op. cit.*, p.136; Rivera, *op. cit.*, p.70; Allen, *The Rockefeller File, op. cit.*, p.47, 48.

[54] A. Ralph Epperson, *The Unseen Hand: An Introduction to the Conspiratorial View of History* (Tucson, AZ: Publius Press, 1985), p.221.

[55] *Ibid.*

[56] Wardner, *Unholy Alliances, op. cit.*, p.154.

[57] *Ibid.*

[58] Epperson, *op. cit.*, p.221.

[59] Allen, *The Rockefeller File, op. cit.*, p.47.

[60] Wardner, *Unholy Alliances, op. cit.*, p.154.

[61] *Ibid.*, p.156.

[62] Bundy, *Collectivism in the Churches, op. cit.*, p.43.

[63] Wardner, *Unholy Alliances, op. cit.*, p.159. See also: Rivera, *op. cit.*, p.225.

[64] Epperson, *op. cit.*, p.221; William McIlhany, "The WCC: A Haven for Marxists?," *Family Protection Scoreboard*, p.21; *The NCC/WCC—Communism's Helpers, op. cit.*, p.11; Peter Collier and David Horowitz, *The Rockefellers: An American Dynasty* (NY: Holt, Rinehart and Winston, n.d.), p.155; Rivera, *op. cit.*, p.225; Cairns, *op. cit.*, p.488; Manschreck, *op. cit.*, p.465; William Martin, *A Prophet with Honor: The Billy Graham Story* (NY: William Morrow and Company, Inc., 1991), p.51; Ursala Niebuhr, Editor, *Remembering Reinhold Niebuhr* (New York, NY: HarperSanFrancisco, 1991), p.71; Wardner, *Unholy Alliances, op. cit.*, p.159; Rael Jean Isaac, "Do You Know Where Your Church Offerings Go?," *Reader's Digest* (January 1983, Vol. 122, No. 729), p.121; William R. Denslow, *10,000 Famous Freemasons* (Vol. III) (n.p., 1959), p.299; Bundy, *Collectivism in the Churches, op. cit.*, p.47; Claire Chambers, *The SIECUS Circle: A Humanist Revolution* (Belmont, MA: Western Islands, 1977), p.258.

[65] Kenneth Scott Latourette, *A History of Christianity* (New York, NY: Harper and Row, 1953), p.1423; Cairns, *op. cit.*, p.488.

[66] "The Right Place for a Mass Murdering Atheist to Speak," *Christian News* (September 18, 2000, Vol. 38, No. 34), p.4.

[67] Claire Chambers, *The SIECUS Circle: A Humanist Revolution* (Belmont, MA: Western Islands, 1977), p.21.

[68] Epperson, *op. cit.*, p.221-222. See also: Homer Duncan, *The Ecumenical Movement in Light of the Holy Scriptures* (Lubbock, TX: MC International Publications, 1980 Edition), p.68.

[69] Homer Duncan, *The Ecumenical Movement in Light of the Holy Scriptures* (Lubbock, TX: MC International Publications, 1980 Edition), p.68.

[70] Gary Allen, *Rockefeller: Campaigning for the New World Order* (n.p., n.d.), p.9; Shirley Correll, "Who Are the Gods of the New World Order and What Is a Spiritual U. N.?" (Part IV), *The Florida Forum* (Spring 2001), p.16.

[71] Peter Collier and David Horowitz, *The Rockefellers: An American Dynasty* (NY: Holt, Rinehart and Winston, n.d.), p.155. See also: Richard N. Ostling, "National Council of Churches Falls upon Hard Times," *Christian News* (November 29, 1999, Vol. 37, No. 44), p.7; Texe Marrs, *Dark Majesty: The Secret Brotherhood and the Magic of a Thousand Points of Light* (Austin, TX: Living Truth Publishers, 1992), p.206. See also: Evan Thomas and Martha Brant, "A Son's Restless Journey," *Newsweek* (August 7, 2000, Vol. 136, No. 6), p.37.

[72] *Ibid.*

[73] Gaines, *op. cit.*, p.187, 459, 463, 540, 544, 547, 746, 848.

[74] Chambers, *op. cit.*, p.347. Wardner, *Unholy Alliances, op. cit.*, p.175.

[75] Wardner, *Unholy Alliances, op. cit.*, p.175.

[76] *Ibid.*

[77] Chambers, *op. cit.*, p.348.

[78] *Ibid.* See also: "John Davidson Rockefeller, Jr.," Softkey Multimedia Inc., Infopedia (1996); "John Davidson Rockefeller, Jr.," Softkey Multimedia Inc., Multipedia (1995); Alan Morrison, *The Serpent and the Cross: Religious Corruption in an Evil Age* (Birmingham, England: K & M Books, 1994), p.580; Allen, *Rockefeller: Campaigning for the New World Order, op. cit.*, p.9; Jim Marrs, *Rule by Secrecy: The Hidden History That Connects the Trilateral Commission, the Freemasons, and the Great Pyramids* (New York, NY: HarperCollins Publishers, Inc., 2000), p.49, 99, 100.

[79] Stanley Meisler, *United Nations: The First Fifty Years* (New York, NY: The Atlantic Monthly Press, 1995), p.35. See also: "United Nations," Softkey Multimedia Inc., Infopedia (1996).

[80] Springmeier, *Bloodlines of the Illuminati, op. cit.*, p.222.

[81] Texe Marrs, *Dark Majesty: The Secret Brotherhood and the Magic of a Thousand Points of Light* (Austin, TX: Living Truth Publishers, 1992), p.206. See also: "Pax Christi Catholic Anti-War Movement," *Calvary Contender* (April 1, 2001, Vol. 18, No. 7); Evan Thomas and Martha Brand, "A Son's Restless Journey," *Newsweek* (August 7, 2000, Vol. 136, No. 6), p.37; "Castro Is Applauded at Riverside Church," *Calvary Contender* (October 15, 2000, Vol. 17, No. 20), p.2.

[82] "Pax Christi Catholic Anti-War Movement," *Calvary Contender* (April 1, 2001, Vol. 18, No. 7), p.1.

[83] Marrs, *Dark Majesty, op. cit.*, p.191. See also: *World Federalist* (Spring 1989, Vol. 14, No. 2), p.2.

[84] "Castro Is Applauded at Riverside Church," *Calvary Contender* (October 15, 2000, Vol. 17, No. 20), p.2; Bundy, *Collectivism in the Churches, op. cit.*, p.256.

[85] Perry F. Rockwood, "The Revised Standard Version," *O Timothy* (1985, Vol. 2, Issue 3).

[86] Springmeier, *The Top 13 Illuminati Bloodlines, op. cit.*, p.156.

[87] "ELCA Publishes Book by Marxist 'Theological Atheist,'" *Christian News* (June 4, 2001, Vol. 39, No. 23), p.15.

[88] Rockwood, *op. cit.;* David W. Cloud, "The Attack upon the Blood Atonement," *O Timothy* (1987, Vol. 4, Issue 1).

[89] Brad K. Gsell, *The Legacy of Billy Graham* (Charlotte, NC: Fundamental Presbyterian Publication, n.d.), p.2. See also: Collier and Horowitz, *op. cit.*, p.152.

[90] Ad in *The Christian Century* (April 4, 2001, Vol. 118, No. 11), p.25.

[91] Duncan, *op. cit.*, p.66.

[92] Stormer, *None Dare Call It Treason, op. cit.*, p.126; John A. Stormer, *The Death of a Nation* (Florissant, MO: Liberty Bell Press, 1968), p.101; *Ibid.;* Richard Wurmbrand, *Marx and Satan* (Westchester, IL: Crossway Books, 1986), p.130; Wardner, *Unholy Alliances, op. cit.*, p.159-160. See also: *IPS Packet* (Independence, MO: Price Publishing Company, n.d.), p.19; Noebel, *Is the NCC Really Soft on Communism, op. cit.*, p.7; William McIlhany, "The WCC: A Haven for Marxists?," *Family Protection Scoreboard*, p.21; Chambers, *op. cit.*, p.21.

[93] Cairns, *op. cit.*, p.488.

[94] *Policy Review* (Fall 1994, No. 70), p.59.

[95] Chambers, *op. cit.*, p.21. See also: Paper from the Committee of Christian Laymen, Inc. of Woodland Hills (March 1970, No. 189), p.1; W. Cleon Skousen, *The Communist Attack on U. S. Police* (Salt Lake City, UT: The Ensign Publishing Company, 1966), p.45.

[96] Paper from the Committee of Christian Laymen, Inc. of Woodland Hills (March 1970, No. 189), p.1.

[97] Mari Jo Buhle, Paul Buhle, and Dan Georgakas, Editors, *Encyclopedia of the American Left* (New York, NY: Oxford University Press, 1998, Second Edition), p.57, 294.

[98] Edgar C. Bundy, *How Liberals and Radicals Are Manipulating Evangelicals* (Miami Shores, FL: Edgar Bundy Ministries, Inc., 1982), p.9.

[99] *Christian Anti-Communism Crusade* (July 15, 1993), p.8.

[100] Paper from the Committee of Christian Laymen, Inc. of Woodland Hills (March 1970, No. 189), p.1.

[101] "W. E. B. Dubois, a Founder of the NAACP," *Christian News* (October 30, 2000, Vol. 38, No. 40), p.2.

[102] Paper from the Committee of Christian Laymen, Inc. of Woodland Hills (March 1970, No. 189), p.1.

[103] Buhle, Buhle, and Georgakas, *op. cit.*, p.201, 241, 242.

[104] *Ibid.*, p.154.

[105] Paper from the Committee of Christian Laymen, Inc. of Woodland Hills (March 1970, No. 189), p.1.

[106] *Ibid.*

[107] *Ibid.*

[108] Chambers, *op. cit.*, p.125. See also: *Ibid.*

[109] Paper from the Committee of Christian Laymen, Inc. of Woodland Hills (March 1970, No. 189), p.1.

[110] *Ibid.*

[111] *Ibid.*

[112] *Ibid.* See also: *Now Is the Dawning of the New Age New World Order, op. cit.*, p.108; "To Socialism by Way of Tax-Exempt Foundations," *The Florida Forum* (Summer 1997), p.23; Rene A. Wormser, *Foundations: Their Power and Influence* (New York, NY: Devin-Adair Company, 1977 Edition), p.114, 115, 116, 117; *World Goodwill Commentary: Race Relations in an Interdependent World* (January 1983, No. 16), p.9.

[113] *Now Is the Dawning of the New Age New World Order, op. cit.*, p.108. See also: "To Socialism by Way of Tax-Exempt Foundations," *The Florida Forum* (Summer 1997), p.23; Planetary Citizens (Letter dated April 17, 1985).

[114] Paper from the Committee of Christian Laymen, Inc. of Woodland Hills (March 1970, No. 189), p.1.

[115] Buhle, Buhle, and Georgakas, *op. cit.*, p.56.

[116] *Ibid.*, p.336.

[117] *Ibid.*, p.337.

[118] *Last Trumpet Newsletter* (August 2000, Vol. 19, Issue 8), p.2-3; W. Cleon Skousen, *The Communist Attack on U. S. Police* (Salt Lake City, UT: The Ensign Publishing Company, 1966), p.45.

[119] *Ibid.*

[120] Paper from the Committee of Christian Laymen, Inc. (June 30, 1964, No. 102), p.1.

[121] Rael Jean Isaac, "Do You Know Where Your Church Offerings Go?," *Reader's Digest* (January 1983, Vol. 122, No. 729), p.121-122.

[122] *Ibid.*, p.120-121. See also: *IPS Packet* (Independence, MO: Price Publishing Company, n.d.), p.4.

[123] "Disrespect for Traditional Religion," *The Florida Forum* (Spring 2001), p.5.

[124] Tom DeWeese, "Radical Greens Use Churches to Force Senate Support of UN's Global Warming Treaty." See also: Carl McIntire, "Perversion and Subversion in the World Council of Churches," *O Timothy* (1988, Vol. 5, Issue 6); Chuck Colson with Ellen Santilli Vaughn, *The Body* (Dallas, TX: Word Publishing, 1996 Edition), p.210.

[125] Chuck Colson with Ellen Santilli Vaughn, *The Body* (Dallas, TX: Word Publishing, 1996 Edition), p.210.

[126] *Ibid.;* "Marxist Terrorists Help Snare RLDS Hierarchy's Program," *IPS Packet* (Independence, MO: Price Publishing Company, n.d.), p.4, 5, 6; Rush Limbaugh, *The Way Things Ought to Be* (New York, NY: Pocket Books, 1992), p.256; Texe Marrs, *Millennium: Peace, Promises, and the Day They Take Our Money Away* (Austin, TX: Living Truth Publishers, 1990), p.100; Beth Spring, "The Government's Heavy Hand Falls on Believers," *Christianity Today* (December 13, 1985, Vol. 29, No. 18), p.51; Brochure from Quixote Center, p.1; David Mark Price, *Secret* (Wichita, KS: Sunset Research Group, 1994), p.4; John A. Stormer, *None Dare Call It Treason...25 Years Later* (Florissant, MO: Liberty Bell Press, 1992), p.7, 432; "Church Workers Still Support Communism in Nicaragua," *The Christian World Report* (December 1990, Vol. 2, No. 9), p.27.

[127] Texe Marrs, *Millennium: Peace, Promises, and the Day They Take Our Money Away* (Austin, TX: Living Truth Publishers, 1990), p.100.

[128] Colson with Vaughn, *op. cit.*, p.210.

[129] Isaac, *op. cit.*, p.124.

[130] "NCC Near Death, but Wants Resurrection," *Calvary Contender* (July 1, 2000, Vol. 17, No. 13), p.1.

[131] Chambers, *op. cit.*, p.21. See also: Wardner, *Unholy Alliances, op. cit.*, p.164; *What About the National Council of Churches?* (Hatfield, PA: Brethren Revival Fellowship Witness, 1967), p.9. See also: John A. Stormer, *None Dare Call It Treason...25 Years Later* (Florissant, MO: Liberty Bell Press, 1992), p.550.

[132] *Ibid.*, p.21, 261.

[133] "Disrespect for Traditional Religion," *op. cit.*, p.14. See also: W. L. King, "S.I.E.C.U.S., Sex, and Subversion," p.3.

[134] Chambers, *op. cit.*, p.260.

[135] W. L. King, "S.I.E.C.U.S., Sex, and Subversion," p.1.

[136] Chambers, *op. cit.*, p.259.

[137] *Ibid.*, p.11.

[138] *Ibid.*, p.17.

[139] *Ibid.*, p.14.

[140] *Ibid.*, p.15.

[141] *Ibid.*

[142] *Ibid.*

[143] *Ibid.;* W. L. King, "S.I.E.C.U.S., Sex, and Subversion," p.2.

[144] *Ibid.*

[145] "Disrespect for Traditional Religion," *op. cit.*, p.14.

[146] Paper from Thanksgiving Square; David R. Barnhart, *Contending for the Faith* (Eagan, MN: Abiding Word Publications, 1994), p.121, 123.

[147] Chambers, *op. cit.*, p.296.

[148] *Ibid.*, p.162.

[149] *World Council of Churches: The Shaky Ship Sails On...* (Los Osos, CA: Fundamental Evangelistic Association, 1999), p.4.

[150] *Ibid.*

[151] *Ibid.*

[152] Alan Morrison, *The Serpent and the Cross: Religious Corruption in an Evil Age* (Birmingham, England: K & M Books, 1994), p.529, 530. See also: *These Times* (1982), p.12.

[153] *Ibid.*, p.530.

[154] *Ibid.*, p.531.

[155] *Ibid.*, p.530.

[156] *Seventh-Day Adventists Believe...A Biblical Exposition of 27 Fundamental Doctrines* (Hagerstown, MD: Review and Herald Publishing Association, 1988), p.371-372.

[157] Rivera, *op. cit.*, p.224. See also: Duncan, *op. cit.*, p.67; Bundy, *Collectivism in the Churches, op. cit.*, p.211; Gaines, *op. cit.*, p.1001; "A Horrible Statement," *Christian News* (February 12, 2001, Vol. 39, No. 7), p.16.

[158] *Ibid.;* John Edward Millheim, "KGB, Secret Police and the World Council of Churches," *Christian News* (February 1, 1993, Vol. 31, No. 5), p.15; "WCC Used by Communists," *Christian News* (September 9, 1991, Vol. 29, No. 32), p.23.

[159] Bundy, *Collectivism in the Churches, op. cit.*, p.211.

[160] *The NCC/WCC—Communism's Helpers, op. cit.*, p.12.

[161] Gaines, *op. cit.*, p.255.

[162] *Ibid.*, p.755.

[163] *Ibid.*, p.768.

[164] "A Horrible Statement," *Christian News* (February 12, 2001, Vol. 39, No. 7), p.16.

[165] *IRFWP Newsletter* (Spring 1998, Vol. 6, No. 1), p.3, 23; "Moon Says He Is the Messiah," *Christian News* (May 31, 1993, Vol. 31, No. 22), p.1.

[166] Duncan, *op. cit.*, p.67.

[167] "WCC President Dies During Papal Audience," *Christian News* (March 20, 2000, Vol. 38, No. 12), p.22; Piers Compton, *The Broken Cross: The Hidden Hand in the Vatican* (Cranbrook, Western Australia: Veritas Publishing Company Pty. Ltd., 1984), p.158.

[168] M. H. Reynolds, *The World Council of Churches: An Ecumenical Tower of Babel* (Los Osos, CA: Fundamental Evangelistic Association, 1983), p.4; *IPS Packet* (Independence, MO: Price Publishing Company, n.d.), p.4; Piers Compton, *The Broken Cross: The Hidden Hand in the Vatican* (Cranbrook, Western Australia: Veritas Publishing Company Pty. Ltd., 1984), p.158, 160; Wardner, *Unholy Alliances, op. cit.*, p.171; "WCC President Dies During Papal Audience," *Christian News* (March 20, 2000, Vol. 38, No. 12), p.22; John Edward Millheim, "KGB, Secret Police and the World Council of Churches," *Christian News* (February 1, 1993, Vol. 31, No. 5), p.14.

[169] John Edward Millheim, "KGB, Secret Police and the World Council of Churches," *Christian News* (February 1, 1993, Vol. 31, No. 5), p.15. See also: "WCC President Dies During Papal Audience," *Christian News* (March 20, 2000, Vol. 38, No. 12), p.22.

[170] *Ibid.*; Wardner, *Unholy Alliances, op. cit.*, p.171.

[171] Rivera, *op. cit.*, p.224. See also: Bundy, *Collectivism in the Churches, op. cit.*, p.152, 210.

[172] "The Deception on Religion in China and AP Features," *Christian News* (October 4, 1999, Vol. 37, No. 36), p.9.

[173] Bundy, *Collectivism in the Churches, op. cit.*, p.209.

[174] *The NCC/WCC—Communism's Helpers, op. cit.*, p.12.

[175] *Ibid.*, p.209-210.

[176] Gaines, *op. cit.*, Inside back flap.

[177] *Ibid.*, p.339.

[178] *Ibid.*

[179] Carl McIntire, "Perversion and Subversion in the World Council of Churches," *O Timothy* (1988, Vol. 5, Issue 6). See also: "Ecumenical Leaders Work for a One-World Government and Religion," *O Timothy* (1989, Vol. 6, Issue 5).

[180] *Ibid.* See also: "The KGB and the Russian Orthodox Church," *O Timothy* (1992, Vol. 9, Issue 7).

[181] "The KGB and the Russian Orthodox Church," *O Timothy* (1992, Vol. 9, Issue 7).

[182] McIntire, *op. cit.*

[183] David A. Noebel, *The Marxist Minstrels: A Handbook on Communist Subversion of Music* (Tulsa, OK: American Christian College Press, 1974), p.138.

[184] *Ibid.*, p.129.

[185] Buhle, Buhle, and Georgakas, *op. cit.*, p.739. See also: *Global 2000: An Interview with Mr. and Mrs. William Bowen* (Oklahoma City, OK: Southwest Radio Church, 1984), p.43.

[186] "Turret of the Times," *Christian News* (September 14, 1992, Vol. 30, No. 33), p.11.

[187] "Clinton Honors 'Best-Loved Commie,'" *AIM Report* (December 1994, 23-24), p.1.

[188] Noebel, *The Marxist Minstrels, op. cit.*, p.130. For more information about Seeger being a Communist, see: *Global 2000: An Interview with Mr. and Mrs. William Bowen* (Oklahoma City, OK: Southwest Radio Church, 1984), p.43; *Ibid.*, p.1, 2; "Common Cause Honors Communist Pete Seeger," *Christian News* (July 19, 1999, Vol. 37, No. 29), p.1; "Rome Is in a State of Total Disarray," *Christian News* (October 20, 1997, Vol. 35, No. 38), p.7; *Who's Running Our Schools?* (Save Our Schools Research and Education Foundation, n.d.), p.60; "Turret of the Times," *Christian News* (September 14, 1992, Vol. 30, No. 33), p.11; "The Anti-Christian Unitarian Theology of Marty's Christian Century," John A. Stormer, *None Dare Call It Treason...25 Years Later* (Florissant, MO: Liberty Bell Press, 1992), p.462; *Christian News* (February 10, 1997, Vol. 35, No. 6), p.22; "Toward a Fourth Psychology Revisited: Part VIII: Omega Institute," *Distant Drums* (August 1995, Vol. 16, No. 1), p.5-6; "Dying to Live," *Christian News* (February 26, 2001, Vol. 39, No. 9), p.7.

[189] "Clinton Honors 'Best-Loved Commie,'" *op. cit.*

[190] Letter from January 1987; Paper from Planetary Citizens.

[191] Noebel, *The Marxist Minstrels, op. cit.*, p.138, 244.

[192] "Pope Foreseen As Leader of World Church," *Midnight Call* (March 1993), p.20.

[193] Morrison, *op. cit.*, p.533.

[194] Edgar C. Bundy, *Billy Graham: Performer?, Politician?, Preacher?, Prophet?* (Wheaton, IL: Church League of America, 1982), p.47.

[195] *Ibid.*

[196] *Ibid.*

[197] William R. Denslow, *10,000 Famous Freemasons* (Vol. I) (n.p., 1957), p.168.

[198] *Unholy Alliances* p.79

[199] *Ibid.*, p.165, 167.

[200] *Ibid.*, p.200.

[201] *Ibid.*, p.201.

[202] *Ibid.*, p.165.

[203] William R. Denslow, *10,000 Famous Freemasons* (Vol. II) (n.p., 1958), p.247.

[204] Wardner, *Unholy Alliances, op. cit.*, p.156.

[205] *Ibid.*

[206] Denslow, (Vol. I), *op. cit.*, p.55.

[207] Denslow, (Vol. II) *op. cit.* p.111.

[208] *Ibid.*, p.144.

[209] *Ibid.*, p.204.

[210] William R. Denslow, *10,000 Famous Freemasons* (Vol. III) (n.p., 1959), p.76.

[211] *Ibid.*, p.145.

[212] William R. Denslow, *10,000 Famous Freemasons* (Vol. IV) (n.p., 1961), p.86.

[213] *Ibid.*, p.258.

[214] *Ibid.*, p.390.

[215] "Garfield Bromley Oxnam," Softkey Multimedia Inc., Infopedia (1996). See also: William Martin, *A Prophet with Honor: The Billy Graham Story* (NY: William Morrow and Company, Inc., 1991), p.276; Bundy, *Collectivism in the Churches, op. cit.*, p.49; Berit Kjos, "Conforming the Church to the New Millennium," *Prophecy Corner and the Nosh Box* (November 2000), p.8.

[216] Denslow, (Vol. III) *op. cit.*, p.299; "Bishop Oxnam Invites the Pope to Live Our Liberty," *The New Age Magazine* (December 1949, Vol. 57, No. 12), p.716.

[217] W. S. McBirnie, *The Coming "World Church": Why It Is Feared by True Christians* (Independence, MO: Gospel Tract Society, Inc., n.d.), p.3.

[218] Wardner, *Unholy Alliances, op. cit.*, p.157; See also: John A. Stormer, *The Death of a Nation* (Florissant, MO: Liberty Bell Press, 1968), p.91-92.

[219] *The NCC/WCC—Communism's Helpers, op. cit.*, p.7.

[220] *Ibid.*, p.5.

[221] Gsell, *The Legacy of Billy Graham, op. cit.* See also: David W. Cloud, "Billy Graham's Disobedience to the Word of God" (Updated March 2, 1999), p.6.

[222] Bundy, *Collectivism in the Churches, op. cit.*, p.75. See also: D. W. Cloud, "Some Frightening Facts About Billy Graham," *O Timothy* (1984, Vol. 1, Issue, 4); "Billy Graham's Disobedience," *O Timothy* (1995, Vol. 12, Issue 11); David W. Cloud, "Billy Graham's Disobedience to the Word of God."

[223] David W. Cloud, "Billy Graham's Disobedience to the Word of God."

[224] Gsell, *The Legacy of Billy Graham, op. cit.*, p.22.

[225] M. H. Reynolds, Jr., *The Truth About the World Council of Churches* (Los Osos, CA: Fundamental Evangelistic Association, n.d.), p.4; "Ecumenist Tells Churches to Take Stronger Action Against 'Global Capitalism,'" *Christian News* (June 26, 2000, Vol. 38, No. 26), p.3; "Episcopal Bishop Worships in a Buddhist Temple," *O Timothy* (1989, Vol. 6, Issue 5); "WCC President Dies During Papal Audience," *Christian News* (March 20, 2000, Vol. 38, No. 12), p.22; G. R. Beirnes, Editor, "Liberals Seek Catholic Membership in WCC-NCC," *The Midnight Cry* (April 1967, Vol. 28, No. 4), p.8.

[226] David W. Cloud, "Billy Graham's Disobedience to the Word of God," "WCC's 50th Anniversary, Orthodox Rife?," *Calvary Contender* (June 1, 1998, Vol. 15, No. 1), p.2.

[227] D. W. Cloud, "Some Frightening Facts About Billy Graham," (n.p., n.d.). See also: D. W. Cloud quoting Philip Potter in "Some Frightening Facts About Billy Graham," *O Timothy* (1984, Vol. 1, Issue 4).

[228] Reynolds, Jr., *The Truth About the World Council of Churches, op. cit.*, p.4.

[229] "WCC's 50th Anniversary, Orthodox Rife?," *Calvary Contender* (June 1, 1998, Vol. 15, No. 11), p.2; "WCC to Meet in Zimbabwe," *Calvary Contender* (November 15, 1998, Vol. 15, No. 24), p.2.

[230] Epperson, *op. cit.*, p.222.

[231] John Cotter, *A Study in Syncretism* (Flesherton, Ontario: Canadian Intelligence Publications, n.d.), p.67.

[232] David W. Cloud, "Billy Graham's Disobedience to the Word of God" (n.p., n.d.); D. W. Cloud, "Some Frightening Facts About Billy Graham" (n.p., n.d.).

[233] D. W. Cloud, "Some Frightening Facts About Billy Graham" (n.p., n.d.); D. W. Cloud, "Some Frightening Facts About Billy Graham," *O Timothy* (1984, Vol. 1, Issue 4).

[234] D. W. Cloud, "Some Frightening Facts About Billy Graham," *O Timothy* (1984, Vol. 1, Issue 4).

[235] M. H. Reynolds, Jr., *Billy Graham, the Pope, and the Bible* (Los Osos, CA: Fundamental Evangelistic Association, n.d.), p.4; M.H. Reynolds, "Planting the Seeds of Ecumenical Apostasy in the Name of Evangelism," *Foundation* (1983, Vol. 4, No. 4); D. W. Cloud, "Some Frightening Facts About Billy Graham," *O Timothy* (1984, Vol. 1, Issue 4).

[236] M. H. Reynolds, "Planting the Seeds of Ecumenical Apostasy in the Name of Evangelism," *Foundation* (1983, Vol. 4, No. 4); *Ibid.;* D. W. Cloud, "Some Frightening Facts About Billy Graham," *O Timothy* (1984, Vol. 1, Issue 4); John Ashbrook, "Billy Graham—The Mouthpiece of New Evangelicalism," *O Timothy* (1993, Vol. 10, Issue 1). See also: Rick Miesel, "Billy Graham: General Teachings/Activities" (Biblical Discernment Ministries, Revised January 1994).

[237] *Ibid.* See also: William Martin, *A Prophet with Honor: The Billy Graham Story* (NY: William Morrow and Company, Inc., 1991), p.327.

[238] Cotter, *op. cit.,* p.60.

[239] D. W. Cloud, "Some Frightening Facts About Billy Graham," *O Timothy* (1984, Vol. 1, Issue 4).

[240] Allen Dickerson, "Passive Fundamentalism" *O Timothy* (1995, Vol. 12, Issue 6).

[241] D. W. Cloud, *O Timothy* (1984, Vol. 1, Issue 4).

[242] Reynolds, Jr., *Billy Graham, the Pope, and the Bible, op. cit.,* p.4.

[243] McIntire, *op. cit.*

[244] Jan Karel Van Baalen, *The Chaos of Cults* (Grand Rapids, MI: Wm. B. Eerdmans Publishing Company, 1962), p.336.

[245] *Christian News* (February 28, 1994, Vol. 32, No. 9), p.11

[246] "A Sampling of Resources Written and Recommended by the National Network of Presbyterian College Women," *The Presbyterian Layman* (January/February 1999, Vol. 32, No. 1), p.5; Parker T. Williamson, "Controversial ReImagining Leader Retiring from WCC," *The Presbyterian Layman* (January/February 1999, Vol. 32, No. 1); Parker T. Williamson, "Sophia Upstages Jesus at the 1998 ReImagining Revival," *The Presbyterian Layman* (May/June 1998, Vol. 31, No. 3), p.1; "WCC Promotes Demoted Lundy," *Calvary Contender* (March 15, 1995, Vol. 12, No. 6), p.2; "The Ecumenical Movement Rolls On...Lutherans and Muslims Hold Joint Conference in Wisconsin...," *The Vine and Branches* (Summer 1998, Vol. 13, Issue 3), p.8; William Thorkelson, "New 'Re-Imagining' Meeting Scheduled in Wake of Controversy," *Christian News* (October 31, 1994, Vol. 32, No. 40), p.11.

[247] *Ibid.* See also: "The Ecumenical Movement Rolls On...Lutherans and Muslims Hold Joint Conference in Wisconsin...," *The Vine and Branches* (Summer 1998, Vol. 13, Issue 3), p.8.

[248] William T. James, Editor, *Foreshocks of Antichrist* (Eugene, OR: Harvest House Publishers, 1997), p.119; "Pope Foreseen As Leader of World Church," *op. cit.,* p.20; David W. Cloud, "Billy Graham's Disobedience to the Word of God" (Updated March 2, 1999), p.7.

[249] David W. Cloud, "Billy Graham's Disobedience to the Word of God" (Updated March 2, 1999), p.7.

[250] "Pope Foreseen As Leader of World Church," *op. cit.,* p.20. See also: David W. Cloud, "Billy Graham's Disobedience to the Word of God" (Updated March 2, 1999), p.7.

[251] David W. Cloud, "Billy Graham's Disobedience to the Word of God" (Updated March 2, 1999), p.7. See also: *Ibid.*

[252] Ursala Niebuhr, Editor, *Remembering Reinhold Niebuhr* (New York, NY: HarperSanFrancisco, 1991), p.261.

[253] Cotter, *op. cit.,* p.45-46.

[254] *Ibid.,* p.62. See also: "Defending the Institutions Against the New Lenins," *The Daily Telegraph* (April 3, 1979); Richard Wurmbrand, *Marx and Satan* (Westchester, IL: Crossway Books, 1986), p.130; "Church Coffers Fund Marxist Revolution," *The Christian World Report* (June 1989, Vol. 1, No. 4), p.1.

[255] Billy Graham, *Just As I Am: The Autobiography of Billy Graham* (Harpers Collins Worldwide, 1997), p.694.

[256] *Ibid.* See also: David W. Cloud, "Billy Graham's Disobedience to the Word of God" (Updated March 2, 1999), p.7.

[257] Denslow, (Vol. II) *op. cit.,* p.51.

[258] Gaines, *op. cit.,* p.244.

[259] Softkey Multimedia Inc., Infopedia, "Geoffrey Francis Fisher" (1996).

[260] Marcus Braybrooke, *A Wider Vision: A History of the World Congress of Faiths* (Oxford, England: Oneworld Publications, 1996), p.128.

[261] "Pope Foreseen As Leader of World Church," *op. cit.*

[262] *Ibid.*

[263] Softkey Multimedia Inc., Infopedia, "Martin Niemoeller" (1996).

[264] Barbara Aho quoting from William Shirer, http://watch.pair.com/pray.html. See also: Softkey Multimedia Inc., Infopedia, "Martin Niemoeller" (1996).

[265] *Ibid.* See also: Softkey Multimedia Inc., Infopedia, "Martin Niemoeller" (1996).

[266] Letter from Planetary Citizens dated April 17, 1985; Letter from Planetary Citizens dated January 1987.

[267] Paper from the Institute for 21st Century Studies, p.4; "China Brands Unregistered Churches 'Evil Cults,'" *Christian News* (January 17, 2000, Vol. 38, No. 3), p.12.

[268] *Ibid.* See also: David Barnhart, "A Fierce Battle Raging in Christendom," *Christian News* (October 3, 1994, Vol. 32, No. 36), p.17.

[269] Brochure from The Temple of Understanding, p.2; *Temple of Understanding Newsletter* (Fall 1998), p.2; *Temple of Understanding Newsletter* (Fall 1995), p.2.

[270] Letter from Whole Earth Papers dated April 14, 1988).

[271] *Breakthrough* (Winter/Summer 1990, Vol. 11, No.2-4), p.2; *Breakthrough* (Spring/Summer 1987, Vol. 8, No.3-4), p.2.

[272] William Swing, "Reactions from Religious Leaders: United Religions International Tour," *Christian News* (May 5, 1997, Vol. 35, No. 18), p.6; Speech by William E. Swing at the North American Interfaith Network Conference (August 10, 1996).

[273] Gaines, *op. cit.*, p.559.

[274] *Ibid.*, p.933-934.

[275] *Ibid.*, p.934.

[276] See: Springmeier, *The Top 13 Illuminati Bloodlines, op. cit.*, p.8; "The CFR Admits It's Been in Control," *Christian World Report* (July/August 1994), p.4; *Now Is the Dawning of the New Age New World Order, op. cit.*, p.48, 91-92; Jim Marrs, *Rule by Secrecy: The Hidden History That Connects the Trilateral Commission, the Freemasons, and the Great Pyramids* (New York, NY: HarperCollins Publishers, Inc., 2000), p.83; "Another Major Player: The Ford Foundation," *The Florida Forum* (Summer 1996), p.11; Joan Veon, *Prince Charles: The* Sustainable *Prince* (Oklahoma City, OK: Hearthstone Publishing, Ltd., 1997), p.21, 22, 23, 24; William T. Still, *New World Order: The Ancient Plan of Secret Societies* (Lafayette, LA: Huntington House, Inc., 1990), p.152; Rivera, *op. cit.*, p.91; Robertson, *op. cit.*, 111-112.

[277] List of Planetary Citizens from a letter dated April 17, 1985; Letter from the Planetary Citizens dated January 1987; Paper from the Planetary Citizens; *Secret Records Revealed: The Men, the Money and the Methods Behind the New World Order* (Oklahoma City, OK: Hearthstone Publishing, Ltd., 1999), p.131.

[278] J. Gordon Melton, Jerome Clark, and Aidan A. Kelly, *New Age Almanac* (Detroit, MI: Visible Ink, 1991), p.205; Marilyn Ferguson, *The Aquarian Conspiracy: Personal and Social Transformation in the 1980s* (Los Angeles, CA: J. P. Tarcher, Inc., 1980), p.137; Jane Gumprecht, *New Age Health Care: Holy or Holistic* (Orange, CA: Promise Publishing, 1988), p.57-58; Dave Hunt and T. A. McMahon, *America: The Sorcerer's New Apprentice: The Rise of New Age Shamanism* (Eugene, OR: Harvest House Publishers, 1988), p.86-87.

[279] *CIB Bulletin* (September 1990, Vol. 6, No. 9), p.1.

[280] *Ibid.*, quoting James I. McCord.

[281] *Now Is the Dawning of the New Age New World Order, op. cit.*, quoting Arnold Toynbee, p.415; *"Secret Records" Revealed: The Men, the Money, and the Methods Behind the New World Order* quoting Arnold Toynbee (Marlborough, NH: The Plymouth Rock Foundation, 1994), p.16; Newsletter from Radio Liberty (May 2001), p.3; *Secret Records Revealed: The Men, the Money and the Methods Behind the New World Order* quoting Arnold Toynbee (Oklahoma City, OK: Hearthstone Publishing, Ltd., 1999), p.50; "The *'One World'* Movement" quoting Arnold Toynbee in *The Florida Forum* (Summer 1998), p.6.

[282] *"Secret Records" Revealed: The Men, the Money, and the Methods Behind the New World Order* (Marlborough, NH: The Plymouth Rock Foundation, 1994), p.34; *Ibid.*, p.244-245; *Secret Records Revealed: The Men, the Money and the Methods Behind the New World Order* quoting Arnold Toynbee (Oklahoma City, OK: Hearthstone Publishing, Ltd., 1999), p.115; . See also: Epperson, quoting Arnold Toynbee, *op. cit.*, p.368.

[283] Arnold Toynbee, *The Religious Background of the Present Environmental Crisis* (Reprinted from the International Journal of Environmental Studies, 1971), p.4.

[284] See: Margot Adler, *Drawing Down the Moon: Witches, Druids, Goddess-Worshippers, and Other Pagans in America Today* (New York, NY: The Viking Press, 1979), p.17-18; Arnold Toynbee, *The Religious Background of the Present Environmental Crisis* (Reprinted from the International Journal of Environmental Studies, 1971), p.8.

[285] Toynbee, *op. cit.*, p.8.

[286] Morning Glory and Otter G'Zell, pamphlet from the Covenant of the Goddess, p.6.

[287] Lawrence LeShan, *How to Meditate: A Guide to Self-Discovery* (Boston, MA: Little, Brown and Company, 1974), p.196.

[288] George W. Blount quoting Arnold Toynbee in *Peace Through World Government* (Durham, NC: Moore Publishing Company, 1974), p.30-31.

[289] *O Timothy* (1986, Vol. 3, Issue 7); D. W. Cloud, "Some Frightening Facts About Billy Graham," *O Timothy* (1984, Vol. 1, Issue 4). See also: "The Move by Christian Leaders to Sanction Islam," *The Vine and Branches* (Summer 1998, Vol. 13, Issue 3), p.7.

[290] *Ibid.*; "Episcopal Bishop Worships in a Buddhist Temple," *O Timothy* (1989, Vol. 6, Issue 5). See also: McIntire *op. cit.*; *World Council of Churches: The Shaky Ship Sails On, op. cit.*, p.9.

[291] *Ibid.* See also: *The Christian World Report* (June 1989, Vol. 1, No. 4), p.1; Brad K. Gsell, "Pagan Indian Rites and Legends Observed at WCC Assembly," *Christian News* (June 4, 2001, Vol. 39, No. 23), p.17; "Indians' 'Sacred Fire' Evokes Peace and Barbs," *Christian News* (June 4, 2001, Vol. 39, No. 23), p.17.

[292] *Christian News* (June 4, 2001, Vol. 39, No. 23), p.17.

[293] Brad K. Gsell, "Pagan Indian Rites and Legends Observed at WCC Assembly," *Christian News* (June 4, 2001, Vol. 39, No. 23), p.17. See also: Joe Pitt, "The Israel Pole Story," *Christian News* (June 4, 2001, Vol. 39, No. 23), p.17.

[294] *World Council of Churches: The Shaky Ship Sails On, op. cit.*, p.9.

[295] "ELCA Publishes Book by Marxist 'Theological Atheist,'" *op. cit.*, p.15; "Lutherans Publish Book by 'Theological Atheist,'" *Christian News* (July 16, 2001, Vol. 39, No. 29), p.2. See also: "ELCA Publishes Book by Dorothee Soelle," *Calvary Contender* (July 1, 2001, Vol. 18, No. 13), p.1.

[296] M. H. Reynolds, Jr., "World Conference on Mission and Evangelism, San Antonio, Texas, May 22-June 1, 1989," *World Council of Churches: The Shaky Ship Sails On, op. cit.*, p.14; Morrison, *op. cit.*, p.537.

[297] Morrison, *op. cit.*, p.537-538; *O Timothy*, "The World Council of Churches and Pagan Religions" (1994, Vol. 11, Issue 6); Cotter, *op. cit.*, p.77.

[298] "World Assembly to Give Grand Thanks," *Dallas Morning News* (February 28, 1999), p.8.

[299] "The Temple of Understanding" (n.d.), Unnumbered page. See also: *Temple of Understanding Newsletter* (Fall 1998), p.2; *Temple of Understanding Newsletter* (Fall 1995), p.2; Brochure from the Temple of Understanding (Received March 12, 1991), p.2.

[300] Paper from Thanksgiving Square; Letter from Thanksgiving Square dated February 2, 1999.

[301] *IRFWP Newsletter* (Spring 1998, Vol. 6, No. 1), p.24.

[302] *Ibid.* p.3, 23; *IRFWP Newsletter* (Fall 1998, Vol. 6, No. 2), p.2; *United Religions* (Fall 1997, Issue 4), p.17.

[303] Reynolds, Jr., "World Conference on Mission and Evangelism," *op. cit.*, p.14.

[304] *Ibid.*

[305] Selena Fox, "Around Circle Sanctuary," *Circle Network News* (Spring 1988, Vol. 10, No. 1), p.5.

[306] "Episcopal Bishop Worships in a Buddhist Temple," *O Timothy* (1989, Vol. 6, Issue 5).

[307] *Ibid.* See also: "News Briefs," *CIB Bulletin* (June 1989, Vol. 5, No. 6), p.4.

[308] Gary H. Kah, *The Demonic Roots of Globalism* (Lafayette, LA: Huntington House Publishers, 1995), p.127.

[309] *Ibid.*, p.127-128.

[310] William R. Denslow, *Freemasonry and the American Indian* (n.p., 1956), p.i.

[311] *The New Age Movement—Age of Aquarius—Age of Antichrist* (Oklahoma City, OK: Southwest Radio Church, 1982), p.25.

[312] Herman Otten, "Get Out of the WCC," *Christian News*, (February 1, 1993, Vol. 31, No. 5), p.13; *One in Christ* (Received November 17, 1994 from the National Council of Churches); Texe Marrs, "Unmasking the New Age Cults and Religions," *Flashpoint* (November/December 1990), p.1; *1993 Church World Service Annual Report* (New York, NY: Church World Service, 1993), p.16; Texe Marrs, *Texe Marrs Book of New Age Cults and Religions* (Austin, TX: Living Truth Publishers, 1990), p.308; Brochure from Church World Service; Darrell Turner, "Graham Happy to Fellowship at the NCC's Interchurch Center," *Christian News* (September 9, 1991, Vol. 29, No. 32), p.23.

[313] *Ibid.*

[314] Robert A. Morey, *The Origins and Teachings of Freemasonry* (Southbridge, MA: Crowne Publications, Inc., 1990), p.97.

[315] "Truth Is One; Paths Are Many" (Brochure from Himalayan Academy Publications), p.3.

[316] Morey, *The Origins and Teachings of Freemasonry, op. cit.*, p.96-97. See also: James L. Holly, *The Southern Baptist Convention and Freemasonry* (Beaumont, TX: Mission and Ministry to Men, Inc., 1992), p.21.

[317] Denslow, (Vol. IV) *op. cit.*, p.211; Charles H. Vail, *The Ancient Mysteries and Modern Masonry* (Macoy Publishing and Masonic Company, 1909), p.226; James L. Holly, *The Southern Baptist Convention and Freemasonry* (Beaumont, TX: Mission and Ministry to Men, Inc., 1992), p.21; Albert Pike, *Morals and Dogma of the Ancient and Accepted Scottish Rite of Freemasonry* (Richmond, VA: L. H. Jenkins, Inc., 1871), p.823; Colin F. W. Dyer, *Symbolism in Craft Freemasonry* (Middlesex, England: A Lewis [Masonic Publishers] Ltd., 1976), p.44; Morey, *The Origins and Teachings of Freemasonry, op. cit.*, p.97.

[318] Francois Ribadeau Dumas (Translated by Elisabeth Abbott), *Cagliostro: Scoundrel or Saint?* (NY: The Orion Press, 1967), p.53.

[319] *Ibid.*, p.34; Samuel Warren, Compiler, *A Compendium of Swedenborg's Theological Writings* (New York, NY: Swedenborg Foundation, Inc., 1979 Edition), p.xxxv.

[320] Texe Marrs, *Texe Marrs Book of New Age Cults and Religions* (Austin, TX: Living Truth Publishers, 1990), p.307-308; "Truth Is One; Paths Are Many" (Brochure from Himalayan Academy Publications), p.3; *Free Inquiry* (Winter 1987/88, Vol. 8, No. 1), p.26; Robert Sessler, *To Be God of One World: The French Revolution Globalized* (Merlin, OR: Let There Be Light Publications, 1992), p.160; Samuel Warren, Compiler, *A Compendium of Swedenborg's Theological Writings* (New York, NY: Swedenborg Foundation, Inc., 1979 Edition), p.xxxii, xxxiv.

[321] *Ibid.*, p.308; "Easy Roads to Hell," (Tract printed by the Pilgrim Tract Society), p.4.

[322] *Ibid.* See also: Colin Wilson, *The Occult: A History* (NY: Random House, 1971), p.278, 281.

[323] Pamphlet from the Council for a Parliament of the World's Religions (Received October 3, 1994).

[324] Mary E. Hunt, "Feminist Ecumenism: Models for the Mainstream," *The Christian Century* (October 30, 1991, Vol. 108, No. 31), p.1000.

[325] Berit Kjos, *A Twist of Faith* (Green Forest, AR: New Leaf Press, 1997), p.110; "Liberal Women Try to Create Gods in Their Own Image," *Christian News* (February 28, 1994, Vol. 32, No. 9), p.11; *Ibid.*

[326] Wardner, *Unholy Alliances, op. cit.*, p.249.

[327] "President of World Council of Churches Says Mary Not a Virgin," *O Timothy* (1986, Vol. 3, Issue 7).

[328] "WCC Conference Honors Sophia Goddess, Gives Ovation to Lesbians," *The Evangelical Methodist* (June 1994, Vol. 73, No. 6), p.4; David W. Cloud, "WCC Conference Honors Sophia Goddess, Gives Ovation to Lesbians," *O Timothy* (1994, Vol. 11, Issue 3).

[329] "NCC Official Endorses PP Sex-Ed Video," *Calvary Contender* (September 15, 1997, Vol. 14, No. 18), p.1.

[330] "Abortion Bill: Graham and Pope Vs. NCC and Clinton," *Calvary Contender* (June 1, 1996, Vol. 13, No. 11), p.1.

[331] *Ibid.*

[332] *Ibid.*

[333] "Clipped Comments," *The Presbyterian Layman* (July/August 2000, Vol. 33, No. 4), p.4.

[334] "NCC Greets Homosexual Church Leader," *Calvary Contender* (February 15, 1999, Vol. 16, No. 4), p.1. See also: *Foundation* (January-February 2000, Vol. 21, Issue 1), p.42.

[335] "Homosexual Activist Is Pres. of Calif. Council of Churches," *Calvary Contender* (April 15, 2001, Vol. 18, No. 8), p.1; "Victory of Shame," *The Witness* (April 2001, Vol. 41, No. 4), p.2.

[336] "Victory of Shame," *The Witness* (April 2001, Vol. 41, No. 4), p.2.

[337] *Foundation* (January-February 2000, Vol. 21, Issue 1), p.42.

[338] David W. Cloud, "Some Questions for Desmond Tutu," *O Timothy* (1987, Vol. 4, Issues 3-4).

[339] *The NCC/WCC—Communism's Helpers, op. cit.*, p.18.

[340] Cloud, "Some Questions for Desmond Tutu," *op. cit.* See also: *Christian News* (December 14, 1998, Vol. 36, No. 46), p.3.

[341] Wardner, *Unholy Alliances, op. cit.*, p.171; Reynolds, *The World Council of Churches, op. cit.*, p.3.

[342] Reynolds, *The World Council of Churches, op. cit.*, p.3.

[343] *Christian News* (December 14, 1998, Vol. 36, No. 46), p.3; "Canaan Banana to Serve Goal Term After Appeal Fails," *Christian News* (June 5, 2000, Vol. 38, No. 23), p.3.

[344] *Secret Records Revealed: The Men, the Money and the Methods Behind the New World Order* (Oklahoma City, OK: Hearthstone Publishing, Ltd., 1999), p.62; *The Road to Socialism and the New World Order* (Highland City, FL: Florida Pro Family Forum, Inc., 1995), p.23; "American Malvern," *Time* (March 16, 1942); Bundy, *Collectivism in the Churches, op. cit.*, p.166, 321.

[345] Reynolds, *The World Council of Churches, op. cit.*, p.2.

[346] *Ibid.*, p.2-3.

[347] Dorothy J. Gaiter, "Former NAACP Director Chavis Says He Is Joining Farrakhan's Nation of Islam," *The Wall Street Journal* (February 24, 1997), p.B9; Texe Marrs, "Has the Entire Christian Establishment Finally Just Gone Berserk?," *Power of Prophecy* (April 2001, Vol. 2001-04), p.2.

[348] "Racial Justice Activist Named to Transition Team," *Christian News* (December 28, 1992, Vol. 30, No. 48), p.16.

[349] Texe Marrs, "Has the Entire Christian Establishment Finally Just Gone Berserk?," *Power of Prophecy* (April 2001, Vol. 2001-04), p.2.

[350] Gaiter, *op. cit.*

[351] *Ibid.* See also: Marrs, "Has the Entire Christian Establishment Finally Just Gone Berserk?," *op. cit.*, p.2.

[352] *Ibid.*

[353] *Ibid.* See also: "The Move by Christian Leaders to Sanction Islam," *The Vine and Branches* (Summer 1998, Vol. 13, Issue 3), p.7.

[354] Robert A. Morey, *Islam Unveiled: The True Desert Storm* (Shermans Dale, PA: The Scholars Press, 1991), p.48-49. See also: M. Esther Harding, *Woman's Mysteries: Ancient and Modern* (NY: G. P. Putnam's Sons, 1971), p.218.

[355] *Ibid.*, p.46.

[356] Stephen Knight, *The Brotherhood: The Secret World of the Freemasons* (Briarcliff Manor, NY: Stein and Day, 1984), p.236.

[357] Paper from PIOUS, p.15.

[358] Abdul Jalil, "25 Most Frequently Asked Questions about Islam" (Received October 14, 1995), p.3.

[359] "NAE Head Don Argue Popular with NCC & Clinton," *Calvary Contender* (April 15, 1997, Vol. 14, No. 8), p.2.

[360] William McIlhany, "The WCC: A Haven for Marxists?," *Family Protection Scoreboard*, p.21.

[361] Bundy, *Billy Graham: Performer?, Politician?, Preacher?, Prophet?, op. cit.*, p.40.

[362] "WCC's Russian Clergy Were KGB Men," *Calvary Contender* (August 15, 1992, Vol. 9, No. 16), p.2; "German Takes Over at WCC," *Associated Press* (September 19, 1992); Joseph A. Harriss, "The Gospel According to Marx," *Christian News* (February 1, 1993, Vol. 31, No. 5), p.12, 14; "German Theologian to Lead World Council," *Associated Press* (August 29, 1992); John A. Stormer, *None Dare Call It Treason...25 Years Later* (Florissant, MO: Liberty Bell Press,

1992), p.560; *The NCC/WCC—Communism's Helpers, op. cit.*, p.8; "New Dynamics," *One World* (April 1990, No. 154), p.23; Joseph A. Harriss, "The Gospel According to Marx," *Reader's Digest* (February 1993), p.72; David W. Cloud, "World Council of Churches Baptizes Heathenism," *Plains Baptist Challenger* (June 1994), p.1; Willmer Thorkelson, "Will Orthodox Exit the WCC?," *Christianity Today* (April 8, 1991, Vol. 35, No. 4), p.66; Morrison, *op. cit.*, p.532-533; "New Dynamics," *One World* (April 1990, No. 154), p.23; "Recognize Those Outside Church, Says WCC Leader," *Christian News* (April 12, 1993), Vol. 31, No. 15), p.11.

[363] Morrison, *op. cit.*, p.532-533.

[364] Paper from Thanksgiving Square.

[365] Joseph A. Harriss, "The Gospel According to Marx," *Reader's Digest* (February 1993), p.72; Joseph A. Harriss, "The Gospel According to Marx," *Christian News* (February 1, 1993, Vol. 31, No. 5), p.12.

[366] *The NCC/WCC—Communism's Helpers, op. cit.*, p.8.

[367] Epperson, *op. cit.*, p.222.

[368] John A. Stormer, *None Dare Call It Treason...25 Years Later* (Florissant, MO: Liberty Bell Press, 1992), p.560. See also: Harriss, *Reader's Digest, op. cit.*; Joseph A. Harriss, "The Gospel According to Marx," *Christian News* (February 1, 1993, Vol. 31, No. 5), p.12.

[369] Paper from Thanksgiving Square in Dallas, Texas.

[370] *Ibid.*

[371] Texe Marrs, "New Agers Meet to Plan World Takeover," *Flashpoint* (January 1990), p.1. See also: David W. Cloud, "The Day of Prayer for World Peace," *O Timothy* (1994, Vol. 11, Issue 3); Wilson Ewin, *Under the New World Order: Evangelicals, Catholics and Israel: Conspiracy of the Ages* (Compton, Quebec: Quebec Baptist Missions, n.d.), p.103; James, *op. cit.*, p.110.

[372] Wilson Ewin, *Under the New World Order: Evangelicals, Catholics and Israel: Conspiracy of the Ages* (Compton, Quebec: Quebec Baptist Missions, n.d.), p.103.

[373] "South Africa: Targeted by Devilish Powers," *O Timothy* (1987, Vol. 4, Issues 3-4).

[374] "World Council of Churches Supports Terrorism and Violence," *O Timothy* (1988, Vol. 5, Issue 4).

[375] Graham, *op. cit.* p.374-375.

[376] George Zeller, *Billy Graham: Ecumenical Evangelism* (Middletown, CT: Middletown Bible Church, n.d.), p.11; Bundy, *Billy Graham: Performer?, Politician?, Preacher?, Prophet?, op. cit.*, p.41.

[377] *Ibid.*; Bundy, *Billy Graham: Performer?, Politician?, Preacher?, Prophet?, op. cit.* p.40.

[378] Bundy, *Billy Graham: Performer?, Politician?, Preacher?, Prophet?, op. cit.*, p.40.

[379] *Ibid.*, p.41.

[380] *Ibid.*, p.7-8.

[381] "South Africa: Targeted by Devilish Powers," *op cit.*

[382] See: *Flashpoint* (February 1995), p.2.

[383] "Leader of African National Congress Threatens Whites," *O Timothy* (1990, Vol. 7, Issue 7).

[384] "New Dynamics," *One World* (April 1990, No. 154), p.23.

[385] *Ibid.*

[386] *Ibid.*

[387] "World Council of Churches 50th Anniversary," *The ACCC Report* (February 1999), p.3.

[388] See: "Assembly Resolutions," *One World* (April 1990, No. 154), p.16.

[389] "South Africa: Targeted by Devilish Powers," *op. cit.*; "Leader of African National Congress Threatens Whites," *op. cit.*; "South African Communists Wield New Power," *America's Future* (July/August 1994, Vol. 36, No. 7/8), p.2; "Who Is Mandela?," *Midnight Call* (September 1990), p.15; Cloud, "Some Questions for Desmond Tutu," *op. cit.*

[390] *Ibid.* See also: "An Update on South Africa," *O Timothy* (1988, Vol. 5, Issue 2).

[391] "Communist Mandela Given Hero's Welcome in Canada, U. S.," *The Christian World Report* (July 1990, Vol. 2, No. 6), p.3.

[392] http://members.nbci.com/_XMCM/katfortuna/FCWP02200Interview.html. See also: Wayne Peterson, *Extraordinary Times, Extraordinary Beings: Experiences of an American Diplomat with Maitreya and the Masters of Wisdom* (Henderson, NV: Emergence Press, 2001), p.179.

[393] "Communist Mandela Given Hero's Welcome in Canada, U. S.," *op. cit.*

[394] "News of Interest to Christians," *Sword of the Lord* (November 23, 1990, Vol. 56, No. 24), p.2.

[395] "Rockefeller Gives Money to South African Communists," *Christian Anti-Communism Crusade* (August 15, 1993, Vol. 33, No. 16), p.6. See also: "Rockefeller Bankrolls Communism in South Africa?," *Christian World Report* (December 1990, Vol. 2, No. 9), p.7.

[396] "Black South African Mayor Exposes Nelson Mandela," *O Timothy* (1990, Vol. 7, Issue 7).

[397] "Communist Mandela Given Hero's Welcome in Canada, U. S.," *op. cit.*, p.3.

[398] Tom Watson, *The Evangelical Eroding of the Deity of Christ* (Southlake, TX: Countryside Bible Church, 1996), p.2.

[399] McIlhany, *op. cit.*, p.21. See also: "WCC Funds African Marxists," *Christian Inquirer* (November 1984), p.5; "South Africa: Targeted by Devilish Powers," *op. cit.* See also: "An Update on South Africa," *O Timothy* (1988, Vol. 5, Issue 2); "Leader of African National Congress Threatens Whites," *op. cit.;* "South African Communists Wield New Power," *America's Future* (July/August 1994, Vol. 36, No. 7/8), p.2; Texe Marrs, *Circle of Intrigue* (Austin, TX: Living Truth Ministries, 1995), p.68; "Our Common Future: Rock Stars and World Leaders Join in the Largest Consciousness Raising Media Event of All Time...," *The Omega-Letter* (June 1989, Vol. 4, No. 5), p.8; Stormer, *None Dare Call It Treason...25 Years Later, op. cit.* p.19; "Rockefeller Gives Money to Help South African Communists," *op. cit.*, p.6.

[400] Harriss, *Reader's Digest, op. cit.*, p.68. See also: Joseph A. Harriss, "The Gospel According to Marx," *Christian News* (February 1, 1993, Vol. 31, No. 5), p.12.

[401] "South Africa: Targeted by Devilish Powers," *op. cit.* See also: *Ibid.*

[402] "An Update on South Africa," *O Timothy* (1988, Vol. 5, Issue 2).

[403] "Black South African Mayor Exposes Nelson Mandela," *op. cit.* See also: "Who Is Mandela?," *Midnight Call* (September 1990), p.15; "World Council of Churches Youth Meeting Praises Terrorism and Murder in South Africa," *O Timothy* (1986, Vol. 3, Issue 7).

[404] Cloud, "Some Questions for Desmond Tutu," *op. cit.* See also: "Who Is Mandela?," *Midnight Call* (September 1990), p.15.

[405] "Christians Warned," *The Witness* (April 1994, Vol. 34, No. 4), p.2.

[406] "Who Is Mandela?," *Midnight Call* (September 1990), p.15; "Communist Mandela Given Hero's Welcome in Canada, U. S.," *op. cit.*, p.3.

[407] *Ibid.*

[408] "Rockefeller Gives Money to South African Communists," *op. cit.*, p.6.

[409] *Last Trumpet Newsletter* (June 1994, Vol. 13, Issue 6), p.3.

[410] *Ibid.*

[411] Robert L. Slimp, "American Christian Media Supports ANC/Communists," *Christian News* (June 10, 1996, Vol. 34, No. 24), p.10.

[412] "South African Communists Wield New Power," *America's Future* (July/August 1994, Vol. 36, No. 7/8), p.3; *Last Trumpet Newsletter* (June 1994, Vol. 13, Issue 6), p.3.

[413] *Ibid.*, p.2.

[414] "Billy Graham Offers Prayers for Mandela," *Christian News* (June 13, 1994, Vol. 32, No. 24), p.3.

[415] "NCC: New Leaders, New Woes," *Calvary Contender* (December 1, 1999, Vol. 16, No. 23), p.2; Jeffery L. Sheler, "Christians, Unite!," *U. S. News & World Report* (November 15, 1999), p.100.

[416] "Andy Young Is New President of NCC," *Calvary Contender* (February 15, 1998, Vol. 15, No. 4).

[417] John H. Adams, "WCC-backed Mugabe Puts Zimbabwe in Bloodbath," *The Presbyterian Layman* (May/June 2000, Vol. 33, No. 3), p.1; A. Richard Harmet, Executive Editor, *The World Book Year Book* (Chicago, IL: World Book-Childcraft International, Inc., 1980), p.454; Harriss, *Reader's Digest, op. cit.*, p.68; "World Council of Churches 50th Anniversary," *The ACCC Report* (February 1999), p.3.

[418] "Andy Young Is New President of NCC?," *op. cit.*

[419] Adams, *op. cit.*, p.1.

[420] *Ibid.*

[421] *Ibid.*, p.14. See also: Richard Wurmbrand, *Marx and Satan* (Westchester, IL: Crossway Books, 1986), p.130.

[422] *Ibid.* See also: "World Council of Churches 50th Anniversary," *The ACCC Report* (February 1999), p.2.

[423] "WCC's 50th Anniversary, Orthodox Rife?," *op. cit.;* Tom A. Hudgens, *Let's Abolish War* (Denver, CO: BILR Corporation, 1986), p.78; "A Dozen Good Reasons to Get *US* Out of the United Nations," (1995), p.5; "State of the World Forum Toward a New Civilization," *Mindszenty Report* (March 1996, Vol. 37, No. 3), p.3; "State of the World Forum," *Wisconsin Report* (September 21, 1995, Vol. 20, No. 36), p.3.

[424] Harriss, *Reader's Digest, op. cit.*, p.69. See also: Rivera, *op. cit.*, p.225; Joseph A. Harriss, "The Gospel According to Marx," *Christian News* (February 1, 1993, Vol. 31, No. 5), p.12.

[425] John A. Stormer, *The Death of a Nation* (Florissant, MO: Liberty Bell Press, 1968), p.93.

[426] Kurt Koch (Translated by Michael Freeman) *Occult ABC* (Germany: Literature Mission Aglasterhausen, Inc., 1978), p.141.

[427] *IPS Packet* (Independence, MO: Price Publishing Company, n.d.), p.19; Stormer, *The Death of a Nation, op. cit.*, p.94.

[428] "Taking the Fire out of Hell," *Christian News* (September 27, 1999, Vol. 37, No. 35), p.10.

[429] Wardner, *Unholy Alliances, op. cit.*, p.157.

[430] Rockwood, *op. cit.*

[431] "Taking the Fire out of Hell," *op. cit.*

[432] "SBC Reaffirms Commitment to Liberal Ecumenical Organization," Watch unto Prayer (September 2, 1998).

[433] Duncan, *op. cit.,* p.28.

[434] "Newbigin, Wiersbe to Speak at Samford," *Calvary Contender* (July 1, 1997, Vol. 14, No. 13), p.2. See also: "Newbigin Dies," *Calvary Contender* (March 15, 1998, Vol. 15, No. 6), p.2; "World Council of Churches 50th Anniversary," *The ACCC Report* (February 1999), p.4.

[435] *Ibid.;* "Newbigin Dies," *Calvary Contender* (March 15, 1998, Vol. 15, No. 6), p.2; David W. Cloud, "Billy Graham's Disobedience to the Word of God" (Updated March 2, 1999), p.6.

[436] David W. Cloud, "Billy Graham's Disobedience to the Word of God" (Updated March 2, 1999), p.6.

[437] Gsell, *The Legacy of Billy Graham, op. cit.,* p.23.

[438] "Newbigin, Wiersbe to Speak at Samford," *op. cit.*

[439] Gsell, *The Legacy of Billy Graham, op. cit.,* p.23.

[440] David W. Cloud, "Two Homosexuals and the New International Version" (1997); Marissa Heinen, "Revived Paganism for a One-World Religion," *The Christian World Report* (September 1990, Vol. 2, No. 8), p.3; David R. Barnhart, *Contending for the Faith* (Eagan, MN: Abiding Word Publications, 1994), p.52.

[441] Leaflet from the Cosmic Study Center.

[442] "Mollenkott, Homosexuality, Bible Translation," *Calvary Contender* (November 1, 1993, Vol. 10, No. 21), p.2; Kjos, *A Twist of Faith, op. cit.,* p.32; "Mollenkott a Lesbian...and More!," *Calvary Contender* (April 1, 1993, Vol. 10, No. 7), p.2; "Virginia Mollenkott," *Christian News* (February 17, 1997, Vol. 35, No. 7), p.23; David W. Cloud, "Two Homosexuals and the NIV" (December 4, 1997); Gail Riplinger, *The Language of the King James Bible: Discover Its Hidden Built-in Dictionary* (Ararat, VA: A.V. Publications Corporation, 1998), p.114.

[443] Gail Riplinger, *The Language of the King James Bible: Discover Its Hidden Built-in Dictionary* (Ararat, VA: A.V. Publications Corporation, 1998), p.114.

[444] "Is the New International Version the Sodomites (sic) Version?," *The Perilous Times* (September 1993, Vol. 15, No. 7), p.8; Gail Riplinger, *Which Bible Is God's Word?: Answers to Common Questions Concerning Modern Versions and Translations* (Oklahoma City, OK: Hearthstone Publishing, Ltd., 1994), p.81; "NIV to Go 'Gender-Neutral?,'" *Calvary Contender* (April 15, 1997, Vol. 14, No. 8), p.2; R. A. Partlow, *Satan's Subtle Sabotage of God's Holy Word* (Erie, PA: The Stable, 1997), p.113, 121; "Mollenkott, Homosexuality, Bible Translation," *op. cit.;* David W. Cloud, "Two Homosexuals and the NIV" (December 4, 1997); *Ibid.,* p.114, 115.

[445] Carol P. Christ, *Laughter of Aphrodite: Reflections on a Journey to the Goddess* (New York, NY: Harper and Row Publishers, Inc., 1987), p.112.

[446] Virginia Ramey Mollenkott, "Whore-ishly Implementing the Political Vision of the Christ-Sophia," *CLOUTreach* (Summer/Autumn 1995, Vol. 4, No. 3), p.1; Riplinger, *The Language of the King James Bible, op. cit.,* p.114, 115; "Is the New International Version the Sodomites (sic) Version?," *op. cit.,* p.8; James, *op. cit.,* p.60; Kjos, *A Twist of Faith, op. cit.,* p.32; "Pro-Homosexual New Evangelicals?," *Calvary Contender* (August 15, 1998, Vol. 15, No. 16), p.1; Brenda Scott and Samantha Smith, *Trojan Horse: How the New Age Movement Infiltrates the Church* (Lafayette, LA: Huntington House Publishers, 1993), p.150; "NIV to Go 'Gender-Neutral?,'" *Calvary Contender* (April 15, 1997, Vol. 14, No. 8), p.2; "Mollenkott a Homosexual," *Calvary Contender* (September 15, 1997, Vol. 14, No. 18); David W. Cloud, "WCC Conference Honors Sophia Goddess, Gives Ovation to Lesbians," *O Timothy* (1994, Vol. 11, Issue 3); "Mollenkott, Homosexuality, Bible Translation," *op. cit.;* "Mollenkott a Lesbian...and More!," *Calvary Contender* (April 1, 1993, Vol. 10, No. 7), p.2; *The Christian Century* (November 20-27, 1991, Vol. 108, No. 34), p.1119; "Events," *CLOUTreach* (Spring 1997, Vol. 6, No. 2), p.5; "Jesus Christ Was Really a Woman," *Christian News* (July 21, 1997, Vol. 35, No. 29), p.1; *Christian News* (October 14, 1991, Vol. 29, No. 37), p.13; "Virginia Mollenkott," *Christian News* (November 25, 1996, Vol. 34, No. 44), p.6; "Virginia Mollenkott," *Christian News* (February 17, 1997, Vol. 35, No. 7), p.23; David W. Cloud, "Two Homosexuals and the NIV" (December 4, 1997); Flyer from Kirkridge (1997); "Gay, Lesbian and Christian," *Kirkridge* (Spring/Summer 1988), p.8; "Gay, Lesbian and Christian," *Kirkridge* (Spring/Summer 1987), p.7; "WCC Conference Honors Sophia Goddess, Gives Ovation to Lesbians," *op. cit.,* p.4; Judith Allen Shelly, "The Feminist Gospel: The Movement to Unite Feminism with the Church," *Journal of Christian Nursing* (Summer 1993), p.43; Ad from *The Other Side* (Received July 22, 1991); *The Other Side* (March 1988, Vol. 24, No. 2, Issue 190), p.39.

[447] "Gay, Lesbian and Christian," *Kirkridge* (Spring/Summer 1988); Flyer from Kirkridge (1987); "Gay, Lesbian and Christian," *Kirkridge* (Spring/Summer 1987); *The Christian Century* (November 20-27, 1991, Vol. 108, No. 34), p.1119; "Events," *CLOUTreach* (Spring 1997, Vol. 6, No. 2), p.5; *The Other Side* (March 1988, Vol. 24, No. 2, Issue 190), p.39.

[448] "Virginia Mollenkott," *Christian News* (February 17, 1997, Vol. 35, No. 7), p.23; Paper from Evangelical and Ecumenical Women's Caucus (Received December 28, 1996).

[449] Gail Riplinger, *Which Bible is God's Word?: Answers to Common Questions Concerning Modern Versions and Translations* (Oklahoma City, OK: Hearthstone Publishing, Ltd., 1994), p.81. See also: "Virginia Mollenkott," *Christian News* (November 25, 1996, Vol. 34, No. 44), p.6.

[450] David W. Cloud, "Virginia Mollenkott," Fundamental Baptist Information Service (January 25, 1997).

[451] *Ibid.*

[452] Samuel Weiser (Catalog for 1984-1985), p.5; *Sojourners* (April 1986), p.40.

[453] Cloud, "Virginia Mollenkott," *op. cit.;* Cloud, "Two Homosexuals and the New International Version," *op. cit.*

[454] Cloud, "Two Homosexuals and the New International Version," *op. cit.*

[455] "Is the New International Version the Sodomites (sic) Version?," *op. cit.*, p.8; Ashbrook, *New Neutralism II, op. cit.*, p.63; "Mollenkott a Lesbian...and More!," *Calvary Contender* (April 1, 1993, Vol. 10, No. 7), p.2; "Virginia Mollenkott," *Christian News* (February 17, 1997, Vol. 35, No. 7), p.23; Paper from Evangelical and Ecumenical Women's Caucus (Received December 28, 1996); David W. Cloud, "Two Homosexuals and the NIV," (December 4, 1997); "Gay, Lesbian and Christian," *Kirkridge* (Spring/Summer 1988), p.8; *The Other Side* (January/February 1988); *The Other Side* (March 1988, Vol. 24, No. 2, Issue 190), p.39.

[456] "Mollenkott a Lesbian...and More!," *Calvary Contender* (April 1, 1993, Vol. 10, No. 7), p.2.

[457] "Virginia Mollenkott," *Christian News* (February 17, 1997, Vol. 35, No. 7), p.23.

[458] David W. Cloud, "Two Homosexuals and the NIV" (December 4, 1997).

[459] "Virginia Mollenkott," *Christian News* (November 25, 1996, Vol. 34, No. 44), p.6.

[460] *Ibid.*

[461] "Virginia Mollenkott," *Christian News* (February 17, 1997, Vol. 35, No. 7), p.23.

[462] *Ibid.*

[463] *Ibid.*

[464] *Ibid.*; "Is the New International Version the Sodomites (sic) Version?," *op. cit.*, p.8; Cloud, "Virginia Mollenkott," *op. cit.*

[465] "Is the New International Version the Sodomites (sic) Version?," *op. cit.*, p.8.

[466] "Mollenkott a Homosexual," *Calvary Contender* (September 15, 1997, Vol. 14, No. 18).

[467] *The Evangelical Methodist* (2000, Vol. 78, No. 2), p.6. See also: http://www.religionproject.org/declaration.html, p.1.

[468] Riplinger, *The Language of the King James Bible, op. cit.*, p.114, 115; Cloud, "Two Homosexuals and the New International Version" *op. cit.*

[469] "Mollenkott a Homosexual," *op. cit.*; "NIV to Go 'Gender-Neutral?,'" *Calvary Contender* (April 15, 1997, Vol. 14, No. 8); "Mollenkott, Homosexuality, Bible Translation," *op. cit.*; "Virginia Mollenkott," *Christian News* (November 25, 1996, Vol. 34, No. 44), p.6; "Virginia Mollenkott," *Christian News* (February 17, 1997, Vol. 35, No. 7), p.23; "WCC Conference Honors Sophia Goddess, Gives Ovation to Lesbians," *op. cit.*, p.4.

[470] "Jesus Christ Was Really a Woman," *Christian News* (July 21, 1997, Vol. 35, No. 29), p.1; "Virginia Mollenkott," *Christian News* (February 17, 1997, Vol. 35, No. 7), p.23. See also: Virginia Ramey Mollenkott, *Women, Men, and the Bible* (Nashville, TN: Abingdon, 1977), p.52, 58, 59, 60, 66, 82; Virginia Mollenkott, "Women and the Bible," *Sojourners* (February 1976); Cloud, "Two Homosexuals and the New International Version," *op. cit.*; Virginia Mollenkott, "Women and the Bible," *Sojourners* (June 1977).

[471] Riplinger, *The Language of the King James Bible, op. cit.*, p.114. See also: Virginia Mollenkott, "Jesus Christ Was Really a Woman," *op. cit.*; "Virginia Mollenkott," *Christian News* (February 17, 1997, Vol. 35, No. 7), p.23.

[472] David W. Cloud, "WCC Conference Honors Sophia Goddess, Gives Ovation to Lesbians," *O Timothy* (1994, Vol. 11, Issue 3).

[473] James, *op. cit.*, p.60; Kjos, *A Twist of Faith, op. cit.*, p.32.

[474] "Liberal Women Try to Create Gods in Their Own Image," *Christian News* (February 28, 1994, Vol. 32, No. 9), p.11; Cloud, "Two Homosexuals and the New International Version," *op. cit.* See also: "Virginia Mollenkott," *Christian News* (November 25, 1996, Vol. 34, No. 44), p.6; "Virginia Mollenkott," *Christian News* (February 17, 1997, Vol. 35, No. 7), p.23.

[475] Mollenkott, "Whore-ishly Implementing the Political Vision of the Christ-Sophia," *op. cit.*, p.1.

[476] "WCC and Catholicism," *Calvary Contender* (February 1, 1999, Vol. 16, No. 3), p.2; "German Takes Over at WCC," *Associated Press* (September 19, 1992); "What Is the WCC?," *Calvary Contender* (April 1, 1998, Vol. 15, No. 7), p.2; *Christian News* (February 1, 1993, Vol. 31, No. 5), p.14; *Foundation* (July-September 1995, Vol. 16, Issue 4), p.10; "World Council of Churches Says 'Stop Evangelizing,'" *The Vine and Branches* (Summer 2001, Vol. 16, Issue 3), p.16; "Gimme That One-World Religion," *The Day Drawing Near* (Fall 1996), p.1; Harriss, *Reader's Digest, op. cit.*, p.72; "German Theologian to Lead World Council," *Associated Press* (August 29, 1992); "World Council of Churches Ecumenical Women's Decade Festival," *The ACCC Report* (January 1999), p.1; "World Council of Churches 50th Anniversary," *The ACCC Report* (February 1999), p.2; "Recognize Those Outside Church, Says WCC Leader," *Christian News* (April 12, 1993), Vol. 31, No. 15), p.11.

[477] T. Aho, "World Council of Churches to Propose New Ecumenical Forum," *Despatch Magazine* (September 1998, Vol. 10, No. 3), p.45; "What Is the WCC?," *Calvary Contender* (June 15, 2001, Vol. 18, No. 12), p.2.

[478] *O Timothy* (1986, Vol. 3, Issue 7); T. Aho, "World Council of Churches to Propose New Ecumenical Forum," *Despatch Magazine* (September 1998, Vol. 10, No. 3), p.45.

[479] Harriss, *Reader's Digest, op. cit.*, p.72. See also: "World Council of Churches 50th Anniversary," *The ACCC Report* (February 1999), p.2; "German Takes Over at WCC," *Associated Press* (September 19, 1992); Roland Rasmussen, "Back Billy Graham?—Californian Baptist Pastor says No," *Sword of the Lord* (October 18, 1963); Joseph A. Harriss, "The Gospel According to Marx," *Christian News* (February 1, 1993, Vol. 31, No. 5), p.12; Epperson, *op. cit.*, p.222; Richard Price and Larry Harlacher, "RLDS Hierarchy Espouses the WCC and NCC," *WCC Packet* (Independence, MO: Price Publishing Company, n.d.), p.18; D. W. Cloud, "Some Frightening Facts About Billy Graham," *O Timothy* (1984, Vol. 1, Issue 4); "World Council of Churches Youth Meeting Praises Terrorism and Murder In South Africa," *O Timothy* (1986, Vol. 3, Issue 7); "World Council of Churches Supports Terrorism and Violence," *op. cit.*; "World Council of

Churches Seeks to Build a New One World Order," *O Timothy* (1986, Vol. 3, Issue 7); "National and World Council of Churches Call for UN Intervention in America's Internal Affairs," *O Timothy* (1995, Vol. 12, Issue 5).

[480] "50th Meeting of the World Council of Churches Central Committee," *The ACCC: A Special Report* (October 1999), p.3.

[481] *World Goodwill Occasional Paper* (Received September 16, 1998), p.9.

[482] "Reconciliation or Jesus?," *The Presbyterian Layman* (May/June 2001, Vol. 34, No. 4), p.17.

[483] *World Council of Churches: The Shaky Ship Sails On, op. cit.*, p.29.

[484] David W. Cloud, "Bishop K. H. Ting—China's Master of Deceit," *O Timothy* (1986, Vol. 3, Issue 3); Bundy, *How Liberals and Radicals Are Manipulating Evangelicals, op. cit.*, p.5; "Evangelical, WCC Reps Join in Evangelism Consultation," *Foundation* (July-September 1995, Vol. 16, Issue 4), p.15.

[485] *Foundation* (July-September 1995, Vol. 16, Issue 4), p.10; "Jesus Christ Is Not the Only Way to God, WCC Says," *The Omega-Letter* (September 1989, Vol. 4, No. 8), p.10.

[486] M. H. Reynolds, "AD 2000 Ecumenical Evangelism: A Warning!," *Foundation* (July-September 1995, Vol. 16, Issue 4), p.10.

[487] "Jesus Christ Is Not the Only Way to God, WCC Says," *The Omega-Letter* (September 1989, Vol. 4, No. 8), p.10.

[488] "United Methodist Theologian Urges Methodists Not to Evangelize," *The Vine and Branches* (Spring 1999, Vol. 14, Issue 2), p.10; *Religion for Peace* (February 1995, Issue 65-A), p.4; Paper from Thanksgiving Square; Texe Marrs, *Ravaged by the New Age: Satan's Plan to Destroy Our Kids* (Austin, TX: Living Truth Publishers, 1989), p.75.

[489] Texe Marrs quoting S. Wesley Ariarajah in *Ravaged by the New Age: Satan's Plan to Destroy Our Kids* (Austin, TX: Living Truth Publishers, 1989), p.75.

[490] Paper from Thanksgiving Square.

[491] Swing, *op. cit.*, p.6.

[492] Parker T. Williamson, "Interfaith Dialogue: 'My God, Your God, Our God, No God,'" *The Presbyterian Layman* (January/February 1999, Vol. 32, No. 1), p.9.

[493] *Ibid.* See also: "World Council of Churches Ecumenical Women's Decade Festival," *The ACCC Report* (January 1999), p.1; Parker T. Williamson, "WCC to Study Diversity of Sexuality," *The Presbyterian Layman* (January/February 1999, Vol. 32, No. 1), p.17.

[494] "World Council of Churches Ecumenical Women's Decade Festival," *The ACCC Report* (January 1999), p.1.

[495] *Ibid.*

[496] *Ibid.*, p.2.

[497] "World Council of Churches 50th Anniversary," *The ACCC Report* (February 1999), p.2.

[498] *Ibid.*, p.4.

[499] "'Your Silence Will Not Protect You...Celebrating Spirit, Seeking Racial Justice,'" *CLOUTreach* (Spring 2001, Vol. 10, No. 2), p.1.

[500] Dee Dee Risher, "Marga Buhrig: Working for Women from Within," *The Other Side* (January/February 1988), p.12; Samantha Smith, "Gorby's Disappearing Act," *Hope for the World* (Spring 1998), p.6.

[501] *Ibid.*

[502] *Ibid.*, p.13.

[503] "Key Players in the Sex Education Game," *AFA Journal* (October 1990, Vol. 14, No. 9), p.13; *The Grab for Power: A Chronology of the NEA* (Marlborough, NH: Plymouth Rock Foundation, 1993), p.24; George Grant, *Grand Illusions: The Legacy of Planned Parenthood* (Nashville, TN: Thomas Nelson, Inc., 1998 Edition), p.51, 77, 116, 350, 352; Springmeier, *The Top 13 Illuminati Bloodlines, op. cit.*, p.239; *Chronology of Education with Quotable Quotes* (Highland City, FL: Pro Family Forum, Inc., 1994 Updated, bound volume), p.91; *Christian News* (November 9, 1992, Vol. 30, No. 41), p.9; "Panorama," *Christian News* (November 11, 1991, Vol. 29, No. 41), p.11; "The American Family Under Attack," *An American Commentary* (Oklahoma City, OK: Hearthstone Publishing, Ltd., 1993), p.22; "Population Control and the 'New Age' Religion," *An American Commentary* (Oklahoma City, OK: Hearthstone Publishing, Ltd., 1993), p.57; Letter from James Dobson dated February 13, 1992, p.4; "What Is Planned Parenthood Teaching Children?," *End-Times News Digest* (April 1990, Issue 139), p.5; *Now Is the Dawning of the New Age New World Order, op. cit.*, p.262-263; Rush Limbaugh, *The Way Things Ought to Be* (New York, NY: Pocket Books, 1992), p.75; F. V. Scott, "The New American Gothic Planned Parenthood," *Passport Magazine* (July-August 1988), p.8; "Political Dirty Tricks Foil Minnesota Bill," *The Christian World Report* (April 1990, Vol. 2, No. 4), p.22.

[504] Springmeier, *The Top 13 Illuminati Bloodlines, op. cit.*, p.239; *Now Is the Dawning of the New Age New World Order, op. cit.*, p.262-263; George Grant, *Grand Illusions: The Legacy of Planned Parenthood* (Nashville, TN: Thomas Nelson, Inc., 1998 Edition), p.51; *SEA Letter* (March 8, 1986), n.p.; F. V. Scott, "The New American Gothic Planned Parenthood," *Passport Magazine* (July-August 1988), p.8.

[505] "The New Right: Part II: The Religion Heritage of America: Instrument of BROTHERHOOD," *Distant Drums* (December 1980, Vol. 2, No. 5), p.9.

[506] *Ibid.*

[507] *Ibid.*

[508] *Ibid.*

[509] *Council on Foreign Relations: Annual Report July 1, 1987-June 30, 1988,* p.174; *Council on Foreign Relations: Annual Report July 1, 1994-June 30, 1995,* p.145; *Council on Foreign Relations: Annual Report July 1, 1990-June 30, 1991,* p.180; *President Clinton Will Continue the New World Order* (Oklahoma City, OK: Southwest Radio Church, 1993), p.27.

[510] Berit Kjos, "Character Training for Global Citizens," *The Christian Conscience* (June 1997, Vol. 3, No. 5), p.51.

[511] "New Liberal Religious/Political Group Deplores 'False Choices,' Redefines Evangelism," *Christian News* (July 1, 1996, Vol. 34, No. 27), p.23; *Mindszenty Report* (March 1996, Vol. 37, No. 3), p.2; *The Cry for Renewal: Biblical Faith and Spiritual Politics* (May 23, 1995), p.2.

[512] *Secret Records Revealed, op. cit.,* p.143; "The Question Now Isn't Just Poverty. For Many, It Is Survival," *The Washington Spectator* (August 1, 2001, Vol. 27, No. 15), p.1; *President Clinton Will Continue the New World Order* (Oklahoma City, OK: Southwest Radio Church, 1993), p.27; "The Children's Defense Fund: Together We Stand for Children," p.9; "Caux 1996: An International Learning Community," *Breakthroughs* (March-April 1996), p.1; Brochure for Character Education Partnership, (February 1994), p.6; *"Secret Records" Revealed, op. cit.,* p.40; *Breakthroughs* (September-October 1996), p.1; "The Tangled Web," *The Christian Conscience* (January/February 1997, Vol. 3, No. 1), p.17; *Character Counts* (1994, Special Issue), p.15; Kjos, "Character Training for Global Citizens," *op. cit.,* p.51; *Children's Defense Fund Annual National Conference,* p.1; Berit Kjos, "'The State of the World' According to Gorbachev," *Christian News* (October 28, 1996, Vol. 34, No. 40), p.1; Billy James Hargis, "Gorbachev Plots His Quiet Takeover," *Christian Crusade* (November 1996, Vol. 44, No. 11), p.7; Letter from MRA dated November 22, 1996), p.1; Robert M. Vandervoort, "Radicals Use Children to Advance Big Government Agenda," *The Florida Forum* (Summer 1997), p.1; *Dallas Morning News* (October 14, 1995); *Temple Awards for Creative Altruism: Update on Recipients 1987-1989,* unnumbered page); "Liberals Find Meaning in Spiritual Politics: Summit Seeks Room on Left for Religion," *The Washington Times* (April 16, 1996), p.A12; "Book Review," *The Florida Forum* (Summer 1994), p.9; *Mindszenty Report* (March 1996, Vol. 37, No. 3), p.2; *The Cry for Renewal: Biblical Faith and Spiritual Politics* (May 23, 1995); Ben Keppel, "Race, Poverty, and the Symbolism of the Child," *Research Reports from the Rockefeller Archive Center* (Spring 1998), p.2; *Sojourners* (March/April 1995, Vol. 24, No. 1), p.7.

[513] *Secret Records Revealed, op. cit.,* p.143; *"Secret Records" Revealed, op. cit.,* p.40.

[514] Samantha Smith, "Gorby's Disappearing Act," *Hope for the World* (Spring 1998), p.6.

[515] *Ibid.*

[516] "World Council of Churches Promotes Female Gods and Revolution," *O Timothy* (1988, Vol. 5, Issue 4).

[517] *Ibid.*

[518] *Caux: Healing the Past—Forging the Future* (Luzerne, Switzerland: Fondation Pour le Rearmament Moral, 1996), p.47; James, *op. cit.,* p.66, 217; Kjos, *A Twist of Faith, op. cit.,* p.178.

[519] James, *op. cit.,* p.217-218.

[520] *Ibid.,* p.218.

[521] Kjos, *A Twist of Faith, op. cit.,* p.179.

[522] *Ibid.*

[523] John H. Adams, "WCC Speaker Tells UN That 'Gods' Are to Be Found in World," *The Presbyterian Layman* (September/October 2000), p.15.

[524] *Ibid.*

[525] *Ibid.*

[526] *Secret Records Revealed, op. cit.,* p.62.

[527] Paper from the Masonic Service Association (April 15, 1969).

[528] Rivera, *op. cit.,* p.89; *Secret Records Revealed, op. cit.,* p.62.

[529] *Council on Foreign Relations: Annual Report July 1, 1987-June 30, 1988,* p.172; *Council on Foreign Relations: Annual Report July 1, 1992-June 30, 1993,* p.164; *Council on Foreign Relations: Annual Report July 1, 1994-June 30, 1995,* p.143; *Ibid.,* p.89, 100; James W. Wardner, *The Planned Destruction of America* (Debary, FL: Longwood Communications, 1994), p.72, 74, 76, 129, 172; "The Agenda of the Invisible Government," *The Prophecy Newsletter* (1985, Vol. 1, No. 3), n.p.; *Secret Records Revealed, op. cit.,* p.62; Gary Kah, *En Route to Global Occupation* (Lafayette, LA: 1992), p.61; Robert Gaylon Ross, Sr., *Who's Who of the Elite* (San Marcos, TX: RIE, 1995), p.110; James R. Patrick, Editor, *America 2000/Goals 2000* (Moline, IL: Citizens for Academic Excellence, 1994), p.620.

[530] Robert Gaylon Ross, Sr., *Who's Who of the Elite* (San Marcos, TX: RIE, 1995), p.110; James R. Patrick, Editor, *America 2000/Goals 2000* (Moline, IL: Citizens for Academic Excellence, 1994), p.620; "The Agenda of the Invisible Government," *The Prophecy Newsletter* (1985, Vol. 1, No. 3), n.p.; *Secret Records Revealed, op. cit.,* p.62; James W. Wardner, *The Planned Destruction of America* (Debary, FL: Longwood Communications, 1994), p.72, 74, 172.

[531] *Ibid.*

[532] *Secret Records Revealed, op. cit.,* p.62. See also: *Ibid.,* p.110, 203; Charles C. Haynes, Editor, *Finding Common Ground* (Nashville, TN: The Freedom Forum First Amendment Center, 1994), p.2.7; Gary Kah, *En Route to Global Occupation* (Lafayette, LA: 1992), p.61; James W. Wardner, *The Planned Destruction of America* (Debary, FL: Longwood Communications, 1994), p.76, 129, 172; Rivera, *op. cit.,* p.89, 100.

[533] Chambers, *op. cit.,* p.174.

[534] George Grant, *Grand Illusions: The Legacy of Planned Parenthood* (Nashville, TN: Thomas Nelson, Inc., 1998 Edition), p.216.

[535] G. Archer Weniger, "Dr. Billy Graham and the National Council of Churches," p.3.

[536] Chambers, *op. cit.*, p.172.

[537] Stormer, *None Dare Call It Treason...25 Years Later, op. cit.*, p.470.

[538] *Ibid.*, p.470-471. See also: Wardner, *Unholy Alliances, op. cit.*, p.173.

[539] McIntire, *op. cit.*

[540] McIlhany, *op. cit.*, p.21.

[541] Wardner, *Unholy Alliances, op. cit.*, p.136; Bundy, *Billy Graham: Performer?, Politician?, Preacher?, Prophet?, op. cit.*, p.83. See also: William Martin, *A Prophet with Honor: The Billy Graham Story* (NY: William Morrow and Company, Inc., 1991), p.421-422; "Billy Graham Does Political Favor for President Clinton," *Flashpoint* (September 1997, Vol. 97-9), p.2; Rick Miesel, "Billy Graham: General Teachings/Activities" (Biblical Discernment Ministries, Revised January 1994); J. W. Wardner, "Unholy Alliances—The Order—The Illuminati Pedigree," *Despatch Magazine* (September 1998, Vol. 10, No. 3), p.28; "Billy Graham: Fellowship with Apostasy," *The BDM Letter* (November 1993, Vol. 2, No. 9), p.2; David Bay, "Meet the Real Reverand (sic) Billy Graham—He Is Not the Person Whom You Thought You Knew!" (Received February 10, 2000), p.4.

[542] Bundy, *Billy Graham: Performer?, Politician?, Preacher?, Prophet?, op. cit.*, p.83.

[543] Wardner, *Unholy Alliances, op. cit.*, p.157.

[544] *Ibid.*, p.156.

[545] "In Globo Cogitare et in Loco Agree (sic) (Thinking Globally and Acting Locally)" (Part III), *Distant Drums* (May 1983, Vol. 5, No. 2), p.6. See also: *Distant Drums* (December 1980, Vol. 2, No. 5), p.8; "The Pseudo Right Revisited Toward a New Federalist—Opiate of the Proletariat," *Distant Drums* (December 1983), p.3, 4.

[546] *Distant Drums* (December 1980, Vol. 2, No. 5), p.8; "The Pseudo Right Revisited Toward a New Federalist—Opiate of the Proletariat," *Distant Drums* (December 1983), p.3, 4.

[547] "In Globo Cogitare et in Loco Agree (sic)" (Part III), *op. cit.*, p.6; "The Pseudo Right Revisited Toward a New Federalist—Opiate of the Proletariat," *Distant Drums* (December 1983), p.3.

[548] *The Witness* (November 1996, Vol. 79, No. 11), p.24.

[549] *Ibid.*

[550] Rivera, *op. cit.*, p.227.

[551] Jim Fields, "The Changing Face of Christianity," *The Evangelical Methodist* (May 2001, Vol. 79, No. 5), p.5.

[552] Arthur Simon, *Bread for the World* (Grand Rapids, MI: William B. Eerdmans Publishing Company, 1984, Revised Edition), p.159; Stormer, *The Death of a Nation, op. cit.*, p.91; Joan Veon, *Prince Charles: The* Sustainable *Prince* (Oklahoma City, OK: Hearthstone Publishing, Ltd., 1997), p.102; Cotter, *op. cit.*, p.66, 79; "Rev. Eugene Blake, 78, Church Leader," *The Washington Times* (August 2, 1985), p.8B; *Distant Drums* (March 1986, Vol. 8, No. 1), p.6; Ashbrook, *New Neutralism II, op. cit.*, p.22; Chambers, *op. cit.*, p.277.

[553] Noebel, *Is the NCC Really Soft on Communism, op. cit.*, p.10.

[554] "World Council of Churches," Softkey Multimedia Inc., Infopedia (1996).

[555] William Martin, *A Prophet with Honor: The Billy Graham Story* (NY: William Morrow and Company, Inc., 1991), p.276; *O Timothy* (1985, Vol. 2, Issue 3); Hartzell Spence, *The Story of America's Religions* (NY: Holt, Rinehart and Winston, 1964), p.61; "Rev. Eugene Blake, 78, Church Leader," *The Washington Times* (August 2, 1985), p.8B; "World Council of Churches" Softkey Multimedia Inc., Infopedia (1996); Bundy, *Collectivism in the Churches, op. cit.*, p.65.

[556] Cotter, *op. cit.*, p.66, 72. See also: "The Temple of Understanding," *Wisconsin Report* (October 25, 1984, Vol. 9, No. 42), p.4.

[557] *Ibid.*, p.66.

[558] Wilbert Forker, Editor, *The Templeton Foundation Prize for Progress in Religion* (Edinburgh: Scottish Academic Press, 1988), p.277; John Templeton, *Possibilities for Over One Hundredfold More Spiritual Information: The Humble Approach in Theology and Science* (Philadelphia, PA: Templeton Foundation Press, 2000), p.202; Joan Veon, *Prince Charles: The* Sustainable *Prince* (Oklahoma City, OK: Hearthstone Publishing, Ltd., 1997), p.102.

[559] Paper from the Planetary Citizens; *Distant Drums* (March 1986, Vol. 8, No. 1), p.6.

[560] Mr. Garry Davis, quoted in "World Government Meets," *Midnight Call* (May 1990), p.17. See also: *Global 2000: An Interview with Mr. and Mrs. William Bowen* (Oklahoma City, OK: Southwest Radio Church, 1984), p.51.

[561] William M. Bowen, Jr. *Globalism: America's Demise* (Shreveport, LA: Huntington House, Inc., 1984), p.92-93. See also: "The U.N. & Education," *The Florida Forum* (Fall 2000), p.23; Jamie Brendan, "United Nations Millennium Forum," p.10; "Muller on World Citizenship," *The Perilous Times* (August 2001, Vol. 22, No. 12), p.2.

[562] Letter from Planetary Citizens dated September 1988. See also: David Spangler, *Emergence: The Rebirth of the Sacred* (NY: Dell Publishing, 1984), p.37; Melton, Clark, Kelly, *op. cit.*, p.426; "Intentional Communities: Seeds for a New Civilization," *The Christian Conscience* (December 1995, Vol. 1, No. 11), p.34. *Now Is the Dawning of the New Age New World Order, op. cit.*, p.148; Constance Cumbey, *A Planned Deception: The Staging of a New Age "Messiah"* (East Detroit, MI: Pointe Publishing, Inc., 1985), p.34; *Distant Drums* (May 1986, Vol. 8, No. 2), p.2; Gary Kah, *En Route to Global Occupation* (Lafayette, LA: Huntington House Publishers, 1992), p.41; List of Planetary Citizens from a letter dated April 17, 1985; Texe Marrs, *Dark Secrets of the New Age: Satan's Plan for a One World Religion* (Westchester, IL: Crossway Books, 1987), p.51.

[563] "The U. N.'s Grab for Power," *The Florida Forum* (Spring 2000), p.8.

[564] Des Griffin, *Fourth Reich of the Rich* (South Pasadena, CA: Emissary Publications, 1978), p.150.

[565] Letter from Planetary Citizens dated April 17, 1985; Letter from Planetary Citizens dated January 1987; *Is the Antichrist in the World Today?* (Oklahoma City, OK: Southwest Radio Church, 1982), p.14.

[566] David Spangler, *Reflections on the Christ* (Scotland: Findhorn Publications, 1977), p.43-44.

[567] *Ibid.*, p.45.

[568] Ashbrook, *New Neutralism II, op. cit.*, p.22.

[569] *Ibid.*

[570] "Rev. Eugene Blake, 78, Church Leader," *The Washington Times* (August 2, 1985), p.8B.

[571] *Ibid.*

[572] Ashbrook, *New Neutralism II, op. cit.*, p.22.

[573] McIlhany, *op. cit.*, p.21.

[574] Chambers, *op. cit.*, p.262.

[575] *Ibid.*

[576] "Rev. Eugene Blake, 78, Church Leader," *op. cit.*, p.8B.

[577] Bundy, *Billy Graham: Performer?, Politician?, Preacher?, Prophet?, op. cit.* p.89.

[578] *Global 2000: An Interview with Mr. and Mrs. William Bowen* (Oklahoma City, OK: Southwest Radio Church, 1984), p.43; Chambers, *op. cit.*, p.336, 363.

[579] Letter from Planetary Citizens dated September 1988. See also: David Spangler, *Emergence: The Rebirth of the Sacred* (NY: Dell Publishing, 1984), p.37; Melton, Clark, Kelly, *op. cit.*, p.426; "Intentional Communities: Seeds for a New Civilization," *The Christian Conscience* (December 1995, Vol. 1, No. 11), p.34; *Now Is the Dawning of the New Age New World Order, op. cit.*, p.148; Constance Cumbey, *A Planned Deception: The Staging of a New Age "Messiah"* (East Detroit, MI: Pointe Publishing, Inc., 1985), p.34; *Distant Drums* (May 1986, Vol. 8, No. 2), p.2; Gary Kah, *En Route to Global Occupation* (Lafayette, LA: Huntington House Publishers, 1992), p.41; List of Planetary Citizens from a letter dated April 17, 1985; Texe Marrs, *Dark Secrets of the New Age: Satan's Plan for a One World Religion* (Westchester, IL: Crossway Books, 1987), p.51.

[580] *Global 2000, op. cit.*, p.43; *ACLU* (Report of Activities 1984-85), p.32; "Who Is Behind the ACLU?," *The Perilous Times* (December 1993, Vol. 15, No. 10), p.1; "Planetary Initiative for the World 'They' Choose," *The Prophecy Newsletter* (1985, Vol. 1, No. 8), p.8; Chambers, *op. cit.*, p.363.

[581] *President Clinton Will Continue the New World Order* (Oklahoma City, OK: Southwest Radio Church, 1993), p.24; "Planetary Initiative for the World 'They' Choose," *The Prophecy Newsletter* (1985, Vol. 1, No. 8), p.8; William T. Still, *New World Order: The Ancient Plan of Secret Societies* (Lafayette, LA: Huntington House, Inc., 1990), p.187; Allen, *The Rockefeller File, op. cit.*, p.83; *Ibid.*; Wardner, *Unholy Alliances, op. cit.*, p.205; Chambers, *op. cit.*, p.363.

[582] Gary Kah, *En Route to Global Occupation* (Lafayette, LA: Huntington House Publishers, 1992), p.41.

[583] *Global 2000, op. cit.*, p.43.

[584] Chambers, *op. cit.*, p.336, 363.

[585] "Planetary Initiative for the World 'They' Choose," *The Prophecy Newsletter* (1985, Vol. 1, No. 8), p.8; Marrs, *Dark Majesty, op. cit.*, p.137.

[586] Blount, *op. cit.*, p.12.

[587] "Planetary Initiative for the World 'They' Choose," *op. cit.*, p.8.

[588] William T. Still, *New World Order: The Ancient Plan of Secret Societies* (Lafayette, LA: Huntington House, Inc., 1990), p.187; Allen, *The Rockefeller File, op. cit.*, p.83; *Which Will It Be: Wars—and More Wars? or a World of Lasting Peace Under Law?* (World Federalist Association, n.d.), p.5; Blount, *op. cit.*, p.12.

[589] Blount, *op. cit.*, p.12. See also: Chambers, *op. cit.*, p.363; Pamphlet from the World Association for World Federation, p.8.

[590] *How To Avoid Incineration in a Nuclear Holocaust* (Washington, DC: World Federalist Association, n.d.), p.5; Undated letter from the World Federalist Association; *World Federalist* (Spring 1989, Vol. 14, No. 2), p.2, 5; Tom A. Hudgens, *Let's Abolish War* (Denver, CO: BILR Corporation, 1986), p.73; "Planetary Initiative for the World 'They' Choose," *The Prophecy Newsletter* (1985, Vol. 1, No. 8), p.8; *"Secret Records" Revealed, op. cit.*, p.46; Marrs, *Dark Majesty, op. cit.*, p.137; Marrs, *Millennium, op. cit.*, p.61; Chambers, *op. cit.*, p.363. See also: *Which Will It Be: Wars—and More Wars? or a World of Lasting Peace Under Law?* (World Federalist Association, n.d.), p.5; J. Melton, Clark, Kelly, *op. cit.*, p.425; *Ibid.*

[591] *"Secret Records" Revealed, op. cit.*, p.46; "The United States Is Not a 'Democracy,'" *An American Commentary* (Oklahoma City, OK: Hearthstone Publishing, Ltd., 1993), p.11.

[592] *President Clinton Will Continue the New World Order, op. cit.*, p.24.

[593] John Barela, *Mysteries Unveiled* (Oklahoma City, OK: Southwest Radio Church, n.d.), p.20.

[594] "Willem Adolf Visser 'T Hooft" Softkey Multimedia Inc., Infopedia (1996); "The World Council of Churches on World Order," *The Whole Earth Papers: Christian Voices on World Order* (1978, Vol. 1, No. 10), p.31; Graham, *op. cit.*, p.125; "Dietrich Bonhoeffer: Heroic Christian Thinker & Martyr or Poor Deceived False Prophet?" (Biblical Discernment Ministries, n.d.), p.4; Niebuhr, *op. cit.*, p.193; Bundy, *Collectivism in the Churches, op. cit.*, p.219; Cotter, *op. cit.*, p.61;

G. R. Beirnes, Editor, "Liberals Seek Catholic Membership in WCC-NCC," *The Midnight Cry* (April 1967, Vol. 28, No. 4), p.8.

595 Bundy, *Collectivism in the Churches, op. cit.*, p.211.

596 Barela, *op. cit.*, p.20.

597 *What About the National Council of Churches?* (Hatfield, PA: Brethren Revival Fellowship Witness, 1967, Vol. 2, No. 1), p.10.

598 Rivera, *op. cit.*, p.244. See also: G. R. Beirnes, Editor, "Liberals Seek Catholic Membership in WCC-NCC," *The Midnight Cry* (April 1967, Vol. 28, No. 4), p.8.

599 McBirnie, *op. cit.*, p.4.

600 Berit Kjos, "Conforming the Church to the New Millennium," *Prophecy Corner and the Nosh Box* (November 2000), p.8.

601 Cotter, *op. cit.*, p.61, 78. See also: Bundy, *Collectivism in the Churches, op. cit.*, p.171; Shirley Correll, "Who Are the Gods of the New World Order and What Is a Spiritual U. N.?" (Part IV), *The Florida Forum* (Spring 2001), p.16; Morrison, *op. cit.*, p.545, 580.

602 "The World Council of Churches on World Order," *The Whole Earth Papers: Christian Voices on World Order* (1978, Vol. 1, No. 10), p.31.

603 *Ibid.*, p.32.

604 *Ibid.*, p.31.

605 "Backslidden Prophets," *The Omega-Letter* (February 1988, Vol. 3, No. 2), p.13; *Blueprint for Building the New World Order* (Dearborn, MI: The Omega-Letter/Christian World Report, n.d.), p.24.

606 Martin, *op. cit.*, p.327; Sam Wellman, *Billy Graham: The Great Evangelist* (Uhrichsville, OH: Barbour Book, 1996), p.79.

607 Graham, *op. cit.*, p.125.

608 John S. Torell, "Betrayal," *The Dove*, (Autumn/Winter 1995, Vol. 16, No. 3), p.10.

609 Graham, *op. cit.*, p.125.

610 Gsell, *The Legacy of Billy Graham, op. cit.*, p.20. See also: Martin, *op. cit.*, p.327. See also: "Billy Graham: Fellowship with Apostasy," *The BDM Letter* (November 1993, Vol. 2, No. 9), p.2.

611 Graham, *op. cit.*, p.125.

612 G. Archer Weniger, *Modernism of National Council of Churches* (Murfreesboro, TN: Sword of the Lord Publishers, 1961), p.3, 8.

613 *Ibid.*, p.6. See also: Noebel, *Is the NCC Really Soft on Communism, op. cit.*, p.10; *The NCC/WCC—Communism's Helpers, op. cit.*, p.5.

614 *Ibid.* See also: Bundy, *Collectivism in the Churches, op. cit.*, p.51.

615 Weniger, "Dr. Billy Graham and the National Council of Churches," *op. cit.*, p.3.

616 Bundy, *Collectivism in the Churches, op. cit.*, p.51.

617 Weniger, *Modernism of National Council of Churches, op. cit.*, p.6.

618 *Ibid.*

619 *Ibid.*, p.8. See also: Gsell, *The Legacy of Billy Graham, op. cit.*, p.20.

620 *Ibid.*, p.9-10. See also: Weniger, "Dr. Billy Graham and the National Council of Churches," *op. cit.*, p.2.

621 Zeller, *op. cit.*, p.9.

622 Gsell, *The Legacy of Billy Graham, op. cit.*, p.21.

623 Weniger, *Modernism of National Council of Churches, op. cit.*, p.22.

624 "50th Meeting of the World Council of Churches Central Committee," *The ACCC* (October 1999), p.1.

625 Weniger, *Modernism of National Council of Churches, op. cit.*, p.10. See also: G. Archer Weniger, "Dr. Billy Graham and the National Council of Churches," p.2.

626 Martin, *op. cit.*, p.221. See also: *Christian Perspectives* (Fall/Winter 1997, Vol. 10, No. 2), p.3; John Ashbrook, *Billy Graham's Catholic Connection;* Gsell, *The Legacy of Billy Graham, op. cit.*, p.20.

627 Collier and Horowitz, *op. cit.*, p.150.

628 Gsell, *The Legacy of Billy Graham, op. cit.*, p.20-21.

629 Graham, *op. cit.*, p.295; Martin, *op. cit.*, p.239.

630 Gsell, *The Legacy of Billy Graham, op. cit.*, p.23; Bundy, *Billy Graham: Performer?, Politician?, Preacher?, Prophet?, op. cit.*, p.14.

631 *Ibid.;* Bundy, *Billy Graham: Performer?, Politician?, Preacher?, Prophet?, op. cit.*, p.14. See also: Cotter, *op. cit.*, p.41, 61; Bundy, *Collectivism in the Churches, op. cit.*, p.234.

[632] Cotter, *op. cit.*, p.41, 61. See also: *The Road to Socialism and the New World Order* (Highland City, FL: Florida Pro Family Forum, Inc., 1995), p.24; Bundy, *Collectivism in the Churches, op. cit.*, p.234-235.

[633] Bundy, *Collectivism in the Churches, op. cit.*, p.235.

[634] *The Road to Socialism and the New World Order* (Highland City, FL: Florida Pro Family Forum, Inc., 1995), p.24.

[635] Cotter, *op. cit.*, p.61. See also: *Ibid.;* "The Vietnamese Syndicate's Connection to the Illuminati," *A Newsletter from a Follower of Jesus Christ* (September 1995, Vol. 4, No. 5), p.49.

[636] "Billy Graham Gave the Apostate National Council of Churches the Greatest Boost It Has Had in Many Years," *Foundation* (June-August 1991), p.34; Darrell Turner, "Graham Happy to Fellowship at the NCC's Interchurch Center," *Christian News* (September 9, 1991, Vol. 29, No. 32), p.1.

[637] Bundy, *Collectivism in the Churches, op. cit.*, p.255-256.

[638] Wardner, *Unholy Alliances, op. cit.*, p.194; Denslow, (Vol. IV) *op. cit.*, p.99; Henry C. Clausen, *Masons Who Helped Shape Our Nation* (The Supreme Council, 33°, Ancient and Accepted Scottish Rite of Freemasonry Southern Jurisdiction, U. S. A., 1976), p.44.

[639] Graham, *op. cit.*, p.180-181.

[640] *Ibid.*, p.282.

[641] *Ibid.*

[642] Bundy, *Billy Graham: Performer?, Politician?, Preacher?, Prophet?, op. cit.*, p.98.

5. BIBLES FOR BETRAYAL

[1] Antony C. Sutton, *America's Secret Establishment: An Introduction to the Order of Skull & Bones* (Billings, MT: Liberty House Press, 1986), p.28.

[2] David A. Noebel, *Is the NCC Really Soft on Communism?* (Tulsa, OK: Christian Crusade, n.d.), p.17.

[3] "Ting Has Been a Puppet of Communism from the Beginning," *O Timothy* (1994, Vol. 2, Issue 5); "China Brands Unregistered Churches 'Evil Cults,'" *Christian News* (January 17, 2000, Vol. 38, No. 3), p.1; Carl McIntire, "Perversion and Subversion in the World Council of Churches," *O Timothy* (1988, Vol. 5, Issue 6); "K. H. Ting—The Master of Chinese Communist Propaganda," *O Timothy* (1994, Vol. 2, Issue 5).

[4] Paul Kauffman, "The Lack of Bibles in China—The Real Reason," *O Timothy* (1994, Vol. 2, Issue 5); Carl McIntire, "Perversion and Subversion in the World Council of Churches," *O Timothy* (1988, Vol. 5, Issue 6); "K. H. Ting—The Master of Chinese Communist Propaganda," *O Timothy* (1994, Vol. 2, Issue 5).

[5] "Religions Cooperating for Peace: The World Conference on Religion and Peace" (Received July 3, 1995), p.4; "WCRP" (Received November 3, 1995), p.5.

[6] "Ting Has Been a Puppet of Communism from the Beginning," *op. cit.;* David W. Cloud, "Bishop K. H. Ting—China's Master of Deceit," *O Timothy* (1986, Vol. 3, Issue 3); *Christian News* (December 20, 1993, Vol. 31, No 47), p.3; "Not All Are Deceived by Communist China's 'New Face': An Australian Journalist Reports China's Deceitful Plan," *O Timothy* (1994, Vol. 2, Issue 5); "China Brands Unregistered Churches 'Evil Cults,'" *Christian News* (January 17, 2000, Vol. 38, No. 3), p.12; "K. H. Ting—The Master of Chinese Communist Propaganda," *O Timothy* (1994, Vol. 2, Issue 5).

[7] "Bishop Ting Praises Socialism—Blasts Historic Christianity," *Christian News* (July 19, 1999, Vol. 37, No. 29), p.25. See also: "Ting Praises Socialism, Blasts Christianity," *Calvary Contender* (August 15, 1999, Vol. 16, No. 16), p.1.

[8] "Ting Has Been a Puppet of Communism from the Beginning," *op. cit.;* David W. Cloud, "Bishop K. H. Ting—China's Master of Deceit," *O Timothy* (1986, Vol. 3, Issue 3); *Ibid.;* "A Loyal Chinese Marxist Invites LCMS President," *Christian News* (Oct. 4, 1999, Vol. 37, No. 36), p.10; "China Brands Unregistered Churches 'Evil Cults,'" *Christian News* (January 17, 2000, Vol. 38, No. 3), p.12; *Christian News* (December 20, 1993, Vol. 31, No. 47), p.3.

[9] *Ibid.;* "A Loyal Chinese Marxist Invites LCMS President," *Christian News* (Oct. 4, 1999, Vol. 37, No. 36), p.10; David W. Cloud, "Bishop K. H. Ting—China's Master of Deceit," *O Timothy* (1986, Vol. 3, Issue 3); "China Brands Unregistered Churches 'Evil Cults,'" *Christian News* (January 17, 2000, Vol. 38, No. 3), p.12; *Christian News* (December 20, 1993, Vol. 31, No. 47), p.3.

[10] *Christian News* (October 4, 1999, Vol. 37, No. 36), p.9; "Han Continues to Defend Communists," *Christian News* (April 3, 2000, Vol. 38, No. 14), p.16; "China Christian Council Controlled by Communists," *Calvary Contender* (August 15, 2000, Vol. 17, No. 16), p.1; "The Truth About China Does Not Count in the LLL or LCMS," *Christian News* (July 17, 2000, Vol. 38, No. 29), p.19; "Bishop Ting Praises Socialism—Blasts Historic Christianity," *op. cit.*, p.25; Carl McIntire, "Perversion and Subversion in the World Council of Churches," *O Timothy* (1988, Vol. 5, Issue 6); "Who Is Telling the Truth About China? The LLL and LCMS or the U. S. State Department and Karnes?," *Christian News* (May 8, 2000, Vol. 38, No. 19), p.1; "Billy Graham Turns Blind Eye to the Serious Persecution in China," *O Timothy* (1989, Vol. 6, Issue 5).

[11] David W. Cloud, "Bishop K. H. Ting—China's Master of Deceit," *O Timothy* (1986, Vol. 3, Issue 3).

[12] *Christian News* (December 20, 1993, Vol. 31, No. 47), p.3.

[13] Cloud, "Bishop K. H. Ting—China's Master of Deceit," *op. cit.*

[14] *Ibid.;* "K. H. Ting Is a Theological Liberal," *O Timothy* (1994, Vol. 2, Issue 5).

[15] *Ibid.;* James W. Wardner, *Unholy Alliances* (n.p., 1996), p.163.

[16] "China Brands Unregistered Churches 'Evil Cults,'" *Christian News* (January 17, 2000, Vol. 38, No. 3), p.12. See also: Eddie Karnes, "Choose Sides," *Christian News* (January 17, 2000, Vol. 38, No. 3), p.13; Newsletter from Radio Liberty (July 2000), p.5; Kurt Koch (Translated by Michael Freeman) *Occult ABC* (Germany: Literature Mission Aglasterhausen, Inc., 1978), p.141; Stanley Monteith, *Brotherhood of Darkness* (Oklahoma City, OK: Hearthstone Publishing, 2000), p.45, 102.

[17] "Mao the Worst Mass Murderer Ever," *Christian News* (November 29, 1999, Vol. 37, No. 44), p.26; "Mao the Worst Mass Murderer Ever," *Calvary Contender* (December 1, 1999, Vol. 16, No. 23), p.1. See also: Denise L. Behreandt, "Permanent Normal Torture of Religions," *The New American* (June 19, 2000, Vol. 16, No. 13), p.26.

[18] Cloud, "Bishop K. H. Ting—China's Master of Deceit," *op. cit.*

[19] *Ibid.*

[20] *Ibid.* See also: "Ting Has Been a Puppet of Communism from the Beginning," *op. cit.* See also: "China Brands Unregistered Churches 'Evil Cults,'" *op. cit.*, p.12.

[21] "Working with Communist Approved Churches," *Christian News* (February 26, 2001, Vol. 39, No. 9), p.21.

[22] "Ting Has Been a Puppet of Communism from the Beginning," *op. cit.*

[23] *Ibid.*

[24] "A Loyal Chinese Marxist Invites LCMS President," *Christian News* (Oct. 4, 1999, Vol. 37, No. 36), p.10; Cloud, "Bishop K. H. Ting—China's Master of Deceit," *op. cit.*

[25] *Ibid.;* Cloud, "Bishop K. H. Ting—China's Master of Deceit," *op. cit.* See also: "The LCMS Has Gone 'Whimpish,'" *Christian News* (July 8, 2001, Vol. 39, No. 28), p.21.

[26] *Ibid.;* Cloud, "Bishop K. H. Ting—China's Master of Deceit," *op. cit.*

[27] Cloud, "Bishop K. H. Ting—China's Master of Deceit," *op. cit.*

[28] ""China Brands Unregistered Churches 'Evil Cults,'" *op. cit.*, p.12.

[29] "Bishop Ting Praises Socialism—Blasts Historic Christianity," *op. cit.*, p.24; "Ting Praises Socialism, Blasts Christianity," *Calvary Contender* (August 15, 1999, Vol. 16, No. 16), p.1.

[30] "Han Continues to Defend Communists," *Christian News* (April 3, 2000, Vol. 38, No. 14), p.16.

[31] "Ting Has Been a Puppet of Communism from the Beginning," *op. cit.* See also: M. H. Reynolds, Jr., "World Conference on Mission and Evangelism, San Antonio, Texas, May 22-June 1, 1989," *World Council of Churches: The Shaky Ship Sails On...* (Los Osos, CA: Fundamental Evangelistic Association, 1999), p.15.

[32] "K. H. Ting—The Master of Chinese Communist Propaganda," *O Timothy* (1994, Vol. 2, Issue 5).

[33] "Ting Has Been a Puppet of Communism from the Beginning," *op. cit.*, quoting from *FEA News & Views* (November/ December 1979). See also: Cloud, "Bishop K. H. Ting—China's Master of Deceit," *op. cit.*

[34] Cloud, "Bishop K. H. Ting—China's Master of Deceit," *op. cit.* See also: "Ting Has Been a Puppet of Communism from the Beginning," *op. cit.;* Carl McIntire, "Perversion and Subversion in the World Council of Churches," *O Timothy* (1988, Vol. 5, Issue 6); "K. H. Ting Is a Theological Liberal," *O Timothy* (1994, Vol. 2, Issue 5).

[35] Eddie Karnes, "Understanding Evangelism in China," *Christian News* (July 8, 2001, Vol. 39, No. 28), p.21.

[36] "The Deception on Religion in China and AP Features," *Christian News* (October 4, 1999, Vol. 37, No. 36), p.9; Carl McIntire, "Perversion and Subversion in the World Council of Churches," *O Timothy* (1988, Vol. 5, Issue 6).

[37] "China Persecutes Christians," *Calvary Contender* (August 15, 1997, Vol. 14, No. 16); *Christian News* (December 20, 1993, Vol. 31, No 47), p.3; "K. H. Ting Tells Lies," *O Timothy* (1994, Vol. 2, Issue 5); "Han Continues to Defend Communists," *op. cit.*, p.16; "China Brands Unregistered Churches 'Evil Cults,'" *op. cit.*, p.12; Cloud, "Bishop K. H. Ting—China's Master of Deceit," *op. cit.;* "World Vindicates Pastor Otten on China," *Christian News* (February 26, 2001, Vol. 39, No. 9), p.23; Eddie Karnes, "Dr. Billy Graham and Dr. Oswald Hoffman, Thank You, But..." (Part I), *Christian News* (February 12, 2001, Vol. 39, No. 7), p.14; Carl McIntire, "Perversion and Subversion in the World Council of Churches," *O Timothy* (1988, Vol. 5, Issue 6).

[38] "LCMS and LLL Supporting Liberals and Communists in China," *Christian News* (March 19, 2001, Vol. 39, No. 12), p.15.

[39] Billy Graham, *Just As I Am: The Autobiography of Billy Graham* (Harpers Collins Worldwide, 1997), p.600; Pamphlet from East Gates Ministries International (Received March 16, 1998); Cloud, "Bishop K. H. Ting—China's Master of Deceit," *op. cit.*

[40] *Ibid.*, p.601; "Mao the Worst Mass Murderer Ever," *Christian News, op. cit.*, p.26; "The Convicted and the Compromised," *The Day Drawing Near* (July 2000, Vol. 2, No. 2), p.2.

[41] "China Brands Unregistered Churches 'Evil Cults,'" *op. cit.*, p.12; Jonathan Chao, "How Evangelical Is the Three Self People's Movement: An Open Letter to Christianity Today," *O Timothy* (1994, Vol. 2, Issue 5); "Chinese Government Targets Seminarians," *Moody* (January-February 2001, Vol. 101, No. 3), p.41; "K. H. Ting—The Master of Chinese Communist Propaganda," *op. cit.*

[42] *Ibid.;* Jonathan Chao, "How Evangelical Is the Three Self People's Movement: An Open Letter to Christianity Today," *O Timothy* (1994, Vol. 2, Issue 5).

[43] Steven Snyder, "Why China's Christians Suffer," *Christian News* (November 1, 1999, Vol. 37, No. 40), p.3.

[44] "China Brands Unregistered Churches 'Evil Cults,'" *op. cit.*, (quoting from "History of the Three-Self Movement in China" by Gary Hart in *Faith for the Family,* April 1986), (January 17, 2000, Vol. 38, No. 3), p.12. See also: Cloud,

"Bishop K. H. Ting—China's Master of Deceit," *op. cit.;* Gary D. Hart, "Religious Freedom in Red China," *O Timothy* (1989, Vol. 6, Issue 6); "LCMS and LLL Supporting Liberals and Communists in China," *op. cit.*, p.15.

[45] Eddie Karnes, "What Has Changed in China?," *Christian News* (May 8, 2000, Vol. 38, No. 19), p.8.

[46] Nina Shea, *In the Lion's Den* (Nashville, TN: Broadman & Holman Publishers, 1997), p.59.

[47] Snyder, *op. cit.*, p.3. See also: "Mao the Worst Mass Murderer Ever," *Christian News, op. cit.*, p.26; "Persecution of Christians in China Continues," *O Timothy* (1994, Vol. 2, Issue 5).

[48] ""China Brands Unregistered Churches 'Evil Cults,'" *op. cit.*, p.12. See also: "K. H. Ting—The Master of Chinese Communist Propaganda," *op. cit.*

[49] "Persecution of Christians in China Continues," *O Timothy* (1994, Vol. 2, Issue 5). See also: "Persecution of Christians," quoting from *The Bible League* in *Christian News* (November 20, 2000, Vol. 38, No. 43), p.20.

[50] *Ibid.*

[51] *Ibid.*

[52] "China Brands Unregistered Churches 'Evil Cults,'" *op. cit.*, p.12; Jonathan Chao, "How Evangelical Is the Three Self People's Movement: An Open Letter to Christianity Today," *O Timothy* (1994, Vol. 2, Issue 5).

[53] Snyder, *op. cit.*, p.3. See also: "China," *Women of Vision 2000* (2000, First Quarter), p.4.

[54] "Persecution of Christians in China Continues," *op. cit.*

[55] Pamphlet from East Gates Ministries International (Received March 16, 1998). See also: Allen D. Hanson, "Bible Distribution in China," *Christian News* (September 20, 1999, Vol. 37, No. 34), p.17.

[56] "K. H. Ting—The Master of Chinese Communist Propaganda," *op. cit.;* Jonathan Chao, "How Evangelical Is the Three Self People's Movement: An Open Letter to Christianity Today," *O Timothy* (1994, Vol. 2, Issue 5); Cloud, "Bishop K. H. Ting—China's Master of Deceit," *op. cit.*

[57] Allen D. Hanson, "Bible Distribution in China," *Christian News* (September 20, 1999, Vol. 37, No. 34), p.17; "The Deception on Religion in China and AP Features," *op. cit.*, p.9; Cloud, "Bishop K. H. Ting—China's Master of Deceit," *op. cit.*

[58] "LCMS and LLL Supporting Liberals and Communists in China," *op. cit.*, p.15.

[59] "Ting Has Been a Puppet of Communism from the Beginning," *op. cit.;* Cloud, "Bishop K. H. Ting—China's Master of Deceit," *op. cit.;* "Bishop Ting Praises Socialism Blasts Historic Christianity," *op. cit.*, p.25; "A Loyal Chinese Marxist Invites LCMS President," *op. cit.*, p.10; "China Brands Unregistered Churches 'Evil Cults,'" *op. cit.*, p.12; *Christian News* (October 4, 1999, Vol. 37, No. 36), p.9; "Han Continues to Defend Communists," *op. cit.*, p.16.

[60] *East Gates Connection* (January-March 2000), p.5; "LCMS and LLL Mission Money Supporting Pro-Abortionist and Pro-Communists in China," *Christian News* (October 4, 1999, Vol. 37, No. 36), p.10; "Who Told the Truth About China?," *Christian News* (July 30, 201, Vol. 39, No. 31), p.4; Eddie Karnes, "Deceiving God's Elect on China," *Christian News* (January 29, 2001, Vol. 39, No. 5), p.23; "The International Day of Prayer for the Persecuted Church," *Christian News* (July 30, 2001, Vol. 39, No. 31), p.18; "Communist Puppets Are Hoodwinking Lutherans," *Christian News* (November 15, 1999, Vol. 37, No. 42), p.21; "China Christian Council to Lead Delegation to UCC Nat'l Office," *Christian News* (July 16, 2001, Vol. 39, No. 29), p.11; "Han Continues to Defend Communists," *op. cit.*, p.1; "LCMS and LLL Supporting Liberals and Communists in China," *op. cit.*, p.15; Eddie Karnes, "Dr. Billy Graham and Dr. Oswald Hoffman, Thank You, But..." (Part I), *Christian News* (February 12, 2001, Vol. 39, No. 7), p.16; "Bishop Ting Praises Socialism—Blasts Historic Christianity," *op. cit.*, p.25; Eddie Karnes, "Christian News Is Reliable," *Christian News* (March 26, 2001, Vol. 39, No. 13), p.15, 16; "Nau Authors New Book for China," *Christian News* (February 26, 2001, Vol. 39, No. 9), p.21.

[61] Graham, *Just As I Am, op. cit.*, p.603.

[62] "LCMS and LLL Mission Money Supporting Pro-Abortionist and Pro-Communists in China," *Christian News* (October 4, 1999, Vol. 37, No. 36), p.10.; "The International Day of Prayer for the Persecuted Church," *Christian News* (July 30, 2001, Vol. 39, No. 31), p.18; "China Christian Council Controlled by Communists," *Calvary Contender* (August 15, 2000, Vol. 17, No. 16), p.1; "Communist Puppets Are Hoodwinking Lutherans," *Christian News* (November 15, 1999, Vol. 37, No. 42), p.21; "Han Continues to Defend Communists," *op. cit.*, p.1, 16; "Bishop Ting Praises Socialism—Blasts Historic Christianity," *op. cit.*, p.25; "LLL and LCMS Still Backing Communist-Controlled China Christian Council," *Christian News* (February 5, 2001, Vol. 39, No. 6), p.1.

[63] *Christian News* (December 20, 1993, Vol. 31, No. 47), p.3.

[64] "Ting Has Been a Puppet of Communism from the Beginning," *op. cit.;* "China Brands Unregistered Churches 'Evil Cults,'" *op. cit.*, p.1.

[65] "China Brands Unregistered Churches 'Evil Cults,'" *op. cit.*, p.1; "Bishop Ting Praises Socialism—Blasts Historic Christianity," *op. cit.*, p.25; "LCMS and LLL Supporting Liberals and Communists in China," *op. cit.*, p.15. See also: "The International Day of Prayer for the Persecuted Church," *Christian News* (July 30, 2001, Vol. 39, No. 31), p.18.

[66] *Ibid.;* "The International Day of Prayer for the Persecuted Church," *Christian News* (July 30, 2001, Vol. 39, No. 31), p.18.

[67] *Ibid.;* "LCMS and LLL Supporting Liberals and Communists in China," *op. cit.*, p.15.

[68] "LCMS and LLL Supporting Liberals and Communists in China," *op. cit.*, p.15.

[69] "China Brands Unregistered Churches 'Evil Cults,'" *op. cit.*, p.1. See also: Cloud, "Bishop K. H. Ting—China's Master of Deceit," *op. cit.;* Eddie Karnes, "Stop the China Scam," *Christian News* (December 11, 2000, Vol. 38, No. 46),

p.16; "K. H. Ting—The Master of Chinese Communist Propaganda," *op. cit.*

[70] *Ibid.;* Gary D. Hart, "Religious Freedom in Red China," *O Timothy* (1989, Vol. 6, Issue 6). See also: "K. H. Ting—The Master of Chinese Communist Propaganda," *op. cit.*

[71] Gary D. Hart, "Religious Freedom in Red China," *O Timothy* (1989, Vol. 6, Issue 6).

[72] *Ibid.*

[73] "China Church Cracking Down on House Churches," *Christian News* (February 12, 2001, Vol. 39, No. 7), p.15.

[74] "Ting Has Been a Puppet of Communism from the Beginning," *op. cit.*

[75] David P. Gaines, *The World Council of Churches: A Study of Its Background and History* (Peterborough, New Hampshire, Richard R. Smith Company, Inc., 1966), p.1001.

[76] Eddie Karnes, "Ways to Get Bibles to the Chinese Without Getting Arrested (Part II)," *Christian News* (May 29, 2000, Vol. 38, No. 22), p.14. See also: Eddie Karnes, "Christian News Is Reliable," *Christian News* (March 26, 2001, Vol. 39, No. 13), p.15.

[77] Kenny Joseph, "Useful Idiots," *Christian News* (October 4, 1999, Vol. 37, No. 36), p.8.

[78] Kauffman, *op. cit.*

[79] *Ibid.*

[80] "LCMS and LLL Supporting Liberals and Communists in China," *op. cit.*, p.15.

[81] Joseph, *op. cit.*

[82] *Ibid.;* Karnes, "What Has Changed in China?," *op. cit.*, p.8. See also: Hart, "Religious Freedom in Red China," *op. cit.*

[83] *Ibid.* See also: Eddie Karnes, "Speak Out for China's Persecuted 100 Million House Church Christians," *Christian News* (November 13, 2000, Vol. 38, No. 42), p.21.

[84] "LCMS Supporting the Wrong Side in China," *Christian News* (June 28, 1999, Vol. 37, No. 26), p.21.

[85] Joseph, *op. cit.* See also: *Christian News* (June 28, 1999, Vol. 37, No. 26); Eddie Karnes, "Deceiving God's Elect on China," *Christian News* (January 29, 2001, Vol. 39, No. 5), p.23.

[86] Eddie Karnes, "Choose Sides," *Christian News* (January 17, 2000, Vol. 38, No. 3), p.13.

[87] "Chinese Christians Held Hostage Also," *Christian News* (April 23, 2001, Vol. 39, No. 17), p.22.

[88] *Ibid.*

[89] "Communist Puppets Are Hoodwinking Lutherans," *Christian News* (November 15, 1999, Vol. 37, No. 42), p.21.

[90] William Swing, "Reactions from Religious Leaders: United Religions International Tour," *Christian News* (May 5, 1997, Vol. 35, No. 18), p.6.

[91] Jonathan Chao, "How Evangelical Is the Three Self People's Movement: An Open Letter to Christianity Today," *O Timothy* (1994, Vol. 2, Issue 5). See also: Cloud, "Bishop K. H. Ting—China's Master of Deceit," *op. cit.*

[92] *Ibid.*

[93] *Ibid.*

[94] *Ibid.*

[95] *Ibid.*

[96] Graham, *Just As I Am, op. cit.*, p.599-600, 602-603.

[97] *East Gates Connection* (January-March 2000), p.5; "LCMS and LLL Mission Money Supporting Pro-Abortionist and Pro-Communists in China," *op. cit.*, p.10; "Communist Puppets Are Hoodwinking Lutherans," *op. cit.*, p.21; "Han Continues to Defend Communists," *op. cit.*, p.1; "Bishop Ting Praises Socialism—Blasts Historic Christianity," *op. cit.*, p.25.

[98] Sam Wellman, *Billy Graham: The Great Evangelist* (Uhrichsville, OH: Barbour Book, 1996), p.190.

[99] Graham, *Just As I Am, op. cit.*, p.601.

[100] *President Clinton Will Continue the New World Order* (Oklahoma City, OK: Southwest Radio Church, 1993), p.2, 42; *"Secret Records" Revealed: The Men, the Money, and the Methods Behind the New World Order* (Marlborough, NH: The Plymouth Rock Foundation, 1994), p.42; Newsletter from Radio Liberty (July 2001), p.3; Texe Marrs, *Dark Majesty: The Secret Brotherhood and the Magic of a Thousand Points of Light* (Austin, TX: Living Truth Publishers, 1992), p.200; David Allen Rivera, *Final Warning: A History of the New World Order* (Harrisburg, PA: Rivera Enterprises, 1994 Edition), p.178; David Carrico, *The Occult Meaning of the Great Seal of the United States* (Evansville, IN: Followers of Jesus Christ, 1991), p.78; Eric Barger, "The New World Order Under Clinton: Establishment Insiders and Political Deceit," *The Christian World Report* (May 1993, Vol. 8, No. 3), p.8; Jim Marrs, *Rule by Secrecy: The Hidden History That Connects the Trilateral Commission, the Freemasons, and the Great Pyramids* (New York, NY: HarperCollins Publishers, Inc., 2000), p.21, 98.

[101] *Secret Records Revealed: The Men, the Money and the Methods Behind the New World Order* (Oklahoma City, OK: Hearthstone Publishing, Ltd., 1999), p.146; *"Secret Records" Revealed: The Men, the Money, and the Methods Behind the New World Order* (Marlborough, NH: The Plymouth Rock Foundation, 1994), p.42; Newsletter from Radio Liberty (July 2001), p.3; Texe Marrs, *Circle of Intrigue* (Austin, TX: Living Truth Ministries, 1995), p.218; James W. Wardner, *Unholy Alliances* (n.p., 1996), p.130; Eric Barger, "The New World Order Under Clinton: Establishment Insiders and Political Deceit," *The Christian World Report* (May 1993, Vol. 8, No. 3), p.8.

[102] Texe Marrs, *Circle of Intrigue* (Austin, TX: Living Truth Ministries, 1995), p.218; Texe Marrs, *Dark Majesty: The Secret Brotherhood and the Magic of a Thousand Points of Light* (Austin, TX: Living Truth Publishers, 1992), p.200; David Allen Rivera, *Final Warning: A History of the New World Order* (Harrisburg, PA: Rivera Enterprises, 1994 Edition), p.178; Newsletter from Radio Liberty (July 2001), p.3; Gary Kah, *En Route to Global Occupation* (Lafayette, LA: Huntington House Publishers, 1992), p.39; Eric Barger, "The New World Order Under Clinton: Establishment Insiders and Political Deceit," *The Christian World Report* (May 1993, Vol. 8, No. 3), p.8.

[103] Sutton, *op. cit.*, p.48; David Carrico, *The Occult Meaning of the Great Seal of the United States* (Evansville, IN: Followers of Jesus Christ, 1991), p.78.

[104] *Council on Foreign Relations: Annual Report July 1, 1987-June 30, 1988*, p.166; *Council on Foreign Relations: Annual Report July 1, 1990-June 30, 1991*, p.173; *Secret Records Revealed, op. cit.*, p.146; *President Clinton Will Continue the New World Order, op. cit.*, p.2, 42; *"Secret Records" Revealed: The Men, the Money, and the Methods Behind the New World Order* (Marlborough, NH: The Plymouth Rock Foundation, 1994), p.42; Eric Barger, "The New World Order Under Clinton: Establishment Insiders and Political Deceit," *The Christian World Report* (May 1993, Vol. 8, No. 3), p.8.

[105] "The Bilderberg Meetings—AD 2000," *Despatch Magazine* (September 2000, Vol. 12:3), p.52.

[106] Gary Kah, *En Route to Global Occupation* (Lafayette, LA: Huntington House Publishers, 1992), p.39.

[107] *President Clinton Will Continue the New World Order, op. cit.*, p.2; Newsletter from Radio Liberty (July 2001), p.3; Eric Barger, "The New World Order Under Clinton: Establishment Insiders and Political Deceit," *The Christian World Report* (May 1993, Vol. 8, No. 3), p.8.

[108] *Ibid.*; David Allen Rivera, *Final Warning: A History of the New World Order* (Harrisburg, PA: Rivera Enterprises, 1994 Edition), p.178 .

[109] *Ibid.*, p.42; *Secret Records Revealed, op. cit.*, p.146; *"Secret Records" Revealed: The Men, the Money, and the Methods Behind the New World Order* (Marlborough, NH: The Plymouth Rock Foundation, 1994), p.42; Newsletter from Radio Liberty (July 2001), p.3.

[110] *Secret Records Revealed, op. cit.*, p.146; *Ibid.*; Jim Marrs, *Rule by Secrecy: The Hidden History That Connects the Trilateral Commission, the Freemasons, and the Great Pyramids* (New York, NY: HarperCollins Publishers, Inc., 2000), p.98; Texe Marrs, *Millennium: Peace, Promises, and the Day They Take Our Money Away* (Austin, TX: Living Truth Publishers, 1990), p.45; Sutton, *op. cit.*, p.48; Newsletter from Radio Liberty (July 2001), p.3; David Carrico, *The Occult Meaning of the Great Seal of the United States* (Evansville, IN: Followers of Jesus Christ, 1991), p.78, 81; Marrs, *Circle of Intrigue, op. cit.*, p.218; Texe Marrs, *Dark Majesty: The Secret Brotherhood and the Magic of a Thousand Points of Light* (Austin, TX: Living Truth Publishers, 1992), p.200; James W. Wardner, *Unholy Alliances* (n.p., 1996), p.124, 130.

[111] Stanley Monteith, *Brotherhood of Darkness* (Oklahoma City, OK: Hearthstone Publishing, 2000), p.78.

[112] "Satanic Activities of Secret Societies," quoting from *Esquire* in The Cutting Edge.

[113] "Satanic Activities of Secret Societies," The Cutting Edge.

[114] James Wardner, *Unholy Alliances* (n.p., 1996), p.124-125.

[115] Texe Marrs, *Dark Majesty: The Secret Brotherhood and the Magic of a Thousand Points of Light* (Austin, TX: Living Truth Publishers, 1992), p.200; Jim Marrs, *Rule by Secrecy: The Hidden History That Connects the Trilateral Commission, the Freemasons, and the Great Pyramids* (New York, NY: HarperCollins Publishers, Inc., 2000), p.98.

[116] Graham, *Just As I Am, op. cit.*, p.606-607.

[117] *Council on Foreign Relations: Annual Report July 1, 1987-June 30, 1988*, p.179; *Council on Foreign Relations: Annual Report July 1, 1994-June 30, 1995*, p.151.

[118] "Freedom from Religious Persecution: Freedom House: A CFR Front," http://watch.pair.com/pray.html, November 3, 1998.

[119] Jim Marrs, *Rule by Secrecy: The Hidden History That Connects the Trilateral Commission, the Freemasons, and the Great Pyramids* (New York, NY: HarperCollins Publishers, Inc., 2000), p.42.

[120] "Freedom from Religious Persecution: Freedom House: A CFR Front," http://watch.pair.com/pray.html, November 3, 1998; http://watch.pair.com/pray.html, November 8, 1998.

[121] Mari Jo Buhle, Paul Buhle, and Dan Georgakas, Editors, *Encyclopedia of the American Left* (New York, NY: Oxford University Press, 1998, Second Edition), p.709.

[122] Charles C. Haynes, Editor, *Finding Common Ground* (The Freedom Forum First Amendment Center: Nashville, TN: 1994), Inside Back Cover.

[123] *Secret Records Revealed, op. cit.*, p.117-118; Newsletter from Radio Liberty (July 2000), p.5-6. See also: Wardner, *Unholy Alliances, op. cit.*, p.163.

[124] Fritz Springmeier, "Billy Graham and the Bible," *Christian News* (July 27, 1992, Vol. 30, No. 30), p.8.

[125] *Ibid.*

[126] Edward Jay Epstein, *Dossier: The Secret History of Armand Hammer* (NY: Random House, 1996), p.20.

[127] *Council on Foreign Relations: Annual Report July 1-June 1, 1988*, p.176.

[128] Letter from the World Federalist Association, dated June 13, 1989).

[129] Epstein, *op. cit.*, p.42, 46, 162, 171, 181.

[130] *Ibid.*, p.87-88.

[131] Armand Hammer with Neil Lyndon, *Hammer* (New York, NY: G. P. Putnam's Sons, 1987), p.71; Joan Veon, *Prince Charles: The* Sustainable *Prince* (Oklahoma City, OK: Hearthstone Publishing, Ltd., 1997), p.46; David Mark Price, *Secret* (1994), p.3; "Watch Al Gore Closely," *The McAlvany Intelligence Advisor* (November 1992), p.6; "Schuller Promotes Pope and Comrade," *Omega-Letter* (March 1988, Vol. 3, No. 3), p.15; Gary Allen, *The Rockefeller File* (Seal Beach, CA: '76 Press, 1976), p.118; David Allen Rivera, *Final Warning: A History of the New World Order* (Harrisburg, PA: Rivera Enterprises, 1994 Edition), p.202; Epstein, *op. cit.*, p.20-21, 68, 88; *Omega-Letter* (March 1991, Vol. 6, No. 3), p.16. See also: George Grant, *Grand Illusions: The Legacy of Planned Parenthood* (Nashville, TN: Thomas Nelson, Inc., 1998 Edition), p.109.

[132] Epstein, *op. cit.*, p.41.

[133] *Ibid.*, p.21, 35.

[134] Hammer with Lyndon, *op. cit.*, p.48; "Al Gore and the Communist Bagman: A Sordid Family Affair," *Flashpoint* (March 1993), p.2; Shirley Correll, "On Stealing Elections and the Electoral College," *The Florida Forum* (Fall 2000), p.12; Steve Weinberg, *Armand Hammer: The Untold Story* (Boston, MA: Little, Brown and Company, 1989); David Mark Price, *Secret* (1994), p.3; Joan Veon, *Prince Charles: The* Sustainable *Prince* (Oklahoma City, OK: Hearthstone Publishing, Ltd., 1997), p.46; "Watch Al Gore Closely," *The McAlvany Intelligence Advisor* (November 1992), p.6; John Elvin, "The Hammer-Gore Connection" (Part 1), *The Schwarz Report* (July 2000, Vol. 40, No. 7), p.6; John Elvin, "Armand Hammer: Soviet Agent," *The Schwarz Report* (August 2000, Vol. 40, No. 8), p.1; "Schuller Promotes Pope and Comrade," *Omega-Letter* (March 1988, Vol. 3, No. 3), p.15; John E. Ashbrook, *New Neutralism II: Exposing the Gray of Compromise* (Mentor, OH: Here I Stand Books, 1992), p.57; *The Omega Letter* (March 1991, Vol. 6, No. 3), p.16; Gary Allen, *The Rockefeller File* (Seal Beach, CA: '76 Press, 1976), p.118; David Allen Rivera, *Final Warning: A History of the New World Order* (Harrisburg, PA: Rivera Enterprises, 1994 Edition), p.202.

[135] Epstein, *op. cit.*, p.60.

[136] *Ibid.*

[137] *Ibid.*, p.64.

[138] "Schuler (sic) and Gorbachev," *Christian News* (January 22, 2001, Vol. 39, No. 4), p.8.

[139] "Is There an Elite Who Would Rule Us?," *The Florida Forum* (Summer 2000), p.26.

[140] Epstein, *op. cit.*, p.65, 80.

[141] *Ibid.*, p.80.

[142] "Al Gore and the Communist Bagman: A Sordid Family Affair," *Flashpoint* (March 1993), p.2. See also: Texe Marrs, "The Green Man or the Son of Skull & Bones...Who Will Be Our Next President," *Power of Prophecy* (January 2000, Vol. 2000-01), p.1-2. See also: *Ibid.*, p.8, 64, 76.

[143] Epstein, *op. cit.*, p.8, 287.

[144] *Ibid.*, p.333.

[145] *Ibid.*, p.333-335.

[146] *Unholy Alliances* (n.p., 1996), p.130. See also: David Carrico, *The Occult Meaning of the Great Seal of the United States* (Evansville, IN: Followers of Jesus Christ, 1991), p.78; Marrs, *Rule by Secrecy, op. cit.*, p.98.

[147] David Mark Price, *Secret* (Wichita, KS: Sunset Research Group, 1994), p.1. See also: Marrs, *Rule by Secrecy, op. cit.*, p.98.

[148] *Ibid.*, p.3.

[149] *Ibid.*, p.4.

[150] John E. Ashbrook, *New Neutralism II: Exposing the Gray of Compromise* (Mentor, OH: Here I Stand Books, 1992), p.57; Epstein, *op. cit.*, p.25.

[151] Shirley Correll, "On Stealing Elections and the Electoral College," *The Florida Forum* (Fall 2000), p.12.

[152] p.614-615.

[153] "Ting Has Been a Puppet of Communism from the Beginning," *op. cit.*

[154] "Communist Puppets Are Hoodwinking Lutherans," *op. cit.*, p.21.

[155] *Ibid.*

[156] *Ibid.*

[157] Letter from East Gates International, dated May 1999.

[158] *East Gates Connection* (January-March 2000), p.5.

[159] Pamphlet from East Gates Ministries International (Received March 16, 1998).

[160] Karnes, "Choose Sides," *op. cit.*, p.13.

[161] *Ibid.*; Eddie Karnes, "Speak Out for China's Persecuted 100 Million House Church Christians," *Christian News* (November 13, 2000, Vol. 38, No. 42), p.21; Eddie Karnes, "Dr. Billy Graham and Dr. Oswald Hoffmann, Thank You, But..." (Part II), *Christian News* (March 5, 2001, Vol. 39, No. 10), p.19.

[162] Pamphlet from East Gates Ministries International (Received March 16, 1998).

[163] "Communist Puppets Are Hoodwinking Lutherans," *op. cit.*, p.21. See also: ""China Brands Unregistered Churches 'Evil Cults,'" *op. cit.*, p.12; Eddie Karnes, "Speak Out for China's Persecuted 100 Million House Church Christians," *Christian News* (November 13, 2000, Vol. 38, No. 42), p.21; Karnes, "Choose Sides," *op. cit.*, p.13; Eddie Karnes, "The Big Lie on China's MFN and WTO," *Christian News* (May 22, 2000, Vol. 38, No. 21), p.10; Eddie Karnes, "Stop the China Scam," *Christian News* (December 11, 2000, Vol. 38, No. 46), p.16; Eddie Karnes, "Deceiving God's Elect on China," *Christian News* (January 29, 2001, Vol. 39, No. 5), p.23; Eddie Karnes, "Dr. Billy Graham and Dr. Oswald Hoffman, Thank You, But..." (Part I), *Christian News* (February 12, 2001, Vol. 39, No. 7), p.14.

[164] "Huaiyin Church Building Project," *East Gates Connection* (January-March 2000), p.3.

[165] *Ibid.*

[166] Letter from East Gates International, dated April 2001.

[167] Tom White, "'Banning' Millennium in China," *Christian News* (March 19, 2001, Vol. 39, No. 12), p.15. See also: "LCMS and LLL Supporting Liberals and Communists in China," *op. cit.*, p.15.

[168] "Ting Praises Socialism, Blasts Christianity," *Calvary Contender* (August 15, 1999, Vol. 16, No. 16).

[169] Karnes, "Ways to Get Bibles to the Chinese Without Getting Arrested," *op. cit.*, p.14.

[170] Cloud, "Bishop K. H. Ting—China's Master of Deceit," *op. cit.*

[171] "K. H. Ting Tells Lies," *O Timothy* (1994, Vol. 2, Issue 5).

[172] "China Clamps Down on Its Seminaries," *Christian News* (November 20, 2000, Vol. 38, No. 43), p.20.

[173] Hart, *op. cit.*Issue 6).

[174] gopher://gopher.wheaton.edu:70/00/Wheaton_Archives/BGC/Guides/Coll/318/3-histba.txt (Printed out on November 16, 1999).

[175] John C. Pollock, *A Foreign Devil in China: The Story of Dr. L. Nelson Bell, An American Surgeon in China* (Minneapolis, MN: World Wide Publications, 1971), p.66.

[176] *Ibid.*, p.96.

[177] *Ibid.*, p.18.

[178] *Ibid.*, p.30.

[179] *Ibid.* See also: gopher://gopher.wheaton.edu:70/00/Wheaton_Archives/BGC/Guides/Coll/318/3-histba.txt (Printed out on November 16, 1999).

[180] *Ibid.*, p.33-34.

[181] Francis S. Washburn, Jr., "An Open Letter to Billy Graham," *Life Advocate* (December 1992), p.29, 30.

[182] *Ibid.*, p.29; "Billy Graham Speaks Out," *Freedom Writer* (May/June 1997). See also: "Billy Graham Says 'Save the Earth, Not Babies!,'" *Flashpoint* (August 1995), p.2; "Turret of the Times," *Christian News* (April 5, 1993, Vol. 31, No. 14), p.2.

[183] "Billy Graham Says 'Pagans Saved Through Nature,'" *Flashpoint* (August 1995), p.1. See also: "Billy Graham Says 'Save the Earth, Not Babies!,'" *Flashpoint* (August 1995), p.2.

[184] George Grant, *Grand Illusions: The Legacy of Planned Parenthood* (Nashville, TN: Thomas Nelson, Inc., 1998 Edition), p.218.

[185] Wellman, *op. cit.*, p.57.

[186] Graham, *Just As I Am, op. cit.*, p.686.

[187] *Ibid.*

[188] "A Word from Ned Graham," *East Gates Connection* (January-March 2000), p.1.

[189] William McIlhany, "The WCC: A Haven for Marxists?," *Family Protection Scoreboard*, p.21.

[190] "LCMS and LLL Supporting Liberals and Communists in China," *op. cit.*, p.15.

[191] David W. Cloud, "Roman Catholic Bishop Helps Dedicate New United Bible Societies Translation," *O Timothy* (1992, Vol. 9, Issue 11). See also: David W. Cloud, "Goal of New Orleans '87—Apostate and Compromised Church Leaders Making Plans to Unite and Create a 'Christian' World," *O Timothy* (1987, Vol. 4, Issue 10-11); David W. Cloud, "The Graceless Bible for the Bart Simpson Generation," *O Timothy* (1991, Vol. 8, Issue 6); "Beware of the United Bible Societies," *The Perilous Times* (April/May 2001, Vol. 22, No. 10), p.8.

[192] David W. Cloud, "Dynamic Equivalency: Death Knell of Pure Scripture" *O Timothy* (1990).

[193] *Ibid.*

[194] *Ibid.*

[195] *Ibid.*

[196] *Ibid;* David W. Cloud, "Goal of New Orleans '87—Apostate and Compromised Church Leaders Making Plans to Unite and Create a 'Christian' World," *O Timothy* (Vol. 4, Issue 10-11).

[197] *Ibid.;* David W. Cloud, "Goal of New Orleans '87—Apostate and Compromised Church Leaders Making Plans to Unite and Create a 'Christian' World," *O Timothy* (Vol. 4, Issue 10-11).

[198] Cloud, "Dynamic Equivalency: Death Knell of Pure Scripture," *op. cit.*

[199] *Ibid.*

[200] *Ibid.*

[201] "American Bible Society Rejects Historicity of Genesis," *Christian News* (March 26, 2001, Vol. 39, No. 13), p.18; "Q & A," *The Berean Call* (May 2001), p.3.

[202] Cloud, "Dynamic Equivalency," *op. cit.*

[203] N. W. Hutchings, "Which Bible Is God's Word?," *The Gospel Truth* (July 1986, Vol. 27, No. 8), p.2.

[204] David W. Cloud, "Bible Societies Continue to Produce Corrupted Scriptures," *O Timothy* (1991, Vol. 8, Issue 2). See also: "Beware of the United Bible Societies," *The Perilous Times* (April/May 2001, Vol. 22, No. 10), p.8.

[205] *1993 Church World Service Annual Report* (New York, NY: Church World Service, 1993), p.16.

[206] Cloud, "Dynamic Equivalency," *op. cit.*

[207] *Ibid.*

[208] "Britishers Prefer Modernistic Paraphrase," *O Timothy* (1991, Vol. 8, Issue 8). See also: David W. Cloud, "Goal of New Orleans '87—Apostate and Compromised Church Leaders Making Plans to Unite and Create a 'Christian' World," *O Timothy* (1987, Vol. 4, Issue 10-11); David W. Cloud, "Wycliffe Bible Translators: Whither Bound?," *O Timothy* (1991); *Ibid.;* D. W. Cloud, "Some Frightening Facts About Billy Graham," *O Timothy* (1984, Vol. 1, Issue 4); David W. Cloud, "The Attack upon the Blood Atonement," *O Timothy* (1987, Vol. 4, Issue 1).

[209] D. W. Cloud quoting Robert Bratcher in "Some Frightening Facts About Billy Graham," *O Timothy* (1984, Vol. 1, Issue 4).

[210] D. W. Cloud, "Some Frightening Facts About Billy Graham," *O Timothy* (1984, Vol. 1, Issue 4).

[211] *Ibid.*

[212] "More A. B. S. Blasphemy," *Calvary Contender* (September 1, 1992, Vol. 9; No. 17), p.2; "American Bible Society Rapping and Cursing," *O Timothy* (1992, Vol. 9, Issue 11).

[213] William R. Denslow, *10,000 Famous Freemasons* (Vol. III) (n.p., 1959), p.343.

[214] *Ibid.*, p.129.

[215] Allen E. Roberts, *Frontier Cornerstone* (OH: The Grand Lodge of Free and Accepted Masons of Ohio, 1980), p.92.

[216] *Secret Records Revealed, op. cit.*, p.53; Joan Veon, *Prince Charles: The* Sustainable *Prince* (Oklahoma City, OK: Hearthstone Publishing, Ltd., 1997), p.24; Amy Donohue, "How John Templeton Got Rich," *Philadelphia* (October 1996), p.85; Paper from the John Templeton Foundation (January 11, 1996), p.1; "John Marks Templeton," *Progress in Theology* (June 1996, Vol. 4, No. 2), p.2.

[217] "Charles Colson to Join Mother Teresa and Pagan Religious Leaders at Parliament of the World's Religions," *O Timothy* (1993, Vol. 10, Issue 6); David W. Cloud, *Flirting with Rome: Evangelical Entanglement with Roman Catholicism (Volume 4—The Charismatics)* (Oak Harbor, WA: Way of Life Literature, 1993).

[218] *Progress in Theology* (June 1996, Vol. 4, No. 2), p.2; "Q & A," *The Berean Call* (May 2001), p.3.

[219] "Charles Colson to Join Mother Teresa and Pagan Religious Leaders at Parliament of the World's Religions," *op. cit.; Progress in Theology* (June 1996, Vol. 4; No. 2), p.2; David W. Cloud, *Flirting with Rome: Evangelical Entanglement with Roman Catholicism (Volume 4—The Charismatics)* (Oak Harbor, WA: Way of Life Literature, 1993).

[220] David W. Cloud, "Norman Vincent Peale: Apostle of Self-Esteem," *O Timothy* (1994, Vol. 11, Issue 2).

[221] "Metzger a Liberal," *Calvary Contender* (January 1, 1997, Vol. 14, No. 1), p.2. See also: David W. Cloud, "Evangelical Doublespeak and the Blood of Christ," *O Timothy* (1987, Vol. 4, Issue 1); *Christian News* (February 24, 1997, Vol. 35, No. 8).

[222] *Christian News* (February 24, 1997, Vol. 35, No. 8).

[223] *Ibid.*

[224] Perry F. Rockwood, "The Revised Standard Version," *O Timothy* (1985, Vol. 2, Issue 3); R. A. Partlow, *Satan's Subtle Sabotage of God's Holy Word* (Erie, PA: The Stable, 1997), p.57, 162. See also: Rael Jean Isaac, "Do You Know Where Your Church Offerings Go?," *Reader's Digest* (January 1983, Vol. 122, No. 729), p.121; *Intelligence Newsletter* (July-August 1991), p.7; William Martin, *A Prophet with Honor: The Billy Graham Story* (NY: William Morrow and Company, Inc., 1991), p.219; John A. Stormer, *None Dare Call It Treason* (Florissant, MO: Liberty Bell Press, 1964), p.127-128; Richard N. Ostling, "National Council of Churches Falls upon Hard Times," *Christian News* (November 29, 1999, Vol. 37, No. 44), p.7; *Christian News* (February 24, 1997, Vol. 35, No. 8).

[225] John A. Stormer, *None Dare Call It Treason* (Florissant, MO: Liberty Bell Press, 1964), p.128.

[226] *Ibid.*, p.127-128; *Unholy Alliances* p.160.

[227] *Ibid.*, p.128.

[228] *Ibid.*, p.127-128; *Unholy Alliances* p.160.

[229] *Unholy Alliances* p.160.

[230] Rockwood, *op. cit.*

[231] *Ibid.*

[232] *Ibid.*

[233] *Ibid.*

[234] *Ibid.*

[235] *Ibid.*

[236] *Ibid.* See also: David W. Cloud, "Can Evangelicals Be Trusted on Bible Versions?," *O Timothy* (1995, Vol. 12, No. 6); David W. Cloud, "Fundamentalism, Modernism, and New-Evangelicalism," *O Timothy* (1995, Vol. 12, No. 1).

[237] *Ibid.*

[238] *Ibid.*

[239] Stormer, *op. cit.*, p.128.

[240] Rockwood, *op. cit.*

[241] *Ibid.*

[242] *Ibid.*

[243] *Ibid.*

[244] *Ibid.*

[245] *Ibid.*

[246] *Ibid.*

[247] *Ibid.*

[248] *Ibid.*

[249] *Ibid.*

[250] *Ibid.*

[251] *Ibid.*

[252] *Ibid.*

[253] *Ibid.*

[254] Stormer, *op. cit.*, p.128; *Ibid.*

[255] Rockwood, *op. cit.*

[256] *Ibid.*

[257] *Ibid.*

[258] *Ibid.*

[259] *Ibid.*

[260] Hutchings, *op. cit.*, p.3.

[261] David W. Cloud, "Billy Graham's Disobedience to the Word of God," cited by Perry Rockwood.

[262] Hanson, *op. cit.*, p.17. See also: "Communist Puppets Are Hoodwinking Lutherans," *op. cit.*, p.21; *Christian News* (May 29, 2000, Vol. 38, No. 22), p.14.

[263] Eddie Karnes, "Dr. Billy Graham and Dr. Oswald Hoffman, Thank You, But..." (Part I), *Christian News* (February 12, 2001, Vol. 39, No. 7), p.14.

[264] "Communist Puppets Are Hoodwinking Lutherans," *op. cit.*, p.21.

[265] "Christianity Today Is No Longer the Conservative Evangelical Publication It Was When It Began," *Christian News* (April 21, 1997, Vol. 35, No. 16), p.2; *Christian News* (January 17, 2000, Vol. 38, No. 3), p.3.

[266] David W. Cloud, "Evangelical Doublespeak and the Blood of Christ," *O Timothy* (1987, Vol. 4, Issue 1).

[267] *Ibid.*

[268] *East Gates Connection* (January-March 2000), p.4; Letter from East Gates International dated Christmas 1999, p.2.

[269] *Ibid.*

[270] *Samaritan's Purse* (January 2000), p.3.

[271] *Ibid.*

[272] "NewsNotes," *Calvary Contender* (August 1, 1997, Vol. 14, No. 15), p.2.

[273] Wardner, *Unholy Alliances, op. cit.*, p.136; J. W. Wardner, "Unholy Alliances—The Order—The Illuminati Pedigree," *Despatch Magazine* (September 1998, Vol. 10, No. 3), p.28. See also: Edgar C. Bundy, *Billy Graham: Performer?, Politician?, Preacher?, Prophet?* (Wheaton, IL: Church League of America, 1982), p.70.

[274] Eddie Karnes, "Can You Buy Bibles in China? Yes and No!," *Christian News* (January 15, 2001, Vol. 39, No. 3), p.15; "Billy Graham Does Political Favor for President Clinton," *Flashpoint* (September 1997, Vol. 97-9), p.2; Denise L. Behreandt, "Permanent Normal Torture of Religions," *The New American* (June 19, 2000, Vol. 16, No. 13), p.23.

[275] Letter from Ned Graham dated March 2000, p.1. See also: Letter from Ned Graham dated May/June 2000, p.1; *The Auger News Letter* (May 2000), p.3.

[276] "House Approves China Trade Bill," *The News-Item* (May 25, 2000), p.1. See also: William F. Jasper, "China Trade: The CFR Steamroller," *The New American* (June 19, 2000, Vol. 16, No. 13), p.23; "World Trade: An Integral Step Toward World Government," *The Proclaimer* (Issue 2, 2000, Vol. 8, No. 2), p.7; James Dobson, *Dr. James Dobson Discusses America's Choice: Nine Key Issues That Will Shape Our Future*, (Colorado Springs, CO: Focus on the Family, 2000), p.14.

[277] Denise L. Behreandt, "Permanent Normal Torture of Religions," *The New American* (June 19, 2000, Vol. 16, No. 13), p.26.

[278] "Chinese Communist Party Structure," *Newsletter from a Christian Ministry* (April 1, 1993, Vol. 2, No. 6), p.25.

[279] "'Evangelicals' Honor Red China Premier," *Calvary Contender* (May 15, 1999, Vol. 16, No. 10), p.2.

[280] *Council on Foreign Relations: Annual Report July 1, 1990-June 20, 1991*, p.28.

[281] *State of the World Forum: Toward a New Civilization* (San Francisco, CA: Gorbachev Foundation USA, n.d.), p.1.

[282] Monteith, *op. cit.*, p.133.

[283] Graham, *Just As I Am, op. cit.*, p.606, 621.

[284] "U. S. State Department Confirms China's Persecution of Christians," *Christian News* (March 12, 2001, Vol. 39, No. 11), p.2. See also: Eddie Karnes, "Boycott the China Olympics 2008," *Christian News* (July 23, 2001, Vol. 39, No. 30), p.19.

[285] *Flashpoint* (September 1997, Vol. 97-9), p.2; "Grahams Side with Red China," *Calvary Contender* (August 1, 1997, Vol. 14, No. 15), p.2. See also: "Whither Religious Freedom in Hong Kong?," *Calvary Contender* (July 15, 1997, Vol. 14, No. 14), p.1.

[286] Karnes, "Choose Sides," *op. cit.*, p.13.

[287] "China," *Women of Vision 2000* (2000, First Quarter), p.4.

[288] Karnes, "Choose Sides," *op. cit.*, p.13; Eddie Karnes, "Speak Out for China's Persecuted 100 Million House Church Christians," *Christian News* (November 13, 2000, Vol. 38, No. 42), p.21; Eddie Karnes, "Dr. Billy Graham and Dr. Oswald Hoffmann, Thank You, But..." (Part II), *Christian News* (March 5, 2001, Vol. 39, No. 10), p.19.

[289] "Billy Graham Turns Blind Eye to the Serious Persecution in China," *O Timothy* (1989, Vol. 6, Issue 5).

[290] Letter from Ned Graham dated May/June 2000, p.1.

[291] Letter from East Gates International dated May 1999.

[292] "China Signs UN Treaty, Arrests Christians," *Calvary Contender* (December 15, 1998, Vol. 25, No. 24), p.1.

[293] Shea, *op. cit.*, p.61. See also: Shelvia Dancy, "China Stepping Up Crackdown on Religion," *Christian News* (December 25, 2000), Vol. 38, No. 48), p.23; Eddie Karnes, "America's Televangelists of Deception on China," *Christian News* (July 30, 2001, Vol. 39, No. 31), p.18; "China and the Kings of the East," *Prophetic Observer* (Mary 2001, Vol. 8, No. 5), p.4; "China Destroying Churches," *Christian News* (January 1, 2001, Vol. 39, No. 1), p.2; Eddie Karnes, "Boycott the China Olympics 2008," *Christian News* (July 23, 2001, Vol. 39, No. 30), p.19.

[294] "China Revealing Its Red Color," *Christian News* (January 15, 2001, Vol. 39, No. 3), p.3; "China Revealing Its Red Color," *Calvary Contender* (January 1, 2001, VOL. 18, No. 1), p.1. See also: Eddie Karnes, "Dr. Billy Graham and Dr. Oswald Hoffman, Thank You, But..." (Part I), *op. cit.*, p.14; "Chinese Underground," *U. S. News & World Report* (June 11, 2001, Vol. 130, No. 23); "Churches Demolished in Wenzhou, China," *Herald of His Coming* (April 2001, Vol. 60, No. 4), p.11; "Government Report Confirms the Bible League Findings of Persecution in China," *Christian News* (April 9, 2001, Vol. 39, No. 15), p.17.

[295] "China and the Kings of the East," *Prophetic Observer* (Mary 2001, Vol. 8, No. 5), p.3.

[296] Shea, *op. cit.*, p.3.

[297] "Six More House Church Leaders Arrested and Sentenced," *The Proclaimer* (Issue 2, 2000, Vol. 8, No. 2), p.9.

[298] *Ibid.* See also: Eddie Karnes, "Boycott the China Olympics 2008," *Christian News* (July 23, 2001, Vol. 39, No. 30), p.19.

[299] "Report: China Arrests Christians," *Christian News* (September 18, 2000, Vol. 38, No. 34), p.31; "U. S. Missionaries Detained in China," *Christian News* (September 18, 2000, Vol. 38, No. 34), p.31; "Increased Crackdown on Chinese Christians," *Christian News* (September 18, 2000, Vol. 38, No. 34), p.30; "LCMS and LLL Supporting Liberals and Communists in China," *op. cit.*, p.16; "China: House Churches Under Siege," *Pray!* (November/December 2000, Issue 21), p.44; "130 Evangelical Christians Arrested in China," *Christian News* (November 20, 2000, Vol. 38, No. 43), p.20.

[300] "China Targets House Church Christians," *Christian News* (October 30, 2000, Vol. 38, No. 40), p.6.

[301] Behreandt, *op. cit.*, p.24.

[302] "Authorities Crack Down on Guangdong Christians," *Christian News* (May 29, 2000, Vol. 38, No. 22), p.13.

[303] *Ibid.*

[304] "Billy Graham Turns Blind Eye to the Serious Persecution in China," *op. cit.*, quoting from *Pulse* (July 22, 1988, Vol. 23, No. 14).

[305] "China: House Churches Under Siege," *Pray!* (November/December 2000, Issue 21), p.44; "Persecution of Christians," quoting from *The Bible League* in *Christian News* (November 20, 2000, Vol. 38, No. 43), p.20.

[306] Snyder, *op. cit.*, p.3.

[307] "Persecuted Christians—What's Really Happening?," *East Gates Connection* (Received December 30, 2000), p.15.

[308] "Persecution of Christians in China Continues," *op. cit.* See also: "Billy Graham Turns Blind Eye to the Serious Persecution in China," *op. cit.*, quoting from *Pulse* (July 22, 1988, Vol. 23, No. 14); "Persecution of Christians," quoting from *The Bible League* in *Christian News* (November 20, 2000, Vol. 38, No. 43), p.20.

[309] *Ibid.* See also: Shea, *op. cit.*, p.60; "Persecution of Christians," quoting from *The Bible League* in *Christian News* (November 20, 2000, Vol. 38, No. 43), p.20; "Chinese Christian Leader Released from Prison," *Christian News* (September 18, 2000, Vol. 38, No. 34), p.19.

[310] *Ibid.*

[311] David Aikman, "The Global Picture," *Charisma* (March 1998); *Christian News* (May 29, 2000, Vol. 38, No. 22), p.13.

[312] "Persecution of Christians," quoting from *The Bible League* in *Christian News* (November 20, 2000, Vol. 38, No. 43), p.20.

[313] Aikman, *op. cit.*, p.13.

[314] Forwarded by the Word Warriorette, March 6, 1998. See also: Brad K. Gsell, *The Legacy of Billy Graham* (Charlotte, NC: Fundamental Presbyterian Publication, n.d.), p.43.

[315] "Billy Graham Does Political Favor for President Clinton," *Flashpoint* (September 1997, Vol. 97-9), p.2; "The Convicted and the Compromised," *The Day Drawing Near* (July 2000, Vol. 2, No. 2), p.2.

[316] William Martin, *A Prophet with Honor: The Billy Graham Story* (NY: William Morrow and Company, Inc., 1991), p.13.

[317] *Ibid.*, p.496-497. See also: Edgar C. Bundy, *Billy Graham: Performer?, Politician?, Preacher?, Prophet?* (Wheaton, IL: Church League of America, 1982), p.148.

[318] Graham, *Just As I Am, op. cit.*, p.481.

[319] Martin, *op. cit.*, p.496; Edgar C. Bundy, *Billy Graham: Performer?, Politician?, Preacher?, Prophet?* (Wheaton, IL: Church League of America, 1982), p.166; Jim Gallagher, "How the Soviets Duped Billy Graham," *Chicago Tribune* (May 16, 1982).

[320] D. W. Cloud, "Some Frightening Facts About Billy Graham," *O Timothy* (1984, Vol. 1, Issue 4). See also: M. H. Reynolds, Jr., *Billy Graham, the Pope, and the Bible* (Los Osos, CA: Fundamental Evangelistic Association, n.d.), p.4.

[321] Graham, *Just as I Am, op. cit.*, p.508.

[322] Cloud, "Bishop K. H. Ting—China's Master of Deceit," *op. cit.*

[323] *Christian News* (October 25, 1999, Vol. 37, No. 39), p.1; Eddie Karnes, "Speak Out for China's Persecuted 100 Million House Church Christians," *Christian News* (November 13, 2000, Vol. 38, No. 42), p.21; Eddie Karnes, "Deceiving God's Elect on China," *Christian News* (January 29, 2001, Vol. 39, No. 5), p.23; "Communist Puppets Are Hoodwinking Lutherans," *op. cit.*, p.21. See also: *Ibid.;* Karnes, "Can You Buy Bibles in China? Yes and No!," *op. cit.*, p.15; "K. H. Ting Tells Lies," *op. cit.;* Eddie Karnes, "Christian News Is Reliable," *Christian News* (March 26, 2001, Vol. 39, No. 13), p.15, 16.

[324] Eddie Karnes, "Speak Out for China's Persecuted 100 Million House Church Christians," *Christian News* (November 13, 2000, Vol. 38, No. 42), p.21; Karnes, "Can You Buy Bibles in China? Yes and No!," *op. cit.*, p.15; Eddie Karnes, "Christian News Is Reliable," *Christian News* (March 26, 2001, Vol. 39, No. 13), p.15, 16.

[325] Edgar C. Bundy, *Billy Graham: Performer?, Politician?, Preacher?, Prophet?*, quoting from the May 10, 1982 issue of the *Chicago Sun-Times* (Wheaton, IL: Church League of America, 1982), p.157.

[326] Graham, *Just As I Am, op. cit.*, p.509.

[327] *Ibid.*

[328] *Ibid.*, p.511-512.

[329] "Franklin Graham: Rebel with a Cause," *Calvary Contender* (April 1, 1999, Vol. 16, No. 7).

[330] David W. Cloud, *Flirting with Rome: Evangelical Entanglement with Roman Catholicism (Volume 1—Billy Graham)* (Oak Harbor, WA: Way of Life Literature, 1993).

[331] Larry Witham, "Graham to Launch Revival in Moscow," *The Washington Times* (June 21, 1991).

[332] Cloud, "Some Frightening Facts About Billy Graham," *op. cit.*

[333] *Ibid.*

[334] Bundy, *op. cit.*, p.110, 111-112.

[335] Wilson Ewin, *Under the New World Order: Evangelicals, Catholics and Israel: Conspiracy of the Ages* (Compton, Quebec: Quebec Baptist Missions, n.d.), p.65.

[336] Cloud, "Some Frightening Facts About Billy Graham," *op. cit.*

[337] Graham, *Just As I Am, op. cit.*, p.488.

[338] *Ibid.*

[339] *Ibid.*

[340] Brad K. Gsell, *The Legacy of Billy Graham* (Charlotte, NC: Fundamental Presbyterian Publication, n.d.), p.43.

[341] "Communist Puppets Are Hoodwinking Lutherans," *op. cit.*, p.21.

[342] Letter from East Gates International dated November 2000, p.1.

[343] *Ibid.*

[344] *Ibid.*

[345] Letter from Ned Graham dated March 2000, p.1.

[346] *Ibid.* See also: Letter from East Gates International dated May 1999.

[347] "Communist Puppets Are Hoodwinking Lutherans," *op. cit.*, p.21, quoting from the November 6, 1999 issue of *World.*

[348] *Ibid.*

[349] *Ibid.*

[350] *Ibid.*

[351] *Ibid.*

[352] *Ibid.*

[353] "Man of the Century," *Christian News*, (March 20, 2000, Vol. 38, No. 12), p.2.

[354] "Graham Defends Divorced Son Guilty of Adultery," *Christian News* (January 17, 2000, Vol. 38, No. 3), p.17.

[355] *Ibid.* See also: "Man of the Century," *op. cit.*, p.2.

[356] Billy Graham, *Unto the Hills: Thoughts for Every Day* (Dallas, TX: Word Publishing, 1986), p.2.

[357] *Christian News* (September 9, 1996, Vol. 34, No. 33), p.5.

[358] *Ibid.*

[359] *Ibid.*; "Gorbachev Speaks to 17,000 in St. Louis," *Christian News* (October 28, 1996, Vol. 34, No. 40).

[360] Marrs, *Dark Majesty, op. cit.*, p.133; "New Age Satanism Flourishes in Russia," *Flashpoint* (February 1990), p.4; "So. Baptist University Hosts Gorbachev," *The Perilous Times* (November/December 2000, Vol. 22, No. 7), p.8; "Oral Roberts Embraces Wealth, Mikhail Gorbachev, and the Democratic Party," *Flashpoint* (May 1996, Vol. 96-5), p.3; Samantha Smith, "Gorby's Disappearing Act," *Hope for the World* (Spring 1998), p.4; Virginia Meves, "Now the Question! How Is It in Your Church? Does the Light of Christ Shine or.....?," *Wisconsin Report* (November 28, 1996, Vol. 21, No. 46), p.3; Cathy Adams, "What About G. W. Bush's Record?," on the July 24, 2000 program of Radio Liberty; Texe Marrs, *Days of Hunger, Days of Chaos: The Coming Great Food Shortages in America* (Austin, TX: Rivercrest Publishing, 1999), p.140; "Russian Strategic Deception: The 'New' Communist Threat," *The McAlvany Intelligence Advisor* (January 1994), p.1; Texe Marrs, *Mystery Mark of the New Age: Satan's Design for World Domination* (Westchester, IL: Crossway Books, 1988), p.231; "The War and the Prophetic Words," *Midnight Call* (April 1991), p.10.

[361] *Christian News* (February 9, 1998, Vol. 36, No. 6), p.19.

[362] *Christian News* (September 9, 1996, Vol. 34, No. 33), p.5.

[363] *Ibid.*

[364] *The News & Observer* (June 24, 2001), p.11A.

[365] Samantha Smith, "Gorby's Disappearing Act" by Samantha Smith, *Hope for the World* (Spring 1998), p.4; "Soviet Union and World Government," *The Omega-Letter* (October 1988, Vol. 3, No. 9), p.7; "Soviet Goals Have Not Changed," *The Christian World Report* (December 1989, Vol. 1, No. 9), p.4; Don McAlvany, *Confronting Our Nation's Problems: The Financial, Political, and Spiritual Decline of America* (Oklahoma City, OK: Southwest Radio Church, n.d.), p.8.

[366] "Russian Strategic Deception: The 'New' Communist Threat," *The McAlvany Intelligence Advisor* (January 1994), p.1.

[367] Ewin, *Under the New World Order, op. cit.*, p.5. See also: "What Are Other Investigators Saying?," *Despatch Magazine* (June 2001, Vol. 13:2), p.53.

[368] "The War and the Prophetic Words," *Midnight Call* (April 1991), p.10.

[369] Ewin, *Under the New World Order, op. cit.*, p.9, 12.

[370] *Ibid.*, p.9-10.

[371] Wilson Ewin, *Evangelism: The Trojan Horse of the 1990's* (Compton, Quebec: Quebec Baptist Missions, 1992).

[372] Martin, *op. cit.*, p.529. See also: Graham, *Just As I Am, op. cit.*, p.546.

[373] Ewin, *Under the New World Order, op. cit.*, p.7.

[374] Ewin quoting from *Time* in *Ibid.*

[375] Edward E. Plowman, "Graham School Bridges Soviet Church Divisions," *Christianity Today* (August 19, 1991, Vol. 35, No. 9), p.40-41.

[376] Martin, *op. cit.*, p.529. See also: Graham, *Just As I Am, op. cit.*, p.546.

[377] "The War and the Prophetic Words," *op. cit.*, p.10.

[378] "Gorbachev Pushes One-World Marxist Utopia," *The Evangel* (March 2001, Vol. 48, No. 3), p.9.

[379] *Secret Records Revealed, op. cit.*, p.175-176.

[380] Epstein, *op. cit.*, p.59.

[381] "The Cedar Chest," *The Evangelical Methodist* (March 2000, Vol. 77, No. 10), p.7.

[382] Virginia Meves, "Now the Question! How Is It in Your Church? Does the Light of Christ Shine or.....?," *Wisconsin Report* (November 28, 1996, Vol. 21, No. 46), p.3.

[383] http://members.nbci.com/_XMCM/katfortuna/FCWP02200Interview.html

[384] *Ibid.*

[385] Wayne Peterson, *Extraordinary Times, Extraordinary Beings: Experiences of an American Diplomat with Maitreya and the Masters of Wisdom* (Henderson, NV: Emergence Press, 2001), p.100.

[386] "Atheist Speaks at Schuller's Church," *Calvary Contender* (November 15, 2000, Vol. 17, No. 22), p.1.

[387] Abhay K. Pati, "Health and Healing—An Interview with Benjamin Creme," *IJHHM* (Winter 1984), p.12; See also: Benjamin Creme, *The Reappearance of the Christ and the Masters of Wisdom* (North Hollywood, CA: Tara Center, 1980), p.53-54; *The World Teacher, Maitreya, Is Now Here* (North Hollywood, CA: Tara Center, n.d.), p.1; *The New Age Movement—Age of Aquarius—Age of Antichrist* (Oklahoma City, OK: Southwest Radio Church, 1982), p.17; Texe Marrs, *Dark Secrets of the New Age: Satan's Plan for a One World Religion* (Westchester, IL: Crossway Books, 1987), p.208.

[388] Benjamin Creme, *The Reappearance of the Christ and the Masters of Wisdom* (North Hollywood, CA: Tara Center, 1980), p.28.

[389] *Ibid.*, p.99. See also: Pati, *op. cit.*, p.11; Flyer from Tara Center; Flyer from World Goodwill; *The Remey Letter* (Autumn-Winter 1990-1991, Vol. 11, No. 4), p.1.

[390] Peterson, *op. cit.*, p.170.

[391] Alice A. Bailey, *The Externalisation of the Hierarchy* (New York, NY: Lucis Publishing Company, 1989 Edition), p.612.

[392] "The Art of Self-realization," *Share International* (Special Information Issue), p.6.

[393] *Ibid.*

[394] Dave Hunt and T. A. McMahon, *The Seduction of Christianity: Spiritual Discernment in the Last Days* (Eugene, OR: Harvest House Publishers, 1985), p.56.

[395] "The Rule of Law," *The Emergence* (June 1999, Vol. 17, No. 5), p.1.

[396] Buhle, Buhle, and Georgakas, *op. cit.*, p.795.

[397] Benjamin Creme, *Network News* (April/May 1987), Vol. 4, Nos. 4-5), p.1.

[398] "Maitreya—A Latter Day Deception," *The Christian World Report* (June 1991, Vol. 3, No. 6), p.7.

[399] "Maitreya's Message: Share and Save the World," *The Christ Is Now Here*, p.5.

[400] Bailey, *op. cit.*, p.191. See also: Constance Cumbey, *A Planned Deception: The Staging of a New Age "Messiah"* (East Detroit, MI: Pointe Publishing, Inc., 1985), p.57.

[401] Don McAlvany, *Confronting Our Nation's Problems: The Financial, Political, and Spiritual Decline of America* (Oklahoma City, OK: Southwest Radio Church, n.d.), p.13.

[402] "No! Steps to Create Peace" (New York, NY: Socialist Party, n.d.), p.7.

[403] See: Ashbrook, *op. cit.*, p.49.

[404] Tom Sine, *The Mustard Seed Conspiracy* (Waco, TX: Word Books, 1981), p.202.

[405] Ashbrook, *op. cit.*, p.49. See also: Jeremy Rifkin with Ted Howard, *The Emerging Order: God in the Age of Scarcity* (NY: G.P. Putnam's Sons, 1979), p.268-269; Tom Sine, *The Mustard Seed Conspiracy* (Waco, TX: Word Books, 1981), p.202; Trish Rector, "Who Is Jay Gary?," *Bold Truth* (February 15, 1993 [sic]), p.8.

6. THE ENVIRONMENT, ASTROLOGY, AND HOMOSEXUALITY

[1] *Christianity Today* (November 22, 1993, Vol. 37, No. 14), p.47; *The Omega-Letter* (April 1990, Vol. 5, No. 4), p.15; Henry Lamb, "The Rise of Global Green Religion," *Eco♦Logic* (1997 Special Report), p.3; Bill Lockwood, "United Nations—United Religion," *Christian News* (December 30, 1996, Vol. 34, No. 49), p.16; Tom DeWeese, "Radical Greens Use Churches to Force Senate Support of UN's Global Warming Treaty"; Brochure from Earthconnection, p.1; "How Do Eco-Ethics and E. S. D. Relate?," *EcoLetter* (Fall 1995), p.9; Brochure from Caring for Creation, announcing a National Conference on Environmental Awareness and Action, April 22-24, 1994; Cheryl Cook, Enid M. Gorman, and Lorette Picciano-Hanson, Editors, *A Directory of Environmental Activities and Resources in the North American Religious Community* (New York, NY: Joint Appeal by Religion and Science for the Environment, 1992), p.15; Randy Frame, "Christianity and Ecology: A Better Mix Than Before," *Christianity Today* (April 23, 1990, Vol. 34, No. 7), p.38; "Environmental Paganism," *The Midnight Cry* (September 1992), p.19; Texe Marrs, "Rockefeller Money, the Illuminati, and the Breeding of the New 'Super Man,'" *Flashpoint* (July 1993), p.1; David Briggs, "20 at Interfaith Parliament Sign

Document on Values," *The Charlotte Observer* (September 1, 1993); Letter from the National Religious Partnership for the Environment; Paper from the National Religious Partnership for the Environment, p.1; Joel Beversluis, Compiler, "URI Joins a Diverse Field of Interreligious Organizations," *United Religions* (Fall 1997, Issue 4), p.16; Paper from The World Conference on Religion and Peace (Received November 3, 1995), p.2; "NCC Establishes Pillars of Peace for 21st Century," *Media Spotlight* (2000, Vol. 23, No. 2), p.5.

[2] "How Do Eco-Ethics and E. S. D. Relate?," *EcoLetter* (Fall 1995), p.9.

[3] Dave Hunt, "Nature or Personal Creator?," *The Berean Call* (March 1994), p.1. See also: Dave Hunt, "The Greening of the Cross," *The Berean Call* (July 1997), p.1; "Green Cross," *Don Bell Reports* (January 26, 1990, Vol. 37, No. 2), p.1; Cheryl Cook, Enid M. Gorman, and Lorette Picciano-Hanson, Editors, *A Directory of Environmental Activities and Resources in the North American Religious Community* (New York, NY: Joint Appeal by Religion and Science for the Environment, 1992), p.24; Texe Marrs, "Al Gore's Hidden Ties with an Occult, Globalist Group," *Flashpoint* (January 1993), p.1; "A Very Successful Start," *World Goodwill Newsletter* (1988, No. 3), p.3.

[4] Paper from the National Religious Partnership for the Environment, p.2.

[5] Rick Miesel, "Youth with a Mission: Ecumenical (Catholic/Charismatic) Evangelism"; Rick Miesel, "InterVarsity Christian Fellowship: A Fellowship of Neo-Evangelicals."

[6] Texe Marrs, "Christianity Afflicted with Doctrines of Devils," *Flashpoint* (December 1996, Vol. 96-12), p.2; Wanda Marrs, *New Age Lies to Women* (Austin, TX: Living Truth Publishers, 1989), p.20, 44; Kathleen R. Hayes, "Feminism, Goddess Movement Infect Christendom, Church," *NRI Trumpet* (March 1989); *Bold Truth* (April 1993), p.12; "Planetary Initiative for the World 'They' Choose," *Prophecy Newsletter* (1985, Vol. 1, No. 8), p.11; Dave Hunt, "The Greening of the Cross," *The Berean Call* (July 1997), p.2; Brenda Scott and Samantha Smith, *Trojan Horse: How the New Age Movement Infiltrates the Church* (Lafayette, LA: Huntington House Publishers, 1993), p.69.

[7] Cheryl Cook, Enid M. Gorman, and Lorette Picciano-Hanson, Editors, *A Directory of Environmental Activities and Resources in the North American Religious Community* (New York, NY: Joint Appeal by Religion and Science for the Environment, 1992), p.162.

[8] Brenda Scott and Samantha Smith, *Trojan Horse: How the New Age Movement Infiltrates the Church* (Lafayette, LA: Huntington House Publishers, 1993), p.153.

[9] Cook, Gorman, and Picciano-Hanson, *op. cit.*, p.163-165.

[10] Albert James Dager, "The World Christian Movement—Part 3: Toward the New World Order," *Media Spotlight* (1999, Vol. 22, No.3), p.8; Albert James Dager, *The World Christian Movement: A Great Delusion Leading to the Religio-Political State of the Anti-Christ* (Redmond, WA: Sword Publishers, 2001), p.155.

[11] "Ron Blue to Speak at IFCA Meeting," *Calvary Contender* (April 1, 1996, Vol. 13, No. 7), p.2; "Christianity Today Promotes Leftist," *Christian News* (May 4, 1992, Vol. 30, No. 18), p.14, 15; *"Christianity Today* Promotes Sider," *Calvary Contender* (July 1, 1992, Vol. 9, No. 13), p.2; "WEF Honors 'Brother Andrew,'" *Calvary Contender* (July 1, 1997, Vol. 14, No. 13); "Church Workers Still Support Communism in Nicaragua," *The Christian World Report* (December 1990, Vol. 2, No. 9), p.27; John W. Robbins, "Ronald Sider Contra Deum," *Christian News* (May 4, 1992, Vol. 30, No. 18), p.15; "New Liberal Religious/Political Group Deplores 'False Choices,' Redefines Evangelism," *Christian News* (July 1, 1996, Vol. 34, No. 27), p.23; "Evangelical & Ecumenical Women's Caucus," (Brochure from Evangelical & Ecumenical Women's Caucus, n.d.), p.3; *Eternity* (January 1985, Vol. 36, No. 1), p.21; Kathleen Hayes, "Evangelicals for Social Action: Developing a Biblical Agenda for Public Life," *The Other Side* (April 1986, Vol. 22, No. 3, Issue 171), p.10.

[12] *Eternity* (January 1985, Vol. 36, No. 1).

[13] Kathleen Hayes, "Evangelicals for Social Action: Developing a Biblical Agenda for Public Life," *The Other Side* (April 1986, Vol. 22, No. 3, Issue 171), p.10.

[14] Albert James Dager, *The World Christian Movement: A Great Delusion Leading to the Religio-Political State of the Anti-Christ* (Redmond, WA: Sword Publishers, 2001), p.155, 163.

[15] *Ibid.*, p.163.

[16] *Ibid.*, p.162.

[17] *Ibid.*, p.162-163.

[18] *Ibid.*, p.163.

[19] *Ibid.*, p.167.

[20] Hayes, "Evangelicals for Social Action," *op. cit.*, p.10. See also: Brochure from Evangelical and Ecumenical Women's Caucus (Received December 28, 1996), p.3; John E. Ashbrook, *New Neutralism II: Exposing the Gray of Compromise* (Mentor, OH: Here I Stand Books, 1992), p.50; "Christianity Today Promotes Sider," *Calvary Contender* (July 1, 1992, Vol. 9, No. 13), p.2; "Christianity Today Promotes Leftist," *Christian News* (May 4, 1992, Vol. 30, No. 18), p.15.

[21] John E. Ashbrook, *New Neutralism II: Exposing the Gray of Compromise* (Mentor, OH: Here I Stand Books, 1992), p.50; See also: Edgar C. Bundy, *How Liberals and Radicals Are Manipulating Evangelicals* (Miami Shores, FL: Edgar Bundy Ministries, Inc., 1982), p.69; "Christianity Today Promotes Leftist," *Christian News* (May 4, 1992, Vol. 30, No. 18), p.15; Paul Fisher, "The Church and the New World Order," *National Educator* (August 1995), p.16; *Ibid.*

[22] Ronald J. Sider, *Rich Christians in an Age of Hunger* (Downers Grove, IL: Inter-Varsity Press, 1977), p.23.

[23] "Christianity Today Promotes Leftist," *Christian News* (May 4, 1992, Vol. 30, No. 18), p.15. See also: Hayes, "Evangelicals for Social Action," *op. cit.*, p.10.

[24] *Ibid.*

[25] "*Ibid.*

[26] *Ibid.*, p.16. See also: "Christianity Today Promotes Sider," *Calvary Contender* (July 1, 1992, Vol. 9, No. 13), p.2.

[27] *Ibid.* See also: "Christianity Today Promotes Sider," *Calvary Contender* (July 1, 1992, Vol. 9, No. 13), p.2.

[28] "Christianity Today Promotes Sider," *Calvary Contender* (July 1, 1992, Vol. 9, No. 13), p.2. See also: "Christianity Today Promotes Leftist," *op. cit.*, p.14.

[29] "Christianity Today Promotes Leftist," *op. cit.*, p.15.

[30] *The Cry for Renewal: Biblical Faith and Spiritual Politics* (May 23, 1995), p.2; Albert James Dager, "The World Christian Movement—Part 3: Toward the New World Order," *Media Spotlight* (1999, Vol. 22, No. 3), p.7; "New Liberal Religious/Political Group Deplores 'False Choices,' Redefines Evangelism," *Christian News* (July 1, 1996, Vol. 34, No. 27), p.23.

[31] "Christianity Today Promotes Sider," *Calvary Contender* (July 1, 1992, Vol. 9, No. 13), p.2. See also: "Christianity Today Promotes Leftist," *op. cit.*, p.14.

[32] "Christianity Today Promotes Leftist," *op. cit.*, p.14.

[33] *Christianity Today* (March 6, 1995, Vol. 39, No. 3), p.4.

[34] ""Christianity Today Promotes Leftist," *op. cit.*, p.14.

[35] *Ibid.*

[36] *Ibid.*, p.15.

[37] *Ibid.*

[38] Paul Fisher, "The Church and the New World Order," *National Educator* (August 1995), p.16.

[39] Ashbrook, *New Neutralism II, op. cit.*, p.50; See also: Edgar C. Bundy, *How Liberals and Radicals Are Manipulating Evangelicals* (Miami Shores, FL: Edgar Bundy Ministries, Inc., 1982), p.69; "Christianity Today Promotes Leftist," *op. cit.*, p.15; *Ibid.;* Hayes, "Evangelicals for Social Action," *op. cit.*, p.10.

[40] Brochure from Sojourners (Received August 23, 1996).

[41] J. W. Wardner, "Billy Graham, Freemasonry & the Communists," *Despatch Magazine* (September 1998, Vol. 10, No. 3), p.28; James W. Wardner, *Unholy Alliances* (n.p., 1996), p.137.

[42] Edgar C. Bundy, *Billy Graham: Performer?, Politician?, Preacher?, Prophet?* (Wheaton, IL: Church League of America, 1982), p.146, 149. See also: Billy Graham, *Approaching Hoofbeats: The Four Horsemen of the Apocalypse* (Minneapolis, MN: Grason, 1983), p.133; Billy Graham, *Just As I Am: The Autobiography of Billy Graham* (Harpers Collins Worldwide, 1997), p.499-502, Wilson Ewin, *The Emerging 666 Peace and the Abolition of Nuclear War* (n.p., 1984), p.18; D. W. Cloud, "Some Frightening Facts About Billy Graham," *O Timothy* (1984, Vol. 1, Issue 4); Wilson Ewin, *Evangelism: The Trojan Horse of the 1990's* (Compton, Quebec: Quebec Baptist Missions, 1992); Rick Miesel, "Billy Graham: General Teachings/Activities" (Biblical Discernment Ministries, Revised January 1994).

[43] D. W. Cloud, "Some Frightening Facts About Billy Graham," *O Timothy* (1984, Vol. 1, Issue 4).

[44] Billy Graham, *Just As I Am: The Autobiography of Billy Graham* (Harpers Collins Worldwide, 1997), p.499. See also: Billy Graham, *Approaching Hoofbeats: The Four Horsemen of the Apocalypse* (Minneapolis, MN: Grason, 1983), p.133.

[45] M. H. Reynolds, "Planting the Seeds of Ecumenical Apostasy in the Name of Evangelism," *Foundation* (1983, Vol. 4, No. 4).

[46] *Ibid.*

[47] Cloud, "Some Frightening Facts About Billy Graham," *op. cit.*

[48] Graham, *Just As I Am, op. cit.*, p.505.

[49] *Ibid.;* Billy Graham, *Approaching Hoofbeats: The Four Horsemen of the Apocalypse* (Minneapolis, MN: Grason, 1983), p.142.

[50] *Ibid.*, p.500.

[51] Carol Houst, "Playing with Fire," *Thoughtline* (April 1999), p.9.

[52] "In Memoriam, Dr. John Humphrey," *Religion for Peace* (June 1995, Issue 66), p.11; Cornelia R. Ferreira, "One-World Church Expected Next Year: San Francisco Chosen As Headquarters," *Wisconsin Report* (November 28, 1996, Vol. 21, No. 46), p.6.

[53] Cornelia R. Ferreira, "One-World Church Expected Next Year: San Francisco Chosen As Headquarters," *Wisconsin Report* (November 28, 1996, Vol. 21, No. 46), p.6.

[54] "Sovereignty in the Global Age," *World Goodwill Newsletter* (1998, No. 4), p.5.

[55] Dominic Dibble, "Transforming the Planet—A Question of Goodwill *The Festival Week of the New Group of World Servers* (New York, NY: Lucis Trust, n.d.), p.10.

[56] Willy Peterson, *The Leavening: A New Age Primer for Christian Parents* (Linwood, KS: 1995), p.213.

[57] Robert Muller, *New Genesis: Shaping a Global Spirituality* (Garden City, NY: Image Books, 1984), p.41.

[58] *Ibid.*, p.87.

[59] See: "Second Hollister Awards Ceremony," *Temple of Understanding Newsletter* (Fall 1998), p.4; United Religions Draft Charter June 1998-June 1999 (Received December 12, 1998).

[60] Paul Kurtz, *Humanist Manifestos I and II* (Buffalo, NY: Prometheus Books, 1973), p.19.

[61] *Ibid.*

[62] *Ibid.*, p.18.

[63] *Ibid.*, p.13.

[64] *Ibid.*, p.9.

[65] *Ibid.*

[66] *Ibid.*, p.15.

[67] *Ibid.*, p.16.

[68] *Ibid.*, p.9.

[69] *Ibid.*, p.7.

[70] "The United Nations: Its Origins and Milestones" (Received March 22, 1995).

[71] *Ibid.*

[72] *Ibid.*

[73] *Ibid.*

[74] Patricia Pitchon, "The Changing Role of the United Nations," *The Emergence Quarterly* (Autumn 1999, No. 28), p.3.

[75] "Humanist Manifesto 2000: A Call for a New Planetary Humanism," *Free Inquiry* (Fall 1999, Vol. 19, No. 4), p.4.

[76] *Ibid.*, p.11.

[77] *Christian News* (February 1, 1993, Vol. 31, No. 5), p.12.

[78] Alan Geyer, *The Idea of Disarmament! Rethinking the Unthinkable* (Elgin, IL: The Brethren Press and the Churches' Center for Theology and Public Policy, 1982), p.221-222.

[79] *Ibid.*, p.222.

[80] Anatoliy Golitsyn, *New Lies for Old* (Atlanta, GA: Clarion House, 1990 Edition), p.294, Clyde L. Manschreck, *A History of Christianity: Readings in the History of the Church from the Reformation to the Present* (Englewood Cliffs, NJ: Prentice-Hall, Inc., 1964), p.500.

[81] "WCC Calls for Gun Control, Disarmament," *Calvary Contender* (June 1, 1999, Vol. 16, No. 11), p.1.

[82] "The World Council of Churches on World Order," *The Whole Earth Papers: Christian Voices on World Order* (1978, Vol. 1, No. 10), p.30-31.

[83] Letter from Coalition for a New Foreign Policy.

[84] *Ibid.*

[85] "WCC Calls for Gun Control, Disarmament," *op. cit.* See also: Golitsyn, *op. cit.*, p.90.

[86] Reynolds, *op. cit.* See also: Cloud, "Some Frightening Facts About Billy Graham," *op. cit.*

[87] Paper from the Environmental Stewardship Team.

[88] Henry Lamb, "The Rise of Global Green Religion," *Eco♦Logic* (1997 Special Report), p.3. See also: "Environmental Ecumenism," *Christianity Today* (November 22, 1993, Vol. 37, No. 14), p.47.

[89] Joel Beversluis, Compiler, "URI Joins a Diverse Field of Interreligious Organizations," *United Religions* (Fall 1997, Issue 4), p.16; *Ibid.;* Miesel, "Youth with a Mission," *op. cit.;* "Environmental Ecumenism...," *Christianity Today* (November 22, 1993, Vol. 37, No. 14), p.47; Hunt, "Nature or Personal Creator?," *op. cit.*, p.1; Letter from the National Religious Partnership for the Environment; Paper from the National Religious Partnership for the Environment; Tom DeWeese, "Radical Greens Use Churches to Force Senate Support of UN's Global Warming Treaty"; William Norman Grigg, "Earth Worship in the Church," *The New American* (December 13, 1993), p.35; Bill Lockwood, "United Nations—United Religion," *Christian News* (December 30, 1996, Vol. 34, No. 49), p.16; *Eco♦Logic* (November/December 1995, No. 29), p.26; Ron Sider, "The Place of Humans in the Garden of God," *Green Cross* (Summer 1995, Vol. 1, No. 3), p.16.

[90] Letter from the National Religious Partnership for the Environment. See also: "Environmental Ecumenism," *Christianity Today* (November 22, 1993, Vol. 37, No. 14), p.47.

[91] Hunt, "Nature or Personal Creator?," *op. cit.*, p.1; Rick Miesel, "InterVarsity Christian Fellowship: A Fellowship of Neo-Evangelicals." See also: *Eco♦Logic* (1997, Special Report), p.2; *Eco♦Logic* (May 1995, No. 26), p.15.

[92] *The Prophecy Club Newsletter* (April 1995), p.3.

[93] Bill Lockwood, "United Nations—United Religion," *Christian News* (December 30, 1996, Vol. 34, No. 49), p.16.

[94] Wanda Marrs, *New Age Lies to Women* (Austin, TX: Living Truth Publishers, 1989), p.48-49. See also: "Satan Goes to Washington," *Flashpoint* (March 1990), p.6; "Oppose New Age Funding Legislation," *The Christian World Report* (August 1989, Vol. 1, No. 6), p.19; "Is Al Gore a Moderate?," *Calvary Contender* (August 1, 1992, Vol. 9, No. 15), p.1; "Senator Albert Gore Pushes New Age Agenda," *Flashpoint* (September 1990), p.2; "Seven Reasons Why I Did Not Vote for Al Gore," *The Voice in the Wilderness* (February 2001), p.7.

[95] "Who's Who in the Clinton Administration," *Wisconsin Report* (February 18, 1993, Vol. 18, No. 8), p.4. See also: "Green Cross," *Don Bell Reports* (January 26, 1990, Vol. 37, No. 2), p.1; Hunt, "Nature or Personal Creator?," *op. cit.*, p.1; Texe Marrs, "Al Gore's Hidden Ties with an Occult, Globalist Group," *Flashpoint* (January 1993), p.1; Scott and Smith, *op. cit.*, p.87.

[96] *What's Next* (Fall 1992, Vol. 14, No. 3), p.7; *What's Next* (September 1979), Vol. 4, No. 2), p.2; Paper from the Congressional Clearinghouse on the Future (1982), p.1; "Congressional Clearinghouse on the Future," *What's Next* (Fall 1985), Vol. 9, No. 8), p.5; James R. Patrick, Editor, *America 2000/Goals 2000* (Moline, IL: Citizens for Academic Excellence, 1994), p.383; *What's Next* (November 1979, Vol. 4, No. 5), p.2; *What's Next* (November 1982, Vol. 7, No. 3), p.2; "Toward a Fourth Psychology Revisited: Part VIII: Omega Institute," *Distant Drums* (August 1995, Vol. 16, No. 1), p.2; "Transformation Toward New Age Synthesis," *Distant Drums* (May 1986, Vol. 8, No. 2), p.7.

[97] Analysis sent to me by a friend. See also: *Now Is the Dawning of the New Age New World Order* (Oklahoma City, OK: Hearthstone Publishing, Ltd., 1991), p.192; Paper from the Congressional Clearinghouse on the Future (1982), p.4; *Chronology of Education with Quotable Quotes* (Highland City, FL: Pro Family Forum, Inc., 1994, Updated, bound volume), p.70; Douglas R. Groothuis, *Unmasking the New Age* (Downers Grove, IL: Intervarsity Press, 1986), p.121-122.

[98] "The Twilight Zone in Washington," *U. S. News & World Report* (December 5, 1988), p.24.

[99] Paper from the World Future Society (Received September 20, 1995), p.4.

[100] *Ibid.*, p.2.

[101] List of participants in the State of the World Forum, p.15.

[102] "Gores Entertain Homosexuals," *Calvary Contender* (May 1, 1995, Vol. 12, No. 9), p.1; "The Bottom Line," *Intelligence Newsletter* (May-June 1996), p.5. See also: "Gore Is Head of the Table at HRC Dinner," *The Advocate* (September 15, 1998), Issue 768), p.15.

[103] *Ibid.*

[104] *Ibid.*

[105] *Ibid.*

[106] "Gore Praises Perversity?," *Calvary Contender* (November 15, 1997, Vol. 14, No. 22), p.1.

[107] Letter from the American Family Association, p.2.

[108] *World Prayer and Share Letter* (August 1991), p.3.

[109] "Tax-Funded Indecency Sinks to New Low," *The Christian World Report* (March 1990, Vol. 2, No. 3), p.2; "NEA Anti-Obscenity Pledge Ruled 'Unconstitutional,'" *The Christian World Report* (March 1991, Vol. 3, No. 3), p.2.

[110] "NEA Gives Grant for 'Lesbian Art,'" *The Christian World Report* (February 1991, Vol. 3, No. 2), p.2. See also: "*Ibid*

[111] "Dying for a Desecrated Flag?," *The Christian World Report* (February 1991, Vol. 3, No. 2), p.1. See also: Phyllis Schlafly, "Latest NEA Outrages," *The Christian World Report* (June 1991, Vol. 3, No. 6), p.14; "It's Your Money," *The Voice in the Wilderness* (February 1992), p.13; "NEA Anti-Obscenity Pledge Ruled 'Unconstitutional,'" *The Christian World Report* (March 1991, Vol. 3, No. 3), p.2.

[112] *Ibid.*; "NEA Gives Grant for 'Lesbian Art,'" *op. cit.*, p.2.

[113] "NEA Anti-Obscenity Pledge Ruled 'Unconstitutional,'" *The Christian World Report* (March 1991, Vol. 3, No. 3), p.2. See also: Phyllis Schlafly, "Latest NEA Outrages," *The Christian World Report* (June 1991, Vol. 3, No. 6), p.14.

[114] *World Prayer and Share Letter* (August 1991), p.3. See also: Phyllis Schlafly, "Latest NEA Outrages," *The Christian World Report* (June 1991, Vol. 3, No. 6), p.14; Berit Kjos, "Using Art to Change Beliefs," *Free World Research Report* (November 1993, Vol. 2, No. 11), p.4.

[115] 1990 Calendar of Events from the Wise Woman Center Gazette.

[116] *Ibid.*

[117] *Ibid.*

[118] "NEA Funds Book Depicting Jesus As Homosexual Pedophile," *AFA Journal* (March 1992, Vol. 16, No. 3), p.23.

[119] "Get Out of the Kitchen," *World* (February 8, 1992, Vol. 6, No. 34), p.13; "Tax-Funded Indecency Sinks to New Low," *op. cit.*, p.2; Lynn and Sarah Leslie, "Resurrecting Pagan Rites" (Part 2), *The Christian Conscience* (January 1996, Vol. 2, No. 1), p.24; "New Age Church Active," *Flashpoint* (March 1991), p.4.

[120] "NEA Funds Book Depicting Jesus As Homosexual Pedophile," *op. cit.*, p.23; "Tax-Funded Indecency Sinks to New Low," *op. cit.*, p.1; Berit Kjos, "Using Art to Change Beliefs," *Free World Research Report* (November 1993, Vol. 2, No. 11), p.4. See also: Phyllis Schlafly, "Latest NEA Outrages," *The Christian World Report* (June 1991, Vol. 3, No. 6), p.14.

[121] "Tax-Funded Indecency Sinks to New Low," *op. cit.*, p.1.

[122] John A. Stormer, *None Dare Call It Treason...25 Years Later* (Florissant, MO: Liberty Bell Press, 1992), p.37. See also: "National Endowment of the Arts Sinks to All-Time Low," *The Voice in the Wilderness* (March 1992), p.8; "'Art' Display Profanes Christ," *The Christian World Report* (July 1989, Vol. 1, No. 5), p.6.

[123] *Ibid.* See also: "NEA Gets More Funds," *Calvary Contender* (July 1, 1993, Vol. 10, No. 13), p.1; "Homosexuals Reflect on Help from President Bush," *The Christian World Report* (April 1991, Vol. 3, No. 4), p.2.

[124] "Your Tax Dollar At Work," *Midnight Call* (August 1991), p.11.

[125] *Ibid.* See also: "Tax-Funded Indecency Sinks to New Low," *op. cit.*, p.1.

[126] "NEA-Funded Blasphemy," *The Christian World Report* (March 1990, Vol. 2, No. 3), p.3. See also: "Tax-Funded Indecency Sinks to New Low," *op. cit.*, p.1.

[127] Berit Kjos, "Using Art to Change Beliefs," *Free World Research Report* (November 1993, Vol. 2, No. 11), p.4.

[128] *Ibid.*

[129] "NEA Funds Book Depicting Jesus As Homosexual Pedophile," *op. cit.*, p.1.

[130] "NEA Funds Involved in Play Depicting Jesus As 'Gay,'" *Calvary Contender* (July 15, 1998, Vol. 15, No. 14).

[131] "Senator Albert Gore Pushes New Age Agenda," *Flashpoint* (September 1990), p.2.

[132] Al Gore, *Earth in the Balance: Ecology and the Human Spirit* (New York, NY: Houghton Mifflin Company, 1992), p.24, 30; "Who's Who in the Clinton Administration," *op. cit.*, p.4; Texe Marrs, "The Green Man or the Son of Skull & Bones...Who Will Be Our Next President?," *Power of Prophecy* (January 2000, Vol. 2000-01), p.2.

[133] *Ibid.*, p.24, 30; Matt, Michael J. "Al Gore—A Truly Frightening Environmentalist," *Christian News* (October 12, 1992, Vol. 30, No. 37), p.9; Barela, John. *The New Covenant of Bill Clinton & Al Gore* (Tulsa, OK: Mark 4 Marketing, Inc., 1992), p.65.

[134] *Ibid.*, p.260; "Seven Reasons Why I Did Not Vote for Al Gore," *Calvary Contender* (January 1, 2001, Vol. 18, No. 1), p.7; "The Bottom Line, *Intelligence Newsletter* (May-June 1996), p.3; Lockwood, *op. cit.*, p.16; Texe Marrs, "The Green Man or the Son of Skull & Bones...Who Will Be Our Next President?," *Power of Prophecy* (January 2000, Vol. 2000-01), p.2; "News Alert," *The Berean Call* (October 1992), p.4.

[135] Samantha Smith, "Eco-Kids Learn Paganism," *The End Times and Victorious Living* (May/June 1996, Vol. 10, No. 3), p.11.

[136] Gore, *op. cit.*, p.384-385.

[137] Texe Marrs, "The Green Man or the Son of Skull & Bones...Who Will Be Our Next President?," *Power of Prophecy* (January 2000, Vol. 2000-01), p.2.

[138] "News Alert," *The Berean Call* (October 1992), p.4. See also: *Ibid.*; Gore, *op. cit.*, p.260.

[139] "The Bottom Line," *Intelligence Newsletter* (May-June 1996), p.4.

[140] John Barela, *The New Covenant of Bill Clinton & Al Gore* (Tulsa, OK: Mark 4 Marketing, Inc., 1992), p.65.

[141] Gore, *op. cit.*, p.12.

[142] Marrs, "The Green Man or the Son of Skull & Bones," *op. cit.*, p.2.

[143] "The Bottom Line," *op. cit.*, p.3.

[144] Alicia C. Shepard, "Billy Graham Goes Global in 'Capstone' of His Career," *Christian News* (February 27, 1995, Vol. 33, No. 9), p.18; "Billy Graham and Al Gore Team Up to Save the Earth," *Flashpoint* (August 1995), p.2. See also: Wardner, "Billy Graham, Freemasonry & the Communists," *op. cit.*, p.29; "Billy Graham Says 'Save the Earth, Not Babies!,'" *Flashpoint* (August 1995), p.2.

[145] Wardner, "Billy Graham, Freemasonry & the Communists," *op. cit.*, p.29. See also: "Billy Graham Says 'Save the Earth, Not Babies!,'" *Flashpoint* (August 1995), p.2.

[146] Brochure from the Washington National Cathedral and the Omni-Shoreham.

[147] "Wallis Revitalizes Social Activism," *Calvary Contender* (July 1, 1997, Vol. 14, No. 13); Adelle M. Banks, "Graham Ministry Spans Half a Century," *Christian News* (May 13, 1996, Vol. 34, No. 20), p.6; Tom Watson, *The Evangelical Eroding of the Deity of Christ* (Southlake, TX: Countryside Bible Church, 1996), p.2, 7; "Savor South African Miracle, NCC General Secretary Says," *Eculink* (Summer 1994, No. 41), p.3; David W. Cloud, "The Preachers Who Influenced Bill Clinton," *Christian News* (March 26, 2001, Vol. 39, No. 13), p.17; "Campbell Prays With UFMCC 'For Healing,'" *Eculink* (Summer 1994, No. 41), p.6; "The National Council of Churches Has Chosen a Roman Catholic Woman," *Foundation* (July-September 1995, Vol. 16, Issue 4), p.37; Letter from the Interfaith Alliance dated April 13, 1995, p.6; "Call to Renewal," *Mindszenty Report* (March 1996, Vol. 37, No. 3), p.2; Monica Langley, "Burning Need," *Wall Street Journal* (August 8, 1996), p.A12; "New Books for Children," *The Perilous Times* (February 1999, Vol. 20, No. 12); *The Temple of Understanding* (Summer 1996), p.3; *Wisconsin Report* (November 6, 1997, Vol. 22, No. 43); Tucker Carlson, "Fidel's National Council of Churches," *The Schwarz Report* (June 2000, Vol. 40, No. 6), p.5; "New Liberal Religious/ Political Group Deplores 'False Choices,'" *Christian News* (July 1, 1996, Vol. 34, No. 27), p.23; Wesley Granberg-Michaelson, "Toward a Politics of Compassion," p.3; "Religions Cooperating for Peace: The World Conference on Religion and Peace" (Received July 3, 1995), p.2.

[148] Tom DeWeese, "Radical Greens Use Churches to Force Senate Support of UN's Global Warming Treaty."

[149] Letter from the National Religious Partnership for the Environment, p.1.

[150] *The Temple of Understanding* (Summer 1996), p.3; *Wisconsin Report* (November 6, 1997, Vol. 22, No. 43); The World Conference on Religion and Peace (Received July 3, 1995), p.4; "WCRP" (Received November 3, 1995), p.5.

[151] "Religions Cooperating for Peace: The World Conference on Religion and Peace" (Received July 3, 1995), p.2; "WCRP" (Received November 3, 1995), p.2.

[152] *Ibid.*, p.3.

[153] "Campbell Prays With UFMCC 'For Healing,'" *Eculink* (Summer 1994), No. 41), p.6. See also: David W. Cloud, "The Preachers Who Influenced Bill Clinton," *Christian News* (March 26, 2001, Vol. 39, No. 13), p.17.

[154] Enrique Rueda, *The Homosexual Network: Private Lives and Public Policy* (Old Greenwich, CT: The Devin Adair Company, 1982), p.157.

[155] *Ibid.*, p.285, 436.

[156] *Ibid.*, p.505.

[157] Tom Watson, *The Evangelical Eroding of the Deity of Christ* (Southlake, TX: Countryside Bible Church, 1996), p.2.

[158] Tucker Carlson, "Fidel's National Council of Churches," *The Schwarz Report* (June 2000, Vol. 40, No. 6), p.6.

[159] David W. Cloud, "The Preachers Who Influenced Bill Clinton," *Christian News* (March 26, 2001, Vol. 39, No. 13), p.17.

[160] "New Liberal Religious/Political Group Deplores 'False Choices,' Redefines Evangelism," *Christian News* (July 1, 1996, Vol. 34, No. 27), p.23; *The Cry for Renewal, op. cit.*, p.2; *Mindszenty Report* (March 1996, Vol. 37, No. 3), p.2; "People of Faith: A Call to Action" (Received September 3, 1996), p.1.

[161] Letter from the Interfaith Alliance dated April 13, 1995, p.6.

[162] *Ibid.*, p.2. See also: Adele M. Stan, "Keeping Faith," *Mother Jones* (May/June 1996), p.26.

[163] Adele M. Stan, "Keeping Faith," *Mother Jones* (May/June 1996), p.88.

[164] *Ibid.*

[165] Pamphlet titled "The Council of Conservative Citizens' Guide to *Martin Luther King, Jr. Holiday,"* p.6; *The NCC/WCC—Communism's Helpers* (Virginia Beach, VA: Good New Baptist Church, p.9; Jesse Helms, *The King Holiday and Its Meaning* (St. Louis, MO: Council of Conservative Citizens, 1998), p.18; Ralph Reed, *Active Faith: How Christians Are Changing the Soul of American Politics* (New York, NY: Free Press, 1996), p.60; Pamphlet titled "The Council of Conservative Citizens' Guide to *Martin Luther King, Jr. Holiday,"* p.6; "Jackson Needs Leave of Absence," *Christian News* (February 12, 2001, Vol. 39, No. 7), p.20; "King Honored As National Hero," *Sojourners* (May 1986), p.12; "Two United Methodist Leaders Close to MLK Welcome Verdict," *Christian News* (January 1, 2000, Vol. 38, No. 1), p.7.

[166] Stan, *op. cit.*, p.26.

[167] *Ibid.*

[168] William J. Murray, *My Life Without God* (Nashville, TN: Thomas Nelson Publishers, 1982), p.85; Claire Chambers, *The SIECUS Circle: A Humanist Revolution* (Belmont, MA: Western Islands, 1977), p.21.

[169] Brochure from the National Coalition Against Censorship (Received September 11, 1997), p.5; "Censorship in Our Schools," Distributed by the National Coalition Against Censorship (Received September 11, 1997), p.5; Letter from Judy Blume of the National Coalition Against Censorship dated July 1990.

[170] Susan N. Wilson, "Different Families Matter," *Censorship News* (1994, Issue 4, No. 55), p.4.

[171] *Ibid.*

[172] *Ibid.*

[173] "Public Libraries and Art Displays," *Censorship News* (1994, Issue 5, No. 56), p.3. See also: "A Kiss Is Just a Kiss," *Censorship News* (Winter 1997, No. 68), p.3.

[174] Kurtz, *op. cit.*, p.13, 16, 17; Albert Ellis, "Is Religiosity Pathological?," *Free Inquiry* (Spring 1988, Vol. 8, No. 2), p.27; Ron Marr quoting J. L Moreno in "The Unbelievable Truth About Your Public Schools" (Niagara Falls, NY: Operation Clean Up, n.d.), p.2; "Do These Women Speak for You?," (Pamphlet by Concerned Women for America, n.d.), p.2; "Advertising Atheism," *Freethought Today* (August 1986, Vol. 3, No. 6), p.3; *Freethought Today* (October 1986, Vol. 3, No. 8), p.10; Texe Marrs, *America Shattered* (Austin, TX: Living Truth Publishers, 1991), p.34; Dee Jepsen, *Women: Beyond Equal Rights* (Waco, TX: Word Books, 1984), p.60; Eli S. Chesen, *Religion May Be Hazardous to Your Health* (New York, NY: Peter H. Wyden, Inc., 1972), p.93; *Mind/Body Medicine* (1995, Vol. 1, No. 3), p.155; Mel and Norma Gabler, *Humanism in Textbooks* (Longview, TX: n.p., 1983), p.4; David M. Virkler, *The Word and the World Presenting...A Commentary on Secular Humanism* (Towaco, New Jersey: Dedication Evangelism, Inc., 1984), p.2-3.

[175] "Critical Thinking and Religion in the Schools," *An American Commentary* (Oklahoma City, OK: Hearthstone Publishing, Ltd., 1993), p.100. See also: *Now Is the Dawning of the New Age New World Order* (Oklahoma City, OK: Hearthstone Publishing, Ltd., 1991), p.182; *The Florida Forum* (Spring 1998); "Residential Psychodrama Training Weekend," *Oasis Center* (April-June 1989), p.12, 13; Claire Chambers, *The SIECUS Circle: A Humanist Revolution* (Belmont, MA: Western Islands, 1977), p.134; Phil Phillips, *Turmoil in the Toybox* (Lancaster, PA: Starburst Publishers, 1986), p.136; Ann Herzer, "Politics of the Radical Center," *Wisconsin Report* (November 17, 1994, Vol. 19, No. 45), p.2.

[176] Ron Marr quoting J. L. Moreno in "The Unbelievable Truth About Your Public Schools" (Niagara Falls, NY: Operation Clean Up, n.d.). See also: Phil Phillips, *Turmoil in the Toybox* (Lancaster, PA: Starburst Publishers, 1986), p.136.

[177] "Critical Thinking and Religion in the Schools," *An American Commentary* (Oklahoma City, OK: Hearthstone Publishing, Ltd., 1993), p.100.

[178] William J. Bowen, Jr. quoting Paul Brandwein in *Globalism: America's Demise* (Shreveport, LA: Huntington House, Inc., 1984), p.18.

[179] Kurtz, *op. cit.*, p.13; Homer Duncan, *Humanism in the Light of Holy Scripture* (Lubbock, TX: Missionary Crusader, Third Printing, 1982), p.13.

[180] *The Omega-Letter* (April 1990, Vol. 5, No. 4), p.15.

[181] "New Creation Institute, Au Sable in Join Effort," *Notes from Au Sable Institute of Environmental Studies* (Spring 1989, Vol. 2, No. 1), p.1.

[182] Letter from the National Religious Partnership for the Environment. See also: Beversluis, *op. cit.*, p.16.

[183] Lamb, *op. cit.*, p.2.

[184] *Ibid.*, p.3.

[185] Letter from the National Religious Partnership for the Environment, p.1.

[186] *The Prophecy Club Newsletter* (April 1995), p.3; "Religious Visionary to Retire," *New Age Journal* (November/December 1996, Vol. 13, Issue 6), p.30.

[187] Robert Sessler, *To Be God of One World: The French Revolution Globalized* (Merlin, OR: Let There Be Light Publications, 1992), p.142. See also: Miesel, "Youth with a Mission," *op. cit.;* Rick Miesel, "InterVarsity Christian Fellowship: A Fellowship of Neo-Evangelicals"; Hunt, "Nature or Personal Creator?," *op. cit.,* p.1.

[188] Jon Naar, "The Green Cathedral: In This Crusading Congregation, Ecology Is 'God's Work," *The Amicus Journal* (Winter 1993), p.22. See also: Marrs, *New Age Lies to Women, op. cit.,* p.44.

[189] J. Gordon Melton, Jerome Clark, and Aidan A. Kelly, *New Age Almanac* (Detroit, MI: Visible Ink, 1991), p.75; Chinook Learning Center (1990 Catalog), Inside Front Cover; "Unfinished Cathedral's 100th Year Celebrated," *Christian News* (January 18, 1993, Vol. 31, No. 3), p.23; "Environmental Ecumenism," *Christianity Today* (November 22, 1993, Vol. 37, No. 14), p.47; *Now Is the Dawning of the New Age New World Order* (Oklahoma City, OK: Hearthstone Publishing, Ltd., 1991), p.144; *Constance Cumbey's New Age Monitor* (August-December 1987, Vol. 2, Nos. 3-7), p.30; Texe Marrs, *Dark Majesty: The Secret Brotherhood and the Magic of a Thousand Points of Light* (Austin, TX: Living Truth Publishers, 1992), p.137; "Transformation Toward New Age Synthesis," *Distant Drums* (March 1986, Vol. 8, No. 1), p.7; "Green Cross," *Don Bell Reports* (January 26, 1990, Vol. 37, No. 2), p.1; Announcement from the Chinook Learning Center, p.5; "Cosmolatry: The Worship of Gaia," *Eco◆Logic* (May 1995, No. 26), p.14; Lamb, *op. cit.,* p.3; *Ibid.;* David Spangler, *Emergence: The Rebirth of the Sacred* (NY: Dell Publishing, 1984), p.ix, 51; Cook, Gorman, and Picciano-Hanson, *op. cit.,* p.24; Texe Marrs, "Al Gore's Hidden Ties with an Occult, Globalist Group," *Flashpoint* (January 1993), p.1; "A Very Successful Start," *World Goodwill Newsletter* (1988, No. 3), p.3; Marrs, *New Age Lies to Women, op. cit.,* p.20, 44; "Religious Visionary to Retire," *New Age Journal* (November/December 1996, Vol. 13, Issue 6), p.30; "The Oxford Conference: An Update on the Emerging Coalition of Political and Spiritual Leaders," *Omega-Letter* (July/August 1988, Vol. 3, No. 7), p.15; Sessler, *op. cit.,* p.142; Texe Marrs, *Ravaged by the New Age: Satan's Plan to Destroy Our Kids* (Austin, TX: Living Truth Publishers, 1989), p.74; "Moscow to Host Second Summit of Political and Religious Leaders," *The Christian World Report* (January 1990, Vol. 2, No. 1), p.3; "Work in Australia and New Zealand," *Yoga Vedanta* (October/November/December 1994, Vol. 3, No. 4), p.15; Dager, "The World Christian Movement—Part 3." *op. cit.,* p.15.

[190] Nan Robertson, *Getting Better: Inside Alcoholics Anonymous* (New York, NY: William Morrow and Company, Inc., 1988), p.86-87; Catalog from Gramavision, p.4; Marrs, *New Age Lies to Women, op. cit.,* p.44; David Spangler, *Emergence: The Rebirth of the Sacred* (NY: Dell Publishing, 1984), p.43; Texe Marrs, "Al Gore's Hidden Ties with an Occult, Globalist Group," *Flashpoint* (January 1993), p.1; Sue Serrone, "Canyon to Cathedral," *Festivals* (October/November 1986), p.6; Texe Marrs, *Ravaged by the New Age: Satan's Plan to Destroy Our Kids* (Austin, TX: Living Truth Publishers, 1989), p.74; *Ibid.*

[191] David Spangler, *Emergence: The Rebirth of the Sacred* (NY: Dell Publishing, 1984), p.53.

[192] David Spangler, *Reflections on the Christ* (Scotland: Findhorn Publications, 1977), p.43-44; Marrs, *New Age Lies to Women, op. cit.,* p.44.

[193] "Environmental Ecumenism," *Christianity Today* (November 22, 1993, Vol. 37, No. 14), p.47; Cook, Gorman, and Picciano-Hanson, *op. cit.*

[194] Cook, Gorman, and Picciano-Hanson, *op. cit.,* p.24. See also: Lamb, *op. cit.,* p.10; "Religious Visionary to Retire," *New Age Journal* (November/December 1996, Vol. 13, Issue 6), p.30.

[195] "Transformation Toward New Age Synthesis," *Distant Drums* (March 1986, Vol. 8, No. 1), p.7.

[196] *Ibid.*

[197] Letter from Planetary Initiative for the World We Choose, p.1.

[198] Texe Marrs, *Dark Majesty: The Secret Brotherhood and the Magic of a Thousand Points of Light* (Austin, TX: Living Truth Publishers, 1992), p.137.

[199] "Green Cross," *Don Bell Reports* (January 26, 1990, Vol. 37, No. 2), p.1; "Cosmolatry: The Worship of Gaia," *Eco◆Logic* (May 1995, No. 26), p.14; Lamb, *op. cit.,* p.3; Cook, Gorman, and Picciano-Hanson, *op. cit.,* p.24; Texe Marrs, "Al Gore's Hidden Ties with an Occult, Globalist Group," *Flashpoint* (January 1993), p.1; "Shared Vision," *The Omega-Letter* (April 1988, Vol. 3, No. 4), p.5; "The Oxford Conference: An Update on the Emerging Coalition of Political and Spiritual Leaders," *The Omega-Letter* (July/August 1988, Vol. 3, No. 7), p.15; "Moscow to Host Second Summit of Political and Religious Leaders," *The Christian World Report* (January 1990, Vol. 2, No. 1), p.3; Scott and Smith, *op. cit.,* p.107.

[200] Scott and Smith, *op. cit.,* p.84.

[201] "The Oxford Conference: An Update on the Emerging Coalition of Political and Spiritual Leaders," *The Omega-Letter* (July/August 1988, Vol. 3, No. 7), p.15.

[202] Texe Marrs, "Al Gore's Hidden Ties with an Occult, Globalist Group," *Flashpoint* (January 1993), p.1.

[203] Hunt, "Nature or Personal Creator?," *op. cit.,* p.1. See also: Wayne Griswold, "The Fallacy of New Age Environmental Concerns."

[204] "A Very Successful Start," *World Goodwill Newsletter* (1988, No. 3), p.3; Lamb, *op. cit.,* p.3, 10; "Cosmolatry: The Worship of Gaia," *Eco◆Logic* (May 1995, No. 26), p.14; "An Emerging Coalition: Political and Religious Leaders Come Together," *The Omega-Letter* (Special Report), p.3; Paper from the Temple of Understanding (n.d.), unnumbered page; Brochure from the Temple of Understanding (Received March 12, 1991), p.1; "The Very Reverend James Parks Morton Introducing His Holiness the Dalai Lama," *Temple of Understanding Newsletter* (Fall 1998), p.3; Letter from the Temple of Understanding dated November 1997, p.1; *The Temple of Understanding Newsletter* (Fall 1995), p.6; "Work in Australia and New Zealand," *Yoga Vedanta* (October/November/December 1994, Vol. 3, No. 4), p.15.

[205] Texe Marrs, *Ravaged by the New Age: Satan's Plan to Destroy Our Kids* (Austin, TX: Living Truth Publishers, 1989), p.74.

[206] "Shared Vision," *Omega-Letter* (April 1988, Vol. 3, No. 4), p.5.

[207] Letter from the National Religious Partnership for the Environment, p.1.

[208] Gore, *op. cit.*, Back Cover.

[209] Naar, *op. cit.* See also: Hunt, "Nature or Personal Creator?," *op. cit.*, p.1; Dave Hunt, *Global Peace and the Rise of Antichrist* (Eugene, OR: Harvest House Publishers, 1990), p.170.

[210] "Carl Sagan, Celebrated Author and Astronomer, Dies at 62," *Christian News* (December 30, 1996, Vol. 34, No. 49), p.1.

[211] *ACLU* (Report of Activities 1984-85), p.32; "In Perils of the ACLU," *The Perilous Times* (December 1993, Vol. 15, No. 10), p.4.

[212] *Council on Foreign Relations: Annual Report July 1, 1990-June 30, 1991,* p.190; *Council on Foreign Relations: Annual Report July 1, 1992-June 30, 1993,* p.175; *Council on Foreign Relations: Annual Report July 1, 1994-June 30, 1995,* p.155.

[213] Gary Kah, *En Route to Global Occupation* (Lafayette, LA: Huntington House Publishers, 1992), p.32, 37, 38, 39; Texe Marrs, *Millennium: Peace, Promises, and the Day They Take Our Money Away* (Austin, TX: Living Truth Publishers, 1990), p.41; James R. Patrick, Editor, *America 2000/Goals 2000* (Moline, IL: Citizens for Academic Excellence, 1994), p.584; A. Ralph Epperson, *The Unseen Hand: An Introduction to the Conspiratorial View of History* (Tucson, AZ: Publius Press, 1985), p.197; Des Griffin, *Fourth Reich of the Rich* (South Pasadena, CA: Emissary Publications, 1978), p.126; William T. Still, *New World Order: The Ancient Plan of Secret Societies* (Lafayette, LA: Huntington House, Inc., 1990), p.156, 191; Gary Allen, *Rockefeller: Campaigning for the New World Order* (n.p., n.d.), p.15; *Blueprint for Building the New World Order* (Dearborn, MI: The Omega-Letter/Christian World Report, n.d.), p.6; David Carrico, *The Occult Meaning of the Great Seal of the United States* (Evansville, IN: Followers of Jesus Christ, 1991), p.71; Chey Simonton, "The Rockefeller/Heritage Connection," *Christian Conscience* (December 1996, Vol. 2, No. 11), p.36; "Bryer (sic) Is Bad News for Christians," *Christian News* (July 18, 1994, Vol. 32, No. 29), p.20; Claire Chambers, *The SIECUS Circle: A Humanist Revolution* (Belmont, MA: Western Islands, 1977), p.34; James W. Wardner, *Unholy Alliances* (n.p., 1996), p.57, 165, 245; Joseph R. Chambers, *Spirit of Babylon: A New World Order* (Charlotte, NC: Paw Creek Ministries, n.d.), p.1.

[214] "Oxford Conference," *op. cit.*, p.15.

[215] "Carl Sagan: 'Educated Fool' Faces Death," *Calvary Contender* (April 1, 1996, Vol. 13, No. 7), p.1; "Evolutionist Carl Sagan Argues for 'Science Over Superstition,'" *Christian News* (March 18, 1996, Vol. 34, No. 12), p.1; "Evolutionist Carl Sagan Argues for 'Science Over Superstition,'" *Christian News* (December 30, 1996, Vol. 34, No. 49), p.5; *Creation* (August 1984), p.12; John D. Morris, "Evolution and the Wages of Sin," *Impact* (November 1990), p.i.

[216] *Ibid.*; "Evolutionist Carl Sagan Argues for 'Science Over Superstition,'" *Christian News* (March 18, 1996, Vol. 34, No. 12), p.1; *Creation* (August 1984), p.12; Brochure from the Washington National Cathedral and the Omni-Shoreham Hotel; "Evolutionist Carl Sagan Argues for 'Science Over Superstition,'" *Christian News* (December 30, 1996, Vol. 34, No. 49), p.5.

[217] "Carl Sagan, Celebrated Author and Astronomer, Dies at 62,," *op. cit.*, p.1; "Evolutionist Carl Sagan Argues for 'Science Over Superstition,'" *Christian News* (December 30, 1996, Vol. 34, No. 49), p.5. See also: "Evolutionist Carl Sagan Argues for 'Science Over Superstition,'" *Christian News* (March 18, 1996, Vol. 34, No. 12), p.1.

[218] Brochure from the American Humanist Association, p.1; *Creation* (August 1984), p.12; Marrs, "Al Gore's Hidden Ties with an Occult, Globalist Group," *op. cit.*, p.1.

[219] "Carl Sagan: 'Educated Fool' Faces Death," *op. cit.*; "Transformation Toward New Age Synthesis," *op. cit.*, p.12; *Free Inquiry* (Summer 1988, Vol. 8, No. 3), p.63; *Free Inquiry* (Fall 1990, Vol. 10, No. 4), p.63.

[220] *Ibid.*

[221] *Ibid.* See also: "Evolutionist Carl Sagan Argues for 'Science Over Superstition,'" *Christian News* (March 18, 1996, Vol. 34, No. 12), p.1.

[222] "Tony Robbins, New Age Guru," *Calvary Contender* (January 15, 1998), p.1; "State of the World Forum Toward a New Civilization," *Mindszenty Report* (March 1996, Vol. 37, No. 3), p.3; "News Alert," *The Berean Call* (October 1992), p.4; John Henry Western, "World's Elite Gather to Talk Depopulation," *The Interim* (April 1996), p.6; "State of the World Forum," *Wisconsin Report* (September 21, 1995, Vol. 20, No. 36), p.3.

[223] Wayne Griswold, "The Fallacy of New Age Environmental Concerns," p.1; Marrs, "Al Gore's Hidden Ties with an Occult, Globalist Group," *op. cit.*, p.1; "Gorbachev's International Green Cross," *The McAlvany Intelligence Advisor* (March 1995), p.13; Berit Kjos, "Gorbachev's New Global Pulpit," *The Christian World Report* (July 1993, Vol. 8, No. 5), p.2.

[224] Marrs, "Al Gore's Hidden Ties with an Occult, Globalist Group," *op. cit.*, p.1.

[225] "The Greening of American Faith," *The Voice in the Wilderness* (November 1994), p.13; Dave Hunt, "The Greening of the Cross," *The Berean Call* (July 1997), p.1; Dave Hunt, *Global Peace and the Rise of Antichrist* (Eugene, OR: Harvest House Publishers, 1990), p.170.

[226] Brochure from the Planetary Society entitled "You're Invited to Become a Member"; "Futureworld Expo in San Francisco," *Utopian Classroom* (Spring 1985, Vol. 13, Issue 1), p.1.

[227] "Shared Vision," *op. cit.*, p.5-6. See also: Gary F. Zeolla, "Sci-Fi, ETs, and the Ways of God," *Darkness to Light* (1995, Vol. 5, No. 1, Issue 18); David Allen Lewis and Robert Shreckhise, *UFO: End-Time Delusion* (Green Forest, AR: New Leaf Press, 1991), p.131.

[228] *Americans for Religious Liberty* (Silver Spring, MD: Americans for Religious Liberty, n.d.), p.4.

[229] *Ibid.*, p.3, 6.

[230] *Ibid.*, p.6-7.

[231] Brochure from the Washington National Cathedral and the Omni-Shoreham Hotel. See also: "The Rise of the Global Green Religion," *Eco◆Logic* (1997), p.5; "Sacred Environmentalism" (Received January 16, 1994), p.2; Paper from the National Religious Partnership for the Environment, p.1; "The Greening of American Faith," *op. cit.*, p.13; Ron Sider, "The Place of Humans in the Garden of God," *Green Cross* (Summer 1995, Vol. 1, No. 3), p.16.

[232] "The Rise of the Global Green Religion," *Eco◆Logic* (1997), p.5.

[233] "Green Cross," *op. cit.*, p.1.

[234] Dave Hunt, "The Greening of the Cross," *The Berean Call* (July 1997), p.1; Hunt, "Nature or Personal Creator?," *op. cit.*, p.1; "News Alert," *The Berean Call* (October 1992), p.4; Dave Hunt, *Global Peace and the Rise of Antichrist* (Eugene, OR: Harvest House Publishers, 1990), p.170.

[235] Dave Hunt, *Global Peace and the Rise of Antichrist* (Eugene, OR: Harvest House Publishers, 1990), p.170.

[236] Donald S. McAlvany, quoted in *Now Is the Dawning of the New Age New World Order* (Oklahoma City, OK: Hearthstone Publishing, Ltd., 1991), p.265.

[237] "Green Cross," *op. cit.*, p.1.

[238] Stanley Monteith, *Brotherhood of Darkness* (Oklahoma City, OK: Hearthstone Publishing, 2000), p.133; "The Earth Charter of the N.W.O.," *Despatch Magazine* (March 2001, Vol. 13, No. 1), p.14; "What Are Other Investigators Saying?," *Despatch Magazine* (June 2001, Vol. 13:2), p.52.

[239] "The Earth Charter of the N.W.O.," *Despatch Magazine* (March 2001, Vol. 13, No. 1), p.14.

[240] *Ibid.*

[241] "'Mr. Bush, the World Doesn't Want to Be American,'" *Despatch Magazine* (March 2001, Vol. 13, No. 1), p.19.

[242] *Ibid.*, p.20.

[243] "The Earth Charter of the N.W.O.," *op. cit.*, p.14.

[244] *Ibid.*

[245] Joan Peros, "Local 'Visioning,'" on the May 9, 2000 program of Radio Liberty.

[246] Graham, *Just As I Am*, *op. cit.*, p.505; Billy Graham, *Approaching Hoofbeats: The Four Horsemen of the Apocalypse* (Minneapolis, MN: Grason, 1983), p.142.

[247] "The U. N. & Education," *The Florida Forum* (Fall 2000), p.27.

[248] Peterson, *The Leavening*, *op. cit.*, p.24; Berit Kjos, "Clinton's War on Hate Crimes," *The Christian Conscience* (April 1998, Vol. 4, No. 3), p.28; Willy Peterson, *Angels Don't Write These Books: A Warning to Conservative Christians About New Age Conspirator, Dr. Nick Begich* (Bonner Springs, KS: n.d.), p.15; "Intentional Communities: Seeds for a New Civilization," *Christian Conscience* (December 1995, Vol. 1, No. 11), p.33; "Toward a Fourth Psychology Revisited: Part VIII: OMEGA Institute," *Distant Drums* (August 1995, Vol. 16, No. 1), p.2; "In Globo Cogitare et in Loco Agere," (Part III), *Distant Drums* (May 1983, Vol. 5, No. 2), p.10; "Intentional Communities: Seeds for the New World Order," *The Florida Forum* (Winter 1998), p.10; "Interview: Corinne McLaughlin and Gordon Davidson," *World Goodwill Newsletter* (1995, No. 3), p.2; Brochure from Sirius; *Stillpoint* (Spring/Summer 1985), p.13; Berit Kjos, "1995—United Nations 50th Anniversary Celebrations Began Earth Day—April—California Conference 1995—'Celebrating the Spirit,'" *Wisconsin Report* (August 24, 1995, Vol. 20, No. 32), p.4, 5.

[249] *Ibid.*; "Intentional Communities: Seeds for a New Civilization," *Christian Conscience* (December 1995, Vol. 1, No. 11), p.33; "Toward a Fourth Psychology Revisited: Part VIII: OMEGA Institute," *Distant Drums* (August 1995, Vol. 16, No. 1), p.2; "In Globo Cogitare et in Loco Agere," (Part III), *Distant Drums* (May 1983, Vol. 5, No. 2), p.10; "Intentional Communities: Seeds for the New World Order," *The Florida Forum* (Winter 1998), p.10; Brochure from Sirius; *Stillpoint* (Spring/Summer 1985), p.13.

[250] Corinne McLaughlin and Gordon Davidson, *Spiritual Politics: Changing the World from the Inside Out* (NY: Ballantine Books, 1994), p.100; *Now Is the Dawning of the New Age New World Order*, *op. cit.*, p.272-273; *Watch Unto Prayer* (Spring 1998), p.6; Constance Cumbey, *A Planned Deception: The Staging of a New Age "Messiah"* (East Detroit, MI: Pointe Publishing, Inc., 1985), p.34; Catalog from the Flower Essence Society, p.17; Paul Hawken, *The Magic of Findhorn* (New York, NY: Harper and Row, 1975), p.181, 186; *The 1988 Guide to New Age Living* (Winter 1988), p.9; Elliott Miller, *A Crash Course on the New Age Movement: Describing and Evaluating a Growing Social Force* (Grand Rapids, MI: Baker Book House, 1989), p.157; David Spangler, *Revelation: The Birth of a New Age* (Middleton, WI: The Lorian Press, 1976), p.11, 17, 21.

[251] *Stillpoint* (Spring/Summer 1985), p.13. See also: Berit Kjos, "1995—United Nations 50th Anniversary Celebrations Began Earth Day—April—California Conference 1995—'Celebrating the Spirit,'" *Wisconsin Report* (August 24, 1995, Vol. 20, No. 32), p.5.

[252] Berit Kjos, "1995—United Nations 50th Anniversary Celebrations Began Earth Day—April—California Conference 1995—'Celebrating the Spirit,'" *Wisconsin Report* (August 24, 1995, Vol. 20, No. 32), p.5; Berit Kjos, "Clinton's War on Hate Crimes," *The Christian Conscience* (April 1998, Vol. 4, No. 3), p.28; "Intentional Communities: Seeds for a New Civilization," *Christian Conscience* (December 1995, Vol. 1, No. 11), p.32; "Intentional Communities: Seeds for the New World Order," *The Florida Forum* (Winter 1998), p.10; *Stillpoint* (Spring/Summer 1985), p.13.

[253] Berit Kjos, "Clinton's War on Hate Crimes," *The Christian Conscience* (April 1998, Vol. 4, No. 3), p.28. See also: *Ibid.*

[254] "Interview: Corinne McLaughlin and Gordon Davidson," *World Goodwill Newsletter* (1995, No. 3), p.2; McLaughlin and Davidson, *op. cit.*, p.477; Pamphlet from the Center for Visionary Leadership (Received February 10, 2001), p.5.

[255] "Intentional Communities: Seeds for a New Civilization," *Christian Conscience* (December 1995, Vol. 1, No. 11), p.32.

[256] Brochure from Sirius.

[257] Brochure from the Center for Visionary Leadership (Received February 10, 2001); David Becker, "Booknotes," *Christian News* (October 31, 1994, Vol. 32, No. 40), p.2.

[258] McLaughlin and Davidson, *op. cit.*, p.47.

[259] *Ibid.*, p.386.

[260] Peter Lalonde, "Building the New World Order: One Piece at a Time," *Prophecy Newsletter* (1986), p.3-4; *Blueprint: For Building the New World Order* (Dearborn, MI: The Omega-Letter/Christian World Report, n.d.), p.3-4. See also: *Now Is the Dawning of the New Age New World Order, op. cit.*, p.420, 421; Paper from the Congressional Clearinghouse on the Future (1982), p.2; "Congressional Clearinghouse on the Future," *What's Next* (Fall 1985, Vol. 9, No. 8), p.5; "Special Report on the World Future Society's Worldview '84," *The Prophecy Newsletter* (n.d.), p.5.

[261] Homer A. Jack, "A Nuclear Freeze Is a SANE Proposal," *The Christian Century* (December 16, 1987), p.1133; Jeffrey K. Hadden and Charles E. Swann, *Prime Time Preachers: The Rising Power of Televangelism* (Reading, MA: Addison-Wesley Publishing Company, Inc., 1981), p.139.

[262] Brochure from 20/20/ Vision; *Ibid.*, p.1134; "Pseudo Right Revisited Toward a New Federalist—Opiate of the Proletariat," *Distant Drums* (December 1983), p.2; Brochure from the World Future Society; "Special Report on the World Future Society's Worldview '84," *The Prophecy Newsletter* (n.d.), p.5; John H. Adams, "NCC Leader's Strange Tack," *The Presbyterian Layman* (January/February 2001, Vol. 34, No. 1), p.22.

[263] "Special Report on the World Future Society's Worldview '84," *The Prophecy Newsletter* (n.d.), p.5.

[264] "NCC: New Leaders, New Woes," *Calvary Contender* (December 1, 1999, Vol. 16, No. 23), p.2; "National Council of Churches Hails Evangelical Bylaw Change," *Christian News* (March 27, 2000, Vol. 38, No. 13), p.1; "Deficit-Plagued NCC Faces Shaky Future," *The Presbyterian Layman* (July 2001, Vol. 34, No. 5), p.3, p.7; *Christian News* (November 27, 2000, Vol. 38, No. 44), p.2; John H. Adams, "'I Want to Apologize,'" *The Presbyterian Layman* (January/February 2001, Vol. 34, No. 1), p.6; "Pattillo Chosen for NCC Staff," *Calvary Contender* (March 15, 2001, Vol. 18, No. 6), p.2; "Habitat for Humanity, NCC Join Hands," *Christian Century* (Vol. 118, No. 12), p.9; "Deficit-Plagued NCC Receives Favorable Review," *The Presbyterian Layman* (July 2001, Vol. 34, No. 5); "Big Severance Package to NCC's Former Leader," *Calvary Contender* (July 1, 2001, Vol. 18, No. 13), p.2.

[265] *Christian News* (November 27, 2000, Vol. 38, No. 44), p.2.

[266] *Ibid.*; "NCC & Same-Sex 'Marriage,'" *Calvary Contender* (December 1, 2000, Vol. 17, No. 23), p.2; John H. Adams, "'I Want to Apologize,'" *The Presbyterian Layman* (January/February 2001, Vol. 34, No. 1), p.6; John H. Adams, "NCC Leader's Strange Tack," *The Presbyterian Layman* (January/February 2001, Vol. 34, No. 1), p.22.

[267] *Ibid.*

[268] "NCC & Same-Sex 'Marriage,'" *Calvary Contender* (December 1, 2000, Vol. 17, No. 23), p.2. See also: *Christian News* (November 27, 2000, Vol. 38, No. 44), p.2.

[269] John H. Adams, "'I Want to Apologize,'" *The Presbyterian Layman* (January/February 2001, Vol. 34, No. 1), p.6.

[270] *Ibid.* See also: John H. Adams, "NCC Leader's Strange Tack," *The Presbyterian Layman* (January/February 2001, Vol. 34, No. 1), p.22.

[271] Jeffrey K. Hadden and Charles E. Swann, *Prime Time Preachers: The Rising Power of Televangelism* (Reading, MA: Addison-Wesley Publishing Company, Inc., 1981), p.139.

[272] Letter from Americans for Democratic Action, Inc., dated April 21, 1988.

[273] C. H. 'Max' Freedman, "Hatchet-Job on Wildmon Shows Moral Bankruptcy of His Foes," *AFA Journal* (October 1990, Vol. 14, No. 9), p.12; *"Secret Records" Revealed: The Men, the Money, and the Methods Behind the New World Order* (Marlborough, NH: The Plymouth Rock Foundation, 1994), p.23; *Secret Records Revealed: The Men, the Money, and the Methods Behind the New World Order* (Oklahoma City, OK: Hearthstone Publishing, Ltd., 1999), p.73; Claire Chambers, *The SIECUS Circle: A Humanist Revolution* (Belmont, MA: Western Islands, 1977), p.63, 239; Rueda, *op. cit.*, p.411; John A. Stormer, *None Dare Call It Treason* (Florissant, MO: Liberty Bell Press, 1964), p.146.

[274] Rueda, *op. cit.*, p.411.

[275] *Ibid.*, p.423.

[276] Brochure from the World Future Society, p.4; *Futurevision* (World Future Society, Received May 9, 1996), p.33; "The Campaign Against National Sovereignty" *The Florida Forum* (Winter 1999), p.18.

[277] Hunt, "The Greening of the Cross," *op. cit.*, p.1.

[278] "Spiritual and Parliamentary Leaders Meet in Rio," *World Goodwill Newsletter* (1992, No. 4), p.6.

[279] Hunt, "The Greening of the Cross," *op. cit.*, p.1. See also: Dave Hunt, "Nature or Personal Creator?," *The Berean Call* (March 1994), p.1; Hunt, *Global Peace and the Rise of Antichrist, op. cit.*, p.170; Dwight L. Kinman, *The World's Last Dictator* (Woodburn, OR: Solid Rock Books, Inc. 1995), p.164.

[280] *Ibid.*

[281] Wilson D. Wallis, "Occult," *The World Book Encyclopedia* (Vol. 13) (Chicago 54, IL: Field Enterprises Educational Corporation, 1961 Edition), p.487.

[282] Bart J. Bok, "Astrology," *The World Book Encyclopedia* (Vol. 1) (Chicago 54, IL: Field Enterprises Educational Corporation, 1961 Edition), p.675.

[283] *The World Book Encyclopedia* (Vol. 12) (Chicago 54, IL: Field Enterprises Educational Corporation, 1961 Edition), p.47.

[284] Catalog from Publishers' Clearing Bureau, p.25.

[285] Robert A. Morey, *Horoscopes and the Christian* (Minneapolis, MN: Bethany House Publishers, 1981), p.18.

[286] "The Twilight Zone in Washington," *op. cit.*, p.24.

[287] J. Edward Decker, *The Question of Freemasonry* (Lafayette, LA: Huntington House Publishers, 1992), p.36; J. Edward Decker *Freemasonry: Satan's Door to America?* (Issaquah, WA: Free the Masons Ministries, n.d.), p.2.

[288] Personal conversation with Dr. Stanley Monteith on October 4, 1999.

[289] John Ankerberg and John Weldon, *The Facts on Astrology: What the Bible, Science, and Common Sense Tell Us About Astrology* (Eugene, OR: Harvest House Publishers, 1991), p.3. See also: McLaughlin and Davidson, *op. cit.*, p.277.

[290] McLaughlin and Davidson, *op. cit.*, p.277.

[291] *Ibid.*

[292] Graham, *Just As I Am, op. cit.*, p.537.

[293] World of Prophecy tape by Texe Marrs.

[294] Graham, *Just As I Am, op. cit.*, p.539.

[295] "RNC Chairman Joins in Honoring Rev. Billy Graham. Reagan Freedom Award Recognizes Former President's 'Greatest Gift,'" *Christian News* (April 10, 2000, Vol. 38, No. 15), p.20.

[296] *Ibid.*

[297] *Ibid.*

[298] Charles Yoh, "The New Age vs Christianity," *The Evangelist of Truth* (April 1990, Vol. 56, No. 4), p.3.

[299] *Ibid.*, p.1.

[300] Letter on file from Alice Braemer to *Christianity Today,* dated September 29, 1979. See also: Nona Dearth, "Abandoning Occult for Christ," *The Patriot Ledger* (November 10, 1979); "The Occultic Nature of The 21st Century Bridge!," *Last Trumpet Newsletter* (January 1997, Vol. 16, Issue 1), p.2.

[301] Albert James Dager, *Inner Healing: A Biblical Analysis* (Santa Ana, CA: Tri-Level Press, 1986), p.52.

[302] *Ibid.*

[303] *Ibid.* See also: Albert James Dager, *The Vineyard: History, Teachings and Practices* (Redmond, WA: Media Spotlight, 1996).

[304] Dave Hunt and T.A. McMahon quoting Ruth Carter Stapleton in *The Seduction of Christianity: Spiritual Discernment in the Last Days* (Eugene, OR: Harvest House Publishers, 1985), p.184.

[305] "Taking the Fire Out of Hell," *Christian News* (September 27, 1999, Vol. 37, No. 35), p.10; David W. Cloud, "How to Stop the Crime Epidemic," *O Timothy* (1994, Vol. 11, Issue 12).

[306] Ruth Carter Stapleton, *The Experience of Inner Healing* (Waco, TX: Bantam Books, 1977), p.8, 12, 51, 64, 112, 124, 181, 182, 183, 184; *The Prophecy Newsletter* (1986, Vol. 2, No. 1), p.6; Jon Trott and Eric Pement, "Visualization and Imaging: Dangerous Trends in Christian Meditation," *Cornerstone* (Vol. 14, Issue 74), p.18.

[307] *Ibid.*, p.181-184.

[308] Albert James Dager, *The Vineyard: History, Teachings and Practices* (Redmond, WA: Media Spotlight, 1996).

[309] Stapleton, *op. cit.*, p.183.

[310] *Ibid.*, p.84.

[311] *The Prophecy Newsletter* (1986, Vol. 2, No. 1), p.6.

[312] Hunt and McMahon, *The Seduction of Christianity, op. cit.*, p.183; Stapleton, *op. cit.*, p.12-13.

[313] Dager, *Inner Healing, op. cit.*, p.51; "First Amendment Case," *Christian News* (December 23, 1996, Vol. 34, No. 48), p.20.

[314] *Ibid.*, p.59.

[315] *Ibid.*

[316] Graham, *Just As I Am, op. cit.*, p.79.

[317] *Ibid.*, p.23.

[318] John D. Christian, *Gladiator: A Masterpiece of Nazi Propaganda* (Postscript) (New Zealand, Underground Press, 2001), p.13.

[319] *Ibid.*, p.12.

[320] Graham, *Just As I Am, op. cit.*, (picture section following p.296). See also: *Ibid.*

[321] James P. Boyd, *Bible Dictionary* (NY: Ottenheimer Publishers, Inc., 1958), p.18.

[322] *Illustrated Davis Dictionary of the Bible* (Nashville, TN: Royal Publishers, Inc., 1973), p.88; H. D. M. Spence and Joseph S. Exell, Editors, *The Pulpit Commentary* (Vol. 13) (Grand Rapids, MI: Eerdmans Publishing Company, 1950), p.163.

[323] Boyd, *op. cit.*, p.15. See also: *Listen My Children* (October 1989), p.7; William J. Schnoebelen, *Halloween: Tis the*

Season to Be Evil... (Issaquah, WA: Saints Alive in Jesus, n.d.), p.2; David L. Brown, *The Dark Side of Halloween and the Bewitching of America* (Oak Creek, WI: Logos Communication Consortium, Inc., 1998), p.12.

[324] Eric Maple, *The Complete Book of Witchcraft and Demonology* (Cranbury, NJ: A. S. Barnes and Company, Inc., 1966 Edition), p.32; *Illustrated Davis Dictionary of the Bible, op. cit.*, p.87; Texe Marrs, *Mystery Mark of the New Age: Satan's Design for World Domination* (Westchester, IL: Crossway Books, 1988), p.91; Thomas Bulfinch, *Bulfinch's Mythology: The Age of Fable or Stories of Gods and Heroes* (Garden City, NY: Doubleday and Company, Inc., 1948), p.384; William J. Schnoebelen, *Halloween: Tis the Season to Be Evil...* (Issaquah, WA: Saints Alive in Jesus, n.d.), p.2; Helena Petrovna Blavatsky, *Isis Unveiled,* Vol. I: Science (New York, NY: Trow's Printing and Bookbinding Company, 1877), p.552; *Listen My Children* (October 1989), p.6; W. J. McK. McCormick, *Christ, the Christian, and Freemasonry* (Belfast, Ireland: Great Joy Publications, 1984), p.87; William O. Peterson, Editor, *Masonic Quiz Book: "Ask Me Another, Brother"* (Chicago, IL: Charles T. Powner Company, 1950), p.254, 255; Marrs, *New Age Lies to Women, op. cit.*, p.231, 232; George Oliver, *Signs and Symbols* (NY: Macoy Publishing and Masonic Supply Company, 1906), p.23; Albert Pike, *The Magnum Opus* (Kila, MT: Kessinger Publishing Company, 1992), xxiii...15, p.xxviii...2.

[325] *Ibid.;* Lewis Spence, *Myths and Legends of Babylonia and Assyria* (London, England: George G. Harrap and Company, 1916), p.95; *Listen My Children* (October 1989), p.6.

[326] Helena Petrovna Blavatsky, *Isis Unveiled,* Vol. I: Science (New York, NY: Trow's Printing and Bookbinding Company, 1877), p.263, 552, 578; Albert Pike, *Morals and Dogma of the Ancient and Accepted Scottish Rite of Freemasonry* (Richmond, VA: L. H. Jenkins, Inc., 1871), p.368, 457; Christian, *op. cit.*, p.12; Thomas Bulfinch, *Bulfinch's Mythology: The Age of Fable or Stories of Gods and Heroes* (Garden City, NY: Doubleday and Company, Inc., 1948), p.384; Malcolm Duncan, *Duncan's Ritual of Freemasonry* (NY: David McKay Company, Inc., n.d.), p.226, 250; David L. Brown, *The Dark Side of Halloween and the Bewitching of America* (Oak Creek, WI: Logos Communication Consortium, Inc., 1998), p.12; William J. Schnoebelen, *Halloween: Tis the Season to Be Evil...* (Issaquah, WA: Saints Alive in Jesus, n.d.), p.2; *Listen My Children* (October 1989), p.6, 7; William Schnoebelen, *Masonry: Beyond the Light* (Chino, CA: Chick Publications, 1991), p.57; W. J. McK. McCormick, *Christ, the Christian, and Freemasonry* (Belfast, Ireland: Great Joy Publications, 1984), p.87; Edmond Ronayne, *The Master's Carpet (Mah-Hah-Bone)* (n.p., 1879), p.362; William O. Peterson, Editor, *Masonic Quiz Book: "Ask Me Another, Brother"* (Chicago, IL: Charles T. Powner Company, 1950), p.254, 255; Marrs, *New Age Lies to Women, op. cit.*, p.109, 231, 232; George Oliver, *Signs and Symbols* (NY: Macoy Publishing and Masonic Supply Company, 1906), p.22-23; Albert Pike, *The Magnum Opus* (Kila, MT: Kessinger Publishing Company, 1992), p.xxiii...15; Clifton L. Fowler, *Santa Claus and Christmas* (Denver, CO: Institute Publishing Company, 1928), p.23; Albert Churchward, *Signs and Symbols of Primordial Man* (London, England: George Allen and Company, Ltd., 1913), p.181.

[327] Stephen Knight, *The Brotherhood: The Secret World of the Freemasons* (Briarcliff Manor, NY: Stein and Day, 1984), p.236; *Ibid.*, p.552.

[328] *Listen My Children* (October 1989), p.6.

[329] Texe Marrs, "Inaugural Weirdness: Bill Clinton Takes Americans into 'the Twilight Zone,'" *Flashpoint* (March 1993), p.1; J. W. Wardner, "Unholy Alliances—The Order—The Illuminati Pedigree," *Despatch Magazine* (September 1998, Vol. 10, No. 3), p.29.

[330] David Becker, "Gay and Lesbian Band to March at Clinton-Gore Inaugural," *Christian News* (December 28, 1992, Vol. 30, No. 48), p.1. See also: Wardner, "Billy Graham, Freemasonry & the Communists," *op. cit.*, p.28.

[331] Marrs, "Inaugural Weirdness," *op. cit.*, p.1.

[332] Jeff Godwin, *Dancing with Demons: The Music's Real Master* (Chino, CA: Chick Publications, 1988), p.109.

[333] Eric Barger, *From Rock to Rock: The Music of Darkness Exposed!* (Lafayette, LA: Huntington House, Inc., 1990), p.131.

[334] *Ibid.*

[335] Godwin, *Dancing with Demons, op. cit.*, p.109. See also: Mike Johnson, *Rock Music Revealed* (n.p., n.d.), p.6; *Ibid.;* David W. Cloud, *Mom and Dad Sleep While the Children Rock in Satan's Cradle* (Oak Harbor, WA: Way of Life Literature, 1991 Edition); http://www.inherownwords.com/witches.htm.

[336] http://www.inherownwords.com/witches.htm.

[337] David W. Cloud, *Mom and Dad Sleep While the Children Rock in Satan's Cradle* (Oak Harbor, WA: Way of Life Literature, 1991 Edition).

[338] Barger, *op. cit.*, p.131.

[339] Mike Johnson, *Rock Music Revealed* (n.p., n.d.), p.6. See also: Godwin, *Dancing with Demons, op. cit.*, p.108.

[340] Barger, *op. cit.*, p.131.

[341] Godwin, *Dancing with Demons, op. cit.*, p.112.

[342] *Ibid.*, p.112-113. See also: Barger, *op. cit.*, p.131.

[343] *Ibid.*, p.342; Jeff Godwin, *What's Wrong with Christian Rock?* (Chino, CA: Chick Publications, 1990), p.281.

[344] *Ibid.*, p.108-109. See also: Jeff Godwin, *Rock & Roll Religion* (Bloomington, IN: The Rock Ministries, 1995), p.49.

[345] http://www.queenofrock.com/articles/stevie_wonder_mccalls_jan_1999.htm. See also: http://www.nicksfix.com/azrepub7.htm.

[346] *Ibid.*

[347] "Church Leaders Praise Bill Clinton's 'Spirituality,'" *Christian News* (November 13, 2000, Vol. 38, No. 42), p.2.

[348] Graham, *Just As I Am, op. cit.*, p.656.

[349] Ian Paisley, "Billy Graham's Tragic Romeward Run," *O Timothy* (1993, Vol. 10, Issue 9).

[350] Marrs, "Inaugural Weirdness," *op. cit.*, p.1.

[351] "Lansbury Honored by NRB," *Calvary Contender* (June 1, 1993, Vol. 10, No. 11), p.1.

[352] Marrs, "Inaugural Weirdness," *op. cit.*, p.1.

[353] "Readers' Forum," *Colorado Christian News* (January 1995, Vol. 6, Issue 6), p.8.

[354] Marrs, "Inaugural Weirdness," *op. cit.*, p.2. See also: "Participants Announced for Inauguration," *Christian News* (December 28, 1992, Vol. 30, No. 48), p.1.

[355] "Graham: 'Other Paths to God?,'" *Calvary Contender* (November 15, 1996, Vol. 13, No. 22), p.2; Marrs, "Christianity Afflicted with Doctrines of Devils," *op. cit.*, p.1. See also: Robert Murphy, "Getting Together," *The News and Observer* (November 12, 1996), p.10A.

[356] Colin Greer, "'Our Task Is to Do All We Can—Not to Sit and Wait,'" *Parade* (October 20, 1996), p.4. See also: *Ibid.*; "Graham: 'Other Paths to God?,'" *Calvary Contender* (March 15, 1996, Vol. 13, No. 6), p.2; Marrs, "Christianity Afflicted with Doctrines of Devils," *op. cit.*, p.1; *Flashpoint* (January 1997, Vol. 97-1), p.2; Robert Murphy, "Getting Together," *The News and Observer* (November 12, 1996), p.10A.

[357] Robert Murphy, "Getting Together," *The News and Observer* (November 12, 1996), p.10A.

[358] Greer, *op. cit.*, p.4. See also: "Graham: 'Other Paths to God?,'" *Calvary Contender* (November 15, 1996, Vol. 13, No. 22), p.2; *The Berean Call* (May 1998); "Noted Evangelist Issues Conflicting Views on Salvation," *Christian News* (November 25, 1996), Vol. 34, No. 44), p.11; "Graham: 'Other Paths to God?,'" *Calvary Contender* (March 15, 1996, Vol. 13, No. 6), p.2; "New Gospel Emerging," *Media Spotlight* (1997, Vol. 20, No. 2), p.24; "Evangelicals and Catholics: Coming Together," *The Day Drawing Near* (March 1999, Vol. 1, No. 6), p.2; "Billy Graham Is Featured on the Cover of the October 20 *Parade* Magazine," *Christian News* (November 4, 1996, Vol. 34, No. 41), p.2.

[359] George Catlin, *Christianity and the New Age* (n.p., 1998), p.3.

[360] Greer, *op. cit.*, p.4. See also: Norman Langley and Leon Freilich, "What Really Happened Between the President and America's Leading Preacher in the Countdown to War: How Billy Graham Brought Light to George Bush's Darkest Hour," *Star* (February 5, 1991), p.6.

[361] George W. Cornell, "Clinton Has Ties with 2 Religions" *Associated Press* (January 16, 1993).

[362] Graham, *Just As I Am*, *op. cit.*, p.450. See also: *A Prophet with Honor*, p.355; Sam Wellman, *Billy Graham: The Great Evangelist* (Uhrichsville, OH: Barbour Book, 1996), p.171; Greer, *op. cit.*, p.5.

[363] *A Prophet with Honor*, p.355.

[364] Graham, *Just As I Am*, *op. cit.*, p.592.

[365] *Ibid.* See also: Sam Wellman, *Billy Graham: The Great Evangelist* (Uhrichsville, OH: Barbour Book, 1996), p.199-200.

[366] "Graham at Harvard Praises Dalai Lama," *Calvary Contender* (November 1, 1999, Vol. 16, No. 21). See also: "NewsNotes," *Calvary Contender* (August 1, 1997, Vol. 14, No. 15), p.2; Dennis W. Costella, "Should We All Get Together?," *Foundation* (January-February 2000, Vol. 21, Issue 1), p.5; "Turret of the Times," *Christian News* (October 30, 2000, Vol. 38, No. 40), p.3; "Harvard's 'Gay' Chaplain Peter Gomes," *Calvary Contender* (April 15, 1997, Vol. 14, No. 8), p.1; "Turret of the Times," *Christian News* (March 16, 1992, Vol. 30, No. 11), p.3; Robin Estrin, "Harvard Preacher Takes New Look at Bible," *Christian News* (January 27, 1997, Vol. 35, No. 4), p.2.

[367] Robin Estrin, "Harvard Preacher Takes New Look at Bible," *Christian News* (January 27, 1997, Vol. 35, No. 4), p.2.

[368] "Turret of the Times," *Christian News* (March 16, 1992, Vol. 30, No. 11), p.3.

[369] "NewsNotes," *Calvary Contender* (August 1, 1997, Vol. 14, No. 15), p.2.

[370] John Ashbrook, "Billy Graham—The Mouthpiece of New Evangelicalism," *O Timothy* (1993, Vol. 10, Issue 1).

[371] "Graham at Harvard Praises Dalai Lama," *op. cit.*

[372] *Ibid.*

[373] John Templeton, *Possibilities for Over One Hundredfold More Spiritual Information: The Humble Approach in Theology and Science* (Philadelphia, PA: Templeton Foundation Press, 2000), p.202.

[374] Dave Hunt and T. A. McMahon, *America: The Sorcerer's New Apprentice: The Rise of New Age Shamanism* (Eugene, OR: Harvest House Publishers, 1988), p.281; Berit Kjos, "From the UNITED NATIONS to the UNITED RELIGIONS" (Received March 20, 1996); Wilbert Forker, Editor, *The Templeton Foundation Prize for Progress in Religion* (Edinburgh, Scotland: Scottish Academic Press, 1988), p.89; Howard C. Cutler, "The Mindful Monk," *Psychology Today* (June 2001, Vol. 34, No. 3), p.34, 36, 38; Alan Morrison, *The Serpent and the Cross: Religious Corporation in an Evil Age* (Birmingham, England: K & M Books, 1994), p.153, 569; Texe Marrs, *Texe Marrs Book of New Age Cults and Religions* (Austin, TX: Living Truth Publishers, 1990), p.174, 175, 224; Texe Marrs, "Texe Marrs Asks Chuck Colson: 'Will You Sell Your Soul to the Devil for a Million Dollars?,'" *Flashpoint* (June 1993), p.1; "Masonic Treachery in High Places: The Wicked Deeds of Bill Clinton, Bob Dole, Al Gore, Jack Kemp, Jesse Helms, and Barry Goldwater," *Flashpoint* (November 1996, Vol. 96-11), p.5; Hunt, *Global Peace and the Rise of Antichrist*, *op. cit.*, p.129, 152; Marrs, "Al Gore's Hidden Ties with an Occult, Globalist Group," *op. cit.*, p.1; Texe Marrs, "New Agers Meet to Plan World Takeover," *Flashpoint* (January 1990), p.1; *The Watchman Expositor* (1998, Vol. 15, No. 5), p.6, 27; David R. Barnhart, *Contending for the Faith* (Eagan, MN: Abiding Word Publications, 1994), p.115; *CIB Bulletin*, (September 1990, Vol. 6, No. 9), p.1; *Dallas Morning News* (July 27, 1996), p.4-G; Paper from Thanksgiving Square; J. Melton, Clark, and Kelly, *op. cit.*, p.283-284; William T. James, Editor, *Foreshocks of Antichrist* (Eugene, OR: Harvest House Publishers, 1997), p.110; William Swing, "Reactions from Religious Leaders: United Religions International Tour," *Christian News* (May 5, 1997, Vol. 35, No. 18), p.6; Marrs, *Dark Majesty*, *op. cit.*, p.137; Ernst-Ulrich Franzen, "Golden Rule Called Universal: World Religious Parliament Readers 'Global Ethic' Declaration," *Milwaukee Sentinel* (September 4, 1993); *Temple of Understanding Newsletter* (Fall 1998), p.3.

[375] "The Bottom Line," *op. cit.*, p.4. See also: Hunt, *Global Peace and the Rise of Antichrist, op. cit.*, p.152; "The Parliament of World Religions: Comments by People We Trust," *Flashpoint* (September 1993), p.2; Alex Jack, "Glimpses of an Unseen Friend," *Macromuse* (Summer/Fire 1985, Issue 20), p.17; *The Watchman Expositor* (1998, Vol. 15, No. 5), p.27.

[376] Glenn H. Mullin, "A Meeting with Kun-Don, the Holy One," *American Theosophist* (Fall 1984), p.380.

[377] Brochure from Wisdom Publications, Inc.

[378] Wilbert Forker, Editor, *The Templeton Foundation Prize for Progress in Religion* (Edinburgh, Scotland: Scottish Academic Press, 1988), p.222. See also: "Sisters of St. Joseph Host Buddhist Ceremony," *The Omega-Letter* (May 1990, Vol. 5, No. 5), p.8; *Harmonia Mundi*, p.14; Alex Jack, "Glimpses of an Unseen Friend," *Macromuse* (Summer/Fire 1985, Issue 20), p.17.

[379] Texe Marrs, *Texe Marrs Book of New Age Cults and Religions* (Austin, TX: Living Truth Publishers, 1990), p.176; Hunt and McMahon, *The Seduction of Christianity, op. cit.*, p.183; Stapleton, *op. cit.*, p.140.

[380] "Buddhist Occultism," *Calvary Contender* (July 1, 2001, Vol. 18, No. 13), p.1.

[381] "Intentional Communities: Seeds for a New Civilization," *The Christian Conscience, op. cit.*, p.34.

[382] Letter from Planetary Initiative for the World We Choose; *Now Is the Dawning of the New Age New World Order, op. cit.*, p.267; Marrs, *Dark Majesty, op. cit.*, p.137.

[383] "Pope Calls Increased Dialogue Among World Religions a 'Sign of Hope' at End of Century," *Foundation* (November-December 1999), p.47.

[384] "Second Hollister Awards Ceremony," *op. cit.*, p.1, 2; Letter from The Temple of Understanding dated November 1997, p.2; James W. Wardner, *Unholy Alliances* (n.p., 1996), p.170; Alan Morrison, *The Serpent and the Cross: Religious Corruption in an Evil Age* (Birmingham, England: K & M Books, 1994), p.537; Hunt, *Global Peace and the Rise of Antichrist, op. cit.*, p.129; David R. Barnhart, *Contending for the Faith* (Eagan, MN: Abiding Word Publications, 1994), p.120; *Now Is the Dawning of the New Age New World Order, op. cit.*, p.143; Lamb, *op. cit.*, p.3.

[385] Dager, "The World Christian Movement—Part 3." *op. cit.*, p.15.

[386] *Ibid.*, p.13-14.

[387] William Swing, "Reactions from Religious Leaders: United Religions International Tour," *Christian News* (May 5, 1997, Vol. 35, No. 18), p.6.

[388] Marcus Braybrooke, *A Wider Vision: A History of the World Congress of Faiths* (Oxford, England: Oneworld Publications, 1996), p.172.

[389] Swing, *op. cit.*, p.6; Speech by William E. Swing at the North American Interfaith Network Conference (August 10, 1996).

[390] "Well Hello, Dalai," *Endtime* (September/October 1999), p.28.

[391] "The Very Reverend James Parks Morton Introducing His Holiness the Dalai Lama," quoting from the Dalai Lama's speech "A Human Approach to World Peace," *Temple of Understanding Newsletter* (Fall 1998), p.3.

[392] *Temple of Understanding Newsletter* (Fall 1998), p.3.

[393] "Dalai Lama Disappoints India's Christians," *Mission Frontiers* (March 2001, Vol. 23, No. 1), p.43.

[394] *Ibid.*

[395] "Gratitude: The Adamant of Existence," *World Goodwill* (2000, No. 4), p.6.

[396] "Texe Marrs Asks Chuck Colson: 'Will You Sell Your Soul to the Devil for a Million Dollars?,'" *Flashpoint* (June 1993), p.1; Albert James Dager, "Parliament of the World's Religions to Meet: Chuck Colson Receives Templeton Prize," *Media Spotlight* (Vol. 15, No. 1), p.1; Ernst-Ulrich Franzen, "Golden Rule Called Universal: World Religious Parliament Readers 'Global Ethic' Declaration," *Milwaukee Sentinel* (September 4, 1993); Patricia Rice, "Parliament of Religions in South Africa Pushes Peace," *Christian News* (February 14, 2000, Vol. 38, No. 7), p.3.

[397] Paper from Thanksgiving Square; *Watch Unto Prayer* (Spring 1998), p.6.

[398] *World Goodwill Newsletter* (1988, No. 3), p.1.

[399] Texe Marrs, "New Agers Meet to Plan World Takeover," *Flashpoint* (January 1990), p.1. See also: William T. James, Editor, *Foreshocks of Antichrist* (Eugene, OR: Harvest House Publishers, 1997), p.110; Wilson Ewin, *Under the New World Order: Evangelicals, Catholics and Israel: Conspiracy of the Ages* (Compton, Quebec: Quebec Baptist Missions, n.d.), p.103; David W. Cloud, "The Day of Prayer for World Peace," *O Timothy* (1994, Vol. 11, Issue 3).

[400] Swing, *op. cit.*, p.6; Berit Kjos, "From the UNITED NATIONS to the UNITED RELIGIONS" (Received March 20, 1996).

[401] *Last Trumpet Newsletter* (October 1997, Vol. 16, Issue 10), p.2. See also: Envelope from the United Religions Initiative (Received December 21, 1999); Wendy B. Howard, *The Alpha Course: Friend or Foe?* (Landsborough, Queensland: Endtime Ministries, 1999), p.30; "'United Religions' Like 'United Nations,'" *Calvary Contender* (April 1, 1996, Vol. 13, No. 7), p.1.

[402] Envelope from the United Religions Initiative (Received December 21, 1999).

[403] *Last Trumpet Newsletter* (September 1999, Vol. 18, Issue 9), p.2.

[404] Speech by William E. Swing at the North American Interfaith Network Conference (August 10, 1996).

[405] David B. Reagan, "The Apostate One World Religion," *Voice in the Wilderness* (August 2001), p.3, 14.

[406] *Last Trumpet Newsletter* (October 1997, Vol. 16, Issue 10), p.2; Virginia Meves, "Now the Question! How Is It in Your Church? Does the Light of Christ Shine or.....?," *Wisconsin Report* (November 28, 1996, Vol. 21, No. 46), p.3; Shirley Correll, "Who Are the Gods of the New World Order and What Is a Spiritual U. N.?" (Part IV), *The Florida Forum* (Spring 2001), p.15; *Ibid.*, p.14; Wendy B. Howard, *The Alpha Course: Friend or Foe?* (Landsborough, Queensland: Endtime Ministries, 1999), p.30; *Secret Records Revealed: The Men, the Money and the Methods Behind the New World Order* (Oklahoma City, OK: Hearthstone Publishing, Ltd., 1999), p.168; "The Disarmament of America," *The Florida Forum* (Spring 1996), p.1; *Last Trumpet Newsletter* (September 1999, Vol. 18, Issue 9), p.2; *The McAlvany Intelligence Advisor* (March 1995), p.13; John F. McManus, "Still Traveling the Red Road," *The New American* (December 13, 1993, Vol. 9, No. 25), p.21; Hunt, "Nature or Personal Creator?," *op. cit.*, p.1; Richard Scheinin, "Bringing Together the 'United Religions,'" *San Jose Mercury News* (February 6, 1996), p.11B; *Last Trumpet Newsletter* (August 1999, Vol. 18, Issue 8), p.2; Cornelia R. Ferreira, "One-World Church Starts Up United Religions on Track—with Modifications," *Wisconsin Report* (November 6, 1997, Vol. 22, No. 43), p.1; Richard Scheinin, "United Faiths: Call Arises for Spiritual U.N. to Cooperate in the Names of God," *San Jose Mercury News* (June 17, 1995), p.1E; "Utopian Dreams: The Early Futurists and Their Influence Today," *Christian Conscience* (February 1996, Vol. 2, No. 2), p.9; "United Religions Initiative 2000," *Calvary Contender* (September 1, 1997), p.1; Edward Epstein, "Gorbachev to Convene MTG in S.F.—Invitees—Bush, Thatcher, Tutu," *Wisconsin Report* (September 21, 1995, Vol. 20, No. 36), p.1; Berit Kjos, "From the UNITED NATIONS to the UNITED RELIGIONS"; Don Lattin, "Religions of World Celebrate with Prayers to Dozen Deities," *San Francisco Chronicle* (June 26, 1995), p.A1; "Gorbachev's International Green Cross," *The McAlvany Intelligence Advisor* (March 1995), p.13; Samantha Smith, "What Is the New Age and How Is It Affecting Us?," *The Prophecy Club Newsletter* (April 1995), p.3; Berit Kjos, "Gorbachev's New Global Pulpit," *The Christian World Report* (July 1993, Vol. 8, No. 5), p.2; Ferreira, "One-World Church Expected Next Year," *op. cit.*, p.1; Don Lattin, "Bishop Pushes Presidio Interfaith Group," *San Francisco Chronicle* (January 23, 1996); *Mindszenty Report* (March 1996, Vol. 37, No. 3), p.3; "The Disarmament of America," *The Florida Forum* (Spring 1996), p.21.

[407] *Last Trumpet Newsletter* (October 1997, Vol. 16, Issue 10), p.2. See also: *Last Trumpet Newsletter* (September 1999, Vol. 18, Issue 9), p.2.

[408] Berit Kjos, "'The State of the World' According to Gorbachev," *Christian News* (October 28, 1996, Vol. 34, No. 40), p.17; *The McAlvany Intelligence Advisor* (March 1995), p.13; Samantha Smith, "Gorby's Disappearing Act," *Hope for the World* (Spring 1998), p.4.

[409] Samantha Smith, "Gorby's Disappearing Act," *Hope for the World* (Spring 1998), p.4; *The McAlvany Intelligence Advisor* (March 1995), p.13.

[410] *The McAlvany Intelligence Advisor* (March 1995), p.13.

[411] "Ruling Elite Working Toward World Govt.," *The Daily Record* (October 17, 1995), p.4. See also: *Secret Records Revealed: The Men, the Money and the Methods Behind the New World Order* (Oklahoma City, OK: Hearthstone Publishing, Ltd., 1999), p.168.

[412] David R. Barnhart, *Contending for the Faith* (Eagan, MN: Abiding Word Publications, 1994), p.115. See also: Marrs, *Texe Marrs Book of New Age Cults and Religions, op. cit.*, p.174, 175.

[413] "Second Hollister Awards Ceremony," *op. cit.*, p.1.

[414] Carol Houst, "Synthesis of the Signs," *Thoughtline* (November 2000), p.3-4.

[415] Joseph Fort Newton, *River of Years: An Autobiography* (Philadelphia, PA: J. B. Lippincott Company, 1946), p.330.

[416] Nancy Wilson, *The Ecumenical Ministry and Witness of Metropolitan Community Churches* (Los Angeles, CA: Universal Fellowship of Metropolitan Community Churches, March 1987 Revision), p.1; *Universal Fellowship Today* (Los Angeles, CA: Universal Fellowship of Metropolitan Community Churches, 1984), p.2; "Two Same-Sex Couples Legally Tie Knot," *Calvary Contender* (February 15, 2001, Vol. 18, No. 4), p.1; "The Church That AIDS Built?," *The Christian World Report* (June 1989, Vol. 1, No. 4), p.22; *Universal Fellowship Today* (Los Angeles, CA: Universal Fellowship Press, n.d.), p.2.; "Outgoing NAE Chief Says NCC Policy Change a Factor in Resignation," *Calvary Contender* (August 15, 2001, Vol. 18, No. 16), p.2; Sherre L. Boothman, "Being Lesbian, Feminist Christian and a Survivor of Childhood Abuse: A Christian Clergywoman Finds Her Voice," *CLOUTReach* (Spring 1994, Vol. 3, No. 1), p.1; "NCC Greets Homosexual Church Leader," *Calvary Contender* (February 15, 1999, Vol. 16, No. 4), p.1; Mari Jo Buhle, Paul Buhle, and Dan Georgakas, Editors, *Encyclopedia of the American Left* (New York, NY: Oxford University Press, 1998, Second Edition), p.260; E. L. Bynum, "The Bible and the Homosexual," *O Timothy* (1989, Vol. 6, Issue 7); Scott Malcolmson, "Sex and Death in Key West," *Mother Jones* (February/March 198, Vol. 13, No. 2), p.36; Jim Seale, "The Gay Reformation," *New Age Journal* (March 1985), p.62; "Campbell Prays with UFMCC 'for Healing,'" *op. cit.*, p.6; "Ed Dobson and Homosexuals," *Calvary Contender* (September 15, 1997, Vol. 14, No. 18), p.2; "United Church of Christ Leader Calls Sodomite Parade a 'Marvelous Moment'", *O Timothy* (1993, Vol. 10, Issue 6); *The Evangelical Methodist* (2000, Vol. 78, No. 2), p.6; William R. Wineke, "Gay Clergyman Decries 'Urge to Purge,'" *Christian News* (April 21, 1997, Vol. 35, No. 16), p.11; "National Council of Churches Head Supports Homosexuals", *O Timothy* (1994, Vol. 11, Issue 11); Barnhart, *op. cit.*, p.81; "Schuller Trains Homosexual Pastors?" *Calvary Contender* (June 15, 1997, Vol. 14, No. 12), p.1; Claire Martin, "Food for Thought," *Denver Post* (March 1996), p.2E; *Foundation* (January-February 2000, Vol. 21, Issue 1), p.42; "ACLU Award to Mel White," *Calvary Contender* (February 15, 1998, Vol. 15, No. 4), p.1; "Ford Foundation Gives Gay-Oriented Denomination $100,000 Grant," *Christian News* (October 26, 1998, Vol. 36, No. 39), p.17; "Homosexual Heads Hawaii Council of Churches," *O Timothy* (1994, Vol. 12, Issue 1); *Calvary Contender* (July 1, 1994, Vol. 11, No. 13), p.1; "Readers' Response," *The Christian Century* (February 3-10, 1988), p.138; Deborah Kovach Caldwell, "Issues in FAST FORWARD: A Look into the '96 Spiritual Scene," *Dallas Morning News* (December 30, 1995), p.3G; Kittredge Cherry and James Mitulski, "We Are the Church Alive, the Church with AIDS," *The Christian Century* (January 27, 1988, Vol. 105, No. 3), p.85-88; Paper from Sacred Space X (Received January 27, 1997); "Virginia Mollenkott," *Christian News* (November 25, 1996, Vol. 34, No. 44), p.6; Adams, "'I Want to Apologize,'" *op. cit.*, p.6; "Five Tips for Social Action," *Freedom Writer Magazine* (March 1996, Vol. 13, No. 2), p.11; "Homosexual Churches Increase," *The Shepherd's Letter* (Spring 1993), p.9; "Virginia Mollenkott," *Christian*

News (February 17, 1997, Vol. 35, No. 7), p.23; John S. Torell, "Betrayal," *The Dove* (Autumn/Winter 1995, Vol. 16, No. 3), p.24; *The Evangelical Methodist* (May 1998, Vol. 77, No. 5), p.3; John H. Adams, "NCC Leader's Strange Tack," *The Presbyterian Layman* (January/February 2001, Vol. 34, No. 1), p.22; Nancy Leigh DeMoss, Executive Editor, *The Rebirth of America* (Arthur S. DeMoss Foundation, 1986), p.106; *The National and International Religion Report* (April 25, 1988, Vol. 2, No. 8), p.1; David W. Cloud, "Two Homosexuals and the New International Version," *O Timothy* (1997); Ben Irwin, *The Bible and Homosexuality: Confronting the Challenge to Scriptural Authority* (Washington, DC: Family Research Council, n.d.), p.2.

[417] Ben Irwin, *The Bible and Homosexuality: Confronting the Challenge to Scriptural Authority* (Washington, DC: Family Research Council, n.d.), p.2.

[418] Jim Seale, "The Gay Reformation," *New Age Journal* (March 1985), p.61-62.

[419] *Ibid.*, p.62-63.

[420] "The Church That AIDS Built?," *The Christian World Report* (June 1989, Vol. 1, No. 4), p.22, quoting from the *San Francisco Chronicle,* dated February 27, 1989.

[421] *Ibid.*

[422] Wilson, *The Ecumenical Ministry, op. cit.*, p.2.

[423] *Ibid.*

[424] "Campbell Prays with UFMCC 'for Healing,'" *op. cit.*, p.6.

[425] *Ibid.*

[426] "National Council of Churches Head Supports Homosexuals," *O Timothy* (1994, Vol. 11, Issue 11).

[427] Campbell Prays with UFMCC 'for Healing,'" *op. cit.*, p.6.

[428] "Catholics Urged to Hear Billy Graham," *O Timothy* (1991, Vol. 8, Issue 8-9).

[429] Ashbrook, "Billy Graham—The Mouthpiece of New Evangelicalism," *op. cit.*

[430] "Catholics Urged to Hear Billy Graham," *op. cit.* See also: Darrell Turner, "Graham Happy to Fellowship at the NCC's Interchurch Center," *Christian News* (September 9, 1991, Vol. 29, No. 32), p.23.

[431] James W. Wardner, *Unholy Alliances* (n.p., 1996), p.136; Wardner, "Billy Graham, Freemasonry & the Communists," *op. cit.*, p.28.

[432] "Billy Graham Gave the Apostate National Council of Churches the Greatest Boost It Has Had in Many Years," *Foundation* (June-August 1991), p.34; Rick Miesel, "Billy Graham: General Teachings/Activities" (Biblical Discernment Ministries, Revised January 1994).

[433] *Ibid.*

[434] John S. Torell, "Betrayal," *The Dove* (Autumn/Winter 1995, Vol. 16, No. 3), p.24.

[435] *Ibid.*, quoting from *The Sacramento Bee.*

[436] *Ibid.*, p.25.

[437] *Just Out* (August 1992, Vol. 9, No. 10), p.2.

[438] "A Powerful (and Surprising) Ally Is Coming to Oregon," *Just Out* (August 1992, Vol. 9, No. 10), p.1-2.

[439] Wilson Ewin, *The Assimilation of Evangelist Billy Graham into the Roman Catholic Church* (n.p., 1992), p.19.

[440] *Ibid.* See also: "Graham Sidesteps Measure 9," *The Oregonian* (September 22, 1992).

[441] *Ibid.* See also: Rick Miesel, "Billy Graham: General Teachings/Activities" (Biblical Discernment Ministries, Revised January 1994); "Graham Sidesteps Measure 9," *The Oregonian* (September 22, 1992).

[442] "Graham Ignores Abortion and Sodomy," *Christian View of the News* (October 10, 1994, Vol. 19, No. 19). See also: "Apostate Graham Ignores Abortion and Sodomy," *The Perilous Times* (November 1994, Vol. 16, No. 9), p.6; "Billy Graham Is a Great Deceiv-er," *Flashpoint* (May 1998, Vol. 98-5), p.1; Bundy, *Billy Graham: Performer?, Politician?, Preacher?, Prophet?, op. cit.*, p.93.

[443] "'Fundamentalist' Bible College for Homosexuals," *Christian News* (July 26, 1999), p.8. See also: *Christian News* (December 26, 1994, Vol. 32, No. 48), p.2; "Billy Graham Says 'Save the Earth, Not Babies!,'" *Flashpoint* (August 1995), p.2; *Christian News* (December 26, 1994, Vol. 32, No. 48), p.2.

[444] *American Family Association Journal* quoting from the February 15-21, 1987 issue of *Gay Community News.* See also: Scott Lively and Kevin Abrams, *The Pink Swastika* (Keizer, OR: Founders Publishing Corporation, 1995), p.194-199.

[445] "Billy Graham Is a Great Deceiver," *Flashpoint* (May 1998, Vol. 98-5), p.1.

[446] *Ibid.*

[447] *Ibid.* See also: Bundy, *Billy Graham: Performer?, Politician?, Preacher?, Prophet?, op. cit.*, p.93.

[448] Scott Lively and Kevin Abrams, *The Pink Swastika* (Keizer, OR: Founders Publishing Corporation, 1995), p.197.

[449] Texe Marrs, "The Scandal of Christian Ghostwriting," *Flashpoint* (July 1996, Vol. 96-7), p.1; "Sodomite at the Gate," *Pointy Hat News* (May/June 1994), p.3; "Five Tips for Social Action," *Freedom Writer Magazine* (March 1996, Vol. 13, No. 2), p.11; Lynn Rosellini, "An Unlikely Friendship, a Historic Meeting: Jerry Falwell and Mel White Join Forces," *U.S. News & World Report* (November 1, 1999), p.68; "Gay Mel White Wrote Books with

Evangelicals," *Calvary Contender* (August 15, 1993, Vol. 10, No. 16), p.2; "'I Am A Homosexual,'" *Christian News* (July 26, 1993, Vol. 31, No. 30), p.18; "Gay Clergyman Receives a ACLU National Civil Liberties Award," *Christian News* (January 19, 1998, Vol. 36, No. 3), p.3.

[450] Lynn Rosellini, "An Unlikely Friendship, a Historic Meeting: Jerry Falwell and Mel White Join Forces," *U. S. News & World Report* (November 1, 1999), p.68.

[451] Marrs, "The Scandal of Christian Ghostwriting," *op. cit.*, p.1; Billy Graham, *Approaching Hoofbeats: The Four Horsemen of the Apocalypse* (Minneapolis, MN: Grason, 1983), p.11; *Ibid.;* "Five Tips for Social Action," *Freedom Writer Magazine* (March 1996, Vol. 13, No. 2), p.11; "Sodomite at the Gate," *Pointy Hat News* (May/June 1994), p.3; "Gay Mel White Wrote Books with Evangelicals," *Calvary Contender* (August 15, 1993, Vol. 10, No. 16), p.2; "'I Am A Homosexual,'" *Christian News* (July 26, 1993, Vol. 31, No. 30), p.18.

[452] "Five Tips for Social Action," *Freedom Writer Magazine* (March 1996, Vol. 13, No. 2), p.11.

[453] Marrs, "The Scandal of Christian Ghostwriting," *op. cit.*, p.1; *Ibid.;* "ACLU Award to Mel White," *Calvary Contender* (February 15, 1998, Vol. 15, No. 4), p.1; "Sodomite at the Gate," *Pointy Hat News* (May/June 1994), p.3; "Gay Mel White Wrote Books with Evangelicals," *Calvary Contender* (August 15, 1993, Vol. 10, No. 16), p.2; Rosellini, *op. cit.*, p.68; "'I Am A Homosexual,'" *Christian News* (July 26, 1993, Vol. 31, No. 30), p.18; "Gay Clergyman Receives a ACLU National Civil Liberties Award," *Christian News* (January 19, 1998, Vol. 36, No. 3), p.3.

[454] *Ibid.*, p.1, 2; "Sodomite at the Gate," *Pointy Hat News* (May/June 1994), p.3; "Gay Mel White Wrote Books with Evangelicals," *Calvary Contender* (August 15, 1993, Vol. 10, No. 16), p.2; "Five Tips for Social Action," *op. cit.*, p.11.

[455] "Gay Mel White Wrote Books with Evangelicals," *Calvary Contender* (August 15, 1993, Vol. 10, No. 16), p.2; "ACLU Award to Mel White," *Calvary Contender* (February 15, 1998, Vol. 15, No. 4), p.1; "'I Am A Homosexual,'" *Christian News* (July 26, 1993, Vol. 31, No. 30), p.18.

[456] *Ibid.;* "ACLU Award to Mel White," *Calvary Contender* (February 15, 1998, Vol. 15, No. 4), p.1. See also: "Pro-Homosexual New Evangelicals?," *Calvary Contender* (August 15, 1998, Vol. 15, No. 16), p.1; "'I Am A Homosexual,'" *Christian News* (July 26, 1993, Vol. 31, No. 30), p.18.

[457] "Five Tips for Social Action," *op. cit.*, p.11; "ACLU Award to Mel White," *Calvary Contender* (February 15, 1998, Vol. 15, No. 4), p.1; *Ibid.;* William R. Wineke, "Gay Clergyman Decries 'Urge to Purge,'" *Christian News* (April 21, 1997, Vol. 35, No. 16), p.11. See also: "PFLAG Supports Reverend Mel White in Bearing Witness," *PFLAGpole* (Spring 1995), p.4; Adelle M. Banks and Ira Rifkin, "With a Nation's Prayers, Clinton's Inaugural Sounds Reconciling Note," *Christian News* (January 27, 1997, Vol. 35, No. 4), p.7; "'I Am A Homosexual,'" *Christian News* (July 26, 1993, Vol. 31, No. 30), p.18 (caption under picture).

[458] Marrs, "The Scandal of Christian Ghostwriting," *op. cit.*, p.1.

[459] Personal conversation on November 20, 1998.

[460] "Sodomite at the Gate," *Pointy Hat News* (May/June 1994), p.3.

[461] *The Evangelical Methodist* (2000, Vol. 78, No. 2), p.6.

[462] "Interfaith Vigil Against Hate Violence Is Oct. 7," *Haverford Press* (September 15, 1999), p.17.

[463] "Gay Mel White Wrote Books with Evangelicals," *op. cit.*, p.2; "Gay Clergyman Receives a ACLU National Civil Liberties Award," *Christian News* (January 19, 1998, Vol. 36, No. 3), p.3.

[464] William R. Wineke, "Gay Clergyman Decries 'Urge to Purge,'" *Christian News* (April 21, 1997, Vol. 35, No. 16), p.11.

[465] *Ibid.*

[466] "Helpful Books for Your Counseling Ministry," *Return to the Word* (Winter 1997, Vol. 3, No. 1), p.7.

7. QUOTABLE QUOTES AND OTHER NOTES

[1] "Billy Graham," *The BDM Letter* (November 1993, Vol. 2, No. 9), p.2; "Billy Graham Says 'Pagans Saved Through Nature,'" *Flashpoint* (August 1995), p.1; John Ashbrook, "Billy Graham—The Mouthpiece of New Evangelicalism," *O Timothy* (1993, Vol. 10, Issue 1); Rick Miesel, "Billy Graham: General Teachings/Activities" (Biblical Discernment Ministries, Revised January 1994); Edgar C. Bundy, *Billy Graham: Performer?, Politician?, Preacher?, Prophet?* (Wheaton, IL: Church League of America, 1982), p.119; J. W. Wardner, "Billy Graham, Freemasonry & the Communists," *Despatch Magazine* (September 1998, Vol. 10, No. 3), p.28; John E. Ashbrook, *New Neutralism II: Exposing the Gray of Compromise* (Mentor, OH: Here I Stand Books, 1992), p.29.

[2] William Martin, *A Prophet with Honor: The Billy Graham Story* (NY: William Morrow and Company, Inc., 1991), p.13.

[3] *Ibid.*, p.576.

[4] David W. Cloud, "Billy Graham's Disobedience to the Word of God," *O Timothy;* "'Evangelicals' Disbelieve in Hell," *Calvary Contender* (December 15, 1993), p.2; D. W. Cloud, "Some Frightening Facts About Billy Graham," *O Timothy* (1984, Vol. 1, Issue 4); "Graham, Women Preachers, Hell," *Calvary Contender* (June 15, 1997, Vol. 14, No. 12). See also: E. L. Bynum, "Pope Says No Fire in Hell So Does Billy Graham," *The Evangelical Methodist* (September 2000, Vol. 78, No. 5), p.4; "Pope Says Hell Is Self-Inflicted," *Calvary Contender* (September 1, 1999, Vol. 16, No. 17), p.2; Rick Miesel, "Billy Graham: General Teachings/Activities" (Biblical Discernment Ministries, Revised January 1994); *Power of Prophecy* (February 2001, Vol. 2001-02), p.4; "Six Mistakes of Man," *The Evangelical Methodist* (December 1993, Vol. 72, No. 10), p.3; David W. Cloud, "Billy Graham's Disobedience," *O Timothy* (1995, Vol. 12, Issue 11); "Religious Changes of Dr. Billy Graham," *A Christian View of the News* (December 25, 1993, Vol. 18, No. 24), p.1.

[5] David W. Cloud quoting from Billy Graham's book in "Billy Graham's Disobedience," *O Timothy* (1995, Vol. 12, Issue 11). See also: Billy Graham, *Approaching Hoofbeats: The Four Horsemen of the Apocalypse* (Minneapolis, MN: Grason, 1983), p.202.

[6] "Graham Doesn't Preach Hell Fire Is Literal," quoting from *Time* in *Plains Baptist Challenger* (June 1994), p.7; "Graham Doesn't Preach Hell Fire Is Literal," *Calvary Contender* (January 1, 1994, Vol. 11, No. 1), p.2; Rick Miesel, "Billy Graham: General Teachings/Activities" (Biblical Discernment Ministries, Revised January 1994); William P. Grady, *Final Authority: A Christian's Guide to the King James Bible* (Knoxville, TN: Grady Publications, Inc., 1993), p.185.

[7] *The Berean Call* (February 1999), p.3. See also: "Billy Graham Says 'Pagans Saved Through Nature,'" *Flashpoint* (August 1995), p.1.

[8] "In Perils of Dr. Billy Graham, the WCC & NCC and Evangelicals and Roman Catholics Together," *The Perilous Times* (June 2000, Vol. 22, No. 4), p.4.

[9] "God? Or Just Good Business?," *The Nosh Box* (April 2001, Vol. 6, Issue 4), p.3.

[10] "The 'Born Again' Jesus Deception," *The End Times and Victorious Living* (March/April 2001, Vol. 15, No. 2), p.3.

[11] Rick Miesel, "Billy Graham: General Teachings/Activities" (Biblical Discernment Ministries, Revised January 1994).

[12] "God? Or Just Good Business?," *op. cit.*

[13] *The Berean Call* (April 2001), p.5.

[14] David W. Cloud, "Billy Graham's Disobedience to the Word of God," (Updated March 2, 1999), p.8.

[15] *The Lutheran Standard* (October 10, 1961), p.13-15. Quotation verified by Rev. Wendell Anderson, Billy Graham Evangelistic Association, 9/19/91. See also: "For Adults Only?" *Time* (October 27, 1961); Wilson Ewin, *The Assimilation of Evangelist Billy Graham into the Roman Catholic Church* (Compton, Quebec: Quebec Baptist Missions, 1992), p.11-12; David W. Cloud, "Billy Graham's Disobedience to the Word of God"; Rick Miesel, "Billy Graham: General Teachings/Activities" (Biblical Discernment Ministries, Revised January 1994); Cloud, David W. *Flirting with Rome: Evangelical Entanglement with Roman Catholicism (Volume 1—Billy Graham)* (Oak Harbor, WA: Way of Life Literature, 1993); David W. Cloud, "Billy Graham's Disobedience," *O Timothy* (1995, Vol. 12, Issue 11).

[16] *The Berean Call* (February 1999); *The Berean Call* (August 1998).

[17] *The Berean Call* (August 1998).

[18] Edgar C. Bundy, *Billy Graham: Performer?, Politician?, Preacher?, Prophet?* quoting from *Christian Times* (Wheaton, IL: Church League of America, 1982), p.65.

[19] Jose Martinez, "Leary's Legacy Murky But Memorable at Harvard," *Christian News* (June 10, 1996), Vol. 34, No. 24), p.8; *Fields Within Fields...Within Fields* (1970, Vol. 3, No. 1), p.28; Randall N. Baer, *Inside the New Age Nightmare* (Lafayette, LA: Huntington House, Inc., 1989), p.7.

[20] Patti Lalonde, "From Psychedelics to Hi-Tech: Virtual Reality: The LSD of the 90's?," *The Omega-Letter* (November 1991, Vol. 6, No. 10), p.5.

[21] Bundy quoting from the October 5, 1971 issue of *Chicago Daily News* in *Billy Graham: Performer?, Politician?, Preacher?, Prophet?, op. cit.*, p.77.

[22] "Billy Graham Backs Off Support of Teen Hotline," *The News & Observer* (August 13, 1993), p.3A.

[23] *Ibid.*

[24] *Ibid.*

[25] *Ibid.*

[26] *The Berean Call* (April 2001), p.5.

[27] Rick Miesel, "Promise Keepers: Ecumenical 'Macho-Men' for Christ?" (Biblical Discernment Ministries, Revised March 1996); Albert James Dager, "Promise Keepers: Is What You See What You Get?" *Media Spotlight* (Received November 10, 1994), p.6; "Promise Keepers and Psychoheresy," *Psychoheresy Awareness Letter* (July/August 1994, Vol. 2, No. 4), p.6.

[28] Lee Grady, "The Last Temptation of Christ: Historical Fiction or Blasphemous Hatred?," *Bridgebuilder* (November/December 1988), p.27.

[29] *Ibid.*

[30] *The American Heritage Dictionary* (Third Edition, Version 3.6a) (SoftKey International, 1994).

[31] Lawrence Meredith, "The Gospel According to Kazantzakis: How Close Did Scorsese Come?," *The Christian Century* (September 14-21, 1988), p.799.

[32] *Ibid.*, p.802.

[33] Texe Marrs, "The Billy Graham Dilemma," *Flashpoint* (March 1992), p.3.

[34] James W. Wardner, *Unholy Alliances* (n.p., 1996), p.125; J. W. Wardner, "Unholy Alliances—The Order—The Illuminati Pedigree," *Despatch* (September 1998, Vol. 10, No. 3), p.29; Martin, *op. cit.*, caption under picture between p.480 and 481; William P. Grady, *Final Authority: A Christian's Guide to the King James Bible* (Knoxville, TN: Grady Publications, Inc., 1993), p.185.

[35] John Ashbrook quoting from *News-Herald* in "Billy Graham—The Mouthpiece of New Evangelicalism," *O Timothy* (1993, Vol. 10, Issue 1); John E. Ashbrook, *New Neutralism II: Exposing the Gray of Compromise* (Mentor, OH: Here I Stand Books, 1992), p.31-32.

[36] *Ibid.*

[37] *Ibid.*

[38] John D. Christian, *Gladiator: A Masterpiece of Nazi Propaganda* (New Zealand, Underground Press, 2000), p.20. See also: Texe Marrs, *Power of Prophecy* (July 28, 2001 program).

[39] "Star Tracks," *People* (March 23, 1998), p.10.

[40] Bundy, *Billy Graham: Performer?, Politician?, Preacher?, Prophet?, op. cit.*, p.51, 64.

[41] "Missing the Real Message of Moses," *Christian News* (December 14, 1998, Vol. 36, No. 46), p.6. See also: "'Prince of Egypt' Receiving Rave Reviews," *Christian News* (December 28, 1998, Vol. 36, No. 48), p.5.

[42] *Ibid.* See also: Steve Rabey, "Prince-ly Promotions: Animated Moses Film Yields a Flood of Products," *Christian News* (December 14, 1998, Vol. 36, No. 46), p.6; "'Prince of Egypt' Receiving Rave Reviews," *Christian News* (December 28, 1998, Vol. 36, No. 48), p.5.

[43] *Ibid.* See also: "The Prince of Egypt Movie," *The Perilous Times* (February 1999, Vol. 20, No. 12), p.8; Tom Neven, "Hollywood Gets One Right," *Focus on the Family* (December 1998, Vol. 22, No. 12), p.12; "'Prince of Egypt' Receiving Rave Reviews," *Christian News* (December 28, 1998, Vol. 36, No. 48), p.5.

[44] Steve Rabey, "Prince-ly Promotions: Animated Moses Film Yields a Flood of Products," *Christian News* (December 14, 1998, Vol. 36, No. 46), p.6; Tom Neven, "Hollywood Gets One Right," *Focus on the Family* (December 1998, Vol. 22, No. 12), p.12; "The Prince of Egypt Movie," *The Perilous Times* (February 1999, Vol. 20, No. 12), p.8.

[45] "Missing the Real Message of Moses," *op. cit.*

[46] "'Prince of Egypt' Receiving Rave Reviews," *Christian News* (December 28, 1998, Vol. 36, No. 48), p.5.

[47] Berit Kjos, "The Prince of Egypt," *Christian News* (January 4, 1999, Vol. 37, No. 1), p.21; *Ibid.;* Tom Neven, "Hollywood Gets One Right," *Focus on the Family* (December 1998, Vol. 22, No. 12), p.12; "The Prince of Egypt Movie," *The Perilous Times* (February 1999, Vol. 20, No. 12), p.8.

[48] See: "'Prince of Egypt' Receiving Rave Reviews," *op. cit.;* "The Exodus 13th or 15th Century B.C.," *Christian News* (January 4, 1999, Vol. 37, No. 1), p.23.

[49] Paige Patterson, "Prince of Egypt Worthy of Evangelical 'Greenbacks,'" *Christian News* (February 8, 1999, Vol. 37, No. 6), p.11; Tom Neven, "Hollywood Gets One Right," *Focus on the Family* (December 1998, Vol. 22, No. 12), p.12; Kjos, "The Prince of Egypt," *op. cit.*, p.22.

[50] Kjos, "The Prince of Egypt," *op. cit.*, p.22.

[51] "The Prince of Egypt Movie," *The Perilous Times* (February 1999, Vol. 20, No. 12), p.8; "Movies," *Media Spotlight* (1998, Vol. 21, No. 4), p.15.

[52] Kjos, "The Prince of Egypt," *op. cit.*, p.22.

[53] "Movies," *Media Spotlight* (1998, Vol. 21, No. 4), p.15.

[54] *Ibid.* See also: Patterson, *op. cit.*

[55] Kjos, "The Prince of Egypt," *op. cit.*, p.22.

[56] Texe Marrs, *Power of Prophecy* (July 28, 2001 program).

[57] "The Prince of Egypt," *Christian News* (January 4, 1999, Vol. 37, No. 1), p.21.

[58] John Pollock, *Crusades: 20 Years with Billy Graham* (Minneapolis, MN: World Wide Publications, 1969), p.243.

[59] *Ibid.*, p.243-244.

[60] Billy Graham, *Just As I Am: The Autobiography of Billy Graham* (Harpers Collins Worldwide, 1997), p.334.

[61] Jay Klopfenstein, "Can Buying a Bible Contribute to Pornography and Licentiousness,?" *Christian News* (December 20, 1993, Vol. 31, No. 47), p.20. See also: "NIV Owner Big Pornography Publisher," *O Timothy* (1994, Vol. 11, Issue 6); Texe Marrs, *Millennium: Peace, Promises, and the Day They Take Our Money Away* (Austin, TX: Living Truth Publishers, 1990), p.170; "Jesus Junk (Another Jesus)," *The Perilous Times* (January 1996, Vol. 17, No. 11), p.6; Gail Riplinger, *Which Bible Is God's Word?: Answers to Common Questions Concerning Modern Versions and Translations* (Oklahoma City, OK: Hearthstone Publishing, Ltd., 1994), p.19.

[62] "Freedom Writer Index," *Freedom Writer* (July/August 1997, Vol. 14, No. 4), p.13; "NewsNotes," *Calvary Contender* (August 1, 1997, Vol. 14, No. 15), p.2.

[63] *CIB Bulletin* (May 1990, Vol. 6, No. 5), p.2; Texe Marrs, "Global Explosion of Religious Apostasy," *Flashpoint* (July 1998, Vol. 98-7), p.1; Dave Hunt, "Religious Unity and the New World Order," *The Omega-Letter* (July 1990, Vol. 5, No. 6), p.16.

[64] Texe Marrs, "Global Explosion of Religious Apostasy," *Flashpoint* (July 1998, Vol. 98-7), p.1.

[65] "Media Controlled by the Few," *Flashpoint* (March 1998, Vol. 98-3), p.3.

[66] Klopfenstein, *op. cit.;* "People in the News," *U. S. News & World Report* (June 7, 1999), p.14; Greg Butterfield, "Who Are the Rich Behind Gingrich, Inc.?"; "NIV Owner Big Pornography Publisher," *O Timothy* (1994, Vol. 11, Issue 6); Gail Riplinger, *The Language of the King James Bible: Discover Its Hidden Built-in Dictionary* (Ararat, VA: A. V. Publications Corp., 1998), p.128; Texe Marrs, *Circle of Intrigue* (Austin, TX: Living Truth Ministries, 1995), p.281.

[67] *Ibid.;* "NIV Owner Big Pornography Publisher," *O Timothy* (1994, Vol. 11, Issue 6). See also: "Media Controlled by the Few," *op. cit.*

[68] "People in the News," *U. S. News & World Report* (June 7, 1999), p.14.

[69] Gail Riplinger, *The Language of the King James Bible: Discover Its Hidden Built-in Dictionary* (Ararat, VA: A. V. Publications Corp., 1998), p.128. See also: Gail Riplinger, *Which Bible Is God's Word?: Answers to Common Questions Concerning Modern Versions and Translations* (Oklahoma City, OK: Hearthstone Publishing, Ltd., 1994), p.19.

[70] Cornelia R. Ferreira, "One-World Church Expected Next Year: San Francisco Chosen As Headquarters," *Wisconsin Report* (November 28, 1996, Vol. 21, No. 46), p.3; *State of the World Forum: Toward a New Civilization* (San Francisco, CA: Gorbachev Foundation USA, n.d.), p.1; John Henry Western, "World's Elite Gather to Talk Depopulation," *The Interim* (April 1996), p.6.

[71] Jeff Godwin quoting Victor Bryditzki in *What's Wrong with Christian Rock?* (Chino, CA: Chick Publications, 1990), p.151. See also: Gary Allen, *The Rockefeller File* (Seal Beach, CA: '76 Press, 1976), p.69-70.

[72] Martin, *op. cit.*, p.226.

[73] *Council on Foreign Relations: Annual Report July 1, 1992-June 30, 1993,* p.160; *Council on Foreign Relations: Annual Report July 1, 1994-June 30, 1995,* p.140; Robert Gaylon Ross, Sr., *Who's Who of the Elite* (San Marcos, TX: RIE, 1995), p.227.

[74] *Religion Broadcasting* (November 1991), p.30.

[75] *Council on Foreign Relations: Annual Report July 1, 1992-June 30, 1993,* p.173; *Council on Foreign Relations: Annual Report July 1, 1994-June 30, 1995,* p.152.

[76] "Graham Receives Recognition for Distinguished Achievement," *Religious Broadcasting* (November 1991), p.30.

[77] William R. Denslow, *10,000 Famous Freemasons* (Vol. IV) (n.p., 1961), p.234.

[78] Fritz Springmeier, *Bloodlines of the Illuminati* (Westminster, CO: Ambassador House, 1999), p.471.

[79] "The New Right" (Part III), *Distant Drums* (March 1981, Vol. 3, No. 1), p.7; *Ibid.*

[80] See: *Ibid.*, p.417, 479.

[81] *Ibid.*, p.471.

[82] Denslow, *10,000 Famous Freemasons, op. cit.* (Vol. IV) p.234.

[83] "Graham Receives Recognition for Distinguished Achievement," *op. cit.*

[84] *Council on Foreign Relations: Annual Report July 1, 1994-June 30, 1995,* p.145.

[85] *Ibid.;* p.149; *Council on Foreign Relations: Annual Report July 1, 1987-June 30, 1988,* p.105; *Council on Foreign Relations: Annual Report July 1, 1992-June 30, 1993,* p.170.

[86] *Ibid.*, p.154; *Council on Foreign Relations: Annual Report July 1, 1987-June 30, 1988,* p.182; *Council on Foreign Relations: Annual Report July 1, 1990-June 30, 1991,* p.189; *Council on Foreign Relations: Annual Report July 1, 1992-June 30, 1993,* p.174; Texe Marrs, *Circle of Intrigue* (Austin, TX: Living Truth Ministries, 1995), p.282; Gary Kah, *En Route to Global Occupation* (Lafay-ette, LA: Huntington House Publishers, 1992), p.56; James W. Wardner, *The Planned Destruction of America* (Debary, FL: Longwood Communications, 1994), p.127; David Allen Rivera, *Final Warning: A History of the New World Order* (Harrisburg, PA: Rivera Enterprises, 1994), p.100; Dwight L. Kinman, *The World's Last Dictator* (Woodburn, OR: Solid Rock Books, Inc. 1995), p.18; Wardner, *Unholy Alliances, op. cit.*, p.198; Robert Sessler, *To Be God of One World: The French Revolution Globalized* (Merlin, OR: Let There Be Light Publications, 1992), p.121.

[87] *Ibid.*, p.155; *Council on Foreign Relations: Annual Report July 1, 1987-June 30, 1988,* p.183; *Council on Foreign Relations: Annual Report July 1, 1990-June 30, 1991,* p.190; *Council on Foreign Relations: Annual Report July 1, 1992-June 30, 1993,* p.175; Wardner, *Unholy Alliances, op. cit.*, p.198; Dwight L. Kinman, *The World's Last Dictator* (Woodburn, OR: Solid Rock Books, Inc. 1995), p.18.

[88] *Impacting Society...Yesterday...Today...Tomorrow* (Amherst, NY: American Humanist Association, n.d.), n.p.

[89] *The Shepherd's Letter* (Spring 1994), p.10.

[90] Wardner, *Unholy Alliances, op. cit.*, p.229.

[91] "The Bilderberg Meetings—AD 2000," *Despatch Magazine* (September 2000, Vol. 12:3), p.52; Gary Allen, *The Rockefeller File* (Seal Beach, CA: '76 Press, 1976), p.81; *Council on Foreign Relations: Annual Report July 1, 1987-June 30, 1988,* p.178.

[92] Graham, *Just As I Am, op. cit.*, p.500-501.

[93] Robert Gaylon Ross, Sr., *Who's Who of the Elite* (San Marcos, TX: RIE, 1995), p.5, 134, 206; Texe Marrs, *Circle of Intrigue* (Austin, TX: Living Truth Ministries, 1995), p.280.

[94] Texe Marrs, *Circle of Intrigue* (Austin, TX: Living Truth Ministries, 1995), p.280.

[95] "The Erosion of Morality," *The Christian World Report* (June 1991, Vol. 3, No. 6), p.12; "Dinkins Appoints Lesbians," *The Christian World Report* (December 1990, Vol. 2, No. 9), p.26.

[96] Frederick A. O. Schwarz, Jr., "'Liberty': Schwarz Gets Our First Annual Award," *Lambda Update* (Fall 1987), p.12.

[97] "Free Condoms Distributed in New York City Schools," *The Christian World Report* (December 1990, Vol. 2, No. 9), p.26.

[98] *Democratic Left* (November/December 1984, Vol. 12, No. 6), p.12.

[99] John A. Stormer, *None Dare Call It Treason...25 Years Later* (Florissant, MO: Liberty Bell Press, 1992), p.431, 477.

[100] "World Federalist Association to Present Award to Walter Cronkite," *News and Announcement* (September 1999), p.1. See also: "Prophetic Insights," *Power of Prophecy* (July 2000, Vol. 2000-07), p.3

[101] *Cronkite: A Reporter's Life*, p.128.

[102] "Prophetic Insights," *Power of Prophecy* (July 2000, Vol. 2000-07), p.3.

[103] "Order of DeMolay Helps Shape Futures of Young Men," *Charity: A Masonic Ideal* (January 1996), p.10; *The Pennsylvania Youth Foundation* (Elizabethtown, PA: The Pennsylvania Youth Foundation, n.d.), p.2; Robert L. Harder, "DeMolay Thriving," *The Scottish Rite Journal* (February 1992, Vol. 100, No. 2), p.37; Thomas C. Raum, Jr., "Today's Young People: Where Will They Learn About the Tools of Life?," *The Scottish Rite Journal* (March 1994, Vol. 102, No. 3), p.46; Dale V. Sandstrom, "DeMolay Fast Facts," *The Scottish Rite Journal* (March 1994, Vol. 102, No. 3), p.6; "Elected But Not Yet Inducted into the DeMolay Hall of Fame," *The Scottish Rite Journal* (March 1994, Vol. 102, No. 3), p.52.

[104] Philip Weiss, "Inside Bohemian Grove," *Spy* (November 1989), p.64.

[105] "Paul Harvey Promotes Global Religion," *The Perilous Times* (November 1998), p.11-12.

[106] "Order of DeMolay Helps Shape Futures of Young Men," *op. cit.;* William J. Mollere, "Five-Star Performance: DeMolay and Its Founder," *The Scottish Rite Journal* (March 1994, Vol. 102, No. 3), p.23; "Members of the DeMolay Hall of Fame," *The Scottish Rite Journal* (March 1994, Vol. 102, No. 3), p.51.

[107] *Ibid.;* William J. Mollere, "Five-Star Performance: DeMolay and Its Founder," *The Scottish Rite Journal* (March 1994, Vol. 102, No. 3), p.23; Robert L. Harder, "DeMolay Thriving," *The Scottish Rite Journal* (February 1992, Vol. 100, No. 2), p.37; Thomas C. Raum, Jr., "Today's Young People: Where Will They Learn About the Tools of Life?," *The Scottish Rite Journal* (March 1994, Vol. 102, No. 3), p.45; "Elected But Not Yet Inducted into the DeMolay Hall of Fame," *The Scottish Rite Journal* (March 1994, Vol. 102, No. 3), p.52.

[108] Forrest D. Haggard, *The Clergy and the Craft* (Ovid Bell Press, Inc., 1970), p.64.

[109] *Ibid.*, quoting Billy Graham, p.127. See also: "Billy Graham—A Mason Without the Apron," *HRT Ministries Inc. Newsletter* (July/August/September 1990, Vol. 3, No. 3).

[110] "Members of the DeMolay Hall of Fame," *The Scottish Rite Journal* (March 1994, Vol. 102, No. 3), p.51; Gary Alan Yerace. Installation Address as Worshipful Master of the Elmer Timberman Lodge #54 (Address given on December 7, 1996), p.12; C. Fred Kleinknecht, "The Cornerstone for Our Next Generation," *The Scottish Rite Journal* (March 1994, Vol. 102, No. 3), p.5; Dale V. Sandstrom, "DeMolay Fast Facts," *The Scottish Rite Journal* (March 1994, Vol. 102, No. 3), p.6; William J. Mollere, "Five-Star Performance: DeMolay and Its Founder," *The Scottish Rite Journal* (March 1994, Vol. 102, No. 3), p.23; Marrs, *Circle of Intrigue, op. cit.*, p.26; *President Clinton Will Continue the New World Order* (Oklahoma City, OK: Southwest Radio Church, 1993), p.33.

[111] Graham, *Just As I Am, op. cit.*, p.651.

[112] *Ibid.*, p.652.

[113] William R. Denslow, *10,000 Famous Freemasons* (Vol. II) (n.p., 1958), p.37.

[114] *President Clinton Will Continue the New World Order* (Oklahoma City, OK: Southwest Radio Church, 1993), unnumbered page, p.1; "Who Controls American Education?," *The Blumenfeld Education Letter* (February 1994), p.2, 4; James Leasor, *Rhodes and Barnato: The Premier and the Prancer* (London, England: Leo Cooper, 1997), p.257; "Time to Rescind North Carolina's Resolution for World Government," *The Citizen* (May 19, 1997), p.8; "Dialectics: Perpetual Process of the Ruling Elite," *Christian Conscience* (September 1995, Vol. 1, No. 8), p.35; *Chronology of Education with Quotable Quotes* (Highland City, FL: Pro Family Forum, Inc., 1994, Updated, bound volume), p.10; *"Secret Records" Revealed: The Men, the Money, and the Methods Behind the New World Order* (Marlborough, NH: The Plymouth Rock Foundation, 1994), p.2, 5, 42; *Secret Records Revealed: The Men, the Money and the Methods Behind the New World Order* (Oklahoma City, OK: Hearthstone Publishing, Ltd., 1999), p.9, 68, 110, 146; "Could It Be Possible That Rush Is a Closet 'Kook?,'" *The Times Leader* (March 23, 1996, Vol. 4, No. 93), p.4; "Clinton Taps 'Fresh Thinking' Activists," *The Daily Item* (December 12, 1992, Vol. 55, No. 346), p.13; Texe Marrs, "Bill Clinton and the Bilderberger Conspiracy," *Flashpoint* (September 1992), p.1; "The Disarmament of America," *The Florida Forum* (Spring 1996), p.21; "Rockefeller Influence on Education Yesterday and Today," *The Florida Forum* (Spring 1996), p.7; Jessica Lipnack and Jeffrey Stamps, "Networking the World: People, Corporation, Communities, and Nations," *The Futurist*, p.9; Joan Veon, *Prince Charles: The* Sustainable *Prince* (Oklahoma City, OK: Hearthstone Publishing, Ltd., 1997), p.24; Wardner, *Unholy Alliances, op. cit.*, p.128; J. Royce Thomason, "Just What Is a Rhodes Scholarship," *The Voice in the Wilderness* (July 1994), p.7; David Allen Rivera, *Final Warning: A History of the New World Order* (Harrisburg, PA: Rivera Enterprises, 1994), p.89; "Who's Who in the Clinton Administration," *Wisconsin Report* (February 18, 1993, Vol. 18, No. 8), p.4; "One More Step Toward World Government," *The Christian World Report* (March 1994, Vol. 9, No. 3), p.7; "Rhodes to the New World Order," *The Christian World Report* (March/April 1993, Vol. 8, No. 2), p.12.

[115] *Ibid.*, p.1. See also: "One More Step Toward World Government," *The Christian World Report* (March 1994, Vol. 9, No. 3), p.7.

[116] *Ibid.;* James R. Patrick, Compiler and Editor, *America 2000/Goals 2000* (Moline, IL: Citizens for Academic Excellence, 1994), p.620; Eric Barger, "The New World Order Under Clinton: Establishment Insiders and Political Deceit," *The Christian World Report* (May 1993, Vol. 8, No. 3), p.8; "Clinton and the New World Order," *An American Commentary* (Oklahoma City, OK: Hearthstone Publishing, Ltd., 1993), p.127; Texe Marrs, *Big Sister Is Watching You* (Austin, TX: Living Truth Publishers, 1993), p.172; "Dialectics: Perpetual Process of the Ruling Elite," *Christian Conscience* (September 1995, Vol. 1, No. 8), p.35; Texe Marrs, "Bill Clinton and the Bilderberger Conspiracy," (Part II) *Flashpoint* (October 1992), p.1; James W. Wardner, *The Planned Destruction of America* (Debary, FL: Longwood Communications, 1994), p.65; *Secret Records Revealed: The Men, the Money and the Methods Behind the New World Order* (Oklahoma City, OK: Hearthstone Publishing, Ltd., 1999), p.9; Texe Marrs, *Days of Hunger, Days of Chaos: The Coming Great Food Shortages in America* (Austin, TX: Rivercrest Publishing, 1999), p.156; Larry Abraham and Franklin Sanders, *The Greening* (Atlanta, GA: Soundview Publications, n.d.), p.103; *"Secret Records" Revealed: The Men, the Money, and the Methods Behind the New World Order* (Marlborough, NH: The Plymouth Rock Foundation, 1994), p.2; J. Royce

Thomason, "Just What Is a Rhodes Scholarship," *The Voice in the Wilderness* (July 1994), p.7; David Allen Rivera, *Final Warning: A History of the New World Order* (Harrisburg, PA: Rivera Enterprises, 1994), p.100; Marrs, *Circle of Intrigue, op. cit.*, p.121, 190, 278; "Who's Who in the Clinton Administration," *Wisconsin Report* (February 18, 1993, Vol. 18, No. 8), p.4.

[117] *President Clinton Will Continue the New World Order, op. cit.*, p.1; Eric Barger, "The New World Order Under Clinton: Establishment Insiders and Political Deceit," *The Christian World Report* (May 1993, Vol. 8, No. 3), p.8; James W. Wardner, *The Planned Destruction of America* (Debary, FL: Longwood Communications, 1994), p.65, 87; Texe Marrs, *Days of Hunger, Days of Chaos: The Coming Great Food Shortages in America* (Austin, TX: Rivercrest Publishing, 1999), p.156; *Secret Records Revealed: The Men, the Money and the Methods Behind the New World Order* (Oklahoma City, OK: Hearthstone Publishing, Ltd., 1999), p.9; "Dialectics: Perpetual Process of the Ruling Elite," *Christian Conscience* (September 1995, Vol. 1, No. 8), p.35; "Who's Who in the Clinton Administration," *Wisconsin Report* (February 18, 1993, Vol. 18, No. 8), p.4; James R. Patrick, Compiler and Editor, *America 2000/Goals 2000* (Moline, IL: Citizens for Academic Excellence, 1994), p.620; Marrs, *Circle of Intrigue, op. cit.*, p.121, 278; *"Secret Records" Revealed: The Men, the Money, and the Methods Behind the New World Order* (Marlborough, NH: The Plymouth Rock Foundation, 1994), p.2; Texe Marrs, "Bill Clinton and the Bilderberger Conspiracy," (Part II) *Flashpoint* (October 1992), p.1; J. Royce Thomason, "Just What Is a Rhodes Scholarship," *The Voice in the Wilderness* (July 1994), p.7.

[118] Texe Marrs, "Bill Clinton and the Bilderberger Conspiracy," (Part II) *Flashpoint* (October 1992), p.1; *Ibid.*, p.1, 18; Texe Marrs, *Days of Hunger, Days of Chaos: The Coming Great Food Shortages in America* (Austin, TX: Rivercrest Publishing, 1999), p.156; Texe Marrs, "Bill Clinton and the Bilderberger Conspiracy," *Flashpoint* (September 1992), p.1; "Dialectics: Perpetual Process of the Ruling Elite," *Christian Conscience* (September 1995, Vol. 1, No. 8), p.35; Marrs, *Circle of Intrigue, op. cit.*, p.29, 121, 278; J. Royce Thomason, "Just What Is a Rhodes Scholarship," *The Voice in the Wilderness* (July 1994), p.7; Eric Barger, "The New World Order Under Clinton: Establishment Insiders and Political Deceit," *The Christian World Report* (May 1993, Vol. 8, No. 3), p.8; "Who's Who in the Clinton Administration," *Wisconsin Report* (February 18, 1993, Vol. 18, No. 8), p.4; "Bush and Clinton: Bilderberger Twins?," *Flashpoint* (May 1992), p.2; James W. Wardner, *The Planned Destruction of America* (Debary, FL: Longwood Communications, 1994), p.167.

[119] UPI news report, 12:00 p.m. (September 23, 1998).

[120] Wardner, *Unholy Alliances, op. cit.*, p.187.

[121] *Ibid.*, p.125.

[122] *Last Trumpet Newsletter* (January 1997, Vol. 16, Issue 1), p.3.

[123] *Ibid.*

[124] Political Deceit," *The Christian World Report* (May 1993, Vol. 8, No. 3), p.8. Concerning Hillary Clinton's contacting the dead, see: "Psychic Guide Sees No Cause for Uproar," *The Washington Times* (June 25, 1996), p.A10; Kenneth L. Woodward, "Soul Searching," *Newsweek* (July 8, 1996), p.33; "Hillary's Other Side," *Newsweek* (July 1, 1996), p.21.

[125] Martin, *op. cit.*, p.577; John E. Ashbrook, *New Neutralism II: Exposing the Gray of Compromise* (Mentor, OH: Here I Stand Books, 1992), p.31; "The Worshiping Heathen," *Christian News* (January 18, 1993, Vol. 31, No. 3), p.6; Bundy, *Billy Graham: Performer?, Politician?, Preacher?, Prophet?, op. cit.*, p.115; "Heaven: Guess Who's Coming," *Christian News* (February 19, 2001), p.9; Ashbrook, "Billy Graham—The Mouthpiece of New Evangelicalism," *op. cit.* See also: Rick Miesel, "Billy Graham: General Teachings/Activities" (Biblical Discernment Ministries, Revised January 1994).

[126] Cecile S. Holmes, "The Gospel According to Elvis," *Christian News* (February 19, 2001), p.10.

[127] *Ibid.*

[128] "The Worshiping Heathen," *Christian News* (January 18, 1993, Vol. 31, No. 3), p.6.

[129] See: "Drugs Killed Elvis, Doctor Says," reprinted from *St. Louis Post-Dispatch* in *Christian News* (February 19, 2001), p.9; *Ibid.*

[130] "The Worshiping Heathen," *op. cit.*

[131] *Ibid.* See also: "Star-Struck," *Newsweek* (April 9, 2001, Vol. 137, No. 15), p.52.

[132] *Ibid.*

[133] *Ibid.*

[134] *Ibid.*

[135] David W. Cloud, *Mom and Dad Sleep While the Children Rock in Satan's Cradle* (Oak Harbor, WA: Way of Life Literature, 1991 Edition).

[136] *Ibid.*, quoting Bob Greene.

[137] See: "Many Who Think They Are Saved Will Not Be Raptured" (Letter from Noah W. Hutchings dated June 2001), p.3.

[138] William Schnoebelen, "The Curse Causeless," *Liberator* (July-August 1999, Vol. 8, No. 4), p.3.

[139] *Ibid.* See also: Albert James Dager, *The World Christian Movement: A Great Delusion Leading to the Religio-Political State of the Anti-Christ* (Redmond, WA: Sword Publishers, 2001), p.75-78.

[140] Graham, *Just As I Am, op. cit.*, p.451.

[141] Martin, *op. cit.*, p.352; Sam Wellman, *Billy Graham: The Great Evangelist* (Uhrichsville, OH: Barbour Book, 1996), p.170.

[142] *Ibid.*, p.371.

[143] Graham, *Just As I Am, op. cit.*, p.456

[144] Martin, *op. cit.*, p.279.

[145] Graham, *Just As I Am, op. cit.*, p.457.

[146] Jerry D. Knapper, "What Happens to Christians When They Die?," *The Front Page* (October 1993, Vol. 7, No. 10), p.4. See also: Sam Wellman, *Billy Graham: The Great Evangelist* (Uhrichsville, OH: Barbour Book, 1996), p.206.

[147] Graham, *Just As I Am, op. cit.*, p.464.

[148] *Ibid.*, p.465.

[149] *Ibid.*, p.466.

[150] Bundy, *Billy Graham: Performer?, Politician?, Preacher?, Prophet?, op. cit.*, p.52. See also: Martin, *op. cit.*, p.312.

[151] Sam Wellman, *Billy Graham: The Great Evangelist* (Uhrichsville, OH: Barbour Book, 1996), p.162.

[152] A Ralph Epperson quoting Lyndon Johnson in *The Unseen Hand: An Introduction to the Conspiratorial View of History* (Tucson, AZ: Publius Press, 1985), p.49.

[153] *Ibid.*

[154] Wardner, *Unholy Alliances, op. cit.*, p.149.

[155] John Coleman, *The Conspirators' Hierarchy: The Committee of 300* (Carson City, Nevada: Joseph Publishing Company, Third Edition, 1994), p.330.

[156] Epperson, *op. cit.*, p.250.

[157] Bundy, *Billy Graham: Performer?, Politician?, Preacher?, Prophet?, op. cit.*, p.52. See also: Martin, *op. cit.*, p.311.

[158] Wellman, *op. cit.*, p.175.

[159] "Washington Has Never Seen Anything Like It—Since the Last Time," *U. S. News & World Report* (February 2, 1998, Vol. 124, No. 4), p.20.

[160] *Knoxville News-Sentinel* (September 15, 1991), p.A8. See also: Martin, *op. cit.*, p.299, 597; Personal conversation with Texe Marrs on June 25, 2001.

[161] Texe Marrs, *Power of Prophecy* (July 21, 2001 program).

[162] Graham, *Just As I Am, op. cit.*, p.692.

[163] *Ibid.*, p.693.

[164] *Ibid.*

[165] Martin, *op. cit.*, p.130.

[166] *Ibid.*, p.460; *Christianity Today* (June 3, 1977).

[167] *Ibid.*

[168] David W. Cloud, *Flirting with Rome: Evangelical Entanglement with Roman Catholicism (Volume 1—Billy Graham)* (Oak Harbor, WA: Way of Life Literature, 1993).

[169] Jeffrey K. Hadden and Charles E. Swann, *Prime Time Preachers: The Rising Power of Televangelism* (Reading, MA: Addison-Wesley Publishing Company, Inc., 1981), p.21-22. See also: McCurdy Lipsey, "Some Little-Known Details About Graham Crusades Might Surprise You," *Christian News* (June 5, 2000, Vol. 38, No. 23), p.3; Wellman, *op. cit.*, p.80-81; Bundy, *Billy Graham: Performer?, Politician?, Preacher?, Prophet?, op. cit.*, p.125.

[170] Rick Miesel, "Billy Graham: General Teachings/Activities" (Biblical Discernment Ministries, Revised January 1994).

[171] McCurdy Lipsey, "Some Little-Known Details About Graham Crusades Might Surprise You," *Christian News* (June 5, 2000, Vol. 38, No. 23), p.3.

[172] *Ibid.*

[173] Wilson Ewin, *The Assimilation of Evangelist Billy Graham into the Roman Catholic Church* (Compton, Quebec: Quebec Baptist Missions, 1992), p.4; Rick Miesel, "Billy Graham: General Teachings/Activities" (Biblical Discernment Ministries, Revised January 1994); Wilson Ewin, *Today's Evangelicals Embracing the World's Deadliest Cult* (Compton, Quebec: Quebec Baptist Missions, n.d.), p.38; Cloud, *Flirting with Rome (Volume 1—Billy Graham), op. cit.*; Wilson Ewin, *Evangelism: The Trojan Horse of the 1990's* (Compton, Quebec: Quebec Baptist Missions, 1992); Wilson Ewin, *Under the New World Order: Evangelicals, Catholics and Israel: Conspiracy of the Ages* (Compton, Quebec: Quebec Baptist Missions, n.d.), p.73. See also: Robert F. Kofahl, "Graham Believes Men Can Be Saved Apart from Name of Christ," *Christian News* (October 20, 1997, Vol. 35, No. 38), p.15; Albert James Dager, *The World Christian Movement: A Great Delusion Leading to the Religio-Political State of the Anti-Christ* (Redmond, WA: Sword Publishers, 2001), p.75; *Media Spotlight* (1997, Vol. 20, No. 2), p.25.

[174] Rick Miesel, "Billy Graham: General Teachings/Activities" (Biblical Discernment Ministries, Revised January 1994). See also: Cloud, *Flirting with Rome (Volume 1—Billy Graham), op. cit.*

[175] Wilson Ewin, *Evangelism: The Trojan Horse of the 1990's* (Compton, Quebec: Quebec Baptist Missions, 1992), p.9.

[176] "America's Bishop," *Catholic Digest* (August 2001, Vol. 65, No. 10), p.83.

[177] Cloud quoting Fulton J. Sheen in *Flirting with Rome (Volume 1—Billy Graham), op. cit.*

[178] Cornelius K. Rand, "Purgatory: Fact or False?," *The Voice of the Nazarene* (December 1962, Vol. 11, No. 12), p.7.

[179] D. Guide, "'Celebrating' the Death of Christ: The Mockery of the Mass," *The Battle Cry* (November/December 1992), p.7.

[180] Wilson Ewin, *Under the New World Order: Evangelicals, Catholics and Israel: Conspiracy of the Ages* (Compton, Quebec: Quebec Baptist Missions, n.d.), p.29.

[181] "America's Bishop," *op. cit.*, p.83.

[182] *Ibid.*

[183] J. Gordon Melton, *The Encyclopedia of American Religions* (Vol. 2) (Wilmington, NC: McGrath Publishing Company, 1978), p.56.

[184] Alan Morrison, *The Serpent and the Cross: Religious Corruption in an Evil Age* (Birmingham, England: K & M Books, 1994), p.107-108. See also: Dave Hunt and T. A. McMahon, *The Seduction of Christianity: Spiritual Discernment in the Last Days* (Eugene, OR: Harvest House Publishers, 1985), p.151; Dave Hunt, *Beyond Seduction: A Return to Biblical Christianity* (Eugene, OR: Harvest House Publishers, 1987), p.51.

[185] Video Catalog for 1987-1988 from Wishing Well Distributing Company, p.2.

[186] *Ibid.*, p.20.

[187] Wardner, *Unholy Alliances, op. cit.*, p.223.

[188] Morrison, *op. cit.*, p.175; John Cotter, *A Study in Syncretism* (Flesherton, Ontario: Canadian Intelligence Publications, n.d.), p.35; Gary Kah, *En Route to Global Occupation* (Lafayette, LA: Huntington House Publishers, 1992), p.41; Robert Sessler, *To Be God of One World: The French Revolution Globalized* (Merlin, OR: Let There Be Light Publications, 1992), 128; Dave Hunt, and T. A. McMahon, *The Seduction of Christianity: Spiritual Discernment in the Last Days* (Eugene, OR: Harvest House Publishers, 1985), p.77.

[189] Dave Hunt, and T. A. McMahon, *The Seduction of Christianity: Spiritual Discernment in the Last Days* (Eugene, OR: Harvest House Publishers, 1985), p.77.

[190] *Now Is the Dawning of the New Age New World Order* (Oklahoma City, OK: Hearthstone Publishing, Ltd., 1991), p.137.

[191] Morrison, *op. cit.*, p.564.

[192] *Ibid.*

[193] *Now Is the Dawning of the New Age New World Order, op. cit.*, p.137; John Cotter, *A Study in Syncretism* (Flesherton, Ontario: Canadian Intelligence Publications, n.d.), p.35.

[194] *Ibid.*; John Cotter, *A Study in Syncretism* (Flesherton, Ontario: Canadian Intelligence Publications, n.d.), p.35; Rhea Fulmer, Teri Jeter, and Wanda Riner, "Robert Muller's Vision for 2000 A. D.," *The Christian Conscience* (May 1995, Vol. 1, No. 5), p.34; Morrison, *op. cit.*, p.175; Robert Sessler, *To Be God of One World: The French Revolution Globalized* (Merlin, OR: Let There Be Light Publications, 1992), 128.

[195] *Ibid.*; Brenda Scott and Samantha Smith, *Trojan Horse: How the New Age Movement Infiltrates the Church* (Lafayette, LA: Huntington House Publishers, 1993), p.140.

[196] Albert James Dager, *Inner Healing: A Biblical Analysis* (Santa Ana, CA: Tri-Level Press, 1986), p.35.

[197] *Now Is the Dawning of the New Age New World Order, op. cit.*, p.137; Morrison, *op. cit.*, p.175; *An American Commentary* (Oklahoma City, OK: Hearthstone Publishing, Ltd., 1993), p.55; Walter Hoffmann, Editor, *A New World Order: Can It Bring Security to the World's People?* (Washington, DC: World Federalist Association, 1991), p.122.

[198] "News Alert," *The Berean Call* (October 1992), p.4; *Now Is the Dawning of the New Age New World Order, op. cit.*, p.137; Dager, *Inner Healing, op. cit.*, p.35; Hunt and McMahon, *The Seduction of Christianity, op. cit.*, p.77; Robert Sessler, *To Be God of One World: The French Revolution Globalized* (Merlin, OR: Let There Be Light Publications, 1992), 128, 166. See also: Rhea Fulmer, Teri Jeter, and Wanda Riner, "Robert Muller's Vision for 2000 A. D.," *The Christian Conscience* (May 1995, Vol. 1, No. 5), p.34; Morrison, *op. cit.*, p.564; Warren Smith, "Sign of the Times: Evangelicals and New Agers Together," *SCP Journal* (19:2/3), p.58; Gary Kah, *En Route to Global Occupation* (Lafayette, LA: Huntington House Publishers, 1992), p.41.

[199] Hunt and McMahon, *The Seduction of Christianity, op. cit.*, p.80. See also: Rhea Fulmer, Teri Jeter, and Wanda Riner, "Robert Muller's Vision for 2000 A. D.," *The Christian Conscience* (May 1995, Vol. 1, No. 5), p.34.

[200] Gary Kah, *En Route to Global Occupation* (Lafayette, LA: Huntington House Publishers, 1992), p.41. See also: *Now Is the Dawning of the New Age New World Order, op. cit.*, p.137.

[201] Brenda Scott and Samantha Smith, *Trojan Horse: How the New Age Movement Infiltrates the Church* (Lafayette, LA: Huntington House Publishers, 1993), p.141.

[202] John Templeton, *Possibilities for Over One Hundredfold More Spiritual Information: The Humble Approach in Theology and Science* (Philadelphia, Pennsylvania: Templeton Foundation Press, 2000), p.133.

[203] "Teilhard de Chardin: Christianity and Evolution," *SCP Journal* (19:2/3), p.56.

[204] *Ibid.*

[205] *Ibid.*

[206] *Ibid.*

[207] "Turret of the Times," quoting from *The Remnant* in *Christian News* (February 24, 1997, Vol. 35, No. 8), p.3.

[208] "Pope Says Unbelievers Saved if Live (sic) a Good Life," *Calvary Contender* (January 1, 2001, Vol. 18, No. 1), p.6; *Christian News* (January 6, 1997, Vol. 35, No. 1); Franklyn M. McAfee, "Creation, Evolution or Creationary Evolution?," *Soul* (July-August 1996, Vol. 47, No. 4), p.6; Maureen Fiedler and Linda Rabben, Editors, *Rome Has Spoken...: A Guide to Forgotten Papal Statements, and How They Have Changed Through the Centuries* (New York, NY: The Crossroad Publishing Company, 1998), p.180, 181, 182, 184; "Theistic Evolution," *The Day Drawing Near* (Spring 1997), p.5; "The Pope and Darwin," *U. S. News & World Report* (November 4, 1996, Vol. 121, No. 18), p.12; "Cardinal: Adam, Eve Possibly Not Human," *Veritas* (December 1996, Vol. 28, No. 12), p.4; *The Berean Call* (February 1999); "Ratzinger Revealed As Heretic," *Veritas* (December 1996, Vol. 28, No. 12), p.4; Rick Miesel, "Roman Catholicism: General Notes" (Biblical Discernment Ministries, Revised August 1997).

[209] "The Pope and Darwin," *U. S. News & World Report* (November 4, 1996, Vol. 121, No. 18), p.12. See also: Franklyn M. McAfee, "Creation, Evolution or Creationary Evolution?," *Soul* (July-August 1996, Vol. 47, No. 4), p.7.

[210] Rick Miesel quoting Edward Daschbach in "Roman Catholicism: General Notes" (Biblical Discernment Ministries, Revised August 1997).

[211] "Cardinal: Adam, Eve Possibly Not Human," *Veritas* (December 1996, Vol. 28, No. 12), p.4; Rick Miesel, "Roman Catholicism: General Notes" (Biblical Discernment Ministries, Revised August 1997).

[212] *Ibid.*

[213] Franklyn M. McAfee, "Creation, Evolution or Creationary Evolution?," *Soul* (July-August 1996, Vol. 47, No. 4), p.7.

[214] Amy Welborn, "Why There Are Still Apes," *Our Sunday Visitor* (June 17, 2001), p.16.

[215] *Ibid.*

[216] Edward F. Blick, *Correlation of the Bible and Science* (Oklahoma City, OK: Southwest Radio Church, 1988 Edition), p.2.

[217] *Christian News* (January 6, 1997, Vol. 35, No. 1).

[218] *The Berean Call* (February 1999).

[219] Martin, *op. cit.,* p.212.

[220] *The Berean Call* (April 2001), p.5.

[221] "Pope Says Hell Is Self-Inflicted," *Calvary Contender* (September 1, 1999, Vol. 16, No. 17), p.2; E. L. Bynum, "Pope Says No Fire in Hell So Does Billy Graham," *The Evangelical Methodist* (September 2000, Vol. 78, No. 5), p.4.

[222] *Ibid.;* E. L. Bynum, "Pope Says No Fire in Hell So Does Billy Graham," *The Evangelical Methodist* (September 2000, Vol. 78, No. 5), p.4.

[223] E. L. Bynum, "Pope Says No Fire in Hell So Does Billy Graham," *The Evangelical Methodist* (September 2000, Vol. 78, No. 5), p.4.

[224] "Pope Says Unbelievers Saved if Live (sic) a Good Life," *op. cit.* See also: "Pope Says Christianity Is Not the Only True and Saving Faith," *The Voice in the Wilderness* (February 2001), p.6; *Power of Prophecy* (February 2001, Vol. 2001-02), p.4; Peggy Polk, "Pope Says Unbelievers Will Be Saved if They Live a Just Life," *Christian News* (December 18, 2000, Vol. 38, No. 47), p.1; Bruce Johnston, "Heaven Open to Everyone, Says Pope," *Christian News* (December 18, 2000, Vol. 38, No. 47), p.12; "Pope Says Belief in Jesus Not Necessary for Salvation," *The Vine and Branches* (Winter 2001, Vol. 16, Issue 1), p.9; "Popular Pope Is a Universalist," *Christian News* (January 30, 1995, Vol. 33, No. 5).

[225] Peggy Polk, "Pope Says Unbelievers Will Be Saved if They Live a Just Life," *Christian News* (December 18, 2000, Vol. 38, No. 47), p.1.

[226] "Pope John Paul II Receives a Mark in His Forehead by a Pagan Shiva Priestess," Cutting Edge Ministries. See also: Elizabeth McDonald, *Alpha: The Unofficial Guide* (Cambridge, England: St. Matthew Publishing, Ltd., 2001), p.12.

[227] Anton Szandor LaVey, *The Satanic Bible* (NY: Avon Books, 1969), p.60, 145. See also: Joseph Campbell, *The Masks of God: Creative Mythology* (New York, NY: The Viking Press, 1968), p.204, 411.

[228] J. S. M. Ward, *Freemasonry and the Ancient Gods* (London, England: Simpkin, Marshall, Hamilton, Kent and Company Ltd., 1921), p.15.

[229] Alain Danielou, *The Gods of India* (New York, NY: Inner Traditions International Ltd., 1985), p.217.

[230] Robert Hieronimus, *America's Secret Destiny: Spiritual Vision and the Founding of a Nation* (Rochester, VT: Destiny Books, 1989), p.82. See also: Alexander Cannon, *The Power of Karma: In Relation to Destiny* (E. P. Dutton and Company, Inc., 1937), p.88-89; Darshan Singh, *Helping Factors on the Spiritual Path* (Delhi, India: n.p., n.d.), p.2-3; J.E. Cirlot, Translated by Jack Sage, *A Dictionary of Symbols* (New York, NY: Philosophical Library, Inc., 1972), p.100; Lucie Lamy, *Egyptian Mysteries* (n.p., 1981), p.16.

[231] Sandra L. Koch, *Combating the New Age Movement: A Christian Warfare Manual* (Boca Raton, FL: Foundation Tabernacle Ministries, Inc., n.d.). See also: Robert S. Liichow, *The Two Roots of Today's Revival* (Kearney, Nebraska: Morris Publishing, 1997), p.209-212.

[232] Catalog from Samuel Weiser (1989/1990), p.66.

[233] Jane Gumprecht quoting Alice Bailey in *New Age Health Care: Holy or Holistic* (Orange, CA: Promise Publishing, 1988), p.190.

[234] Alice A. Bailey, *The Soul: Quality of Life* (NY: Lucis Publishing Company, 1974), p.201. See also: Alice A. Bailey, *A Treatise on White Magic or the Way of the Disciple* (NY: Lucis Publishing Company, 1951), p.213.

[235] Richard P. McBrien, *Lives of the Popes: The Pontiffs from St. Peter to John Paul II* (New York, NY: HarperSanFrancisco,

1997), p.441; Albert James Dager, *The World Christian Movement: A Great Delusion Leading to the Religio-Political State of the Anti-Christ* (Redmond, WA: Sword Publishers, 2001), p.146-147; "Pope Prays for Earth Summit," *O Timothy* (1992, Vol. 9, Issue 8); David W. Cloud, "The Day of Prayer for World Peace," *O Timothy* (1994, Vol. 11, Issue 3); "Roman Catholicism/General Notes" (Biblical Discernment Ministries, Revised August 1997); William T. James, Editor, *Foreshocks of Antichrist* (Eugene, OR: Harvest House Publishers, 1997), p.110; *Flashpoint* (April 1993); Michael Hoffman, *Researcher* (Vol. 4, No. 3).

[236] "Roman Catholicism/General Notes" (Biblical Discernment Ministries, Revised August 1997). See also: *Flashpoint* (April 1993); Ewin, *Under the New World Order, op. cit.*, p.39, 103; Michael Hoffman, *Researcher* (Vol. 4, No. 3); Elizabeth McDonald, *Alpha: The Unofficial Guide* (Cambridge, England: St. Matthew Publishing, Ltd., 2001), p.11; William T. James, Editor, *Foreshocks of Antichrist* (Eugene, OR: Harvest House Publishers, 1997), p.110.

[237] Elizabeth McDonald, *Alpha: The Unofficial Guide* (Cambridge, England: St. Matthew Publishing, Ltd., 2001), p.11.

[238] "Roman Catholicism/General Notes" (Biblical Discernment Ministries, Revised August 1997).

[239] *Ibid.*

[240] William T. James, Editor, *Foreshocks of Antichrist* (Eugene, OR: Harvest House Publishers, 1997), p.110. See also: "Pope, Voodoo Worshippers, Contextual Evangelism," *Calvary Contender* (March 15, 1993, Vol. 10, No. 6), p.2; "Voodoo Chiefs Meet Catholic Chief," *Midnight Call* (April 1993), p.16; "Roman Catholicism/General Notes" (Biblical Discernment Ministries, Revised August 1997).

[241] *Power of Prophecy* (April 2001, Vol. 2001-04), p.5; "Gone Berserk," *Power of Prophecy* (May 2001, Vol. 2001-05), p.6; Texe Marrs quoting from *Christian News* on *Power of Prophecy* (March 17, 2001 program).

[242] Rick Miesel, "Roman Catholicism: General Notes" (Biblical Discernment Ministries, Revised August 1997). See also: *The Berean Call* (October 1994), p.4.

[243] Texe Marrs, *Texe Marrs Book of New Age Cults and Religions* (Austin, TX: Living Truth Publishers, 1990), p.296; Dave Hunt and T. A. McMahon, *America: The Sorcerer's New Apprentice: The Rise of New Age Shamanism* (Eugene, OR: Harvest House Publishers, 1988), p.60; Johanna Michaelsen, *Like Lambs to the Slaughter* (Eugene, OR: Harvest House Publishers, 1989), p.114; Rick Miesel, "Roman Catholicism: General Notes" (Biblical Discernment Ministries, Revised August 1997).

[244] *The Silva Mind Control Method* (Complete Program Transcripts with Jose Silva, George Desau, David Hunt, and John Weldon) (Chattanooga, TN: The John Ankerberg Show, 1986), p.1; Rick Miesel, "Roman Catholicism: General Notes" (Biblical Discernment Ministries, Revised August 1997); Randall N. Baer, *Inside the New Age Nightmare* (Lafayette, LA: Huntington House, Inc., 1989), p.9, 11; Peter Lalonde, "Religion in the Public Schools," *Christian Inquirer* (Vol. 15, No. 6), p.9; Texe Marrs, "Unmasking the New Age Cults and Religions," *Flashpoint* (November/December 1990), p.1; Don Matzat, *Inner Healing: Deliverance or Deception?* (Eugene, OR: Harvest House Publishers, 1987), p.82; Johanna Michaelsen, *Like Lambs to the Slaughter* (Eugene, OR: Harvest House Publishers, 1989), p.114; Texe Marrs, *Mystery Mark of the New Age: Satan's Design for World Domination* (Westchester, IL: Crossway Books, 1988), p.154-155; Constance Cumbey, *A Planned Deception: The Staging of a New Age "Messiah"* (East Detroit, MI: Pointe Publishing, Inc., 1985), p.49; Robert Sessler, *To Be God of One World: The French Revolution Globalized* (Merlin, OR: Let There Be Light Publications, 1992), p.134; Dave Hunt and T. A. McMahon, *America: The Sorcerer's New Apprentice: The Rise of New Age Shamanism* (Eugene, OR: Harvest House Publishers, 1988), p.60; *Ibid.*, p.296; Kurt Koch, (Translated by Michael Freeman). *Occult ABC* (Germany: Literature Mission Aglasterhausen, Inc., 1978), p.25; Texe Marrs, *Dark Secrets of the New Age: Satan's Plan for a One World Religion* (Westchester, IL: Crossway Books, 1987), p.111; Hunt and McMahon, *The Seduction of Christianity, op. cit.*, p.138-139; Clifford Wilson and John Weldon, *Psychic Forces and Occult Shock: A Biblical View* (Chattanooga, TN: Global Publishers, 1987), p.387.

[245] Randall N. Baer, *Inside the New Age Nightmare* (Lafayette, LA: Huntington House, Inc., 1989), p.9, 11.

[246] Dave Hunt and T. A. McMahon, *America: The Sorcerer's New Apprentice: The Rise of New Age Shamanism* (Eugene, OR: Harvest House Publishers, 1988), p.63, 261.

[247] Constance Cumbey, *A Planned Deception: The Staging of a New Age "Messiah"* (East Detroit, MI: Pointe Publishing, Inc., 1985), p.49; Texe Marrs, *Mystery Mark of the New Age: Satan's Design for World Domination* (Westchester, IL: Crossway Books, 1988), p.154.

[248] Texe Marrs, *Mystery Mark of the New Age: Satan's Design for World Domination* (Westchester, IL: Crossway Books, 1988), p.154.

[249] *Ibid.*, p.155.

[250] Cloud, *Flirting with Rome (Volume 1—Billy Graham), op. cit.*

[251] Jack T. Chick, *Smokescreens: Who Is the "Whore" of Revelation? A Biblical and Historical Answer* (Chino, CA: Chick Publications, 1983); David W. Cloud, "Christian Leaders and the Pope," *O Timothy* (1991, Vol. 8, Issue 2); "The Pope...Spiritual Leader or Anti-Christ?," *The Protestant Challenge* (January-February 1997, Vol. 24, No. 1), p.8; David W. Cloud, "A Most Infamous Day in Church History: The Day of Prayer for World Peace," *O Timothy* (1994, Vol. 11, Issue 3); Rick Miesel, "Billy Graham: General Teachings/Activities" (Biblical Discernment Ministries, Revised January 1994); D. W. Cloud, "Papal Supremacy," *O Timothy* (1987, Vol. 4, Issue 7); *Ibid.* See also: "Catholic-Lutheran Unity," *Calvary Contender* (January 15, 2000), p.2.

[252] David W. Cloud, *Is the Roman Catholic Changing?* (Oak Harbor, WA: Way of Life Literature, 1995 Edition).

[253] "Graham's Affinity with Catholicism," *Calvary Contender* (June 1, 2001, Vol. 18, No. 11), p.2; Robert Sullivan and the Editors of *Life. Pope John Paul II: A Tribute* (Time, Inc., 1999).

[254] D. W. Cloud, "Some Frightening Facts About Billy Graham," *O Timothy* (1984, Vol. 1, Issue 4).

[255] For example, see: *Midnight Call* (August 1992), p.13; *Preparing Families for the Third Millennium...* (1997), p.2; Richard M. Bennett, *"We Ought to Obey God Rather Than Men,"* (Portland, OR: Berean Beacon, 1994).

[256] "Mary's Era," *National Catholic Register* (October 22-28, 2000, Vol. 76, No. 43), p.1; Raymond J. De Souza, "In Special Act, Pope Puts Mary's Seal on Great Jubilee," *National Catholic Register* (October 22-28, 2000, Vol. 76, No. 43), p.4. See also: Rick Miesel, "Roman Catholicism: General Notes" (Biblical Discernment Ministries, Revised August 1997).

[257] Raymond J. De Souza, "In Special Act, Pope Puts Mary's Seal on Great Jubilee," *National Catholic Register* (October 22-28, 2000, Vol. 76, No. 43), p.4.

[258] "Pope Entrusts 'Whole Church' to Mary," *Calvary Contender* (July 1, 2001, Vol. 18, No. 13), p.1.

[259] *Ibid.*

[260] Rick Miesel, "Roman Catholicism: General Notes" (Biblical Discernment Ministries, Revised August 1997).

[261] Keith A. Fournier, *Evangelical Catholics* (Nashville, TN: Thomas Nelson, Inc., 1990), p.25-26.

[262] "Mary" (on disk). See also: William G. McLoughlin, and Robert N. Bellah, *Religion in America* (Boston, MA: Houghton Mifflin Company, 1968), p.50.

[263] Cloud, *Is the Roman Catholic Changing?, op. cit.*

[264] Mary Ann Maccri, "A Call to Roman Catholics," *End of the World Chronicle* (March/April 1999, Vol. 2, Issue 2), p.7.

[265] Dave Hunt, *Whatever Happened to Heaven?* (Eugene, OR: Harvest House Publishers, 1988), p.113; *The Omega-Letter* (April 1990, Vol. 5, No. 4), p.13; *CIB Bulletin* (December 1989, Vol. 5, No. 12), p.1; Peter Lalonde, *One World Under Antichrist* (Eugene, OR: Harvest House Publishers, 1991), p.59-60; Ralph Edward Woodrow, *Babylon Mystery Religion: Ancient and Modern* (Riverside, CA: Ralph Woodrow Evangelistic Association, Inc., 1990 Edition), p.13-14; Fritz Springmeier, *The Top 13 Illuminati Bloodlines* (Portland, OR: n.p., 1995), p.16; Rick Miesel, "Roman Catholicism—Christian or Pagan" (Biblical Discernment Ministries, Revised August 1997). See also: Charles G. Berger, *Our Phallic Heritage* (New York, NY: Greenwich Book Publishers, Inc., 1966), p.154.

[266] Michael Howard, *The Occult Conspiracy: The Power of Secret Societies in World History* (New York, NY: MFJ Books, 1989), p.22. See also: Esther M. Harding, *Woman's Mysteries: Ancient and Modern* (NY: G. P. Putnam's Sons, 1971), p.184-185.

[267] Charles G. Berger, *Our Phallic Heritage* (New York, NY: Greenwich Book Publishers, Inc., 1966), p.154-155.

[268] Ralph Edward Woodrow, *Babylon Mystery Religion: Ancient and Modern* (Riverside, CA: Ralph Woodrow Evangelistic Association, Inc., 1990 Edition), p.27-28.

[269] Charles Chiniquy, *50 Years in the 'Church' of Rome: The Conversion of a Priest* (Chino, CA: Chick Publications, 1985 Edition), p.43-44. See also: Michael Howard, *op. cit.,* p.22; Guy Emmanuel Abraham, *Chronology of Important Events in the Life of Jesus Christ* (Silver Spring, MD: Home Bible Study Group, 2001), p.24.

[270] Michael Howard, *op. cit.,* p.24.

[271] Woodrow, *op. cit.,* p.79.

[272] Corrado Pallenberg, *Inside the Vatican* (New York City 11, NY: Hawthorn Books, Inc., 1960), p.233, 241.

[273] *Ibid.*, p.234.

[274] *The American Heritage Dictionary* (Third Edition, Version 3.6a) (SoftKey International, 1994). See also: *Webster's Seventh New Collegiate Dictionary* (Springfield, MA: G. & C. Merriam Company, 1967), p.72; J. E. Cirlot (Translated by Jack Sage), *A Dictionary of Symbols* (NY: Dorset Press, 1991 Edition), p.22; Thomas Bulfinch, *Bulfinch's Mythology: The Age of Fable or Stories of Gods and Heroes* (Garden City, NY: Doubleday and Company, Inc., 1948), p.338.

[275] J. E. Cirlot (Translated by Jack Sage), *A Dictionary of Symbols* (NY: Dorset Press, 1991 Edition), p.22. See also: Thomas Bulfinch, *Bulfinch's Mythology: The Age of Fable or Stories of Gods and Heroes* (Garden City, NY: Doubleday and Company, Inc., 1948), p.338.

[276] George Oliver, *Signs and Symbols* (NY: Macoy Publishing and Masonic Supply Company, 1906), p.33.

[277] *Webster's Seventh New Collegiate Dictionary* (Springfield, MA: G. & C. Merriam Company, 1967), p.124. See also: *The American Heritage Dictionary,* (Third Edition, Version 3.6a) (SoftKey International, 1994).

[278] *Ibid.*

[279] Chiniquy, *50 Years in the 'Church' of Rome, op. cit.,* p.43-44. See also: Michael Howard, *op. cit.,* p.22; Guy Emmanuel Abraham, *Chronology of Important Events in the Life of Jesus Christ* (Silver Spring, MD: Home Bible Study Group, 2001), p.24; Woodrow, *op. cit.,* p.79.

[280] "Patriotic Civil Religion," *The Little Cloud Report* (October 1994), p.7.

[281] D. Guide, "Did You Know?," *Battle Cry* (November/December 1992), p.3.

[282] *Ibid.* See also: J. S. M. Ward, *Who Was Hiram Abiff?* (London, England: The Baskerville Press, Ltd., 1925), p.22, 72, 73; L. Kean, "The Idolatry of the Churches," *O Timothy* (1987, Vol. 4, Issue 12).

[283] Patti Lalonde, "The Bondage of Religion," *The Omega-Letter* (July 1990, Vol. 5, No. 6), p.18-19.

[284] David W. Cloud, "The Sinaiticus and Vaticanus Manuscripts Were Found in Demonized Places," *O Timothy* (1994, Vol. 11, Issue 6).

[285] Cloud, *Flirting with Rome (Volume 1—Billy Graham), op. cit.;* Cloud, *Is the Roman Catholic Changing?, op. cit.* See also: D. W. Cloud, "Papal Supremacy," *O Timothy* (1987, Vol. 4, Issue 7); Rick Miesel, "Billy Graham: General Teachings/

Activities" (Biblical Discernment Ministries, Revised January 1994); D. W. Cloud, *Is the Roman Catholic Changing?* (1984); Brad K. Gsell, *The Legacy of Billy Graham* (Charlotte, NC: Fundamental Presbyterian Publication, n.d.), p.33; David W. Cloud, "Christian Leaders and the Pope," *O Timothy* (1991, Vol. 8, Issue 2).

[286] "Graham Meets Again with Pope," *Calvary Contender* (April 15, 1993, Vol. 10, No. 8), p.2; "Pope Prays for Earth Summit," *O Timothy* (1992, Vol. 9, Issue 8); Jewel van der Merwe, "The River Is Wide, but the Way Is Narrow," *Discernment* (March/April 1997, Vol. 8, No. 3) p.2; "Evangelicals and Catholics: Coming Together," *The Day Drawing Near* (March 1999, Vol. 1, No. 6), p.2; Brad K. Gsell, *The Legacy of Billy Graham* (Charlotte, NC: Fundamental Presbyterian Publication, n.d.), p.33; D. W. Cloud, "Some Frightening Facts About Billy Graham," *O Timothy* (1984, Vol. 1, Issue 4). See also: "Pope Is Graham's 'Man of the Century,'" *Calvary Contender* (January 15, 2000), p.1; "The Pope...Spiritual Leader or Anti-Christ?," *The Protestant Challenge* (January-February 1997, Vol. 24, No. 1), p.8; Martin, *op. cit.*, p.461; *Ibid.*; M. H. Reynolds, "AD 2000 Ecumenical Evangelism: A Warning!," *Foundation* (July-September 1995, Vol. 16, Issue 4), p.7; Perry F. Rockwood, *The Charismatic Renewal in the Roman Catholic Church* (Halifax, Nova Scotia: The Peoples Gospel Hour, n.d.), p.2; "Romeward Bound Continues," *Dorea Ministries* (January-March 1992), p.8; M. H. Reynolds, Jr., *Billy Graham, the Pope, and the Bible* (Los Osos, CA: Fundamental Evangelistic Association, n.d.), p.7; "Man of the Century," *Christian News* (March 20, 2000, Vol. 38, No. 12), p.2; "Catholic-Lutheran Unity," *Calvary Contender* (January 15, 2000), p.2; "Graham Says He Admires Pope's Attempts at Religious Reconciliation," *Foundation* (January-February 2000, Vol. 21, Issue 1), p.40; "How Can Catholic Church Deceive So Many?," *Calvary Contender* (March 15, 1996, Vol. 13, No. 6); "Billy Graham 'Delighted' Pope Came to Denver," *Christian News* (September 27, 1993, Vol. 31, No. 35); "Billy Graham," *The BDM Letter* (November 1993, Vol. 2, No. 9), p.2.

[287] "Billy Graham," *The BDM Letter* (November 1993, Vol. 2, No. 9), p.2.

[288] Graham, *Just As I Am, op. cit.*, p.489. See also: Cloud, *Flirting with Rome (Volume 1—Billy Graham), op. cit.*

[289] "Pope Voices Concern Over Catholic Defection," *Christianity Today* (June 18, 1990), p.60.

[290] Rick Miesel, "Billy Graham: General Teachings/Activities" (Biblical Discernment Ministries, Revised January 1994).

[291] "Popular Pope Is a Universalist," *Christian News* (January 30, 1995, Vol. 33, No. 5), p.3; Cloud, *Is the Roman Catholic Changing?, op. cit.*; Ian Paisley, "Billy Graham's Tragic Romeward Run," *O Timothy* (1993, Vol. 10, Issue 9).

[292] "*CT* Promotes Pope Video," *Calvary Contender* (April 15, 1998, Vol. 15, No. 8).

[293] "Graham Says He Admires Pope's Attempts at Religious Reconciliation," *Foundation* (January-February 2000, Vol. 21, Issue 1), p.40-41; "Man of the Century," *Christian News* (March 20, 2000, Vol. 38, No. 12), p.2; "Pope Is Graham's 'Man of the Century,'" *Calvary Contender* (January 15, 2000), p.1.

[294] "Pope Calls Increased Dialogue Among World Religions a 'Sign of Hope' at End of Century," *Foundation* (November-December 1999), p.17.

[295] McDonald, *op. cit.*, p.10.

[296] *The Evangelical Methodist* (March 2000, Vol. 77, No. 10), p.2.

[297] Rick Miesel, "Roman Catholicism: General Notes" (Biblical Discernment Ministries, Revised August 1997). See also: "Vatican Paper Rakes Fundamentalist Views While Evangelicals and Catholics Join Forces," *The Front Page* (October 1993, Vol. 7, No. 10), p.4; Maureen Fiedler and Linda Rabben, Editors, *Rome Has Spoken...: A Guide to Forgotten Papal Statements, and How They Have Changed Through the Centuries* (New York, NY: The Crossroad Publishing Company, 1998), p.39.40.

[298] Maureen Fiedler and Linda Rabben, Editors, *Rome Has Spoken...: A Guide to Forgotten Papal Statements, and How They Have Changed Through the Centuries* (New York, NY: The Crossroad Publishing Company, 1998), p.33.

[299] *Ibid.* See also: David R. Barnhart, "The Spirit Still Speaks to the Churches!: Part 1—The Church at Ephesus," *The Vine and Branches* (Summer 2001, Vol. 16, Issue 31), p.5.

[300] Rick Miesel, "Roman Catholicism: General Notes" (Biblical Discernment Ministries, Revised August 1997).

[301] Martin, *op. cit.*, p.460; Cloud, *Flirting with Rome (Volume 1—Billy Graham), op. cit.*

[302] Roy Livesey, *Understanding the New Age: World Government and World Religion* (Chichester, England: New Wine Press, 1989), p.104.

[303] *Ibid.*

[304] "Pope Defends Document on Salvation," *National Catholic Register* (October 15-21, 2000, Vol. 76, No. 42), p.5.See also: "Indian Catholics Back *Dominus Iesus,* Archbishop Says," *National Catholic Register* (October 22-28, 2000, Vol. 76, No. 43), p.6; "Justification? Can We Protestants Dialogue???," *Despatch Magazine* (June 2001, Vol. 13:2), p.30.

[305] *Ibid.*

[306] "Indian Catholics Back *Dominus Iesus,* Archbishop Says," *National Catholic Register* (October 22-28, 2000, Vol. 76, No. 43), p.6.

[307] "True Bible-Believers Denounced at Papal Conference," *Power of Prophecy* (March 2000, Vol. 2000-03), p.3.

[308] "Catholics Make Evangelicals Leave Town in Mexico," *Calvary Contender* (June 15, 2001, Vol. 18, No. 12), p.1.

[309] Wilson Ewin, *The Vatican-Moscow Alliance and Its Effect Upon Christians* (n.p., n.d.), p.12-13.

[310] D. W. Cloud, "Some Frightening Facts About Billy Graham," *O Timothy* (1984, Vol. 1, Issue 4).

[311] "Billy Graham Speaks in North Korea, Delivers Message from the Pope," *O Timothy* (1992, Vol. 9, Issue 6); Rick Miesel, "Billy Graham: General Teachings/Activities" (Biblical Discernment Ministries, Revised January 1994); Wesley Pruden, "Preaching Christ in Pyongyang," *The Washington Times* (April 5, 1992); Cloud, *Flirting with Rome (Volume 1—Billy Graham), op. cit.*; Larry Witham, "U. S. Evangelist Invited to Preach in North Korea," *The Washington Times* (March 28, 1992), p.A3.

[312] *Ibid.;* Cloud, *Flirting with Rome (Volume 1—Billy Graham), op. cit.;* Rick Miesel, "Billy Graham: General Teachings/ Activities" (Biblical Discernment Ministries, Revised January 1994).

[313] Cloud, *Flirting with Rome (Volume 1—Billy Graham), op. cit.*

[314] "Billy Graham Does Political Favor for President Clinton," *Flashpoint* (September 1997, Vol. 97-9), p.2.

[315] "Billy Graham Speaks in North Korea, *op. cit.;* Rick Miesel, "Billy Graham: General Teachings/Activities" (Biblical Discernment Ministries, Revised January 1994).

[316] *Ibid.;* Rick Miesel, "Billy Graham: General Teachings/Activities" (Biblical Discernment Ministries, Revised January 1994).

[317] Graham, *Just As I Am, op. cit.*, p.497.

[318] *Ibid.*, p.630-631. See also: Wellman, *op. cit.*, p.205.

[319] "North Korea: A Little Crack in the Door," *Samaritan's Purse* (July 2000), p.1.

[320] *Flashpoint* (September 1997, Vol. 97-9), p.2.

[321] Ian Paisley, "Billy Graham's Tragic Romeward Run," *O Timothy* (1993, Vol. 10, Issue 9); Cloud, *Is the Roman Catholic Changing?, op. cit.;* D. W. Cloud, "Papal Supremacy," *O Timothy* (1987, Vol. 4, Issue 7); David W. Cloud, "Christian Leaders and the Pope," *O Timothy* (1991, Vol. 8, Issue 2); Ewin, *Evangelism, op. cit.*, p.8; D. W. Cloud, *Is the Roman Catholic Changing?* (1984).

[322] "Cosmolatry: The Worship of Gaia," *Eco♦Logic* (May 1995, No. 26), p.14; Dave Hunt, *Global Peace and the Rise of Antichrist* (Eugene, OR: Harvest House Publishers, 1990), p.152; "The Temple of Understanding," *Wisconsin Report* (November 1, 1984, Vol. 9, No. 43), p.6; Wardner, *Unholy Alliances, op. cit.*, p.170; "An Emerging Coalition: Political and Religious Leaders Come Together," *The Omega-Letter* (Special Report), p.4; Brochure from The Temple of Understanding, unnumbered page; Brochure from The Temple of Understanding (Received March 12, 1991), p.1; Letter from The Temple of Understanding (Dated November 1997), p.2.

[323] Message from Our Lady of the Roses Shrine in Bayside, New York; Piers Compton, *The Broken Cross: The Hidden Hand in the Vatican* (Cranbrook, Western Australia: Veritas Publishing Company Pty. Ltd., 1984), p.104, 112, 122, 148.

[324] Richard Wurmbrand, *Marx and Satan* (Westchester, IL: Crossway Books, 1986), p.100-101.

[325] John T. Sekellick, "A Priestly Education in Rome, *The Catholic Answer* (July/August 1998, Vol. 12, No. 3), p.56; "Broken Cross: Hidden Hand in the Vatican—Book Review for the Coming New World Order" (Radio Show Transcript); Robert Muller, *New Genesis: Shaping a Global Spirituality* (Garden City, NY: Image Books, 1984), p.45; Piers Compton, *The Broken Cross: The Hidden Hand in the Vatican* (Cranbrook, Western Australia: Veritas Publishing Company Pty. Ltd., 1984), p.64; "Jesus' Flock or Satan's Herd,?" *Voice in the Wilderness* (March 196, Vol. 3, Issue 3), p.3; "The Robert Muller School: World Core Curriculum" (no other info available), p.15.

[326] "Broken Cross: Hidden Hand in the Vatican—Book Review for the Coming New World Order" (Radio Show Transcript). See also: McBrien, *op. cit.*, p.379.

[327] *Ibid.* See also: Livesey, *Understanding the New Age, op. cit.*, p.92; Piers Compton, *The Broken Cross: The Hidden Hand in the Vatican* (Cranbrook, Western Australia: Veritas Publishing Company Pty. Ltd., 1984), p.68.

[328] Robert Muller, *New Genesis: Shaping a Global Spirituality* (Garden City, NY: Image Books, 1984), p.101.

[329] Des Griffin, *Fourth Reich of the Rich* (South Pasadena, CA: Emissary Publications, 1978), p.150.

[330] "The U. N.'s Grab for Power," *The Florida Forum* (Spring 2000), p.8.

[331] "Broken Cross: Hidden Hand in the Vatican, *op. cit.;* Piers Compton, *The Broken Cross: The Hidden Hand in the Vatican* (Cranbrook, Western Australia: Veritas Publishing Company Pty. Ltd., 1984), p.71.

[332] Piers Compton, *The Broken Cross: The Hidden Hand in the Vatican* (Cranbrook, Western Australia: Veritas Publishing Company Pty. Ltd., 1984), p.114.

[333] *Ibid.*, p.114-115.

[334] *Ibid.*, p.115.

[335] *Ibid.*, p.53.

[336] "Ticking Time Bomb," *The Voice in the Wilderness* (February 1992), p.8; Mari Jo Buhle, Paul Buhle, and Dan Georgakas, Editors, *Encyclopedia of the American Left* (New York, NY: Oxford University Press, 1998, Second Edition), p.18; *Now Is the Dawning of the New Age New World Order, op. cit.*, p.108; *NEA: The Grab for Power: A Chronology of the National Education Association* (Oklahoma City, OK: Hearthstone Publishing, 2000), p.28-29; J. Royce Thomason, "Will We Survive It All?," *The Voice in the Wilderness* (February 1992), p.6; Walter Otten, "A Rose by Any Other Name...or Any Organization Bred by IAF Is Still the Offspring of Saul Alinsky or Immovable Church Bureaucracy," *Christian News* (October 13, 1997, Vol. 35, No. 37), p.9.

[337] Saul D. Alinsky, *Rules for Radicals: A Practical Primer for Realistic Radicals* (Vintage Books, 1971), unnumbered page; *The Grab for Power: A Chronology of the NEA* (Marlborough, NH: Plymouth Rock Foundation, 1993), p.13; "Texas, Other States and the IAF," *The Christian Conscience* (May 1996, Vol. 2, No. 5), p.42; *Chronology of Education with Quotable Quotes* (Highland City, FL: Pro Family Forum, Inc., 1994, Updated, bound volume), p.49; *Secret Records Revealed: The Men, the Money and the Methods Behind the New World Order* (Oklahoma City, OK: Hearthstone Publishing, Ltd., 1999), p.237; "Twenty Years of Federal 'Change Agentry,'" *An American Commentary* (Oklahoma City, OK: Hearthstone Publishing, Ltd., 1993), p.89; "The Industrial Areas Foundation (IAF)," *The Florida Forum* (Summer 1996), p.6; *NEA: The Grab for Power: A Chronology of the National Education Association* (Oklahoma City, OK: Hearthstone Publishing, 2000), p.29.

[338] Compton, *op. cit.*, p.53.

[339] *Ibid.*, p.53-54.

[340] Saul D. Alinsky, *Rules for Radicals: A Practical Primer for Realistic Radicals* (NY: Random House, 1971), p.94.

[341] *Secret Records Revealed: The Men, the Money and the Methods Behind the New World Order* (Oklahoma City, OK: Hearthstone Publishing, Ltd., 1999), p.237.

[342] *Now Is the Dawning of the New Age New World Order, op. cit.*, p.108; "A Disturbing Look Inside the NEA," *An American Commentary* (Oklahoma City, OK: Hearthstone Publishing, Ltd., 1993), p.80; *Chronology of Education with Quotable Quotes* (Highland City, FL: Pro Family Forum, Inc., 1994, Updated, bound volume), p.49; *The Grab for Power: A Chronology of the NEA* (Marlborough, NH: Plymouth Rock Foundation, 1993), p.14; "Twenty Years of Federal 'Change Agentry,'" *An American Commentary* (Oklahoma City, OK: Hearthstone Publishing, Ltd., 1993), p.89; *NEA: The Grab for Power: A Chronology of the National Education Association* (Oklahoma City, OK: Hearthstone Publishing, 2000), p.29.

[343] Paper from the Committee of Christian Laymen, Inc. (September 10, 1970, No. 196), p.2.

[344] "Broken Cross: Hidden Hand in the Vatican, *op. cit.* See also: David Bay, "Traditional Roman Catholic Church Proven to Be a Practice of White Magic witchcraft—Words and Symbols Tell the Story!" (Cutting Edge Ministries, n.d.), p.5, 10; Compton, *op. cit.*, p.72.

[345] *Ibid.*

[346] "A Pontiff Freemason" (Tract from In His Grip Ministries, Inc.).

[347] *Ibid.*

[348] *Ibid.*

[349] *Ibid.*

[350] "Freemasonry Unmasked in the Vatican," *Flashpoint* (May 1994), p.3.

[351] John Cotter, *A Study in Syncretism* (Flesherton, Ontario: Canadian Intelligence Publications, n.d.), p.48.

[352] *Despatch Magazine* (September 1994, Vol. 6:3), p.8; Claire Chambers, *The SIECUS Circle: A Humanist Revolution* (Belmont, MA: Western Islands, 1977), p.434; Letter dated November 1997 from the Temple of Understanding; Brochure from the Temple of Understanding.

[353] "The New Right: Part II: The Religious Heritage of America: Instrument of Brotherhood," *Distant Drums* (December 1980, Vol. 2, No. 5), p.11; *Distant Drums* (November 1982, Vol. 4, No. 5), p.11.

[354] Cotter, *op. cit.*, p.48; Nicholas Piediscalzi, *Teaching About World Religions: NCRPE Curriculum Resource Guide* (Minneapolis, MN: World Religion Curriculum, 1987), p.23; Dagobert D. Runes, *Treasury of Philosophy* (New York, NY: Philosophical Library, 1955), p.1203.

[355] Dave Hunt, *A Woman Rides the Beast* (Eugene, OR: Harvest House, 1994), p.417.

[356] James, *op. cit.*, p.101.

[357] *Now Is the Dawning of the New Age New World Order, op. cit.*, p.148-149.

[358] *Secret Records Revealed, op. cit.*, p.108; *The Road to Socialism and the New World Order* (Highland City, FL: Florida Pro Family Forum, Inc., 1995), p.30.

[359] "What Are Other Investigators Saying?," *Despatch Magazine* (June 2001, Vol. 13:2), p.52.

[360] "Salvation by Sanctifying Grace Demo," *Constantly Evolving Catholicism* (September 1995), p.5.

[361] "Graham Worries Heaven May Be Wrong Place for Him," *Calvary Contender* (January 15, 2000), p.2.

[362] Rick Miesel, "Billy Graham: General Teachings/Activities" (Biblical Discernment Ministries, Revised January 1994).

[363] "Graham's Hedonistic Paradise," *Calvary Contender* (February 15, 1999, Vol. 16, No. 4), p.1; *The Berean Call* (February 1999); Bynum, *op. cit.*, p.6, 8.

[364] "Protestants, Catholics, and Jews to Pray to Same God?," *Calvary Contender* (March 1, 1993, Vol. 10, No. 5), p.2; "Protestants, Catholics and Jews Pray to Same God?," *Christian News* (July 26, 1993, Vol. 31, No. 30), p.17.

[365] Letter from the Billy Graham Evangelistic Association dated August 1995, p.2.

[366] D. W. Cloud, "Papal Supremacy," *O Timothy* (1987, Vol. 4, Issue 7). See also: David W. Cloud, "Christian Leaders and the Pope," *O Timothy* (1991, Vol. 8, Issue 2); Paisley, *op. cit.* See also: Cloud, *Is the Roman Catholic Changing?, op. cit.;* Wilson Ewin, *Today's Evangelicals Embracing the World's Deadliest Cult* (Compton, Quebec: Quebec Baptist Missions, n.d.), p.55; Martin, *op. cit.*, p.310; Cloud, *Flirting with Rome (Volume 1—Billy Graham), op. cit.;* Ewin, *Evangelism, op. cit.;* Rick Miesel, "Billy Graham: General Teachings/Activities" (Biblical Discernment Ministries, Revised January 1994); D. W. Cloud, *Is the Roman Catholic Changing?* (1984).

[367] McBrien, *op. cit.*, p.253.

[368] Woodrow, *op. cit.*, p.88. See also: Livesey, *Understanding the New Age, op. cit.*, p.91; Charles Chiniquy, *The Priest, the Woman, and the Confessional* (Chino, CA: Chick Publications, n.d.), p.139.

[369] *Ibid.* See also: Livesey, *Understanding the New Age, op. cit.*, p.91.

[370] Livesey, *Understanding the New Age, op. cit.*, p.91; Compton, *op. cit.*, p.38-39.

[371] McBrien, *op. cit.*, p.369.

[372] See: *Secret Records Revealed, op. cit.*, p.77; *President Clinton Will Continue the New World Order, op. cit.*, p.14; *The*

Road to Socialism and the New World Order (Highland City, FL: Florida Pro Family Forum, Inc., 1995), p.51; "The U.N. & Education," *The Florida Forum* (Fall 2000), p.23.

[373] Bartholomew F. Brewer with Alfred W. Furrell, *Pilgrimage* (Greenville, SC: Bob Jones University Press, 1986), p.148.

[374] *Ibid.*, p.146.

[375] Livesey, *Understanding the New Age, op. cit.*, p.88. See also: Compton, *op. cit.*, p.35, 37.

[376] William G. McLoughlin, and Robert N. Bellah, *Religion in America* (Boston, MA: Houghton Mifflin Company, 1968), p.421. See also: McBrien, *op. cit.*, p.373-374; Compton, *op. cit.*, p.44.

[377] Brewer with Furrell, *op. cit.*, p.148-149.

[378] Ewin, *Under the New World Order, op. cit.*, p.27. See also: McBrien, *op. cit.*, p.373.

[379] *Ibid.*, p.102.

[380] Pallenberg, *op. cit.*, p.83.

[381] *Ibid.*, p.86.

[382] Livesey, *Understanding the New Age, op. cit.*, p.89-91. See also: Compton, *op. cit.*, p.34; Michael Howard, *op. cit.*, p.151, 183.

[383] Michael Howard, *op. cit.*, p.151. See also: "Freemasonry Unmasked in the Vatican," *op. cit.*, p.3; Compton, *op. cit.*, p.40.

[384] "Freemasonry Unmasked in the Vatican," *op. cit.*, p.3.

[385] David R. Barnhart, *Contending for the Faith* (Eagan, MN: Abiding Word Publications, 1994), p.120; *Now Is the Dawning of the New Age New World Order, op. cit.*, p.143; "The Temple of Understanding," *Despatch Magazine* (September 1994, Vol. 6:3), p.8; Henry Lamb, "The Rise of Global Green Religion," *Eco◆Logic* (1997 Special Report), p.3; "The Temple of Understanding," *Wisconsin Report* (October 25, 1984, Vol. 9, No. 42), p.4; "The Temple of Understanding," *Wisconsin Report* (November 1, 1984, Vol. 9, No. 43), p.6; Wardner, *Unholy Alliances, op. cit.*, p.170; "An Emerging Coalition: Political and Religious Leaders Come Together," *The Omega-Letter* (Special Report), p.4; Albert James Dager, "The World Christian Movement—Part 3: Toward the New World Order," *Media Spotlight* (1999, Vol. 22, No. 3), p.13; Brochure from The Temple of Understanding, unnumbered page; Brochure from The Temple of Understanding (Received March 12, 1991), p.1; "Second Hollister Awards Ceremony," *Temple of Understanding Newsletter* (Fall 1998), p.1; Letter from The Temple of Understanding (Dated November 1997), p.2.

[386] *Now Is the Dawning of the New Age New World Order, op. cit.*, p.148; Wardner, *Unholy Alliances, op. cit.*, p.205.

[387] *Ibid.*; Martin, *op. cit.*, p.310; Wilson Ewin, "The Church of Rome: Its Beginning, Evolution, Struggle for World Control and Impending Destruction" *O Timothy* (1989, Vol. 6, Issue 2); John Samaha, "Understanding the Eastern Christian Churches," *The Catholic Answer* (July/August 2001, Vol. 15, No. 3), p.46; Fiedler and Rabben, *op. cit.*, p.55, 62, 66; John Paul II (Translated by Jenny and Martha McPhee), *Crossing the Threshold of Hope* (NY: Alfred A. Knopf, 1994), p.141, 147; Scott Anderson and Jon Lee Anderson, *Inside the League: The Shocking Expose of How Terrorists, Nazis, and Latin American Death Squads Have Infiltrated the World Anti-Communist League* (New York, NY: Dodd, Mead & Company, 1986), p.75; David W. Cloud, "The Day of Prayer for World Peace," *O Timothy* (1994, Vol. 11, Issue 3); Roy Livesey, *Understanding Deception, New Age Teaching in the Church* (Chichester, England: New Wine Press, 1987), p.153, 159; "As the Third Millennium Draws Near 'Tertio Mellennio Adveniente,'" *Despatch Magazine* (June 1995, Vol. 7, No. 2), p.41; David L. Harris, "Evangelism: The Ultimate Deception," *The New Age Adversary Bulletin and Old Time Gospel Advocate* (June 1994, Vol. 9, No. 6), p.1; *A Gift of Prophecy: The Phenomenal Jeane Dixon* (NY: William Morrow and Company, 1965), p.167; Ewin, *The Vatican-Moscow Alliance, op. cit.*, p.12; "As the Third Millennium Draws Near: Tertio Mellennio Adveniente," (Apostolic Letter of Pope John Paul II released on November 13, 1994), p.8; Vinson Synan and Ralph Rath, *Launching the Decade of Evangelization* (South Bend, IN: North American Renewal Service Committee, 1990), p.90; M. Edmund Hussey, "Needed: A Theology of Priesthood," *Origins* (February 4, 1988, Vol. 17, No. 34), p.579; Muller, *New Genesis, op. cit.*, p.101.

[388] Brewer with Furrell, *op. cit.*, p.157. See also: "Comments Regarding 'Evangelicals and Catholics Together,'" *Christians Evangelizing Catholics* (April 1995), p.6; Clyde L. Manschreck, *A History of Christianity: Readings in the History of the Church from the Reformation to the Present* (Englewood Cliffs, NJ: Prentice-Hall, Inc., 1964), p.468; McLoughlin, and Bellah, *op. cit.*, p.421; McBrien, *op. cit.*, p.375.

[389] "Comments Regarding 'Evangelicals and Catholics Together," *Christians Evangelizing Catholics* (April 1995), p.6. See also: "The Roman Connection: The 'Sovereign Drug,'" *Dorea Ministries* (January-March 1992), p.13; "The Present-Day Official Teaching of the Roman Catholic Church" (Article by Evangelical Outreach), p.7.

[390] Dave Hunt, "A Cult Is a Cult," *CIB Bulletin* (June 1991, Vol. 7, No. 6), p.1. See also: D. W. Cloud, *Is the Roman Catholic Changing?* (1984); "The Roman Connection: The 'Sovereign Drug,'" *Dorea Ministries* (January-March 1992), p.13; Cloud, *Is the Roman Catholic Changing?, op. cit.*

[391] Cloud, *Is the Roman Catholic Changing?, op. cit.*; "The Present-Day Official Teaching of the Roman Catholic Church" (Article by Evangelical Outreach), p.7; Brewer with Furrell, *op. cit.*, p.41; "Justification? Can We Protestants Dialogue???," *Despatch Magazine* (June 2001, Vol. 13:2), p.30; T. A. McMahon, "Why Evangelize Roman Catholics?," *The Berean Call* (June 2001), p.2; D. W. Cloud, *Is the Roman Catholic Changing?* (1984).

[392] Brewer with Furrell, *op. cit.*, p.41. See also: Robert A. Champagne, "Evangelical Catholics," *Dorea Ministries* (Winter 1992, Vol. 4), p.16.

[393] Wendy B. Howard, *The Alpha Course: Friend or Foe?* (Landsborough, Queensland: Endtime Ministries, 1999), p.19.

[394] Cloud, *Is the Roman Catholic Changing?, op. cit.* See also: "The Present-Day Official Teaching of the Roman

Catholic Church" (Article by Evangelical Outreach), p.8; David W. Cloud, "Roman Catholicism Still Follows the Council of Trent," *O Timothy* (1992, Vol. 9, Issue 6); Dave Hunt, *Global Peace and the Rise of Antichrist* (Eugene, OR: Harvest House Publishers, 1990), 143; D. W. Cloud, *Is the Roman Catholic Changing?* (1984).

[395] Robert A. Champagne, "Evangelical Catholics," *Dorea Ministries* (Winter 1992, Vol. 4), p.16.

[396] Ewin, *Today's Evangelicals Embracing the World's Deadliest Cult, op. cit.*, p.16.

[397] "The Present-Day Official Teaching of the Roman Catholic Church" (Article by Evangelical Outreach), p.8; Richard M. Bennett, *"We Ought to Obey God Rather Than Men,"* (Portland, OR: Berean Beacon, 1994), p.8; Tony Caputo, "Et Tu Impe," *Bold Truth Press Inc.* (November 5, 1993), p.8.

[398] *Ibid.*

[399] *Ibid.*, p.7.

[400] "Thus Saith Vatican Council II," *Fighting the Good Fight* (November/December 1994), p.2; T. A. McMahon, "Why It Matters" (Part II), *The Berean Call* (November 1999), p.1; *Ibid.*, p.1; Dave Hunt, "The Gospel Betrayed," *The Berean Call* (May 1994), p.2; *The Berean Call* (October 1993), p.3; Ewin, *Today's Evangelicals Embracing the World's Deadliest Cult, op. cit.*, p.16.

[401] Brewer with Furrell, *op. cit.*, p.55; "The Present-Day Official Teaching of the Roman Catholic Church," *op. cit.*, p.8.

[402] Michael Paulson, "Confession Is Good for the Mind, Too," *Catholic Digest* (June 2001, Vol. 65, No. 8), p.8.

[403] Henry G. Graham, *Where We Got the Bible: Our Debt to the Catholic Church* (Rockford, IL: Tan Books and Publishers, Inc., 1987 Edition), p.15.

[404] *Ibid.*

[405] *Our Sunday Visitor* (February 22, 1998, Vol. 86, No. 43), p.20.

[406] Fiedler and Rabben, *op. cit.*, p.41.

[407] *Ibid.*, p.32.

[408] *Ibid.*

[409] Karl Keating, "Q and A," *Be* (November-December 2000), p.2.

[410] Fiedler and Rabben, *op. cit.*, p.165.

[411] "The Present-Day Official Teaching of the Roman Catholic Church," *op. cit.*, p.7; Brewer with Furrell, *op. cit.*, p.42. See also: David W. Cloud, "Roman Catholicism Still Follows the Council of Trent," *O Timothy* (1992, Vol. 9, Issue 6); Woodrow, *op. cit.*, p.116; T. A. McMahon, "Why Evangelize Roman Catholics?," *The Berean Call* (June 2001), p.2; Jeff Mardis, "The Greatest Words Ever Spoken by Mary: A Message to Roman Catholics" (Campbellsville, KY: The Contender, 2000), p.6; Cloud, *Is the Roman Catholic Changing?, op. cit.*

[412] Jeff Mardis, "The Greatest Words Ever Spoken by Mary: A Message to Roman Catholics" (Campbellsville, KY: The Contender, 2000), p.6.

[413] *Ibid.*, p.7.

[414] Brewer with Furrell, *op. cit.*, p.42. See also: Chiniquy, *50 Years in the 'Church' of Rome, op. cit.*, p.80.

[415] Chiniquy, *50 Years in the 'Church' of Rome, op. cit.*, p.80.

[416] T. A. McMahon, "Why It Matters" (Part II), *The Berean Call* (November 1999), p.1.

[417] Fiedler and Rabben, *op. cit.*, p.14, 55, 93.

[418] T. A. McMahon, "Why Evangelize Roman Catholics?," *The Berean Call* (June 2001), p.2.

[419] *Catechism of the Catholic Church* (New York, NY: Image Books, 1995), p.379. See also: Hugh Farrell, "The Charismatic Phenomenon in the Church of Rome," *O Timothy* (1986, Vol. 3, Issue 4); "The Present-Day Official Teaching of the Roman Catholic Church," *op. cit.*, p.3; D. W. Cloud, "Some Frightening Facts About Billy Graham," *O Timothy* (1984, Vol. 1, Issue 4); David W. Cloud, "The Roman Catholic Mass," *O Timothy* (1995, Vol. 12, Issue 4); Woodrow, *op. cit.*, p.118; "Can a Good Catholic Be Saved?," *O Timothy* (1995, Issue 12, Issue 12); David W. Cloud, "The New Catholic Catechism," *O Timothy* (1995, Vol. 12, Issue 1); "On the Mass," *The Gospel Standard* (June 1994, Vol. 43, No. 10), p.4; Cloud, *Is the Roman Catholic Changing?, op. cit.*

[420] "The Present-Day Official Teaching of the Roman Catholic Church," *op. cit.*, p.3.

[421] Richard Bennett, Compiler, quoting Anthony Wilhelm in *The Bible and Vatican Council II: A Comparison* (Portland, OR: Berean Beacon, n.d.), p.2.

[422] Richard M. Bennett, *"We Ought to Obey God Rather Than Men,"* (Portland, OR: Berean Beacon, 1994), p.10.

[423] *Ibid.*

[424] *Catechism of the Catholic Church, op. cit.*, p.379.

[425] Pallenberg, *op. cit.*, p.41.

[426] Roy Livesey, *Understanding Deception, New Age Teaching in the Church* (Chichester, England: New Wine Press, 1987), p.160. See also: Cloud, *Is the Roman Catholic Changing?, op. cit.*

[427] Cloud, *Is the Roman Catholic Changing?, op. cit.*

[428] Edmond Paris, *The Secret History of the Jesuits* (Chino, CA: Chick Publications, 1975), p.167. See also: "Catholic Church and the Death Penalty," *Calvary Contender* (August 1, 2001, Vol. 19, No. 15), p.1.

[429] McBrien, *op. cit.*, p.350-351, 459. See also: "Short Reviews," *The Catholic Answer* (July/August 2001, Vol. 15, No. 3), p.30-31; Russell Shaw, "Why the Pope Rules," *Our Sunday Visitor* (February 22, 1998, Vol. 86, No. 43), p.7.

[430] "On Papal Primacy," *Our Sunday Visitor* (July 29, 2001, Vol. 90, No. 13), p.10.

[431] *Ibid.*

[432] *Ibid.*

[433] Richard Scheinin, "United Faiths: Call Arises for Spiritual U. N. to Cooperate in the Names of God," *San Jose, CA Mercury News* (June 17, 1995), p.11e; Eugene Daniels, *A Protestant Looks at the Catholic Church in Mission* (Monrovia, CA: MARC, 1993), p.7; John Paul II (Translated by Jenny and Martha McPhee), *Crossing the Threshold of Hope* (NY: Alfred A. Knopf, 1994), p.147; *The Problems of Humanity: The Building of Right Human Relations: The Problem of the Churches* (New York, NY: World Goodwill, n.d.), p.15.

[434] Muller, *New Genesis, op. cit.*, p.101. See also: "Jesus' Flock or Satan's Herd,?" *Voice in the Wilderness* (March 196, Vol. 3, Issue 3), p.3.

[435] "Q & A," *The Berean Call* (December 1998), p.4; Rick Miesel, "Billy Graham: General Teachings/Activities" (Biblical Discernment Ministries, Revised January 1994); Ewin, *Evangelism, op. cit.;* David W. Cloud, "Christian Leaders and the Pope," *O Timothy* (1991, Vol. 8, Issue 2).

[436] *Ibid.;* Ewin, *The Assimilation of Evangelist Billy Graham into the Roman Catholic Church, op. cit.*, p.7; David W. Cloud, "Christian Leaders and the Pope," *O Timothy* (1991, Vol. 8, Issue 2); Ewin, *Evangelism, op. cit.;* Cloud, *Flirting with Rome (Volume 1—Billy Graham), op. cit.*

[437] *The Communion of Saints: Sanctity Through the Centuries* (Still River, MA: n.p., 1967), p.63.

[438] *Ibid.*

[439] Paisley, *op. cit.*

[440] Graham, *Just As I Am, op. cit.*, p.302.

[441] *Ibid.*, p.296.

[442] Cloud, *Flirting with Rome (Volume 1—Billy Graham), op. cit.;* Wellman, *op. cit.*, p.161.

[443] Graham, *Just As I Am, op. cit.*, p.357.

[444] *Ibid.*, p.368.

[445] John W. Robbins, "Contemporary Religion Vs. the Gospel," *Christian News* (April 24, 1995, Vol. 33, No. 17), p.12.

[446] Paisley, *op. cit.*

[447] Cloud, *Flirting with Rome (Volume 1—Billy Graham), op. cit.*

[448] "How Billy Graham Protected the Jesuits," *Newsletter from a Christian Ministry* (September 1, 1993, Vol. 2, No. 12), p.79.

[449] "Billy Graham," *BDM Newsletter* (November 1993, Vol. 2, No. 9). p.2.

[450] Cloud, *Flirting with Rome (Volume 1—Billy Graham), op. cit.*

[451] *Ibid.*

[452] *Ibid.*

[453] *Ibid.* See also: Brad K. Gsell, *The Legacy of Billy Graham* (Charlotte, NC: Fundamental Presbyterian Publication, n.d.), p.32.

[454] *Ibid.;* Rick Miesel, "Billy Graham: General Teachings/Activities" (Biblical Discernment Ministries, Revised January 1994); "The Pope...Spiritual Leader or Anti-Christ?," *The Protestant Challenge* (January-February 1997, Vol. 24, No. 1), p.8; Chick, *op. cit.*, p.57.

[455] "All of That Means Nothing to Me Any More," *Foundation* (October-December 1988), p.22.

[456] Cloud, *Flirting with Rome (Volume 1—Billy Graham), op. cit.*

[457] Graham, *Just As I Am, op. cit.*, p.429.

[458] Cloud, *Flirting with Rome (Volume 1—Billy Graham), op. cit.* See also: M. H. Reynolds, "AD 2000 Ecumenical Evangelism: A Warning!," *Foundation* (July-September 1995, Vol. 16, Issue 4), p.27; Perry F. Rockwood, *The Charismatic Renewal in the Roman Catholic Church* (Nova Scotia, Canada: The Peoples Gospel Hour, n.d.), p.5; Brad K. Gsell, *The Legacy of Billy Graham* (Charlotte, NC: Fundamental Presbyterian Publication, n.d.), p.32; Tricia Tillin, "Testing Evangelism," *Mainstream* (Spring 1994), p.5; Ewin, *The Assimilation of Evangelist Billy Graham into the Roman Catholic Church, op. cit.*, p.17.

[459] *Council on Foreign Relations: Annual Report July 1, 1987-June 30, 1988,* p.172; *Council on Foreign Relations: Annual Report July 1, 1990-June 30, 1991,* p.177; *Council on Foreign Relations: Annual Report July 1, 1992-June 30, 1993,* p.163; *Council on Foreign Relations: Annual Report July 1, 1994-June 30, 1995,* p.143.

[460] Templeton, *op. cit.*, p.205.

[461] Brochure from the Arms Control Association.

[462] "The Most Important Arms Agreement of the Nuclear Age Is in Danger...," (Brochure from the National Campaign to Save the ABM Treaty).

[463] Basil Hume, *One in Christ: Unity and Diversity in the Church Today* (New York, NY: Catholic Common Ground Initiative, 1999), back cover; Cornelia R. Ferreira, "The Global Ethic: From Golden Rule to Common Ground," *Wisconsin Report* (May 14, 1998), p.1.

[464] Albert James Dager, "Parliament of the World's Religions to Meet: Chuck Colson Receives Templeton Prize," *Media Spotlight* (Vol. 15, No. 1), p.1; Barnhart, *Contending for the Faith, op. cit.*, p.114; Morrison, *op. cit.*, p.553.

[465] Morrison, *op. cit.*, p.554.

[466] "Radical Feminist Agenda," quoting from *Chicago Sun-Times* in *The Koinonia Chronicle* (April 1996, Vol. 3), p.4.

[467] "The Son of Perdition," *Point Hat News* (May/September 1995), p.5.

[468] Dwight L. Kinman quoting from *The Oregonian* in *The World's Last Dictator* (Woodburn, OR: Solid Rock Books, Inc., 1995), p.161.

[469] Hume, *op. cit.*, p.7.

[470] Fournier, *op. cit.*, p.iv.

[471] *Ibid.*, p.161. See also: John Paul II (Edited by Peter Canisus Johannes Van Lierde; Translated by Firman O'Sullivan (New York, NY: Penguin Group, 1994), p.67.

[472] Keating, *op. cit.*, p.2.

[473] Fiedler and Rabben, *op. cit.*, p.57.

[474] Cloud, *Is the Roman Catholic Changing?, op. cit.*; Albert James Dager, *The World Christian Movement: A Great Delusion Leading to the Religio-Political State of the Anti-Christ* (Redmond, WA: Sword Publishers, 2001), p.142.

[475] Fiedler and Rabben, *op. cit.*, p.56.

[476] Paul VI, "Decree on Ecumenism: Unitatis Redintegratio" (no other info available), p.1, 3, 11. See also: Cloud, *Is the Roman Catholic Changing?, op. cit.*, quoting from Vatican II.

[477] Cloud, *Is the Roman Catholic Changing?, op. cit.*, quoting Benjamin Luther. See also: Cloud, "Papal Supremacy," *op. cit.*

[478] "Charismatics and Roman Catholics," *Dorea Ministries* (January-March 1992), p.15-16. See also: J. Royce Thomason, "Evangelization, A.D. 2000," *The Voice of the Nazarene* (November/December 1991, Vol. 38, No. 5), p.3.

[479] Richard M. Bennett, Dominus Iesus: Rome Exalts Her Throne: A Kiss of Death for the Ecumenists," *The Protestant Challenge* (2001, No. 2), p.3. See also: Keating, *op. cit.*, p.2.

[480] *Ibid.* See also: "Catholics Say They Are Superior," *Calvary Contender* (October 1, 2000, Vol. 17, No. 19), p.2.

[481] Hunt, *Whatever Happened to Heaven?, op. cit.*, p.159; Robert A. Morey, "A Refutation of Roman Catholicism," *The Researcher* (January/February 1993), p.4; Dave Hunt, "A City on Seven Hills," *O Timothy* (1995, Vol. 12, Issue 3).

[482] Keating, *op. cit.*, p.2.

[483] Robbins, *op. cit.*, p.5.

[484] Paolo Ricca quoting Paul IV in "New Possibilities for the Papacy?," *Theology Digest* (Spring 1999, Vol. 46, No. 1), p.49.

[485] *Ibid.*

[486] Cloud, "Papal Supremacy," *op. cit.* See also: Pallenberg, *op. cit.*, p.108.

[487] Pallenberg, *op. cit.*, p.108.

[488] Cloud, "Papal Supremacy," *op. cit.*

[489] *Ibid.*, quoting Loraine Boettner.

[490] *Ibid.*

[491] McBrien, *op. cit.*, p.297.

[492] Pallenberg, *op. cit.*, p.94, 98; Dave Hunt, *Global Peace and the Rise of Antichrist* (Eugene, OR: Harvest House Publishers, 1990), p.153.

[493] *Ibid.*, p.98.

[494] "Charismatics Believe God Is Building Bridges," *O Timothy* (1995, Vol. 12, Issue 4); "Pastor of Thailand's Largest Church Is in Fellowship with Rome," *O Timothy* (1991, Vol. 8, Issue 10-12); David W. Cloud, "Jack Hayford and Rome," *O Timothy* (1995, Vol. 12, Issue 7); "European Christians Being Swept into Ecumenism and Pentecostalism," *O Timothy* (1991, Vol. 8, Issue 10-12); "John Wimber, Jack Hayford, and the Catholics," *O Timothy* (1991, Vol. 8, Issue 6); David W. Cloud, "Contemporary Christian Music and Rome," (Part II), *The Evangelical Methodist* (June 1999, Vol. 77, No. 6), p.2; David W. Cloud, "Paul Yonggi Cho and Rome," *O Timothy* (1995, Vol. 12, Issue 6); Brochure from the Congress on the Holy Spirit and World Evangelization; "Catholics, Protestants Join Forces," *O Timothy* (1995, Vol. 12, Issue 11); "Orlando '95 Celebrates Unity in the Holy Spirit," *Focus Express* (November 1995); David W. Cloud, *Flirting with Rome: Evangelical Entanglement with Roman Catholicism (Volume 4—The Charismatics)* (Oak Harbor, WA: Way of Life Literature, 1993); Nancy Kellar, "From Generation to Generation You Will Be My Witnesses," *Focus* (Winter 1995, Vol. 20, No. 1), p.10.

[495] Karl Keating, "Q & A," *Be* (July-August 2001), p.2.

[496] "G-C Woman Pastor Defines Best/Worst Witness," *Calvary Contender* (October 1, 1995, Vol. 12, No. 19); "Billy Graham to Speak at Ockenga Testimonial Dinner; All Invited to March 30 Event," *Contact* (Winter 1979, Vol. 9, No. 2); *Hilltop* (1977); "The Inauguration of Robert E. Cooley," *Contact* (Winter 1981-82, Vol. 12, No. 1); M. H. Reynolds, "Mixing Truth and Error at Urbana '90," "New Chancellor and President Named," *Hilltop* (Winter 1996-1997, Vol. 8, No. 3), p.1; *Foundation*, p.13; Paul Fisher, "The Church and the New World Order," *National Educator* (August 1995), p.16; "News Notes," *Hilltop* (Summer 1996, Vol. 8, No. 2), p.3; Graham, *Just As I Am, op. cit.*, p.471; "Urbana '96," *Hilltop* (Winter 1996-1997, Vol. 8, No. 3), p.4; "Colson, Palau to Gordon-Conwell Board," *Calvary Contender* (September

15, 1999, Vol. 16, No. 18), p.2; Graham, *Just As I Am, op. cit.*, p.471.

[497] *Ibid.* See also: "Colson, Palau to Gordon-Conwell Board," *Calvary Contender* (September 15, 1999, Vol. 16, No. 18), p.2; "Colson, Palau to Gordon-Conwell Board," *Despatch Magazine* (September 1999, Vol. 11, No. 3), p.39.

[498] "Colson, Palau to Gordon-Conwell Board," *Calvary Contender* (September 15, 1999, Vol. 16, No. 18), p.2; "Colson, Palau to Gordon-Conwell Board," *Despatch Magazine* (September 1999, Vol. 11, No. 3), p.39.

[499] "The Inauguration of Robert E. Cooley," *Contact* (Winter 1981-82, Vol. 12, No. 1); *Hilltop* (1977); Paul Fisher, "The Church and the New World Order," *National Educator* (August 1995), p.16; "Mary French Rockefeller Endowed Chair in New Testament Established," *Hilltop;* "Mary French Rockefeller, Trustee, Dies at 86," *Hilltop* (Summer 1997, Vol. 9, No. 1), p.5.

[500] M. Sabeheddin, "The Rockefeller-UFO Connection: An Alien Conspiracy?," *New Dawn* (March-April, 1996, No. 35).

[501] "Meet Maurice Strong," *Eco◆Logic* (November/December 1995, No. 29), p.6.

[502] "Three New Trustees Appointed to Gordon-Conwell Board," *Hilltop* (1977).

[503] Sabeheddin, *op. cit.*

[504] *Ibid.*

[505] *Ibid.*

[506] "Author Makes Transition," *Sparrow Hawk Villager* (July-September 2001, Vol. 21, No. 3), p.5.

[507] Texe Marrs, *Dark Majesty: The Secret Brotherhood and the Magic of a Thousand Points of Light* (Austin, TX: Living Truth Publishers, 1992), p.105.

[508] "Intentional Communities: Seeds for a New Civilization," *The Christian Conscience* (December 1995, Vol. 1, No. 11), p.33; *Now Is the Dawning of the New Age New World Order, op. cit.*, p.318; David Spangler, *Emergence: The Rebirth of the Sacred* (NY: Dell Publishing, 1984), p.4, 118; Ed Rowe, *New Age Globalism* (Herndon, VA: Growth Publishing, 1985), p.32.

[509] Scott and Smith, *op. cit.*, p.93.

[510] "Cathedral Not-So-Divine," *The New American* (January 23, 1995), p.11.

[511] *Now Is the Dawning of the New Age New World Order, op. cit.*, p.318-319. See also: "Intentional Communities, *op. cit.*, p.33.

[512] "Cathedral Not-So-Divine," *op. cit.*, p.11.

[513] Matthew Fox, *The Coming of the Cosmic Christ* (New York, NY: Harper & Row, Inc., 1988), Acknowledgement page; Texe Marrs, "Greedy 'Christian' Leaders Taken in by New Age Hucksters," *Flashpoint* (October 1995, Vol. 95-10), p.1; Marrs, *Circle of Intrigue, op. cit.*, p.59; Warren Smith, "Sign of the Times: Evangelicals and New Agers Together," *SCP Journal* (19:2/3), p.62.

[514] Texe Marrs, "Greedy 'Christian' Leaders Taken in by New Age Hucksters," *Flashpoint* (October 1995, Vol. 95-10), p.1.

[515] Marrs, *Circle of Intrigue, op. cit.*, p.59; Warren Smith, "Sign of the Times: Evangelicals and New Agers Together," *SCP Journal* (19:2/3), p.62.

[516] "Friend, Can You Spare A...?," *Creation* (July/August 1986, Vol. 2, No. 3), p.38.

[517] "Mary French Rockefeller, Trustee, Dies at 86," *Hilltop* (Summer 1997, Vol. 9, No. 1), p.5; Claire Chambers, *The SIECUS Circle: A Humanist Revolution* (Belmont, MA: Western Islands, 1977), p.390.

[518] Claire Chambers, *The SIECUS Circle: A Humanist Revolution* (Belmont, MA: Western Islands, 1977), p.389.

[519] *Ibid.*

[520] *Ibid.*, p.390.

[521] "Three New Trustees Appointed to Gordon-Conwell Board," *op. cit.*

[522] Claire Chambers, *op. cit.*, p.390.

[523] Templeton, *op. cit.*, p.191.

[524] "Humility Theology Information Center Advisory Board," *Progress in Theology* (June 1996, Vol. 4, No. 2), p.2.

[525] "Faculty News," *Hilltop* (Summer 1997, Vol. 9, No. 1), p.10.

[526] *Ibid.*

[527] "Alumni/ae Notes," *Hilltop* (Summer 1997, Vol. 9, No. 1), p.6.

[528] Lovelace's, Mott's, and Cooley's names were included in the "Partial List of Signers of 'An Evangelical Declaration on the Care of Creation'" as of October 17, 1995; "Partial List of Signers of 'An Evangelical Declaration on the Care of Creation'" as of March 1, 1996.

[529] Edgar C. Bundy, *How Liberals and Radicals Are Manipulating Evangelicals* (Miami Shores, FL: Edgar Bundy Ministries, Inc., 1982), p.82, 89.

[530] *Ibid.*, p.19.

[531] *Ibid.*

[532] "Mary French Rockefeller Endowed Chair in New Testament Established," *Hilltop.*

[533] "Three New Trustees Appointed to Gordon-Conwell Board," *op. cit.*

[534] "New Chancellor and President Named," *Hilltop* (Winter 1996-1997, Vol. 8, No. 3), p.2.

[535] Roger A. McCaffrey, Editor, *Sursum Corda!* (Fort Collins, CO: Foundation for Catholic Reform, n.d.), p.3.

[536] *Ibid.*, p.13.

[537] "$1 Million Scholarship Endowment Awarded by The Billy Graham Evangelistic Association," *Hilltop* (Summer 1999, Vol. 11, No. 2), p.4.; "Colson, Palau to Gordon-Conwell Board," *Calvary Contender, op. cit.*, p.2; "Colson, Palau to Gordon-Conwell Board," *Despatch Magazine* (September 1999, Vol. 11, No. 3), p.39.

[538] M. H. Reynolds, "Mixing Truth and Error at Urbana '90," *Foundation,* p.13.

[539] "Gordon-Conwell Awarded $442,150 for Program in Evangelical Leadership," *Hilltop* (Summer 1997, Vol. 9, No. 1), p.1.

[540] "$2.27 Million Grant to Equip Urban Ministries Received by Gordon-Conwell," *Hilltop.*

[541] Graham, *Just As I Am, op. cit.*, p.289, 368, 426, 646.

[542] *Ibid.*, p.646. See also: Bundy, *Billy Graham: Performer?, Politician?, Preacher?, Prophet?, op. cit.*, p.99-100.

[543] *Ibid.* See also: Martin, *op. cit.*, p.467.

[544] Bundy, *Billy Graham: Performer?, Politician?, Preacher?, Prophet?, op. cit.*, p.104.

[545] Martin, *op. cit.*, p.468.

[546] Bundy quoting *Chicago Tribune* in *Billy Graham: Performer?, Politician?, Preacher?, Prophet?, op. cit.*, p.101.

[547] *Ibid.* See also: Hadden and Swann, *op. cit.*, p.21-22; Wellman, *op. cit.*, p.186; Martin, *op. cit.*, p.468; Ashbrook, "Billy Graham—The Mouthpiece of New Evangelicalism," *op. cit.*

[548] *Ibid.*, p.101-102. See also: Martin, *op. cit.*, p.467.

[549] Martin, *op. cit.*, p.467. See also: Wellman, *op. cit.*, p.186.

[550] *Ibid.*, p.468-469.

[551] Bundy, *Billy Graham: Performer?, Politician?, Preacher?, Prophet?, op. cit.*, p.104.

[552] *Ibid.*, p.103

[553] Graham, *Just As I Am, op. cit.*, p.647. See also: Martin, *op. cit.*, p.467.

[554] Paper from Planetary Citizens.

[555] David P. Gaines, *The World Council of Churches: A Study of Its Background and History* (Peterborough, NH: Richard R. Smith Company, Inc., 1966), p.559.

[556] Donald C. Kerr, "Pilgrim Feet, Patriot Dream," *The Scottish Rite Journal* (November 1994, Vol. 102, No. 11), p.27; Graham, *Just As I Am, op. cit.*, p.647.

[557] Gaines, *op. cit.*, 1966), p.934.

[558] Graham, *Just As I Am, op. cit.*, p.677; Martin, *op. cit.*, p.472.

[559] Martin, *op. cit.*, p.472.

[560] Eddie Karnes, "Boycott the China Olympics 2008," *Christian News* (July 23, 2001, Vol. 39, No. 30), p.19.

[561] "Communist Puppets Are Hoodwinking Lutherans," *Christian News* (November 15, 1999, Vol. 37, No. 42), p.21, quoting from the November 6, 1999 issue of *World.*

[562] Graham, *Just As I Am, op. cit.*, p.675; Jim Jones, "Billy Graham's Organization in Good Hands—His Son's," *The News and Observer* (December 8, 2000), p.2F. See also: "Graham Meetings," *Calvary Contender* (January 15, 2001, Vol. 18, No. 2), p.2; "Billy Graham Takes Failing Health in Stride, Plans More Crusades Next Year," *The News and Observer* (November 1, 2000), p.11A; "BBF Gives Graham Book to Preachers," *Calvary Contender* (April 1, 1999, Vol. 16, No. 7), p.2; "Franklin Graham Named CEO of His Father's Evangelical Association," *The Vine and Branches* (Winter 2001, Vol. 16, Issue 1), p.10; Christine Wicker, "The Son Also Rises: Franklin Graham to Preach at First Baptist Church," *The Dallas Morning News*, p.1G; "Franklin Graham to Speak at Liberty," *Calvary Contender* (May 1, 1996, Vol. 23, No. 9), p.2; "People and Events," *Moody* (January-February 2001, Vol. 101, No. 3), p.38; "Franklin Graham Named CEO of Father's Evangelical Association," *Christian News* (November 27, 2000, Vol. 38, No. 44), p.2; Brad K. Gsell, *The Legacy of Billy Graham* (Charlotte, NC: Fundamental Presbyterian Publication, n.d.), p.46; Adelle M. Banks, "Graham Ministry Spans Half a Century," *Christian News* (May 13, 1996, Vol. 34, No. 20), p.6; "The Prodigal Graham," *New Man* (October 1996, Vol. 3, No. 7), p.12; Wellman, *op. cit.*, p.205.

[563] Marcia Ford, "New Era Scam Involved Millions in Donor Funds," *Christian News* (July 31, 1995, Vol. 33, No. 31), p.5; "College Loses Twice in Financial Scandals," *The News-Item* (July 5, 1995, Vol. 27), No. 224), p.16; "Evangelicals May Lose Millions in Ponzi Scheme," *Calvary Contender* (June 15, 1995, Vol. 12, No. 12), p.1. See also: "Major Ministries Jolted by Scandal," *Christian News* (July 3, 1995, Vol. 33, No. 27), p.3; "Groups with Trust, Faith," *Morning Call* (May 28, 1995); *Focus on the Family* (July 1995), p.4-6; Russ Bellant, *The Religious Right in Michigan Politics* (Silver Spring, MD: Americans for Religious Liberty, 1996), p.62.

[564] "College Loses Twice in Financial Scandals," *The News-Item* (July 5, 1995, Vol. 27), No. 224), p.16.

[565] "New Era Founder Gets 12 Years," *Calvary Contender* (November 15, 1997, Vol. 14, No. 22), p.1.

[566] Marrs, "Greedy 'Christian' Leaders Taken in by New Age Hucksters," *op. cit.*, p.2; Amy Donohue, "How John Templeton Got Rich," *Philadelphia* (October 1996), p.125.

[567] *Ibid.*

[568] "More on New Era Scam," *Calvary Contender* (August 1, 1995), p.1. See also: *Focus on the Family* (July 1995), p.4.

[569] Ashbrook, "Billy Graham—The Mouthpiece of New Evangelicalism," *op. cit.*

[570] "Charismatic Adulterer," *Christian News* (January 11, 1993, Vol. 31, No. 2), p.7; George R. Brunk, "Counterfeit Revival," *Christian News* (June 9, 1997, Vol. 35, No. 23), p.20.

[571] *Ibid.*; "Praising a Twice Divorced Woman 'Pastor,'" *Christian News* (March 8, 1993, Vol. 31, No. 10), p.9; "National Religious Broadcasters: 55th Annual Convention and Exposition," *The ACCC Report* (July 1998), p.3; "Patty's (sic) Critics Are Few, Despite Affair," *Christian News* (October 30, 1995, Vol. 33, No. 40), p.3; George R. Brunk, "Counterfeit Revival," *Christian News* (June 9, 1997, Vol. 35, No. 23), p.20; Benny Hinn, *The Anointing* (Nashville, TN: Thomas Nelson Publishers, 1992), p.62-63, 65.

[572] Benny Hinn, *The Anointing* (Nashville, TN: Thomas Nelson Publishers, 1992), p.62; Rebekah Scott, "The Legacy of Kathryn Kuhlman," *Christian News* (July 24, 1995, Vol. 33, N. 30), p.2; George R. Brunk, "Counterfeit Revival," *Christian News* (June 9, 1997, Vol. 35, No. 23), p.20.

[573] *Ibid.*, p.63; "Charismatic Adulterer," *op. cit.*, p.7.

[574] George R. Brunk, "Counterfeit Revival," *Christian News* (June 9, 1997, Vol. 35, No. 23), p.20; Rebekah Scott, "The Legacy of Kathryn Kuhlman," *Christian News* (July 24, 1995, Vol. 33, N. 30), p.2.

[575] Rebekah Scott, "The Legacy of Kathryn Kuhlman," *Christian News* (July 24, 1995, Vol. 33, N. 30), p.2.

[576] *Ibid.*

[577] John S. Torell, "Betrayal," *The Dove* (Autumn/Winter 1995, Vol. 16, No. 3), p.4; David W. Cloud, "Charismatics and the Pope of Rome," *O Timothy* (1989, Vol. 6, Issues 3-4); Ed and Mary Tarkowski, "Is Christian America's Manifest Destiny Being Fulfilled?" (Received May 7, 1994), p.6; David W. Cloud, *Flirting with Rome: Evangelical Entanglement with Roman Catholicism (Volume 4—The Charismatics)* (Oak Harbor, WA: Way of Life Literature, 1993).

[578] "Charismatic Adulterer," *op. cit.*, p.7.

[579] *Ibid.*

[580] "Graham Museum Honors First Pope As an Evangelist," *Christian News* (July 23, 2001, Vol. 39, No. 30), p.22.

[581] *Ibid.*

[582] Woodrow, *op. cit.*, p.63. See also: Rick Miesel, "Roman Catholicism: General Notes" (Biblical Discernment Ministries, Revised August 1997).

[583] *Ibid.*; Rick Miesel, "Roman Catholicism: General Notes" (Biblical Discernment Ministries, Revised August 1997).

[584] "Halloween: Kids' Treat or Pagan Trick?," *Battle Cry* (July/August 1991), p.4.

[585] "The Papacy and the 'Rock' of Matthew 16," *Jesus People Newsletter* (1999, Vol. 27, Issue 2), p.17.

[586] "Graham Museum Honors First Pope As an Evangelist," *op. cit.*, p.22.

[587] Matthew Fox, *Original Blessing: A Primer in Creation Spirituality* (Santa Fe, NM: Bear & Company, 1983), p.221.

[588] Jay Gary, *The Star of 2000: Our Journey Toward Hope* (Colorado Springs, CO: Bimillennial Press, 1994), p.100.

[589] "Brother Wind, Sister Earth," *Maryknoll* (January 1990, Vol. 84, No. 1), p.3-6. See also: Friedrich Rest, *Our Christian Symbols* (Philadelphia, PA: The Christian Education Press, 1954), p.73-74; *Ibid.*, p.100-101.

[590] Matthew Fox, *Original Blessing: A Primer in Creation Spirituality* (Santa Fe, NM: Bear & Company, 1983), p.309.

[591] Fox, *The Coming of the Cosmic Christ, op. cit.*, p.50, 134. See also: *Ibid.*, p.123; Matthew Fox, *Whee! We, Wee All the Way Home...A Guide to the New Sensual Spirituality,* (Wilmington, NC: Consortium Books, 1976), p.79; Michael Fox, "Panentheism: Where Animal Rights and Deep Ecology Meet," *Creation* (July/August 1986, Vol. 2, No. 3), p.16.

[592] William Kilpatrick and Gregory and Suzanne M. Wolfe, *Books That Build Character: A Guide to Teaching Your Child Moral Values Through Stories* (New York, NY: Simon & Schuster, 1994), p.244. See also: "Brother Wind, Sister Earth," *op. cit.*, p.6.

[593] Cheryl Cook, Enid M. Gorman, Lorette Picciano-Hanson, Editors, *A Directory of Environmental Activities and Resources in the North American Religious Community* (New York, NY: Joint Appeal by Religion and Science for the Environment, 1992), p.24. See also: Henry Lamb, "The Rise of Global Green Religion," *Eco♦Logic* (1997 Special Report), p.10; "Unfinished Cathedral's 100th Year Celebrated," *Christian News* (January 18, 1993, Vol. 31, No. 3), p.23; "Religious Visionary to Retire," *New Age Journal* (November/December 1996, Vol. 13, Issue 6), p.30.

[594] Robert Muller, *Framework for Preparation for the Year 2000, the 21st Century and the Third Millennium* (Hamden, CT: Albert Schweitzer Institute/Quinnipiac College Press, 1994), p.29.

[595] Cloud, *Flirting with Rome (Volume 1—Billy Graham), op. cit.*; Rick Miesel, "Billy Graham: General Teachings/ Activities" (Biblical Discernment Ministries, Revised January 1994); "The Pope...Spiritual Leader or Anti-Christ?," *The Protestant Challenge* (January-February 1997, Vol. 24, No. 1), p.8; Chick, *op. cit.*, p.57.

[596] Bundy, *Billy Graham: Performer?, Politician?, Preacher?, Prophet?, op. cit.*, p.129.

[597] David W. Cloud, *The Living Bible: Blessing or Curse?* (Oak Harbor, WA: Way of Life Literature, 1991). See also: "Graham Promotes Bad Bible Version," *Calvary Contender* (August 1, 1995), p.2; Bundy, *Billy Graham: Performer?,*

Politician?, Preacher?, Prophet?, op. cit., p.13; Edgar C. Bundy, *Collectivism in the Churches: A Documented Account of the Political Activities of the Federal, National, and World Councils of Churches* (Wheaton, IL: The Church League of America, 1958), p.133.

[598] David W. Cloud, "Billy Graham's Disobedience to the Word of God"; David W. Cloud, "Graham Thankful for the Phillips' Version," *O Timothy* (1995, Vol. 12, Issue 7).

[599] "Heresy and Apostasy," quoting Milton Jones in *Calvary Contender* (October 1, 1999, Vol. 16, No. 19), p.2.

[600] David W. Cloud, "Graham Thankful for the Phillips' Version," *O Timothy* (1995, Vol. 12, Issue 7).

[601] *The Living Bible Paraphrased: A Review* (Nova Scotia, Canada: The Peoples Gospel Hour, n.d.), p.3, 8; Cloud, *The Living Bible, op. cit.;* "Graham Promotes Bad Bible Version," *Calvary Contender* (August 1, 1995), p.2; William P. Grady, *Final Authority: A Christian's Guide to the King James Bible* (Knoxville, TN: Grady Publications, Inc., 1993), p.19.

[602] David W. Cloud, "Billy Graham's Disobedience to the Word of God." See also: Cloud, *The Living Bible, op. cit.;* R. A. Partlow, *Satan's Subtle Sabotage of God's Holy Word* (Erie, PA: The Stable, 1997), p.117.

[603] *The Living Bible Paraphrased, op. cit.*, p.11.

[604] *Ibid.*, p.12.

[605] Cloud, *The Living Bible, op. cit.*

[606] *Ibid.*

[607] Ad for the New Living Translation in *Ministries Today* (September/October 2000), p.33.

[608] "Graham Promotes Bad Bible Version," *Calvary Contender* (August 1, 1995), p.2.

[609] R. A. Partlow, *Satan's Subtle Sabotage of God's Holy Word* (Erie, PA: The Stable, 1997), p.64.

[610] "Graham Promotes Bad Bible Version," *op. cit.*, p.2.

[611] Letter from the Billy Graham Evangelistic Association (Dated February 1995), p.4. See also: "The Message," *The BDM Letter* (March/April 1995, Vol. 4, No. 2), p.3.

[612] "The Message," *The BDM Letter* (March/April 1995, Vol. 4, No. 2), p.3.

[613] Barbara Aho, "The 19th Century Occult Revival," *The Christian Conscience* (July/August 1997, Vol. 3, No. 6), p.23; Cecil J. Carter, *The Thinking, Theories and Theology of Drs. Westcott and Hort* (1978).

[614] *The Living Bible Paraphrased, op. cit.*, p.4; *Ibid.*, p.27, 28; Cecil J. Carter, *The Thinking, Theories and Theology of Drs. Westcott and Hort* (1978).

[615] David W. Cloud, "The Apostasy of the English Revised Version," *O Timothy* (1995, Vol. 12, Issue 10).

[616] William P. Grady, *Final Authority: A Christian's Guide to the King James Bible* (Knoxville, TN: Grady Publications, Inc., 1993), p.240.

[617] Cloud, "The Apostasy of the English Revised Version," *op. cit.*

[618] *Ibid.*

[619] *Ibid.*

[620] *Ibid.*

[621] *The Living Bible Paraphrased, op. cit.*, p.5.

[622] Joseph R. Chambers, "Modern Bible Versions: The De-Absolutionizing of God's Word," *USA Today's Front Page* (June 1994), p.15.

[623] Cecil J. Carter, *The Thinking, Theories and Theology of Drs. Westcott and Hort* (1978).

[624] Cloud, "The Apostasy of the English Revised Version," *op. cit.*

[625] *Ibid.*

[626] *Ibid.*

[627] *Ibid.;* Carter, *op. cit.*

[628] Carter, *op. cit.; The Living Bible Paraphrased, op. cit.*, p.5.

[629] *Ibid.*

[630] Cloud, "The Apostasy of the English Revised Version," *op. cit.*

[631] Carter, *op. cit.;* William P. Grady, *Final Authority, op. cit.*, p.231. See also: *The Living Bible Paraphrased, op. cit.*, p.5.

[632] *The Living Bible Paraphrased, op. cit.*, p.5.

[633] Carter, *op. cit.;* Gail Riplinger, *Which Bible Is God's Word?: Answers to Common Questions Concerning Modern Versions and Translations* (Oklahoma City, OK: Hearthstone Publishing, Ltd., 1994), p.81.

[634] Gail Riplinger, *Which Bible Is God's Word?: Answers to Common Questions Concerning Modern Versions and Translations* (Oklahoma City, OK: Hearthstone Publishing, Ltd., 1994), p.81.

[635] Aho, *op. cit.*, p.21, 27.

[636] *Ibid.*

[637] *Ibid.*

[638] *Ibid.*

[639] See: "Billy Graham's Disobedience to the Word of God" by David W. Cloud (Updated March 2, 1999), p.9.

[640] "Questions and Answers," *Share International* (Special Information Issue), p.26.

[641] Shirley Correll, "Who Are the Gods of the New World Order and What Is a Spiritual U. N.?" (Part IIIg) *The Florida Forum* (Winter 2000), p.21.

[642] "What Are Other Investigators Saying?," *op. cit.*, p.53.

[643] "Bulletin Inserts," quoting from *Old Union Reminder* in *Pulpit Helps* (July 1998, Vol. 24, No. 7), p.17.

[644] Texe Marrs, "The Awful Truth About Billy Graham" (2-tape set).

8. AMSTERDAM 2000

[1] "'The Most Internationally Representative Gathering, Secular or Religious, in Human History' Officially Being in Amsterdam," *Christian News* (August 7, 2000, Vol. 38, No. 32), p.2; Matt Friedman, "Like Amsterdam, Is America Headed for Quick Descent?," *AFA Journal* (November-December 2000, Vol. 24, No. 10), p.20; "Ecumenical Confusion and Deception at Graham Conference," *Christian News* (August 7, 2000, Vol. 38, No. 32), p.25; "Billy Graham's Amsterdam 2000: A Special First-Hand Report by Ralph Colas," *Calvary Contender* (August 15, 2000, Vol. 17, No. 16), p.2; "Graham to 'Pass the Torch' in Amsterdam," *Calvary Contender* (August 1, 2000, Vol. 17, No. 15), p.1.

[2] "Billy Graham's Amsterdam 2000: A Special First-Hand Report by Ralph Colas," *Calvary Contender* (August 15, 2000, Vol. 17, No. 16), p.2; "Graham to 'Pass the Torch' in Amsterdam," *Calvary Contender* (August 1, 2000, Vol. 17, No. 15), p.1; *Ibid.;* "Ecumenical Confusion and Deception at Graham Conference," *Christian News* (August 7, 2000, Vol. 38, No. 32), p.25.

[3] "Billy Graham's Last Scheduled International Event to Be His Most Technologically Advanced," *Christian News* (June 19, 2000, Vol. 38, No. 25), p.2; "Ecumenical Confusion and Deception at Graham Conference," *Christian News* (August 7, 2000, Vol. 38, No. 32), p.25.

[4] "'Evangelicals' Disbelieve in Hell," *Calvary Contender* (December 15, 1993, Vol. 10, No. 25), p.2; "New Evangelical Scholars Explain Away Hell," *The Christian World Report* (May 1991, Vol. 3, No. 5), p.15; "Taking the Fire Out of Hell," *Christian News* (September 27, 1999, Vol. 37, No. 35), p.10; *The Evangelical Methodist* (December 1993, Vol. 72, No. 10), p.3; "New Evangelical Scholars Explain Away Hell," *The Gospel Standard* (November 1991, Vol. 41, No. 5), p.15; "Six Mistakes of Man," *The Evangelical Methodist* (December 1993, Vol. 72, No. 10), p.3; Albert James Dager, *The World Christian Movement: A Great Delusion Leading to the Religio-Political State of the Anti-Christ* (Redmond, WA: Sword Publishers, 2001), p.112; Letter from the American Council of Christian Churches dated May 2000; "Billy Graham's Amsterdam 2000 Shows Solidarity Amid Diversity," *Christian News* (July 3, 2000, Vol. 38, No. 27), p.26; "Hell: Eternal Torment or Annihilation?," *Calvary Contender* (November 1, 2000, Vol. 17, No. 21), p.2; "Exposure of Apostasy & Compromise," *The Perilous Times* (May 2000, Vol. 22, No. 3), p.8.

[5] "Taking the Fire Out of Hell," *Christian News* (September 27, 1999, Vol. 37, No. 35), p.10.

[6] Roy McCloughry, "Basic Stott: Candid Comments on Justice, Gender, and Judgment," *Christianity Today* (January 8, 1996), p.25. See also: "Amsterdam 2000," *The ACCC Report* (August 2000), p.3; Bill Randles, *Beware the New Prophets: A Caution Concerning the Modern Prophetic Movement* (Marion, IA: n.p., 1999), p.111-112.

[7] Texe Marrs, *Ravaged by the New Age: Satan's Plan to Destroy Our Kids* (Austin, TX: Living Truth Publishers, 1989), p.75.

[8] McCloughry, *op. cit.*, p.28.

[9] Edgar C. Bundy, *How Liberals and Radicals Are Manipulating Evangelicals* (Miami Shores, FL: Edgar Bundy Ministries, Inc., 1982), p.5, 15, 16, 18; *Christian News* (July 1, 1996, Vol. 34, No. 27), p.23; "On the Left: Religion, Politics & One-Worldism," *Mindszenty Report* (March 1996, Vol. 37, No. 3), p.1; "Read All About It: Words to Live By," *World Christian* (November/December 1987, Vol. 6, No. 6), p.34; "More Communist Praise," *The Christian World Report* (December 1990, Vol. 2, No. 9), p.27; Ben Irwin, *The Bible and Homosexuality: Confronting the Challenge to Scriptural Authority* (Washington, DC: Family Research Council, n.d.), p.5.

[10] *Ibid.*, p.18.

[11] *Sojourners* (December 1985), p.27; "Virginia Mollenkott," *Christian News* (February 17, 1997, Vol. 35, No. 7), p.23.

[12] Virginia Mollenkott, "Women and the Bible," Reprinted from *Sojourners* (February 1976 and June 1977), p.1; Bundy, *How Liberals and Radicals Are Manipulating Evangelicals, op. cit.*, p.15, 18; *Sojourners* (April 1986), p.40; *Sojourners* (December 1985), p.43.

[13] *Sojourners* (January 1990, Vol. 19, No. 1), p.6; *Sojourners* (October 1989, Vol. 18, No. 9), p.2; *Sojourners* (December 1985), p.2.

[14] Alan Morrison, *The Serpent and the Cross: Religious Corruption in an Evil Age* (Birmingham, England: K & M Books, 1994), p.313.

[15] *Utne Reader* (March/April 1996); Paper from the Summit on Ethics and Meaning (Received March 14, 1996); Letter from Political Research Associates dated January 25, 2000; Letter from Political Research Associates dated November 28, 2000; Ben Irwin, *The Bible and Homosexuality: Confronting the Challenge to Scriptural Authority* (Washington, DC: Family Research Council, n.d.), p.5.

[16] Ben Irwin, *The Bible and Homosexuality: Confronting the Challenge to Scriptural Authority* (Washington, DC: Family Research Council, n.d.), p.5.

[17] *Utne Reader* (March/April 1996); *Christian News* (February 26, 1996, Vol. 34, No. 9), p.17.

[18] Irwin, *op. cit.*, p.5.

[19] "Marxist Terrorists Help Shape RLDS Hierarchy's Program," *IPS Packet* (Independence, MO: Price Publishing Company, n.d.), p.7.

[20] *Ibid.*

[21] *Ibid.*

[22] *Ibid.*

[23] *Sojourners* (January 1990, Vol. 19, No. 1), p.6; *Sojourners* (October 1989, Vol. 18, No. 9), p.2; *Sojourners* (March/April 1995, Vol. 24, No. 1), p.4; *Sojourners* (December 1985), p.2; Bundy, *How Liberals and Radicals Are Manipulating Evangelicals, op. cit.*, p.23.

[24] Bundy, *How Liberals and Radicals Are Manipulating Evangelicals, op. cit.*, p.23; "Multinational Corporations and the Loss of Sovereignty," *The Florida Forum* (Spring 1998), p.14; David Mark Price, *Secret* (Wichita, KS: Sunset Research Group, 1994), p.4, 5, 35; John A. Stormer, *None Dare Call It Treason...25 Years Later* (Florissant, MO: Liberty Bell Press, 1992), p.385.

[25] David Mark Price, *Secret* (Wichita, KS: Sunset Research Group, 1994), p.4. See also: "Marxist Terrorists Help Shape RLDS Hierarchy's Program," *op. cit.*, p.5.

[26] "Marxist Terrorists Help Shape RLDS Hierarchy's Program," *op. cit.*, p.5.

[27] *Ibid.*

[28] *Ibid.*, p.6.

[29] *Ibid.*, p.8.

[30] "On the Left: Religion, Politics & One-Worldism," *Mindszenty Report* (March 1996, Vol. 37, No. 3), p.1.

[31] "Marxist Terrorists Help Shape RLDS Hierarchy's Program," *op. cit.*, p.6; *Council on Foreign Relations: Annual Report July 1, 1987-June 30, 1988*, p.171; *Council on Foreign Relations: Annual Report July 1, 1992-June 30, 1993*, p.163; *Council on Foreign Relations: Annual Report July 1, 1994-June 30, 1995*, p.142.

[32] Bundy, *How Liberals and Radicals Are Manipulating Evangelicals, op. cit.*, p.23.

[33] *Sojourners* (March/April 1995, Vol. 24, No. 1), p.64.

[34] Tom Sine, "A Hijacked Heritage," *Sojourners* (March/April 1995, Vol. 24, No. 1), p.20.

[35] *Sojourners* (December 1989, Vol. 18, No. 11), p.36; *Sojourners* (October 1989, Vol. 18, No. 9), p.42.

[36] *Sojourners* (March 1985), p.40, 41, 48.

[37] Clark Pinnock, "The Inspiration and Interpretation of the Bible," Reprinted from *Sojourners* (October 1980), p.2.

[38] Mollenkott, *op. cit.*, p.3.

[39] "Christianity Today Promotes Leftist," *Christian News* (May 4, 1992, Vol. 30, No. 18), p.15.

[40] Newspaper ad received May 12, 2001.

[41] David W. Cloud, "Evangelical Leaders Befriend the Mother of Harlots," *O Timothy* (1988, Vol. 5, Issue 4); David W. Cloud, "Evangelical Entanglement with Romanism: How Serious Is the Back-to-Rome Movement?," *Foundation* (January/February 1987), p.5; John E. Ashbrook, *New Neutralism II: Exposing the Gray of Compromise* (Mentor, OH: Here I Stand Books, 1992), p.61; Wilson Ewin, *Today's Evangelicals Embracing the World's Deadliest Cult* (Compton, Quebec: Quebec Baptist Missions, n.d.), p.65-66.

[42] Dennis W. Costella, "Should We All Get Together?," *Foundation* (January-February 2000, Vol. 21, Issue 1), p.3.

[43] Cloud, "Evangelical Leaders Befriend the Mother of Harlots," *op. cit.* See also: David W. Cloud, *Flirting with Rome: Evangelical Entanglement with Roman Catholicism* (Oak Harbor, WA: Way of Life Literature, 1993).

[44] Billy Graham, *Just As I Am: The Autobiography of Billy Graham* (Harpers Collins Worldwide, 1997), p.614-615. See also: "A Word from Ned Graham," *East Gates Connection* (January-March 2000), p.1; Allen D. Hanson, "Bible Distribution in China," *Christian News* (September 20, 1999, Vol. 37, No. 34), p.17. "Communist Puppets Are Hoodwinking Lutherans," *Christian News* (November 15, 1999, Vol. 37, No. 42), p.21; *Christian News* (May 29, 2000, Vol. 38, No. 22), p.14.

[45] Cloud, "Evangelical Leaders Befriend the Mother of Harlots," *op. cit.* See also: David W. Cloud, *Flirting with Rome: Evangelical Entanglement with Roman Catholicism* (Oak Harbor, WA: Way of Life Literature, 1993); David W. Cloud, "Evangelical Entanglement with Romanism: How Serious Is the Back-to-Rome Movement?," *Foundation* (January/February 1987), p.5.

[46] Wendy B. Howard, *The Alpha Course: Friend or Foe?* (Landsborough, Queensland: Endtime Ministries, 1999), p.18, 29-30; Brooks Egerton, "'If God Himself Gave Freedom,'" *Dallas Morning News* (March 20, 1999), p.1G; Wendy B. Howard, "The First Religion and Cultural Diversity Conference, Melbourne, July 1997," *Despatch Magazine* (August 8, 1997), p.1; "Well Hello, Dalai," *Endtime* (September/October 1999), p.28; "World Assembly to Give Grand Thanks," *Dallas Morning News* (February 28, 1999), p.8; Dan Shine, "Leaders Want Global Thanksgiving for All Faiths," *Dallas Morning News* (February 2, 1995), p.1G.

[47] *Ibid.*, p.18, 29-30; "Cardinal Arinze Speaks Out on Family," *Countdown to the Year 2000* (1995, Issue No. 2), p.5, 6; *Preparing Families for the Third Millennium...* (1997), p.8; "Representatives of More Than 20 Religions Open Vatican

Meeting," *Christian News* (November 1, 1999, Vol. 37, No. 40), p.15; Wendy B. Howard, "The First Religion and Cultural Diversity Conference, Melbourne, July 1997," *Despatch Magazine* (August 8, 1997), p.1; Andy Neckar, "Rome and Hindus: Together in Pagan Pageantry," *Christian News and Re-Views* (September 25, 1998); *Religion for Peace* (February 1995, Issue 65-A), p.1, 4, 5; Cornelia R. Ferreira, "One-World Church Starts Up United Religions on Track—with Modifications," *Wisconsin Report* (November 6, 1997, Vol. 22, No. 43), p.3; Cornelia R. Ferreira, "One-World Church Expected Next Year: San Francisco Chosen As Headquarters," *Wisconsin Report* (November 28, 1996, Vol. 21, No. 46), p.6.

[48] "Cardinal Arinze Speaks Out on Family," *Countdown to the Year 2000* (1995, Issue No. 2), p.6.

[49] "Vatican Seeks Ties with Hindus," *Calvary Contender* (November 15, 1998, Vol. 15, No. 24), p.1.

[50] "Representatives of More Than 20 Religions Open Vatican Meeting," *Christian News* (November 1, 1999, Vol. 37, No. 40), p.15. See also: Carl McIntire, "Perversion and Subversion in the World Council of Churches," *O Timothy* (1988, Vol. 5, Issue 6).

[51] Carl McIntire, "Perversion and Subversion in the World Council of Churches," *O Timothy* (1988, Vol. 5, Issue 6).

[52] Paper from Thanksgiving Square; Letter from Thanksgiving Square, dated February 2, 1999; "World Assembly to Give Grand Thanks," *Dallas Morning News* (February 28, 1999), p.8; Wendy B. Howard, "The First Religion and Cultural Diversity Conference, Melbourne, July 1997," *Despatch Magazine* (August 8, 1997), p.1; Cornelia R. Ferreira, "One-World Church Expected Next Year: San Francisco Chosen As Headquarters" *Wisconsin Report* (November 28, 1996, Vol. 21, No. 46), p.6.

[53] Dan Shine, "Leaders Want Global Thanksgiving for All Faiths," *Dallas Morning News* (February 2, 1995), p.1G.

[54] Brooks Egerton, "'If God Himself Gave Freedom,'" *Dallas Morning News* (March 20, 1999), p.3G.

[55] Cornelia R. Ferreira, "One-World Church Expected Next Year: San Francisco Chosen As Headquarters," *Wisconsin Report* (November 28, 1996, Vol. 21, No. 46), p.6.

[56] "Fundamentalists a Problem for UR," *Calvary Contender* (November 15, 1997, Vol. 14, No. 22); Howard, *The Alpha Course, op. cit.*, p.18, 29-30; W. B. Howard, "The First Religion and Cultural Diversity Conference, Melbourne, July 1997," *Despatch Magazine* (August 8, 1997), p.1.

[57] Cornelia R. Ferreira, "One-World Church Starts Up United Religions on Track—with Modifications," *Wisconsin Report* (November 6, 1997, Vol. 22, No. 43), p.3-4. See also: David B. Reagan, "The Apostate One World Religion," *Voice in the Wilderness* (August 2001), p.14.

[58] Ferreira, "One-World Church Expected Next Year, *op. cit.*, p.6.

[59] Graham, *Just As I Am, op. cit.*, p.505; Billy Graham, *Approaching Hoofbeats: The Four Horsemen of the Apocalypse* (Minneapolis, MN: Grason, 1983), p.142.

[60] Ferreira, "One-World Church Expected Next Year, *op. cit.*, p.6.

[61] *Ibid.*

[62] "Profound Thanks," *Religion for Peace* (February 1995, Issue 65-A), p.5. See also: Ferreira, "One-World Church Starts Up United Religions on Track, *op. cit.*, p.3; *Ibid.*, p.3, 6.

[63] *Ibid.* See also: Ferreira, "One-World Church Expected Next Year, *op. cit.*, p.6.

[64] "Quotes to Ponder," *Voice in the Wilderness* (March 2000), p.11.

[65] Howard, *The Alpha Course, op. cit.*, p.18, 29-30; Ferreira, "One-World Church Starts Up United Religions on Track, *op. cit.*, p.3; David B. Reagan, "The Apostate One World Religion," *Voice in the Wilderness* (August 2001), p.14.

[66] "Anglican Betrayal Stalled: Capitulation to Rome Does Not God Ahead for Now!," *The Protestant Challenge* (2000, No. 2/3), p.2; Peggy Polk, "Vatican Declares Only the Roman Catholic Church Brings Salvation," *Christian News*, (September 25, 2000, Vol. 38, No. 35), p.14; "European Christians Being Swept into Ecumenicism and Pentecostalism," *O Timothy* (1991, Vol. 8, Issue 10-12); "Pastor of Thailand's Largest Church Is in Fellowship with Rome," *O Timothy* (1991, Vol. 8, Issue 10-12); "More Muslims Than Anglicans in England?," *Calvary Contender* (July 1, 1997, Vol. 14, No. 13), p.1; "Key Anglican Parish in London Defects to Rome," *O Timothy* (1993, Vol. 10, Issue 6).

[67] Howard, *The Alpha Course, op. cit.*, p.30.

[68] *Ibid.*, p.18.

[69] David B. Reagan, "The Apostate One World Religion," *Voice in the Wilderness* (August 2001), p.3; Marcus Braybrooke, *A Wider Vision: A History of the World Congress of Faiths* (Oxford, England: Oneworld Publications, 1996), p.172.

[70] "United Religions Initiative 2000," *Christian News* (May 5, 1997, Vol. 35, No. 18), p.6; Speech by William E. Swing at the North American Interfaith Network Conference (August 10, 1996).

[71] "World Assembly to Give Grand Thanks," *Dallas Morning News* (February 28, 1999), p.8; Paper from Thanksgiving World Assembly advertising a March 15, 1999 Assembly.

[72] *Ibid.*

[73] "Named to Canterbury," *The Christian Century* (August 8-15, 1990, Vol. 107, No. 23), p.728.

[74] Ed Briggs, "Archbishop of Canterbury Urges Tolerance in Sexuality Debate," *Christian News* (February 10, 1997, Vol. 35, No. 6), p.11. See also: "Q & A," *The Berean Call* (July 2001), p.4.

[75] *Ibid.*

[76] "'The Most Internationally Representative Gathering,'" *op. cit.*, p.2.

[77] *The Evangelical Methodist* (2000, Vol. 78, No. 4), p.3. See also: "Exposure of Apostasy & Compromise," *The Perilous Times* (May 2000, Vol. 22, No. 3), p.8.

[78] *Ibid.*

[79] "Pope Foreseen As Leader of World Church," *Midnight Call* (March 1993), p.20.

[80] William T. James, Editor, *Foreshocks of Antichrist* (Eugene, OR: Harvest House Publishers, 1997), p.117-118.

[81] "Archbishop of Canterbury Lashes Out at Fundamentalists," *O Timothy* (1994, Vol. 11, Issue 5).

[82] Morrison, *op. cit.*, p.554.

[83] *Ibid.*, p.553. See also: James W. Wardner, *Unholy Alliances* (n.p., 1996), p.177-178.

[84] *Ibid.*, quoting George Carey, p.554.

[85] "Q & A," *The Berean Call* (July 2001), p.4.

[86] "Anglican Leaders Dialogue with Druids," *Christian News* (July 3, 2000, Vol. 38, No. 27), p.24.

[87] David W. Cloud, "Charismatics Join Hands with World Council Heretics," *O Timothy* (1991, Vol. 8, Issue 5).

[88] Willmer Thorkelson, "Will Orthodox Exit the WCC?," *Christianity Today* (April 8, 1991, Vol. 35, No. 4), p.66. See also: "Praying for Renewal," *One World* (November 1990, Vol. 160), p.8.

[89] *Ibid.*

[90] Robert Sessler, *To Be God of One World: The French Revolution Globalized* (Merlin, OR: Let There Be Light Publications, 1992), p.156-157.

[91] David W. Cloud, "World Council of Churches Baptizes Heathenism," *Plains Baptist Challenger* (June 1994), p.1.

[92] *Ibid.*, p.1-2. See also: Joseph A. Harriss, "The Gospel According to Marx," *Christian News* (February 1, 1993, Vol. 31, No. 5), p.12; Joseph A. Harriss, "The Gospel According to Marx," *Reader's Digest* (February 1993), p.68; "Salvation Army and the International Millennial Congress," *Despatch Magazine* (September 2000, Vol. 12:3), p.55.

[93] "Salvation Army and the International Millennial Congress," *Despatch Magazine* (September 2000, Vol. 12:3), p.55.

[94] Shirley Correll, "Who Are the Gods of the New World Order and What Is a Spiritual U. N.?" (Part IV), *The Florida Forum* (Spring 2001), p.15.

[95] "The Ecumenical Bandwagon Rolls on to Its Final Doom," *The Voice in the Wilderness* (September 2000), p.7.

[96] "Anglican—Catholic—Consultation—Important Gathering," *Despatch Magazine* (June 2000, Vol. 12, No. 2), p.10.

[97] "Anglican Betrayal Stalled, *op. cit.*, p.2.

[98] "The Service for Diana's Funeral," *Despatch Mini News;* John M. Drickamer, "I Wish It Had Been Christian," *Christian News* (September 15, 1997, Vol. 35, No. 33), p.6.

[99] *Ibid.*

[100] *Last Trumpet Newsletter* (July 2001, Vol. 20, Issue 7), p.2.

[101] *Ibid.*

[102] "Billy Graham's Amsterdam 2000: A Special First-Hand Report by Ralph Colas, *op. cit.*, p.2; "Graham to 'Pass the Torch' in Amsterdam," *Calvary Contender* (August 1, 2000, Vol. 17, No. 15), p.1; "Billy Graham's Last Scheduled International Event, *op. cit.*, p.2; "Ecumenical Confusion and Deception at Graham Conference," *Christian News* (August 7, 2000, Vol. 38, No. 32), p.25; "Billy Graham's Amsterdam 2000 Shows Solidarity Amid Diversity," *Christian News* (July 3, 2000, Vol. 38, No. 27), p.26; "Exposure of Apostasy & Compromise," *The Perilous Times* (May 2000, Vol. 22, No. 3), p.8.

[103] *Ibid.*

[104] Edgar C. Bundy, *Collectivism in the Churches: A Documented Account of the Political Activities of the Federal, National, and World Councils of Churches* (Wheaton, IL: The Church League of America, 1958), p.230-231.

[105] "Exposure of Apostasy & Compromise," *The Perilous Times* (May 2000, Vol. 22, No. 3), p.8; "Ecumenical Confusion and Deception at Graham Conference," *Christian News* (August 7, 2000, Vol. 38, No. 32), p.25.

[106] Graham, *Just As I Am, op. cit.*, p.275.

[107] "Amsterdam 2000," *The ACCC Report* (August 2000), p.3.

[108] Paper listing Promise Keepers Speakers for 1997, p.35.

[109] "BWA Heroes," *Calvary Contender* (December 15, 1999, Vol. 16, No. 24), p.2; "Kim Nominated as BWA President," *Calvary Contender* (September 1, 1999, Vol. 16, No. 17), p.2; "Billy Kim a Friend of Cho," *Calvary Contender* (April 1, 1993, Vol. 10, No. 7), p.2; "More on Billy Kim," *Calvary Contender* (May 1, 1993, Vol. 10, No. 9), p.2; "Billy Kim Says Doctrine Is Not What Unites BWA," *Calvary Contender* (September 15, 2000, Vol. 17, No. 18), p.2. See also: "Affiliated Groups Gather at SBC Meeting," *Calvary Contender* (June 15, 2001, Vol. 18, No. 12), p.2.

[110] "BWA Cozy with Castro," *Calvary Contender* (September 15, 2000, Vol. 17, No. 18), p.2; "CC Editor's Reply to a So. Baptist," *Calvary Contender* (October 1, 2000, Vol. 17, No. 19), p.2. See also: "Falwell's Church a Member of SBC for 'Several Years,'" *Calvary Contender* (June 1, 2001, Vol. 18, No. 11), p.2.

[111] "Castro To Address Baptists," *The Voice in the Wilderness* (December 2000), p.14.

[112] "Amsterdam 2000," *op. cit.*, p.4.

[113] "BWA Cozy with Castro," *op. cit.*, p.2; "BWA Met in Cuba," *Calvary Contender* (August 1, 2000, Vol. 17, No. 15), p.2. See also: *Ibid.*

114 "Baptist World Alliance Says Ecumenicism More Important Than Doctrine," *Christian News* (January 15, 2001, Vol. 39, No. 3), p.3.

115 The Way of Life web site http://wayoflife.org/~dcloud. See also: *Ibid.*

116 "Pope Prays for Earth Summit," *O Timothy* (1992, Vol. 9, Issue 8). See also: David W. Cloud, "The Day of Prayer for World Peace," *O Timothy* (1994, Vol. 11, Issue 3).

117 *Ibid.;* David W. Cloud, "The Day of Prayer for World Peace," *O Timothy* (1994, Vol. 11, Issue 3).

118 David W. Cloud, "The Day of Prayer for World Peace," *O Timothy* (1994, Vol. 11, Issue 3).

119 *Ibid.*

120 "'Lutheran Hour News' Features Zhidkov, Propagandist for Reds," *Christian News* (February 21, 2001, Vol. 39, No. 7), p.15.

121 McIntire, *op. cit.;* David W. Cloud, "Flirting with Rome: Evangelical Entanglement with Roman Catholicism (Volume 3—The Southern Baptist Convention)," *O Timothy* (1993); "Ecumenicalism," *The Perilous Times* (January 2001, Vol. 22, No. 8), p.8. See also: "The Openness Debate," *Calvary Contender* (March 15, 2001, Vol. 18, No. 6), p.2; "Pattillo Chosen for NCC Staff," *Calvary Contender* (March 15, 2001, Vol. 18, No. 6), p.2.

122 David W. Cloud, "Flirting with Rome: Evangelical Entanglement with Roman Catholicism (Volume 3—The Southern Baptist Convention)," *O Timothy* (1993).

123 *Ibid.*

124 "Doctrine on Display," *The Perilous Times* (February 1999, Vol. 20, No. 12), p.9. See also: "Doctrine Divides," *Calvary Contender* (April 1, 2000, Vol. 17, No. 7), p.2.

125 William Martin, *A Prophet with Honor: The Billy Graham Story* (NY: William Morrow and Company, Inc., 1991), p.272; Graham, *Just As I Am, op. cit.*, p.359, 360; "Graham Promotes BWA," *Calvary Contender* (August 15, 1997, Vol. 14, No. 16), p.1.

126 Cloud, "Flirting with Rome: Evangelical Entanglement with Roman Catholicism (Volume 3—The Southern Baptist Convention)" *O Timothy* (1993).

127 D. W. Cloud, "Some Frightening Facts About Billy Graham," *O Timothy* (1984, Vol. 1, Issue 4).

128 "Graham Promotes BWA," *Calvary Contender* (August 15, 1997, Vol. 14, No. 16), p.1.

129 "BWA Heroes," *op. cit.*

130 David W. Cloud, "Bishop K. H. Ting—China's Master of Deceit," *O Timothy* (1986, Vol. 3, Issue 3).

131 Joseph A. Walkes, Jr., *Jno. G. Lewis, Jr.—End of an Era: The History of the Prince Hall Grand Lodge of Louisiana 1842-1979* (n.p., 1986), p.269.

132 Interfaith Witness Department, *A Study of Freemasonry* (Atlanta, GA: Home Mission Board, Southern Baptist Convention, n.d.), p.65; D. D. Tidwell, "Dr. George W. Truett," *Scottish Rite Journal* (February 1993, Vol. 101, No. 2), p.31.

133 *Ibid.*, p.66.

134 "Billy Kim a Friend of Cho," *Calvary Contender* (April 1, 1993, Vol. 10, No. 7), p.2; "Kim Nominated As BWA President," *Calvary Contender* (September 1, 1999, Vol. 16, No. 17), p.2; "SOLM Careless Associations?," *Calvary Contender* (December 15, 1997, Vol. 14, No. 24), p.2.

135 "Kim Nominated As BWA President," *Calvary Contender* (September 1, 1999, Vol. 16, No. 17), p.2; *Ibid.;* "More on Billy Kim," *Calvary Contender* (May 1, 1993, Vol. 10, No. 9), p.2; "NAE Features Cho As Speaker," *Calvary Contender* (March 1, 2001, Vol. 18, No. 5), p.2; "Schuller Meets with Cho and Pope," *Calvary Contender* (August 15, 1998, Vol. 15, No. 16), p.2; "BWA Heroes," *op. cit.* See also: Martin and Deidre Bobgan, *Hypnosis: Medical, Scientific, or Occultic* (Santa Barbara, CA: EastGate Publishers, 2001), p.28.

136 John Ashbrook, "Billy Graham—The Mouthpiece of New Evangelicalism," *O Timothy* (1993, Vol. 10, Issue 1); M.H. Reynolds, "Planting the Seeds of Ecumenical Apostasy in the Name of Evangelism," *Foundation* (1983, Vol. 4, No. 4); *The BDM Letter* (September 1993, Vol. 2, No. 7), p.2; John E. Ashbrook, *New Neutralism II: Exposing the Gray of Compromise* (Mentor, OH: Here I Stand Books, 1992), p.79; Rick Miesel, "Billy Graham: General Teachings/Activities" (Biblical Discernment Ministries, Revised January 1994).

137 http://www.fullnet.net/np/archives/cyberj/synan.html, printed out on November 16, 1999.

138 "Kim Nominated As BWA President," *op. cit.;* "Billy Kim a Friend of Cho," *op. cit.;* "More on Billy Kim," *Calvary Contender* (May 1, 1993, Vol. 10, No. 9), p.2; "CC Editor's Reply to a So. Baptist," *Calvary Contender* (October 1, 2000, Vol. 17, No. 19), p.2; "BWA Heroes," *op. cit.*

139 "Mother Teresa" (Biblical Discernment Ministries—Revised March 1996); James W. Wardner, *Unholy Alliances* (n.p., 1996), p.180.

140 Dave Hunt, "A New Christianity?," *The Berean Call* (February 2000), p.1; Dave Hunt, "What's Happening to the Faith?," *The Berean Call* (May 1998), p.1; "Tutu Wants WCC to Favor Homosexuality?," *Calvary Contender* (April 1, 1998, Vol. 15, No. 7), p.2; "Catholics May Name King 'Martyr for the Faith,'" *Calvary Contender* (February 1, 2000), p.1; "American Baptist Meeting Features Tutu, Campolo," *Calvary Contender* (March 1, 1995, Vol. 12, No. 5), p.2; "Tutu Wants Homosexual Priests," *Calvary Contender* (June 1, 1996, Vol. 13, No. 11), p.1; "Kim Nominated As BWA President," *op. cit.;* "WCC Faith & Order Commission Conference," *Calvary Contender* (September 15, 1993, Vol. 10, No. 18), p.2; William McCall, "Ecumenism, 'Global Spirituality' and Mother Teresa," *Christian Inquirer* (April 1985),

p.26; "Scholars Seek New Image of God," *Christian News* (March 27, 2000, Vol. 38, No. 13), p.13; Jonathan Petre, "Tutu Writes Foreword for Book of Christian Liturgies for Gays," *Christian News* (May 6, 1996, Vol. 34, No. 19), p.11; "The Open Conspiracy," *Don Bell Reports* (February 21, 1986, Vol. 33, No. 8), p.3; "NCEA 1985 'and the Strange Gods of Syncretism,'" *Distant Drums* (June 1985, Vol. 7, No. 2), p.10; Don Lattin, "Religions of World Celebrate with Prayers to Dozen Deities," *San Francisco Chronicle* (June 26, 1995), p.A1; *Eternity* (January 1985, Vol. 36, No. 1), Back Cover; "Tutu Blasts Christians, Promotes Blasphemy," *Flashpoint* (September 1990), p.6; Gary H. Kah, *The Demonic Roots of Globalism* (Lafayette, LA: Huntington House Publishers, 1995), p.127; Brochure from World Goodwill; Gary Kah, *En Route to Global Occupation* (Lafayette, LA: Huntington House Publishers, 1992), p.189; "State of the World Forum Toward a New Civilization," *Mindszenty Report* (March 1996, Vol. 37, No. 3), p.3; "Man of Peace," *The Omega-Letter* (October 1988, Vol. 3, No. 9), p.17; Gerard J. Hekker, "The Day of the African Child," *Religion for Peace* (June 1995, Issue 66), p.9; *The Prophecy Newsletter* (1985, Vol. 1, No. 5), p.6; *Religion for Peace* (Autumn 1992, Issue 63), p.2; *The Shepherd's Letter* (Spring 1993), p.13; Graham Fraser, "Maurice Strong Wins Prize for Peace: Canadian Garners U Thant Award," *The Globe and Mail* (May 4, 1996), p.A-13; Berit Kjos, "From the United Nations to the United Religions" (Received March 20, 1996); The United Religions Initiative, Modified on January 12, 1998; Richard Scheinin, "Bringing Together the 'United Religions,'" *San Jose Mercury News* (February 6, 1996), p.11B; Letter from the United Religions (Received March 20, 1996); James W. Wardner, *Unholy Alliances* (n.p., 1996), p.180; Edward Epstein, "Gorbachev to Convene MTG in S.F.—Invitees—Bush, Thatcher, Tutu," *Wisconsin Report* (September 21, 1995, Vol. 20, No. 36), p.1; Ferreira, "One-World Church Expected Next Year, *op. cit.*, p.1; "World Council of Churches Youth Meeting Praises Terrorism and Murder in South Africa," *O Timothy* (1986, Vol. 3, Issue 7); "South Africa: Targeted by Devilish Powers," *O Timothy* (1987, Vol. 4, Issue 3-4); James H. Dearmore, "Who Built Modern South Africa," *O Timothy* (1987, Vol. 4, Issue 3-4); David W. Cloud, "Some Questions for Desmond Tutu," *O Timothy* (1987, Vol. 4, Issue 3-4); "A Missionary Speaks Against Desmond Tutu's View of South Africa," *O Timothy* (1987, Vol. 4, Issue 3-4); "Interview with Isaac Mokoena, South African Christian Leader" *O Timothy* (1987, Vol. 4, Issue 3-4); David W. Cloud, "Liberation Theology: Christianized Marxism," *O Timothy* (1988, Vol. 5, Issue 1); "Desmond Tutu—the Cursing Archbishop!," *O Timothy* (1988, Vol. 5, Issue 4); "Ecumenical Leaders Work for a One-World Government and Religion," *O Timothy* (1989, Vol. 6, Issue 5); William Oltmans, "Who Are the Real Terrorists in South Africa," *O Timothy* (1989, Vol. 6, Issue 7); David W. Cloud, "Anglican Bishop Honored After Acknowledging Ambiguous Sexuality," *O Timothy* (1995, Vol. 12, Issue 9).

[141] *Ibid.*; "Tutu Wants WCC to Favor Homosexuality?," *Calvary Contender* (April 1, 1998, Vol. 15, No. 7), p.2; William McCall, "Scholars Seek New Image of God," *Christian News* (March 27, 2000, Vol. 38, No. 13), p.13; Jonathan Petre, "Tutu Writes Foreword for Book of Christian Liturgies for Gays," *Christian News* (May 6, 1996, Vol. 34, No. 19), p.11; "The Open Conspiracy," *Don Bell Reports* (February 21, 1986, Vol. 33, No. 8), p.3; "NCEA 1985 'and the Strange Gods of Syncretism,'" *Distant Drums* (June 1985, Vol. 7, No. 2), p.10; *Eternity* (January 1985, Vol. 36, No. 1), Back Cover; "Tutu Blasts Christians, Promotes Blasphemy," *Flashpoint* (September 1990), p.6; Gary Kah, *En Route to Global Occupation* (Lafayette, LA: Huntington House Publishers, 1992), p.189; "Man of Peace," *The Omega-Letter* (October 1988, Vol. 3, No. 9), p.17; *The Shepherd's Letter* (Spring 1993), p.13; "600 Honor Sir John Templeton at Dinner," *The Independent* (Vol. 9, No. 1), p.1; The United Religions Initiative, Modified on January 12, 1998; Letter from the United Religions (Received March 20, 1996); Edward Epstein, "Gorbachev to Convene MTG in S.F.—Invitees—Bush, Thatcher, Tutu," *Wisconsin Report* (September 21, 1995, Vol. 20, No. 36), p.1; Ferreira, "One-World Church Expected Next Year, *op. cit.*, p.1; James H. Dearmore, "Who Built Modern South Africa," *O Timothy* (1987, Vol. 4, Issue 3-4); David W. Cloud, "Some Questions for Desmond Tutu," *O Timothy* (1987, Vol. 4, Issue 3-4).

[142] "Ecumenical Leaders Work for a One-World Government and Religion," *O Timothy* (1989, Vol. 6, Issue 5); "The Open Conspiracy," *Don Bell Reports* (February 21, 1986, Vol. 33, No. 8), p.3; "NCEA 1985 'and the Strange Gods of Syncretism,'" *Distant Drums* (June 1985, Vol. 7, No. 2), p.10; Gerard J. Hekker, "The Day of the African Child," *Religion for Peace* (June 1995, Issue 66), p.9; *Religion for Peace* (Autumn 1992, Issue 63), p.2; Howard, *The Alpha Course, op. cit.*, p.8; Cornelia R. Ferreira, "One-World Church Starts Up United Religions on Track, *op. cit.*, p.1.

[143] Gary Kah, *En Route to Global Occupation* (Lafayette, LA: Huntington House Publishers, 1992), p.77.

[144] *Religion for Peace* (Autumn 1992, Issue 63), p.2.

[145] William McCall, "Ecumenism, 'Global Spirituality' and Mother Teresa," *Christian Inquirer* (April 1985), p.26; "Mother Teresa" (Biblical Discernment Ministries—Revised March 1996).

[146] *Ibid.* See also: *Distant Drums* (November 1989, Vol. 11, No. 3), p.8. *The Prophecy Newsletter* (1985, Vol. 1, No. 5), p.6.

[147] The United Religions Initiative, Modified on January 12, 1998; Howard, *The Alpha Course, op. cit.*, p.8; "Desmond Tutu," *Christian News* (March 5, 2001, Vol. 39, No. 10), p.6; Ferreira, "One-World Church Expected Next Year, *op. cit.*, p.1, 2; Berit Kjos, "From the United Nations to the United Religions" (Received March 20, 1996); Richard Scheinin, "Bringing Together the 'United Religions,'" *San Jose Mercury News* (February 6, 1996), p.11B); Letter from the United Religions (Received March 20, 1996); Don Lattin, "Religions of World Celebrate with Prayers to Dozen Deities," *San Francisco Chronicle* (June 26, 1995), p.A1.

[148] Ferreira, "One-World Church Starts Up United Religions on Track, *op. cit.*, p.1; List of Participants in the State of the World Forum.

[149] List of Participants in the State of the World Forum; "State of the World Forum Toward a New Civilization," *Mindszenty Report* (March 1996, Vol. 37, No. 3), p.3.

[150] *Council on Foreign Relations: Annual Report July 1, 1990-June 30, 1991*,, p.26.

[151] William McCall, "Scholars Seek New Image of God," *Christian News* (March 27, 2000, Vol. 38, No. 13), p.13.

[152] "The Open Conspiracy," *Don Bell Reports* (February 21, 1986, Vol. 33, No. 8), p.3.

[153] "Australia and the 2001 N.W.O. Planetary Events," *Despatch Magazine* (March 2001, Vol. 13, No. 1), p.13.

[154] "Tutu Wants WCC to Favor Homosexuality?," *Calvary Contender* (April 1, 1998, Vol. 15, No. 7), p.2; Jonathan

Petre, "Tutu Writes Foreword for Book of Christian Liturgies for Gays," *Christian News* (May 6, 1996, Vol. 34, No. 19), p.11; "Tutu's Modernism," *Christian News* (November 6, 2000, Vol. 38, No. 41), p.16; "Tutu Wants Homosexual Priests," *Calvary Contender* (June 1, 1996, Vol. 13, No. 11), p.1; "Liberal Lutherans Still Praise Tutu," *Christian News* (March 5, 2001, Vol. 39, No. 10), p.6.

155 Jonathan Petre, "Tutu Writes Foreword for Book of Christian Liturgies for Gays," *Christian News* (May 6, 1996, Vol. 34, No. 19), p.11; "Tutu Wants Homosexual Priests," *Calvary Contender* (June 1, 1996, Vol. 13, No. 11), p.1; "Desmond Tutu," *Christian News* (March 5, 2001, Vol. 39, No. 10), p.6.

156 David W. Cloud, "Anglican Bishop Honored After Acknowledging Ambiguous Sexuality," *O Timothy* (1995, Vol. 12, Issue 9).

157 *Ibid.*

158 "Tutu's Modernism," *Christian News* (November 6, 2000, Vol. 38, No. 41), p.16.

159 "Tutu Wants WCC to Favor Homosexuality?," *op. cit.*, p.2; "American Baptist Meeting Features Tutu, Campolo," *Calvary Contender* (March 1, 1995, Vol. 12, No. 5), p.2; "Interview with Isaac Mokoena, South African Christian Leader" *O Timothy* (1987, Vol. 4, Issue 3-4); David W. Cloud, "Liberation Theology: Christianized Marxism," *O Timothy* (1988, Vol. 5, Issue 1); "WCC Faith and Order Commission Conference," *Calvary Contender* (September 15, 1993, Vol. 10, No. 18), p.2; William Oltmans, "Who Are the Real Terrorists in South Africa," *O Timothy* (1989, Vol. 6, Issue 7).

160 William Oltmans, "Who Are the Real Terrorists in South Africa," *O Timothy* (1989, Vol. 6, Issue 7); James W. Wardner, *Unholy Alliances* (n.p., 1996), p.180; *The Shepherd's Letter* (Spring 1993), p.13.

161 *The Shepherd's Letter* (Spring 1993), p.13.

162 "Who Is Mandela?," *Midnight Call* (September 1990), p.15; "Communist Mandela Given Hero's Welcome in Canada, U. S.," *The Christian World Report* (July 1990, Vol. 2, No. 6), p.3.

163 *The Shepherd's Letter, op. cit.*, p.13; "Man of Peace," *The Omega-Letter* (October 1988, Vol. 3, No. 9), p.17.

164 *Ibid.*

165 "Desmond Tutu—the Cursing Archbishop!," *O Timothy* (1988, Vol. 5, Issue 4); *The Shepherd's Letter, op. cit.*, p.13; Oltmans, *op. cit.*

166 *The Shepherd's Letter, op. cit.*, p.13; James W. Wardner, *Unholy Alliances* (n.p., 1996), p.180; David W. Cloud, "Liberation Theology: Christianized Marxism" *O Timothy* (1988, Vol. 5, Issue 1); "American Baptist Meeting Features Tutu, Campolo," *Calvary Contender* (March 1, 1995, Vol. 12, No. 5), p.2; David W. Cloud, "Liberation Theology: Christianized Marxism," *O Timothy* (1988, Vol. 5, Issue 1); "WCC Faith & Order Commission Conference," *Calvary Contender* (September 15, 1993, Vol. 10, No. 18), p.2; *Ibid.*

167 *Ibid.*

168 "Man of Peace," *The Omega-Letter* (October 1988, Vol. 3, No. 9), p.17.

169 *Ibid.*

170 News report when Desmond Tutu was in Philadelphia, Pennsylvania on January 14, 1986.

171 "Tutu Blasts Christians, Promotes Blasphemy," *Flashpoint* (September 1990), p.6; *The Shepherd's Letter, op. cit.* p.13; "Man of Peace," *op. cit.*, p.17; "Tutu's Modernism," *op. cit.*, p.16; "Desmond Tutu—the Cursing Archbishop!," *op. cit.*

172 "WCC Faith & Order Commission Conference," *Calvary Contender* (September 15, 1993, Vol. 10, No. 18), p.2.

173 "Exposure of Apostasy & Compromise," *op. cit.*, p.8; "Ecumenical Confusion and Deception at Graham Conference," *Christian News* (August 7, 2000, Vol. 38, No. 32), p.25.

174 *Evangelicals and Catholics Together: The Christian Mission in the Third Millennium* (March 29, 1994); "Who Will Evangelize Catholics?," *Calvary Contender* (June 15, 1997, Vol. 14, No. 12), p.2; David W. Cloud, *Is the Roman Catholic Changing?* (Oak Harbor, WA: Way of Life Literature, 1995 Edition); Michal J. Paquette, "Evangelicals, Catholics Issue Joint Mission Statement," *Christian News* (April 11, 1994, Vol. 32, No. 15), p.17; "Bill Bright and Catholics," *Calvary Contender* (January 1, 1999, Vol. 16, No. 1), p.2; Letter from J. Royce Thomason dated January 1995; Dave Hunt, "The Gospel Betrayed," *The Berean Call* (May 1994), p.1; Albert James Dager, "Evangelicals and Catholics Together: The New Ecumenical Accord in Light of Vatican II," *Media Spotlight* (Vol. 15, No. 2), p.8; "Catholics Seduce New Evangelicals," *Calvary Contender* (June 1, 1998, Vol. 15, No. 11), p.1; *The BDM Letter* (March/April 1995, Vol. 4, No. 2), p.2; "Catholics Seduce New Evangelicals," *Calvary Contender* (June 1, 1998, Vol. 15, No. 11), p.1.

175 Paper from Campus Crusade for Christ International.

176 Graham, *Just As I Am, op. cit.*, p.231.

177 "Roy Rogers Confesses to Soap Addiction" (April 27, 1993), p.B6.

178 *Christian News.*

179 "His 'Toronto Blessing' Endorsement Brings Broadcaster Criticism," *Christian News,* (April 17, 1995, Vol. 33, No. 16), p.2.

180 *Christian News* (April 24, 1995, Vol. 33, No. 17), p.11.

181 "In Globo Cogitare et in Loco Agree (sic) (Thinking Globally and Acting Locally)" (Part 3), *Distant Drums,* (May 1983, Vol. 5, No. 2), p.4.

182 Dave Hunt, "Religious Unity and the New World Order," *The Omega-Letter,* (July 1990, Vol. 5, No. 6), p.16.

183 Dave Hunt and T. A. McMahon, *The Seduction of Christianity: Spiritual Discernment in the Last Days* (Eugene, OR: Harvest House Publishers, 1985), p.28.

[184] Ken Ham, "What's Wrong with 'Progressive Creation?,'" (Florence, KY: Answers in Genesis), p.b.

[185] Rick Miesel quoting Hugh Ross in "Hugh Ross," Computer Discernment Notebook (on disk). See also: *Reasons To Believe* Web Site (Updated July 8, 1997), quoted in "What's Wrong with 'Progressive Creation?'" by Ken Ham (Florence, KY: Answers in Genesis), p.c.

[186] *Reasons To Believe* Web Site (Updated July 8, 1997), quoted in "What's Wrong with 'Progressive Creation?'" by Ken Ham (Florence, KY: Answers in Genesis), p.c.

[187] *The Berean Call* (February 1999).

[188] "Bill Bright Wins Templeton," *Allentown Morning Call* (March 9, 1996).

[189] John Templeton, *Possibilities for Over One Hundredfold More Spiritual Information: The Humble Approach in Theology and Science* (Philadelphia, PA: Templeton Foundation Press, 2000), p.201; Adelle M. Banks, "Campus Crusade Founder Wins $1 Million Prize," *Christian News* (March 18, 1996, Vol. 34, No. 12), p.15; "The Templeton Prize for Religious Excellence," *Despatch Magazine* (June 2001, Vol. 13:2); Judy Pinalto, "Unholy Hands on the Bible," American Freedom Network (Guest on Henry Feinberg's June 14, 1996 Program); "Bill Bright Gets $1 Million Templeton Prize," *Calvary Contender* (April 1, 1996, Vol. 13, No. 7), p.1; "Barbour Wins Templeton Prize," *Calvary Contender* (July 15, 1999, Vol. 16, No. 14); Joan Veon, *Prince Charles: The* Sustainable *Prince* (Oklahoma City, OK: Hearthstone Publishing, Ltd., 1997), p.102; "Ailing Bill Bright, Busy, Receives Awards," *Calvary Contender* (May 1, 2001, Vol. 18, No. 9), p.2.

[190] "Bill Bright and the Templeton Prize," *C.E.C. Journal* (May 1996), p.3.

[191] *Ibid.*

[192] Dave Hunt, "Progress in Religion?," *The Berean Call* (May 1996), p.1.

[193] *Ibid.*

[194] Hunt, "Progress in Religion?," *op. cit.*, p.1. See also: "John Marks Templeton," *Progress in Religion* (June 1996, Vol. 4, No. 2), p.2.

[195] *Ibid.*, p.2.

[196] Fact Sheet from Washington for Jesus '88; Cloud, "Flirting with Rome: Evangelical Entanglement with Roman Catholicism," *O Timothy* (1993).

[197] Brochure from March for Jesus.

[198] Jay Gary, *The Star of 2000: Our Journey Toward Hope* (Colorado Springs, CO: Bimillennial Press, 1994), p.3-5, etc.

[199] *Inside Music* (June 1991, Vol. 3, No. 3), p.22; "#1 'Christian' Rock Group Unmasked," *Flashpoint* (September 1990), p.3.

[200] "Music Videos with a Gospel Message," *Charisma and Christian Life* (June 1991, Vol. 16, No. 11), p.64.

[201] Dave Hunt, "Evangelizing the World," *CIB Bulletin* (July 1991, Vol. 7, No. 7), p.2.

[202] M. H. Reynolds, Jr., *AD 2000 Ecumenical Evangelism—A Warning!* (n.p., n.d.), p.11.

[203] "Gone Berserk," World of Prophecy (September 30, 2000). See also: "Gone Berserk," *Power of Prophecy* (May 2001, Vol. 2001-05), p.6.

[204] Charles W. Dunn, *Campus Crusade: Its Message and Methods* (Greenville, SC: Bob Jones University Press, Inc., 1980), p.9.

[205] "Digging in the Walls," *O Timothy,*(1995, Vol. 12, Issue 10).

[206] *Ibid.*

[207] "Billy Graham's Last Scheduled International Event, *op. cit.*, p.2.

[208] "Amsterdam 2000," *op. cit.*, p.4.

[209] "Charles Stanley's Handbook for Christian Living," *Christian News* (March 5, 2001, Vol. 39, No. 10), p.3; "Stanley's Handbook for Christian Living," *Calvary Contender* (April 1, 2001, Vol. 18, No. 7), p.2.

[210] Chuck Colson with Ellen Santilli Vaughn, *The Body* (Dallas, TX: Word Publishing, 1996 Edition), p.26; John E. Ashbrook, *New Neutralism II: Exposing the Gray of Compromise* (Mentor, OH: Here I Stand Books, 1992), p.69.

[211] *Ibid.*, Jacket Flap; "Why Do Colson and Evangelicals Think Catholics Are Saved?," *Calvary Contender* (November 15, 1999, Vol. 16, No. 22), p.2; Wilson Ewin, *Under the New World Order: Evangelicals, Catholics and Israel: Conspiracy of the Ages* (Compton, Quebec: Quebec Baptist Missions, n.d.), p.22, 23; "Evangelicals and Catholics Together: The Christian Mission in the Third Millennium," *O Timothy* (1994, Vol. 11, Issue 5); "Colson a Speaker at Westminster," *Calvary Contender* (September 15, 1995, Vol. 12, No. 18), p.2; David W. Cloud, *Is the Roman Catholic Changing?* (Oak Harbor, WA: Way of Life Literature, 1995 Edition); "Colson at PK-Memphis," *Calvary Contender* (November 15, 1996, Vol. 13, No. 22), p.2; "SBC Reaction to Catholic-Evangelical Paper," *Calvary Contender* (June 15, 1994, Vol. 11, No. 12), p.2; "Comments Regarding 'Evangelicals and Catholics Together,'" *Christians Evangelizing Catholics* (April 1995), p.5; "Colson's Prison Fellowship Honors RC Priest Neuhaus," *Calvary Contender* (March 15, 1998, Vol. 15, No. 6), p.2; "Priest Richard Neuhaus Exposed—He's a Marxist Heretic!," *Flashpoint* (November 1994), p.2; "Who Will Evangelize Catholics?," *Calvary Contender* (June 15, 1997, Vol. 14, No. 12), p.2; *Christian News* (April 11, 1994, Vol. 32, No. 15), p.1; Albert James Dager, "Evangelicals and Catholics Together: The New Ecumenical Accord in Light of Vatican II," *Media Spotlight* (Vol. 15, No. 2), p.3; *Christian View of the News* (October 10, 1994, Vol. 19, No. 19); *The BDM Letter* (March/April 1995, Vol. 4, No. 2), p.2; Letter from J. Royce Thomason dated January 1995; "Catholics Seduce New Evangelicals," *Calvary Contender* (June 1, 1998, Vol. 15, No. 11), p.1; Tom Watson, *The Redefining of a Christian* (Southlake, TX: Countryside Bible Church, 1995); "Chuck Colson's Historic Secret Mission: Undo the Protestant Reformation," *Flashpoint* (November 1994), p.1.

[212] *Ibid.*, p.83-84.

[213] "Priest Richard Neuhaus Exposed—He's a Marxist Heretic!," *Flashpoint* (November 1994), p.2; *The BDM Letter* (March/April 1995, Vol. 4, No. 2), p.2; David R. Barnhart, *Contending for the Faith* (Eagan, MN: Abiding Word Publications, 1994), p.126; John E. Ashbrook, *New Neutralism II: The Gray of Compromise* (Mentor, OH: Here I Stand Books, 1992), p.96; *The Berean Call* (May 1998), p.2; "Colson's Prison Fellowship Honors RC Priest Neuhaus," *Calvary Contender* (March 15, 1998, Vol. 15, No. 6), p.2; Letter from J. Royce Thomason dated January 1995; "Catholics Seduce New Evangelicals," *Calvary Contender* (June 1, 1998, Vol. 15, No. 11), p.1; "Catholic Priest to Speak at Asbury Seminary," *Calvary Contender* (February 1, 1997, Vol. 14, No. 3), p.2; *Christian News* (April 11, 1994, Vol. 32, No. 15), p.1; "Turret of the Times," *Christian News* (April 21, 1997, Vol. 35, No. 16), p.2; "Turret of the Times," *Christian News* (May 5, 1997, Vol. 35, No. 18), p.2.

[214] "LCMS Pastors and Laymen Asking—Who Invited Neuhaus and Dawn?," *Christian News* (March 28, 1994, Vol. 32, No. 13), p.12. See also: "Priest Richard Neuhaus Exposed—He's a Marxist Heretic!," *op. cit.*, p.2; Letter from J. Royce Thomason dated January 1995.

[215] "Priest Richard Neuhaus Exposed—He's a Marxist Heretic!," *op. cit.*, p.2.

[216] "LCMS Pastors and Laymen Asking—Who Invited Neuhaus and Dawn?," *op. cit.*, p.13.

[217] "Priest Richard Neuhaus Exposed—He's a Marxist Heretic!," *op. cit.*, p.2.

[218] *Ibid.* See also: "LCMS Pastors and Laymen Asking—Who Invited Neuhaus and Dawn?," *op. cit.*, p.12.

[219] "LCMS Pastors and Laymen Asking—Who Invited Neuhaus and Dawn?," *op. cit.*, p.12.

[220] "Priest Richard Neuhaus Exposed—He's a Marxist Heretic!," *op. cit.*, p.2.

[221] "LCMS Pastors and Laymen Asking—Who Invited Neuhaus and Dawn?," *op. cit.*, p.13; "Billy Graham's Last Scheduled International Event, *op. cit.*, p.7; "Turret of the Times," *Christian News* (July 19, 1999, Vol. 37, No. 29), p.2.

[222] David W. Cloud, "Evangelical Catholics," *O Timothy* (1992, Vol. 9, Issue 7); John E. Ashbrook, *New Neutralism II: Exposing the Gray of Compromise* (Mentor, OH: Here I Stand Books, 1992), p.69; David W. Cloud, *Is the Roman Catholic Changing?* (Oak Harbor, WA: Way of Life Literature, 1995 Edition).

[223] Keith A. Fournier, *Evangelical Catholics* (Nashville, TN: Thomas Nelson, Inc., 1990), p.vi.; Cloud, "Flirting with Rome: Evangelical Entanglement with Roman Catholicism," *O Timothy* (1993).

[224] Colson with Vaughn, *op. cit.*, p.376.

[225] "Colson's Prison Fellowship Honors RC Priest Neuhaus," *Calvary Contender* (March 15, 1998, Vol. 15, No. 6), p.2.

[226] "Why Do Colson and Evangelicals Think Catholics Are Saved?," *Calvary Contender* (November 15, 1999, Vol. 16, No. 22), p.2; "Prison Fellowship Now Headed by Catholic," *Calvary Contender* (July 15, 1998, Vol. 15, No. 14), p.1.

[227] "*Ibid.*

[228] Cloud, "Flirting with Rome: Evangelical Entanglement with Roman Catholicism," *O Timothy* (1993).

[229] Albert James Dager, *Inner Healing: A Biblical Analysis* (Santa Ana, CA: Tri-Level Press, 1986), p.52.

[230] "Colson at PK-Memphis," *Calvary Contender* (November 15, 1996, Vol. 13, No. 22), p.2. See also: Gordon Loux and Ronald E. Wilson, *You Can Be a Point of Light* (Portland, OR: Multnomah Press, 1991), p.10.

[231] Colson with Vaughn, *op. cit.*, p.73.

[232] *Ibid.* See also: Larry Spargimino, "From Rome with Love," *Prophetic Observer* (March 1999, Vol. 6, No. 3), p.3.

[233] Graham, *Just As I Am, op. cit.*, p.277. See also: Billy Graham, *Approaching Hoofbeats: The Four Horsemen of the Apocalypse* (Minneapolis, MN: Grason, 1983), p.196-197; David W. Cloud, *Flirting with Rome: Evangelical Entanglement with Roman Catholicism (Volume I—Billy Graham)* (Oak Harbor, WA: Way of Life Literature, 1993).

[234] "BBF Gives Graham Book to Preachers," *Calvary Contender* (April 1, 1999, Vol. 16, No. 7), p.2.

[235] Templeton, *op. cit.*, p.198.

[236] Hunt, "Evangelizing the World," *op. cit.*, p.2.

[237] David W. Cloud, "Mother Teresa's Successor Worships Hindu Idols," *Christian News* (January 24, 2000), p.7. See also: Dave Hunt, *Global Peace and the Rise of Antichrist* (Eugene, OR: Harvest House Publishers, 1990), p.149; William P. Grady, *Final Authority: A Christian's Guide to the King James Bible* (Knoxville, TN: Grady Publications, Inc., 1993), p.192; Sessler, *op. cit.*, p.153; Quote from Desmong Doig in "Mother Teresa: Loving Idol Worshiper," *The Battle Cry* (July/August 1991), p.1.

[238] *Ibid.*, quoting from "Mother Teresa Touched Other Faiths," Associated Press, September 7, 1997 in *Christian News* (January 24, 2000), p.7.

[239] *Christians Evangelizing Catholics* (February 1993), p.1.

[240] Cloud, "Mother Teresa's Successor Worships Hindu Idols," *op. cit.;* p.7; D. W. Cloud, "Is Mother Teresa a True Christian?," *Christian News* (September 15, 1997, Vol. 35, No. 33), p.9.

[241] "United Religions Initiative 2000," *op. cit.*, p.6; Speech by William E. Swing at the North American Interfaith Network Conference (August 10, 1996).

[242] Albert James Dager, "The World Christian Movement—Part 3: Toward the New World Order," *Media Spotlight* (1999, Vol. 22, No.3), p.14; Albert James Dager, *The World Christian Movement: A Great Delusion Leading to the Religio-Political State of the Anti-Christ* (Redmond, WA: Sword Publishers, 2001), p.178.

[243] "Gratitude: The Adamant of Existence," *World Goodwill* (2000, No. 4), p.6.

[244] McCall, "Ecumenism, 'Global Spirituality' and Mother Teresa," *op. cit.*, p.26.

[245] Cloud, "Mother Teresa's Successor Worships Hindu Idols," *op. cit.*, p.7.

[246] Colson with Vaughn, *op. cit.*, Back Cover and Jacket Flap; Templeton, *op. cit.*, p.201; "Getting Out of Jail Free: A Conversation with Charles Colson," *Research News & Opportunities in Science and Theology* (July/August 2001, Vol. 1, No. 11/12), p.6; Texe Marrs, "Texe Marrs Asks Chuck Colson: 'Will You Sell Your Soul to the Devil for a Million Dollars?,'" *Flashpoint* (June 1993), p.1; "The Templeton Prize for Religious Excellence," *Despatch Magazine* (June 2001, Vol. 13:2); Wilson Ewin, *Under the New World Order: Evangelicals, Catholics and Israel: Conspiracy of the Ages* (Compton, Quebec: Quebec Baptist Missions, n.d.), p.22, 23; Judy Pinalto, "Unholy Hands on the Bible," American Freedom Network (Guest on Henry Feinberg's June 14, 1996 Program); *The Berean Call* (August 1993), p.4; "Colson at PK—Memphis," *Calvary Contender* (November 15, 1996, Vol. 13, No. 22), p.2; "Chuck Colson Organization Spreading Misinformation," *O Timothy* (1994, Vol. 11, Issue 2); Joan Veon, *Prince Charles: The* Sustainable *Prince* (Oklahoma City, OK: Hearthstone Publishing, Ltd., 1997), p.102; Tom Watson, *The Redefining of a Christian* (Southlake, TX: Countryside Bible Church, 1995), p.2; "Charles Colson to Join Mother Teresa and Pagan Religious Leaders at Parliament of the World's Religions," *O Timothy* (1993, Vol. 10, Issue 6); David W. Cloud, *Flirting with Rome: Evangelical Entanglement with Roman Catholicism (Volume 4—The Charismatics)* (Oak Harbor, WA: Way of Life Literature, 1993); Texe Marrs, "Chuck Colson: The Pied Piper of Ecumenicism," *Flashpoint* (October 1993), p.2.

[247] "Templeton Is Awarded to Physicist," *Reading Eagle* (March 11, 1995); Joan Veon, *Prince Charles: The* Sustainable *Prince* (Oklahoma City, OK: Hearthstone Publishing, Ltd., 1997), p.102; "Books of Interest Endorsed by the John Templeton Foundation" (Paper from the John Templeton Foundation dated January 11, 1996), p.1; "Barbour Wins Templeton Prize," *Calvary Contender* (July 15, 1999, Vol. 16, No. 14); Harry Bruinius, "Templeton Winner Coaxed Science and Religion to Talk," *Christian Science Monitor* (March 11, 1999), p.18.

[248] Fritz Springmeier, "The World Parliment (sic) of Religions—The Visible Creation of a World Church," *Newsletter from a Christian Ministry* (September 1, 1993, Vol. 2, No. 12), p.55; *Council on Foreign Relations: Annual Report July 1, 1987-June 30, 1988,* p.172; *Council on Foreign Relations: Annual Report July 1, 1992-June 30, 1993,* p.164; *"Secret Records" Revealed: The Men, the Money, and the Methods Behind the New World Order* (Marlborough, NH: The Plymouth Rock Foundation, 1994), p.36; Robert Gaylon Ross, Sr., *Who's Who of the Elite* (San Marcos, TX: RIE, 1995), p.109; *Secret Records Revealed: The Men, the Money and the Methods Behind the New World Order* (Oklahoma City, OK: Hearthstone Publishing, Ltd., 1999), p.125; Texe Marrs, *Circle of Intrigue* (Austin, TX: Living Truth Ministries, 1995), p.276.

[249] Texe Marrs, *Circle of Intrigue* (Austin, TX: Living Truth Ministries, 1995), p.276.

[250] Joan Veon, *Prince Charles: The* Sustainable *Prince* (Oklahoma City, OK: Hearthstone Publishing, Ltd., 1997), p.24; *"Secret Records" Revealed: The Men, the Money, and the Methods Behind the New World Order* (Marlborough, NH: The Plymouth Rock Foundation, 1994), p.36; *Secret Records Revealed: The Men, the Money and the Methods Behind the New World Order* (Oklahoma City, OK: Hearthstone Publishing, Ltd., 1999), p.125.

[251] Springmeier, "The World Parliment (sic) of Religions," *op. cit.*, p.55.

[252] Texe Marrs, "Texe Marrs Asks Chuck Colson: 'Will You Sell Your Soul to the Devil for a Million Dollars?,'" *Flashpoint* (June 1993), p.2; "Charles Colson to Join Mother Teresa and Pagan Religious Leaders at Parliament of the World's Religions," *O Timothy* (1993, Vol. 10, Issue 6).

[253] Tom Watson, *The Redefining of a Christian* (Southlake, TX: Countryside Bible Church, 1995), p.3; "Chuck Colson Organization Spreading Misinformation," *O Timothy* (1994, Vol. 11, Issue 2).

[254] *The Berean Call* (August 1993), p.3-4; "Chuck Colson Organization Spreading Misinformation," *O Timothy* (1994, Vol. 11, Issue 2).

[255] *Ibid.*, p.4.

[256] David Barnhart, "A Fierce Battle Raging in Christendom," *Christian News* (October 3, 1994, Vol. 32, No. 36), p.17.

[257] James W. Wardner, *Unholy Alliances* (n.p., 1996), p.177.

[258] Marrs, "Texe Marrs Asks Chuck Colson, *op. cit.*, p.1-2.

[259] Texe Marrs, "Chuck Colson: The Pied Piper of Ecumenicism," *Flashpoint* (October 1993), p.2.

[260] *Report from the Planetary Commission* (May 1, 1986).

[261] Morrison, *op. cit.*, p.181.

[262] John Randolph Price, *The Planetary Commission* (Boerne, TX: The Quartus Foundation for Spiritual Research, Inc., 1984), p.69.

[263] Texe Marrs, *Mystery Mark of the New Age: Satan's Design for World Domination* (Westchester, IL: Crossway Books, 1988), p.157.

[264] Wanda Marrs, *New Age Lies to Women* (Austin, TX: Living Truth Publishers, 1989), p.43

[265] Price, *The Planetary Commission, op. cit.*, p.37.

[266] Marrs quoting John Randolph Price in *Circle of Intrigue, op. cit.*, p.100.

[267] Price, *The Planetary Commission, op. cit.*, p.163; Texe Marrs, *Dark Secrets of the New Age: Satan's Plan for a One World Religion* (Westchester, IL: Crossway Books, 1987), p.13; Morrison, *op. cit.*, p.181.

[268] *Ibid.*

[269] *Ibid.*, p.60.

[270] *Ibid.*, p.81.

[271] *Ibid.*

[272] *Ibid.*, p.84.

[273] *Ibid.*, p.99.

[274] *Ibid.*, p.147.

[275] *Ibid.*, p.37.

[276] Marrs, *Circle of Intrigue, op. cit.*, p.100; Marrs, *New Age Lies to Women, op. cit.*, p.38.

[277] Marrs, *New Age Lies to Women, op. cit.*, p.38.

[278] "The Healer Within," *World Goodwill Newsletter* (1987, No. 2), p.8; *Now Is the Dawning of the New Age New World Order* (Oklahoma City, OK: Hearthstone Publishing, Ltd., 1991), p.358; Marrs, *Mystery Mark of the New Age, op. cit.*, p.157.

[279] Marrs, *Mystery Mark of the New Age, op. cit.*, p.177.

[280] Price, *The Planetary Commission, op. cit.*, p.157-158. See also: *Ibid.*

[281] Marrs, "Chuck Colson: The Pied Piper of Ecumenicism," *op. cit.* p.2.

[282] Gordon Loux and Ronald E. Wilson, *You Can Be a Point of Light* (Portland, OR: Multnomah Press, 1991), p.10.

[283] *Ibid.*

[284] J. Gordon Melton, Jerome Clark, and Aidan A. Kelly, *New Age Almanac* (Detroit, MI: Visible Ink, 1991), p.10-11.

[285] *Ibid.*, p.10. See also: *Now Is the Dawning of the New Age New World Order* (Oklahoma City, OK: Hearthstone Publishing, Ltd., 1991), p.275.

[286] "The Great Invocation: A Mantram for the New Age and for All Humanity" (Received February 13, 1999), p.1.

[287] *Reader's Digest* (October 1982), p.203.

[288] *Transmission* (April 1983, No. 1), p.3. See also: Benjamin Creme, *The Reappearance of the Christ and the Masters of Wisdom* (North Hollywood, CA: Tara Center, 1980), p.39-41; *The Prophecy Newsletter* (1985, Vol. 1, No. 6), p.12.

[289] Alice A. Bailey, *Discipleship in the New Age* (Vol. I) (NY: Lucis Publishing Company, 1972), p.462. See also: Texe Marrs, *Dark Majesty: The Secret Brotherhood and the Magic of a Thousand Points of Light* (Austin, TX: Living Truth Publishers, 1992), p.78.

[290] *Now Is the Dawning of the New Age New World Order* (Oklahoma City, OK: Hearthstone Publishing, Ltd., 1991), p.123.

[291] *Ibid.*, p.174.

[292] Alice A. Bailey, *The Rays and the Initiations* (New York, NY: Lucis Trust, 1960), p.49.

[293] Alice A. Bailey, *A Treatise on White Magic or the Way of the Disciple* (NY: Lucis Publishing Company, 1951), p.100.

[294] Texe Marrs, *Dark Majesty: The Secret Brotherhood and the Magic of a Thousand Points of Light* (Austin, TX: Living Truth Publishers, 1992), p.78-79.

[295] See: *The Problems of Humanity: The Building of Right Human Relations: Study Three: The Problem of International Unity* (New York, NY: World Goodwill, n.d.), p.44; Bernard Gunther, *Energy Ecstasy* (Van Nuys, CA: Newcastle Publishing Company, Inc., 1978), p.28; Alice A. Bailey, *The Externalization of the Hierarchy* (New York, NY: Lucis Publishing Company, 1957), p.48, 353; Bailey, *A Treatise on White Magic, op. cit.*, p.93, 96; Alice A. Bailey, *The Light of the Soul: Its Science and Effect* (NY: Lucis Publishing Company, 1965), p.83; Benjamin Creme, *The Reappearance of the Christ and the Masters of Wisdom* (North Hollywood, CA: Tara Center, 1980), p.39-41; Two Disciples, *The Rainbow Bridge* (Escondido, CA: The Triune Foundation, 1981), p.88, 191; Paper from Seven Ray Institute; *Transmission* (April 1983, No. 1), p.3; Letter from Triangles dated September 1994), p.1. Exposing this phrase (from a Christian perspective), see: "Look Who's Bringing in a New Curriculum," *Christian Conscience* (December 1997, Vol. 3, No. 10), p.30; *Now Is the Dawning of the New Age New World Order, op. cit.*, p.274, 275; *President Clinton Will Continue the New World Order* (Oklahoma City, OK: Southwest Radio Church, 1993), p.5; *The Road to Socialism and the New World Order* (Highland City, FL: Florida Pro Family Forum, Inc., 1995), p.28-29; *The New World Order* (Milford, PA: America's Future, Inc., 1992), p.6; "The Triple Play," *Don Bell Reports* (May 31, 1991, Vol. 38, No. 11), p.1-2; Marrs, *Circle of Intrigue, op. cit.*, p.86; *The New Age Movement—Age of Aquarius—Age of Antichrist* (Oklahoma City, OK: Southwest Radio Church, 1982), p.16; Patti Lalonde, "Educating for Service in the New Age," *Christian Parent Alert* (January 1992, Vol. 2, No. 1), p.4; *The Prophecy Newsletter* (1985, Vol. 1, No. 6), p.12; Marrs, *Ravaged by the New Age, op. cit.*, p.85.

[296] *Now Is the Dawning of the New Age New World Order, op. cit.*, p.28; *The Road to Socialism and the New World Order* (Highland City, FL: Florida Pro Family Forum, Inc., 1995), p.28-29.

[297] *The Road to Socialism and the New World Order* (Highland City, FL: Florida Pro Family Forum, Inc., 1995), p.29

[298] Patti Lalonde, "Educating for Service in the New Age," *Christian Parent Alert* (January 1992, Vol. 2, No. 1), p.4.

[299] "The United Nations and the Path to Unity and Right Relations," *World Goodwill Newsletter* (1995, No. 2), p.2.

[300] Warren Smith, "M. Scott Peck: Community and the Cosmic Christ," *Christian Conscience* (November 1995, Vol. 1, No. 10), p.25.

[301] Marrs, "Chuck Colson: The Pied Piper of Ecumenicism," *op. cit.*, p.2.

[302] *Ibid.*

[303] "Conference Addresses Globalization and the Family," *Acton Notes* (January 2001, Vol. 11, No. 1), p.6; "James Dobson, Charles Colson Visit Vatican, Praise Roman Catholic Church," *Christian News* (February 26, 2001, Vol. 39, No. 9), p.15; "Dobson and Colson Visit the Pope," *Christian News* (January 8, 2001, Vol. 39, No. 2), p.2; "James Dobson, Chuck Colson, and the Pope!," *Despatch Magazine* (March 2001, Vol. 13, No. 1), p.30.

[304] *Ibid.*

[305] Dave Hunt, "The Gospel Betrayed," *The Berean Call* (May 1994), p.1.

[306] Colson with Vaughn, *op. cit.*, p.243; Rick Miesel, "Colson: General Teachings/Activities" (on disk).

[307] *Catholics and Purgatory* (New Haven, CT: Catholic Information Service, Knights of Columbus, n.d.), p.6.

[308] David W. Cloud, "The Catholic Church Still Grants Indulgences," *O Timothy* (1991, Vol. 8, Issue 2).

[309] Hunt, "The Gospel Betrayed," *op. cit.*, p.2; Rick Miesel, "Colson: General Teachings/Activities" (on disk). *The Berean Call* (Octo-ber 1993), p.3; Wilson Ewin, *Today's Evangelicals Embracing the World's Deadliest Cult* (Compton, Quebec: Quebec Baptist Missions, n.d.), p.16. See also: David W. Cloud, *Is the Roman Catholic Changing?* (Oak Harbor, WA: Way of Life Literature, 1995 Edition).

[310] David W. Cloud quoting from Vatican Documents in *Is the Roman Catholic Changing?* (Oak Harbor, WA: Way of Life Literature, 1995 Edition). See also: "Thus Saith Vatican Council II," *Fighting the Good Fight* (November/December 1994), p.2.

[311] *Catechism of the Catholic Church* (New York, NY: Image Books, 1995), p.291, 413, 417; Cloud, "The Catholic Church Still Grants Indulgences," *op. cit.;* David W. Cloud, "The New Catholic Catechism," *O Timothy* (1995, Vol. 12, Issue 1); *Ibid.*

[312] *Ibid.*, p.417. See also: Richard P. McBrien, *Lives of the Popes: The Pontiffs from St. Peter to John Paul II* (New York, NY: HarperSanFrancisco, 1997), p.231; Dave Hunt, *Whatever Happened to Heaven?* (Eugene, OR: Harvest House Publishers, 1988), p.157-158; "The Present-Day Official Teaching of the Roman Catholic Church," (Article by Evangelical Outreach), p.8; *The Evangelical Methodist* (April 2001, Vol. 79, No. 3), p.6.

[313] *Ibid.*, p.413. See also: *Catholic Word Book* (New Haven, CT: Catholic Information Service, Knights of Columbus, n.d.), p.23; Letter from Legionaries of Christ (Received September 19, 1998; "Thus Saith Vatican Council II," *Fighting the Good Fight* (November/December 1994), p.2.

[314] "Catholic-Lutheran Unity," *Calvary Contender* (January 15, 2000), p.2. See also: "LWF General Secretary: Consultation on Indulgences," *Christian News* (February 26, 2001, Vol. 39, No. 9), p.11, *The Evangelical Methodist* (April 2001, Vol. 79, No. 3), p.6.

[315] "Pope Offers Early Salvation?," *Calvary Contender* (January 1, 1999, Vol. 16, No. 1), p.1.

[316] "Authority," *C. E. C. Journal* (March/April 2001), p.8.

[317] Richard P. McBrien, *Lives of the Popes: The Pontiffs from St. Peter to John Paul II* (New York, NY: HarperSanFrancisco, 1997), p.240-241; Dave Hunt, *Whatever Happened to Heaven?* (Eugene, OR: Harvest House Publishers, 1988), p.161.

[318] Ralph Edward Woodrow quoting from *The Catholic Encyclopedia* in *Babylon Mystery Religion: Ancient and Modern* (Riverside, CA: Ralph Woodrow Evangelistic Association, Inc., 1990 Edition), p.58. See also: *Catholics and Purgatory, op. cit.*, p.7.

[319] "Ecumenical Consultation on Indulgences," *Despatch Magazine* (March 2001, Vol. 13, No. 1), p.32.

[320] *Ibid.*

[321] Cloud quoting from Vatican II Documents in *Is the Roman Catholic Changing?, op. cit.* See also: "The Present-Day Official Teaching of the Roman Catholic Church," (Article by Evangelical Outreach), p.8; "Thus Saith Vatican Council II," *Fighting the Good Fight* (November/December 1994), p.2.

[322] Marrs, "Chuck Colson: The Pied Piper of Ecumenicism," *op. cit.*, p.2. See also: "L'Engle a New Ager," *Calvary Contender* (January 15, 1998), p.1; "Abominations Masquerading As 'Christian' Books," *Flashpoint* (February 1992), p.2; Berit Kjos, "What Kind of Message Is *The Message?," Christian News* (December 20, 1993, Vol. 31, No. 47), p.18; Marrs, *New Age Lies to Women, op. cit.*, p.149; "Colson: General Teachings/Activities" (Biblical Discernment Ministries) (on disk).

[323] Brenda Scott and Samantha Smith, *Trojan Horse: How the New Age Movement Infiltrates the Church* (Lafayette, LA: Huntington House Publishers, 1993), p.161. See also: Marrs, *Ravaged by the New Age, op. cit.*, p.188.

[324] *Ibid.*, p.191.

[325] Madeleine L'Engle, *The Rock That Is Higher: Story As Truth* (Wheaton, IL: Harold Shaw Publishers, 1993), p.90.

[326] Scott and Smith, *op. cit.*, p.162.

[327] *Ibid.*

[328] *Ibid.*, p.179.

[329] *Ibid.*

[330] L'Engle, *op. cit.*, p.147.

[331] Scott and Smith, *op. cit.*, p.181.

[332] *Ibid.*, p.179.

[333] L'Engle, *op. cit.*, p.128, 237.

[334] *Ibid.*, p.135. See also p.122, 130 for more references referring to God as a woman.

[335] *Ibid.*, p.240.

[336] "Abominations Masquerading As 'Christian' Books," *Flashpoint* (February 1992), p.2.

[337] *Ibid.*

[338] *Ibid.*

[339] *Ibid.*, p.188.

[340] L'Engle, *op. cit.*, p.208-209.

[341] *Ibid.*, p.173.

[342] Scott and Smith, *op. cit.*, p.165.

[343] *Ibid.*, p.165-166.

[344] *Ibid.*, p.109.

[345] Clifford Wilson and John Weldon, *Psychic Forces and Occult Shock: A Biblical View* (TN: Global Publishers, 1987), p.186-187; *News & Views* (June 1988), p.1; Charles H. Vail, *The Ancient Mysteries and Modern Masonry* (Macoy Publishing and Masonic Company, 1909), p.39; Texe Marrs, *Dark Secrets of the New Age: Satan's Plan for a One World Religion* (Westchester, IL: Crossway Books, 1987), p.114; Melton, Clark, and Kelly, *op. cit.*, p.51.

[346] Melton, Clark, and Kelly, *op. cit.*, p.69; *The Watchman Expositor* (1998, Vol. 15, No. 5), p.19; Douglas Shah, *The Meditators* (Plainfield, NJ: Logos International, 1975), p.98; Texe Marrs, *Dark Secrets of the New Age: Satan's Plan for a One World Religion* (Westchester, IL: Crossway Books, 1987), p.114; John Blofeld, *The Tantric Mysticism of Tibet* (Boston, MA: Shambhala Publications, Inc., 1970), p.89.

[347] Sri Chinmoy, *Selfless Service-Light*, p.25; Al G. Manning, *Helping Yourself with Psycho-Cosmic Power* (West Nyack, NY: Parker Publishing Company, Inc., 1968), p.21.

[348] Alain Danielou, *The Gods of India* (New York, NY: Inner Traditions International Ltd., 1985), p.174. See also: J.S.M. Ward and W. G. Stirling, *The Hung Society or the Society of Heaven and Earth* (Vol. I) (London, England: The Baskerville Press, Limited, 1925), p.118; Helena Petrovna Blavatsky, *Isis Unveiled*, Vol. I: Science (New York, NY: Trow's Printing and Bookbinding Company, 1877), p.xxxvi.

[349] Wilson and Weldon, *op. cit.*, p.186-187. See also: Benjamin Creme, *The Reappearance of the Christ and the Masters of Wisdom* (North Hollywood, CA: Tara Center, 1980), p.148; "Transformation Toward New Age Synthesis," *Distant Drums* (March 1986, Vol. 8, No. 1), p.8; Ira Progoff, *The Practice of Process Meditation: The Intensive Journal Way to Spiritual Experience* (New York, NY: Dialogue House Library, 1980), p.204; John Blofeld, *The Tantric Mysticism of Tibet* (Boston, MA: Shambhala Publications, Inc., 1970), p.88, 250; Texe Marrs, *Dark Secrets of the New Age: Satan's Plan for a One World Religion* (Westchester, IL: Crossway Books, 1987), p.114; *News & Views* (June 1988), p.1; Pat Means, *The Mystical Maze: A Guidebook Through the Mindfields of Eastern Mysticism* (Campus Crusade for Christ, Inc., 1976), p.134, 247-248.

[350] Danielou, *op. cit.*, p.334-335, 337.

[351] Scott and Smith, *op. cit.*, p.163.

[352] *Ibid.*, p.169.

[353] *Ibid.*, p.180-181. For other references about "Namaste," see: *Tolerance, Goodwill, Peace* (New York, NY: World Goodwill, n.d.), p.15; Corinne McLaughlin and Gordon Davidson, *Spiritual Politics: Changing the World from the Inside Out* (NY: Ballantine Books, 1994), p.62; Samantha Smith, "Gorby's Disappearing Act," *Hope for the World* (Spring 1998), p.5.

[354] *Ibid.*, p.168.

[355] Marrs, *Ravaged by the New Age, op. cit.*, p.186.

[356] Scott and Smith, *op. cit.*, p.170.

[357] *Ibid.*, p.44.

[358] Marrs, *Ravaged by the New Age, op. cit.*, p.188. See also: "Press Release—Trojan Horse," *Bold Truth* (April 1993), p.12; Marrs, *New Age Lies to Women, op. cit.*, p.149.

[359] Paper listing the participants in the State of the World Forum; George Chaplin, "Lecture in May Will Focus on Need to Preserve Planet," *The Honolulu Advertiser* (April 12, 1997), p.B3; Samantha Smith, "Gorby's Disappearing Act," *Hope for the World* (Spring 1998), p.5; Scott and Smith, *op. cit.*

[360] "The Forum at Grace Cathedral," *URI News Update* (December 1996), p.2.

[361] Paper listing the participants in the State of the World Forum.

[362] George Chaplin, "Lecture in May Will Focus on Need to Preserve Planet," *The Honolulu Advertiser* (April 12, 1997), p.B3.

[363] "Abominations Masquerading As 'Christian' Books," *op. cit.*, p.2; "Press Release—Trojan Horse," *Bold Truth* (April 1993), p.12.

[364] Scott and Smith, *op. cit.*, p.x, back cover. See also: "Press Release—Trojan Horse," *Bold Truth* (April 1993), p.12.

[365] *Ibid.*, p.x. See also: "Abominations Masquerading As 'Christian' Books," *op. cit.*, p.2.

[366] *Ibid.*, p.x.

[367] *Ibid.*, p.159.

[368] "The Lion, the Witch, and the VCR," *Breakpoint with Chuck Colson* (May 18-22, 1992, No. 221), p.3.

[369] *Ibid.*

[370] Colson with Vaughn, *op. cit.*, p.338.

[371] *Ibid.*

[372] Texe Marrs, *Texe Marrs Book of New Age Cults and Religions* (Austin, TX: Living Truth Publishers, 1990), p.274.

[373] *Ibid.* See also: Corinne McLaughlin and Gordon Davidson, *Spiritual Politics: Changing the World from the Inside Out* (NY: Ballantine Books, 1994), p.265.

[374] *Ibid.*, p.274-275.

[375] "Reviews," *Connecting Link* (November/December 1989, Vol. 1, No. 5), p.47. See also: Machaelle Small Wright, "Why Bother? A Matter of Spiritual Integrity, A Matter of the Heart," *Connecting Link* (January/February 1990, Issue 6), p.6; *2001: A Vision from the Future Visualization 2001* (n.p., n.d.), p.7; Marrs, *Texe Marrs Book of New Age Cults and Religions, op. cit.*, p.274.

[376] *Ibid.*

[377] Machaelle Small Wright, "Why Bother? A Matter of Spiritual Integrity, A Matter of the Heart," *Connecting Link* (January/February 1990, Issue 6), p.8.

[378] *What? When? Where? Why? Who? in Freemasonry* (Silver Spring, MD: Masonic Service Association of the United States, 1986 Edition), p.37; Blue Star, "Pagan Deities: Echoes of the Old Ones," *Circle Network News* (Spring 1986, Vol. 8, No. 1), p.7; Johanna Michaelsen, *Like Lambs to the Slaughter* (Eugene, OR: Harvest House Publishers, 1989), p.255-256, 316; Marrs, *Ravaged by the New Age, op. cit.*, p.117; J. E. Cirlot, Translated by Jack Sage, *A Dictionary of Symbols* (New York, NY: Philosophical Library, Inc., 1972), p.134, 249; Jack M. Roper, "Pan: Pagan God and Nature Demon," *The Christian World Report* (October 1992, Vol. 7, No. 8), p.27; Stephanie Ericsson, "Simply Divine: A Beginner's Guide to Oracles—Tarot Cards, Rune Stones, the *I Ching*, and Other Tools of Personal Spirituality," *Utne Reader* (March/April 1992, No. 50), p.111; Jeff Godwin, *Dancing with Demons: The Music's Real Master* (Chino, CA: Chick Publications, 1988), p.4; Jeff Godwin, *Rock & Roll Religion* (Bloomington, IN: The Rock Ministries, 1995), p.63; "Who Do You Think This Is?," *Despatch Magazine* (December 1997, Vol. 9, No. 4), p.53; Kathleen Hayes, "The Horned God Pan is Patron of Witches," *NRI Trumpet* (July 1987), p.3; 1988 Catalog from Papa Jim, p.105; Catalog from International Imports, p.115.

[379] Catalog from International Imports, p.115. See also: J. E. Cirlot, Translated by Jack Sage, *A Dictionary of Symbols* (NY: Dorset Press, 1991), p.81, 143; Melton, Clark, and Kelly, *op. cit.*, p.402; David Spangler, *Reflections on the Christ* (Scotland: Findhorn Publications, 1977), p.116; Findhorn Community, *The Findhorn Garden* (New York, NY: Harper and Row, 1975), p.7-8, 17, 128; Paul Hawken, *The Magic of Findhorn* (New York, NY: Harper and Row, 1975), p.136-137.

[380] Robin Lane Fox, *Pagans and Christians* (NY: Alfred S. Knopf, Inc., 1986), p.118; Jeff Godwin, *Dancing with Demons: The Music's Real Master* (Chino, CA: Chick Publications, 1988), p.4; George Ryley Scott, *Phallic Worship: A History of Sex and Sexual Rites* (London, England: Senate, 1966), p.218; Jeff Godwin, *The Devil's Disciples: The Truth About Rock* (Chino, CA: Chick Publications, 1985), p.51; Paul Hamlyn, *Greek Mythology* (London, England: Paul Hamlyn Limited, 1967), p.52; *What? When? Where? Why? Who? in Freemasonry, op. cit.*, p.37; Milton Alberto Pottenger, *Symbolism* (Sacramento, CA: Symbol Publishing Company, 1905), p.184-185; Jeff Godwin, *Rock & Roll Religion* (Bloomington, IN: The Rock Ministries, 1995), p.51, 63, 203; Manly Palmer Hall, *The Secret Teachings of All Ages* (Los Angeles 27, CA: The Philosophical Research Society Press, 1945), p.xxxv; Eliphas Levi, Translated by Arthur Edward Waite, *The History of Magic Including a Clear and Precise Exposition of Its Procedure, Its Rites and Its Mysteries* (London, England: Cathedral House, 1922), p.191-192; *New Larousse Encyclopedia of Mythology* (Prometheus Press, 1972 Edition), p.124, 161; *New Times* (September/October 1985, No. 854), p.28; 1988 Catalog from Papa Jim II, Inc., p.108; S. R. Parchment, *Ancient Operative Masonry* (San Francisco, CA: San Francisco Center—Rosicrucian Fellowship, 1930), p.64; "Halloween and Witchcraft," *Christian Parent Alert* (October 1991, Vol. 1, No. 3), p.13; Charles G. Berger, *Our Phallic Heritage* (New York, NY: Greenwich Book Publishers, Inc., 1966), p.32, 46; Catalog from Pyramid Books and the New-Age Collection, p.3; Catalog from Sounds True (Winter 1992, Vol. 4, No. 1), Inside Front Cover; Laurie Cabot with Tom Cowan, *Power of the Witch: The Earth, the Moon, and the Magical Path to Enlightenment* (New York, NY: Delacorte Press, 1989), p.66; Jack M. Roper, "Pan: Pagan God and Nature Demon," *The Christian World Report* (October 1992, Vol. 7, No. 8), p.26; *The World Book Encyclopedia* (Vol. 14) (Chicago 54, IL: Field Enterprises Educational Corporation, 1961 Edition), p.93.

[381] J. E. Cirlot, Translated by Jack Sage, *A Dictionary of Symbols* (NY: Dorset Press, 1991), p.81, 134, 143, 249; Harry E. Wedeck, *Treasury of Witchcraft* (New York, NY: Philosophical Library, 1961), p.249. See also: *Complete Occult Digest A to Z* (North Hollywood, CA: International Imports, 1984), p.115; Eliphas Levi, Translated by Arthur Edward Waite, *The History of Magic Including a Clear and Precise Exposition of Its Procedure, Its Rites and Its Mysteries* (London, England: Cathedral House, 1922), p.192; Paul Hamlyn, *Greek Mythology* (London, England: Paul Hamlyn Limited, 1967), p.114; Marrs, *Texe Marrs Book of New Age Cults and Religions, op. cit.*, p.61, 231-232; Charles G. Berger, *Our Phallic Heritage* (New York, NY: Greenwich Book Publishers, Inc., 1966), p.46; Laurie Cabot with Tom Cowan, *Power of the Witch: The Earth, the Moon, and the Magical Path to Enlightenment* (New York, NY: Delacorte Press, 1989), p.65; Jack M. Roper, "Pan: Pagan God and Nature Demon," *The Christian World Report* (October 1992, Vol. 7, No. 8), p.26; Catalog from Pyramid Books and the New-Age Collection, p.3; Jeff Godwin, *Dancing with Demons: The Music's Real Master* (Chino, CA: Chick Publications, 1988), p.4; *What? When? Where? Why? Who? in Freemasonry, op. cit.*, p.37; *New Larousse Encyclopedia of Mythology* (Prometheus Press, 1972 Edition), p.161; 1988 Catalog from

Papa Jim II, Inc., p.105; *New Times* (September/October 1985, No. 854), p.28; *Ibid.;* Anton Szandor LaVey, *The Satanic Bible* (NY: Avon Books, 1969), p.59, 145; Jeff Godwin, *Rock & Roll Religion* (Bloomington, IN: The Rock Ministries, 1995), p.63; Thomas Bulfinch, *Bulfinch's Mythology: The Age of Fable or Stories of Gods and Heroes* (Garden City, NY: Doubleday and Company, Inc., 1948), p.181; Thomas Bulfinch, *Bulfinch's Mythology* (NY: Thomas Y. Crowell Company, Inc., 1970), p.957; Manly Palmer Hall, *The Secret Teachings of All Ages* (Los Angeles 27, CA: The Philosophical Research Society Press, 1945), p.xxxv.

[382] Anton Szandor LaVey, *The Satanic Bible* (NY: Avon Books, 1969), p.59. See also: Kathleen Hayes, "The Horned God Pan is Patron of Witches," *NRI Trumpet* (July 1987), p.3; Charles G. Berger, *Our Phallic Heritage* (New York, NY: Greenwich Book Publishers, Inc., 1966), p.25; Jack M. Roper, "Pan: Pagan God and Nature Demon," *The Christian World Report* (October 1992, Vol. 7, No. 8), p.27.

[383] S. R. Parchment, *Ancient Operative Masonry* (San Francisco, CA: San Francisco Center—Rosicrucian Fellowship, 1930), p.64.

[384] Charles G. Berger, *Our Phallic Heritage* (New York, NY: Greenwich Book Publishers, Inc., 1966), p.32. See also: Paul Hamlyn, *Greek Mythology* (London, England: Paul Hamlyn Limited, 1967), p.119; Thomas Bulfinch, *Bulfinch's Mythology: The Age of Fable or Stories of Gods and Heroes* (Garden City, NY: Doubleday and Company, Inc., 1948), p.181.

[385] Fox, *op. cit.*, p.130; Jeff Godwin, *The Devil's Disciples: The Truth About Rock* (Chino, CA: Chick Publications, 1985), p.51.

[386] Berger, *op. cit.*, p.32. See also: Thomas Bulfinch, *Bulfinch's Mythology: The Age of Fable or Stories of Gods and Heroes* (Garden City, NY: Doubleday and Company, Inc., 1948), p.181; *New Larousse Encyclopedia* (Prometheus Press, 1972 Edition), p.161.

[387] Stewart Farrar, *What Witches Do: The Modern Coven Revealed* (Custer, WA: Phoenix Publishing Company, 1983, Revised Edition), p.33; William J. Petersen, *Those Curious New Cults* (New Canaan, CT: Keat Publishing, Inc., 1973), p.80; *Flashpoint* (November 1989), p.6; Johanna Michaelsen, *Like Lambs to the Slaughter* (Eugene, OR: Harvest House Publishers, 1989), p.316; Marrs, *Ravaged by the New Age, op. cit.*, p.117; Jack M. Roper, "Pan: Pagan God and Nature Demon," *The Christian World Report* (October 1992, Vol. 7, No. 8), p.26; Eric Maple, *The Complete Book of Witchcraft and Demonology* (Cranbury, NJ: A. S. Barnes and Company, Inc., 1966 Edition), Picture facing p.145; Brochure from Nuit Unlimited Imports, p.3; *Fate* (October 1990, Vol. 43, No. 9 [sic]), p.56; William Schnoebelen, *Masonry: Beyond the Light* (Chino, CA: Chick Publications, 1991), p.169-170; LaVey, *op. cit.*, p.136, 58, 145; William O. Peterson, Editor, *Masonic Quiz Book: "Ask Me Another, Brother"* (Chicago, IL: Charles T. Powner Company, 1950), p.72; Eric Barger, *From Rock to Rock: The Music of Darkness Exposed!* (Lafayette, LA: Huntington House, Inc., 1990), p.164; Cirlot, *op. cit.*, p.80; Maurice Bessy, *A Pictorial History of Magic and the Supernatural* (NY: Hamlyn Publishing Group Limited, 1964), p.163; Frank Gaynor, Editor, *Dictionary of Mysticism* (NY: Philosophical Library, 1953), p.24, 159; Rex R. Hutchens and Donald W. Monson, *The Bible in Albert Pike's Morals and Dogma* (Washington, DC: Supreme Council, 33°, 1992), p.251.

[388] Jack M. Roper, "Pan: Pagan God and Nature Demon," *The Christian World Report* (October 1992, Vol. 7, No. 8), p.26.

[389] *Ibid.*, p.27.

[390] Marrs, *Texe Marrs Book of New Age Cults and Religions, op. cit.*, p.275.

[391] Benjamin Creme, *The Reappearance of the Christ and the Masters of Wisdom* (North Hollywood, CA: Tara Center, 1980), p.116; Alice A. Bailey, *The Unfinished Autobiography* (NY: Lucis Publishing Company, 1951), p.134; *Ibid.;* Constance Cumbey, *The Hidden Dangers of the Rainbow: The New Age Movement and Our Coming Age of Barbarism* (Shreveport, LA: Huntington House, Inc., Revised Edition, 1983), p.95-96; Mac Dominick, et. al., "The New Age Movement—Satan's Counterfeit of the Truth"; Texe Marrs, *Dark Secrets of the New Age: Satan's Plan for a One World Religion* (Westchester, IL: Crossway Books, 1987), p.79, 80.

[392] *The World Book Encyclopedia* (Vol. 18) (Chicago 54, IL: Field Enterprises Educational Corporation, 1961 Edition), p.251; *Webster's Seventh New Collegiate Dictionary,* 1967, p.502; Joseph Carr, *The Lucifer Connection* (Lafayette, LA: Huntington House, Inc., 1987), p.139; Manly Palmer Hall, *America's Assignment with Destiny* (Los Angeles, CA: Philosophical Research Society, Inc., 1951), p.19; Arthur Edward Waite, *The Brotherhood of the Rosy Cross: A History of the Rosicrucians* (NY: Barnes & Noble, Inc., 1993), p.641; Texe Marrs, *Dark Secrets of the New Age: Satan's Plan for a One World Religion* (Westchester, IL: Crossway Books, 1987), p.76; E. C. Slipher, "Venus," *The World Book Encyclopedia* (Vol. 18) (Chicago 54, IL: Field Enterprises Educational Corporation, 1961 Edition), p.251; Arthur Edward Waite, *A New Encyclopedia of Freemasonry and of Cognate Instituted Mysteries: Their Rites, Literature and History* (Vol. I) (NY: Weathervane Books, 1970), p.ix; Manly Palmer Hall, *The Secret Teachings of All Ages* (Los Angeles 27, CA: The Philosophical Research Society Press, 1945), p.lxviii; J. S. M. Ward, *Who Was Hiram Abiff?* (London, England: The Baskerville Press, Ltd., 1925), p.129; Rex R. Hutchens and Donald W. Monson, *The Bible in Albert Pike's Morals and Dogma* (Washington, DC: Supreme Council, 33°), 1992), p.102; Sessler, *op. cit.*, p.137; Willy Peterson, *The Leavening: A New Age Primer for Christian Parents* (Linwood, KS: n.p., 1995), p.167, 205.

[393] Joseph Carr quoting Helena Petrovna Blavatsky, *The Lucifer Connection* (Lafayette, LA: Huntington House, Inc., 1987), p.139.

[394] John J. Robinson, *A Pilgrim's Path: One Man's Road to the Masonic Temple* (New York, NY: M. Evans and Company, Inc., 1993), p.48.

[395] George Catlin, *Christianity and the New Age* (n.p., 1998), p.10.

[396] Arthur Edward Waite, *A New Encyclopedia of Freemasonry and of Cognate Instituted Mysteries: Their Rites, Literature and History* (Vol. I) (NY: Weathervane Books, 1970), p.ix.

[397] *Ibid.*, p.76; J. S. M. Ward, *Who Was Hiram Abiff?* (London, England: The Baskerville Press, Ltd., 1925), p.25, 56, 220; Catalog from Just Us & Associates (Received July 23, 1993), unnumbered page; Arthur Edward Waite, *The Mysteries of Magic: A Digest of the Writings of Eliphas Levi* (Chicago, IL: De Laurence, Scott & Company, 1909), p.212; F. de P. Castells, *The Apocalypse of Freemasonry: A Constructive Scheme of Interpretation of the Symbolism of the Masonic Lodge* (Dartford, England: Snowden Brothers, 1924), p.92; Charles Bensinger, *Chaco Journey: Remembrance and Awakening* (Santa Fe, NM: Timewindow Publications, 1988), p.63; Geoffrey Parrinder, Editor, *World Religions: From Ancient History to the Present* (New York, NY: Facts on File Publications, 1983), p.116, 117.

[398] Percival George Woodcock, *Short Dictionary of Mythology* (NY: Philosophical Library, 1953), p.87. See also: Michael Howard, *The Occult Conspiracy: The Power of Secret Societies in World History* (New York, NY: MFJ Books, 1989), p.14.

[399] *Ibid.*, p.61.

[400] Arthur Edward Waite quoting Eliphas Levi, *The Mysteries of Magic: A Digest of the Writings of Eliphas Levi* (Chicago, IL: De Laurence, Scott and Company, 1909), p.76-77; Helena Petrovna Blavatsky, *Isis Unveiled*, Vol. I: Science (New York, NY: Trow's Printing and Bookbinding Company, 1877), p.138; Brochure from Nuit Unlimited Imports, p.3; Parchment, *op. cit.*, p.41; George Ryley Scott, *Phallic Worship: A History of Sex and Sexual Rites* (London, England: Senate, 1966), p.23; Rex R. Hutchens, *A Bridge to Light* (Washington, DC: Supreme Council, 33° Ancient and Accepted Scottish Rite of Freemasonry, Southern Jurisdiction, 1988), p.201, 205; William Schnoebelen, *Masonry: Beyond the Light* (Chino, CA: Chick Publications, 1991), p.169; Rex R. Hutchens and Donald W. Monson, *The Bible in Albert Pike's Morals and Dogma* (Washington, DC: Supreme Council, 33°, 1992), p.251; Catalog from Occult Emporium, p.26; Cirlot, *op. cit.*, p.80; Brochure from The Wicca describing a course in witchcraft; *Complete Occult Digest A to Z* (North Hollywood, CA: International Imports, 1984), p.95, 106; Eric Maple, *The Complete Book of Witchcraft and Demonology* (Cranbury, NJ: A. S. Barnes and Company, Inc., 1966 Edition), Caption under picture facing p.145.

[401] Brochure from Nuit Unlimited Imports, p.3; Catalog from Occult Emporium, p.26; Brochure from The Wicca describing a course in witchcraft; *Complete Occult Digest A to Z* (North Hollywood, CA: International Imports, 1984), p.95, 106; Eric Maple, *The Complete Book of Witchcraft and Demonology* (Cranbury, NJ: A. S. Barnes and Company, Inc., 1966 Edition), Caption under picture facing p.145; Cirlot, *op. cit.*, p.80.

[402] Michael Howard, *The Occult Conspiracy: The Power of Secret Societies in World History* (New York, NY: MFJ Books, 1989), p.38. See also: George Ryley Scott, *Phallic Worship: A History of Sex and Sexual Rites* (London, England: Senate, 1966), p.220.

[403] A. N. Wilson: *C. S. Lewis: A Biography* (New York, NY: W. W. Norton & Company, 1990), p.322.

[404] *Ibid.*

[405] Duane Winters, *A Search for Light in a Place of Darkness: A Study of Freemasonry* (no other info available), p.64; Jack T. Chick, *The Curse of Baphomet* (Chino, CA: Chick Publications, 1991), p.10.

[406] Charles Clyde Hunt, *Some Thoughts on Masonic Symbolism* (NY: Macoy Publishing and Masonic Supply Company, 1930), p.91; Ronald Hutton, *The Triumph of the Moon: A History of Modern Pagan Witchcraft* (Oxford, England: Oxford University Press, 1999), p.32, 33; George Ryley Scott, *Phallic Worship: A History of Sex and Sexual Rites* (London, England: Senate, 1966), p.220; Hugh A. Moran and David H. Kelley, *The Alphabet and the Ancient Calendar Signs* (Palo Alto, CA: Daily Press, 1969), p.90, 91; Arthur Edward Waite, *The Brotherhood of the Rosy Cross: A History of the Rosicrucians* (NY: Barnes & Noble, Inc., 1993), p.86; Milton Alberto Pottenger, *Symbolism* (Sacramento, CA: Symbol Publishing Company, 1905), p.74, 75, 154; Paul Hamlyn, *Greek Mythology* (London, England: Paul Hamlyn Limited, 1967), p.88; Woodrow, *op. cit.*, p.24; Berger, *op. cit.*, .70; Thomas H. Burgoyne, *The Light of Egypt or the Science of the Soul and the Stars* (Vol. 1) (Denver 20, CO: Astro Philosophical Publishing Company, 1963 reprint), p.215, 220, 263; Lynn and Sarah Leslie, "Resurrecting Pagan Rites" (Part 2), *The Christian Conscience* (January 1996, Vol. 2, No. 1), p.22; Howard, *The Occult Conspiracy, op. cit.*, p.27; Armandine F. Kelly, "The Full Rose Moon," *Festivals* (June/July 1986), p.21; Woodcock, *op. cit.*, p.150; J. S. M. Ward, *Freemasonry and the Ancient Gods* (London, England: Simpkin, Marshall, Hamilton, Kent & Co., Ltd., 1921), p.44, 232; Geoffrey Parrinder, Editor, *World Religions: From Ancient History to the Present* (New York, NY: Facts on File Publications, 1983), p.164, 169; *The Good Newsletter* (May 1995, Issue 8), p.5; Anthony Frewin, *The Book of Days* (London, England: William Collins Sons & Co., Ltd., 1979), p.109, 110; Robert A. Morey, *Horoscopes and the Christian* (Minneapolis, MN: Bethany House Publishers, 1981), p.9-10; Waite, *The Mysteries of Magic, op. cit.*, p.213; David Stevenson, *The Origins of Freemasonry: Scotland's Century, 1590-1710* (Cambridge, England: Cambridge University Press, 1988), p.97; *Necronomicon* (New York, NY: Avon Books, 1977), p.xxxiv; "Church Notes," *The Aurea Flamma—OTB* (July 1986), p.2; Arthur Edward Waite, *The Brotherhood of the Rosy Cross: Being Records of the House of the Holy Spirit in Its Inward and Outward History* (New Hyde Park, NY: University Books, 1961), p.86; *The Webster's New Book of Word Histories;* Starhawk, *The Spiral Dance: A Rebirth of the Ancient Religion of the Great Goddess* (New York, NY: Harper-Collins Publishers, 1989), p.92, 258; Audrey Lavin, "The Sins of the Swaggarts," *Star* (1988, Vol. 15, Issue 8), p.8; Cirlot, *op. cit.*, p.359; *PRS Journal* (Spring 1983), p.46; G. O. Marx, "Why I Don't Want to Be Your Valentine," *The Voice in the Wilderness* (February 1992), p.14, 15; Laurie Cabot with Tom Cowan, *Power of the Witch: The Earth, the Moon, and the Magical Path to Enlightenment* (New York, NY: Delacorte Press, 1989), p.246.

[407] George Ryley Scott, *Phallic Worship: A History of Sex and Sexual Rites* (London, England: Senate, 1966), p.34.

[408] Berger, *op. cit.*, p.70; Texe Marrs, *Dark Secrets of the New Age: Satan's Plan for a One World Religion* (Westchester, IL: Crossway Books, 1987), p.76.

[409] Paul R. Cannon, "Venereal Disease," *The World Book Encyclopedia* (Vol. 18) (Chicago 54, IL: Field Enterprises Educational Corporation, 1961 Edition), p.239; Woodrow, *op. cit.*, p.134; *Ibid.*, p.93.

[410] Albert James Dager, "C. S. Lewis: The Man and His Myths," *Media Spotlight* (1985); Texe Marrs, "Witchcraft Invades Christianity," Intelligence Examiner (tape).

[411] "Who Do You Think This Is?," *Despatch Magazine* (December 1997, Vol. 9, No. 4), p.53.

[412] Texe Marrs, "Witchcraft Invades Christianity: Sorcery and Magic Seduce Many into Depths of Satan," *Power of*

Prophecy (December 2000, Vol. 2000-12), p.1. See also: Dager, "C. S. Lewis," *op. cit.;* Texe Marrs, "Witchcraft Invades Christianity," Intelligence Examiner (tape); *Ibid.;* Marrs, *Texe Marrs Book of New Age Cults and Religions, op. cit.*, p.275-276.

413 *Ibid.*

414 Dager, "C. S. Lewis," *op. cit.*

415 *Ibid.*

416 "Who Do You Think This Is?," *op. cit.*, p.53.

417 *Ibid.*

418 "C. S. Lewis: One of the Greatest Communicators of the Christian Faith or Deceived Deceiver?" (Compilation of different sources, n.d.).

419 "Special Christmas Offerings from Ariel Press and Books of Light" (Catalog), p.7; *The Mystic Trader* (Fall 1985), p.28; *The Mystic Trader* (Winter 1984), p.28; *One Books,* p.6.

420 Marrs, *Texe Marrs Book of New Age Cults and Religions, op. cit.*, p.275.

421 Correll, *op. cit.*, p.28.

422 Marrs, *Texe Marrs Book of New Age Cults and Religions, op. cit.*, p.275.

423 *The Mystic Trader* (Winter 1984), p.28.

424 "C. S. Lewis: One of the Greatest Communicators of the Christian Faith or Deceived Deceiver?," *op. cit.*

425 Marrs, *Texe Marrs Book of New Age Cults and Religions, op. cit.*, p.275; "Was C. S. Lewis a Christian?," *Calvary Contender* (September 15, 1998, Vol. 15, No. 18), p.2; *"CT* Praised C. S. Lewis," *Calvary Contender* (May 1, 2001, Vol. 18, No. 9), p.2.

426 "C. S. Lewis Acceptable to Mormons," *The Perilous Times* (July 1999, Vol. 21, No. 5), p.9. See also: J. I. Packer, J.I. "Still Surprised by Lewis," *Christianity Today* (September 7, 1998); "C. S. Lewis: One of the Greatest Communicators of the Christian Faith or Deceived Deceiver?," *op. cit.*

427 Marrs, "Witchcraft Invades Christianity," *op. cit.*, p.1; Texe Marrs, "Witchcraft Invades Christianity," Intelligence Examiner (tape). See also: "C. S. Lewis: General Teachings/Activities" (Biblical Discernment Ministries, 1994) (on disk); David W. Cloud, "C. S. Lewis and Evangelicals Today," *Christian News* (April 30, 2001, Vol. 39, No. 18), p.22.

428 "C. S. Lewis: General Teachings/Activities" (Biblical Discernment Ministries, 1994) (on disk). See also: David W. Cloud, "C. S. Lewis and Evangelicals Today," *Christian News* (April 30, 2001, Vol. 39, No. 18), p.22.

429 "Was C. S. Lewis a Christian?," *Calvary Contender* (September 15, 1998, Vol. 15, No. 18), p.2; *"CT* Praised C. S. Lewis," *Calvary Contender* (May 1, 2001, Vol. 18, No. 9), p.2; David W. Cloud, "C. S. Lewis and Evangelicals Today," *Christian News* (April 30, 2001, Vol. 39, No. 18), p.22.

430 "C. S. Lewis: General Teachings/Activities" (Biblical Discernment Ministries, 1994) (on disk); David W. Cloud, "C.S. Lewis and Evangelicals Today," *Christian News* (April 30, 2001, Vol. 39, No. 18), p.22. See also: "C. S. Lewis Acceptable to Mormons," *op. cit.*, p.9; J. I. Packer, J. I. "Still Surprised by Lewis," *Christianity Today* (September 7, 1998); "C. S. Lewis: One of the Greatest Communicators of the Christian Faith or Deceived Deceiver?," *op. cit.*

431 Richard N. and Joan K. Ostling quoting C. S. Lewis in *Mormon America: The Power and the Promise* (New York, NY: HarperSanFrancisco, 1999), p.308.

432 *Ibid.*, p.xvi, 308. See also: "Was C. S. Lewis a Christian?," *op. cit.*, p.2.

433 *Ibid.* See also: "C. S. Lewis Acceptable to Mormons," *op. cit.*, p.9.

434 Miles J. Stanford, "False Fare," in "C. S. Lewis: One of the Greatest Communicators of the Christian Faith or Deceived Deceiver?" (Compilation of different sources, n.d.), p.1.

435 Lloyd C. Button, "No Longer a Mormon" (Minneapolis, MN: Religious Analysis Service, Inc.), pp. 3-4.

436 David W. Cloud, "C. S. Lewis and Evangelicals Today," *Christian News* (April 30, 2001, Vol. 39, No. 18), p.22.

437 "Evangelicals Are Divided Over Series," *The Presbyterian Layman* (September/October 2000), p.17; Berit Kjos, "Harry Potter Lures Kids to Witchcraft with Praise from Christian Leaders," *Prophecy Corner and The Nosh Box* (October 2000).

438 "Bewitched by Harry Potter," *Christian News* (November 29, 1999, Vol. 37, No. 44), p.2; Marrs, "Witchcraft Invades Christianity," *op. cit.*, p.2; Berit Kjos, "Harry Potter Lures Kids to Witchcraft with Praise from Christian Leaders," *Prophecy Corner and The Nosh Box* (October 2000).

439 David W. Cloud, "Harry Potter Witchcraft Church Service" *Christian News* (September 25, 2000, Vol. 38, No. 35), p.13. See also: Art Toalston, "Latest 'Harry Potter' Book Meets Cautionary Response from Christians," *Christian News* (July 17, 2000, Vol. 38, No. 29), p.11; "*Harry Potter* Books," *Calvary Contender* (August 1, 2001, Vol. 19, No. 15), p.1; "The Harry Potter Books," *The Perilous Times* (January 2001, Vol. 22, No. 8), p.9; "Educator Calls for Warning Stickers on 'Harry Potter' Books," *Christian News* (April 23, 2001, Vol. 39, No. 17), p.2; "Still Think Harry Potter Is Harmless?," *Calvary Contender* (February 1, 2001, Vol. 18, No. 3), p.1; Esther Saunders and Joseph Youannas, "Harry Potter: A Modern Day Pied Piper," *Christian News* (February 26, 2001, Vol. 39, No. 9), p.17; "Harry Potter and the Bible," *Calvary Contender* (March 15, 2001, Vol. 18, No. 6), p.1.

440 *Last Trumpet Newsletter* (December 2000, Vol. 19, Issue 12), p.3.

441 *Ibid.*

442 *Ibid.*

[443] Marrs, "Witchcraft Invades Christianity," *op. cit.*, p.2. See also: Art Toalston, "Latest 'Harry Potter' Book Meets Cautionary Response from Christians," *Christian News* (July 17, 2000, Vol. 38, No. 29), p.11; "Beware of Harry Potter," *Christian News* (March 12, 2001, Vol. 39, No. 11), p.2.

[444] "Harry's Magic," *Christian News* (September 25, 2000, Vol. 38, No. 35), p.13.

[445] "Still Think Harry Potter Is Harmless?," *Calvary Contender* (February 1, 2001, Vol. 18, No. 3), p.1.

[446] Cloud, "Harry Potter Witchcraft Church Service," *op. cit.*, p.13.

[447] "Bewitched by Harry Potter," *op. cit.*, p.2.

[448] "Evangelicals Are Divided Over Series," *op. cit.*, p.17. See also: "Canterbury Is No Hogswarts," *Christian News* (July 17, 2000, Vol. 38, No. 29), p.2.

[449] Bruce Nolan, "Harry Potter Casts No Spell on Christian Booksellers," *Christian News* (July 24, 2000, Vol. 38, No. 30), p.21.

[450] *"CT* Praised C. S. Lewis," *Calvary Contender* (May 1, 2001, Vol. 18, No. 9), p.2; Cloud, "C. S. Lewis and Evangelicals Today," *op. cit.*, p.22.

[451] Cloud, "C. S. Lewis and Evangelicals Today," *op. cit.*, p.22.

[452] Sam Wellman, *Billy Graham: The Great Evangelist* (Uhrichsville, OH: Barbour Book, 1996), p.134.

[453] *Christian News* (December 4, 2000, Vol. 38, No. 45), p.3.

[454] Graham, *Just As I Am, op. cit.*, p.290.

[455] *Christianity Today* (March 6, 1995, Vol. 39, No. 3), p.4.

[456] "Christianity Today Is No Longer the Conservative Evangelical Publication It Was When It Began," *Christian News* (April 21, 1997, Vol. 35, No. 16), p.2; *Christianity Today* (March 6, 1995, Vol. 39, No. 3), p.4; "Roman Catholic Editors of Christianity Today," *Christian News* (May 5, 1997, Vol. 35, No. 18), p.2; "Rome and the Pope Still Deny Justification by Faith Alone," *Christian News* (December 19, 1994, Vol. 32, No. 47), p.11.

[457] "Canterbury Is No Hogswarts," *Christian News* (July 17, 2000, Vol. 38, No. 29), p.2.

[458] Laurie Goodstein, "Christian Leaders Counter Religious Right," *Philadelphia Inquirer* (May 24, 1995); Paul Fisher, "A Syndicated Conspiracy Against God and Man?," *The Observer* (January 17, 1996).

[459] "Ecumenical Confusion and Deception at Graham Conference," *Christian News* (August 7, 2000, Vol. 38, No. 32), p.25; *Evangelicals and Catholics Together: The Christian Mission in the Third Millennium* (March 29, 1994); Albert James Dager, "Evangelicals and Catholics Together: The New Ecumenical Accord in Light of Vatican II," *Media Spotlight* (Vol. 15, No. 2), p.8; *The BDM Letter* (March/April 1995, Vol. 4, No. 2), p.2; Letter from J. Royce Thomason dated January 1995; Tom Watson, *The Evangelical Eroding of the Deity of Christ* (Southlake, TX: Countryside Bible Church, 1996), p.7; "Bill Bright and Catholics," *Calvary Contender* (January 1, 1999, Vol. 16, No. 1), p.2; "Evangelicals and Catholics: Coming Together," *The Day Drawing Near* (March 1999, Vol. 1, No. 6), p.2; Rick Miesel, "Roman Catholicism: General Notes" (Biblical Discernment Ministries, Revised August 1997); Cloud, *Is the Roman Catholic Changing?, op. cit.;* Dave Hunt, "What's Happening to the Faith?," *The Berean Call* (May 1998), p.2.

[460] *Ibid.;* p.25; "Evangelicals and Catholics: Coming Together," *The Day Drawing Near* (March 1999, Vol. 1, No. 6), p.2.

[461] T. A. McMahon, "The 'Evangelical' Seduction," *The Berean Call* (April 1996), p.1.

[462] "Ecumenical Confusion and Deception at Graham Conference," *op. cit.*, p.25; Cloud, "Flirting with Rome: Evangelical Entanglement with Roman Catholicism,c" *O Timothy* (1993).

[463] Robert M. Zins, "Book Review," *Theo-Logical* (1997), p.10.

[464] *Ibid.*

[465] *Ibid.*

[466] "Hell: Eternal Torment or Annihilation?," *Calvary Contender* (November 1, 2000, Vol. 17, No. 21), p.2; "Taking the Fire out of Hell," *op. cit.*, p.10.

[467] "Packer Criticizes Fundamentalists," *Calvary Contender* (September 15, 1998, Vol. 15, No. 18), p.2.

[468] *Ibid.*

[469] Paul Fisher, "A Syndicated Conspiracy Against God and Man?," *The Observer* (January 17, 1996), p.13. See also: Letter from Evangelicals for Social Action received April 16, 1996, p.2.

[470] Wesley Granberg-Michaelson, "Toward a Politics of Compassion," *The Cry for Renewal: Biblical Faith and Spiritual Politics* (May 23, 1995), p.3; Laurie Goodstein, *op. cit.;* Dager, "The World Christian Movement—Part 3, *op. cit.*, p.7.

[471] Goodstein, *op. cit.*

[472] Packer's name was included in the "Partial List of Signers of 'An Evangelical Declaration on the Care of Creation'" as of March 1, 1996.

[473] Matthew Carolan, "Environmental Piety No Substitute for Technique," *Religion and Liberty* (March/April 2001), p.9.

[474] Cloud, "C. S. Lewis and Evangelicals Today," *op. cit.*, p.22; "Evangelicals Praising 'Patron Saint' C. S. Lewis," *Christian News* (September 14, 1998, Vol. 36, No. 33), p.14.

[475] "Amsterdam 2000," *op. cit.*, p.1; "Billy Graham's Amsterdam 2000 Shows Solidarity Amid Diversity," *Christian News* (July 3, 2000, Vol. 38, No. 27), p.26; "Graham to 'Pass the Torch' in Amsterdam," *Calvary Contender* (August 1, 2000, Vol. 17, No. 15); "Billy Graham's Last Scheduled International Event, *op. cit.*, p.2.

[476] "America's Top Evangelists Show Interest in Alpha Rise," *Alpha News* (December 2000-March 2001, No. 8), p.10;

"Q & A," *The Berean Call* (July 2001), p.4; "Alpha: A Model for Dynamic Growth in the Local Church" (Brochure received January 11, 2001); Ken Ham, "'Alpha'—a Misnomer!," *The Christian News* (May 21, 2001, Vol. 39, No. 21), p.22; "Alpha to America," *The Day Drawing Near* (July 2000, Vol. 2, No. 2), p.8; "'Alpha Course' Warning," *Calvary Contender* (December 15, 1998, Vol. 25, No. 24), p.1.

[477] Howard, *The Alpha Course, op. cit.*, p.8.

[478] "'Alpha Course' Warning," *Calvary Contender* (December 15, 1998, Vol. 25, No. 24), p.1. See also: "Beware of the 'The Alpha Course,'" *Calvary Contender* (March 1, 1998, Vol. 15, No. 5), p.1; Carol Woster, *Woster's Religious Almanac* (Columbia Falls, MT: Christian Wall Center, 1999), p.4; "Preserved Forever by God Almighty!," *Despatch Magazine* (June 2001, Vol. 13:2), p.35; "Q & A," *The Berean Call* (July 2001), p.4.

[479] "Beware of the 'The Alpha Course,'" *Calvary Contender* (March 1, 1998, Vol. 15, No. 5), p.1.

[480] Cloud, "C. S. Lewis and Evangelicals Today," *op. cit.*, p.22.

[481] Howard, *The Alpha Course, op. cit.*, .17.

[482] "The World Council of Churches on World Order," *The Whole Earth Papers: Christian Voices on World Order* (1978, Vol. 1, No. 10), p.31.

[483] Howard, *The Alpha Course, op. cit.*, p.20-21; "Alpha to America," *The Day Drawing Near* (July 2000, Vol. 2, No. 2), p.8.

[484] *Ibid.*, p.20-21. See also: "Q & A," *The Berean Call* (July 2001), p.4; Elizabeth McDonald, *Alpha: The Unofficial Guide* (Cambridge, England: St. Matthew Publishing, Ltd., 2001), p.118.

[485] *Ibid.*, p.21. See also: Elizabeth McDonald, *Alpha: The Unofficial Guide* (Cambridge, England: St. Matthew Publishing, Ltd., 2001), p.118.

[486] Bill Randles quoting from *Time* in *Beware the New Prophets: A Caution Concerning the Modern Prophetic Movement* (Marion, IA: n.p., 1999), p.106.

[487] "Alpha to America," *The Day Drawing Near* (July 2000, Vol. 2, No. 2), p.8. See also: *Ibid.*

[488] Debra Bouey, "Pensacola Pendemonium (sic)," quoting from the March-April 1997 issue of *Foundation* in *The Christian Conscience* (June 1997, Vol. 3, No. 5), p.6.

[489] Elizabeth McDonald, *Alpha: The Unofficial Guide* (Cambridge, England: St. Matthew Publishing, Ltd., 2001), p.112.

[490] Brochure from Burdines Travel and Cruises, p.2; Letter from New Age Books and Games, Inc.

[491] "How to Get What You Want From Life..." (Brochure from Life Dynamics), p.3; Bernie S. Siegel, *Love, Medicine and Miracles* (New York, NY: Harper and Row Publishers, 1986), p.148; "On...Being at Alpha," p.2, 3, 4. For Christian resources warning about alpha, see: Don Matzat, *Inner Healing: Deliverance or Deception?* (Eugene, OR: Harvest House Publishers, 1987), p.124-126; Carr, *op. cit.*, p.66; Kurt Koch, (Translated by Michael Freeman). *Occult ABC* (Germany: Literature Mission Aglasterhausen, Inc., 1978), p.24-25; *The Silva Mind Control Method* (Complete Program Transcripts with Jose Silva, George Desau, David Hunt, and John Weldon) (Chattanooga, TN: The John Ankerberg Show, 1986), p.3-4; Tanya C. Turner, "Television: America's Babysitter and Its 'Dumbing Down' Effect," *The End Times and Victorious Living* (September/October 1997, Vol. 11, No. 5), p.12-13.

[492] Laurie Cabot with Tom Cowan, *Power of the Witch: The Earth, the Moon, and the Magical Path to Enlightenment* (New York, NY: Delacorte Press, 1989), p.173.

[493] *Ibid.*, p.174-175, 187.

[494] McDonald, *op. cit.*, p.66-67.

[495] Kristyna Arcarti, *Interpreting Signs and Symbols: A Beginner's Guide* (London, England: Hodder and Stoughton Educational, 1997), p.140.

[496] See: Martin and Deidre Bobgan, *Hypnosis: Medical, Scientific, or Occultic* (Santa Barbara, CA: EastGate Publishers, 2001), p.81-82.

[497] McDonald, *op. cit.*, p.67.

[498] Martin and Deidre Bobgan quoting Michael Harner in *Hypnosis: Medical, Scientific, or Occultic* (Santa Barbara, CA: EastGate Publishers, 2001), p.82.

[499] *Ibid.*, p.29; Morrison, *op. cit.*, p.432.

[500] *Ibid.*, quoting Michael Yapko, p.73, 115-116.

[501] Don Matzat, *Inner Healing: Deliverance or Deception?* (Eugene, OR: Harvest House Publishers, 1987), p.124.

[502] Cabot with Cowan, *op. cit.*, p.173.

[503] "Alpha to America," *op. cit.*, p.8.

[504] *Ibid.*

[505] "Bright and Campolo Join Praise for Alpha," *Alpha News* (August-November 2000, No. 7), p.1; "Billy Graham Invites Alpha," *Alpha News* (April-July 2000, No. 6), p.1; Ken Ham, "'Alpha'—a Misnomer!," *The Christian News* (May 21, 2001, Vol. 39, No. 21), p.22; *Wisconsin Report* (July 27, 2000), p.7; *Christian News*, "Alpha Course Workshop at Amsterdam 2000" (September 18, 2000, Vol. 38, No. 34), p.2; "Alpha Course Workshop at Amsterdam," *Calvary Contender* (September 1, 2000, Vol. 17, No. 17), p.1.

[506] "Billy Graham Invites Alpha," *Alpha News* (April-July 2000, No. 6), p.1.

[507] McDonald, *op. cit.*, p.69.

[508] *Ibid.*, p.72.

[509] *Ibid.*, p.7.

[510] "Deception: 'What Killed the Rat?,'" *Calvary Contender* (March 15, 2000, Vol. 17, No. 6), p.1. See also: "Good to Remember," *The Perilous Times* (February 1999, Vol. 20, No. 12), p.9.

[511] McDonald, *op. cit.*, p.6.

[512] *Ibid.*

[513] "Bright and Campolo Join Praise for Alpha," *op. cit.*, p.1, 24; "America's Top Evangelists Show Interest in Alpha Rise," *op. cit.*, p.10; "Alpha: A Model for Dynamic Growth in the Local Church" (Brochure received January 11, 2001).

[514] *Ibid.*; "America's Top Evangelists Show Interest in Alpha Rise," *op. cit.*, p.10; "Alpha: A Model for Dynamic Growth in the Local Church" (Brochure received January 11, 2001).

[515] *Ibid.*, p.1.

[516] *Ibid.*; *Alpha News* (August-November 2000, No. 7), p.24.

[517] *Ibid.*; *Alpha News* (August-November 2000, No. 7), p.24.

[518] *Ibid.*; *Alpha News* (August-November 2000, No. 7), p.24.

[519] *Alpha News* (August-November 2000, No. 7), p.24.

[520] *Ibid.*; "Billy Graham Invites Alpha," *op. cit.*, p.1.

[521] "Alpha to America," *op. cit.*, p.8; *Alpha News* (August-November 2000, No. 7), p.24; "Q & A," *The Berean Call* (July 2001), p.4.

[522] *Ibid.*; "Billy Graham Invites Alpha," *op. cit.*, p.1; *Alpha News* (August-November 2000, No. 7), p.24.

[523] "Yonggi Cho and Billy Kim Praise 'Excellent Program,'" *Alpha News* (December 2000-March 2001, No. 8), p.10.

[524] *Ibid.*

[525] *Alpha News* (August-November 2000, No. 7), p.24; "Billy Graham Invites Alpha," *op. cit.*, p.1.

[526] "Cedar Replaced Ford at L.C.W.E.," *Calvary Contender* (August 15, 1992, Vol. 9, No. 16), p.2.

[527] "Alpha to America," *op. cit.*, p.8; "Q & A," *The Berean Call* (July 2001), p.4.

[528] "Bright and Campolo Join Praise for Alpha," *op. cit.*, p.1; *Ibid.*; "Q & A," *The Berean Call* (July 2001), p.4; "Leighton Ford's New Ministry," *Calvary Contender* (October 15, 2000, Vol. 17, No. 20), p.2; *Alpha News* (August-November 2000, No. 7), p.24.

[529] James Hefley, *God Goes to High School* (Waco, TX: Word Books, 1970), p.32, 66; "Leighton Ford's New Ministry," *Calvary Contender* (October 15, 2000, Vol. 17, No. 20), p.2.

[530] Bundy, *How Liberals and Radicals Are Manipulating Evangelicals, op. cit.*, p.74; "Dallas Seminary Doings," *Calvary Contender* (February 1, 1998, Vol. 15, No. 3), p.2; Martin, *A Prophet with Honor, op. cit.*, p.571; Texe Marrs, *Millennium: Peace, Promises, and the Day They Take Our Money Away* (Austin, TX: Living Truth Publishers, 1990), p.40; "Leighton Ford's New Ministry," *Calvary Contender* (October 15, 2000, Vol. 17, No. 20), p.2.

[531] Letter from Evangelicals for Social Action, p.6.

[532] Hunt, "Evangelizing the World," *op. cit.*, p.2. See also: John E. Ashbrook, *New Neutralism II: Exposing the Gray of Compromise* (Mentor, OH: Here I Stand Books, 1992), p.79-80.

[533] "Leighton Ford's New Ministry," *Calvary Contender* (October 15, 2000, Vol. 17, No. 20), p.2.

[534] "Graham Says All Denoms Have Same God," *Calvary Contender* (February 1, 1998, Vol. 15, No. 3), p.2.

[535] *Ibid.*

[536] *Ibid.*

[537] "Leighton Ford's New Ministry," *op. cit.*, p.2.

[538] Bundy, *How Liberals and Radicals Are Manipulating Evangelicals, op. cit.*, p.74; "Christianity Today Promotes Leftist," *op. cit.*, p.15.

[539] Texe Marrs, *Millennium: Peace, Promises, and the Day They Take Our Money Away* (Austin, TX: Living Truth Publishers, 1990), p.40.

[540] "Alpha: A Model for Dynamic Growth in the Local Church" (Brochure received January 11, 2001); "Q & A," *The Berean Call* (July 2001), p.4; Howard, *The Alpha Course, op. cit.*, p.17; Ken Ham, "'Alpha'—a Misnomer!," *The Christian News* (May 21, 2001, Vol. 39, No. 21), p.22; *Alpha News* (August-November 2000, No. 7), p.24; "Billy Graham Event Hears of 'Alpha Revolution,'" *Alpha News* (December 2000-March 2001, No. 8), p.1.

[541] "Billy Graham Event Hears of 'Alpha Revolution,'" *Alpha News* (December 2000-March 2001, No. 8), p.1.

[542] *Ibid.*

[543] "America's Top Evangelists Show Interest in Alpha Rise," *op. cit.*, p.10.

[544] Howard, *The Alpha Course, op. cit.*, p.19.

[545] *The Evangelical Methodist* (2000, Vol. 78, No. 4), p.3.

[546] Howard, *The Alpha Course, op. cit.*, p.18.

547 *Ibid.*

548 "Ecumenical Confusion and Deception at Graham Conference," *op. cit.*, p.25.

549 See: Carol Houst, "Playing with Fire," *Thoughtline* (April 1999), p.8, 10; "World Citizenship: A Global Ethic for Sustainable Development," *One Country* (July-September 1993, Vol. 5, Issue 2), p.2; "Review," *One Country* (October-December 1993, Vol. 5, Issue 3), p.16; "Sovereignty in the Global Age," *World Goodwill Newsletter* (1998, No. 4), p.4; *World Goodwill Newsletter* (1998, No. 3), p.1, 2; , "U. N. & Vatican Unity" quoting Robert Muller in *Despatch Magazine* (June 2001, Vol. 13:2), p.32; *Problems of Humanity: The Building of Right Human Relations: Study Three: The Problem of International Unity* (New York, NY: World Goodwill, n.d.), p.1; Robert Muller, *New Genesis: Shaping a Global Spirituality* (Garden City, NY: Image Books, 1984), p.113-114; "United Religions Draft Charter June 1998-June 1999" (Received December 12, 1998); Dominic Dibble, "Transforming the Planet—A Question of Goodwill," *The Festival Week of the New Group of World Servers* (New York, NY: Lucis Trust, n.d.), p.11; Dan Wheatley, "Unity in Diversity," *The Festival Week of the New Group of World Servers* (New York, NY: Lucis Trust, n.d.), p.11, 12, 13; Corinne McLaughlin, and Gordon Davidson, *Spiritual Politics: Changing the World from the Inside Out* (NY: Ballantine Books, 1994), p.20, 49, 149, 183, 238, 293; Natalie N. Banks, *The Golden Thread* (New York, NY: Lucis Publishing Company, 1999 Edition), p.45; "Human Development, Human Rights—Pathways to Freedom," *World Goodwill* (2001, No. 2), p.1; "Synthesis and the Meaning of Unity-and-Diversity," *Thoughtline* (June 1998), p.1; "World Citizenship: A Global Ethic for Sustainable Development," (From the Baha'i International Community), p.1; Daniel Martin, "The Earth Charter: A Religious Voice," *Creation Spirituality* (March/April 1992), p.36; "Festivals of the Season," *Festivals* (June/July 1986), p.28; Alexander Cannon, *The Power of Karma: In Relation to Destiny* (E.P. Dutton and Company, Inc., 1937), p.173; Personal Letter from Dale Ramsdell dated April 23, 1985); Paper from Thanksgiving Square; "More Reflections from Stanford," *United Religions* (Fall 1997, Issue 4), p.9; David P. Gaines, *The World Council of Churches: A Study of Its Background and History* (Peterborough, NH: Richard R. Smith Company, Inc., 1966), p.340; "Work in Australia and New Zealand," *Yoga Vedanta* (October/November/December 1994, Vol. 3, No. 4), p.15.

550 John E. Ashbrook, *New Neutralism II: Exposing the Gray of Compromise* (Mentor, OH: Here I Stand Books, 1992), p.30; Ashbrook, "Billy Graham—The Mouthpiece of New Evangelicalism," *op. cit.*

551 Gil Rugh, *Faithfulness Amid Conflict: The Church's Battle Against Heresy* (Lincoln, NE: Sound Words Communications, 1990), p.1.

552 "World Citizenship: A Global Ethic for Sustainable Development," *One Country* (July-September 1993, Vol. 5, Issue 2), p.2.

553 "Sovereignty in the Global Age," *World Goodwill Newsletter* (1998, No. 4), p.4.

554 *World Goodwill Newsletter* (1998, No. 3), p.1.

555 *Problems of Humanity: The Building of Right Human Relations: Study Three: The Problem of International Unity* (New York, NY: World Goodwill, n.d.), p.1.

556 "United Religions Draft Charter June 1998-June 1999" (Received December 12, 1998). See also: "Transition Activities," *World Goodwill Newsletter* (1999, No. 1), p.10; Saran van Gelder, "Making Peace Among Religions," *Yes!* (Fall 1998), p.26.

557 Dan Wheatley, "Unity in Diversity," *The Festival Week of the New Group of World Servers* (New York, NY: Lucis Trust, n.d.), p.12-13.

558 Corinne McLaughlin, and Gordon Davidson, *Spiritual Politics: Changing the World from the Inside Out* (NY: Ballantine Books, 1994), p.183-184.

559 *Watch Unto Prayer* (Spring 1998), p.6; *Constance Cumbey's New Age Monitor* (August-December 1987, Vol. 2, Nos. 3-7), p.6; Johanna Michaelsen, *Like Lambs to the Slaughter* (Eugene, OR: Harvest House Publishers, 1989), p.44; "Synthesis and the Meaning of Unity-and-Diversity," *Thoughtline* (June 1998), p.1.

560 "Synthesis and the Meaning of Unity-and-Diversity," *Thoughtline* (June 1998), p.1.

561 *Ibid.*

562 Carol Houst, "Playing with Fire," *Thoughtline* (April 1999), p.10.

563 Johanna Michaelsen quoting from *Toward a Maitreyan Revolution* in *Like Lambs to the Slaughter* (Eugene, OR: Harvest House Publishers, 1989), p.170.

564 *The Problems of Humanity: The Building of Right Human Relations: The Problem of the Churches* (New York, NY: World Goodwill, n.d.), p.30; *The New World Religion* (New York, NY: World Goodwill, n.d.), p.2.

565 *The New World Religion* (New York, NY: World Goodwill, n.d.), p.14. See also: "A Selection Compilation from the Books of Alice A. Bailey on the Aquarian Age" (Vol. II) quoting from p.182 of *The Reappearance of the Christ*, (Jersey City, NJ: Aquarian Age Community), p.40; "Answer to the Question," *Christian Conscience* (January 1996, Vol. 2, No. 1), p.4; "Alice A. Bailey on 'the Christ' and 'the Coming World Religion,'" *SCP Journal* (19:2/3), p.60.

566 "A Selection Compilation from the Books of Alice A. Bailey on the Aquarian Age" (Vol. II) quoting from p.573 of *The Externalisation of the Hierarchy*, (Jersey City, NJ: Aquarian Age Community), p.14-15.

567 Natalie N. Banks, *The Golden Thread* (New York, NY: Lucis Publishing Company, 1999 Edition), p.40.

568 Fritz Springmeier, *Bloodlines of the Illuminati* (Westminster, CO: Ambassador House, 1999), p.345.

569 *World Goodwill Newsletter* (1993, No. 4), p.2.

570 Jim Marrs quoting Manly P. Hall in *Rule by Secrecy: The Hidden History That Connects the Trilateral Commission, the Freemasons, and the Great Pyramids* (New York, NY: HarperCollins Publishers, Inc., 2000), p.261.

571 "A Selection Compilation from the Books of Alice A. Bailey on the Aquarian Age" (Vol. II) quoting from p.152 of

Destiny of the Nations, (Jersey City, NJ: Aquarian Age Community), p.14-15.

[572] Wardner, *op. cit.,* p.228.

[573] *Ibid.,* p.227-228.

[574] *Ibid.,* p.228.

[575] Flyer from World Goodwill announcing World Invocation Day, June 2, 1985.

[576] Colson with Vaughn, *op. cit.,* p.23.

[577] "Express Excerpts," *Focus Express* (Winter 2000/2001), p.1.

[578] *Ibid.*

[579] *Focus Express* (May/June 1997), p.2.

[580] "Polls Show That Americans Believe No One Is Perfect—Including God!," *The Christian World Report* (February 1995, Vol. 10, No. 2), p.17. See also: "High Percentage of Born-Again Christians Question Biblical Teachings," *The Vine and Branches* (2000, Vol. 15, Issue 5), p.12.

[581] *Ibid.* See also: "High Percentage of Born-Again Christians Question Biblical Teachings," *The Vine and Branches* (2000, Vol. 15, Issue 5), p.12.

[582] Colson with Vaughn, *op. cit.,* p.36. See also: "On Being 'Born-Again,'" *Focus Express* (January/February 2000), p.1; "Reborn but Not Remade?," *Focus Express* (June/June/August 2000), p.1.

[583] Tom Watson, *The Evangelical Eroding of the Deity of Christ* (Southlake, TX: Countryside Bible Church, 1996), unnumbered page. See also: "Polls Show That Americans Believe No One Is Perfect," *op. cit.,* p.17; Craig Branch, "Chicken Soup or Witch's Brew," *The Watchman Expositor,* p.18.

[584] *The Robert Muller School: World Core Curriculum Manual* (1986), Preface; Constance Cumbey, *A Planned Deception: The Staging of a New Age "Messiah"* (East Detroit, MI: Pointe Publishing, Inc., 1985), p.34; Correll, *op. cit.,* p.17.

[585] *Chronology of Education with Quotable Quotes* (Highland City, FL: Pro Family Forum, Inc., 1994, Updated, bound volume), p.77; *Now Is the Dawning of the New Age New World Order, op. cit.,* p.217, 272; "Transformation Toward New Age Synthesis," *Distant Drums* (May 1986, Vol. 8, No. 2), p.2; "Dr. Paul Cedar Pulls Endorsement from *Star of 2000,*" Report from Broadcasters United for Revival and Reformation, p.2; *Don Bell Reports* (January 10, 1986), Vol. 33, No. 2), p.3.

[586] Robert Muller, *New Genesis: Shaping a Global Spirituality* (Garden City, NY: Image Books, 1984), p.183. See also: Rhea Fulmer, Teri Jeter, and Wanda Riner, "Robert Muller's Vision for 2000 A. D.," *The Christian Conscience* (May 1995, Vol. 1, No. 5), p.34.

[587] Alice A. Bailey, *Discipleship in the New Age* (Vol. II) (NY: Lucis Publishing Company, 1955), p.v.

[588] *Ibid.,* p.62. See also: Marrs, *Millennium, op. cit.,* p.224.

[589] Marrs, *Millennium, op. cit.,* p.224.

[590] *Building and Bridging: The New Group of World Servers,* a booklet compiled from the books by Alice A. Bailey, written in collaboration with Djwhal Khul, p.9.

[591] *The Problems of Humanity: The Building of Right Human Relations: The Problem of the Churches, op. cit.,* p.10-11.

[592] *Blueprint for Building the New World Order* (Dearborn, MI: The Omega-Letter/Christian World Report, n.d.), p.21.

[593] Muller, *op. cit.,* p.177, 178; *Chronology of Education with Quotable Quotes, op. cit.,* p.77; "The U. N. & Education," *The Florida Forum* (Fall 2000), p.26; Newsletter from Radio Liberty (July 2001), p.3.

[594] Dwight L. Kinman quoting Robert Muller in *The World's Last Dictator* (Woodburn, OR: Solid Rock Books, Inc. 1995), p.81.

[595] *The Problems of Humanity: The Building of Right Human Relations: The Problem of the Churches, op. cit.,* p.5.

[596] *Ibid.*

[597] *Ibid.,* p.15-16.

[598] Barbara Marx Hubbard, quoted in *The Omega-Letter* (October 1988, Vol. 3, No. 9), p.12. See also: Wilson Ewin, *Under the New World Order: Evangelicals, Catholics and Israel: Conspiracy of the Ages* (Compton, Quebec: Quebec Baptist Missions, n.d.), p.19.

[599] Alice A. Bailey, *Education in the New Age* (NY: Lucis Publishing Company, 1954), p.111-112.

[600] *Shamballa: The Centre Where the Will of God Is Known* (New York, NY: World Goodwill, n.d.).

[601] *Predictions to the Year 2000* (Monterey, CA: Angel Press, 1977), p.13-14. See also: *The Path of Light* (Franklin, MI: Harmony Horizons, Inc., n.d.), p.25-26.

[602] Ruth Montgomery, *Threshold to Tomorrow,* (New York, NY: G. P. Putnam's Son, 1982), p.262.

[603] Ruth Montgomery, *Strangers Among Us* (NY: Coward, McCann and Geoghegan, 1979), p.126.

[604] "Exposing the New Age," tape by Randall Baer, 1989.

[605] *The Globalists: The Power Elite Exposed* (Oklahoma City, Oklahoma: Hearthstone Publishing, 2001), p.114.

[606] Alice A. Bailey quoting S. Radhakrishnan in *From Bethlehem to Calvary: The Initiations of Jesus* (NY: Lucis Trust Publishing Company, 1965), p.275.

[607] R. P. Lawrie Krishna, *Kalki Avatar: Revelation of Christ Jesus at His Second Coming* (Vol. 2) (Medway, OH: Manujothi Ashram Publications, 1987), p.125.

[608] Mortimer J. Adler, quoted in *The Omega-Letter* (December 1989, Vol. 5, No. 11), p.7.

[609] "A New Inquisition," *The Omega-Letter* (December 1989, Vol. 5, No. 11), p.7-8.

[610] "Problems of Humanity," *op. cit.,* p.17.

[611] Alice A. Bailey, *Preparation for the Reappearance of the Christ,* p.5-6. (This was taken from a small booklet based on Alice A. Bailey's book by the same title.)

[612] *Despatch Magazine* (June 2001, Vol. 13:2), p.33.

[613] Marrs quoting Christopher Hyatt in *Mystery Mark, op. cit.* p.154.

[614] *Ibid.,* p.154-155.

[615] Alice A. Bailey, *Preparation for the Reappearance of the Christ,* p.12.

[616] *Ibid.,* p.13.

[617] David Haddon and Vail Hamilton, *TM Wants You!* (Grand Rapids, MI: Baker Book House, 1976), p.131. See also Dave Hunt, *The Cult Explosion* (Eugene, OR: Harvest House Publishers, 1980), p.92.

[618] W. E. Vine, *Vine's Expository Dictionary of New Testament Words* (Lynchburg, VA: The Old-Time Gospel Hour, n.d.), p.855.

[619] Constance Cumbey quoting Dick Sutphen in *The Hidden Dangers of the Rainbow: The New Age Movement and Our Coming Age of Barbarism* (Shreveport, LA: Huntington House, Inc., 1983), p.198.

[620] *F. A. Newsletter,* (June 1986), p.1.

[621] *Ibid.,* p.3.

[622] "March Ahead of Time," *Kingdom Voice* (August 1990), p.11.

[623] William J. Bowen, Jr. quoting Paul Brandwein in *Globalism: America's Demise* (Shreveport, LA: Huntington House, Inc., 1984), p.18.

BIBLIOGRAPHY

NOTE: I have quoted from hundreds upon hundreds of sources. Some of the following sources have good information but are not doctrinally sound. Quoting from a source does not imply doctrinal agreement in any way.

(The following is a partial listing of the reference materials that were used in preparing this book.)

"#1 'Christian' Rock Group Unmasked," *Flashpoint* (September 1990).

"$1 Million Scholarship Endowment Awarded by The Billy Graham Evangelistic Association," *Hilltop* (Summer 1999, Vol. 11, No. 2).

"$2.27 Million Grant to Equip Urban Ministries Received by Gordon-Conwell," *Hilltop.*

"1,000 Attend Rabbi's Funeral" (July 11, 1992).

"130 Evangelical Christians Arrested in China," *Christian News* (November 20, 2000, Vol. 38, No. 43).

1988 Guide to New Age Living, The (Winter 1988).

"1993 Biennial Session Banquet Honorees," *The Scottish Rite Journal* (January 1994, Vol. 102, No. 1).

1993 Church World Service Annual Report (New York, NY: Church World Service, 1993).

2001: A Vision from the Future Visualization 2001 (n.p., n.d.).

"50th Meeting of the World Council of Churches Central Committee," *The ACCC* (October 1999).

"600 Honor Sir John Templeton at Dinner," *The Independent* (Vol. 9, No. 1).

"A Disturbing Look Inside the NEA," *An American Commentary* (Oklahoma City, OK: Hearthstone Publishing, Ltd., 1993).

"A Dozen Good Reasons to Get *US* Out of the United Nations," (1995).

A Gift of Prophecy: The Phenomenal Jeane Dixon (NY: William Morrow and Company, 1965).

"A Guinea Pig Remembers," *Wisconsin Report* (January 28, 1993, Vol. 18, No. 5).

"A Horrible Statement," *Christian News* (February 12, 2001, Vol. 39, No. 7).

"A Kiss Is Just a Kiss," *Censorship News* (Winter 1997, No. 68).

"A Lot of What's Best in America...Is Socialist" (New York, NY: Socialist Party, n.d.).

"A Loyal Chinese Marxist Invites LCMS President," *Christian News* (Oct. 4, 1999, Vol. 37, No. 36).

"A Missionary Speaks Against Desmond Tutu's View of South Africa," *O Timothy* (1987, Vol. 4, Issue 3-4).

"A New Era Begins," *Forecasts and Commentary from Maitreya, the World Teacher* (March 20, 1990).

"A New Inquisition," *The Omega-Letter* (December 1989, Vol. 5, No. 11).

A Newsletter from a Follower of Christ (January 1995, Vol. 4, No. 1).

"A Powerful (and Surprising) Ally Is Coming to Oregon," *Just Out* (August 1992, Vol. 9, No. 10).

"A Sampling of Resources Written and Recommended by the National Network of Presbyterian College Women," *The Presbyterian Layman* (January/February 1999, Vol. 32, No. 1).

"A Season for Non-Violence," *Temple of Understanding Newsletter* (Fall 1998).

"A Selection Compilation from the Books of Alice A. Bailey on the Aquarian Age," (Jersey City, NJ: Aquarian Age Community).

"A Universal Declaration of Human Responsibilities," *World Goodwill Occasional Paper* (Received September 16, 1998).

"A Very Successful Start," *World Goodwill Newsletter* (1988, No. 3).

"A Word from Ned Graham," *East Gates Connection* (January-March 2000).

"A World Religion," *The Witness* (April 1991, Vol. 31, No. 4).

"AAL Helps Create Film on Bonhoeffer," *Christian News* (May 15, 2000, Vol. 38, No. 20).

"Abernathy Attacked by Blacks for King Revelations," *The Christian World Report* (December 1989, Vol. 1, No. 9).

"Abominations Masquerading As 'Christian' Books," *Flashpoint* (February 1992).

"Abortion Bill: Graham and Pope Vs. NCC and Clinton," *Calvary Contender* (June 1, 1996, Vol. 13, No. 11).

"Abraham Flexner and the Rhodes Connection," *The Christian Conscience* (February 1996, Vol. 2, No. 2).

Abraham, Guy Emmanuel. *Chronology of Important Events in the Life of Jesus Christ* (Silver Spring, MD: Home Bible Study Group, 2001).

Abraham, Larry and Sanders, Franklin. *The Greening* (Atlanta, GA: Soundview Publications, n.d.).

ACCC Report, The (August 2000).

ACCC Report, The (July 1998).

"Accounts of Torture in China on the Rise," *Christian News* (February 26, 2001, Vol. 39, No. 9).

ACLU (Report of Activities 1984-85).

"ACLU's Attack on God," Interview by Dr. Stan Monteith with William Donahue on August 22, 2000.

"ACLU Award to Mel White," *Calvary Contender* (February 15, 1998, Vol. 15, No. 4).

"Actor in Jesus Film Is Not a Believer," *O Timothy* (1995, Vol. 12, Issue 10).

Adams, Cathy. "What About G. W. Bush's Record?," on the July 24, 2000 program of Radio Liberty.

Adams, George R. *A Trilogy: Inner Journey to the East, Meditations of a Master Mason Along the Way, Masonry for the Millennium* (Glen Echo, MD: SELFormation Corporation, Inc., 1999).

Adams, John H. "'I Want to Apologize,'" *The Presbyterian Layman* (January/February 2001, Vol. 34, No. 1).

Adams, John H. "NCC Leader's Strange Tack," *The Presbyterian Layman* (January/February 2001, Vol. 34, No. 1).

Adams, John H. "Sophia Speaker: Put More Women in Canon," *The Presbyterian Layman* (July/August 1998, Vol. 33, No. 4).

Adams, John H. "WCC-backed Mugabe Puts Zimbabwe in Bloodbath," *The Presbyterian Layman* (May/June 2000, Vol. 33, No. 3).

Adams, John H. "WCC Speaker Tells UN That 'Gods' Are to Be Found in World," *The Presbyterian Layman* (September/October 2000).

Adeney, Frances. "'Re-Visioning' Reality," *SCP Newsletter* (June-July 1981, Vol. 7, No. 2).

Adler, Margot. *Drawing Down the Moon: Witches, Druids, Goddess-Worshippers, and Other Pagans in America Today* (New York, NY: The Viking Press, 1979).

"Advertising Atheism," *Freethought Today* (August 1986, Vol. 3, No. 6).

"Affiliated Groups Gather at SBC Meeting," *Calvary Contender* (June 15, 2001, Vol. 18, No. 12).

"Agenda of the Invisible Government, The," *The Prophecy Newsletter* (Vol. 1, No. 3).

Aho, Barbara. "The 19th Century Occult Revival," *The Christian Conscience* (July/August 1997, Vol. 3, No. 6).

Aho, T. "World Council of Churches to Propose New Ecumenical Forum," *Despatch Magazine* (September 1998, Vol. 10, No. 3).

Aikman, David. "The Global Picture," *Charisma* (March 1998).

"Ailing Bill Bright, Busy, Receives Awards," *Calvary Contender* (May 1, 2001).

"Al Gore and the Communist Bagman: A Sordid Family Affair," *Flashpoint* (March 1993).

Alexander, Caroline. "The World of the Occult and Its Infiltration into Modern Society," *The Perilous Times* (July/August 2000, Vol. 22, No. 5).

Alexander-Moegerle, Gil. *James Dobson's War on America* (Amherst, NY: Prometheus Books, 1997).

Algeo, John. "One Life: A Theosophical View of the Global Challenge," *The Quest* (Autumn 1993, Vol. 6, No. 3).

"Alice A. Bailey on 'the Christ' and 'the Coming World Religion,'" *SCP Journal* (19:2/3).

Alinsky, Saul D. *Rules for Radicals: A Practical Primer for Realistic Radicals* (NY: Random House, 1971).

Alinsky, Saul D. *Rules for Radicals: A Practical Primer for Realistic Radicals* (Vintage Books, 1971).

"All of That Means Nothing to Me Any More," *Foundation* (October-December 1988).

"All Souls Pastor Retained," *The Christian Century* (November 6, 1991, Vol. 108, No. 32).

Allen, Gary. *Jimmy Carter, Jimmy Carter* (Seal Beach, CA: '76 Press, 1976).

Allen, Gary. *Rockefeller: Campaigning for the New World Order* (n.p., n.d.).

Allen, Gary. *The C.F.R.: Conspiracy to Rule the World* (n.p., n.d.).

Allen, Gary. *The Rockefeller File* (Seal Beach, CA: '76 Press, 1976).

"'Alpha Course' Warning," *Calvary Contender* (December 15, 1998, Vol. 25, No. 24).

"Alpha Course Workshop at Amsterdam," *Calvary Contender* (September 1, 2000, Vol. 17, No. 17).

Alpha News (August-November 2000, No. 7).

"Alpha: A Model for Dynamic Growth in the Local Church" (Brochure received January 11, 2001).

"Alumni/ae Notes," *Hilltop* (Summer 1997, Vol. 9, No. 1).

"America Subverted by the A.C.L.U.," *Christian World Report* (July 1989, Vol. 1, No. 5).

"America's Bishop," *Catholic Digest* (August 2001, Vol. 65, No. 10).

America's Hour of Decision: Revival Campaigns and Life Story of Billy Graham (Wheaton, IL: Van Kampen Press, 1951).

"America's Top Evangelists Show Interest in Alpha Rise," *Alpha News* (December 2000-March 2001, No. 8).

"American Baptist Meeting Features Tutu, Campolo," *Calvary Contender* (March 1, 1995, Vol. 12, No. 5).

"American Bible Society Rapping and Cursing," *O Timothy* (1992, Vol. 9, Issue 11).

"American Bible Society Rejects Historicity of Genesis," *Christian News* (March 26, 2001, Vol. 39, No. 13).

American Heritage Dictionary, The (Third Edition, Version 3.6a) (SoftKey International, 1994).

American Family Association Journal.

"American Family Under Attack, The," *An American Commentary* (Oklahoma City, OK: Hearthstone Publishing, Ltd., 1993).

"American Malvern," *Time* (March 16, 1942).

"AmerRuss: The Illuminati Plot to Merge the United States and Russia," *Power of Prophecy* (February 2001, Vol. 2001-02).

"Amsterdam 2000," *The ACCC Report* (August 2000).

"Amy Grant and Husband Separate," *Calvary Contender* (February 1, 1999, Vol. 16, No. 3).

"Amy Grant at 'Christian Rock Festival,'"*Calvary Contender* (March 1, 1993, Vol. 10, No. 5).

"Amy Grant Remarries, Terry Separates," *Calvary Contender* (April 1, 2000, Vol. 17, No. 7).

"Amy Grant, Gary Chapman Separate," *Dallas Morning News* (January 9, 1999).

An American Commentary (Oklahoma City, OK: Hearthstone Publishing, Ltd., 1993).

"An Emerging Coalition: Political and Religious Leaders Come Together," *The Omega-Letter* (Special Report).

"An Intimate Portrait of John Paul II," *U. S. News & World Report* (September 27, 1999).

"An Update on South Africa," *O Timothy* (1988, Vol. 5, Issue 2).

Anderson, David E. "Religious Groups Support Gay Rights March," *Christian News* (March 8, 1993, Vol. 31, No. 10).

Anderson Scott, and Anderson, Jon Lee. *Inside the League: The Shocking Expose of How Terrorists, Nazis, and Latin American Death Squads Have Infiltrated the World Anti-Communist League* (New York, NY: Dodd, Mead & Company, 1986).

"Andy Young Is New President of NCC?," *Calvary Contender* (February 15, 1998, Vol. 15, No. 4).

Angers, Jefferson M., Editor. *Council for National Policy Annual Directory 1984-85* (Baton Rouge, LA: Council for National Policy, 1984).

"Anglican Betrayal Stalled: Capitulation to Rome Does Not God Ahead for Now!," *The Protestant Challenge* (2000, No. 2/3).

"Anglican Leaders Dialogue with Druids," *Christian News* (July 3, 2000, Vol. 38, No. 27).

"Anglican—Catholic—Consultation—Important Gathering," *Despatch Magazine* (June 2000, Vol. 12, No. 2).

Ankerberg, John and Weldon, John. *The Facts on Astrology: What the Bible, Science, and Common Sense Tell Us About Astrology* (Eugene, OR: Harvest House Publishers, 1991).

Ankerberg, John and Weldon, John, *The Facts on Spirit Guides: How to Avoid the Seduction of the Spirit World and Demonic Powers* (Eugene, OR: Harvest House Publishers, 1988).

"Another Major Player: The Ford Foundation," *The Florida Forum* (Summer 1996).

"Answer to the Question," *Christian Conscience* (January 1996, Vol. 2, No. 1).

"Anti-Christian Unitarian Theology of Marty's Christian Century, The," *Christian News* (February 10, 1997, Vol. 35, No. 6).

Applebome, Peter. "Nurturing New Seeds in a Garden of Hopes," *The New York Times National* (January 29, 1990).

Apocalypse Chronicles, The (Winter 1998, Vol. 5, No. 2).

"Apostasy and Deception," *CIB Bulletin* (November 1991, Vol. 7, No. 11).

"Apostate Graham Ignores Abortion and Sodomy," *The Perilous Times* (November 1994, Vol. 16, No. 9).

Arcarti, Kristyna. *Interpreting Signs and Symbols: A Beginner's Guide* (London, England: Hodder and Stoughton Educational, 1997).

"Archbishop of Canterbury Lashes Out at Fundamentalists," *O Timothy* (1994, Vol. 11, Issue 5).

Archibald, George. "Conservative Blacks Fault GOP for Not Overcoming Party Image As the Enemy," *The Washington Times* (December 2, 1985).

"Are These the Only Choices I've Got?" (New York, NY: Socialist Party, n.d.).

"'Art' Display Profanes Christ," *The Christian World Report* (July 1989, Vol. 1, No. 5).

"Art of Self-realization, The," *Share International* (Special Information Issue).

"As Mainstream Accepts King, Young Blacks Turn to Malcolm," *Associated Press* (January 17, 1993).

"As the Third Millennium Draws Near: Tertio Mellennio Adveniente," (Apostolic Letter of Pope John Paul II released on November 13, 1994).

"As the Third Millennium Draws Near 'Tertio Mellennio Adveniente,'" *Despatch Magazine* (June 1995, Vol. 7, No. 2).

Ashbrook, John. "Billy Graham—The Mouthpiece of New Evangelicalism," *O Timothy* (1993, Vol. 10, Issue 1).

Ashbrook, John. *Billy Graham's Catholic Connection.*

Ashbrook, John E. *New Neutralism II: Exposing the Gray of Compromise* (Mentor, OH: Here I Stand Books, 1992).

"Assembly Resolutions," *One World* (April 1990, No. 154).

"Atheist Speaks at Schuller's Church," *Calvary Contender* (November 15, 2000, Vol. 17, No. 22).

Auger News Letter, The (January 2000).

Auger News Letter, The (May 2000).

"Australia and the 2001 N.W.O. Planetary Events," *Despatch Magazine* (March 2001, Vol. 13, No. 1).

"Author Makes Transition," *Sparrow Hawk Villager* (July-September 2001, Vol. 21, No. 3).

"Authorities Crack Down on Guangdong Christians," *Christian News* (May 29, 2000, Vol. 38, No. 22).

"Authority," *C. E. C. Journal* (March/April 2001).

"Awful Truth About Jesse Jackson, The (Part I)," *Flashpoint* (March 2001, Vol. 2001-03).

"Backslidden Prophets," *The Omega-Letter* (February 1988, Vol. 3, No. 2).

Baer, Randall N. *Inside the New Age Nightmare* (Lafayette, LA: Huntington House, Inc., 1989).

Baigent, Michael and Leigh, Richard. *The Temple and the Lodge* (NY: Arcade Publishing, Inc., 1989).

Bailey, Alice A. *A Treatise on White Magic or the Way of the Disciple* (NY: Lucis Publishing Company, 1951).

Bailey, Alice A. *Discipleship in the New Age* (Vol. I) (NY: Lucis Publishing Company, 1972).

Bailey, Alice A. *Discipleship in the New Age* (Vol. II) (NY: Lucis Publishing Company, 1955).

Bailey, Alice A. *Education in the New Age* (NY: Lucis Publishing Company, 1954).

Bailey, Alice A. *From Bethlehem to Calvary: The Initiations of Jesus* (NY: Lucis Trust Publishing Company, 1965).

Bailey, Alice A. *Preparation for the Reappearance of the Christ.* (This was taken from a small booklet based on Alice Bailey's book by the same title.)

Bailey, Alice A. *The Externalisation of the Hierarchy* (New York, NY: Lucis Publishing Company, 1989 Edition).

Bailey, Alice A. *The Light of the Soul: Its Science and Effect* (NY: Lucis Publishing Company, 1965).

Bailey, Alice A. *The Soul: Quality of Life* (NY: Lucis Publishing Company, 1974).

Bailey, Alice A. *The Rays and the Initiations* (New York, NY: Lucis Trust, 1960).

Bailey, Alice A. *The Reappearance of the Christ* (New York, NY: Lucis Publishing Company, 1948).

Bailey, Alice A. *The Unfinished Autobiography* (NY: Lucis Publishing Company, 1951).

Bailey, Keith. "Masonry: Returning to Its Ancient Spiritual Roots," "Festival Week of the New Group of World Servers" (December 19, 21, and 28, 1998).

Baker, Virginia Birt. "Who's Who in the U. S. Government?," *Wisconsin Report* (February 18, 1993, Vol. 18, No. 8).

"Ban Jackson and All Adulterers from the Pastoral Ministry," *Christian News* (January 29, 2001, Vol. 39, No. 5).

Banks, Adelle M. "Billy, Ruth Graham Receive Congressional Gold Medal," *Christian News* (May 13, 1996, Vol. 34, No. 20).

Banks, Adelle M. "Campus Crusade Founder Wins $1 Million Prize," *Christian News* (March 18, 1996, Vol. 34, No. 12).

Banks, Adelle M. "Clinton, Others Praise Graham at Washington Dinner," *Christian News* (May 13, 1996, Vol. 34, No. 20).

Banks, Adelle M. "Graham Ministry Spans Half a Century," *Christian News* (May 13, 1996, Vol. 34, No. 20).

Banks, Adelle M. "Struggling to Honor King in a Shifting Racial Climate," *Christian News* (January 19, 1998, Vol. 36, No. 3).

Banks, Adelle M. and Rifkin, Ira. "With a Nation's Prayers, Clinton's Inaugural Sounds Reconciling Note," *Christian News* (January 27, 1997, Vol. 35, No. 4).

Banks, Natalie N. *The Golden Thread* (New York, NY: Lucis Publishing Company, 1999 Edition).

"Baptist Leader Apologizes but Refuses to Step Down," *Christian News* (December 15, 1997, Vol. 35, No. 46).

"Baptist Leader Denied Two Previous Unions at Time of Third Marriage," *Christian News* (September 15, 1997, Vol. 35, No. 33).

"Baptist Leader Surprises Jewelers ," *Christian News* (September 15, 1997, Vol. 35, No. 33).

"Baptist World Alliance Says Ecumenicism More Important Than Doctrine," *Christian News* (January 15, 2001, Vol. 39, No. 3).

Barbera, Michael. "Christian Groups Lay Aside Differences in Battle Against Poverty," *National Catholic Register* (December 28, 1997-January 3, 1998, Vol. 73, No. 52).

"Barbour Wins Templeton Prize," *Calvary Contender* (July 15, 1999, Vol. 16, No. 14).

Barela, John. *Mysteries Unveiled* (Oklahoma City, OK: Southwest Radio Church, n.d.).

Barela, John. *The New Covenant of Bill Clinton & Al Gore* (Tulsa, OK: Mark 4 Marketing, Inc., 1992).

Barger, Eric. *From Rock to Rock: The Music of Darkness Exposed!* (Lafayette, LA: Huntington House, Inc., 1990).

Barger, Eric. "The New World Order Under Clinton: Establishment Insiders and Political Deceit," *The Christian World Report* (May 1993, Vol. 8, No. 3).

Barnhart, David. "A Fierce Battle Raging in Christendom," *Christian News* (October 3, 1994, Vol. 32, No. 36).

Barnhart, David R. *Contending for the Faith* (Eagan, MN: Abiding Word Publications, 1994).

Barnhart, David R. "Islam: The Cross or the Crescent?," *The Vine and Branches* (Summer 1998, Vol. 13, Issue 3).

Barnhart, David R. "The Spirit Still Speaks to the Churches!: Part 1—The Church at Ephesus," *The Vine and Branches* (Summer 2001, Vol. 16, Issue 31).

Barr, K. E. *Unholy Alliances 2000* (Kansas City, MO: Barr Press, 1994).

"Barth, a Socialist, Praised by Evangelicals," *Calvary Contender* (June 1, 1998, Vol. 15, No. 11).

Battle Cry (March/April 1991).

Baxter, Jr., Irvin. "What the U. N. Doesn't Want You to Know."

Bay, David. "Meet the Real Reverand (sic) Billy Graham—He Is Not the Person Whom You Thought You Knew!"

Bay, David. "Traditional Roman Catholic Church Proven to Be a Practice of White Magic Witchcraft—Words and Symbols Tell the Story!" (Cutting Edge Ministries, n.d).

"Bayard Rustin at Notre Dame," *The Review of the News* (December 3, 1969).

"Baylor Honors Chuck Swindoll," *Calvary Contender* (March 1, 1997, Vol. 14, No. 5).

"BBF Gives Graham Book to Preachers," *Calvary Contender* (April 1, 1999, Vol. 16, No. 7).

BDM Letter, The (March/April 1995, Vol. 4, No. 2).

BDM Letter, The (November 1993, Vol. 2, No. 9).

BDM Letter, The (October 1993, Vol. 2, No. 8).

BDM Letter, The (September 1993, Vol. 2, No. 7).

"Be Informed About the Talmud," *Christian News* (March 5, 2001, Vol. 39, No. 10).

Beardsley, John. "DC Talk Examined," *The Christian Conscience* (June 1996, Vol. 2, No. 6).

Becker, David. "Booknotes," *Christian News* (October 31, 1994, Vol. 32, No. 40).

Becker, David. "Gay and Lesbian Band to March at Clinton-Gore Inaugural," *Christian News* (December 28, 1992, Vol. 30, No. 48).

Behreandt, Denise L. "Permanent Normal Torture of Religions," *The New American* (June 19, 2000, Vol. 16, No. 13).

Beirnes, G. R., Editor. "Liberals Seek Catholic Membership in WCC-NCC," *The Midnight Cry* (April 1967, Vol. 28, No. 4).

Bellant, Russ. *The Religious Right in Michigan Politics* (Silver Spring, MD: Americans for Religious Liberty, 1996).

Bennett, Richard, Compiler. *The Bible and Vatican Council II: A Comparison* (Portland, OR: Berean Beacon, n.d.).

Bennett, Richard M. *"We Ought to Obey God Rather Than Men,"* (Portland, OR: Berean Beacon, 1994).

Bensinger, Charles. *Chaco Journey: Remembrance and Awakening* (Santa Fe, NM: Timewindow Publications, 1988).

Benson, Herbert with Klipper, Miriam Z. *The Relaxation Response* (New York, NY: William Morrow and Company, Inc., 1975).

Berean Call, The (April 1998).

Berean Call, The (April 2001).

Berean Call, The (August 1993).

Berean Call, The (August 1998).

Berean Call, The (February 1999).

Berean Call, The (January 1998).

Berean Call, The (July 1999).

Berean Call, The (June 1997).

Berean Call, The (May 1998).

Berean Call, The (October 1993).

Berean Call, The (October 1994).

Berger, Charles G. *Our Phallic Heritage* (New York, NY: Greenwich Book Publishers, Inc., 1966).

Bessy, Maurice. *A Pictorial History of Magic and the Supernatural* (NY: Hamlyn Publishing Group Limited, 1964).

Betancourt, Mike, Compiler. "Promise Keepers: Should Fundamentalists Get Involved?," *O Timothy* (n.d.).

Bettson, Bob. "Ailing Graham Still Draws Record Crowds," *Observer* (August 1995).

Beversluis, Joel, Compiler. "URI Joins a Diverse Field of Interreligious Organizations," *United Religions* (Fall 1997, Issue 4).

"Beware of 'Comparative Religion,'" *Christian News* (September 26, 1998, Vol. 26, No. 35).

"Beware of Harry Potter," *Christian News* (March 12, 2001, Vol. 39, No. 11).

"Beware of the United Bible Societies," *Christian News* (March 19, 2001, Vol. 39, No. 12).

"Beware of the United Bible Societies," *The Perilous Times* (April/May 2001, Vol. 22, No. 10).

"Bewitched by Harry Potter," *Christian News* (November 29, 1999, Vol. 37, No. 44).

"Bible Burning Planned By 'Arts' Group," *The Christian World Report* (November 1990, Vol. 2, No. 9).

"Big Severance Package to NCC's Former Leader," *Calvary Contender* (July 1, 2001, Vol. 18, No. 13).

"Bilderberg Meetings—AD 2000, The," *Despatch Magazine* (September 2000, Vol. 12:3).

"Bill Bright and Catholics," *Calvary Contender* (January 1, 1999, Vol. 16, No. 1).

"Bill Bright and the Templeton Prize," *C.E.C. Journal* (May 1996).

"Bill Bright Gets $1 Million Templeton Prize," *Calvary Contender* (April 1, 1996, Vol. 13, No. 7).

"Bill Bright Wins Templeton," *Allentown Morning Call* (March 9, 1996).

"Billy Graham and Al Gore Team Up to Save the Earth," *Flashpoint* (August 1995).

"Billy Graham Backs Off Support of Teen Hotline," *The News and Observer* (August 13, 1993).

"Billy Graham 'Delighted' Pope Came to Denver," *Christian News* (September 27, 1993, Vol. 31, No. 35).

"Billy Graham Does Political Favor for President Clinton," *Flashpoint* (September 1997, Vol. 97-9).

"Billy Graham Endorser of Evil," *The Perilous Times* (February 1994, Vol. 15, No. 12).

"Billy Graham Event Hears of 'Alpha Revolution,'" *Alpha News* (December 2000-March 2001, No. 8).

"Billy Graham Gave the Apostate National Council of Churches the Greatest Boost It Has Had in Many Years," *Foundation* (June-August 1991).

"Billy Graham Invites Alpha," *Alpha News* (April-July 2000, No. 6).

"Billy Graham Is a Great Deceiver," *Flashpoint* (May 1998, Vol. 98-5).

"Billy Graham Is Featured on the Cover of the October 20 *Parade* Magazine," *Christian News* (November 4, 1996, Vol. 34, No. 41).

"Billy Graham Offers Prayers for Mandela," *Christian News* (June 13, 1994, Vol. 32, No. 24).

"Billy Graham Praises Bill Clinton," *Flashpoint* (April 1994).

"Billy Graham Praises Clinton," *Christian View of the News* (October 10, 1994, Vol. 19, No. 19).

"Billy Graham Praises the Pope," *Christian News* (July 9, 2001, Vol. 39, No. 28).

"Billy Graham Says 'Save the Earth, Not Babies!,'" *Flashpoint* (August 1995).

"Billy Graham Speaks in North Korea, Delivers Message from the Pope," *O Timothy* (1992, Vol. 9, Issue 6).

"Billy Graham Speaks Out," *Freedom Writer* (May/June 1997).

"Billy Graham Takes Failing Health in Stride, Plans More Crusades Next Year," *The News and Observer* (November 1, 2000).

"Billy Graham to Get Award in Charlotte," *The News and Observer* (February 1, 1990).

"Billy Graham to Speak at Liberty University Commencement," *Christian News* (April 21, 1997, Vol. 35, No. 16).

"Billy Graham to Speak at Ockenga Testimonial Dinner; All Invited to March 30 Event," *Contact* (Winter 1979, Vol. 9, No. 2).

"Billy Graham Turns Blind Eye to the Serious Persecution in China," *O Timothy* (1989, Vol. 6, Issue 5).

"Billy Graham: Fellowship with Apostasy," *The BDM Letter* (November 1993, Vol. 2, No. 9).

"Billy Graham—A Mason Without the Apron," *HRT Ministries Inc. Newsletter* (July/August/September 1990, Vol. 3, No. 3).

"Billy Graham's Amsterdam 2000 Shows Solidarity Amid Diversity," *Christian News* (July 3, 2000, Vol. 38, No. 27).

"Billy Graham's Amsterdam 2000: A Special First-Hand Report by Ralph Colas," *Calvary Contender* (August 15, 2000, Vol. 17, No. 16).

"Billy Graham's Disobedience," *O Timothy,* (1995, Vol. 12, Issue 11).

"Billy Graham's Last Scheduled International Event to Be His Most Technologically Advanced," *Christian News* (June 19, 2000, Vol. 38, No. 25).

"Billy Kim a Friend of Cho," *Calvary Contender* (April 1, 1993, Vol. 10, No. 7).

"Billy Kim Says Doctrine Is Not What Unites BWA," *Calvary Contender* (September 15, 2000, Vol. 17, No. 18).

"BIOLA Has Rock Concert," *Calvary Contender* (June 15, 1992, Vol. 9, No. 12).

"Bishop Oxnam Invites the Pope to Live Our Liberty," *The New Age Magazine* (December 1949, Vol. 57, No. 12).

"Bishop Ting Praises Socialism—Blasts Historic Christianity," *Christian News* (July 19, 1999, Vol. 37, No. 29).

"Black South African Mayor Exposes Nelson Mandela," *O Timothy* (1990, Vol. 7, Issue 7).

Blanton, Raymond. "In Perils of the ACLU," *The Perilous Times* (December 1993, Vol. 15, No. 10).

Blau, Joseph Leon. *The Christian Cabala* (Port Washington, NY: Kennikat Press, Inc., 1944).

Blavatsky, Helena Petrovna. *Isis Unveiled,* Vol. I: Science (New York, NY: Trow's Printing and Bookbinding Company, 1877).

Blick, Edward F. *Correlation of the Bible and Science* (Oklahoma City, OK: Southwest Radio Church, 1988 Edition).

Blofeld, John. *The Tantric Mysticism of Tibet* (Boston, MA: Shambhala Publications, Inc., 1970).

Blount, George W. *Peace Through World Government* (Durham, NC: Moore Publishing Company, 1974).

Blue Star, "Pagan Deities: Echoes of the Old Ones," *Circle Network News* (Spring 1986, Vol. 8, No. 1).

Blueprint for Building the New World Order (Dearborn, MI: The Omega-Letter/Christian World Report, n.d.).

Blumenthal, Sidney. "Edgar Forges Campaign with Help in Hollywood: Underdog in Senate Race Trades on Image," *The Washington Post* (October 23, 1986).

Bobgan, Martin and Deidre. *Hypnosis: Medical, Scientific, or Occultic* (Santa Barbara, CA: EastGate Publishers, 2001).

Bok, Bart J. "Astrology" (Vol. 1) *The World Book Encyclopedia* (Chicago 54, IL: Field Enterprises Educational Corporation, 1961 Edition).

Bold Truth (April 1993).

Bold Truth (February 13, 1994).

"Bonhoeffer Denied Christianity" *Calvary Contender* (July 15, 2000, Vol. 17, No. 14).

"Bonhoeffer Lauded by Evangelicals," *Calvary Contender* (June 15, 1998, Vol. 15, No. 12).

"Book Review," *Christian News* (October 28, 1991, Vol. 29, No. 39).

"Book Review," *The Florida Forum* (Summer 1994).

"Books," *The Christian Century* (October 22, 1986).

Bookstore Journal (November 1991).

Boothman, Sherre L. "Being Lesbian, Feminist Christian and a Survivor of Childhood Abuse: A Christian Clergywoman Finds Her Voice," *CLOUTreach* (Spring 1994, Vol. 3, No. 1).

"'Born Again' Jesus Deception," The, *The End Times and Victorious Living* (March/April 2001, Vol. 15, No. 2).

"Bottom Line, The," *Intelligence Newsletter* (May-June 1996).

Bouey, Debra. "On Appealing to John Wesley," *The Christian Conscience* (January/February 1998, Vol. 4, No. 1).

Bouey, Debra. "Pensacola Pendemonium (sic)," *The Christian Conscience* (June 199, Vol. 3, No. 5).

Bovee, Vic. "Unitarian Churches," *The World Book Encyclopedia* (1961 Edition, Vol. 18).

Bowen, William M., Jr. *Globalism: America's Demise* (Shreveport, LA: Huntington House, Inc., 1984).

Boyd, Herb. "What King Left Behind," *The Guardian* (April 13, 1988, Vol. 40, No. 28).

Boyd, James P. *Bible Dictionary* (NY: Ottenheimer Publishers, Inc., 1958).

Branch, Craig. "Chicken Soup or Witch's Brew?," *The Watchman Expositor.*

Braun, Sr., William. "Habitat's Cash Cow," *Christian Conscience* (July/August 1997, Vol. 3, No. 6).

Braybrooke, Marcus. *A Wider Vision: A History of the World Congress of Faiths* (Oxford, England: Oneworld Publications, 1996).

Breakthrough (Spring/Summer 1987, Vol. 8, No. 3-4).

Breakthrough (Winter/Summer 1990, Vol. 11, No. 2-4).

Breakthrough News (Fall 1994).

Breakthroughs (September-October 1996).

Brendan, Jamie. "United Nations Millennium Forum."

Brewer, Bartholomew F. with Furrell, Alfred W. *Pilgrimage* (Greenville, SC: Bob Jones University Press, 1986).

Briggs, David. "20 at Interfaith Parliament Sign Document on Values," *The Charlotte Observer* (September 1, 1993).

Briggs, David. "In Shadow of Armageddon, Preacher at 73 Tiring but Plans to Keep Working," *The Knoxville News-Sentinel* (September 15, 1991).

Briggs, Ed. "Archbishop of Canterbury Urges Tolerance in Sexuality Debate," *Christian News* (February 10, 1997, Vol. 35, No. 6).

"Bright and Campolo Join Praise for Alpha," *Alpha News* (August-November 2000, No. 7).

"Britishers Prefer Modernistic Paraphrase," *O Timothy* (1991, Vol. 8, Issue 8).

Broadway, Bill. "Franklin Graham Set for Bush Invocation," *The News and Observer* (January 16, 2001).

"Broken Cross: Hidden Hand in the Vatican—Book Review for the Coming New World Order" (Radio Show Transcript).

"Brother Wind, Sister Earth," *Maryknoll* (January 1990, Vol. 84, No. 1).

"Brotherhood of Mormon" (Part II), *Distant Drums* (June 1985, Vol. 7, No. 2).

Brown, David L. *The Dark Side of Halloween and the Bewitching of America* (Oak Creek, WI: Logos Communication Consortium, Inc., 1998).

"Brownsville Revival High Pressure Appeals," *Calvary Contender* (April 15, 1998, Vol. 15, No. 8).

"Brownsville Revival: An Insider's Report," *Calvary Contender* (October 15, 1998).

Bruinius, Harry. "Templeton Winner Coaxed Science and Religion to Talk," *Christian Science Monitor* (March 11, 1999).

Brunk, George R. "Counterfeit Revival," *Christian News* (June 9, 1997, Vol. 35, No. 23).

"Bryer (sic) Is Bad News for Christians," *Christian News* (July 18, 1994, Vol. 32, No. 29).

"Buddhist Occultism," *Calvary Contender* (July 1, 2001, Vol. 18, No. 13).

Buhle, Mari Jo, Buhle, Paul, and Georgakas, Dan, Editors. *Encyclopedia of the American Left* (New York, NY: Oxford University Press, 1998, Second Edition).

Building and Bridging: The New Group of World Servers, a booklet compiled from the books by Alice Bailey, written in collaboration with Djwhal Khul (a demonic spirit guide).

Bulfinch, Thomas. *Bulfinch's Mythology* (NY: Thomas Y. Crowell Company, Inc., 1970).

Bulfinch, Thomas. *Bulfinch's Mythology: The Age of Fable or Stories of Gods and Heroes* (Garden City, NY: Doubleday and Company, Inc., 1948).

"Bulletin Inserts," quoting from *Old Union Reminder* in *Pulpit Helps* (July 1998, Vol. 24, No. 7).

"Bulletin Inserts," quoting from *Sword of the Lord* in *Pulpit Helps* (May 1995, Vol. 20, No. 5).

Bundy, Edgar C. *Billy Graham: Performer?, Politician?, Preacher?, Prophet?* (Wheaton, IL: Church League of America, 1982).

Bundy, Edgar C. *Collectivism in the Churches: A Documented Account of the Political Activities of the Federal, National, and World Councils of Churches* (Wheaton, IL: The Church League of America, 1958).

Bundy, Edgar C. *How Liberals and Radicals Are Manipulating Evangelicals* (Miami Shores, FL: Edgar Bundy Ministries, Inc., 1982).

Burgoyne, Thomas H. *The Light of Egypt or the Science of the Soul and the Stars* (Vol. 1) (Denver 20, CO: Astro Philosophical Publishing Company, 1963 reprint).

Burhoe, Ralph Wendell. "Religion's Importance As Seen in Natural History," *Religious Humanism* (n.d.).

"Bush and Clinton: Bilderberger Twins?," *Flashpoint* (May 1992).

Butler, E. M. *The Myth of the Magus* (NY: MacMillan Company, 1948).

Button, Lloyd C. "No Longer a Mormon" (Minneapolis, MN: Religious Analysis Service, Inc.).

"BWA Cozy with Castro," *Calvary Contender* (September 15, 2000, Vol. 17, No. 18).

"BWA Ecumenism," *Calvary Contender* (August 15, 1998, Vol. 15, No. 16).

"BWA Heroes," *Calvary Contender* (December 15, 1999, Vol. 16, No. 24).

"BWA Met in Cuba," *Calvary Contender* (August 1, 2000, Vol. 17, No. 15).

Bynum, E. L. "Pope Says No Fire in Hell So Does Billy Graham," *The Evangelical Methodist* (September 2000, Vol. 78, No. 5).

Bynum, E. L. "The Bible and the Homosexual," *O Timothy* (1989, Vol. 6, Issue 7).

"C. S. Lewis Acceptable to Mormons," *The Perilous Times* (July 1999, Vol. 21, No. 5).

"C. S. Lewis: General Teachings/Activities" (Biblical Discernment Ministries, 1994).

"C. S. Lewis: One of the Greatest Communicators of the Christian Faith or Deceived Deceiver?" (Compilation of different sources, n.d.).

Cabot, Laurie with Cowan, Tom. *Power of the Witch: The Earth, the Moon, and the Magical Path to Enlightenment* (New York, NY: Delacorte Press, 1989).

Cairns, Earle E. *Christianity Through the Centuries: A History of the Christian Church* (Grand Rapids, MI: Zondervan Publishing House, 1954).

Caldwell, Deborah Kovach. "Issues in FAST FORWARD: A Look into the '96 Spiritual Scene," *Dallas Morning News* (December 30, 1995).

"Call to Renewal," *Mindszenty Report* (March 1996, Vol. 37, No. 3).

Calvary Contender (July 1, 1989).

Calvary Contender (July 1, 1993, Vol. 10, No. 13).

Calvary Contender (July 1, 1994, Vol. 11, No. 13).

Calvary Contender (July 15, 1998, Vol. 15, No. 14).

Calvary Contender (May 15, 1999, Vol. 16, No. 10).

"Campaign Against National Sovereignty, The," *The Florida Forum* (Winter 1999).

"Campbell Prays with UFMCC 'for Healing,'" *Eculink* (Summer 1994, No. 41).

Campbell, Joseph. *The Masks of God: Creative Mythology* (New York, NY: The Viking Press, 1968).

"Campolo a Bad Role Model for Youth," *Calvary Contender* (June 1, 1998, Vol. 15, No. 11).

"Campolo Reaffirms Belief in Universalist Theology, Cites Graham to Support His Position," *Foundation* (November-December 1999).

"Campolo Teaches 'Socialism' to So. Baptist Teens," *Calvary Contender* (March 15, 1992, Vol. 9, No. 6).

"Campolo Teaches 'Socialism' to So. Baptist Teens," *Christian News* (October 19, 1992, Vol. 30, No. 38).

"Campolo Won't Say Jesus Only Way to Heaven," *Calvary Contender* (August 15, 1999, Vol. 16, No. 16).

"Campolo Won't Say Jesus Only Way to Heaven," *Prophecy Corner and the Nosh Box* (August 1999, Vol. 4, Issue 8).

Campolo, Tony. *How to Rescue the Earth Without Worshiping Nature* (Nashville, TN: Thomas Nelson Publishers, 1992).

"Campolo: Clinton's 'Socialist' Friend," *Calvary Contender* (May 15, 1994, Vol. 11, No. 10).

"Campolo's Confusing Attempt to Clarify," *Calvary Contender* (October 1, 1999, Vol. 16, No. 19).

"Campus Crusade for Christ," *CovertAction Information Bulletin* (Spring 1987, No. 27).

"Campus Crusade's Ecumenical Tribute to Jesus," *Calvary Contender* (January 15, 2000, Vol. 17, No. 2).

"Can a Good Catholic Be Saved?," *O Timothy* (1995, Issue 12, Issue 12).

"Canaan Banana to Serve Goal Term After Appeal Fails," *Christian News* (June 5, 2000, Vol. 38, No. 23).

Cannon, Alexander, *The Power of Karma: In Relation to Destiny* (E.P. Dutton and Company, Inc., 1937).

Cannon, Paul R. "Venereal Disease," *The World Book Encyclopedia* (Vol. 18) (Chicago 54, IL: Field Enterprises Educational Corporation, 1961 Edition).

"Canterbury Is No Hogswarts," *Christian News* (July 17, 2000, Vol. 38, No. 29).

"Canterbury Objects to Vatican Eucharist Ban," *Christian Century* (April 11, 2001, Vol. 118, No. 12).

"'Captain Planet' Worse Than Imagined," *The Christian World Report* (December 1990, Vol. 2, No. 9).

Caputo, Tony. "Et Tu Impe," *Bold Truth Press Inc.* (November 5, 1993).

"Cardinal Arinze Speaks Out on Family," *Countdown to the Year 2000* (1995, Issue No. 2).

"Cardinal Suenens Dies at 91," *Calvary Contender* (August 15, 1996, Vol. 13, No. 16).

"Cardinal: Adam, Eve Possibly Not Human," *Veritas* (December 1996, Vol. 28, No. 12).

"Carl Sagan, Celebrated Author and Astronomer, Dies at 62," *Christian News* (December 30, 1996, Vol. 34, No. 49).

"Carl Sagan: 'Educated Fool' Faces Death," *Calvary Contender* (April 1, 1996, Vol. 13, No. 7).

Carle, Erica. "Six Generational to Serfdom," *The Florida Forum* (Spring 2001).

Carle, Erica. "Who Cares About the Constitution?," *The Florida Forum* (Summer 2000).

Carlson, Tucker. "Fidel's National Council of Churches," *The Schwarz Report* (June 2000, Vol. 40, No. 6).

Carolan, Matthew. "Environmental Piety No Substitute for Technique," *Religion and Liberty* (March/April 2001).

Carpenter, Joel A. *Revive Us Again: The Reawakening of American Fundamentalism* (New York, NY: Oxford University Press, 1997).

Carr, Joseph. *The Lucifer Connection* (Lafayette, LA: Huntington House, Inc., 1987).

Carr, William G. *One World in the Making: The United Nations* (Ginn and Company, 1946).

Carrico, David L. *Lucifer—Eliphas Levi—Albert Pike and the Masonic Lodge* (Evansville, IN: Followers of Jesus Christ, 1991).

Carrico, David L. *Manly P. Hall: The Honored Masonic Author* (Evansville, IN: Followers of Jesus Christ, 1992).

Carrico, David L. *The Gulf War, George Bush, the World Order, the Vision of the United Nations Founders* (Evansville, IN: Followers of Jesus Christ, 1991).

Carrico, David L. *The Occult Meaning of the Great Seal of the United States* (Evansville, IN: Followers of Jesus Christ, 1991).

"Carter Comments on Conversion," *Calvary Contender* (March 15, 1997, Vol. 14, No. 5).

"Carter Cuts SBC Ties," *Calvary Contender* (November 15, 2000, Vol. 17, No. 22).

Carter, Cecil J. *The Thinking, Theories and Theology of Drs. Westcott and Hort* (1978).

Carter, Darlene. "A Very Outspoken Interview with Dick and Tara Sutphen," *Self-Help Update* (Issue #31).

Carter, Jimmy. *Living Faith* (Times Books, 1996).

Cascione, Jack. "Visit to Glories of Christmas Show at Crystal Cathedral," *Christian News* (January 22, 2001, Vol. 39, No. 4).

Castells, F. de P. *The Apocalypse of Freemasonry: A Constructive Scheme of Interpretation of the Symbolism of the Masonic Lodge* (Dartford, England: Snowden Brothers, 1924).

"Castro Applauded at Church," *The Voice in the Wilderness* (December 2000).

"Castro Is Applauded at Riverside Church," *Calvary Contender* (October 15, 2000, Vol. 17, No. 20).

"Castro To Address Baptists," *The Voice in the Wilderness* (December 2000).

Catechism of the Catholic Church (New York, NY: Image Books, 1995).

"Cathedral Not-So-Divine," *The New American* (January 23, 1995).

"Catholic Cardinal Promotes Graham Crusade," *O Timothy* (1992, Vol. 9, Issue 9).

"Catholic Church and the Death Penalty," *Calvary Contender* (August 1, 2001, Vol. 19, No. 15).

"Catholic Priest to Speak at Asbury Seminary," *Calvary Contender* (February 1, 1997, Vol. 14, No. 3).

Catholic Word Book (New Haven, CT: Catholic Information Service, Knights of Columbus, n.d.).

"Catholic-Lutheran Unity," *Calvary Contender* (January 15, 2000).

Catholics and Purgatory (New Haven, CT: Catholic Information Service, Knights of Columbus, n.d.).

"Catholics 'Honor' Amy Grant," *Calvary Contender* (June 1, 1994, Vol. 11, No. 11).

"Catholics Make Evangelicals Leave Town in Mexico," *Calvary Contender* (June 15, 2001, Vol. 18, No. 12).

"Catholics May Name King 'Martyr for the Faith,'" *Calvary Contender* (February 1, 2000).

"Catholics Say They Are Superior," *Calvary Contender* (October 1, 2000, Vol. 17, No. 19).

"Catholics Seduce New Evangelicals," *Calvary Contender* (June 1, 1998, Vol. 15, No. 11).

"Catholics Urged to Hear Billy Graham," *O Timothy* (1991, Vol. 8, Issue 8-9).

"Catholics, Protestants Join Forces," *O Timothy* (1995, Vol. 12, Issue 11).

Catlin, George. *Christianity and the New Age* (n.p., 1998).

"Caux 1996: An International Learning Community," *Breakthroughs* (March-April 1996).

Caux: Healing the Past—Forging the Future (Luzerne, Switzerland: Fondation Pour le Rearmament Moral, 1996).

"CC Editor's Reply to a So. Baptist," *Calvary Contender* (October 1, 2000, Vol. 17, No. 19).

"CCM: At The Crossroads," *Calvary Contender* (April 1, 1999, Vol. 16, No. 7).

"Cedar Chest, The," *The Evangelical Methodist* (March 2000, Vol. 77, No. 10).

"Cedar Replaced Ford at L.C.W.E.," *Calvary Contender* (August 15, 1992, Vol. 9, No. 16).

"Censorship in Our Schools," Distributed by the National Coalition Against Censorship (Received September 11, 1997).

Cerio, Gregory; Clift, Eleanor; and Leonard, Elizabeth Ann. "Playing a Losing Game?," *Newsweek* (May 4, 1992).

Cerminara, Gina. *Many Lives, Many Loves* (NY: William Morrow and Company, Inc., 1963).

"CFR Admits It's Been in Control, The," *Christian World Report* (July/August 1994).

Chambers, Claire. *The SIECUS Circle: A Humanist Revolution* (Belmont, MA: Western Islands, 1977).

Chambers, Joseph R. "Modern Bible Versions: The De-Absolutionizing of God's Word," *USA Today's Front Page* (June 1994).

Chambers, Joseph R. *Spirit of Babylon: A New World Order* (Charlotte, NC: Paw Creek Ministries, n.d.).

Champagne, Robert A. "Evangelical Catholics," *Dorea Ministries* (Winter 1992, Vol. 4).

"Champions of Mental Health," *Psychology Today* (June 2001, Vol. 34, No. 3).

Chao, Jonathan. "How Evangelical Is the Three Self People's Movement: An Open Letter to Christianity Today," *O Timothy* (1994, Vol. 2, Issue 5).

Chaplin, George. "Lecture in May Will Focus on Need to Preserve Planet," *The Honolulu Advertiser* (April 12, 1997).

Character Counts (1994, Special Issue).

Charisma and Christian Life (June 1988, Vol. 13, No. 11).

"Charismatic Adulterer," *Christian News* (January 11, 1993, Vol. 31, No. 2).

"Charismatic Professor to Pastor Nation's Foremost Liberal Church," *Ministries Today* (May/June 1989).

"Charismatics and Roman Catholics," *Dorea Ministries* (January-March 1992).

"Charismatics Believe God Is Building Bridges," *O Timothy* (1995, Vol. 12, Issue 4).

"Charles Colson to Join Mother Teresa and Pagan Religious Leaders at Parliament of the World's Religions," *O Timothy* (1993, Vol. 10, Issue 6).

"Charles Stanley's Handbook for Christian Living," *Christian News* (March 5, 2001, Vol. 39, No. 10).

Cherry, Kittredge and Mitulski, James. "We Are the Church Alive, the Church with AIDS," *The Christian Century* (January 27, 1988, Vol. 105, No. 3).

Chesen, Eli S. *Religion May Be Hazardous to Your Health* (New York, NY: Peter H. Wyden, Inc., 1972).

Cheshire, William P. "Margaret Sanger: Weeding Out Misfits to Get Thoroughbreds," *Wisconsin Report* (November 14, 1991, Vol. 16, No. 44).

Chick, Jack T. *Smokescreens: Who Is the "Whore" of Revelation? A Biblical and Historical Answer* (Chino, CA: Chick Publications, 1983).

Chick, Jack T. *The Curse of Baphomet* (Chino, CA: Chick Publications, 1991).

Chicone, Christie L. "1,900 Catholics Respond to Billy Graham's Call," *The Catholic Standard and Times* (July 16, 1992).

Children's Defense Fund Annual National Conference.

"Children's Defense Fund: Together We Stand for Children."

"China and the Kings of the East," *Prophetic Observer* (Mary 2001, Vol. 8, No. 5).

"China Brands Unregistered Churches 'Evil Cults,'" *Christian News* (January 17, 2000, Vol. 38, No. 3).

"China Christian Council Controlled by Communists," *Calvary Contender* (August 15, 2000, Vol. 17, No. 16).

"China Christian Council to Lead Delegation to UCC Nat'l Office," *Christian News* (July 16, 2001, Vol. 39, No. 29).

"China Church Cracking Down on House Churches," *Christian News* (February 12, 2001, Vol. 39, No. 7).

"China Clamps Down on Its Seminaries," *Christian News* (November 20, 2000, Vol. 38, No. 43).

"China Destroying Churches," *Christian News* (January 1, 2001, Vol. 39, No. 1).

"China Persecutes Christians," *Calvary Contender* (August 15, 1997, Vol. 14, No. 16).

"China Revealing Its Red Color," *Calvary Contender* (January 1, 2001, Vol. 18, No. 1).

"China Revealing Its Red Color," *Christian News* (January 15, 2001, Vol. 39, No. 3).

"China Signs UN Treaty, Arrests Christians," *Calvary Contender* (December 15, 1998, Vol. 25, No. 24).

"China Targets House Church Christians," *Christian News* (October 30, 2000, Vol. 38, No. 40).

"China," *Women of Vision 2000* (2000, First Quarter).

"China: House Churches Under Siege," *Pray!* (November/December 2000, Issue 21).

"Chinese Christian Leader Released from Prison," *Christian News* (September 18, 2000, Vol. 38, No. 34).

"Chinese Christians Held Hostage Also," *Christian News* (April 23, 2001, Vol. 39, No. 17).

"Chinese Communist Party Structure," *Newsletter from a Christian Ministry* (April 1, 1993, Vol. 2, No. 6).

"Chinese Government Targets Seminarians," *Moody* (January-February 2001, Vol. 101, No. 3).

"Chinese Underground," *U. S. News & World Report* (June 11, 2001, Vol. 130, No. 23).

Chiniquy, Charles. *50 Years in the 'Church' of Rome: The Conversion of a Priest* (Chino, CA: Chick Publications, 1985 Edition).

Chiniquy, *The Priest, the Woman, and the Confessional* (Chino, CA: Chick Publications, n.d.).

Chinmoy, Sri. *Selfless Service-Light.*

Chopra, Deepak. *Ageless Body Timeless Mind* (New York, NY: Harmony Books, 1993).

Christ, Carol P. *Laughter of Aphrodite: Reflections on a Journey to the Goddess* (New York, NY: Harper and Row Publishers, Inc., 1987).

"Christendom Is Ending," *Christian News* (September 25, 2000, Vol. 38, No. 35).

Christian Anti-Communism Crusade (July 15, 1993).

Christian Century, The (April 4, 2001, Vol. 118, No. 11).

Christian Century, The (November 20-27, 1991, Vol. 108, No. 34).

"Christian Century...Mouthpiece for Modernism, The," *Christian News* (February 10, 1997, Vol. 35, No. 6).

"Christian Legacy of Martin Luther King, The," *Christianity Today* (June 16, 1989, Vol. 33, No. 9).

Christian News (April 11, 1994, Vol. 32, No. 15).

Christian News (April 24, 1995, Vol. 33, No. 17).

Christian News (December 4, 2000, Vol. 38, No. 45).

Christian News (December 14, 1998, Vol. 36, No. 46).

Christian News (December 20, 1993, Vol. 31, No 47).

Christian News (December 26, 1994, Vol. 32, No. 48).

Christian News (February 1, 1993, Vol. 31, No. 5).

Christian News (February 9, 1998, Vol. 36, No. 6).

Christian News (February 10, 1997, Vol. 35, No. 6).

Christian News (February 12, 2001, Vol. 39, No. 7).

Christian News (February 24, 1997, Vol. 35, No. 8).

Christian News (February 26, 1996, Vol. 34, No. 9).

Christian News (February 28, 1994, Vol. 32, No. 9).

Christian News (February 28, 2000, Vol. 38, No. 9).

Christian News (January 3, 2000, Vol. 38, No. 1).

Christian News (January 6, 1997, Vol. 35, No. 1).

Christian News (January 17, 2000, Vol. 38, No. 3).

Christian News (July 1, 1996, Vol. 34, No. 27).

Christian News (March 6, 2000, Vol. 38, No. 10).

Christian News (May 29, 2000, Vol. 38, No. 22).

Christian News (November 9, 1992, Vol. 30, No. 41).

Christian News (November 27, 2000, Vol. 38, No. 44).

Christian News (October 4, 1999, Vol. 37, No. 36).

Christian News (October 14, 1991, Vol. 29, No. 37).

Christian News (October 25, 1999, Vol. 37, No. 39).

Christian News (October 28, 1991, Vol. 29, No. 39).

Christian News (September 9, 1996, Vol. 34, No. 33).

Christian Perspectives (Fall/Winter 1997, Vol. 10, No. 2).

Christian View of the News (October 10, 1994, Vol. 19, No. 19).

"Christian Witnessing to an Alternative," *The Witness* (November 1996, Vol. 79, No. 11).

Christian World Report, The (February 1991, Vol. 3, No. 2).

Christian World Report, The (June 1989, Vol. 1, No. 4).

Christian, John D. *Gladiator: A Masterpiece of Nazi Propaganda* (New Zealand, Underground Press, 2000).

Christian, John D. *Gladiator: A Masterpiece of Nazi Propaganda* (Postscript) (New Zealand, Underground Press, 2001).

"Christianity Afflicted with Doctrines of Devils," *Flashpoint* (December 1996, Vol. 96-12).

Christianity Today (April 25, 1994).

Christianity Today (February 8, 1980).

Christianity Today (January 8, 1996).

Christianity Today (November 22, 1993, Vol. 37, No. 14).

"Christianity Today Is No Longer the Conservative Evangelical Publication It Was When It Began," *Christian News* (April 21, 1997, Vol. 35, No. 16).

"Christianity Today Promotes Leftist," *Christian News* (May 4, 1992, Vol. 30, No. 18).

"*Christianity Today* Promotes Sider," *Calvary Contender* (July 1, 1992, Vol. 9, No. 13).

"Christianity Today's Smokescreen About Immoral Article," *Christian News* (June 19, 2000, Vol. 38, No. 25).

"Christians and Muslims for Peace," *Endtime* (September/October 1999).

Christians Evangelizing Catholics (February 1993).

"Christians Interested in Salvation," *Christian News* (May 13, 1996, Vol. 34, No. 20).

"Christians Warned," *The Witness* (April 1994, Vol. 34, No. 4).

Chronology of Education with Quotable Quotes (Highland City, FL: Pro Family Forum, Inc., 1994, Updated, bound volume).

"Chuck Colson Organization Spreading Misinformation," *O Timothy* (1994, Vol. 11, Issue 2).

"Chuck Colson's Historic Secret Mission: Undo the Protestant Reformation," *Flashpoint* (November 1994).

"Church Coffers Fund Marxist Revolution," *The Christian World Report* (June 1989, Vol. 1, No. 4).

"Church Leaders Praise Bill Clinton's 'Spirituality,'" *Christian News* (November 13, 2000, Vol. 38, No. 42).

"Church Notes," *The Aurea Flamma—OTB* (July 1986).

"Church That AIDS Built?, The," *The Christian World Report* (June 1989, Vol. 1, No. 4).

"Church Workers Still Support Communism in Nicaragua," *The Christian World Report* (December 1990, Vol. 2, No. 9).

"Churches Demolished in Wenzhou, China," *Herald of His Coming* (April 2001, Vol. 60, No. 4).

Churchward, Albert. *Signs and Symbols of Primordial Man* (London, England: George Allen and Company, Ltd., 1913).

CIB Bulletin (December 1989, Vol. 5, No. 12).

CIB Bulletin (January 1990, Vol. 6, No. 1).

CIB Bulletin (January 1991, Vol. 7, No. 1).

CIB Bulletin (July 1987, Vol. 3, No. 7).

CIB Bulletin (May 1989, Vol. 5, No. 5).

CIB Bulletin (May 1990, Vol. 6, No. 5).

CIB Bulletin, (September 1990, Vol. 6, No. 9).

Cirlot, J. E., Translated by Sage, Jack. *A Dictionary of Symbols* (New York, NY: Philosophical Library, Inc., 1972).

Claire, Merwyn. "The Festival Week of the New Group of World Servers," *Diamond Light* (1998, No. 3).

Clausen, Henry C. *Masons Who Helped Shape Our Nation* (The Supreme Council, 33°, Ancient and Accepted Scottish Rite of Freemasonry Southern Jurisdiction, U. S. A., 1976).

Clausen, Henry C. *To a Non-Mason: You Must Seek Masonic Membership!* (Washington, D.C.: The Supreme Council, 33°, Mother Council of the World, Southern Jurisdiction, USA, 1977).

Clemetson, Lynette and McRoberts, Flynn. "A Confession from Jesse," *Newsweek* (January 29, 2001, Vol. 137, No. 5).

Clift, Eleanor and Leonard, Elizabeth Ann. "Playing a Losing Game?," *Newsweek* (May 4, 1992).

"Clinton and the New World Order," *An American Commentary* (Oklahoma City, OK: Hearthstone Publishing, Ltd., 1993).

"Clinton Desires to Serve God," *Christian News* (May 12, 1997, Vol. 35, No. 19).

"Clinton Honors 'Best-Loved Commie,'" *AIM Report* (December 1994, 23-24).

"Clinton: Saint, or Socialist?," *Calvary Contender* (May 15, 1994, Vol. 11, No. 10).

"Clinton Taps 'Fresh Thinking' Activists," *The Daily Item* (December 12, 1992, Vol. 55, No. 346).

"Clinton's Cynicism Toward Repentance," *Calvary Contender* (September 15, 1998, Vol. 15, No. 18).

"Clipped Comments," *The Presbyterian Layman* (July/August 2000, Vol. 33, No. 4).

Cloud, D. W. "Is Mother Teresa a True Christian?," *Christian News* (September 15, 1997, Vol. 35, No. 33).

Cloud, D. W. "Is Mother Teresa a True Christian?," *O Timothy* (1985, Vol. 2, Issue 1).

Cloud, D. W. *Is the Roman Catholic Changing?* (1984).

Cloud, D. W. "Papal Supremacy," *O Timothy* (1987, Vol. 4, Issue 7).

Cloud, D. W. "Some Frightening Facts About Billy Graham," *O Timothy* (1984, Vol. 1, Issue 4).

Cloud, D. W. "The Church and Its Music," *O Timothy* (1984, Vol. 1, Issue 1).

Cloud, David W. "Amy Grant Says Being Sexy Is Good," *O Timothy* (1991, Vol. 8, Issue 10-12).

Cloud, David W. "Anglican Bishop Honored After Acknowledging Ambiguous Sexuality," *O Timothy* (1995, Vol. 12, Issue 9).

Cloud, David W. "Bible Societies Continue to Produce Corrupted Scriptures," *O Timothy* (1991, Vol. 8, Issue 2).

Cloud, David W. "Billy Graham's Disobedience to the Word of God."

Cloud, David W. "Billy Graham's Disobedience to the Word of God" (Updated March 2, 1999).

Cloud, David W. "Billy Graham's Disobedience," *O Timothy* (1995, Vol. 12, Issue 11).

Cloud, David W. "Bishop K. H. Ting—China's Master of Deceit," *O Timothy* (1986, Vol. 3, Issue 3).

Cloud, David W. "C. S. Lewis and Evangelicals Today," *Christian News* (April 30, 2001, Vol. 39, No. 18).

Cloud, David W. "Can Evangelicals Be Trusted on Bible Versions?," *O Timothy* (1995, Vol. 12, No. 6).

Cloud, David W. "Charismatics and the Pope of Rome," *O Timothy* (1989, Vol. 6, Issues 3-4).

Cloud, David W. "Charismatics Join Hands with World Council Heretics," *O Timothy* (1991, Vol. 8, Issue 5).

Cloud, David W. "Christian Leaders and the Pope," *O Timothy* (1991, Vol. 8, Issue 2).

Cloud, David W. "Contemporary Christian Music and Rome," (Part II), *The Evangelical Methodist* (June 1999, Vol. 77, No. 6).

Cloud, David W. "Contemporary Christian Music and the Rock Beat," *O Timothy* (1988, Vol. 5, Issue 8).

Cloud, David W. "Dynamic Equivalency: Death Knell of Pure Scripture" *O Timothy* (1990).

Cloud, David W. "Evangelical Catholics," *O Timothy* (1992, Vol. 9, Issue 7).

Cloud, David W. "Evangelical Doublespeak and the Blood of Christ," *O Timothy* (1987, Vol. 4, Issue 1).

Cloud, David W. "Evangelical Entanglement with Romanism: How Serious Is the Back-to-Rome Movement?," *Foundation* (January/February 1987).

Cloud, David W. "Evangelical Leaders Befriend the Mother of Harlots," *O Timothy* (1988, Vol. 5, Issue 4).

Cloud, David W. "Evangelicals and Modernist Robert Schuller," *O Timothy* (1993, Vol. 10, Issue 7).

Cloud, David W. *Flirting with Rome: Evangelical Entanglement with Roman Catholicism (Volume 1—Billy Graham)* (Oak Harbor, WA: Way of Life Literature, 1993).

Cloud, David W. *Flirting with Rome: Evangelical Entanglement with Roman Catholicism (Volume 4—The Charismatics)* (Oak Harbor, WA: Way of Life Literature, 1993).

Cloud, David W. "Flirting with Rome: Evangelical Entanglement with Roman Catholicism (Volume 3—The Southern Baptist Convention)," *O Timothy* (1993).

Cloud, David W. "Fundamentalism, Modernism, and New-Evangelicalism," *O Timothy* (1995, Vol. 12, No. 1).

Cloud, David W. "Goal of New Orleans '87—Apostate and Compromised Church Leaders Making Plans to Unite and Create a 'Christian' World," *O Timothy* (1987, Vol. 4, Issue 10-11).

Cloud, David W. "Harry Potter Witchcraft Church Service" *Christian News* (September 25, 2000, Vol. 38, No. 35).

Cloud, David W. "How to Stop the Crime Epidemic," *O Timothy* (1994, Vol. 11, Issue 12).

Cloud, David W. *Is the Roman Catholic Changing?* (Oak Harbor, WA: Way of Life Literature, 1995 Edition).

Cloud, David W. "Jack Hayford and Rome," *O Timothy* (1995, Vol. 12, Issue 7).

Cloud, David W. "Jerry Falwell Praises Modernist Bonhoeffer," *O Timothy* (1993, Vol. 10, Issue 8).

Cloud, David W. "Jimmy Carter Leaves the Southern Baptist Convention—Again," *Christian News* (November 6, 2000, Vol. 38, No. 41).

Cloud, David W. "Liberation Theology: Christianized Marxism," *O Timothy* (1988, Vol. 5, Issue 1).

Cloud, David W. "Modernism in the Southern Baptist Convention," *O Timothy* (1994, Vol. 11, Issue 1).

Cloud, David W. *Mom and Dad Sleep While the Children Rock in Satan's Cradle* (Oak Harbor, Washington, Way of Life Literature, 1991 Edition).

Cloud, David W. "Mother Teresa's Successor Worships Hindu Idols," *Christian News* (January 24, 2000).

Cloud, David W. "Norman Vincent Peale: Apostle of Self-Esteem," *Christian News* (May 12, 1997, Vol. 35, No. 19).

Cloud, David W. "Norman Vincent Peale: Apostle of Self-Esteem," *O Timothy* (1994, Vol. 11, Issue 2).

Cloud, David W. "Paul Yonggi Cho and Rome," *O Timothy* (1995, Vol. 12, Issue 6).

Cloud, David W. "Some Questions for Desmond Tutu," *O Timothy* (1987, Vol. 4, Issues 3-4).

Cloud, David W. "Roman Catholic Bishop Helps Dedicate New United Bible Societies Translation," *O Timothy* (1992, Vol. 9, Issue 11).

Cloud, David W. "Roman Catholic Church Awards Amy Grant," *O Timothy* (1994, Vol. 11, Issue 6).

Cloud, David W. "Roman Catholicism Still Follows the Council of Trent," *O Timothy* (1992, Vol. 9, Issue 6).

Cloud, David W. "The Apostasy of the English Revised Version," *O Timothy* (1995, Vol. 12, Issue 10).

Cloud, David W. "The Attack upon the Blood Atonement," *O Timothy* (1987, Vol. 4, Issue 1).

Cloud, David W. "The Catholic Church Still Grants Indulgences," *O Timothy* (1991, Vol. 8, Issue 2).

Cloud, David W. "The Course of This Church Age," *O Timothy* (1985, Vol. 2, Issue 3).

Cloud, David W. "The Day of Prayer for World Peace," *O Timothy* (1994, Vol. 11, Issue 3).

Cloud, David W. "The Graceless Bible for the Bart Simpson Generation," *O Timothy* (1991, Vol. 8, Issue 6).

Cloud, David W *The Living Bible: Blessing or Curse?* (Oak Harbor, WA: Way of Life Literature, 1991).

Cloud, David W. "The New Catholic Catechism," *O Timothy* (1995, Vol. 12, Issue 1).

Cloud, David W. "The Positive Jesus," *O Timothy* (1995, Vol. 12, Issue 10).

Cloud, David W. "The Preachers Who Influenced Bill Clinton," *Christian News* (March 26, 2001, Vol. 39, No. 13).

Cloud, David W. "The Roman Catholic Mass," *O Timothy* (1995, Vol. 12, Issue 4).

Cloud, David W. "The Sinaiticus and Vaticanus Manuscripts Were Found in Demonized Places," *O Timothy* (1994, Vol. 11, Issue 6).

Cloud, David W. "Two Homosexuals and the New International Version" (1997).

Cloud, David W. "Two Homosexuals and the NIV" (December 4, 1997).

Cloud, David W. "Virginia Mollenkott," Fundamental Baptist Information Service (January 25, 1997).

Cloud, David W. "WCC Conference Honors Sophia Goddess, Gives Ovation to Lesbians," *O Timothy* (1994, Vol. 11, Issue 3).

Cloud, David W. "What Is Judaism?," *O Timothy* (1988, Vol. 5, Issue 2).

Cloud, David W. "World Council of Churches Baptizes Heathenism," *Plains Baptist Challenger* (June 1994).

Cloud, David W. "World Council of Churches Promotes Female Gods," *O Timothy* (1992, Vol. 9, Issue 1).

Cloud, David W. "World Vision and Rome," *O Timothy* (1995, Vol. 12, Issue 2).

Cloud, David W. "Wycliffe Bible Translators: Whither Bound?," *O Timothy* (1991).

Clymer, R. Swinburne. *The Mysteries of Osiris or Ancient Egyptian Initiation* (Quakertown, PA: The Philosophical Publishing Company, 1951, Revised Edition).

Coleman, John. *The Conspirators' Hierarchy: The Committee of 300* (Carson City, NV: Joseph Publishing Company, Third Edition, 1994).

"College Loses Twice in Financial Scandals," *The News-Item* (July 5, 1995, Vol. 27), No. 224).

Collier, Peter and Horowitz, David. *The Rockefellers: An American Dynasty* (NY: Holt, Rinehart and Winston, n.d.).

Collins, B. F. "Religious Freedom Restoration Act of 1993: Beware the Greeks Bearing Gifts," *The Florida Forum* (Fall 1994).

Collum, Danny with Horton, Myles. "Building Democracy in the Mountains" *Sojourners* (April 1986).

"Colson a Speaker at Westminster," *Calvary Contender* (September 15, 1995, Vol. 12, No. 18).

"Colson at PK-Memphis," *Calvary Contender* (November 15, 1996, Vol. 13, No. 22).

Colson, Chuck with Vaughn, Ellen Santilli. *The Body* (Dallas, TX: Word Publishing, 1996 Edition).

"Colson, Palau to Gordon-Conwell Board," *Calvary Contender* (September 15, 1999, Vol. 16, No. 18).

"Colson, Palau to Gordon-Conwell Board," *Despatch Magazine* (September 1999, Vol. 11, No. 3).

"Colson: General Teachings/Activities," Biblical Discernment Ministries.

"Colson's Prison Fellowship Honors RC Priest Neuhaus," *Calvary Contender* (March 15, 1998, Vol. 15, No. 6).

"Columbia University," Softkey Multimedia Inc., Infopedia (1996).

"Comments Regarding 'Evangelicals and Catholics Together,'" *Christians Evangelizing Catholics* (April 1995).

"Common Cause Honors Communist Pete Seeger," *Christian News* (July 19, 1999, Vol. 37, No. 29).

Common Sense for Today (November/December 1995).

Communion of Saints: Sanctity Through the Centuries, The (Still River, MA: n.p., 1967).

"Communion Service at Promise Keepers Clergy Conference," *Christian News* (April 1, 1996, Vol. 34, No. 14).

"Communism, Socialism and the New World Religion," *The Florida Forum* (Winter 1998).

"Communist Mandela Given Hero's Welcome in Canada, U. S.," *The Christian World Report* (July 1990, Vol. 2, No.6).

"Communist Puppets Are Hoodwinking Lutherans," *Christian News* (November 15, 1999, Vol. 37, No. 42).

Complete Occult Digest A to Z (North Hollywood, CA: International Imports, 1984).

Compton, Piers. *The Broken Cross: The Hidden Hand in the Vatican* (Cranbrook, Western Australia: Veritas Publishing Company Pty. Ltd., 1984).

"Comrades Seeger and King, Our 'Heroes,'" *Christian News* (June 23, 1997).

"Congressional Clearinghouse on the Future," *What's Next* (Fall 1985), Vol. 9, No. 8).

Conspirators' Hierarchy: The Committee of 300, The (Carson City, NV: Joseph Publishing Company, 1994).

Constance Cumbey's New Age Monitor (August-December 1987, Vol. 2, Nos. 3-7).

Contact (Winter 1981-82, Vol. 12, No. 1).

Continuum (Fall/Winter 1995/96).

Continuum (Spring/Summer 1996).

"Contradictions and Ambiguities," *Christian News* (January 29, 2001, Vol. 39, No. 5).

"Convicted and the Compromised, The," *The Day Drawing Near* (July 2000, Vol. 2, No. 2).

"Convicted Baptist Leader Seeking Divorce," *Christian News* (April 23, 2001, Vol. 39, No. 17).

Cook, Cheryl, Gorman, Enid M., and Picciano-Hanson, Lorette, Editors. *A Directory of Environmental Activities and Resources in the North American Religious Community* (New York, NY: Joint Appeal by Religion and Science for the Environment, 1992).

Cook, Wes, Editor. *Masonic Curiosa from the Desk of H. L. Haywood* (Fulton, MO: The Ovid Bell Press, Inc., 1968).

"'Copping a 'Tude,'" *Voice in the Wilderness* (March 2001, Vol. 8, Issue 3).

Cornell, George W. "Clinton Has Ties with 2 Religions" *Associated Press* (January 16, 1993).

Correll, Shirley. "On Stealing Elections and the Electoral College," *The Florida Forum* (Fall 2000).

Correll, Shirley. "Who Are the Gods of the New World Order and What Is a Spiritual U. N.?" (Part I), *The Florida Forum* (Winter 1998).

Correll, Shirley. "Who Are the Gods of the New World Order and What Is a Spiritual U. N.?" (Part III), *The Florida Forum* (Summer 2000).

Correll, Shirley. "Who Are the Gods of the New World Order and What Is a Spiritual U. N.?" (Part IIIg), *The Florida Forum* (Winter 2000).

Correll, Shirley. "Who Are the Gods of the New World Order and What Is a Spiritual U. N.?" (Part IV), *The Florida Forum* (Spring 2001).

Correll, Shirley. "Will the Communist Plans for America Be Fulfilled in Louisville?," *The Florida Forum* (Winter 2000).

Cosijns, Lucien F. "Interfaith Dialogue Guidelines," *IRFWP Newsletter* (Spring 1998, Vol. 6, No. 1).

"Cosmolatry: The Worship of Gaia," *EcoiLogic* (May 1995, No. 26).

Costella, Dennis W. "Should We All Get Together?," *Foundation* (January-February 2000, Vol. 21, Issue 1).

Cotter, John. *A Study in Syncretism* (Flesherton, Ontario: Canadian Intelligence Publications, n.d.).

"Could It Be Possible That Rush Is a Closet 'Kook?,'" *The Times Leader* (March 23, 1996, Vol. 4, No. 93).

Council of Conservative Citizens' Guide to Martin Luther King, Jr. Holiday (Jasper, AL: n.p., n.d.).

Council on Foreign Relations: Annual Report July 1, 1987-June 30, 1988.

Council on Foreign Relations: Annual Report July 1, 1990-June 30, 1991.

Council on Foreign Relations: Annual Report July 1, 1992-June 30, 1993.

Council on Foreign Relations: Annual Report July 1, 1994-June 30, 1995.

Cowles, John H. "Italian Masonry Under Fascist Regime," *The New Age Magazine* (January 1926, Vol. 34, No. 1).

Creation (August 1984).

Creation Spirituality (March/April 1992).

"Creative Partnership Initiatives with the AD2000 Movement," *Mission Frontiers* (July-August 1993, Vol. 15, No. 7-8).

Creme, Benjamin. *Network News* (April/May 1987), Vol. 4, Nos. 4-5).

Creme, Benjamin. *The Reappearance of the Christ and the Masters of Wisdom* (North Hollywood, CA: Tara Center, 1980).

Creme, Benjamin. "Spirit of Sanctity," *The Emergence* (January/February 1995, Vol. 13, No. 1).

Crisis, The (October 1992, Vol. 99, No. 7).

"Critical Thinking and Religion in the Schools," *An American Commentary* (Oklahoma City, OK: Hearthstone Publishing, Ltd., 1993).

"Crowds Flock to 'Pensacola Outpouring,'" *Calvary Contender* (March 15, 1997, Vol. 14, No. 5).

Cry for Renewal: Biblical Faith and Spiritual Politics, The (May 23, 1995).

"CT Praised C. S. Lewis," *Calvary Contender* (May 1, 2001, Vol. 18, No. 9).

"CT Praises Liberal Catholic Theologian," *Calvary Contender* (October 15, 1998, Vol. 15, No. 20).

"*CT* Promotes Pope Video," *Calvary Contender* (April 15, 1998, Vol. 15, No. 8).

Cumbey, Constance. *A Planned Deception: The Staging of a New Age "Messiah"* (East Detroit, MI: Pointe Publishing, Inc., 1985).

Cumbey, Constance. *The Hidden Dangers of the Rainbow: The New Age Movement and Our Coming Age of Barbarism* (Shreveport, LA: Huntington House, Inc., Revised Edition, 1983).

Cutler, Howard C. "The Mindful Monk," *Psychology Today* (June 2001, Vol. 34, No. 3).

Dager, Albert James. "C. S. Lewis: The Man and His Myths," *Media Spotlight* (1985).

Dager, Albert James. "Evangelicals and Catholics Together: The New Ecumenical Accord in Light of Vatican II," *Media Spotlight* (Vol. 15, No. 2).

Dager, Albert James. "Holy Laughter: Rodney Howard-Browne and the Toronto Blessing," *Media Spotlight* (Special Report).

Dager, Albert James. *Inner Healing: A Biblical Analysis* (Santa Ana, CA: Tri-Level Press, 1986).

Dager, Albert James. *Out on a Limb* (Costa Mesa, CA: Media Spotlight, 1987).

Dager, Albert James. "Parliament of the World's Religions to Meet: Chuck Colson Receives Templeton Prize," *Media Spotlight* (Vol. 15, No. 1).

Dager, Albert James. "Promise Keepers: Is What You See What You Get?" *Media Spotlight* (Received November 10, 1994).

Dager, Albert James. "Promise Keepers' D.C. Covenant Agenda for Churches Revealed," *Media Spotlight* (1997, Vol. 20, No. 2).

Dager, Albert James. *The Vineyard: History, Teachings and Practices* (Redmond, WA: Media Spotlight, 1996).

Dager, Albert James. *The World Christian Movement: A Great Delusion Leading to the Religio-Political State of the Anti-Christ* (Redmond, WA: Sword Publishers, 2001).

Dager, Albert James. "The World Christian Movement: Evangelism Vs. Evangelization," *Media Spotlight* (1999, Vol. 22, No. 1).

Dager, Albert James. "World Christian Movement—Part 3: Toward the New World Order, The," *Media Spotlight* (1999, Vol. 22, No. 3).

"Dalai Lama Disappoints India's Christians," *Mission Frontiers* (March 2001, Vol. 23, No. 1).

Dallas Morning News (July 27, 1996).

Dallas Morning News (October 14, 1995).

"Dallas Seminary Doings," *Calvary Contender* (February 1, 1998, Vol. 15, No. 3).

Dancy, Shelvia. "China Stepping Up Crackdown on Religion," *Christian News* (December 25, 2000, Vol. 38, No. 48).

Danielou, Alain. *The Gods of India* (New York, NY: Inner Traditions International Ltd., 1985).

Daniels, Eugene. *A Protestant Looks at the Catholic Church in Mission* (Monrovia, CA: MARC, 1993).

Day Drawing Near, The (March 1999, Vol. 1, No. 6).

"DC Talk Mixes Secular & 'Sacred,'" *Calvary Contender* (September 1, 1996, Vol. 13, No. 17).

de Riencourt, Amaury. *The Eye of Shiva: Eastern Mysticism and Science* (William Morrow and Company, Inc., 1980).

de Souza, Marshall, "IRFWP United Kingdom" *IRFWP Newsletter* (Spring 1998, Vol. 6, No. 1).

De Souza, Raymond J. "In Special Act, Pope Puts Mary's Seal on Great Jubilee," *National Catholic Register* (October 22-28, 2000, Vol. 76, No. 43).

Dearmore, James H. "Who Built Modern South Africa," *O Timothy* (1987, Vol. 4, Issue 3-4).

Dearth, Nona. "Abandoning Occult for Christ," *The Patriot Ledger* (November 10, 1979).

"Deception of Billy Graham, The," *Newsletter from a Christian Ministry* (July 1, 1993, Vol. 2, No. 10).

"Deception on Religion in China and AP Features, The," *Christian News* (October 4, 1999, Vol. 37, No. 36).

"Deception: 'What Killed the Rat?,'" *Calvary Contender* (March 15, 2000, Vol. 17, No. 6).

"Deceptive New Age 'Service' and 'Light', The," *The Christian World Report* (February 1991, Vol. 3, No. 2).

Decker, J. Edward. *Freemasonry: Satan's Door to America?* (Issaquah, WA: Free the Masons Ministries, n.d.).

Decker, J. Edward. *The Question of Freemasonry* (Issaquah, WA: Free the Masons Ministries, n.d.).

Decker, J. Edward. *The Question of Freemasonry* (Lafayette, LA: Huntington House Publishers, 1992).

"Defending the Institutions Against the New Lenins," *The Daily Telegraph* (April 3, 1979).

"Deficit-Plagued NCC Faces Shaky Future," *The Presbyterian Layman* (July 2001, Vol. 34, No. 5).

"Deficit-Plagued NCC Receives Favorable Review," *The Presbyterian Layman* (July 2001, Vol. 34, No. 5).

Democratic Left (November/December 1984, Vol. 12, No. 6).

"Democrats Endorse Gay/Lesbian Rights," *Task Force Report* (Winter 1988).

"DeMolay Hall of Fame," *The Scottish Rite Journal* (March 1994, Vol. 102, No. 3).

DeMoss, Nancy Leigh. Executive Editor, *The Rebirth of America* (Arthur S. DeMoss Foundation, 1986).

Denslow, William R. *10,000 Famous Freemasons* (Vol. I) (n.p., 1957).

Denslow, William R. *10,000 Famous Freemasons* (Vol. II) (n.p., 1958).

Denslow, William R. *10,000 Famous Freemasons* (Vol. III) (n.p., 1959).

Denslow, William R. *10,000 Famous Freemasons* (Vol. IV) (n.p., 1961).

Denslow, William R. *Freemasonry and the American Indian* (n.p., 1956).

"Desmond Tutu," *Christian News* (March 5, 2001, Vol. 39, No. 10).

"Desmond Tutu—the Cursing Archbishop!," *O Timothy* (1988, Vol. 5, Issue 4).

Despatch Magazine (June 2001, Vol. 13:2).

Despatch Magazine (September 1994, Vol. 6:3).

Despatch Magazine (September 1996, Vol. 8, No. 3).

DeWeese, Tom. "Radical Greens Use Churches to Force Senate Support of UN's Global Warming Treaty."

"Dialectics: Perpetual Process of the Ruling Elite," *Christian Conscience* (September 1995, Vol. 1, No. 8).

Dibble, Dominic. "Transforming the Planet—A Question of Goodwill," *The Festival Week of the New Group of World Servers* (New York, NY: Lucis Trust, n.d.).

"Did You Know?," *The Good Newsletter* (November/December 1996, Vol. 2, Issue 12).

"Dietrich Bonhoeffer," Softkey Multimedia Inc., Infopedia (1996).

"Dietrich Bonhoeffer," *The BDM Letter* (July/August 1995, Vol. 4, No. 4).

"Dietrich Bonhoeffer: Heroic Christian Thinker & Martyr or Poor Deceived False Prophet?" (Biblical Discernment Ministries, n.d.).

"Digging in the Walls," *O Timothy,*(1995, Vol. 12, Issue 10).

"Dinkins Appoints Lesbians," *The Christian World Report* (December 1990, Vol. 2, No. 9).

"Disarmament of America, The," *The Florida Forum* (Spring 1996).

"Disrespect for Traditional Religion," *The Florida Forum* (Spring 2001).

Distant Drums (August 1995, Vol. 16, No. 1).

Distant Drums (December 1980, Vol. 2, No. 5).

Distant Drums (March 1981, Vol. 3, No. 1).

Distant Drums (March 1986, Vol. 8, No. 1).

Distant Drums (May 1986, Vol. 8, No. 2).

Distant Drums (November 1982, Vol. 4, No. 5).

Distant Drums (November 1989, Vol. 11, No. 3).

"Divorce Rampant Among Contemporary Christian Musicians," *Christian News* (January 15, 2001, Vol. 39, No. 3).

Dobbs, Zygmund. *Keynes at Harvard: Economic Deception As a Political Credo* (West Sayville, NY: Probe Research, Inc., 1969 Edition).

"Dobson Touts Ecumenical Hero Dietrich Bonhoeffer," *Despatch Magazine* (September 1998, Vol. 10, No. 3).

Dobson, James. *Dr. James Dobson Discusses America's Choice: Nine Key Issues That Will Shape Our Future*, (Colorado Springs, CO: Focus on the Family, 2000).

"Doctrine Divides," *Calvary Contender* (April 1, 2000, Vol. 17, No. 7).

"Doctrine on Display," *The Perilous Times* (February 1999, Vol. 20, No. 12).

Dominick, Mac, et. al., "The New Age Movement—Satan's Counterfeit of the Truth."

Don Bell Reports (August 15, 1994, Vol. 41, No. 16).

Don Bell Reports (January 10, 1986), Vol. 33, No. 2).

Don Bell Reports (September 13, 1993, Vol. 40, No. 18).

Donaldson, Scott. *Archibald MacLeish: An American Life* (New York, NY: Houghton Mifflin Company, 1992).

Donohue, Amy. "How John Templeton Got Rich," *Philadelphia* (October 1996).

"Don't Call Schuller a Christian," *Prophecy Corner and the Nosh Box* (August 1999, Vol. 4, Issue 8).

"Dr. Billy Graham, the WCC and NCC and Evangelicals and Roman Catholics" (Received October 22, 1999).

"Dr. Paul Cedar Pulls Endorsement from *Star of 2000,*" Report from Broadcasters United for Revival and Reformation.

Drickamer, John M. "I Wish It Had Been Christian," *Christian News* (September 15, 1997, Vol. 35, No. 33).

"Drugs Killed Elvis, Doctor Says," reprinted from *St. Louis Post-Dispatch* in *Christian News* (February 19, 2001).

"Drunken Revival Churches Having Trouble," *Christian News* (January 15, 2001, Vol. 39, No. 3).

Dulles, John Foster, *War or Peace* (NY: The Macmillan Company, 1950).

Dumas, Francois Ribadeau. (Translated by Abbott, Elisabeth.) *Cagliostro: Scoundrel or Saint?* (NY: The Orion Press, 1967).

Duncan, Homer. *Humanism in the Light of Holy Scripture* (Lubbock, TX: Missionary Crusader, Third Printing, 1982).

Duncan, Homer. *The Ecumenical Movement in Light of the Holy Scriptures* (Lubbock, TX: MC International Publications, 1980 Edition).

Duncan, Malcolm. *Duncan's Ritual of Freemasonry* (NY: David McKay Company, Inc., n.d.).

Dunn, Charles W. *Campus Crusade: Its Message and Methods* (Greenville, SC: Bob Jones University Press, Inc., 1980).

"Dwight David Eisenhower," Softkey Multimedia Inc., Infopedia (1996).

Dyer, Colin F. W. *Symbolism in Craft Freemasonry* (Middlesex, England: A Lewis [Masonic Publishers] Ltd., 1976).

"Dying for a Desecrated Flag?," *The Christian World Report* (February 1991, Vol. 3, No. 2).

"Dying to Live," *Christian News* (February 26, 2001, Vol. 39, No. 9).

"E. V. Hill a PK Speaker," *Calvary Contender* (February 15, 1996, Vol. 13, No. 4).

"E. V. Hill Defends Lyons," *Christian News* (September 29, 1997, Vol. 35, No. 35).

"E. V. Hill Supports Lyons," *Calvary Contender* (November 15, 1997, Vol. 14, No. 22).

"Earth Charter of the N.W.O., The," *Despatch Magazine* (March 2001, Vol. 13, No. 1).

East Gates Connection (January-March 2000).

"Eastern College," *Calvary Contender* (May 15, 1997, Vol. 14, No. 10).

"Easy Roads to Hell," (Tract printed by the Pilgrim Tract Society).

Eckstrom, Kevin. "NCC, Habitat for Humanity, Launch Partnership," *Christian News* (June 18, 2001, Vol. 39, No. 25).

Eco◆Logic (1997).

Eco◆Logic (May 1995, No. 26).

Eco◆Logic (November/December 1995, No. 29).

"Ecumenical Bandwagon Rolls on to Its Final Doom, The," *The Voice in the Wilderness* (September 2000).

"Ecumenical Confusion and Deception at Graham Conference," *Christian News* (August 7, 2000, Vol. 38, No. 32).

"Ecumenical Consultation on Indulgences," *Despatch Magazine* (March 2001, Vol. 13, No. 1).

"Ecumenical Leaders Work for a One-World Government and Religion," *O Timothy* (1989, Vol. 6, Issue 5).

"Ecumenical Movement Rolls On...Lutherans and Muslims Hold Joint Conference in Wisconsin..., The," *The Vine and Branches* (Summer 1998, Vol. 13, Issue 3).

"Ecumenical Prayer Call," *The Perilous Times* (September 1993, Vol. 15, No. 7).

"Ecumenicalism," *The Perilous Times* (January 2001, Vol. 22, No. 8).

"Ecumenism, 'Global Spirituality' and Mother Teresa," *Christian Inquirer* (April 1985).

"Ecumenist Tells Churches to Take Stronger Action Against 'Global Capitalism,'" *Christian News* (June 26, 2000, Vol. 38, No. 26).

"Ed Dobson and Homosexuals," *Calvary Contender* (September 15, 1997, Vol. 14, No. 18).

"Editor's Testimony to LCMS Convention Committee," *Christian News* (July 16, 2001, Vol. 39, No. 29).

"Educator Calls for Warning Stickers on 'Harry Potter' Books," *Christian News* (April 23, 2001, Vol. 39, No. 17).

Egerton, Brooks. "'If God Himself Gave Freedom,'" *Dallas Morning News* (March 20, 1999).

El-Amin, Mustafa. *Freemasonry: Ancient Egypt and the Islamic Destiny* (Jersey City, NJ: New Mind Productions, 1988).

"ELCA Fills Minds of Youth with Anti-Christian Theology," *Christian News* (September 25, 2000, Vol. 38, No. 35).

"ELCA Publishes Book by Dorothee Soelle," *Calvary Contender* (July 1, 2001, Vol. 18, No. 13).

"ELCA Publishes Book by Marxist 'Theological Atheist,'" *Christian News* (June 4, 2001, Vol. 39, No. 23).

"Elected But Not Yet Inducted into the DeMolay Hall of Fame," *The Scottish Rite Journal* (March 1994, Vol. 102, No. 3).

"Elian Revisited," *Prophetic Observer* (March 2001, Vol. 8, No. 3).

Ellis, Albert. "Is Religiosity Pathological?," *Free Inquiry* (Spring 1988, Vol. 8, No. 2).

Elvin, John. "Armand Hammer: Soviet Agent," *The Schwarz Report* (August 2000, Vol. 40, No. 8).

Elvin, John. "The Hammer-Gore Connection" (Part 1), *The Schwarz Report* (July 2000, Vol. 40, No. 7).

Engle, Randy. "The Roots of Sex Education," *Free World Report* (December 1993, Vol. 2, No. 12).

"Environmental Ecumenism," *Christianity Today* (November 22, 1993, Vol. 37, No. 14).

"Environmental Paganism," *The Midnight Cry* (September 1992).

"Episcopal Bishop Worships in a Buddhist Temple," *O Timothy* (1989, Vol. 6, Issue 5).

Epperson, A. Ralph. *The Unseen Hand: An Introduction to the Conspiratorial View of History* (Tucson, AZ: Publius Press, 1985).

Epstein, Edward. "Gorbachev to Convene MTG in S.F.—Invitees—Bush, Thatcher, Tutu," *Wisconsin Report* (September 21, 1995, Vol. 20, No. 36).

Epstein, Edward Jay. *Dossier: The Secret History of Armand Hammer* (NY: Random House, 1996).

Ericsson, Stephanie. "Simply Divine: A Beginner's Guide to Oracles—Tarot Cards, Rune Stones, the *I Ching,* and Other Tools of Personal Spirituality," *Utne Reader* (March/April 1992, No. 50).

"Erosion of Morality, The," *The Christian World Report* (June 1991, Vol. 3, No. 6).

Estrin, Robin. "Harvard Preacher Takes New Look at Bible," *Christian News* (January 27, 1997, Vol. 35, No. 4).

Eternity (January 1985, Vol. 36, No. 1).

"European Christians Being Swept into Ecumenicism and Pentecostalism," *O Timothy* (1991, Vol. 8, Issue 10-12).

Evangelical Methodist, The (April 2001, Vol. 79, No. 3).

Evangelical Methodist, The (2000, Vol. 78, No. 2).

Evangelical Methodist, The (2000, Vol. 78, No. 4).

Evangelical Methodist, The (December 1993, Vol. 72, No. 10).

Evangelical Methodist, The (March 2000, Vol. 77, No. 10)

Evangelical Methodist, The (May 1998, Vol. 77, No. 5).

"Evangelical, WCC Reps Join in Evangelism Consultation," *Foundation* (July-September 1995, Vol. 16, Issue 4).

"Evangelicals and Catholics: Coming Together," *The Day Drawing Near* (March 1999, Vol. 1, No. 6).

Evangelicals and Catholics Together: The Christian Mission in the Third Millennium (March 29, 1994).

"Evangelicals and Catholics Together: The Christian Mission in the Third Millennium," *O Timothy* (1994, Vol. 11, Issue 5).

"Evangelicals Are Divided Over Series," *The Presbyterian Layman* (September/October 2000).

"Evangelicals May Lose Millions in Ponzi Scheme," *Calvary Contender* (June 15, 1995, Vol. 12, No. 12).

"Evangelicals Promote Catholics More Than Catholics?," *Calvary Contender* (March 15, 2001, Vol. 18, No. 6).

"'Evangelicals' Disbelieve in Hell," *Calvary Contender* (December 15, 1993, Vol. 10, No. 25).

"'Evangelicals' Honor Red China Premier," *Calvary Contender* (May 15, 1999, Vol. 16, No. 10).

"Evangelicals Praising 'Patron Saint' C. S. Lewis," *Christian News* (September 14, 1998, Vol. 36, No. 33).

"Evangelism," *Time* (June 10, 1966).

Evangelist of Truth (April 2001, Vol. 67, No. 4).

Evans, M. Stanton. "Dr. King and the Communists," *Human Events* (February 1, 1986, Vol. 46, No. 5).

"Events," *CLOUTreach* (Spring 1997, Vol. 6, No. 2).

"Evolutionist Carl Sagan Argues for 'Science Over Superstition,'" *Christian News* (December 30, 1996, Vol. 34, No. 49).

"Evolutionist Carl Sagan Argues for 'Science Over Superstition,'" *Christian News* (March 18, 1996, Vol. 34, No. 12).

Ewin, Wilson. *Evangelism: The Trojan Horse of the 1990's* (Compton, Quebec: Quebec Baptist Missions, 1992).

Ewin, Wilson. *The Assimilation of Evangelist Billy Graham into the Roman Catholic Church* (Compton, Quebec: Quebec Baptist Missions, 1992).

Ewin, Wilson. "The Church of Rome: Its Beginning, Evolution, Struggle for World Control and Impending Destruction" *O Timothy* (1989, Vol. 6, Issue 2).

Ewin, Wilson. *The Emerging 666 Peace and the Abolition of Nuclear War* (n.p., 1984).

Ewin, Wilson. *The Spirit of Pentecostal-Charismatic Unity* (Norton, VT: n.p., n.d.).

Ewin, Wilson. *The Vatican-Moscow Alliance and Its Effect Upon Christians* (n.p., n.d.).

Ewin, Wilson. *Today's Evangelicals Embracing the World's Deadliest Cult* (Compton, Quebec: Quebec Baptist Missions, n.d.).

Ewin, Wilson. *Under the New World Order: Evangelicals, Catholics and Israel: Conspiracy of the Ages* (Compton, Quebec: Quebec Baptist Missions, n.d.).

"Exodus 13th or 15th Century B.C., The," *Christian News* (January 4, 1999, Vol. 37, No. 1).

"EXPLORIS: Grand Opening and Connecting the Dots...," *The Florida Forum* (Summer 1999).

"Exposing the New Age," tape by Randall Baer (1989).

"Exposure of Apostasy & Compromise," *The Perilous Times* (May 2000, Vol. 22, No. 3).

"Express Excerpts," *Focus Express* (Winter 2000/2001).

Externalisation of the Hierarchy: Emergence of the Kingdom of God on Earth, The (New York, NY: School for Esoteric Studies, n.d.).

F. A. Newsletter, (June 1986).

"Facts to Consider Concerning AD 2000 Evangelism," *Foundation* (July-September 1995, Vol. 16, Issue 4).

"Faculty News," *Hilltop* (Summer 1997, Vol. 9, No. 1).

Fagan, Myron. Transcript of "Illuminati and the Council on Foreign Relations."

"Falwell Lends a Hand to Habitat," *Calvary Contender* (November 1, 1999, Vol. 16, No. 21).

"Falwell's BBF Address," *Calvary Contender* (March 15, 1999, Vol. 16, No. 6).

"Falwell's Church a Member of SBC for 'Several Years,'" *Calvary Contender* (June 1, 2001, Vol. 18, No. 11).

"Family Album," *Eculink* (Summer 1994), No. 41).

Farah, Joseph. "Jesse: Black, Blue and Red?," *The Schwarz Report* (May 2001, Vol. 41, No. 5).

Farrar, Stewart. *What Witches Do: The Modern Coven Revealed* (Custer, WA: Phoenix Publishing Company, 1983, Revised Edition).

Farrell, Hugh. "The Charismatic Phenomenon in the Church of Rome," *O Timothy* (1986, Vol. 3, Issue 4).

Fate (October 1990, Vol. 43, No. 9 [sic]).

"Federal Agents Confiscate Church and Forcibly Remove Pastor and Members—Fulfilling the Plan of the Communist Internationle," *The Florida Forum* (Winter 2000).

Ferguson, Marilyn. *The Aquarian Conspiracy: Personal and Social Transformation in the 1980s* (Los Angeles, CA: J. P. Tarcher, Inc., 1980).

Ferreira, Cornelia R. "One-World Church Starts Up United Religions on Track—with Modifications," *Wisconsin Report* (November 6, 1997, Vol. 22, No. 43).

Ferreira, Cornelia R. "One-World Church Expected Next Year: San Francisco Chosen As Headquarters," *Wisconsin Report* (November 28, 1996, Vol. 21, No. 46).

Ferreira, Cornelia R. "The Global Ethic: From Golden Rule to Common Ground," *Wisconsin Report* (May 14, 1998).

"Festival Week of the New Group of World Servers" (December 19, 21, and 28, 1998).

"Festivals of the Season," *Festivals* (June/July 1986).

Fiedler, Maureen, and Rabben, Linda, Editors. *Rome Has Spoken...: A Guide to Forgotten Papal Statements, and How They Have Changed Through the Centuries* (New York, NY: The Crossroad Publishing Company, 1998).

Fields, Jim. "The Changing Face of Christianity," *The Evangelical Methodist* (May 2001, Vol. 79, No. 5).

Fields Within Fields...Within Fields (1970, Vol. 3, No. 1).

Findhorn Community, *The Findhorn Garden* (New York, NY: Harper and Row, 1975).

"Finding Heaven on Earth," *The New Age Journal* (January/February 1988, Vol. 4, Issue 1).

Finnegan, Kathy. *Goals 2000: Restructuring Our Schools...Restructuring Society* (Oklahoma City, OK: Hearthstone Publishing, Ltd., 1996).

"First Amendment Case," *Christian News* (December 23, 1996, Vol. 34, No. 48).

Fisher, Paul. "A Syndicated Conspiracy Against God and Man?," *The Observer* (January 17, 1996).

Fisher, Paul. "The Church and the New World Order," *National Educator* (August 1995).

"Five Tips for Social Action," *Freedom Writer Magazine* (March 1996, Vol. 13, No. 2).

Flashpoint (February 1995).

Flashpoint (January 1997, Vol. 97-1).

Flashpoint (May 1998, Vol. 98-5).

Flashpoint (November 1989).

Flashpoint (September 1997, Vol. 97-9).

"Flight Attendant to Sue Schuller," *Calvary Contender* (October 15, 1997, Vol. 14, No. 20).

Florida Forum, The (Fall 1994, Special Edition).

Florida Forum, The (Spring 1998).

Focus Express (May/June 1997).

Focus on the Family (July 1995).

Foer, Franklin. "Running on Their Faith: Bush and Gore Are Making Religion a Big Issue, and Praying Voters Buy the Sermon," *U.S. News & World Report* (December 6, 1999).

"Follow Up on Graham Crusade," *Christian View of the News* (November 10, 1994, Vol. 19, No. 21).

"Following the Money (Still)," *Eco◆Logic* (January/February 1996, No. 30).

"Food for Thought on Music," *The Day Drawing Near* (July 2000, Vol. 2, No. 2).

"For Adults Only?" *Time* (October 27, 1961).

"For Jesse Jackson and His Campaign," *The Nation* (April 16, 1988, Vol. 246, No. 15).

"Ford Foundation Gives Gay-Oriented Denomination $100,000 Grant," *Christian News* (October 26, 1998, Vol. 36, No. 39).

Ford, Marcia. "New Era Scam Involved Millions in Donor Funds," *Christian News* (July 31, 1995, Vol. 33, No. 31).

Forker, Wilbert, Editor. *The Templeton Foundation Prize for Progress in Religion* (Edinburgh: Scottish Academic Press, 1988).

"Forum at Grace Cathedral, The," *URI News Update* (December 1996).

Foundation (January-February 2000, Vol. 21, Issue 1).

Foundation (July-September 1995, Vol. 16, Issue 4).

Foundation (June-August 1991).

"Four Die Waiting for Healing," *The Voice in the Wilderness* (December 2000).

Fournier, Keith A. *Evangelical Catholics* (Nashville, TN: Thomas Nelson, Inc., 1990).

Fowler, Clifton L. *Santa Claus and Christmas* (Denver, CO: Institute Publishing Company, 1928).

Fox, Matthew. *Original Blessing: A Primer in Creation Spirituality* (Santa Fe, NM: Bear & Company, 1983).

Fox, Matthew. *The Coming of the Cosmic Christ* (New York, NY: Harper & Row, Inc., 1988).

Fox, Matthew. *Whee! We, Wee All the Way Home...A Guide to the New Sensual Spirituality,* (Wilmington, NC: Consortium Books, 1976).

Fox, Michael. "Panentheism: Where Animal Rights and Deep Ecology Meet," *Creation* (July/August 1986, Vol. 2, No. 3).

Fox, Robin Lane. *Pagans and Christians* (NY: Alfred S. Knopf, Inc., 1986).

Fox, Sam. "Psychic Letters from Jesus," *Alpha...and Beyond.* Reprinted from the *Weekly World News* April 24, 1984.

Fox, Selena. "Around Circle Sanctuary," *Circle Network News* (Spring 1988, Vol. 10, No. 1).

Frady, Marshall. *Jesse: The Life and Pilgrimage of Jesse Jackson* (NY: Random House, Inc., 1996).

Frame, Randy. "Christianity and Ecology: A Better Mix Than Before," *Christianity Today* (April 23, 1990, Vol. 34, No. 7).

"Franklin Graham Named CEO of Father's Evangelical Association," *Christian News* (November 27, 2000, Vol. 38, No. 44).

"Franklin Graham Named CEO of His Father's Evangelical Association," *The Vine and Branches* (Winter 2001, Vol. 16, Issue 1), p.10.

"Franklin Graham to Speak at Liberty," *Calvary Contender* (May 1, 1996, Vol. 23, No. 9).

"Franklin Graham: Rebel with a Cause," *Calvary Contender* (April 1, 1999, Vol. 16, No. 7).

"Franklin Graham's Ecumenical Festivals," *Voice in the Wilderness* (December 2000).

Franzen, Ernst-Ulrich. "Golden Rule Called Universal: World Religious Parliament Readers 'Global Ethic' Declaration," *Milwaukee Sentinel* (September 4, 1993).

Fraser, Graham. "Maurice Strong Wins Prize for Peace: Canadian Garners U Thant Award," *The Globe and Mail* (May 4, 1996).

"Free Condoms Distributed in New York City Schools," *The Christian World Report* (December 1990, Vol. 2, No. 9).

Free Inquiry (Fall 1990, Vol. 10, No. 4)

Free Inquiry (Summer 1988, Vol. 8, No. 3).

Free Inquiry (Winter 1987/88, Vol. 8, No. 1).

Free Inquiry (Winter 1988/89, Vol. 9, No. 1).

Freedland, Nat. *The Occult Explosion* (NY: G. P. Putnam's and Sons, 1972).

Freedman, C. H. 'Max.' "Hatchet-Job on Wildmon Shows Moral Bankruptcy of His Foes," *AFA Journal* (October 1990, Vol. 14, No. 9).

"Freedom Writer Index," *Freedom Writer* (July/August 1997, Vol. 14, No. 4).

Freemasonry and Religion (The Supreme Council, 33°, Ancient and Accepted Scottish Rite of Freemasonry, Mother Jurisdiction of the World, Southern Jurisdiction, U. S. A., 1977).

"Freemasonry Unmasked in the Vatican," *Flashpoint* (May 1994).

Freethought Today (October 1986, Vol. 3, No. 8).

Frewin, Anthony. *The Book of Days* (London, England: William Collins Sons & Co., Ltd., 1979).

Friedman, Matt. "Like Amsterdam, Is America Headed for Quick Descent?," *AFA Journal* (November-December 2000, Vol. 24, No. 10).

"Friend, Can You Spare A...?," *Creation* (July/August 1986, Vol. 2, No. 3).

Full Moon Story, The (Manhattan Beach, CA: Arcana Workshops, September 1974 Edition).

Fulmer, Rhea, Jeter, Teri, and Riner, Wanda. "Robert Muller's Vision for 2000 A. D.," *The Christian Conscience* (May 1995, Vol. 1, No. 5).

"'Fundamentalist' Bible College for Homosexuals," *Christian News* (July 26, 1999).

"Fundamentalists a Problem for UR," *Calvary Contender* (November 15, 1997, Vol. 14, No. 22).

"Futureworld Expo in San Francisco," *Utopian Classroom* (Spring 1985, Vol. 13, Issue 1).

"G-C Woman Pastor Defines Best/Worst Witness," *Calvary Contender* (October 1, 1995, Vol. 12, No. 19).

Gabler, Mel and Norman. *Humanism in Textbooks* (Longview, TX: n.p., 1983).

Gaines, David P. *The World Council of Churches: A Study of Its Background and History* (Peterborough, NH: Richard R. Smith Company, Inc., 1966).

Gaiter, Dorothy J. "Former NAACP Director Chavis Says He Is Joining Farrakhan's Nation of Islam," *The Wall Street Journal* (February 24, 1997).

"Garfield Bromley Oxnam," Softkey Multimedia Inc., Infopedia (1996).

Garling, Brian. *Global Checkmate by the New Age-New World Order* (Landsborough, Queensland: Endtime Ministries, 1993).

Gary, Jay and Olgy. *The Countdown Has Begun: The Story of the Global Consultation on AD 2000* (Rockville, VA: AD 2000 Global Service Office, 1989).

Gary, Jay. *The Star of 2000: Our Journey Toward Hope* (Colorado Springs, CO: Bimillennial Press, 1994).

"Gay Clergyman Receives a ACLU National Civil Liberties Award," *Christian News* (January 19, 1998, Vol. 36, No. 3).

"Gay Mel White Wrote Books with Evangelicals," *Calvary Contender* (August 15, 1993, Vol. 10, No. 16).

"Gay, Lesbian and Christian," *Kirkridge* (Spring/Summer 1987).

"Gay, Lesbian and Christian," *Kirkridge* (Spring/Summer 1988).

Gaynor, Frank, Editor. *Dictionary of Mysticism* (NY: Philosophical Library, 1953).

Geisst, Charles R. *Monopolies in America: Empire Builders and Their Enemies from Jay Gould to Bill Gates* (Oxford, England: Oxford University Press, 2000).

Gendron, Mike. "Roman Catholicism: Scripture vs. Tradition."

"German Takes Over at WCC," *Associated Press* (September 19, 1992).

"German Theologian to Lead World Council," *Associated Press* (August 29, 1992).

"Get Out of the Kitchen," *World* (February 8, 1992, Vol. 6, No. 34).

"Getting Out of Jail Free: A Conversation with Charles Colson," *Research News & Opportunities in Science and Theology* (July/August 2001, Vol. 1, No. 11/12).

"Getting Together," *The News and Observer* (November 12, 1996).

Geyer, Alan. *The Idea of Disarmament! Rethinking the Unthinkable* (Elgin, IL: The Brethren Press and the Churches' Center for Theology and Public Policy, 1982).

"Gimme That One-World Religion (Part II)," *The Day Drawing Near* (Spring 1997).

"Gimme That One-World Religion," *The Day Drawing Near* (Fall 1996).

Global 2000: An Interview with Mr. and Mrs. William Bowen (Oklahoma City, OK: Southwest Radio Church, 1984).

"Global Connections," *EFA Today* (January-March 1993, Issue No. 2).

"Global Evangelization Course to Be Offered Along the Front Range," *Colorado Christian News* (January 1995, Vol. 6, Issue 6).

"Global Mind Linking" (Part III), *Bold Truth* (Fall 1991).

Globalists: The Power Elite Exposed, The (Oklahoma City, OK: Hearthstone Publishing, 2001).

"Goal for the Year 2000," (May 2, 1991).

"God? Or Just Good Business?," *The Nosh Box* (April 2001, Vol. 6, Issue 4).

Godwin, Jeff. *Dancing with Demons: The Music's Real Master* (Chino, CA: Chick Publications, 1988).

Godwin, Jeff. *Rock & Roll Religion* (Bloomington, IN: The Rock Ministries, 1995).

Godwin, Jeff. *The Devil's Disciples: The Truth About Rock* (Chino, CA: Chick Publications, 1985).

Godwin, Jeff. *What's Wrong with Christian Rock?* (Chino, CA: Chick Publications, 1990).

Godwin, John. *Occult America* (Garden City, NY: Doubleday and Company, Inc., 1972).

Golitsyn, Anatoliy. *New Lies for Old* (Atlanta, GA: Clarion House, 1990 Edition).

Goldwyn, Ron. "Clinton's Spiritual Adviser Feeling Fallout from Scandal," *Philadelphia Daily News* (April 9, 1999).

"Gone Berserk," World of Prophecy (September 30, 2000).

"Gone Berserk," *Power of Prophecy* (May 2001, Vol. 2001-05).

Good Newsletter, The (May 1995, Issue 8).

"Good to Remember," *The Perilous Times* (February 1999, Vol. 20, No. 12).

Goodstein, Laurie. "Christian Leaders Counter Religious Right," *Philadelphia Inquirer* (May 24, 1995).

"Goodwill Games and Ted Turner," *Despatch Magazine* (March 2001, Vol. 13, No. 1).

"Gorbachev on Schuller's 'Hour of Power,'" *Prophecy Corner and the Nosh Box* (November 2000).

"Gorbachev Pushes One-World Marxist Utopia," *The Evangel* (March 2001, Vol. 48, No. 3).

"Gorbachev Speaks to 17,000 in St. Louis," *Christian News* (October 28, 1996, Vol. 34, No. 40).

"Gorbachev to Convene Meeting in S.F. in Fall—Invitees include Bush, Thatcher, Tutu," *San Francisco Chronicle* (February 3, 1995).

"Gorbachev's International Green Cross," *The McAlvany Intelligence Advisor* (March 1995).

"Gorby's Favorites," *The Christian World Report* (September 1990, Vol. 2, No. 8).

"Gordon-Conwell Awarded $442,150 for Program in Evangelical Leadership," *Hilltop* (Summer 1997, Vol. 9, No. 1).

"Gordon-Conwell Leadership Changes," *Calvary Contender* (February 15, 1997, Vol. 14, No. 4).

"Gore Is Head of the Table at HRC Dinner," *The Advocate* (September 15, 1998, Issue 768).

"Gore Praises Perversity?," *Calvary Contender* (November 15, 1997, Vol. 14, No. 22).

Gore, Al. *Earth in the Balance: Ecology and the Human Spirit* (New York, NY: Houghton Mifflin Company, 1992).

"Gores Entertain Homosexuals," *Calvary Contender* (May 1, 1995, Vol. 12, No. 9).

"Government Report Confirms the Bible League Findings of Persecution in China," *Christian News* (April 9, 2001, Vol. 39, No. 15).

Grab for Power: A Chronology of the NEA, The (Marlborough, NH: Plymouth Rock Foundation, 1993).

Grady, Lee. "The Last Temptation of Christ: Historical Fiction or Blasphemous Hatred?," *Bridgebuilder* (November/December 1988).

Grady, William P. *Final Authority: A Christian's Guide to the King James Bible* (Knoxville, TN: Grady Publications, Inc., 1993).

"Graham Admits Alcohol Use," *The Perilous Times* (March 1995, Vol. 17, No. 1).

"Graham and Catholic Universalism," *Calvary Contender* (October 15, 1997, Vol. 14, No. 20).

"Graham and Masonry," *Christian News* (July 27, 1992, Vol. 30, No. 30).

"Graham Asks Roman Catholic Diocese to Help Referrals," *Battle Cry* (July/August 1991).

"Graham at Harvard Praises Dalai Lama," *Calvary Contender* (November 1, 1999, Vol. 16, No. 21).

"Graham Continues to Send to Catholicism," *The Flaming Torch* (April/May/June 1998, Vol. 39, No. 2).

"Graham Crusade in Minneapolis Breaks Attendance Records," *The Vine and Branches* (Mid-Summer 1996, Vol. 11, Issue 4).

"Graham Crusades Now Feature Rock Music," *Calvary Contender* (August 1, 1995).

"Graham Defends Divorced Son Guilty of Adultery," *Christian News* (January 17, 2000, Vol. 38, No. 3).

"Graham Doesn't Preach Hell Fire Is Literal," *Calvary Contender* (January 1, 1994, Vol. 11, No. 1).

"Graham Doesn't Preach Hell Fire Is Literal," *Plains Baptist Challenger* (June 1994).

"Graham Draws Many Back to Christ, Church," *Christian News* (November 15, 1999).

"Graham Ignores Abortion and Sodomy," *Christian View of the News* (October 10, 1994, Vol. 19, No. 19).

"Graham Meetings," *Calvary Contender* (January 15, 2001, Vol. 18, No. 2).

"Graham Meets Again with Pope," *Calvary Contender* (April 15, 1993, Vol. 10, No. 8).

"Graham Museum Honors First Pope As an Evangelist," *Christian News* (July 23, 2001, Vol. 39, No. 30).

"Graham Promotes Bad Bible Version," *Calvary Contender* (August 1, 1995).

"Graham Promotes BWA," *Calvary Contender* (August 15, 1997, Vol. 14, No. 16).

"Graham Receives Recognition for Distinguished Achievement," *Religious Broadcasting* (November 1991).

"Graham Says All Denoms Have Same God," *Calvary Contender* (February 1, 1998, Vol. 15, No. 3).

"Graham to 'Pass the Torch' in Amsterdam," *Calvary Contender* (August 1, 2000, Vol. 17, No. 15).

"Graham Says He Admires Pope's Attempts at Religious Reconciliation," *Foundation* (January-February 2000, Vol. 21, Issue 1).

"Graham Sidesteps Measure 9," *The Oregonian* (September 22, 1992).

"Graham Team Denies Sending Roman Catholics Back to Romanism," *O Timothy* (1994, Vol. 11, Issue 12).

"Graham Turned 2,000 Inquirers over to the Catholic Church in New England," *O Timothy* (1992, Vol. 9, Issue 6).

"Graham Worries Heaven May Be Wrong Place for Him," *Calvary Contender* (January 15, 2000).

"Graham Youth Rally in Atlanta," *Calvary Contender* (January 1, 1995, Vol. 12, No. 1).

Graham, Billy. *Approaching Hoofbeats: The Four Horsemen of the Apocalypse* (Grason: Minneapolis, MN: 1983).

Graham, Billy. *Just As I Am: The Autobiography of Billy Graham* (Harpers Collins Worldwide, 1997).

Graham, Billy. *The Jesus Generation* (Grand Rapids, MI: Zondervan Publishing House, 1971).

Graham, Billy. *Unto the Hills: Thoughts for Every Day* (Dallas, TX: Word Publishing, 1986).

Graham, Henry G. *Where We Got the Bible: Our Debt to the Catholic Church* (Rockford, IL: Tan Books and Publishers, Inc., 1987 Edition).

"Graham, Women Preachers, Hell," *Calvary Contender* (June 15, 1997, Vol. 14, No. 12).

"Graham: 'Other Paths to God?,'" *Calvary Contender* (March 15, 1996, Vol. 13, No. 6).

"Graham: 'Other Paths to God?,'" *Calvary Contender* (November 15, 1996, Vol. 13, No. 22).

"Graham's Affinity with Catholicism," *Calvary Contender* (June 1, 2001, Vol. 18, No. 11).

"Graham's Atlanta Crusade," *Calvary Contender* (November 15, 1994, Vol. 11, No. 20).

"Graham's Hedonistic Paradise," *Calvary Contender* (February 15, 1999, Vol. 16, No. 4).

"Graham's Music at Tampa," *Calvary Contender* (January 1, 1999, Vol. 16, No. 1).

"Graham's Nashville Crusade," *Calvary Contender* (July 15, 2000, Vol. 17, No. 14).

"Graham's Quebec Crusade Unites English Protestants, French Catholics," *Calvary Contender* (September 1, 1998, Vol. 15, No. 17).

"Graham's Rock Music Friends Say 'Thanks," *Calvary Contender* (August 15, 2001, Vol. 18, No. 16).

"Graham's Unscriptural Means, Unscriptural Goal," *Calvary Contender* (March 15, 1996, Vol. 13, No. 6).

"Grahams Side with Red China," *Calvary Contender* (August 1, 1997, Vol. 14, No. 15).

Granberg-Michaelson, Wesley. "Toward a Politics of Compassion," *The Cry for Renewal: Biblical Faith and Spiritual Politics* (May 23, 1995).

"Grand Rapids Prof Promotes Pensacola Book," *Calvary Contender* (September 15, 1998, Vol. 15, No. 18).

Grant, George. *Grand Illusions: The Legacy of Planned Parenthood* (Nashville, TN: Thomas Nelson, Inc., 1998 Edition).

"Grant, Gill Marry," *Christian News* (April 3, 2000, Vol. 38, No. 14).

"Gratitude: The Adamant of Existence," *World Goodwill* (2000, No. 4).

"Great Invocation: A Mantram for the New Age and for All Humanity" (Received February 13, 1999).

Green Cross (Summer 1995, Vol. 1, No. 3).

Green Cross (Winter 1995, Vol. 1, No. 2).

Green Cross (Winter 1996, Vol. 2, No. 1).

"Green Cross," *Don Bell Reports* (January 26, 1990, Vol. 37, No. 2).

"Greening of American Faith, The," *The Voice in the Wilderness* (November 1994).

Greer, Colin. "'Our Task Is To Do All We Can—Not To Sit And Wait,'" *Parade* (October 20, 1996).

Griffin, Des, *Fourth Reich of the Rich* (South Pasadena, CA: Emissary Publications, 1978).

Griffin, Ralph G. "Bush Heralds a 'New World Order,'" *The Christian World Report* (March 1991, Vol. 3, No. 3).

Grigg, William Norman. "A Global School Board," *The New American* (January 23, 1995).

Grigg, William Norman. "Earth Worship in the Church," *The New American* (December 13, 1993).

Grigg, William Norman. "Whose Child Is This?," *The New American* (November 28, 1994, Vol. 10, No. 24).

Griswold, Wayne. "Fallacy of New Age Environmental Concerns, The."

Groothuis, Douglas R. *Unmasking the New Age* (Downers Grove, IL: Intervarsity Press, 1986).

Grose, Peter. *Gentleman Spy: The Life of Allen Dulles* (New York, NY: Houghton Mifflin Company, 1994).

"Group Invocation and the Three Spiritual Festivals," *World Goodwill Newsletter* (1999, No. 2).

"Group Promotes Tolerance Between Faiths, Cultures," *The News-Item* (April 27, 1996).

"Groups Endorse Homosexual March," *AFA Journal* (June 1993, Vol. 17, No. 6).

"Groups Promoting Democratic Rights, Civil Liberties, Social Justice, Equality & Pluralism."

"Groups Represented," *World Goodwill Newsletter* (1988, No. 4).

"Groups with Trust, Faith," *Morning Call* (May 28, 1995).

"Growing Global Religion Blending Christianity with Other Religions Finds Growing Acceptance, The," *The Vine and Branches* (Spring 1999, Vol. 14, Issue 2).

Gsell, Brad K. "Pagan Indian Rites and Legends Observed at WCC Assembly," *Christian News* (June 4, 2001, Vol. 39, No. 23).

Gsell, Brad K. *The Legacy of Billy Graham* (Charlotte, NC: Fundamental Presbyterian Publication, n.d.).

Guardian, The (November 30, 1988, Vol. 41, No. 10).

"Guardian Angel," *U. S. News & World Report* (May 5, 1997).

Gudel, Joseph P. "A New Reformation?: The Faulty Gospel of Robert Schuller," *Passport Magazine* (January-February 1988).

Guide, D. "'Celebrating' the Death of Christ: The Mockery of the Mass," *The Battle Cry* (November/December 1992).

Guide, D. "Did You Know?," *Battle Cry* (November/December 1992).

Gumprecht, Jane. *New Age Health Care: Holy or Holistic* (Orange, CA: Promise Publishing, 1988).

Gunther, Bernard. *Energy Ecstasy* (Van Nuys, CA: Newcastle Publishing Company, Inc., 1978).

Gurstein, Rochelle, "Signs of the Times," *The New Republic* (July 30, 2001, Issue 4515).

"Habitat for Humanity a Global Religion," *Calvary Contender* (January 1, 1997, Vol. 14, No. 1).

"Habitat for Humanity Is About Money," *Calvary Contender* (September 1, 1997).

"Habitat for Humanity Promotes Ecumenical Movement," *Calvary Contender* (December 1, 1994, Vol. 11, No. 21).

"Habitat for Humanity, NCC Join Hands," *Christian Century* (April 11, 2001, Vol. 118, No. 12).

Hadden, Jeffrey K. and Swann, Charles E. *Prime Time Preachers: The Rising Power of Televangelism* (Reading, MA: Addison-Wesley Publishing Company, Inc., 1981).

Haddon, David and Hamilton, Vail. *TM Wants You!* (Grand Rapids, MI: Baker Book House, 1976).

Haggard, Forrest D. *The Clergy and the Craft* (Ovid Bell Press, Inc., 1970).

Hall, Manly Palmer. *America's Assignment with Destiny* (Los Angeles, CA: Philosophical Research Society, Inc., 1951).

Hall, Manly Palmer. *The Lost Keys of Freemasonry* (Richmond, VA: Macoy Publishing and Masonic Supply Company, Inc., 1976 Edition).

Hall, Manly Palmer. *The Mystical Christ: Religion As a Personal Spiritual Experience* (Los Angeles 27, CA: The Philosophical Research Society, Inc., 1956 Edition).

Hall, Manly Palmer. *The Secret Teachings of All Ages* (Los Angeles 27, CA: The Philosophical Research Society Press, 1945).

"Halloween and Witchcraft," *Christian Parent Alert* (October 1991, Vol. 1, No. 3).

"Halloween: Kids' Treat or Pagan Trick?," *Battle Cry* (July/August 1991).

Ham, Ken. "'Alpha'—a Misnomer!," *The Christian News* (May 21, 2001, Vol. 39, No. 21).

Ham, Ken. "What's Wrong with 'Progressive Creation?,'" (Florence, KY: Answers in Genesis).

Hamilton, Marsha and Couchman, Judith. "Building Houses with Love," *Christian Life* (May 1987, Vol. 49, No. 1).

Hamlyn, Paul. *Greek Mythology* (London, England: Paul Hamlyn Limited, 1967).

Hammer, Armand with Lyndon, Neil. *Hammer* (New York, NY: G. P. Putnam's Sons, 1987).

"Han Continues to Defend Communists," *Christian News* (April 3, 2000, Vol. 38, No. 14).

Hanh, Thich Nhat. "Every Breath You Take," *New Age Journal* (November/December 1990, Vol. 7, Issue 6).

Hanson, Allen D. "Bible Distribution in China," *Christian News* (September 20, 1999, Vol. 37, No. 34).

Harder, Robert L. "DeMolay Thriving," *The Scottish Rite Journal* (February 1992, Vol. 100, No. 2).

Harding, M. Esther. *Woman's Mysteries: Ancient and Modern* (NY: G. P. Putnam's Sons, 1971).

Hargis, Billy James. "Gorbachev Plots His Quiet Takeover," *Christian Crusade* (November 1996, Vol. 44, No. 11).

Harmet, A. Richard, Executive Editor. *The World Book Year Book* (Chicago, IL: World Book-Childcraft International, Inc., 1980).

Harmonia Mundi (no other information available).

Harris, David L. "Evangelism: The Ultimate Deception," *The New Age Adversary Bulletin and Old Time Gospel Advocate* (June 1994, Vol. 9, No. 6).

Harrison, John B. and Sullivan, Richard E. *A Short History of Western Civilization* (NY: Alfred A. Knopf, 1960).

Harriss, Joseph A. "The Gospel According to Marx," *Christian News* (February 1, 1993, Vol. 31, No. 5).

Harriss, Joseph A. "The Gospel According to Marx," *Reader's Digest* (February 1993).

"Harry Potter and the Bible," *Calvary Contender* (March 15, 2001, Vol. 18, No. 6).

"*Harry Potter* Books," *Calvary Contender* (August 1, 2001, Vol. 19, No. 15).

"Harry Potter Books, The," *The Perilous Times* (January 2001, Vol. 22, No. 8).

"Harry's Magic," *Christian News* (September 25, 2000, Vol. 38, No. 35).

Hart, Gary D. "Religious Freedom in Red China," *O Timothy* (1989, Vol. 6, Issue 6).

"Harvard's 'Gay' Chaplain Peter Gomes," *Calvary Contender* (April 15, 1997, Vol. 14, No. 8).

Hawken, Paul. *The Magic of Findhorn* (New York, NY: Harper and Row, 1975).

Hayes, Kathleen R. "All Rhodes Lead To One World Government" (1993).

Hayes, Kathleen R. "Feminism, Goddess Movement Infect Christendom, Church," *NRI Trumpet* (March 1989).

Hayes, Kathleen R. "The Horned God Pan is Patron of Witches," *NRI Trumpet* (July 1987).

Hayes, Kathleen. "Evangelicals for Social Action: Developing a Biblical Agenda for Public Life," *The Other Side* (April 1986, Vol. 22, No. 3, Issue 171).

Haynes, Charles C., Editor. *Finding Common Ground* (Nashville, TN: The Freedom Forum First Amendment Center, 1994).

Haywood, H. L. *More About Masonry* (Chicago 16, IL: The Masonic History Company, 1948).

"Healer Within, The," *World Goodwill Newsletter* (1987, No. 2).

"Heaven: Guess Who's Coming," *Christian News* (February 19, 2001).

Hefley, James C. "Johnny Cash Live!," *The Christian Reader* (November/December 1983).

Hefley, James. *God Goes to High School* (Waco, TX: Word Books, 1970).

Heinen, Marissa. "Revived Paganism for a One-World Religion," *The Christian World Report* (September 1990, Vol. 2, No. 8).

Hekker, Gerard J. "The Day of the African Child," *Religion for Peace* (June 1995, Issue 66).

"Hell: Eternal Torment or Annihilation?," *Calvary Contender* (November 1, 2000, Vol. 17, No. 21).

Helms, Jesse. *The King Holiday and Its Meaning* (St. Louis, MO: Council of Conservative Citizens, 1998).

"Helpful Books for Your Counseling Ministry," *Return to the Word* (Winter 1997, Vol. 3, No. 1).

"Heresy and Apostasy," *Calvary Contender* (October 1, 1999, Vol. 16, No. 19).

Herzstein, Robert E. *Henry R. Luce: A Political Portrait of the Man Who Created the American Century* (New York, NY: Macmillan Publishing Company, 1994).

Herzer, Ann. "Politics of the Radical Center," *Wisconsin Report* (November 17, 1994, Vol. 19, No. 45).

Heuer, Michael H. "People for the American Way: What Is It?," *Faith for the Family* (July/August 1985, Vol. 14, No. 6).

Hieronimus, Robert. *America's Secret Destiny: Spiritual Vision and the Founding of a Nation* (Rochester, VT: Destiny Books, 1989).

"High Percentage of Born-Again Christians Question Biblical Teachings," *The Vine and Branches* (2000, Vol. 15, Issue 5).

Highland, Jean, Editor. *The Words of Martin Luther King, Jr.* (Selected by Coretta Scott King) (New York, NY: Newmarket Press, 1987).

"Hilary (sic) Clinton's Religious Beliefs," *Christian News* (April 12, 1993), Vol. 31, No. 15).

"Hillary's Other Side," *Newsweek* (July 1, 1996).

Hilltop (1977).

Hinn, Benny. *The Anointing* (Nashville, TN: Thomas Nelson Publishers, 1992).

Hinton, William G. "Freemasonry, Politics, and Religion," *Scottish Rite Journal* (February 1993, Vol. 101, No. 2).

"His 'Toronto Blessing' Endorsement Brings Broadcaster Criticism," *Christian News,* (April 17, 1995, Vol. 33, No. 16).

Hockenos, Paul. "Jackson Spirit Takes Hold in New York," *The Guardian* (April 13, 1988, Vol. 40, No. 28).

Hoffmann, Walter, Editor. *A New World Order: Can It Bring Security to the World's People?* (Washington, D.C.: World Federalist Association, 1991).

Holly, James L. *The Southern Baptist Convention and Freemasonry* (Beaumont, TX: Mission and Ministry to Men, Inc., 1992).

Holmes, Cecile S. "The Gospel According to Elvis," *Christian News* (February 19, 2001).

"Homosexual Activist Is Pres. of Calif. Council of Churches," *Calvary Contender* (April 15, 2001, Vol. 18, No. 8).

"Homosexual Churches Increase," *The Shepherd's Letter* (Spring 1993).

"Homosexual Heads Hawaii Council of Churches," *O Timothy* (1994, Vol. 12, Issue 1).

"Homosexuals Reflect on Help from President Bush," *The Christian World Report* (April 1991, Vol. 3, No. 4).

Hook, Brian R. "Leaders Explore Globalization at State of the World Forum," *Progress in Theology* (December 2000, Vol. 8, No. 8).

Hosenball, Mark and Thomas, Evan. "Jesse and Al's Food Fight," *Newsweek* (April 9, 2001, Vol. 137, No. 15).

"House Approves China Trade Bill," *The News-Item* (May 25, 2000).

House, Edward Mandell. *Philip Dru: Administrator* (Appleton, WI: Robert Welch University Press, 1998 reprint).

Houst, Carol. "Playing with Fire," *Thoughtline* (April 1999).

Houst, Carol. "Synthesis of the Signs," *Thoughtline* (November 2000).

"How Billy Graham Protected the Jesuits," *Newsletter from a Christian Ministry* (September 1, 1993, Vol. 2, No. 12).

"How Can Catholic Church Deceive So Many?," *Calvary Contender* (March 15, 1996, Vol. 13, No. 6).

"How Do Eco-Ethics and E. S. D. Relate?," *EcoLetter* (Fall 1995).

How to Avoid Incineration in a Nuclear Holocaust (Washington, D.C.: World Federalist Association, n.d.).

Howard, Michael. *The Occult Conspiracy: The Power of Secret Societies in World History* (New York, NY: MFJ Books, 1989).

Howard, Wendy B. *The Alpha Course: Friend or Foe?* (Landsborough, Queensland: Endtime Ministries, 1999).

Howard, Wendy B. "The First Religion and Cultural Diversity Conference, Melbourne, July 1997," *Despatch Magazine* (August 8, 1997).

HRT Ministries Inc. Newsletter (January/February/March 1991, Vol. 4, No. 1).

"Huaiyin Church Building Project," *East Gates Connection* (January-March 2000).

Hudgens, Tom A. *Let's Abolish War* (Denver, CO: BILR Corporation, 1986).

"Human Development, Human Rights—Pathways to Freedom," *World Goodwill* (2001, No. 2).

"Humanist Manifesto 2000: A Call for a New Planetary Humanism," *Free Inquiry* (Fall 1999, Vol. 19, No. 4).

"Humanist, Positive Religion" *Calvary Contender* (December 1, 2000, Vol. 17, No. 23).

Hume, Basil. *One in Christ: Unity and Diversity in the Church Today* (New York, NY: Catholic Common Ground Initiative, 1999).

"Humility Theology Information Center Advisory Board," *Progress in Theology* (June 1996, Vol. 4, No. 2).

Hunt, Charles Clyde. *Some Thoughts on Masonic Symbolism* (NY: Macoy Publishing and Masonic Supply Company, 1930).

Hunt, Dave. "A City on Seven Hills," *O Timothy* (1995, Vol. 12, Issue 3).

Hunt, Dave. "A Cult Is a Cult," *CIB Bulletin* (June 1991, Vol. 7, No. 6).

Hunt, Dave. "A New Christianity," *The Berean Call* (February 2000).

Hunt, Dave. *A Woman Rides the Beast* (Eugene, OR: Harvest House, 1994).

Hunt, Dave. *Beyond Seduction: A Return to Biblical Christianity* (Eugene, OR: Harvest House Publishers, 1987).

Hunt, Dave. "Evangelizing the World," *CIB Bulletin* (July 1991, Vol. 7, No. 7).

Hunt, Dave. *Global Peace and the Rise of Antichrist* (Eugene, OR: Harvest House Publishers, 1990).

Hunt, Dave. "Nature or Personal Creator?," *The Berean Call* (March 1994).

Hunt, Dave. "Progress in Religion?," *The Berean Call* (May 1996).

Hunt, Dave. "Religious Unity and the New World Order," *The Omega-Letter* (July 1990, Vol. 5, No. 6).

Hunt, Dave. "'Stand Fast in the Faith' I Corinthians 16:13," *Berean Call* (December 1994).

Hunt, Dave. *The Cult Explosion* (Eugene, OR: Harvest House Publishers, 1980).

Hunt, Dave. "The Gospel Betrayed," *The Berean Call* (May 1994).

Hunt, Dave. "The Greening of the Cross," *Berean Call* (July 1997).

Hunt, Dave. "Time & Eternity," *The Berean Call* (January 1996).

Hunt, Dave. "What's Happening to the Faith?," *The Berean Call* (May 1998).

Hunt, Dave. *Whatever Happened to Heaven?* (Eugene, OR: Harvest House Publishers, 1988).

Hunt, Dave. "Why Christ Came," *The Berean Call* (December 1995).

Hunt, Dave and McMahon, T. A. *America: The Sorcerer's New Apprentice: The Rise of New Age Shamanism* (Eugene, OR: Harvest House Publishers, 1988).

Hunt, Dave and McMahon, T. A. *The Seduction of Christianity: Spiritual Discernment in the Last Days* (Eugene, OR: Harvest House Publishers, 1985).

Hunt, Mary E. "Feminist Ecumenism: Models for the Mainstream," *The Christian Century* (October 30, 1991, Vol. 108, No. 31).

Hussey, M. Edmund. "Needed: A Theology of Priesthood," *Origins* (February 4, 1988, Vol. 17, No. 34).

Hutchens, Rex R. *A Bridge to Light* (Washington, D.C.: Supreme Council, 33° Ancient and Accepted Scottish Rite of Freemasonry, Southern Jurisdiction, 1988).

Hutchens, Rex R. and Monson, Donald W. *The Bible in Albert Pike's Morals and Dogma* (Washington, DC: Supreme Council, 33°, 1992).

Hutchings, N. W. "Which Bible Is God's Word?," *The Gospel Truth* (July 1986, Vol. 27, No. 8).

Hutton, Ronald. *The Triumph of the Moon: A History of Modern Pagan Witchcraft* (Oxford, England: Oxford University Press, 1999).

"Hybels Featured at Schuller Meeting," *Calvary Contender* (February 15, 2001, Vol. 18, No. 4).

"'I Am A Homosexual,'" *Christian News* (July 26, 1993, Vol. 31, No. 30).

"ICCRE Family: News from Around the Country, The," *The Spirit of the Earth* (Fall 1995, Vol. 3, No. 2).

Illustrated Davis Dictionary of the Bible (Nashville, TN: Royal Publishers, Inc., 1973).

Impacting Society...Yesterday...Today...Tomorrow (Amherst, NY: American Humanist Association, n.d.).

"'Impressions' Curriculum Angers Parents," *The Christian World Report* (July 1990, Vol. 2, No. 6).

"In Globo Cogitare et in Loco Agree (sic) (Thinking Globally and Acting Locally)" (Part III), *Distant Drums* (May 1983, Vol. 5, No. 2).

"In Memoriam, Dr. John Humphrey," *Religion for Peace* (June 1995, Issue 66).

"In Perils of Corruptions: The Amplified Version," *The Perilous Times* (November 1994, Vol. 16, No. 9).

"In Perils of Dr. Billy Graham, the WCC & NCC and Evangelicals and Roman Catholics Together," *The Perilous Times* (June 2000, Vol. 22, No. 4).

"In Perils of the ACLU," *The Perilous Times* (December 1993, Vol. 15, No. 10).

"Inauguration of Robert E. Cooley, The," *Contact* (Winter 1981-82, Vol. 12, No. 1.

"Increased Crackdown on Chinese Christians," *Christian News* (September 18, 2000, Vol. 38, No. 34).

"Indian Catholics Back *Dominus Iesus*, Archbishop Says," *National Catholic Register* (October 22-28, 2000, Vol. 76, No. 43).

"Indians' 'Sacred Fire' Evokes Peace and Barbs," *Christian News* (June 4, 2001, Vol. 39, No. 23).

"Industrial Areas Foundation (IAF), The," *The Florida Forum* (Summer 1996).

Inside Music (June 1991, Vol. 3, No. 3).

"Intentional Communities: Seeds for a New Civilization," *The Christian Conscience* (December 1995, Vol. 1, No. 11).

"Intentional Communities: Seeds for the New World Order," *The Florida Forum* (Winter 1998).

"Interfaith Vigil Against Hate Violence Is Oct. 7," *Haverford Press* (September 15, 1999).

Interfaith Witness Department, *A Study of Freemasonry* (Atlanta, GA: Home Mission Board, Southern Baptist Convention, n.d.).

"International Day of Prayer for the Persecuted Church, The," *Christian News* (July 30, 2001, Vol. 39, No. 31).

"Interview with Isaac Mokoena, South African Christian Leader" *O Timothy* (1987, Vol. 4, Issue 3-4).

"Interview: Corinne McLaughlin and Gordon Davidson," *World Goodwill Newsletter* (1995, No. 3).

IRFWP Newsletter (Spring 1998, Vol. 6, No. 1).

IRFWP Newsletter (Fall 1998, Vol. 6, No. 2).

"Irrepressible Mussolini," *The New Age Magazine* (July 25, Vol. 33, No. 7).

Irwin, Ben. *The Bible and Homosexuality: Confronting the Challenge to Scriptural Authority* (Washington, DC: Family Research Council, n.d.).

Irwin, Victoria. "US Socialist Leader Says He Prefers Jackson But Is Comfortable with Dukakis," *The Christian Science Monitor* (July 21, 1988, Vol. 80, No. 165).

"Is Al Gore a Moderate?," *Calvary Contender* (August 1, 1992, Vol. 9, No. 15).

Is the Antichrist in the World Today? (Oklahoma City, OK: Southwest Radio Church, 1982).

"Is the New International Version the Sodomites (sic) Version?," *The Perilous Times* (September 1993, Vol. 15, No. 7).

"Is There an Elite Who Would Rule Us?," *The Florida Forum* (Summer 2000).

Isaac, Rael Jean. "Do You Know Where Your Church Offerings Go?," *Reader's Digest* (January 1983, Vol. 122, No. 729).

"It's Your Money," *The Voice in the Wilderness* (February 1992).

Jack, Alex. "Glimpses of an Unseen Friend," *Macromuse* (Summer/Fire 1985, Issue 20).

Jack, Homer A. "A Nuclear Freeze Is a SANE Proposal," *The Christian Century* (December 16, 1987).

"Jackson Returns to Public Stage, Thanks Family, Supporters," *Christian News* (January 29, 2001, Vol. 39, No. 5).

"Jackson's 'Rainbow' Includes Pink Adviser," *Human Events* (May 10, 1986).

Jacobs, Sean. "Forgiveness on the Agenda," *Breakthroughs* (February 2001).

Jalil, Abdul. "25 Most Frequently Asked Questions About Islam."

"James Dobson, Chuck Colson, and the Pope!," *Despatch Magazine* (March 2001, Vol. 13, No. 1).

"James Dobson, Charles Colson Visit Vatican, Praise Roman Catholic Church," *Christian News* (February 26, 2001, Vol. 39, No. 9).

James, William T., Editor. *Foreshocks of Antichrist* (Eugene, OR: Harvest House Publishers, 1997).

"Jars of Clay at Creation 97," *Calvary Contender* (February 15, 1997, Vol. 14, No. 4).

"Jars of Clay No Christian Band," *Calvary Contender* (September 15, 1998, Vol. 15, No. 18).

"Jars of Clay," *Calvary Contender* (February 15, 1998, Vol. 15, No. 4).

Jasper, William F. "China Trade: The CFR Steamroller," *The New American* (June 19, 2000, Vol. 16, No. 13).

Jenkins, Karen. "Home at Last: Habitat Offers the Ultimate Hospitality," *World Christian* (September/October 1987, Vol. 6, No. 5).

Jepsen, Dee. *Women: Beyond Equal Rights* (Waco, TX: Word Books, 1984).

"Jesse Jackson and Communism," *Calvary Contender* (March 1, 1995, Vol. 12, No. 5).

"Jesse Jackson Fathers Child out of Wedlock," *The News-Item* (January 19, 2001).

"Jesse Jackson Is the Best Candidate for the Gay and Lesbian Community," *National & International Religion Report* (April 25, 1988, Vol. 2, No. 8).

"Jesse Jackson Likens Clinton to Noah," *The Voice in the Wilderness* (January 1993).

"Jesse Jackson Scandal, The," *Calvary Contender* (February 1, 2001, Vol. 18, No. 3).

"Jesse Jackson—A One World Propagandist?," *Flashpoint* (February 1992)

"Jesse Jackson's Confession Shocks America!," *The Sacred Name Broadcaster* (January 2001, Vol. 33, No. 10).

"Jesse's Movement," *The Nation* (April 2, 1988, Vol. 246, No. 13).

"Jesus Christ Is Not the Only Way to God, WCC Says," *The Omega-Letter* (September 1989, Vol. 4, No. 8).

"Jesus Christ Was Really a Woman," *Christian News* (July 21, 1997, Vol. 35, No. 29).

"Jesus' Image That of a Female," *The Voice of the Nazarene* (November/December 1994, Vol. 31, No. 12).

"Jesus Junk (Another Jesus)," *The Perilous Times* (January 1996, Vol. 17, No. 11).

"Jesus' Flock or Satan's Herd,?" *Voice in the Wilderness* (March 196, Vol. 3, Issue 3).

"Jimmy Carter Leaves the Southern Baptist Convention—Again," *Christian News* (November 6, 2000, Vol. 38, No. 41).

"John Davidson Rockefeller, Jr.," Softkey Multimedia Inc., Infopedia (1996).

"John Davidson Rockefeller, Jr.," Softkey Multimedia Inc., Multipedia (1995).

"John Foster Dulles," Softkey Multimedia Inc., Infopedia (1996).

"John MacArthur Update," *The BDM Letter* (March/April 1995, Vol. 4, No. 2).

"John Marks Templeton," *Progress in Theology* (June 1996, Vol. 4, No. 2).

John Paul II (Edited by Peter Canisus Johannes Van Lierde; Translated by Firman O'Sullivan (New York, NY: Penguin Group, 1994).

John Paul II (Translated by Jenny and Martha McPhee), *Crossing the Threshold of Hope* (NY: Alfred A. Knopf, 1994).

"John Wimber, Jack Hayford, and the Catholics," *O Timothy* (1991, Vol. 8, Issue 6).

Johnson, Mike. *Rock Music Revealed* (n.p., n.d.).

Johnston, Bruce. "Heaven Open to Everyone, Says Pope," *Christian News* (December 18, 2000, Vol. 38, No. 47).

Jones, Jim. "Billy Graham's Organization in Good Hands—His Son's," *The News and Observer* (December 8, 2000).

Joseph, Kenny. "Useful Idiots," *Christian News* (October 4, 1999, Vol. 37, No. 36).

Josephson, Emanuel M. *The Truth About Rockefeller* (New York City, NY: Chedney Press, 1964).

"Judaism's Strange Gods," *Christian News* (October 9, 2000, Vol. 38, No. 37).

Just Out (August 1992, Vol. 9, No. 10).

"Justification? Can We Protestants Dialogue???," *Despatch Magazine* (June 2001, Vol. 13:2).

"K. H. Ting Is a Theological Liberal," *O Timothy* (1994, Vol. 2, Issue 5).

"K. H. Ting Tells Lies," *O Timothy* (1994, Vol. 2, Issue 5).

"K. H. Ting—The Master of Chinese Communist Propaganda," *O Timothy* (1994, Vol. 2, Issue 5).

Kah, Gary. *En Route to Global Occupation* (Lafayette, LA: Huntington House Publishers, 1992).

Kah, Gary H. *The Demonic Roots of Globalism* (Lafayette, LA: Huntington House Publishers, 1995).

Kallen, H. M. "Theosophist," *The World Book Encyclopedia* (1961 Edition, Vol. 17).

Kanz, David C., Guzman, Ingrid, and Smith, Steven P. *An Urgent Report: Celebration 2000 and Jay Gary* (Milwaukee, WI: VCY/America Radio Network, 1995).

Kanz, David C. *The New Global Missions Agenda: InterVarsity Christian Fellowship and New Age Politics* (Oak Creek, WI: Logos Communication Consortium, 1996).

"Karen Burton Mains," *Bold Truth* (October 1995).

Karnes, Eddie. "America's Televangelists of Deception on China," *Christian News* (July 30, 2001, Vol. 39, No. 31).

Karnes, Eddie. "Boycott the China Olympics 2008," *Christian News* (July 23, 2001, Vol. 39, No. 30).

Karnes, Eddie. "Can You Buy Bibles in China? Yes and No!," *Christian News* (January 15, 2001, Vol. 39, No. 3).

Karnes, Eddie. "Choose Sides," *Christian News* (January 17, 2000, Vol. 38, No.3).

Karnes, Eddie. "Christian News Is Reliable," *Christian News* (March 26, 2001, Vol. 39, No. 13).

Karnes, Eddie. "Deceiving God's Elect on China," *Christian News* (January 29, 2001, Vol. 39, No. 5).

Karnes, Eddie. "Dr. Billy Graham and Dr. Oswald Hoffman, Thank You, But..." (Part I), *Christian News* (February 12, 2001, Vol. 39, No. 7).

Karnes, Eddie. "Dr. Billy Graham and Dr. Oswald Hoffmann, Thank You, But..." (Part II), *Christian News* (March 5, 2001, Vol. 39, No. 10).

Karnes, Eddie. "Speak Out for China's Persecuted 100 Million House Church Christians," *Christian News* (November 13, 2000, Vol. 38, No. 42).

Karnes, Eddie. "Stop the China Scam," *Christian News* (December 11, 2000, Vol.38, No. 46).

Karnes, Eddie. "The Big Lie on China's MFN and WTO," *Christian News* (May 22, 2000, Vol. 38, No. 21).

Karnes, Eddie. "Understanding Evangelism in China," *Christian News* (July 8, 2001, Vol. 39, No. 28).

Karnes, Eddie. "Ways to Get Bibles to the Chinese Without Getting Arrested (Part II)," *Christian News* (May 29, 2000, Vol. 38, No. 22).

Karnes, Eddie. "What Has Changed in China?," *Christian News* (May 8, 2000, Vol. 38, No. 19).

Kauffman, Paul. "The Lack of Bibles in China—The Real Reason," *O Timothy* (1994, Vol. 2, Issue 5).

Kean, L. "The Idolatry of the Churches," *O Timothy* (1987, Vol. 4, Issue 12).

Kearns, Kenneth M. "A Visit by J. C. Penney, 33°," *Scottish Rite Journal* (August 1992, Vol. 100, No. 8).

Keating, Karl. "Q & A," *Be* (July-August 2001).

Keating, Karl. "Q & A," *Be* (November-December 2000).

Kellar, Nancy. "From Generation to Generation You Will Be My Witnesses," *Focus* (Winter 1995, Vol. 20, No. 1).

Kelley, Kevin J. "A Socialist in the House?," *The Guardian* (April 13, 1988, Vol. 40, No. 28).

Kelley, Kevin J. "Jackson Radically Altering Political Landscape," *The Guardian* (May 4, 1988).

Kelly, Armandine F. "The Full Rose Moon," *Festivals* (June/July 1986).

"Ken Medema at GARBC-Approved School," *Calvary Contender* (May 1, 2000, Vol. 17, No. 9).

Kennedy, D. James with Wise, Norman. *The Great Deception* (Fort Lauderdale, FL: TCRM Publishing, 1985).

Kennedy, Edwin O. "Union Theological Seminary," *The World Book Encyclopedia* (Vol. 18) (Chicago 54, IL: Field Enterprises Educational Corporation, 1961).

"Kenneth Copeland 33rd Degree Mason Exposed," *Despatch Magazine* (December 1997, Vol. 9:4).

Keppel, Ben. "Race, Poverty, and the Symbolism of the Child," *Research Reports from the Rockefeller Archive Center* (Spring 1998).

Kerr, Donald C. "Pilgrim Feet, Patriot Dream," *Scottish Rite Journal* (November 1994, Vol. 102, No. 11).

Kerr, Howard and Crow, Charles L., Editors. *The Occult in America: New Historical Perspectives* (Urbana, IL: University of Illinois Press, 1983).

"Key Anglican Parish in London Defects to Rome," *O Timothy* (1993, Vol. 10, Issue 6).

"Key Players in the Sex Education Game," *AFA Journal* (October 1990, Vol. 14, No. 9).

Keys, Donald. *Spirituality at the United Nations* (Jersey City, NJ: Aquarian Age Community, n.d.).

"KGB and the Russian Orthodox Church, The," *O Timothy* (1992, Vol. 9, Issue 7).

Kilpatrick, William and Wolfe, Gregory and Suzanne M. *Books That Build Character: A Guide to Teaching Your Child Moral Values Through Stories* (New York, NY: Simon & Schuster, 1994).

"Kim Nominated as BWA President," *Calvary Contender* (September 1, 1999, Vol. 16, No. 17).

"King Holiday a Travesty," *Calvary Contender* (February 15, 1992, Vol. 9, No. 4).

King Holiday and Its Meaning, The (Saint Louis, MO: Council of Conservative Citizens, 1998).

"King Honored As National Hero," *Sojourners* (May 1986).

"King No Role Model," *Calvary Contender* (February 15, 1998, Vol. 15, No. 4).

King, W. L. "S.I.E.C.U.S., Sex, and Subversion."

"King's Sexual Orgies" *Christian News* (January 24, 2000).

Kinman, Dwight L. *The World's Last Dictator* (Woodburn, OR: Solid Rock Books, Inc. 1995).

Kirkridge (Spring/Summer 1988).

Kjos, Berit. "1995—United Nations 50th Anniversary Celebrations Began Earth Day—April—California Conference 1995—'Celebrating the Spirit,'" *Wisconsin Report* (August 24, 1995, Vol. 20, No. 32).

Kjos, Berit. *A Twist of Faith* (Green Forest, AR: New Leaf Press, 1997).

Kjos, Berit. *Brave New Schools* (Eugene, OR: Harvest House Publishers, 1995).

Kjos, Berit. "Celebrating the Spirit," *The Christian Conscience* (September 1995, Vol. 1, No. 8).

Kjos, Berit. "Character Training for Global Citizens," *The Christian Conscience* (June 1997, Vol. 3, No. 5).

Kjos, Berit. "Clinton's War on Hate Crimes," *The Christian Conscience* (April 1998, Vol. 4, No. 3)

Kjos, Berit. "Conforming the Church to the New Millennium," *Christian News* (February 28, 2000, Vol. 38, No. 9).

Kjos, Berit. "Conforming the Church to the New Millennium," *Prophecy Corner and the Nosh Box* (November 2000).

Kjos, Berit. "From the UNITED NATIONS to the UNITED RELIGIONS."

Kjos, Berit. "Gorbachev's New Global Pulpit," *The Christian World Report* (July 1993, Vol. 8, No. 5).

Kjos, Berit. "Harry Potter Lures Kids to Witchcraft with Praise from Christian Leaders," *Prophecy Corner and The Nosh Box* (October 2000).

Kjos, Berit. "The Prince of Egypt," *Christian News* (January 4, 1999, Vol. 37, No. 1).

Kjos, Berit. "'The State of the World' According to Gorbachev," *Christian News* (October 28, 1996, Vol. 34, No. 40).

Kjos, Berit. "Using Art to Change Beliefs," *Free World Research Report* (November 1993, Vol. 2, No. 11).

Kjos, Berit. "What Kind of Message Is *The Message?,*" *Christian News* (December 20, 1993, Vol. 31, No. 47).

Kleinknecht, C. Fred. "The Cornerstone for Our Next Generation," *The Scottish Rite Journal* (March 1994, Vol. 102, No. 3).

Klopfenstein, Jay. "Can Buying a Bible Contribute to Pornography and Licentiousness,?" *Christian News* (December 20, 1993, Vol. 31, No. 47).

Knapper, Jerry D. "What Happens to Christians When They Die?," *The Front Page* (October 1993, Vol. 7, No. 10).

Knight, Stephen. *The Brotherhood: The Secret World of the Freemasons* (Briarcliff Manor, NY: Stein and Day, 1984).

Knoxville News-Sentinel (September 15, 1991).

Koch, Kurt. (Translated by Michael Freeman.) *Occult ABC* (Germany: Literature Mission Aglasterhausen, Inc., 1978).

Koch, Sandra L. *Combating the New Age Movement: A Christian Warfare Manual* (Boca Raton, FL: Foundation Tabernacle Ministries, Inc., n.d.).

Kofahl, Robert F. "Graham Believes Men Can Be Saved Apart from Name of Christ," *Christian News* (October 20, 1997, Vol. 35, No. 38).

Krishna, R. P. Lawrie. *Kalki Avatar: Revelation of Christ Jesus at His Second Coming* (Vol. 2) (Medway, OH: Manujothi Ashram Publications, 1987).

Kurtz, Paul. *Humanist Manifestos I and II* (Buffalo, NY: Prometheus Books, 1973).

Kyle, Ted. "Pagan Earth Mother Reemerges As 'Christian' Sophia Cult," *Pulpit Helps* (March 1995, Vol. 20, No. 3).

"L'Engle a New Ager," *Calvary Contender* (January 15, 1998).

L'Engle, Madeleine. *The Rock That Is Higher: Story As Truth* (Wheaton, IL: Harold Shaw Publishers, 1993).

Laubach, Frank C. "The Mightiest Force in the World," *Plus: The Magazine of Positive Thinking* (February 1988, Vol. 39, No. 2).

Ladies' Home Journal (December 1985).

Lalonde, Patti, "Educating for Service in the New Age," *Christian Parent Alert* (January 1992, Vol. 2, No. 1).

Lalonde, Patti, "From Psychedelics to Hi-Tech: Virtual Reality: The LSD of the 90's?," *The Omega-Letter* (November 1991, Vol. 6, No. 10).

Lalonde, Patti. "The Bondage of Religion," *The Omega-Letter* (July 1990, Vol. 5, No. 6).

Lalonde, Peter. "Building the New World Order: One Piece at a Time," *Prophecy Newsletter* (1986).

Lalonde, Peter. *One World Under Antichrist* (Eugene, OR: Harvest House Publishers, 1991).

Lalonde, Peter. "Religion in the Public Schools," *Christian Inquirer* (Vol. 15, No. 6).

Lamb, Henry. "The Rise of Global Green Religion," *Eco✦Logic* (1997 Special Report).

Lamont, Corliss. *The Philosophy of Humanism* (NY: Frederick Unger Publishing Company, 1949).

Lamy, Lucie. *Egyptian Mysteries* (n.p., 1981).

Langley, Monica. "Burning Need," *Wall Street Journal* (August 8, 1996).

Langley, Norman and Freilich, Leon. "What Really Happened Between the President and America's Leading Preacher in the Countdown to War: How Billy Graham Brought Light to George Bush's Darkest Hour," *Star* (February 5, 1991).

"Lansbury Honored by NRB," *Calvary Contender* (June 1, 1993, Vol. 10, No. 11).

Laurentin, Rene. (Translated by O'Connell, Matthew J.) *Catholic Pentecostalism: An In-Depth Report on the Charismatic Renewal by a Renowned International Theologian* (Garden City, NY: Doubleday & Company, Inc., 1977).

Last Trumpet Newsletter (April 2001, Vol. 20, Issue 4).

Last Trumpet Newsletter (August 1999, Vol. 18, Issue 8).

Last Trumpet Newsletter (August 2000, Vol. 19, Issue 8).

Last Trumpet Newsletter (August 2001, Vol. 20, Issue 7 [sic]).

Last Trumpet Newsletter (December 2000, Vol. 19, Issue 12).

Last Trumpet Newsletter (January 1997, Vol. 16, Issue 1).

Last Trumpet Newsletter (July 2001, Vol. 20, Issue 7).

Last Trumpet Newsletter (June 1994, Vol. 13, Issue 6).

Last Trumpet Newsletter (October 1997, Vol. 16, Issue 10).

Last Trumpet Newsletter (September 1999, Vol. 18, Issue 9).

Lattin, Don. "Bishop Pushes Presidio Interfaith Group," *San Francisco Chronicle* (January 23, 1996).

Lattin, Don. "Religions of World Celebrate with Prayers to Dozen Deities," *San Francisco Chronicle* (June 26, 1995).

Latourette, Kenneth Scott. *A History of Christianity* (New York, NY: Harper and Row, 1953).

LaVey, Anton Szandor. *The Satanic Bible* (NY: Avon Books, 1969).

Lavin, Audrey. "The Sins of the Swaggarts," *Star* (1988, Vol. 15, Issue 8).

Lawrence, Malcolm. "Education Expert Announces 'Lame-Brain Awards,'" *Human Events* (May 3, 1986, Vol. 46, No. 18).

"Lawsuit Filed Over 'Impressions' Curriculum," *The Christian World Report* (February 1991, Vol. 3, No. 2).

"LCMS and LLL Mission Money Supporting Pro-Abortionist and Pro-Communists in China," *Christian News* (October 4, 1999, Vol. 37, No. 36).

"LCMS and LLL Supporting Liberals and Communists in China," *Christian News* (March 19, 2001, Vol. 39, No. 12).

"LCMS Has Gone 'Whimpish,' The," *Christian News* (July 8, 2001, Vol. 39, No. 28).

"LCMS Pastors and Laymen Asking—Who Invited Neuhaus and Dawn?," *Christian News* (March 28, 1994, Vol. 32, No. 13).

"LCMS Seminary President Praises Fortress Press," *Christian News* (December 4, 2000, Vol. 38, No. 45).

"LCMS Supporting the Wrong Side in China," *Christian News* (June 28, 1999, Vol. 37, No. 26).

"Leader of African National Congress Threatens Whites," *O Timothy* (1990, Vol. 7, Issue 7).

Leasor, James. *Rhodes and Barnato: The Premier and the Prancer* (London, England: Leo Cooper, 1997).

"Leighton Ford's New Ministry," *Calvary Contender* (October 15, 2000, Vol. 17, No. 20).

LeShan, Lawrence. *How to Meditate: A Guide to Self-Discovery* (Boston, MA: Little, Brown and Company, 1974).

"Leslie Weatherhead, Methodist Modernist," *Calvary Contender* (April 1, 2001, Vol. 18, No. 7).

Leslie, Lynn and Sarah. "Resurrecting Pagan Rites" (Part 2), *The Christian Conscience* (January 1996, Vol. 2, No. 1).

Leslie, Sarah H. "The Feminist As Oppressor," *The Christian Conscience* (March 1995, Vol. 1, No. 3).

"Let's Not Follow 'Orders,'" *The Christian World Report* (April 1991, Vol. 3, No. 4).

Levi, Eliphas. Translated by Waite, Arthur Edward. *The History of Magic Including a Clear and Precise Exposition of Its Procedure, Its Rites and Its Mysteries* (London, England: Cathedral House, 1922).

Leviton, Richard. "The Imagination of Pentecost: Rudolf Steiner and Contemporary Spirituality," *The Quest* (Autumn 1993, Vol. 6, No. 3).

Lewis, C. S. *Perelandra* (New York, NY: Macmillan Publishing Company, 1944).

Lewis, David Allen and Shreckhise, Robert. *UFO: End-Time Delusion* (Green Forest, AR: New Leaf Press, 1991).

"Liberal Lutherans Still Praise Tutu," *Christian News* (March 5, 2001, Vol. 39, No. 10).

"Liberal Who Parades As Evangelical," *The Perilous Times* (July 1999, Vol. 21, No. 5).

"Liberal Women Try to Create Gods in Their Own Image," *Christian News* (February 28, 1994, Vol. 32, No. 9).

"Liberals Find Meaning in Spiritual Politics: Summit Seeks Room on Left for Religion," *The Washington Times* (April 16, 1996).

"Lieberman, Gore, and God," *Power of Prophecy* (September 2000, Vol. 2000-09).

"Lieberman, The Talmud, The Noahide Laws and Judeo-Christians," *Christian News* (September 18, 2000, Vol. 38, No. 34).

Liichow, Robert S. *The Two Roots of Today's Revival* (Kearney, NE: Morris Publishing, 1997).

Limbaugh, Rush. *The Way Things Ought to Be* (New York, NY: Pocket Books, 1992).

"Lion, the Witch, and the VCR, The," *Breakpoint with Chuck Colson* (May 18-22, 1992, No. 221).

Lionni, Paolo. *The Leipzig Connection: The Systematic Destruction of American Education* (Sheridan, OR: Heron Books, 1993).

Lipnack, Jessica and Stamps, Jeffrey. "Networking the World: People, Corporation, Communities, and Nations," *The Futurist.*

Lipsey, McCurdy, "Some Little-Known Details About Graham Crusades Might Surprise You," *Christian News* (June 5, 2000, Vol. 38, No. 23).

Listen My Children (October 1989).

Lively, Scott and Abrams, Kevin. *The Pink Swastika* (Keizer, OR: Founders Publishing Corporation, 1995).

Livesey, Roy. *Understanding Deception, New Age Teaching in the Church* (Chichester, England: New Wine Press, 1987).

Livesey, Roy. *Understanding the New Age: World Government and World Religion* (Chichester, England: New Wine Press, 1989).

Living Bible Paraphrased: A Review, The (Nova Scotia, Canada: The Peoples Gospel Hour, n.d.).

"LLL and LCMS Still Backing Communist-Controlled China Christian Council," *Christian News* (February 5, 2001, Vol. 39, No. 6).

Lockwood, Bill. "United Nations—United Religion," *Christian News* (December 30, 1996, Vol. 34, No. 49).

Lofton, John. "Could Jackson Be Next?," *Christian News* (January 29, 2001, Vol. 39, No. 5).

Lofton, John. "Tony Campolo's Wife Says We Should 'Celebrate' Homosexual Marriages and That Our Lord Violated God's Law!," *Christian News* (April 11, 1994, Vol. 32, No. 15).

"Look Who's Bringing in a New Curriculum," *Christian Conscience* (December 1997, Vol. 3, No. 10).

Loux, Gordon and Wilson, Ronald E. *You Can Be a Point of Light* (Portland, OR: Multnomah Press, 1991).

Luckhoo, Lionel. *The Quran Is Not the Word of God* (Dallas, TX: Luckhoo Ministries, n.p.).

"'Lutheran Hour News' Features Zhidkov, Propagandist for Reds," *Christian News* (February 21, 2001, Vol. 39, No. 7).

Lutheran Standard, The (October 10, 1961).

"Lutherans Publish Book by 'Theological Atheist,'" *Christian News* (July 16, 2001, Vol. 39, No. 29).

"LWF General Secretary: Consultation on Indulgences," *Christian News* (February 26, 2001, Vol. 39, No. 9).

Lyons, Arthur. *Satan Wants You: The Cult of Devil Worship in America* (New York, NY: The Mysterious Press, 1988).

Maccri, Mary Ann. "A Call to Roman Catholics," *End of the World Chronicle* (March/April 1999, Vol. 2, Issue 2).

MacKenzie, Norman, Editor. *Secret Societies* (NY: Holt, Rinehart and Winston, 1967).

"Mafia, The," *Newsletter from a Christian Ministry* (September 1, 1993, Vol. 2, No. 12).

"Magic," *World Book Encyclopedia* (Vol. 12) (Chicago 54, IL: Field Enterprises Educational Corporation, 1961).

"Maitreya—A Latter Day Deception," *The Christian World Report* (June 1991, Vol. 3, No. 6).

"Maitreya's Message: Share and Save the World," *The Christ Is Now Here.*

"Major Ministries Jolted by Scandal," *Christian News* (July 3, 1995, Vol. 33, No. 27).

"Malcolm Muggeridge Still a Liberal," *Sword of the Lord* (March 31, 1989, Vol. 55, No. 7).

Malcolmson, Scott. "Sex and Death in Key West," *Mother Jones* (February/March 198, Vol. 13, No. 2).

"Man of Peace," *The Omega-Letter* (October 1988, Vol. 3, No. 9).

"Man of the Century," *Christian News* (March 20, 2000, Vol. 38, No. 12).

Manning, Al G. *Helping Yourself with Psycho-Cosmic Power* (West Nyack, NY: Parker Publishing Company, Inc., 1968).

Manschreck, Clyde L. *A History of Christianity: Readings in the History of the Church from the Reformation to the Present* (Englewood Cliffs, NJ: Prentice-Hall, Inc., 1964).

"Mao the Worst Mass Murderer Ever," *Christian News* (November 29, 1999, Vol. 37, No. 44).

Maple, Eric. *The Complete Book of Witchcraft and Demonology* (Cranbury, NJ: A. S. Barnes and Company, Inc., 1966 Edition).

"March Ahead of Time," *Kingdom Voice* (August 1990).

Mardis, Jeff. "The Greatest Words Ever Spoken by Mary: A Message to Roman Catholics" (Campbellsville, KY: The Contender, 2000).

"'Marketing Christianity' & 'Purpose Driven Church,'" Transcript of Radio Liberty Audio, *Despatch Magazine* (June 2001, Vol. 13:2).

Marr, Ron. "The Unbelievable Truth About Your Public Schools" (Niagara Falls, NY: Operation Clean Up, n.d.).

Marrs, Jim. *Rule by Secrecy: The Hidden History That Connects the Trilateral Commission, the Freemasons, and the Great Pyramids* (New York, NY: HarperCollins Publishers, Inc., 2000).

Marrs, Texe. "Al Gore's Hidden Ties with an Occult, Globalist Group," *Flashpoint* (January 1993).

Marrs, Texe. *America Shattered* (Austin, TX: Living Truth Publishers, 1991).

Marrs, Texe. *Big Sister Is Watching You* (Austin, TX: Living Truth Publishers, 1993).

Marrs, Texe. "Bill Clinton and the Bilderberger Conspiracy," *Flashpoint* (September 1992).

Marrs, Texe. "Bill Clinton and the Bilderberger Conspiracy," (Part II) *Flashpoint* (October 1992).

Marrs, Texe. "Christianity Afflicted with Doctrines of Devils," *Flashpoint* (December 1996, Vol. 96-12).

Marrs, Texe. "Chuck Colson: The Pied Piper of Ecumenicism," *Flashpoint* (October 1993).

Marrs, Texe. *Circle of Intrigue* (Austin, TX: Living Truth Ministries, 1995).

Marrs, Texe. *Dark Majesty: The Secret Brotherhood and the Magic of a Thousand Points of Light* (Austin, TX: Living Truth Publishers, 1992).

Marrs, Texe. *Dark Secrets of the New Age: Satan's Plan for a One World Religion* (Westchester, IL: Crossway Books, 1987).

Marrs, Texe. *Days of Hunger, Days of Chaos: The Coming Great Food Shortages in America* (Austin, TX: Rivercrest Publishing, 1999).

Marrs, Texe. "Global Explosion of Religious Apostasy," *Flashpoint* (July 1998, Vol. 98-7).

Marrs, Texe. "Greedy 'Christian' Leaders Taken in by New Age Hucksters," *Flashpoint* (October 1995, Vol. 95-10).

Marrs, Texe. "Has the Entire Christian Establishment Finally Just Gone Berserk?," *Power of Prophecy* (April 2001, Vol. 2001-04).

Marrs, Texe. "Heroism and Cowardice in the Lion's Den," *Flashpoint* (April 1994).

Marrs, Texe. "Inaugural Weirdness: Bill Clinton Takes Americans into 'the Twilight Zone,'" *Flashpoint* (March 1993).

Marrs, Texe. *Millennium: Peace, Promises, and the Day They Take Our Money Away* (Austin, TX: Living Truth Publishers, 1990).

Marrs, Texe. *Mystery Mark of the New Age: Satan's Design for World Domination* (Westchester, IL: Crossway Books, 1988).

Marrs, Texe. "New Agers Meet to Plan World Takeover," *Flashpoint* (January 1990).

Marrs, Texe. *Power of Prophecy* (February 10, 2001 program).

Marrs, Texe. *Power of Prophecy* (July 21, 2001 program).

Marrs, Texe. *Power of Prophecy* (July 28, 2001 program).

Marrs, Texe. *Power of Prophecy* (March 17, 2001 program).

Marrs, Texe. *Ravaged by the New Age: Satan's Plan to Destroy Our Kids* (Austin, TX: Living Truth Publishers, 1989).

Marrs, Texe. "Rockefeller Money, the Illuminati, and the Breeding of the New 'Super Man,'" *Flashpoint* (July 1993).

Marrs, Texe. "Secrets #60," *Power of Prophecy* (June 9, 2001 program).

Marrs, Texe. "Texe Marrs Asks Chuck Colson: 'Will You Sell Your Soul to the Devil for a Million Dollars?,'" *Flashpoint* (June 1993).

Marrs, Texe. *Texe Marrs Book of New Age Cults and Religions* (Austin, TX: Living Truth Publishers, 1990).

Marrs, Texe. "The Awful Truth About Billy Graham" (2-tape set).

Marrs, Texe. "The Billy Graham Dilemma," *Flashpoint* (March 1992).

Marrs, Texe. *The Dragon's Hot Breath: Unmasking the Awful Truth About "Christian" Rock Music* (Austin, TX: Living Truth Ministries, n.d.).

Marrs, Texe. "The Green Man or the Son of Skull & Bones...Who Will Be Our Next President," *Power of Prophecy* (January 2000, Vol. 2000-01).

Marrs, Texe. *The New Rome: Germany, The Fourth Reich, and the New Age Movement* (Austin, TX: Living Truth Publishers, 1999).

Marrs, Texe. "The Scandal of Christian Ghostwriting," *Flashpoint* (July 1996, Vol. 96-7).

Marrs, Texe. "The World Is More Queer Than Most People Think," *Power of Prophecy* (June 2001, Vol. 2001-06).

Marrs, Texe. "Unmasking the New Age Cults and Religions," *Flashpoint* (November/December 1990).

Marrs, Texe. "Witchcraft Invades Christianity: Sorcery and Magic Seduce Many into Depths of Satan," *Power of Prophecy* (December 2000, Vol. 2000-12).

Marrs, Wanda. *New Age Lies to Women* (Austin, TX: Living Truth Publishers, 1989).

Martin, Claire. "Food for Thought," *Denver Post* (March 1996).

Martin, Daniel. "The Earth Charter: A Religious Voice," *Creation Spirituality* (March/April 1992).

Martin, Rick. "The Most Powerful Man in the World? The 'Black' Pope Count Hans Kolvenbach—The Jesuit's General," *Free American Newsmagazine* (July 2000).

Martin, Walter. *Kingdom of the Cults.*

Martin, William. *A Prophet with Honor: The Billy Graham Story* (NY: William Morrow and Company, Inc., 1991).

Martinez, Jose. "Leary's Legacy Murky But Memorable at Harvard," *Christian News* (June 10, 1996), Vol. 34, No. 24).

Marx, G. O. "Why I Don't Want to Be Your Valentine," *The Voice in the Wilderness* (February 1992).

"Marxist Terrorists Help Snare RLDS Hierarchy's Program," *IPS Packet* (Independence, MO: Price Publishing Company, n.d.).

"Mary French Rockefeller Endowed Chair in New Testament Established," *Hilltop.*

"Mary French Rockefeller, Trustee, Dies at 86," *Hilltop* (Summer 1997, Vol. 9, No. 1).

"Mary's Era," *National Catholic Register* (October 22-28, 2000, Vol. 76, No. 43).

"Maryland Coalition of Concerned Parents," *Watch* (Spring 1989).

"Masonic Treachery in High Places: The Wicked Deeds of Bill Clinton, Bob Dole, Al Gore, Jack Kemp, Jesse Helms, and Barry Goldwater," *Flashpoint* (November 1996, Vol. 96-11).

Master, The. "The Emergence of Maitreya," *Network News* (April/May 1987, Vol. 4, No. 4-5).

Mateer, Robert. "In Memory," *Christian Perspectives* (Fall/Winter 1997, Vol. 10, No. 2).

Matt, Michael J. "Al Gore—A Truly Frightening Environmentalist," *Christian News* (October 12, 1992, Vol. 30, No. 37).

Matzat, Don. *Inner Healing: Deliverance or Deception?* (Eugene, OR: Harvest House Publishers, 1987).

"May Is the Month of 100th Birthday!!!," *Powerlines* (May 1998).

McAfee, Franklyn M. "Creation, Evolution or Creationary Evolution?," *Soul* (July-August 1996, Vol. 47, No. 4).

McAlvany Intelligence Advisor, The (March 1995).

McAlvany Intelligence Advisor, The (November 1992).

McAlvany, Don. *Confronting Our Nation's Problems: The Financial, Political, and Spiritual Decline of America* (Oklahoma City, OK: Southwest Radio Church, n.d.).

McBirnie, W. S. *The Coming "World Church": Why It Is Feared by True Christians* (Independence, MO: Gospel Tract Society, Inc., n.d.).

McBrien, Richard P. *Lives of the Popes: The Pontiffs from St. Peter to John Paul II* (New York, NY: HarperSanFrancisco, 1997).

McCaffrey, Roger A., Editor. *Sursum Corda!* (Fort Collins, CO: Foundation for Catholic Reform, n.d.).

McCall, William. "Ecumenism, 'Global Spirituality' and Mother Teresa," *Christian Inquirer* (April 1985).

McCall, William. "Scholars Seek New Image of God," *Christian News* (March 27, 2000, Vol. 38, No. 13).

McCloughry, Roy. "Basic Stott: Candid Comments on Justice, Gender, and Judgment," *Christianity Today* (January 8, 1996).

McCormick, W. J. McK. *Christ, the Christian, and Freemasonry* (Belfast, Ireland: Great Joy Publications, 1984).

McDonald, Elizabeth. *Alpha: The Unofficial Guide* (Cambridge, England: St. Matthew Publishing, Ltd., 2001).

McDowell, Josh and Stewart, Don. *Understanding the Occult* (San Bernardino, CA: Here's Life Publishers, Inc., 1982).

McIlhany, William. "The WCC: A Haven for Marxists?," *Family Protection Scoreboard.*

McIntire, Carl. "'One World Worship': The UN Uses Religion, but They Are Making Their Own," *Christian News* (May 15, 1995, Vol. 33, No. 20).

McIntire, Carl. "Perversion and Subversion in the World Council of Churches," *O Timothy* (1988, Vol. 5, Issue 6).

McKechnie, Dale. "The New Group of World Servers: Vanguard of the New Age: Signs of the New World Religion," "Festival Week of the New Group of World Servers" (December 19, 21, and 28, 1998).

McKeever, Jeani. "God Is Alive and Well and Visiting America!," *END-Times News Digest* (March 1997, Issue 222).

McLaughlin, Corinne and Davidson, Gordon. *Spiritual Politics: Changing the World from the Inside Out* (NY: Ballantine Books, 1994).

McLean, Terence D. "Whatever Happened to Godly Music?," *Christian News* (September 29, 1997).

McLoughlin, William G. and Bellah, Robert N. *Religion in America* (Boston, MA: Houghton Mifflin Company, 1968).

McMahon, T. A. "The 'Evangelical' Seduction," *The Berean Call* (April 1996).

McMahon, T. A. "Why Evangelize Roman Catholics?," *The Berean Call* (June 2001).

McMahon, T. A. "Why It Matters" (Part II), *The Berean Call* (November 1999).

McManus, John F. "Still Traveling the Red Road," *The New American* (December 13, 1993, Vol. 9, No. 25).

McManus, John F. "The Council on Foreign Relations: Early History Shows Its Subversive Designs," *America 2000/Goals 2000* 1994.

Means, Pat. *The Mystical Maze: A Guidebook Through the Mindfields of Eastern Mysticism* (Campus Crusade for Christ, Inc., 1976).

"Media Controlled by the Few," *Flashpoint* (March 1998, Vol. 98-3).

Media Spotlight (Received 1995).

Media Spotlight (Vol. 20, No. 2).

"Meet Maurice Strong," *Eco◆Logic* (November/December 1995, No. 29).

Meisler, Stanley. *United Nations: The First Fifty Years* (New York, NY: The Atlantic Monthly Press, 1995).

Melton, J. Gordon. *The Encyclopedia of American Religions* (Vol. 2) (Wilmington, NC: McGrath Publishing Company, 1978).

Melton, J. Gordon, Clark, Jerome and Kelly, Aidan A. *New Age Almanac* (Detroit, MI: Visible Ink, 1991).

"Members of the DeMolay Hall of Fame," *The Scottish Rite Journal* (March 1994, Vol. 102, No. 3).

Meredith, Lawrence. "The Gospel According to Kazantzakis: How Close Did Scorsese Come?," *The Christian Century* (September 14-21, 1988).

"Message, The," *The BDM Letter* (March/April 1995, Vol. 4, No. 2).

"Methodist Church to Remain in NCC," *The Vine and Branches* (Summer 2000, Vol. 15, Issue 3).

"Metzger a Liberal," *Calvary Contender* (January 1, 1997, Vol. 14, No. 1).

Meves, Virginia. "Now the Question! How Is It in Your Church? Does the Light of Christ Shine or.....?," *Wisconsin Report* (November 28, 1996, Vol. 21, No. 46).

Michaelsen, Johanna. *Like Lambs to the Slaughter* (Eugene, OR: Harvest House Publishers, 1989).

Michaelsen, Johanna. *The Beautiful Side of Evil* (Eugene, OR: Harvest House Publishers, 1982).

Midnight Call (August 1992).

"Midrash—What Is It?," *Despatch Magazine* (June 2000, Vol. 12, No. 2).

Miesel, Rick. "Billy Graham: General Teachings/Activities" (Biblical Discernment Ministries, Revised January 1994).

Miesel, Rick. "Colson: General Teachings/Activities" (Biblical Discernment Ministries) (on disk).

Miesel, Rick. "Hugh Ross," Computer Discernment Notebook.

Miesel, Rick. "InterVarsity Christian Fellowship: A Fellowship of Neo-Evangelicals" (Biblical Discernment Ministries, n.d.).

Miesel, Rick. "Promise Keepers: Ecumenical 'Macho-Men' for Christ?" (Biblical Discernment Ministries, Revised March 1996).

Miesel, Rick. "Robert Schuller" (Biblical Discernment Ministries).

Miesel, Rick. "Roman Catholicism: General Notes" (Biblical Discernment Ministries, Revised August 1997).

Miesel, Rick. "Roman Catholicism—Christian or Pagan" (Biblical Discernment Ministries, Revised August 1997).

Miesel, Rick. "Youth with a Mission: Ecumenical (Catholic/Charismatic) Evangelism" (Biblical Discernment Ministries, n.d.).

Miller, Elliott. *A Crash Course on the New Age Movement: Describing and Evaluating a Growing Social Force* (Grand Rapids, MI: Baker Book House, 1989).

Millheim, John Edward. "KGB, Secret Police and the World Council of Churches," *Christian News* (February 1, 1993, Vol. 31, No. 5).

Mills, Robert P. "Habitat for Humanity Builds on Christian Foundations," *The Presbyterian Layman* (March/April 2001, Vol. 34, No. 2).

Mind/Body Medicine (1995, Vol. 1, No. 3).

Mindszenty Report (March 1996, Vol. 37, No. 3).

Ministries Today (September/October 2000).

"Missing the Real Message of Moses," *Christian News* (December 14, 1998, Vol. 36, No. 46).

"Modernists Among 'Greatest Preachers,'" *Calvary Contender* (January 15, 2000).

Moholy-Nagy, Siby. "Gargoyle," *The World Book Encyclopedia* (Vol. 7) (Chicago 54, IL: Field Enterprise Educational Corporation, 1961 Edition).

"Mollenkott, Homosexuality, Bible Translation," *Calvary Contender* (November 1, 1993, Vol. 10, No. 21).

Mollenkott, Virginia. "Jesus Christ Was Really a Woman," *Christian News* (July 21, 1997, Vol. 35, No. 29).

Mollenkott, Virginia. "Women and the Bible," *Sojourners* (February 1976).

Mollenkott, Virginia. "Women and the Bible," *Sojourners* (June 1977).

Mollenkott, Virginia Ramey. "Whore-ishly Implementing the Political Vision of the Christ-Sophia," *CLOUTreach* (Summer/Autumn 1995, Vol. 4, No. 3).

Mollenkott, Virginia Ramey. *Women, Men, and the Bible* (Nashville, TN: Abingdon, 1977).

"Mollenkott a Homosexual," *Calvary Contender* (September 15, 1997, Vol. 14, No. 18).

"Mollenkott a Lesbian...and More!," *Calvary Contender* (April 1, 1993, Vol. 10, No. 7).

Mollere, William J. "Five-Star Performance: DeMolay and Its Founder," *The Scottish Rite Journal* (March 1994, Vol. 102, No. 3).

Monteith, Stanley. *Brotherhood of Darkness* (Oklahoma City, OK: Hearthstone Publishing, 2000).

Monteith, Stanley. "Brotherhood of Darkness," *Prophetic Observer* (January 2001, Vol. 8, No. 1).

Montgomery, Ruth. *A Gift of Prophecy: The Phenomenal Jeane Dixon* (NY: William Morrow & Company, 1965).

Montgomery, Ruth. *Strangers Among Us* (NY: Coward, McCann and Geoghegan, 1979).

Montgomery, Ruth. *Threshold to Tomorrow,* (New York, NY: G. P. Putnam's Son, 1982).

"Moody Founder's Week Features Ecumenicals," *Calvary Contender* (December 15, 1995).

"Moon Says He Is the Messiah," *Christian News* (May 31, 1993, Vol. 31, No. 22).

Mooney, Lucindi Frances. *Storming Eastern Temples: A Psychological Explanation of Yoga* (Wheaton, IL: The Theosophical Publishing House, 1976).

"Moralphobic," *Christian News* (November 11, 1991, Vol. 29, No. 41).

Moran, Hugh A. and Kelley, David H. *The Alphabet and the Ancient Calendar Signs* (Palo Alto, CA: Daily Press, 1969).

"More A. B. S. Blasphemy," *Calvary Contender* (September 1, 1992, Vol. 9, No. 17).

"More Communist Praise," *The Christian World Report* (December 1990, Vol. 2, No. 9).

"More in Common Then (sic) You Think," *The Voice in the Wilderness* (November 1999).

"More Muslims Than Anglicans in England?," *Calvary Contender* (July 1, 1997, Vol. 14, No. 13).

"More on Billy Kim," *Calvary Contender* (May 1, 1993, Vol. 10, No. 9).

"More on New Era Scam," *Calvary Contender* (August 1, 1995).

"More Questions and Answers," *F. A. Newsletter* (June 86).

"More Reflections from Stanford," *United Religions* (Fall 1997, Issue 4).

Morey, Robert A. "A Refutation of Roman Catholicism," *The Researcher* (January/February 1993).

Morey, Robert A. *Horoscopes and the Christian* (Minneapolis, MN: Bethany House Publishers, 1981).

Morey, Robert A. *Islam Unveiled: The True Desert Storm* (Shermans Dale, PA: The Scholars Press, 1991).

Morey, Robert A. *The Origins and Teachings of Freemasonry* (Southbridge, MA: Crowne Publications, Inc., 1990).

Morris, John D. "Evolution and the Wages of Sin," *Impact* (November 1990).

Morris, S. Brent, Editor. *Heredom: The Transactions of The Scottish Rite Research Society* (Vol. 5) (Washington, D.C.: The Scottish Rite Research Center, 1996).

Morrison, Alan. *The Serpent and the Cross: Religious Corruption in an Evil Age* (Birmingham, England: K & M Books, 1994).

"Moscow to Host Second Summit of Political and Religious Leaders," *The Christian World Report* (January 1990, Vol. 2, No. 1).

Moseley, Leonard. *Dulles: A Biography of Elmer, Allen, and John Foster Dulles* (1970).

"'Most Internationally Representative Gathering, Secular or Religious, in Human History' Officially Being in Amsterdam, The," *Christian News* (August 7, 2000, Vol. 38, No. 32).

"Mother Teresa," Biblical Discernment Ministries—Revised 3/96).

"Mother Teresa: Loving Idol Worshiper," *The Battle Cry* (July/August 1991).

Mothers' Watch (Summer 1995, Vol. 1, No. 4).

"Move by Christian Leaders to Sanction Islam, The," *The Vine and Branches* (Summer 1998, Vol. 13, Issue 3).

"Movies," *Media Spotlight* (1998, Vol. 21, No. 4).

"'Mr. Bush, the World Doesn't Want to Be American,'" *Despatch Magazine* (March 2001, Vol. 13, No. 1).

"Mrs. Tony Compolo (sic) Promotes Homosexual Weddings," *Christian News* (September 26, 1994, Vol. 32, No. 35).

MSA "Freemasonry's Servant": How It Works (Silver Spring, MD: The Masonic Service Association of the United States, n.d.).

"MTV Bans Madonna Video," *The Christian World Report* (March 1991, Vol. 3, No. 3).

"Muller on World Citizenship," *The Perilous Times* (August 2001, Vol. 22, No. 12).

Muller, Robert. *First Lady of the World* (Anacortes, WA: World Happiness and Cooperation, 1991).

Muller, Robert. *Framework for Preparation for the Year 2000, the 21st Century and the Third Millennium* (Hamden, CT: Albert Schweitzer Institute/Quinnipiac College Press, 1994).

Muller, Robert. *New Genesis: Shaping a Global Spirituality* (Garden City, NY: Image Books, 1984).

Muller, Robert. "Religions and Spiritual Traditions: The World Needs You Very Much!," *World Goodwill* (1994, No. 1).

Muller, Robert. *The Birth of a Global Civilization* (Anacortes, WA: World Happiness and Cooperation, 1991).

Mullin, Glenn H. "A Meeting with Kun-Don, the Holy One," *American Theosophist* (Fall 1984).

"Multinational Corporations and the Loss of Sovereignty," *The Florida Forum* (Spring 1998).

Murphy, Joseph M. *Santeria: African Spirits in America* (Boston, MA: Beacon Press, 1993 Edition).

Murphy, Robert. "Getting Together," *The News and Observer* (November 12, 1996).

Murray, William J. *My Life Without God* (Nashville, TN: Thomas Nelson Publishers, 1982).

"Music Videos with a Gospel Message," *Charisma and Christian Life* (June 1991, Vol. 16, No. 11).

Mystic Trader, The (Fall 1985).

Mystic Trader, The (Winter 1984).

Naar, Jon. "The Green Cathedral: In This Crusading Congregation, Ecology is 'God's Work,'" *The Amicus Journal* (Winter 1993).

"NAE '96 Speakers," *Calvary Contender* (March 1, 1996, Vol. 13, No. 5).

"NAE Features Cho As Speaker," *Calvary Contender* (March 1, 2001, Vol. 18, No. 5).

"NAE Head Don Argue Popular with NCC & Clinton," *Calvary Contender* (April 15, 1997, Vol. 14, No. 8).

"NAE's World Relief Gets Big Bucks from U. S. Government to Distribute Condoms?," *Calvary Contender* (April 15, 1998, Vol. 15, No. 8).

"NAE's World Relief Gets Big Bucks from U. S. Government to Distribute Condoms?," *Christian News* (October 5, 1998, Vol. 36, No. 36).

"Named to Canterbury," *The Christian Century* (August 8-15, 1990, Vol. 107, No. 23).

National and International Religion Report, The (April 25, 1988, Vol. 2, No. 8).

"National and World Council of Churches Call for UN Intervention in America's Internal Affairs," *O Timothy* (1995, Vol. 12, Issue 5).

"National Baptists Forgive Lyons," *Calvary Contender* (October 15, 1997, Vol. 14, No. 20).

"National Council of Churches Hails Evangelical Bylaw Change," *Christian News* (March 27, 2000, Vol. 38, No. 13).

"National Council of Churches Has Chosen a Roman Catholic Woman, The," *Foundation* (July-September 1995, Vol. 16, Issue 4).

"National Council of Churches Head Supports Homosexuals", *O Timothy* (1994, Vol. 11, Issue 11).

"National Council of Churches Turns to Evangelicals and Roman Catholics," *The Vine and Branches* (2000, Vol. 15, Issue 5).

"National Endowment of the Arts Sinks to All-Time Low," *The Voice in the Wilderness* (March 1992).

"National Enquirer Bombshell: Jesse Jackson Love Child; Mistress Paid in Cash," *Christian News* (January 22, 2001, Vol. 39, No. 4).

"National Religious Broadcasters: 55th Annual Convention and Exposition," *The ACCC Report* (July 1998).

"Nau Authors New Book for China," *Christian News* (February 26, 2001, Vol. 39, No. 9).

"Navy Chaplains Take on a New Role," *Breakthroughs* (February 2001).

"NCC & Same-Sex 'Marriage,'" *Calvary Contender* (December 1, 2000, Vol. 17, No. 23).

"NCC a Sinking Ship?," *Calvary Contender* (January 1, 2000, Vol. 17, No. 1).

"NCC Establishes Pillars of Peace for 21st Century," *Media Spotlight* (2000, Vol. 23, No. 2).

"NCC Greets Homosexual Church Leader," *Calvary Contender* (February 15, 1999, Vol. 16, No. 4).

"NCC Near Death, but Wants Resurrection," *Calvary Contender* (July 1, 2000, Vol. 17, No. 13).

"NCC Official Endorses PP Sex-Ed Video," *Calvary Contender* (September 15, 1997, Vol. 14, No. 18).

"NCC Turns to Evangelicals, Catholics for Financial Help," *Calvary Contender* (September 15, 2000).

"NCC, Habitat Form New Partnership," *Calvary Contender* (July 15, 2001, Vol. 18, No. 14).

"NCC, Young Find No Persecution in China," *Calvary Contender* (January 15, 1999, Vol. 16, No. 2).

"NCC: New Leaders, New Woes," *Calvary Contender* (December 1, 1999, Vol. 16, No. 23).

NCC/WCC—Communism's Helpers, The (Virginia Beach, VA: Good News Baptist Church, n.d.).

"NCEA 1985 'and the Strange Gods of Syncretism,'" *Distant Drums* (June 1985, Vol. 7, No. 2).

"NEA Anti-Obscenity Pledge Ruled 'Unconstitutional,'" *The Christian World Report* (March 1991, Vol. 3, No. 3).

"NEA Funds Book Depicting Jesus As Homosexual Pedophile," *AFA Journal* (March 1992, Vol. 16, No. 3).

"NEA Funds Involved in Play Depicting Jesus As 'Gay,'" *Calvary Contender* (July 15, 1998, Vol. 15, No. 14).

"NEA Gets More Funds," *Calvary Contender* (July 1, 1993, Vol. 10, No. 13).

"NEA Gives Grant for 'Lesbian Art,'" *The Christian World Report* (February 1991, Vol. 3, No. 2).

NEA: The Grab for Power: A Chronology of the National Education Association (Oklahoma City, OK: Hearthstone Publishing, 2000).

"NEA-Funded Blasphemy," *The Christian World Report* (March 1990, Vol. 2, No. 3).

Neckar, Andy. "Rome and Hindus: Together in Pagan Pageantry," *Christian News and Re-Views* (September 25, 1998).

Necronomicon (New York, NY: Avon Books, 1977).

"Needed: America-First Locally Controlled Education" (n.d.).

"Neo-Orthodox Christianity," *The Watchman Expositor* (1998, Vol. 15, No. 5).

Neven, Tom. "Hollywood Gets One Right," *Focus on the Family* (December 1998, Vol. 22, No. 12).

New Age Adversary Bulletin and Old Time Gospel Advocate, The (January 1993, Vol. 8, No. 1).

"New Age Church Active," *Flashpoint* (March 1991).

New Age Journal (March/April 1987, Vol. 3, Issue 2).

New Age Journal (September/October 1987, Vol. 3, Issue 5).

New Age Magazine, The (December 1929).

New Age Movement—Age of Aquarius—Age of Antichrist, The (Oklahoma City, OK: Southwest Radio Church, 1982).

"New Age Politics and Education," *The Emergence* (January 1992, Vol. 9, No. 1).

"New Age Satanism Flourishes in Russia," *Flashpoint* (February 1990).

"New Books for Children," *The Perilous Times* (February 1999, Vol. 20, No. 12).

New Call to Peacemaking: A Cooperative Program of Brethren, Friends and Mennonites (Elkhart, IN: n.d.).

"New Chancellor and President Named," *Hilltop* (Winter 1996-1997, Vol. 8, No. 3).

"New Creation Institute, Au Sable in Join Effort," *Notes from Au Sable Institute of Environmental Studies* (Spring 1989, Vol. 2, No. 1).

"New Dynamics," *One World* (April 1990, No. 154).

"New Era Auction Scheduled Monday," *Reading Eagle* (October 1, 1995).

"New Era Founder Gets 12 Years," *Calvary Contender* (November 15, 1997, Vol. 14, No. 22).

"New Evangelical Scholars Explain Away Hell," *The Christian World Report* (May 1991, Vol. 3, No. 5).

"New Findings on Religious Behavior and Attitudes," *Christian World Report* (May 1991, Vol. 3, No. 5).

"New Gospel Emerging," *Media Spotlight* (1997, Vol. 20, No. 2).

"New Group of World Servers and the Sacred Mysteries, The," *Diamond Light* (1998, No. 3).

New Larousse Encyclopedia of Mythology (Prometheus Press, 1972 Edition).

"New Liberal Religious/Political Group Deplores 'False Choices,' Redefines Evangelism," *Christian News* (July 1, 1996, Vol. 34, No. 27).

"New Red Hats—and the Next Pope?," *Newsweek* (January 22, 2001).

"New Right: Part II: The Religious Heritage of America: Instrument of Brotherhood, The" *Distant Drums* (December 1980, Vol. 2, No. 5).

"New Right, The" (Part III), *Distant Drums* (March 1981, Vol. 3, No. 1).

New Times (September/October 1985, No. 854).

"New World Order and the Rise of Antichrist, The," *The Omega Letter* (April 1991, Vol. 6, No. 4).

New World Order, The (Milford, PA: America's Future, Inc., 1992).

New World Order: A Critique and Chronology, The (Milford, PA: America's Future, Inc., n.d.).

New World Religion, The (New York, NY: World Goodwill, n.d.).

"Newbigin Dies," *Calvary Contender* (March 15, 1998, Vol. 15, No. 6).

"Newbigin, Wiersbe to Speak at Samford," *Calvary Contender* (July 1, 1997, Vol. 14, No. 13).

News (October 19, 1994).

"News Alert," *The Berean Call* (January 1995).

"News Alert," *The Berean Call* (October 1992).

News & Observer, The (June 24, 2001).

News & Views (June 1988).

"News & Views," *Plains Baptist Challenger* (May 1993, Vol. 52, No. 5).

"News Bits from Here and There," *Voice in the Wilderness* (March 2000).

"News Briefs," *CIB Bulletin* (December 1989, Vol. 5, No. 12).

"News Briefs," *CIB Bulletin* (June 1989, Vol. 5, No. 6).

"News Notes," *Hilltop* (Summer 1997, Vol. 8, No. 2).

"News of Interest to Christians," *Sword of the Lord* (November 23, 1990, Vol. 56, No. 24).

Newsletter from a Christian Ministry (July 1, 1993, Vol. 2, No. 10).

Newsletter from a Christian Ministry (October 1992, Vol. 1, No. 8).

Newsletter from Radio Liberty (April 2001).

Newsletter from Radio Liberty (August 2000).

Newsletter from Radio Liberty (July 2000).

Newsletter from Radio Liberty (July 2001).

Newsletter from Radio Liberty (May 2001).

Newsletter from Radio Liberty (September 1999).

"NewsNotes," *Calvary Contender* (August 1, 1997, Vol. 14, No. 15).

Newton, Joseph Fort. *River of Years: An Autobiography* (Philadelphia, PA: J. B. Lippincott Company, 1946).

Newton, Joseph Fort *The Builders: A Story and Study of Masonry* (Cedar Rapids, IA: The Torch Press, 1914).

Nickel, Jake. "Graham Crusade Features Father and Son for First Time," *Mennonite Reporter* (November 27, 1995).

Niebuhr, Gustav. "Tucker Case May Split Evangelical Christians," *New York Times* (February 4, 1998).

Niebuhr, Ursala, Editor. *Remembering Reinhold Niebuhr* (New York, NY: HarperSanFrancisco, 1991).

"NIV Owner Big Pornography Publisher," *O Timothy* (1994, Vol. 11, Issue 6).

"NIV to Go 'Gender-Neutral?,'" *Calvary Contender* (April 15, 1997, Vol. 14, No. 8).

"No! Steps to Create Peace" (New York, NY: Socialist Party, n.d.).

"Noahide Laws: Religion of a New World Order," *GANPAC Brief* (February 1992, No. 112).

Noebel, David A. *Is the NCC Really Soft on Communism?* (Tulsa, OK: Christian Crusade, n.d.).

Noebel, David A. *The Marxist Minstrels: A Handbook on Communist Subversion of Music* (Tulsa, OK: American Christian College Press, 1974).

Nolan, Bruce. "Harry Potter Casts No Spell on Christian Booksellers," *Christian News* (July 24, 2000, Vol. 38, No. 30).

Noll, Richard A. "The Tetelestai Initiative: Paid in Full" (Part IV), *Midnight Call* (July 2000).

"Norman Mattoon Thomas," Softkey Multimedia Inc., Infopedia (1996).

"Norman Vincent Peale to be Honored on National T.V.," *Christian News* (January 22, 2001, Vol. 39, No. 4).

"Norman Vincent Peale Was Gourgas Medalist," *The Northern Light* (February 1994, Vol. 25, No. 1).

"North Korea: A Little Crack in the Door," *Samaritan's Purse* (July 2000).

"Not All Are Deceived by Communist China's 'New Face': An Australian Journalist Reports China's Deceitful Plan," *O Timothy* (1994, Vol. 2, Issue 5).

"Not Just Another Denomination," *The Omega-Letter* (October 1989, Vol. 4, No. 9).

"Noted Evangelist Issues Conflicting Views on Salvation," *Christian News* (November 25, 1996), Vol. 34, No. 44).

Now Is the Dawning of the New Age New World Order (Oklahoma City, OK: Hearthstone Publishing, Ltd., 1991).

"NRB Cuts Ties with NAE," *Calvary Contender* (March 1, 2001, Vol. 18, No. 5).

O Timothy (1984, Vol. 1, Issue 4).

O Timothy (1985, Vol. 2, Issue 3).

O Timothy (1986, Vol. 3, Issue 7).

O Timothy (1987, Vol. 4, Issues 3-4).

O Timothy (1994, Vol. 11, Issue 11).

O Timothy (1995, Vol. 12, Issue 11).

Observer, The (January 17, 1996)

"Occultic Nature of The 21st Century Bridge!, The," *Last Trumpet Newsletter* (January 1997, Vol. 16, Issue 1).

Olinger, Dan. "Moon's Message to America," *Faith for the Family* (July/August 1985, Vol. 14, No. 6).

Oliver, George. *Signs and Symbols* (NY: Macoy Publishing and Masonic Supply Company, 1906).

Oltmans, William. "Who Are the Real Terrorists in South Africa," *O Timothy* (1989, Vol. 6, Issue 7).

Omega-Letter, The (April 1989, Vol. 4, No. 3).

Omega-Letter, The (April 1990, Vol. 5, No. 4).

Omega-Letter, The (March 1991, Vol. 6, No. 3).

"On Being 'Born-Again,'" *Focus Express* (January/February 2000).

"On Papal Primacy," *Our Sunday Visitor* (July 29, 2001, Vol. 90, No. 13).

"On the Left: Religion, Politics & One-Worldism," *Mindszenty Report* (March 1996, Vol. 37, No. 3).

"On the Mass," *The Gospel Standard* (June 1994, Vol. 43, No. 10).

One Books (no other information available).

One in Christ (New York, NY: NCC Department of Communication, Received November 17, 1994).

"One More Step Toward World Government," *The Christian World Report* (March 1994, Vol. 9, No. 3).

"*'One World'* Movement, The" *The Florida Forum* (Summer 1998).

"Open Conspiracy, The," *Don Bell Reports* (February 21, 1986, Vol. 33, No. 8).

"Openness Debate, The," *Calvary Contender* (March 15, 2001, Vol. 18, No. 6).

"Oppose New Age Funding Legislation," *The Christian World Report* (August 1989, Vol. 1, No. 6).

"Oral Roberts Embraces Wealth, Mikhail Gorbachev, and the Democratic Party," *Flashpoint* (May 1996, Vol. 96-5).

"Order of DeMolay Helps Shape Futures of Young Men," *Charity: A Masonic Ideal* (January 1996).

"Orlando '95 Celebrates Unity in the Holy Spirit," *Focus Express* (November 1995).

Ostling, Richard N. and Joan K. *Mormon America: The Power and the Promise* (New York, NY: HarperSanFrancisco, 1999).

Ostling, Richard N. "National Council of Churches Falls upon Hard Times," *Christian News* (November 29, 1999, Vol. 37, No. 44).

Other Side, The (April 1986, Vol. 22, No. 3, Issue 171).

Other Side, The (January/February 1988).

Other Side, The (March 1988, Vol. 24, No. 2, Issue 190).

Otten, Herman. "Get Out of the WCC," *Christian News,* (February 1, 1993, Vol. 31, No. 5).

Otten, Walter. "A Rose by Any Other Name...or Any Organization Bred by IAF Is Still the Offspring of Saul Alinsky or Immovable Church Bureaucracy," *Christian News* (October 13, 1997, Vol. 35, No. 37).

"Our Common Future: Rock Stars and World Leaders Join in the Largest Consciousness Raising Media Event of All Time...," *The Omega-Letter* (June 1989, Vol. 4, No. 5).

Our Sunday Visitor (February 22, 1998, Vol. 86, No. 43).

"Outgoing NAE Chief Says NCC Policy Change a Factor in Resignation," *Calvary Contender* (August 15, 2001, Vol. 18, No. 16).

Overby, Barbara L. "Spiritual Philanthropy: A Communist Perspective," *The Bridging Tree* (Winter 2000-2001, Vol. 4, Issue 1).

"Oxford Conference: An Update on the Emerging Coalition of Political and Spiritual Leaders," *Omega-Letter* (July/August 1988, Vol. 3, No. 7).

"Packer Criticizes Fundamentalists," *Calvary Contender* (September 15, 1998, Vol. 15, No. 18).

Packer, J. I. "Still Surprised by Lewis," *Christianity Today* (September 7, 1998).

Paisley, Ian. "Billy Graham's Tragic Romeward Run," *O Timothy* (1993, Vol. 10, Issue 9).

Pallenberg, Corrado. *Inside the Vatican* (New York City 11, NY: Hawthorn Books, Inc., 1960).

Palmer, John L. "Vision 2013 and Habitat for Humanity in Tennessee," *The Scottish Rite Journal* (June 1998, Vol. 106, No. 6).

"Panorama," *Christian News* (November 11, 1991, Vol. 29, No. 41).

"Papacy and the 'Rock' of Matthew 16, The," *Jesus People Newsletter* (1999, Vol. 27, Issue 2).

Paquette, Michal J. "Evangelicals, Catholics Issue Joint Mission Statement," *Christian News* (April 11, 1994, Vol. 32, No. 15).

Parchment, S. R. *Ancient Operative Masonry* (San Francisco, CA: San Francisco Center—Rosicrucian Fellowship, 1930).

Paris, Edmond. *The Secret History of the Jesuits* (Chino, CA: Chick Publications, 1975).

Parker, Kimberly. "The Abortion Connection: Linking Schools to Health Care," *The Christian Conscience* (May 1995, Vol. 1, No. 5).

Parks, Rosa with Redd, Gregory J. *Quiet Strength: The Faith, the Hope, and the Heart of a Woman Who Changed a Nation* (Grand Rapids, MI: Zondervan Publishing House, 1994).

"Parliament of World Religions Meets to Discuss Need for Unity Based on 'Global Ethic,'" *Foundation* (January-February 2000, Vol. 21, Issue 1).

"Parliament of World Religions: Comments by People We Trust," *Flashpoint* (September 1993).

"Parliament of World's Religions Event in New York," *Christian News* (September 20, 1999).

Parrinder, Geoffrey, Editor. *World Religions: From Ancient History to the Present* (New York, NY: Facts on File Publications, 1971, 1983).

"Participants Announced for Inauguration," *Christian News* (December 28, 1992, Vol. 30, No. 48), p.1.

Partlow, R. A. *Satan's Subtle Sabotage of God's Holy Word* (Erie, PA: The Stable, 1997).

Passport (October/November 1987).

"Pastor of Thailand's Largest Church Is in Fellowship with Rome," *O Timothy* (1991, Vol. 8, Issue 10-12).

Path of Light, The (Franklin, MI: Harmony Horizons, Inc., n.d.).

Pati, Abhay K. "Health and Healing—An Interview with Benjamin Creme," *IJHHM* (Winter 1984).

Patrick, James R. Compiler and Editor, *America 2000/Goals 2000* (Moline, IL: Citizens for Academic Excellence, 1994).

"Patriotic Civil Religion," *The Little Cloud Report* (October 1994).

Patterson, Paige. "Prince of Egypt Worthy of Evangelical 'Greenbacks,'" *Christian News* (February 8, 1999, Vol. 37, No. 6).

"Pattillo Chosen for NCC Staff," *Calvary Contender* (March 15, 2001, Vol. 18, No. 6).

Patton, Ron. "The Depopulation Agenda," *Endure to the End* (October 1994, Vol. 1, Issue 1).

"Patty's (sic) Critics Are Few, Despite Affair," *Christian News* (October 30, 1995, Vol. 33, No. 40).

"Paul Harvey Promotes Global Religion," *The Perilous Times* (November 1998).

"Paul Johannes Tillich," Softkey Multimedia Inc., Infopedia (1996).

Paul VI. "Decree on Ecumenism: Unitatis Redintegratio" (no other info available).

Paull, Robert C., Editor. *Achievement Skills: Guidelines for Personal Growth* (Teacher's Guide) (Thomas Jefferson Research Center, 1984).

Paulson, Michael. "Confession Is Good for the Mind, Too," *Catholic Digest* (June 2001, Vol. 65, No. 8).

"Pax Christi Catholic Anti-War Movement," *Calvary Contender* (April 1, 2001, Vol. 18, No. 7).

"Peace at the Expense of Purity," *Calvary Contender* (April 1, 1999, Vol. 16, No. 7).

"'Peace' Prize That the World Gives, The," *The Christian World Report* (February 1991, Vol. 3, No. 2).

Peale, Norman Vincent. "No More Stress or Tension," *Plus, The Magazine of Positive Thinking* (Pawling, NY: Foundation for Christian Living, May, 1986).

Peale, Norman Vincent. "What Freemasonry Means to Me," *The Scottish Rite Journal* (February 1993, Vol. 101, No. 2).

Peale, Ruth Stafford. "A Life of Faith and Love: Remembering Norman Vincent Peale 33°, Grand Cross," *The Scottish Rite Journal* (September 1995, Vol. 104, No. 9).

"Peale's 100th Anniversary," *Calvary Contender* (June 15, 1998, Vol. 15, No. 14).

Pennsylvania Youth Foundation, The (Elizabethtown, PA: The Pennsylvania Youth Foundation, n.d.).

Penzel, Klaus, Editor. *Philip Schaff: Historian and Ambassador of the Universal Church* (Macon, GA: Mercer University Press, 1991).

"People," *U. S. News & World Report* (May 13, 1996, Vol. 120, No. 19).

"People and Events," *Moody* (January-February 2001, Vol. 101, No. 3).

"People for the American Way Defends New Age Impressions Curriculum," *Christian Parent Alert* (August 1991, Vol. 1, No. 1).

"People in the News," *U. S. News & World Report* (June 7, 1999).

"People of Faith: A Call to Action" (Received September 3, 1996).

Peros, Joan. "Local 'Visioning,'" on the May 9, 2000 program of Radio Liberty.

"Persecuted Christians—What's Really Happening?," *East Gates Connection* (Received December 30, 2000).

"Persecution of Christians," *Christian News* (November 20, 2000, Vol. 38, No. 43).

"Persecution of Christians in China Continues," *O Timothy* (1994, Vol. 2, Issue 5).

Petersen, William J. *Those Curious New Cults* (New Canaan, CT: Keat Publishing, Inc., 1973).

Peterson, Wayne. *Extraordinary Times, Extraordinary Beings: Experiences of an American Diplomat with Maitreya and the Masters of Wisdom* (Henderson, NV: Emergence Press, 2001).

Peterson, William O., Editor. *Masonic Quiz Book: "Ask Me Another, Brother"* (Chicago, IL: Charles T. Powner Company, 1950).

Peterson, Willy. *Angels Don't Write These Books: A Warning to Conservative Christians About New Age Conspirator, Dr. Nick Begich* (Bonner Springs, KS: n.d.).

Peterson, Willy. *The Leavening: A New Age Primer for Christian Parents* (Linwood, KS: n.p., 1996, Third Edition).

Petre, Jonathan. "Tutu Writes Foreword for Book of Christian Liturgies for Gays," *Christian News* (May 6, 1996, Vol. 34, No. 19).

"PFLAG Supports Reverend Mel White in Bearing Witness," *PFLAGpole* (Spring 1995).

Phillips, Phil. *Turmoil in the Toybox* (Lancaster, PA: Starburst Publishers, 1986).

"Philosophy Behind School-to-Work (and Goals 2000), The," *The Florida Forum* (Summer 1997).

Piediscalzi, Nicholas. *Teaching About World Religions: NCRPE Curriculum Resource Guide* (Minneapolis, MN: World Religion Curriculum, 1987).

Pike, Albert. *Morals and Dogma of the Ancient and Accepted Scottish Rite of Freemasonry* (Richmond, VA: L. H. Jenkins, Inc., 1871).

Pike, Albert. *The Magnum Opus* (Kila, MT: Kessinger Publishing Company, 1992).

Pinalto, Judy. "Unholy Hands on the Bible," American Freedom Network (Guest on Henry Feinberg's June 14, 1996 Program).

Pinnock, Clark. "The Inspiration and Interpretation of the Bible."

Pitchon, Patricia. "The Changing Role of the United Nations," *The Emergence Quarterly* (Autumn 1999, No. 28).

Pitt, Joe. "The Israel Pole Story," *Christian News* (June 4, 2001, Vol. 39, No. 23).

"Plan of Love and Light: Excerpts Presented by the Tibetan Master Within the Books of Alice A. Bailey, The," (Jersey City, NJ: Aquarian Age Community).

"Planetary Initiative for the World 'They' Choose," *The Prophecy Newsletter* (1985, Vol. 1, No. 8).

"Planned Parenthood's Supremacist Roots," *The Christian World Report* (September 1990, Vol. 2, No. 8).

Plowman, Edward E. "Graham School Bridges Soviet Church Divisions," *Christianity Today* (August 19, 1991, Vol. 35, No. 9).

Policy Review (Fall 1994, No. 70).

"Political Dirty Tricks Foil Minnesota Bill," *The Christian World Report* (April 1990, Vol. 2, No. 4).

"Political Pluralism Sells Out," *Voice in the Wilderness* (December 2000).

Polk, Peggy. "Pope Says Unbelievers Will Be Saved If They Live a Just Life," *Christian News* (December 18, 2000, Vol. 38, No. 47).

Polk, Peggy. "Vatican Declares Only the Roman Catholic Church Brings Salvation," *Christian News,* (September 25, 2000, Vol. 38, No. 35).

Pollack, Andrew. "Moon's Church Tied to Bush Sponsor," *The Oregonian* (September 4, 1995).

Pollock, John C. *A Foreign Devil in China: The Story of Dr. L. Nelson Bell, An American Surgeon in China* (Minneapolis, MN: World Wide Publications, 1971).

Pollock, John. *Crusades: 20 Years with Billy Graham* (Minneapolis, MN: World Wide Publications, 1969, Special Billy Graham Crusade Edition).

"Polls Show That Americans Believe No One Is Perfect—Including God!," *The Christian World Report* (February 1995, Vol. 10, No. 2).

Polsgrove, Carol. "Unbroken Circle," *Sierra* (January/February 1992, Vol. 77, No. 1).

"Pope and Darwin, The," *U. S. News & World Report* (November 4, 1996, Vol. 121, No. 18).

"Pope Calls for 'Ecological Conversion,'" *Christian News* (February 12, 2001, Vol. 39, No. 7).

"Pope Calls Increased Dialogue Among World Religions a 'Sign of Hope' at End of Century," *Foundation* (November-December 1999).

"Pope Defends Document on Salvation," *National Catholic Register* (October 15-21, 2000, Vol. 76, No. 42).

"Pope Entrusts 'Whole Church' to Mary," *Calvary Contender* (July 1, 2001, Vol. 18, No. 13).

"Pope Foreseen As Leader of World Church," *Midnight Call* (March 1993).

"Pope John Paul II Receives a Mark in His Forehead by a Pagan Shiva Priestess" (Cutting Edge Ministries, n.d.).

"Pope Is Graham's 'Man of the Century,'" *Calvary Contender* (January 15, 2000).

"Pope Offers Early Salvation?," *Calvary Contender* (January 1, 1999, Vol. 16, No. 1).

"Pope Praises Buddhist Leader," *O Timothy* (1992, Vol. 9, Issue 4).

"Pope Says Belief in Jesus Not Necessary for Salvation," *The Vine and Branches* (Winter 2001, Vol. 16, Issue 1).

"Pope Says Christianity Is Not the Only True and Saving Faith," *The Voice in the Wilderness* (February 2001).

"Pope Says Hell Is Self-Inflicted," *Calvary Contender* (September 1, 1999, Vol. 16, No. 17).

"Pope Says Unbelievers Saved If Live (sic) a Good Life," *Calvary Contender* (January 1, 2001, Vol. 18, No. 1).

"Pope...Spiritual Leader or Anti-Christ?, The," *The Protestant Challenge* (January-February 1997, Vol. 24, No. 1).

"Pope Voices Concern Over Catholic Defection," *Christianity Today* (June 18, 1990).

"Pope, Voodoo Worshippers, Contextual Evangelism," *Calvary Contender* (March 15, 1993, Vol. 10, No. 6).

"Popular Pope Is a Universalist," *Christian News* (January 30, 1995, Vol. 33, No. 5).

"Population Control and the 'New Age' Religion," *An American Commentary* (Oklahoma City, OK: Hearthstone Publishing, Ltd., 1993).

Pottenger, Milton Alberto. *Symbolism* (Sacramento, CA: Symbol Publishing Company, 1905).

Power of Prophecy (February 2001, Vol. 2001-02).

"Praising a Twice Divorced Woman 'Pastor,'" *Christian News* (March 8, 1993, Vol. 31, No. 10).

"Praying for Renewal," *One World* (November 1990, Vol. 160).

Predictions to the Year 2000 (Monterey, CA: Angel Press, 1977).

Preparing Families for the Third Millennium... (1997).

Presbyterian Layman, The (January/February 1999, Vol. 32, No. 1).

"Present-Day Official Teaching of the Roman Catholic Church, The" (Article by Evangelical Outreach).

"Preserved Forever by God Almighty!," *Despatch Magazine* (June 2001, Vol. 13:2).

President Clinton Will Continue the New World Order (Oklahoma City, OK: Southwest Radio Church, 1993).

"President Clinton Beatifies an African Marxist," *Christian News* (July 26, 1993, Vol. 31, No. 30).

"President of World Council of Churches Says Mary Not a Virgin," *O Timothy* (1986, Vol. 3, Issue 7).

"President's Letter, The," *Spiritual Advisory Council Newsletter* (May/June 1989, Vol. 15, No. 5 & 6).

"Press Release—Trojan Horse," *Bold Truth* (April 1993).

Price, David Mark. *Secret* (Wichita, KS: Sunset Research Group, 1994).

Price, John Randolph. *The Planetary Commission* (Boerne, TX: The Quartus Foundation for Spiritual Research, Inc., 1984).

Price, Richard and Harlacher, Larry. "RLDS Hierarchy Espouses the WCC and NCC," *WCC Packet* (Independence, MO: Price Publishing Company, n.d.).

"Priest Richard Neuhaus Exposed—He's a Marxist Heretic!," *Flashpoint* (November 1994).

"'Prince of Egypt' Receiving Rave Reviews," *Christian News* (December 28, 1998, Vol. 36, No. 48).

"Prince of Egypt Movie, The," *The Perilous Times* (February 1999, Vol. 20, No. 12).

"Prince of Egypt, The," *Christian News* (January 4, 1999, Vol. 37, No. 1).

"Prison Fellowship Now Headed by Catholic," *Calvary Contender* (July 15, 1998, Vol. 15, No. 14).

"Pro-Homosexual New Evangelicals?," *Calvary Contender* (August 15, 1998, Vol. 15, No. 16).

Problems of Humanity: The Building of Right Human Relations: Study Three: The Problem of International Unity (New York, NY: World Goodwill, n.d.).

Problems of Humanity: The Building of Right Human Relations: The Problem of the Churches, The (New York, NY: World Goodwill, n.d.).

"Prodigal Graham, The," *New Man* (October 1996, Vol. 3, No. 7).

"Profound Thanks," *Religion for Peace* (February 1995, Issue 65-A).

Progoff, Ira. *The Practice of Process Meditation: The Intensive Journal Way to Spiritual Experience* (New York, NY: Dialogue House Library, 1980).

"Program Is a Platform We Use to Help People," *USA Today* (March 23, 1989).

Progress in Theology (June 1996, Vol. 4, No. 2).

"'Progressive' Educators' Plans Fulfilled Today," *The Florida Forum* (Spring 1996).

"Progressive National Baptist Convention Affirm Jackson," *The Voice in the Wilderness* (May 2001).

"Project Green," *Religion for Peace* (Autumn 1992, Issue 63).

"Promise Keepers and Psychoheresy," *Psychoheresy Awareness Letter* (July/August 1994, Vol. 2, No. 4).

"Promise Keepers," *The BDM Letter* (May/June 1996, Vol. 5, No. 3).

"Promise Keepers' D.C. Covenant Agenda for Churches Revealed," *Media Spotlight* (1997, Vol. 20, No. 2).

Prophecy Club Newsletter, The (April 1995).

Prophecy Newsletter, The (1985, Vol. 1, No. 3).

Prophecy Newsletter, The (1985, Vol. 1, No. 5).

Prophecy Newsletter, The (1985, Vol. 1, No. 6).

Prophecy Newsletter, The (1985, Vol. 1, No. 8).

Prophecy Newsletter, The (1986, Vol. 2, No. 1).

"Prophetic Insights," *Power of Prophecy* (July 2000, Vol. 2000-07).

"Protestantism, "*The World Book Year Book* (Chicago, IL: World Book—Childcraft International, Inc., 1978).

"Protestants, Catholics and Jews Pray to Same God?," *Christian News* (July 26, 1993, Vol. 31, No. 30).

"Protestants, Catholics, and Jews to Pray to Same God?," *Calvary Contender* (March 1, 1993, Vol. 10, No. 5).

PRS Journal (Spring 1983).

Pruden, Wesley, "Preaching Christ in Pyongyang," *The Washington Times* (April 5, 1992).

"Pseudo Right Revisited Toward a New Federalist—Opiate of the Proletariat," *Distant Drums* (December 1983).

"Psychic Guide Sees No Cause for Uproar," *The Washington Times* (June 25, 1996).

"Public Libraries and Art Displays," *Censorship News* (1994, Issue 5, No. 56).

"Public School Sex Education: A Report," *AFA Journal* (October 1990, Vol. 14, No. 9).

"Q & A," *The Berean Call* (December 1998).

"Q & A," *The Berean Call* (July 2001).

"Q & A," *The Berean Call* (May 2001).

"Quest for Synthesis: A Call to World Leadership, The," *World Goodwill* (2000, No. 3).

"Question Now Isn't Just Poverty. For Many, It Is Survival," The," *The Washington Spectator* (August 1, 2001, Vol. 27, No. 15).

"Questions and Answers," *Share International* (Special Information Issue).

Quigley, Carroll. *The Anglo-American Establishment* (New York, NY: Books in Focus, Inc., 1981).

Quigley, Carroll. *Tragedy and Hope: A History of the World in Our Time* (NY: The Macmillan Company, 1966).

"Quote of the Day: Former Sen. Harris Wofford," *Christian News* (January 15, 2001, Vol. 39, No. 3).

"Quotes to Ponder," *Voice in the Wilderness* (March 2000).

Rabey, Steve. "Christian Singer Appeals to Fans of Secular Pop Music: Is Amy Grant Sending Mixed Messages?," *Christianity Today* (November 8, 1985).

Rabey, Steve. "Prince-ly Promotions: Animated Moses Film Yields a Flood of Products," *Christian News* (December 14, 1998, Vol. 36, No. 46).

Racer, David G., Jr. *Not for Sale: The Rev. Sun Myung Moon and One American's Freedom* (St. Paul, MN: Tiny Press, 1989).

"Racial Justice Activist Named to Transition Team," *Christian News* (December 28, 1992, Vol. 30, No. 48).

"Radical Feminist Agenda," *The Koinonia Chronicle* (April 1996, Vol. 3).

Raehm, Ray. "Why Neither George Bush Nor Albert Gore Seems Willing or Able to Derail the Ongoing Cultural Revolution in America," *The Florida Forum* (Fall 2000).

Rainbow Connection, The (April 1995).

"Rally to the Defense of KFUO," *Christian News* (January 2, 1995, Vol. 33, No. 1).

"Ralph Reed/'Christian Coalition' Preaching Another Gospel Which Is Christ Denial,"*Christian News* (January 23, 1995, Vol. 33, No. 4).

Rand, Cornelius K. "Purgatory: Fact or False?," *The Voice of the Nazarene* (December 1962, Vol. 11, No. 12).

Randles, Bill. *Beware the New Prophets: A Caution Concerning the Modern Prophetic Movement* (Marion, IA: n.p., 1999).

Rasmussen, Roland. "Back Billy Graham?—Californian Baptist Pastor says No," *Sword of the Lord* (October 18, 1963).

"Ratzinger Revealed As Heretic," *Veritas* (December 1996, Vol. 28, No. 12).

Raum, Thomas C., Jr. "Today's Young People: Where Will They Learn About the Tools of Life?," *The Scottish Rite Journal* (March 1994, Vol. 102, No. 3).

Ray, Ronald. "Kinsey's Legal Legacy," *The New American* (January 19, 1998).

"Read All About It: Words to Live By," *World Christian* (November/December 1987, Vol. 6, No. 6).

Reader's Digest (October 1982).

"Readers' Forum," *Colorado Christian News* (January 1995, Vol. 6, Issue 6).

"Readers' Response," *The Christian Century* (February 3-10, 1988).

Reagan, David B. "The Apostate One World Religion," *Voice in the Wilderness* (August 2001).

"Reborn but Not Remade?," *Focus Express* (June/June/August 2000).

"Recognize Those Outside Church, Says WCC Leader," *Christian News* (April 12, 1993, Vol. 31, No. 15).

"Reconciliation or Jesus?," *The Presbyterian Layman* (May/June 2001, Vol. 34, No. 4).

Rector, Trish. "Who Is Jay Gary?," *Bold Truth* (February 15, 1993 [sic]).

Reed, Ralph. *Active Faith: How Christians Are Changing the Soul of American Politics* (New York, NY: Free Press, 1996).

Reese, W. L. *Dictionary of Philosophy and Religion: Eastern and Western Thought* (Atlantic Highlands, NJ: Humanities Press, Inc., 1980).

"Rehabilitation of Communism, The" *The Schwarz Report* (October 2000, Vol. 40, No. 10).

"Reinhold Niebuhr," Softkey Multimedia Inc., Infopedia (1996).

Reisman, Judith A. *Kinsey: Crimes and Consequences* (Arlington, VA: The Institute for Media Education, Inc., 1998).

Reisman, Judith A. and Ray, Eunice Van Winkle. "Kaiser Foundation's Sexual Propaganda," *The Florida Forum* (Fall 2000).

Religion for Peace (Autumn 1992, Issue 63).

Religion for Peace (February 1995, Issue 65-A).

"Religions Cooperating for Peace: The World Conference on Religion and Peace" (Received July 3, 1995).

"Religious Changes of Dr. Billy Graham," *A Christian View of the News* (December 25, 1993, Vol. 18, No. 24).

"Religious Unity and the New World Order," *The Omega-Letter* (July 1990, Vol. 5, No. 6).

"Religious Visionary to Retire," *New Age Journal* (November/December 1996, Vol. 13, Issue 6).

Remey Letter, The (Autumn-Winter 1990-1991, Vol. 11, No. 4).

"Report: China Arrests Christians," *Christian News* (September 18, 2000, Vol. 38, No. 34).

Report from the Planetary Commission (May 1, 1986).

"Representatives of More Than 20 Religions Open Vatican Meeting," *Christian News* (November 1, 1999, Vol. 37, No. 40).

"Residential Psychodrama Training Weekend," *Oasis Center* (April-June 1989).

Rest, Friedrich. *Our Christian Symbols* (Philadelphia, PA: The Christian Education Press, 1954).

"Rev. Eugene Blake, 78, Church Leader," *The Washington Times* (August 2, 1985).

"Review," *One Country* (October-December 1993, Vol. 5, Issue 3).

"Review of Reviews: Music: Stevie Nicks," *The Week* (May 25, 2001, Vol. 1, Issue 6).

"Reviews," *Connecting Link* (November/December 1989, Vol. 1, No. 5).

Reynolds, Jr., M. H. *AD 2000 Ecumenical Evangelism—A Warning!* (n.p., n.d.).

Reynolds, Jr., M. H. *Billy Graham, the Pope, and the Bible* (Los Osos, CA: Fundamental Evangelistic Association, n.d.).

Reynolds, Jr., M. H. *The Truth About the World Council of Churches* (Los Osos, CA: Fundamental Evangelistic Association, n.d.).

Reynolds, Jr., M. H. "World Conference on Mission and Evangelism, San Antonio, Texas, May 22-June 1, 1989," *World Council of Churches: The Shaky Ship Sails On...* (Los Osos, CA: Fundamental Evangelistic Association, 1999).

Reynolds, M. H. "AD 2000 Ecumenical Evangelism: A Warning!," *Foundation* (July-September 1995, Vol. 16, Issue 4).

Reynolds, M. H. "Mixing Truth and Error at Urbana '90," *Foundation.*

Reynolds. M. H. *The World Council of Churches: An Ecumenical Tower of Babel* (Los Osos, CA: Fundamental Evangelistic Association, 1983).

Reynolds, M. H. "Planting the Seeds of Ecumenical Apostasy in the Name of Evangelism," *Foundation* (1983, Vol. 4, No. 4).

"Rhodes to the New World Order," *The Christian World Report* (March/April 1993, Vol. 8, No. 2).

Ricca, Paolo. "New Possibilities for the Papacy?," *Theology Digest* (Spring 1999, Vol. 46, No. 1).

Rice, Patricia. "Parliament of Religions in South Africa Pushes Peace," *Christian News* (February 14, 2000, Vol. 38, No. 7).

Rifkin, Jeremy with Howard, Ted. *The Emerging Order: God in the Age of Scarcity* (NY: G.P. Putnam's Sons, 1979).

"Right Place for a Mass Murdering Atheist to Speak, The" *Christian News* (September 18, 2000, Vol. 38, No. 34).

Rini, Suzanne M. *Beyond Abortion: A Chronicle of Fetal Experimentation* (Rockford, IL: Tan Books and Publishers, Inc., 1993).

Riplinger, G. A. *New Age Bible Versions* (Munroe Falls, OH: A. V. Publications, 1993).

Riplinger, Gail. *The Language of the King James Bible: Discover Its Hidden Built-in Dictionary* (Ararat, VA: A.V. Publications Corporation, 1998).

Riplinger, Gail. *Which Bible Is God's Word?: Answers to Common Questions Concerning Modern Versions and Translations* (Oklahoma City, OK: Hearthstone Publishing, Ltd., 1994).

Risher, Dee Dee. "Marga Buhrig: Working for Women from Within," *The Other Side* (January/February 1988).

Rivera, David Allen. *Final Warning: A History of the New World Order* (Harrisburg, PA: Rivera Enterprises, 1994).

"RNC Chairman Joins in Honoring Rev. Billy Graham. Reagan Freedom Award Recognizes Former President's 'Greatest Gift,'" *Christian News* (April 10, 2000, Vol. 38, No. 15).

Road to Socialism and the New World Order, The (Highland City, FL: Florida Pro Family Forum, Inc., 1995).

"Road to Socialism?, The" *Herald-Press* (Mary 16, 1996).

Robbins, John W. "Contemporary Religion Vs. the Gospel," *Christian News* (April 24, 1995, Vol. 33, No. 17).

Robbins, John W. "Contemporary Religion Vs. the Gospel," *Christian News* (December 2, 1996, Vol. 34, No. 45).

Robbins, John W. "Ronald Sider Contra Deum," *Christian News* (May 4, 1992, Vol. 30, No. 18).

Robert Muller School: World Core Curriculum Manual, The (1986).

"Robert Schuller Addressed 15,000 Muslim at the Abou Nour Mosque," *Foundation* (January-February 2000, Vol. 21, Issue 1).

Roberts, Allen E. *Frontier Cornerstone* (OH: The Grand Lodge of Free and Accepted Masons of Ohio, 1980).

Roberts, Allen E. *Masonic Trivia and Facts* (Highland Springs, VA: Anchor Communications, 1994).

Robertson, Nan. *Getting Better: Inside Alcoholics Anonymous* (New York, NY: William Morrow and Company, Inc., 1988).

Robertson, Pat. *The New World Order* (Dallas, TX: Word Publishing, 1991).

Robinson, John J. *A Pilgrim's Path: One Man's Road to the Masonic Temple* (New York, NY: M. Evans and Company, Inc., 1993).

"Rockefeller Bankrolls Communism in South Africa?," *Christian World Report* (December 1990, Vol. 2, No. 9).

"Rockefeller Gives Money to Help South African Communists," *Christian Anti-Communism Crusade* (August 15, 1993, Vol. 33, No. 16).

"Rockefeller Influence on Education Yesterday and Today," *The Florida Forum* (Spring 1996).

Rockwood, Perry F. *The Charismatic Renewal in the Roman Catholic Church* (Halifax, Nova Scotia: The Peoples Gospel Hour, n.d.).

Rockwood, Perry F. "The Revised Standard Version," *O Timothy* (1985, Vol. 2, Issue 3).

Rodman, Rosamond C., Editor. *The United Nations in an Interdependent World: Past, Present, Future* (New York, NY: Global Education Associates, 1995).

"Roman Catholic Editors of Christianity Today," *Christian News* (May 5, 1997, Vol. 35, No. 18).

"Roman Connection: The 'Sovereign Drug,' The," *Dorea Ministries* (January-March 1992).

"Romanism, Ecumenicalism and Protestantism," *Bold Truth* (November 5, 1993).

Romanofsky, Peter, Editor. *The Greenwood Encyclopedia of American Institutions: Social Service Organizations* (Greenwood Press: Westport, CT: 1978).

"Rome and the Pope Still Deny Justification by Faith Alone," *Christian News* (December 19, 1994, Vol. 32, No. 47).

"Rome Is in a State of Total Disarray," *Christian News* (October 20, 1997, Vol. 35, No. 38).

"Romeward Bound Continues," *Dorea Ministries* (January-March 1992).

"Ron Blue to Speak at IFCA Meeting," *Calvary Contender* (April 1, 1996, Vol. 13, No. 7).

Ronayne, Edmond. *The Master's Carpet (Mah-Hah-Bone)* (n.p., 1879).

Roper, Jack M. "Pan: Pagan God and Nature Demon," *The Christian World Report* (October 1992, Vol. 7, No. 8).

"Rosa Parks: 'She Sat Down and the World Turned Around,'" *U. S. News & World Report* (August 20-27, 2001, Vol. 131, No. 7).

Rosellini, Lynn. "An Unlikely Friendship, a Historic Meeting: Jerry Falwell and Mel White Join Forces," *U. S. News & World Report* (November 1, 1999).

Rosenfeld, Megan. "Once Again, a President Calls on Billy Graham," *The News and Observer* (January 18, 1991).

Ross, Robert Gaylon, Sr. *Who's Who of the Elite* (San Marcos, TX: RIE, 1995).

Ross, Nancy Wilson. *Three Ways of Ancient Wisdom* (New York, NY: Simon and Schuster, 1966).

Rowe, Ed. *New Age Globalism* (Herndon, VA: Growth Publishing, 1985).

"Roy Rogers Confesses to Soap Addiction" (April 27, 1993).

Rueda, Enrique. *The Homosexual Network: Private Lives and Public Policy* (Old Greenwich, CT: The Devin Adair Company, 1982).

Rugh, Gil. *Faithfulness and Conflict: The Church's Battle Against Heresy* (Lincoln, NE: Sound Words Communications, 1990).

"Rule of Law, The," *The Emergence* (June 1999, Vol. 17, No. 5).

"Ruling Elite Working Toward World Govt.," *The Daily Record* (October 17, 1995).

Runes, Dagobert D. *Treasury of Philosophy* (New York, NY: Philosophical Library, 1955).

"Russian Strategic Deception: The 'New' Communist Threat," *The McAlvany Intelligence Advisor* (January 1994).

Sabeheddin, M. "The Rockefeller-UFO Connection: An Alien Conspiracy?," *New Dawn* (March-April, 1996, No. 35).

Saloma, John S. III. *Ominous Politics: The New Conservative Labyrinth* (NY: Hill and Wang, 1984).

"Salvation Army and the International Millennial Congress," *Despatch Magazine* (September 2000, Vol. 12:3).

"Salvation by Sanctifying Grace Demo," *Constantly Evolving Catholicism* (September 1995).

Samaha, John. "Understanding the Eastern Christian Churches," *The Catholic Answer* (July/August 2001, Vol. 15, No. 3).

Samaritan's Purse (January 2000).

Samuelson, Eric. *Fabian Society.*

"San Antonio Express-News," *The Berean Call* (June 1997).

Sandstrom, Dale V. "DeMolay Fast Facts," *The Scottish Rite Journal* (March 1994, Vol. 102, No. 3).

Sanoff, Alvin P. with Scherer, Ron. "Behind Merger Mania in Book Publishing," *U. S. News & World Report* (December 10, 1984, Vol. 97, No. 24).

"Satan Goes to Washington," *Flashpoint* (March 1990).

"Satan, the Illuminati and the Destruction of Fatherhood," *Newsletter from a Christian Ministry* (July 1, 1993, Vol. 2, No. 10).

"Satanic Activities of Secret Societies" (The Cutting Edge, n.d.).

Saunders, Esther and Youannas, Joseph. "Harry Potter: A Modern Day Pied Piper," *Christian News* (February 26, 2001, Vol. 39, No. 9).

"Savor South African Miracle, NCC General Secretary Says," *Eculink* (Summer 1994, No. 41).

"Says King Was a Communist Traitor," *Christian News* (January 24, 2000).

"SBC Reaction to Catholic-Evangelical Paper," *Calvary Contender* (June 15, 1994, Vol. 11, No. 12).

"SBC Reaffirms Commitment to Liberal Ecumenical Organization," Watch unto Prayer, (September 2, 1998).

Scales, Richard. "Allegations Unchallenged," *Christian News* (January 29, 2001, Vol. 39, No. 5).

Scheinin, Richard. "Bringing Together the 'United Religions,'" *San Jose Mercury News* (February 6, 1996).

Scheinin, Richard. "United Faiths: Call Arises for Spiritual U.N. to Cooperate in the Names of God," *San Jose Mercury News* (June 17, 1995).

Schimmel, Joe. "Sweet to the Ears—Deadly to the Soul," *CIB Bulletin* (October/November 1992, Vol. 8, No. 10).

Schindler, Julius E. "Despotism vs. Popular Government," *The New Age Magazine* (November 1929, Vol. 37, No. 11).

Schlafly, Phyllis. "Latest NEA Outrages," *The Christian World Report* (June 1991, Vol. 3, No. 6).

Schmitt, Wilhelm E. "Some Facts About 'Martin Luther' King Apparently Missed by a Wheaton College Professor," *Christian News* (October 26, 1992, Vol. 30, No. 39).

Schmitt, Wilhelm E. "Some Facts About 'Martin Luther' King, Jr. Ignored by the National Capital Planning Commission," *Christian News* (January 1, 2000, Vol. 38, No. 1).

Schnoebelen, William. *Masonry: Beyond the Light* (Chino, CA: Chick Publications, 1991).

Schnoebelen, William. "The Curse Causeless," *Liberator* (July-August 1999, Vol. 8, No. 4).

Schnoebelen, William J. and Spencer, James R. *White Sepulchers: The Hidden Language of the Mormon Temple* (Boise, ID: Through the Maze, 1990).

Schnoebelen, William J. *Halloween: Tis the Season to Be Evil...* (Issaquah, WA: Saints Alive in Jesus, n.d.).

"Scholars Seek New Image of God," *Christian News* (March 27, 2000, Vol. 38, No. 13).

Schoonover, Melvin E. "William Stringfellow's Quest for Truth," *Sojourners* (December 1985).

"Schuler (sic) and Gorbachev," *Christian News* (January 22, 2001, Vol. 39, No. 4).

"Schuller and Rome," *Christian News* (October 9, 2000, Vol. 38, No. 37).

"Schuller Has Catholic Speaker," *Calvary Contender* (November 15, 1998, Vol. 15, No. 24).

"Schuller Meets with Cho and Pope," *Calvary Contender* (August 15, 1998, Vol. 15, No. 16).

"Schuller Promotes Pope and Comrade," *Omega-Letter* (March 1988, Vol. 3, No. 3).

"Schuller Rides High," *The Omega-Letter* (July 1989, Vol. 4, No. 6).

"Schuller Rides High," *The Omega-Letter* (March 1991, Vol. 6, No. 3).

"Schuller Speaks for Moonies, Mormons," *Calvary Contender* (January 1, 1999, Vol. 16, No. 1).

"Schuller Trains Homosexual Pastors?," *Calvary Contender* (June 15, 1997, Vol. 14, No. 12).

"Schuller, Mother Teresa, and the New Age," *O Timothy* (Vol. 11, Issue 2, 1994).

Schuller, Robert H. *Self-Esteem: The New Reformation* (Waco, TX: Word Books, 1982).

Schwarz, Fred C. "The Communist Front," *The Schwarz Report* (September 2000, Vol. 40, No. 9).

Schwarz, Fred C. "The Leninist Use of Force and Violence," *The Schwarz Report* (November 2000, Vol. 40, No. 11).

Schwarz, Frederick A. O., Jr. "'Liberty': Schwarz Gets Our First Annual Award," *Lambda Update* (Fall 1987).

Scott, Brenda and Smith, Samantha. *Trojan Horse: How the New Age Movement Infiltrates the Church* (Lafayette, LA: Huntington House Publishers, 1993).

Scott, F. V. "The New American Gothic Planned Parenthood," *Passport Magazine* (July-August 1988).

Scott, George Ryley. *Phallic Worship: A History of Sex and Sexual Rites* (London, England: Senate, 1966).

Scott, Rebekah, "The Legacy of Kathryn Kuhlman," *Christian News* (July 24, 1995, Vol. 33, N. 30).

Seale, Jim. "The Gay Reformation," *New Age Journal* (March 1985).

Sears, Gordon. *Apostasy and Deception in Christian Music* (Coldwater, MI: Song Fest, 1998).

"Second Hollister Awards Ceremony," *Temple of Understanding Newsletter* (Fall 1998).

"Secret Records" Revealed: The Men, the Money, and the Methods Behind the New World Order (Marlborough, NH: The Plymouth Rock Foundation, 1994).

Secret Records Revealed: The Men, the Money and the Methods Behind the New World Order (Oklahoma City, OK: Hearthstone Publishing, Ltd., 1999).

Seeger, Elizabeth. *Eastern Religions* (NY: Thomas Y. Cromwell Company, 1973).

Sekellick, John T. "A Priestly Education in Rome, *The Catholic Answer* (July/August 1998, Vol. 12, No. 3).

"Senator Albert Gore Pushes New Age Agenda," *Flashpoint* (September 1990).

Serrone, Sue. "Canyon to Cathedral," *Festivals* (October/November 1986).

"Service for Diana's Funeral, The," *Despatch Mini News.*

Sessler, Robert. *To Be God of One World: The French Revolution Globalized* (Merlin, OR: Let There Be Light Publications, 1992).

"Seven Reasons Why I Did Not Vote for Al Gore," *The Voice in the Wilderness* (February 2001).

Seventh-Day Adventists Believe...A Biblical Exposition of 27 Fundamental Doctrines (Hagerstown, MD: Review and Herald Publishing Association, 1988).

Shah, Douglas. *The Meditators* (Plainfield, NJ: Logos International, 1975).

Shamballa: The Centre Where the Will of God Is Known (New York, NY: World Goodwill, n.d.).

"Shame, Shame on the Christian Establishment," World of Prophecy (October 11, 1997).

"Shared Vision," *The Omega-Letter* (April 1988, Vol. 3, No. 4).

Shaw, Jim Shaw McKenney, Tom. *The Deadly Deception: Freemasonry Exposed...by One of Its Top Leaders* (Lafayette, LA: Huntington House, Inc.).

Shaw, Russell. "Why the Pope Rules," *Our Sunday Visitor* (February 22, 1998, Vol. 86, No. 43).

Shea, George Beverly with Bauer, Fred. *Then Sings My Soul* (Minneapolis, MN: World Wide Publications, 1968).

Shea, Nina. *In the Lion's Den* (Nashville, TN: Broadman & Holman Publishers, 1997).

Sheedy, "Ask Me a Question," *Our Sunday Visitor* (February 14, 1993, Vol. 81, No. 42).

Sheler, Jeffery L. "Christians, Unite!," *U.S. News & World Report* (November 15, 1999).

Shelly, Judith Allen. "The Feminist Gospel: The Movement to Unite Feminism with the Church," *Journal of Christian Nursing* (Summer 1993).

Shepard, Alicia C. "Billy Graham Goes Global in 'Capstone' of His Career," *Christian News* (February 27, 1995, Vol. 33, No. 9).

Shepherd's Letter, The (Spring 1993).

Shepherd's Letter, The (Spring 1994).

Sherrill, Robert, "Billy Graham," *Collier's Encyclopedia* (1988 Edition).

Shine, Dan. "Leaders Want Global Thanksgiving for All Faiths," *Dallas Morning News* (February 2, 1995).

Shoemaker, Sam, et. al. *Steps to a New Beginning* (1993).

"Short Reviews," *The Catholic Answer* (July/August 2001, Vol. 15, No. 3).

"Should Christians Cooperate with Roman Catholics in Evangelism?," *The Evangelical Methodist* (December 1993, Vol. 72, No. 10).

Shriver, George. *Philip Schaff: Christian Scholar and Ecumenical Prophet* (Macon, GA: Mercer University Press, 1987).

Sider, Ron. "The Place of Humans in the Garden of God," *Green Cross* (Summer 1995, Vol. 1, No. 3).

Sider, Ronald J. *Rich Christians in an Age of Hunger* (Downers Grove, IL: Inter-Varsity Press, 1977).

Siegel, Bernie S. *Love, Medicine and Miracles* (New York, NY: Harper and Row Publishers, 1986).

Silva Mind Control Method, The (Complete Program Transcripts with Jose Silva, George Desau, David Hunt, and John Weldon) (Chattanooga, TN: The John Ankerberg Show, 1986).

Simon, Arthur. *Bread for the World* (Grand Rapids, MI: William B. Eerdmans Publishing Company, 1984, Revised Edition).

Simonton, Chey. "The Rockefeller/Heritage Connection," *Christian Conscience* (December 1996, Vol. 2, No. 11).

Sine, Tom. "A Hijacked Heritage," *Sojourners* (March/April 1995, Vol. 24, No. 1).

Sine, Tom. *The Mustard Seed Conspiracy* (Waco, TX: Word Books, 1981).

Singh, Darshan. *Helping Factors on the Spiritual Path* (Delhi, India: n.p., n.d.).

"Sisters of St. Joseph Host Buddhist Ceremony," *The Omega-Letter* (May 1990, Vol. 5, No. 5).

"Six Mistakes of Man," *The Evangelical Methodist* (December 1993, Vol. 72, No. 10).

"Six More House Church Leaders Arrested and Sentenced," *The Proclaimer* (Issue 2, 2000, Vol. 8, No. 2).

Skeptical Inquirer, The (Spring 1988, Vol. 12, No. 3).

Skousen, W. Cleon. *The Communist Attack on U. S. Police* (Salt Lake City, UT: The Ensign Publishing Company, 1966).

Slimp, Robert L. "American Christian Media Supports ANC/Communists," *Christian News* (June 10, 1996, Vol. 34, No. 24).

Slipher, E. C. "Venus," *The World Book Encyclopedia* (Vol. 18) (Chicago 54, IL: Field Enterprises Educational Corporation, 1961 Edition).

Smith, Samantha. "Eco-Kids Learn Paganism," *The End Times and Victorious Living* (May/June 1996, Vol. 10, No. 3).

Smith, Samantha. "Gorby's Disappearing Act," *Hope for the World* (Spring 1998).

Smith, Samantha. "What Is the New Age and How Is It Affecting Us?," *The Prophecy Club Newsletter* (April 1995).

Smith, Warren. "M. Scott Peck: Community and the Cosmic Christ," *Christian Conscience* (November 1995, Vol. 1, No. 10).

Smith, Warren. "Sign of the Times: Evangelicals and New Agers Together," *SCP Journal* (19:2/3).

Snider, Brian. "A Review Article on the 'Stand in the Gap' Promise Keepers Rally in Washington," *Christian News* (December 1, 1997, Vol. 35, No. 44).

Snow, Anita. "Harlem Backers Applaud Castro," *The Schwarz Report* (November 2000, Vol. 40, No. 11).

Snyder, Steven. "Why China's Christians Suffer," *Christian News* (November 1, 1999, Vol. 37, No. 40).

"So. Baptist University Hosts Gorbachev," *The Perilous Times* (November/December 2000, Vol. 22, No. 7).

"So, How Much Did Schuller Pay Gorbachev Who Gets $75-$100,000 Per Talk?," *Christian News* (January 22, 2001, Vol. 39, No. 4).

"Social Gospel," Softkey Multimedia Inc., Infopedia (1996).

"Sodomite at the Gate," *Pointy Hat News* (May/June 1994).

Sojourners (April 1986).

Sojourners (December 1985).

Sojourners (December 1989, Vol. 18, No. 11).

Sojourners (January 1990, Vol. 19, No. 1).

Sojourners (March 1985).

Sojourners (March/April 1995, Vol. 24, No. 1).

Sojourners (October 1989, Vol. 18, No. 9).

"Sojourners Forms Coalition," *Call to Action News* (March-April 1996, Vol. 18, No. 1).

"SOLM Careless Associations?," *Calvary Contender* (December 15, 1997, Vol. 14, No. 24).

Solomon, Linda Ilene. "Village of Peace," *New Age Journal* (March/April 1992, Vol. 9, Issue 2).

"Solstice Library," *Solstice* (May/June 1989, Issue 36).

"Something to Think About: Forty-Five Communist Goals," (Knoxville, TN: The Evangelist of Truth, n.d.).

"Son of Perdition, The," *Point Hat News* (May/September 1995).

"South Africa: Targeted by Devilish Powers," *O Timothy* (1987, Vol. 4, Issues 3-4).

"South African Communists Wield New Power," *America's Future* (July/August 1994, Vol. 36, No. 7/8).

"Sovereignty in the Global Age," *World Goodwill Newsletter* (1998, No. 1).

"(Soviet) American Education Today," *The Christian Conscience* (June 1995, Vol. 1, No. 6).

"Soviet Goals Have Not Changed," *The Christian World Report* (December 1989, Vol. 1, No. 9).

"Soviet Union and World Government," *The Omega-Letter* (October 1988, Vol. 3, No. 9).

Spangler, David. *Emergence: The Rebirth of the Sacred* (NY: Dell Publishing, 1984).

Spangler, David. *Reflections on the Christ* (Scotland: Findhorn Publications, 1977).

Spangler, David. *Revelation: The Birth of a New Age* (Middleton, WI: The Lorian Press, 1976).

Spargimino, Larry, "Fido, Come Forth!," *Prophetic Observer* (April 2001, Vol. 8, No. 4)

"Speakers at Schuller's Institute," *Christian News* (March 19, 2001, Vol. 39, No. 12).

"Special Report on the World Future Society's Worldview '84," *The Prophecy Newsletter* (n.d.).

Speech by William E. Swing at the North American Interfaith Network Conference (August 10, 1996).

Spence, H. D. M. and Exell, Joseph S., Editors, *The Pulpit Commentary* (Vol. 13) (Grand Rapids, MI: Eerdmans Publishing Company, 1950).

Spence, Hartzell. *The Story of America's Religions* (NY: Holt, Rinehart and Winston, 1957).

Spence, Lewis. *Myths and Legends of Babylonia and Assyria* (London, England: George G. Harrap and Company, 1916).

"Spiritual and Parliamentary Leaders Meet in Rio," *World Goodwill Newsletter* (1992, No. 4).

"Spiritual Work of the United Nations and the Spiritual Welfare of the Planet: The Promise of the New Millennium: Revelation of the Soul in Humanity," Summary Report of April 1, 1999 meeting.

Spring, Beth. "The Government's Heavy Hand Falls on Believers," *Christianity Today* (December 13, 1985, Vol. 29, No. 18).

Springmeier, Fritz. "Billy Graham Is Indeed Popular....," *Christian News* (July 27, 1992, Vol. 30, No. 30).

Springmeier, Fritz. *Bloodlines of the Illuminati* (Westminster, CO: Ambassador House, 1999).

Springmeier, Fritz. *The Top 13 Illuminati Bloodlines* (Portland, OR: n.p., 1995).

Springmeier, Fritz. *The Watchtower and the Masons* (Portland, OR: n.p., 1992).

Springmeier, Fritz. "The World Parliment (sic) of Religions—The Visible Creation of a World Church," *Newsletter from a Christian Ministry* (September 1, 1993, Vol. 2, No. 12).

Stackhouse, Max L. *Public Theology and Political Economy: Christian Stewardship in Modern Society* (Grand Rapids, MI: Wm. B. Eerdmans Publishing Company for Commission on Stewardship, National Council of the Churches of Christ in the U. S. A., 1987).

"Stan Mooneyham," *Christianity Today* (July 22, 1991, Vol. 35, No. 8).

Stan, Adele M. "Keeping Faith," *Mother Jones* (May/June 1996).

Standridge, William C. *Can We Cooperate with Catholics* (Greensboro, North Carolina, n.d.).

Stanford, Miles J. "False Fare," in "C. S. Lewis: One of the Greatest Communicators of the Christian Faith or Deceived Deceiver?" (Compilation of different sources, n.d.).

"Stanley's Handbook for Christian Living," *Calvary Contender* (April 1, 2001, Vol. 18, No. 7).

Stapleton, Ruth Carter. *The Experience of Inner Healing* (Waco, TX: Bantam Books, 1977).

"Star Tracks," *People* (March 23, 1998).

"Star-Struck," *Newsweek* (April 9, 2001, Vol. 137, No. 15).

Starhawk, *The Spiral Dance: A Rebirth of the Ancient Religion of the Great Goddess* (New York, NY: Harper-Collins Publishers, 1989).

Starnes, Todd. "Carter States Affirmation of Homosexual Ordination," *Christian News* (October 30, 2000, Vol. 38, No. 40).

"State of the World Forum," *Wisconsin Report* (September 21, 1995, Vol. 20, No. 36).

State of the World Forum: Toward a New Civilization (San Francisco, CA: Gorbachev Foundation USA, n.d.).

"State of the World Forum Toward a New Civilization," *Mindszenty Report* (March 1996, Vol. 37, No. 3).

Steiner, Rudolf (Translated by Max Gysi). *The Way of Initiation* (NY: Macoy Publishing and Masonic Supply Company, 1910).

"Steve Hill's Testimony," *Calvary Contender* (November 15, 1997, Vol. 14, No. 22).

"Steve Hill's Weak Testimony," *Calvary Contender* (May 15, 1999, Vol.. 16, No. 10).

Stevenson, David. *The Origins of Freemasonry: Scotland's Century, 1590-1710* (Cambridge, England: Cambridge University Press, 1988).

"Still Think Harry Potter Is Harmless?," *Calvary Contender* (February 1, 2001, Vol. 18, No. 3).

Still, William T. *New World Order: The Ancient Plan of Secret Societies* (Lafayette, LA: Huntington House, Inc., 1990).

Stillpoint (Spring/Summer 1985).

Stockwell, Foster "Niebuhr: Relevant Theologian," *The World Book Year Book*, (Chicago 54, IL: Field Enterprises Educational Corporation, 1972).

Stormer, John A. *None Dare Call It Treason* (Florissant, MO: Liberty Bell Press, 1964).

Stormer, John A. *None Dare Call It Treason...25 Years Later* (Florissant, MO: Liberty Bell Press, 1992).

Stormer, John A. *The Death of a Nation* (Florissant, MO: Liberty Bell Press, 1968).

"Strange Things in New Orleans," *O Timothy* (1987, Vol. 4, Issues 8-9).

"Strength of the Weak—Toward a Christian Feminism Identity, The," *Christian News* (June 4, 2001, Vol. 39, No. 23).

Sullivan, Robert and the Editors of *Life*. *Pope John Paul II: A Tribute* (Time, Inc., 1999).

"Summit on Ethics and Meaning, The," *Christian News* (February 26, 1996, Vol. 34, No. 9).

Surburg, Raymond F. "An Evaluation of Dietrich Bonhoeffer's Life and Theology After Half of a Century," *Christian News* (May 15, 2000, Vol. 38, No. 20).

Sutton, Antony C. *America's Secret Establishment: An Introduction to the Order of Skull & Bones* (Billings, MT: Liberty House Press, 1986).

Sutton, Antony C. *How the Order Controls Education* (Phoenix, AZ: Research Publications, Inc., 1983).

Svoboda, Peter. "Jesse Jackson, the Democrats, and the 1988 Elections," *Solidarity.*

Swimme, Brian and Berry, Thomas. *The Universe Story: From the Primordial Flaring Forth to the Ecozoic Era—a Celebration of the Unfolding of the Cosmos* (New York, NY: Harper Collins Publishers, 1992).

Swing, William. "Reactions from Religious Leaders: United Religions International Tour," *Christian News* (May 5, 1997, Vol. 35, No. 18).

Sword of the Lord (March 31, 1989, Vol. 55, No. 7).

Synan, Vinson and Rath, Ralph. *Launching the Decade of Evangelization* (South Bend, IN: North American Renewal Service Committee, 1990).

"Synthesis and the Meaning of Unity-and-Diversity," *Thoughtline* (June 1998).

"Synthesizing New Evangelicals, The," *Bold Truth* (May 1995), p.5.

"T. W. Wilson, Longtime Associate to Billy Graham Dies at 82," *Christian News* (June 4, 2001, Vol. 39, No. 23).

"Taking the Fire out of Hell," *Christian News* (September 27, 1999, Vol. 37, No. 35).

"Tangled Web, The," *The Christian Conscience* (January/February 1997, Vol. 3, No. 1)

Tarkowski, Ed. "One Minute of Instant Global Cooperation to be Realized Through WAM?," *Alabama Discernment Ministries Newsletter* (June 1996).

Tarkowski, Ed. "Prayer Circles: Tools of Empowering Intimacy/Accountability Groups: Part Four: The 'Revival's' Prayer Circles of Power," *The Christian Conscience* (June 1998, Vol. 4, No. 5).

Tarkowski, Ed and Mary. "Is Christian America's Manifest Destiny Being Fulfilled?" (Received May 7, 1994).

"Tavistock and Internationalizing via Education," *The Christian Conscience* (May 1998, Vol. 4, No. 4).

"Tavistock and Internationalizing via Education," *The Florida Forum* (Spring 1998).

"Tax-Funded Indecency Sinks to New Low," *The Christian World Report* (March 1990, Vol. 2, No. 3).

"Teilhard de Chardin: Christianity and Evolution," *SCP Journal* (19:2/3).

Temple Awards for Creative Altruism: Update on Recipients 1987-1989.

"Temple of Understanding, The," *Despatch Magazine* (September 1994, Vol. 6:3).

"Temple of Understanding, The," *Wisconsin Report* (November 1, 1984, Vol. 9, No. 43).

"Temple of Understanding, The," *Wisconsin Report* (October 25, 1984, Vol. 9, No. 42).

Temple of Understanding Newsletter, The (Fall 1995).

Temple of Understanding Newsletter, The (Fall 1998).

Temple of Understanding Newsletter, The (Summer 1996).

"Templeton Dies," *Calvary Contender* (August 15, 2001, Vol. 18, No. 16).

"Templeton Foundation Press Launched," *Progress in Theology* (January/February 1997, Vol. 5, No. 1).

"Templeton Is Awarded to Physicist," *Reading Eagle* (March 11, 1995).

"Templeton Prize for Religious Excellence, The," *Despatch Magazine* (June 2001, Vol. 13:2).

Templeton, John. *Possibilities for Over One Hundredfold More Spiritual Information: The Humble Approach in Theology and Science* (Philadelphia, PA: Templeton Foundation Press, 2000).

"Tennessee Waltzes," *Town and Country Magazine* (April 1995).

"Testimony of a Modernist," *O Timothy* (1994, Vol. 11, Issue 12).

"Texas, Other States and the IAF," *The Christian Conscience* (May 1996, Vol. 2, No. 5).

"Texe Marrs Asks Chuck Colson: 'Will You Sell Your Soul to the Devil for a Million Dollars?,'" *Flashpoint* (June 1993).

"'The Rev.' Jesse Jackson Blasphemes," *Calvary Contender* (August 15, 1992, Vol. 9, No. 16).

"Theistic Evolution," *The Day Drawing Near* (Spring 1997).

"Theology of Martin Luther King, The," *Christian News* (April 13, 1998, Vol. 36, No. 15).

"Theology of Robert Schuller, The," *Christian News* (January 22, 2001, Vol. 39, No. 4).

These Times (1982).

Thomas, Cal. *Book Burning* (Westchester, IL: Crossway Books, 1983).

Thomas, Evan and Brant, Martha. "A Son's Restless Journey," *Newsweek* (August 7, 2000, Vol. 136, No. 6).

Thomas, F W "The Black Plague of Apostasy."

Thomason, J. Royce. "Comments on Gore, *The Voice in the Wilderness* (January 1993).

Thomason, J. Royce. "Editorial," *The Voice in the Wilderness* (March 1993).

Thomason, J. Royce. "Evangelization, A.D. 2000," *The Voice of the Nazarene* (November/December 1991, Vol. 38, No. 5).

Thomason, J. Royce. "Just What Is a Rhodes Scholarship," *The Voice in the Wilderness* (July 1994).

Thomason, J. Royce. "Will We Survive It All?," *The Voice in the Wilderness* (February 1992).

Thorkelson, William. "New 'Re-Imagining' Meeting Scheduled in Wake of Controversy," *Christian News* (October 31, 1994, Vol. 32, No. 40).

Thorkelson, Willmer. "Will Orthodox Exit the WCC?," *Christianity Today* (April 8, 1991, Vol. 35, No. 4).

"Thousands Rock with Evangelist," *The Ledger* (November 6, 2000).

Three Meditation Festivals of Spring: A World Religion for the New Age, The (Received April 2, 1996).

"Three New Trustees Appointed to Gordon-Conwell Board," *Hilltop* (1977).

"Thus Saith Vatican Council II," *Fighting the Good Fight* (November/December 1994).

"Thy Strong Word," *Christian News* (October 16, 2000, Vol. 38, No. 38).

"Ticking Time Bomb," *The Voice in the Wilderness* (February 1992).

Tidwell, D. D. "Dr. George W. Truett," *The Scottish Rite Journal* (February 1993, Vol. 101, No. 2).

Tillin, Tricia. "Testing Evangelism," *Mainstream* (Spring 1994).

"Time to Rescind North Carolina's Resolution for World Government," *The Citizen* (May 19, 1997).

"Ting Has Been a Puppet of Communism from the Beginning," *O Timothy* (1994, Vol. 2, Issue 5).

"Ting Praises Socialism, Blasts Christianity," *Calvary Contender* (August 15, 1999, Vol. 16, No. 16).

"To Socialism by Way of Tax-Exempt Foundations," *The Florida Forum* (Summer 1997).

Toalston, Art. "Latest 'Harry Potter' Book Meets Cautionary Response from Christians," *Christian News* (July 17, 2000, Vol. 38, No. 29).

Tolerance, Goodwill, Peace (New York, NY: World Goodwill, n.d.).

"Tony Campolo Excoriates Religious Right," *Christian News* (December 19, 1994, Vol. 32, No. 47).

"Tony Robbins, New Age Guru," *Calvary Contender* (January 15, 1998).

Torell, John S. "Betrayal," *The Dove* (Autumn/Winter 1995, Vol. 16, No. 3).

"Totem Pole Ceremony at World Council of Churches Assembly," *Christian News* (June 4, 2001, Vol. 39, No. 23).

"Toward a Fourth Psychology Revisited: Part VIII: Omega Institute," *Distant Drums* (August 1995, Vol. 16, No. 1).

"Towards a Global Ethic (An Initial Declaration)," *USA Weekend.*

"Towards an Inclusive Religious Spirit," *World Goodwill Newsletter* (1994, No. 1).

Tower, Jay. "ACLU: Its Subversive Past and Evil Vision for America's Future," *Christian Crusade* (May 1993, Vol. 41, No. 5).

Toynbee, Arnold. *The Religious Background of the Present Environmental Crisis* (Reprinted from the International Journal of Environmental Studies, 1971).

"Transformation Toward New Age Synthesis," *Distant Drums* (March 1986, Vol. 8, No. 1).

"Transition Activities," *World Goodwill Newsletter* (1999, No. 1).

"Transition Activities," *World Goodwill Newsletter* (1999, No. 2).

Transmission (April 1983, No. 1).

Tresner, Jim. "Conscience and the Craft," *The Scottish Rite Journal* (February 1993, Vol. 101, No. 2).

Trinterud, L. J. "Reinhold Niebuhr," *The World Book Encyclopedia* (Vol. 13), (Chicago 54, IL: Field Enterprises Education Corporation, 1961).

"Triple Play, The," *Don Bell Reports* (May 31, 1991, Vol. 38, No. 11).

Trott, Jon and Pement, Eric. "Visualization and Imaging: Dangerous Trends in Christian Meditation," *Cornerstone* (Vol. 14, Issue 74).

"True Bible-Believers Denounced at Papal Conference," *Power of Prophecy* (March 2000, Vol. 2000-03).

Trumpet Messenger, The (February 1990, No. 15).

Trussell, Jacqueline. "Making a Joyful Noise," *CPWR Journal* (November 1993, Vol. 5, No. 6), p.7.

"Truth About China Does Not Count in the LLL or LCMS, The," *Christian News* (July 17, 2000, Vol. 38, No. 29).

Tucker, Cynthia. "Jackson Needs Leave of Absence," *Christian News* (February 12, 2001, Vol. 39, No. 7).

Tuleja, Tad. "Red-Letter Days: On the Origins of Holiday Rituals," *Utne Reader* (November/December 1987).

Turner, Darrell. "Graham Happy to Fellowship at the NCC's Interchurch Center," *Christian News* (September 9, 1991, Vol. 29, No. 32).

Turner, Tanya C. "Television: America's Babysitter and Its 'Dumbing Down' Effect," *The End Times and Victorious Living* (September/October 1997, Vol. 11, No. 5).

"Turret of the Times," *Christian News* (April 5, 1993, Vol. 31, No. 14).

"Turret of the Times," *Christian News* (April 21, 1997, Vol. 35, No. 16).

"Turret of the Times," *Christian News* (February 1, 1993, Vol. 31, No. 5).

"Turret of the Times," *Christian News* (February 5, 2001, Vol. 39, No. 6).

"Turret of the Times," *Christian News* (February 17, 1991, Vol. 30, No. 7).

"Turret of the Times," *Christian News* (February 24, 1997, Vol. 35, No. 8).

"Turret of the Times," *Christian News* (July 19, 1999, Vol. 37, No. 29).

"Turret of the Times," *Christian News* (March 16, 1992, Vol. 30, No. 11).

"Turret of the Times," *Christian News* (May 5, 1997, Vol. 35, No. 18).

"Turret of the Times," *Christian News* (November 11, 1991, Vol. 29, No. 41).

"Turret of the Times," *Christian News* (October 30, 2000, Vol. 38, No. 40).

"Turret of the Times," *Christian News* (September 14, 1992, Vol. 30, No. 33).

"Tutu Blasts Christians, Promotes Blasphemy," *Flashpoint* (September 1990).

"Tutu Wants Homosexual Priests," *Calvary Contender* (June 1, 1996, Vol. 13, No. 11).

"Tutu Wants WCC to Favor Homosexuality?," *Calvary Contender* (April 1, 1998, Vol. 15, No. 7).

"Tutu's Modernism," *Christian News* (November 6, 2000, Vol. 38, No. 41).

"Twenty Years of Federal 'Change Agentry,'" *An American Commentary* (Oklahoma City, OK: Hearthstone Publishing, Ltd., 1993).

"Twilight Zone in Washington, The," *U. S. News & World Report* (December 5, 1988).

Two Disciples, *The Rainbow Bridge* (Escondido, CA: The Triune Foundation, 1981).

"Two Paths Open Before Us: An Interview with Dr. Karan Singh," *World Goodwill Newsletter* (1994, No. 1).

"Two Same-Sex Couples Legally Tie Knot," *Calvary Contender* (February 15, 2001, Vol. 18, No. 4).

"Two United Methodist Leaders Close to MLK Welcome Verdict," *Christian News* (January 1, 2000, Vol. 38, No. 1).

"U. N. & Education, The," *The Florida Forum* (Fall 2000).

"U. N. & Vatican Unity," *Despatch Magazine* (June 2001, Vol. 13:2).

"U. N.'s Grab for Power, The," *The Florida Forum* (Spring 2000).

"U. S. Missionaries Detained in China," *Christian News* (September 18, 2000, Vol. 38, No. 34).

"U. S. State Department Confirms China's Persecution of Christians," *Christian News* (March 12, 2001, Vol. 39, No. 11).

"Unfinished Cathedral's 100th Year Celebrated," *Christian News* (January 18, 1993, Vol. 31, No. 3).

"Union Seminary's New Leader Is a Unitarian," *Christian News* (September 9, 1991, Vol. 29, No. 32).

"Union Theological Seminary," Softkey Multimedia Inc., Infopedia (1996).

"Unitarian Churches Using Wicca Rituals," *Christian News* (February 26, 2001, Vol. Vol. 39, No. 9).

"Unitarians Promote Free Sex!," *Christian News* (January 17, 2000, Vol. 38, No. 3).

"Unitarians Say Paganism Fits Well with Their Tradition," *The Christian World Report* (November 1989, Vol. 1, No. 8).

"United Flight Attendant to Sue Schuller for $5 Million," *Christian News* (September 15, 1997, Vol. 35, No. 33).

"United Church of Christ Leader Calls Sodomite Parade a 'Marvelous Moment'", *O Timothy* (1993, Vol. 10, Issue 6).

"United Methodist Theologian Urges Methodists Not to Evangelize," *The Vine and Branches* (Spring 1999, Vol. 14, Issue 2).

"United Nations and the Path to Unity and Right Relations, The," *World Goodwill Newsletter* (1995, No. 2).

"United Nations," Softkey Multimedia Inc., Infopedia (1996).

"United Nations: Its Origins and Milestones" (Received March 22, 1995).

United Religions (Fall 1997, Issue 4).

"United Religions Initiative 2000," *Calvary Contender* (September 1, 1997).

"United Religions Initiative 2000," *Christian News* (May 5, 1997, Vol. 35, No. 18).

"'United Religions' Like 'United Nations,'" *Calvary Contender* (April 1, 1996, Vol. 13, No. 7).

"United States Is Not a 'Democracy,' The," *An American Commentary* (Oklahoma City, OK: Hearthstone Publishing, Ltd., 1993).

Universal Fellowship Today (Los Angeles, CA: Universal Fellowship of Metropolitan Community Churches, 1984).

"Update Report: Historic ~ Millennium Summit Sept. 2000," *Despatch Magazine* (September 2000, Vol. 12:3).

"Urbana '96 Reports," *Calvary Contender* (April 1, 1997, Vol. 14, No. 7).

"Urbana '96," *Hilltop* (Winter 196-1997, Vol. 8, No. 3).

Utah Evangel (March 1987).

Utne Reader (March/April 1996).

"Utopian Dreams: The Early Futurists and Their Influence Today," *Christian Conscience* (February 1996, Vol. 2, No. 2).

USA Today (March 23, 1989).

Vail, Charles H. *The Ancient Mysteries and Modern Masonry* (Macoy Publishing and Masonic Company, 1909).

Van Baalen, Jan Karel, *The Chaos of Cults* (Grand Rapids, MI: Wm. B. Eerdmans Publishing Company, 1962).

van der Merwe, Jewel. "The River Is Wide, but the Way Is Narrow," *Discernment* (March/April 1997, Vol. 8, No. 3).

Van Dongen, Susan. "An Ever-Widening Circle of Light," *TimeOff* (June 30, 2000).

Vandervoort, Robert M. "Radicals Use Children to Advance Big Government Agenda," *The Florida Forum* (Summer 1997).

van Gelder, Saran "Making Peace Among Religions," *Yes!* (Fall 1998).

"Vast Left-Wing Conspiracy, The," *The Christian Conscience* (May 1998, Vol. 4, No. 4).

"Vatican Paper Rakes Fundamentalist Views While Evangelicals and Catholics Join Forces," *The Front Page* (October 1993, Vol. 7, No. 10).

"Vatican Seeks Ties with Hindus," *Calvary Contender* (November 15, 1998, Vol. 15, No. 24).

Veon, Joan. *Prince Charles: The* Sustainable *Prince* (Oklahoma City, OK: Hearthstone Publishing, Ltd., 1997).

"Very Reverend James Parks Morton Introducing His Holiness the Dalai Lama, The," *Temple of Understanding Newsletter* (Fall 1998).

"Victory of Shame," *The Witness* (April 2001, Vol. 41, No. 4).

"Vietnamese Syndicate's Connection to the Illuminati, The," *A Newsletter from a Follower of Jesus Christ* (September 1995, Vol. 4, No. 5).

Vine and Branches, The (Summer 1998, Vol. 13, Issue 3).

Vine, W. E. *Vine's Expository Dictionary of New Testament Words* (Lynchburg, VA: The Old-Time Gospel Hour, n.d.).

"Virginia Mollenkott," *Christian News* (February 17, 1997, Vol. 35, No. 7).

"Virginia Mollenkott," *Christian News* (November 25, 1996, Vol. 34, No. 44).

Virkler, David M. *The Word and the World Presenting...A Commentary on Secular Humanism* (Towaco, NJ: Dedication Evangelism, Inc., 1984).

Voice of Reason (Fall 1994, No. 51).

"Voodoo Chiefs Meet Catholic Chief," *Midnight Call* (April 1993).

"W. C. C. Speaker Admits to Syncretism," *Calvary Contender* (April 1, 1992, Vol. 9, No. 7).

"W. E. B. Dubois, a Founder of the NAACP," *Christian News* (October 30, 2000, Vol. 38, No. 40).

Waite, Arthur Edward. *A New Encyclopedia of Freemasonry and of Cognate Instituted Mysteries: Their Rites, Literature and History* (Vol. I) (NY: Weathervane Books, 1970).

Waite, Arthur Edward. *The Brotherhood of the Rosy Cross: A History of the Rosicrucians* (NY: Barnes & Noble, Inc., 1993).

Waite, Arthur Edward. *The Brotherhood of the Rosy Cross: Being Records of the House of the Holy Spirit in Its Inward and Outward History* (New Hyde Park, NY: University Books, 1961).

Waite, Arthur Edward. *The Mysteries of Magic: A Digest of the Writings of Eliphas Levi* (Chicago, IL: De Laurence, Scott & Company, 1909).

Walkes, Joseph A., Jr., *Jno. G. Lewis, Jr.—End of an Era: The History of the Prince Hall Grand Lodge of Louisiana 1842-1979* (n.p., 1986).

Wallechinsky, David, Wallace, Amy, and Wallace, Irving. *The Book of Predictions* (New York, NY: William Morrow and Company, Inc., 1981).

"Wallis Revitalizes Social Activism," *Calvary Contender* (July 1, 1997, Vol. 14, No. 13).

Wallis, Jim. "A Life of Commitment and Compassion," *Sojourners* (December 1989, Vol. 18, No. 11).

Wallis, Jim. "Biblical Faith and Spiritual Politics," *The Cry for Renewal: Biblical Faith and Spiritual Politics* (May 23, 1995).

Wallis, Wilson D. "Occult," *The World Book Encyclopedia* (1961 Edition, Vol. 13).

Walsh, Thomas G. "Faith and Interfaith," *IRFWP Newsletter* (Spring 1998, Vol. 6, No. 1).

"Walter Rauschenbusch," Softkey Multimedia Inc., Infopedia (1996).

Walton, Rus. *One National Under God* (Nashville, TN: Thomas Nelson Publishers, 1987).

"War and Peace: The Turbulent Times of Thich Nhat Hanh," *New Age Journal* (November/December 1990, Vol. 7, Issue 6).

"War and the Prophetic Words, The," *Midnight Call* (April 1991).

Ward J. S. M. and Stirling, W. G. *The Hung Society or the Society of Heaven and Earth* (Vol. I) (London, England: The Baskerville Press, Limited, 1925).

Ward, J. S. M. *Freemasonry and the Ancient Gods* (London, England: Simpkin, Marshall, Hamilton, Kent & Co., Ltd., 1921).

Ward, J. S. M. *Who Was Hiram Abiff?* (London, England: The Baskerville Press, Ltd., 1925).

Wardner, J. W. "Billy Graham, Freemasonry & the Communists," *Despatch Magazine* (September 1998, Vol. 10, No. 3).

Wardner, J. W. "Unholy Alliances—The Order—The Illuminati Pedigree," *Despatch Magazine* (September 1998, Vol. 10, No. 3).

Wardner, James W. *The Planned Destruction of America* (Debary, FL: Longwood Communications, 1994).

Wardner, James W. *Unholy Alliances* (n.p., 1996).

Warren, Samuel, Compiler. *A Compendium of Swedenborg's Theological Writings* (New York, NY: Swedenborg Foundation, Inc., 1979 Edition).

"Was C. S. Lewis a Christian?," *Calvary Contender* (September 15, 1998, Vol. 15, No. 18).

Washburn, Francis S., Jr., "An Open Letter to Billy Graham," *Life Advocate* (December 1992).

"Washington Has Never Seen Anything Like It—Since the Last Time," *U. S. News & World Report* (February 2, 1998, Vol. 124, No. 4).

"Watch Al Gore Closely," *The McAlvany Intelligence Advisor* (November 1992).

Watch Unto Prayer (Spring 1998).

Watchman Expositor, The (1998, Vol. 15, No. 5).

Watson, Richard L., Jr. "Norman Mattoon Thomas," *World Book Encyclopedia* (Vol. 17) (Chicago 54, IL: Field Enterprises Educational Corporation, 1961).

Watson, Tom. *The Evangelical Eroding of the Deity of Christ* (Southlake, TX: Countryside Bible Church, 1996).

Watson, Tom. *The Redefining of a Christian* (Southlake, TX: Countryside Bible Church, 1995).

Waymer, Bob. *A. Philip Randolph: A Short Biography* (Atlanta, GA: The Elloree Company, 1990).

"WCC and Catholicism," *Calvary Contender* (February 1, 1999, Vol. 16, No. 3).

"WCC Calls for Gun Control, Disarmament," *Calvary Contender* (June 1, 1999, Vol. 16, No. 11).

"WCC Conference Honors Sophia Goddess, Gives Ovation to Lesbians," *The Evangelical Methodist* (June 1994, Vol. 73, No. 6).

"WCC Faith & Order Commission Conference," *Calvary Contender* (September 15, 1993, Vol. 10, No. 18).

"WCC Funds African Marxists," *Christian Inquirer* (November 1984).

WCC Packet (Independence, MO: Price Publishing Company, n.d.).

"WCC President Dies During Papal Audience," *Christian News* (March 20, 2000, Vol. 38, No. 12).

"WCC Promotes Demoted Lundy," *Calvary Contender* (March 15, 1995, Vol. 12, No. 6).

"WCC Promotes Left Wing Revolutionary Causes and Universalism," *Christian News* (May 23, 1994, Vol. 32, No. 21).

"WCC to Meet in Zimbabwe," *Calvary Contender* (November 15, 1998, Vol. 15, No. 24).

"WCC Used by Communists," *Christian News* (September 9, 1991, Vol. 29, No. 32).

"WCC's 50th Anniversary, Orthodox Rife?," *Calvary Contender* (June 1, 1998, Vol. 15, No. 1).

"WCC's Russian Clergy Were KGB Men," *Calvary Contender* (August 15, 1992, Vol. 9, No. 16).

"WCRP Prepares for a New Center on Religion and Conflict," *Religion for Peace* (June 1995, Issue 66).

"WCRP Sixth World Assembly Held in Rome and Riva Del Garda, Italy, November 1994," *Religion for Peace* (February 1995, Issue 65-A).

We Affirm: National Religious Organizations' Statements on Abortion Rights (Washington, DC: Religious Coalition for Abortion Rights, n.d.).

Webb, Miki. "Invoking the Heart of L. A.," *Thoughtline* (February 1999).

Webber, David F. and Hutchings, N. W. *Satan's Kingdom and the Second Coming* (Oklahoma City, OK: Southwest Radio Church, 1983).

Webster's New Book of Word Histories, The.

Webster's Seventh New Collegiate Dictionary (Springfield, MA: G. & C. Merriam Company, 1967).

Wedeck, Harry E. *Treasury of Witchcraft* (New York, NY: Philosophical Library, 1961).

"WEF Honors 'Brother Andrew,'" *Calvary Contender* (July 1, 1997, Vol. 14, No. 13).

Weinberg, Steve. *Armand Hammer: The Untold Story* (Boston: Little, Brown and Company, 1989).

Weiss, Philip. "Inside Bohemian Grove," *Spy* (November 1989).

Welborn, Amy. "Why There Are Still Apes," *Our Sunday Visitor* (June 17, 2001), p.16.

"Well Hello, Dalai," *Endtime* (September/October 1999).

Wellman, Sam. *Billy Graham: The Great Evangelist* (Uhrichsville, OH: Barbour Book, 1996).

Weniger, G. Archer. "Dr. Billy Graham and the National Council of Churches."

Weniger, G. Archer. *Modernism of National Council of Churches* (1961).

Western, John Henry. "World's Elite Gather to Talk Depopulation," *The Interim* (April 1996).

"What Are Other Investigators Saying?," *Despatch Magazine* (June 2001, Vol. 13:2).

"Where Did the New Age Come From?," *The Front Page* (September 1993, Vol. 7, No. 9).

What About the National Council of Churches? (Hatfield, PA: Brethren Revival Fellowship Witness, 1967).

"What Billy Graham and Roman Catholics Believe," *Flashpoint* (August 1995).

"What Is Planned Parenthood Teaching Children?," *End-Times News Digest* (April 1990, Issue 139).

"What Is the WCC?," *Calvary Contender* (April 1, 1998, Vol. 15, No. 7).

"What Is the WCC?," *Calvary Contender* (June 15, 2001, Vol. 18, No. 12).

"What Kind of Man Was Martin Luther King, Jr.?," *Common Sense for Today* (November/December 1995).

What? When? Where? Why? Who? in Freemasonry (Silver Spring, MD: Masonic Service Association of the United States, 1956).

What? When? Where? Why? Who? in Freemasonry (Silver Spring, MD: Masonic Service Association of the United States, 1986 Edition).

What's Next (Fall 1992, Vol. 14, No. 3).

What's Next (November 1979, Vol. 4, No. 5).

What's Next (November 1982, Vol. 7, No. 3)

What's Next (September 1979), Vol. 4, No. 2).

Wheatley, Dan. "Unity in Diversity," *The Festival Week of the New Group of World Servers* (New York, NY: Lucis Trust, n.d.).

"When Tolerance Is Compromise," *Voice in the Wilderness* (December 2000).

Which Will It Be: Wars—and More Wars? or a World of Lasting Peace Under Law? (World Federalist Association, n.d.).

"White House Honors Memory of Anti-Communist Chambers," *Christian News* (July 23, 2001, Vol. 39, No. 30).

"White House Ignores NEA Indecency," *The Christian World Report* (April 1990, Vol. 2, No. 4).

White, Jack E. "The End of the Rainbow," *Christian News* (February 5, 2001, Vol. 39, No. 6).

White, Lew. *Fossilized Customs: The Pagan Sources of Popular Customs* (Louisville, KY: Strawberry Islands Publishers, 2000).

White, Tom. "'Banning' Millennium in China," *Christian News* (March 19, 2001, Vol. 39, No. 12).

"Whither Religious Freedom in Hong Kong?," *Calvary Contender* (July 15, 1997, Vol. 14, No. 14).

"Who Controls American Education?," *The Blumenfeld Education Letter* (February 1994).

"Who Do You Think This Is?," *Despatch Magazine* (December 1997, Vol. 9, No. 4).

"Who Is Behind the ACLU?," *The Perilous Times* (December 1993, Vol. 15, No. 10).

"Who Is Mandela?," *Midnight Call* (September 1990).

"Who Is Telling the Truth About China? The LLL and LCMS or the U. S. State Department and Karnes?," *Christian News* (May 8, 2000, Vol. 38, No. 19).

"Who Told the Truth About China?," *Christian News* (July 30, 201, Vol. 39, No. 31).

"Who Will Evangelize Catholics?," *Calvary Contender* (June 15, 1997, Vol. 14, No. 12).

Who's Running Our Schools? (Save Our Schools Research and Education Foundation, n.d.).

"Who's Who in the Clinton Administration," *Wisconsin Report* (February 18, 1993, Vol. 18, No. 8).

"Whom Can I Believe?," *O Timothy* (1987, Vol. 4, Issue 3-4).

"Why Do Colson and Evangelicals Think Catholics Are Saved?," *Calvary Contender* (November 15, 1999, Vol. 16, No. 22).

"Wicca Stories Are 'Bunk,' Historians Say," *Christian News* (January 29, 2001, Vol. 39, No. 5).

Wicker, Christine. "The Son Also Rises: Franklin Graham to Preach at First Baptist Church," *The Dallas Morning News*.

"Willem Adolf Visser 'T Hooft" Softkey Multimedia Inc., Infopedia (1996).

"William Randolph Hearst," Softkey Multimedia Inc., Infopedia (1996).

Williams, Charles. "The Clinton/Marxist Connections: Derek Schearer (sic) & the Institute for Policy Studies," *Wisconsin Report* (July 8, 1993, Vol. 18, No. 27).

Williamson, Parker T. "Controversial ReImagining Leader Retiring from WCC," *The Presbyterian Layman* (January/February 1999, Vol. 32, No. 1).

Williamson, Parker T. "Interfaith Dialogue: 'My God, Your God, Our God, No God,'" *The Presbyterian Layman* (January/February 1999, Vol. 32, No. 1).

Williamson, Parker T. "Litanies of Oppression Prompt Spasms of Repentance: Padare Participants Lament the Exclusion of Witch Doctors," *The Presbyterian Layman* (January/February 1999, Vol. 32, No. 1).

Williamson, Parker T. "Mandela Urges Christians to Build a Democratic Africa," *The Presbyterian Layman* (January/February 1999, Vol. 32, No. 1).

Williamson, Parker T. "Mugabe Hails WCC As Faithful Ally in Marxist Struggle," *The Presbyterian Layman* (January/February 1999, Vol. 32, No. 1).

Williamson, Parker T. "Sophia Upstages Jesus at the 1998 ReImagining Revival," *The Presbyterian Layman* (May/June 1998, Vol. 31, No. 3).

Williamson, Parker T. "WCC to Study Diversity of Sexuality," *The Presbyterian Layman* (January/February 1999, Vol. 32, No. 1).

"Willow: Bringing the Star Wars Message to a Whole New Generation," *Omega-Letter* (July/August 1988, Vol. 3, No. 7).

Wilson, A. N. *C. S. Lewis: A Biography* (New York, NY: W. W. Norton & Company, 1990).

Wilson, Clifford and Weldon, John. *Psychic Forces and Occult Shock: A Biblical View* (Chattanooga, TN: Global Publishers, 1987).

Wilson, Colin. *Beyond the Occult: A Twenty Year Investigation into the Paranormal* (New York, NY: Carroll and Graf Publishers, Inc., 1989).

Wilson, Colin. *The Occult: A History* (New York, Random House, 1971).

Wilson, Nancy. *The Ecumenical Ministry and Witness of Metropolitan Community Churches* (Los Angeles, CA: Universal Fellowship of Metropolitan Community Churches, March 1987 Revision).

Wilson, Susan N. "Different Families Matter," *Censorship News* (1994, Issue 4, No. 55).

Wineke, William R. "Gay Clergyman Decries 'Urge to Purge,'" *Christian News* (April 21, 1997, Vol. 35, No. 16).

Winters, D. Duane. *A Search for Light in a Place of Darkness: A Study of Freemasonry* (no other information is available).

Wisconsin Report (July 27, 2000).

Wisconsin Report (November 1, 1984, Vol. 9, No. 43).

Wisconsin Report (November 6, 1997, Vol. 22, No. 43).

Witham, Larry. "Graham to Launch Revival in Moscow," *The Washington Times* (June 21, 1991).

Witham, Larry. "U. S. Evangelist Invited to Preach in North Korea," *The Washington Times* (March 28, 1992).

Witness, The (November 1996, Vol. 79, No. 11).

Wood, Debbie. "Latins Say 'Si' to World Evangelization: Latinoamerica 2000," *Mission Frontiers* (January/February 1997, Vol. 19, No. 1-2).

Wood, Rick. "Taking Jesus to the World," *Mission Frontiers* (November-December 1997, Vol. 19, No. 11-12).

Woodcock, Percival George. *Short Dictionary of Mythology* (NY: Philosophical Library, 1953).

Woodrow, Ralph Edward. *Babylon Mystery Religion: Ancient and Modern* (Riverside, CA: Ralph Woodrow Evangelistic Association, Inc., 1990 Edition).

Woodward, Kenneth L. "Soul Searching," *Newsweek* (July 8, 1996).

Words of Desmond Tutu, The (Selected and Introduced by Naomi Tutu) (New York, NY: Newmarket Press, 1996).

"Work in Australia and New Zealand," *Yoga Vedanta* (October/November/December 1994, Vol. 3, No. 4).

"Working with Communist Approved Churches," *Christian News* (February 26, 2001, Vol. 39, No. 9).

"World Assembly to Give Grand Thanks," *Dallas Morning News* (February 28, 1999).

World Book Encyclopedia, The (Vol. 12) (Chicago 54, IL: Field Enterprises Educational Corporation, 1961 Edition).

World Book Encyclopedia, The (Vol. 14) (Chicago 54, IL: Field Enterprises Educational Corporation, 1961 Edition).

World Book Encyclopedia, The (Vol. 17) (Chicago 54, IL: Field Enterprises Educational Corporation, 1961 Edition).

World Book Encyclopedia, The (Vol. 18) (Chicago 54, IL: Field Enterprises Educational Corporation, 1961 Edition).

"World Citizenship: A Global Ethic for Sustainable Development," *One Country* (July-September 1993, Vol. 5, Issue 2).

"World Council Finds Spirituality in Pagan Practices," *O Timothy* (1994, Vol. 11, Issue 3).

"World Council of Churches 50th Anniversary," *The ACCC Report* (February 1999).

"World Council of Churches Ecumenical Women's Decade Festival," *The ACCC Report* (January 1999).

"World Council of Churches on World Order, The," *The Whole Earth Papers: Christian Voices on World Order* (1978, Vol. 1, No. 10).

"World Council of Churches Promotes Female Gods and Revolution," *O Timothy* (1988, Vol. 5, Issue 4).

"World Council of Churches Says 'Stop Evangelizing,'" *The Vine and Branches* (Summer 2001, Vol. 16, Issue 3).

"World Council of Churches Seeks to Build a New One World Order," *O Timothy* (1986, Vol. 3, Issue 7).

"World Council of Churches Supports Terrorism and Violence," *O Timothy* (1988, Vol. 5, Issue 4).

"World Council of Churches Youth Meeting Praises Terrorism and Murder in South Africa," *O Timothy* (1986, Vol. 3, Issue 7).

"World Council of Churches," Softkey Multimedia Inc., Infopedia (1996).

World Council of Churches: The Shaky Ship Sails On... (Los Osos, CA: Fundamental Evangelistic Association, 1999).

World Federalist (Spring 1989, Vol. 14, No. 2).2.

"World Federalist Association to Present Award to Walter Cronkite," *News and Announcement* (September 1999).

World Federalist Bicentennial Edition (1987).

World Goodwill Commentary: Race Relations in an Interdependent World (January 1983, No. 16).

World Goodwill Newsletter (1988, No. 3).

World Goodwill Newsletter (1993, No. 4).

World Goodwill Newsletter (1994, No. 1).

World Goodwill Newsletter (1998, No. 3).

World Goodwill Occasional Paper (Received September 16, 1998).

"World Government Meets," *Midnight Call* (May 1990).

World Prayer and Share Letter (August 1991).

"World Religious Leaders Meet at UN," *Calvary Contender* (September 15, 2000, Vol. 17, No. 18).

World Teacher, Maitreya, Is Now Here (North Hollywood, CA: Tara Center, n.d.).

"World Trade: An Integral Step Toward World Government," *The Proclaimer* (Issue 2, 2000, Vol. 8, No. 2).

"World Vindicates Pastor Otten on China," *Christian News* (February 26, 2001, Vol. 39, No. 9).

Wormser, Rene A. *Foundations: Their Power and Influence* (New York, NY: Devin-Adair Company, 1977 Edition).

"Worshiping Heathen, The," *Christian News* (January 18, 1993, Vol. 31, No. 3).

Woster, Carol. *Woster's Religious Almanac* (Columbia Falls, MT: Christian Wall Center, 1999).

WPTF Newsletter (Winter 1984, No. 4).

Wright, Machaelle Small. "Why Bother? A Matter of Spiritual Integrity, A Matter of the Heart," *Connecting Link* (January/February 1990, Issue 6).

Wurmbrand, Richard. *Marx and Satan* (Westchester, IL: Crossway Books, 1986).

Yanconelli, Mike. "Door Editor Defends Mrs. Campolo," *Christian News* (April 11, 1994, Vol. 32, No. 15).

Yarker, John. *The Arcane Schools* (Belfast, Ireland: William Tait, 1909).

Yerace, Gary Alan. Installation Address as Worshipful Master of the Elmer Timberman Lodge #54 (Address given on December 7, 1996).

Yoga Vedanta (October/November/December 1994, Vol. 3, No. 4).

Yoh, Charles. "The New Age vs Christianity," *The Evangelist of Truth* (April 1990, Vol. 56, No. 4).

"Yonggi Cho and Billy Kim Praise 'Excellent Program,'" *Alpha News* (December 2000-March 2001, No. 8).

"'Your Silence Will Not Protect You...Celebrating Spirit, Seeking Racial Justice,'" *CLOUTreach* (Spring 2001, Vol. 10, No. 2).

"Your Tax Dollar At Work," *Midnight Call* (August 1991).

Zeller, George. *Billy Graham: Ecumenical Evangelism* (Middletown, CT: Middletown Bible Church, n.d.).

Zeolla, Gary F. "Sci-Fi, ETs, and the Ways of God," *Darkness to Light* (1995, Vol. 5, No. 1, Issue 18).

Zimmer, Heinrich. *Philosophies of India* (Princeton, NJ: Princeton University Press, 1974 Edition).

Zins, Robert M. "Book Review," *Theo-Logical* (1997).

INDEX

H

N

Mormonism, Masonry, and Godhood

Can Angels Be Trusted?

The Church o f Jesus Christ of Latter-day Saints (Mormons) began on April 6, 1830. In this book Dr. Burns covers many of the key Mormon doctrines as well as looking closely at Mormon's founder, Joseph Smith.

This well-documented book answers questions such as the following:

— What **talisman** was found on Joseph Smith when he died?
— Was Joseph Smith involved in **magical and occultic practices?**
— Is there a **Masonic connection?**
— What takes place inside the Mormon Temple?
— Was God once a man?
— Is **polygamy** necessary to attain heaven?
— How can a Mormon attain **godhood?**
— What does Mormonism teach about **baptism for the dead?**
— Was Jesus married?
— Was Jesus crucified because He was a polygamist?

A SCRIPTURAL VIEW OF HELL

Dr. Cathy Burns

Does the Bible teach soul sleep?
Is Hell eternal?
Is Hell the grave?
Are the wicked annihilated?
Is there fire in Hell?
Is Hell a place of torment?
All of these questions are answered Scripturally in this small book.

For your gift of $4.95 plus $1.05 postage and handling.

40 pages • ISBN: 1-891117-11-4

STARTLING FACTS ABOUT AA UNCOVERED

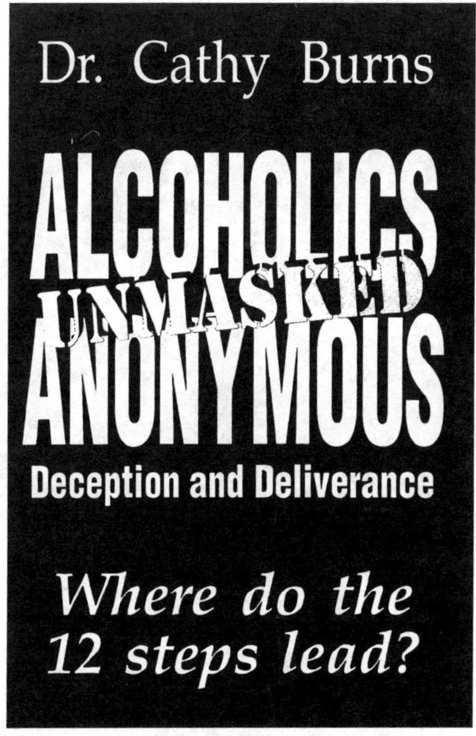

Dr. Cathy Burns
ALCOHOLICS
UNMASKED
ANONYMOUS
Deception and Deliverance
Where do the
12 steps lead?

- Who is the Higher Power of AA?
- Were AA's founders Christians or occultists?
- How is the New Age involved?
- How successful is AA's treatment program?
- Is alcoholism a sin or a disease?

Don't you think it's time to learn about Bill Wilson's adulterous affairs, LSD experimentation, as well as his and Dr. Bob Smith's interest in seances and spiritualism?

128 pages • $5.95 • ISBN 1-56043-449-X

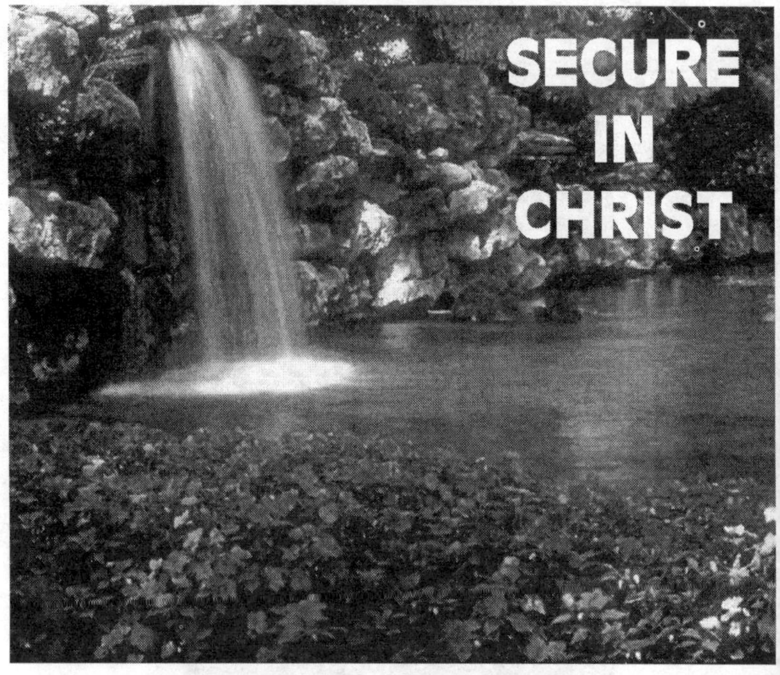

SECURE IN CHRIST

In this most fascinating and Scripturally-oriented book you will find approximately 1000 Bible verses to meditate upon. It will enlighten you as you search the Scriptures and will encourage a closer walk with the Lord.

This book will also strengthen your spiritual outlook on life as you see how the Lord wants you to cast all your care upon Him and walk hand in hand in fellowship with Him as He leads you into the deep truth of His Word.

"Now unto Him that is able to keep you from falling, and to present you faultless before the presence of His glory with exceeding joy" (Jude 1:24).

For your gift of $6.95 plus $1.25 postage and handling.

136 pages • ISBN: 1-891117-10-6

Pathway to Peace

This book has been prepared to help souls find the to salvation and to find rest and true peace through ying God's never-failing words to our hearts. A great essing tool!

For your gift of $2.50 plus $1.25 postage and handling.
50 books for $50.00 plus $6.00 postage and handling.

72 pages • ISBN: 1-891117-14-9

SHOCKING TRUTH REVEALED

√ Does Masonry pr
mote astrology and reincarn
tion?

√ Are Masonry a
Christianity compatible?

√ What do the Maso
symbols represent?

√ Who is the **REAL** g
of Masonry?

Discover hidden meanings, sexual overtones, the god they concea
and much more. Fully documented with 276 footnotes.

64 pages • $4.95 (plus $1.25 postage) • ISBN 0-00-540512-2

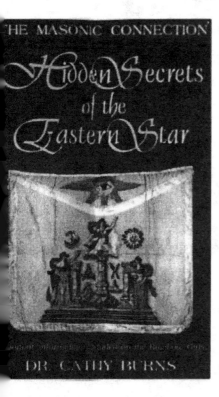

Tongues, Prosperity, & Godhood

This important book looks at the issue of speakin in tongues from a Biblical perspective. The chapter title are: 1. Do All Speak in Tongues?; 2. Baptism in the Hol Ghost; 3. Sinful Lives and Tongues; 4. Signs and Wonders 5. Prosperity and Riches; 6. The Power of Words; 7. Ca We Create Our Own Reality?; 8. What Is Visualization 9. A Look at Inner Healing; 10. Are You a God?; 11. Misfit Removed; 12. Renegades Excluded!; 13. Thy Kingdo Come!; and 14. Will the Church Be Raptured?

For your gift of only $8.95 plus $1.25 postage and handling.

ISBN: 1-891117-18-1

A ONE WORLD ORDER IS COMING

"Peace, peace, we must have peace at any cost," is the cry being heard from every quarter today. If we don't soon agree to have a peaceful world, we may all die in a nuclear holocaust. So, what will it take to have a peaceful co-existence? The answer given is the establishment of a one world government. In addition to a one world government, there will be a one world religion and a one world economy. What is also needed in a one world government is a leader. Who will this leader be?

In spite of many plans for this one world government, there is still one obstacle in the way. What—or **WHO**—is this obstacle?

Each of these topics is discussed in detail in this book and then compared to the Bible to see how prophecy is being fulfilled.

For your gift of $5.95 plus $1.25 postage and handling.

116 pages • ISBN: 1-891117-00-9

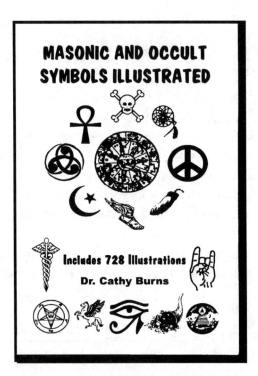

ORDER BLANK

BOOKS:

____*A One World Order Is Coming* (116 pages)..................$ 5.95
____*A Scriptural View of Hell* (40 pages).............................$ 4.95
____*Alcoholics Anonymous Unmasked* (320 pages)............$11.95
____*Billy Graham and His Friends* (800 pages)..................$21.95
____*Hidden Secrets of Masonry* (64 pages)..........................$ 4.95
____*Hidden Secrets of the Eastern Star* (512 pages)............$15.95
____*Masonic and Occult Symbols Illustrated* (552 pages)..$21.95
____*Mormonism, Masonry, and Godhood* (132 pages)........$ 6.95
____*Pathway to Peace* (72 pages).....................................$2.50
____*Secure in Christ* (136 pages)..$ 6.95
____*Tongues, Prosperity, and Godhood* (192 pages).............$8.95

BOOKLETS: ....$ .50 each

____ Astrology and Your Future
____ Different Types of Friendship
____ Dowsing Is in the Bible!
____ Eastern Star Goddesses
____ Explanation of Some Occult Terms
____ Hidden Dangers of Reflexology
____ Hypnosis: Cure or Curse?
____ Questions and Answers About the New Age Movement
____ To Catholics with Love
____ What Is Your I.Q.?

ARTICLES: ....$ .50 each

____ Chart Your Course with Orion International
____ Divination
____ I Have Sinned
____ Jason Winters and His Herbal Tea

____ March for Jesus (WHICH Jesus?)
____ New Age Love
____ Should We Name Names?
____ The Rapture—When Will It Occur?
____ Unity or D-i-v-i-s-i-o-n?
____ What Is Miscegenation?
____ Witchcraft in the Church
____ Ye Shall Not Surely Die

MORE ARTICLES:

____ Jay Gary: The Millennium Doctor.................................$4.00
____ Unholy Laughter? (2 part series)...................................$1.00

TRACTS: ....$ .05 each

____ A Perfect Church (Malcolm Burns)
____ ABC's of Salvation
____ Divorce and Remarriage
____ I've Been Cheated! (Jean Burns)
____ My God Cannot Do Everything
____ Treasure of All Ages (Jean Burns)
____ What Are You Missing? (Jean Burns)
____ What Is Sin?

______ **SUBTOTAL**
______ **POSTAGE** (10% of order [$1.00 mininum; $6.00 maximum])
______ **ADDITIONAL DONATION**
______ **TOTAL ENCLOSED**

For orders, or a complete list of literature available, write to:

SHARING

212 East Seventh Street (#B)

Mt. Carmel, PA 17851-2211